AN
AMERICAN
HISTORY

NEW YORK

APPLETON · CENTURY · CROFTS

EDUCATIONAL DIVISION

AN
AMERICAN
HISTORY

Rebecca Brooks Gruver
Hunter College
of the City University
of New York

MEREDITH CORPORATION

Designed by Louis Orsini
Cartography by Harold Faye

PREFACE

The history of America has been told many times and from many points of view. However, in the last few years the argument has been advanced that the past record of the United States is no longer relevant to the cataclysmic problems faced by the present generation. Yet even a cursory survey of that record indicates that although the nation's problems have multiplied, the nature of man has changed very little, if at all. Thus, if the challenges that confront the United States are to be met, a grasp of how she has reached her present circumstances, and why certain attitudes are held on different subjects by large numbers of Americans, would seem to be of great relevance to the formulation of any viable answer to present-day issues.

Most Americans have always been interested in their history even when their knowledge of factual detail has been lacking. The United States abounds with historical societies, museums, restorations, and programs designed to perpetuate the remembrance of the nation's past. Even the college freshman, who may think that he does not want to study American history in college because he has already been exposed to it in elementary or high school, or because he was bored by its being taught as a catalogue of facts and dates, will show a renewed interest in the subject if it is presented in a clear and challenging manner.

At no time in the history of the United States has it been more important for Americans of college age to study the history of their country analytically. Textbooks that rely on massive factual detail at the expense of analysis, or that seek to be highly interpretative without adequate factual information, do not satisfy this requirement.

THE PLAN OF THE BOOK

This new American history textbook is designed to meet the needs of both instructors and students in introductory courses at the college level. A consistent effort has been made to treat the American past in a comprehensive manner. While there is broad and incisive coverage of political and diplomatic events, equal attention has also been given to the evolution of the American economy from a simple agrarian society to its present position of industrial leadership.

The development of business enterprise has been presented in such a way as to show its influence on other important sectors of the economy, such as labor and agriculture. The impact on modern America of the country's ethnic diversity and racial problems has been described in some detail. Finally, the social and intellectual history of the nation also has been given broad coverage. There is special emphasis throughout the text on American manners and mores, literary and artistic movements, and religious and philosophical schools of thought. The general outlook of the American people on a particular subject, such as government regulations of business or the desire for an isolationist foreign policy, has been fully explained in an effort to provide a background for understanding national policy on proposals related to that subject.

The book is graphically appealing and easily adapted to either a one-semester or a two-semester introductory course. It has been broken down into six essentially equal parts, with the midpoint of coverage ending after the Civil War. There are particularly useful annotated bibliographies at the end of each chapter, along with a supplementary reading list at the end of the book. The large number of maps and illustrations within each chapter and in the five portfolios have been chosen for their visual impact and with special attention to their relevance to the text. In particular, the portfolios illustrate aspects of American culture more easily grasped visually than verbally.

WHY ANOTHER AMERICAN HISTORY TEXTBOOK?

This textbook satisfies the increasing demand by college instructors for a more sophisticated approach to the study of America's past. The utmost effort has been made to present the important facts of America's journey from simple colonial settlements to her present position of world prominence in clear and readable language. While the connection between events and movements has been stressed, the unembellished record of the nation's past deeds and purposes has been left to speak for itself. The fascinating story of the conquest and settlement of a vast and richly endowed continent by peoples of diverse ethnic, racial and religious backgrounds has been told both respectfully and realistically. Events and points of view usually considered highly praiseworthy have not been presented to the exclusion of those for which the country has been criticized by many Americans, as well as by friendly and unfriendly critics abroad. In short, the book has been made as objective, clear, and comprehensive as possible.

At the same time, the controversial nature of much of the country's past has not been overlooked. Historical debates over the causes and results of significant aspects of American history have been incorporated at relevant points throughout the text. The viewpoints of individual historians have been discussed to indicate controversial attitudes on such subjects as Puritanism, Jacksonian democracy, America's entry into World War I, and the New Deal. Wherever possible the latest scholarship also has been included in the text, although it has not been possible to cite specific historians in many cases. Throughout the book there are also contrasting quotations from original sources to indicate that even participants in events frequently saw them from differing points of view.

Readability

The only good textbook is one that students can and will read, yet the complaint most frequently made by teachers and students alike about introductory textbooks is that they lack readability. A first step in producing this book, therefore, was to define "readability" in the context of the teaching situation, and determine how it might be achieved. After much discussion and analysis, and with the help of professionals, it was decided that readability depends essentially on organization and on the relevance of language. Briefly, clear and familiar language makes a book readable. The result is a book that is more interesting and useful to students and a better teaching tool for professors.

ACKNOWLEDGMENTS

I especially would like to express my appreciation for the expert editorial advice and choice of graphics made by Miss Betsy H. Wyckoff, the Product Development Editor at Appleton-Century-Crofts. I also am greatly indebted to the care taken by the Assistant Editor, Mrs. Jessica Vega, in an effort to make the final book accurate and consistent.

Rebecca Brooks Gruver

CONTENTS

THE EVOLUTION OF DEMOCRACY

NATIONALISM AND SECTIONALISM

EMERGENCE OF INDUSTRIAL AMERICA

WORLD POWER AND DOMESTIC REFORM

THE CHALLENGES OF MATURITY

portfolios

maps

AN
AMERICAN
HISTORY

1

FROM COLONIES TO INDEPENDENT NATION

The Meeting of

Dutch traders meet with the Indians.

Two Worlds

1

*So we stood looking about us
. . . and we saw the fresh water
that comes from Chapultepec
which supplies the city, and we
saw the bridge on the three
causeways which were built at
certain distances apart through
which the water of the lake flowed
in and out from one side to the
other, and we beheld on that
great lake a great multitude of
canoes, some coming with
supplies of food and others
returning loaded with cargoes of
merchandise; and we saw that
from every house of that great
city of all the other cities that
were built in the water it was
impossible to pass from house to
house, except by drawbridges
which were made of wood or in
canoes; and we saw in those cities
Cues and oratories like towers
and fortresses and all gleaming
white, and it was a wonderful
thing to behold; then the houses
with flat roofs, and on the
causeways other small towers and
oratories which were like
fortresses.*

*After having examined and
considered all that we had seen
we turned to look at the great
market place and the crowds of
people that were in it, some
buying and others selling, so that
the murmur and hum of their
voices and words that they used
could be heard more than a
league off. Some of the soldiers
among us who had been in
many parts of the world, in
Constantinople, and all over
Italy, and in Rome, said that so
large a market place and so full
of people, and so well regulated
and arranged, they had never
beheld before.*

—Bernal Diaz del Castillo,
The Discovery and Conquest of Mexico

1

CONQUISTADORS MEET THE AZTECS

The Spanish conquistadors were not the first men to journey to the Western Hemisphere. Although no remains have been found in the New World of the creatures who evolved into *Homo sapiens,* there is evidence that Asiatic peoples began migrating westward before the dawn of recorded history. Scientists disagree about the exact time of the first arrivals, with estimates ranging from 12,000 to 35,000 years ago, but most experts agree that they came across the Bering Straits, from Siberia to Alaska. Probably they traveled on foot, for during the last Ice Age, which ended about 10,000 years ago, sea levels were as much as 300 feet lower than they are today, and a land bridge emerged from the ocean connecting the tip of northeast Asia with Alaska. According to current theories, the Asians journeyed—perhaps in a series of migrations—

Spanish conquistadores and their Indian bearers.

across this land bridge. In any event, when the land bridge was submerged again at the end of the Ice Age, all overland passage came to a halt.

Some anthropologists believe later travelers navigated across the Pacific. Natives of northeast Asia, from what is now Japan, are thought to have sailed to the cost of Ecuador about 3,000 B.C., bringing with them pottery and perhaps domesticated cotton. Still later, between A.D. 500 and 1,000, when the first Asians landed in the Polynesian islands, some may have drifted farther east to the Western Hemisphere and remained.

PRE-COLUMBIAN CULTURE

By the fifteenth century the New World was populated by millions of people, organized into thousands of political units, some of them quite primitive but others among the most advanced cultures in the world.

THE AZTECS OF MEXICO

The ruling people of Mexico, the Aztecs, had inherited a remarkable intellectual history from an earlier Central American civilization, the Mayan. The Aztecs possessed a system of hieroglyphic writing and astronomical knowledge so precise that priests were able to predict eclipses and devise an accurate calendar. They had developed sophisticated architectural styles distinguished by temples, baths, and observatories covered with arched vaults. The Aztec capital, Tenochtitlán (now Mexico City), covered about 8 square miles, had about sixty thousand citizens, and was built around a pyramid 200 feet in height. They were also experts at irrigating and terracing agricultural lands, produced intricately designed pottery and sculpture, and were familiar with the use of zero in mathematics. However, none of the tribes of the New World

had discovered how to use the wheel, and because horses did not exist in the Western Hemisphere until they were introduced by the Europeans, all transport depended on human beings or boats.

THE INCAS OF PERU

When the Spanish conquistadors arrived in South America in the sixteenth century, they found an advanced civilization flourishing in Peru. The rulers of this civilization were the Incas who controlled a vast empire of seven million people that extended some 2,000 miles along the Pacific Coast of South America. The people of this area had possessed an advanced culture since about 200 B.C., one that for hundreds of years was the equal in complexity of any of the civilizations of Europe and Asia. The Indians built extensive irrigation systems and aqueducts and enriched their crops with fertilizer. They developed many edible plants, including the white potato. Textile weaving was one of the highest achievements of South American culture; llama or alpaca wool was woven, embroidered, and braided into fabrics ornamented with designs dyed as many as 190 different hues on a single piece of cloth. Under the

The Great Temple of Tenochtitlan reconstructed by Ignacio Marquina from descriptions by Spanish conquerors and existing Aztec monuments.

3

Incas, all property was owned by the government or the state religious organization. Every aspect of life, from public health to the transportation of food from one end of the empire to the other, was controlled by the emperor and his family. This ruling class presided over its holdings with great ceremony; surrounded by numerous wives and servants, they wore gold and silver and were borne about on litters.

THE INDIANS
OF NORTH AMERICA

The inhabitants of the hemisphere north of Mexico were less highly centralized than their neighbors to the south, less wealthy, and less technologically advanced. At the time of Columbus' arrival there were about one million Indians in the United States and Canada. Among them were marked differences in tribal life, and their culture in general, particularly in the matter of religion, differed from that of the Indians of Central and South America. They were more likely, for example, to practice healing ceremonies than the rites of human sacrifice and self-torture used by certain of the Mexican Indian tribes. In the Pacific Northwest, the tribes liked to show off their wealth and disposed of it with a free hand. They frequently gave feasts, called "potlatches," during which they gave away or destroyed their belongings. The more blankets, baskets, hides, or slaves that a man divested himself of, the higher his prestige among his fellow tribesmen. Their preoccupation with private property extended even to tunes, which the "owner" and no one else might sing.

However, many of the tribes along the eastern seaboard had no concept of private property. The hunting territories of such tribes were owned in common by all the members of the tribe. They had so little understanding of the European meaning of private property that when they "sold"

land to Europeans, they would innocently try to repossess it later. The Europeans thought they had gained complete possession of the ground; the Indians thought that they had merely leased hunting rights. This misunderstanding repeatedly led to bitter struggles.

These woodland Indians of the Northeast belonged primarily to tribes speaking the language of the Algonquin, Iroquois, or Siouan families. They usually lived in villages in rectangular houses covered with bark or in cone-shaped wigwams. They subsisted by raising corn, squash, and beans and increased their food supply by hunting deer and fishing. The Iroquois displayed a shrewd grasp of politics, which in the sixteenth century enabled five Iroquois tribes to band together into a powerful league that quickly became the strongest political force in North America, with a governing council that was democratic in structure. The League had the bad fortune, however, to support the losing side in the American Revolution. Its support of the English caused most of its members to be exiled to Canada after the war.

The Southeastern tribes, the Creeks, Chickasaws, Choctaws, and Cherokees, had living patterns similar to those of the Indians of the Northeast. However, unlike the Iroquois, they were never able to cooperate closely with each other. Once their territory was taken over by the white man, one tribe might be bribed by the English, for instance, to attack another tribe that had become allied with the Spanish.

Along the Mississippi River, a highly developed tribe, the Natchez, ruled by an absolute monarch called the Great Sun, was discovered by the French. Believed by his followers to be descended from the sun, this ruler was treated with all the slavish respect of an Incan emperor, and like an Incan monarch, was both a religious and political leader. He was borne on a litter, his house rested atop a huge mound, and when he died his wife and retainers were

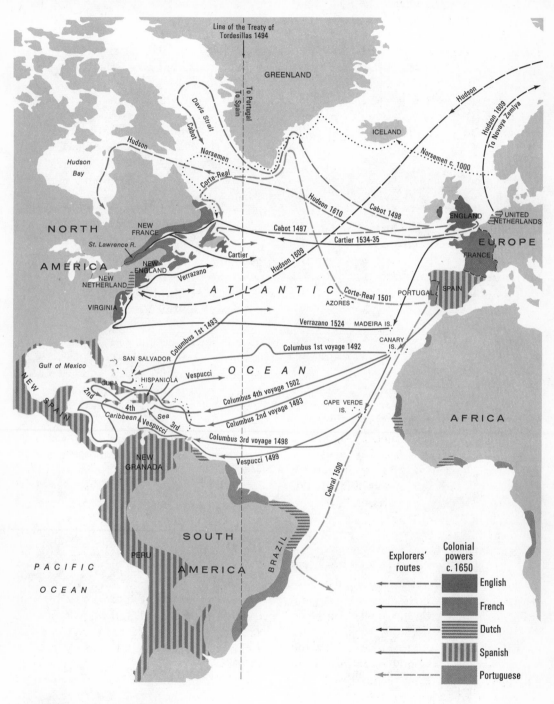

Line of the Treaty of
Tordesillas 1494

GREENLAND

ICELAND

Davis Strait

Cabot

To Portugal
To Spain

Hudson

Hudson 1609
To Novaya Zemlya

Norsemen

Hudson
Bay

Corte-Real

Norsemen c. 1000

Hudson 1610

Cabot 1498

NORTH

NEW
FRANCE

Cabot 1497

Cartier 1534-35

ENGLAND

UNITED
NETHERLANDS

EUROPE

St. Lawrence R.

Cartier

FRANCE

AMERICA

NEW
ENGLAND

Hudson 1609

ATLANTIC

NEW
NETHERLAND

Verrazano

Corte-Real 1501

PORTUGAL

SPAIN

VIRGINIA

AZORES

Columbus 1st 1493

Verrazano 1524

MADEIRA IS.

CANARY
IS.

SAN SALVADOR

Columbus 1st voyage 1492

Gulf of Mexico

NEW SPAIN

CUBA

HISPANIOLA

Vespucci

OCEAN

2nd

4th

Caribbean

Sea

Vespucci

3rd

Columbus 4th voyage 1502

Columbus 2nd voyage 1493

CAPE VERDE
IS.

AFRICA

Columbus 3rd voyage 1498

NEW
GRANADA

Vespucci 1499

PERU

SOUTH

Cabral 1500

PACIFIC

AMERICA

BRAZIL

OCEAN

Explorers'
routes

Colonial
powers
c. 1650

English

French

Dutch

Spanish

Portuguese

VOYAGES OF DISCOVERY

killed, so they might continue to serve their master in the next world. Farming, hunting, and fishing provided these southeastern people with abundant foods, and they dined on such exotic fare as bear ribs and root jelly. Two dishes that were destined to become part of American Southern cooking, hominy and corn bread, were invented by these Indians.

In the heartland of the United States, between the Mississippi River and the Rocky Mountains, lived the Plains Indians. They dwelt in circular huts covered with earth, grass, or animal hides. They grew corn, gathered wild rice, and hunted buffalo. The hunting of buffalo became more widespread after Europeans brought horses to the New World. Before then it was done on foot, a difficult and unreliable method on the open plains, where buffalo could spot a hunter at a great distance and flee. Many of the characteristics of the Indians pictured in Hollywood movies were derived from these Plains Indians, and even then the movie version is only vaguely true. These tribes wore warbonnets of eagle feathers and ornamented their clothing with beads and porcupine quills. Their chiefs earned their preeminence through courage or wisdom, but exerted only an advisory influence over their followers. The limited power of many Indian chieftains was understood by few European colonists. Frequently a colonist would reach an agreement with a chief, but if the chief failed to make his tribe abide by the agreement, Europeans often regarded the failure as a treacherous breach of faith.

Of all the Indian tribes in the United States, perhaps the most advanced in Western terms when the Europeans arrived were

The Algonquin Indians raised various grain crops in addition to hunting. They lived in rectangular bark-covered houses, as depicted in this sixteenth century watercolor by John White.

the tribes of the Southwest—the Hopis, the Zuñis, and the Pueblos. Grouped together as the Pueblo people (after the Spanish word *pueblo,* which means "town"), these tribes were peace-loving farmers who lived in modernistic-looking apartment buildings built into cliff walls or on the top of plateaus. Constructed of stone or adobe (dried mud), some of these buildings were four stories high and looked down upon spacious streets and squares. Located under the squares were hidden chambers in which priests held secret meetings. Pueblo culture was saturated with religion. The men devoted as much as half of their time to performing rituals with brilliantly colored prayer sticks and feathered masks. These ceremonies were directed toward helping the community by magically healing the sick, bringing rain during periods of drought, and establishing peace and harmony. So community-minded were the Pueblos that all wealth was divided equally. No distinctions in money, work, or prestige were allowed among the inhabitants of any village.

INDIAN CONTRIBUTIONS TO EUROPEAN CULTURE

One of the most valuable gifts the red man gave the settler was a range of foods the European had never before known. Most important was maize, or Indian corn, which became a staple food in many parts of the world. Corn was an American innovation, discovered thousands of years ago when Indian farmers began to cultivate tiny cobs of wild corn until eventually, after much trial and error, big, plump yellow maize was developed. Easy and economical to grow, corn was an enormous boon to the early European settlers. Other foods first found in the Americas were squash, white and sweet potatoes, many varieties of beans, peanuts, peppers, vanilla, tomatoes, pumpkins, avocados, pineapples,

7

and cacao (the plant processed into chocolate).

The Indians made many contributions to later civilization in the Western Hemisphere. About sixty drugs originated in the Americas. From these drugs were derived cocaine, novocaine, and quinine, to mention a few. Many utilitarian objects which came into wide use were designed by the Indians, notably canoes, snowshoes, sleds, parkas, moccasins, and hammocks. And today, when pollution threatens to destroy the American countryside, experts are studying the ways in which the Indians coexisted with nature for thousands of years in perfect balance and harmony.

FIRST COLONIZATION IN THE AMERICAS

Ships preparing for departure to America from a port in Lisbon, Portugal.

Before the compass was known to Europeans, a Norse captain, Leif Ericson, happened upon the New World. Setting out from Greenland about A.D. 1000, he came upon Labrador and Nova Scotia. The Norse, however, had no interest in these vast territories and the discovery of lands lying in the west was soon recalled only in folk tales.

The next explorations of the Western Hemisphere by Europeans came later, beginning with Christopher Columbus. These long voyages would not have been possible without new advances in navigation and technical skills.

Columbus' first journey, and all the Spanish voyages to the New World that followed, owed a large debt to earlier Portuguese advances in navigation. Portugal had set Europe a striking example of courage and intelligence in the exploits of its explorers of the fifteenth century. The figure most responsible for Portugal's success was Prince Henry the Navigator. He consulted the greatest geographers, astronomers, mapmakers, and mathematicians of his day. Equipped with the knowledge of these experts and the writings of ancient Greek and Roman geographers, Prince Henry's captains explored the western coast of Africa and discovered the archipelago lying off the coast of Africa made up of the Azores, the Madeiras, and the Canaries. By 1488, Bartholomeu Dias had reached the southern tip of Africa and found the eastward sea route to India. The Orient remained the goal of the Portuguese, as of all other explorers, for the next two centuries because of its rich supplies of spices. The Orient also possessed jewels and other luxury goods, and gold and silver. Spices were more highly prized, however, for in the days before refrigeration, meats spoiled quickly, particularly in warm climates, and spices were added to meat dishes not so much to enhance the flavor as to disguise it.

Portuguese triumphs encouraged the sailors of other nations. The introduction of the magnetic compass made navigation simpler for long voyages, as did improvements in the design of ocean-going vessels (a new, highly maneuverable sailing vessel called the caravel began to be used by all Portuguese and Spanish navigators in the Middle Ages).

"By the marvelous daring of Christopher Columbus," a European wrote in 1516, "almost another world has been discovered and added to the company of Christians." Columbus himself never realized that he had found this new world. He was certain that by sailing west he had simply charted a new way of reaching China, Japan, and India. Although he sailed four times to the Americas between 1492 and 1500 and saw Cuba, Haiti, a host of little Caribbean islands, and parts of Central and South America, the only land he was willing to admit *might* be new was South America, which he thought was probably the Garden of Eden.

COLUMBUS

Christopher Columbus was born in 1451 in the Italian town of Genoa, the son of a poor wool weaver. He began sailing when still a boy and as a young man started to dream of one day leading an expedition across the Atlantic to the Orient, or as Europeans of his day called it, "the Indies." He first proposed such a journey to the King of Portugal. At that time Portugal was the European country most interested in exploration, and Portuguese navigators had already explored much of the western coast of Africa. After reviewing Columbus' proposal, a committee of the king's mathematicians, astronomers, and geographers decided, correctly, that Columbus had underestimated the length of the voyage from Europe to Asia—and turned him down.

Columbus had based his calculations on those of the ancient Greek philosopher, Aristotle, who mistakenly wrote that one could cross from Spain to the Indies in a few days. Another authority used by Columbus was a medieval Moslem geographer named Alfragan. Columbus misread and mistranslated Alfragan, estimating that the world was 25 percent smaller than it actually is. Armed with these erroneous facts, Columbus approached the rulers of Spain, Isabella of Castile and Ferdinand of Aragon. After four tedious years of arguing with Spanish experts, Columbus finally received the queen's approval to undertake a voyage across the Atlantic. He was assigned three ships named the *Nina,* the *Pinta* and the *Santa Maria,* a crew of ninety men and boys, and a budget equaling about $14,000.

THE FIRST VOYAGE

Columbus set sail from Spain on August 3, 1492, stopping briefly at the Canary Islands. Early in September he began the long Atlantic crossing. Columbus knew little or nothing about celestial navigation (the science of locating a ship's position by its relation to the position of the stars). He gauged his direction with a compass and estimated his speed by watching bubbles or weeds floating by. The voyage over was uneventful except for a minor mutiny on October 10 aboard the flagship, the *Santa Maria,* which Columbus quickly quelled. After traveling more than 3,000 miles in

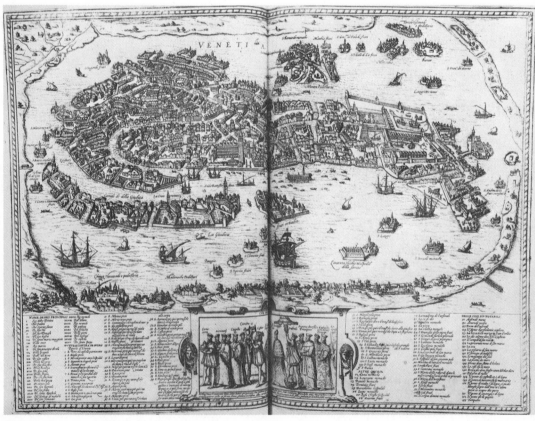

Sixteenth-century Venice.

33 days, a lookout on the *Pinta* sighted land at 2 A.M. on October 12. The first bit of land discovered in the New World was one of the Bahamas, which Columbus named San Salvador ("Holy Saviour"); it is now called Watlings Island.

When the crew went ashore, they were startled to see naked people running toward them. Columbus later wrote his patrons, Ferdinand and Isabella: "In order that we might win good friendship, because I knew that they were a people who could better be freed and converted to our Holy Faith by love than by force, I gave to some of them red caps and to some glass beads, which they hung on their necks, and many other things of slight value, in which they took much pleasure; they remained so much our friends that it was a marvel; and later they came swimming to the ships' boats in which we were, and brought us parrots and cotton thread in skeins and darts and many other things. . . . They ought to be good servants and of good skill, for I see that they repeat very quickly all that is said to them; and I believe that they would easily be made Christians, because it seemed to me that they belonged to no religion."

This pleasant encounter between the people of two different worlds in no way suggested what was soon to come: within a few years the Spanish would exterminate or exploit millions of Indians and plunder their land for gold.

THE ADMIRAL'S DELUSIONS

Columbus was so eager to believe that he had landed in Asia that he ignored all evidence to the contrary. Every day he and his men encountered something new, goods

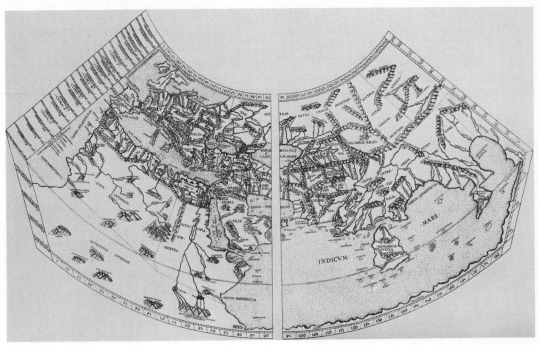

A map published in Rome in 1490 which erroneously shows China directly west of Europe. The error led Columbus to believe that he could reach India by sailing west from Europe.

and foods never before seen by European travelers, even in the Orient. Columbus and his crew saw hammocks and were much impressed with these simple, comfortable swinging beds. In Cuba they saw Indians smoking cigars which the natives called *tobacos;* soon thousands of Europeans would be smoking the new plant. The Europeans tasted new foods such as sweet potatoes, pineapples, and strange nuts and fruits. On a second voyage they saw their first cannibals. On a third, they met Central Americans who turned their backs when they spoke, habitually chewed a herb that rotted their teeth, and lived on pineapple wine and sardines.

None of these extraordinary findings could convince Columbus that his New World was not the fabled Orient. When the people of Cuba advised him to look for gold in the center of Cuba ("Cubanacan"), he thought they were talking of "El Gran Can," the Great Khan whom a Venetian traveler, Marco Polo, had met in China in the thirteenth century. Columbus sent into the interior a delegation led by an interpreter who could speak Arabic (Arabic was then considered the mother of all languages and Columbus felt certain it would be understood by the Chinese Emperor). After this fruitless expedition, Columbus pursued the notion that the western end of Cuba was Malaya and that an island the Indians called Cibao was Japan or at least Sheba (a land mentioned in the Old Testament).

Although many Europeans gradually came to suspect that Columbus had found a new world, he himself never realized this and today the fact that we still call natives of the Western Hemisphere "Indians," and refer to the islands of the Caribbean as "the West Indies," bears witness to the great admiral's mistake. The full extent of Columbus' error was not known until 1521, well after his death, when the Spanish navigator Ferdinand Magellan headed an expedition that sailed around the world for the first time. Although Magellan died in

the Philippines, his crew came back with clear reports that indicated the full extent of the globe.

SPANISH SETTLEMENTS

Within a few years after Columbus' first trip to America, Spanish ships were regularly crossing the Atlantic, carrying supplies and colonists to the New World and bringing cargoes of gold and silver back to Europe. In fact, on Columbus' second voyage in 1493, he led a fleet of seventeen ships and some 1,500 colonists and laid the foundations for Spain's empire in the Western Hemisphere. These expeditions were motivated by two equally strong impulses: greed for gold and religious idealism. In one of his letters to Ferdinand and Isabella, Columbus explicitly wrote: "I say that Your Highnesses ought not to consent that any foreigner do business or set foot here, except Christian Catholics, since this was the end and the beginning of the enterprise, that it should be for the enhancement and glory of the Christian religion, nor should anyone who is not a good Christian come to these parts." Such sentiments appealed greatly to the pious Isabella, who relished the idea that the millions of inhabitants of "the Indies" could be converted to Catholicism and saved. Even the gold that poured into her coffers she intended for religious deeds. Isabella longed to renew the Crusades to free Jerusalem from the control of the Moslems.

Religious idealism, however, did not occupy the thoughts of most of the Spanish conquistadors who followed Columbus. They subjugated more and more inhabitants of the New World through the most ruthless of tactics, and once they secured control over a new region, exploited its people and riches without scruple. Almost every year a new territory was added to the Spanish domains. Columbus himself explored many of the Caribbean islands: his principal discoveries were Cuba, Puerto Rico, and Hispaniola. In 1498, Amerigo Vespucci, a Florentine who lived in Seville, sailed under the Spanish flag along the coast of South America. (His glowing account of his voyage led a German geographer to publish, in 1507, a map of this vast new land mass and label it with the Latinized form of Amerigo's name—*America*.) Ponce de Leon sailed along the east coast of Florida in 1512, becoming the first European to set foot on what is now the United States. A year later Vasco Nuñez de Balboa penetrated the jungles of Panama and when he came out on the other side, discovered the Pacific Ocean. Between 1519 and 1521, Hernando Cortes conquered the Aztecs of Mexico. Ten years later Francisco Pizarro overcame the Incas of Peru. Thus, half a century after Columbus' first voyage, Spain was in control of a vast empire.

The means used to obtain this empire were almost always disastrous to the Indians and invariably enriched the Spanish. The two richest territories captured, Mexico and Peru, were seized by unusually small forces. Cortes, leading only a few hundred men, made a prisoner of the Aztec ruler, Montezuma, and ruled through him. According to a Spanish account of 1519, titled with unconscious irony, *The Pleasant History of the Conquest of the West Indies,* Cortes first befriended the Mexican king and then imprisoned him: "There was never Greek nor Roman, nor any other nation since the names of kings was ordained, did give the like enterprise as Hernando Cortes did, in taking Montezuma prisoner in his own house, being a most mighty king in a most strong fort among infinite people, Cortes having but only 450 companions." Outraged by Cortes' plundering of Montezuma's treasures, as well as by heavy Spanish taxes, the Mexican people rose up and killed their king. This uprising gave Cortes an excellent excuse for completing his conquest of Mexico. His conduct of the venture was governed by greed. Later Spaniards carved

out huge estates for themselves in Mexico and conscripted Indian laborers to till their fields, but this was not for Cortes who asserted openly, "I came to get gold, not to till the soil like a peasant."

Pizarro was moved by similar considerations in his conquest of Peru. After hearing Indian rumors of the wealth of the Peruvian capital of Cuzco, Pizarro, imitating Cortes, made friendly overtures to the Inca monarch, Atahuallpa. When Atahuallpa came to the Spanish camp with a retinue of unarmed men, the Spanish opened fire on the Indians and captured their king. The booty extracted by Pizarro's men from Inca temples and treasuries exceeded even the plunder of Mexico.

Why did these two empires fall so easily before the small bands of Spanish adventurers? First, the Spanish were mounted on horses and used powerful weapons. Gunpowder was unknown to the Indians. Second, both the Aztecs and the Incas had religious legends about white-skinned gods; they feared the newcomers as "men from Heaven." Third, the Indians had no immunity to the bacteria and viruses brought to the New World by the Spanish. In the century after the conquest of Mexico, the population was decimated by disease. In Hispaniola (the island now comprising Haiti and the Dominican Republic), which had over one million Indians in 1492, smallpox reduced the population within 20 years to one hundred thousand. One of the most important reasons for the defeat of the Aztecs and the Incas may have been that their leaders had been in power for only a short time, and both, being of a despotic character, commanded little popular support.

TREATY OF TORDESILLAS

Ferdinand and Isabella had immediately sensed the value, if not the full extent, of their new domains and secured exclusive title to them through a number of diplomatic moves. The first step occurred on

May 4, 1493, when Pope Alexander VI (who happened to be Spanish) granted to Spain all lands west of a north-south line drawn through the Atlantic Ocean (38 degrees longitude). At the same time, Portugal was presented with all lands ruled by non-Christians lying to the east of this line. In effect, this decision handed the Western Hemisphere to Spain, and Africa and Asia to Portugal. The Portuguese, however, were not entirely satisfied, and the next year they signed the Treaty of Tordesillas with Spain. This treaty shifted the line farther west, to 46 degrees 30 minutes. The new line sliced off the eastern bulge of South America, giving Brazil to the Portuguese.

The Portuguese did not, at first, apply themselves as assiduously as the Spanish to developing their new possessions. The Spanish had good reason to devote themselves single-mindedly to the venture. Before the end of the sixteenth century, gold and silver from Mexico and Peru were adding thirty million dollars' worth of treasure every year to the European economy, and a fifth of that sum went by law into the royal coffers. By the middle of the century, two fabulously rich silver mines had been discovered, the Zacatecas in Mexico and the Potosí in Bolivia. Potosí soon became the most thriving mining city in the world, attracting a population of 120,000, more people than in any European city except London and Paris. Aided by recent technological advances in extracting silver ore from its compounds, Spanish miners were able to ship back to Europe in the 1590s more than ten million ounces of silver a year.

The wealth of Spain was further enriched by cattle hides from the colonies and crops of tobacco and sugar. The revenues from these products eventually surpassed even the value of New World silver and gold. Spanish overseers compelled millions of Indians to plant and harvest tobacco and sugar cane. When this labor force was thinned by disease, the Spanish turned to the use of imported slave labor. Throughout the Ca-

Early drawing of a confrontation between the South American Indians and the Spanish.

ribbean and in parts of South America, Negro slaves were brought from Africa by Portuguese or Dutch traders to serve in the fields (enslavement of Indians was forbidden by the Spanish government).

America was too dazzling a jewel for the Spanish monarchy to allow very much self-government there. To the end of extending strong royal control the king imposed a complex hierarchy of officials upon South America and Mexico. In Lima, a viceroy governed all of South America except for Brazil (which was Portuguese) and Venezuela. Another viceroy situated in Mexico City represented the crown in Mexico, Central America, the Caribbean islands and the West Indies. In the major cities, Spanish courts of law administered justice. Still smaller governmental units were under the control of agents appointed by Spain's monarch. From Spain, two large councils administered colonial policy. All of this bureaucratic machinery enhanced the prestige of the Spanish king at home and, at least in theory, ensured his personal direction of affairs in the colonies. Spanish America became the first important colonial possession. True, the Portuguese and Dutch were becoming masters in parts of Africa and Asia, but they were establishing trading posts, not true colonies. Spain, by contrast, sent thousands of her nationals to live in America. These men intermarried with the Indians, built cities, churches, and universities, and raised families that regarded the New World as their native land.

RIVAL CLAIMS TO AMERICA

Spain's title to America did not go unchallenged. The Spanish had come to the New World looking for a short sea route to the Indies. They discovered instead more abundant quantities of gold and silver than even the Orient possessed. These discoveries whetted the appetite of the other European powers—France, The Netherlands, and England—for precious metals and overseas empires. The consolidation of strong nation-states in Western Europe by the sixteenth century isolated Europeans from each other and created a strong sense of nationalism within each country. A race among these nations for power, wealth, prestige, and competition for empire could hardly have been avoided.

FRENCH EXPLORATIONS

In 1524, Francis I, King of France, sent an Italian navigator named Giovanni Verrazano to North America. Three years earlier Magellan's men had returned from their trip around the world establishing unquestionably that America was not India, but rather a huge land mass blocking the way to the Orient. Having only a hazy knowledge of North America, geographers imagined a Northwest Passage that might be discovered through the continent, or north of it. Verrazano was ordered to search for this shortcut. He cruised along the Atlantic Coast of North America, from the Gulf of Mexico to the St. Lawrence River, but failed to find a passage to Asia.

Undaunted, Francis I dispatched Jacques Cartier on three voyages in 1534, 1535, and 1541, but this time the quest was not so much for the elusive passage to the Orient as for gold and diamonds, which the French confidently expected to find in a northern kingdom said to be called "Saguenay." Although Cartier sailed up the St. Lawrence as far as Montreal, the fabled city was not to be found, for in fact it never existed. The French, however, were more successful in their search for riches during this period, when they raided Spanish galleons bearing silver and gold back to Europe. The French corsairs became such a potent threat to Spanish ships that Spain built a fort at St. Augustine, Florida, in 1565, to guard the entrance to the Caribbean, thus becoming the first European settlement in what would become the United States.

In the second half of the sixteenth century, France was internally divided by civil wars and religious conflicts, which prevented the French from taking an interest in the New World until 1603. In that year, Samuel de Champlain sailed up the St. Lawrence River, and in 1608 built a fort at Quebec, the first permanent French settlement in North America. Soon French traders were exchanging brandy and firearms for furs, particularly beaver, which was turned into felt hats for fashionable French ladies and gentlemen. By the 1680s, French explorers, traders, and priests had gained control over much of eastern Canada, the Great Lakes, and the Mississippi Valley, which in 1682 they named "Louisiana" after their king, Louis XIV. The king never succeeded in convincing Frenchmen to settle North America in large numbers

in this era. French settlements were never much more than sparsely populated fur-trading centers.

DUTCH EXPLOITS

Like the first French voyage to the New World, the first Dutch exploration set out to discover a Northwest Passage to the Pacific leading to India. In 1609, 85 years after Verrazano's unsuccessful mission, Holland dispatched an Englishman, Henry Hudson, in his ship the *Half Moon*. Hudson sailed up what was to be called the Hudson River and explored much of the Canadian wilderness surrounding the body of water now called Hudson's Bay.

The Dutch continued to search for a westward sea route to the Orient. Yet in 1498, more than a hundred years earlier, the Portuguese navigator, Vasco da Gama

Indians bringing beaver pelts to the French.

had found a much shorter route from Europe to Asia, around the southern tip of Africa. Why didn't the Dutch follow the same route? To answer this question we need only recall that the Pope had assigned all of Africa and Asia to the Portuguese, who zealously protected their sea route around Africa and across the Indian Ocean against all rivals. Portugal, however, could not possibly guard every access to the Orient by invaders from across the Pacific. Knowing this, the French, Dutch, and English all wanted to discover a Northwest Passage to the Orient through North America. (The southwest passage around the southern tip of South America, which Magellan had charted, was too perilous and took too long.)

After their initial failure, the Dutch quickly forgot about the Northwest Passage and settled down to something at which they were expert, raid and trade. In the first few decades of the seventeenth century, the Dutch pirated so many Spanish ships, ransacking them for gold and silver, that by 1630 The Netherlands had virtually destroyed Spanish shipping and established a monopoly of its own. As Spanish control over the Caribbean began to wane, the Dutch moved in and took over the islands of Curaçao and St. Eustatius. For a while, they also occupied hundreds of miles of the coast of Brazil. These outposts in Latin America and the Caribbean served as convenient centers for selling slaves (who were bought by the Dutch from Portuguese slave traders in Africa).

In North America, the Dutch set up fur-trading posts in Manhattan and Albany. In 1626, a group of merchants representing the Dutch West India Company purchased Manhattan from the local Indians for goods worth only a few dollars. By 1629 the company was granting great estates (patroonships) along the Hudson River to Dutchmen who, it was envisioned, would become permanent residents of the valley. This plan to attract settlers never became popu-

lar, however. In 1664 the English captured all Dutch holdings in North America.

Even after the Dutch lost their possessions they remained an economic force. The Netherlands had a population of only two million in the middle of the seventeenth century, but its people were the most enterprising merchants in the world. The trading network of the Dutch spread like a web over all the globe. Amsterdam, the Dutch commercial center, reflected its cosmopolitan interests in its books, which were printed in every European language, and in its lively French and English language newspapers. Aggressive and practical, Dutch merchants were not prevented from becoming immensely wealthy by the fact that their nation was tiny and devoid of natural resources. The Dutch were middlemen. They bought spices, cotton, and tea in the Orient, and sugar, tobacco, and furs in America, and sold them in Europe. They also merchandised the products of the Continent, transporting lumber and copper from northern to southern Europe, and returning with wine and silk. The Dutch merchants were so successful that they shifted the center of European trade from the Mediterranean, where it had been since the Middle Ages, to the Atlantic. Commanding access to the Baltic Sea, the Rhine River, and the English Channel, Amsterdam became the nerve center of the world's shipping routes.

ENGLISH VOYAGES

The English first came to the shores of the New World, like all others, in search of the nonexistent Northwest Passage. In 1497, only 5 years after Columbus' first voyage, John Cabot sailed to the mouth of the St. Lawrence River, looking for a route to China. Others took up the same task, Martin Frobisher in 1576, John Davis in 1585, and between 1602 and 1632, a series of other captains in search of the passage in the Arctic. Although the Northwest Passage turned out to be a will-of-the-wisp, English explorers were *still* searching for it a hundred years later, as late as 1746, only 30 years before the Declaration of Independence.

All of these early English ventures accomplished nothing. Early explorers and colonists were looking for monetary gain alone, and greed seemed not to be a sufficiently sound motive for establishing a permanent settlement in North America. Later colonists, motivated by the desire to escape poverty and prison, to gain land, or practice religion without persecution, were more successful in establishing permanent settlements.

THE EUROPEAN BACKGROUND

Why did Europeans come to the Western Hemisphere? Why did they stay and create colonies? What function were the colonies supposed to serve? How did many of the struggles raging in Europe spill over into the New World and shape its destiny? None of these questions can be answered without taking a closer look at the great changes that were taking place in the Old World.

THE COMMERCIAL REVOLUTION

Colonization of the New World occurred only when the time was ripe for it in Europe. Before the fifteenth century, when Columbus found the New World and thousands of adventurers were drawn to its exotic shores, there was little interest in colonization in faroff territories. The excitement that began in 1492 can be explained in part by the economic change that occurred in Europe between the eleventh and fifteenth centuries.

In A.D. 1000, most of Europe was divided into small duchies, principalities, and estates ruled by a powerful hereditary nobility. The chief economic unit was the manor, a castle and village, surrounded by

fields. The manor was almost completely self-supporting. All the food products or labor required to sustain it were supplied by the villagers themselves. These villagers were serfs, or servants whose lives were dominated by their local lord, for they were his personal property. Serfs were in bondage to the soil and were never permitted to leave the manor. They married only with the lord's consent and when they died most of their pitiful belongings were seized by him. In return for a guarantee of personal safety, much of the serf's time was devoted to serving his master primarily in plowing and tilling his fields several months a year, repairing the fortifications of his castle, and fighting as foot soldiers in his frequent battles with neighboring lords.

THE CRUSADES

These conditions began to change slowly about the time of the Crusades. Between 1095 and 1291, many Christian nobles and their retainers, under the leadership of successive Popes, attempted to recover Palestine, and particularly the holy city of Jerusalem, from the Moslems, and to liberate Middle Eastern Christians being held captive by Islam. The Moslems, followers of the religious leader Mohammed, had joined together in effective armies and spread the Islamic faith over all of North Africa, and most of Spain by the eighth century. By the end of the tenth century, the Moslems had conquered Greece, Persia, and much of India, and were threatening to overrun Europe itself.

The Christian offensive against the Moslems was ultimately unsuccessful, but the Crusades had an important effect upon European trade and, indirectly, changed the European way of life. The Italian trade centers of Pisa, Genoa, and Venice profited greatly from the transportation of Crusaders and pilgrims to the Holy Land on ships that returned laden with luxury goods: fine

Damascus steel, silks from China, spices from the Indies, and rugs and costly dyed fabrics from the Levant (the name given by the Europeans to the Middle East, meaning, "the land where sun rises"). Following the failure of the Crusades, Levantine trade routes fell under the control of the Turks, who had taken the leadership in the Islamic drive on Europe. Normal trade routes were disrupted and as a result the cost of oriental goods leaped upward. Europeans began to look for new routes to the Indies to avoid encounters with the Turks.

Most modern historians believe the Crusades caused the quickening of European trade; a few, however, disagree, believing that the Crusades resulted from the growth of Italian shipping and the creation of more orderly and stable European governments. Regardless of which theory is correct, the time of the Crusades was one of significant economic change.

THE RISE OF CITIES

Cities grew larger and more influential partly as a result of the increase in European trade during the Crusades. To raise funds for the long voyage to the Holy Land, feudal knights sold towns the right to incorporate. For a large fee, townsfolk were able to buy from their ruling baron or bishop a charter granting them the right to levy taxes, enroll a militia, and name their own officials. The growth of cities in turn encouraged the expansion of commerce. An increase in city dwellers saw the development of more craftsmen to produce goods for trade, and expanding trade heightened the demand for manufactured goods. Nobles eager to buy the new products raised money for this purpose by selling freedom to their serfs. More and more of these freed serfs moved into the towns, thus increasing their population.

Seventeenth-century Amsterdam.

19

A conception of Americans by Europeans who had never been to the New World.

MERCHANTS

As trade between towns, countries, and even continents increased, the merchant became an increasingly important figure. In the medieval period, goods changed hands, usually by the barter method rather than by money payment, at tiny fairs held in small towns. (Roads were poor, transportation slow, bandits were everywhere on the highways, and every petty official taxed the products passing through his territory.) Transporting goods from one small duchy to another was costly. The only items brought from distant regions were small luxury items such as Saracen carpets, dyes from the Middle East, and silks and glass from Syria. During and after the Crusades, however, long-distance trade became safer and cheaper. Money came into widespread use, providing the means for more people to pay for goods without relying on the barter system.

During the fifteenth and sixteenth centuries, while the New World was being colonized, the merchant class rose to a position of great importance. The new sea routes to the Orient and the Americas brought a great upsurge in trade, especially in such bulk commodities as lumber, rice, tea, and sugar. Heavy industries, such as the building of ships and manufacture of cannons, were stimulated by colonization. Emphasis slowly shifted from small groups of craftsmen making goods intended primarily for local consumption, to the production of goods intended for distant markets. At the same time that the economy expanded, the population of Europe more than doubled.

Intercontinental trade, as well as increased trade between European trading centers, enlarged the role of the middleman or merchant. The merchant of this day often functioned also as a banker and manufacturer. He might make the goods he sold, but if he did not, he frequently financed their production. The Medici family of Florence, for example, were merchants who not only bought and sold goods but manufactured Italian silk, became international bankers, and even managed mines owned by the Pope. Merchants became so influential that by the sixteenth century they stood at the very pinnacle of society, outranked only by noblemen.

How did these successful European merchants affect the development of America? In two direct ways: by their subsequent dependence on America for resources and commerce and by making colonization possible in the first place. The merchants succeeded in building international trade until it became a mainstay of the European economy, so that the discovery of America was of great importance, offering as it did a source of new raw materials for European industry, as well as a potentially large market. Also, the rise of the merchant class gave many Europeans the means to finance the expensive colonization of the Western Hemisphere. As described in the next chapter, the first English colonies in North America were backed by English merchants who pooled their resources. Not the English government, but private companies, with the crown's approval, were the sponsors of the first settlers of North America.

LABORERS

Less directly, the ascendancy of European merchants affected America's future by creating a large group of discontented, impoverished laborers ready to forsake the Old World and try their luck in the New. Soon after Columbus discovered America, the Spanish began to bring back to Europe shiploads of gold and silver. So much precious metal flowed into circulation that widespread inflation resulted. Prices rose in the sixteenth century, but wages lagged far behind. In 1560 workers in Spain, France, Germany, and England were earning as much as 50 percent less, in terms of purchasing power, than their grandparents had earned a hundred years earlier. Merchants, however, benefited from the rise in prices, for the value of their goods kept pace with the rise in prices. As a result, the gulf between the wealthy middle class and poor laborers widened year by year.

Discontented workers tried to form primitive labor unions and strike for higher wages, but in almost every case government authorities suppressed them, or industrialists banded together and agreed never to employ troublemakers. Other social factors were working against laborers. In the twelfth and thirteenth centuries, a craftsman could get a job with a master jeweler, tinsmith, or carpenter. For years the young man would serve his master as an apprentice and finally graduate to the status of journeyman. If he worked hard and learned his trade well, a man who started out as an apprentice could expect someday to become a master craftsman himself. Such success stories were not at all uncommon. But by the sixteenth century this system had broken down. Master craftsmen tended increasingly to simply hand their positions down to their sons so that journeymen had little hope of ever reaching the status of master. Unable to grasp a share of the riches pouring in from the New World, many disgruntled laborers were willing to risk unknown hazards for American wealth.

THE RISE OF NATIONAL MONARCHIES

Another development of the fifteenth and sixteenth centuries that was to prove as influential as the ascendancy of the merchant class, and which had an equal impact on the New World, was the consolidation of power by the kings of France, Spain, and England. In the Middle Ages, kings were dependent on the cooperation of their nobles and each feudal lord had almost absolute control over his own lands. He could start a war whenever he chose, tax his subjects, and administer laws as he saw fit. Shortly before Columbus' discovery of America, however, the position of the king began to change.

SPAIN

In Spain royalty gained power first by uniting the nation geographically. In 1450, Spain was more an idea than a reality. The country was divided into three separate realms, the Christian kingdoms of Aragon in the Northeast, Castile in the center of the peninsula, and the Moslem state of Granada in the South. By their marriage in 1469, Ferdinand, heir to the throne of Aragon, and Isabel, future queen of Castile brought together two pieces of this jigsaw puzzle. The third was added when the army of the king and queen caused Granada to capitulate on January 2, 1492, only 6 months before Columbus sailed. Ferdinand and Isabella strengthened their power by consolidating Spain. Nevertheless, royal power was still not as strong as it was to become in the centuries that followed. One problem in the fifteenth century was that the people of Castile and Aragon spoke languages so dissimilar they could not understand one another. Also, Ferdinand and Isabella were quite different in temperament: she was one of the most pious Catholic monarchs ever to reign, obsessed with the idea of purifying the Spanish monasteries and priesthood of corruption; he, on the other hand, was only vaguely religious and far more interested in meddling in international political intrigues. Despite their conflicts, the king and queen became powerful figures at the beginning of the sixteenth century. Their heirs continued to control the Spanish throne, partly because of the immense wealth reaching them from the New World.

FRANCE

Immense gains in royal power were also achieved in France. There, power gradually shifted from the townsmen, nobles, and Catholic bishops to the monarch. The growing middle class produced by the economic transformation of Europe became the natural ally of the ambitious royal houses of Europe. The middle class had wealth for the fifteenth-century kings to tap in building centralized power. In return the monarchs offered the townspeople protection and support of trade, as well as administrative and military positions. The nobility, fearing that strong centralized power in France would weaken their own influence, offered more resistance to royal pretensions, but were gradually forced to yield the power of taxation over their lands so that taxation became the exclusive right of the French king. Nobles finally were willing to surrender this prerogative to the king in exchange for their own immunity from taxation. Since noblemen and clergymen did not pay taxes, the burden fell partly on the middle class, but mainly on the peasants.

The French king needed these tax revenues to support his armies. Before the fifteenth and sixteenth centuries, European kings had seldom maintained professional armies. But in a time of almost constant warfare between European states, the French king built a permanent military force composed largely of paid soldiers, the bulk of whom were foreigners (Germans in particular). Spanish rulers began to maintain similar large forces of mercenaries. Armies of this type increased royal authority and helped kings rule, rather than simply reign.

The French monarchy also strengthened its control of the state by limiting the power of the Catholic Church in regard to nonreligious affairs (a policy also begun in Spain and England). Church authority over official appointments in France was removed to royal hands. The king's need for revenue to maintain an army and purchase goods on the commercial market also dictated a policy of greater control over Church funds and an end to the large flow of gold and silver into Vatican coffers. No fifteenth-century monarch challenged the centuries-old religious authority of Rome, but the kings demanded reduction of the Church's influence over secular matters.

Finally, the French king was able to forge his nation into a centralized state, with himself at the head, by more directly administering his laws. The number of royal officers greatly increased, and the royal will was expressed in even the smallest towns by the king's judges and administrators, who were known as the king's lieutenants. In the past, every town, bishopric, or feudal estate had had its own rules and regulations; now the law of the king became the law of France.

ENGLAND

In England, the crown had used tactics similar to those of the French kings to unite the realm. In addition, the king's law was upheld in every locality by justices of the peace. Unlike their counterparts in France (the king's lieutenants) who were salaried, the English justices of the peace served without pay. Although voluntary service developed a tradition of public spirit, amateur status made it easier for the justices to ignore the king when they disapproved of a royal law and the king could not force his unpaid public servants to execute laws they objected to. The English king's authority was also checked by Parliament. Whereas the people's representatives in France counted for little (they did not even meet between 1484 and 1560), the English Parliament was a force to be reckoned with. Parliament's strength was in its control of taxation. Unlike France, where only part of the population was taxed, England taxed all of its citizens. In return for their money, however, the nobility and wealthy merchants had established their right to have a voice in government. This right was later to be expressed in England's American colonies by the slogan, "No taxation without representation."

23

In sixteenth-century France and Spain, then, the rulers were on their way to becoming absolute monarchs; in England, the throne was being shaped into a constitutional monarchy. In spite of these differences, all three monarchies were stronger than ever before and out of their sovereignty came the birth of the modern state. At last, France, Spain, and England were able to act as nations, not simply as collections of small principalities.

How did the new kind of European monarchy and concept of nationhood affect America? In the case of Spain, for example, the king's right to tax supplied funds to send expeditions to the New World, his right to maintain an army gave him the military strength to protect his American colonies, and his right to make laws enabled him to regulate trade between the mother country and her possessions in the Western Hemisphere.

Economic and political changes in Europe, important as they were, do not give us the whole background for the colonization of North America. To round out the picture we must look at one of the greatest upheavals in European history, the Protestant Reformation.

Today, when even the most devout people make countless daily decisions without

Martin Luther preaching. Popes and monks are in the mouth of Hell, on the right, and salvation in the form of the crucifix is on the left.

referring to religious doctrine for guidance, it may be hard to understand the obsession with religion, even the fine points of religious ritual, that dominated all earlier centuries. Columbus regarded his discovery of the New World as a triumph for Christendom, and Popes were powerful enough to assign whole continents to the nations they favored. One man's protest against Catholic theology and the influence of the Papal hierarchy at a strategic moment changed the course of history. That man was Martin Luther, a sixteenth-century German monk, gifted with an eloquent pen and ruled by powerful religious convictions.

MARTIN LUTHER

Initially, Luther never intended to break with the Catholic Church. However, a private crisis of faith led him into open opposition to the central tenets of Catholicism. He was troubled by the thought that his own sinfulness was so pervasive that none of the outward observances of the Catholic Church, basically the seven sacraments, could bring him the inner grace of God and enable him to find peace of mind. Through a study of the Scriptures he found a solution in the idea that absolute faith in God's love was all one needed in order to be able to accept all that resulted from God's will, whatever it might be.

This idea, known as "justification by faith," brought Luther into open conflict with Rome on matters of doctrine and church organization. In 1517 he began to question the Church's right to allow the sale of an indulgence. According to Catholic theology, Christ, Mary, and the saints had accumulated excess grace, which they had bestowed on the Church. The Church's power to dispense this additional grace to its members is called an indulgence. If a person received an indulgence, it was believed, the number of days he would have to pass in purgatory before entering heaven

Sieben köpffe Martini Luthers
Vom Hochwirdigen Sacrament des Altars / Durch
Doctor Jo. Cocleus.

Luther caricatured by his enemies as a seven-headed monster.

would be reduced. In theory, priests were not to sell indulgences, but at this period in history Catholics were strongly urged to make a cash offering upon receiving these "Papal letters."

Luther was offended by one particularly vulgar purveyor of indulgences, Johann Tetzel, who shamelessly announced that an indulgence was an "easy conscience ticket" and a surefire method of assuring not only one's own salvation but also that of deceased relatives. Luther abhorred the entire practice and in 1517 posted his famous "Ninety-five Theses" to the church door in Wittenberg, where he taught at the university. He wanted scholars and churchmen to debate the question. Luther addressed his local archbishop, saying that he doubted the validity of indulgences and grieved "at the very false ideas which the people conceive from them, and which are spread abroad in common talk on every side—namely that unhappy souls believe that, if they buy letters of indulgences, they are sure of salvation; also, that as soon as they have thrown their contribution into the chest, souls forthwith fly out of purgatory. . . ." After all, the acceptance of the indulgence did not prove that a man had inner faith.

The Church replied to Luther's careful address with a stern rebuttal. As Luther himself recorded, "I hoped the Pope would protect me, for I had so fortified my theses with proofs from the Bible and papal decretals that I was sure he would condemn Tetzel and bless me. But when I expected a benediction from Rome, there came thunder and lightning instead, and I was treated like a sheep who had roiled the wolf's water. Tetzel went scot-free, and I must submit to be devoured." Instead of accepting the Pope's condemnation, Luther struck back and called for a public examination of the whole issue. The debate stirred up by Luther won him the widespread support of many of the German people. It also revealed that his differences with orthodox theology were much more extreme than even he had imagined.

In quick response, Luther denied the authority of the Pope, of church councils, of even the early Christians. In any matter of religion, Luther stated, the final authority was the Bible itself. In 1520, while the Pope was drawing up the papal bull that expelled Luther from the Church and declared him a heretic, Luther was reaching all of Germany with his fiery religious tracts (published by the recently invented printing press). In one, he appealed to the princes of Germany to join his cause and break with Rome. Germany at that time was a group of small states and cities under the feudal rule of Charles V, the Holy Roman Emperor, who reigned over a group of loosely joined countries: the German states, The Netherlands, Spain, Portugal, parts of Italy, Bohemia, Hungary, and Austria. Ger-

Der Bapst kan allein auslegen
Die Schrifft ⁊ vnd irthum ausfegen
Wie der Esel allein pfeiffen=
kan: vnd die noten recht greiffen;
                    Mart. Luth. D,1545.

Sixteenth-century woodcut depicts the Pope as an ass.

man princes found Protestantism a perfect excuse for breaking away from both the Italian papacy (which they resented on nationalistic grounds) and the Holy Roman Empire. By 1555, most of northern Germany had become unalterably Lutheran and independent.

Luther's true impact, however, lay in his revolutionary religious ideas. The name "Protestant" at first referred simply to those German princes who had *protested* the Holy Roman Emperor's attempts to persecute Luther and his followers, but the word came to express the fundamental challenge Luther presented to the traditional Catholic Church. Luther felt that centuries of papal decisions needed to be cast aside and that Christians, who had been prohibited by the Church from reading Scripture, had to study the Bible and rely on its guidance. To this end, he translated the Bible into German. To Luther, every Christian was a priest; in fact, he believed no distinction should exist between priests and laymen before God. After consulting Scripture, Luther decided that marriage did not have a sacramental quality. Of the other seven sacraments recognized by Catholics, Luther accepted only two, baptism and communion.

In the new Lutheran churches, the service was conducted in the language of the people rather than in Latin. The congregation sang hymns; fasts, saints, and sacred relics were banished; and clergymen were permitted to marry.

JOHN CALVIN

The teachings of another European theologian, John Calvin, were to have a far greater impact than Lutheranism on religious life in the New World. Calvin, a stern Frenchman who lived from 1509 to 1564, became the spiritual leader of the Swiss city of Geneva and tried to turn it into a model Christian community. He believed he was doing this when he established penalties for citizens who invited others to have a drink and ruled that, "If anyone sing immoral, dissolute or outrageous songs, or dance the *virollet* or other dance, he shall be put in prison for three days and then sent to the consistory."

Calvin, a generation younger than Luther, agreed with many of the ideas of the great German religious leader, but differed from him in two important respects. Calvin emphasized, far more than Luther, the doctrine of predestination. According to this doctrine, God knew beforehand which human beings would be saved and admitted into heaven, and which would be condemned to hell forever. No matter what an individual did in his lifetime, no matter how frequently he prayed or how hard he strove to live morally, his efforts would have no effect on his fate. His salvation or damnation had been decided, or "predestined" by God from the dawn of creation. Far from being discouraged by this doctrine, Calvin's followers believed that *they* had been chosen by God, and that the proof of their election to heaven was in the spotlessly pure lives they led on earth. As a consequence, Calvinists examined their own actions—and their neighbors'—with tireless insistence, earnestly searching out every sign of moral corruption as they defined it.

The second way Calvin differed from Luther was in his approach to politics. Whereas Luther entertained a profound respect for the German governmental authorities and in fact turned the administration of his church over to the rulers of every locality, Calvin believed the church should govern the state, not the reverse. Ideally, every community would be concerned only with carrying out God's will and the citizenry would conduct their affairs according to principles drawn from the Scriptures. The goal of a true Calvinist was glorification of God through purification of the body politic as well as the individual spirit.

These two doctrines—the theory of predestination and the vision of the community of saints—were put to practice in the colonies of New England during the rigid era of Puritan control.

In the twentieth century, historians have been fascinated by the possible connection between Calvinism and the rise of capitalism. According to the German sociologist, Max Weber, who published *The Protestant Ethic and the Spirit of Capitalism* in 1904, Calvin had taught that every man's occupation was assigned to him by God. If a man was a butcher or baker, it was because God had given him the job. Furthermore, if a baker made a great deal of money, this was evidence that he was one of the elect, one of those predestined for salvation. Weber contended that these theories encouraged the sort of tenacious ambition and frugality that are essential to modern capitalism. Critics of Weber point out that Calvinism sprung up not only among wealthy capitalists but also in such economically backward areas as Scotland and rural areas of The Netherlands. In fact, in more prosperous localities, such as Amsterdam, Calvinism quickly became diluted. All the early capitalist institutions in Amsterdam such as centralized banking had arisen before Calvin began preaching. Regardless of those who disagreed with Weber's main thesis, the fact remains that the intense individualism of Calvinist theology had an appeal to the growing middle class, many of whom invested heavily in colonization ventures. It should also be remembered that the Calvinists admired material success without vulgar display as a likely indication of a man's godliness.

THE REFORMATION IN ENGLAND

Like many other areas of northern Europe, England broke away from the Catholic Church, but the rebellion in England, at least at first, was more a result of the personal and political goals of its king, Henry VIII, than a real doctrinal disagreement. Henry was a devout Catholic as a young man. Because of an attack he wrote against Luther's views, the Pope rewarded him with the title "Defender of the Faith." The Venetian ambassador to England reported that the king was "very religious, heard three masses daily when he hunted, and sometimes five on other days."

Henry, a member of the Tudor family, became more interested, however, in assuring the continuity of his family's power than in defending the faith. Henry's wife, Catherine of Aragon, had borne no living son. Henry married Catherine in 1509 and one stillborn child or miscarriage had followed another. Finally, in 1516, Catherine

27

bore a daughter, Mary, but the king felt a daughter was not a worthy heir to the throne. Furthermore, England had never been governed by a woman, and a queen, by marrying a foreign prince, could deliver England into the hands of her husband's country. To Henry, a male heir was essential, and he resumed his suit to have his marriage annulled by the Pope. The king's plan to remarry was also aided by his infatuation with a young lady-in-waiting at the court, Anne Boleyn.

The Pope, however, was not in a position to grant Henry's request, since at the time he was a prisoner of war of Charles V, the Holy Roman Emperor. Charles, as it happened, was the nephew of Henry's wife, Catherine. If the Pope were to grant an annulment, his secretary wrote Henry, "The Church cannot escape utter ruin, as it is entirely in the power of the Emperor's servants."

Determined to remarry, with or without the Pope's consent, Henry persuaded Parliament to abolish all ties between Rome and England and to declare the king the only supreme head on earth of the Church of England. This law, called the Act of Supremacy, instituted the Church of England in 1534. In the next few years, Henry seized the properties that belonged to Catholic bishops and monasteries and parceled them out to his followers, thus strengthening his support among the new landed middle class, the gentry, many of whom were also wealthy businessmen.

Although the king was now the spiritual head of the Church of England, the new religion differed little from Catholicism. Priests were still forbidden to marry, churchgoers still had to confess to priests, bishops still ruled and sat in the House of Lords in Parliament, and the Mass remained unchanged, except that it was said in English. Henry's hatred now extended equally to Protestant and Catholic dissenters against his policy. The king demonstrated his impartial displeasure by burning heretics in pairs, binding a Catholic to a Lutheran and having them both thrown into the flames.

After a time, the king obtained the son he sought, but only after beheading Anne Boleyn, who had given him only a daughter, and marrying Jane Seymour. (Henry married six times in all.) When Henry died in 1547, his ten-year-old son, Edward VI, a boy raised as a Protestant, ascended the throne. After reigning only 6 years, he died and the crown passed to his half-sister, Mary, the daughter of Catherine of Aragon. Mary remained true to her mother's faith, and Catholicism was briefly restored in England during her reign. Those subjects who refused to return to the fold were either burned as heretics (thus earning the queen the name "Bloody Mary") or fled to Protestant strongholds in Europe. On the Continent, about eight hundred of these exiles absorbed the ideas of Calvinism in Frankfort, Strasbourg, Zurich, and Geneva.

At the end of Mary's 5-year reign, the third of Henry VIII's children ascended the throne, and the exiles returned, filled with far more radical ideas than most earlier English Protestants had ever held.

Elizabeth I was a brilliant and enigmatic woman who brought England to a peak of power, pride, wealth, and artistic glory. During her reign, England reduced the might of Spain, became a world trade center, and produced the greatest poet and playwright of any age, William Shakespeare. Under Elizabeth, the Church of England, which had veered from one extreme doctrinal position to another within two decades, was finally stabilized in essentially its present form. The Thirty-Nine Articles, approved by the queen in 1571, provided for a church that retained many Catholic forms of ritual as well as the entire ecclesiastical hierarchy of bishops, but the Articles did make many concessions to Calvinists. The doctrine of predestination was endorsed, and only baptism and the Lord's Supper were recognized as legitimate sacraments.

The worship of saints was prohibited, and priests were permitted to marry (although Elizabeth was somewhat uneasy about archbishops marrying).

These moderate concessions did not satisfy the more radical Calvinists. Although they were divided even among themselves, they were in agreement that the Church of England must be *purified* of "popish" reminders of Catholicism. In essential questions of theology, these "Puritans" had few quarrels to pick with the Thirty-Nine Arti-

cles. They firmly believed, nevertheless, that the administration of church affairs should be taken out of the hands of bishops and given to groups made up of both clerics and laymen. Puritans resented the queen's control over the Church. As a later Puritan historian wrote, they thought it "unreasonable that the religion of a whole nation should be at the disposal of a single lay person." Anglicans (as members of the Church of England were called) were willing to recognize the Pope as a legitimate bishop, if not

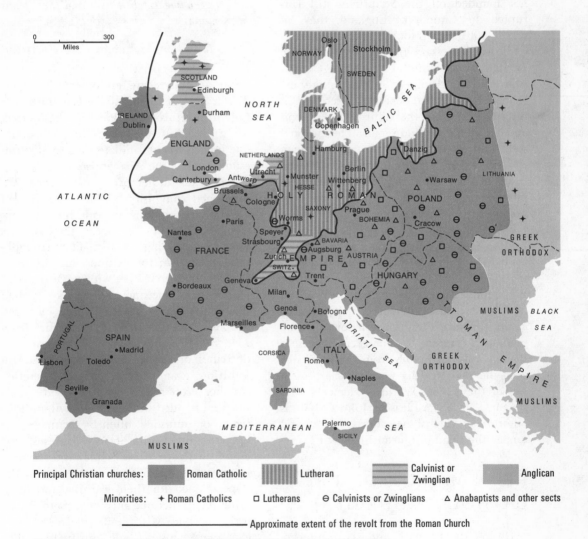

Principal Christian churches: Roman Catholic   Lutheran   Calvinist or Zwinglian   Anglican

Minorities: ✦ Roman Catholics   □ Lutherans   ⊖ Calvinists or Zwinglians   △ Anabaptists and other sects

———— Approximate extent of the revolt from the Roman Church

RELIGIOUS GROUPS · SIXTEENTH CENTURY EUROPE

as the head of the entire Christian church. The Puritans, by contrast, wanted to do away with the office of bishop entirely. Finally, in the manner of Luther and Calvin, the Puritans acknowledged the individual's conscience and the Bible as the only sources of wisdom in religious matters. All early practices of the first Christians, all the centuries of accumulated laws and literature, all the rulings of Popes, and all the ceremonies had to be cast aside, according to the Puritans. Customs, rituals, and notions not founded on the Scriptures still corrupted the Church of England, they insisted, and Puritans took it upon themselves to do the necessary purging. Most of the Puritans were willing to reform the Church from within. Another, smaller, more extreme faction, called Separatists, recoiled in utter disgust from the Church of England and declared it beyond repair. They wanted to break from it totally and start their own church, the only *true* church in their eyes, to which they would only admit those people they regarded as having had a real conversion to Calvinism.

The Puritans were among the first English settlers of New England and they brought with them the unremitting zeal that had characterized their movement since Elizabethan times. Strict avoidance of all frivolity, whether dancing, drinking, or gambling; an endless concern for not only one's own conduct but for everyone else's; the exclusion of luxury from the houses of even the very wealthy were all characteristics of these New World settlements that stemmed from the ideas of John Calvin as absorbed by Englishmen shortly before and during the reign of Queen Elizabeth I.

REFORMATION OF THE CATHOLIC CHURCH

During the fifteenth and sixteenth centuries, religious tolerance was almost completely unknown. Every sect, no matter how

A woodcut showing a battle fought in 1588 between the English fleet and the Spanish Armada.

small or how persecuted, longed to vanquish and persecute all other Christians. The Lutherans despised the Calvinists, the Calvinists returned the favor. Catholics took up arms against all Protestants, and everyone longed to exterminate such small Protestant sects as the Anabaptists.

Relentless intolerance threw Europe into prolonged convulsions. While Luther and Calvin were making inroads into the ancient structure of Catholicism, the Catholics were not standing by idly. They strengthened their own foundations, first by purifying their church from within. During this period, the Pope and priests alike applied themselves to their vocations with increased purpose. The Council of Trent met from 1545 to 1563 and reaffirmed the principal doctrines of Catholicism. The Italian Inquisition examined all possible heretics, whether Protestants, Jews, or lapsed Catholics, and handed them over to civil authorities to be punished, often by death. A new monastic order, the Society of Jesus, was established, and its disciples, the Jesuits, made themselves the personal agents of the Pope. Famed for their learning and discipline, many became missionaries to America, Asia, and Africa and led lives of such exemplary modesty and purity that they raised the public's respect for both the papacy and the Church itself.

When this newly fortified Catholic Church ran headlong into the Protestants, a complex series of wars fanned out over the Continent and kept Europe in constant upheaval between 1559 and 1648. The Protestant Netherlands, after several years of struggle against their Spanish rulers, declared their independence in 1581. Long warfare between the two nations continued, ending in 1648 with international recognition of Dutch freedom. Protestant England and Catholic Spain exchanged blows in 1588. Spain had sent its navy, the "Invincible Armada," to overrun England and return it to the Catholic Church. The invasion was stopped when the English decisively defeated the Spanish fleet and thereby freed their nation forever from the threat of Spanish domination and Catholicism. Civil wars between Protestants (Huguenots) and Catholics divided France from 1562 to 1598, when the Protestants were finally granted the right to practice their faith in peace. Between 1618 and 1648 the Thirty Years' War began as a struggle between Protestants and Catholics, as well as between various Protestant factions, and ended as a conflict over territory between the French and the Holy Roman Empire. The treaty which concluded the war, the Peace of Westphalia (1648), made France a major power in European politics and ended once and for all European religious wars. Never again would countries in Europe take up arms against one another in the name of religion.

ENGLAND: THE MOTHER COUNTRY

Although England entered into hostilities with Spain and made military alliances with various Protestant powers, on the English side of the Channel peace was maintained. This relative stability allowed a variety of English institutions, values, and customs to have the opportunity to develop, producing the strong sense of purpose that was to lead to the settlement of North America by Englishmen.

As discussed earlier, England's first voyage to America was in 1497 when John Cabot sailed to the mouth of the St. Lawrence River. The first permanent settlement was not established, however, until 1607. The primary cause for this delay was the preoccupation of the Tudor family, which had only recently attained the English throne, with the task of securing its power during the sixteenth century.

The hundred-year delay was to have a significant effect on the American colonies, shaping their character to the important changes that had taken place in the mother country. The sixteenth century saw the birth of nationalism in western Europe, the rise of modern capitalism, and the foundation of Protestanism. Out of the English

31

version of this experience, the North American colonies would become a nation, not simply a chain of independent commonwealths, economically capitalist and predominately Protestant in religion.

A HERITAGE OF REPRESENTATIVE GOVERNMENT

Not only did the American colonies ultimately become an independent nation, but they became so with representative political institutions patterned after those of England. Representative government had its roots in English history. As early as 1215, some of the great nobles and churchmen of England presented the document known as Magna Carta to the king. Against his will, it compelled him to rule with their "common counsel." Their number was expanded after 1265 to include the well-to-do landed and urban middle class and this body became known as Parliament, although its early character was markedly different from that of Parliament today. Over the next two centuries, Parliament's power grew and, in the middle of the fourteenth century, it was formally separated into two houses, the hereditary House of Lords and the elected House of Commons.

In the sixteenth century, Parliament continued to grow in influence and self-confidence, meeting frequently. Although the Tudors were strong monarchs, they ruled according to no firm theory of government, and for most major decisions relied on the sanction of Parliament. However, Elizabeth's successor, James I (the first monarch of the Stuart house, which ruled England in the seventeenth century), claimed to rule by "divine right" and without restriction. Parliament was to limit itself to offering counsel to the monarch. In practice, however, Parliament was able to curb royal authority because the House of Commons controlled England's purse strings. The king's income was suffering (revenues from royal estates, for example, had dropped by 25 percent) and the king was forced to turn to Parliament for tax money. But Commons refused to cooperate unless the king relinquished a few of his "divine" rights to the people. In 1621, Commons resolved: "That the liberties, franchises, privileges and jurisdictions of Parliament are the ancient and undoubted birthright and inheritance of the subjects of England." The king was so furious that he dissolved the session.

When Charles I, the son of James I, ascended the throne in 1625, he faced an even more resolute and rebellious Parliament. The new king also dissolved Parliament and ruled for 11 years on his own authority. He imposed new duties on merchants and introduced other extraordinary measures to raise revenues. Parliament in 1628 presented him with the Petition of Right, asking that "no man hereafter be compelled to make or yield any gift, loan, benevolence, tax, or such like charge, without common consent by Act of Parliament." The king angrily accepted the petition, but late in the 1630s Charles, trying to force the Scottish people to change from the Presbyterian to the Anglican church service, had to call on Parliament for money to finance his armies. Parliament refused and the king dissolved it. Within a few months he was in such desperate straits that he had to convene Parliament again. This time the legislators sat without interruption for 20 years and defied the king in every way. Because the king was unwilling to give in to Parliament's demands, not only to control taxation but to regulate the church and make many important political appointments, in May, 1641, a Parliamentary session took steps to raise its own army. At the same session, two laws were passed that set a precedent for America in protecting representational government. First, Parliament's members resolved that they would meet once every 3 years, regardless of the king's pleasure and, second, Parliament could never be dissolved without its own consent. Subsequently, Parliament started a civil war against Charles, imprisoned him, and finally, to the horror of all of Europe, beheaded him in 1649.

A HERITAGE OF CAPITALISM

As representative government gradually developed in America, it followed the English pattern, but the influence of capitalism on the colonies made itself felt at the very beginning. The first American colonies were financed by private enterprise with royal approval. Sir Humphrey Gilbert, the first Englishman to try to start a permanent colony, was backed by a private corporation of nobles, merchants, and religious dissenters. His two attempts to plant settlements in Newfoundland, in 1578 and again in 1583, both ended in disaster (Gilbert's ship went down in mid-Atlantic). His half-brother, Sir Walter Raleigh, planned the second permanent settlement and also received private financing. The investors wanted a base from which English ships could raid Spanish vessels laden with treasure, as well as a settlement that would grow food and tobacco, and trade with the Indians. Their interest in colonization was first and foremost financial. In 1585, the settlers landed on Roanoke Island near a rich coast they named Virginia after their virgin queen, Elizabeth I. After a year, this venture failed. In 1586, when Sir Francis Drake sailed into the harbor, the ragged, starving survivors of Roanoke all joined him and returned to England. Raleigh tried again to colonize America the following year and the new settlers met a mysterious and probably tragic fate. An English ship that visited Roanoke in 1590 found that they had vanished without a trace.

These first failures, and the successful ventures that followed in the seventeenth century, were all financed through a new economic institution, the joint-stock company. In the past, individual merchants of wealth, or the government, had been the only sources of capital for costly projects. But the joint-stock company, a Dutch innovation adopted by the English, enlisted the support of numerous capitalists. Each stockholder bought only a small portion of the company. If it failed, he was not necessarily hurt severely, for, like most investors, he usually owned stocks in several companies and his other investments might be profitable. Colonization of the New World became an attractive source of investment, and with the financial backing of the joint-stock companies, the English emigrants who

"The Tree of Classes" progresses from Popes and Kings to merchants, laborers, and peasants at the base of the tree.

crossed the Atlantic brought with them the new capitalistic spirit of the early seventeenth century, rather than the lingering medieval economic ideas of the century before.

If economic changes wrought in the sixteenth century brought great wealth to merchants (who were the majority of stockholders in these companies), it ruined other groups, particularly poor farmers. During the 1500s England became a great wool center and as a consequence, sheepherding became a major industry. Land was suddenly enclosed which, under the old medieval system, lords had allowed all the people to use for grazing. Little farms were consolidated into great grazing pastures and large numbers of farmers were turned off the land and shunted into the cities. Urban overpopulation became a serious problem as bands of unemployed ruffians wandered about the cities terrorizing their more prosperous fellow citizens. These homeless, unemployed people made up a large percentage of those who came to the colonies for new opportunities. Among others who came to America because they were disgruntled with England for various reasons were the second sons of country gentry who had no chance to inherit their father's wealth, since by law all property must go to the eldest son; poor farmers who eked out a living by tanning leather, shoeing horses, or performing countless other small, poorly paid services; and even a few nobles, who resented the rise of the wealthy new merchant class.

A HERITAGE OF PROTESTANTISM

Many colonists also came to America for religious motives. Since Henry VIII's time, both the more extreme Protestants, the Puritans, and the Catholics had found England hostile to their beliefs. Under James I and Charles I matters worsened. James had

rejected a Puritan petition to reform the Anglican Church, saying, "If this be all your party hath to say, I will make them conform themselves or else harry them out of the land." Similarly, after drawing English Catholics out of hiding by promising them tolerance, James I renewed persecution against them on a greater scale. Charles I was equally harsh with dissenters. Also, he reissued a law originated by James which particularly embittered the straitlaced Puritans. This law was the Declaration of Sports and it forbade the English people to be disturbed in such recreations as "May games, Whitsun ales, or morris dances, and setting up of May-poles, or other sports therewith used. . . ." More serious was Charles's dismissal of Parliament, an act which stood in the way of reform, either of the government or of the Anglican Church. From 1629 to 1649, persecution of Puritans in England led to the so-called "Great Migration" in search of a more hospitable environment. Many Puritans moved to The Netherlands, where they were accorded total religious freedom. In 1620, the Pilgrims sailed for America. Soon other Puritans followed and, in 1630, founded the Massachusetts Bay Colony.

Thus, the religious, political, and economic developments of the sixteenth and seventeenth centuries made it almost inevitable that American colonies would be predominantly Protestant, that political life would be based on English institutions, and that the economy would be capitalistic.

The Divine Right of Kings

66 *The State of Monarchie is the supremest thing upon earth: For Kings are not only Gods Lieutenants upon earth, and sit upon Gods throne, but even by God himselfe they are called Gods. There bee three principall similitudes that illustrates the state of Monarchie. One taken out of the word of God; and the two others out of Policie and Philosophie. In the Scriptures Kings are called Gods, and so their power after a certaine relation compared to the Divine power. Kings are are also compared to Fathers of families: for a King is trewly Parens patriae, the politique father of his family. And lastly, Kings are compared to the head of this Microcosme of the body of man.*

Kings are justly called Gods, for that they exercise a manner or resemblance of Divine power upon earth: For if you will consider the Attributes of God, you shall see how they agree in the person of a King. God hath power to create, or destroy, make, or unmake at his pleasure, to give life, or send death, to judge all, and to be judged nor accomptable to none; To raise low things, and to make high things low at his pleasure, and to God are both soule and body due. And the like power have Kings: They make and unmake their subjects: they have power of raising and casting downe, of life and death; judges over all their subjects, and in all causes and yet accomptable to none but God onely. . . . 99

—*The Political Works of James I*

A Heritage of Representation in Government

66 *12. No scutage or aid shall be imposed on our kingdom, unless by common counsel of our kingdom, except for ransoming our person, for making of our oldest son a knight, and for once marrying our eldest daughter, and for these purposes there shall not be levied more than a reasonable aid. . . .*
14. And for obtaining the common counsel of the kingdom, a rent, the assessment of an aid (except in the three cases aforesaid) or of a scutage, we will cause to be summoned the arshbishops, bishops, abbots, earls and greater barons severally by our letters; and we will moreover cause to be summoned generally through our sheriffs and bailiffs, all others who hold of us in chief, . . .

38. No Bailiff for the future shall, upon his own unsupported complaint, put anyone to his "law," without credible witnesses brought for this purpose.

39. No freeman shall be taken or imprisoned or disseised, or exiled or in any way destroyed, nor will we go upon him nor send upon him, except by the lawful judgment of his peers or by the law of the land.

40. To no one will we sell, to no one will we refuse or delay, right or justice. 99

—*Magna Carta*

Readings

GENERAL WORKS

Brandon, William, *The American Heritage Book of Indians*. New York, Dell, 1961—A well-illustrated survey of the Indians of both North and South America.

Brebner, J. B., *The Explorers of North America, 1492–1806*. New York, Macmillan, 1933—A classic general history of the exploration of North America from Columbus through Lewis and Clark.

Cheyney, E. P., *The Dawn of a New Era*. New York, Harper & Row, 1936 (Paper: Harper Torch Books, 1962)—An older general introduction to the history of the late Middle Ages suggesting that the period showed signs of the coming transition to modern times.

Debo, Angie, *A History of the Indians of the United States*. Norman, Okla., University of Oklahoma Press, 1970—An in-depth historical survey of the Indians of the United States (including the Eskimos and Aleuts of Alaska) which isolates and analyzes the problems that have beset these people since their first contacts with Europeans.

Driver, Harold E., *Indians of North America*. Chicago, University of Chicago Press, 1961 (Paper, 1964)—A thorough survey of Indian anthropology with chapters on subjects ranging from farming techniques to Indian music.

Ferguson, Wallace K., *Europe in Transition, 1300–1520*. Boston, Houghton Mifflin, 1962 —A survey of European history which contends that the Renaissance marked the transition from a Medieval to a modern Western European civilization.

Gibson, Charles, *Spain in America*. New York, Harper & Row, 1966—A summary and interpretation of the impact of Spanish exploration and colonization. Gibson analyzes the relations between the Spanish colonies in South America and the British and French colonies in North America.

Horgan, Paul, *Conquistadors in North American History*. New York, Farrar, Straus and Giroux, 1936 (Paper: Fawcett, 1969)—A history of Spanish explorers and conquerors in America which balances accounts from Spanish sources with Indian accounts of the invasions.

McNeill, William H., *The Rise of the West*. Chicago, University of Chicago Press, 1963 —A broad interpretation of world history which seeks to explain how and why European societies in the fifteenth and sixteenth centuries came to explore and ultimately dominate much of the world.

Notestein, Wallace, *The English People on the Eve of Colonization*. New York, Harper & Row Torchbooks, 1954—A social history of early seventeenth-century English life. Notestein emphasizes the conditions which led to the migration to America.

Nowell, Charles E., *The Great Discoveries and the First Colonial Empires*. Ithaca, N.Y., Cornell University Press, 1954—A brief essay on the Age of Discovery and settlement that compares the experiences of different European nations.

Reynolds, Robert L., *Europe Emerges: Transition Toward an Industrial World-Wide Society*. Madison, Wis., University of Wisconsin Press, 1961—An outline of the development of Europe between 600 and 1750 which stresses the importance of technological innovations and businessmen's initiative to Europe's rise to world power.

SPECIAL STUDIES

Bindoff, S. T., *Tudor England*. Baltimore, Md., Penguin, 1950—A brief, well-organized general survey of English history from 1485 to 1603. Bindoff emphasizes the impact of economic and political developments on a nation not far removed from the Middle Ages.

Boxer, C. R., *The Dutch Seaborne Empire: 1600–1800*. New York, Knopf, 1965—Boxer relates the Dutch period of naval and commercial power to the drives of the Calvinist Dutch middle class and emphasizes the lack of national unity as a cause of the decline of the Dutch empire.

Byrne, M. St. Clare, *Elizabethan Life in Town and Country*. New York, Barnes & Noble, 1961—An older, but still important, work of social history which deals with such subjects as Elizabethan dress, manners, architecture, and theater.

Coe, Michael D., *Mexico*. New York, Praeger, 1962—A well-illustrated general history of Mexico before the Spanish conquest. Coe emphasizes the importance of peoples other than the Aztecs.

Hemming, John, *The Conquest of the Incas*. New York, Harcourt Brace & Jovanovich, 1970—A new interpretation of the Spanish conquest which uses much material from Indian sources.

Jones, Gwyn, *A History of the Vikings*. New York, Oxford University Press, 1968—A thorough recent history of the Vikings which points out the importance of Scandinavia in Medieval Europe. The author combines conventional history with archaeology.

Mason, J. Alden, *The Ancient Civilization of Peru*. Baltimore, Md., Penguin, 1957—An anthropological and historical study which deals with both Inca and pre-Inca cultures. Contains many photographs.

Mattingly, Garrett, *The Armada*. Boston, Houghton Mifflin, 1959 (Paper: Sentry Edition, 1962)—A detailed narrative of the English and European factors leading to the defeat of Spanish naval power in 1588. Mattingly agrees with older historians that the English victory ensured that the drive of Catholic Spain to dominate North Europe and England would not succeed.

Parkman, Francis, *Pioneers of France in the New World*. Boston, Little, Brown, 1900—Originally written in 1865, this is the story of French explorers in North America. Parkman was an outstanding nineteenth-century American historian known for his vivid and eloquent style.

Parry, J. H., *The Spanish Seaborne Empire*. New York, Knopf, 1966—Although the growth of the Spanish Empire in the 1500s took place in the context of a mother country which was Medieval in outlook and institutions, a central bureaucracy was able to direct the remarkable expansion of Spanish power.

Powicke, F. Maurice, *The Reformation in England*. New York, Oxford University Press, 1961—A series of lectures on aspects of the English Reformation by a distinguished Medieval historian. Powicke emphasizes the point that in England the Reformation was the result of governmental policy, not of a popular movement.

Prescott, William H., *Prescott's Histories: The Rise and Decline of the Spanish Empire*. Edited by Irwin R. Blacker. New York, Viking, 1963—An abridged collection of the great nineteenth-century American historian's massive works on Spanish conquests in the New World.

Rowse, A. L., *The England of Elizabeth.* New York, Macmillan, 1961—A general overview of Elizabethan English society which stresses the importance and value of that society's contributions to the modern world.

Simpson, Alan, *Puritanism in Old and New England.* Chicago, University of Chicago Press, 1955 (Paper: Phoenix Books, 1961) —Although Simpson admired both the realism and the courage of many Puritans, he criticizes both the English and the Massachusetts Puritans for being moral absolutists.

Weber, Max, *The Protestant Ethic and the Spirit of Capitalism.* New York, Scribner's, 1958—A classic sociological investigation of the ways in which Calvinist theology influenced capitalistic values such as devotion to work and thrift.

PRIMARY SOURCES

Bainton, Roland, *The Age of the Reformation.* New York, D. Van Nostrand, 1956— An essay followed by a selection of primary source documents. Bainton maintains that the Reformation was responsible for the best values of modern Western society.

Diaz del Castillo, Bernal, *The Discovery and Conquest of Mexico.* Edited by Genaro Garcia. Translated by A. P. Maudslay. New York, Farrar, Straus & Cudahy, 1956 (Paper: Farrar, Straus and Giroux, 1965)— This is a firsthand account of the Spanish conquest of Mexico, written by an explorer and adventurer who had enlisted as a soldier under Cortes. Although Diaz del Castillo was influenced by popular romantic myths of sixteenth-century Spain, his his-

tory is an excellent source for the story of the conquest.

Komroff, Manuel, ed., *The Travels of Marco Polo.* New York, Random House, 1953— The story of the expedition across Asia to China of Marco Polo, thirteenth-century Venetian adventurer.

Leon-Portilla, M., *The Broken Spears: The Aztec Account of the Conquest of Mexico.* Boston, Beacon Press, 1962—The story of Cortes' expedition from the Indian point of view. The Aztecs' interpretations of their defeat are in part surprisingly sophisticated and in part tragically naive.

Viereck, Philip, ed., *The New Land.* New York, John Day, 1967—Firsthand accounts of discoveries and explorations in the New World from the Norsemen through the Pilgrims. Well illustrated, with editor's notes and commentary.

BIOGRAPHIES

Bainton, Roland, *Here I Stand.* New York, Abingdon, 1950 (Paper: New American Library, 1955)—A biography of Martin Luther which stresses his religious and theological impact on the world.

Hackett, Francis, *The Personal History of Henry VIII.* New York, Modern Library, 1945—A highly popular biography of the English monarch which portrays Henry VIII as a fascinating but cruel ruler.

Morison, S. E., *Admiral of the Ocean Sea.* Boston, Atlantic Monthly–Little, Brown, 1942—A prize-winning biography of Christopher Columbus. In researching his subject, Morison crossed the Atlantic in a sailing ship, retracing Columbus' route to the New World.

Neale, J. E., *Queen Elizabeth.* London, Jonathan Cape, 1935 (Paper: Doubleday Anchor, 1957)—A standard biography of the last of the Tudor monarchs. Under Queen Elizabeth's rule, the English reached new heights in both commerce and culture and initiated schemes for colonizing the New World.

Rowse, A. L., *Sir Walter Raleigh: His Family and Private Life*. New York, Harper & Row, 1964—A biography of the Elizabethan who played many important roles in Queen Elizabeth's court and in colonization efforts.

Williamson, J. A., *Sir Francis Drake*. New York, Macmillan, 1962—A brief biography of the Elizabethan sailor and warrior by a distinguished British historian of the age of discovery.

HISTORICAL NOVELS

Cather, Willa, *Shadows on the Rock*. New York, Knopf, 1931—A novel in which the problems of seventeenth-century colonial Quebec are seen through the eyes of a child.

Forester C. S., *To the Indies*. Boston, Little, Brown, 1940—A novel about Columbus' third voyage to the West Indies. The central figure of the book is a lawyer sent by King Ferdinand to investigate Columbus' activities.

Hugo, Victor, *Notre Dame de Paris*. New York, Modern Library, 1941—Set in late fifteenth-century France, the two leading characters are Quasimodo, the dwarf who rings the bells in the great Cathedral of Notre Dame, and Esmeralda, a Spanish dancer. The novel reflects nineteenth-century romantic notions about the late middle ages.

Kingsley, Charles, *Westward Ho!* New York, Airmont, 1968—A Victorian novel set in

Elizabethan times which pictured British exploration as a venture creating national unity, pride, and sense of purpose.

Scott, Walter, *Kenilworth*. New York, Airmont, 1968—One of Scott's Waverly novels, set in Elizabethan England. The plot is loosely based on the marriage of Dudley, a leading court figure, to Amy Robsart, and her death.

Scott, Walter, *Quentin Durward*. New American Library, 1963—A novel set in fifteenth-century France. The theme is the death of chivalry and the decay of what Scott considered the best in the Medieval tradition.

Shellabarger, Samuel, *Captain from Castile*. Boston, Little, Brown, 1945—A historical adventure novel based on Hernando Cortes' conquest of Mexico.

Shute, Nevil, *An Old Captivity*. New York, W. Morrow, 1940—A love story set in an archeological expedition to Greenland. The real story parallels a long dream sequence in which the hero and heroine take part in Leif Ericson's explorations.

RELATED RESOURCES

Bushnell, G. H. S., *The First Americans*. New York, McGraw-Hill, 1968—A brief modern summary of the archaeology and history of the Americans before Columbus. Bushnell concentrates on the Central American civilizations. Well illustrated in both color and black-and-white photos and drawings.

Lehner, Ernst and Johanna, *How They Saw the New World*, Gerard L. Alexander, ed. New York, Tudor, 1966—A collection, with commentaries, of maps, illustrations, and brochures about the New World. The maps and pictures often tell as much about their authors' ideas as about the things they drew.

in Henry Hudson discovered this Country Ao 1609 and sold it to y Hollanders & Letters Patents being granted to some Merch.ts by y States
called An. 10. called New Nether- -land & but S.r Samuell Argal Royal Governour of Virginia gave them disturbance he those . . . . their Plantation

Colonizing the New World

The mildnesse of the aire, the fertilitie of the soile, and the situation of the rivers are so propitious to the nature and use of man as no place is more convenient for pleasure, profit, and mans sustenance. . . . The waters, Isles, and shoales, are full of safe harbours for ships of warre or marchandize, for boats of all sortes, for transportation or fishing, etc. The Bay and rivers have much marchandable fish and places for Salt coats, building of ships, making of iron, etc.

. . . . So then here is a place a nurse for souldiers, a practise for marriners, a trade for marchants, a reward for the good, and that which is most of all a businesse (most acceptable to God) to bring such poore infidels to the true knowledge of God and his holy Gospell.

—Captain John Smith,
Narratives of Early Virginia

New York, originally called New Amsterdam, was settled by the Dutch in 1626 as a base from which to raid the Spanish gold-bearing galleons. This engraving shows New York in 1717, 47 years after the English seized New Amsterdam from the Dutch. New York has always been an important port-city originally because of its accessibility to the fur producing regions of the north.

BEGINNINGS ON THE CHESAPEAKE

Two motives impelled Englishmen to leave their native soil for the New World—they sought wealth or a place to practice their religion free from persecution. Most colonists arrived with only the vaguest notion of what life would be like 3,000 miles from home. Was North America wintry or tropical? Were the Indians noble savages or cruel pagans? Did lush vegetation and rivers of gold await them, or barren land and poverty? They could only guess the answers to such questions and wonder what the quality of life would be like in the New World. Some colonists, for example, expected greater liberties than they had ever enjoyed in England, while others anticipated stern martial law. Through bitter experience, the first settlers learned that the barest essentials of living had to be eked out of the land and that a stable form of government would be slow in evolving. Despite their difficulties, the remarkable fact remains that England, which had no colonies anywhere in the world at the beginning of the seventeenth century, by the end of the century had twenty colonies along the Atlantic Coast of North America and in the West Indies, populated by a quarter of a million settlers.

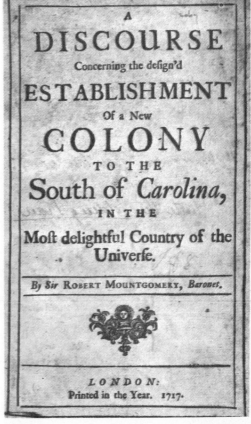

An advertisement describing the wonders of colonial life in America to the British. In order to entice the British to colonize the New World, often desolate, uninhabited lands were described as cover with "rubies and pearls."

In 1604, the first of the Stuart kings, James I, signed a peace treaty with Spain that won him little popularity among his subjects but which inaugurated a 20-year period of peace, prosperity, and enormous confidence in England. There were patriotic but greedy supporters of the war with Spain who would have preferred continuing their raids on Spanish shipping under the cover of war, but for England as a nation, the treaty with Spain fostered prosperity by ensuring stability at home and security at sea. The king himself was little interested in merchants or in their projects, but his influential group of advisors, the Privy Council, was intrigued with every aspect of navigation, colonization, and business; moreover, many of the members were investors in the first companies to finance American colonies.

The first English settlements in North America were undertaken by private business organizations known as joint-stock companies, corporations which accumulated capital by issuing stock to many shareholders, who assumed no risks beyond the percentage of their investment. In 1606, two companies petitioned the king for a charter to settle Virginia (the name in those days for the entire Atlantic seaboard from Florida to Maine). The king granted their petition, thereby making two separate grants of land: the Virginia Company of Plymouth was given the northern half of the Atlantic seaboard (38–45 degrees); the Virginia Company of London received the southern half (34–41 degrees).

A FALSE START
IN MAINE

The Plymouth Company's activities were short-lived. After sending two ships to explore the coast, the company dispatched 120 men in the *Gift of God* and *Mary and John,* which landed on August 7, 1607 in the area of the future colony of Maine, at the mouth of the Kennebec River. They chose a place for their settlement, or "plantation" a short distance up the river, and during the next 2 months the men built a fort and attempted to establish friendly relations with the Indians. Due to petty quarrels, however, they quickly lost the respect of the Indians, who refused to trade with them. The president of the plantation, George Popham, whom a contemporary described as "an honest man but old and of an unwieldy body," turned out to be so polite, meek and timorous that he was "fearful to offend or contest with others that will or do oppose him."

Lacking a strong leader, fragmented by bickering, and short on food and supplies, the settlers were further demoralized by the dreadfully cold Maine winter, particularly since they had expected a tropical climate. When several of the important men connected with the enterprise died and a fire demolished the storehouse and other buildings, the colonists abandoned their outpost, packed their belongings, and returned to England.

THE SETTLEMENT
OF JAMESTOWN

The plantation started by the second joint-stock company, the London Company, encountered even more severe hardships, but it endured to become the first successful colony. The cost of the success, however, was staggering; four-fifths of the colonists who came to Jamestown between 1607 and 1624 died and the company spent roughly seven million dollars without receiving any profit. The final blow to the company came in 1624 when it lost its charter and the king took over the budding colony.

The Jamestown settlers sailed for the New World from England in December, 1606, on three ships, the *Susan Constant,* the *Godspeed,* and the *Discovery.* There were 144 colonists, all men. When the vessels arrived in Virginia 4 months later, thirty-nine had died at sea and one, Captain John Smith, had been put in the brig for mutinous grumblings. No one on the voyage ever knew exactly who would govern the settlement. The company had sent along a sealed steel box, which contained the names of seven investors in the company who were to take charge of the colony. When the box was opened upon arrival, one of the members was revealed to be the aforementioned John Smith. The other designated members immediately voted, as the charter permitted them to do, to remove Smith from the resident council. Smith's later rise to leadership in the colony proved that he was not a man to be easily suppressed.

The colony had been planned for three purposes, all of them financial: to discover a passage to China through the mainland of North America, to trade with the Indians, and to mine gold, copper, and iron. To work toward these ends, the settlers immediately established a base some 30 miles up the James River. The site was selected to conceal the town from roving Spanish vessels, but unfortunately the land was swampy and a source of malaria, as well as distant from all natural wells. While one group started to build a fort, another party proceeded up the river, in search of the route to China.

The exploring party failed to find the Northwest Passage, but it did come across an Indian town called Powhatan. The Indians alternated between periods of friendliness, during which they helped the English with gifts of food, and periods of hostility. During the first few weeks, a band of Indians attacked the fort, hurt seventeen men and killed one boy, retreating only when one of the ships fired a shot that struck a branch in a tree above them and caused the "savages to retire."

Within the colony itself, the council and its president had little power to maintain order. The king had retained the right to influence the ruling of the colony through a Virginia company council in England which sent instructions to the resident council in Virginia. The eight members of the resident council in Jamestown had no authority to originate orders, and no power to enforce those from England. Indeed, this was no government at all.

The settlers, almost half of them English gentlemen unused to physical labor, all wanted to turn a quick profit. They neglected tilling the fields and providing for the winter ahead and began to feverishly mine the "gold" of Virginia—which turned out to be only the most ordinary of minerals, iron pyrite. "No talk, no hope, nor work," wrote Captain John Smith in despair, "but dig gold, wash gold, refine gold. load gold." By the autumn of 1607, half of

This early woodcut illustrates a popular myth about the marriage of Captain John Smith and the Indian Princess, Pocahontas. Smith is being held on the floor, menaced by Indian braves. Pocahontas is begging her father, Chief Powhatan, for Smith's life. According to the myth, Pocahontas wins the argument and is given Smith as a reward.

the settlers had died. The colonists who had so hopefully dug gold were now digging graves. As the winter progressed, more and more colonists perished from disease or starvation. One colonist described how three or four men might die in a night: "In the morning their bodies trailed out of their cabins like dogs to be buried." Only the help of the Indians and their "kings" enabled a few to survive. One early settler wrote: "It pleased God, after a while, to send those people which were our mortal enemies to relieve us with victuals, as bread, corn, fish and flesh in great plenty, which was the setting up of our feeble men, otherwise we had all perished. Also, we were frequented by diverse kings in the country, bringing us store of provision to our great comfort."

Relief from England failed to arrive and decorum declined so far that, at one time, the president of the council was charged with raiding the hen house and drinking too much of the communal brandy. When a ship from England arrived in January, 1608, bringing supplies and 120 settlers, only 38 of the original 144 colonists were still alive.

CAPTAIN JOHN SMITH

During the next winter only twelve colonists died and the colony began to prosper. This improvement was due to the leadership of John Smith, who was elected president of the council in September. Smith stopped the disorganized search for gold and saw to it that buildings were repaired, crops planted, livestock nurtured, and slackers punished. If a rough-and-ready "adventurer" (as the settlers were called) swore too much, Smith ordered a glass of water to be poured down his sleeve. He established peaceful relations with the Indians, even to the point of offering himself in marriage to the daughter of the chief of the Powhatans. According to one version of the story, the Indian princess, Pocahontas,

had been visiting Jamestown in the nude and doing cartwheels down the streets, and that Smith took a fancy to her. Another legendary account has it that she saved Smith's life by warning him of an Indian plot and so won his heart. Cynics of the time circulated rumors that Smith planned to marry Pocahontas and make himself Emperor of Virginia. Reports of Smith's harsh rule and rumored plans reached the London Company, and he was sent back to England for trial.

Although Smith was removed from office, his achievements showed the London Company the advantage of having a strong governor instead of a weak council to rule the colony. Accordingly, the king of England granted the colony a new charter in 1609, calling for an all-powerful administrator and reducing the council to merely an advisory capacity.

In order to encourage new emigrants to America, under the new charter the company promised to transport settlers free of charge in return for 7 years of unpaid labor on lands owned by the stockholders. If the settler could pay his own way, he would receive a share of stock in the enterprise. For the first 7 years, until 1616, all the settlers would work together for the company. At the end of that period, all profits would be divided equally and every shareholder would receive 100 acres as a bonus.

This plan sounded so promising that six hundred settlers signed up. The trip was financed by a national lottery held in England; losers in the lottery were consoled in verse: "Let no man think that he shall lose, / though he no prize possess. / His substance to Virginia goes, / Which God no doubt will bless. . . ."

THE STARVING TIME

The promised blessings seemed an eternity away during the winter of 1609 to 1610. Food became so scarce that the settlers were reduced to eating dogs, cats, rats, snakes, and boiled shoes. One man even killed his wife and "powdered" (that is, salted) her to eat, "for which he was executed, as he well deserved," one colonist wrote, adding with grim humor, "whether she was better roasted, boiled or carbonadoed, I know not, but of such a dish as powdered wife I never heard of."

Back in England, to silence reports of starvation and cannibalism, the Virginia Company hired preachers to present a rosier picture of the New World to their parishioners. One overly zealous minister extolled Virginia's "abundance of mulberries, minerals, rubies, pearls, gems, grapes, deer, fowls" and "ashes for soap." Not only were all such riches lacking in Virginia, but even the strong governor the colony had been promised failed to arrive (he was delayed when his ship was wrecked off Bermuda). Once again anarchy reigned until 1611, when order was restored under Governor Thomas Dale, a stern Puritan.

THE HOUSE OF BURGESSES

During the governorship of Dale and his successor, Samuel Argall, life at Jamestown took a turn for the better. A profitable crop for the colonists, tobacco, resulted from the agricultural experiments of John Rolfe, who produced a new strain of the plant. When this Virginia strain was later judged too bitter, the farmers imported a milder variety from the West Indies. By 1617 Jamestown was able to ship 20,000 pounds of tobacco to England. Another boon was the arrival of women. In 1620, ninety young women, guaranteed by the company to be "pure and spotless," came over to be the wives of the men, who had to pay 120 pounds of tobacco for each woman.

The colony's new prosperity aroused demands for more economic freedom and a relaxation of the harsh one-man rule. This resulted in a new charter in 1619 granting the colony more economic and political freedom. In addition, 10 free acres were given to all who had settled there before 1616. The new document stated that settlers transported to America at the company's expense would be required to work the land for 7 years to pay off their obligations. Those who paid their own way over would be granted 50 acres of land, called a "headright," and 50 additional acres for any person they brought with them. This granting of free land to settlers was to become a practice in all the colonies. The severe discipline that had prevailed under the autocratic governers was relaxed by the charter and the settlers were assured all the legal rights of Englishmen back home.

The greatest innovation in the new charter was permission to the colonists to elect representatives to an assembly called the House of Burgesses. Thus, on July 30, 1619, before any other permanent English colony was planted, Virginians met in the first representative assembly of the New World. The group was permitted to make laws for the entire colony, and henceforth all directives sent by the London Company would have to be ratified by the representatives. This strong provision for self-government was the work of Sir Edwin Sandys, the company's treasurer, a man known for his tolerance and learning and his opposition to any extension of the king's power.

Sandys introduced other new schemes. Under his direction the company began to sell private plantations to small groups. They settled in semi-independent villages (each of which had two representatives in the House of Burgesses). He also convinced the company to send, at its own expense, tradesmen and artisans (glassblowers, ironmongers, shipbuilders) so that the colony could diversify its business interests and protect itself against the disaster of a possible tobacco crop failure. But Sandys in his enthusiasm for emigration to America failed to make certain that Virginia was outfitted with food, housing, and supplies for the arrivals. More than 3,500 settlers were lured by Sandys to Virginia; 3 years

The Reality of Virginia

" *This was that time, which still to this day we called the starving time; it were too vile to say, and scarce to be believed, what we endured: but the occasion was our own, for want of providence industry and government, and not the barrenness and defect of the Country, as is generally supposed; for till then in three years, for the numbers were landed us, we had never from England provision sufficient for six months, though it seemed by the bills of loading sufficient was sent us, such a glutton is the Sea, and such good fellows the Mariners; we as little tasted of the great proportion sent us, as they of our want and miseries, yet notwithstanding they ever overswayed and ruled the business, though we endured all that is said, and chiefly lived on what this good Country naturally afforded. Yet had we been in Paradise itself with these Governors, it would not have been much better with us; yet there was amongst us, who had they had the government as Captain Smith appointed, but that they could not maintain it, would surely have kept us from those extremities of miseries. This in ten days more, would have supplanted us all with death.*

But God that would not this Country should be unplanted, sent Sir Thomas Gates, and Sir George Sommers with one hundred and fifty people most happily preserved by the Bermudas to preserve us: strange it is to say how miraculously they were preserved in a leaking ship, as at large you may read in the insuing History of those Islands. "

—Captain John Smith, The Generall
Historie of Virginia, 1624:
The Fourth Booke

The Pilgrims' Trial

" *But here I cannot but stay and make a pause, and stand half amazed at this poor people's present condition; and so I think will the reader too, when he well considers the same. Being thus passed the vast ocean, and a sea of troubles before in their preparation . . . they had now no friends to welcome them, nor inns to entertain or refresh their weatherbeaten bodies, no houses or much less towns to repair to, to seek for succor. It is recorded in scripture as a mercy to the apostle and his shipwrecked company, that the barbarians showed them no small kindness in refreshing them, but these savage barbarians, when they met with them . . . were readier to fill their sides full of arrows than otherwise. And for the season it was winter, and they that know the winters of that country know them to be sharp and violent, & subject to cruel & fierce storms, dangerous to travel to known places, much more to search an unknown coast. Besides, what could they see but a hideous & desolate wilderness, full of wild beasts & wild men? and what multitudes there might be of them they knew not. . . . If it be said they had a ship to succor them, it is true, but what heard they daily from the master & company? . . . It is true, indeed, the affections & love of their brethren at Leyden was cordial & entire towards them, but they had little power to help them, or themselves. . . . What could now sustain them but the spirit of God & his grace? May not & ought not the children of these fathers, rightly say: Our fathers were Englishmen which came over this great ocean, and were ready to perish in this wilderness. . . .* "

—William Bradford,
Of Plymouth Plantation,
The Pilgrims in America

on Newfoundland. Soon afterward, Calvert set out for this New World to govern the small settlement of his coreligionists already growing there. However, he soon found it too cold and too exposed to French raids. He applied to King Charles I for an estate in a warmer climate. The king granted him land on the Chesapeake Bay, north of Virginia.

A FEUDAL ESTATE

The royal charter that created Maryland (which the king named after his own wife, Queen Henrietta Maria) was a throwback to the Middle Ages. Like those feudal estates discussed in Chapter 1, Maryland was in theory completely subject to the will of Lord Baltimore. Baltimore owned all of the colony's ten million acres. He was free to make laws, appoint officials, try criminals, bequeath titles, and tax trade almost without restriction. Indeed, Lord Baltimore theoretically had more power in his own colony than the king exercised in England. In return for all these favors, Baltimore had only to promise the king one-fifth of all the gold and silver discovered in Maryland, and two Indian arrowheads a year.

But life in Maryland never followed this medieval pattern, partly because of the people who came to settle it and partly because of the wisdom of its proprietors. George Calvert died before he actually received the king's charter. When the document was finally fixed with the king's seal in 1632, the colony went to George's son, Cecil, the second Lord Baltimore. In November, 1633, two Jesuit priests, seventeen gentlemen, their wives and children, and about two hundred other settlers set sail on the *Ark* and the *Dove* for America. The enterprise was headed by Cecil's brother, Leonard Calvert.

The Calvert brothers were intelligent and tolerant administrators who based their successful colonization to a large extent on the experience of the older Virginia settle-

ment. Each settler was given 100 acres, plus another hundred for his wife and each servant and 50 acres for each child over sixteen. Gentlemen who brought five other people along were permitted to establish manors of 2,000 acres. Those who qualified were usually close friends of Baltimore and fellow Catholics. Class divisions, defined by the size of a man's property holdings, were thus created by the granting of free land to settlers under precedents established by earlier Virginia charters. A new social structure arose that was quite unlike the single-class society of yeoman farmers that had predominated in Virginia until the second half of the seventeenth century.

The troubles the Virginians had had with the Indians (in particular the massacre of 1622) served to warn the Maryland colonists of the dangers of dealing carelessly with the tribes. Accordingly, the Marylanders were careful to purchase land for their first town, St. Mary's, from friendly local Indians (who were only too glad to sell it, since they were moving south to escape their enemies, the Susquehannas).

The Virginians had suffered intolerably in their early years. They had starved because they had not planted crops but rather abandoned themselves to a fruitless search for gold. They had grown ill because the site of Jamestown was so unhealthy. By contrast, the Marylanders brought adequate supplies with them (and purchased more from Virginia), and carefully cultivated vegetable gardens. By this time, the Indians knew how to cultivate corn and the settlers learned from them how to cultivate their own corn fields. They constructed sound fortifications and chose a site for St. Mary's with an excellent harbor and plenty of fresh water. Ambitious farmers wanted to devote their fields entirely to the most profitable product, tobacco, but the governor, imitating a 1624 Virginia law, insisted that they also cultivate at least 2 acres of corn. later, all but about 900 were dead from disease or starvation.

The final blow to the company came on March 22, 1622, when the Indians, alarmed by the encroachment of Englishmen on their lands, massacred 347 settlers. The week before the attack, the Indians insinuated themselves into the life of the colony by breakfasting with the settlers every day and trading peacefully; then suddenly, on signal, they rose up and slaughtered their hosts. With equal cunning, the colonists later carried out reprisals in kind. They invited 250 Indians to a peace conference and offered them poisoned wine which killed them all. The massacre and the approaching bankruptcy of the company, which had not yet seen a real return on its investment, made the future of the colony uncertain. The following year, a royal commission investigated the company's management of the settlement. As a result, in 1624 a trial was held in London, and the court ordered the company's privileges revoked. The colony was handed over to the king and his privy council.

A first royal governor, Francis Wyatt, was dispatched immediately. The House of Burgesses was dissolved; the king was having trouble with Parliament and did not want to encourage independence among his subjects on the other side of the Atlantic. Under the governor, however, self-determination reappeared in another form. He brought together a group of former representatives from the House of Burgesses which began to function as the governor's council. This body wielded almost as much power as the House of Burgesses. In 1629, the House of Burgesses again began to meet, but without official sanction. It met this way until 1639, when a crown commission recognized its permanent right to exist.

Although the Jamestown colony turned out to be a financial disaster and 4,600 settlers perished, an enduring settlement was built. Farms began to flourish, children were being raised in the New World, the Indian threat was diminishing and, after 1629, annual assemblies were meeting and passing laws whether or not they had the king's approval.

MARYLAND: A PROPRIETARY GRANT

The colony that was settled to the north of Virginia was a private, not a business, enterprise. Virginia had been devised as a profit-making venture by a joint-stock company. Maryland, on the other hand, began as a vast feudal estate granted to a single nobleman, Lord Calvert, who envisioned the colony as a refuge for persecuted Catholics like himself.

George Calvert was not born a nobleman, but through his education at Oxford, connections, and hard work, he rose to be secretary of state in the king's privy council. While occupying that position, he took a great interest in schemes to settle the New World, serving as one of those commissioners who dissolved the London Company and made Virginia a royal colony.

Another very important change occurred in Calvert's life during his years of service to the throne—he converted to Catholicism. As a Catholic, Calvert was of little use to the government. His religion made him unpopular in an Anglican country, subject to suspicion in his dealings with Catholic countries such as Spain, and technically disloyal, since no Catholic could take the Oath of Supremacy that recognized the monarch as supreme head of both church and state. Accordingly, Calvert stepped down from power. Nevertheless, he remained a royal favorite. The king personally excused him from the necessity of taking the Oath of Supremacy. He also made Calvert a noble, with the title of Baron Baltimore of Baltimore (an estate in Ireland).

As early as 1623 Calvert received a charter from the king for a huge tract of land

RELIGIOUS FREEDOM

In order to prevent the religious intolerance that had wracked England for a century, Lord Baltimore ordered "no scandal or offense to be given to any of the Protestants" by the Catholics. Although the Calverts intended Maryland as a refuge for Catholics, Protestants outnumbered Catholics from the start. This potentially explosive situation was held in check by a number of other measures instituted by the Calverts. In 1649 an official "Toleration Act" was made law, banning all religious insults. (Catholics were forbidden to call Protestants "heretics" and Protestants could not scream "popish priest" at a Catholic.) More important, the law provided that no person who admitted belief in Jesus Christ would be molested for his religious beliefs. This act was an important step toward the religious freedom that ultimately would become a fundamental civil liberty in the United States.

REPRESENTATIONAL GOVERNMENT

Seeds of representative government were also taking root in Maryland. Its charter had guaranteed Lord Baltimore and his heirs nearly total control over the administration of the government, but with the "advice, assent, and approbation of freemen." To receive this assent, the governor convened an assembly 3 years after the colony was settled. The assemblymen, however, immediately balked at the notion of simply rubber-stamping the laws handed down to them. Like the members of Parliament back in England, the assemblymen wanted the right to initiate legislation. They also demanded the right of freedom from arrest for any rebellious remarks they might make during a session (setting a precedent for the concept of congressional immunity later stated in the Constitution). Although Lord Baltimore rejected in principle the assembly's right to draft laws of its own, he soon discovered that he had

to bow to the people's will if he wanted his statutes approved. Before long, legislation was being suggested by the assembly, and most of the proprietor's proposals were rewritten by the people's representatives. By 1650 Maryland had a strong legislature, divided into two houses. In this way, Maryland arrived at a form of government similar to that of Virginia: each had a governor and upper house, or council of local property holders (in Virginia appointed by the king and in Maryland by the proprietor), and an assembly made up of two men from each of the local counties elected by the colonists themselves (the House of Burgesses in Virginia and the House of Commons in Maryland).

LIFE IN THE CHESAPEAKE BAY AREA

Although Virginia was a royal colony after the 1620s, and Maryland the personal property of the Calverts, life was essentially similar in the two settlements. Occasionally, Virginia would pass an anti-Catholic law or Maryland would try to undersell Virginia in tobacco, but in general the interests of the two colonies became closely intertwined. Part of the reason for this interdependence was in the nature of the Chesapeake Bay area itself.

The bay, which is nearly 200 miles long and 22 miles wide, is fed by scores of little waterways—some real rivers, others only creeks. This immense system of natural "roads" produced two distinct features of life in the area. One was that tobacco was cheap to transport since no plantation was more than a few hundred feet away from the water. Farmers could ship their half-ton hogsheads of tobacco easily in canoes to Jamestown or St. Mary's, or oceangoing vessels could enter the deep rivers and pick up cargoes at individual wharves for many miles into the interior, where the produce was transferred to vessels sailing for England. Second, rapid transportation and to-bacco farming discouraged the growth of villages and encouraged the settlement of farms. As a consequence, the bay area was extremely hard to rule. ("For how is it possible to govern a people so dispersed?" complained one English official.)

The Bay area was hard to administer in the first few years for another reason: a large part of the population was made up of those considered "undesirables." As early as 1618, the city of London had sent over to Virginia one hundred homeless children, and in 1619 another hundred vagrants, paupers, and thieves were also shipped over—"fellons and other desperate villanes," as one Virginia document described them. However, by the latter part of the seventeenth century, most of those who came were farmers or artisans, and one fourth were women.

Slaves made up a part of the Chesapeake Bay population from almost its earliest days. By 1670 some two thousand blacks had been brought from Africa or the West Indies to Virginia (which had a population of 40,000 white settlers by that time). Although huge tobacco plantations employing extensive slave labor did not become characteristic of Southern life until the eighteenth century, Virginia had already legalized life-long slavery by 1661.

BACON'S REBELLION

As the colonists pushed inland, the Indians stepped up their attacks on white outposts. Frontier plantations (which had moved only 50 miles inland from Jamestown by 1670) suffered repeated raids from Indians. The frontiersmen, mostly old-time settlers who had abandoned the coast to newer arrivals, appealed in vain to the royal governor, William Berkeley, for help.

Berkeley and his friends were engaged in profitable trade with the Indians. Moreover, Berkeley was afraid of stirring up a full-scale war between Indians and colo-nists. His indecision aroused the wrath of the frontiersmen. They despised Berkeley on other counts as well. He was the agent who administered oppressive new English taxes and laws and he had not called for an election of members to the House of Burgesses in 15 years. In the eyes of the frontiersmen, many of whom had been in Virginia since the early days, Berkeley and his circle represented a group of newcomers who were more interested in serving the crown than in aiding Virginia and who favored Jamestown over the hinterland in the government of the colony.

As a result, a rebellion broke out against Berkeley, led by his cousin (by marriage), Nathaniel Bacon. Backed by older, established frontier planters Bacon took the law in his own hands and slaughtered two neighboring Indian tribes. Berkeley labeled Bacon a rebel and ordered him to stop his raids on the Indians. Bacon responded by rallying five hundred men and marching on Jamestown. The frightened governor and House of Burgesses were forced to grant Bacon's request for an army with which he could continue his fight against the Indians. The House also enacted "Bacon's Laws" which were measures intended to destroy Berkeley's power and reestablish the position of the older settlers whom Bacon represented.

The differences between Bacon and Berkeley became more serious. When Bacon returned to the frontier, Berkeley once more branded him as a rebel; in revenge, Bacon marched on Jamestown and burned it. But suddenly, in October, 1676, Bacon died of dysentery and his rebellion collapsed. Berkeley executed twenty of Bacon's followers before the king's commissioners arrived in Jamestown to remove him from office. The brief but chaotic rebellion caused England to tighten her controls over the colonies of Chesapeake Bay by increasing the authority of the royal governors. This began a long period of controversy between Virginians and their governors.

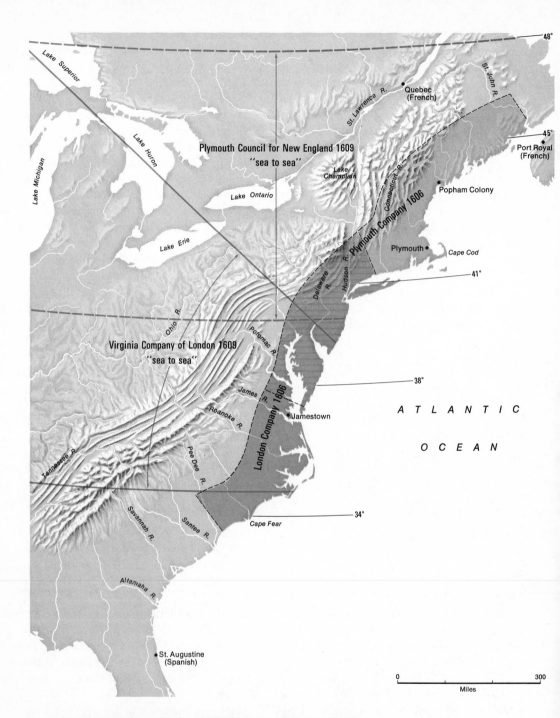

EARLY COLONIAL LAND GRANTS · 1606 TO 1620

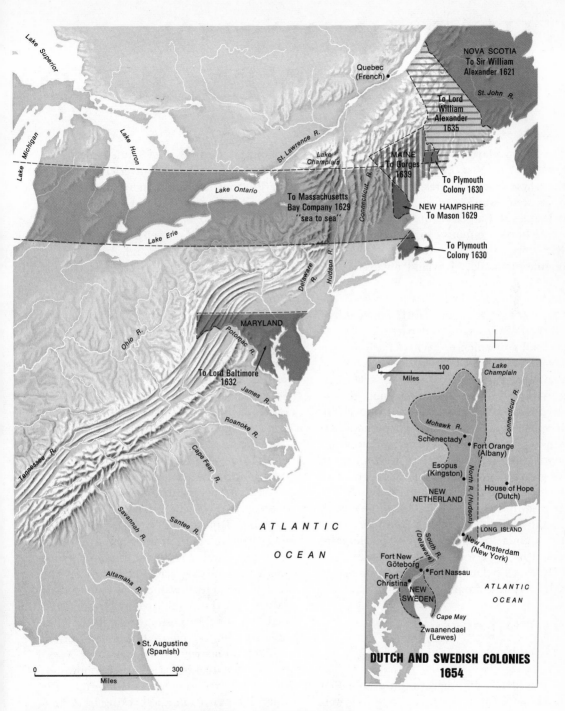

Quebec (French)

NOVA SCOTIA
To Sir William
Alexander 1621

St. John R.

To Lord
William
Alexander
1635

Lake
Champlain

St. Lawrence R.

MAINE
To Gorges
1639

To Plymouth
Colony 1630

Lake Ontario

To Massachusetts
Bay Company 1629
"sea to sea"

NEW HAMPSHIRE
To Mason 1629

Lake Erie

To Plymouth
Colony 1630

Connecticut R.

Delaware R.

Hudson R.

Ohio R.

MARYLAND

Potomac R.

To Lord Baltimore
1632

James R.

Roanoke R.

Cape Fear R.

Tennessee R.

Savannah R.

Santee R.

Altamaha R.

A T L A N T I C

O C E A N

St. Augustine
(Spanish)

0   300
Miles

DUTCH AND SWEDISH COLONIES 1654

0   100
Miles

Lake
Champlain

Mohawk R.

Schenectady

Fort Orange
(Albany)

Connecticut R.

Esopus
(Kingston)

House of Hope
(Dutch)

NEW
NETHERLAND

North R. (Hudson)

LONG ISLAND

South R.
(Delaware)

New Amsterdam
(New York)

Fort New
Göteborg

Fort Nassau

Fort
Christina

NEW
SWEDEN

A T L A N T I C
O C E A N

Cape May

Zwaanendael
(Lewes)

EARLY COLONIAL LAND GRANTS • 1620 TO 1639

THE FOUNDING OF NEW ENGLAND

Religion played a far greater role in the settlement of New England than it did in the Chesapeake Bay area. Maryland, as we have seen, was designed as a refuge for beleaguered Catholics, but since Catholics were always a minority in the colony, Lord Baltimore and his successors never attempted to make Maryland an exclusively Catholic settlement, built upon Catholic dogma. Virginia was a stronghold of the Church of England and a 1643 law required all non-Anglicans to "depart the colony with all convenience." When Puritans and Quakers attempted to settle in Virginia, they were eased out, so that by 1660, Virginia could claim less opposition to the Anglican faith than existed in England. Despite such conformity—or perhaps because of it—religion was never an important motivation for the settlers who came to Virginia. Virginia offered no more religious freedom than did England; its church was, at least in theory, identical with the church in the mother country. Adventurers came to Virginia for profit, not for the hope of practicing a persecuted faith in peace.

In New England, however, religion played a leading role from the start.

THE PILGRIMS' ARRIVAL

The first Englishmen to settle New England came for religious reasons but were backed by merchants—thus combining once again the two elements that, singly or in combination, always figured so importantly in the colonization of the New World: religion and economics. The Spaniards had conquered Central and South America in order to gain gold and convert Indians; but the Pilgrims had much more modest ambitions. They wanted simply to repay the merchants who had financed their voyage and to practice their religion far from the oppressive hand of England.

The Pilgrims, as we discovered in the previous chapter, were Separatists—that is, Puritans who wished not to reform the Church of England but to break from it altogether. The sect had arisen in a little town called Scrooby in northern England among a group of well-to-do farmers. The people of Scrooby had so tormented the Separatists in their midst that the Separatists fled to Holland, known for its tolerance, where they eventually settled in the town of Leyden. But life in The Netherlands did not completely suit the Separatists. Most were farmers, and city life seemed strange and unnatural to them. Moreover, their children were growing up speaking Dutch and some were drifting away from the faith of their parents. Catholic Spain—and the Spanish Inquisition—was trying to conquer Holland. What the Leyden Separatists wanted was land of their own, where they could live by farming, and maintain English customs and the English language, but be removed from persecution.

They found what they wanted in America. Before making the voyage, however, they had to obtain permission from the English government and backing from English merchants. The king, after exacting a promise that the Leyden Separatist group or Pilgrims, as they called themselves, would remain loyal to him personally, promised not to molest them so long as "they carried themselves peaceably." The London Company of Virginia in 1620 granted the Pilgrims a patent, permitting them to settle in Virginia. The money for the venture came from a hardware dealer of questionable character named Thomas Weston and several of his fellow merchants, who banded together in a joint-stock company. The agreement between the company and the Pilgrims stated that in return for funding the passage over, the colonists would divide all profits equally with the merchants after 7 years. The financial affairs of the company would be managed by officers residing both in London and in the New World.

Thirty-five Separatists, some from Leyden and some from London, sailed from England in August, 1620. They started out in two ships, the *Speedwell* and the *Mayflower*, but the first ship quickly sprang a leak, and both had to turn back. Finally in September 102 persons set out in the *Mayflower,* only a third of them Pilgrims, and the majority "strangers," as the Pilgrims called those not of their faith. Among the "strangers" were John Alden, a sympathizer of the persecuted Pilgrims, and Captain Miles Standish, who helped prevent a mutiny when the *Mayflower* sighted land, not in Virginia but on the cold, rocky New England coast.

Finding themselves outside of the jurisdiction of the London Company of Virginia and their patent useless, the Pilgrims, who

A Currier and Ives print of the landing of the Pilgrims at Plymouth in December, 1620. By spring, half of the 102 Pilgrims had died. Those who survived did so through the help of the Indian in the picture, Squanto, who befriended the Pilgrims and taught them to fish and plant corn.

were in the minority, feared that the "strangers" (some of whom were an "undesirable lot" according to the Pilgrim leader and historian, William Bradford) would "use their own liberty" and run wild. To prevent chaos, the Pilgrims, while still aboard ship, drew up the famous Mayflower Compact, a document scarcely two hundred words long. In it, the forty-one men who signed it said they were forming a "body politic" and that they would obey whatever laws the group passed. The compact was not a constitution, only a temporary measure until such time as the Pilgrims could obtain a patent from the rightful possessors of New England.

The legal landlords of New England were a company of forty aristocrats called the Council of New England. They were led by Sir Ferdinando Gorges, who had won from the king a royal charter supplanting the old charter granted to the Virginia Company of Plymouth. Like the earlier Plymouth Company, the Council of New England did little to settle its vast holdings beyond discussing how the land would some day be divided into feudal estates—when and if it were colonized. The unexpected and unplanned arrival of the Pilgrims was not at all what Gorges and his associates had had in mind, but on June 1, 1621, the Council issued a patent to Pierce and Associates, the firm representing Weston's London merchants, and the Pilgrims now in America.

The Pilgrims landed on December 21, 1620, at Plymouth in New England. Never did an enterprise face more difficulties. By spring, half of the settlers had died, and the survivors were saved from starvation only by the help of a friendly Indian named Squanto, who taught these intense, pious

people how to fish and plant corn. The pilgrims gathered sometime in October, 1621, to give thanks to God for their first harvest. They had little else to cheer them. When the London merchants sent the *Mayflower* to Plymouth the following November, it brought no supplies, only thirty-five more mouths to feed. As late as the 1640s Plymouth could claim only one plow. The Pilgrims had brought no livestock with them on their original voyage, and 6 years later there was still only one cow to every six people and one goat to every three. The region produced scarcely any useful commodities other than furs, lumber, and fish.

The possibility of getting a return on their investment seemed so remote to the London merchants that they were willing to sell their interest to the Pilgrims on November 15, 1626. The purchase, however, placed the tiny, impoverished community under an enormous debt that took 17 years to pay off.

In its formative years Plymouth was governed by William Bradford, who ruled the community with absolute authority from 1620 to 1657 (except for a period of 5 years). During his administration Plymouth became a self-supporting colony and new towns were added. The problems of government became increasingly complex and in 1636 the "Great Fundamentals" were drawn up. This was the first system of laws that originated in the colonies; it created representative government for the Pilgrims. The laws provided that two deputies would be elected from each town to a single-bodied legislature that sat with the governor and his assistants.

The expedition of Pilgrims originated in Holland, after obtaining a patent from the King of England for a tract of land in Virginia. Although they started out in two ships, only the Mayflower completed the trip. Carrying 102 persons, the Mayflower, was extremely overcrowded during the 63-day trip.

Bradford's position rested on very shaky ground, since the settlers were never able to obtain a charter from the king and their patent from the Council of New England was a rather vague document that said nothing about the establishment of a civil government. Finally, in 1691, Plymouth and the villages it had spawned were absorbed against their will into the much more flourishing Massachusetts Bay colony that had grown up around the city of Boston.

THE MASSACHUSETTS BAY COMPANY

Whereas the Pilgrim venture was small, poorly financed, and sustained only by courage and religious conviction, the Massachusetts Bay Company was, by contrast, made up of many well-to-do merchants and nobles with keen business sense. These settlers arrived in New England 10 years after the Pilgrim crossing, in a great fleet of eleven ships (seven carrying about seven hundred people, the rest carrying livestock and supplies).

These triumphant newcomers were Puritans. Like the Pilgrims, they despised the "popish practices" that in their estimation continued to infect the Church of England. But unlike the Pilgrims, they remained loyal to that Church, wanting only to reform it, not break away from it altogether. Another difference between the two groups was that the Pilgrims continued to recognize the king of England as their sovereign, while the Puritans wanted to escape his authority altogether. The Puritans were Calvinists and like Calvin, they longed to build a self-governed community of saints. The New England Puritans had an unshakable conviction that God would favor their migration. "We doubt not but God will be with us," one Puritan wrote, "and if God be with us, who can be against us?"

Their spiritual confidence was matched by their common sense. For example, the

Puritans sailed in March, 1630, departing in the spring so that they would be able to plant a crop before winter set in. They laid in a large supply of limes in order to prevent an outbreak of scurvy during the voyage. When they landed at Salem, they were met by four hundred settlers who had come over in two groups (in 1628 and 1629) to prepare the way for those who followed. Most important, the Puritans established from the outset the right to rule themselves.

The Puritans were granted a royal charter by King Charles I which formed them into a joint-stock company called the Massachusetts Bay Company. The charter gave twenty-six investors the right to land which lay approximately between the Merrimac and the Charles rivers, the area between what is now Boston and the border of Maine. Essentially, this charter resembled earlier charters that had been granted the Virginia Company of London, except that it granted the new company virtual self-control over its affairs. There was no provision in the document insisting that the charter or company headquarters remain in England.

This was the first time in the history of joint-stock companies that the headquarters of an enterprise moved from the mother country to the colonies. The Puritans realized that if they took the charter and a number of the twenty-six investors *with* them to America, they would be a legally separate and self-governing body politic, free from all interference by royal governors and English officials (including the members of Parliament). The Puritans could make their own laws, decide on their own taxes, establish their own school system, administer their own justice and, most importantly, determine their own religious life.

The 1630 migration, therefore, was unlike any earlier English movement of settlers. The Puritans, united in religious purpose and well financed, carried with them all of the governmental machinery they would need to rule themselves in America. Only a small office continued to represent the company in London, and it had little power. When John Winthrop, the first governor of the Company, stepped off his ship, the *Jewel,* he carried the charter with him into the New World. The Puritan dream of founding an independent City of God finally had been realized.

Soon after landing, the Puritans decided that Salem would not do for their holy city simply because "It pleased them not," as one wrote in a letter. Many decided on Boston as a suitable site, while others settled the towns of Charlestown, Medford, Watertown, Roxbury, and Dorchester. Even with the precautions against hunger taken by the new settlers, nearly two hundred people died the first winter from starvation, but fresh supplies came in February and by the middle of 1631 additional Puritans had arrived in New England, bringing with them guns, saws, and window glass. The Puritans, except for their first difficult winter, never suffered the horrors of Jamestown or Plymouth.

THE GREAT MIGRATION

During the next 10 years, 15-20,000 more Puritans flooded into New England, while many more fled to the English colonies in the West Indies. This influx of Puritans into the New World was called the "Great Migration." What were the Puritans trying to escape? Why did so many of them leave England between 1630 and 1640?

The answers lie in the bitter struggles that took place between King Charles I and Parliament. The king eventually dissolved Parliament, thereby crushing Puritan hopes of church and state reform. Moreover, the king was displaying an increasing impatience with all sects that refused to conform to the Church of England. Puritan ministers were turned out of their churches. Puritan books were burned. Government officials who happened to be Puritans felt the weight of royal displeasure.

Political and religious oppression in England was matched by economic decline. Prices and unemployment rose. Rents for farmland were fixed by law, and landlords found that these sums were worth much less during the current period of inflation. Many of the leading Puritans were country squires; these disgruntled landlords saw their property losing its value every day and they concluded that a mighty disaster was about to demolish the entire country. They believed evil and corruption stalked the land. As John Winthrop wrote, it was better to "avoid the plague when it is foreseen than to tarry till it should overtake us."

A PURITAN GOVERNMENT

The Puritan leaders were determined to keep the vices of the Old World out of the New. In order to ensure that the Massachusetts Bay Company would remain as pure as humanly possible, they instituted a strong government closely modeled after Puritan religious ideals. These settlers were not interested in democracy. Only the virtuous deserved a voice in the administration of colony affairs. Accordingly, only male church members were permitted to vote. By requiring church membership for the right to vote, the Puritan leaders, in violation of the Massachusetts Bay Company Charter, tried to prevent the colony from ever losing its religious character.

Becoming a church member was no easy matter. It was an arduous process during which a candidate had to demonstrate that he had been specially touched by God's grace and overcome by a revelation of the true meaning of being a Christian. A congregation could reject an applicant because of such crimes as "rash carriage and speeches savoring of self confidence," or for being "too much addicted to the world," or for overcharging for grain. Puritan theology may have seemed harsh and exclusive to later generations of Americans, but, in fact, Puritans as a group were more interested

in carrying out God's glory in a settlement dedicated to Him than in merely establishing themselves as personally among the elect. This sense of purpose gave them courage in the new and often hostile environment of New England, as we shall see in the next chapter.

The New England settlers, unlike their counterparts in Virginia and Maryland, did not settle on individual farms but in towns. They felt safer in numbers, and most important, town living made it easier to practice their religion. The center of each town was the meeting house (often serving as a town hall as well) which stood at one end of the village green. The inhabitants of the town lived in houses surrounding the green. Their farms, wooded areas for hunting, fishing, pasturage, and firewood were close by the town.

Shortly after arriving in the New World, the administrators of the Massachusetts Bay Company were forced to turn their trading company into a commonwealth. Originally Governor Winthrop, his lieutenant governor, and a handful of other stockholders had held absolute power over both the company and the colony (which, in the unusual provisions of the charter, were really only two aspects of the same venture). In the language of seventeenth-century English business, all stockholders were "freemen," that is, voting members of a company. But more than one hundred adult males (all Puritans of good standing) did not hold stock and were therefore excluded from participation in government. Under pressure from them, Winthrop and his aides decided to extend the meaning of "freeman" so that they too were able to vote for the governor's assistants, who, along with the governor and lieutenant governor, made up a legislative and judicial body. This assembly was called the General Court, and met four times a year to create new laws.

Representative government slowly took form in the Massachusetts Bay Colony. In 1632 the freemen gained the right to elect the governor directly, and in 1634 a growing number of communities insisted that each town be represented by two or three deputies in the General Court, all elected annually by the freemen. As the years passed by, the governor's absolute (albeit, highly ethical) rule was more and more restricted by the citizens. At first the deputies had no real power to enforce their decisions against the will of the governor and his assistants. But in 1644 an argument over a pig changed all this. A poor widow who ran a boarding house and a rich merchant and moneylender got into an argument over who owned a plain white sow. The governor's assistants (called magistrates) favored the moneylender, while most of the people's deputies took the side of the poor woman, Mrs. Sherman. The magistrates had the right to veto all decisions made by the deputies. Suddenly a raging debate broke out over the magistrates' authority, with deputies demanding an equal voice. Governor Winthrop, alarmed by the demand, pointed out that if the magistrates lost their right to veto the actions of the deputies, the colony would degenerate into a democracy and that according to the Holy Scriptures, "there is no such government in Israel." The deputies stood fast, and in 1644 the General Court was divided into two houses. The upper house consisted of the governor and his magistrates, the lower (still known as the General Court) of the deputies. Each house had to approve of the proposals made by the other. Thereby, over the question of a pig, Massachusetts ultimately gained a bicameral, or two-house, legislature. One of the original features of the Puritan commonwealth—government by magistrates who acted as the spokesmen of God—had been destroyed.

Winthrop was also outflanked by the people on another issue of great importance to him. He had always opposed a codification of laws, partly because he feared that a written body of statutes would provide evidence for their enemies in England against the Puritan rule in Massachusetts, and partly because he believed only those laws should be written down that actually appeared in the Bible. But the people were unwilling to let Winthrop continue governing as a self-appointed spokesman for God and the Divine will. In 1641 the deputies pushed through a Body of Liberties, which provided for trial by jury. In 1648, this code was extended into The Laws and Liberties, which lessened punishments for criminals and debtors, and simplified and strengthened the court system. Specific punishments were established for specific crimes. The governor's arbitrary authority was abolished.

While only freemen, that is, male church members, could vote for members of the General Court, in the towns even nonfreemen could hold local offices and vote in the general town meeting and hold local offices, such as "hog reeve," fire warden, or "fense mender." Such town meetings became an important instrument for direct participation in government, and even now in many small communities of New England, townsmen vote directly on local issues.

THE EXPANSION OF NEW ENGLAND

Twentieth-century students of the colonial period sometimes find it difficult to understand how seriously the Puritans took small points of religious doctrine, and yet Rhode Island, for example, was founded solely over a theological argument.

RHODE ISLAND

Massachusetts was a Puritan Commonwealth whose government was viewed as an instrument for securing the religious foundation of daily life. Church attendance was compulsory for all citizens, although, as we have seen, not all citizens were deemed worthy to be church members: this law was designed to convert the unregenerate or at least keep them from further temptation. The Ten Commandments were the basis for all commonwealth laws. Taxes were levied to pay ministers' salaries. Voting was based on church membership and property ownership.

In 1631, a highly intelligent and pious young minister named Roger Williams moved to New England and soon began questioning the assumptions upon which the commonwealth was structured. Williams was a Separatist like the Pilgrims. He believed that the Church of England was beyond redemption and attacked the Puritans' attachment to it. Although the Puritans desperately wanted to reform the Church of England to rid it of bishops and such "popish practices" as kneeling and incense, they nevertheless regarded it as their sacred mother, and permitted New Englanders to attend Anglican church services when they went home to England on visits. Williams considered this loose bond unacceptable. He demanded a complete break. He also contended that the Massachusetts law requiring compulsory church attendance brought "unregenerate" sinners into houses of worship. He could find no precedent in the Scriptures for such a practice. According to Williams, only those who were

One of the earliest Puritan houses made from tree bark, in Salem, Mass. Because the Puritans brought no glass or carpenter's tools with them, they were forced to work with available materials and primitive tools.

regenerate, who had been "born again" into God's love, should be admitted to church services. But exactly who was regenerate? This question tormented Williams so much that finally he decided that only he and his wife were regenerate beyond a shadow of a doubt.

Politically, young Williams was even more of a trouble-maker. He felt that the king of England's claim to America was ridiculous. The English did not own the land, nor had they discovered it. Properly speaking, the land belonged to the Indians, and the English should have bought it from them. The Puritans in Massachusetts had paid the Indians for lands under cultivation which they took from them but had helped themselves to undeveloped territory, which they regarded as free for the taking. He attacked the Massachusetts government on yet another score. Why should people pay taxes to support ministers? What right did the General Court and the governor have to legislate the Ten Commandments? In what passage from the Bible did Puritans find their justification for such high-handed procedures?

All of these doubts raised by Williams threatened to disrupt the cohesiveness of the colony and the magistrates banished him in 1635. With a few followers, he fled south and founded a new colony, Providence, Rhode Island. There he had a chance to fulfill his own beliefs. The new colony broke with the Church of England. The civil government was not allowed to interfere with religious matters at all. Williams' persistent doubts over exactly who had been redeemed led him to institute religious freedom. In the Massachusetts Bay Colony, Catholics and Protestant sects other than the Puritans were not allowed to practice their religion, but in Rhode Island Williams came to believe that since it was unclear which was the *true* religion, all groups should be allowed to seek after ultimate wisdom in their own fashion. For the first time in America genuine religious freedom was practiced.

Another overly scrupulous Puritan, Anne Hutchinson, was banished from Massachusetts about the same time as Williams. Mrs. Hutchinson, who had a large following, discussed theology at least once a week in her house. She believed that good works and moral behavior had nothing to do with salvation. Quite the contrary; God might reveal his divine truths to a sinner and keep an upright man in darkness forever. The Puritans held a different belief. They subscribed to the notion that a sudden revelation was necessary for salvation, but they thought such a revelation, or conversion, could occur only to those who had led exemplary lives. Mrs. Hutchinson's "heresy" threatened to divide the colony. According to her theory, neither church attendance, sessions of prayer, nor moral behavior, nor even the clergy were necessary. All of the laws of the society were useless in promoting the most important goal—salvation. In 1638, Anne Hutchinson was banished. Like Roger Williams, she fled with her family to Rhode Island, where she founded Portsmouth.

In 1640, Roger Williams applied for a charter to the overwhelmingly Puritan Parliament, which King Charles I had been forced to recall. The charter was granted in 1644. It provided for an assembly based on representation from the towns and a governor with assistants, much like the Massachusetts Bay government. But there was one notable difference—in Rhode Island the right to vote was not confined to church members.

CONNECTICUT, NEW HAMPSHIRE, AND MAINE

Other Puritan colonies also sprang up in New England. They were not always primarily the result of religious quarrels, although occasionally congregations started new settlements because they found life in Boston or other older towns either too strict or too wicked and licentious (Boston, after all, had two taverns). In 1636, Thomas Hooker, a minister from Cambridge, led his congregation to the Connecticut Valley and established four towns there, including Hartford and Springfield. This group had moved westward in search of better land and a less oppressive religious atmosphere. The colony was modeled after Massachusetts, but here, as in Rhode Island, suffrage was no longer restricted to church members. The Fundamental Orders of Connecticut of 1639, the first written constitution in the New World, left voter qualifications up to the individual towns. In 1638 John Davenport and Theophilus Eaton established New Haven, a strict little religious colony south of Hartford. Hartford and New Haven banded together as Connecticut and obtained a charter from the English government in 1662, the year before Portsmouth and Providence received their second charter as Rhode Island. Connecticut and Rhode Island retained their charters, under which they continued to elect all their officials, throughout the colonial period.

Puritan settlers in the colony of New Hampshire, to the north of Massachusetts, were separated from the Bay colony in 1679 by the British government. Massachusetts Bay colonists had also penetrated into the area of Maine, and Massachusetts incorporated these settlements under her jurisdiction in 1658. The area remained a part of Massachusetts until 1820, when Maine became a separate state in the American union.

In spite of the religious and economic forces that drew the New England colonies apart, they found they had common goals requiring a certain amount of cooperation. The first attempt of American colonies to work together for common goals occurred in 1643, when Massachusetts Bay, Connecticut, New Haven, and Plymouth created "The Confederation of the United Colonies of New England" which lasted until 1684. Its members feared possible danger from French and Dutch settlers in North America, and Massachusetts dreamed of uprooting the Rhode Island heretics, but the chief purpose of this union was to stave off Indian attacks. The Indians, alarmed by the rapid expansion of Puritan settlements, made frequent raids on frontier villages. These attacks brought on reprisals, and the resulting strife with the Indians led to a bloody, year-long war between the colonists of the New England Confederation and the followers of the chieftain known as King Philip. In 1675, at about the same time that frontier pressures erupted in Bacon's rebellion in Virginia, the Confederation was being tested in King Philip's War. Some five hundred colonists and at least a thousand Indians were killed. Many captured warriors were sent as slaves to the West Indies. With the frontier relatively quiet, the New England Confederation fell into disuse.

Although the economy of New England had originally depended on farming and unlimited trade in lumber and fur, by the middle of the seventeenth century agriculture had been superseded by commerce. The merchant became the key figure in the New England economy, and many New England merchants achieved great wealth. Fishing also became a source of New England wealth, and great quantities of seafood were exported to Europe. The Puritan settlers of the New World found no single commodity as valuable as tobacco, which had enriched the Virginians, or sugar, which had become the basis of the West Indian economy. This deprivation, however, proved to be a blessing in disguise, forcing the people of New England to make commerce their business and to diversify their economy.

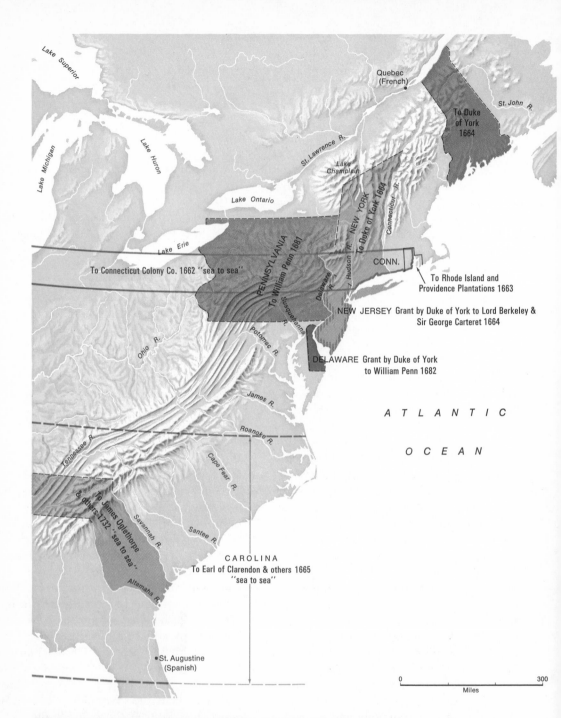

To Duke
of York
1664

Quebec
(French)

St. John R.

Lake Superior

Lake Michigan

Lake Huron

Lake Ontario

St. Lawrence R.

Lake Champlain

Connecticut R.

Lake Erie

NEW YORK

To Duke of York 1664

Hudson R.

CONN.

To Connecticut Colony Co. 1662 "sea to sea"

PENNSYLVANIA
To William Penn 1681

Susquehanna R.

Delaware R.

To Rhode Island and
Providence Plantations 1663

NEW JERSEY Grant by Duke of York to Lord Berkeley &
Sir George Carteret 1664

Ohio R.

Potomac R.

DELAWARE Grant by Duke of York
to William Penn 1682

James R.

A T L A N T I C

Tennessee R.

Roanoke R.

O C E A N

Cape Fear R.

To James Oglethorpe
& others 1732 "sea to sea"

Savannah R.

Santee R.

CAROLINA
To Earl of Clarendon & others 1665
"sea to sea"

Altamaha R.

St. Augustine
(Spanish)

0   300
Miles

EARLY COLONIAL LAND GRANTS · 1662 TO 1732

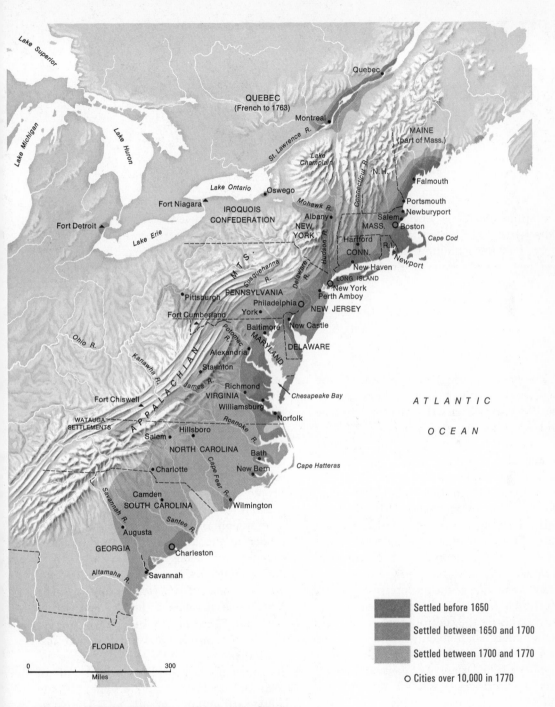

Lake Superior

Lake Michigan

Lake Huron

Quebec

QUEBEC
(French to 1763)

Montreal

St. Lawrence R.

MAINE
(part of Mass.)

Lake Champlain

Lake Ontario   Oswego

Fort Niagara

Mohawk R.

**IROQUOIS
CONFEDERATION**

Fort Detroit

Lake Erie

N.H.

Falmouth

Portsmouth
Newburyport
Salem

Connecticut R.

Albany

**NEW
YORK**

Hartford

MASS. Boston

Cape Cod

CONN.

Hudson R.

R.I.

New Haven

Newport

Susquehanna R.

Pittsburgh

M T S.

PENNSYLVANIA

Delaware R.

LONG ISLAND

New York

Perth Amboy

Philadelphia

Fort Cumberland

York

NEW JERSEY

Potomac R.

Baltimore

New Castle

MARYLAND

DELAWARE

Alexandria

Staunton

James R.

Richmond

VIRGINIA

Fort Chiswell

Williamsburg

Chesapeake Bay

A P P A L A C H I A N

Ohio R.

Kanawha R.

**WATAUGA
SETTLEMENTS**

Norfolk

Roanoke R.

A T L A N T I C

O C E A N

Salem

Hillsboro

NORTH CAROLINA

Bath

Cape Fear R.

New Bern

Cape Hatteras

Charlotte

Camden

SOUTH CAROLINA

Savannah R.

Santee R.

Wilmington

Augusta

GEORGIA   Charleston

Altamaha R.   Savannah

FLORIDA

0   300

Miles

Settled before 1650

Settled between 1650 and 1700

Settled between 1700 and 1770

O Cities over 10,000 in 1770

COLONIAL SETTLEMENT · 1650 TO 1770

THE PROPRIETARY GRANTS

Virginia and New England were originally settled by joint-stock companies, but the rest of the Atlantic seaboard was parceled out by the king of England to his favorites, much as Maryland had been granted to Lord Baltimore.

NEW YORK

The area between New England and the Chesapeake settlements was bestowed in 1664 by King Charles II on his brother, the Duke of York. However, part of the land was already in the possession of England's commercial rival, the Dutch. As early as 1624 a Dutch outpost had been established at Albany, and in 1626 New Amsterdam was founded on Manhattan Island. Originally the Dutch planned to populate the entire Hudson Valley with immense feudal estates called patroonships, but only one, Rensselaerswyck, was actually successful.

By the middle of the seventeenth century, the Dutch and the English had become the chief rivals for the control of sea trade. The Netherlands boasted only a tiny population of two million, but its merchant fleet dominated the Orient, its fishermen reigned over the North Sea, its wool mills outproduced and undersold English producers. Partly because their population was so small, and partly because North America promised little immediate return on an investment, the Dutch were never especially dedicated to colonizing the Hudson River Valley. Nonetheless, they used New Amsterdam as a base from which their ships could raid gold-bearing Spanish galleons, or compete in commerce with English merchant vessels. Moreover, the Hudson River Valley was the chief entrance to the fur regions of the interior.

By the 1670s Great Britain had, through a series of naval engagements, reduced Dutch sea power, driving the Dutch out of North America and eliminating this rival to her control of the profitable tobacco trade with Virginia and commercial contracts with New England. In April, 1664, an English officer, Colonel Richard Nicholls, leading four ships, was able to seize the unprepared Dutch colony of 10,000 people on Manhattan without a fight.

From its very beginnings, New York was a cosmopolitan city. At the time of its surrender to the English, eighteen languages were already being spoken in Manhattan and so many religious sects prevailed that one governor wrote: "Here be not many of the Church of England; few Roman Catholics; abundance of Quakers . . . ; Singing Quakers, Ranting Quakers; Sabbatarians; Antisabbatarians; some Anabaptists; some independents; some Jews; in short, of all sorts and opinions there are some, and the most part of none at all. . . . The most prevailing opinion is that of the Dutch Calvinists." So sophisticated were rich young ladies that they followed Parisian fashions and spoke several languages. The Dutch had provided a few schools, a fire patrol, and a small police force in the town. There were also some thirty taverns doing a thriving business by 1680 and rents were already considered outrageously high.

Until 1691 the colony of New York was ruled by a governor and his council, appointed by the proprietor, and only in the last decade of the seventeenth century did the colony receive a representative government of its own. The economy also lagged behind that of New England; New Yorkers were slow to exploit the advantages of their farm lands and their superb harbor at the mouth of the Hudson.

NEW JERSEY

Besides New York, three other English colonies were carved out of the land under the Duke of York's jurisdiction: New Jersey, Pennsylvania, and Delaware. In 1664, after the Duke of York received the grant to New York from his brother, the king, he immediately gave part of his territories to two of his friends, Sir George Carteret and Lord John Berkeley. As a compliment to Carteret, who had once served as governor of the Isle of Jersey, Lord Berkeley named the territory New Jersey. In 1676 the territories belonging to the two friends were formally divided. Lord Berkeley's half, which he had sold to a group of Quakers, was named West Jersey. Carteret, who inherited with his land a settlement of Puritans in the southeast, called his half East Jersey. In 1702 the king of England rejoined the two sections officially and made New Jersey a royal colony, sharing New York's governor until 1738.

PENNSYLVANIA AND DELAWARE

We have seen how large a part religious idealism played in the settlement of New England. The same fervor—though ex-

pressed by a strange sect that the Puritans despised—led to the founding of Pennsylvania in 1681.

The proprietor of the new colony was William Penn, the son of a wealthy English admiral. Even as a young man, Penn was friendly with the future King Charles II and his brother, the Duke of York. He received his education at Oxford and was sent on a luxurious two-year grand tour of the Continent. Everything about his upbringing suggested that he would be a great gentleman, rich, powerful, and an intimate of the king.

Penn had a highly developed moral sense and in 1666, while managing his father's estates in Ireland, he became interested in the Quaker faith, or Society of Friends, as the sect called itself. (The term Quaker was coined by its enemies because the Friends spoke so much about "trembling" before God.) Quakerism was one of the nearly two hundred obscure sects that had emerged in England during the middle of the seventeenth century. While the others vanished almost as quickly as they had appeared, the Society of Friends endured.

THE QUAKERS

English Protestants, both Anglicans and Puritans, were infuriated by the religious doctrines of the Quakers. The founder of the Society of Friends was George Fox. After a deep religious revelation changed his life in 1646, Fox began to preach a form of Christian mysticism. Somewhat like Anne Hutchinson, Fox felt that men could communicate directly with God, not needing the intervention of clergymen and church services. Unlike the Puritans, who believed that only a small minority of humanity was predestined for salvation, Fox contended that *every* human being had a spark of divinity. All people possessed an "inner light," and if they could but learn to detect its brilliance within them, they would have immediate contact with God.

67

Unlike the Puritans, who insisted that all of God's revelations were in the Bible, Fox taught that these revelations were continuously occurring to living men and women. To experience God's will, one need not consult the Bible (although Fox felt that studying it was useful); one could discover divine wisdom equally well within his own heart. Fox assumed that religion was not an intellectual matter, but rather an emotional, even irrational pursuit. The Quakers thus turned away from the doctrine of predestination and accepted the ideal of ultimate universal perfection.

Such notions seemed wild and wicked to the Puritans and Anglicans, who were equally incensed by the strange public behavior of the Quakers. Believing that all men were created equal by God (since all possessed the inner light), the Friends refused to doff their caps to noblemen or bow to the king. Similarly, they refused to use the polite word "you" which Englishmen in the seventeenth century employed when addressing their superiors; the Quakers called everyone "thee"—which seemed shockingly disrespectful. Even worse, the Quakers refused to pay taxes for the support of the Church of England and its clergy and claimed exemption from military service because they were opposed to war. They continued to hold their own illegal services, which were characterized by a rejection of all forms and ceremonies.

Hundreds of Quakers were arrested in England, including William Penn, who spent 2 years in jail. Refusing to pay fines or to resist arrest, more than 8,000 Friends were thrown in prison between 1660 and 1685.

In America they fared little better at first. In Virginia Quakerism was illegal and two Friends in 1660 were lashed, then banished. Quakers felt called upon by their conscience to testify against the Puritans in New England. The Quakers were as intolerant of the Puritans as the Puritans were of the Friends, but the Puritans were in the ma-

John Winthrop on Liberty

66 *There is a twofold liberty, natural (I mean as our nature is now corrupt) and civil or federal. The first is common to man with beasts and other creatures. By this, man, as he stands in relation to man simply, hath liberty to do what he lists; it is a liberty to evil as well as to good. This liberty is incompatible and inconsistent with authority, and cannot endure the least restraint of the most just authority . . . The other kind of liberty I call civil or federal, it may also be termed moral, in reference to the covenant between God and man, in the moral law, and the politic covenants and constitutions, amongst men themselves. This liberty is the proper end and object of authority, and cannot subsist without it; and it is a liberty to that only which is good, just, and honest. This liberty you are to stand for, with the hazard (not only of your goods, but) of your lives, if need be. Whatsoever crosseth this, is not authority, but a distemper thereof. This liberty is maintained and exercised in a way of subjection to authority; it is of the same kind of liberty wherewith Christ hath made us free . . . If you stand for your natural corrupt liberties, and will do what is good in your own eyes, you will not endure the least weight of authority, but will murmur, and oppose, and be always striving to shake off that yoke; but if you will be satisfied to enjoy such civil and lawful liberties, such as Christ allows you, then will you quietly and cheerfully submit unto that authority which is set over you, in all the administration of it, for your good.*

—John Winthrop's Journal, History of New England

William Penn on Liberty and Property

*In England the Law is both the measure
and the bound of every Subject's duty
and allegiance, each man having a fixed
Fundamental Right born with him, as to
freedom of his person and property in
his estate, which he cannot be deprived
of, but either by his consent, or some crime,
for which the law has imposed such a
penalty or forfeiture . . .*

*This original happy Frame of Government
is truly and properly called an
Englishman's Liberty, a Privilege not
exempt from the law, but to be freed in
person and estate from arbitrary violence
and oppression. A greater inheritance
(saith Judge Coke) is derived to every
one of us from our laws than from our
parents. For without the former, what
would the latter signify? And this Birthright of Englishmen shines most
conspicuously in two things:*

1. Parliaments.
2. Juries.

*By the First the Subject has a share by
his chosen Representatives in the
Legislative (or law-making) Power; for
no new laws gind the people of England,
but such as are by common consent agreed
on in that great Council.*

*By the Second, he has a share in the
executive part of the law, no causes
being tried, nor any man adjudged to lose
life, member or estate, but upon the
verdict of his Peers or Equals his neigh-
bours, and of his own condition. . . .*

—*William Penn,*
**The Excellent Privileges
of Liberty and Property**

jority. Demonstrating against Puritanism in New England, the Quakers broke bottles in churches in order to underline symbolically how empty the services were. Sometimes Friends would burst noisily into a Puritan church and hysterically denounce the minister. Frequently Quaker women walked naked through New England streets to register their protest. Such outrageous acts aroused fury in the Puritans. They fined people for reading Quaker tracts, banished Quakers as witches, branded and whipped Quakers, drove red-hot irons through Quakers' tongues, attempted to sell Quaker children as slaves to sugar farmers in the West Indies, and hanged half a dozen noisy Quaker adults.

WILLIAM PENN

Although many Friends seemed to take an almost masochistic pleasure in their martyrdom, William Penn longed for a refuge for his coreligionists. In 1681 he received a grant for a region north of Maryland from his old friend, Charles II. Penn's father, the old admiral, had once lent Charles a great sum of money which the king had never repaid. Although the king seldom felt called on to pay his debts, he now regarded the debt as a good excuse for granting the land to his persecuted Quaker friend. Some evidence indicates that Charles urged Penn to settle the new territory as quickly as possible; securing the safety of his friend and ridding his kingdom of so many malcontents all in one blow obviously appealed to the monarch. As Penn was to write later, "The government at home was glad to be rid of us at so cheap a rate as a little parchment to be practiced in a desert three thousand miles off."

Penn wanted to call the colony New Wales, but an influential Welshman indignantly objected. Then Penn suggested Sylvania (land of woods); his own name was immediately prefixed to the new designation, and much as Penn objected to it, it stuck. The chief port on the Delaware River he named Philadelphia, which in Greek means "brotherly love." In this new land, so aptly named, Penn, like the Puritans who had come to America before him, hoped to create an ideal Christian community.

Penn was so certain Quakerism would thrive in freedom and attract believers through its simplicity and unmistakable access to the truth that he made religious freedom for all those who believed in God one of the cornerstones of his "holy experiment." Religious liberty was matched by civil freedom; together they formed what Penn called "Soul Liberty." An Anglican clergyman exclaimed, "Africa never more abounded with New Monsters than Pennsylvania does with New Sects." In keeping with their solicitude for all humanity, the

Friends formed committees to help the poor, the Indians, and the slaves. Because of the friendship they extended to the Indians, peace with them was maintained for seventy-five years.

Penn was not only a wise legislator but a gifted publicist. He wrote promotional literature about the economic and religious advantages of the colony and circulated the brochures throughout Europe. By 1684 fifty shiploads of settlers from England, Wales, Holland, Germany, and Ireland had come to Pennsylvania.

Penn drew up the Frame of Government

Pennsylvania, begun as an exile colony for the Quakers, became the center for religious tolerance for all faiths. William Penn, shown in this engraving making a peace treaty with the Indians, founded the colony, and in only 8 years attracted over 20,000 settlers.

in 1682 as a framework for the administration of the colony. He himself would choose the governor, but a bicameral legislature would be elected by all freemen (ownership of a small amount of land or the payment of taxes made a male citizen a "freeman"). The upper house, called the council, had the right to initiate all legislation; the lower house, called the assembly, could only approve or disapprove of the bills handed down to it. The assembly attacked this provision from the beginning. For four years, from 1692 to 1696, Penn lost his charter to Pennsylvania (he had supported King James II, who, as we shall note later in this chapter, had been exiled), and while the colony was under royal control, the assembly finally won the right to initiate legislation. When Penn regained his colony, he accepted the new order of things; in fact, the power of the governor to veto legislation was the only restriction on an otherwise all-powerful legislature.

The Charter of Liberties, enacted in 1701, confirmed this legislative supremacy. In addition to restricting the governor's privileges and creating a one-house unicameral legislature, the Charter also gave three counties their own representative assembly. These three counties, between Maryland and the Delaware Bay, later became the colony of Delaware but continued to be administered by the governor of Pennsylvania until the Revolution.

So practical, enterprising and understanding was Penn that his colony thrived almost immediately. Only 8 years after Pennsylvania was founded, 20,000 settlers were living in this remarkable community. They produced large quantities of wheat, flour, beef, and pork. Philadelphia became a prosperous commercial center. Penn himself, however, did not prosper. His tenants rebelled against paying the rents they owed him, and a dishonest agent made his financial problems even more severe. In 1701, Penn was sent to a debtor's prison, where he died in 1718.

Over 2,500 families lived in Pennsylvania in 1754. The city of "Brotherly Love" was a major attraction to settlers coming to Pennsylvania.

THE CAROLINAS

In 1663, a year before Carteret and Berkeley received a royal charter to New Jersey, they were part of a group of eight aristocrats who were granted Carolina. This land, which lay between the colony of Virginia and the Spanish outpost of St. Augustine in Florida, was supposed to serve two functions. First, it would stand as a bulwark against further Spanish encroachments into North America. Second, the proprietors hoped that commodities could be produced in the warm climate that could not be grown in England—silk, in particular. (Mulberry trees were imported several times, but a silk industry was never established.)

From the very beginning the northern and southern parts of Carolina were treated as two separate districts. Settlement was rather slow in each part. The proprietors did not want to undertake the expense of transporting colonists from the mother country to Carolina; they hoped to populate their lands with settlers who were already in the New World—in Virginia, New England, and in the West Indies. Few Puritans from New England, however, wanted to enter a territory and that offered few natural attractions where they would have to live with people who did not share their religious notions. There were probably a few squatters in the area that became North Carolina by the 1650s and a few Virginians were persuaded by Lord Berkeley to migrate south, but the new territory had nothing to offer them that they could not get on better terms in Virginia. By the end of the seventeenth century there were only four or five thousand settlers in the colony of North Carolina, most of them eking out a living from farming tobacco and corn and raising livestock near Albermarle Sound.

Many of the immigrants who settled in the Carolinas came from Barbados and Jamaica. Those two islands had originally been colonized by poor English farmers, but over the years these small landholders were driven out as great sugar-growing estates were consolidated and English yeomen were replaced by African slaves. Seeking a new place where they could find work, eight hundred white settlers from the West Indies came to live in South Carolina near Cape Fear by 1666. Within a few years, however, they became discouraged by frequent storms and by their belief that the soil was barren. Most of them dispersed into North Carolina, Virginia, and New England, while some returned to Barbados.

The entire project of populating the Carolinas seemed doomed until 1669, when Anthony Ashley Cooper, one of the eight proprietors, brought over three ships of colonists from England. They built a fort on the Ashley River. By 1672 there were two hundred colonists in South Carolina, and in the 1680s a small group of French Protestants and Scots joined them. The principal city, Charles Town (soon called Charleston), was built at the junction of two rivers which the immodest proprietor had named after himself, the Ashley and the Cooper.

The Fundamental Constitutions of Carolina devised by the proprietors made rank in government dependent upon the size of a man's property, providing for two-fifths of the property to be held by the proprietors as hereditary estates. Its main effect was to put large landed estates into the hands of a few men. The government, headed by an appointed governor, had a two-house legislature; the upper house, representing the nobility, retained the sole right to introduce legislation. Gradually, however, the Constitutions were liberalized; the lower house fought for, and slowly won, more power as in the other colonies. By the end of the century, the Constitutions had faded from practice.

The Carolina colonies grew slowly and developed different types of societies. At the end of the century only about 3,000 people were living in North Carolina and 5,000 in South Carolina. After 1664, North Carolina had its own government, becoming a separate colony in 1691. It was mainly made up of poor, fiercely individualistic farmers who raised vegetables, tobacco, and livestock, and made naval stores. South Carolina's economy was based on the export of rice and deerskins; life was orderly, conservative, aristocratic, and cosmopolitan. Both Carolinas were made royal colonies in the 1720s after numerous complaints by the settlers that the proprietors failed to aid them against the Spanish and Indians.

GEORGIA

On the southern border of South Carolina a new colony was created in 1732 when George II granted Georgia (named after himself) to a group of English philanthro-pists, headed by James Oglethorpe. The king wanted to use Georgia as yet another military outpost against the Spanish in Florida; Oglethorpe and his humanitarian colleagues wanted to use it as a refuge for the debtors being kept in English prisons.

The colony was conceived in highly idealistic terms. No Georgians were to become extremely wealthy; farmers, the trustees decided, could own no more than 500 acres. Slavery was prohibited, as were rum and brandy.

Savannah, Ga., in 1734. The colony was originally a place of exile for English debtors who were serving prison sentences. Thus, many laws prohibiting rum, brandy, slaves, and the amount of land a man could own were put into effect for the former prisoners. However, in less than one generation, Georgians were able to repeal these restrictive laws.

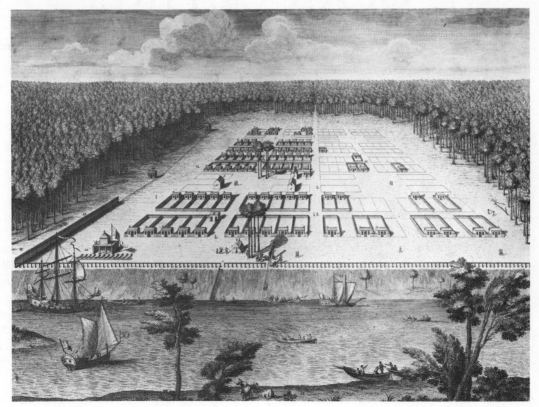

The heterogeneous group of Scots, Welsh, Germans, and English who came to Georgia did not accept these restrictions gracefully. As a result of their protests, the law against rum was rescinded in 1742 and in 1750 slavery became legal, along with the right to dispose of land as an individual wished. The restriction to 500 acres was lifted. Georgia did not thrive, however, and in 1751, the colony was turned over to the crown to become a royal colony.

The proprietary colonies of the Carolinas and Georgia never had a coherent, sectional character. Unlike New England, where English Puritans were in the majority and lent the region a distinct unity, the three southernmost colonies had a far more fragmented population. Except for a few Virginians who had drifted down into North Carolina, most Carolinians came directly from England, France, or the West Indies. Georgia was populated by an even greater mixture of nationalities.

THE DEVELOPMENT OF AN EMPIRE

During the first half of the seventeenth century, the English government took little interest in their American colonies. When it did, the constant disputes between the monarchy and the Parliament diverted its attention to matters closer to home. It was not until the decade of the Commonwealth and Protectorate under the Puritan General Oliver Cromwell that England began to turn her thoughts again toward the regulation of her struggling colonies along the Atlantic seaboard of North America. Moreover, the internal stability produced by the return of the Stuarts to the throne in 1660 set the stage for a much more forceful imperial policy. The settlement of the entire Atlantic seaboard by parcelling out the uninhabited areas (and even lands already settled by the Dutch) to royal favorites as proprietary grants was one aspect of this policy. The other aspect was the greater enforcement of a mercantilistic policy by the passage of a series of navigation acts to regulate colonial trade for the profit of England.

THE MERCANTILIST THEORY

While the colonies were working out their individual destinies, in England the power struggle between the king and Parliament ended with the beheading of Charles I and the ascension in 1649 of Cromwell to the office of Lord Protector, the office which replaced the monarchy until 1660. A new era began, and Parliament turned its attention more to the nation's economy. The result was the initiation of a series of protective trade measures known as the navigation acts. Few things were to have greater effect on relations between the mother country and her New World colonies than these acts.

Starting in the sixteenth century, economists began to argue that trade must not be allowed to follow its own course without restrictions. On the contrary, the government must carefully regulate all commerce with one end in mind—increasing its own supplies of precious metals in order to end economic dependence on other nations. Gold and silver were considered of absolute value, the only true way to measure wealth, and in fact, were synonymous with wealth. One of the main reasons Spain colonized the New World was to add to its supply of gold bullion. England, France, and The Netherlands, however, did not find great quantities of precious metals in their colonies. They therefore concluded that they could get bullion by a favorable balance of trade, that is, by exporting more than they imported.

England saw her American colonies as a very useful part of this system. There were many products that England needed but did not grow: hemp for ships' ropes, indigo for the manufacture of dyes, and tobacco were only a few examples. If England bought these products from foreign countries, English gold would drain off into foreign lands. But if England could buy these products from its own colonies, the trade, and the gold, would all be kept in the British empire. Equally important, the colonies would serve as a market for manufactured goods made in the mother country. America had vast natural resources, but few people consuming them; England had many people and limited resources. The plan was for America to exchange its resources for England's goods, recycling the wealth within the empire.

Besides accumulating as much hard cash as possible, British mercantilism also worked to protect native industry and agriculture from all competition and to encourage the growth of English shipping.

THE NAVIGATION LAWS

To encourage its merchant marine, and also to make sure that no English gold trickled unnecessarily into the hands of foreign shippers, the English Parliament, during Cromwell's rule, enacted the Navigation Act of 1651. It included the following regulations: (1) all goods bought in England could be transported to the colonies only in English ships; (2) foreign goods could be brought to England only in English vessels or in ships belonging to the country where the product had been actually grown or made. This act was designed particularly to restrict the activities of Dutch shipowners, who were serving as busy middlemen in world trade.

In 1660, the Parliament, sensing a popular desire for a return to traditional institutions, invited Charles I's son, Charles II, to ascend the throne. The period from 1660 to 1685 was called the Stuart Restoration. Despite the general reaction against the regime of Cromwell, during this period Charles II and his Anglican royalist parliament continued and expanded Cromwell's trade policies. The 1651 act had permitted the colonies to export to and import directly from the other countries of Europe. A new act in 1660 stipulated that now *all* goods, no matter where made, had to be shipped to the colonies on English or colonial ships. The majority of sailors and the master of the ship had to be either Englishmen or English colonials. Certain "enumerated articles" such as sugar, tobacco, and cotton could not be sold directly by colonists to the Continent. These products had to be shipped to England, where Europeans could then buy them (after paying English duties).

Another, stronger law was passed in 1663. Under this act, not only did all goods imported to America from Europe have to be carried in English ships, but they had to pass through England before coming to the colonies (with the exception of salt, slaves, and wine). This law brought additional duties—and gold—to England.

English officials discovered that colonial shippers were occasionally getting around the navigation laws by pretending to customs officials that they were simply carrying "enumerated articles," such as tobacco, from one colony to another (trade between the colonies was not subject to the navigation acts), when actually they were smuggling goods into European ports. To close this loophole, the Navigation Act of 1673 stipulated that American captains had to pay duty when they embarked, rather than when they arrived. To collect these export duties, a staff of customs officials was to be stationed in all important colonial ports.

The navigation acts were further enlarged in the ensuing decades, mainly by modifying the list of enumerated articles so that the manufacture as well as the trade of certain colonial products would be controlled. The Wool Act of 1699 forbade the export of certain colonial textiles; in 1704 rice was made an enumerated article; in 1705 naval stores were added to the list and bounties were placed on their production; in 1721 copper and furs were added to the enumerated list. The Hat Act of 1732 outlawed the exportation of American-made hats. The Iron Act of 1750 forbade erecting new colonial iron mills for manufacturing products out of raw iron, while it encouraged the production of pig and bar iron by removing all duties on their importation into England.

HISTORICAL INTERPRETATIONS OF MERCANTILISM

What effect did these strong mercantilist regulations have on the growth or decline of colonial trade? Historians have debated the question for decades. In the 1830s

George Bancroft, a prominent American historian, wrote a *History of the United States* in which British mercantilism was pictured as pure selfishness on the part of the English, a cold-blooded plan to ruthlessly exploit American natural resources and stunt the American economy. In fact, Bancroft argued that American resentment against the navigation acts had been one of the principal causes of the Revolution.

Fifty years later, George L. Beer and Charles M. Andrews took a quite different point of view. They contended that the navigation acts had protected American industries and encouraged American shipping more than they had dampened the colonial economy. True, certain minor industries, such as hat making, had been forbidden in order to prevent competition with the English hat industry. This seemed a small price to pay for guaranteeing the colonies other markets, and occasionally monopolies, in England. Furthermore, they wrote, colonials were assured a part in the extremely lucrative shipping between the British empire and the rest of the world. These historians rejected the notion that the navigation acts had played an important part in bringing on the American Revolution (as did L. A. Harper's important studies of the navigation acts written during the New Deal era).

In the late 1930s, the historian Louis M. Hacker, then a Marxist, pictured the mercantilistic laws as an attempt of one capitalist state, England, to suppress another, America. British regulations against American manufacturing and trade with nations outside the Empire were restrictions that the colonies had to throw off, Hacker argued, if it was to fulfill its own capitalistic destiny.

Hacker's arguments seemed to be refuted in the 1950s when Oliver M. Dickerson showed, through an examination of seventeenth- and eighteenth-century pamphlets, newspapers, and essays, that the colonists rarely objected to the navigation laws until

1763, when the British began to exploit the colonies.

The relevant mass of evidence is at once enormous and insufficient. While thousands of contemporary writings remain, figures for shipping and commerce are incomplete. At this time it seems unlikely that more data will be uncovered; more probably, the interpretations of future historians will depend upon more sophisticated analysis of the information we already have—and the biases of the historians making the interpretations.

ENFORCING THE NAVIGATION ACTS

To administer the navigation acts, the English instituted a tougher, more direct way of governing the colonies. In the first half of the seventeenth century, the colonies enjoyed a large measure of independence. They were ignored because they were not especially lucrative and there were as yet relatively few settlers. Moreover, 3,000 miles of ocean and weeks of sailing time separated England and America, and orders were difficult to communicate or enforce. Most important, as we have noted, endless disputes between Parliament and the throne over control of the English government prevented the creation of a responsible policy of colonial administration.

In the second half of the century, however, and particularly after the Stuart Restoration, Britain settled down to the business of running the Empire. In 1675, a committee of King Charles II's Privy Council was created to enforce the navigation acts and oversee all aspects of colonial rule. This body was at first called the Lords of Trade and renamed the Board of Trade in 1696. One of its first acts was to send an agent to New England to investigate smuggling and other evasions of the navigation acts which had been reported to it. This agent, Edward Randolph, filed a report that condemned almost every aspect of life in Massachusetts. Hating the colonists as much as they hated him, Randolph reported that French ships were entering New England ports illegally and openly flouting the navigation laws, and that colonial merchants were fully cooperating with the French. Public officers were neglecting to take oaths of allegiance to the king, and the Church of England was virtually nonexistent in New England. He also charged that Massachusetts had annexed Maine and New Hampshire, without royal permission and against the will of the people in those colonies.

THE DOMINION OF NEW ENGLAND

Alarmed by Randolph's reports, the Lords of Trade annulled the charter of the Massachusetts Bay Company in 1684. The following year James II became king, and one of the first acts of his reign was to consolidate all of New England, New York, and New Jersey into one vast governmental unit that was larger than England itself. His aim was to centralize rule in the empire while pursuing a similar course at home. The area, as the Dominion of New England, was to be ruled from Boston by a royal governor.

On December 20, 1686, Sir Edmund Andros sailed into Boston aboard the *Kingfisher* to become the first and only Dominion governor. Three hours after his arrival, he antagonized the Puritans by holding an Anglican service. That was only the first of a long list of grievances he inflicted upon the colonials. Above all, he was resented because he possessed dictatorial powers. James II had personally eliminated a representative assembly provision from the new constitution for the Dominion; only a council of officials appointed by him could limit Andros' authority. The governor and his advisors could make laws, dispense justice, and levy taxes as they saw fit—without the consent of those they governed.

Andros enraged merchants by imposing a heavy duty on imported rum, brandy, and wine. Then he infuriated landowners by creating a direct tax on real estate; by 1688 he had questioned the validity of all New England land titles and announced to all property owners that they had to obtain new patents from the king. He dedicated himself to enforcing the navigation acts and had offenders tried by judges who were experts in maritime law, rather than by juries.

All of Andros' measures spelled the end of the old Puritan dominance over New England. Their religion was no longer the exclusive faith of the province. Their rights to their land, to trial by jury, to representative government were all in jeopardy. The Puritans had come to America to rule themselves in a completely independent community; now they were reduced to dependents of the crown. New England merchants were no longer allowed to continue their smuggling. Andros had stifled their profitable, if illegal, trade with the Spanish, French, and Dutch.

THE GLORIOUS REVOLUTION

The reign of Edmund Andros—and the identity of the Dominion of New England—ceased when James II abdicated the throne of England in 1688. James had followed two foolish policies since taking up the scepter: he had tried to be an absolute monarch, a return to the discredited concept of "divine right," and he had tried to reestablish the Roman Catholic Church. The first objective aroused the ire of even his very conservative Parliament, which was determined not to lose the prerogatives it had consolidated over the last century. James's sympathy with Catholicism alarmed an overwhelmingly Protestant England. So unpopular did James become that several prominent Englishmen boldly invited William of Orange, a Protestant Dutch prince who was married to James II's elder daughter, Mary, to come to England and seize the throne. The "revolution" turned out to be merely a peaceful and triumphant procession. James II fled the country having lost the support of all influential people, including the army. Parliament crowned the foreign prince as William III, with Mary as coruler to maintain a link with English monarchs. Parliament gave him the crown on its own conditions, however. William had to pledge to abide by a Bill of Rights drawn up by Parliament. The bill denied the king the right to suspend laws, levy taxes, or maintain a standing army without Parliament's consent. The Parliament, in an effort to end religious strife, also passed the Toleration Act in 1689, permitting all Protestants to worship openly. The "Glorious Revolution," which brought William III to power, established beyond all doubt that the ultimate source of authority in England lay in Parliament and not in the king.

As word of James II's abdication spread throughout New England, the colonists carried out a small rebellion of their own. The royal governor, Andros, was imprisoned. Connecticut, Plymouth, and Rhode Island began to rule themselves again. In New York, a German named Jacob Leisler ousted Andros' assistant and governed the colony for almost 2 years in the name of the new king, backed by his own private militia. However, when a royal governor, appointed by William III, finally arrived in New York in 1691 to take over, Leisler briefly resisted surrendering his position. The royal governor summarily denounced him as a traitor and had him hanged.

THE ENGLISH SYSTEM

The Glorious Revolution was a turning point in American colonial history. After 1688 Britain would never again attempt to consolidate the colonies into larger administrative units. The triumph of Parliament in England had established the principle of representative government, even for the colonies. Never again would royal governors attempt to rule without a colonial legislature.

The governmental machinery of almost every colony was altered in the years following the Glorious Revolution. Maryland was taken away from Lord Baltimore in 1689 and made a royal colony (the Baltimores regained possession only in 1715, when the fourth Lord Baltimore made a politically wise decision to convert to the Anglican Church). New Jersey became a royal colony in 1702, South Carolina in 1721, and North Carolina in 1729. William III granted Massachusetts a new charter in 1691. The new charter enlarged the colony by giving it Plymouth and Maine, but it restricted the people's political power to a certain extent. Massachusetts no longer could elect its own governor. From now on he would be appointed by the king. Even the laws passed by the assembly would be subject to review in England. On the other hand, following England's example, Massachusetts was also forced to practice religious toleration by giving up the religious qualification for voting, which enlarged the electorate.

The total effect of these changes was to increase the number of royal colonies and strengthen the authority of royal governors, although in theory the king retained direct control over America. He appointed the governors, as well as most of the upper houses of the colonial legislatures. One out of every twenty laws passed by colonial assemblies during the eighteenth century was vetoed by the king. The Anglican faith was actively promoted by royal governors, who were instructed to see that the state church was strengthened everywhere in America. Vice-admiralty courts, presided over by royal, not colonial judges, were empowered to try offenders against the navigation acts. The number of colonial goods that could be shipped to England—but to England only—was increased. Colonial produce, such as wheat, flour, and fish, and colonial manufactured goods, such as woolen cloth, were placed under more rigorous restrictions by the later navigation acts. These items could not be exported from the colonies at all, not even to England, since they were in direct competition with English goods.

Thus, by the end of the seventeenth century, the colonies had undergone a transformation. Most of those colonies originally owned by joint-stock companies or individual proprietors had come under royal jurisdiction. Freewheeling shippers who had once ignored British commercial restrictions were now to be hemmed in on every side by a battery of laws and an army of customs officials who hampered their smuggling operations.

However, the new order brought prosperity to the colonies. The religious toleration act established by Parliament soon put a stop to the most outrageous attacks on dissenters such as Quakers and Catholics. Dangerous commercial rivals, such as Dutch shippers, were no longer allowed to interfere in colonial trade. American merchants were guaranteed an important place in the thriving British system of commerce. Although royal control was occasionally oppressive, in many ways it simplified regulations and promoted harmony among the various colonies. Moreover, even with the British trade regulations, widespread smuggling was still possible. For the moment, at least, most colonials were willing to accept the demands, as well as the rewards, of belonging to a mighty empire.

Readings

GENERAL WORKS

Adams, James T., *The Founding of New England*. Boston: Atlantic Monthly Press, 1921 (Paper: Atlantic Monthly-Little, Brown, 1965)—An early and influential history of seventeenth century New England which reflects the distaste Adams and others of his generation felt for Puritan values.

Andrews, Charles M., *The Colonial Period of American History*. New Haven: Yale University Press, 1964—A 4-volume classic of American colonial history. Andrews was among the first Americans to argue that British mercantilism was a benevolent force in American colonial life.

Craven, Wesley F., *The Southern Colonies in the Seventeenth Century*. Baton Rouge, La.: Louisiana State University Press, 1949 —In writing a history of the South in a period before sectional consciousness had developed, Craven emphasizes aspects such as settlement patterns and local government which later contributed to Southern uniqueness.

Langdon, George, *Pilgrim Colony: A History of New Plymouth, 1620–1691*. New Haven: Yale University Press, 1966—A history of the colony of New Plymouth from 1620 to its merger with Massachusetts in 1691. Langdon feels that the earlier settlers of Plymouth continued to dominate the colony's life down to the time of its amalgamation.

Nettels, Curtis P., *The Roots of American Civilization*. New York: Appleton-Century-Crofts, 1963—A standard textbook of colonial history. Nettels finds conflict between aristocratic and democratic tendencies and between imperial and local control to have been the main themes of the age.

Parkman, Francis, *Pioneers of France in the New World*. Boston: Little, Brown, 1900— Written originally in 1865, this is the story of French explorers in North America. Parkman, one of the greatest nineteenth century American historians, was known for his vivid and eloquent style.

Tolles, Frederick B., *Meeting House and Counting House: The Quaker Merchants of Colonial Philadelphia 1682–1763*. Chapel Hill, N.C.: University of North Carolina Press, 1948 (Paper: W. W. Norton, 1963)—An exploration of the religious beliefs and daily practices of Quaker merchants in early Pennsylvania. Though sympathetic to the merchants' contributions, Tolles maintains that they could not keep up the spiritual traditions of the earlier Quakers.

Wertenbaker, T. J., *The First Americans*. New York: Macmillan, 1927—An older history of colonial America in the seventeenth century. Wertenbaker argues that the influence of the American wilderness on settlers in Virginia and Maryland led to a sense of individualism and a democratic spirit.

Wertenbaker, T. J., *The Middle Colonies*. New York: Scribner's, 1938—In this social history of colonial New York, New Jersey, Pennsylvania, and Delaware, Wertenbaker emphasizes the effect the diverse origins of the colonists had on the development of American traditions of independence and democracy.

Wertenbaker, T. J., *The Old South*. New York: Scribner's, 1942—A social history of the South during the colonial period, emphasizing the diversity within the region and the ways in which southern culture was expressed in art and architecture.

Wertenbaker, T. J., *The Puritan Oligarchy*. New York: Scribner's, 1947 (Paper, 1970)—

A critical history of colonial Massachusetts. The New Englanders who contributed to democratic traditions were, Wertenbaker claims, not the Puritans but those who dared to oppose their power.

SPECIAL STUDIES

Bailyn, Bernard, *The New England Merchants in the Seventeenth Century.* Cambridge: Harvard University Press, 1955 (Paper: Harper & Row Torchbook, 1964) —A study of the ideals and policies of the New England merchants. Bailyn points out the importance of their ties to Europe, their struggles to become a unified group, and the growth of a business ideology among them.

Crane, V. W., *The Southern Frontier, 1670–1732.* Ann Arbor: University of Michigan Press, 1956—A history of southern expansion between 1670 and 1732. Crane emphasizes the relationship of Indian trade to frontier history.

Harper, L. A., *The English Navigation Laws.* New York: Octagon Books, 1964—A study of the English navigation acts as exercises in governmental "social engineering." Harper concludes that they were on the whole beneficial and did not cause American disenchantment with their dependent status in the British empire.

Morgan, Edmund S., *The Puritan Family.* New York: Harper Torchbook, 1966—A discussion of the effects of Puritan religious thought and the social conditions of seventeenth century Massachusetts on family life. Morgan suggests that the Puritan family was used to transmit and enforce the values of the larger society.

Morgan, Edmund S., *Visible Saints.* New York: New York University Press, 1963 (Paper: Cornell University Press, 1970)— A history of the changing Puritan concepts of how to judge whether a man or woman had been saved from damnation and how to decide who should be given full church membership.

Morison, Samuel E., *Builders of the Bay Colony.* Boston: Houghton Mifflin, 1964— Morison presents a series of biographical sketches of early Massachusetts Bay leaders, including such people as John Winthrop and Anne Bradstreet.

Morison, Samuel E., *The Intellectual Life of Colonial New England.* New York: New York University Press, 1956 (Paper: Cornell University Press, 1960)—Morison emphasizes that early New England had a thriving cultural life and that Puritanism did not stifle intellectual and artistic creativity.

Smith, Abbot E., *Colonists in Bondage: White Servitude and Convict Labor in America 1607–1776.* Chapel Hill, N.C.: University of North Carolina Press, 1947— A study of the white settlers who came to America as indentured servants, exchanging a period of their labor for transportation to the New World. Smith calculates that perhaps more than half of the white immigrants who came to the colonies came in bondage.

Vaughan, Alden T., *New England Frontier, Puritans and Indians 1620–1675.* Boston: Little, Brown, 1965—A history of Puritan-Indian relations which gives the Puritans credit for their efforts at cooperation with Indians. Divisions within both groups produced conflicts with divisions not always along racial lines.

Washburn, Wilcomb E., *The Governor and the Rebel: A History of Bacon's Rebellion in Virginia.* Chapel Hill, N.C.: University of North Carolina Press, 1967—Washburn revises the standard account of Bacon's Rebellion in this book. He maintains that the rebel leader was no democrat and that greed and racist attitudes towards Indians were at the heart of the revolt.

Willison, George E., *Behold Virginia*. New York: Harcourt Brace Jovanovich, 1951— A popular history of Virginia from the initial colonization attempts through the American Revolution. Stresses the early difficulties of the first settlers.

Wright, Louis B., *The First Gentlemen of Virginia*. San Marino, Calif.: The Huntington Library, 1940 (Paper: University Press of Virginia, 1964)—Wright traces the development of the Virginia aristocracy. He concludes that the Virginia gentry were distinguished by their intellect as well as their wealth.

PRIMARY SOURCES

Beverly, Robert, *The History and Present State of Virginia*, Louis B. Wright, ed. Charlottesville, Va.: University Press of Virginia, 1968—Beverly was a wealthy Virginia planter, who wrote one of the first and best accounts of the geography and political history of Virginia. Critical of royal governors and of fellow colonists, he nevertheless painted a highly attractive picture of Virginia life.

Bradford, William, *Of Plymouth Plantation*, Samuel E. Morison, ed. New York: Knopf, 1952—Bradford was the governor and leading figure in the early years of the Plymouth colony. Half journal and half history, *Of Plymouth Plantation* is the best source for the story of that colony.

Lankgord, John, ed., *Captain John Smith's America: Selections from his Writings.*

New York: Harper & Row, 1967—The adventurous leader of the Jamestown expedition was a close observer of Virginia. He describes the settlement and settlers as well as the wilderness and the Indians they encountered.

Miller, Perry and Thomas H. Johnson, eds., *The Puritans: A Source Book of Their Writings.* New York: Harper & Row Torchbooks, 1969—In the authors' long introduction to this broad selection of documents they defend Puritanism against charges of fanaticism and irrationality. The Puritans were realistic, they claim, in their concept of religion's role in man's life.

Morton, Thomas, *The New English Canaan*, Charles F. Adams, ed. New York: B. Franklin, 1966—An account of the Puritan settlement at Merrymount.

Percy, George. *Observations Gathered Out of a Discourse of the Plantation of the Southern Colony of Virginia by the English, 1606.* Charlottesville, Va.: University Press of Virginia, 1967—In 1609 Percy succeeded John Smith as governor of Virginia. His *Discourse* is the best account of the voyage and initial settlement of the Jamestown colony.

Tolles, Frederick B. and E. G. Alderfer, eds., *The Witness of William Penn.* New York: Macmillan, 1957—A selection of the writings of William Penn which show both the religious and secular aspects of his life and thought.

Winthrop, John, *Winthrop's Journal*, James K. Hosmer, ed. New York: Scribner's, 1908 —The journal covers the years 1630 to 1649 and is one of the most important sources for the study of colonial Massachusetts. As governor, Winthrop supplies great detail on the daily duties of running the colony.

BIOGRAPHIES

Barbour, Philip, *Pocahontas and Her World*. Boston: Houghton Mifflin, 1970—A new treatment of the story of the Indian princess and her involvement in the lives of the leaders of the Virginia settlement. Through his story, Barbour shows the greed and conflict which characterized early Virginia life.

Barbour, Philip L., *The Three Worlds of Captain John Smith*. Boston: Houghton Mifflin, 1964—An attempt to separate fact from legend in a biography of one of the leaders of the Virginia colony. Smith is approached as adventurer, colonist, and promoter.

Miller, Perry, *Roger Williams: His Contribution to the American Tradition*. New York: Atheneum, 1962—A brief biography of the founder of Rhode Island which challenges the idea that Williams was a democrat and believer in civil liberties. All of Williams' social opinions, Miller claims, were secondary to his religious interests.

Morgan, Edmund S., *The Puritan Dilemma: The Story of John Winthrop*. Boston: Little, Brown, 1958—A biography of John Winthrop which discusses the effects of Puritan religious thought on questions of governmental powers and organization.

Peare, Catherine O., *William Penn*. New York: Holt, Rinehart and Winston, 1958 (Paper: University of Michigan, Ann Arbor Books, 1966)—An admiring popular biography of the great Quaker leader. Peare devotes much attention to Penn's earlier life in England.

Smith, Bradford, *Captain John Smith*. Philadelphia: Lippincott, 1953—The author defends Captain Smith against charges that the accounts of his adventures were dishonest and discusses Smith's travels in Hungary and Turkey.

Winslow, Ola E., *Master Roger Williams*. New York: Macmillan, 1957—A biography which balances the older interpretation of Williams as a democrat with the more recent picture of him as a man preoccupied with religious concerns.

HISTORICAL NOVELS

Barth, John, *The Sot-Weed Factor*. New York: Grosset & Dunlap, 1964—This is a long, comic but fundamentally philosophical novel set in seventeenth-century London and Maryland. A sot-weed factor was a tobacco merchant and this is what the bumbling hero, Ebenezer Cooke, sets out to become in the New World.

Cannon, Le Grand, Jr., *Come Home at Even*. New York: Holt, 1951—A novel set in seventeenth-century England and Massachusetts.

Forbes, Esther, *Paradise*. New York: Harcourt Brace Jovanovich, 1937—A historical novel which traces the fortunes of a group of emigrants to Massachusetts from 1639 until King Philip's War with the Indians.

Hawthorne, Nathaniel, *The Scarlet Letter*. New York: New American Library, 1970—This famous novel, set in seventeenth-century Massachusetts, is an exploration of the penalties Puritan society imposes on sinning and the individual's reactions to having sinned.

Johnston, Mary, *To Have and to Hold*. New York: McGraw-Hill, 1953—Historical romance set in colonial Virginia. The arrival of a shipload of potential brides provides the plot against a background of Indian conflict.

Shaping

A large self-sufficient estate, the plantation used slave labor to raise great quantities of tobacco, rice, indigo, and cotton. This painting shows the plantation mansion surrounded by the slave quarters, barns, laundry buildings, a kitchen and, a grist mill. Crops were stored in a warehouse on the waterfront so that they could be easily transferred to oceangoing ships.

an Identity 3

After a foreigner from any part of Europe is arrived, and become a citizen; let him devoutly listen to the voice of our great parent, which says to him, "Welcome to my shores, distressed European; bless the hour in which thou didst see my verdant fields, my fair navigable rivers, and my green mountains!—If thou wilt work, I have bread for thee; if thou wilt be honest, sober, and industrious, I have greater rewards to confer on thee—ease and independence. I will give thee fields to feed and clothe thee; a comfortable fireside to sit by, and tell thy children by what means thou hast prospered; and a decent bed to repose on. I shall endow thee beside with the immunities of a freeman. If thou wilt carefully educate thy children, teach them gratitude to God, and reverence to that government, that philanthropic government, which has collected here so many men and made them happy. I will also provide for thy progeny; and to every good man this ought to be the most holy, the most powerful, the most earnest wish he can possibly form, as well as the most consolatory prospect when he dies. Go thou and work and till; thou shalt prosper, provided thou be just, grateful, and industrious.

—St. John de Crèvecoeur,
Letters from an American Farmer

PATTERNS OF LIFE

During the seventeenth and eighteenth centuries, the American colonies developed a distinct character of their own, an economic and cultural identity that, although patterned after European models, evolved into forms uniquely American. Most of the free population of the pre-Revolutionary colonies was of English descent, but by 1765 30 percent of the 1,850,000 people living in America came from a *non*-English background. This mixed heritage, the 3,000 mile separation between the mother country and the New World, the ever-present pull of the frontier on American life, as well as the evolution of novel social institutions in a wilderness environment made the American a new sort of man.

At the time of the Revolution the American's standard of living was the highest in the world. About 5 percent of the population, including the wealthy planters, merchants, and lawyers, were regarded as the "better sort" or aristocracy. The vast majority of Americans, about 70 percent, were yeoman farmers who owned their own land or were skilled craftsmen and small businessmen in the towns. They were the eighteenth-century equivalent of a middle class. The other 25 percent of the population were poor farmers, indentured servants, tenants on great estates, or day laborers. With some effort, many of these people also entered the middle class. A poor peasantry never existed in colonial America on a large scale.

Furthermore, the religious laws of the early settler were more tolerant and his government more truly democratic than those in Europe. To be sure, the colonial American generally regarded himself as a European, and he reflected this in many of his customs, habits, and attitudes. Yet there were distinctive differences that would in time grow sharper and finally lead to a break with Britain.

The vast majority of early Americans were farmers, but farming in the Southern colonies bore little resemblance to agriculture as practiced in New England or in New York, New Jersey, or Pennsylvania. In order to understand the quality of daily life in the various regions, it is necessary to look at the social and economic systems of the three major colonial regions.

THE SOUTHERN COLONIES

In the early seventeenth century, proprietors and private companies soon learned that the most certain way to lure settlers to the rigorous and dangerous life of the New World was by promising them property under the headright system. This system was based on the condition that the land given away be cultivated. Before the day of mechanized farm equipment, the job of clearing land, ploughing, and harvesting crops was backbreaking work and one person could seldom care for more than 50 acres. Accordingly, King James I, after taking over direct control of Virginia in 1624, granted the "right" to 50 acres to every adult person, or "head," entering the colony. The settler did not truly own the land, it was merely licensed to him on condition that he cultivate it, and live in some sort of house on the property. The grantor—whether it was the king, a nobleman like Lord Baltimore, or a joint-stock company—usually collected a small tax from the settler. This sum, called a quitrent, was as little as a shilling every year for 50 acres. Even this small sum, however, became increasingly difficult to collect. It has been estimated that by the time the Revolution began, landlords were receiving only half of the quitrent money entitled to them.

INDENTURED SERVANTS

Despite the promised reward of "free" land for coming to America, most Europeans who wanted to immigrate found that they could not afford the passage to the New World. However, an immigrant who agreed to become an indentured servant was given passage to America. Such a servant agreed to work for a period, usually 4 or 5 years, without pay. At the end of his servitude, his employers usually gave him a new suit of clothes and some agricultural equipment. He was now free to seek his fortune and with luck he would save enough money to buy his own farm within a few years. Or he might become a "squatter" on land that no one had yet claimed. Squatting created many legal problems when someone wanted to buy the land; so the squatters began to claim "squatters' rights," the privilege of buying the land from the legal owner without paying for the improvements they had made upon it. If a squatter happened to be dispossessed, he could journey farther west and begin to farm a new piece of land. In the Carolinas, indentured servants were often given small plots of land when their service was completed. Few indentured servants rose to positions of privilege or social distinction; most remained yeoman farmers or artisans.

Indentured servitude was very common in America. By 1683, for example, fully one-sixth of the population was indentured. If one excludes New England, where the system was never used extensively, the astonishing fact is that more than half of all those who migrated to the colonies in the eighteenth century came as indentured servants.

THE PLANTATION SYSTEM

Small farms worked by a few hands were typical in the early days of the Southern colonies, but with the beginning of the eighteenth century, large plantations owned by a small percentage of the population and farmed by scores of slaves became increasingly important to the economy. The reason for this development lay in the nature of the South's main crops—tobacco, rice, and indigo.

Tobacco became the major export of Virginia, and later Maryland, after the crown granted the colonists a monopoly of the English market in 1617. Production skyrocketed from 2,500 pounds in 1616 to almost 30 million pounds a year in the late seventeenth century. By the time of the Revolution, Southerners were growing more than one hundred million pounds yearly. So abundant were American tobacco crops that the supply soon exceeded England's demand and prices dropped sharply in the late seventeenth century. The only farmers who could still make a large profit were those who grew tobacco on vast estates or plantations. Therefore, the Southern plantation developed rapidly. In addition to being a low-cost "factory" for producing tobacco, the plantation enjoyed a special advantage. Tobacco wore out the soil rapidly, stripping it of valuable minerals in a decade or two. Small farmers had no recourse but to continue planting and replanting their few acres, until the earth became exhausted. Plantation owners, by contrast, could afford to rotate crops and let some of their fields lie fallow (unplanted) every year.

THE INTRODUCTION OF SLAVERY

Plantation owners also found another way to increase their profits: the use of Africans imported into the colonies as slave labor. The institution of slavery suited

COLONIAL OVERSEAS TRADE

◄─────────── Triangular trade

Southern agriculture perfectly. Unlike an indentured servant, a slave did not finish his service after a few years—he worked for life. The owner did not have to feed or house slaves as well as he did his servants. Moreover, when an indentured servant finished his service, he was free to set himself up as a possible small-scale rival to his former benefactor. Slaves offered no threat of competition. Finally, slaves could be forced to do exhausting, even unhealthy work which no free man would undertake. A slave could literally be worked to death,

since he needed to survive only 6 or 7 years to return the investment the owner had made in him.

Inevitably, Southern farmers turned to the use of slaves from Africa. It was impossible to force slavery on European immigrants who came for the most part by their own consent since they demanded more freedom than they had in Europe, not less. A few Indians were enslaved, but Indians proved difficult to capture in large numbers. The tribal unit protected its own, and the Indians were skillful and courageous warriors who were so familiar with the geography of the continent that it was hard to hunt them down. The black man, on the other hand, was utterly unprepared by his African cultural background, and too shocked psychologically by the experience of his enslavement, to offer strong resistance.

The blacks who were brought to America usually came from tiny villages along the 3,000-mile length of the West Coast of Africa. They came from many tribes, spoke scores of different dialects, and varied greatly in appearance, skills, and cultural attainments.

The Portuguese began the slave trade as early as 1441 and dominated it until the second half of the seventeenth century, when the Dutch, English, and French began to engage in this lucrative enterprise. After 1713, Great Britain was powerful enough to establish a monopoly over the trade.

European slave traders all operated in the same way. They would establish a coastal trading center in Africa and build a corral in which they imprisoned slaves until they collected a full shipload. Coastal tribes would generally raid villages in the interior and capture slaves for the European traders. The captives were bound and carried, sometimes in chains, to the trading center, where the coastal tribesmen exchanged them for European firearms, precious metals, intoxicating drinks, or trinkets. Then the European traders branded the slaves, packed them tightly into ships, and set sail for the West Indies. The crossing lasted about 50 days, and during the hot, miserable "middle passage" one of every eight slaves usually died. The shock of this brutal and barbarous train of events weakened the African and left him ill prepared for conditions in a new and strange environment.

Black slaves were first used in the West Indies and South America, primarily to grow sugar on plantations. By 1655 Jamaica was the chief slave market in the Western world. In the colonies, the first African laborers appeared in August, 1619, when a Dutch frigate sailed into the harbor at Jamestown, Virginia, carrying twenty blacks. In the early seventeenth century, the legal distinction between slavery and indentured servitude had not been defined for blacks.

It gradually became the custom to hold black workers for life as farms grew larger and mass agriculture became more profitable. After 1660, one colony after another passed laws legalizing the status of slavery for those of African descent. By 1700, slavery had become a major source of labor in the Southern colonies. By 1756, 120,000 blacks made up 41 percent of the population in Virginia, and in Maryland, blacks comprised 29 percent of the population. In Georgia, slavery was not legalized until 1750, but 25 years later blacks in bondage outnumbered whites. Only North Carolina, the poorest of the Southern colonies, had few slaves.

Slavery was not confined to the South. There were slaves in all thirteen of the original colonies, although they never made up more than a small fraction of the total population. In general, New England's slave codes were far milder than those in the South (most northern slaves, for instance, were entitled to trial by jury and had the

A slave market in Zanzibar, an island off the coast of Africa. Slaves were taken from the interior by African coastal tribes who sold them to the European traders for firearms, liquor, and trinkets.

A poster advertising healthy, small-pox immune black slaves for sale. Slaves brought over from Africa spent the 50-day trip packed like cattle in the European ships. One out of eight slaves died during the passage.

right to sue and to testify in court). Slaves were numerous in only one northern colony —Rhode Island. Merchants from Rhode Island played an active part in the slave trade and often brought home to Newport those slaves they were unable to sell in the South.

In Virginia, where slaves were used on tobacco plantations, few farmers controlled more than four or five slaves before the Revolution. In Essex County, Virginia, in fact, almost half of the estates in 1750 had no slaves; 30 percent had from two to five slaves, and only one plantation had fifty.

Rice cultivation in South Carolina and Georgia required slave labor from its very beginning, for free men would not submit to its unhealthy conditions. Rice was grown in low-lying coastal areas or near rivers where the fields could be flooded. Slaves had to ply their way through humid swamps, frequently exposing themselves to

malaria.

Rice was first introduced to South Carolina in 1696. Seventy-five years later, planters were exporting some 65 million pounds of rice a year and profits exceeded even those of tobacco growing. In the 1740s, the South discovered still another valuable cash crop, indigo, which was used to make blue dyes for the British woolen industry. This plant was grown in the South Carolina uplands, where rice could not be cultivated, during months when the rice paddies did not require tending, and proved to be a successful complement to the rice crop.

AFRICAN CULTURE

While the slave trade had little effect on most of Africa, it cost the coastal tribes of West Africa about fifteen million of their population over a 400-year period. Weakened by inept rulers, attacks by roving Arab bandits from North Africa, famine, and plague, the people of West Africa were easy prey to European slave traders. The slave trade separated families, broke tribal patterns, and caused taboos to be violated.

Europeans ignorantly assumed that their own civilization was infinitely superior to anything ever produced by Africa. It is now known, however, that unique and sophisticated nations flourished in West Africa as early as A.D. 700. In the fourteenth century, the West African kingdom of Mali had reached a high point of wealth, learning, and humanity. As an Arab traveler wrote: "The Negroes . . . have a greater abhorrence of injustice than any other people. There is complete security in their country." Another traveler was equally rapturous over the empire of Songhay a century later. He wrote about Songhay's "stately temple," its "princely palace," and particularly its "great store of doctors, judges, priests and other learned men." In western Nigeria, the art works of the Ife culture (A.D. 1000–1400), and the striking bronze statues of the kingdom of Benin (A.D. 1500–

RAFFLE

Mr. Joseph Jennings respectfully informs his friends and the public that, at the request of many acquaintances, he has been induced to purchase from Mr. Osborne, of Missouri, the celebrated

DARK BAY HORSE, "STAR,"

Aged five years, square trotter and warranted sound; with a new light Trotting Buggy and Harness; also, the dark, stout

MULATTO GIRL, "SARAH,"

Aged about twenty years, general house servant, valued at *nine hundred dollars*, and guaranteed, and

Will be Raffled for

At 4 o'clock P. M., February first, at the selection hotel of the subscribers. The above is as represented, and those persons who may wish to engage in the usual practice of raffling, will, I assure them, be perfectly satisfied with their destiny in this affair.
The whole is valued at its just worth, fifteen hundred dollars; fifteen hundred

CHANCES AT ONE DOLLAR EACH.

The Raffle will be conducted by gentlemen selected by the interested subscribers present. Five nights will be allowed to complete the Raffle. BOTH OF THE ABOVE DESCRIBED CAN BE SEEN AT MY STORE, No. 78 Common St., second door from Camp, at from 9 o'clock A. M. to 2 P. M.
Highest throw to take the first choice; the lowest throw the remaining prize, and the fortunate winners will pay twenty dollars each for the refreshments furnished on the occasion.
N. B. No chances recognized unless paid for previous to the commencement.

JOSEPH JENNINGS.

A poster advertising a horse and a slave-girl for raffle. An estimated 15 million Africans were sold into slavery during 400 years of trade.

1600), along the Atlantic Coast were expressions of advanced culture.

These states developed complex political and economic systems and a humane social order. Political life was tribal, and often several tribes combined to form a kingdom. A king headed such a confederation, with ministers representing him in the various provinces. The ministers and advisers acted as the king's advisory council. In the tribe, the family unit was important, with polygamy a common practice. The family might also include slaves taken as captives of war. While slaves could be sold, sacrificed, or freed, they usually became an integral part of the family unit and were almost free in status. Religious life consisted of the worship of nature, ancestors, and certain magical practices. Occupations were varied, including farming, cattle raising, mining, trade, and crafts.

Despite the oppressive conditions of slave life, blacks were able to transplant some of their culture to the New World, bringing with them their heritage of music, dancing, folklore, and handicrafts. Negro spirituals, animal tales, crafts made their influence felt on America's cultural life, in time becoming recognized as American art forms.

THE
NEW ARISTOCRACY
AND CITY LIFE

Although most of these rural "aristocrats" came from fairly humble origins in England, they used their newly acquired wealth to create an exclusive society. While small farmers made up the greater part of the population, plantation owners were the most influential people in the South.

Some of the more wealthy planters lived in huge, architecturally symmetrical mansions, distinguished by high columns, and facing a river. Surrounding each great house were barns, slave quarters, a laundry, and a kitchen. Within the mansion, most of the expensive furnishings were usually imported from England. Almost no fine crafts flourished in the South, except in Charlestown. The biggest southern industry at this time was barrelmaking.

Southern planters often entertained one another on their magnificent estates. Weekend visits stretched into month-long stays. Balls, particularly after weddings, ran into 3 days of dancing, drinking, and feasting. Horse racing and cockfights engaged the gentlemen, while the ladies played cards or performed in musicals. Hospitality was so lavish that one family and its guests in one year consumed 27,000 pounds of pork, 150 gallons of brandy, and 550 bushels of wheat. All this socializing inevitably led to matchmaking. By the time of the Revolution, most of the great planters were related by marriage.

Plantation owners were not only leaders of society, but also the chief political figures. The distinct class differences which arose in the South, based on the amount of land owned by a man, thus placed power in the hands of the wealthy. Although small farmers might grumble about the arrogant ways and wasteful pleasures of the rich, they were usually quiet at election time, for most of the elected representatives of the Southern colonies were leading planters. In Virginia, North Carolina, and Georgia, owning land was absolutely essential for voting. In South Carolina, voters had to have either land or money. Of those entitled to vote, the majority were too indifferent to politics to bother. Thus the active electorate was reduced to a group of fairly well-to-do, concerned white men, and this group out of custom and necessity elected the great planters they respected. On minor local levels also, politics was class-conscious. County officials such as justices of the peace, sheriffs, and judges were appointed by the governor, who inevitably chose officeholders from among his own upper-class acquaintances. The subdivisions of the counties, known as parishes, were under the control of the most important laymen in the Church of England. They assumed not only the maintenance of the parish church, but also control of the political life of the area. These men were at first elected by the members of the church, but by the latter part of the seventeenth century the controlling positions were taken as a matter of right by certain wealthy families in each parish.

Because Southern life was rural, the only city of consequence to arise during the early plantation days was Charleston, South Carolina. In the summer months, wealthy planters and their families made a general departure from their rice paddies and poured into the cool, seaside town. There, as might be expected, the gentry's tastes were well attended to. Henry Gignilliat's tavern on Broad Street advertised banquets of "about 40 dishes," and lesser establishments announced the arrival of traveling shows, such as the exhibition in 1738 of a

mysterious ape, the "ourangnogang (or Man of the Woods) tho' this was a female of that Species." A pastry cook from London set up shop in 1736 and baked delicate pastries for parties, cooked roasts for dinners, and prepared pickles for more ordinary repasts. John Paul Grimke, a jeweler, assured customers that he had on hand "a fresh assortment of Brilliant and Rose Diamonds, Rubies, Emeralds, Saphirs, Jacints, Topz's, Amethists . . . and some ready made rings." Wigmakers, barbers, and London tailors were on hand to attend the gentlemen, and cabinetmakers and upholsterers to decorate townhouses in the latest English styles.

BACK COUNTRY HARDSHIPS

While plantation owners treated themselves to the highest refinements of leisure, settlers in the interior faced the constant hardships of disease and Indian attacks, particularly in the Carolina back country. Many pioneers on the frontier of the Chesapeake settlements lived at an almost subhuman level. A traveling preacher reported with horror that many people had given up farming and were simply eking out a meager living by herding wild swine and cattle. He was even more startled by their behavior: many of the men were "swapping their wives as cattle, and living in a state of nature, more irregularly and unchastely than the Indians."

As settlers poured into the back country, subsistence farming, growing food for survival rather than for profit, gradually developed. Life continued to be hard for the frontier families, who usually lived in log cabins that offered poor shelter. Nevertheless, the population grew, trade expanded, and by the middle of the eighteenth century, thriving communities had developed where trade routes crossed. At Fredericksburg and Hagerstown, Maryland; at Martinsburg and Winchester, Virginia; and at Charlotte, North Carolina, grist mills and country stores, and bakers, masons, and other tradesmen served the needs of the backwoods farmers.

Despite social differences, the American colonies in general were far more democratic than England. In America there was no hereditary nobility. A Virginia planter or a Massachusetts merchant might consider himself an "aristocrat," even if he had no title, no birthright to lands, and no position in the government. His children would inherit his rank in society only if they inherited his wealth. Money guaranteed social position far more in the New World than in the Old, and there were many more opportunities for gaining or losing it.

Except for slaves, most Americans could hope to make their way up the social ladder. At the top of the social system, there was a small percentage of rich men, but none had the prestige of the English aristocracy. Americans during the colonial period were as conscious of social distinctions as Europeans. Gulfs still separated those spoken of as "the better sort," the "middling sort," and the "meaner sort." But the classic American rags-to-riches success story was already a reality and many industrious youths and immigrants rose in a few years from the bottom to the top of the social ladder.

THE MIDDLE COLONIES

North of Maryland and south of New England lay the four colonies of Delaware, New York, Pennsylvania, and New Jersey. Sugar, rice, indigo, and, as a rule, tobacco could not be grown easily in these temperate regions. Corn was usually the first crop a newcomer cultivated. It was an easy plant to grow, required little attention, provided abundant nourishment, and served as fodder for livestock. After a farmer began to prosper, he generally turned to the cultivation of such crops as wheat, barley, and oats.

During the eighteenth century, the Middle colonies became the breadbasket of America. Wheat was harvested in such surplus that great quantities were shipped out of Philadelphia and New York to New England and the West Indies. By 1765, Philadelphia was exporting more than 350,000 bushels of wheat a year and 18,000 tons of flour. Meat products from the Middle colonies found a market in southern Europe, while workhorses and thoroughbreds raised in the Middle colonies were transported for sale to New England and the Southern colonies.

Intercolonial trade had two effects: it increased specialization and it tied the colonies together. The Northern colonies, for example, imported rice and tobacco from the South and sugar from the West Indies, while the Southern colonies purchased from the North not only wheat but rum and fish. This interdependence allowed each region to market what it could produce most efficiently and formed links between the colonies that would soon take on political overtones.

LAND SPECULATION

As in the Southern colonies, land was distributed in the central regions by means of the headright system. However, a man could claim only the land which he actually cleared, planted, and lived on. The system worked smoothly in Pennsylvania and New Jersey, but in New York it broke down and became cover for land speculation. For example, political corruption allowed one clever man to piece together an enormous manor of 300,000 acres, which he had no intention of farming himself. One early eighteenth-century royal governor, Lord Cornbury, handed one of his cronies a patent to a million acres. By law, grants were limited to 2,000 acres, but the law was conveniently ignored.

Land speculators in New York sometimes resold their huge holdings, but more often they rented them to tenant farmers. The rents established by New York landlords in-

cluded additional obligations that were a throwback to the Middle Ages. Typically land might be leased in return for 10 bushels of wheat, "four fat hens," and a few days' work on the landlord's own property. The landlords also reserved all milling and mineral rights for themselves. Sometimes they even established private courts on their property.

Not all land speculators were scoundrels. Many were honest and hard-working tradesmen, preachers, and farmers. Thousands of people in the Middle colonies, no matter how honest or poor, were consumed by land fever. As one New York observer commented, "An unaccountable thirst for large tracts of land without the design of cultivation hath prevailed over the inhabitants of this and the neighboring provinces with a singular rage. Patents have been lavishly granted (to give it no worse term) upon the pretense of fair Indian purchases, some of which the Indians have alleged were never made but forged. . . . They say that the surveyors have frequently run patents vastly beyond even the pretended conditions or limits of sale."

IMMIGRATION

Only about a quarter of a million people lived in America in 1700, but by the 1760s the population was nearly two million. About a third of this number had been born abroad and most of the newest arrivals were non-English immigrants.

From their very beginnings, the colonies had attracted and absorbed foreigners. When the British annexed New York, they inherited a settlement influenced by the Dutch. Danes, Finns, and Swedes infiltrated the Delaware Valley in the seventeenth cen-

Eighteenth-century Philadelphia. By the time of the American Revolution, Philadelphia was the largest, richest city in the colonies.

tury. In 1683, William Penn induced a friend of his, Francis Daniel Pastorius, to lead a group of his German followers to Pennsylvania where the newcomers founded Germantown, north of Philadelphia.

These arrivals were a mere trickle compared to the deluge that flooded America after 1713. Impoverished by wars on the Continent and hounded by religious persecution, thousands of Germans came to America seeking economic opportunity and the freedom to practice their faith. Another pressure that forced Europeans to emigrate was the rising population in the Old World. During the eighteenth century the Continent's population doubled, while the amount of farmable land remained fixed.

Almost half of the Germans who came to the colonies eventually settled in Pennsylvania, there becoming the "Pennsylvania Dutch" (Dutch was the English mispronunciation of the German word for German, "Deutsch"). At first some Germans went to New York where they learned that landlords were reluctant to sell farms, preferring to rent them. However, as reports of New York's restrictions on land holding were printed in German newspapers German immigrants began to avoid New York, which helps explain why New York's population increased very slowly during the eighteenth century. About 20 percent of the German immigrants settled in the Southern colonies and only 1 percent dared to confront Puritan intolerance and exclusiveness in New England.

Pennsylvania attracted immigrants because it promised nearly complete religious freedom, a generous land policy, and soil that was so similar to Germany's that newcomers could plant the same crops with the same success and foresee the same farming

problems they had known in Europe. A minority of the Germans were "plain people" or Mennonites (Amish), Moravians, and Dunkards, who were pacifists and wished to avoid contact with the rest of the world. The vast majority, however, were more worldly and quickly immersed themselves in politics and commerce. They were frequently skilled craftsmen who practiced their trades in Philadelphia. By the time of the Revolution, Philadelphia was the largest and richest city in the colonies, with more people than any city in England except London.

Another substantial wave of immigrants arrived from Ireland. A few were true Irishmen, but most were Scotch-Irish, that is, Presbyterian Scots who had moved to northern Ireland early in the seventeenth century. They came for many reasons. Early in the eighteenth century a series of economic, political, and natural disasters plagued northern Ireland. Parliament had outlawed the importation into England of Irish beef and wool and in 1704 had barred all Presbyterians from public office. In 1714, drought struck northern Ireland. Four years of bad crops followed. In 1717, landlords of Irish properties doubled or trebled rents. Scots by the thousands pulled up stakes and headed for America. At first they went to New England, but the Puritans gave them a cold reception. One Puritan minister saw the new arrivals as "formidable attempts of Satan and his Sons to unsettle us." Rebuffed by Massachusetts, the Scotch-Irish headed south to Pennsylvania. From there they pushed west to the Appalachian Mountains and moved along them into the Southern uplands, becoming the New World's most rugged frontiersmen.

THE ISOLATION OF FARM LIFE

In Europe, farmers lived in villages, as a rule. In America, with the exception of New England, farms were scattered far apart, often separated by forests of hard-

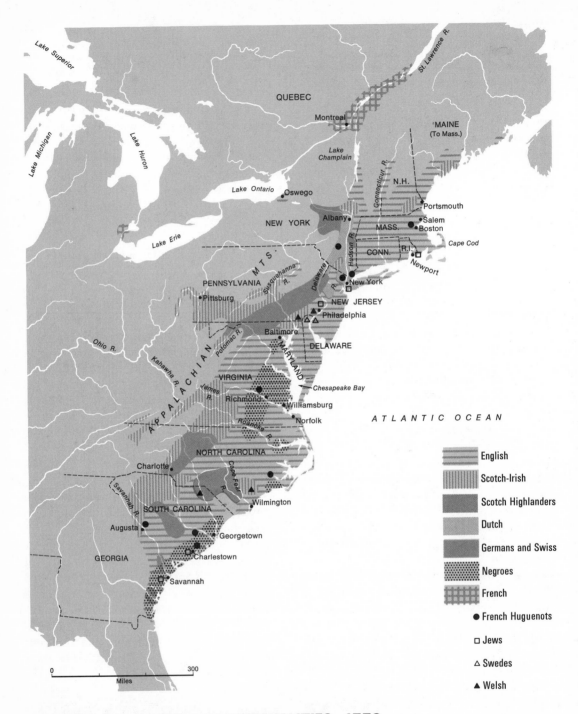

Lake Superior

Lake Michigan

Lake Huron

QUEBEC

Montreal

St. Lawrence R.

MAINE
(To Mass.)

Lake Champlain

Lake Ontario

Oswego

Lake Erie

NEW YORK

Albany

Connecticut R.

N.H.

Portsmouth

Salem
Boston

MASS.

Hudson R.

CONN.

R.I.

Newport

Cape Cod

PENNSYLVANIA

Pittsburg

Susquehanna R.

Delaware R.

New York

NEW JERSEY

Philadelphia

Ohio R.

Kahawha R.

APPALACHIAN MTS.

Potomac R.

Baltimore

DELAWARE

MARYLAND

Chesapeake Bay

VIRGINIA

James R.

Richmond

Williamsburg

Roanoke R.

Norfolk

ATLANTIC OCEAN

NORTH CAROLINA

Charlotte

Cape Fear R.

Savannah R.

SOUTH CAROLINA

Wilmington

Augusta

Georgetown

GEORGIA

Charlestown

Savannah

0   300
Miles

Legend:

- English
- Scotch-Irish
- Scotch Highlanders
- Dutch
- Germans and Swiss
- Negroes
- French
- ● French Huguenots
- □ Jews
- △ Swedes
- ▲ Welsh

COLONIAL SETTLEMENT BY NATIONALITIES · 1770

wood trees that their owners treasured as an additional source of income. In fact, farms were so spread out that many were beyond traveling distance to a church. Itinerant missionaries, or "circuit riders," as they were called, rode long lonely miles preaching to gruff, sometimes unfriendly, farmers.

Since there were few towns, farmers in the Middle colonies carried on their civic duties through much larger, looser governmental units—the counties (a practice similar to that of the Southern colonies). Once a month, farmers would ride to the county

courthouse to vote, take part in drills of the local militia, or pursue legal business. The county courthouse registered births, marriages, and deaths; tried cases; recorded wills and deeds; and licensed taverns. County judges also authorized the building of new roads, established charities to care for the poor and for orphaned children and decided when and where new ferry lines should be opened up.

Because they were so isolated, rural families had to turn to one another for most of their practical and spiritual needs. The family made its own furniture, raised most

Life in Urban America

. . . [Philadelphia] must certainly be the object of every one's wonder and admiration. It is situated upon a tongue of land, a few miles above the confluence of the Deleware and Schuilkill; and contains about 3,000 houses, and 18 or 20,000 inhabitants. It is built north and south upon the banks of the Delaware; and is nearly two miles in length, and three quarters of one in breadth. The streets are laid out with great regularity in parallel lines, intersected by others at right angles, and are handsomely built: on each side there is a pavement of broad stones for foot passangers; and in most of them a causeway in the middle for carriages. Upon dark nights it is well lighted, and watched by a patrole: there are many fair houses and public edifices in it. . . . The city is in a very flourishing state, and inhabited by merchants, artists, tradesmen, and persons of all occupations. There is a public market held twice a week, upon Wednesday and Saturday, almost equal to that of Leadenhall; and a tolerable one every day besides. The streets are crowded with people, and the river with vessels. "

—Andrew Burnaby, Travels through the Middle Settlements in North America in the years 1759 and 1760

The Small Farmer

" None of my ancestors, on either side, were either rich or great, but had the character of honesty and industry, by which they lived in credit among their neighbors, free from real want, and above the frowns of the world. . . . Meat, bread and milk was the ordinary food of all my acquaintance. I suppose the richer sort might make use of those and other luxuries, but to such people I had no access. We were accustomed to look upon, what were called gentle folks, as beings of a superior order. For my part, I was quite shy of them, and kept off at a humble distance. A periwig, in those days, was a distinguishing badge of gentle folk—and when I saw a man riding the road, near our house, with a wig on, it would so alarm my fears, and give me such a disagreeable feeling, that, I dare say, I would run off, as for my life. Such ideas of the difference between gentle and simple, were, I believe, universal among all of my rank and age. . . . "

—Devereux Jarratt, The Life of the Reverend Devereux Jarratt of its food, and wove and sewed most of its clothes. The parents taught their children how to read and do simple arithmetic since, outside of New England, there were few schools in colonial America.

Colonial families were large. Parents frequently had ten or twelve children. For example, Benjamin Franklin came from a family of seventeen and John Marshall had fourteen brothers and sisters. Large families were considered desirable because children were needed to work on the farm. As soon as a boy reached seven years of age, he was helping his father in the field. Little girls attended their mother in the kitchen or at the sewing table as soon as they were old enough to follow orders. Adult women often labored in the fields beside the men. Throughout the eighteenth century, America suffered from a great labor shortage and this labor shortage accounted for the importation of slaves, the encouragement of foreign immigration, and large families.

However, numerous children were rarely a permanent solution to a family's labor problems. Unlike England, where a son usually brought his wife to live with his parents, America offered too much free land to keep the young at home. Newlyweds usually got their own farms early in life. Servants were as hard to keep as grown children. In England, a maid or butler generally served a family for life, but in America labor was so scarce that families were forced to pay servants wages that were three or four times greater than in London. Servants soon were able to amass enough money to start farms of their own.

THE NEW ENGLAND COLONIES

Of the colonies' three main regions along the Atlantic Coast, New England was the most closely knit. By the middle of the eighteenth century, New England boasted a population of half a million, little of it drawn from the recent waves of immigration. During the entire pre-Revolutionary era, New England remained predominantly Puritan and ethnically English. True, there were differences among the various denominations of Puritan background over religious doctrine which sometimes led to sharp disputes; nevertheless, the area possessed a more unified and distinctive regional character than any other part of America.

THE TOWNSHIPS

The solid Puritan and English background of New England was not the only factor that gave the region its distinct character. Another factor that promoted unity in New England was the method by which unsettled land was distributed. Unlike the Southern and Middle colonies, where pioneers staked out remote farms which they had received as their headright, or which they had seized illegally simply by "squatting" on other people's land, in New England the process was orderly, legal, and community-minded. The immigrants to this area settled in towns. New England's colonial governments granted virgin lands not to individuals but to *groups* of settlers. A group usually received a 36-square-mile tract called a township. Near the center of the tract, the citizens erected a village around a town square. Here all the farmers lived in a true community, with a church and a school. The land around the village was divided into farms, pasture, and woodlands. The farms were parceled out to each family, but the pastures and the timberlands were held in common by the villagers as a group.

The widespread growth of towns encouraged two developments: specialized crafts and local government. Even small towns could support such skilled craftsmen as carpenters, tailors, weavers, and blacksmiths. (Some villages built their fortunes on one craft in particular; for instance, in the 1760s, Lynn, Massachusetts, was manufac-

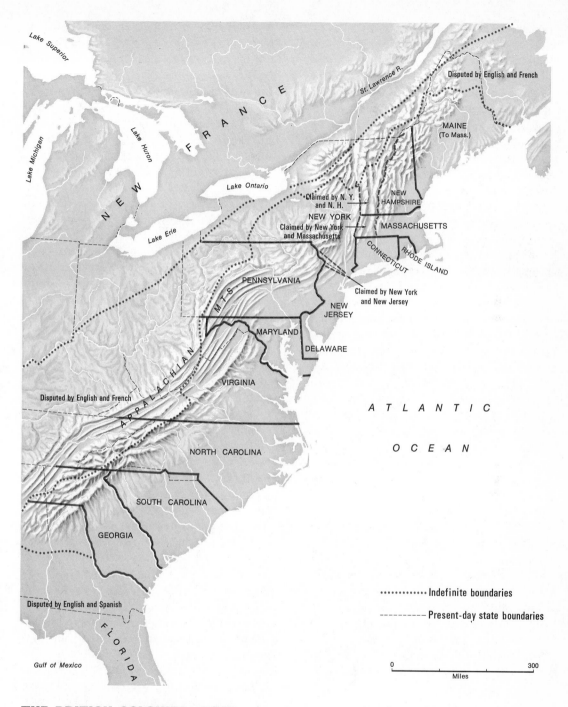

Lake Superior

Lake Michigan

Lake Huron

NEW FRANCE

St. Lawrence R.

Disputed by English and French

MAINE
(To Mass.)

Lake Ontario

Lake Erie

Claimed by N. Y.
and N. H.

NEW
HAMPSHIRE

NEW YORK

Claimed by New York
and Massachusetts

MASSACHUSETTS

CONNECTICUT

RHODE ISLAND

PENNSYLVANIA

A
P
P
A
L
A
C
H
I
A
N

M.T.S.

NEW
JERSEY

Claimed by New York
and New Jersey

MARYLAND

DELAWARE

Disputed by English and French

VIRGINIA

ATLANTIC

OCEAN

NORTH CAROLINA

SOUTH CAROLINA

GEORGIA

Disputed by English and Spanish

FLORIDA

Gulf of Mexico

············ Indefinite boundaries

--------- Present-day state boundaries

0   300
Miles

THE BRITISH COLONIES · 1750

turing 80,000 pairs of shoes a year!) During the long winters, farm families kept themselves busy by making bone buttons, leather pants, and string bags. The success of Northern manufacturing, coupled with a shortage of labor, made the workingman's lot a happy one. His wages were considerably higher than those paid a laborer in England and his importance to the economy worked to prevent the development of an underprivileged working class.

New Englanders took a lively role in municipal affairs. Local issues were voted on by all male adult members of the township. But participation in government went beyond merely voting. Every New England town had a number of public offices to fill, and at some time in his life, almost every townsman served in at least one of these positions. So intense was interest in local politics that the average New Englander tended to neglect the larger issues of colonial or provincial affairs. These matters he left to his elected representatives in the colonial assembly. Usually these representatives were of the "better sort," that is, merchants, lawyers, and prosperous farmers, and once they received a seat in the assembly they were usually reelected time and again.

THE CITIES

Despite the diligent efforts of New England farmers, the region could not feed itself. The ground was simply too rocky, the growing season too short, and the amount of workable land too small. Throughout the eighteenth century New England had to import large quantities of pork and flour from the Middle colonies. New England had no single staple crop nor any important mineral resources.

Yet the area prospered. Its wealth was founded not on the bounty of the soil, but on the energy of its merchants, craftsmen, and fishermen. In the seventeenth century the Northern colonies were indisputably the masters of New World commerce. In

the eighteenth century their dominance was threatened by New York and Pennsylvania, but New England merchants always controlled a substantial part of the business of shipping goods to and from America. At the time of the Revolution, they owned about a thousand seagoing vessels.

New England's commerce was built on what has been called "the triangular trade." The three corners of the triangle were: New England itself, the West Indian islands in the Caribbean, and finally, southern Europe and Africa. About 7,500 New Englanders were directly or indirectly connected with the fishing industry. These men made great catches of fish, which were then dried. The best fish were shipped to southern Europe and the fish on the "refuse ship" were sent to feed slaves in the West Indies.

In the Caribbean, fish was exchanged for molasses, more than 80 percent of which was bought from the French-owned islands in the West Indies, since British islands such as Jamaica had drastically declined in their sugar production in the eighteenth century. New England ships, loaded with molasses, headed back home. By 1763 there were in New England 150 distilleries which converted molasses into rum. The rum was then transported to the West Coast of Africa where it was exchanged for slaves, ivory, and gold dust. The slaves were then conveyed to the West Indies, where they were sold to plantation owners. With the profits, the merchants bought more molasses. Some historians have presented the triangular trade as a neat, precise pattern (molasses to New England, rum to Africa, slaves to the West Indies), but in fact few ships ever followed exactly that route, reasonable as it might have been. There were many criss-crossings back and forth across the triangle. Sometimes New England's vessels stopped off in southern Europe to load up on wine or salt. At other times, they docked in England.

Thriving commerce created thriving cities, and the most important of these was Boston. By 1722 Boston had a dozen major shipyards, forty-two principal streets, three thousand houses, and sixteen thousand citizens. Except for sailors and stevedores, most Bostonians were upper or middle-class lawyers, clergymen, merchants, shipbuilders and shopkeepers, or self-employed craftsmen. There were few poor laborers in Boston, or in any other American city.

Despite the strictness of Puritan morality, Boston was much like any city in England. The Puritan ban against frivolous amusements was strong enough to ensure that no plays or concerts were performed in the city, but several merchants were rich enough to afford coaches, fine houses, and expensive furniture. An English traveler described how the well-to-do Bostonians diverted themselves:

For their domestic amusements, every afternoon, after drinking tea, the gentlemen and ladies walk the Mall, and from thence adjourn to one another's houses to spend the evening. . . . But, notwithstanding plays and such like diversions do not obtain here, they don't seem to be dispirited nor moped for want of them; for both the ladies and gentlemen dress and appear as gay, in common, as courtiers in England on a coronation or birthday. And the ladies here visit, drink tea, and indulge every little piece of gentility, to the height of the mode; and neglect the affairs of their families with as good a grace as the finest ladies in London.

Boston State House in 1801. Trades such as shipbuilding, clockmaking, gold and silver handiwork, and other specialized crafts were prosperous in Boston in the early 1700s.

In the area of fashion, Boston sophistication often conflicted with Puritan other-worldliness. In the seventeenth century, Bostonian gentlemen began to wear wigs, spending as much as $250 on their long, powdered, false locks. When hundreds of New Englanders were massacred in Indian attacks in 1676, many stern preachers attributed the disaster to God's anger at his seeing the presumed elect making such a display of themselves.

Prosperous Boston offered a living to tradesmen and craftsmen of every variety. Besides the necessary occupations of carpentry, bricklaying, and leather-tanning, Boston enjoyed the services of America's finest goldsmiths and silversmiths, a London clockmaker, and one amazingly adaptive craftsman, George Brownell, who advertised:

All sorts of Millinery Work done; making up Dresses and flowering of Muslin, making of furbelow'd Scarffs, and quilting and cutting of Gentlewomen's Hair in the newest Fashion; and also young Gentlewomen and Children taught all sorts of Fine Works, as Feather-work, Filigre, and Painting on Glass, Embroidering in a new Way, Turkeywork and Dancing cheaper than was ever taught in Boston. Brocaded work for Handkerchiefs and short aprons upon Muslin; artificial Flowers work'd with a needle.

Women who were shopping or gentlemen conducting business were carried about in sedan chairs or in carriages, often accompanied by slaves. Boston had more than a thousand blacks in bondage during the eighteenth century. But in spite of its air of wealth and luxury, by the 1740s the growth rate of Boston fell behind its great northern rivals, Philadelphia, Newport, and New York, where the population was growing rapidly. Portsmouth, Rhode Island took over much of Boston's shipbuilding industry and Newport's shipowners, who controlled half of America's slave trade, diverted a great deal of business from Boston.

Boston, like other cities, began to experience problems that farmers did not have to face. An underground drainage system had to be built. (City officials, elected by the townsmen, supervised construction of the sewers, which were paid for by private individuals.) The Boston city government also found it necessary to build jails, pay doctors to visit its few poor families, and after the city was ravaged by several serious fires, to organize a public fire department of twenty men and six engines. These firefighters were helped by the first unpaid colonial fire company, the Boston "Fire Society" of 1717. The society was made up of twenty gentlemen volunteers who brought to each fire two buckets and two large bags in which they carried away valuable goods from burning houses in order to prevent pillage. Such volunteer associations sprang up in other cities and became a familiar feature of colonial life.

THE FRONTIER SPIRIT

Although America's five main cities—Newport, Boston, Philadelphia, New York, and Charleston—seemed like transplanted English communities, America was unlike any place in Europe. America was different partly because of its odd mixture of religions and nationalities, but also because many of its inhabitants were constantly confronting the wilderness.

One famous American historian, Frederick Jackson Turner, considered the frontier the *most* decisive factor in the formation of the American character. In 1893, Turner wrote:

American social development has been continually beginning over again on the frontier. This perennial rebirth, this fecundity of American life, this expansion westward with its new opportunities, its continuous touch with the simplicity of primitive society, furnish the forces dominating Amer-

Early colonial craftsmen did not think of themselves as artists. For the woodcarver or artisan with a knack for limning or illustrating, their work consisted of simple jobs to be done: A sign for the tavernkeeper to hang above his door, a weathervane to be cut out of metal for a farmer and, aside from the inevitable cradles, chests, and coffins, there were toys to be carved for the children. If a prosperous merchant wanted his likeness painted, the sign painter was ready, as a sideline, to oblige by limning "a counterfeit presentment."

Early American Folk Art

Weathervane.

*In this way, craftsmen unself-consciously and sponta-
neously produced America's folk art. Objects of great
charm were carved by skilled but untrained hands, and
needlewomen with infinite patience for handiwork produced the samplers and embroidered cloths that have
been left as reminders of the American experience. Pictures were painted by untutored artists of such child-
like simplicity in their representation of men and nature
that the sophisticated critics of the twentieth century
termed them American primitives and enshrined them
in museum collections.*

*One such amateur was Edward Hicks of Bucks
County, Pennsylvania. A Quaker preacher, Hicks spent
a lifetime in conflict with his irrepressible desire to
paint. At first he earned a living as a sign and carriage
painter, later he became a minister and farmer. To appease his Quaker guilt because he painted pictures in his
spare time, he concentrated on religious and patriotic
subjects. Gloomily, he described painting as, "the inseparable companion of voluptuousness and pride,"
adding a prediction that it "presaged the downfall of
empires and kingdoms, and . . . stands now enrolled
among the premonitory systems of the rapid decline of
the American republic." In a Calvinist society, few were
likely to disagree with him.*

Some seventeenth and eighteenth century limners took to the road to peddle their gift for portraiture. Some sculpted gravestones, adorning them with death's-heads, cherubs, and mermaids and, in a later period, with portraits of the deceased. An itinerant carver of another sort was the legendary toymaker Wilhelm Schimmel, a burly, eccentric old German who roamed Pennsylvania by horse and buggy, whittling his carvings as he went.

Colonial America also produced folk sculpture carved by blacksmiths, carpenters, and stone-cutters. One of the most renowned folk artists was "Deacon" Shem Drowne, a coppersmith who made weathervanes, pump heads and signs for shops, and figureheads for sailing vessels. Under the hand of such carvers as Drowne, American figureheads, at first influenced by European design traditions, became freer and bolder in character, acquiring an authentically Yankee spirit as they proudly rode the clipper ships that proclaimed Revolutionary America's growing sea and mercantile power. Later, when the advent of the steam engine changed the shape of prows, full-blown curved maidens were replaced by upright figures, and gradually the disappearance of the figurehead marked the end of an era. The makers of ship ornaments then turned their talents to carving

cigar store Indians and other
wooden figures ordered by shopkeepers.

The wooden Indian was not the only figure used to
advertise tobacco shops. Jockeys, ladies of fashion, soldiers, sailors, turks, Egyptians, and Scotsmen also lured
buyers into shops. They were among America's earliest
advertising trademarks in a day when much of the populace was still illiterate. One could recognize the cobbler
by the hanging boot, the apothecary by the mortar and
pestle, and the milliner by a lady's bonnet.

These were the only sculptures and pictures known
by the ordinary people of a raw land. In time, wealthy
American colonists would import art and gradually the
nation would develop a fine arts culture. The folk
craftsman would yield to the industrial revolution and
his unique skills would be enveloped by the methods
of mass production.

Henry Ward Beecher. Carved by farmer by the name of
Corbin after Beecher visited his home.

Carving of George Washington.

Circus group by William T. Hornaday.

Appliqué bedspread.

Mahantango Valley farm.

Wooden splint box.

Early nineteenth-century painting of quilting bee.

Chalkwork church.

Pennsylvania German earthenware dish, 1786.

The Residence of David Twining by Edward Hicks.

Fireman of the Eureka Brigade, woodcarving.

Gravestone, Plymouth.

Gravestone, Boston.

Decorated powder horn.

Needlework of Adam and Eve, 1760.

Figurehead of Andrew Jackson carved for the Constitution.

Figurehead of ship Creole.

ican character. . . . Thus the advance of the frontier has meant a steady movement away from the influence of Europe, a steady growth of independence on American lines.

Today many historians contend that Turner has overemphasized the importance of the frontier. Some stress the persistence of the English and European cultural heritage as the most important factor in shaping life in the New World. Others have claimed that the cities contributed as much, and perhaps more than the wilderness, to the creation of a uniquely American way of life.

In any case, the fact remains that the development of life in the New World was influenced significantly by geography. To illustrate, land travel was impractical over the long distances separating one city from another. Roads were expensive to build and maintain. As late as 1723 Benjamin Franklin, in going from Boston to Philadelphia, preferred going by boat down the Atlantic coast to New York and up the Delaware River than traveling by road. The American forests, while providing for lumber, discouraged intensive farming on a large scale. The Appalachian Mountains, and the French and Indians beyond, inhibited westward expansion until after the Revolution.

The terrain even determined where cities would be established. The Dutch, immediately after arriving in New York, founded Albany 150 miles up the Hudson, but a century passed before towns were established only a few miles inland from a waterway or the Atlantic Coast.

The immenseness of the wilderness hindered the preservation of many traditional English institutions and aspirations. To use a trivial example, Virginians who tried to import the English sport of fox-hunting had to abandon the effort in the colonial period. The fox simply disappeared into the forest. The runaway fox is symbolic of the difficulties encountered in attempts to transplant upper-class customs from the Old World to the New. Peasants could no longer be kept as servile menials on a lord's estate. As we have seen, several attempts to start manorial estates in the colonies never went beyond the planning stage. Where so much cheap land was available, and labor was so scarce and highly paid, few would plow another man's fields for long.

Although early American cities were the cultural and economic stronghold of the country, the drive by settlers to the frontiers of the colonies never ceased. By the time of the Revolution, the pioneers had pushed as far west as the Appalachian Mountains.

THE
IMPACT
OF
RELIGION

The most striking facts about religion in colonial America were that: the colonies were overwhelmingly Protestant (there were about 25,000 Catholics and 2,000 Jews at the time of the Revolution, out of a total population of about 1.5 million); there were numerous denominations; and many people attended no church at all. By the middle of the eighteenth century, the percentage of nonchurchgoers was greater in the colonies than in any European country. The main reason for the existence of so many "non-professing Christians," as they were called, is that great areas of the country were too poor or too sparsely settled to support a church. In 1701, for example, although there were 12,000 people living in the Carolinas, there were no ministers from the Church of England. As late as 1729, a Virginian wrote about the capital of North Carolina: "I believe this is the only Metropolis in the Christian or Mahometan World, where there is neither Church, Chappel, Mosque, Synagogue, or any other place of Publick Worship of any Sect or Religion whatsoever."

ANGLICANS IN THE SOUTH

The Church of England, sometimes called the Anglican Church, was by no means the strongest religious institution in the colo-

nies. In 1775, there were 668 Congregational (Puritan) churches in America, 588 Presbyterian churches, and only 495 Anglican places of worship. The Baptists had 494 churches and the Quakers, 310.

In places where the Church of England might be expected to flourish, it failed to gain genuine support. It was, to be sure, the established religion from Maryland to Georgia by 1758. The citizens were obligated to support Anglican ministers financially and many Southerners swore allegiance to the Church but grumbled about paying these salaries.

The Church's position in the South was further weakened by the fact that an American bishop was never appointed for the colonies. The Bishop of London, who was in charge of America, never crossed the Atlantic to visit his charge. Moreover, in the Anglican faith, as in the Catholic, a priest could only be ordained by a bishop. Since ordination required sailing to London, few aspirants made the trip. As a consequence, they were not "real" ministers at all, and colonial congregations felt free to run their churches and hire and fire their spiritual leaders as they chose. Frequently, a layman conducted the service, and many Anglican church services had a tone that was almost Puritan.

Along the frontier, the Anglican Church made an even smaller impression. Most of the back country was populated with Scotch-Irish Presbyterians, Welsh Baptists, and Germans who belonged to a variety of sects. Occasionally Anglican ministers would travel into pioneer settlements, but they did not always receive a gracious welcome. One such clergyman reported that a group of Presbyterians "hired a band of rude fellows to come to service who brought with them fifty-seven dogs (for I counted them), which in time of service they set fighting, and I was obliged to stop." The disturbances stopped only when the minister concluded by thanking the "fifty-seven Presbyterians" for attending his sermon.

PURITANS IN THE NORTH

The Bible Commonwealth established by the Puritans in Massachusetts was a strong fortress in the seventeenth century. The founders of the colony had come to America in search of religious freedom, but once they secured it, they were not at all eager to extend tolerance to other sects. As Richard Mather wrote in 1643:

The discipline appointed by Jesus Christ for his churches is not arbitrary, that one church may set up and practice one form, and another another form, as each one shall please, but is one and the same for all churches. . . . And if that discipline which we here practice, be (as we are persuaded of it) the same which Christ hath appointed, and therefore unalterable, we see not how another can be lawful.

Convinced that they were in the right, that they had recreated in America a society that bore a close resemblance to the original community of Christ and his followers, the Puritans were determined to exclude all heretics and chasten all sinners in their midst. Seventeenth-century laws provided for whipping, branding, and execution of non-Puritans, under certain circumstances. Under these laws, four Quakers met death in Massachusetts during 1659 and 1660. The Puritans were not opposed to liquor and sex, as modern Americans tend to imagine. Wine was something that God had provided for man's pleasure and sexual enjoyment between husband and wife was a thoroughly permissible blessing. But drunkenness was the handiwork of the devil, and one of the first words Puritan children learned to spell was "fornication."

Whereas the Anglican Church in the South was a pale imitation of the mother church in England, the Puritan commonwealth was an experiment without precedent, a purely American phenomenon. By the beginning of the eighteenth century, however, the peak of Puritan control had been passed. Bostonians became increasingly absorbed in making money. They went to church as a ritual, observing the outward appearance of a moral life. Few children of church members could prove that they had experienced the religious conversion necessary for church membership so that Puritan control of the colony was threatened by lack of members from the younger generation. Consequently, in 1662, the colony's leaders felt compelled to change the requirement for church membership, adopting the so-called "Half-way Covenant," which permitted the children of members to be baptized, thereby obtaining a half-way membership entitling them to have their own children baptized. Full membership was still reserved, however, for those who had experienced a religious conversion and only they could receive communion.

The Half-way Covenant stopped dissent within the colony for a while, but in 1699 hostility against old-line Puritanism again arose. A group of well-to-do merchants broke away from the Boston congregation and started the Brattle Street Church. The new congregation gave its emphatic approval to the Half-way Covenant, insisted that baptism could not be denied to any child, and argued that any person who attended a church and made contributions to it was entitled to help select the minister—even if that person was not an official church member. Conservatives in the community tried to stop the spread of such reform measures, but as an anonymous rhyme put it: "The old strait gate is now out of date, The street it must be broad."

WITCH TRIALS

Meanwhile, the Puritan oligarchy, or ruling class, received other blows that weakened its control over the colony. Its legal

Two original documents from the Salem witchcraft trials. The first is the testimony of a Mrs. Ann Putnam and her daughter against a "witch" called Rebekah. The second is a court indictment against Abigail Hobbs for "covenanting with the Devil." Evidence such as this was enough to sentence a person to hanging.

DEPOSITIONS OF MRS. ANN PUTNAM AND ANN PUTNAM, JR. BEFORE MAGISTRATES HATHORNE AND CORWIN, SALEM VILLAGE, MAY 31, 1692.—

INDICTMENT AGAINST ABIGAIL HOBBS OF TOPSFIELD, "FOR COVENANTING WITH THE DEVIL" 1692.

control was curbed by the charter of 1691 making Massachusetts a royal colony and its respected position was further undermined by the hysteria that accompanied— and the remorse that followed—the Salem witch trials. In 1689, one of Boston's most eloquent and respected theologians, Cotton Mather, published a widely read book about witchcraft. This was an intellectual and purely speculative book, but 3 years after it was published it had disastrous consequences in a small village outside of Salem, Massachusetts. Some young girls who had been overexcited by voodoo stories they had heard from a West Indian woman began to shout at odd moments and twitch nervously. A doctor examined them and announced that they were under a witch's spell. The villagers began to accuse one another wildly, beginning a craze for witch hunting that quickly spread to neighboring villages and Boston itself.

The trials began in June, 1692. By September, twenty "witches" identified by the girls were dead and 150 suspects jailed. Most officials and intellectuals kept silent at first, but gradually a few brave souls stepped forward to speak out against the executions. Finally, the Governor, Lord Phips, lost patience when his own wife was accused of being a witch. He ordered the prisoners released from jail. Several of the girls who had first made accusations confessed that they had lied. Cotton Mather, even though he warned the court not to accept the evidence presented by "witches," guiltily admonished himself for not "appearing with *vigor* to stop the proceedings of the judges when the inexplicable storm from the invisible world assaulted the country."

EVALUATING PURITANISM

Historians have disagreed sharply about the nature and extent of Puritan influence on American culture. Some have said the Puritans obstructed freedom of thought and religion, while others maintained that they established the foundations of American democracy. Opposing viewpoints such as these may reflect the historian's reaction to his own environment since students of the past frequently have adopted interpretations of past events to suit their present needs. For instance, most nineteenth-century American critics of the Puritans frankly idolized certain personalities. John Gorham Palfrey was outstanding in this respect, as can be seen by his five-volume *History of New England*. Palfrey, a descendent of the Puritans, found little to condemn in his forefathers, and regarded John Winthrop, in particular, as a genius for his part in establishing the idea of self-government.

By the twentieth century, however, an anti-Puritan attitude developed. In the 1920s critics such as H. L. Mencken saw the narrow-minded ideas of their own day as the cultural result of the Puritan outlook. In addition, three scholars of this period—James Truslow Adams, Vernon L. Parrington, and Thomas J. Wertenbaker—were all strongly affected by the economic and social inequities in the America of their day. They began to look for parallel conflicts in earlier American history and found the roots of some of these modern ills in the Puritan past. They condemned the early New England settlers for their oppressive control over the individual's public and private life, for the dominance of the middle class over the less fortunate in society, and for their authoritarian religious concepts.

In the 1930s, a group of historians at Harvard wrote more sympathetically about the Puritans. Perhaps the best known of these scholars is Samuel Eliot Morison. He praised the Puritan contribution to American culture, believing that the settlers of Massachusetts carried European intellectual accomplishments to the wilderness. While other colonists often became half-savage in their struggles with the obstinate land, he wrote, the Puritans were able, through self-

discipline and great energy, to found Harvard College only a few years after arriving in Boston. Morison pointed out that the Puritans created a public elementary school system, printed, imported, and read a great many books, and were in touch with most of the new scientific and artistic movements flowering in England.

Morison and such colleagues as Perry Miller and Clifford K. Shipton constructed a view of the Puritans which emphasized their intellectual sophistication. After World War II, a new group of historians, called the neo-conservative school, revised this interpretation. The neo-conservatives wrote at a time when America's security seemed threatened by the Cold War and by a widespread fear of subversion from within. Such historians as Daniel Boorstin emphasized that the institutions in the United States founded by the practical-minded Puritans were still strong and powerful. They felt that the Puritans' pragmatic approach to problems was unique and had characterized the American people ever since.

THE GREAT AWAKENING

Shocked by the apathy toward formal religion, many ministers in the early eighteenth century embarked upon a crusade to bring about conversions among colonial Americans and hopefully make them formal churchgoers. Religious life in America underwent a revival by the 1740s and this hastened the decline of the more tradition-bound denominations.

As early as 1725 a Dutch Reformed minister in New Jersey named Theodore Frelinghusen was inspiring his congregation with sermons that betrayed a new fervent, emotional note, an insistence upon faith rather than reason. In the 1730s, Jonathan Edwards, the most outstanding preacher of the so-called Great Awakening in New England, began to exhort his parishioners in brilliant, highly charged oratory to remember that suffering awaited sinners in hell. He urged men to surrender themselves with emotion to God's mercy. The most important figure in the entire movement, however, was the English revivalist, George Whitefield, who made his first speaking tour through the colonies in 1739 and quickly became the best known man of his generation in America.

One of Whitefield's sermons outside of Philadelphia attracted ten thousand people and in almost every town he drew such large crowds that the meetings had to be held outside the church. Aside from his great abilities as a speaker, Whitefield ex-

cited his audiences with his emotional intensity. Roaming preachers who imitated his style whipped up mass hysteria wherever they went. Zealous men and women burst into shouts or tears, promised to reform their lives, or experienced shattering revelations of divine light. Carried away, congregations would often exhibit the most extraordinary behavior, as one observer noted:

Some would stand in the pulpit exhorting, some in the body of the seats, some in the pews, and some up in the gallery; and oftentimes, several of them would speak together; so that some praying, some exhorting, and testifying, some singing, some screaming, some crying, some laughing, and some scolding, made the most amazing confusion that ever was heard.

Regardless of the emotional excesses of the Great Awakening, it had far-reaching consequences. Traveling evangelists assured their listeners that education had nothing to do with salvation and even criticized local ministers for being too well educated. Several churches split into two groups. Both

Religious fervor and superstitious folklore, combined with Cotton Mather's ill-timed book on witches, brought about the Salem witch trials in 1692. Mather's book, published in 1689, was an intellectual and speculative account of witchcraft, but hysteria took hold of the New England people when reports of actual hexing began. This engraving shows the frenzied trial of a supposed witch, George Jacobs.

. . . and when we got to Middletown old meeting house, there was a great multitude, it was said to be 3 or 4,000 of people, assembled together. . . . Everything, men, horses, and boats seemed to be struggling for life. The land and banks over the river looked black with people and horses; all along the 12 miles I saw no man at work in his field, but all seemed to be gone. When I saw Mr. Whitefield come upon the scaffold, he looked almost angelical; a young, slim, slender youth, before some thousands of people with a bold undaunted countenance. And my hearing how God was with him everywhere as he came along, it solemnized my mind and put me into a trembling fear before he began to preach; for he looked as if he was clothed with authority from the Great God, and a sweet solemn solemnity sat upon his brow, and my hearing him preach gave me a heart wound. By God's blessing, my old foundation was broken up, and I saw that my righteousness would not save me.

—*Nathan Cole,* Spiritual Travels

Skepticism of the Great Awakening

"*But it may justly be question'd whether extraordinary Warmth in the Passions, when there is not answerable Light in the Mind, is so much owing to the SPIRIT OF GOD, as some may be ready to imagine. For is it reasonable to think that the Divine SPIRIT in dealing with Men in a Way of Grace, and in Order to make them good Christians, would give their Passions the chief Sway over them? Would not this be to invert their Frame? To place the Dominion in those Powers, which were made to be kept in Subjection? And would the alwise GOD introduce such a State of Things in the human Mind? Can this be the Effect of the Out-pouring of his SPIRIT? It ought not to be supposed. One of the most essential Things necessary in the new-forming Men, is the Reduction of their Passions to a proper Regimen, i.e. The Government of a sanctified Understanding: And 'till this is effected, they may be called New Creatures, but they are far from deserving this Character.*"

—*Charles Chauncy,* Seasonable Thoughts on the State of Religion in Massachusetts

Presbyterians and Congregationalists were forced either to stay with the older, conservative wing of their faiths or join the "new side" calling for a spiritual democracy. In an excess of anti-intellectualism, many radical congregations fired their ministers for being too learned. The established denominations, particularly Presbyterians and Baptists, gained many new adherents, and a new group, later known as Methodists, disenchanted with the formalism of the Church of England, made great headway in the back country of America.

The Great Awakening may also have had political and social side effects. As the Anglican Church weakened, so did respect for British authority—especially in Virginia. The growth of membership in the dissent-

ing churches also prepared the way for the separation of church and state and ultimately for religious freedom everywhere. It became increasingly difficult to obtain financial support for the Church of England in the Southern colonies and the Congregational Church in New England when these churches could no longer claim the allegiance of a majority of the settlers. The new religious awakening provided a social outlet for pent-up emotions. Attitudes of racial exclusiveness may also have been softened by the doctrine of the sinfulness of all men and the Methodist and Quaker emphasis on universal salvation. The Quakers, in fact, were the first religious denomination to attack slavery as opposed to the will of God. New religious seminaries appeared to carry on the religious revival. The most famous of these were the College of New Jersey (Presbyterian), Dartmouth (Congregational), Rutgers (Dutch Reformed), and the College of Rhode Island (Baptist).

THE SECULAR MIND

While the ordinary people of America were submitting to an epidemic of revivalism, the intellectual elite was embracing a new religion of its own—the cult of reason. For a small number of rich, educated, and influential men, a new way of looking at the world was being developed in the eighteenth century—the philosophy of the Enlightenment.

THE ENLIGHTENMENT

Whereas Puritan theology had seen man as essentially an evil creature dependent on the mercy of God, the philosophy of the Enlightenment taught that man was basically good and capable of becoming better through reason and education. The two leading figures of the Enlightenment in England were Sir Isaac Newton and John Locke. Building on the ideas and experiments of such earlier scientists as Coper-

nicus and Galileo and on mathematical discoveries of his own, Newton published his *Principia Mathematica* in 1687 in which he explained a great law which controlled the movement of the universe, the law of gravity. Ever since the Greek and Roman period, men believed there was a natural law of order and harmony controlling the universe although it could not be defined in exact terms. Now, Newton described this law with precise simplicity. He discovered that every particle of matter was subject to the forces of gravity. The far-reaching implications of the discovery of the law of gravity were expressed by his contemporary, Alexander Pope, when he declared: "Nature and Nature's laws lay hid in night, God said: 'Let Newton be,' and there was light." Everything seemed possible to human reason.

Unlike generations of philosophers before him who had attempted to explain the universe by turning to Aristotle or the Scriptures, Newton used the scientific method of arriving at correct knowledge through investigation, experiment, and rational analysis of specific data. If such great advances could be made in understanding one aspect of life, his contemporaries concluded, certainly in other areas of human experience—politics, morality, religion—man's reason could discover laws which would establish the proper order and harmony.

Accepting the implications of Newton's discovery, John Locke wrote his *Essay on Human Understanding*. In this treatise, published in 1690, Locke argued that man's mind was not already filled at birth with sin or any other definite ideas, but was rather a blank slate. When a child came into the world, he was totally receptive, an empty page which his experience would eventually fill. All the knowledge engraved on man's mind came through his senses, from observation and experiment, Locke said.

Locke's essay struck some Americans as a

strong argument against the belief that man was born evil and predestined for either salvation or damnation. At the same time, the *Essay* seemed to underline the necessity for careful scientific study. If man's senses were the only avenues through which he gained knowledge, then he must make sure that his sense impressions were reliable.

Subsequently, Locke wrote two treatises on government in which he described what he saw as a rational model for civil rule guided by man's reason. According to Locke, men were born free under the natural law of the universe and endowed with the natural rights, of life, liberty, and property. But a society without organization would hinder men from enjoying their rights, for the nature of man was selfish and violent as well as rational and man's freedom could be trampled on by aggressive neighbors. Locke believed that men were rational enough to overcome this danger, however, by forming a contract among themselves to protect their natural rights. To a man of Locke's background, the parliamentary system of government in England appeared as the most rational type of political system. Thus, his political philosophy called for a government with divided powers and majority rule under law. There would be executive, legislative, and judicial branches of government, each with power to prevent the other two from creating a tyranny. Locke believed, however, that the legislature with representation based on the popular will should be the most important branch of government. Its laws should be passed by the majority of its members and should apply equally to all the citizenry. If, under some extreme circumstance, the government did not operate to protect the natural rights of man, was there a remedy? Yes, said Locke, the remedy was for the people to take back the power that they had delegated to the government under the contract. In other words, Locke believed government was an artificial creation of man himself, and if man was dissatisfied with it,

he could modify it. Under extreme circumstances he could revolt against it. Thus, John Locke's political philosophy offered strong support for the concept of the right of revolution against established authority.

For educated Americans, Locke's theory of government had the same clarity as Newton's explanation of the laws of the universe. In both theories, God had created a natural order which included man and a grand design for the universe, and had then quietly retired. God did not intervene in people's lives. He was like a clockmaker who, once having built and wound his perfect machine, sat back and watched it tick. The scientist and the political philosopher need only study nature to see God's great plan.

This nonreligious faith in man's potential which was a result of the period of the Enlightenment, was called Deism. It was in startling contrast to the beliefs fostered during the same period by the Great Awakening. For the revivalists of the Awakening, God was a personal deity intensely involved in the fate of every one of his creatures. God could either sweep a sinner off to heaven or hurl him screaming into hell. While the deists pictured God as a retired clockmaker, utterly indifferent once his work was done, the revivalists saw him as a stern father, passionately concerned over the deeds of his wayward children.

Whereas the Awakening exerted its greatest appeal upon uneducated farmers, Enlightenment ideas at first held sway primarily over the social and intellectual elite of the cities. By the time of the Revolution, however, many Enlightenment ideas had filtered down to the great masses of the people. Even for those who had never heard of Newton or Locke, the idea that man was perfectible (an idea also preached by Baptists, Methodists, and Quakers), that government could be fashioned into a system that rationally fitted men's needs and respected their freedoms, that the pursuit of scientific investigation could lead to a better life for everyone—all of these Enlightenment attitudes were growing familiar to the public at large. In frontier settlements, Americans had learned the necessity for experimentation, for practicality, for cooperation. This knowledge was only a step away from the Enlightenment's emphasis upon scientific inquiry and a rational government responsible to the people. Ultimately, when the English began to enact laws that seemed tyrannical and unjust, Americans felt justified in rebelling. They were not breaking the law, but rather conforming to the natural law of the universe as taught by Locke.

EDUCATION

Although many colonists had been concerned about schools since the early seventeenth century, the Enlightenment brought a new emphasis upon education. In this regard the South differed from the North. Virginia made the first attempt to establish a college, but these early plans were stopped by the Indian massacre of 1622. In 1693 the first Southern college, William and Mary, was founded at Williamsburg, Virginia. On the elementary level, the South lagged behind the other colonies. Grammar schools did not exist and well-to-do planters had to hire private tutors for their children. Sometimes a few neighboring families would band together and hire one tutor to instruct all their youngsters (Thomas Jefferson learned Latin and Greek at such an improvised elementary school). Women and blacks of both sexes seldom received any education at all, and most backwoods farmers could neither read nor write. At the end of the seventeenth century, only 55 percent of the white men in Virginia could sign their own names, whereas 90 percent of New England men could demonstrate at least that simple proof of literacy. South Carolina tried several times to start a public school system, but without success. The South's lack of adequate schooling seemed advantageous to at least one man: Governor Berkeley of Virginia thanked God in 1671 that "there are no free schools nor printing in Virginia . . . for learning has brought disobedience, and heresy, and sects into the world, and printing has divulged them, and libels against the best government. God keep us from both!"

In the Middle colonies, the level of education reached a slightly higher level. Here too, public school systems did not exist, although in New York City fourteen private schools were thriving by 1762. Moreover, in Pennsylvania the Quakers had established church schools of their own, as had the Scotch-Irish. The eighteenth century brought several important colleges to the Middle colonies: the College of New Jersey (Princeton, 1746), (Rutgers, 1766), (University of Pennsylvania, 1755), and King's College (Columbia, 1754).

Education received its greatest encouragement in New England. Puritan theology required each man to be sufficiently schooled to read and interpret the Bible and make independent religious judgments. In 1636, only 6 years after the Puritans arrived in Massachusetts, they founded a college. The school started out with only one house, one professor, an acre of land, and revenues from the local ferry service. When a Bostonian named John Harvard died in 1638 and left four hundred books and half his money to the college, the Board of Overseers decided to name the institution after him. Originally Harvard was built to train new ministers, but the college did not specialize in religious instruction. In 1738, John Winthrop (great-grandson of Governor Winthrop) began to teach science and mathematics there. John Locke's *Essay on Human Understanding* was part of Harvard's curriculum as early as 1742. The other New England colonies followed Massachusetts' example, if somewhat slowly: Yale was founded in Connecticut in 1701 and Brown in Rhode Island in 1764.

Elementary education also played a prominent part in New England life. In 1647 the Massachusetts assembly ordered all towns of fifty families or more to hire an instructor to teach children to read. The instructor was to be paid out of public funds. Some of these schools were free, some demanded a small tuition and in all of them, the children of the poor could attend without paying anything. School attendance was not compulsory, but learning to read was. Parents were not required to send their children to school, but if they did not, they had to teach their youngsters at home. None of the grammar schools was run by the Puritan church. They were all created by the government, not by religious groups or private donors.

In writing about early America, historians are often tempted to picture the colonial period as one of unbroken progress, with a succession of more and more humane laws, increasingly active commerce, and greater wisdom. In the field of education, at least, the facts belie this interpretation. Although there were *more* schools throughout the colonies in the eighteenth century than in the seventeenth, they had definitely declined, becoming less effective, and the national rate of illiteracy was rising. Third and fourth generation Americans may have been better adapted than their forefathers to life in the wilderness, but fewer could read, and those in school were receiving inferior instruction.

Although pre-Revolutionary schools were generally not very good, at least they were freer than most institutions of learning in Europe. Almost every American college was theoretically tied to a particular religious denomination, but none was controlled by any given sect. Men of various denominations sat on the board of directors in each college and students of different faiths were admitted to every school.

Despite their independent positions, most universities were closely traditional in their curricula. As in European schools, students learned Latin, Greek, Hebrew, rhetoric, and moral philosophy. Few courses prepared graduates for actual professional careers other than the ministry (and only 25 percent of the college graduates followed this career). For example, no American college taught law or medicine. If a young man wanted to become a lawyer, he had to apprentice himself to an older professional and read law books on his own. Of the 3,500 doctors in America on the eve of the Revolution, only 200 held medical degrees and these they had earned abroad.

SCIENTIFIC ADVANCES

The colleges did, however, teach science and mathematics, but most of America's outstanding scientists were in no way connected with universities and many had not even attended school. Botany and zoology were two fields in which American amateurs excelled. John Bartram collected and catalogued plants from Florida to the Great Lakes. Dr. John Mitchell of Virginia discovered twenty-two new classes of plants. Perhaps the leading naturalist at this time was Dr. Alexander Garden of South Carolina, for whom the gardenia is named. Garden was famous throughout Europe for his genius at classifying plants.

An outstanding contribution to medicine was made by the Puritan minister, Cotton Mather. When Mather read in an English journal that the people of Turkey inoculated themselves against smallpox (the most deadly disease in colonial times), he remembered that his slave, Onesimus, once told him that he had been given in Africa "something of the smallpox" that "would forever preserve him from it." This gave Mather the idea of injecting live smallpox germs into Bostonians as a prevention against the disease. A storm of controversy broke out after he introduced the strange new practice, but a lowered casualty rate in the next epidemic proved the value of inoculation. Mather thus made one of America's greatest contributions to medical knowledge prior to the nineteenth century.

America's greatest scientific genius during the colonial period, however, was Benjamin Franklin, a true child of the Enlightenment. Wary of religious "superstitions," convinced that the universe was governed by discoverable laws, intensely curious about every aspect of his environment, Franklin was passionately devoted to science. He was responsible for many practical inventions: the Franklin stove, bifocal spectacles, the lightning rod, and the grocery store's long arm (a pole with a moveable clamp for fetching cans—or books—from high shelves). His experiment with a kite and key during a storm gave the first definite proof that electricity was not simply a force released through man's intervention, but was something that coursed freely through nature. After Franklin's discovery, any physicist attempting to give an explanation of natural phenomena had to take into account the role of electricity.

Benjamin Franklin was responsible for such inventions as the bifocal eyeglass lens, the grocery store portable arm, and the Franklin stove. He is shown here performing his famous lightning experiment with a key and a kite.

DEVELOPMENT OF THE ARTS

LIBRARIES, LITERATURE, AND NEWSPAPERS

Some of the best writers in the colonial period were ministers, such as the New England leader of the Great Awakening, Jonathan Edwards, and religious literature composed the bulk of colonial reading matter. John Wise of Massachusetts wrote a rousing defense of Puritanism in his book, *The Churches Quarrel Espoused* (1710). As one critic has remarked, "No other American author of the colonial time is the equal of John Wise in the union of great breadth of power and thought with great splendor of style." The energetic Cotton Mather, in addition to his treatise on witchcraft, authored a church history of New England.

The leading historian of New England, however, was Thomas Hutchinson, whose *History of the Colony of Massachusetts Bay* is generally considered straightforward and scrupulously fair.

Benjamin Franklin was probably the most prolific colonial writer; his *Poor Richard's Almanac,* a collection of pithy sayings, is still admired today, as is his autobiography. But even Franklin could not make a living as a writer. In fact, no American was able to support himself on his literary earnings during this period.

Public libraries were founded in many towns during the pre-Revolutionary era. As might be expected, most volumes dealt with religious subjects, but every collection also contained works on science and history, as

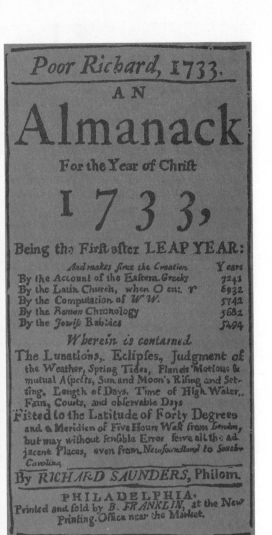

A facsimile of the title page of Poor Richard's Almanak, *"printed and fold by B. Franklin" in 1733.*

well as a few books on medicine and farming. Some private individuals amassed impressive personal libraries at a time when books were scarce and costly possessions. Cotton Mather owned 3,000 books and William Byrd II of Virginia had 4,000. Most educated people, however, seldom owned more than 100 volumes.

In 1704, America's first successful newspaper, the *Boston News Letter,* was published. By 1763, twenty-three newspapers were being printed in the colonies. Most

"Poor Richard" was a remarkable person with a witty, common sense philosophy of life. These three illustrations taken from the Almanak *are examples of Poor Richard's sayings.*

115

articles dealt with news from England rather than with local affairs. The colonists already had a general idea of what was happening at home, but they were starved for information about the mother country, particularly financial or governmental news that might directly affect their own affairs. In 1729, Franklin took over the *Pennsylvania Gazette* and made some lively innovations such as poems, literary essays, and cartoons which were afterward copied by other colonial newspapers.

Freedom of the press also received a boost in the famous Peter Zenger case in New York City in 1733. Zenger was tried for publishing articles in his paper, *The New York Weekly Journal,* which the governor of the colony claimed were libelous. The publisher was acquitted on the grounds that although the articles were highly critical of the governor, and did indeed lessen his official prestige, they were, in fact, true. This case set an important precedent for publication of controversial articles and paved the way for the freedom of the press granted by the First Amendment to the United States Constitution.

THE VISUAL ARTS

American painters, furniture makers, and architects were quite dependent on English models and styles. One of the most famous painters of the period, John Singleton Copley, did something new that was characteristically American: he showed his subjects working. When Copley painted a portrait of the silversmith Paul Revere, he placed Revere at his workbench wearing work clothes. In England a painter would have posed him in his Sunday best and tried to give the impression that he was really a country squire. But Revere, and Copley, expressed an American pride in manual labor.

In Philadelphia craftsmen turned out beautiful objects fashioned from brass, copper, and wood. Joseph Richardson pro-

duced some of the most expertly crafted silver pieces in the world. Furniture makers made delicate but sturdy Windsor chairs and cabinets in the "Philadelphia Chippendale" style. This type of furniture was borrowed directly from England, like the prevailing architectural design in the colonies, the Georgian style.

CONFLICTS AMONG THE COLONIES

We have seen that the colonies were spread out along the Atlantic seaboard; that most farmers were isolated from one another, except in New England; and that it was tedious and slow to travel overland. Distance, isolation, and poor transportation made each colony a distinct entity. Colonists had little feeling of belonging to a single land. In fact, the term "American" was seldom used. Men like Jefferson would refer to "my country, Virginia," and New Yorkers and Pennsylvanians generally felt a closer allegiance to England than they did to the other colonies. Southerners would speculate on the New England character as though they were studying foreigners.

For example, Jefferson drew up a list of differences between the people of the North and the South. He found the Northerners "cool, sober, laborious, interested" and "superstitious and hypocritical in their reli-

John Singleton Copley painted this portrait of Paul Revere around 1770. Revere, a famous colonial silversmith, is shown in work clothes at his work bench. This innovative style of portrait painting was indicative of the pride felt for manual labor in the Colonies.

gion." Southerners, by contrast, were "fiery, voluptuary, indolent, generous" and "without attachment or pretensions to any religion but that of the heart." In general, aristocrats of the Chesapeake country disliked the plain manners and democratic ways of New England, while John Adams of Massachusetts prided himself and his "countrymen" on their "purer English blood, less mixed with Scotch, Irish, Dutch, French, Danish, Swedish, etc. than any other."

There was little cooperation among the colonies. Maryland tried to undersell Virginia in the tobacco trade. When Indians, stirred up by the French, attacked New England in 1703, the Puritans begged the other colonies for help, and New York, New Jersey, Virginia, and Pennsylvania all refused. Only in 1708, when New Yorkers saw

that they might gain control of the western fur trade if New France and her Indian allies were crushed, did the state offer any aid to the beleaguered New Englanders. Quarrels over borders often broke out between neighboring colonies. The settlers of the Carolinas and Georgia had several bitter disputes over which colony had the right to trade with the Cherokees and Chicksaws.

EASTERN AND WESTERN CONFLICTS

The sharpest disagreements, however, were felt not between the various colonies but between the eastern and western regions within each colony. Although the "frontier" in colonial times was seldom more than a hundred miles inland, the distance was sufficient to generate hostility. People living in the back country faced different problems and had different needs from those living in the more settled counties. Westerners wanted the government to spend money on new roads and strong fortifications against the Indians. Usually the pioneers were poorer than the town dwellers and resented the high rates of interest set by coastal banks.

In many colonies, these conflicts were intensified by the fact that the westerners were of different national origin from the older, established English settlers in the East. The great immigration of the first half of the eighteenth century brought to Pennsylvania thousands of Germans and Scotch-Irish, who pushed into the back country of Virginia in the 1730s, the Carolinas in the next two decades, and Georgia in the 1760s. Unlike the Anglican, wealthier part of the population dwelling in Charleston or Jamestown, these newcomers were Presbyterian or German Pietist, and poor. Often the judges, sheriffs, and other county officials appointed to administer the new counties frankly despised the Germans and Scotch-Irish and zealously served the interests of the governor and his eastern clique of well-to-do merchants and plantation owners.

A political injustice that angered westerners was the control exercised by the seaboard counties over each colony's assembly and the denial of full representation to the back country. In 1760, for example, Pennsylvania's western Lancaster County had twice as many people as the eastern Bucks County, but Bucks County had twice as many representatives. In Virginia and the Carolinas, discrimination against the frontier was even more high-handed and unfair. At the time of the Revolution, the older counties still elected two-thirds of the members of the assembly.

INDIAN WARFARE

The greatest source of contention between the western and eastern regions was the question of how to handle the Indians. From about 1660 to 1760, the most powerful Indian tribes, from the Iroquois in the North to the Cherokees in the South, controlled the Appalachian mountain range and kept colonists from penetrating farther west. On the other side of the mountains lay New France, and the Indians cleverly played the French colonists off against the English. As a consequence, the Indians, particularly the Iroquois Confederation, maintained the balance of power for a century. They were determined to grow rich in trade with the white man, but not to permit further enchoachments into their territories.

The Indians, however, did not represent a solid front against the Europeans. A tribe might make an alliance with the English against another tribe, or join forces with the French in attacking New England. The colonists in western counties clashed with the Indians almost daily. Squatters were stealing Indian lands and driving the game away that was necessary for their survival.

Authorities in England and America did nothing to stop the conflicts. They felt that bloodshed was the price that had to be paid to destroy French control in the North and Spanish dominance in the deep South.

The seaboard counties were often slow in giving concrete support to the embattled westerners. In the last chapter we saw that Nathaniel Bacon raised an illegal army in the western part of Virginia to battle the Indians in defiance of the orders of Governor Berkeley. Bacon's Rebellion finally ended in an attack on Jamestown itself, as the disgruntled frontier farmers showered their rage on an administration they felt had always exploited them and never helped them in their wars with the Indians.

In the eighteenth century a similar uprising took place in Pennsylvania. A band of Scotch-Irish, who called themselves the "Paxton Boys" (they were from the Paxton and Donegal townships of Lancaster County), killed twenty peaceful Conestoga Indians in 1763 as revenge for the raids that another tribe had staged on the settlers' frontier homes. Excited by their success, the Paxton Boys marched toward Philadelphia, determined to force the capital to send troops against the Indians. The Quakers of Philadelphia were pacifists and had maintained peaceful relations with the Indians for decades. Scotch-Irish fierceness seemed to them a problem as great as, or greater than, any ever posed by the red man. Gathering their courage, the Philadelphians delegated Benjamin Franklin and four other men to reason with the Paxton Boys. Ten miles outside the city, Franklin and the other delegates made peace with the mob. Franklin was forced to promise the frontiersmen a bounty for Indian scalps, but in private he referred to the Paxton Boys as "Christian white savages."

In the decades immediately before the American Revolution, an observer might have predicted that a war between westerners and easterners was more likely than a united colonial fight against England. Tempers flared in frontier counties and rhetoric became heated. One frontiersman denounced the eastern ruling class as "cursed hungry Caterpillars, that will eat out the very Bowels of our Commonwealth, if they are not pulled down from their Nests in a very short time." In North Carolina a group of small farmers in the west decided to pull down the "caterpillars" in order to end political corruption. In 1771, some two thousand frontiersmen banded together into an army and engaged in a battle with the governor's militia. The Regulators, as the frontiersmen called themselves, were defeated, but their resentment against the seaboard counties continued. It required a strong common cause such as the Revolution to bring about a partial relaxation of the mounting tensions between the eastern seaboard and the western settlements in colonial America.

A cartoon of the Paxton Boys' march on Philadelphia where they demanded troops to fight the Indians on the frontier. Due to the explosive nature of the situation, the Philadelphians delegated Benjamin Franklin to meet with the Paxton Boys to avert any hostile confrontation with them.

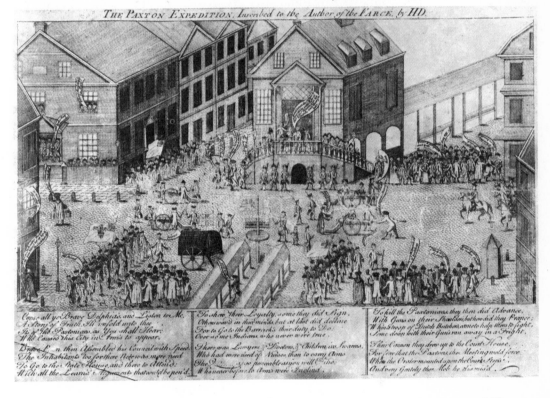

Readings

GENERAL WORKS

Boorstin, D. J., *The Americans: The Colonial Experience.* New York: Random House, 1958—An excellent book on the formation of the American character as expressed in politics, law, society, and religion.

Bridenbaugh, Carl, *Myths and Realities: Societies of the Colonial South.* New Orleans: Louisiana State University Press, 1952 (Paper: Atheneum, 1963)—A discerning account of the social and cultural history of the South in the eighteenth century.

Cunliffe, Marcus, *The Literature of the United States.* Baltimore: Penguin, 1954—A brief overview of literary movements in America, with historical background and some criticisms by the author.

Gipson, L. H., *The British Empire Before the American Revolution,* Vols. 1–11. New York: Knopf, 1936–1965—A monumental and scholarly work which stresses the development of the American colonies as an integral part of the British empire. The emphasis is on the political and constitutional relationship of the colonies to the mother country.

Jones, H. M., *O Strange New World: American Culture—The Formative Years.* New York: Viking, 1964—The first of two volumes presenting a study of the interplay between the cultures of the Old and New Worlds.

Mead, S. E., *The Lively Experiment: The Shaping of Christianity in America.* New York: Harper & Row, 1963—A history of the role of the church in America.

Morison, S. E., ed., *The Parkman Reader.* Boston: Little, Brown, 1955—Selections from the many works of the great nineteenth-century historian, Francis Parkman. The emphasis is on the development of New France and the ultimate clash between France and Britain for control of the North American continent.

Parrington, V. L., *The Colonial Mind. Main Currents in American Thought,* Vol. 1. New York: Harcourt Brace Jovanovich, 1927—A major work that traces the development of American opinion from 1620 to 1800. Parrington's viewpoint is that Jeffersonian idealism is the standard against which all American thought in the colonial period should be measured.

Rossiter, Clinton, *Seedtime of the Republic: The Origin of the American Tradition of Political Liberty.* New York: Harcourt Brace Jovanovich, 1953—An excellent compact analysis of colonial life in the eighteenth century. Rossiter sees the economic, social, religious and political life of the colonies as preparing them for the break with England in the 1770s.

Ver Steeg, C. L., *The Formative Years: 1607–1763*. New York: Hill & Wang, 1964—A compact general history of the American colonies from the European background to the beginning of the revolutionary struggle.

Wright, L. B., *The Cultural Life of the American Colonies: 1607–1763*. New York: Harper & Row, 1957—A comprehensive survey of colonial culture, popularly written yet scholarly in its approach.

SPECIAL STUDIES

Bailyn, Bernard, *Education in the Forming of American Society: Needs and Opportunities for Study*. Chapel Hill, N.C.: University of North Carolina Press, 1960 (Paper: Random House, 1962)—These two scholarly essays present a thorough picture of eighteenth-century education in the colonies.

Bridenbaugh, Carl, *Cities in the Wilderness: The First Century of Urban Life in America, 1625–1742*, New York: Putnam's, 1964 —This detailed but readable study traces the emergence of five urban centers in colonial America in the seventeenth and early eighteenth centuries.

Bridenbaugh, Carl, *The Colonial Craftsman*. Chicago: University of Chicago Press, 1950 —A study of the eighteenth-century artisan and his place in pre-Revolutionary society.

Bridenbaugh, Carl, and Jessica Bridenbaugh, *Rebels and Gentlemen: Philadelphia in the Age of Franklin*. New York: Oxford University Press, 1965—A portrayal of life and culture in Philadelphia between 1740 and 1776.

Brown, R. E., *Middle Class Democracy and the Revolution in Massachusetts, 1691–1780*. Ithaca, New York: Cornell University Press, 1955 (Paper: Harper & Row, 1969)—This study presents the thesis that the revolution was fought to preserve prevalent democratic institutions, not to establish them.

Hansen, M. L., *Atlantic Migration, 1607–1860: A History of the Continuing Settlement of America*, A. M. Schlesinger, ed. Cambridge, Mass.: Harvard University Press, 1940 (Paper: Harper & Row, 1964) —A general account of the great waves of immigration from Europe to America over a 250-year period.

Hindle, Brook, *The Pursuit of Science in*

Revolutionary America, 1735–1789. Chapel Hill, N.C.: University of North Carolina Press, 1956—A scholarly account of scientific interest and achievement in eighteenth-century America.

Jordan, Winthrop D., *White Over Black.* Chapel Hill, N.C.: University of North Carolina Press, 1968 (Paper: Penguin, 1969)—A brilliant study of the development of slavery in colonial America. Jordan shows that the belief in the racial inferiority of Africans preceded the institutionalization of slave labor in America.

Smith, A. E., *Colonists in Bondage: White Servitude and Convict Labor in America, 1607–1776.* Chapel Hill, N.C.: University of North Carolina Press, 1947—A statistical study of bond servants in the British colonies in America.

Starkey, M. L., *The Devil in Massachusetts: A Modern Inquiry into the Salem Witch Trials.* New York: Knopf, 1949 (Paper: Doubleday, 1969)—A dramatic record of the witchcraft hysteria in 1692, with its psychological interpretations.

Sydnor, C. S., *Gentlemen Freeholders: Political Practices in Washington's Virginia.* Chapel Hill, N.C.: University of North Carolina Press, 1952—An engrossing picture of the way in which politics was actually practiced in eighteenth-century Virginia and how the Virginia aristocracy preserved its control of political life in the colony.

Wertenbaker, Thomas J., *The Old South.* New York: Scribner's, 1942—A social history of the South during the colonial period, emphasizing the diversity within the region and the ways in which Southern culture expressed itself in art and architecture.

PRIMARY SOURCES

Bruchey, Stuart, ed., *The Colonial Merchant.* New York: Harcourt Brace Jovanovich, 1965—This book of sources and readings points out the interrelationships between economic interests and national values, pursuits and institutions.

Colden, Cadwallader, *History of the Five Indian Nations.* Ithaca, N.Y.: Cornell University Press, 1958—A colonial teacher and intellectual, Colden wrote the *History of the Five Indian Nations* in 1727, and published a second volume in 1747. Although he felt the Five Nations were vicious enemies, he blamed white men for teaching them their vices instead of their virtues.

Franklin, Benjamin, *Autobiography.* New York: Simon & Schuster, 1970—The classic American success story. Franklin tells how to get ahead in eighteenth-century America, lessons which many still try to follow. The work also illustrates the cosmopolitan nature of life in Philadelphia.

Hall, M. G., L. H. Leder, and M. G. Kammen, eds., *The Glorious Revolution in America: Documents on the Colonial Crisis of 1689.* Chapel Hill, N.C.: University of North Carolina Press, 1964—Selected primary sources related to the colonial situation at the time of the overthrow of James II in England.

Riley, E. M., ed., *The Journal of John*

Harrower: An Indentured Servant in the Colony of Virginia, 1773–1776. Holt, Rinehart & Winston, 1964—An interesting eyewitness account of colonial Virginia.

Sewall, Samuel, *Diary of Samuel Sewall.* New York: Putnam's, 1967—This diary of a Massachusetts merchant and political leader covers over half a century of colonial life (1674–1729). It shows a man with a combination of moral principles and a great desire for business success, qualities which characterized many Puritans of the period.

BIOGRAPHIES

Crane, V. W., *Benjamin Franklin and a Rising People.* Boston: Little, Brown, 1954—A well-written, short study of Franklin's contributions to America and to humanity.

Ketcham, Ralph, *Benjamin Franklin.* New York: Simon & Schuster, 1965—A brief biography which relates Franklin's thought to twentieth-century trends. The author suggests that Franklin might disapprove of current styles of writing and thinking.

McLoughlin, William G., ed., *Isaac Backus and the American Patriotic Tradition.* Boston: Little, Brown, 1967—Backus was the leading Baptist preacher in eighteenth-century America. McLoughlin emphasizes his contribution to the development of ideas of religious toleration and liberty.

Miller, Perry, *Roger Williams: His Contribution to the American Tradition.* New York: Atheneum, 1962—A brief biography of the founder of Rhode Island which challenges the idea that Williams was a democrat and believer in civil liberties. All of Williams' social opinions, Miller claims, were secondary to his religious interests.

Van Doren, C. C., *Benjamin Franklin.* New York: Viking, 1964—This excellent and detailed biography is descriptive rather than interpretive, narrative rather than analytical.

Winslow, O. E., *Jonathan Edwards, 1703–1758: A Biography.* New York: Macmillan, 1940—A complete and scholarly account of the eminent theologian and educator.

HISTORICAL NOVELS

Cooper, James F., *The Deerslayer.* New York: Macmillan, 1962—All of the following books by Cooper are adventure stories depicting life in the eighteenth-century New York frontiers:

The Last of the Mohicans. New York: Airmont, 1964.

The Pathfinder. New York: Airmont, 1964.

The Pioneers. New York: Airmont, 1964.

Johnston, Mary, *Audrey.* Boston: Houghton Mifflin, 1902—A popular historical novel of eighteenth-century Virginia. Johnston had a keen awareness of class distinctions and wrote sympathetically of the colonial elite.

Simms, William Gilmore, *The Yemassee.* Boston: Houghton Mifflin, 1961—This novel by an influential South Carolina author is a tale of adventure dealing with Indian warfare on the Carolina coastline.

An engraving by Paul Revere of the Boston "Massacre." A band of British soldiers fired on a mob that was pelting them with snowballs and clam shells, killing five men and wounding six.

Prelude to Independence

4

In the early ages of the world, according to the scripture chronology there were no kings; the consequence of which was, there were no wars; it is the pride of kings which throws mankind into confusion. . . . If we inquire into the business of a king, we shall find that in some countries they may have none; and after sauntering away their lives without pleasure to themselves or advantage to the nation, withdraw from the scene, and leave their successors to tread the same idle round. . . . In England a king hath little more to do than to make war and give away places; which, in plain terms, is to empoverish the nation and set it together by the ears. A pretty business indeed for a man to be allowed eight hundred thousand sterling a year for, and worshipped into the bargain! Of more worth is one honest man to society, and in the sight of God, than all the crowned ruffians that ever lived.

—Thomas Paine, Common Sense

Between 1690 and 1776 a series of events prepared the way for an outbreak of armed conflict between England and her colonies in North America. Few people on either side of the Atlantic during this decisive period would have predicted that a permanent break would ever occur between Britain and its American possessions.

EIGHTEENTH-CENTURY COLONIAL POLITICS

THE GOVERNOR

By the middle of the eighteenth century all of the original thirteen colonies had been founded. There were three different kinds of colonies: proprietary, charter, and royal. Maryland and Pennsylvania were both proprietary colonies, and the owner, or proprietor, of each colony appointed its governor. (Pennsylvania's governor also served as governor of Delaware, although that colony had its own legislature.) Connecticut and Rhode Island were charter colonies. They had received from the king a charter granting them virtual independence in internal affairs. In both colonies the freemen had the right to elect the governor and members of the council and assembly.

The eight other colonies were royal. They were more closely tied to the crown and the king had the right to appoint chief executive officers.

In the royal colonies, the governor was the direct representative of the crown. The governor enjoyed many of a king's prerogatives, but he also was forced to accept many of the restrictions that were placed upon the monarchy in England during the seventeenth century. In America, provincial legislatures attempted to gain the upper hand over their governors in the same way that Parliament had limited the crown's power in Britain.

Every governor brought with him to the New World two documents from the king: his commission and his instructions. The commission authorized in a public document the form of government in the colony: a governor, a crown-appointed council, and an elected assembly. The instructions were a secret list of objectives for the governor to implement in regulating trade, promoting religion. and sponsoring laws. Its very secrecy placed the governor in a difficult position, requiring him to follow royal instructions but preventing him from disclosing them to the people he ruled. The obligation to play a double role affected every aspect of the governor's position, for he owed his first loyalty to the king and Parliament back in England. He was deeply involved in colonial politics, and appointed judges, justices of the peace, and many other minor officials. (Gradually the British government withdrew some of the governor's powers of appointment as well as his ability to grant large tracts of land.) The governor was also commander-in-chief of the colonists' armed forces. Throughout the eighteenth century, however, his military powers were limited by legislation passed by assemblies. After 1750, he was also limited by the fact that there were more royal troops led by British commanders based in the colonies than colonial troops with their own commanders.

THE GOVERNOR'S COUNCIL

Usually twelve men in each royal colony were appointed to act as the governor's council. Theoretically, the king's Board of Trade in England chose the councilmen, but in practice the Board simply confirmed the recommendations made by the governor himself. Massachusetts, where the council was elected by the assembly, was an exception. The council had three basic functions. First, it acted as the chief advisory body to the governor. The governor could not summon the assembly, appoint judges, or issue paper money without the consent of his council. Second, the council acted within the legislature, where its powers were even greater. The governor's council was the upper house of the legislature, resembling the House of Lords in Parliament or the Senate in the United States Congress. Like the House of Lords, the council had the final say on the wording of all financial legislation and had an equal vote in the passing of all other laws. Finally, the council acted as the highest court in each colony, fulfilling the same function as the Supreme Court in the United States today. Thus, it was a body that exercised executive, legislative, and judicial functions.

THE ASSEMBLY

By the first half of the eighteenth century, the power of the governor's council was on the wane. Authorities in England started to bypass the council and deal directly with the governor alone. Laws became so complex that the councilmen no longer had the time or training to serve effectively as a supreme court. Moreover, within the legislature, the lower house slowly but steadily was wresting power from the council.

The lower house, called the assembly, was elected directly by the freemen of each colony. A freeman was a white male who owned a certain amount of wealth or land and was at least twenty-one. Property qualifications for voting varied from colony to colony. The colony of South Carolina had the least representative government, for government was by the tidewater counties and there was no local government or representation in the populous interior. North Carolina, Virginia, and Maryland established local governments in their interior regions, but small coastal counties had more representatives than the larger and more populous ones. The same situation prevailed in Pennsylvania and New York, so that many artisans in Philadelphia and New York City were denied a voice in government. Only New England had equal representation from all towns and widespread white male suffrage. The percentage of adult males eligible to vote was much larger in America than in England, mainly because land—and hence the right to vote—was much easier to acquire.

Some colonies required one kind of property qualification for voting but another kind for the right to hold office. In South Carolina, for example, an assemblyman had to own at least ten slaves and 500 acres of land or possess an equivalent amount of cash. The theory behind such property qualifications was that only a man of means had the financial independence to resist bribes and enough of a stake in the community to vote responsibly. This theory was seldom questioned during colonial times. Within each colony poor frontiersmen might resent the East Coast aristocracy of wealthy merchants or planters, but time and again the richest and most influential men of every colony were returned to the assembly. Why did most colonials keep voting for the same small group? One reason is that many people were unqualified to hold office. One-quarter of the colonists could not read and one-fifth of those who could read did not speak English. Another reason is that their European background with its strong class structure made most settlers look to the well-to-do as leaders. For centuries in Europe, wealth had always been a prerequisite for power. Finally, in many colonies voting was not a secret process. In Virginia, for example, the candidates were present at the polling places and voters indicated their choices by calling out the candidate's name. Throughout the colonies a man announced his vote before his fellow citizens at a county courthouse, or, in New England, at a town meeting. The less affluent found it greatly to their interest to vote for a rich neighbor upon whom they depended for a host of small favors.

THE QUESTION OF AUTHORITY

How much power did the colonial assemblies have? Were they legally entitled to the power they did command? In a royal colony, who was more important, the governor or the assembly? During the colonial period the answers to these questions were uncertain and a source of ceaseless friction.

Provincial legislatures patterned themselves after the House of Commons in Parliament. They copied Commons' procedures and viewed Commons as a model and a justification of popular rule. The House of Commons, however, did not return the compliment. In fact, the members of Parliament resented having their power challenged by these colonial upstarts. The colonial assemblies believed that their power to rule came from the people they represented. Parliament, however, saw the provincial assemblies as nothing more than bodies whose provisional power came from Parliament it-

One View of Royal Authority

❝ *You ask me, if we have not reason to fear we shall soon be reduced to a worse situation than that of the colonies of France, Spain, or Holland. I may safely affirm that we have not; that we have no reason to fear any evils from a submission to the authority of parliament, equal to what we must feel from its authority being disputed, from an uncertain rule of law and government. For more than seventy years together, the supremacy of parliament was acknowledged, without complaints of grievance. The effect of every measure cannot be foreseen by human wisdom. What can be expected more, from any authority than when the unfitness of a measure is discovered, to make it void? When, upon the united representations and complaints of the American colonies, any acts have appeared to parliament to be unsalutary, have there not been repeated instances of the repeal of such acts? We cannot expect these instances should be carried so far as to be equivalent to a disavowal, or relinquishment of the right itself. Why then, shall we fear for ourselves, and our posterity, greater rigor of government for seventy years to come, than what we and our predecessors have felt, in the seventy years past.*

—Alden T. Vanghan, ed.,
Chronicles of the American Revolution

self. According to Parliament, they had no right to exist, but were permitted to meet at the whim of the mother country. The two conflicting views were summed up by Governor Francis Bernard of Massachusetts: "In Britain the American governments are considered as corporations empowered to make by-laws, existing only during the pleasure of Parliament. In America they claim to be perfect states, not otherwise

A Different View of Royal Authority

Here then, let my countrymen, ROUSE yourselves, and behold the ruin hanging over their heads. If they ONCE admit, that Great-Britain may lay duties upon her exportations to us, for the purpose of levying money on us only, she then will have nothing to do, but to lay those duties on the articles which she prohibits us to manufacture—and the tragedy of American liberty is finished. We have been prohibited from procuring manufactures, in all cases, any where but from Great-Britain, (excepting linens, which we are permitted to import directly from Ireland). We have been prohibited, in some cases, from manufacturing for ourselves; We are therefore exactly in the situation of a city besieged, which is surrounded by the works of the besiegers in every part but one. If that is closed up, no step can be taken, but to surrender at discretion. If Great-Britain can order us to come to her for necessaries we want, and can order us to pay what taxes she pleases before we take them away, or when we have them here, we are as abject slaves . . . 🙶

—*John Dickinson*, Letters from a Farmer in Pennsylvania

dependent upon Great Britain than by having the same King."

In their efforts to resemble the House of Commons, the colonial assemblies had won by 1720 two important rights: the right to propose legislation and the sole right to initiate money bills. This second right put the purse strings in the hands of assemblymen. Unless the assembly designated funds for a governor's salary, he would not be paid. Unless the assembly voted the funds for a military expedition or a road-building program, wars could not be fought and roads could not be constructed.

As a result, in every colony the assembly had two potential adversaries: the governor and the authorities in England. The governor's strongest weapon was his power of veto. Since his salary depended upon the assembly, however, a governor usually employed veto with discretion. The assemblies' conflicts with England were much more confusing, since no one really knew exactly which governmental agency in England was directly responsible for managing colonial affairs. The king had certain claims over the colonies. After all, most of them were *royal* colonies. In 1714, however, a German monarch, George I of Hanover, came to the throne. He and his successor, George II, left the handling of colonial affairs in the hands of their ministers, although all decisions required the consent of the crown. The Board of Trade had the strongest control over colonial administration. By 1730 all colonies except Rhode Island and Connecticut (the charter colonies) had to submit their laws to the Board of Trade for review. If the Board rejected (or "disallowed") a statute, it was revoked. Yet the Board acted slowly and years sometimes went by before the Board reviewed a law. Parliament too, insisted upon its right to control colonial affairs through its advisers to the crown known as the Cabinet, but frequently this right was disputed by the king.

In short, the lines of authority and communication between England and the colonies were often obscure and complex. If a colony wanted to object to an imperial measure, to whom did it object? Was the king in charge, the Board of Trade, the House of Commons, or some particular cabinet member? Colonial politicians could not answer these questions with any certainty.

THE WARS FOR EMPIRE

North America was frequently an arena for the conflicts of four European imperial powers: England, France, Spain, and The Netherlands. France and Spain fought over Florida in the sixteenth century. Spain, while weakened by the defeat of its great Armada in 1588, succeeded in keeping the peninsula as its stronghold. In 1670, however, Spain was compelled to recognize the legitimacy of British control of the Atlantic seaboard of North America. In the seventeenth century, England expelled the Dutch from New Amsterdam, although Dutch ships continued to compete with English merchants for colonial trade until the 1680s. Thus, by the end of the century Spain and The Netherlands were effectively eliminated from the contest for North America.

By the late seventeenth century, the European struggle for world supremacy had narrowed down to England and France. Both countries fought to gain the upper hand in Europe. Neither wanted this conflict to extend to their colonial possessions but their wars repeatedly spilled over into the New World. In North America the French held Canada and the Ohio and Mississippi valleys, and the English occupied the Atlantic seaboard. French and English colonials wrangled over fishing rights in the Northeast, each wanting sole control over the harbors and waters of Maine, Newfoundland, and Nova Scotia. An even bigger cause of contention was the fur trade. Since many fur trappers were Indians—and many hunting grounds were Indian territories—disputes over the fur trade led to alliances between France and the Algonquins and Huron Indians in Canada, and between England and the Iroquois tribes in New York.

THREE FRENCH AND ENGLISH WARS

The first conflict between France and England to spread to the New World was waged between 1689 and 1697, and in it each side enlisted the aid of its Indian allies. Europeans called this the War of the League of Augsburg. The American colonists called it King William's War. In Europe, Britain in alliance with Holland was trying to curb Louis XIV's hunger for power, glory, and more land. The major campaigns took place in Europe and the skirmishes in America consisted mostly of indecisive frontier pillaging along the New York-New England borders. The French managed to seize a few villages in New England as well as Schenectady in New York and New Englanders briefly held Port Royal in Nova Scotia. This indecisive situation did not last long and the peace settlement that ended the war restored all captured territories to their original owners.

The second war broke out 5 years later, in 1702. In Europe it was called the War of the Spanish Succession because England, The Netherlands, and Austria sought to prevent the King of France from "succeeding" to the throne of Spain. In America the colonists called it Queen Anne's War, after their reigning English monarch. The Abenaki Indians, goaded on by their French allies, attacked Deerfield, Massachusetts and spilled a great deal of English blood. For their part, the New Englanders recaptured the French possession, Port Royal, in Nova Scotia. When the war ended in 1713, Nova

Scotia, Newfoundland, and Hudson's Bay were ceded by France to Britain. The powerful Iroquois Indians also allied themselves more closely with England.

The next 30 years proved to be only a temporary respite from war during which both France and Great Britain tried to strengthen their military positions in the New World. France built Fort Toulouse on the border of South Carolina and formed a compact with Spain in 1733 for mutual aid in case of attack. Between 1713 and 1744 both Britain and France strengthened their fortifications around the Great Lakes and upper New York.

The War of the Austrian Succession (1740–1748) was the third Anglo-French clash over European politics to have repercussions in America, where it was known as King George's War. Again tribes allied with the French crossed the St. Lawrence River and attacked English settlements, and again a force from New England marched north, this time to seize Louisbourg on

NORTH AMERICA · 1713

The European power struggle between France and England resulted in three wars within a 60-year period. In King George's War, English ships laid siege to the French fort at Louisbourg in Nova Scotia.

Cape Breton Island, a strategic French fortress that protected the mouth of the St. Lawrence. The loss of Louisbourg was a serious blow to French control of Canada and the interior territories beyond the Appalachians. France regained the fort in the Peace of Aix-la-Chapelle in 1748, but at the cost of giving up its European conquests in the Austrian Netherlands. France was sufficiently worried about its future power in America to completely refortify Louisbourg and to begin building a line of forts along the Appalachians. France was well aware that Massachusetts, Connecticut, Virginia, Pennsylvania, and New York all had pretensions to the Ohio Valley, and she was determined to keep the English colonials from ever realizing their plans.

THE ALBANY CONGRESS

Many political observers in Europe believed that the time had come for a final showdown between France and England. In 1758 a French minister wrote:

The King believes . . . that it is possessions in America that will in the future form the balance of power in Europe, and, that if the English invade that part of the world, as it appears they have the intention of doing, it will result that England will usurp the commerce of the nations, and that she alone will remain rich in Europe.

In this century-long struggle, which nation would ultimately dominate North America? English colonials outnumbered French settlers fifteen to one. Along the Atlantic Coast, towns, farms, and scattered industry flourished; whereas the colony of New France, concentrated around the towns of Quebec and Montreal on the St. Lawrence River, was populated by a small number of soldier-settlers and fur trappers. Yet, the French settlement possessed certain advantages. Although outnumbered, it had a

much larger and more carefully trained army. Also, the French were backed by strong Indian allies, and had built forts in the Ohio Valley to prevent the westward advance of the British.

Not undermined by these facts, Britain acted to shore up its position against French power. The first item of business was to improve relations with the Iroquois confederacy of New York by attending to some of the grievances brought by these tribes against the colonists. The confederacy had been complaining that New York traders were bypassing the Iroquois and dealing directly with other Indian tribes under Iroquois control. Also, speculators from the English colonies had been invading Iroquois lands. The British feared that the Iroquois might desert England and join forces with France.

To still Iroquois grievances and reinforce the alliance with them, the Privy Council in England ordered the colonists to meet with the Indians at Albany, New York. In June, 1754, one hundred and fifty Iroquois leaders convened at Albany, where their allegiance was sought by nineteen delegates from New Hampshire, Massachusetts, Connecticut, Rhode Island, Pennsylvania, Maryland, and New York. Despite a great deal of pomp and ceremony, the Indians left the meeting without giving a specific promise to aid the English in the event of another war with the French. Although the Indians failed to make a commitment, they managed to collect thirty wagonloads of gifts, including guns, scarlet coats, axes, scissors, and silver buttons.

The Albany Congress failed in two ways. Not only were the representatives unable to obtain a promise from the Iroquois, but they failed to establish a proposed alliance among the colonies. On the way to the conference, Benjamin Franklin had devised a scheme for an intercolonial federation, a plan of union calling for a "general government . . . under which the government of each colony may retain its present con-

A metal cut by Benjamin Franklin for the Pennsylvania Gazette, *depicting his proposal to the Albany Congress that the colonies either unite together or die.*

stitution." According to Franklin's plan, each colony would send delegates to a grand council that would handle Indian affairs, dispose of lands in the Ohio Valley, govern frontier territories beyond the boundaries of the present colonies, and levy taxes for an intercolonial army.

The delegates to the Albany Congress accepted the plan and agreed to take it back to the assemblies in their own colonies. All of the colonial assemblies rejected the proposal. The colonies were unwilling to hand over to a federation the right to tax, and the concept of federation was unappealing to some colonies, such as Pennsylvania and Virginia, who were competing with each other for the unclaimed territories in the Ohio Valley. "Everyone cries a union is necessary," Franklin wrote with dry humor to a friend, "but when they come to the manner and form of the union, their weak noodles are perfectly distracted." In England, Franklin added, the proposal was "judged to have too much of the *democratic.*" Britain disliked any measure that might unify the colonies and threaten the crown's domination. Thus, the first colonial attempt to join forces came to nothing.

THE FRENCH AND INDIAN WAR

A major area of rivalry between the British and French, as well as among the colonials, was the Ohio Valley. Virginia land speculators under the name of the Loyal Land Company had obtained a grant in 1748 to 800,000 acres in the Ohio Valley. A rival Virginia corporation, the Ohio Company, also had claims over the unsettled territory (as did Pennsylvania and Connecticut). When a fur trader named George Croghan, representing the Ohio Company, set up a post at Pickawillany in Ohio, the French reacted with alarm to this invasion of territory they regarded as their own. In June, 1752, a French force attacked the post, wiping it out and capturing five English colonials. Suddenly all of the Ohio Company's prospects vanished and Croghan went bankrupt.

Assuming he had rid the Ohio Valley of the British, the new French governor of Canada, the Marquis Duquesne, was exceedingly pleased. To make certain they stayed out, in the following year he constructed a line of forts in western Pennsylvania: Fort Presque Isle (present-day Erie); Fort Le Boeuf (Waterford); and Fort Venango (Franklin).

Not so pleased, however, was the new Lieutenant Governor of Virginia, Robert Dinwiddie. He had instructions to protect the interests of the Ohio Company, moreover, he owned a few shares in the enterprise. Dinwiddie sent a twenty-one-year-old Virginia surveyor named George Washington to inform the French that they were trespassing on property claimed by Virginia. Washington arrived with six other men at Fort Le Boeuf on December 11, 1753, where he was treated with perfect French cordiality—and then rebuffed. According to Washington, the French announced "it was their absolute design to take possession of the Ohio, and by G— they would do it."

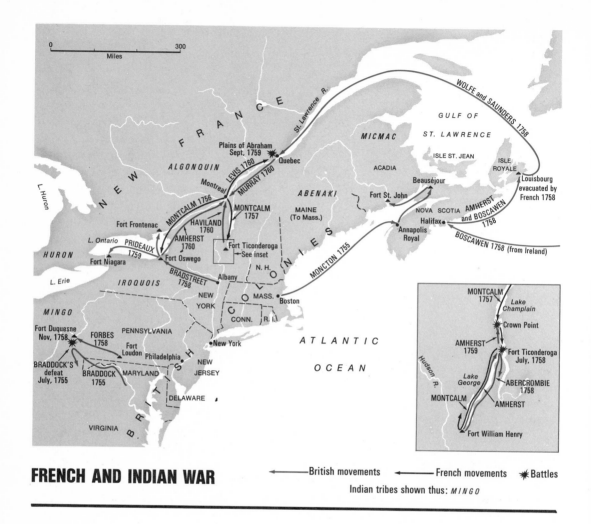

FRENCH AND INDIAN WAR

⟵ British movements ⟵ French movements ✳ Battles

Indian tribes shown thus: *MINGO*

In fact, the French coolly mentioned that they intended to build yet another fort at the point where the Monongahela and the Allegheny rivers join to form the Ohio (at present-day Pittsburgh).

Dinwiddie, resolved to beat the French to this strategic site, dispatched a small work force to build a fort there. To protect this work force, in the spring of 1754 Dinwiddie ordered Washington to set out for the site with two small companies of soldiers. Before they reached the Virginia workers, the French had already driven them out and had begun to erect their own fort (called Fort Duquesne after their governor).

THE WAR BEGINS

Washington, full of enthusiasm but altogether inexperienced in military strategy, was leading his men through the mountains southeast of Pittsburgh when he received word that the Virginians had been expelled by the French. On May 28, 1754, Washington attacked a small group of French scouts, killed ten, and took twenty-one prisoners. The minor attack had major and far-reaching consequences abroad as well as in America. It signaled the beginning of the French and Indian War, which spread the conflict between France and

England to Europe, where it became known as the Seven Years' War.

Following his successful assault on the French and knowing that he was outnumbered, Washington retreated. He improvised a camp at Great Meadows, near present-day Uniontown, Pennsylvania, which he aptly named Fort Necessity. When 500 French soldiers and 400 Indians attacked the Fort on July 3, Washington was unable to drive them back. After 9 hours he surrendered and the enemy forced Washington, who could not read French, to sign a document confessing that he had "assassinated" the leader of the French scouts on May 28. Having tricked the inexperienced young man, his captors released him and his men.

EARLY FRENCH VICTORIES

Virginia's Governor Dinwiddie knew that the colonies could not deal alone with the French threat. He appealed to England for aid, and although France and England were still officially at peace, England sent General Edward Braddock and two regiments of regulars to the New World.

Braddock, a heavy-set, sixty-year-old professional soldier, had never led troops in battle before. He was further handicapped by incorrect information about American geography supplied by the British authorities. Sensing danger the night before his ship sailed for America, he said, "We are sent like lambs to the altar." Once he arrived in the colonies, however, Braddock's courage rose and he became supremely confident. According to Benjamin Franklin, Braddock, referring to Indian attacks, declared, "These savages may, indeed, be a formidable enemy to your raw American militia, but upon the King's regular and disciplined troops, it is impossible they should make any impression."

Braddock arrived in Virginia in the spring of 1755, expecting to swell his ranks with American volunteers and Indian allies but he was sharply disappointed. Only

eight Indians and 1,200 colonials were willing to march with Braddock into Ohio. Furthermore, only paltry sums of money to finance the war effort were voted by New York, Pennsylvania, and Virginia. When Braddock set off into the wilderness he was understandably disgruntled. He was so angry with American "lies and villainy" that he began to make disparaging remarks about the colonists. Perhaps the kindest thing that any colonist said about Braddock himself was said by Washington: "His attachments were warm, his enmities strong, and having no disguise, both appeared in full force. He was generous and disinterested, but plain and blunt in manner, even to rudeness."

As the English troops forded a stream near Fort Duquesne, the French, though greatly outnumbered, attacked. French troops fired on the first lines of redcoats (as the English troops were called). The young English officer in charge ordered a retreat, but the retreating first wave of English soldiers collided with a second wave that was rushing forward to aid their comrades. In the resulting melee, Englishmen fired on Englishmen while the French and their Indian allies picked off their victims one by one. George Washington had two horses shot out from under him and Braddock lost five mounts. By the end of the disastrous skirmish, 976 of Braddock's men had died, and the General himself was fatally wounded.

Following this battle, Britain offered to regard the Allegheny Mountains as the permanent boundary between British and French colonial possessions if France would allow Britain to control all of Nova Scotia. France refused and Britain declared war on France. Britain immediately captured Fort Beausejour in the strategic Bay of Fundy, between New Brunswick and Nova Scotia.

The first 3 years went badly for the English. The French were more familiar with the wilderness, they had more and stronger Indian allies, and their autocratic govern-

An English battle plan for the capture of Fort William Henry on Lake George. General Johnson took the French fort and held it for two years when General Montcalm recaptured it in 1757.

ment enabled them to make more efficient war preparations in New France. The British were less well informed, for in the British colonies, most of the assemblies felt that what happened on the other side of the Appalachians was no business of theirs. In addition, New England suspected that Virginia exaggerated the danger of a French invasion simply to further the interests of the Ohio Company. The only colony badly hit by French attacks was Pennsylvania, and there the pacifist Quakers, who were still in control, were opposed to any military venture whatsoever.

Meanwhile, the Indians were so impressed with the French victory in western Pennsylvania that every tribe north of the Ohio River, except for those in the Iroquois federation, transferred its loyalty to New France. As the war intensified, the British attacked Fort Niagara, located where Lake Erie and Lake Ontario meet, and were repelled, as they were again following an assault against Crown Point on Lake Champlain. In 1756 the French military leader, the Marquis de Montcalm, captured Fort Oswego on Lake Ontario as well as nearby Fort Bull. In 1757 Montcalm took Fort William Henry on Lake George. The war was going so badly for Britain that the Earl of Chesterfield felt moved to write: "The French are masters to do what they please in America. We are no longer a nation. I never yet saw so dreadful a project."

WILLIAM PITT

The tide of events was reversed by William Pitt, a military and political genius, who took over the leadership of the English war effort. Pitt came to power at the end of 1757, declaring: "I believe that I can save this nation and that no one else can." His predecessors had paid little attention to the war in America. Pitt believed that the major English objectives should be command of the seas and possession of Canada and all territories west of the colonies up to the Mississippi River.

To reach this goal, Pitt spared no expense. The British navy quickly blockaded the coast of France. He also dispatched numerous English regiments to the New World, shipped adequate supplies, and promised to repay the colonies for any expenses incurred in fighting the French. (In fact, the colonies received over a million pounds in reparations after the war.) Because Pitt had no patience with mediocre and incompetent officers no matter how many years they had served the crown, he sent new, younger commanding officers to America to lead the English and colonial forces.

Pitt's new armies soon gained the upper hand. In July, 1758, Brigadier General James Wolfe and Major General Jeffrey Amherst took the Louisbourg fortress, thereby ending French control of the Atlantic fishing grounds and the mouth of the St. Lawrence. The victory prompted great bonfire celebrations in London, Philadelphia, Boston, and New York. A fort at the other end of the St. Lawrence, Fort Frontenac, fell a month later. Soon after, the French gave up Fort Duquesne, which the British renamed Fort Pitt.

In the fall of 1759 James Wolfe, who was by now considered the most brilliant of all English generals, captured Quebec. Quebec's high rock cliff facing the river made it almost impregnable, but Wolfe managed to find one undefended route up the stone precipice and one night sent his men on boats floating silently to the base of the path. At dawn the French saw five thousand British regulars lined up for battle on the

The capture of the French city of Quebec by the English in 1759. The French believed Quebec impregnable because of the high rock cliffs facing the river. However, as this eighteenth-century engraving shows, the English succeeded in finding an undefended ravine in the rock cliffs, allowing them to surprise the French and capture Quebec.

Plains of Abraham beside the fort. Wolfe died in the ensuing struggle, as did the French commander, the Marquis de Montcalm, but the English won the day. In 1760 Montreal fell to the English. The Seven Years' War, now a worldwide struggle, would be fought for three more years in Europe, India, and the Caribbean, but for all practical purposes in America it had come to an end.

EFFECTS OF THE WAR

The map of America was radically reshaped by the Treaty of Paris signed in 1763. Britain received all lands north of the Great Lakes (Canada) and all lands east of the Mississippi River, including Florida, which France's ally, Spain, lost in battle to the British during the war. France repaid Spain for having entered the war on her side by granting the Spanish all lands west of the Mississippi. Of its once vast holdings in America, France retained only two islands in the Caribbean, Guadaloupe and Martinique, and two tiny islands in the St. Lawrence, as well as the fishing rights off Newfoundland.

In previous American wars, colonial forces had fought with little assistance from the English. But in the French and Indian War, British money and British soldiers were chiefly responsible for the victory. The colonial assemblies had contributed small amounts to the effort, but most of this money was later returned by the English in reparations. Colonial soldiers had fought poorly compared with trained English troops. One English officer had called the Americans "broken innkeepers, horse jockeys and Indian traders."

So impressive was the English victory that pride in belonging to the British empire had never been higher, as articles and speeches of the day testify. Some Englishmen feared that the Americans might turn their thoughts to independence from the mother country now that the French men-

ace was driven out of Canada, but Benjamin Franklin expressed the view of many colonials when he remarked that a union among the colonies "is not merely improbable, it is impossible." Franklin then added: "When I say such a union is impossible, I mean without the most grievous tyranny and oppression."

English

French

Spanish

NORTH AMERICA · 1763

BRITAIN'S NEW EMPIRE

Victory proved to be an expensive prize, for England now had to assume the financial burden of maintaining a much larger American Empire. Britain's North American possessions, in fact, cost five times more to administer after the war than they had before 1763.

Within the original thirteen colonies themselves new problems had to be faced. The imperial machinery for governing the colonies was no longer adequate to meet the demands of a burgeoning population. Conflicting claims among the various colonies regarding the Ohio Valley had to be reviewed by a new English commission. The French and Indian War was fought over the Ohio Valley, but now that the land was secured, a decision had to be made as to who had the right to inhabit it. Moreover, Britain needed to decide how the new territories of Canada and the Floridas were to be governed.

The complexities of English politics of the day hindered the search for effective solutions to these new problems. George III, who had come to the throne in 1760, participated actively in the British election process in an effort to obtain men in Parliament friendly to his ideas of a strong monarchy. Such members were known as the "King's friends." Another complication was the existence of three important Whig factions that had personal differences with one another, although each was opposed to an increase in the power of the crown. One faction was led by Lord Grenville, another by William Pitt, and the third was a faction that called itself the Rockingham Whigs. The rise and fall from power in the House of Commons of these Whig groups between 1763 and 1770 was an important influence, along with colonial attitudes, on the constantly shifting British policy in those years.

THE PROCLAMATION OF 1763

The first problem the British nation faced after the war was how to handle its vastly enlarged scope of government. Now, in addition to the colonies, there were sprawling new land acquisitions to be controlled: the territory between the Appalachian Mountains and the Mississippi River, as well as Canada and the Floridas.

British relations with the Indians, always tense, deteriorated after the war. Most of the tribes had allied themselves with the French in the hope that a French victory would stop the westward migration of English colonists. An Ottawa chief named Pontiac decided to make a last desperate attempt to stem the English invasion. Pontiac's Rebellion, as his uprising is called, occurred in 1763. The Ottawas and their allies attacked the frontier outpost of Detroit and soon after were again defeated in clashes on the line of English forts and trading posts around the Great Lakes, and along the Appalachian Mountains from Pennsylvania to Virginia.

Although Pontiac's Rebellion failed, the British were so anxious to avoid stirring up the Indians further that they issued the Proclamation of 1763, prohibiting settlers from either crossing the Appalachians or purchasing Indian lands. No white man, in fact, whether a settler, a land speculator, or a fur trader, was to be admitted to the new lands in the West. Colonists who had been planning to migrate west were advised to go either to Quebec or to Florida, England's new acquisitions. These two new colonies were to be provided with representative

Samuel Adams Questions Parliament's Right to Legislate for the Colonies

" *... It is an essential, unalterable right in nature, engrafted into the British constitution, as a fundamental law, and ever held sacred and irrevocable by the subjects within the realm, that what a man has honestly acquired is absolutely his own, which he may freely give, but cannot be taken from him without his consent; that the American subjects may, therefore, exclusive of any consideration of charter rights, with a decent firmness, adapted to the character of free men and subjects, assert this natural and constitutional right.*

It is, moreover, their humble opinion, which they express with the greatest deference to the wisdom of the Parliament, that the Acts made there, imposing duties on the people of this province, with the sole and express purpose of raising a revenue, are infringements of their natural and constitutional rights; because, as they are not represented in the British Parliament, his Majesty's commons in Britain, by those Acts, grant their property without their consent.

—Works of Samuel Adams

government similar to that in the thirteen colonies along the Atlantic seaboard.

The Proclamation enraged the colonies. Some settlers had already migrated to Kentucky. Dozens of land development companies were planning to develop the Ohio Valley. George Washington announced that he had no intention of conforming to the Proclamation, saying, "Any person . . . who neglects the present opportunity of hunting out good lands, and in some measure marking and distinguishing them for his own (in order to keep others from settling them), will never regain it." Washing-

The Supremacy of Parliament from the Declaratory Act

" *... be it declared . . . , That the said colonies and plantations in America have been, are, and of right ought to be, subordinate unto, and dependent upon the imperial crown and parliament of Great Britain; and that the King's majesty, by and with the advice and consent of the lords spiritual and temporal, and commons of Great Brtain, in parliament assembled, had, hath, and of right ought to have, full power and authority to make laws and statutes of sufficient force and validity to bind the colonies and people of America, subjects of the crown of Great Britain, in all cases whatsoever. . . .*

—Declaratory Act

ton promptly sent an agent to protect his claims.

The British had devised the Proclamation as only a temporary measure, but it continued to be enforced year after year, **"** since exclusion of white settlers from the Ohio Valley was the easiest way to handle the Indian problem. The colonists, particularly Virginians, chafed under the restriction. They demanded new farmlands because tobacco farming had badly depleted the soil of Virginia farms, crops were smaller, and erosion was eating away the topsoil. Opposition to the Proclamation became so clamorous that the British began to revise its restrictions in small, piecemeal ways: they made a treaty in 1768 with the Cherokees that extended the western boundary of Virginia; a second treaty with the Creeks enlarged the territory of South Carolina and Georgia; and a third British treaty in 1768, this one with the Iroquois, gave more land to New York. But these compromises and small gains did not appease the land hunger of the colonists. In defiance of the Proclamation, Daniel Boone began to explore the land north of the Ohio River in 1769 and in 1775 he led the first group of settlers into the Midwest.

The Proclamation was intended not only to stop further Indian insurrections but also as a means of keeping the colonists within the area controlled by the royal governors and the whole apparatus of the British government. The British feared that once the colonists slipped beyond the Appalachians, they would become completely ungovernable.

A PROGRAM TO RAISE REVENUE

The British next determined to find a means to extract more money from the colonies, not only to pay Britain's debts but also to enforce the policy of mercantilism more effectively in the colonies.

George Grenville became Chancellor of the Exchequer of England in April, 1763, and he persuaded the Parliament to pass several pieces of legislation that raised American tempers to the boiling point. Already enraged by restrictions against settling the Ohio Valley, the colonists responded first vocally and then with physical violence to attempts to tax them directly.

In Britain itself taxes to cover the expenses of the Seven Years' War had soared so high that landowners were paying a third of their income to the government. Now officials estimated that ten thousand British troops would have to be permanently garrisoned in America to protect the colonies from Indian raids. The British public resented paying for these troops and insisted that the Americans assume a major part of the burden.

THE CURRENCY AND SUGAR ACTS

To deal with the economic problems of the colonies, Grenville persuaded Parlia-

The English Proclamation of 1763 prohibiting settlement on the lands west of the Appalachians enraged the colonists. Daniel Boone, depicted here, leading a band of settlers into this prohibited frontier, openly defied the Proclamation. Boone was the first colonial explorer to open up the Midwest to settlement.

ment to pass two different acts: the Currency Act of April, 1764, and a few days later, the Sugar Act. The Currency Act, although the less irritating of the two, created great financial difficulty for many colonists. It forbade the colonies to issue more paper money or to use any paper as legal tender in payment of debts. This act had its origins in the uneasiness of English businessmen over American paper money. As southern lands became increasingly depleted by tobacco farming, Virginia plantation owners accumulated greater and greater debts, mostly owed to English merchants. Virginia tobacco crops grew smaller, but Virginia aristocrats refused to curtail their expenses or reduce their standard of living. As a consequence, Virginians ran up huge debts with British merchants and shipowners. Jefferson remarked that these debts "had become hereditary from father to son, for many generations, so that the planters were a species of property annexed to certain mercantile houses in London." When the planters paid off these debts with paper money issued in America, English merchants became extremely alarmed. American paper money was usually worth less than its face value. Therefore, English merchants wanted to be paid in gold or silver, and nothing else. The Currency Act imposed a real hardship on the American economy. Not only did it make paying off debts to English merchants more costly, but it also inhibited the growth of American trade. The colonies had always been short of gold and silver. There was little precious metal in North America and laws prohibited the exportation of bullion from England into the colonies. Forbidden to issue paper money, and deprived of hard cash, the colonists found it extremely difficult to conduct business.

The Sugar Act, however, infuriated the colonists far more. In the past, British customs regulations had been designed mainly to ensure the smooth working of the mercantilistic system. Duties and taxes had penalized colonists who wanted to trade with foreign countries and favored colonial merchants who dealt with England. The customs fees were designed to keep business circulating within the empire and to prevent profits from trickling into foreign pockets. Now, however, Grenville hoped to use a series of duties for the specific purpose of raising revenue for the British government. Whereas the old duties had seemed to the colonists an aspect of Britain's foreign policy (an imperial concern that all Americans conceded was a matter that Parliament had the right to decide), these new charges struck the colonists as a very different affair. Grenville imposed duties on the importation into the colonies of sugar, indigo, coffee, wine, woven cloth, and foreign molasses. A duty on foreign molasses (that is, molasses imported from the French instead of the English sugar islands in the Caribbean) had existed since 1733, but colonial ship owners had generally avoided paying it by bribing customs officials. Grenville recognized that the old duty on molasses had been too high. He cut it in half, but he wanted to make sure that every penny of the reduced fee was collected.

Smuggling would become very difficult since now colonial merchants would have to fill out lengthy documents whenever they entered or sailed out of an American port.

The revenue raised by the Sugar Act duties was supposed to pay imperial expenses, however, not nearly enough was raised to solve Britain's budgetary problems. Colonists felt that they were being indirectly taxed by Parliament. They were angered still more by another provision of the Sugar Act: all smugglers could be tried, if the informer desired, not by a common law court using the jury system, but rather by a new admiralty court without jury in Halifax, Nova Scotia. The wording of the act showed that the defendant was presumed guilty until proven innocent—the exact opposite of traditional English legal practice.

THE STAMP ACT

The resentment smoldering among the colonists against the *indirect* taxation of the Sugar Act turned into open rebellion when Parliament tried to tax the colonies *directly*. In February, 1765, Grenville asked Parliament to levy a stamp tax on the colonies. According to this proposal, colonists would have to pay a tax to register every legal document (such as wills and deeds to property). Taxes were also levied on newspapers, pamphlets, almanacs, and even on playing cards and sets of dice. Again, tax dodgers would not be tried in common law courts, where juries made up of fellow colonists would inevitably treat the offenders leniently, but in the stricter admiralty courts, where a royally appointed judge alone handed down the decision. The act became law on March 22, 1765, and was due to go into effect the following November. A few days after the Stamp Act was made law, Parliament put through a third measure, the Quartering Act. According to its provisions, colonial cities where royal troops were stationed had to provide the soldiers with living accommodations in public inns, alehouses, empty buildings, or barns and had to furnish them with candles, firewood, blankets, salt, and liquor.

THE COLONIAL RESPONSE

Grenville's three acts had an immediate impact on the colonies. The Currency Act had made business transactions chaotic. The Sugar Act, with its strict provisions for collection of molasses duties, threatened to destroy New England's rum distillers. English sugar-producing islands could not provide the distillers with enough molasses,

English soldiers tried to enforce the Stamp Act in the colonies by burning all colonial mail that did not bear the English tax stamp. The colonists uniformly ignored the act and not a single English stamp was sold in America.

and enforcement of the import duty made the cost of molasses bought from Martinique and Guadaloupe (the French islands) prohibitively expensive. The Stamp Act appeared as the worst of all three to the colonists, for it deprived Americans not only of money but of their liberties.

The swift colonial response was unexpected. Those most likely to be affected by the legislation were the three most articulate groups in the colonies, the lawyers, the clergy, and the merchants. Protest meetings, speeches, and pamphlets followed with great rapidity. In Boston many artisans and laborers organized into the so-called "Sons of Liberty" to march in protest demonstrations. Other cities followed suit with their own Sons of Liberty. Disciplined actions took place later, but during the protests in 1765 violent eruptions were frequent. Stamp collectors were manhandled into resigning, and in Massachusetts the governor's house was overrun and many valuable items destroyed.

TAXATION WITHOUT REPRESENTATION

Most colonists believed that the Stamp Act was an infringement of their right, as Englishmen, to be taxed by only their elected representatives. The colonies had never been directly taxed by England before; therefore, the Stamp Act raised the question of the relationship of the colonial assemblies to Parliament. Colonists, to be sure, probably would not have received *any* plan of taxation with much enthusiasm, even if imposed by their own assemblies. The Stamp Act, however, was regarded with particular distaste because the colonists were given no voice in its passage into law.

As noted in earlier chapters, Parliament's fight to control taxation was one of the chief issues in its struggle with the monarchy in the seventeenth century. Knowing that whoever controlled the country's purse strings was England's real ruler, the members of Parliament were determined that they, and not the king, would wield that power. Parliament's long struggle was finally successful. When Parliament gave the throne of James II to William of Orange and his wife Mary in 1688, it was following the ideas of John Locke, who asserted that men's property must not be appropriated without their consent, whether that property be land or money. Parliament was stronger than the king, Locke had pointed out. Parliament, representing the people, vested power in the king, but if the king became tyrannical, Parliament could oust him and choose another monarch. At no time did the king have the right to tax; that right remained eternally with the representatives of the people.

This principle of no taxation without representation thus became a cornerstone of English liberty and the colonists assumed that the principle extended to them, at least in legislation providing revenue for the needs of each individual colony. Parliament, however, thought otherwise. It was jealous of the prerogatives it had gained in the "Glorious Revolution" of 1688. Parliament would not admit that each colonial legislature had as much power to legislate for its own people as Parliament itself had in legislating for England. In Parliament's view, the colonial legislatures existed only because of the generosity of the mother country. To pacify the colonists, Grenville agreed in principle that colonists should be taxed only by their representatives, but suggested that every member of Parliament *was* such a representative. According to Grenville, although the colonists did not actually elect any members of Parliament (neither did many Englishmen), Americans had *virtual* representation, since every member represented all of the empire, not merely his own district. Such assertions in the midst of a rising crisis in America over the Stamp Act provoked questions about the structure of the empire and about the protection of individual rights. The prac-

tice had developed in colonial America that a man had to live in a certain district to represent that district; therefore, colonists felt they were not represented in Parliament. They also knew that from a practical standpoint, even if they could elect men to sit in Parliament, their representatives would be greatly outnumbered by the English members. In addition, colonists were aware that admiralty courts were being used in America to deny colonists the traditional Englishman's right to trial by jury.

THE STAMP ACT CONGRESS

"One single act of Parliament set the people a'thinking in six months more than they had done in their whole lives before," wrote James Otis, the leader of the Massachusetts Assembly. Suddenly, colonists everywhere were questioning British policies in a way that probably would not have occurred to them before the Stamp Act crisis. The assemblies of New York and Virginia sent petitions to England objecting to the Sugar Act. By the time the Stamp Act was passed, every colonial assembly was hotly debating what action it should take.

In June, 1765, Massachusetts called for the first intercolonial assembly ever to be summoned by the colonists themselves. This assembly, the Stamp Act Congress, met in New York City the following October. Nine colonies were represented. Of the four colonies that did not send representatives, three —Virginia, Georgia, and North Carolina— failed to do so only because their royal governors had strictly forbidden it.

After the Stamp Act Congress went through the formality of avowing "all due subordination" to Parliament, the representatives set about framing a joint statement that was a strong assertion of colonial autonomy. They resolved: "That the people in these colonies are not and from their local circumstances cannot be, represented in the House of Commons in Great Britain; that the only representatives of the people of these colonies are persons chosen by themselves, and that no taxes ever have been, or can be constitutionally imposed on them, but by their respective legislatures." The congress then petitioned the king and Parliament to repeal the Sugar Act and the Stamp Act and abolish the admiralty courts.

Months before, the colonies had been so suspicious of one another that they had been unable to cooperate in even the smallest detail. Now, however, a new spirit of unity coursed through America. Merchants in every colony agreed to stop importing all British goods, thereby giving real economic bite to their angry words. The colonies were a huge market for British manufactured goods and a total embargo might throw England into a depression, they reasoned. The economic boycott for all practical purposes never extended further south than Philadelphia, but it was an important first step in economic cooperation. At the Stamp Act Congress, a new note was sounded by a representative from South Carolina, who declared that "there ought to be no New England man, no New Yorker known on this continent, but all of us Americans."

The Stamp Act went into force on November first, but mobs intimidated every royal official so thoroughly that no one attempted to sell a single stamp. In fact, not one stamp was ever issued in America. Hundreds of merchants in every port suspended business and when they opened their shops and stores again in late December, they ignored the Stamp Act with a uniformity never before witnessed in America. To a large extent this was the work of a group of conspirators called the Sons of Liberty, an intercolonial organization devoted to resisting the Stamp Act "to the last extremity."

REPEAL OF THE STAMP ACT

By July, 1765, the Grenville ministry had lost the confidence of the king, and the Rockingham Whig faction was asked to form a new government. By August, 1765, news of American revolt against the Stamp Act had reached Britain. The new government was besieged by merchants' petitions calling for repeal of the Stamp Act as injurious to British trade. The king supported repeal to back the Rockingham group in power and prevent the return of Grenville, whom he disliked. Pitt also urged Parliament to repeal the controversial law, going so far as to say: "I rejoice that America has resisted."

Before it ever officially received the petition of the Stamp Act Congress, Parliament rescinded both the Stamp Act and the Sugar Act in March, 1766. Only a one-penny duty on sugar remained. When the news reached the colonies, general rejoicing broke out, but these high spirits were soon dampened. Americans discovered that on the same day Parliament repealed the Stamp Act it had passed a Declaratory Act. This measure reasserted Parliament's right to frame legislation for the colonies without their approval: Parliament could "make laws and statutes of sufficient force and validity to bind the colonies and people of America . . . in all cases whatsoever." This meant that, although Americans had successfully combatted one particular piece of disagreeable legislation, they had not won their crucial argument that *all* such legislation was unconstitutional. On the contrary, Parliament had stated its supremacy over the colonies in the clearest possible terms.

THE TOWNSHEND ACTS

American political thinkers objected to the Stamp Act on the grounds that it was *direct* taxation applied and collected *internally* from within the colonies. Benjamin Franklin went so far as to inform Parliament that the colonists objected only to direct taxes and not to indirect taxes. Although the argument seemed merely an exercise in theory, the members of Parliament finally persuaded themselves that they could

An English cartoon, showing "the funeral procession of Miss American-Stamp," published in London in 1766.

get money more easily out of the recalcitrant colonies by levying a new series of *indirect* taxes on goods taxed and shipped from some *external* port into America.

The duties were proposed in June, 1767, by a new chancellor of the exchequer, Charles Townshend, a man of so frivolous a reputation that the public nicknamed him "Champagne Charlie." The Townshend acts instituted levies on glass, lead, paints, paper, and tea—all products that, under the navigation acts, Americans could import only from England. The acts stated that money from these duties would be used for the salaries of royal officials and called for payment of all duties in gold and silver.

Even more dismaying than these new duties was the establishment of a Board of Customs Commissioners, with headquarters in Boston. These officials could use the hated writs of assistance (general search warrants) to search for smuggled goods. New admiralty courts were also established in four major American ports where the colonists would, as in all military courts, be denied their right to trial by jury. Aggravating matters further, the salaries of the new customs commissioners were to be paid out of fines levied against those shippers convicted in the admiralty courts. This provision made the commissioners independent of Parliament and colonial assemblies and led quickly and inevitably to corruption. In addition, officials were to receive one-third of the total value of every ship and cargo caught violating any British mercantile law. A final blow enraging colonists was Parliament's suspension of the New York

FROM DISCORD TO DISUNION

assembly for refusing to obey the Quartering Act, a move which seemed a direct British attack on colonial self-government.

The members of Parliament had been convinced by Franklin that America objected only to internal taxes, but the fact remained that this argument had always been a rationalization, and that Americans did not want any kind of new taxes. A tax was a tax, and every colonist understood this without much reflection. Now colonial spokesmen had to invent a distinction between supposedly acceptable external taxes and the unacceptable Townshend duties. "Here is no distinction made between internal and external taxes," John Dickinson criticized in his widely circulated *Letters from a Farmer in Pennsylvania*. He maintained that Parliament, of course, had the right to pass the navigation acts, but they were to be distinguished from the Townshend duties because the purpose of the navigation acts was to regulate trade whereas the unlawful purpose of the Townshend duties was to raise revenue—a tenuous argument at best.

Much less violence occurred against the Townshend duties than had taken place in 1765. Demonstrations were peaceful in order not to alienate moderate and conservative opinion from the effort to bring about repeal of the acts. Merchants throughout the colonies worked out an effective boycott of the British goods listed in the acts. People made their own clothes, and paper and paint were manufactured in the colonies. At first the boycott did not affect England, but gradually the slowdown in trade with her most important possession had its influence on Britain's parliamentary leadership.

The Townshend acts, coming close on the heels of the Stamp Act crisis, heightened American suspicions of British motives with a singleness of mind that took the English completely off guard and even surprised Americans themselves. Throughout the French and Indian War the colonies had continued to bicker as usual, indulging in their regional rivalries and admitting a connection to one another only insofar as they were all subjects of the same king. But the continuing threat of British interference with American self-government, as represented by the Townshend duties, caused Americans to begin to think more in terms of unified resistance to British measures. Individually they knew they could do little to resist Parliament, but united they posed a considerable threat to parliamentary supremacy.

A small group of men representing each of the colonies had begun to take a strong stand against British policy at the time of the resistance to the Stamp Act. They were the first to sense not only the economic, but even more keenly, the political implications of British policy for the future of America. The activities of this small group led to widespread organized resistance and eventually, the Revolution. Ultimately, this group was able to win the support of one-third to two-fifths of the moderate and conservative colonists for their demands, first for redress of grievances and finally for complete independence. Over about a decade this patriot party engineered one of the greatest changes of public opinion in world history, shifting the colonies from loyalty to

147

disloyalty to the mother country. A majority of Americans probably never supported the break with England, but a large percentage did and among them were not merely the agitators but a large number of the economic, social, and political leaders of colonial America.

The battle against Parliament in New England was led by three important figures, James Otis, Samuel Adams, and John Adams. They were supported behind the scenes by many merchants and even some of the clergy of the Congregational Church. Otis was a lawyer and a flamboyant, energetic speaker, whose effectiveness was diminished by his lapses into emotional illness. The two Adamses were cousins. At first Samuel was the more influential in shaping events. He leaped upon every grievance against the British and even distorted it (or "improved" it, to use his own word) to incense the public against the mother country. "We cannot make events," Samuel

John Singleton Copley's portrait of Samuel Adams.

Adams once remarked. "Our business is wisely to improve them." He was also the greatest force behind the formation of the Sons of Liberty. Much more sober was John Adams, who in his quiet, dignified way stepped up the growing hostility against Parliament.

The Southern colonies also had clearly identifiable leaders of the resistance to British policy by 1767. In Virginia the fiery Patrick Henry and Richard Henry Lee of the wealthy planter family were outspoken in their attacks on British policy. Thomas Jefferson of western Virginia was still a young law student, but his training in political philosophy made him a student of Locke's arguments regarding the natural rights of man. In Charleston, South Carolina, the formidable Christopher Gadsden worked tirelessly for the patriot cause.

TROUBLE IN MASSACHUSETTS

On the surface the Townshend duties were accepted quietly in the colonies, but anger in Massachusetts against the Townshend acts began to mount until in 1768 the assembly sent a "Circular Letter" written by Samuel Adams to the legislatures of the other colonies complaining about the laws and asserting anew America's right to govern herself. In fact, all over America men of intelligence were debating the question of how much power Parliament should have over the colonies. This debate, which was crucial and needed to be handled with tact and diplomacy, was treated as mere insubordination by Lord North, the new Chancellor of the Exchequer and a favorite of the king. This man, who should have carefully reexamined the imperial system, could scarcely be made to understand that a problem existed. The circular letter was also considered impudent by the Secretary of State, Lord Hillsborough. He ordered the Massachusetts assembly to withdraw it immediately. The king's other advisors were considering a "kind and lenient" circular letter of their own, but Hillsborough acted without their knowledge and even went so far as to tell all the other royal governors to dissolve their assemblies if the legislatures paid any attention whatsoever to the dangerous document from Massachusetts.

The Massachusetts assembly, by a vote of ninety-two to seventeen, refused to rescind its circular letter. Governor Bernard, acting on Hillsborough's orders, dissolved the assembly. In September, 1768, two regiments of royal troops were billeted in Boston to maintain order, in case of violence against the presence of British officials. Regarding the troops sent to Boston as a provocative act, Benjamin Franklin labeled Hillsborough "perverse and senseless."

An unofficial Massachusetts convention met a few days later and resolved that "as Englishmen they have an aversion to an unnecessary standing army, which they look upon as dangerous to their civil liberty." Samuel Adams tried to stir the convention to stronger action, but the delegates refused, and the British troops were received by the town without the occurrence of any trouble.

THE BOSTON MASSACRE

A year and a half later, however, violence suddenly broke out. On March 5, 1770, a band of unemployed laborers attacked a British sentry at the Boston customhouse. The officer on duty, Captain Preston, tried to reason with the crowd. The mob did not disperse, but continued to pelt the soldiers with oyster shells and snowballs. In the confusion, someone shouted "Fire!" and the British fired. Five of the rioters were killed, six others wounded. The first man killed was Crispus Attucks, an unemployed black seaman. Samuel Adams and James Otis ballooned this street brawl into a "massacre" for propaganda purposes, but John Adams defended the British soldiers in court

against a murder indictment and they were acquitted.

By one of those strange coincidences of history, on the very same day the massacre occurred, Parliament repealed all of the Townshend acts. The colonial boycott of British goods had proved effective. Only a symbolic three-penny duty on tea remained. Lord North, who became Prime Minister in 1770, thought it was important to keep the tea tax only to prove to Americans that Parliament *did* have the right to tax the colonies. Although more than half of the members of Parliament believed the tea duty would only stir up more trouble, they let North have his way.

A PERIOD OF PEACE— 1770–1773

The Sons of Liberty tried to hold out for a continued embargo of all English goods until the tea tax was withdrawn, but most Americans were so pleased at the repeal of the other duties that colonial merchants soon began to trade with England as in the past. British-American trade had dropped off badly under the Townshend acts. In fact, the acts had benefited no one: Americans were compelled to do without many goods, British manufacturers watched with dismay as competing American industries began to make the goods under embargo, and Parliament received very little revenue from the customs officers.

The tea tax—and the duties on foreign molasses established under the Sugar Act—continued, but during the period from 1770 to 1773, Americans paid the small amounts without much grumbling. Business was better than it had been in years and all but a handful of colonials seemed to have lost interest in questions of who had the right to tax whom.

Once the colonists stopped quarreling with England, they began to quarrel with one another. Anglicans in New England asked the Church of England to send a bishop to America at long last, a proposal which infuriated Anglicans in the South, who enjoyed running their congregations as they pleased and who did not look forward to the meddling of a bishop. Non-Anglicans in the North and the South were also enraged at the idea of an Anglican bishop in America. The perennial squabbles over lands in the West were renewed. Connecticut invaded northeastern Pennsylvania and set up a county of its own in the disputed territory. Pennsylvanians and Virginians again took up their disputes over lands in the Ohio Valley, even though the Proclamation of 1763 was still in force, forbidding all white men to enter most of the new lands. Tensions between frontiersmen and the East Coast establishment in the Southern colonies surfaced again. The English had mixed feelings about all the bickering. They could not help being slightly pleased to see the "unity" of the colonies divided once more by the old factionalism of self-interest.

However, below this relatively calm surface, the Patriot party in America was ardently at work. Samuel Adams and his colleagues publicized every British mistake or insult. While Adams realized the usefulness of existing institutions as vehicles for pro-test—such as town meetings, assemblies, county courts, churches, local and colonial clubs, and newspapers—he was also looking for a new method of reaching the citizenry with information. As a result, in 1772 he succeeded in forming a committee of correspondence to formulate a list of grievances and persuaded the other towns in Massachusetts to form similar committees. Within 3 months, eighty more committees were formed in Massachusetts, all exchanging written complaints against the English. Other New England colonies also formed committees and eventually there was at least one in each of the colonies except North Carolina and Pennsylvania. One subject of complaint was a new plan for paying the governor of Massachusetts. His salary hitherto had been paid by the assembly, an arrangement which ensured a certain amount of colonial control over the governor. After June, 1772, however, the governor was to be paid directly by the crown, a measure that "exposed the province to a despotic administration of government," ac-

The burning of the Gaspee *in 1772. The* Gaspee *was a British revenue ship that was used to suppress colonial smuggling in New England. Her burning was to become one of the most defiant colonial acts before the American Revolution.*

cording to one correspondence committee. The crown instead of the assembly soon began to pay the salaries of the judges of the Superior Court as well.

An even more inflammatory issue which aided Adams' campaign was an incident involving a British warship, the *Gaspee,* which had been lent to the customs service to suppress smuggling in New England. The ship's captain had harassed farmers and fishermen who traded in the Narragansett Bay, and when the *Gaspee* ran aground in pursuit of a smuggler, local citizens boarded the ship at night, wounded the captain, and burned the ship.

Surprisingly, the British government responded to this outrage against the king's property with mild forbearance, but Americans everywhere heard a false rumor that the suspects in the *Gaspee* affair would be tried in England, not in Massachusetts. The right to be tried in one's native district was one of the oldest English privileges, and in Virginia the House of Burgesses became so incensed at the rumor that it set up correspondence committees all over the colony. By the middle of 1773 all of New England and South Carolina had agreed to correspond with the committees in Virginia. An underground news system had been set up and the groundwork laid for union.

THE INTOLERABLE ACTS

The *Gaspee* affair had been the colonists' fault and Americans had overreacted to it. The event that brought on the final crisis, however, was a grave English miscalculation, a mistake compounded by British arrogance and ignorance.

THE BOSTON TEA PARTY

For almost 175 years the British East India Company had held a monopoly over all trade between India and the rest of the British Empire. Control of this trade had

brought the company enormous prosperity, but in the 1770s the firm fell on hard times and faced bankruptcy. In its warehouses the company had some seventeen million pounds of tea from India. Tea glutted the English market and some politicians suggested that the government should revoke the company's charter and take it over. This proposal struck many members of Parliament as an "attack on the liberties of the people." And yet, what should be done with all that tea? And how could the East India Company be saved?

Lord North came up with what he considered a brilliant scheme, bound to please everyone, particularly the colonists, and to implement it he guided the Tea Act of 1773 quickly through Parliament. This law provided that the government would withdraw its usual import duties on all tea brought *into* England. Moreover, it enabled the company to export tea directly to America, without dealing with both English and American wholesalers. The East India Company would deal directly with colonial retailers, and the simplicity of the new arrangement would make the price of its tea competitive, well below the cost of Dutch tea (which Americans had been drinking illegally for years). In fact, tea would cost less in the colonies than in England, even after the Townshend duty of threepence a pound was collected.

The plan, as anticipated, pleased everyone except the colonists who felt they were being denied freedom of choice. If the English government could eliminate American tea wholesalers, who could stop Parliament from destroying all other colonial middlemen? Worse, the East India Company chose as its agents in America only those merchants who had ignored or opposed the embargo against English goods during the crises over the Stamp Act and Townshend acts. If the Tea Act was allowed to go into effect, Americans thought, England would set up monopolies for wine, spices, cloth—all goods, in fact—and the monopoly would

151

favor only merchants who had passed a loyalty test.

American opposition to the Tea Act was almost unanimous. The British had looked on the bickering among the colonies during the past 3 years as proof that Americans could never act in concert for long. Now, this hope was thoroughly exploded. The committees of correspondence had done their work well. In Charleston the tea was unloaded but immediately locked in public warehouses, where it remained unopened until after the Declaration of Independence. In New York and Philadelphia, ship captains never attempted to deliver their tea. The East India Company's agents were harassed in every port.

In Boston, the governor was determined to land the tea, collect the duty and proceed normally, despite the abnormal tensions in the town. On the night of December 16, 1773, however, between thirty and sixty men boarded three ships in the harbor. They were lightly disguised as Indians in war paint and feathers. They dumped 45 tons of tea into the harbor, while a cheering crowd watched them from the wharf.

In England, Lord North was appalled. He had devised the Tea Act to *please* the colonists, but now he realized there was no way of dealing with these "haughty American republicans." The king announced: "We must master them or totally leave them to themselves and treat them as aliens." The reaction elsewhere in America was equally critical. Most of the other colonists thought the Boston Tea Party was a shameful affair, and as one colonist put it, "calculated to introduce anarchy, confusion and bloodshed among the people." The Boston Tea Party brought to a head the conflict over British authority. The Patriot party had committed violence in the hope of rallying popular support at home against British rule and to see what measures, if any, would be taken by Britain in reply. Americans were not long in receiving the answer.

LORD NORTH'S REVENGE

To punish the Bostonians, Lord North steered through Parliament four measures that Americans promptly dubbed "the intolerable acts." The Boston Port Bill, passed on March 25, 1774, closed the harbor to all shipping until the citizens compensated the East India Company for the destroyed tea and paid the customs officials the required duty. Boston was stunned by the news, which seemed to threaten the city with starvation and poverty unless the citizens bowed to the will of an unyielding English government. The Boston Committee of Correspondence responded by penning a flurry of letters to other committees throughout the colonies. When the news reached Virginia, Thomas Jefferson proposed to the House of Burgesses that June 1 be declared a day of American mourning for the "heavy calamity which threatens destruction to our civil rights, and the evils of civil war." Jefferson's proposal was adopted and on June 1 flags hung at half mast and church bells tolled mournfully in every colony. Fellow Americans who had

The Boston Tea Party resulted from the Tea Act of 1773, which established a monopoly on British tea in the colonies. Enraged at this proposal, a group of colonists, disguised as Indians, dumped 45 tons of British tea into the Boston harbor.

recently denounced the Bostonians for anarchy during the Boston Tea Party now rushed to the city's aid. Charleston sent Boston rice; Philadelphia dispatched a thousand barrels of flour.

While Americans were bemoaning the Boston Port Bill, Parliament was passing three other "intolerable" acts. The Massachusetts Government Act revised the old Massachusetts charter of 1691. From now on the governor's council (the upper house of the legislature) would be appointed by the king, as in all other royal colonies, and not elected by the assembly. If the governor saw fit, he could forbid town meetings from convening except once a year when local officers were elected. Massachusetts was being taken a long way from its seventeenth-century autonomy. This colony, which had started out as virtually self-governing, now had a governor appointed and paid by the king, judges on the royal payroll, and a council chosen by the king.

The Administration of Justice Act provided that any government or customs official who had committed violence in the course of suppressing riots or other disturbances could be tried in England rather than in the colonies by an American jury.

Finally, a new Quartering Act ordered local authorities to provide housing in towns where barracks did not exist, should troops be needed in that town to quell disturbances.

Another act passed at this time was the Quebec Act. Though unrelated to the "intolerable acts," to Americans it seemed another part of England's sinister plan for extending despotic rule and hemming in the colonies. At the end of the French and Indian War, the British government had tried to institute representative government in Canada. Now Quebec was enlarged, so that its borders reached south to the Ohio River and west to the Mississippi, and the whole vast colony was given a permanent government—without a representative assembly. The Catholic Church was to be the established faith for the region, supported by tax money. The Quebec Act was Parliament's attempt to give French-speaking residents a government similar to the one they had enjoyed under France, but Protestants in the colonies objected to the establishment of Catholicism so close to American borders; American land speculators with claims in the Ohio Valley were infuriated that the rich lands had been given to Quebec; and Americans were disturbed that Quebec would be ruled by an autocratic governor, seeing this precedent as a threat to their own free government.

The "intolerable acts" brought the crisis between England and her North American colonies to a point from which there was to be no subsequent retreat by either side. The imperialists in the British Parliament who wanted no compromise with the colonists were in power. For a century and a half Americans had regarded themselves as loyal Englishmen and as recently as 1763 had felt nothing but good will toward the king. Now, the Patriot party in America, which was even thinking of independence, was gradually getting the upper hand.

From the British point of view, Americans had a very provincial attitude and were ignorant of the responsibilities of empire. They had lived with few taxes and great freedom, far from the bureaucratic and financial complexities of London. Now that the colonies were more populous and richer, the time had come for Americans to realize that they would have to submit to taxation.

Most Americans were willing to let Parliament continue to make most of the laws for the colonies which related to imperial matters such as foreign policy and international trading regulations. Parliament, however, insisted stubbornly on treating the colonial governments not as the inherent right of a free people but as subordinate agencies of government in an imperial system—agencies which could be destroyed at will by the Parliament. Assemblies had been suspended and trial by jury set aside. British troops had been stationed on American soil during peacetime. American territorial aspirations in the Ohio Valley were frustrated first by the Proclamation of 1763 and then by the Quebec Act. American merchants were bullied by corrupt customs officials and American overseas trade undermined. Most insulting of all, the Declaratory Act had spelled out in no uncertain terms Parliament's claims to be able to do anything it chose in America, without consulting Americans. This dubious privilege Parliament finally pushed to the limit in the "Intolerable acts." The colonies' answer was a call for an intercolonial congress to meet in September, 1774.

THE FIRST CONTINENTAL CONGRESS

All of the colonies except Georgia sent representatives to the First Continental Congress, which met in Carpenters' Hall, Philadelphia. The group in attendance represented many points of view. The Patriot group came well represented by the two Adamses, Patrick Henry, Richard Henry Lee, and Christopher Gadsden, among others. These men knew what they wanted and worked tirelessly on the moderate and conservative men to win them over. Joseph Galloway balefully observed that Sam Adams "eats little, sleeps little, thinks much and is most decisive and indefatigable in the pursuit of his objects." The moderate and conservative opinion in the colonies had such able spokesmen as George Washington, Payton Randolph, Joseph Galloway, John Dickinson, and John Jay.

The arguments of the Patriots had their effect. The Congress proposed a complete revision of the machinery for governing the colonies that would have given America a grand council to share power with Parliament on colonial matters and a president-

general with the right to veto all parliamentary acts affecting the colonies. Galloway's plan was defeated by a narrow margin of six colonies to five after a much more radical plan advanced by Sam Adams of Massachusetts was adopted. This plan, already adopted in Massachusetts as the Suffolk Resolves, called on the colonies to raise troops and to suspend all trade with Great Britain. These proposals were adopted unanimously. In a move to conciliate to the moderate element at the convention, a new written petition of colonial grievances was also sent to the British government.

Of as much importance was the new trade embargo decided upon under the name of the "Continental Association." Under its provisions, on every level of government—town, county, and provincial—committees would be set up to enforce nonimportation, nonexportation, and nonconsumption of British goods. They were to encourage frugality among the populace and to publish the names of those who violated the agreement, as well as check all customs entries. These committees quickly fell into the hands of the revolutionary elements in the colonies who enforced the boycott rigorously and often violently in the first few months. The creation of this association was of great importance, not because of its effect on Britain, which was little, but because of its effect on opinion in the colonies. More moderate and conservative men now had to decide which side they were going to take. A man like Washington supported the policy of resistance. Joseph Galloway would not, and eventually sided with Britain.

Parliament responded by passing two conflicting measures. One was intended to be a conciliatory act, which permitted each colony to tax itself and *then* hand the money over to England, thus getting around Parliament's direct supervision of tax collection. The other act was punitive; it forbade New England fishermen to fish off

Newfoundland and extended the navigation acts until they covered *all* commerce. New England could now trade only with Britain, no matter what goods were bought or sold. Simultaneously, the government called a halt to the exportation of all British weapons and ammunition to America.

England was ready for war. America was almost ready for independence. As John Adams later wrote of the First Continental Congress, "The revolution was complete, in the minds of the people, and the Union of the colonies, before the war commenced." The war actually began when the governor of Massachusetts, General Gage, sent seven hundred soldiers on April 19, 1775, to Concord to confiscate a supply of weapons stored there by the colonial militia. When the commanding officer, Major John Pitcairn, arrived at the town of Lexington, he found the colonial militia ready to halt his progress. No one knows who fired the first shot, but when the smoke cleared, the Redcoats had killed eight Americans and wounded ten.

Pitcairn hurried on to Concord, where the British seized a few supplies (most of the munitions had already been spirited away by the militia). Two colonial and three British soldiers died. On the way back to Boston, however, Pitcairn faced a real danger. Summoned by riders like Paul Revere, who had ridden across the countryside calling for resistance, four thousand Americans lined the road to Boston and fired on the British regulars from behind rocks and trees. By the time Pitcairn limped back into Boston, 73 of his men had been killed and 174 wounded. That night the colonial militia laid siege to the city.

The first battle of the Revolution took place in Lexington, Mass., when British troops, on their way to Concord to seize a colonial arsenal, were stopped by a colonial militia. The Battle of Lexington resulted in 8 American deaths and 10 wounded. This engraving shows the typical disorder of the highly regimented British troops when confronted with "uncivilized" colonials who would not line up in the open for battle.

155

THE SECOND CONTINENTAL CONGRESS

During 1774 to 1775 royal control over the other colonies was crumbling rapidly. Most of the governors fled to British warships for safety and the assemblies continued to meet outside the authority of British law. Caution was the keynote and mob rule never took over. The assemblies proceeded to raise troops and issue paper money, preparing for the inevitable clash.

A Grant Wood painting of the Midnight Ride of Paul Revere. After the battle of Lexington, British troops, on their way to Boston, went through Concord to seize weapons. The skirmish at Concord resulted in two colonial deaths. In retaliation, 4,000 colonials, who were summoned by Revere and other riders, lined the road to Boston and fired upon the British as they marched by.

In May, 1775, only a month after the battles of Lexington and Concord, the Second Continental Congress assembled in Philadelphia. The streets of the town were festooned with banners proclaiming "Liberty or Death" and an escort of soldiers led a solemn parade the day the delegation from New England arrived. Meeting in the dignified statehouse was a brilliant assembly of the colonies' most gifted men. Some of them had attended the First Congress: John and Sam Adams were the most notable. Among the new faces were Thomas Jefferson, the quiet, very tall, shy Virginian who had just published *A Summary View of the Rights of British America,* in which he had stated that "Kings are the servants, not the proprietors of the people." Benjamin Franklin was present (he had returned from England only 4 days earlier). George Washington came in the blue uniform of the Virginia militia. The president of the Congress was John Hancock, Boston's richest merchant, who, according to rumor, had been one of the "Indians" at the Boston Tea Party.

The Second Continental Congress was expected to make important decisions, although the colonies had not provided it with very much authority. The Congress obviously had no legal power at all in the eyes of the king, and only provisional authority in the eyes of the colonists. Nevertheless, the Congress immediately dealt boldly with the military crisis in Massachusetts. The militia surrounding Boston were formed into a Continental Army and George Washington was appointed commander-in-chief.

BUNKER HILL

Washington left to join his troops on June 23, but 6 days earlier the worst battle of the entire Revolution had already been fought. The Patriots had seized Bunker Hill and Breed's Hill in Charlestown and were preparing to pound Boston with artillery. General Gage ordered his men to retake the hills—and they did, at a terrible cost. More than a thousand English troops fell, virtually half of those in the action. The Patriots lost only about four hundred men. Although the British regained possession of the hill (actually Breed's Hill), Americans counted the so-called Battle of Bunker Hill an American victory.

Meanwhile, the varying views of how to proceed in the crisis facing the colonies were reflected in steps being taken in Philadelphia. On July 5, Congress sent George III the Olive Branch Petition, which denounced Parliament and begged the king to free the colonies of its incompetent management. The very next day, however, Congress approved a Declaration of Causes of Taking-up of Arms, announcing, "the arms we have been compelled by our enemies to assume, we will, in defiance of every hazard . . . employ for the preservation of our liberties; being with one mind resolved to die Freemen rather than live Slaves." A secret Committee of Correspondence was created to write to America's friends abroad for support. Congress also ordered an attack on Canada, created officials to deal with the Indians, authorized the outfitting of a navy, and urged the colonies to appoint Committees of Safety to direct local military operations against the English.

COLONIAL HESITANCY

Despite all these decisive moves, the Congress seemed reluctant to take the final step —an official declaration of independence from England. Colonists had always regarded themselves as Englishmen and only secondarily as "Americans." English liberties were what they had been clamoring for. The terrible word *traitor*—and the realization of what happened to defeated, unsuccessful traitors—weighed heavily on the minds of many Americans. Upper-class Americans feared that a revolution might go too far and not only drive out the English but also expel America's native aristocracy. Once the mob was unleashed, who knew how violent it might become? Finally, no colony in the modern history of the world had ever rebelled against its mother country before. John Adams compared America to a house filled with thirteen clocks where each one must be set so that they would chime at the same time. Although the North and the South were ready for independence, the Middle colonies still longed for reconciliation.

By the end of 1775, all four New England colonies wanted independence. On November 9, Congress had learned that the king had refused to read the Olive Branch Petition and was, instead, sending 20,000 troops to the New World. The king had also proclaimed that every member of the Congress was a traitor. The moderates saw that they would be hanged no matter what position they now took. The soldiers on their way to America, it was learned, were not ordinary English troops, but rather paid German soldiers. The colonists believed that these Hessians would ravage the land, making no distinction between those citizens who remained loyal to the king and those in rebellion. Mercenaries would take whatever they could get from whomever they could overpower.

The final incentive for an open break with England came in January, 1776, when the pamphleteer Thomas Paine published his *Common Sense*. All America was aroused. About 150,000 copies were sold in a few months and those people who did not buy it borrowed a copy from others. Paine, an Englishman who had been living in America for only a year, attacked the king and the very idea of monarchy. He called George III a "royal brute" and declared, "Of more worth is one honest man to society and in the sight of God than all the crowned ruffians who ever lived." Respect for the king had been bred into most Americans almost as strongly as respect for God, but suddenly an eloquent propagandist was calling for the abolishment of all royalty and the establishment of a republican form of government. British society, Paine firmly announced, was corrupt and tended to corrupt America. These striking ideas seemed to most Americans the very essence of common sense, and revolutionaries who had whispered the same sentiments in the dark now discussed them openly.

THE DECLARATION OF INDEPENDENCE

Paine's impassioned attack on England unleashed American patriotism and spurred the Continental Congress forward. In March, Congress directed American ships to raid British vessels. The next month, America's ports were opened to foreign shipping. In May, the colonial assemblies were asked to establish new state governments.

On July 2, 1776, Congress adopted a resolution that had been introduced a month earlier by Richard Henry Lee. The first sentence read:

That these United Colonies are, and of right ought to be, free and independent states, that they are absolved from all allegiance to the British crown, and that all

political connection between them and the state of Great Britain is, and ought to be, totally dissolved.

A committee had been chosen early in June to draw up a document that would justify American independence to the world. Thomas Jefferson, Benjamin Franklin, John Adams, Robert Livingston of New York, and Roger Sherman of Connecticut were appointed to accomplish the important task. Because Jefferson received the largest number of votes, he was the committee chairman and the man responsible for the actual wording of the document. (He tried to get Adams to write it, but Adams considered Jefferson the better writer.) On July 2, the paper was read to the Congress and all the colonies approved it, except New York, which abstained. Since no negative votes had been recorded, Congress spent the next two days editing the manuscript, cutting it by about a third (removing a long passage that blamed American slavery on the king of England). On the fourth of July, "The Unanimous Declaration of the Thirteen United States of America" was sent to the printer. When it was read to the public four days later, a crowd tore the king's coat of arms from over the door of the statehouse and that night abandoned itself to great demonstrations of joy.

The declaration had two parts. The first part, the more important, justified the right of a people to rebel against a government that denied them their natural rights.

The sentiments in this section were indeed self-evident for most educated Americans of the eighteenth century. They knew the great ideas of the Enlightenment as expressed either in the works of John Locke, or as handed down in the dozens of sermons or pamphlets on the foundations of government written in the past hundred years. Jefferson paraphrased the words of Locke's *Two Treatises of Government:* "Men being . . . all free, equal and independent, no

one can be put out of his estate and subjected to the political power of another
without his consent." Moreover, Locke had
reminded his readers that "absolute monarchs are but men." When John Adams,
who rather envied Jefferson, accused him of
having simply mouthed commonplaces in
the declaration, Jefferson modestly replied,
"I did not consider it any part of my charge
to invent new ideas, but to place before
mankind the common sense of the subject,
in terms so plain and firm as to command
their assent. It was intended to be an expression of the American mind."

In the second part of the declaration,
Jefferson listed the crimes against Americans committed by the king. The king was
blamed for dissolving "representative houses
repeatedly for opposing with manly firmness his invasion on the right of the people"; for putting off elections of public
officials; for paying judges directly instead
of allowing colonial assemblies to determine
their salaries and for keeping "among us in
times of peace standing armies, without the
consent of our legislatures." The king was
also accused of "cutting off our trade with
all parts of the world; for imposing taxes
on us without our consent"—and for a host
of other "injuries and usurpations."

The one issue that had been most debated before the Revolution was Parliament's right to tax and otherwise legislate
for the colonies, but, in the declaration
Parliament was not mentioned by name at
all and only once indirectly. George III
was singled out as the tyrant and he alone
was made responsible for British oppression. Since the declaration was directed not
just to Americans but also to the people
of the world as a justification for colonial
action, Jefferson undoubtedly presented it
in a way that would be readily understood
by foreigners. Prussians, Spaniards, Frenchmen could not be expected to understand
complex references to the British parliamentary system, but they would respond
to the denunciation of a tyrannical king.

Moreover, Jefferson did not want to attack a symbol of representative government
when the revolution was being made in the
name of the sanctity of representative institutions.

Interpretation of the Revolution

 *Why did the Continental Congress finally
declare the independence of America?
What motives inspired the delegates?
What were the true reasons for the rupture
and what did the colonists hope to
accomplish? These questions have been
answered in several ways by American
historians in various eras.*

*Through most of the nineteenth century,
American historians piously accepted the
Founding Fathers on their word. The
Revolution had been fought for life,
liberty, and the pursuit of happiness, and
as a blow against tyranny. The outstanding
spokesman of this orthodox, "patriotic"
point of view was George Bancroft, whose
ten-volume* History of the United States
*was issued between the 1830s and 1870s.
Writing during a period when America
was torn apart by its bloody Civil War,
Bancroft summoned up a nostalgic image
of an earlier united nation, a country that
had been guided by the purity of its ideals.*

*Bancroft's morally uplifting
interpretation was discarded by the
historians of the last decade of the
nineteenth century. Relations between
Britain and the United States had become
much friendlier in this period and many
American historians became great admirers
of the British, enthusiastically praising
their accomplishments. These scholars,
known as the imperial school of historians,
were headed by George L. Beer, Charles
M. Andrews, and Lawrence H. Gipson.
Beer studied Britain's commerical policies
during the seventeenth and eighteenth
centuries and concluded that the mercantile*

system, far from restricting American economy, had fostered the colonies' prosperity. Andrews and Gipson both claimed that the Navigation acts had been enlightened and liberal pieces of legislation. Andrews concluded that the Revolution had been fought because, as Americans had evolved toward a concept of greater and greater colonial independence, England had drifted toward a theory of tighter and tighter imperial controls: "On the one side was the immutable, stereotyped system of the mother country, based on precedent and tradition and designed to keep things comfortably as they were; on the other, a vital, dynamic organism, containing the seeds of a great nation, its forces untried, still to be proved."

The imperial school saw the Revolution as a constitutional struggle between two different concepts of what a colony should be, but the progressive historians of the early twentieth century considered the Revolution a class struggle that had been economically determined. The progressives were deeply influenced by the growing socialist movement in America, the ideas of Marx, and the general social unrest of their era. Some of the flavor of their writing can be grasped by the very titles of their books: An Economic Interpretation of the Constitution by Charles A. Beard; Arthur M. Schlesinger's The Colonial Merchants and the American Revolution; and J. Franklin Jameson's The American Revolution Considered as a Social Movement. Beard felt that a true understanding of the nation's early years must include the recognition of a conflict not only between England and America but also between the haves and have-nots within the colonies. Schlesinger argued that rich merchants had started the revolutionary movement because they were losing money as a result of Britain's economic policies following the French and Indian War. Once independence had been declared, however, the rich became more afraid of their poor countrymen than of England and, as a consequence, the merchant class became lukewarm toward the Revolution. Jameson drew attention to the extraordinary advances democracy made during the Revolution. Property qualifications for voting were lowered, the vast estates of Tories (those who remained loyal to the crown) were confiscated and distributed to poor farmers, and lands that had formerly been controlled by England were opened to the mass of Americans. (See Chapter 5.)

After World War II, a school of historians emerged which reflected the conservative climate of opinion in the nation. Robert E. Brown and Daniel J. Boorstin were the best known of these scholars. The progressives had insisted that the Revolution was the culmination of a movement by the masses to gain economic and political equality in an undemocratic society. The neoconservative historians, Brown and Boorstin, challenged the theory that colonial America had been undemocratic. In Middle-Class Democracy and the Revolution Brown set out to demonstrate that at least in Massachusetts the vast majority of men had owned enough property to vote. The purpose of the Revolution had been not a radical *desire for social reform, Brown maintained, but rather a conservative longing for the good old days before the French and Indian War. Boorstin, agreeing with this viewpoint in* The Genius of American Politics, *felt that the colonists rebelled against England because they wanted to retain the* status quo, *which they were quite content to preserve. The English were the radicals, because it was they who wanted to change the existing order.*

Finally, in recent years a variation on this theme has been offered, which interprets the Revolution as a moment in the history of ideas. Bernard Bailyn in his Pamphlets of the American Revolution *regards the Revolution as the climax of a developing theory of politics in America. By studying the writings of scores of colonial thinkers and apologists for the Revolution, Bailyn traces the origin and underlines the importance of ideas that had sprung from English common law, Enlightenment philosophers, and New England Puritanism. American revolutionary thought held that every man's longing for power was a natural but corrupting lust that government had to control lest it infringe on the liberties of other people. The colonists had interpreted the actions of the British government after 1763 as deliberate and sinister efforts to deprive men in both England and America of their liberty. In taking up arms against England, Bailyn concludes, Americans had been most strongly motivated by a love of the rights of Englishmen which by 1776 had been expanded into the universal concept of the rights of man.* ""

Readings

GENERAL WORKS

Andrews, Charles M., *The Colonial Background of the American Revolution*. New Haven: Yale University Press, 1961—In four essays dealing with the relationship between Britain and the colonies, Andrews shows how the Revolution was the inevitable result of conflict of motives and colonial policy originating in the 1600s.

Bancroft, George, *History of the United States of America from the Discovery of the Continent*, Vols. I–VI. Chicago: University of Chicago Press, 1966—Bancroft, regarded as the "Father of American History," spent 40 years (1834–1874) writing this scholarly treatise on the American government and people. It is still a major source work and one of the classic histories of early America.

Gipson, Lawrence H., *The British Empire Before the American Revolution*, Vols. I–XV. New York: Knopf, 1936–1970—This is a monumental and authoritative history of the British Empire in America.

Knollenberg, Bernhard, *Origin of the American Revolution: 1759–1766*. New York: Macmillan, 1965—A study of the events which almost led to rebellion in 1765–1766. The author's thesis is that the Stamp Act crisis was only one of many incidents which finally provoked revolution in 1775.

Miller, John C., *Origins of the American Revolution*. Boston: Little, Brown, 1943—This is a scholarly history of the background of the American Revolution with vivid accounts of the American leaders. It does not follow the thesis of "economic determinism" proposed by Charles Beard, popular in the 1930s and 1940s.

———, *Triumph of Freedom, 1775–1783*. Boston: Little, Brown, 1948—This is a complete account of the American Revolution. The author provides colorful portraits of the people and events of the time.

Morgan, Edmund S., *Birth of the Republic, 1763–1789*. Chicago: University of Chicago Press, 1956—This brief and very readable study of the American Revolutionary period is well balanced, giving the views of both the British and American sides.

Namier, Lewis B., *England in the Age of the American Revolution*. New York: St. Martin's Press, 1961—The volume discusses British politics between 1760 and 1783. Of particular importance is the survey of the political climate at the accession of George III.

Peckham, Howard H., *The Colonial Wars, 1689–1762*. Chicago: University of Chicago Press, 1963—Peckham vividly describes the rivalries among Spain, England, and France in Europe and the effects of these rivalries in the New World. A good narrative history of pre-Revolutionary America.

Trevelyan, George O., *The American Revolution,* Richard B. Morris, ed. New York: David McKay, 1964—This is a condensation of the original six-volume detailed history of the American Revolution by an eminent British historian.

SPECIAL STUDIES

Bailyn, Bernard, *Ideological Origins of the American Revolution.* Cambridge: Harvard University Press, 1967—The author traces the specific attitudes, conceptions, and particular phrases, which together formed the American Revolutionary ideology.

Becker, Carl L., *The Declaration of Independence: A Study in the History of Political Ideas.* New York: Harcourt Brace Jovanovich, 1922—Becker, former professor of European history at Cornell University, discusses the political philosophy and historical basis of the document.

Brown, Robert E., *Middle Class Democracy and the Revolution in Massachusetts, 1691–1780.* Ithaca, N.Y.: Cornell University Press, 1955—The author seeks to document his thesis that the Revolution was fought primarily to preserve an existing democracy, not to institute it.

Green, Jack P., *The Quest for Power: The Lower Houses of Assembly in the Southern Royal Colonies, 1689–1776.* Chapel Hill, N.C.: University of North Carolina Press, 1963—A good study of the growth of colonial assemblies as a focal point of power, how this power was acquired, and how it was later challenged by the British.

Labaree, Benjamin W., *The Boston Tea Party.* Oxford: Oxford University Press, 1964—A thorough study of the events leading up to the Boston Tea Party and the results of that incident in the Revolutionary movement.

Morgan, Edmund S., and Helen M. Morgan, *The Stamp Act Crisis: Prologue to Revolution.* Chapel Hill, N.C.: University of North Carolina Press, 1953 (Paper: Collier Books, 1963)—An intensive study of the two-year period of 1764 and 1765, which saw the beginning of the American revolutionary movement.

Schlesinger, Arthur M., *The Colonial Merchants and the American Revolution.* New York: Atheneum, 1968—This study by an eminent Harvard historian shows how colonial trade interests helped bring about the Revolution by boycotts of British trade restrictions.

PRIMARY SOURCES

Commager, Henry S., and Richard B. Morris, eds., *The Spirit of Seventy-Six: The Story of the American Revolution As Told by*

Participants, Vols. I–II. New York: Harper & Row, 1967—A comprehensive collection of the literature of the period: diaries, journals, letters, orderly books, and official Congressional records.

Fithian, Philip V., *Journal and Letters of Philip V. Fithian, 1773–1774: A Plantation Tutor at the Old Dominion.* Charlottesville, Va.: University Press of Virginia, 1968—Fithian, a young Princeton graduate, wrote of his experiences on a Virginia plantation prior to the Revolution. Fithian's journal contains remarks on political and social issues of the day.

Morgan, Edmund S., *Prologue to Revolution: Sources and Documents on the Stamp Act Crisis.* Chapel Hill, N.C.: University of North Carolina Press, 1959—Original writings and publications from the period (1765) selected to illustrate the growing revolutionary movement in the colonies.

Oliver, Peter, *Peter Oliver's Origin and Progress of the American Revolution: A Tory View,* Douglas Adair, ed. Calif.: Stanford University Press, 1961—Oliver believed that British rule was helpful to the colonies and that the revolutionaries were a dangerous, vulgar mob led by demogogues.

Paine, Thomas, *Common Sense* and *Crisis.* New York: Doubleday, 1970—These two pamphlets were written in 1776 in support of the Revolution and brought Paine immediate recognition as a leading writer in the colonies. *Common Sense* states that American independence would help liberate mankind; *Crisis* urges revolutionaries to stand fast against the British.

BIOGRAPHIES

Chinard, Gilbert, *Honest John Adams.* Boston: Little, Brown, 1933—This is an excellent biography of the revolutionary leader and second President of the United States. The author traces the development of Adams's political theory, drawing largely upon original documents, letters, and diaries.

Crane, Verner W., *Benjamin Franklin and a Rising People,* Oscar Handlin, ed. Boston: Little, Brown, 1954—This is a scholarly study of Franklin's contributions as author, philosopher, scientist, and statesman.

Cunliffe, Marcus, *George Washington: Man and Monument.* Boston: Little, Brown, 1958—The author describes the Washington of popular myth and then attempts to reveal the real person in a rather short biography.

Forbes, Esther, *Paul Revere and the World He Lived In.* Boston: Houghton Mifflin, 1942—This is a popular biography of the silversmith who became a hero for his famous ride in 1775.

Malone, Dumas, *Jefferson and His Time: Jefferson the Virginian,* Vol. I. Boston: Little, Brown, 1948—This first volume of a multi-volume work on Jefferson covers his ancestry and first 41 years of his life. A complete and interesting study.

Miller, John C., *Sam Adams: Pioneer in Propaganda.* Boston: Little, Brown, 1936—A fascinating account of how Adams used propaganda to bring about the Declaration of Independence.

Morison, Samuel E., *John Paul Jones: A Sailor's Biography.* Boston: Little, Brown, 1959—A Pulitzer Prize-winning portrait of the Revolutionary War sea captain, his war cruises and battles.

Washington, George, *Journal of Major George Washington,* James R. Short and Thaddeus W. Tate, Jr., eds. Charlottesville, Va.: University Press of Virginia, 1963—The *Journal,* written in 1753 during a military expedition to the colonial frontier, reflects the French-British crisis in Europe and North America.

HISTORICAL NOVELS

Cannon, Legrand, Jr., *Look to the Mountain.* New York: Holt, Rinehart and Winston, 1942—An historical novel about pioneering in New Hampshire from 1769 to 1777. Political and military events of the period are sharply contrasted with the daily struggle to survive in the wilderness.

Churchill, Winston, *Richard Carvel.* New York: Macmillan, 1914—Not to be confused with the British statesman, Churchill was a turn-of-the-century American who wrote this historical novel of eighteenth-century Maryland.

Forbes, Esther, *Johnny Tremain.* New York: Dell, 1969—The beginnings of the American Revolution in Boston as seen through the eyes of a young apprenticed silversmith. The novel won several literary prizes.

Gordon, Caroline, *Green Centuries.* New York: Scribner's, 1941—This is a novel about life on the frontier of Kentucky and Tennessee before the American Revolution.

Roberts, Kenneth, *Arundel* (1944), *Lydia Bailey* (1947), *Northwest Passage, Oliver Wiswell* (1940), *Rabble in Arms* (1947). New York: Doubleday (Paper: Fawcett, 1970)—These novels about America in the eighteenth century are good fiction based on historical facts. They are vivid accounts of America's heroic men, women, and events.

166

5

The Emergence of a Nation

We hold these truths to be self-evident, that all men are created equal, that they are endowed by their Creator with certain unalienable rights, that among these are life, liberty, and the pursuit of happiness. That to secure these rights, governments are instituted among men, deriving their just powers from the consent of the governed; that whenever any form of government becomes destructive of these ends, it is the right of the people to alter or to abolish it, . . .

—The Declaration of Independence

America had declared its independence, but unlike most other nations embarking on a war, it was a country fighting for its rights before it had a national government. There was a Continental Congress, but it had the authority neither to enact binding legislation nor to tax. America had no army, no navy, no real government, and a population of 2.5 million people. Britain, in contrast, was a mighty power of 10 million people with a highly trained army and the world's best navy.

A British cartoon depicting an American rifleman as wounded, sick, and feebleminded. The words on the cap of the rifleman are the words of Patrick Henry: "Give me liberty or give me death."

167

THE REVOLUTION

America was not only faced with an impressive enemy abroad, but was beset by opposition within from those who remained loyal to the king. An estimated one-fifth to one-third of the population sympathized with the English, and eventually 100,000 Tories (or Loyalists) emigrated from America. Some returned to England but many settled in the Canadian provinces of Quebec and Nova Scotia.

Tories came from all classes. The largest number of known Tories came from among the ranks of officeholders, Anglican clergymen, landowners, and merchants. Many middle- and lower-class farmers from the Middle and Southern colonies may have been Tories because they did not understand what the Revolution was about, because they did not want violence, or because they feared the colonial aristocracy more than they feared the British government. It is believed a majority of the population in New Jersey, New York, North Carolina, and Georgia were Tories. There were also many in Pennsylvania. Loyalist sentiment was weakest in Virginia, Maryland, and New England.

In addition to those Americans who were actively opposed to the Revolution, probably one-fifth to one-third of the population remained uninterested or unmoved by the break with England. Many such Americans simply refused to take part one way or another in the war effort.

RAISING AN ARMY

Before the Continental Congress could be concerned with forging a national spirit and establishing an American government, the men assembled in Philadelphia needed to make certain there would be a nation to govern. They had to create an effective army to drive out the British.

Bunker Hill had demonstrated that American Patriots were not always as ineffective in battle as the British liked to think they were. However, the men encamped around Boston were not a disciplined army, but rather, a hastily assembled gathering of outraged citizens. To weld such scattered units into an efficient fighting instrument, George Washington took command at Cambridge on July 3, 1775. One of Washington's first tasks was to choose a new staff. The militia units were accustomed to electing their own officers, but popularity had proved to have no relation to tactical ability. Washington dismissed many of the unfit officers and appointed his own.

He was unable, however, to control the length of time his men served. Most soldiers were farmers and few could afford to be away from their fields for long. They were willing to serve for a few months, but just when they were beginning to learn how to follow orders or fire a musket, they had to return home to harvest the crops. Indeed, terms of service were so short that although some 400,000 Americans took up arms at one time or another during the 8 years of the war, Washington never had more than 17,000 men serving under him at any one time and his army often numbered less than 5,000 men. Soldiers begged for release from military service on the grounds that their crops would wither and their families go hungry.

Serving in the army was in fact a terrible economic burden for most soldiers. Officers had to pay most of their own expenses and ordinary soldiers were paid very low salaries in paper money issued by the Continental Congress. Because the paper had little backing in gold or silver, it declined in value every year. One of the earliest expressions to come out of the Revolution was that something was "not worth a Continental."

Much more profitable than fighting as a soldier was sailing as a privateer. The various states instructed local shipowners to make pirate raids on English vessels. Some 20,000 sailors took to the high seas as privateers and the majority reaped great fortunes from their labors. During the Revolution Britain lost 2,000 ships and some 12,000

A German rendition of the American soldier. Although over 400,000 Americans served during the Revolution, many men had to leave the army to return home to tend their crops.

sailors to American privateers. The losses damaged both Britain's navy and its economy.

The triumphs of American privateers, however, did nothing to solve Washington's problems. The Continental Congress had no power to draft soldiers or requisition supplies. Only with tact and eloquence was Washington able to convince ten thousand militiamen to remain in service in the Continental Army until the end of 1776. He was dependent on the state governments for an additional backup force of seven thousand militiamen and for the supplies to feed, arm, and house his men. Not only was Washington short of supplies, he also lacked a trained staff. Fortunately, he was aided by a few aristocratic officers from abroad such as Baron Friedrich von Steuben of Prussia, who was particularly helpful in drilling raw recruits, Count Casimir Pulaski of Poland, and the French Marquis de Lafayette.

FINANCING THE WAR

In addition to military deficiencies, the country experienced grave difficulties in financing the war effort. The Revolution was, in essence, a war fought against taxation, yet it was necessary for the Congress to demand money from Americans in order to pay the costs of rebellion. Congress invented three solutions to its economic problems: it borrowed money, it requested money from the states, and it printed paper money. About 8 million dollars was borrowed from American citizens through the sale of national bonds, and foreign governments lent another 8 million. In response to requests, state governments contributed some 5.5 million dollars. Finally, Congress issued more than 240 million dollars' worth of paper money. America, as noted earlier, had always been short of hard money (gold and silver). During the Revolution, when the shortage was aggravated, wealthy Tories

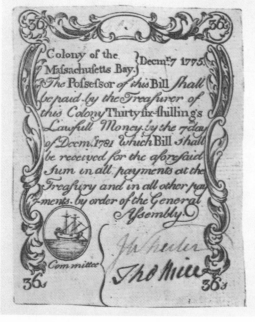

fled with most of the existing supply.

The individual states also issued their own paper money. Soon there were fourteen different currencies in circulation. As more and more paper notes were printed, the buying power of the different currencies fell well below face value. This led to an inflation of prices which was worsened by American entrepreneurs who, thinking only of their own profits, kept hiking the price of war supplies. Far from regarding such profiteering as disloyal, one merchant smugly declared: "It seems to me that the present opportunity of improving our fortunes ought not to be lost, especially as the very means of doing it will contribute to the service of our country."

STRATEGIC ADVANTAGES

Although America was burdened with serious military and financial problems, Britain had certain disadvantages which weighed heavily in favor of the rebels. Britain was 3,000 miles away. In past wars Britain had depended on the colonies to supply its troops with food and ammunition, but now at least in theory, all supplies had to be shipped across the Atlantic. Also, there was no single American city that was so central, so crucially important, that by taking it Britain could win the war. In the French and Indian War, Britain had won Canada by conquering Quebec and Montreal, but in America the English had to deploy their forces over the length of the

A 10-shilling note issued by the Colony of New York in 1771 and a 36-shilling note issued by the Massachusetts Bay Colony in 1775. In order to help Congress finance the war, state governments contributed about $5.5 million through state-backed paper money.

Atlantic coastline and into the interior at selected points. Most of this vast territory was not accessible by road, for few roads existed. As one English officer said, the lack of roads "absolutely prevented us this whole war from going fifteen miles from a navigable river."

Most important, the war had little support from the people of England. Many British politicians had no enthusiasm for what they considered a civil war in the Empire. Britain was still staggering under its debts from other recent wars and powerful enemies on the Continent were eager for another opportunity to show that they could humble her. Should British forces be fighting a costly war thousands of miles away against Americans, who, after all, were for the most part English in origin, when these forces might suddenly be needed to defend the mother country against French or Spanish attacks? To many Englishmen the answer was clearly "no."

FIRST CONFLICTS WITH THE BRITISH

The first major theater of the war was around Boston. The Battle of Bunker Hill had been fought in June, 1775. When dislodged from Breed's Hill the American troops under Washington fortified Dorchester Heights, which overlooked the city from the south. Washington set up fifty-nine cannon and mortars that had been dragged across the country from Fort Ticonderoga, which Ethan Allen and Benedict Arnold had captured in May, 1775. Rather than risk another battle as bloody as Bunker Hill, the English commander, General William Howe, withdrew his forces (and a thousand Bostonian Tories) from the city and sailed to Halifax, Nova Scotia. Thus abandoned, Boston was occupied by Washington on March 17, 1776.

During the opening months of the war, everything seemed to favor the Americans

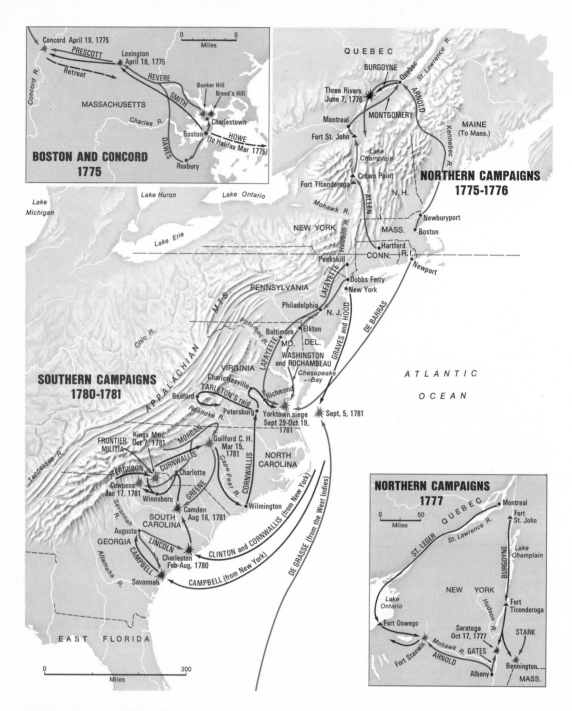

BOSTON AND CONCORD 1775

Concord April 19, 1775
PRESCOTT
Lexington April 19, 1775
Retreat
REVERE
Concord R.
Bunker Hill
Breed's Hill
MASSACHUSETTS
SMITH
Charles R.
Charlestown
Boston
HOWE (to Halifax Mar. 1775)
DAWES
Roxbury
0 Miles 5

NORTHERN CAMPAIGNS 1775-1776

QUEBEC
BURGOYNE
Quebec
St. Lawrence R.
Three Rivers June 7, 1776
ARNOLD
Montreal
MONTGOMERY
MAINE (To Mass.)
Fort St. John
Kennebec R.
Lake Champlain
Fort Ticonderoga
Crown Point
N. H.
ALLEN
Mohawk R.
Hudson R.
Newburyport
NEW YORK
MASS.
Boston
Hartford
CONN.
R.I.
Peekskill
Newport

Lake Michigan
Lake Huron
Lake Ontario
Lake Erie

SOUTHERN CAMPAIGNS 1780-1781

PENNSYLVANIA
LAFAYETTE
Dobbs Ferry
New York
Philadelphia
N. J.
DE BARRAS
Ohio R.
M T S.
Potomac R.
Baltimore
Elkton
MD.
DEL.
WASHINGTON and ROCHAMBEAU
GRAVES and HOOD
VIRGINIA
Charlottesville
LAFAYETTE
Richmond
Chesapeake Bay
A T L A N T I C
O C E A N
APPALACHIAN
Bedford
TARLETON's raid
Roanoke R.
Petersburg
Yorktown siege Sept 29-Oct 19, 1781
Sept. 5, 1781
Kings Mtn. Oct 7, 1781
MORGAN
Guilford C. H. Mar 15, 1781
FRONTIER MILITIA
CORNWALLIS
Cape Fear R.
NORTH CAROLINA
Tennessee R.
FERGUSON
Charlotte
GREENE
CORNWALLIS
Cowpens Jan 17, 1781
Winnsboro
Camden Aug 16, 1781
Wilmington
Savannah R.
SOUTH CAROLINA
Augusta
LINCOLN
GEORGIA
Charleston Feb-Aug, 1780
CLINTON and CORNWALLIS (from New York)
CAMPBELL
Altamaha R.
Savannah
CAMPBELL (from New York)
DE GRASSE (from the West Indies)
E A S T   F L O R I D A

0 Miles 300

NORTHERN CAMPAIGNS 1777

QUEBEC
Montreal
Fort St. John
ST. LEGER
St. Lawrence R.
Lake Champlain
BURGOYNE
NEW YORK
Fort Ticonderoga
Lake Ontario
Hudson R.
Fort Oswego
Saratoga Oct 17, 1777
GATES
STARK
Fort Stanwix
Mohawk R.
ARNOLD
Bennington
Albany
MASS.
0 Miles 50

MILITARY CAMPAIGNS OF THE REVOLUTION

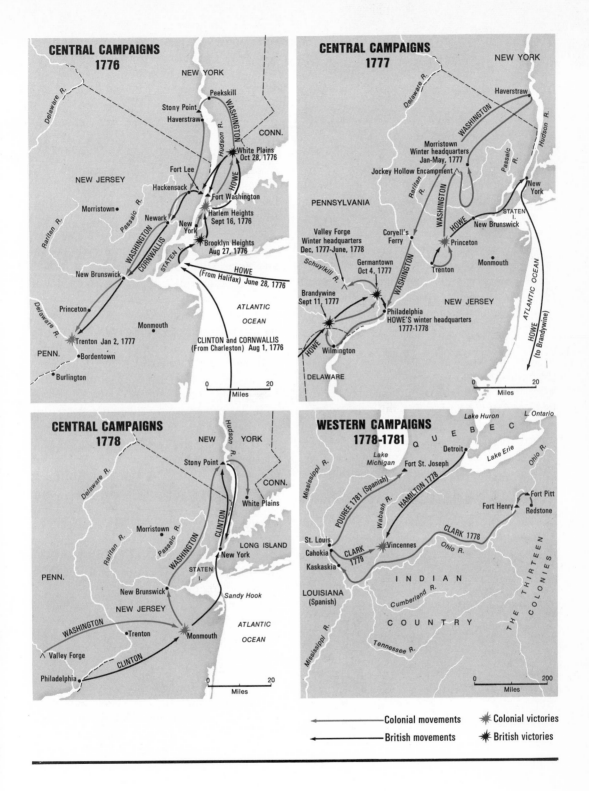

CENTRAL CAMPAIGNS 1776

NEW YORK
Peekskill
Stony Point
Haverstraw
CONN.
Hudson R.
WASHINGTON
Delaware R.
NEW JERSEY
White Plains Oct 28, 1776
Fort Lee
HOWE
Hackensack
Morristown
Passaic R.
Fort Washington
Harlem Heights Sept 16, 1776
Newark
New York
Raritan R.
WASHINGTON
CORNWALLIS
STATEN I.
Brooklyn Heights Aug 27, 1776
New Brunswick
HOWE (From Halifax) June 28, 1776
ATLANTIC OCEAN
Princeton
Delaware R.
Monmouth
Trenton Jan 2, 1777
CLINTON and CORNWALLIS (From Charleston) Aug 1, 1776
PENN.
Bordentown
Burlington
0   20
Miles

CENTRAL CAMPAIGNS 1777

NEW YORK
Delaware R.
Haverstraw
WASHINGTON
Hudson R.
Morristown Winter headquarters Jan-May, 1777
Passaic R.
New York
Jockey Hollow Encampment
Raritan R.
WASHINGTON
HOWE
STATEN I.
New Brunswick
PENNSYLVANIA
Valley Forge Winter headquarters Dec, 1777-June, 1778
Coryell's Ferry
Princeton
Schuylkill R.
Germantown Oct 4, 1777
WASHINGTON
Trenton
Monmouth
Brandywine Sept 11, 1777
NEW JERSEY
Philadelphia HOWE'S winter headquarters 1777-1778
ATLANTIC OCEAN
HOWE (to Brandywine)
HOWE
Wilmington
DELAWARE
0   20
Miles

CENTRAL CAMPAIGNS 1778

NEW YORK
Hudson R.
Stony Point
Delaware R.
CONN.
White Plains
CLINTON
Morristown
Passaic R.
Raritan R.
WASHINGTON
LONG ISLAND
New York
STATEN I.
PENN.
New Brunswick
Sandy Hook
NEW JERSEY
WASHINGTON
Trenton
Monmouth
ATLANTIC OCEAN
Valley Forge
CLINTON
Philadelphia
0   20
Miles

WESTERN CAMPAIGNS 1778-1781

Lake Huron
L. Ontario
QUEBEC
Detroit
Lake Erie
Lake Michigan
Fort St. Joseph
Mississippi R.
POURÉE 1781 (Spanish)
HAMILTON 1778
Wabash R.
Ohio R.
Fort Pitt
Fort Henry
Redstone
St. Louis
Cahokia
CLARK 1778
Vincennes
Ohio R.
Kaskaskia
CLARK 1779
INDIAN
THE THIRTEEN COLONIES
LOUISIANA (Spanish)
Cumberland R.
COUNTRY
Tennessee R.
0   200
Miles

Colonial movements   ✳ Colonial victories
British movements   ✴ British victories

American sympathies before the Revolution were divided between the Tories who favored British rule, and the Patriots who favored independence. In this illustration, a group of Patriots pull down the symbol of British tyranny, a statue of King George III.

in the South. The royal governor of North Carolina had tried to secure that colony for the king, but on February 27, 1776 a thousand Patriots defeated a Tory army at the battle of Moore's Creek Bridge. Four months later, on June 1, the British tried to sail into Charleston, the largest city in the South, but they were unable to get past a fortress that guarded the harbor on Sullivan's Island. The fort was built of spongy palmetto logs and dirt which literally absorbed cannonballs. Even a tremendous barrage from British ships could not destroy it. After a 10-hour duel, the English departed.

In Canada the Americans were not as successful. True, the American general Richard Montgomery captured Montreal, but he and Benedict Arnold failed to take Quebec. Arnold's troops fought bravely, but they were greatly weakened by a long march through Maine, during which the men were reduced at one point to living on boiled candles and roasted moccasins. After the defeat at Quebec, Americans had to give up the hope that Canada would be made the fourteenth state.

THE BRITISH CAMPAIGN AGAINST NEW YORK CITY

English strategy in the early days of the Revolution was to split the colonies in half by seizing New York City. New York, be-

sides occupying a key position, had a large Tory population; half of the 100,000 Tories who were to leave America came from New York State.

To capture New York, the British put together the largest invasion force of the eighteenth century: 34,000 troops, 10,000 sailors, 400 transport vessels, and 30 warships. General William Howe was again in command of the British land forces, a large part of which he had brought with him from Nova Scotia. His brother, Admiral Richard Howe, led the naval contingent.

Washington arrived before the British and fortified Brooklyn Heights, thinking that because these bluffs overlooked the East River and the island of Manhattan they would serve as a strategic vantage point, much as Dorchester Heights had dominated Boston. Washington, however, had only 20,000 men and he himself was relatively inexperienced. The only other time he had ever been in command was in 1754, when he had led a small force in the French and Indian War.

Sir William Howe arrived with his soldiers on August 12, 1776, and camped on Staten Island. Ten days later Admiral Howe arrived with the fleet. The Howes then sent Washington a letter, asking him to submit peacefully to the superior English force. Washington refused to open the letter, which was addressed to "George Washington, Esq., etc., etc.," since it did not recognize his rank as general.

Late in August General Howe embarked from Staten Island and drove Washington out of Brooklyn Heights. After suffering heavy losses, Washington's forces crossed over to Manhattan. Howe again offered to confer with the rebels on ending the war. Congress replied with a delegation comprised of Benjamin Franklin, John Adams, and Edward Rutledge. After dining on "good claret, good bread, cold ham, tongues and mutton," Admiral Howe said sentimentally that "he felt for America as a brother, and, if America should fall, he should feel and lament it like the loss of a brother." To which Benjamin Franklin tartly replied: "My lord, we will do our utmost endeavours to save your lordship that mortification." The Americans made it clear that they would accept nothing less than independence.

In the next encounter, however, Washington's soldiers did not fulfill Franklin's hopes. Howe attacked Manhattan and chased Washington off the island and north to White Plains. Once more defeated, Washington fled to New Jersey. Washington was so dispirited that he admitted, "I think the game is pretty much up." However, in an effort to prevent complete defeat, he designed a new principle of strategy: "We should on all occasions avoid a general action or put anything to the risk, unless compelled by a necessity, into which we ought never to be drawn."

TRENTON AND PRINCETON

In December, 1776, Howe pursued Washington out of New Jersey and across the Delaware River into Pennsylvania. Howe then went into winter quarters. Washington was further discouraged by the knowledge that on December 8 the British had captured Newport, Rhode Island. In less than

After Washington's success at Trenton, a few days later he attacked the British at Princeton.

3 months the enemy had gained control over New York City and most of New Jersey. Washington's army had dwindled to fewer than 8,000 men, and at the beginning of the year most of them would finish their terms of service.

Washington decided on a drastic move. On Christmas night, 1776, as winter winds blew, he crossed the Delaware River with his men, marched them 9 miles to Trenton, and attacked. The enemy was hibernating in its winter camp, never suspecting that Washington would depart from the usual practice of suspending operations during

On Christmas Eve in 1776, Washington attacked the British in Trenton. The attack, shown here as Washington is crossing the Delaware River to Trenton, resulted in a great victory for Washington, who killed the Commanding Officer of the English and took 900 prisoners.

the winter months. In 45 minutes the Americans killed Howe's commanding officer and took 900 prisoners.

Buoyed by this success, Washington attacked Princeton a few days later, on January 3, 1777. By a brilliant bit of strategy he outmaneuvered the enemy and drove the English back to New Brunswick. Neither the victory at Trenton nor the one at Princeton was decisive, but both served to boost American morale, badly in need of encouragement since the defeat in New York.

THE BATTLE OF SARATOGA

A decisive American victory finally did take place during the summer and fall campaign of 1777. The British strategy was to seize Albany, New York. With Albany in their hands, they would control the Hudson, divide the North from the South, and gain access to the back country beyond the Appalachian Mountains.

General John Burgoyne masterminded a three-pronged attack on Albany. From the south, General Howe would lead his forces from New York City up the Hudson to Albany. From the west, Lieutenant Colonel Barry St. Leger would set out from Fort Oswego on Lake Ontario toward Albany. Finally, from the north, Burgoyne himself would descend from Canada and join the other two forces in Albany.

Every contingency was foreseen with mathematical precision, but nothing worked out as it had been planned. General Howe was playing a cat–and–mouse game with Washington in New Jersey and for a long time put off his departure for Albany. Finally, he decided to attack Philadelphia first before fulfilling his part of the Albany strategy. This he did, severely trouncing Washington along the way at the Battle of Brandywine on September 11, before capturing Philadelphia. Washington retaliated in October at Germantown, almost defeating Howe, who still had not set out to meet Burgoyne.

St. Leger was also slow to move his forces,

and when at last he left Fort Oswego and started heading east toward Albany, he was battered all along the way by American skirmishes. He had gone only a third of the way to Albany when he was attacked by Benedict Arnold at Fort Stanwix. Arnold very cleverly negotiated with St. Leger's Indian allies, convincing them to desert the British. Suddenly deprived of his large supporting force of Indians, St. Leger beat a hasty retreat back to Fort Oswego.

Meanwhile Burgoyne was moving clumsily down to Albany, never suspecting that his associates would not be there to greet him. Burgoyne, known as "Gentleman Johnny," had to march at a snail's pace. He led a force of 7,000 men, accompanied by a thousand women. Moreover, he dragged along fifty-two cannon, and a huge baggage train, including thirty carts devoted to his personal luggage. This slow-moving caravan made an easy target. In Vermont the local militia, known as the "Green Mountain Boys," fell on a foraging party of 700 of Burgoyne's redcoats and destroyed them. When the reduced British army reached Saratoga, it met with American forces and fortifications of unexpected and awesome strength. Burgoyne attacked the Americans on September 19, and again on October 7, and both times he was repulsed and suffered very heavy losses. On October 17, 1777, Burgoyne had no choice but to surrender his entire army of some 5,700 men.

The American victory astounded the British. General Howe, who had entered and occupied Philadelphia without a struggle, submitted his resignation to the king when he received the staggering news. A captured British officer declared: "The courage and obstinacy with which the Americans fought were the astonishment of everyone, and we now become fully convinced they are not that contemptible enemy we had hitherto imagined them, incapable of standing a regular engagement. . . ."

Burgoyne's surrender, however, did not seriously reduce the superiority of the British forces in troops and supplies. The most important result of the Battle of Saratoga was that news of it persuaded France to become an open ally of America.

THE FRENCH ALLIANCE

The news of Saratoga prompted not only France but Britain to take a new course of action. Lord North foresaw that the American victory would mean a Franco-American alliance and he took immediate steps to end the war. He proposed to Parliament a series of concessions that would guarantee the colonies virtual home rule. If necessary, all of the acts passed by Parliament after 1763 which had proved objectionable in America would be repealed and the British would pledge that the colonies would never be taxed, not then or in the future.

Parliament, however, delayed acting on the proposals and when they were finally approved and sent to the Continental Congress, it was too late. The Americans had already accepted the French offer to recognize their independence.

THE FRENCH TREATY

According to popular myth, the French rushed to the aid of the Americans out of their love for freedom and democracy. Although the idea of a republic in the New World did appeal to many French aristocrats and intellectuals, to the French Foreign Office the prospective alliance was a well-calculated, strategic move against Britain's powerful position in the world. After the Seven Years' War, Britain had become the most powerful—and most arrogant—nation in the Western world. As Benjamin Franklin wrote: "Every nation in Europe wishes to see Britain humbled, having all in their turns been offended by her insolence. . . ."

The Continental Congress had decided to send Silas Deane (a member of the Congress) and Arthur Lee (a commercial agent from Virginia) to Paris months before independence was declared. Both agents made themselves ridiculous in the sophisticated French capital. Deane pretended to be a figure of great mystery, wrote in invisible ink, and vowed to speak only French in order to throw off the English. This resolve led the French Foreign Minister, the Comte de Vergennes, to remark: "He must be the most silent man in France, for I defy him to say six consecutive words in French." Lee was equally eager to play the secret agent, but he inadvertently managed to hire six British spies, who doubtless found it easy enough to decode Lee's code name, "Mary Johnston."

Such bungling was not sufficient, however, to prevent the French from helping America secretly. Vergennes' policy was influenced by a remarkably versatile Frenchman named Pierre Augustin Caron de Beaumarchais, who had made his fame as the author of two popular, and dangerously democratic, comedies—*The Barber of Seville* and *The Marriage of Figaro*. (They are known today as the plots of two operas by Rossini and Mozart respectively.) Beaumarchais, with the permission of King Louis XVI, set up a fictitious private concern, Roderique Hortalez et Compagnie, through which war supplies were channeled into America. Before the Battle of Saratoga the French were reluctant to help the Americans directly, believing an open alliance would undoubtedly lead to another war with England. Louis XVI, however, could find no objection to aiding the Americans indirectly through the fake company. In the first $2\frac{1}{2}$ years of the war, fourteen ships operated by Hortalez et Compagnie plied back and forth across the Atlantic, supplying the Americans with, among other things, 90 percent of all the gunpowder they used during the war.

To encourage the French to make an open avowal of their support of America, Congress chose Benjamin Franklin to go to Paris 5 months after independence was declared. Congress could not have made a better choice. When he arrived in France in

December, 1776, Franklin was seventy years old, but still vigorous, an experienced diplomat, world-famous for his experiments with electricity, and a great showman. Knowing that the French regarded all Americans as simple, homespun pioneers, Franklin yielded to their fantasies by doffing his wig and donning a fur cap. The cap and its wearer were the sensation of Paris: ladies had their hair piled up into "caps," the *coiffure á la Franklin*. The great man sat for dozens of portraits and Parisians paid good money for a vantage point to view Franklin walking through the streets.

All of Franklin's charm and celebrity was not as effective, however, as the news of the outcome of the Battle of Saratoga. Only upon hearing of the American victory did France decide to declare herself an ally. Even then the French government was not free to make a move without the approval of Spain, for the two nations had signed a compact agreeing to act together in all decisions that might lead to war. Spain was against an alliance with the United States. She had colonies of her own in the New World and feared that the spirit of rebellion might spread from North to South America. Finally, thinking that America might succumb to England's peace offers, France decided to act on her own.

On February 6, 1778, Franklin, Deane, and Lee signed two pacts with the Comte de Vergennes. The first was a treaty of commerce in which France for the first time officially recognized the independence of the North American colonies from Great Britain. The second treaty was an alliance which established three points: both nations would fight until American independence had been won; neither France nor the United States would sign a peace treaty with Britain before receiving the formal consent of the other; and finally, each country promised to respect the holdings of the other in America "mutually from the present time and *forever* against all other powers."

Benjamin Franklin, at 70 years old, was sent as an ambassador to France to secure French support for the Revolution. Franklin, depicted here wearing his famous fur hat, succeeded not only in gaining French support for the war, but also in increasing personal respect and admiration for his own scientific genius.

NEW BRITISH STRATEGIES

The French alliance, though immensely encouraging, did not bring the war to an immediate, successful conclusion. In fact, Washington still had to endure his worst trial: the winter of 1777–1778 at Valley Forge. While General Howe and the British occupying forces wintered in comfort in Philadelphia, Washington and his men endured terrible suffering only 20 miles away. One officer wrote: "All my men except eighteen are unfit for duty for want of shoes, stockings and shirts, breeches and coats. . . . We are becoming exceedingly lousy." An army surgeon summarized the desperate situation in these terse words:

Poor food—hard lodging—cold weather—fatigue—nasty clothes—nasty cookery—vomit half my time—smoked out of my senses—the Devil's in it—I can't endure it. Why are we sent here to starve and freeze?

Almost 2,000 of Washington's men deserted to the British, and the Continental Congress threatened to replace the Commander in Chief with the "hero" of Saratoga, Horatio Gates, a man who actually had little to do with the victory. The local Pennsylvania farmers were selling their crops to the highest bidder, and the highest bidder was usually the British. General Howe probably could have wiped out Washington's dispirited forces with one quick blow, but he had already submitted his resignation and refused to stir himself from comfortable Philadelphia. Howe was replaced in May, 1778, by General Henry Clinton.

Clinton wanted a victory that would lift British spirits, for France had just entered the war, and the Americans had refused the terms offered by a peace commission which had allowed them complete self-government within the British empire. In search of a sure victory, the British turned their eyes southward. Optimistic reports led them to believe that the South was a stronghold of Tory sympathizers who would spontaneously rise up and throw in their lot with the British. Therefore, orders were sent to General Clinton to move the British army to New York, where he would devise a strategy for overrunning the South. On his march to New York, Clinton was attacked by Washington at Monmouth Court House.

A low point in Washington's career came during the winter of 1777-1778 at Valley Forge, when many of his troops who were starving and freezing deserted to the British.

Although Washington did not gain a clear victory, his army's good showing cheered Americans. In the meantime, the Americans had some small success in the West. George Rogers Clark, commanding a force from Virginia, was able to take the towns of Kaskaskia, Cahokia, and Vincennes in the Ohio Valley. Clark was never able to take Detroit nor did his victories give complete control of the Ohio and Illinois country to the Americans, but he succeeded in removing Indian pressure from the areas of Kentucky and West Virginia.

Monmouth was the last major battle in the North. From there the war shifted to South Carolina and Georgia. The Americans hoped to stop the transfer of British troops from New York to Savannah with the help of the French Navy. Congress had let the American Navy, which had never been impressive, dwindle from thirty-four ships to seven. France (and possibly Spain) would contribute the necessary sea power, it was hoped, to vanquish the British. The expected aid was slow in coming, however. The French Vice Admiral d'Estaing arrived in the spring of 1778 with seventeen French ships and 4,000 troops, but he failed to act decisively. In November he sailed south for a warm winter in the French West Indies.

Once French naval might was out of sight, Clinton sent General Archibald Campbell and 3,500 men to Savannah, Georgia. After 6 days the city fell, leading to British control of the entire state.

A year later, Clinton came down from New York to personally conduct the siege of Charleston. After 3 months, the most important city of the South capitulated on May 12, 1780. The British captured 5,000 prisoners, including three generals; the rest of South Carolina surrendered soon after, and Clinton returned to New York in high spirits. Convinced that total victory was now in sight, Clinton left behind 8,000 men under the command of General Cornwallis.

The situation was so alarming that Congress again turned to the "hero" of Saratoga, Horatio Gates, and directed him, against Washington's objections, to take charge of American operations in the South. Washington's low estimation of Gates was soon justified. On August 16, 1780, near Camden, South Carolina, Gates launched a surprise attack on the British but fled the moment the battle seemed to be going against him. Gates's entire force surrendered. Within a 4-month period, Britain had thus captured two sizable American armies, each as large as the ones she had lost at Saratoga. Georgia and South Carolina were firmly in British hands.

Washington's men were living on such scanty rations, even during the summer of 1780, that he had to cut down his army to a scant thousand men for fear a larger number would face starvation. "I have almost ceased to hope," Washington commented gloomily. Then, as the final blow, he learned that Benedict Arnold, his ablest general—possibly the best general to fight in the Revolution on either side—had gone over to the British side.

From this low point, American fortunes could only rise, and rise they did, in the fall of 1780. In September a thousand British troops were badly beaten in North Carolina. Washington, now that the disgraced Horatio Gates had retired, appointed his own protégé, Nathanael Greene, to head American operations in the South. Under Greene, American forces won several battles against Cornwallis, the most notable occurring at King's Mountain in October 1780; at Cowpens, North Carolina, on January 16, 1781; and at Guilford Courthouse the following March. Cornwallis now abandoned the state and moved into Virginia.

THE BATTLE OF YORKTOWN

In the spring and summer of 1781, American troops led by another of Washington's protégés, General Lafayette, and aided by forces under Von Steuben, harassed Cornwallis in Virginia and drove him to York-

town on the coast.

Throughout the war the British had always felt safe on the coast, relying on their vastly superior navy to provide them with supplies and a cover of cannon fire. Over the years the British had learned that once they moved inland, they could win specific battles but never hold territory for long. America was simply too vast, its roads too poor, and its citizens too rebellious to control through might alone.

In August, 1781, Washington was stationed in New York where he waited for the French Navy as Clinton and the British looked on. When he learned that the new French Admiral, the Comte de Grasse, was sailing north from the West Indies with thirty ships and 3,000 marines, Washington gave up ideas for a New York campaign and immediately ordered Greene to keep Cornwallis penned up in Yorktown until he arrived in Virginia.

On September 5, De Grasse crippled the British navy in Chesapeake Bay and sent the English ships hastening to New York City for repairs. On September 28, Washington laid siege to Yorktown with a combined force of 5,700 Continentals; 3,100 militia; and 7,000 French troops. Three weeks later, Cornwallis surrendered his entire force. Seven thousand English soldiers, most of them drunk, handed over their weapons to the Americans while a band played "The World Turned Upside Down." The surrender occurred on October 17, 4 years to the day after "Gentleman Johnny" Burgoyne's defeat at Saratoga.

PEACE NEGOTIATIONS

When Lord North heard the news of the defeat at Yorktown he exclaimed, "Oh, God! It is all over." Britain immediately began to extend peace feelers. Washington had expected the war to continue, but Britain was experiencing serious defeats elsewhere at the hands of other enemies. Spain

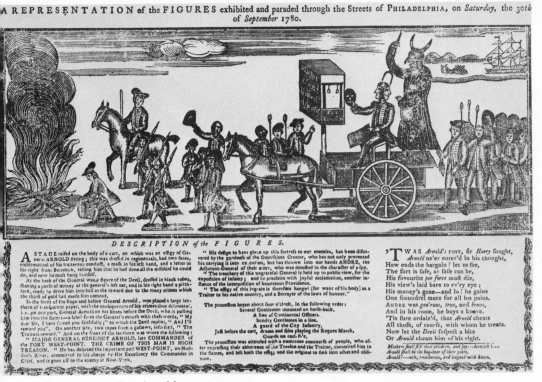

A REPRESENTATION of the FIGURES exhibited and paraded through the Streets of PHILADELPHIA, on *Saturday*, the 30th of *September* 1780.

DESCRIPTION of the FIGURES.

After General Benedict Arnold went to the British a two-faced effigy of Arnold was driven through Philadelphia.

had captured Pensacola, Florida, in May, 1781, and the following February was to take Minorca in the Mediterranean. France had seized several key British islands in the Caribbean. In Africa and Asia the British were also meeting reverses. The English national debt had doubled in 7 years. In March, 1782, Lord North resigned and the new ministry of Lord Rockingham decided to negotiate a peace settlement with the Americans.

The settlement involved not only the United States and Britain, but also France, as well as Spain and Holland, who had both joined in the war against England. Hence the diplomatic negotiations in Paris tended to be complicated and at times confusing. The Continental Congress, naively believing that the French felt nothing but sincere

interest in the problems and future of the United States, instructed American representatives in Paris to conform in all matters to France's wishes. Some members of the Congress also had been bribed by the French government. France did indeed favor an independent United States, but one that was weak and confined to the territory east of the Appalachians.

The American delegation in Paris included Benjamin Franklin, John Jay, and John Adams. Franklin carried the burden of the peace negotiations until the summer of 1782 when he was joined in Paris by John Jay. Adams, who was in The Netherlands negotiating a much needed loan for the United States government, did not arrive in Paris until October.

Jay was a man of great dignity and reserve who had been president of the Continental Congress before embarking on a diplomatic career. Before coming to Paris

181

he had spent 2½ years of neglect and insult as American ambassador to Spain. He made no headway in his efforts to persuade the Spanish government to recognize the new republic and extend it a loan. Jay came to Paris to redeem his own and his country's honor, and he rejected the guidance of the French minister, contrary to Congressional instructions. When Franklin became ill in August of 1782, Jay carried on the negotiations alone for several weeks. He learned that the French were making an undercover trip to London, possibly to deal secretly with the British. He also knew that both Spain and France were determined that the United States should gain as few concessions as possible from Britain, especially in the western territories. Convinced that America's allies were now as dangerous as her enemy, Jay told Franklin that they would be wise to ignore French advice and make the best agreement they could on their own. Franklin was at first cool to Jay's suggestion, but when Adams arrived in Paris and agreed with Jay, Franklin changed his mind. Although they knew the unethical implications of their action, they conferred with the British secretly. In November, 1782, a preliminary treaty was signed between the Americans and British. The formal treaty was then signed by France as well, as stipulated in the French alliance.

THE TREATY

Franklin had at first tried to persuade the British to cede Canada to the United States, but they refused. Britain, however, fully recognized American independence and made generous territorial concessions. The United States received all lands lying between the Great Lakes and the northern border of Florida, and all territory between the Atlantic Coast and the Mississippi River. Florida itself and the region from the Gulf Coast to the Mississippi River, then called West Florida, had been retaken from Britain by Spain during the war. The

NORTH AMERICA · 1783

treaty also recognized the right of both nations to navigate the Mississippi River from its source to its mouth—a provision which would cause great future difficulty, since Spain, which was not a party to the treaty, controlled the mouth of the river. Americans also gained the right to fish off Newfoundland, and even to salt and dry their catches on unsettled parts of the coasts of Labrador and Nova Scotia. The British promised to withdraw their troops from American soil as soon as possible. In return, America made a half-hearted promise to "earnestly recommend" that the states compensate Tories for properties confiscated by Patriots during the war. Negotiators on both sides knew that the "earnest recommendation" would be ignored insofar as possible by the various state governments. The United States also agreed that Americans would pay pre-Revolutionary War debts owed to British merchants, another clause which proved difficult to fulfill.

The French foreign minister was flabbergasted when he learned of the treaty and its provisions. He wrote to Franklin:

I am at a loss, sir, to explain your conduct and that of your colleagues on this occasion . . . You are wise and discreet, sir; you perfectly understand what is due to propriety; you have all your life performed your duties. I pray you to consider how you propose to fulfill those which are due to the King?

Off the record, however, Vergennes communicated his admiration of American diplomatic finesse—and amazement at British generosity.

CREATING A NATION

During the Revolution, the new American states had been slowly evolving new governmental forms. One of the most remarkable aspects of the war, in fact, was the generally peaceful and legal way that colonies became states.

A written constitution struck Americans as essential. For too long they had been governed under the unwritten British constitution. True, the very vagueness of the British system of rule made it flexible and easily adapted to changing social conditions. Its failure, however, lay in the ease

with which unscrupulous politicians could interpret it to serve their own ends. Americans were determined to have their rights stated in black and white and their government's functions clearly defined. The written charters, compacts, the philosophy of the Enlightenment, the English Bill of Rights, and their own long experience with self-government served as excellent guides in forming the new constitutions.

Each state established itself as a republic and between May 10 and May 15, 1776, the Continental Congress recognized the states as independent. By the end of 1777 ten states had transformed their colonial charters into state constitutions.

Of the ten states that had established governments before the end of 1777, only Pennsylvania had called a constitutional convention to write the new document. In all the other states, the assemblies had simply written and approved the new constitutions themselves, without submitting the documents to the people. (Six state assemblies, however, had received special permission from the people to write their states' constitutions.)

Massachusetts broke with this practice in 1780 when it selected delegates to a special convention to form a new state constitution which then presented the convention's recommendations to the voters for ratification. The people of Massachusetts believed that only a popular vote for the constitution could secure a firm basis for the government. If the assembly were free to institute the constitution without referring to the people, then what could prevent the assembly from changing, corrupting, or abolishing the constitution at will? Popular ratification was a principle that would be employed in the formation of future state constitutions and in the creation of the United States Constitution.

Basically the framers of the state constitutions wanted to preserve what they already had—republican government, government based on popular will and the rule

The Continental Congress on July 4, 1776, signed the Declaration of Independence.

of law, not personal whim. The authors of the documents had no desire to make a sharp break with the past. While certain innovations were incorporated into the documents, the tried patterns of colonial government were usually retained, thus creating a striking uniformity in the new state constitutions.

In most cases the new constitutions tried to enhance legislative power at the expense of the executive branch of government. The idea of a strong governor, who wielded a veto power over legislation, was rejected. Royal governors had possessed this privilege, and Americans were suspicious of putting so much power again into one man's hands. Only in New York and Massachusetts did the governor retain the power of veto and even there his veto could be overridden by the legislature. Pennsylvania went so far in its dislike of executive power

as to abolish the office of governor altogether and to give his duties to a twelve-man council.

The lower house of a colonial legislature had, in fact, been the branch of government most responsive to the popular will, since its members were generally elected annually. In their new constitutions the states strengthened the powers of the lower house (except in Pennsylvania, where there was only one house). In most states the judges were appointed by the legislature. Every state but South Carolina continued the practice of annual election of assemblymen (South Carolina's constitution called for elections every 2 years).

Most of the constitutions made innovations falling into four general categories:

1. In imitation of the Virginia constitu-

tion of 1776, most other states also included a bill of rights, guaranteeing protection of life, liberty, and property; the right to trial by jury; moderate bail and humane punishment; rotation in office; free elections; and freedom of speech, assembly, and religion. These ideas were drawn directly from the English constitutional heritage.

2. No state extended the right to vote to all adult men or to any woman. Georgia and Pennsylvania allowed all taxpayers to vote, but the other states continued to maintain property qualifications. (Massachusetts, however, reduced the amount of property required for voting.) "The rich having been used to govern, seem to think it their right," wrote a citizen of New Jersey, adding that the poor, "having hitherto had little or no hand in government, seem to think it does not belong to them to have any." However, the difference between rich and poor had never been so extreme in America as in Europe. For at least one old-fashioned Virginia farmer the Revolution had brought about too much equality, and he protested. "There is more *leveling* than ought to be."

3. A provision for amendment was always to be found in the new documents. The philosophy of the Enlightenment stressed the experimental nature of government. Therefore, the framers of these documents wished to leave them flexible enough to be changed if experience proved some of their provisions faulty.

4. Before the Revolution, and even during the war, conflicts frequently arose between frontiersmen living in the western regions of states and the older and more established East Coast counties. Citizens in the coastal regions had consistently denied full representation in the colonial assemblies to people in west. This inequity continued during and after the Revolution, but the new state constitutions attempted to redress these wrongs at least to some extent. In Pennsylvania, where the more democratic element from the western parts of the

state was quite influential, the new constitution came very close to equalizing representation from all counties, but nowhere in the Middle or Southern states was representation perfectly fair, the eastern counties still being overrepresented. In South Carolina, the conservative Tidewater planters continued to deny westerners an equal voice in the assembly although giving them some representation.

SOCIAL REFORMS

The Revolution also created a relaxation of social ties and a philosophical idealism which encouraged social change. Most of the new constitutions established social reforms or confirmed those which already existed. In several cases, innovations indicated a widening awareness that, in the words of the Declaration, "All men are created equal."

SLAVERY

Slavery had increasingly become part of American life, particularly in the South, and few whites, except Quakers, had questioned its moral propriety. During the Revolution, however, men fighting for their own freedom from the British began to see the injustice in the graver denial of liberty to black people. By the end of the Revolution, all the states except Georgia and South Carolina had passed legislation against the slave trade. Antislavery societies were active in such states as Pennsylvania and New York. In addition, north of Maryland, the abolition of the slave trade soon led to the gradual abolition of slavery itself. The territory of Vermont banned slavery in 1777. In the Massachusetts Constitution of 1780, the first article read: "All men are born free and equal." One slave took the article seriously, sued for his freedom, and won his case. Thereafter all other slaves in the state were automatically free. All the other

185

Northern states provided for the gradual abolition of slavery by the beginning of the nineteenth century. In the South, progress lagged far behind. Many Southerners thought of slavery as a benevolent institution. However, Virginia, which had hitherto forbidden the release of slaves, passed a law in 1782 permitting their owners to manumit them. By 1790, 10,000 Southern slaves had been given their freedom.

PROPERTY

A great change in property ownership took place as a result of the departure from America of about 100,000 Tories. Many of those who fled were from the colonial aristocracy, and considering that there were twenty-four Tory emigrants per thousand persons in America, their loss represented a significant decline in the number of wealthy Americans. Behind them, they left landed estates, which were confiscated by state governments, broken into smaller units, and sold to farmers. Land redistribution in many cases was drastic. For example, 311 persons eventually moved onto the former estate of the Phillips family in New York.

A few small token steps were also taken to increase opportunities to own land. The feudal laws derived from medieval England —the laws of primogeniture (which held that a man's oldest son must invariably inherit all his property) and the law of entail (by which a man could dictate exactly how and to whom his heirs would pass on his property)—were discarded. Quitrents (the small sums farmers paid their feudal "lord") were also removed from the books.

In the democratic spirit of the new states, it became illegal for citizens to accept titles of nobility from foreign nations. Suspected attempts to establish a native aristocracy aroused equal opposition. When officers of the Continental Army formed the Society of the Cincinnati in 1783 (named after Cincinnatus, a Roman farmer who had gone to war to protect the ancient republic), they were severely criticized for creating an elite organization and particularly for making membership in the club hereditary.

The printing of paper money during the Revolution also favored the poor, since it helped debtors and hurt lenders. The paper money declined in purchasing power through inflation, and a debtor who had borrowed a thousand dollars at the beginning of the war could pay it back at the end in currency that was worth a good deal less.

EDUCATION

Five state constitutions paid lip service to the idea of publicly supported education, but by 1800 none of the states had actually implemented such a plan. In New England, town-supported schools became fewer and were usually replaced by private academies. In fact, private secondary schools became the rule in almost every section of the country. Efforts to reform school curricula by replacing the study of Greek and Latin with more practical courses met with only limited success. The classics remained requirements for admission to every university. The number of colleges in the United States doubled after the war. By 1789 there were eighteen schools of higher learning, with at least one in every state but Delaware. American patriotism was reflected in the change of college names: King's College became Columbia, Queen's College became Rutgers.

RELIGION

A further advance in the total separation of church and state (a separation that would be basic to the future Constitution of the United States) was also a result of the American Revolution. When the Declaration of Independence was adopted, every colony except Pennsylvania, New Jersey, Delaware, and Rhode Island had an established church (that is, one supported with tax money levied within each colony). In the South and in the lower counties of New York, the Church of England was established, in New England the Congregational Church. During the Revolution the Church of England stopped receiving state support in the South, but in New England the states continued to support an established religion. However, in New England, under the new state constitutions taxpayers could specify to which Protestant church they wanted their money to go.

The new constitutions also guaranteed religious freedom in their Bills of Rights, but this freedom meant the freedom to belong to any Protestant church, not necessarily the right not to belong to a church at all. For instance, all states required that their elected officials take a religious oath.

Virginia was the first state to abolish these religious restrictions. Thomas Jefferson had written a liberal statute for religious freedom which, through the guidance of James Madison, was adopted by the legislature in 1786. Jefferson's statute stated "no man shall be compelled to frequent or support any religious worship, place, or ministry whatsoever," since "Almighty God hath created the mind free." By 1800 all states except Massachusetts, Connecticut, and New Hampshire had followed Virginia in separating church and state by law.

CREATING A NATIONAL GOVERNMENT

The Declaration of Independence had been ratified after 2 days of debate. The first national constitution, however, was debated for 5 years before it was finally adopted. Called the Articles of Confederation, this document was much weaker than the constitution that was to follow and exceed it in authority, but even so, the government created by the Articles struck many Americans as too strong, and perhaps unnecessary altogether. Men who had just re-

volted against too much centralized government power were not ready willingly to give similar power to another central government. The creation of any kind of permanent centralized authority, under the circumstances, has to be regarded as an achievement.

Many Americans also doubted whether a republican form of government could be adapted to a country as large as the United States. Montesquieu, a sixteenth-century French philosopher, had maintained in *The Spirit of Laws,* which was widely read in America, that a large territory could not be organized as a republic, it could be ruled only by authoritarian power. Indeed, history had provided few examples of successful large republics. The republics of ancient Greece had been city-states; Rome had abandoned republicanism after it became an immense empire; the republic of Switzerland was a tiny country, broken up into still smaller cantons, or districts. In a large nation, the argument ran, the legislature would inevitably sit in a capital far from the electorate, thus growing out of touch with the will of the voters.

Nevertheless, most educated Americans recognized that thirteen independent states could not survive in a world dominated by such powers as Britain, Spain, and France. To raise an army, operate a post office and, most important, conduct foreign affairs, the thirteen states had to have a central government, and this they tried to achieve through the Continental Congress. Representatives to the Congress were elected annually by their state legislatures. Every state had only one vote in Congressional decisions, small states like Rhode Island wielding the same power as such giants as Pennsylvania or Virginia.

To secure the foundations of the national government, however, Congress thought it wise to define its powers in a constitution. A committee presented a first draft of "Articles of Confederation" to Congress as early as July 12, 1776, but Congress bickered over the document for a year, and 4 more years passed before all the states ratified the revised version.

THE ARTICLES OF CONFEDERATION

During the Revolution the large states had agreed to the provision of one vote for each state as only a temporary wartime measure. When the first draft of the Articles proposed to make this procedure permanent, a vehement debate erupted that lasted almost a year. Finally, the rule of one state, one vote was accepted, only because the revised articles stipulated that every major measure had to be passed by a majority of nine of the states (a two-thirds majority); thus the interests of every region (the North, the Middle States, and the South) would be protected.

The controversial first draft of the Articles, framed by John Dickinson, attempted to establish a national government stronger than any American government ever set up by the British. After the Articles were revised, however, federal powers were severely limited. The union was barely more than a "league of friendship" between the states. Each state would retain "its sovereignty, freedom, and independence, and every Power, Jurisdiction and right, which is not by this confederation expressly delegated to the United States, in Congress assembled." So natural was it for Americans to think of their states as independent units that no one, not even the author of the Articles, referred to the United States in the singular. People invariably said, "The United States *are* winning the war."

The Articles provided for a federal system of government but left the most important powers in state hands. Congress was given no power to regulate commerce (which meant it could not impose a tariff) or levy internal taxes. Its lack of power to impose taxes was a crucial decision, for it weakened the power of Congress consider-

Criticism of the Government Under the Articles

66 *We may indeed with propriety be said to have reached almost the last stage of national humiliation. There is scarcely any thing that can wound the pride or degrade the character of an independent nation which we do not experience. Are there engagements to the performance of which we are held by every tie respectable among men? These are the subjects of constant and unblushing violation. Do we owe debts to foreigners and to our own citizens contracted in a time of imminent peril for the preservation of our political existence? These remain without any proper or satisfactory provision for their discharge . . . Are we in a condition to resent or to repel the aggression? We have neither troops, nor treasury, nor government. Are we even in a condition to remonstrate with dignity? . . . Is public credit an indispensable resource in time of public danger? We seem to have abandoned its cause as desperate and irretrievable. Is commerce of importance to national wealth? Ours is at the lowest point of declension. Is respectability in the eyes of foreign powers a safeguard against foreign encroachments? The imbecility of our government even forbids them to treat with us. Our ambassadors abroad are the mere pageants of mimic sovereignty . . . To shorten an enumeration of particulars which can afford neither pleasure nor instruction, it may in general be demanded what indication is there of national disorder, poverty, and insignificance that could befall a community so peculiarly blessed with natural advantages as we are, which does not form a part of the dark catalogue of our public misfortunes.*

—*The Federalist*

188

Support for the Government
Under the Articles

Whoever attentively examines the history of America, and compares it with that of other nations, will find its commencement, its growth, and its present situation, without a precedent.

. . . America stands completely systemised without any of these misfortunes. On the contrary, from the first settlement of the country, the necessity of civil associations, founded upon equality, consent, and proportionate justice have even been universally acknowledged. The means of education always attended to, and the fountains of science brought within the reach of poverty. Hitherto we have commenced society, and advanced in all respects resembling a family, without partial affections, or even a domestic bickering: And if we consider her as an individual, instead of an undue proportion of violent passions and bad habits, we must set her down possessed of reason, genius, and virtue. I premise these few observations because there are too many among us of narrow minds, who live in the practice of blasting the reputation of their own country.

—The Anti-federalist

ably. In addition, the country was to have no chief executive or national judiciary. Congress alone would administer the league of thirteen nations. The authority of Congress included: asking the states for revenue, regulating foreign affairs, sending and receiving ambassadors and making treaties, declaring war and concluding peace, establishing a post office, regulating the coinage, and controlling Indian affairs. All other powers were left in the hands of the states.

Once the Articles had been ratified, Congress, seeing the need for new administra-tive units, created the departments of war, foreign affairs, and finance. Among the first appointees, the most important, efficient, and intelligent department head was the Superintendent of Finance, Robert Morris. When he took office in 1781, the government's credit was foundering, the army was suffering from lack of food and uniforms, and the Continental dollar was almost worthless. Morris managed to alleviate these ills for a few years with help from the privately controlled Bank of North America. He obtained foreign loans to restore America's credit, improved the method for supplying the army, and checked the devaluation of paper money by backing it with borrowed gold.

PROBLEMS OF RATIFICATION

Ratification of the Articles themselves was a long and arduous process. The main obstacle blocking approval by all the states was the question of what to do with the territory beyond the Appalachian Mountains, the western lands. The British had kept most Americans out of this territory by the Proclamation of 1763, but the measure had not kept land speculators from staking out prospective claims, or seven states from demanding vast tracts. These seven "landed" states were Massachusetts, Connecticut, Virginia, the Carolinas, Georgia, and New York. The first six based their claims on their royal charters, which had granted the colonies all territories to the west—in fact, to the Pacific Ocean. New York's rather shadowy claims were based on the argument that since New York governed the Iroquois Indians, it should also govern their lands. The remaining six "landless" states had fixed western boundaries and wanted Congress itself to take charge of the western lands, revoking the claims of the landed states. It seemed to them that the western lands should be a national domain equally accessible to the citizens of all thirteen states.

189

These territorial disputes were bitter. Even during the Revolution, Virginia and Pennsylvania bickered over the Ohio Valley, and Connecticut and Pennsylvania battled over the Wyoming Valley. Three "landless" states—Pennsylvania, New Jersey, and Maryland—had entered into the fray before the Revolution by purchasing territory in the Ohio Valley from the Indians.

Now Maryland, speaking for the six states with fixed boundaries, refused to ratify the Articles of Confederation until the seven landed states renounced their claims to the western lands. Maryland argued that if the landed states received territories in the west, they could sell off these lands and use the profits to free their own citizens from paying taxes. Citizens of the landless states would all flock to the landed states, attracted by the prospect of paying few or no taxes.

This deadlock was finally broken when New York, and soon afterward Virginia, relinquished their western claims. Patriots in Virginia, led by James Madison, preferred giving up the Ohio Valley to standing in the way of a union of the thirteen states. After learning that Virginia had yielded, Maryland finally ratified the Articles of Confederation in February, 1781. Eventually all the landed states surrendered their claims and handed them over to Congress. The Articles went into effect and the first union of the independent states took place. A nation had been born.

AMERICAN NATIONALISM

The creation of the United States was the result of an unusual process. Most peoples that have fought for independence have experienced a strong sense of nationalism first and then gone to war to secure their national freedom. In America, the reverse was true. As one historian has said, "Our nation was the child, not the father, of our revolution."

190

Even after the Revolution, the average American still felt that his first loyalty was to his state. A new sense of being an American, however, was developing and strong fraternal ties were being forged among the citizens of every part of the nation. The Revolution itself had done much to promote this feeling. The Declaration of Independence had been drawn up in the name of the people of the united colonies. The literature of the period from 1764 to 1780 is full of self-conscious statements about American culture and the American past. In 1774 Patrick Henry spoke of being an American. Soldiers had fought for American liberty, not the freedom of Connecticut or New York, and they had often fought for it far from their home states. A common enemy had made Americans realize that they had a common cause. For example, the Virginian John Marshall had joined the Continental Army when he was twenty-one, served in the Middle States and endured the winter of 1777–1778 at Valley Forge. As he later wrote, "I was confirmed in the habit of considering America as my country and Congress as my government."

This party, given in Franklin's honor while he was in France to gain support for the Revolution, turned into a coronation ceremony when he was crowned with a wreath of laurels.

The war not only sent soldiers marching from state to state, but dislocated many civilians, particularly national leaders. The members of Congress left behind their homes—and to a certain extent their provincial concerns—and traveled to Philadelphia, where they conferred together on matters concerning the welfare of the entire nation.

The adoption of an American flag of thirteen stars and thirteen stripes in June, 1777, gave the American people a visible symbol of their unity. The ratification of the Articles of Confederation also conferred prestige on the federal government. As Article XIII declared, "the Union shall be perpetual." The important diplomatic victory in Paris in 1782 increased American pride and confidence in the new republic. Nevertheless, as Franklin remarked in 1787:

The American war is over; but this is far from being the case with the American Revolution. On the contrary, nothing but the first act of the great drama is closed. It remains yet to establish and perfect our new forms of government.

Practical considerations also brought the states together. Now that the United States could no longer depend on Britain for manufactured goods, American industries had to increase their output and cooperate with one another. The increased activity in interstate commerce revealed common interests to American businessmen. Similarly, Americans recognized the folly of having thirteen separate postal systems, or thirteen separate ministries of foreign affairs. A central post office, a centralized diplomacy, a single government that could declare war, deal with the Indians, establish weights and measures, and settle disputes between the states or on the high seas was seen as a necessity.

Finally, Americans of every state felt a national pride in their great leaders, notably Benjamin Franklin, Thomas Jefferson, and George Washington. Franklin had become famous throughout America for his widely read *Poor Richard's Almanack* and throughout the world for his experiments in electricity. In the second half of the eighteenth century, he was considered *the* genius of science by the French and was more celebrated in France than even Newton. His skill in handling the intricate diplomacy of the Revolutionary era crowned him with new laurels when he was already seventy. In Europe Franklin was regarded as an American, not as a Pennsylvanian, and he was regarded in the same way by his fellow citizens.

Jefferson, the author of the Declaration of Independence, was also becoming a figure of national prominence. And undoubtedly the greatest American in the eyes of his contemporaries was George Washington. As a military strategist, a courageous general, and a model of personal integrity and solid republican virtues, Washington was the symbol of a common Americanism.

THE CRITICAL PERIOD

As the years 1783 to 1789 made abundantly clear, the government of the new nation had little power. It was laden with responsibility but had little authority to act decisively. Congress could pass resolutions, but had no way of implementing them. The states frequently ignored the resolutions as well as federal requests for funds. Congress had no power to levy taxes or even to impose tariffs. The delegates to

Congress had little opportunity to exercise their abilities. A delegate was elected for only a 1-year term and could not be re-elected for more than 3 years in every six. The older leaders of Congress during the Revolution—Patrick Henry, Thomas Jefferson, Benjamin Franklin, John Adams, Samuel Adams, John Hancock—all left Congress and their places were taken by younger, less experienced, men.

In order to pass legislation, the Articles of Confederation required a quorum, in this case the presence of the representatives of at least seven states. To make decisions relating to war and peace or to vote appropriations, nine states had to be present. (During the first 4 months of 1784, Congress had a nine-state quorum on only 3 days.) The frequent lack of such quorums continually interrupted Congress, especially since no executive branch of the government existed to provide any sort of continuity. The three department heads (Secretary of War, Superintendent of Finance, and Secretary for Foreign Affairs) assumed some executive responsibility, but these posts were not always filled. For example, after the first Secretary of War, Benjamin Lincoln, resigned in 1783, the position remained vacant until Henry Knox was appointed in 1785.

Geographical as well as political uncertainties handicapped Congress. No permanent capital existed. When a mutiny among the militia in Philadelphia in 1783 frightened Congress away from that city, the delegates wandered about like gypsies, from Princeton to Annapolis, then to Trenton and New York.

Worst of all, Congress was impoverished. By 1786 only a third of the states were paying funds they had promised to deliver annually to Congress, and these were only a fraction of the amount promised. Throughout the 1780s Congress received only one-fourth of the revenue it asked for from the states. The dismal situation of the Confederation Congress prompted John Jay, now

Secretary for Foreign Affairs, to write in a gloomy letter to Washington on June 27, 1786:

Our affairs seem to lead to some crisis, some revolution—something that I cannot foresee or conjecture. I am uneasy and apprehensive; more so than during the war. Then we had a fixed object, and though the means and time of obtaining it were often problematical, yet I did firmly believe we should ultimately succeed, because I was convinced that justice was with us. The case now is altered; we are going and doing wrong, and therefore I look forward to evils and calamities, but without being able to guess at the instrument, nature, or measure of them.

FOREIGN AFFAIRS

The absence of unity among the states and the lack of power in the central government made it extremely difficult to carry on diplomatic relations with foreign powers. The impoverished, ineffective, fragmented new country was scorned abroad. A best-selling pamphlet in England stated:

It will not be an easy matter to bring the American states to act as a nation. They are not to be feared as such by us . . . We might as well dread the effect of combinations among the German as among the American states.

John Adams and Thomas Jefferson—the American ministers to London and Paris, respectively—suffered daily from the humiliations imposed upon them. Adams complained that the British treated him to a "dry decency and cold civility," and confessed: "No step that I can take, no language I can hold will do any good, or indeed much harm." Jefferson echoed the lament: "We are the lowest and most obscure of the whole diplomatic tribe."

PROBLEMS WITH THE ENGLISH

There were several causes of friction between America and Great Britain during the 1780s. One problem was mutual treaty violations. In the peace treaty of 1783, Congress had pledged that British creditors would meet with "no lawful impediment" in collecting the millions of dollars' worth of debts owed them by Americans. However, when Englishmen tried to get their money, American debtors (particularly tobacco planters in the South) flatly refused. "If we are now to pay the debts due to British merchants," demanded George Mason of Virginia, "what have we been fighting for all this while?" Many years later the United States government finally paid Great Britain a sum of money to cover these debts.

Tories met with similar difficulties. The treaty had promised that American authorities would protect Tories against the vengeance of Patriots and stated it would "recommend" that the states supervise the restoration of confiscated Tory property. This resolution was not honored and years later Britain finally awarded five thousand American Tories more than 3 million pounds.

Britain herself violated the treaty of 1783 by refusing to turn over forts along the Great Lakes on American soil. Canadian merchants had urged Britain to hold on to to the forts, to continue the profitable fur trade with the Indians as long as possible. England also felt that the Indians in the area, left to the mercy of the American frontier farmers, would be so angry at the British departure that they might turn on the Canadians in revenge. The Continental Congress, as in all its diplomatic ventures of this period, was helpless—helpless to protect Tories or to drive the English out of American territory. England, knowing that Congress was weak, used the American violations of the treaty as a pretext and announced that she would give up her posts only when the Loyalist properties were re-stored and British merchants had been paid.

Another lingering controversy developed with Britain over Vermont. Both New Hampshire and New York had squabbled over the land between the Connecticut River and Lake Champlain. In 1777, however, the people of Vermont created their own government and went so far as to promise England their neutrality in the Revolution in exchange for British diplomatic recognition. After the war, Vermont's most important leaders—the three Allen brothers, Ethan, Levi, and Ira—considered making such an agreement again, hinting that perhaps they might reunite with the mother country and attach Vermont to Canada. British intrigue with Vermont continued until 1791, when Vermont was admitted as the fourteenth state in the American union.

PROBLEMS WITH THE SPANISH

While Britain dominated the Northwest from its forts along the Great Lakes, Spain retained control over the Southwest through possession of New Orleans and the lower Mississippi River. Following the Revolution England and Spain still exercised strong influence over more than half of America's territory.

The Spanish had resented the meddling of English colonists in Spanish trade as far back as the seventeenth century. In the eighteenth century, Spain refused to aid Americans in their war for independence, for fear the example of an American republic might stir up rebellion in Central and South America. Now Spain claimed the entire Southwest from the Gulf of Mexico to the Ohio River. By 1785 some 50,000 Americans had settled in the areas soon to be the states of Tennessee and Kentucky. These pioneers could not afford to haul their produce by land over the Alleghenies. Economically, the only feasible transportation of their goods was on boats down the Mississippi. Spain, recognizing this necessity, attempted to drive out unwelcome Americans by announcing in 1784 that henceforth the river would be closed to all foreigners. Spain further harassed settlers by arming the Indian tribes of the South-west, which periodically made raids on American villages. At the same time, how-ever, Spain offered western settlers land, religious toleration, and even the use of the Mississippi at low rates if they would swear allegiance to Spain.

The result of Spain's tactics was to make many American settlers in the territories of Tennessee and Kentucky consider breaking off all ties with the ineffective Continental Congress, declaring their independence and negotiating directly with the Spanish for more favorable trading conditions. As early as 1775 Daniel Boone had rejected the pros-pect of statehood for Kentucky, declaring it "entirely against the voice of the people at large." In the 1780s the people of Tennessee began to listen with interest to Spanish overtures. In 1784 George Washington, after journeying hundreds of miles through the back country, reported: "The western settlers (I speak now from my own observa-tion) stand as it were on a pivot. The touch of a feather would turn them any way."

Spain tried to drive a deeper wedge into the union of American states, by encour-aging a conflict of interests between the Northeast and the South and Southwest. Merchants in New England had little use for the western settlers, whom they regarded as boors and ruffians. What concerned New England more was the trade with Spain. During the Revolution, Spain had per-mitted Americans to trade with her empire to a limited degree; now American busi-nessmen were hungering after a larger part of that profitable market. Accordingly, the Spanish envoy, Don Diego de Gardoqui, made an offer to the American Secretary of Foreign Affairs, John Jay. Americans, Gar-doqui said, would be invited to expand their trade with Spain if the United States would recognize Spain's exclusive control over the Mississippi River.

John Jay—and the merchants of Boston, Newport, Philadelphia, and New York—were willing to make a treaty on such a basis. According to rumor, Gardoqui had persuaded Jay to ignore instructions from Congress to demand the right to navigate the entire Mississippi River. The charming Spaniard, it was said, had managed to in-gratiate himself with Mrs. Jay, who had a great hold over her husband. Such atten-tions were, in fact, part of Gardoqui's offi-cial instructions from Madrid. He wrote to the Spanish Foreign office: "Notwithstand-ing my age, I am acting the gallant and accompanying Madame to the official en-tertainments and dances, because she likes it and I will do everything which appeals to me for the King's best interest."

Jay's decision to ignore his instructions, however, was based on his belief that com-merce with Spain was more in the interest of America at that time than the use of the Mississippi River. As he told Congress, the river would be an American possession in due time. All the United States had to do was wait until she was strong enough, per-haps 25 to 30 years, and then she could seize it. In the meantime, why not grasp the benefits of a favorable trading agreement with Spain?

When Jay proposed a treaty meeting Gar-doqui's terms, the Southern delegates in Congress and the whole Southwest erupted in rage. "The prohibition of the navigation of the Mississippi," wrote one indignant pioneer, "has astonished the whole western country. To sell us and make us vassals of the merciless Spaniards is a grievance not to be borne." So furious were the settlers, that Jay had to abandon his talks with Gar-doqui.

Eventually, in 1788, Spain granted Amer-icans the right to navigate the Mississippi (although they had to pay high duties for the privilege). Nevertheless, settlers in the West long remembered with bitterness the East Coast's plan to exchange free passage through the Mississippi for trade concessions with Spain, in defiance of the wishes of Congress.

THE WESTERN LANDS

Opposition to British and Spanish control of the area between the Appalachians and the Mississippi River, as well as the westward movement of Americans finally pushed the Congress toward its most important accomplishment of the Confederation period—the creation of a policy for orderly westward expansion. Legislation passed between 1785 and 1787 pertained specifically to the area above the Ohio River—the Old Northwest. The procedures adopted in this legislation were subsequently applied to the rest of the country as settlers moved across the continent. Although the vast northwest tract of land awarded America by the peace of 1783 was rich and promising, it was almost entirely inhabited by Indian tribes, French traders, and British soldiers. Neither the Indians, the French, nor the soldiers wanted Americans to enter this wooded paradise, but by 1785 Congress was already laying plans for the invasion.

When Virginia ceded to Congress its claims to the Northwest, the state had stipulated that the territory "shall be formed into distinct republican states, which shall become members of the Federal Union, and have the same rights of sovereignty, freedom, and independence of the other States." Accordingly, Congress appointed a committee, headed by Thomas Jefferson, to work out a plan that would meet these requirements. His efforts were not enacted into law, but the Land Ordinance of 1785, and the more important Northwest Ordinance of 1787 which followed it, set up a system under which these goals could be realized.

The Land Ordinance of 1785 provided for a way of surveying the Northwest into 6-mile-square townships. Each township was to be further subdivided into thirty-six sections. Purchasers could buy no less than one section (640 acres) at the price of a dollar an acre. Since the price of 640 dollars was steep for a pioneer farming family, this provision attracted few customers. In later years the price and minimum number of acres was lowered. In the meantime, speculators bought up large tracts of land illegally at lower prices and then resold land in smaller parcels to farmers. Many farmers simply settled on a tract of land in the hope that when it was eventually surveyed and put up for sale, they would have the first opportunity to buy it.

According to the Northwest Ordinance of 1787, the entire Northwest Territory ultimately was to be carved into not more than five and not fewer than three states. These states were to provide public elementary education and be free forever from the institution of slavery. Each territory would be governed at first by a governor, a secretary, and three judges, appointed by Congress. When five thousand free male inhabitants settled in the territory, the second stage of territorial government would begin and those who owned 50 acres could elect a legislature of their own. The governor would appoint a council of men from the territory and the assembly would enact laws for the region that would be subject only to the governor's veto. Moreover, the assembly would send a nonvoting delegate to the Congress. When a potential state had sixty thousand free inhabitants, it would enter the third phase of territorial government. It could be admitted into the Union "on an equal footing with the original states in all respects whatever," as soon as it formed a state constitution similar to the ones in the original thirteen states.

The Ordinance established the basic procedures by which most new territories would become states as the nation advanced to the Pacific. It solved America's problem of how to dispose of her landed empire. The first British empire had foundered on the question of imperial control

Ceded by Mass. 1785

Ceded by Conn. 1786

Ceded by Conn. 1800

Ceded by New York 1782

Ceded by Virginia 1792

Ceded by North Carolina 1790

Ceded by South Carolina 1787

Ceded by Georgia 1802

Ceded by South Carolina 1787, Claimed by Spain until 1795

B R I T I S H   C A N A D A

Lake Superior

Lake Michigan

Lake Huron

Lake Ontario

Lake Erie

St. Lawrence R.

Claimed by Great Britain

MAINE (To Mass.)

VT. (1791)

N. H.

NEW YORK

MASS.

CONN.   R. I.

PENNSYLVANIA

NEW JERSEY

MD.

DEL.

VIRGINIA

NORTH CAROLINA

SOUTH CAROLINA

GEORGIA

Mississippi R.

Ohio R.

L O U I S I A N A (Spanish)

Mississippi R.

S P A N I S H   F L O R I D A

A T L A N T I C

O C E A N

G U L F   O F   M E X I C O

0   300
Miles

Western lands ceded by states

Ceded by Virginia 1784 ("Northwest Territory")

Disputed territories

WESTERN LANDS CEDED BY THE STATES

versus home rule, but the new nation had found a way to avoid the same mistake. In the territorial phases, the Confederation Congress followed the British procedure of an appointed governor and council and elected assembly, but it wisely decided against a policy of indefinite colonial status for the newly settled areas to the west of the original thirteen states. When Ohio became a state in the Union in 1803, her Senators may not have had the prestige or the influence of those from Massachusetts or Virginia, but their votes counted just as much.

ECONOMIC PROBLEMS

During the 1780s the instability of the American economy became the overriding issue. In the same way that financial hardships had led to the Revolution, now economic depression and dislocations in foreign trade following the war were bringing about lack of confidence in the Confederation government.

America had always had an unfavorable balance of trade, but while it was still part of the British Empire this imbalance had

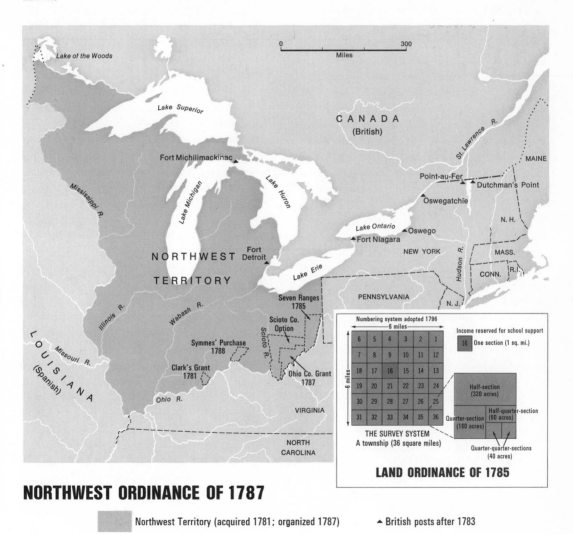

NORTHWEST ORDINANCE OF 1787

Northwest Territory (acquired 1781; organized 1787)   ▲ British posts after 1783

LAND ORDINANCE OF 1785

Numbering system adopted 1796

Income reserved for school support
16 One section (1 sq. mi.)

Half-section (320 acres)

Quarter-section (160 acres)

Half-quarter-section (80 acres)

Quarter-quarter-sections (40 acres)

THE SURVEY SYSTEM
A township (36 square miles)

been a family matter. After the Revolution, between 1784 and 1786, America imported three times as much from Britain as it exported and the imbalance drained almost every ounce of silver and gold out of the United States and into Britain's coffers. Moreover, Britain set high tariff walls around its empire. Americans could import only a few raw materials from Britain in their own ships. No American manufactured goods could be brought in. In addition, they were cut off from the West Indian trade except by smuggling or using British ships, and this was particularly hard on the United States. The shipping industry, halted by the British blockade during the war, was struck once more as American vessels were prevented from returning to familiar trading areas. These losses were compensated only slightly by new markets that American merchants were desperately trying to establish. Trade with France and Holland provided some relief and American businessmen even turned profits in far–off China by selling sea otter skins they had purchased from Indians in the Pacific Northwest.

Nevertheless, the unfavorable balance of trade prevented the stabilization of the American economy, made prices drop as much as 25 percent, caused numerous bankruptcies, and eventually undermined the currency. The obvious solution was for Congress to set up tariffs that would protect native manufacturers, but the Articles of Confederation had specifically forbidden Congress this power. Some states individually passed laws to discourage imports, but these efforts were piecemeal measures that often backfired. One observer said of the New Hampshire tariff law: "It was a blow aimed at Britain but wounds us and our friends."

Several states saw the need for a national tariff system, and as early as 1781, eleven states agreed to give Congress that power. The Articles of Confederation, however, required that any such measure receive the unanimous consent of the states. A similar movement for congressionally controlled trade was defeated by a slim margin a few years later. The nation's economy demanded central control, but the existing governmental machinery was incapable of imposing it.

The lack of foreign trade added further stress to a domestic economy in a state of confusion. During the war years, Congress had resorted to printing more and more paper money to meet its operating expenses. Because no gold existed in a national treasury to back the paper, by 1781 the Continental dollar was almost worthless. Of the 10 million dollars requested from the states, the Congress received about 1.5 million. After the war, the Congress was saddled with a domestic debt of 42 million dollars and a foreign debt of about 12 million. It had to rely on the states for the needed funds, and because only about one-fourth of the sum was honored, the debts could not be paid. Faith in the government's ability to meet its obligations declined. In 1783 Robert Morris resigned the Treasury post in disgust.

The states had their own war debts to meet and some of them also needed the money for rehabilitation because of war damage. As a result, they too continued to print paper money as they had during the war. Soon paper currency dropped sharply in purchasing power, for there was no gold in state treasuries either. To restore credit, the states began imposing heavy taxes on their citizens and some severely restricted the issue of new paper currency. In the postwar years, the average Massachusetts farmer handed over about one-third of his income in state taxes.

POPULAR UNREST

The depression hit merchants in the cities first. Some 90 percent of the population, however, was made up of farmers, and they were only gradually affected by hard times. During the Revolution, and even for a few years after, farmers attained great prosperity, selling their produce at very high prices to both the British and American armies. However, by 1785 the British army had been withdrawn and the American army disbanded. The farmers' market shrank and so did their income. Simultaneously, state legislatures raised taxes. During the war the devalued paper money had permitted debtors, who were usually farmers, to pay their creditors in easily available dollars; now they were called upon to pay their debts and high taxes on a sharply reduced income.

This depression, nevertheless, was not as damaging as some modern historians have stated. Virginia farmers were soon selling larger quantities of tobacco than before the war. Banks were paying handsome dividends to their investors. Many workers were employed in new projects to build roads, canals, bridges, and houses. In fact, the depression that followed the French and Indian War may well have been worse.

TROUBLE IN RHODE ISLAND

The postwar depression, however, was serious enough to many persons. Throughout the country, debtor farmers were begging their state governments for relief. They were asking for three things: stay laws, which would give debtors a period of grace before they had to resume paying their loans; tender laws which would allow them to pay their debts in produce; and more paper money, which would again devalue the currency and favor those with large debts.

In 1785 and 1786 seven of the state governments yielded to these demands. In South Carolina, New York, and Pennsylvania, where issues of paper money were handled with care, the new currency held its value. In other states, unfortunately, devaluation soon set in. (In Georgia, state dollars lost 75 percent of their worth in one year.)

In Rhode Island a new issue of paper money prompted a minor crisis. Creditors distrusted the new notes and refused to accept them. Finally, in a move to force the acceptance of the new money, the Rhode Island assembly, controlled by debtor farmers, passed a law fining creditors for declining payment in paper dollars. In the case of *Trevett vs. Weeden*, trying the constitutionality of the law, the Rhode Island Supreme Court refused to take jurisdiction, and the laws were subsequently repealed.

SHAYS'S REBELLION

In most states political leadership came from conservatives who demanded order in society and who were apprehensive of signs of unrest anywhere in the nation. To them the final proof that the collapse of authority in America was at hand came in 1786, in Massachusetts. Hard times, tight money, and heavy taxes had sent many bankrupt farmers to debtors' prison and caused more to lose their land. The state legislature was in the hands of the wealthy merchants along the Atlantic Coast. In the area of Cape Cod, and in central and western Massachusetts, many towns were too poor to send delegates to the legislature in Boston. In some counties, at times no men could meet the property qualifications for serving in the state government.

Oppressed and underrepresented, about a thousand farmers in the west rose up in violence, led in a haphazard way by Captain Daniel Shays, a veteran of the Revolution. Weary of fruitlessly petitioning an unresponsive legislature to pass stay laws and issue paper money, the rebels took the law into their own hands. Shays's ragged forces attacked the civil courts where hundreds of mortgage foreclosure cases were scheduled. When the rebels menaced federal arsenals, state troops led by General Benjamin Lincoln quelled the disturbances. By the end

199

of February, 1787, Shays had fled the state and his "army" had vanished.

Thomas Jefferson pointed out that it had only been "a *little rebellion*," but George Washington, who feared mob violence, dramatically exclaimed, "What, gracious God, is man! That there should be such inconsistency and perfidiousness in his conduct? We are fast verging to anarchy and confusion!" Perhaps the usually taciturn General was overreacting. Nonetheless, when Massachusetts appealed to Congress to quell the rebellion, Congress had been powerless to help. Washington's horror of the Massachusetts mobs was equaled only by his disgust with Congress, which he described as "a half-starved, limping government, always moving upon crutches and tottering at every step." Many Americans now recognized that the time had come to give the Confederation government more power. American representatives were being insulted in foreign capitals; American manufacturers were suffering from foreign competition; American settlers west of the Appalachians were threatened by the Brit-

In 1786 a Massachusetts veteran, Daniel Shays, led a rebellion against a Massachusetts Civil Court where mortgage foreclosures were being passed. Shays's Rebellion, shown here, did not succeed, but the real problem of losing faith in the state legislatures because of the poor job they were doing was finally realized. America was ready for a Federal Constitution and a Federal Government to lead the states in governing the people.

ish, Spanish, and the Indians; American ships were harassed on the high seas and American goods were barred from British ports. Worst of all, the country was in an economic depression, and although conditions took a turn for the better by 1786, they were still bad enough to cause outbreaks of violence. Against each of these grave national problems, Congress was powerless to take action. Many delegates in Congress had for a long time wanted a strong central government. Now their opportunity to obtain it was at hand.

Readings

GENERAL WORKS

Alden, John R., *The American Revolution, 1775–1783*. New York: Harper & Row, 1954—This book deals primarily with the military campaigns of the American and British forces. The author also considers the political and economic events which played a significant role in the outcome of the Revolution.

Burnett, Edmund C., *The Continental Congress*. New York: Macmillan, 1941 (Paper: W. W. Norton, 1964)—Based primarily on original letters and documents, this book is concerned with the political origins of the United States through the work of the Continental Congress.

de Crèvecoeur, J. Hector, *Letters from an American Farmer*. New York: Dutton, 1969 —The author describes life in a frontier area and discusses political and social development of the times.

Douglas, Elisha P., *Rebels and Democrats*. Chapel Hill, N.C.: University of North Carolina Press, 1955—This study illustrates the struggle for political rights and majority rule during the Revolution.

Jensen, Merrill, *The Articles of Confed-eration: An Interpretation of the Social Constitutional History of the American Revolution, 1774–1781*. Madison, Wis.: University of Wisconsin Press, 1940—The book is concerned with the men who drafted the Articles and what they meant in terms of the Revolution.

Jensen, Merrill, *The New Nation*. New York: Knopf, 1950—A history of the United States during the Confederation, 1781–1789; the author refutes historians who interpreted the period as one of corruption and stagnation.

Morris, Richard B., *The American Revolution Reconsidered*. New York: Harper & Row, 1967—The book consists of four essays by one of the outstanding historians of the Revolutionary period. The essays are a challenge to the accepted theories of the history of this era.

Nagel, Paul C., *One Nation Indivisible: The Union in American Thought, 1776–1861*. New York: Oxford University Press, 1964—Nagel discusses the various meanings the term "union" held for Americans between the Revolutionary and Civil wars. The work contains an important analysis of early Americans.

Nettels, Curtis P., *The Emergence of a National Economy, 1775–1815*. New York:

Holt, Rinehart & Winston, 1969—An economic history of the United States from the Revolution to the end of the war of 1812.

Nye, Russel B., *The Cultural Life of the New Nation, 1776–1830*. New York: Harper & Row, 1960—This volume of cultural history discusses key American ideas and institutions, and traces the development of what we now consider an "American point of view."

Peckham, Howard H., *The War for Independence. A Military History*. Chicago: University of Chicago Press, 1958—This is a compact and colorful account of the American and British military forces during the American Revolution. The author analyzes the strengths and weaknesses of both sides.

Wood, Gordon S., *Creation of the American Republic, 1776–1787*. Chapel Hill, N.C.: University of North Carolina Press, 1969—An interesting thesis in which the author attempts to show how Americans substantially altered existing political thinking while adopting new forms of government.

SPECIAL STUDIES

Bemis, Samuel F., *The Diplomacy of the American Revolution (Foundations of American Diplomacy, 1775–1823)*. New York: Appleton-Century-Crofts, 1935 (Paper: Indiana University Press, 1957)—A leading diplomatic historian discusses America's diplomacy with Spain, France, Austria, and The Netherlands during the Revolutionary War. He emphasizes the skill of the American diplomats.

Jameson, J. Franklin, *The American Revolution Considered as a Social Movement*. Princeton, N.J.: Princeton University Press, 1926 (Paper, 1967)—This short study has made an important contribution to our knowledge of the internal social, economic, and political changes that took place in America during the Revolutionary era.

Main, Jackson T., *The Antifederalists: Critics of the Constitution: 1781–1788*. Chapel Hill, N.C.: University of North Carolina Press, 1970—This study describes the personalities and politics of the group which did not favor a stronger central government. The author's thesis is that the antifederalists actually represented the majority of Americans in the 1780s but were politically outmaneuvered by Madison and his federalist group.

Nelson, William H., *The American Tory*. New York: Oxford University Press, 1962

(Paper: Beacon Press, 1964)—The author seeks to explain why a group of Loyalists remained in America during the Revolution.

Starkey, Marion L., *A Little Rebellion*. New York: Knopf, 1955—This is a history of the event in western Massachusetts which culminated in Shays's Rebellion in 1786. The author describes the social forces and personalities involved in the rebellion.

Whitaker, Arthur P., *The Spanish-American Frontier: 1783–1795; The Westward Movement and the Spanish Retreat in the Mississippi Valley*. Boston: Houghton Mifflin, 1927 (Paper: University of Nebraska Press, 1969)—Commercial and diplomatic intrigues in the backwoods of the colonies after the Revolutionary War are the basic subjects of this volume.

Williamson, Chilton, *American Suffrage: From Property to Democracy, 1760–1860*. Princeton, N.J.: Princeton University Press, 1960—This is an historical survey of early suffrage (right-to-vote) practices in America. The author seeks to show that no one thesis, political party, or group can wholly account for the spread of the franchise.

Zilversmit, Arthur, *The First Emancipation: The Abolition of Slavery in the North*. Chicago: University of Chicago Press, 1967 —The author describes the early status of blacks, attitudes toward them, and why slavery "failed" in the North but persisted in the South.

BIOGRAPHIES

Brant, Irving, *James Madison: Father of the Constitution, 1787–1800*, Vol. II. Indianapolis: Bobbs-Merrill, 1950—The "decade" covered in this last volume is the most important in Madison's career: he was father of the Constitution and Washington's most important executive.

Chinard, Gilbert, *Thomas Jefferson: The Apostle of Americanism*. Boston: Little, Brown, 1929 (Reprinted, University of Michigan Press, 1957)—The author investigates the influences of European thinkers on Jefferson's political philosophy and concludes that Jefferson developed his own ideas independently of French or English thinkers.

Flexner, James T., *George Washington in the American Revolution, 1775–1783*. Boston: Little, Brown, 1968—The author explores Washington's emotions and career against the background of the Revolution.

Mitchell, Broadus, *Alexander Hamilton*, Vol. II. New York: Macmillan, 1957—This objective study of the man who is usually interpreted as Jefferson's antithesis is a good reappraisal. The work is meant to be a definitive biography.

Tyler, Moses C., *Patrick Henry*. Ithaca, N.Y.: Cornell University Press, 1962—This is an admiring biography of the Virginia Revolutionary who opposed ratification of the Constitution as a strong supporter of states' rights.

Van Doren, Carl C., *Benjamin Franklin*. New York: Viking, 1964—This classic biography of Franklin's career is a very detailed, readable account that draws largely on Franklin's own writings.

HISTORICAL NOVELS

Bellamy, Edward, *The Duke of Stockbridge: A Romance of Shays' Rebellion*. Cambridge: Harvard University Press, 1962—A historical romance about Shays' Rebellion in Massachusetts (1780s) by the author of *Looking Backward*.

Boyd, James, *Drums*. New York: Scribner's, 1968—This novel about the American Revolution tells the story of a young Tory who was converted to the causes for independence, joined John Paul Jones's naval expeditions, and later returned to fight in North Carolina.

Brown, Charles B., *Ormond*, Ernest Marchand, ed. Darien, Conn.: Hafner, 1969—A romantic novel of the Revolution by the first professional American writer.

Cooper, James Fenimore, *The Spy*. New York: Oxford University Press, 1968—This was Cooper's second novel, published in 1821. It is a tale of high adventure about Harbey Birch, a secret spy for George Washington in New York.

Edmonds, Walter D., *Drums Along the Mohawk*. Boston: Atlantic Monthly Press–Little, Brown, 1969—This is a novel about the effects of the American Revolution on farmers in the Mohawk Valley of upstate New York.

Lancaster, Bruce, *Guns of Burgoyne*. New York: Stokes, 1939—The defeat of British troops under "Gentleman Johnny" Burgoyne is told through the character of a Hessian soldier fighting with the British.

Simms, Gilmore W., *The Partisan: A Romance of the Revolution*. New York: AMS Press, 1969—Set in the Carolinas during the Revolution, the novel describes the guerrilla warfare carried on by Francis Marion (the "Swamp Fox"). Simms emphasizes the tensions between civilization and nature on the frontier.

2

THE
EVOLUTION
OF
DEMOCRACY

er Lacour delin.

A. Dool

FEDERAL HALL

The Seat of Congress

6

Founding a New Government

[James Wilson] contended strenuously for drawing the most numerous branch of the Legislature immediately from the people. He was for raising the federal pyramid to a considerable altitude, and for that reason wished to give it as broad a basis as possible. No government could long subsist without the confidence of the people. In a republican Government this confidence was peculiarly essential. He also thought it wrong to increase the weight of the State Legislatures by making them the electors of the national Legislature. All interference between the general and local Governments should be obviated as much as possible. On examination it would be found that the opposition of States to federal measures had proceeded much more from the Officers of the States, than from the people at large.

—The Records of the Federal Convention of 1787

Amos Doolittle's engraving depicts the inauguration of George Washington as President of the United States and John Adams as Vice President on the balcony of Federal Hall in New York City.

THE CONSTITUTIONAL CONVENTION

Hard times were at a peak when dissatisfaction erupted into the violence of Shays's Rebellion. The outbreak was short-lived and, in itself, not very serious, but there were those who saw it as a warning of further violence and social upheaval. The ever-worsening depression made many citizens question the worth of a government that could not regulate commerce and had no power to tax. Mortgage foreclosures were driving farmers off their property, and the jails in some areas were overflowing with debtors.

Some felt that a union of all the states was impossible and a scheme was advanced for a division into three separate nations. This effort was described by a concerned citizen, who wrote: "Some of our enlightened men who begin to despair of a more complete union of the states in Congress have secretly proposed an Eastern, Middle, and Southern Confederacy, to be united by an alliance, offensive and defensive."

A conservative group in the army recommended that America be turned into a military dictatorship. General Washington, horrified by the proposal, voiced concern over its implications: "What a triumph for the advocates of despotism to find we are incapable of governing ourselves, and that systems founded on the basis of equal liberty are merely fallacious."

Fortunately a number of influential men throughout the country favored neither several small confederacies nor a military dictatorship, but rather, a stronger central government. Two minor conventions that were assembled to consider interstate problems paved the way for the Convention of 1787, which created the United States Constitution. At the first of these meetings, in 1785, representatives from Virginia and Maryland discussed their rivalry over the navigation of the Potomac River and Chesapeake Bay. In September, 1786, a similar conference was held in Annapolis, Maryland, to discuss commercial problems affecting the entire country. Even though only five states attended, the convention proved of strategic importance because it brought together two staunch nationalists, James Madison of Virginia and Alexander Hamilton of New York. Together they successfully urged the other delegates to call on the state governments and the Confederation Congress to endorse a national meeting to which all states would send delegates. This convention, as Madison put it, would consider how "to devise such further provisions as shall appear to them necessary to render the Constitution of the Federal government adequate to the exigencies of the Union."

George Washington addressing the Constitutional Convention in 1787. Washington was unanimously elected president of the Convention.

THE DELEGATES

The Great Convention was held in Philadelphia and representatives attended from all the states except Rhode Island. They met from May 25 to September 17, 1787, and in those 4 months they created the new Constitution.

Who were these delegates? Of the fifty-five who attended, most were well-to-do; only one, William Few from Georgia, represented the average farmer. Most of the delegates had a college education, in a day when attending a university was unusual even for the wealthy. The most common profession among them was law. The average age was forty-two. Benjamin Franklin, at eighty-one, was by far the oldest member of the convention. Five representatives were in their twenties, and many more in their early thirties. Despite the prevailing youthfulness of the gathering, many had been active in the Revolution. Well over half of the members also had been in the Continental Congress and had held important political positions in their states at one time or another.

With a few exceptions, they were the best men America had for the job. Four had already achieved widespread fame. They were the revered George Washington, who was unanimously elected president of the convention; James Madison, a young and brilliant Virginian who had already been working for several years to strengthen the federal government; New York's Alexander Hamilton, the most ardent advocate in the group of a very strong centralized government; and Benjamin Franklin, the sage of the convention. Among the prominent men who did *not* attend were John Adams, the minister to England, Thomas Jefferson, minister to France, and John Jay, who as Secretary for Foreign Affairs was not considered eligible for election.

Historians sometimes emphasize the disagreements that divided the delegates during the Convention debates to the exclusion of the ideas on which they were united. Underlying their specific recommendations for improving the governmental system was the generally held eighteenth-century concept of the nature and capability of man. They were in full agreement with the philosopher John Locke that man had the capacity for self-government if he could keep his strong aggressive tendencies under control. Moved by this consideration and the conditions in the country, almost all the members of the convention agreed that the Articles needed to be strengthened—or scrapped altogether. A new government should be created which had an independent source of income as well as control over foreign affairs and commerce. In addition, they agreed that the government should have three branches: executive, legislative, and judicial to prevent a concentration of power in the hands of one man or group of men. However, there was also general concurrence that the states should retain some of their former powers, that the central government should be responsible to the ordinary citizen, and that the citizenry should share in the process of electing representatives to the new government.

TWO MAJOR DEBATES

The convention in Philadelphia had originally been called solely to revise the Articles of Confederation, but on May 30 the delegates, urged on by the contingent from Virginia, voted to forge an entirely new constitution. With remarkable unanimity, the delegates quickly approved additional powers for the new government. They gave the national government the right to levy taxes, regulate interstate and foreign commerce, and to raise and maintain an army and navy. At the same time, the states were deprived of the right to coin money, make treaties, or tax imports and exports without the consent of Congress.

These major issues aroused little debate, but two other questions led to weeks of controversy which nearly destroyed the convention. The controversy over both questions concerned the problem of representation in Congress.

THE VIRGINIA PLAN

On the third day of the Constitutional Convention, Edmund Randolph presented a plan for a new government drafted by James Madison. Because both men were Virginians, the proposal was soon called "The Virginia Plan." After this plan was extensively revised and modified, it became the model for the United States Constitution.

The Virginia Plan called for a government with three branches: legislative, executive, and judicial. The legislature would be composed of two houses, a lower house elected by the people and an upper house chosen by the lower house. The seats in both houses would be distributed according to each state's population; the more populous states, in other words, would have more representatives in *both* houses. This differed from the Articles, which provided for only a one-house Congress, and gave one vote to each state, no matter how small or how large. Under the Virginia plan, the legislative branch would have been the most important branch of government, for it would have elected both the executive and judicial departments.

THE NEW JERSEY PLAN

This method of apportioning representatives on the basis of population alone brought an immediate protest from the smaller states. They banded together to present their own views in a proposal introduced by William Paterson of New Jersey. The "New Jersey Plan" essentially called for a continuation of the old form of government, a Congress of one house in which each state would have one vote. Representatives would continue to be elected by the state legislatures, not by the people. The innovations offered by the plan were three: first, Congress would have the power to tax; second, Congress could regulate trade; and third, the government would have an executive branch with authority placed in several men chosen by the Congress, rather than one man.

THE GREAT COMPROMISE

Many of the delegates to the convention believed the New Jersey Plan could not fail to work because it was simply a slight revision of the old form of government. In addition, the plan drew attention to the fear of the smaller states that they would continually be outvoted by the more populous states if representation in Congress were based on the number of citizens in each state.

On the second of July, a committee was appointed to review the question of representation. Three days later it presented a compromise, devised by Benjamin Franklin: Congress would have two houses; in the lower one (to be called the House of Representatives) the states would be represented according to population. This proposal satisfied the larger states. In the other house (now the Senate), the states would all have an equal number of representatives. This part of the plan pleased the smaller states.

Franklin's plan, called the "Great Compromise," effected an important change in attitude. It helped convince the smaller states that the Articles of Confederation should be discarded altogether, not merely revised, and thereby paved the way toward a federal government with true power to act. The only people it displeased were the handful of diehard nationalists who had hoped the new government would com-

pletely do away with the concept of statehood. Hamilton held this view and left the convention in disgust after the Great Compromise was adopted.

THE THREE-FIFTHS COMPROMISE

Once the convention decided the question of representation in the two houses of the legislature, a new question arose: Who should be counted? Southerners wanted their slaves counted as part of their population (although they had no intention of allowing the slaves to vote). Northerners agreed in essence, but then insisted that slaves be counted in deciding each state's share of direct federal taxes. States were to be taxed by the new federal government according to the size of their population; if slaves were counted for *this* purpose, the Southern states would have to foot a larger share of the national bill than if only the free population was counted.

Southerners objected to this stipulation since they had no desire to pay a heavier load of taxes than was strictly necessary. Finally, Franklin's committee worked out another compromise to the effect that three-fifths of the South's slaves would be counted for *both* purposes, voting as well as taxation.

The two compromises saved the convention.

A CONTROVERSY OVER COMMERCE

The North and South were divided on several other questions, all related to the power to be granted the federal government in regulating commerce. The conflicting viewpoints reflected the different sources of income in the two regions. The North made a large part of its money from commerce and manufacturing and, therefore, wanted the federal government to be able to levy tariffs to protect domestic industry.

The South, on the other hand, stood to gain nothing from such tariffs, since there were few industries in Southern states. To them, import duties only meant that Southern consumers would have to pay higher prices for goods.

The South made its money by exporting such staple products as tobacco and rice, and Southerners feared that the new government might legislate high export duties on these items. To ensure that no such legislation would be passed, the South demanded that all acts regulating commerce be passed by a two-thirds majority in Congress. In addition, Southerners were worried that Congress might try to stop the slave trade; they wanted assurance that no such interference would occur.

Thus, in yet another compromise, the convention made several concessions to the South: the government would never levy export taxes, the slave trade would be allowed to continue for twenty more years, and the Northern states promised to return fugitive slaves to their Southern owners. In return, the South made a concession of its own: Congress could pass acts regulating commerce with a simple majority vote.

THE FINAL DOCUMENT

On September 17, thirty-nine of the original fifty-five delegates signed a new Constitution that incorporated many aspects of the various state constitutions and of the Virginia and New Jersey plans, and introduced a few new provisions as well.

One of the most significant innovations was the office of the President. Under English rule there had never been one governor with authority over all the colonies, nor had the Articles of Confederation provided for a chief executive. Thus, there was no precedent for a chief executive for the whole country. After much debate in the convention, the office of President was cre-

ated, and he was given the power to veto legislation (although his veto could be overruled by a two-thirds majority of Congress); he could negotiate treaties (although all treaties required Senate approval by a two-thirds majority); and he was commander-in-chief of the army and navy (although only Congress could declare war or appropriate a military budget).

The President was to be a powerful figure, but almost every one of his powers would be limited to a certain extent by the legislature. This system, by which each branch of the government could limit the power of the other two, was called the system of "checks and balances" and was one of the most distinctive attributes of the new document. The President could veto legislation, but he could not stop meetings of Congress. Congress could override his veto and even impeach a President it believed to be incompetent. The President had control of the armed forces, but only Congress could declare war.

Another notable accomplishment of the Constitution was the relationship established between the federal government and the people. Under the Articles of Confederation, the people had had no direct contact with the government; all representatives had been selected by the state legislatures. Under the new Constitution, however, voters would directly elect members to the House of Representatives. The legislature of each state would select only its two senators (a practice changed in 1913 by the Seventeenth Amendment, which established the direct popular election of senators).

The election of the President was to be accomplished through a new device, an electoral college. Everyone at the Constitutional Convention knew that Washington would be the first President, a choice that met with universal approval. Yet, what would happen after Washington retired? Most of the delegates to the Constitutional Convention were quite suspicious of too much popular control of government. They feared that if the President were popularly elected, he might turn out to be a demagogue who thought mainly of pleasing crowds. If the President were not popularly elected, then how should he be chosen? The strong nationalists wanted an independent executive and were determined that he should not be dependent on the legislature for election. Finally, the electoral college was devised as a compromise in which each state would have the same number of delegates as it had representatives and senators in Congress. These electors were to be chosen in a manner to be determined by each state legislature. They could be popularly elected, for instance, or they could be chosen by the state legislature itself. Once chosen, the electors would then vote for two people. The candidate with the most votes would be President, the one with the second largest number would be Vice-President. If no two men received a clear majority, then the election would be determined by the House of Representatives (something that has happened only twice in American history).

Finally, the Constitution protected many states' rights while setting up a central government much stronger than the previous one. States could continue to maintain police forces, control education, regulate working conditions, and enact civil and criminal laws. Moreover, Article VI of the Constitution made the state courts responsible for carrying out federal law.

Since the Constitution contained compromises and phraseology which could be interpreted in various ways, no member of the convention was completely satisfied with it. Yet, most probably agreed with Benjamin Franklin when he said to Washington: "I consent, Sir, to this Constitution, because I expect no better, and because I am not sure that it is not the best. The opinions I have had of its errors, I sacrifice to the public good."

RATIFICATION

Opposition to Ratification

66 *The writer of these essays has clearly proven, that the president is a King to all intents and purposes, and at the same time one of the most dangerous kind too— an elective King, the commander-in-chief of a standing army, etc. and to these add, that he has a negative over the proceedings of both branches of the legislature: and to complete his uncontrouled sway, he is neither restrained nor assisted by a privy council, which is a novelty in government. I challenge the politicians of the whole continent to find in any period of history a monarch more absolute.*

Who is so base as not to burn with resentment against the conspirators, who have dared to establish such a tyrant over his life, his liberty and property? Is the flame of sacred liberty so entirely extinguished in the American breast as not to be kindled again? No, you mistaken despots, do not let such a preposterous thought madden you into perseverance, lest your persons fall sacrifices to the resentment of an injured country. Stop at once, and join the rest of your fellow citizens. Let another Convention be immediately called, and let a system of government fitted to the pure principles of the Revolution, be framed. Then a general amnesty among all ranks and degrees of your fellow citizens must succeed, and America become the seat of liberty, peace, friendship and happiness; and her government have ample energy and respectability among the nations of the earth; yes, she will thereby be rendered the great arbiter of the world. 99

—*"Philadelphiensis Letter,"*
The Antifederalist

> 66 *The constitution of the executive department of the proposed government, claims next our attention.*
>
> *There is hardly any part of the system which could have been attended with greater difficulty in the arrangement of it than this; and there is, perhaps, none which has been inveighed against with less candor or criticised with less judgment.*
>
> *Here the writers against the Constitution seem to have taken pains to signalize their talent of misrepresentation. . . . The authorities of a magistrate, in few instances greater, in some instances less, than those of a governor of New York, have been magnified into more than royal prerogatives. He has been decorated with attributes superior in dignity and splendor to those of a king of Great Britain. . . .*
>
> *Attempts so extravagant as these to disfigure or, it might rather be said, to metamorphose the object, render it necessary to take an accurate view of its real nature and form: in order as well to ascertain its true aspect and genuine appearance, as to unmask the disingenuity and expose the fallacy of the counterfeit resemblances which have been so insidiously, as well as industriously, propagated. . . . It is impossible not to bestow the imputation of deliberate imposture and deception upon the gross pretence of a similitude between a king of Great Britain and a magistrate of the character marked out for that of the President of the United States. It is still more impossible to withhold that imputation from the rash and barefaced expedients which have been employed to give success to the attempted imposition.* 99

—*"Paper Number 67,"* The Federalist

Even after the Constitution was signed, the document was still a mere piece of paper, not yet the law of the land. In order to become so, it passed through more months of debate.

The framers of the Constitution were realistic enough to expect opposition to the proposed changes and they devised two means to make ratification easier. First, the document provided that the Constitution should not be referred to the state legislatures for approval, but rather to popularly elected conventions in every state. Because the new government proposed to divest the states of much of their power, state legislatures had a vested interest in defeating it; representatives chosen directly by the people would be likely to treat the Constitution far more favorably. Moreover, a popular ratification would implement the opening words of the Constitution: "We the people of the United States . . ." Massachusetts had provided the model for the ratification of the Federal Constitution when earlier it held a popularly elected convention which ratified its state constitution (see Chapter 5), thereby enabling the electorate to give the state government its authoriy in fact as well as in theory.

The second means for hastening ratification was a provision requiring only nine of the states to approve the new form of government to make it effective. The convention in Philadelphia thus rejected the notion of unanimous ratification. Rhode Island had not even sent a delegate to Philadelphia and it was known that in some states powerful forces opposed a strong central government.

FEDERALISTS VERSUS ANTIFEDERALISTS

Those who championed the new Constitution called themselves "Federalists" and labeled the enemies of the new document "Antifederalists." No clear-cut geographic or economic differences can account for the divisions over ratification. In general, the Federalists were from the wealthy, well-educated class, both urban and rural, while many Antifederalists were from the yeoman farmer class. However, these broad economic divisions do not explain why many people belonged to one group rather than the other. The causes of dissension over ratification were inherent in the conflicting political beliefs and economic differences between large and small states.

There was sharp debate over the broad powers given to the federal government under the new constitution. The document did not include a Bill of Rights and many Antifederalists seized upon this omission as clear proof that the new federal government would be tyrannical. Never before had one man possessed as much power over the country as that given the President. Such authority, argued the Antifederalists, might lead the President to declare himself king. Under the Constitution the federal government, as well as the states, would have the right to tax and the poor would be bled dry by tax collectors. Furthermore Antifederalists claimed, the Constitution was the handiwork of the wealthy in the nation who simply wanted more personal power. As Amos Singletary, a Massachusetts farmer, put it:

These lawyers, and men of learning, and moneyed men, that talk so finely, and gloss over matters so smoothly, to make us poor, illiterate people swallow down the pill, expect to get into Congress themselves; they expect to be managers of this Constitution, and get the power and all the money into their own hands, and then they will swallow up all us little folks, like the great leviathan, . . . yes, just as the whale swallowed up Jonah. This is what I am afraid of.

The Antifederalists also raised the old argument of eighteenth-century political thinkers that a republican form of government could not rule a country as large as the United States. Congress would sit in a city far from many of its constituents and would lose touch with their interests. There would be so many special interest groups clamoring for legislation favorable to themselves that Congress would act in a way that pleased no one. Many people still felt their first loyalty to the state governments and feared that under the new system, the states would be sharply downgraded.

THE STATE CONVENTIONS

The small states generally favored the Constitution. They realized that a stronger federal government could protect their economic interests and even their existence in competition with the larger states. They were also pleased that the Constitution had given them an influence disproportionate to their populations in the proposed Senate. Federalists knew, however, that if any one of four large states, Massachusetts, Pennsylvania, New York, and Virginia, failed to ratify the Constitution, the new government might not survive.

As expected, the small state of Delaware ratified first, voting unanimously for the Constitution on December 7, 1787. The important state of Pennsylvania endorsed the new government a few days later by a two-to-one majority even though it had an active and vocal Antifederalist minority. By the middle of January, 1788, three more small states, New Jersey, Georgia, and Connecticut had joined the Federalist fold.

In February, Massachusetts joined the union after a strenuous period of debate and a close vote. Maryland ratified in April and South Carolina in May. On June 21, when New Hampshire approved the Constitution, the requisite nine states had ratified. North Carolina and Rhode Island were still holding out, but all eyes were focused on the two remaining large states, Virginia and New York. Many in these crucial states felt that because they were economically self-sufficient they did not need a federal government to protect their economies. Like many persons in other states, they also feared a powerful federal government.

Washington wrote, "A few short weeks will determine the political fate of America." He pointed out that in Virginia the Antifederalists were employing "every art that could inflame the passions or touch the interest of men." George Mason argued that the federal government would destroy the sovereignty of Virginia, saying: "These two concurrent powers cannot exist long together; the one will destroy the other: the general government being paramount to, and in every respect more powerful than the state governments, the latter must give way to the former." He finally conceded that he would vote for ratification if a Bill of Rights were added to the Constitution. Patrick Henry, however, was not willing to make a single concession. Deeply loyal to Virginia, he seized upon the opening words of the Constitution as proof that it would subvert the states: "The question turns, sir, on that poor little thing—the expression, We, the *people,* instead of the *states,* of America." Playing on every republican's deepest fears, Henry warned, "Your President may easily become your king. Your Senate is so imperfectly constructed that your dearest rights may be sacrificed by what may be a small minority; and a very small minority may continue forever unchangeably this government, although horridly defective." In short, the Antifederalists were more afraid than any Federalist that the people under the new system would be prevented from adequately governing themselves.

Virginia ratified the Constitution by the slim majority of eighty-nine to seventy-nine, largely because the state's governor, Edmund Randolph, dramatically switched his loyalties to the Constitution at the last

minute, declaring, "I am a friend to the Union." Washington, Virginia's most famous native son, also reserved his public endorsement of the Constitution until the crucial last moment.

Madison and Hamilton arranged for the news of Virginia's ratification to be sped by couriers to New York. New York was sharply divided on the question, with the Antifederalists having an overwhelming majority. In general, New York City favored ratification, while the upstate delegates opposed it. In order to plead the cause of the Constitution, John Jay, Alexander Hamilton, and James Madison produced a series of brilliant articles, the *Federalist Papers.* Although these essays may have influenced some members of the New York ratification convention, the members probably were

Benjamin Franklin addressing James Madison at the Constitutional Convention. Franklin was working for a compromise between the Virginia Plan and the plan submitted by New Jersey.

216

swayed far more by the news from Virginia and New Hampshire. In addition, the delegates from New York City vowed to take the city into the union on its own if the convention did not ratify the document. In July, 1788, New York adopted the Constitution by the narrow margin of three votes (30 to 27).

The two remaining states entered the Union only after the new government was already in operation. North Carolina held out until November, 1789, and Rhode Island ratified in May, 1790, only after Congress threatened to deal with the recalcitrant little state as a foreign power.

HISTORICAL VIEWPOINTS

Throughout the nineteenth century, American historians generally looked upon the Founding Fathers as enlightened statesmen who had had to struggle against men with no vision of the great future destiny of the nation. In 1913, however, the historian Charles Beard published *An Economic Interpretation of the Constitution of the United States* in which he presented a case for at least one of the Antifederalist positions, the claim that the Constitution was the work of "moneyed men" whose primary motive had been to protect their own financial interests. Beard referred to the Constitution as "an economic document drawn with superb skill by men whose property interests were immediately at stake." He did not claim that the framers of the Constitution had cynically worked only for their own interests, but he did suggest that their economic interests had shaped their political attitudes. Beard discovered that most of the Founding Fathers held public securities of the United States (the national debt) and therefore stood to gain if the national credit were strengthened.

More than any other historian, Beard succeeded in demoting the delegates to the Philadelphia convention from their status as demigods (a word used by Jefferson at the time to describe the assembly). Throughout the latter nineteenth century, such men as Franklin, Madison, and Washington had been revered without question. Yet, the writings of these men did suggest that Beard's interpretation might have some validity. Washington wrote General Lafayette that he looked forward to a "government of respectability under which life, liberty and property will be secured to us." John Rutledge of South Carolina wrote, "Property is certainly the principal object of society." Similarly, Gouverneur Morris declared, "If property is then the main object of government, certainly it ought to be one measure of the influence due to those who are to be affected by the government."

A closer look at the actual statements of the Founding Fathers, however, offers evidence that they were as devoted to the common good as to their own interests. Pierce Butler of South Carolina, for example, held government securities and stood to profit if the new regime honored wartime debts in full, yet he argued against such a policy "lest it should compel payment as well to the bloodsuckers who had speculated on the distress of others, as to those who had fought and bled for their country." Similarly, Hamilton, who had a strong aristocratic bent and wanted the President and Senators elected for life, nevertheless argued for a large House of Representatives since it "was on so narrow a scale as to be really dangerous, and to warrant a jealousy in the people for their liberties." Moreover, he owned few public securities.

Perhaps of more significance was the enormous prestige of the essays of John Locke. For Locke, one of the main purposes of government was the protection of property; human freedom could be defined and measured only by the amount of protection the government afforded to private property. The founders believed in these ideas, but the security of property was only one part of their larger goal, the protection of the liberty of the American people and the nation as a whole. The men who supported the Constitution wanted a central government able to foster their dream of a nation where men could find individual and political liberty and economic opportunity, and protect it. They also wanted a government which could maintain the nation's self-respect in international affairs. If a stronger central government could achieve this, many founders believed, the republic would fulfill its destiny of greatness.

If Beard's thesis were entirely correct, Antifederalists should all have been champions to the common man and democracy, and Federalists should all have been moneyed aristocrats. The facts belie the thesis. Two leading Antifederalists, for example, were George Mason and Elbridge Gerry, and they were as skeptical of a people's democracy as any New York banker. Gerry was also one of the largest holders of public securities at the convention and he refused to sign the document. Had the Antifederalists represented the mood of the land-hungry farmer, then it should follow that the men who took up arms in Shays's Rebellion would have been Antifederalists. In fact, the delegates from the Shaysite territory in Massachusetts all voted *for* ratification. Similarly, the predominantly agricultural state of New Jersey also endorsed the new government, which would have been unlikely, according to Beard's thesis.

In short, the Antifederalist camp was characterized not so much by its clear-cut economic interests as by vague suspicions that the Constitution would spell the end of states' rights and inaugurate an era of federal tyranny. The new government would be empowered to tax, raise an army, regulate commerce, and sign treaties with foreign powers. All this untried power struck Antifederalists as a dangerous innovation. The republican form of government was still on trial, for most of the world was ruled by monarchies. Could a vast, centralized republic succeed any better than the states in protecting individual liberty? Men on both sides of the issue who cherished freedom hotly debated the question.

THE NEW GOVERNMEN

The new Congress was supposed to convene on March 4, 1789, in New York's City Hall, which had just been luxuriously remodeled by the French architect, Pierre Charles L'Enfant. The House of Representatives, however, was not able to meet until a month later, causing Fisher Ames, a Congressman from Boston, to moan: "The people will forget the new government before it is born." However, by April 6, the Senate had formed a quorum and the two houses of Congress were ready to examine the ballots for President. No one was greatly surprised at the results: Washington had been unanimously elected President and John Adams (just returned from being minister to England), Vice-President.

Washington made a triumphal journey from his Virginia plantation, Mount Vernon, to New York City. Everywhere, parades and cheering crowds greeted the revered "Father of His Country." Washington himself recognized that his new office carried awesome responsibilities. Everything he did in his first months as President would be taken as an omen of things to come. As he said, "There is scarcely an action, the motive of which may not be subject to a double interpretation. There is scarcely any part of my conduct which may not hereafter be drawn into precedent."

Alexander Hamilton played a key role in obtaining New York's ratification of the Constitution. New York held a parade honoring Hamilton with a float that fired a thirteen-gun salute when it passed Washington and his cabinet.

The Vice-President, John Adams, was, according to Benjamin Franklin, "always an honest man, often a wise one, but sometimes, and in some things, absolutely out of his senses." Adams became very involved with the whole question of how to address the President. The simple title of President seemed to him ridiculous. "What will the common people of foreign countries, what will the soldiers and sailors say 'George Washington, President of the United States'? They will despise him to *all eternity*." Called merely the President, he might be confused with the president of a cricket club, Adams argued. He would have preferred "His Highness the President of the United States and Protector of Their Liberties." This controversy occupied the Senate's time from April 23 to May 14, and nothing came of it except that Adams earned himself the unofficial title, "His Rotundity."

Much more influential than the Vice-President, were James Madison and Alexander Hamilton. Madison and Hamilton had been the prime movers behind the ratification of the Constitution and they were now the two most dominant figures, besides Washington, in the first years of the Federalist era. Madison's fellow Virginian, Patrick Henry, had so opposed ratification that after it became a fact he vengefully prevented Madison's election to the Senate. As a consequence, Madison was sent to the House of Representatives, where he quickly became the leading member. In addition, he served as a close personal adviser to the President.

Alexander Hamilton received the important post of Secretary of the Treasury. Unlike Madison, he did not come from an aristocratic background, but was born out of wedlock in the British West Indies, and did not come to the colonies until shortly before the Revolutionary War. He was soon involved in writing articles for the patriot cause. During the war he became Washington's aide-de-camp and married into the wealthy Schuyler family of New York, two associations which greatly influenced his future. After the war he became a successful lawyer in New York and helped found the Bank of New York. Hamilton had an intense personality and a brilliant mind. He loved politics and was a fierce advocate of any cause he supported. Of most importance to the new nation was his incisive understanding of the intricacies of high finance.

WASHINGTON AS PRESIDENT

Stern, dignified, and austere, Washington was an impressive first President who deliberated carefully (some felt *too* carefully) before making a decision. He appointed advisers he believed to be the most highly qualified for the posts, not necessarily because they agreed with him. Washington was well aware that many Antifederalists feared that the President might become a tyrant; accordingly, he took scrupulous care never to overstep his bounds. For example, the Constitution stated that the President must make treaties with "the advice and consent" of the Senate and Washington took the directive at its word. When negotiations with certain Indian tribes were pending, Washington personally went to the Senate, took the Vice-President's chair and asked the Senators for their advice. The senators, evidently intimidated by his presence and unprepared for his sudden demand for advice, hemmed and hawed. Finally, they suggested that the proposals should be studied by a committee of five. Washington stood up in a towering rage, exclaiming: "This defeats every purpose of my coming here," and left abruptly. Despite his dissatisfaction with their response

on this occasion, Washington never neglected to communicate his negotiations on treaties to the Senate, but henceforth in the form of written messages, which was much more his inclination.

Washington was able to allay public fears that he would overstep his powers as defined by the Constitution, yet he could never be mistaken for a man of the people. He had no interest in being styled as a king, but in many ways he lived like one. He traveled in a magnificent coach drawn by six cream-colored horses. His mansion on Broadway in Manhattan was staffed with twenty-one uniformed servants. His birthday was the most important event of the social season. Like the King of England in Parliament, Washington delivered his state of the union speech to Congress personally and then insisted that the members of both houses attend him to his mansion. Washington held receptions on appointed days for dignitaries, as Mrs. Washington did for their wives. Madison complained that the "satellites and sycophants which surrounded him had wound up the ceremonials of the government to such a pitch of stateliness which nothing but his personal character could have supported, and which no character after him could ever maintain."

A CABINET OF ADVISERS

The Constitution had not specifically mentioned that the President would have advisers, but a need for executive departments to aid the President had been foreseen. One of the first acts of the new Congress was to provide for the continuation of the three departments created under the Articles, the Departments of State (formerly Foreign Affairs), War, and Treasury. The Congress also created the offices of Attorney General and Postmaster General. As already noted, Washington appointed Jefferson to head the State Department and Hamilton, the Treasury. As his Secretary of War, he selected Henry Knox, a man of girth (he weighed 300 pounds) with a reputation as a marksman during the Revolution. Edmund Randolph, who had opposed the Constitution during the Virginia ratification convention until the last moment, was rewarded for his farsightedness with the post of Attorney General.

Washington's failure to obtain the advice of the Senate on the matter of the Indian treaty made him turn thereafter to the heads of his executive departments for counsel. Thus began the institution of the Cabinet, which was holding regular meetings by 1793. Washington was a skilled administrator, leaving the work of the individual departments to those in charge of them while keeping an eye on all governmental activities. He asked for the opinions of all department heads on important questions, which occasionally aroused controversy in the administration, but he never hesitated to make the final decisions and take responsibility for them. He was industrious, prompt, systematic, and exacting.

RELATIONS WITH CONGRESS

The President did not, however, play a positive role in relation to the Congress. Washington was so wary of treading on the toes of Congress that he believed the President should never propose or even favor pieces of legislation while they were being debated. He also believed that the Presidential veto should never be invoked except when a proposed bill, in his opinion, was unconstitutional.

Because Washington took little or no initiative in guiding the Congress, Madison, Hamilton, and later Jefferson filled the vacuum. Madison was a member of the House and his natural leadership soon elevated him to a dominant position there. Hamilton, as Secretary of the Treasury, dealt closely with the House, which had the sole right to initiate money bills. In actual fact, Hamilton not only advised the House on financial matters but often even wrote the bills he wanted. He was a man of enormous energy and vast powers of persuasion, and many Representatives constantly deferred to his genius. Jefferson, who became Secretary of State in 1790, had little contact officially with Congress but nevertheless made his presence felt. His close friendship with Madison gradually gave him considerable influence.

THE FIRST CONGRESS

Many members of Congress were well-known to Washington. Indeed, forty-four members of the First Congress had taken part in the Constitutional Convention, a number from his own Virginia, the only state to return Antifederalist senators.

By September, 1789, the new Congress had passed the important Judiciary Act, thereby setting up thirteen federal district courts and three circuit courts of appeal. Congress had set the number of Supreme Court justices at six and Washington appointed John Jay as Chief Justice. During the debates over the Judiciary Act, some Congressmen concerned about states' rights had tried to eliminate the provision for district courts. Madison, however, had persuaded the majority that the enforcement of federal laws should not be entrusted to the state courts alone. The act provided that cases dealing with the Constitution, federal laws, or treaties could be appealed from the state courts to the federal court system. This, in effect, assured that the final authority on any federal matter would be the highest federal court—the Supreme Court. Thus, the doctrine of judicial review, not mentioned in the Constitution, received strong support in one of the first acts of the Congress.

THE BILL OF RIGHTS

The Antifederalists had seized upon the omission of a Bill of Rights in the new

221

constitution as a reason for not ratifying it. While the first Congress was meeting, New York and Virginia called for a second Constitutional Convention to write a new document from an extreme states' rights point of view.

In order to stop such disruptive moves and to honor the promises that Federalists had made to several ratifying conventions, Madison proposed a Bill of Rights as one of the first orders of business in the new Congress. "If we can make the Constitution better in the opinion of those who are opposed to it without weakening its frame, or abridging its usefulness in the judgment of those who are attached to it," Madison said, "we act the part of wise and liberal men to make such alterations as shall produce that effect."

A Bill of Rights had been omitted from the original Constitution for several rea-

James Madison in a portrait by Gilbert Stuart. Madison proposed that a Bill of Rights be the first order of business of the new Congress in an attempt to quell criticism by the anti-Federalists.

sons. First, the Articles of Confederation had not contained a Bill of Rights. Second, the Constitution had not superseded the bills of rights that were included in the constitutions of almost every state. Third, the new federal government had been instituted by the people themselves through their representatives. Why should the people need a guarantee of their liberties in a document they themselves had ratified? Finally, some of the framers of the Constitution had feared that a specific list of rights might be interpreted as excluding other rights that had not been mentioned.

Nevertheless, Madison recognized that a list of liberties would allay the fears of the skeptical so he drew up twelve amendments (the first eight he condensed from a list of forty suggested by the Virginia ratifying convention), only ten of which were ratified. Passed by Congress on September 25, 1789, and in 1791 by three-fourths of the states, the Bill of Rights guaranteed freedom of speech, religion, peaceful assembly, and the press; the right to bear arms; freedom from unreasonable search; no general search warrants; and the right to the protection of certain legal procedures known as the due process of law. The Ninth and Tenth Amendments promised that the federal government would not assume any powers not accorded it in the Constitution, thus confining Congress and the President to their allotted spheres.

HAMILTON'S FISCAL POLICY

Washington had foreseen that the chief problem of the new government would be to establish its authority, which in turn would depend on whether the American people could learn "to distinguish between oppression and the necessary exercise of lawful authority . . . to discriminate the spirit of liberty from that of licentiousness." Americans had fought a long, bitter Revolutionary War to escape economic oppression. The first government they had established did not have the power to tax, and it had failed to support itself or impose order on the disrupted country. Now a second government had been born, but with the right to raise revenue. Would Americans submit to federal customs officers and tax collectors?

Because the new nation was fortunate enough to have a financial expert, Alexander Hamilton, as its first Secretary of the Treasury, it soon had efficient methods for coping with its financial problems.

In this post, Hamilton was the most important official in the new administration, second only to Washington and, according to some critics, more important than even the President. He headed the largest department. Under his control, the Treasury had thirty clerks and almost one thousand customhouse officers and internal revenue agents in its employ, whereas the State Department had only four clerks, and the Department of War only three. Hamilton's

Alexander Hamilton was the new nation's first Secretary of the Treasury.

status was deserving of the official in charge of solving the nation's most pressing problem, a lack of money. The country needed revenue first and credit second, and these two requirements took precedence over all other matters.

Hamilton believed a strong central government was essential. He had a pessimistic view of man's capacity for governing himself well. He feared anarchy and chaos more than the loss of freedom under a too powerful and perhaps arbitrary government. He seemed to believe, however, that the wealthy and well born would be less inclined to govern out of greed and self-interest than other men. In other words, only a few men were fit to hold political office, and political authority should be strong to keep order and command respect at home and abroad.

A sound economy was essential to Hamilton's concept of an orderly government. He considered a nation's economy secure when it was balanced and could pay its debts; that is to say, when it achieved a good credit rating. In order to reach these two goals, he called for an expansion of the commercial and manufacturing sectors, while allowing the predominant agricultural interest to continue developing on its own. Eventually, all areas of the American economy would be equally strong and interdependent. The United States would be almost self-sufficient and not dependent on other countries for its economic needs. To accomplish this, Hamilton wanted to establish a tie between the commercial and manufacturing interests (the monied wealth) and the government through economic policies which would please the businessmen.

From an economic standpoint, Hamilton's fiscal program was a brilliant success. However, his program turned out to be so one-sided that it gradually alienated the agricultural element, which represented over 90 percent of the population at that time. Thus, Hamilton's program led in the long run to political disaster for its supporters.

THE NATIONAL DEBT

Upon examining America's financial position, Hamilton discovered that the country owed about fifty-four million dollars (the combined domestic and foreign debt). Of this total, more than eleven million was owed to Dutch bankers and to the governments of France and Spain. Forty-two million was owed to American citizens who had bought bonds during the war to support the Revolution. Some of these certificates had also been issued to soldiers instead of pay. By 1790, however, few of the original purchasers of these certificates still held them. The certificates had declined in value over the last 10 years as it seemed more and more unlikely that the government would ever redeem them. Speculators, mainly the commercial interests in the eastern seaboard towns, then had bought them at a fraction of their original price.

In his *Report on Public Credit,* presented to Congress on January 14, 1790, Hamilton recommended that these certificates be paid in full. To fund the national debt, Hamilton proposed to replace these old certificates with new ones which could be paid off very slowly beginning in 1791. The plan was not to pay off the total national debt immediately, which the government did not have the means to do, but to establish American credit by showing the ability to pay at least a small amount each year on demand.

Hamilton's bold plan created an uproar. The chief opponent to the plan was Madison, Hamilton's old friend. Madison believed that some method of establishing American credit should be found but objected to Hamilton's scheme for two reasons. First, Madison was a Southerner and four-fifths of the national debt was owed to Northerners. If the entire country were taxed equally to redeem the certificates, the payment would amount to a massive transfer of money from Southern to Northern hands. Second, Madison objected to it on ethical grounds. He felt no hesitation in paying the soldiers and citizens who had bought the certificates *originally;* the soldiers, after all, had served in the army and received the certificates as pay, while the citizens had taken a risk in order to finance the Revolution. But Madison vehemently objected to payment in full to Northern speculators, some of whom had bought the certificates only quite recently at a fraction of their original price (about twenty-five cents on the dollar).

Hamilton firmly defended his original proposal. First, he pointed out that if the government distinguished between one sort of certificate-holder and another, America's credit would remain shaky. Foreign and native investors would not trust a government that did not pay *all* its debts, no matter to whom they were owed. Second, Hamilton believed that the well-to-do speculators who owned most of the certificates (many of them members of Congress) were the only group in America that "thought continentally." The rest of the citizenry, "the community at large," was provincial in its outlook and still felt its first loyalty to the states; little support for a strong federal government could be won from these people. No, the government must court the well-to-do, for only through their support could the new government succeed and the country expand in the areas Hamilton wished to bolster—commerce and manufacturing.

Hamilton won his way. The entire national debt was assumed and his funding system instituted. This action undeniably benefited speculators, but it also had the desired effect of restoring the national credit. Henceforth, citizens and foreign bankers were not afraid to invest in the United States. In the struggle, Madison had lost prestige in Congress and he was no longer its undisputed master. Now Hamilton became increasingly influential in the

House of Representatives. His victory also endeared him to the monied class in the nation. Although Hamilton had not personally profited from funding the national debt, he had allowed news of his plan to leak to friends in high places. These confidants immediately bought up all available shares at prices considerably below their face value.

THE STATE DEBTS

The second part of Hamilton's plan called for the government to assume an additional obligation, that of the debts that each state had incurred during the Revolution. The controversy over assumption (as this part of the plan was called) generated more heat than any other debate over funding of the national debt. In general, Congressmen approved of assumption if their states still had large unpaid wartime debts but disapproved if their states' debts had been paid off.

Maryland, Georgia, and North Carolina voted against assumption because they had only small debts. Pennsylvania owed about two million dollars, and its representatives in Congress were divided over the question. Since New York, New Jersey, Massachusetts, and South Carolina still owed large sums, they voted for assumption. Virginia had already paid a large share of its debts and felt that it should not have to assist states that were less prompt in discharging their obligations.

Congress was deadlocked over the issue of assumption for nearly 6 months. Hamilton wanted the federal government to assume the states' debts because he thought that by doing so he would build up the prestige of the federal government even further. He thought that the states' creditors would become increasingly attached to the national government, and that the influence of the states would gradually wither away.

The outcry against assumption was particularly strident in Virginia. Senator

George Mason declared that Hamilton had "done us more injury than Great Britain and all her fleets and armies." Patrick Henry called the plan unconstitutional. Henry had long predicted that the new federal government was up to no good and now his fellow Virginians honored him as a vindicated prophet.

The controversy was finally resolved in July, 1790. Hamilton agreed that the states which had already paid a large part of their debts would receive a partial reimbursement in the form of an outright grant of money. More important, Hamilton made a deal with Madison and Jefferson. The two Virginians had both opposed Hamilton's plan, but they agreed to support it in return for his promise that the national capital would be moved eventually (after a temporary, ten-year stay in Philadelphia) to the banks of the Potomac River. Jefferson later regretted this compromise, but at the time he thought conceding to Hamilton on the matter of assumption was not too high a price to pay for placing the nation's capital in Virginia.

THE NATIONAL BANK

Hamilton's financial plans for the new federal government did not stop at funding the national debt and assuming the states' wartime debts. He now proposed that Congress charter a national bank. The Bank of the United States would be owned partly by the government, but the major portion of its ten million dollar capital (four-fifths in fact) would be invested by private individuals. In fact, a large amount of this private investment would be made in the newly funded debt. Only a small percentage of investment would consist of gold and silver.

Hamilton argued that a national bank was necessary for a variety of purposes: it would serve as a safe depository for government funds; it would facilitate the collection of taxes; and it would issue a uniform national currency to aid American

The establishment of the first Bank of the United States was a hard-won victory for Hamilton against Jefferson's opposition.

economic expansion. In addition, a national bank would greatly benefit the well-to-do by providing them with easy credit and a safe venture in which to invest. As already noted, although Hamilton himself was a self-made man, he had an immense respect for the wealthy and felt that they alone could be counted on to support the new federal government. As most of the wealthy commercial class lived in the North, every part of Hamilton's financial blueprint (funding, assumption, and the establishment of a national bank) appealed to Northern commercial interests, repelled the Southern and Western landed class, and drove a wedge between the two sections of the nation.

The President had reservations of a different nature about the bank. Washington profoundly respected Hamilton's financial genius, but he was concerned that the proposed national bank might be unconstitutional. The bill authorizing the Bank of the United States had already passed the House of Representatives by a vote of thirty-seven to twenty, but Madison, who opposed it, had succeeded in raising doubts about its constitutionality in Washington's mind. The President then decided to ask Jefferson for his opinion; the Secretary of State also opposed the bank. Citing the Tenth Amendment, which states that "all powers not delegated to the United States by the Constitution . . . are reserved to the states, or the people," Jefferson argued that establishing a national bank was clearly *not* a power delegated to the federal government. If Congress started expanding its powers without authority, the states would rise up in anger and soon Congress would "take possession of a boundless field of power, no longer susceptible to any definition." He maintained that such an institution was not provided for under Article I, Section 8 of the Constitution, which outlined the specific powers of Congress. Even under the last clause of this Article, which allowed the Congress to "make all laws which shall be necessary and proper for carrying into Execution the foregoing Powers," Jefferson could not see that such an institution was "necessary." After all, it was not absolutely essential to the operation of government. Jefferson, Madison, and others of their persuasion came to be known as "strict constructionists," because they believed the federal government should exercise only those powers which were explicitly given to it by the Constitution.

In reply, Hamilton submitted his own *Opinion on the Constitutionality of the Bank* on February 23, 1791. He dismissed Jefferson's strict interpretation and favored a broad, or loose, construction of the Constitution. As Hamilton put it, "the powers contained in a constitution of government, especially those which concern the general administration of the affairs of a country, its finances, trade, defense etc., ought to be construed liberally in advancement of the public good. . . ." Hamilton insisted that the right to set up a bank was implied in the "necessary and proper" clause since "a bank has a natural relation to the power of collecting taxes—to that of regulating trade—to that of providing for the common defense." Collecting taxes, regulating trade, and providing for the common defense were all "powers vested by the Constitution in the government," and therefore the bank was wholly in accord with the Constitution. According to Hamilton, "necessary" did not have to mean what was absolutely essen-

tial, but only that which was convenient.

Throughout American history, men have taken either Jefferson's or Hamilton's position on how the Constitution should be interpreted. For example, in 1819 the Supreme Court adopted Hamilton's broad construction of the "necessary and proper" clause, and by doing so sanctioned the gradual extension of federal authority into countless matters never envisioned by the Founding Fathers. The interpretation placed on the Constitution by politicians has occasionally resulted from abstract beliefs as to whether a strong or a weak central government was in the best interests of the citizenry. However, whether a politician has argued for a strict or a loose construction of the Constitution has usually depended upon how the argument would further his economic and political interests and those of his constituents. It is clear that Hamilton wanted a loose construction of the Constitution because he believed it would further his goals of a strong central government and a strong and diversified economy. We shall soon see why Jefferson was most of the time a staunch defender of a strict interpretation of the document.

Washington was convinced by Hamilton's argument and signed the bank bill. The Bank of the United States succeeded from the beginning of its career. Foreign investments began in the United States and soon the country had a sound credit rating in the world. Although Hamilton's financial plans had created division in the nation, they established widespread confidence in the solvency and reliability of the new government.

ECONOMIC PLANNING

The final contribution Hamilton made as Secretary of the Treasury was embodied in his *Report on the Subject of Manufactures*. The House had asked Hamilton in January, 1790, to draw up a plan that would encourage American manufacturers

and make the United States independent
of other nations, particularly in its production of military supplies. After Hamilton
studied world economic conditions and government economic policies, he submitted
his report in December, 1791. He argued
that other countries were setting up increasingly restrictive mercantilist systems
and that the United States could only follow suit by adopting a closed economic
system of its own. To protect fledgling
American manufacturers, Hamilton proposed to construct a system of tariffs, subsidies, and "bounties," or awards for new
industries.

Once again Hamilton's proposition
aroused sectional controversy. Southerners,
who had few industries and were primarily
agriculturists, resented the plan. The Southern farmer would gain nothing from higher
tariffs; he would simply have to pay higher
prices on manufactured goods. Jefferson in
his *Notes on Virginia* considered the growth
of manufacturing, of cities, and of the urban working class to be a grave threat to
traditional American virtues. According to
Jefferson, "those who labor in the earth
are the chosen people of God," whereas
"the mobs of great cities" were like sores
sapping "the strength of the human body."
Paradoxically, some Northern merchants
joined Southerners in opposing Hamilton's
plan, for they feared high tariffs would discourage trade. The Report was not implemented, although many of Hamilton's specific suggestions were incorporated into the
Tariff Act of May, 1792. All of his proposed
bounties were discarded, except one to encourage the fishing industry. As Hamilton
learned, the United States was not yet ready
to become a great manufacturing center.
It was still predominantly agricultural and
would remain so for some time.

FIRST SIGNS OF
POLITICAL PARTIES

Hamilton's fiscal policies, his admiration
of the rich, his distrust of the common man,

and his clear preference for the North over
the South earned him the political enmity
of both Madison and Jefferson. Whereas
Hamilton disliked the state governments,
Jefferson and Madison were both convinced
that a too-powerful federal government was
a real threat to liberty. Jefferson became
convinced that Hamilton was leading a
royalist plot to overthrow republicanism in
America and was planning to replace it
with a monarchy. In return, Hamilton
called Jefferson's character into question by
describing him as "the most intriguing
man in the United States," a man who
was "cautious and sly, wrapped up in impenetrable silence and mystery." Hamilton
threw his support behind John Fenno, the
publisher of a Philadelphia newspaper, the
Gazette of the United States. He gave him
many Treasury printing contracts and outright loans. Out of "gratitude," Fenno
praised Hamilton as the greatest American
statesman next to Washington. For his part,
Jefferson subsidized Philip Freneau, a well-
known Revolutionary poet. Freneau set up
a rival newspaper in 1791, the *National
Gazette,* which heralded Jefferson as "the
Colossus of Liberty." The two newspapers
exchanged many bitter words, Fenno lam-
pooning Jefferson and Freneau attacking
Hamilton.

Washington tried to stand above the
quarrel, although it greatly disturbed him.
The Founding Fathers had hoped that
America would not have political parties
which they equaled with the rancor of
factions such as those prevalent in eighteenth-century England and in some of the
colonies before the Revolution. Washington
himself disliked being President and longed
to return to the peace of his beloved Mount
Vernon. He had prepared to retire in the
spring of 1792, but Hamilton, Jefferson,
and Madison convinced him to serve another term. Washington reluctantly accepted, and he and John Adams were re-
elected in the fall. Washington persuaded
Hamilton and Jefferson to maintain at
least an outward show of mutual respect.

However, the fierce antagonism that would eventually split Americans into the first political parties subsided only temporarily.

FOREIGN AFFAIRS

The ever-widening gulf between Jefferson and Hamilton also showed in disagreements over American foreign policy.

Jefferson, as Secretary of State, was chiefly concerned with realization of true American independence. While he had a strong personal attachment to France because of his years there as minister, he sought to uphold France's friendship with America on strategic grounds. The only alliance the United States had was with France. France did not menace the country's western borders, as did Spain at the mouth of the Mississippi, and England around the Great Lakes. France might in fact come to the aid of the United States in expelling these two powers from American soil. Jefferson wanted to establish American sovereignty to the Mississippi River, while at the same time keeping the country isolated from the quarrels of Europe.

Hamilton's foreign policy goals were related to the protection of American credit. Hamilton's influence in the Congress prevented the passage of measures favored by Jefferson and Madison which would have cut off all trade with Great Britain until she negotiated a favorable commercial treaty with the United States. Hamilton had always been a great admirer of England. He was, however, against this policy not so much out of love of Britain, but for the practical reason that the main source of revenue to the hard-pressed United States Treasury were tariffs on British goods imported into the country. In this case, the foreign policy favored by Jefferson was subordinated to the needs of Hamilton's Treasury, but his advice gained stronger support from Washington in relations with France.

The year 1789 saw the beginning of the French Revolution, and in 1791 a French republic was proclaimed. At first, Americans of every political persuasion greeted the news of the fall of the French monarchy with exultation. France, America's wartime ally, was now following the example of the United States and freeing herself from the yoke of royal tyranny. The Count de Lafayette later sent Washington the key to the Bastille, a prison in Paris where the Bourbon kings had imprisoned their political enemies. Washington declared the key "a token of victory gained by liberty over despotism."

By the fall of 1792, the first phase of the French Revolution, moderate and middle-class in character, had come to an end and the second and much more violent stage of the great upheaval was under way. France, now under the control of a party anxious to spread the doctrines of the Revolution throughout Europe, was at war with Austria and Prussia. Internally, the constitutional monarchy of 1791 was overthrown by the combined forces of the war party, the workers, and the peasantry. Unrest and fear swept the land and the government resorted to the guillotine to restore order. France's "reign of terror" had begun. In January, 1793, King Louis XVI was beheaded and American conservatives began to fear that this rage for attacks on property, religion, and those in authority in general might spread to the shores of the United States. While Hamilton, Washington, and their followers were horrified at the French excesses, Jefferson remained steadfast in his approval of the goals of the French Revolution. Jefferson deplored the beheadings but announced: "The liberty of the whole earth was depending on the issue of the contest and . . . rather than it should have failed, I would have seen half the earth devastated."

AMERICAN NEUTRALITY

Following the beheading of the French king, Great Britain formed an alliance with Holland, Prussia, and Austria (later joined by Spain) to stop what they considered a threat to European civilization. On February 1, 1793, these powers declared war on France. News of the international war shifted the debate over the merits of the French Revolution to the practical question of whether the United States should become involved in the conflict. The Franco-American Alliance of 1778 required the United States to defend French possessions, such as the French West Indies, against such enemies of France as the British. Americans wondered, would France demand that the United States fulfill this obligation?

Hamilton watched with horror as France's "war of all peoples against all kings" progressed. Involvement in such a conflict with a nation whose policies were alien to everything Hamilton believed in was not only personally repugnant, but it would reach into the American treasury. He argued that the Treaty of 1778 was no longer valid, since it had been made with the French monarch and not with the government now in power. There was no doubt in Hamilton's mind that the United States must abrogate the treaty, proclaim its neutrality, and refuse to receive the French minister.

Jefferson, who had served as America's first minister to France, admired French civilization and particularly the spirit of French democracy, and he strongly disagreed with Hamilton. Like Hamilton, Jefferson realized that for the United States to enter a war against Great Britain would be foolhardy, but he urged Washington not to declare American neutrality without Congressional support. He further argued that the United States should not abrogate the Alliance of 1778 unless American security was directly endangered. The agreement had been made with the French people, not a specific government; it was therefore important for America to set a precedent of living up to international commitments.

Washington finally compromised and accepted the combined advice of his two advisers. He proclaimed American neutrality on April 22, 1793, but without specifically using the word "neutrality." At the same time, the United States did not abrogate the French Alliance and received the French minister to the United States, Citizen Edmond Genêt.

CITIZEN GENÊT

The young French minister, Edmond Genêt, was a hot-blooded idealist who was determined to throw diplomatic caution to the wind and take any risk to aid his country. While France had decided not to press the United States to defend her West Indian Islands, she did wish to use American ports for launching attacks on British merchant ships. In 1793, Genêt arrived in Charleston, South Carolina, a stronghold of pro-French sentiment. Violating American law, Genêt commissioned fourteen Charleston ship captains as privateers for the French. These managed to capture about eighty British ships without the sanction of the United States government. After arriving in Philadelphia, Genêt also planned an abortive expedition against Louisiana to be led by the Revolutionary War hero, George Rogers Clark.

President Washington, deeply displeased, warned Genêt to stop his illegal activities, but Genêt was unperturbed, having enjoyed a triumphal march from Charleston to Philadelphia. Everywhere, Genêt had been met with adoration. In Philadelphia he founded a Democratic Society, dedicated to upholding the cause of France. Soon more than forty other such clubs were formed across the country. Receiving so much popular acclaim, Genêt decided to appeal to public opinion and ignore the President.

Washington was furious, Hamilton was convinced that unless Genêt was stopped Federalist heads would soon be rolling in Philadelphia, and even the pro-French Jefferson lost patience. Jefferson described the reckless Genêt as "all imagination,

THE TIMES, a POLITICAL PORTRAIT

The Cannibals are landing

Stop de wheels of

de gouvernement

Triumph Government: perish all its enemies.—
Traitors, be warned: justice though slow, is sure.

This Federalist cartoon exaggerates Jefferson's pro-French attitude and Washington's anxieties over the state of affairs following the French Revolution in 1790. The French are shown attacking from the left. Washington is trying to advance to meet the French, but Citizen Gênet, Albert Gallatin, and Thomas Jefferson attempt to restrain Washington.

no judgment, passionate, disrespectful and even indecent towards the President." He knew that while the majority of Americans might be pro-French, they certainly did not want to enter the war on her side. Washington demanded that the impudent Genêt be recalled by his government to Paris.

The government that had dispatched Genêt, however, no longer existed. Genêt had represented a political faction called the Girondists. They had been overturned by a new, even more radical group, the Jacobins, who declared that all of Genêt's actions were "criminal maneuvers." The frightened young man realized that a return to France might mean the loss of his head. He begged Washington to grant him asylum in America. Washington relented and a few months later the attractive hothead married the daughter of Governor Clinton of New York and retired to a quiet farm.

BRITISH ATTACKS

The United States had declared its neutrality, but England and France nevertheless seized about six hundred American ships between 1793 and 1794. The provocation for these seizures was quite simple: France captured American vessels headed for England and England took American ships sailing for France. Americans hoped to profit by supplying each of the belligerents with American products, but both European powers were determined to ob-

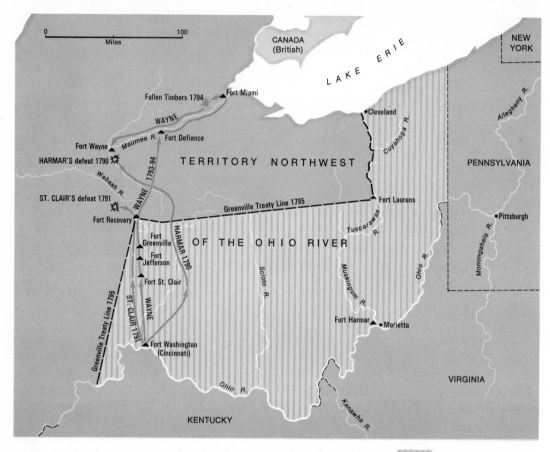

INDIAN WARS IN THE NORTHWEST · 1790 TO 1794

Indian lands ceded in 1795

✳ American victory ✵ Indian victory

struct American trade with the enemy. England was more formidable in this regard since the British navy was the most powerful one in the world. When American ships attempted to trade with the French West Indies, British warships seized some 250 American vessels, tried them in British West Indian admiralty courts, and condemned half of them for violating the rights of neutrals in wartime. In addition, many American sailors were forced (impressed) into the British Navy. To the British, anything that might conceivably aid the French war effort, including food, was contraband

and thus liable to seizure. The United States, however, had insisted since the Revolutionary War that the only contraband were arms and ammunition.

While these seizures inflamed American feelings against the British, England almost drove the United States to declare war by stirring up the Indians in the Northwest. The United States had obtained the entire Northwest in the Peace Treaty of 1783, but as yet, few American settlers had been able to enter the territory. Washington sent Arthur St. Clair in 1791 to crush the Miamis of Ohio, but the Indians, encouraged by the British, had routed St. Clair. In February, 1794, as Major General Anthony Wayne (known as "Mad Anthony" for his fierce leadership in the Revolution) prepared to enter the Northwest, the British governor of Canada again incited the Indians to repel the Americans. Worse still, the British had never removed their troops from American soil; a thousand redcoats were still stationed in the Northwest. In 1794 England was actually beginning to build a new fort in the Ohio country.

War between the United States and Great Britain was a real and immediate danger. American public opinion was inflamed over British conduct, and even Hamilton, the Anglophile, characterized her aggressive acts on the high seas as "atrocious." When the followers of Jefferson in Congress secured a temporary embargo on trade with England in early 1794, Hamilton persuaded the President to send a special negotiator to London to prevent open conflict between the two countries. On April 19, 1794, Congress named Chief Justice John Jay to undertake the mission with instructions to: get the British out of the Northwest, force England to pay for the American ships that had been seized, urge Britain to accept America's rights as a neutral, and negotiate a new commercial treaty with Britain.

JAY'S TREATY

After months of discussion, Jay and the British foreign minister, Lord Grenville, worked out a treaty that the British regarded as too generous to the United States and Jay's fellow Americans considered a national disgrace. At this time, the British war effort was going well, George III's troops had just scored a number of important victories in the war against France, and English intelligence reported that America was pitifully unprepared for a full-scale war. Moreover, Lord Grenville knew that a war with England would mean an end to the import duties American customs offi-

cials collected on British goods entering the United States, for the American government drew most of its revenue from these duties. Thus, such a war would bring the United States close to bankruptcy.

Equally bolstering to English confidence was the retirement of Jefferson, the friend of France and enemy of Britain, from his post as Secretary of State in December, 1793. Exhausted by his long quarrel with Hamilton, Jefferson had decided to leave politics. His retirement left Hamilton's control over American diplomacy stronger than ever and Hamilton was so indiscreet as to communicate to George Hammond, the British minister in America: "I have always preferred a connection with you to that of any other country, *we think in English,* and have a similarity of prejudices and predilections." Furthermore, Hamilton may have directly weakened Jay's position in London by revealing that Washington had decided not to join with the neutral nations of Denmark and Sweden in arming their merchant ships to prevent seizure by England. It is quite unlikely, however, that this information, or any other that Hamilton could have given, would have changed the final outcome of the negotiation. Britain did not want war with the United States, but she was ready to go to war with America rather than make concessions in areas vital to the success of her war effort against revolutionary France.

When Jay signed the Treaty of London on November 19, 1794, America succeeded in attaining only some of her demands. The British agreed to evacuate their forts in the Northwest (which they finally did by 1796). A commercial treaty opened additional trade with the British and also granted American merchants the right to trade freely with the British East Indies. The rivers, lakes, and waters of the American continent were also to be open to both countries. The British promised to compensate American shipowners for vessels recently seized in the West Indies. An arbitration commission ultimately worked out a settlement of both this question and the amount American merchants still owed to British merchants in pre-Revolutionary war debts. These gains were all Jay was able to squeeze out of England. He had no success in convincing the English to respect American rights as a neutral power on the high seas. Jay yielded in accepting the English definition of "contraband," which included not only provisions but also naval stores (such as turpentine and tar), if paid for when confiscated. He also failed to get the British to give up the infuriating practice of impressment.

Of all the articles of the treaty, the one pertaining to American participation in the British West Indian trade was the most controversial. Ever since the Revolution, Britain had excluded Americans from the lucrative trade with the British West Indies, once so important to the American economy. One of Jay's primary goals had been to convince the British to open this trade again to the United States. Britain responded with a plan that was so hedged with restrictions that the American public regarded it as insulting. For example, American ships trading in the Indies could not weigh more than seventy tons and they could only carry their cargoes back to the United States. These terms would deny American merchants a part in the world trade of such valuable Caribbean produce as molasses, coffee, cocoa, sugar, and cotton. Congress rejected this provision before it would consider approving the treaty.

When news of the terms of Jay's treaty leaked out, the American people were indignant. They nicknamed the unfortunate minister "Sir John Jay" and Washington observed that a cry went up against the treaty "like that against a mad dog." To Americans, acceptance of the treaty seemed a humiliation. Yet, rejection of it might mean the outbreak of war with England. Washington stifled his pride and submitted the treaty to the Senate. After a protracted debate, the Senate ratified it on June 24, 1795, by a bare two-thirds majority.

Agreeing to the treaty was one of the most unpopular moves in Washington's career, although as events turned out, it was the wisest. Feeling against it was still so strong a year after it was ratified that when the House voted on the appropriation of money to implement the treaty, the vote was evenly divided. Frederick Muhlenberg finally cast his vote in favor of implementation (and was stabbed for doing so a few days later by his brother-in-law). Despite such violent reactions, the treaty could be credited with two accomplishments: it probably kept the country out of a war which she could ill afford and had little hope of winning, and it allowed America to continue to make immense profits as a neutral nation trading with the two great belligerents, France and England. Removal of British troops, coupled with the Grenville Treaty with the Indians in 1795, also prepared the way for American expansion into the Ohio Valley. From hindsight, the treaty was not a disaster, considering the weakness of the nation. The British could have refused to negotiate at all. In addition, over the next 10 years, relations with Britain improved. The treaty rankled not because better terms were really possible, but because it secured from the hated former Mother Country so much less than the American people thought they should have obtained.

PINCKNEY'S TREATY

Jay's Treaty with England was unpopular, but it helped prepare the groundwork for a treaty with Spain that was an unqualified success. Spain had withdrawn from her alliance with Britain and had made peace with the French. For this desertion, Spain expected British reprisals. What Spain especially feared was a joint British-American attack against Spanish possessions in America: Florida and the Gulf Coast. Even though Spain probably knew the terms of Jay's Treaty, she may have feared a secret article providing for such a military alliance. Moreover, Spain was in a state of bankruptcy and knew she could no longer hope to hold back American expansion in the Mississippi Valley. As a result, Spain tried to placate the United States by signing a treaty with a special American envoy to Madrid, Thomas Pinckney. Pinckney's treaty granted everything America had previously wanted: free navigation of the Mississippi "in its whole length from its source to the ocean"; free use of the port of New Orleans by Americans for 3 years, after which time a new, mutually satisfying arrangement would be made; and Spanish acceptance of the thirty-first parallel as America's southern boundary. Under the treaty's terms, Spain gave up her claims over the disputed areas of the Southwest and even promised to discourage Indian attacks on American settlements. For her part, the United States also pledged to try to pacify the Indians in the area, but made no further commitments.

The Senate accepted Pinckney's Treaty unanimously on March 3, 1796. The treaty removed the possibility that Kentucky and Tennessee, which had become states in 1792 and 1796, might secede from the Union and annex themselves to Spain. Americans in those states desperately needed to transport their farm produce down the Mississippi, and as long as Spain had kept the river closed to American citizens, farmers in the Southwest had contemplated changing their citizenship. The Mississippi was now open to trade. American sovereignty over the Northwest and the Southwest was finally realized through Jay's Treaty and Pinckney's Treaty. The promise of the Treaty of Paris of 1783 had been fulfilled.

DOMESTIC UNREST

While Jay was still negotiating his treaty, the administration faced unrest on the domestic front. In several western areas, there were eruptions of open rebellion against the federal government. To raise money for the assumption of states' debts, tariffs on commerce could not be raised still higher without encouraging smuggling and evasion, Hamilton reasoned. The necessary money had to come, therefore, from an excise tax on domestic products, of which whiskey was the most prominent. Hamilton had engineered the tax through Congress in 1791. Whiskey was a very important product in the West. As long as the Mississippi River remained closed to American traffic, whiskey was the only form in which grain could be transported cheaply overland. Whiskey was also used as money in the West in exchange for other goods. In addition, Hamilton's duties were high, as much as twenty-five cents on every dollar. Western farmers began to protest in 1792, but managed to hold their anger in check until the summer of 1794, when rioting broke out in western Pennsylvania. Government agents were terrorized, federal court proceedings were forcibly interrupted, and the excise inspector for western Pennsylvania was forced to surrender to an unruly mob.

After 2 years of cautious waiting, the President acted boldly to suppress this "Whiskey Rebellion." He called out a force of some thirteen thousand state militia. A contest had developed that tested the authority of the new federal government. Shays's Rebellion had been one of the immediate causes for the abandonment of the Articles of Confederation and the ratification of the new Constitution. Now that a second popular revolt had broken out, would the federal government be able to suppress it?

The man the western farmers loathed most, Alexander Hamilton, led the government's troops. Hamilton was determined to see to it personally that the law and order he had done so much to establish were properly vindicated. To Hamilton's dismay, the whiskey rebels fled out of sight at the approach of such a large army. Only a handful of prisoners were taken, and only two were accused of high treason. Washington pardoned both of them, adjudging one a "simpleton," the other "insane."

Hamilton and Jefferson, by now open political enemies, had quite different reactions to the Whiskey Rebellion. Jefferson scoffed, "An insurrection was announced and proclaimed and armed against, but could never be found." He believed that the proper method of ridding the country of the excise tax was by its repeal. Hamilton, on the other hand, announced that the government had gained "reputation and strength" by the display of military force. He seemed well satisfied that the forces of anarchy had been dispelled.

Alexander Hamilton on the Whiskey Rebellion

" *In compliance with your requisitions, I have the honor to submit my opinion as to the course which it will be advisable for the President to pursue, in regard to the armed opposition recently given in the four western counties of Pennsylvania to the execution of the laws of the United States laying duties upon spirits distilled within the United States, and upon stills . . .*

What in this state of things is proper to be done? The President has, with the advice of the heads of departments and the Attorney-General, caused to be submitted all the evidence of the foregoing facts to the consideration of an associate judge, under the act entitled, "An act to provide for calling forth the militia to execute the laws of the Union, suppress insurrection, and repel invasion."

If the judge shall pronounce that the case described in the second section of that act exists, it will follow that a competent force of militia should be called forth and employed to suppress the insurrection, and support the civil authority in effectuating obedience to the laws and punishment of offenders.

It appears to me that the very existence of government demands this course, and that a duty of the highest nature urges the Chief Magistrate to pursue it. The Constitution and laws of the United States contemplate and provide for it. . . . "

—Letter from Hamilton to Washington

Thomas Jefferson on the Whiskey Rebellion

" *. . . with respect to the transactions against the excise law, it appears to me that you are all swept away in the torrent of governmental opinions, or that we do not know what these transactions have been. We know of none which, according to the definitions of the law, have been anything more than riotous. There was indeed a meeting to consult about a separation. But to consult on a question does not amount to a determination of that question in the affirmative, still less to the acting on such a determination; but we shall see, I suppose, what the court lawyers, and courtly judges, and would-be ambassadors will make of it. The excise law is an infernal one. The first error was to admit it by the Constitution; the 2d, to act on that admission; the 3d and last will be, to make it the instrument of dismembering the Union, and setting us all afloat to chuse which part of it we will adhere to. The information of our militia, returned from the Westward, is uniform, that tho the people there let them pass quietly, they were objects of their laughter, not of their fear; that 1,000 men could have cut off their whole force in a thousand places of the Alleganey; that their detestation of the excise law is universal, and has now associated to it a detestation of the government; and that separation which perhaps was a very distant and problematical event, is now near, and certain, and determined in the mind of every man.*

—Letter from Jefferson to Madison

THE RISE OF POLITICAL PARTIES

By the middle of the 1790's, the political life of the United States was dominated by two of Washington's advisers, Jefferson and Hamilton. Although Jefferson retired from his post as Secretary of State in 1793 and Hamilton left his position as Secretary of the Treasury in January, 1795, both men continued to exert strong influence over their followers.

Jefferson's main complaint against Hamilton and the Federalists was simple: they wanted to make the federal government increasingly strong at the expense of the states. In Jefferson's opinion, the Federalists were conspiring to convert America into a monarchy. Hamilton himself outlined his differences with Jefferson in a remarkably dispassionate summary: "One side appears to believe there is a serious plot to overturn the state governments, and substitute a monarchy to the present republican system. The other side firmly believes there is a serious plot to overturn the general government and elevate the separate powers of the states upon its ruins. Both sides may be wrong. . . ."

Jefferson, the gentleman farmer, also distrusted Hamilton's efforts to make manufacturing and urban life more important than the rural areas. Jefferson felt that America could remain morally pure and true to itself only so long as it remained rural. One of Jefferson's colleagues even went so far as to point out, in his defense of rural life, that the divine intelligence "had selected an agricultural state as a paradise for its first favorites."

There was a more profound difference between the Jeffersonians and the Federalists in regard to their views of man's potential capabilities. Jefferson believed that human nature was made up of both worthy and unworthy instincts, but he had much more faith than the Federalists in the ability of humanity to improve itself through education and experience. Whereas the Federalists believed that "those who own the country ought to run it," Jefferson wanted eventually to extend the vote to every adult white male and do away with all property qualifications (although he did believe that universal education was a necessary prerequisite for universal suffrage). The Federalists' aristocratic bias led them to admire Great Britain and her obvious class distinctions; correspondingly, the Republicans' democratic prejudices made them admirers of the philosophy of the French Revolution.

The Federalists and the Jeffersonians, or Democratic Republicans, were not comparable to modern political parties. They were not as structured nor had they evolved to the point of having national committees or conventions, although there were local committees that nominated candidates. By 1796, the Jeffersonians in Congress created a caucus of leaders to make nominations for the highest offices. They were the first true parties, nevertheless, in that they both followed a clearly formulated set of ideas and sought to administer the government for the benefit of distinct economic groups. The Federalists represented the merchants, shipowners, and financiers of the Northeast, as well as a gradually decreasing number of prosperous Northern farmers and Tidewater planters in the South. The Democratic Republicans, on the other hand, were backed by many artisans and workers in the towns, as well as the small farmers all over the country, and increasingly by the wealthy agricultural interests. Hamilton's financial policies (such as funding, assumption, the enactment of the whiskey excise, and the founding of a national bank) had favored the Northeast, and in general worked against the economic interests of the South and West. Opposition to his policies united the small farmer and the Southern plantation owner against the Federalists.

THE ELECTION OF 1796

While Jefferson was the acknowledged leader of the Democratic Republicans after 1792, most of the work of organization was done by James Madison and James Monroe, another Virginia planter. Committees in the states and the Democratic Republican societies helped create support, too. Only Genêt's mission seemed for a short time to impede the party's steady progress. Hamilton's policies, the Whiskey Rebellion, and above all, Jay's Treaty, solidified support for the candidacy of Thomas Jefferson in 1796.

When Washington stepped down from office in 1796, the nation faced its first real Presidential contest. No one had ever questioned that Washington would be the first chief executive, but now that his administration had ended, politicians began to speculate about the great man's successor. Washington had always imagined that he was above political parties, but in fact, by favoring Hamilton during the last years of his second term, he had clearly allied himself with the Federalists. In fact, most Jeffersonians considered Washington's Farewell Address, which called for an end to partisanship in domestic affairs and also warned against permanent entangling alliances in foreign relations, as only a partisan statement.

Hamilton was rejected by his own party on the grounds that he was too controversial a figure to put up for election. The Federalists decided to back Washington's Vice-President, John Adams, as the logical replacement for the Father of the Country. Thomas Pinckney, negotiator of the Spanish treaty, was nominated as Vice-President. Hamilton certainly did not want to see his old enemy, Jefferson, in either office, but neither did he want Adams as the second President. Adams, being strong-willed, was not likely to follow Hamilton's advice. In addition, Adams had at one time been an intimate friend of Jefferson's.

Hamilton therefore, preferred the more pliable Pinckney. He intrigued to round up the support of all the Northern electors for Pinckney so that the South Carolinian might become President with Adams as Vice-President. The scheme, however, backfired. Hamilton's plotting failed, mainly because he was too indiscreet to nurse a secret plan into full success. Adams was elected President with seventy-one electoral votes, and according to the procedure outlined in the Constitution, Jefferson, with the second highest number of votes, became Vice-President. Adams carried New England and New York, and Jefferson, Pennsylvania and the South and West.

THE NEW ADMINISTRATION

Adams' political philosophy was more moderate than Hamilton's and represented the thinking of a larger proportion of the Federalist voters. However, because he lacked Hamilton's skill at organization, he never mobilized his supporters or dominated his party. His rural background made him somewhat distrustful of the monied group to which Hamilton catered. He favored expansion of commerce, but unlike Hamilton, he did not approve of speculation in land or expansion of bank credit. Moreover, like Jefferson, he believed the only true aristocracy was one of education and talent, not money. He did not, however, believe in the idea that human life would become progressively more enlightened and happy for the mass of humanity. On this point, he and Jefferson could never see eye to eye.

In order to dispel the fears of the Democratic Republicans that the Federalists intended to turn America into a monarchy, Adams made clear in his inaugural address that he was now, and always would be, loyal to the principle of republicanism. As

on after his election, John Adams found mself faced with the serious possibility of ar with France.

a result, a decline in political partisanship seemed to be in the making. Republican newspapers praised Adams' "incorruptible integrity" and Jefferson hailed the "talents and integrity" of the new President.

Party feeling was not to be so easily smothered, however. Madison urged Jefferson to remember the long-term ambitions of the Democratic Republicans. Federalist leaders discouraged Adams from sending Jefferson's ally, Madison, as an envoy to France. Then Adams had to break with Jefferson after a letter came to public attention in which the Vice-President seemed to criticize George Washington. The President had to concede that his administration could not rise above the party battles that had begun during Washington's regime.

Adams not only inherited the factionalism of the previous administration, but also Washington's cabinet: Oliver Wolcott, the Secretary of the Treasury, James McHenry in the War Department, and Timothy Pickering as Secretary of State. All three men were mediocre administrators and all three received constant instruction from Hamilton, now practicing law in New York. To make matters worse, Adams devoted only part of his energies to the business of running a nation; he spent much of his time at home in Quincy, Massachusetts, because of his wife's illness. Since he was not a politician by inclination, Adams never tried to develop a program or mobilize his supporters in Congress in order to direct the Federalist Party to a more moderate course.

CONFLICT WITH FRANCE

During Adams' Presidency, the French, still at war with the English, began to attack American shipping. The French were angry because the United States, while claiming to be neutral or even an ally, consistently seemed to be favoring Britain.

Jay's Treaty, in particular, struck the French as a gift from America to England. The French correctly believed that the Federalists were pro-British. Consequently, Adet, the new French minister to America, tried to bring about the defeat of the Federalists in 1796 by threatening a complete break in Franco-American relations if Adams were elected. Adams was elected, however, and now France's threat was carried out. France captured several American vessels bound for England, refused to receive the American minister, and announced that from then on American sailors serving on British ships would be treated as pirates by French authorities.

To persuade the French to abandon these tactics, Adams sent a three-man commission to Paris. The American delegation failed completely and the French Foreign minister, Talleyrand, offered a humiliating proposal through a matching trio of French agents. These agents, referred to as X, Y, and Z, suggested to the Americans that a bargain could be worked out between the two nations. France would begin official negotiations with the American commission in return for a huge bribe (Talleyrand's personal fortune had been depleted by the Revolution and he hoped to replenish it at America's expense). The French also demanded an apology from the President for

The multi-headed monster in this cartoon represents Talleyrand who is demanding money from American delegates at knifepoint, while his agents, X, Y, and Z perform a sleight of hand.

remarks criticizing the French Revolution, as well as a large loan. "No, no, not a sixpence," declared Charles Pinckney, the senior United States minister to France.

Adams decided that France's demands should be exposed to the American public. He released the commissioners' reports and Pinckney's mild retort was quickly magnified into the overblown slogan, "Millions for defense, but not one cent for tribute!" America's reaction to the news took many forms. The Federalists, who feared the French Revolution and sympathized with Britain, seized upon the occasion as a pretext for demanding war with France.

The Republicans, always pro-French, at first refused to believe Adams. They demanded to see the commission's papers, which Adams willingly agreed to. The documents substantiated France's guilt. Republicans joined Federalists and both agreed on measures to repudiate America's treaties with France, suspend all trade with France, establish a Navy department, and authorize attacks by American vessels on French ships.

Washington came out of retirement and agreed to command the army. Hamilton, delighted at this turn of affairs, insisted that Adams make him a general and Washington's second in command. For the next 2 years an undeclared war was waged on the high seas between the two countries.

The French were anxious to avoid a full-fledged war with the United States. At this time, Napoleon's campaign in North Africa was stalled by the British. Napoleon did not wish to encourage an Anglo-American alliance, which he feared the Federalists might succeed in obtaining as a result of French naval attacks on the United States. Hence, Talleyrand was ordered to reverse French policy. Talleyrand, after all, had only wanted to humiliate the United States and line his own pockets. When he saw what a tempest he had stirred up, he quickly backed down. One of Adams' ministers in Europe reported that France was daily becoming more conciliatory. The President's

son, John Quincy Adams, supported this opinion. Talleyrand humbly assured him that an American envoy to Paris would "undoubtedly be received with the respect due to the representative of a free, independent and powerful nation."

On the other hand, the President's own party was clamoring for a declaration of war. As a means of remaining in power, the members of his cabinet, all under Hamilton's influence, echoed the cry. Adams, however, realized that to declare war against France would cancel out the advantages of neutrality. He put patriotism over popularity in his own party, although his action may not have hurt him as much in the election of 1800 as was believed at the time. Ignoring his party and cabinet, Adams appointed a new three-man commission that reached a compromise in the Convention of 1800 whereby the United States was formally released from the encumbering Alliance of 1778 in return for an end of the American demand for French payment for the losses to American commerce.

THE ALIEN AND SEDITION ACTS

The furor aroused by the XYZ Affair gave the Federalists an opportunity to try to silence political opposition. In June and July, 1798, Congress passed several laws known as the Alien and Sedition Acts. One was a Naturalization Act that increased from 5 to 14 years the period a foreigner had to live in America before he could become eligible for citizenship. Two Alien Acts empowered the President to expel aliens either in time of peace or of war if he believed it necessary for American security. The most controversial law was the Sedition Act, which not only made instigating a conspiracy against the government illegal, but also forbade publishing, or even uttering, any "false, scandalous and malicious" criticism of the government or its top officials.

241

The Federalists used the Sedition Act to silence some of Jefferson's followers. Ten Republicans, mostly newspaper editors, were convicted under the law. Three editors, for example, who favored Jefferson's policies were each given stiff fines and jail sentences. In what are known as the Virginia and Kentucky Resolutions, Jefferson and Madison responded immediately by declaring the Alien and Sedition Acts as flagrant violations of the First Amendment's guarantee of freedom of speech and the press. Madison's resolutions condemning the acts were presented to the Virginia assembly and Jefferson sent a somewhat more extreme statement to the legislature of Kentucky. Jefferson went so far as to propose that it was the right of a majority of the state legislatures to nullify a federal law which they felt was unconstitutional. The basis for this argument was Jefferson's belief that the Constitution was a compact between the states. Because the states had never given up their sovereignty, they, not the Supreme Court, were the final authority on the constitutionality of laws passed by the federal government. Jefferson's theory was not put to a test at that time because other state legislatures either disagreed or ignored the Virginia and Kentucky Resolutions. However, his ideas proved to be a dangerous legacy for the future.

ELECTION OF 1800

As the war scare waned, so did Federalist popularity. Although the public respected Adams for his peaceful stand, the Federalist party now struck many Americans as a war-mongering group. The waging of an undeclared war against France had led to new taxes and an increase in the national debt. Most young, energetic politicians, and many young voters, were attracted by Jefferson's vigorous party, while the older Federalists sank back into what historian John C. Miller has called "opulent apathy."

Wealthy and satisfied, leading Federalists refused to run for political office; they preferred their luxurious privacy to the glare of public life. Washington, the most respected Federalist, died in December, 1799. The split between Adams and Hamilton over whether or not to declare war against France had also weakened the structure of the Federalist Party. Finally, underlying the entire decline of Federalism was the gradual shift of the greater part of the agricultural sector to the Jeffersonian coalition.

The Presidential contest in 1800, between Adams and Jefferson, was very close, but when the electoral votes were counted, the Democratic Republicans had won. However, the way the electoral college had been organized again presented problems. According to the Constitution, whichever man received the most votes would be President, and the runner-up, Vice-President, but republican electors, voting strictly according to party loyalties, had returned as many votes for Jefferson as for his running mate, Aaron Burr, a former New York senator and a skillful if unscrupulous politician. Each man had received seventy-three votes.

The Constitution provided that in such cases the House of Representatives would choose between the two candidates. In the House, a new deadlock occurred. Through thirty-five ballots, neither Jefferson nor Burr was able to win a clear majority. The Federalists detested Jefferson and preferred to vote for the elegant, urbane, and pliable Burr. Most Federalists at this point would have sooner voted for the devil than for the Virginian.

Several factors contributed to a swing to Jefferson on the thirty-sixth ballot. For one thing, Hamilton disliked Burr even more than he did Jefferson. In Hamilton's eyes, Burr was "the most unfit and dangerous

This picture, painted in China after Washington's death, depicts his ascent to heaven.

242

PLURIBUS

SACRED
to the Memory of
WASHINGTON

man of the community." Even more important than Hamilton's efforts to defeat Burr were those of Jefferson's emissaries to several Federalist delegations. Finally the states of Maryland and Vermont changed their vote to Jefferson and he was elected on February 17, 1801, with ten votes to Burr's four. To prevent such a dangerous deadlock from ever recurring, the Twelfth Amendment was drafted, providing for separate ballots for President and Vice-President.

Many Federalists were still filled with horror at the outcome of the election. Their worst nightmare had become a reality. Jefferson, this wild-eyed atheist, this revolutionary, this enemy of stable, centralized government, was now President. Federalist preachers had predicted that if Jefferson were elected, the United States must expect "the just vengeance of insulted heaven." That hour had come and Federalists awaited the holocaust which would destroy constitutional government.

FEDERALIST ACCOMPLISHMENTS

On March 4, 1801, Jefferson was sworn in at the new national capital, the city of Washington, on the banks of the Potomac. Government officials exchanged the comforts of Philadelphia for the mud, mosquitoes, and crowded boardinghouses of the half-built city. In this uncomfortable atmosphere, Jefferson delivered his inaugural address.

The Federalist era had ended. The party's accomplishments were great and enduring. The Federalists had strengthened the national government and rescued its finances. They had brought about official harmony between the United States and Great Britain, established American sovereignty to the Mississippi River, and, in general, maintained American neutrality in the European war. Their defeat, however, was now as certain as their former ascendency. In the Congressional elections, the Federalists lost about forty seats in the House of Representatives. In the new House, sixty-six Republicans would outnumber the remaining forty Federalists.

Why had the Federalists lost? Perhaps chiefly because of their aristocratic prejudices. As Noah Webster put it, "they have attempted to resist the force of current public opinion, instead of falling into the current with a view to direct it. In this they have manifested more integrity than address." After its defeat in 1800, the Federalist Party slowly waned as a national force. The Federalists stood in the way of the forces shaping the future direction of the republic. Most Americans were not interested in having a strong national government to guide their political and economic activities. They believed that the meaning of the American experiment was in the ever-widening opportunity for the mass of people to participate in political life and in the unrestricted economic opportunity opened to each individual. They wanted to achieve these goals on their own or through their state legislatures. The Jeffersonians, not the Federalists, were the embodiment of their ideals.

Thomas Jefferson became America's third President and the first to be inaugurated in Washington. His election marked the end of Federalist strength as a political party.

Readings

GENERAL WORKS

Bowers, Claude G., *Jefferson and Hamilton*. Boston: Houghton Mifflin, 1925—Bowers was both an historian and a Democratic party politician. Not surprisingly, he feels that the contrasting ideals of Jefferson and Hamilton define the central divisions in American history and that Jefferson stood for the more noble position.

Chambers, William N., *Political Parties in a New Nation*. New York: Oxford University Press, 1963—Chambers sees the growth of political parties as a means of making American democracy effective and providing for mass participation in politics. He feels the lessons are applicable to problems of political development in new nations today.

Charles, Joseph, *The Origins of the American Party System*. Williamsburg, Va.: Institute of Early American History and Culture, 1956—Three essays which stress the importance of James Madison in the formation of the Republican Party, Hamilton's influence on Washington, and which point to the Jay Treaty as the issue around which party alliances formed.

Cunningham, Noble E., Jr., *The Jeffersonian Republicans*. Chapel Hill, N.C.: University of North Carolina Press, 1957—Less concerned with Jefferson's ideology and political theory than with organizational problems, this study concentrates on the events to which Jeffersonians responded and their efforts to gain national power.

Dauer, Manning J., *The Adams Federalists*. Baltimore: Johns Hopkins Press, 1953—An analysis which calculates allegiances on roll call votes in Congress and maintains that there was a group of Federalist politicians who rejected Alexander Hamilton and supported John Adams on such issues as policy toward France.

Koch, Adrienne, *Jefferson and Madison: The Great Collaboration*. New York: Knopf, 1950—An account of the fifty-year friendship of the two statesmen. Koch emphasizes the influence of Madison on Jefferson's thought.

Miller, John C., *The Federalist Era*. New York: Harper & Row, 1960—Miller's general summary of the 1789 to 1800 period shows the Federalists to be talented administrators and financial theorists. However, their lack of comprehension of the significance of political democracy led to their downfall.

Schachner, Nathan, *The Founding Fathers.* New York: Putnam, 1954—A political history of the Presidencies of Washington and John Adams. Schachner's approach gives more praise to the Federalists than did some earlier pro-Jefferson authors.

SPECIAL STUDIES

Baldwin, Leland D., *Whiskey Rebels: The Story of a Frontier Uprising.* Pittsburgh: University of Pittsburgh Press, 1939—A history of the revolt of western Pennsylvania's farmers against the excise tax on whiskey. Baldwin also gives a portrait of Hugh Henry Breckenridge, Pennsylvania lawyer, politician, and novelist.

Bemis, Samuel F., *Jay's Treaty.* New Haven: Yale University Press, 1962—A diplomatic history of Jay's treaty negotiations with detailed background information on Anglo-American relations in this period.

Bemis, Samuel F., *Pinckney's Treaty.* New Haven: Yale University Press, 1960—Bemis views Pinckney's Treaty with Spain as a lucky stroke for the United States and poor diplomacy by Spain. Because of pressures brought about by European wars, Spain blundered into giving up a large part of her colonial claims in North America.

Cooke, Jacob E., ed., *Alexander Hamilton: A Profile.* New York: Hill & Wang, 1967—A brief biographical sketch is combined with fourteen essays by modern scholars which analyze Hamilton's career and programs.

DeConde, Alexander, *Entangling Alliance: Politics and Diplomacy Under George Washington.* Durham, N.C.: Duke University Press, 1958—DeConde suggests that the coming to power of the Federalists with their anti-French bias inevitably led to the degeneration of the American alliance with France during Washington's administration. The President, however, did not grasp the significance of the decline in the relationship.

DeConde, Alexander, *The Quasi-War.* New York: Scribner's, 1966—Although during 1797 and 1801 naval skirmishes often pointed toward the outbreak of full-fledged war with France, an uneasy peace remained. DeConde credits Talleyrand, the French diplomat, as well as John Adams, for this achievement.

Gilbert Felix, *The Beginnings of American Foreign Policy: To the Farewell Address.* Princeton, N.J.: Princeton University Press, 1961—A study of the ideas behind early American foreign policy which stresses the continuing tension between idealism and realism and between isolationism and internationalism in American thought.

Kurtz, Stephen G., *The Presidency of John Adams*. Philadelphia: University of Pennsylvania Press, 1957—An account of Adams' administration that emphasizes his moderation and his unwillingness to join with the extreme anti-French Hamilton faction of the Federalist Party.

Perkins, Bradford, *The First Rapprochement: England and the United States*. Berkeley, Calif.: University of California Press, 1967 —British-American relations from 1799 to 1805 are discussed. Perkins credits the Jay Treaty as being the most important factor in the improved relations between the two nations in these years.

Miller, John C., *Crisis in Freedom*. Boston: Little, Brown, 1964—A history of the Alien and Sedition Acts of 1798. Miller views them as an attack upon political opposition which, rather than unify the nation behind an anti-French position, almost brought about civil war.

Whitaker, Arthur P., *The Mississippi Question, 1795–1803*. Gloucester, Mass.: Peter Smith, 1962—Whitaker traces the growing interest in free navigation on the Mississippi and the right of deposit at New Orleans to the expansion of United States trade and commercial activity in the West.

PRIMARY SOURCES

Commager, Henry S., ed., *Selections from th Federalist*. New York: Appleton-Century Crofts, 1949—Written by Alexander Ham ilton, John Jay, and James Madison, *Th Federalist,* was both a work of politica theory and propaganda for the ratificatio of the Constitution.

Cooke, Jacob E., ed., *The Reports of Alex ander Hamilton*. New York: Harper Row, 1964—A reprinting of Hamilton famous reports issued between Januar 1790 and December 1791. They deal wit public credit, a national bank, and th encouragement of manufacturing.

Hazen, Charles D., *Contemporary America Opinion of the French Revolution*. Balt more: Johns Hopkins Press, 1897—An olde work showing the attitudes of Federalist and Republicans to French development The author describes the opinions of bot Americans in France and leaders at home

Koch, Adrienne, and William Peden, eds. *The Life and Selected Writings of Thoma Jefferson*. New York: The Modern Library 1944—A thorough selection from Jeffer son's writings, emphasizing his letters. I also contains the complete text of hi "Autobiography."

Maclay, William, *The Journal of Willia Maclay*. New York: Boni, 1927—Maclay wa a Pennsylvania Senator who kept a journa of the years 1789 to 1791. An early adherent to the position of Madison and Jefferson, Maclay's lively account is biased, but it remains a lively and valuable record of a new system of government beginning to feel its way.

BIOGRAPHIES

Brant, Irving, *James Madison,* Vols. I–VI. Indianapolis: Bobbs-Merrill, 1970—A six-volume biography of James Madison. Brant admires Madison greatly and cites John F. Kennedy's appraisal of him as our "most underrated President."

Chinard, Gilbert, *Honest John Adams.* Boston: Little, Brown, 1933—A biography of the second President by a French author who views Adams as a product of New England Puritanism. Brilliant and principled, Adams was also often vain and stubborn.

Flexner, James T., *George Washington and the New Nation, 1783–1793.* Boston: Little, Brown, 1970—The latest volume in the author's multi-volumed biography of Washington, this work covers the years from the end of the Revolution through his first term as President.

Malone, Dumas, *Jefferson and the Ordeal of Liberty.* Boston: Little, Brown, 1969—The third volume of Malone's biography of Jefferson, this book deals with the period from 1792 to his accession to the Presidency in 1801.

Malone, Dumas, *Jefferson and the Rights of Man.* Boston: Little, Brown, 1951—This is the second volume of Malone's multi-volumed biography of Jefferson. The book covers the years from 1784 to 1792 and deals with Jefferson's service in France and his first years as Secretary of State under Washington.

Miller John C., *Alexander Hamilton: Portrait in Paradox.* New York: Harper Torchbooks, 1959—Miller sees Hamilton's life and policies as devoted to achieving national strength and unity. Ironically, his programs led to a sharp split between North and South which was only temporarily healed during Jefferson's administration.

Monaghan, Frank, *John Jay.* Indianapolis: Bobbs-Merrill, 1935—A biography of the first Chief Justice of the Supreme Court who also was a leading diplomat and politician of the Federalist period.

Walters, Raymond, Jr., *Albert Gallatin.* New York: Macmillan, 1957—A biography of Jefferson's Secretary of the Treasury which discusses Gallatin's roles as party organizer, financier, and diplomat.

The USS Constitution *("Old Ironsides"), under the command of Isaac Hull, confronted and destroyed HMS* Guerriere *in the middle of the Atlantic only two months after the War of 1812 began.*

7

The Jeffersonians in Power

I know, indeed, that some honest men fear that a republican government can not be strong, that this Government is not strong enough; but would the honest patriot, in the full tide of successful experiment, abandon a government which has so far kept us free and firm on the theoretic and visionary fear that this Government, the world's best hope, may by possibility want energy to preserve itself? I trust not. I believe this, on the contrary, the strongest Government on earth. I believe it the only one where every man, at the call of the law, would fly to the standard of the law, and would meet invasions of the public order as his own personal concern. Sometimes it is said that man can not be trusted with the government of himself. Can he, then, be trusted with the government of others? Or have we found angels in the forms of kings to govern him? Let history answer this question.

—Thomas Jefferson,
The First Inaugural Address

DOMESTIC CHANGES

The election of the Jeffersonians in 1800 brought into power the party which embodied the spirit of American nationalism. The result of the election reflected the desire of a majority of Americans for more rapid progress toward political democracy. It gave proof that most voters did not favor a strong central government and that they wanted a policy of laissez-faire on economic questions. Jefferson's victory also represented a protest by the agricultural sector against the disproportionate influence on national politics of the commercial and banking interests. From hindsight, the election could be considered as a victory for the concept that a responsible political opposition had the right not only to exist but to assume power when it obtained majority support. It showed, contrary to Federalist fears, that the Jeffersonians did not plan to overthrow the Constitution or the government established under it. With this election, the modern political party system came into being. At a time of war and repression in Europe, the majority of Americans had voted in free elections for government by the party of their choice. This party assumed power in 1801, if not without unyielding opposition from extreme Federalists, at least without bloodshed.

Jefferson's democratic beliefs were mirrored by his style of living. The Federalist Presidents, Washington and Adams, had been formal and lofty, but Jefferson was as casual as an old shoe. In fact, he literally wore old shoes around the White House, or rather, worn-down slippers. One Federalist Senator mistook him for a servant and noted that Jefferson was dressed in a dirty shirt. The expensive wigs favored by Washington were not for Jefferson, who clipped his own hair short. He conducted the nation's business while cracking nuts and passing sherry to high government officials. At social functions, he ignored the customary rules of precedence, allowing guests to sit wherever they wanted, instead of putting the most important persons at the head of the table, and at times even served dinner himself from a dumbwaiter. These democratic mannerisms irritated the British and Spanish ministers to the extent that they both began to boycott White House banquets. Jefferson explained his behavior by saying, "The principle of society with us is the equal rights of all. . . . Nobody shall be above you, nor you above anybody, *pell mell* is our law."

Under this studied casualness, however, was a poised, refined mind. Jefferson was both an expert in the science of agriculture and a successful lawyer. He was the owner of the country's best library and his 6,500 volumes became the nucleus of the Library of Congress. Jefferson had mastered Greek and Latin before he was eighteen, could read French and Italian, and had studied some forty American Indian languages. His writing style was a model of clarity and eloquence and he wrote prolifically. Between 1760 and 1826 he produced fifty thousand pieces of writing, one of the richest literary legacies left by any man.

Monticello, designed and built by Thomas Jefferson, is illustrated in this 1826 watercolor by Jane Braddick.

Jefferson was known for his "sunny aspect," but observers also noticed in him an underlying current of cynicism, coldness, and even bitterness. These aspects of his personality may have been the result of personal tragedies. He had six children, but between 1772 and 1782 four of them had died. In 1782 his wife also died. Jefferson then threw himself into politics, just as earlier he had devoted his vast energies to such pursuits as birdwatching, horticulture, and mastering the violin.

THE INAUGURATION

Jefferson was probably the most adroit statesman of his day. Federalists had feared that once this radical atheist became President he would undermine all established institutions. In fact, Jefferson made every attempt to reconcile the opposition to his Presidency. In his inaugural address, Jefferson spoke in a whisper and only two or three people sitting quite close to him heard the address. After the ceremony, however, printed copies of the speech were handed out and the public read measured statements expressing not a call to rebellion but the sweet voice of reason: ". . . every difference of opinion is not a difference of principle. We have called by different names brethren of the same principle. We are all republicans; we are all federalists." He declared that "the minority possess their equal rights, which equal law must protect, and to violate would be oppression."

Nevertheless, Jefferson's speech reflected popular demands. Having assured his political enemies that he was fair-minded, he proceeded to outline his basic principles. Like Washington in his Farewell Address, Jefferson warned the nation against entering into "entangling alliances" with European powers, alliances that might lead America into

253

foreign wars. He emphasized his desire to limit the responsibilities of the federal government. Such a course would be wise and frugal, and as much as possible would leave men to their own pursuits. The government would function to keep order, protect liberty, and reduce the national debt. The new President guaranteed his support of the state governments and states' rights; in his view, domestic concerns belonged in state hands. In addition, Jefferson promised to stimulate and protect both agriculture and its "handmaid," commerce.

OLD AND NEW POLICIES

Jefferson regarded his coming to power as "the Revolution of 1800," but his administration did not make many changes in the policies established by his predecessors. The core of Federalism had been Hamilton's economic program: the funding of the national debt, the assumption of the states' Revolutionary debts, and the founding of the First National Bank. Jefferson had fought all three measures while Secretary of State; however, as President he retained all three on the advice of Albert Gallatin, his Secretary of the Treasury. Funding and assumption both went ahead as before and the Bank of the United States continued its operations until 1811, when its charter expired. Concerning Hamilton's financial structure, Jefferson remarked, "We can pay off his debt, but we cannot get rid of his financial system." Many Federalists were suspicious of the President's mild, reasonable behavior and attributed it solely to his "immoderate thirst for popularity." One Federalist diehard said, "In dress, conversation and demeanor, he studiously sought and displayed the arts of a low demagogue seeking gratification of the democracy on whose voices and votes he laid the foundation of his power."

There were several changes made in the federal laws. Jefferson had bitterly opposed the Alien and Sedition Acts passed during Adams' administration. Now his Republican administration refused to renew the Alien Act, which expired in 1801. The Sedition Act also expired in 1801 and Jefferson freed all those citizens who had been imprisoned under it and refunded their fines. The residence requirement for citizenship, which Adams had raised from 5 years to 14, was now reduced to 5.

Jefferson also turned his attention to a promise he had made in his inaugural address—the frugal management of the economy. He and Gallatin had a clear-cut policy in regard to public finance. They both believed that first the United States should pay off the national debt as quickly as possible. By practicing the most rigid economies, Gallatin was able to shrink the national debt during Jefferson's 8 years in office from eighty-three million to fifty-seven million dollars. All federal bonds were thus paid off by 1807. Jefferson's second most important economic goal was to have the United States pay its way by tariffs, revenues from land sales, and postal services. Tariff duties would bring in the most revenue and Jefferson thought these duties would fall mostly on the rich and would not burden the ordinary man. Accordingly, the Congress repealed all excise taxes, including the hated Whiskey Tax. To stay within his tight budget, Jefferson reduced the Army from 4,000 to 2,500 officers and enlisted men. He also pared down naval costs by selling a few ocean-going vessels and halting the construction of others. Gallatin thereby reduced the Navy's annual appropriation from three and a half million to one million dollars for 1802. Jefferson was also able to make minor savings by closing the United States legations in Berlin and The Hague, leaving American ministers in only three European cities—Madrid, Paris, and London.

The effect of these Republican measures was to bring America close to Jefferson's ideal of a nation of citizens "managing their own affairs in their own way and for their own use, unembarrassed by too much regulation, unoppressed by fiscal exactions." Henry Adams, the historian, wrote that Jefferson saw America in 1801 as "an enlarged Virginia"—predominantly rural, frugal, prosperous, and agricultural. Certainly the nation seemed to be prospering. Manufacturing and shipping were booming in the North, while in the South cotton was quickly becoming the most important crop. Three thousand bales of cotton had been picked in 1790, 73,000 in 1800, and 178,000 in 1810. The country's population had swelled by 1800 to well over five million people. Only one cloud darkened this bright picture. One-sixth of that population was in slavery. During the last decades of the eighteenth century a number of plantation owners had freed their slaves. However, the invention of the cotton gin made the expanded production of cotton profitable and revived the dying institution of slavery. Even Jefferson was incapable of rising far above the ruling prejudices of his day. Like Washington and Madison, Jefferson op-

posed slavery in principle and predicted universal emancipation, but he owned slaves himself and believed that the two races could never live together harmoniously if the blacks were freed. He considered blacks inferior to whites except in their ability to perform music, to remember, and to act courageously. In 1814, he politely declined to head an antislavery movement.

THE BARBARY PIRATES

Jefferson had always hated paying tribute to the Barbary pirates. This was another area in which he disagreed with the Federalists, who, like the major European powers, had found it cheaper and easier to pay blackmail to the rulers of Morocco, Algiers, Tunis, and Tripoli than to fight them. To protect some one hundred American vessels from pirate raids, the United States paid approximately one hundred thousand dollars a year, a practice which infuriated Jefferson. "When this idea comes across my mind, my faculties are absolutely suspended between indignation and impatience," he asserted. After the Dey of Algiers publicly humiliated an American naval officer, and the Pasha of Tripoli attempted to squeeze still more money out of the United States, Jefferson firmly refused to pay. The Pasha declared hostilities by chopping down the flagpole in front of the American consulate in May, 1801. Jefferson, in reply, sent a squadron of American vessels to the Mediterranean.

Unfortunately, the President's wish to crush the pirates with American naval might could not be carried out by a Navy greatly weakened by his earlier efforts to economize. The pirates were not overwhelmed and the United States continued to pay a form of tribute until 1815. Nevertheless, following an effective blockade in 1805, America was able to extract better terms from the Pasha of Tripoli than had been granted to any other nation. The

North African Arab States extracted "protection" money for all Mediterranean shipping. When the price was raised, an enraged Jefferson refused to pay. Stephen Decatur was then sent to Tripoli and succeeded in capturing two pirate ships and burning the Philadelphia *to save her from enemy hands.*

Pasha settled with Jefferson for a mere sixty thousand dollars to be paid to the Pasha personally. The war with the Barbary pirates also provided the new American Navy with excellent practice. The officers, including Stephen Decatur, and the crews serving under Commodore Edward Preble learned much about warfare at sea, knowledge they would be able to put to good use in the War of 1812.

WAR ON THE JUDICIARY

When Jefferson assumed power, he was free to appoint men of his own party to important political positions. Jefferson abandoned the idea of choosing a few Cabinet members from the opposition, and filled it completely with Democratic Republicans. Any other government posts that were in the President's power to assign, he also gave to Jeffersonians. He showed partiality to his friends and fellow party members, but made appointments so wisely that no scandal stained his administration. By July, 1803, only 130 of the 316 offices within the President's control were still held by Federalists. Thus, Jefferson had succeeded in equalizing political patronage.

Congress was also in Democratic Republican control. In the House of Representatives, they outnumbered Federalists sixty-nine to thirty-six, and in the Senate, eighteen to thirteen.

The only remaining Federalist stronghold was the judiciary. In the final days of Adams' administration the departing Federalist Congress had rammed through the Judiciary Act of 1801, which reinforced Federalist domination of the courts. The act created a number of minor judicial positions, judgeships, and sixteen new circuit courts, which Adams filled with Federalists. Because he was supposedly still signing the appointments during his last night in office, these new judges were dubbed "midnight justices." Adams also appointed as Chief Justice of the Supreme Court, John Marshall of Virginia, a resolute Federalist loathed by Jefferson.

Jefferson and the new Congress immediately launched an attack on the act, which they saw as an attempt by the Federalists to hold on indefinitely to at least one branch of the federal government. The result was the repeal of the Judiciary Act of 1801, a step which, Jefferson believed, had the effect of removing all of Adams' last-minute appointees. Wherever possible, Jefferson also replaced Federalists in existing judicial positions with his own supporters. In 1802, the Jeffersonians passed their own Judiciary Act which enlarged the number of lower federal courts but created no new judicial positions.

By abolishing Adams' appointments, the Jeffersonians had performed an act of doubtful legality. The Constitution guaranteed that federal judges "shall hold their offices during good behavior." Had Jefferson acted unconstitutionally by removing the new Federalist judges? Did the Constitution permit the executive and legislative branches to control the judiciary by eliminating jobs in this way? If not, would the Supreme Court declare Jefferson's action unconstitutional? Yet, up to this point the Supreme Court had not yet reviewed the constitutionality of any law and many Americans greatly doubted that the Supreme Court had the right to review legislation at all.

Chief Justice Marshall made his position clear in the historically famous case of *Marbury v. Madison*. William Marbury was among the very last of Adams' midnight appointees. His appointment to serve as justice of the peace in the District of Columbia had been signed by Adams on March 2, 1801, and confirmed the next day by the Senate. The papers, however, had not been delivered to Marbury before Jefferson took office on March 4. Informed that his appointment was ineffective, Marbury petitioned the Supreme Court to issue a writ ordering the new Secretary of State, James

Madison, to deliver his commission to him.

Would Chief Justice Marshall issue the writ (called a *mandamus*) and thereby inaugurate open war between the judicial and executive branches of government? Marshall knew that if he failed to issue the writ, he would be admitting that the Court was afraid to challenge the President. If he did issue the *mandamus,* however, it would probably be ignored and the Supreme Court would have no means of forcing Madison to comply. If this occurred, the Court would lose prestige. Caught between two unacceptable alternatives, Marshall finally decided to pursue a third course that at the same time restricted and enlarged the Supreme Court's powers. The Chief Justice first lectured the administration by saying that Marbury had a right to his commission. However, Marbury's request for a *mandamus* had been based on a clause in the Judiciary Act of 1789 by which Congress had granted the Supreme Court the right to issue writs of *mandamus,* a right Congress could not delegate to the Court according to Marshall's interpretation of the Constitution. The clause in the Judiciary Act was therefore unconstitutional. Marshall, in turning down Marbury's request for *mandamus,* seemed to be handing a victory to Jefferson and Madison. Yet at the same time he established the Court's right to pass on the constitutionality of laws passed by Congress. By sacrificing Marbury, Marshall had proclaimed the Supreme Court's authority to invalidate federal laws when they came into conflict with the Constitution. With due respect, a contemporary remarked of Marshall, "His head is one of the best organized of anyone I have known."

Jefferson had been cleverly outmaneuvered by Marshall. Now Jefferson tried another tack to drive out Federalist judges. He ordered the House of Representatives to impeach District Judge John Pickering. On March 2, 1803, the House brought charges against Pickering of "high crimes and misdemeanors" (the Constitutional grounds for removing a judge). He was considered insane and had been delivering drunken harangues from his bench in New Hampshire for the previous 3 years. The Senate quickly voted to remove Pickering from his office, despite the fact that the impeachment trial was of doubtful legality, i.e., an insane man cannot legally be tried on such charges.

The Jeffersonians immediately sought a more clear-cut precedent for their procedure. An hour after Pickering was convicted by the Senate, the House impeached Supreme Court Justice Samuel Chase, another Federalist. Among the eight charges leveled at Chase, one cited a lecture in May, 1803, when he had harangued a grand jury for hours on Jefferson's administration. The Democratic Republicans, Chase had insisted, would bring on a "mobacracy, the worst of all possible governments." Chase had earlier aroused antagonism by giving his whole-hearted support to the Sedition Act under Adams. Although Jefferson exerted every effort to evict Chase, who was generally considered the most narrow-minded Federalist in power, the Senate was unable to convict him. A simple majority was prepared to find Chase guilty of committing "high crimes and misdemeanors," but the two-thirds majority necessary for conviction was impossible to muster and Chase returned triumphant to his bench. Most Senators had agreed that Chase was indiscreet and had not maintained the impartial dignity expected of members of the judiciary, but even many ardent Jeffersonians could not be convinced that his conduct constituted criminal acts for which he could be convicted in a court of law.

Chase's acquittal was fortunate. Had his impeachment been effected, Jefferson might have been tempted to continue his war on Federalist judges and the courts might have lost their independence. Jefferson, in his anger, had come perilously close to suppressing the political opposition. However, during his 8 years in office, he did have the opportunity to appoint three Jeffersonians to the Supreme Court.

THE WESTWARD MOVEMENT

The outstanding achievement of Jefferson's Presidency was the purchase of the Louisiana territory from France, a fabulous bargain by which the United States increased its territory by 140 percent at a cost of only fifteen million dollars.

By 1800 nearly a million American settlers were living in the huge area between the Appalachians and the Mississippi River. The territories of Kentucky and Tennessee had become states in the 1790s, and Ohio became the first state to be carved out of the Northwest Territory in 1803.

To encourage still more settlers to enter the Western lands, Jefferson urged Congress to pass new land acts, lowering the price and the minimum acreage of individual farms. Thus, by 1804, the requirements had been so far reduced that for a down payment of only sixty-five dollars, a man could gain title to 160 acres. To further encourage settlement, in 1806 the Congress authorized the building of the National Road from Cumberland, Maryland, across the Appalachians to Wheeling, Virginia. While only ten miles were completed before 1813, the road was later extended until it reached into Illinois.

Even if roads were well constructed, overland transportation was not cheap, quick, or efficient enough for Western farmers with produce to ship to East Coast markets. What they needed was water transportation, that is, free access to the Mississippi River and its tributaries. Before this access had been acquired in 1795 through Pinckney's Treaty, Spain had controlled the mouth of the Mississippi from its port of New Orleans (New Orleans and the immense territory of Louisiana, stretching as far as the Rockies, had been ceded to the Spanish by the French in 1763, at the end of the Seven Years' War). The Spanish had blocked American use of the harbor. The treaty broke down this barrier, however, and opened the Mississippi to American navigation, allowing Americans to deposit their cargoes on the wharves of New Orleans.

Jefferson had visions of owning New Orleans outright. In fact, he imagined that some day the United States would own all of North America to the Pacific Ocean. It would be one vast, freedom-loving republic, an "empire for liberty." Despite such dreams, Jefferson did not hurry to wrest New Orleans from the Spanish by force. He knew that Spain was a weak nation, powerless to obstruct American navigation of the Mississippi indefinitely.

THE LOUISIANA PURCHASE

Jefferson's ease of mind did not last long. Before he assumed office, Spain had agreed to return the Louisiana Territory (but not the Floridas) to France, under the Treaty of San Ildefonso of 1800. In exchange, Napoleon promised Spain he would not sell the territory to a third power. He also offered to create a handsome little Italian kingdom for one of the Spanish dukes. Eventually, he broke both promises.

Why did France want the territory and why was Spain willing to give it up? France under Napoleon reversed the official policy she had followed since 1763 to again work toward extending her empire to the Western Hemisphere. She wanted the territory of Louisiana with its fertile soil to produce food for the French West Indian sugar islands. Spain decided to transfer the territory to France because her efforts to hold it had grown too costly to her treasury, and because she believed the French when they assured her that Louisiana under France would be a reliable buffer between Spain's other American possessions and the aggressive American settlers to the east.

Louisiana was formally transferred to France in 1802. Before the transfer, the Spanish official at New Orleans proclaimed that the right of Americans to deposit their cargoes in New Orleans was suspended. The Pinckney Treaty of 1795 had stipulated that this right would exist for only 3 years.

America was deeply distressed by this turn of events. Spanish possession of the Mississippi had not been a serious threat, for Spain was a declining power. But France was the strongest country on the continent of Europe, and her ownership of the strategic Port of New Orleans placed the life-

LOUISIANA PURCHASE AND WESTERN EXPLORATION · 1803 TO 1819

The Louisiana Purchase:
The Executive View

———————————

“ *This treaty must of course be laid before both Houses, because both have important functions to exercise respecting it. They, I presume, will see their duty to their country in ratifying and paying for it, so as to secure a good which would otherwise probably be never again in their power. But I suppose they must then appeal to the nation for an additional article to the Constitution, approving and confirming an act which the nation had not previously authorized. The Constitution has made no provision for our holding foreign territory, still less for incorporating foreign nations into our Union. The Executive, in seizing the fugitive occurrence which so much advances the good of their country, have done an act beyond the Constitution. The Legislature, in casting behind them metaphysical subtleties and risking themselves like faithful servants, must ratify and pay for it, and throw themselves on their country for doing for them unauthorized what we know they would have done for themselves had they been in a situation to do it.*

It is the case of a guardian investing the money of his ward in purchasing an important adjacent territory, and saying to him when of age, I did this for your good; I pretend to no right to bind you; you may disavow me and I must get out of the scrape as I can; I thought it my duty to risk myself for you. But we shall not be disavowed by the nation, and their act of indemnity will confirm and not weaken the Constitution, by more strongly marking out its lines. ”

—*Thomas Jefferson,* Letter to John Breckinridge

The Louisiana Purchase:
The Legislative View

———————————

“ *. . . I wish to establish, that this treaty is unconstitutional and void, and that I have, consequently, a right to withhold my vote from any bill which shall be introduced to carry it into effect. I acknowledge, sir, that my opinion ever has been, and still is, that when a treaty is ratified by the constituted authorities, and is a Constitutional treaty, every member of the community is bound by it, as a law of the land; but not so by a treaty which is unconstitutional . . .*

. . . I have no doubt but we can obtain territory either by conquest or compact, and hold it, even all Louisiana, and a thousand times more, if you please, without violating the Constitution. We can hold territory; but to admit the inhabitants into the Union, to make citizens of them, and States, by treaty, we cannot constitutionally do; and no subsequent act of legislation, or even ordinary amendment to our Constitution, can legalize such measures. If done at all, they must be done by universal consent of all the States or partners to our political association. And this universal consent I am positive can never be obtained to such a pernicious measure as the admission of Louisiana, of a world, and such a world, into our Union. This would be absorbing the Northern States, and rendering them as insignificant in the Union as they ought to be, if, by their own consent, the measure should be adopted.

———————————

—*Uriah Tracy,* **Annals of Congress**

line of much of America in the powerful grip of Napoleon. Also, if the Spanish closing of New Orleans to Americans was any indication of the French policy to come, the United States faced a crisis.

Jefferson wrote to Robert R. Livingston, the American minister to France, that there was "on the globe one single spot, the possessor of which is our natural and habitual enemy. It is New Orleans, through which the produce of three-eighths of our territory must pass to market. . . . France placing herself in that door, assumes to us the attitude of defiance." If France gained possession of New Orleans, the United States had no choice, Jefferson thought, but to ally herself with Britain. "The day that France takes possession of New Orleans," he wrote, we must "marry ourselves to the British fleet and nation."

Jefferson wanted neither war nor foreign alliances. He envisioned America as a frugal, peaceful agrarian state and he dreaded the prospect of a long, exhausting, and expensive war with a much stronger European power. Consequently, Jefferson obtained an appropriation of two million dollars from Congress and instructed Livingston in May, 1802, to try to buy New Orleans and West Florida. Livingston discussed the proposal with Talleyrand, Napoleon's foreign minister, but made little headway. In December, 1802, Jefferson took a bolder position by appointing James Monroe as a special envoy to France. Monroe was instructed to offer Napoleon ten million dollars for New Orleans and the Floridas.

Just two days before Monroe arrived in Paris, Napoleon made a sudden reversal of policy and offered the Americans not only New Orleans but the entire territory of Louisiana! Why did Napoleon make this incredible offer? No one is quite certain since few French documents dealing with the matter have been preserved. What seems likely is that Napoleon had second thoughts about colonialism because of French setbacks at this time in the Caribbean island of Santo Domingo (today divided into the nations of Haiti and the Dominican Republic). France had lost control of Santo Domingo in the late 1790s when the slaves there rebelled under their brilliant general, Toussaint L'Ouverture. Napoleon, hoping to rebuild the French empire in America, sent his brother-in-law and thirty thousand French soldiers to retake the island, but he met with disaster. The Santo Domingans outfought the French, and those they did not defeat were vanquished by malaria.

There was another reason for Napoleon's offer to America. He was a skilled military man who realized that in any contest over territory in North America, Britain, with its superior navy, would beat the French. Moreover, since 1799 the chief aim of French New World diplomacy had been to keep the Americans out of the British camp with the least expenditure of money. The Louisiana Purchase would win the friendship of the United States, remove her reason for forming an alliance with Britain, and instead of costing money, would actually bring money into the French treasury.

On April 30, 1803, Livingston and Monroe agreed to a price of fifteen million dollars. A little over eleven million dollars was paid to Napoleon in United States bonds which he immediately sold to bankers in Amsterdam and London for ready cash. The rest of the money was obtained from United States Treasury funds and money borrowed by Gallatin.

In return for this small sum, the United States gained millions of acres of land in a vaguely defined area; the territory was merely stated to be the same as when Spain had possessed it. The United States also inherited a population of 200,000 Spanish, French, and Indians to whom America agreed to grant citizenship and religious freedom.

IMPACT OF THE PURCHASE

Most Americans rejoiced over the Louisiana Purchase. The United States was able to pay one-fourth of the price in cash, and the remainder was paid without the introduction of internal taxes or any other means that would alter the existing federal financial structure. Jeffersonians called the terms a great diplomatic victory and Westerners were highly satisfied to have the Mississippi at last securely in American hands. Only a few unrelenting Federalists raised objections. They argued that France did not have the right to sell Louisiana, since Spain had ceded the territory to her with the stipulation that she must never sell it to a third power. Moreover, some Federalists believed the entire transaction was an affront to Spain. They also questioned whether the President had not exceeded the powers delegated to him by Congress. Republicans countered by reminding them that before the purchase they had called for a war to take New Orleans, but now they were objecting to the purchase of a far greater territory at much less expense. The real worry of the Federalists, however, was that the rural interests in this vast region would some day overwhelm the commercial demands of New England.

Jefferson was perhaps the only Republican truly worried about Federalist objections. As an ardent expansionist, he could foresee great possibilities for the development of a landed empire of free farmers clear to the Rocky Mountains. Yet the President believed in a strict interpretation of the Constitution, and the document did not provide specifically for the acquisition of new territory. Jefferson knew that if he tried to secure a constitutional amendment before making the purchase he would risk loss of the territory. He finally decided he could compromise by buying the territory under the treaty-making power. In later years Jefferson justified his action in these words: "Strict observance to the written laws is doubtless *one* of the high duties of a good citizen, but it is not the *highest*. The laws of necessity, of self-preservation, of saving our country when in danger, are of a higher obligation."

The Senate, with its overwhelming Jeffersonian majority, easily upheld the treaty by a vote of twenty-six to five in October, 1803.

EXPLORATION

Jefferson had great interest in natural science. Therefore when the United States obtained millions of unexplored acres of land, one of his first decisions was to dispatch a team of explorers. Early in 1803 Congress, at his request, granted $2,500 to send an exploring party across Louisiana. The party was led by Jefferson's private secretary, Meriwether Lewis, an experienced wilderness explorer, and William Clark, younger brother of George Rogers Clark. Jefferson issued copious instructions to Lewis, ordering him to note "the soil and face of the country," as well as animal remains of extinct species, "mineral productions of every kind, but particularly metals," and meteorological information of every sort. Jefferson, who had never traveled more than 50 miles west of Monticello, was determined to learn as much as possible about America's new lands. Much of this information was expected, of course, to be of practical value. Lewis and Clark were to find a usable path to the Pacific, learn the territory's geography, study Indian trade possibilities, and determine how to develop the fur trade.

Lewis and Clark left St. Louis in May, 1804, with about forty-five men. The explorers followed the Missouri River up to North Dakota, where they spent the winter. In April, 1805, after shipping back nine boxes full of specimens and curios to their eager President, they started pushing west. They were guided by a French Canadian and his Indian wife, Sacajawea (which meant "Canoe Launcher," not "Bird Woman" as some writers have mistakenly called her). Passing over the Continental Divide in southwestern Montana, the explorers descended to the Pacific via the Columbia River. They reached the ocean in November, 1805, and carved on a tree, "By land from the U. States in 1804 & 5."

*Lewis and Clark meet the Flathead Indians
in this mural by C. M. Russell.*

After spending the winter there, they returned to St. Louis in September, 1806. Because of the tragic suicide of Lewis, the only records of the expedition published were the journal of a team member (1807), a fake account (1809), and a synthetic journal pieced together from actual events (1814). The full Lewis and Clark records were not published until 1904. The highest scientific achievement of their voyage was a map published in 1814. Jefferson was pleased to receive many specimens of wild life and two grizzly bear cubs, which lived for some time in a stone pit on the White House lawn.

Other explorers also began charting the West and settlers and traders moved into the new territory. Thomas Freeman entered the territory in the far Southwest still owned by the Spanish but was forced to turn back by hostile Spanish forces. Between 1805 and 1807 Lieutenant Zebulon Pike explored the upper Mississippi Valley and then the region of present-day Colorado. In Colorado he discovered, but failed

to scale, the peak named after him. He then made his way down into Spanish-held New Mexico where he was arrested, but soon freed, by the Spanish. Although he failed to keep accurate records of his observations, he drew up a map of the far Southwest and brought back the first detailed reports of the Rockies and the Great Plains. By 1812 there were 75,000 people in the territory of Louisiana adjacent to the mouth of the Mississippi River and Louisiana entered

*Sketches taken from Sergeant Patrick Gass'
account of the Lewis and Clark expedition.
The shaggy dog is really a grizzly bear who
has treed a member of the party.*

the Union that year as the eighteenth state. John Jacob Astor and other fur traders began pushing into the newly acquired territory soon after the purchase, but the northern region, with its vague boundaries, lay virtually unsettled for many years to come.

THE ESSEX JUNTO

The Louisiana Purchase spelled disaster to Federalist leaders, who felt certain that the settlers in the new territory would be Jeffersonian Republicans. Most of the nation had already gone over to Jefferson's side, with Federalism still alive only in New England. The most extreme Federalists, led by Senator Timothy Pickering, made a move to secede from the union. "The people of the East," Pickering declared, "cannot reconcile their habits, views and interests with those of the South and West. The latter are beginning to rule with a rod of iron." The proposed Federalist country would include Newfoundland, New England, Pennsylvania, and New York. These plans were proposed by a political group centered in Massachusetts known as the "Essex Junto."

The Junto found little support even among Federalists. Hamilton refused to take part in the plot. Undeterred, Pickering turned to Hamilton's archenemy, Aaron Burr. Burr had become disgruntled with his job as Vice-President. Jefferson openly disliked and distrusted him after the election of 1800 and excluded him from important decision making. Disgusted, Burr looked for power elsewhere by running for governor of New York in 1804. Pickering approached Burr and promised him Federalist support in the election if Burr would agree to bring New York into the "Northern Confederacy." Burr's answer appeared encouraging, if evasive, and the Federalists backed him against Morgan Lewis, the regular Republican candidate. Hamilton, despising Burr, entered the fray on the side of Lewis.

Burr lost overwhelmingly in the state contest, a result which had important consequences. First, the Essex Junto collapsed along with Burr's campaign. Second, Hamilton's view of him as a dangerous man got into public print; and third, Burr demanded a retraction and challenged Hamilton to a duel. Hamilton evaded the demand, saying his remarks were not personal. His own son had died in a duel and he wished to shun the custom, yet he felt his honor was at stake and reluctantly accepted the challenge. The two met with pistols on July 11, 1804, at Weehawken, New Jersey. Hamilton aimed his gun to miss, but Burr's bullet found its mark and Hamilton fell. The great financial wizard of the republic died 30 hours later.

OPPOSITION TO JEFFERSON

In the Presidential election of 1804, Jefferson won by a landslide. His Federalist opponent, Charles Pinckney, received only 14 against Jefferson's 162 electoral votes. The Republican incumbent carried every state except Connecticut and Delaware.

Jefferson had triumphed completely. He had proved to the Federalists that a limited and frugal federal government was possible without political and economic disorder. There had been no lawlessness and internal taxes had been abolished without harm to the nation. "What farmer, what mechanic, what laborer ever sees a taxgatherer in the United States?" the President asked rhetorically in 1805.

There were some dissidents, however, within the Jeffersonian coalition. One group was an extreme states' rights segment of the party led by John Randolph of Roanoke. Randolph, who suffered periodic bouts of insanity, had originally supported Jefferson as a defender of states' rights. But by 1804 Randolph began to express fear that Jefferson was overextending the federal government's powers. For example, he opposed

Jefferson's attempts to buy West Florida from Spain as unconstitutional. In a shrill soprano voice Randolph screamed, "Asking one of the States to surrender part of her sovereignty is like asking a lady to surrender part of her chastity." In Jefferson's administration, and later Madison's, John Randolph was an indefatigable gadfly who lit into every executive plan with neurotic frenzy. His positive defiance, however, won him limited sympathy. Yet he persisted, declaring in 1806, "I found I might cooperate or be an honest man—I have therefore opposed, and will oppose them." "Them," of course being Jefferson and his allies.

The other great opponent of Jefferson was Aaron Burr, by now politically isolated. His failure to be elected governor of New York, and his duel with Hamilton ended Burr's political career. There was talk of indicting him for murder, his private debts were enormous, and he had no public or private prospects. A short, bald dandy, Burr was a descendent of the famous Puritan clergyman, Jonathan Edwards. Burr had studied at Princeton and started his career full of promise but he was dominated from the start by excessive ambition and an unstable mind. John Quincy Adams said of Burr: "Ambition of military fame, ambition of conquest over female virtue was the duplicate ruling passion of his life." Many women succumbed to the magnetism of his "terrible" black eyes, but his military ventures proved less successful.

BURR'S CONSPIRACY

While still Vice-President, Burr asked the British minister, Anthony Merry, to make a deal with him. If England would supply him with half a million dollars, Burr would lead the Western part of the United States in an insurrection and create a separate confederacy. Merry was interested enough to relay news of the proposal to London. Before word came back from England, Burr had already traveled West where he joined forces with General James Wilkinson, the military commandant of the Louisiana Territory appointed by Jefferson. Wilkinson and Burr organized a small band of soldiers on Blennerhassett Island in the Ohio River, where a fellow conspirator, the Irish exile Harman Blennerhassett, lived in splendor.

No one knows exactly what Burr intended to do; Burr himself may not have been quite certain. Perhaps he planned to take New Orleans and use it as a base to

Aaron Burr was a colorful and controversial character. The extent of his conspiratorial guilt has never been fully established. Despite his treachery, he experienced a full measure of grief during his life: his political aspirations were dashed by Jefferson; his daughter disappeared and was assumed dead; he failed to establish a new Mexican empire, and his plans were revealed to the President which led to his arrest and court martial; and, in his eighties, he faced charges of adultery.

INTERNATIONAL PROBLEMS

detach the western states from the Union or to conquer part of Mexico as the first step in forming a new empire from Ohio to Panama with himself as emperor. In any event, Burr began to march south with his soldiers in the winter of 1806. Meanwhile, Wilkinson suddenly panicked and revealed the whole plot to Jefferson. Jefferson ordered Burr's arrest; he was captured while trying to escape into Florida and returned to Virginia for trial.

His trial began in Richmond, Virginia, on August 3, 1807. The presiding judge was Chief Justice John Marshall, who was bitterly hostile to Jefferson. Marshall conducted the trial in a suspiciously partisan manner, leaving a black mark on his otherwise excellent record. First, Marshall tried to subpoena Jefferson himself as a witness, but the President refused on Constitutional grounds (successive Presidents have followed his precedent). Then Marshall defined "treason" so narrowly to the jury that in effect he ensured Burr's acquittal. He pointed out that Burr had not been at Blennerhassett Island when the expedition started out, but had joined it later. After deliberating 25 minutes, the jury found Burr not guilty.

Burr was released on bail. Wanted in six states for either murder or treason, he jumped bail and fled to Europe. There he sought an audience with Napoleon. He thought he could persuade the French to make peace with England, unite in an Anglo-French alliance, and be appointed as the head of an army that would conquer Mexico and eventually the United States, a ridiculous scheme which failed from its inception.

Jefferson's second term in office was as stormy and perilous in foreign affairs as his first had been peaceful. At home he had won support from almost all the people, but abroad trouble lay before him. Jefferson's solutions to the new international problems proved highly controversial and lost him much prestige among his own party members. His second term became so trying that Jefferson wrote a friend: "Never did a prisoner, released from his chains, feel such relief as I shall on shaking off the shackles of power."

THE FRENCH AND BRITISH CONFLICT

Two weeks after Napoleon arranged for the sale of Louisiana to the United States, he renewed hostilities with England. The temporary respite from war provided by the Peace of Amiens of 1802 was at an end. This new conflict, which ravaged all of Europe, lasted off and on for 12 years. For a time, America was able to stay out of it, profiting immensely from her neutrality. Eventually, however, the United States was pulled into the conflict.

Napoleon resumed his war against England on May 18, 1803. Between 1803 and 1812 the United States became the world's most important neutral carrier, the leading wholesaler of tropical produce and virtually the commercial mistress of the Atlantic. In fact, American reexport trade flourished so luxuriantly from 1800 to 1812 that it was not equaled again in real value until the late 1940s. Shipbuilding boomed and American tonnage increased prodigiously.

Between 1803 and 1805, neither Britain nor France interfered with American commerce. American ships were free to deal openly with both belligerents. England and the United States were on fairly good terms, and the French navy, bottled up by Britain, was unable to patrol the Atlantic. France had never had as many ships as England, and those she did have were demolished in October, 1805, by the British fleet in the Battle of Trafalgar off the coast of Spain.

British triumphs on the sea, however, were matched by French victories on land. In November, 1805, Napoleon defeated the combined armies of Russia and Austria at Austerlitz in central Europe. Thus, Napoleon was master of most of the continent, just as England was mistress of the seas.

Because France and England could not strike directly at one another, they turned to commercial warfare. Britain began the economic war of attrition in April, 1806, with an Order in Council which closed the northern coast of Europe to all trade. In November, Napoleon's answer was the Berlin Decree declaring a blockade of the British Isles.

In 1807 Britain retaliated by forbidding all coastal trade between ports under French control and requiring all neutral vessels to procure a British license before entering a European port. Napoleon's answer to these orders was the Milan Decree of December, 1807, which made all ships with a British license subject to immediate seizure.

The sum and substance of these decrees and orders was that they caught the United States in a vise. If American vessels sailed between French ports without a British license, they could be seized by the British; if they entered a French port with a British license they would be seized by the French. Jefferson and other Americans regarded these Anglo-French regulations as insupportable insults. John Quincy Adams labeled Napoleon's decrees as "little more than extortion wearing the mask of prohibi-

tion." It appeared that the British Navy intended to stand by its motto, "The winds and seas are Britain's wide domain, and not a sail but by permission spreads." The commercial warfare that followed gave British merchants the satisfaction of seeing their government undermine America's expanding trade, which had become a threat to British commercial supremacy.

THE IMPACT ON AMERICA

Nearly continuous war was waged between Britain and France from 1792 to 1815. Until 1806 the United States gained the major share of all commerce between the New World and the Old. The United States was able to monopolize this trade because British and French merchant vessels were afraid to sail the Atlantic. French men-of-war were constantly capturing and destroying British ships, and vice versa. Only neutral American ships could sail with little fear.

British merchants, however, resented Americans growing rich at their expense. Since the early 1790s they had pressured their government to enforce the old Rule of 1756, under which a neutral could not engage during time of war in trade that was usually denied it in time of peace. The success of American merchants in evading this rule in the French and Spanish Caribbean Islands in this endeavor had earlier helped bring on the crisis that led to Jay's Treaty.

After 1800, Americans again shipped Cuban sugar or coffee from Martinique directly to the United States. American merchants would unload the tropical cargoes at an American port and pay duties on them. Then they would load the cargoes back on ships (often the very same ships) and dispatch the vessels to France and Spain. The American government encouraged this practice by refunding customs duties on foreign products reexported within a year.

At first the British did not try to stop this bit of subterfuge. In 1805, however, they took action against it. The *Essex*, an American vessel carrying cargo from Spain to Spanish Cuba by way of Salem, Massachusetts, was seized by an English frigate. A British Vice-Admiralty Court announced that henceforth American ships could no longer rely on "mere voluntary *ceremonies*" to get around the Rule of 1756. After this decision, British cruisers seized scores of American merchant vessels, and British men-of-war hovered off the American coast, creating a virtual blockade.

IMPRESSMENT

Britain's high-handed behavior infuriated Americans, but some Yankee merchants pointed out that if only one out of every three American vessels made its way safely from the Caribbean to Europe and back the shipowner would still turn a handsome profit. It was not the interference with neutral rights that shortly drove the United States to the brink of war, but anger over another British practice—impressment.

The British navy impressing American seamen during the War of 1812.

For more than 400 years the British Navy had been forcibly raiding English villages and towns and carrying off able-bodied men to serve in the Navy. The British Navy had a hard time attracting recruits in any less violent way. The pay was poor, the food wretched, and ordinary discipline on shipboard was severe.

When war resumed in 1803, the British Navy was in desperate need of sailors. Under British law, any subject of the king could be impressed into the Royal Navy in an emergency. British regulations also permitted the Navy to stop any neutral vessel on the high seas and capture from it any British subject. Under official sanction, British naval officers began to search American merchant vessels at sea.

In truth, many British sailors were serving on American ships. American commerce was so active and American ships so understaffed that British sailors were offered comparatively high wages and good working conditions. They regularly deserted their own vessels and joined crews on American vessels. In 1804, for example, twelve British men-of-war which had stopped over in Norfolk, Virginia, were detained in the port because their crews had all jumped ship.

When searching for English subjects among American crews, British officers were not particularly scrupulous. Swedes, Danes, and Portuguese sailors on American ships were glibly dubbed "Englishmen" and hauled away. If a sailor said "paise" for "peas" he was undoubtedly Irish and hence, as a British subject, he was summarily impressed into the British Navy. Between 1793 and 1811, the British impressed about ten thousand native-born Americans.

AN AMERICAN EMBARGO

Impressment and British interference with American trade would have driven a man less temperate than Jefferson to threaten a break in diplomatic relations, but he believed that for the United States, prosperity was more important than glory, peace as valuable as honor. The American people were less philosophical than their President in the face of British seizure of more than five hundred American ships and French capture of about two hundred vessels. "We have principles from which we shall never depart," Jefferson insisted. "We do not want war, and all this is very embarrassing."

In 1807, however, the English Navy struck a blow to American pride that caused a great outcry in the new nation and almost defeated the President's policy. In February, a British crew had escaped to the shore of Virginia from an English man-of-war. Four of the deserters had enlisted on an American frigate, the *Chesapeake*. The *Chesapeake* was part of the United States Navy. Under international practice at the time, war ships could stop and search merchant vessels of a neutral power, but not war ships. A hot-headed British admiral stationed in Nova Scotia, however, was so outraged when he heard of the desertion that he ordered the fugitives to be captured. Carrying out this order, the British frigate *Leopard* stopped the *Chesapeake* 10 miles off Norfolk, Virginia, and demanded the right to board the American ship. When the American captain refused, the *Leopard* opened fire, killing three men and wounding eighteen others. The *Chesapeake,* taken by surprise, returned one shot and surrendered. Of the deserters, one was a native-born Englishman and the other three seized were Americans.

The American people rose up in righteous indignation. As far away as Boston, patriots shouted, "Let us whet the sword! Let us bend the bow!" Jefferson wrote: "Never since the battle of Lexington have I seen this country in such a state of exasperation as at present, and even that did not produce such unanimity." The public clamored for war, but Jefferson realized that America had only the tiniest Navy (largely due to Jefferson's own decision in 1801 to cut the Navy's budget). America was in no position to take on British sea-power.

Jefferson, however, felt he had to strike back. To do nothing would be too humiliating to the nation. When Britain refused to accede to his request to end impressment, he turned to an idea he had long cherished, the use of economic coercion as a tool in foreign policy. His supporters forced through Congress, despite Federalist protest, the Embargo Act, in December, 1807. The Embargo Act prohibited *all* exports from the United States by land or by sea. Only coastal trade between American ports was permitted. Because the warring nations, particularly England, depended heavily on the United States for food and other commodities, Jefferson expected the embargo to quickly bring England to her knees.

The embargo did hurt a segment of the British economy. English textile factories, dependent on American cotton, were forced to close down after a time. Thousands of unemployed factory workers, hungry and idle, roamed the English countryside, but had little influence on British foreign policy. Also, a shortage of grains caused a curtailment of the production of alcoholic drinks. Fortunately for England, however, 1808 was a good year for her crops, a boon which greatly offset the effects of the embargo. In addition, the embargo policy also helped wealthy and influential merchants get some of their markets back.

The embargo, however, turned out to create much more hardship in the United States. Grass grew on once bustling wharves. Ships rotted in ports. Exports fell from 108 million dollars in 1807 to 22 million dollars in 1808. Farm prices and the prices of manufactured goods suffered a sharp drop. Once again, embittered New England merchants talked of secession from the union. Pickering, ever the embattled Federalist, asserted: "How are the powers reserved to the states

This cartoon depicts the influence of the Embargo Act passed by Congress in December, 1807, which was enacted in retaliation against Britain's refusal to stop impressment of American seamen into the British Navy.

respectively or to the people, to be maintained, but by the respective states judging for themselves and putting their negatives on the usurpations of the federal government?" It was now the New England Federalists who were the strongest proponents of states' rights! Yankee skippers found devious ways to evade the embargo, and tons of goods were smuggled across the Canadian border. Federal agents who tried to interfere were shot down. Even so, the country faced depression and one New Englander said that Jefferson had resorted to "cutting one's throat to cure the nosebleed." Jefferson later wrote: "I felt the foundation of the government shaken under my feet by the New England townships."

Jefferson, nonetheless, refused to give up his unpopular law. Rather than try to enforce American rights by building a bigger Navy and arming merchant vessels, he obtained from the Congress the Force Act of 1809 which gave federal collectors almost arbitrary power over American trade. Government customs officials were now as hated as British officers had ever been under the navigation laws, and the law proved unworkable, Finally, on March 1, 1809, three days before Jefferson was slated to leave office, a rebellious Congress revoked the Embargo Act and replaced it with a less stringent Nonintercourse Act, which banned trade only with Great Britain and France.

Ironically, the Embargo Act may have had at least one beneficial effect, but one that Jefferson would not have foreseen or wanted. Because Northern merchants were cut off from international trade, they began to invest their capital in manufacturing, thus laying the foundation of America's industrial might. Jefferson, who regarded cities and factories with distaste, had unintentionally encouraged the industrialization of America.

MADISON AS PRESIDENT

Jefferson was weary of politics. He had always disliked the speechmaking, the bickering, the direct confrontations of political life. He also believed, as had Washington, that no President should serve more than two terms. This conviction, combined with a growing weariness with seemingly insoluble international problems, led him to a decision not to seek reelection. He did keep his hand in the game, however. He personally intervened to win the nomination for his close friend, Secretary of State, James Madison.

Madison won the election over his Federalist opponent, C. C. Pinckney of South Carolina, by the decisive majority of 122 to 47 in the Electoral College. Madison sought to continue Jefferson's policies, and retained Jefferson's Secretary of the Treasury, Albert Gallatin.

The new President, unfortunately, did not have the political skill of his brilliant predecessor. A scholarly, even bookish man, Madison was a professed student of political philosophy. One observer remembered his conversation years later as "a stream of history . . . so rich in sentiment and fact, so enlivened by anecdotes and epigrammatic remarks, so frank and confidential . . . that it had an interest and charm, which the conversation of few men now living, could have. . . . His little blue eyes sparkled like stars from under his bushy grey eye-brows and amidst the deep wrinkles of his poor thin face." Despite such accomplishments, Madison was subject to ill health, fits of indecision, and poor judgment. He was no match for stronger, more aggressive politicians. He was the first President to have cabinet choices forced on him by the Congress. Madison wanted Gallatin to be Secretary of State, but the Senate forced a nonentity named Robert Smith on him, and Gallatin remained in the Treasury post. In 1813 when Madison succumbed again to party pressure and appointed an untalented, greedy New Yorker as Secretary of War, Gallatin retired in disgust. After Gallatin's departure, the President was said to have appeared heartbroken.

THE FAILURE OF PEACEABLE COERCION

The great problem facing Madison when he took office was to avoid going to war with Britain. The Embargo Act had failed and the Nonintercourse Act, passed in 1809, had replaced it. This new act was beginning to have effect on the British. Napoleon had sealed off most of continental Europe from trade with the English and America remained the only important foreign consumer of British industrial goods. As a result, British industrialists placed great pressure on the Foreign Minister, George Canning, to repeal Britain's Orders in Council. They argued that as long as the Orders continued to operate, the Americans would not be able to trade openly with England. Canning responded half-heartedly to these pressures. He understood the importance of the United States as a market for British goods and was willing to admit that Britain had no right to search American warships; but he would make no apology for the attack on the *Chesapeake*.

On the report that Madison wished an accommodation with England, Canning opened some European ports to American trade. He also instructed the affable British

271

Minister in Washington, David M. Erskine, to negotiate a settlement of differences with the Americans. Erskine was married to an American woman and was fond of Americans. He took the whole matter in his own hands and concluded an agreement with the Americans that offered terms far more lenient than anything Canning had had in mind. It provided that Britain would withdraw the Orders in Council and ask the United States for no concessions in return. Madison was delighted. He lifted the embargo on June 10, 1809, without waiting for the agreement to be approved in London.

When Canning received news of the generous Erskine agreement, he was furious. He repudiated it, summoned Erskine back to London and replaced him with a disagreeable man who abhorred Americans, thinking of them as "by many degrees more blackguard and ferocious than the mob in other countries." This new minister, Francis James Jackson, found the President a "plain and rather mean-looking man," and his wife, Dolly, "fat and forty, but not fair." His presence further strained Anglo-American relations.

Madison, embarrassed by his haste in lifting the embargo and humiliated by Canning's repudiation of the Erskine agreement, was forced to restore nonintercourse. Unfortunately for America, hundreds of her vessels had already landed tons of produce in England, bringing relief to the long period of hardship that the embargo had imposed on Britain. With its warehouses stocked with food and cotton, England was in a much better position to drive a hard bargain with the United States.

On May 1, 1810, the United States further weakened the policy of economic coercion by taking a new tack. Instead of nonintercourse, America instituted a policy embodied in a measure called Macon's Bill Number 2. This bill restored trade with Britain and France, but offered each of the belligerents an opportunity to be the favored nation. If France would agree to respect America's neutral rights, the United States would suspend trade with Britain; or, if Britain would repeal its Orders in Council, America would reward her by suspending trade with France.

Napoleon immediately saw an opportunity for manipulating the law to the advantage of France. In the famous Cadore letter he professed his love of America and promised that France would repeal its commercial restrictions, but he hedged the promise in a thicket of qualifying clauses that virtually cancelled it out. Madison swallowed the bait. Madison asked Britain for a similar concession and when she refused, Congress reestablished nonintercourse with Britain in February, 1811. Meanwhile, Napoleon was not fulfilling his pledge. On the very day he made his offer, France raised its tariffs on American goods and all American ships in French ports were ordered seized and sold. The resumption of nonintercourse also failed to win concessions from England. Unable to persuade Britain to repeal its Orders in Council, the American minister in London set sail for the United States.

Britain now made a few vague attempts to win American friendship. Two of the three Americans who had been captured from the *Chesapeake* were returned to American soil (the third had died in captivity). An editorial in a Baltimore newspaper was typical of American reaction: "Presented at such a time," it said, "the reparation was like restoring a hair after fracturing the skull." Ironically, on June 16, 1812, Britain, now in dire economic straits, decided to suspend the hated Orders in Council. However, it was too late. On June 1, Madison had asked Congress for a declaration of war. On June 4, the House complied by a divided vote of 79 to 49; the Senate, fourteen days later, voted 19 to 13 to declare war.

WAR HAWKS

Why had Jefferson's policy of peaceful pressure broken down? Which factions in Congress had voted for war? Why was war declared against Britain and not France? Had Napoleon not injured American pride as sorely as the British?

Answers to these questions lie to a great extent in the character of the new Congress. When the Twelfth Congress met on November 4, 1811, its membership had changed considerably. Almost half of the membership of the old House of Representatives (mostly those who had opposed war with Britain) had been voted out of office and replaced by about thirty Congressmen sensitive to American honor. Once in Congress, they became fervidly anti-British as they learned more about British wartime activities. A breakdown of the vote on the declaration of war shows that while the older commercial states on the coast, Rhode Island, Connecticut, New York, New Jersey, and Delaware, voted against war, those that voted for the war were the agrarian Southern states of Ohio, Tennessee, and Kentucky, and the solidly Republican states of Maryland and Pennsylvania. In view of the fact that Madison's war message had stressed, as the principal provocations for war, impressment and the violation of America's rights as a neutral, why did those states directly concerned with trade and shipping vote against the war? And why did the South and West, both dependent on agriculture and presumably less concerned about international trade, align themselves on the side of war?

The leaders of the war faction were a small band of youthful Republicans from the Southern and Western states, called the War Hawks. They were dominated by the new Speaker of the House, Henry Clay of Kentucky, and they clamored for revenge on England. These angry young men, among them Richard M. Johnson of Kentucky, Felix Grundy of Tennessee, and John C. Calhoun of South Carolina, were dismissed by the cantankerous John Randolph as merely "buckskin statesmen." They had little interest in the old question of states' rights and were quite willing to delegate more power to the federal government, particularly in wartime. Citizens of the older, original states still felt intense loyalties to their states and feared that in wartime the federal government might appropriate from the states an ever greater and greater share of authority. The representatives from the West shared no part of this anxiety. These Westerners tended to be nationalistic, eager for America's geographic expansion and economic growth, and furious at the steady diet of British condescension and attacks on American honor since 1806. By the middle of 1812

War Hawks in Congress

66 *An honorable peace is attainable only by an efficient war. My plan would be to call out the ample resources of the country, give them a judicious direction, prosecute the war with the utmost vigor, strike wherever we can reach the enemy, at sea or on land, and negotiate the terms of a peace at Quebec or Halifax. We are told that England is a proud and lofty nation that disdaining to wait for danger, meets it half-way. Haughty as she is, we once triumphed over her, and if we do not listen to the councils of timidity and despair we shall again prevail. In such a cause, with the aid of Providence, we must come out crowned with success; but if we fail, let us fail like men—lash ourselves to our gallant tars, and expire together in one common struggle, fighting for 'seamen's rights and free trade.'* 99

—*Henry Clay,* Annals of Congress

New England Doves

_____

66 *I have understood, and from a pretty direct channel, that the Expedition agt. Canada is postponed, and that it will not proceed this year. The non-intercourse, or rather non-importation law remains in force, but must I conjecture be repealed early in the next Session of Congress. If we make no objection, Engd. will oppose no impediments to supplying us with their manufactures. The only opposition will be from France: indeed the only serious danger to our Country is from that quarter. I regard the war, as a war of party, & not of the Country—those who have made the war will dread the unpopularity of French connexion, and hence my hope that French influence will be kept out.*

The war cannot be carried on by the Militia. A regular army will be enlisted with the utmost difficulty; besides money cannot be raised by Loans: and if Taxes be collected, the popularity of the Party according to Mr. Jefferson's former opinion, must be destroyed. I infer that the war will drag on heavily; that it will become very, and extensively, unpopular; that the dread of French connexion will greatly increase the mass of discontent; that the Congressional Elections will show the perilous unanimity of the Northern States agt. the war, and if England have a wise ministry, we must soon return to Peace. 99

_____

—*Rufus King,* Letter to C. Gore

even the President and his Secretary of State, James Monroe, were becoming more warlike and receptive to the aggressive demands of the War Hawks.

WESTERN PRESSURES FOR WAR

While the strongest prowar sentiment came from Americans described by a Boston newspaper as "backwoodsmen" who had never seen "the ocean but on a map, or conceived the taste of it except from a salt lick," the strongest opposition to war came from New Englanders. Despite the threat to its maritime rights, New England, the nation's commercial shipping center, had a lingering attachment to Britain which influenced its view of the war issue.

New England was the stronghold of Federalism. Its citizens still felt close ties to England and its shipowners still received their greatest profits from trading with Great Britain. Politically and culturally, conservative New Englanders sympathized strongly with England in her great struggle with France. They believed that a war against England would be a blow against the English parliamentary tradition and a triumph for the little giant, Napoleon, who now held all Europe in his autocratic grip. As one New England poet put it:

If England look askance, we boil with rage,
And blood, blood only, can the wound assuage:
Yet whipt, robbed, kicked and spit upon by France,
We treat her with the greater complaisance.

Such considerations did not impress the fiery "backwoodsmen." In a burst of nationalistic pride, they demanded vindication for the years of insult by Britain through impressment and seizure of American ships. They argued that France had seemed to change her ways recently and was no longer interfering with American commerce. As Clay said, "As to France we have no complaint . . . but of the past. Of England we have to complain in all tenses."

AGRICULTURAL DEPRESSION

Westerners and Southerners also had a solid economic reason for despising the English for their attacks on America's ocean commerce and stranglehold on American ports. Although America's farmers did not own the ships that plied the Atlantic, they did grow the food and cotton that filled those ships. A serious depression had settled over the United States since 1808. Prices for Western and Southern tobacco, cotton, and hemp had fallen steadily and farmers blamed this agricultural depression on English commercial restrictions. Henry Clay said in urging war, "We are asserting our right . . . to export cotton, tobacco and other domestic produce to market."

WESTWARD EXPANSION

Maritime problems, however, were not the entire reason for the War of 1812. In part, the war arose out of sentiment to expand America's boundaries, blocked by the Indians, British, and Spanish.

Westerners had suffered greatly from Indian attacks on frontier settlements and most "buckskin statesmen" were certain that England had been behind the Indian raids. As a matter of fact, England had counseled peace to the Indians, but Westerners were convinced that British officials in Canada were paying Indians six dollars apiece for American scalps and supplying them with firewater and firearms to spur them on.

Actually, the Indians were "aroused" because they were daily being plundered of their fields and hunting territories by American frontiersmen. General William Henry Harrison, the governor of the Indiana ter-

ritory, considered Indians "wretched savages" and mere obstructions to American "civilization." He was able to deprive several tribes of their lands through ingenious treaty arrangements. When a Shawnee chief named Tecumseh, and his half-brother Tenskwatawa (called The Prophet), tried to reverse this course of events, General Harrison prepared for an all-out battle. Tecumseh had organized all the tribes east of the Mississippi into a confederacy by 1806. Traveling from the Great Lakes to the Gulf of Mexico, he had leagued a vast number of Indians into a solid union. The Prophet preached to the Indians that God had ordained that the red man should live separately from the white man, safe from his power and his corrupting laws and liquor. So great was the influence of this movement that even Harrison was obliged to say of Tecumseh: "He is one of those uncommon geniuses which spring up occasionally to produce revolutions and overturn the established order of things."

The inevitable clash occurred on November 7, 1811, when Tenskwatawa attacked General Harrison. Harrison had come to wipe out Tecumseh's camp, called Prophetstown, on Tippecanoe Creek near the Wabash River in Indiana. Harrison was able to repel the Indian braves and destroy the camp. Although the battle was indecisive in itself, it served to throw the Indian confederacy into disarray and to alarm the American people. Across the country, outraged citizens, convinced that the English had been backing Tecumseh, shouted, "Look to the Wabash, look to the impressed seamen."

Westerners calling for vengeance against Britain for her support, real or imagined, of hostile Indians, had another reason for desiring a declaration of war. They saw a war as a splendid opportunity, not only to drive the Indians farther west, but for the United States to annex Canada and the Floridas (still held by Spain, now England's ally). Canada, populated by many Tories who had fled America during the Revolution, deserved to be seized, Westerners thought. Once Canada was part of America, the continent would be free of the Union Jack forever. Congressman Harper of New Hampshire saw this as the work of Providence: "To me, sir, it appears that the Author of Nature has marked our limits in the south by the Gulf of Mexico, and on the north by the regions of eternal frost."

This idea was expressed in more concrete terms by Felix Grundy of Tennessee, as "We shall drive the British from our continent. . . . They will no longer have an opportunity of intriguing with our Indian neighbors. . . . That nation will lose her Canadian trade, and, having no resting place in this country, her means of annoying us will be diminished." The acid-tongued John Randolph, who was quite decidedly against the War Hawks and war with England, responded to such outbursts with, "Agrarian cupidity, not maritime rights, urges this war." He complained that in Congress one "heard but one word—like the whip-poorwill, but one eternal monotonous tone—Canada! Canada! Canada!"

THE WAR OF 1812

The United States was so poorly prepared and so deeply divided over the conflict that the War of 1812 was almost a national disaster. First, the country was unprepared financially. Early in 1811 the Bank of the United States had been allowed to expire and now there was no central eco-

nomic institution that could handle the complex job of issuing war bonds. Moreover, when the Bank died, so did the confidence of many investors in the government's ability to redeem the bonds that were finally issued. As a consequence, only half of the eleven million dollars' worth of bonds offered for sale by the government were bought. Congress had equal difficulty raising money from other sources. It did not even consider war taxes until 1813. When Congress doubled tariffs and introduced new excise taxes they were widely disregarded or evaded.

Of even more serious consequence was the inadequacy of the Army and Navy. Jefferson and Gallatin, in their anxiety to reduce the national debt, had reduced the armed forces along with it. As late as 1811, Madison was continuing this policy. The new President had made no recommendation for naval expansion in his message to

News of the defeat of the British war sloop Barbadoes *by the American ship* Argus *in September, 1813, off Halifax.*

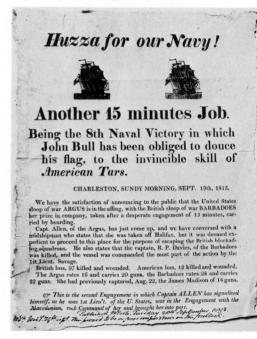

Congress. The following January the same Congress that would vote for war in five months, overwhelmingly defeated a modest proposal to add ten new ships to the Navy. Not until several months after the war had actually started did Congress authorize the building of new frigates, none of which were ready to sail before the end of the war. The United States, in short, was taking on the world's most powerful Navy, which had hundreds of men-of-war, while she owned only a tiny fleet of sixteen vessels! Fortunately, unlike the Army, the Navy, at least, had well-trained officers who had

gained excellent experience in the unde- clared war against France and in the raids on the Barbary pirates.

The War Hawks were not particularly disturbed about the small size of the Navy. They were planning to defeat Britain on land by capturing Canada, an easily obtain- able goal in their opinion. Jefferson, now retired to Monticello, was confident that taking Canada "will be a mere matter of marching." America with its more than seven million people expected little resist- ance, perhaps even happy compliance, from Canada's half million inhabitants. Ameri-

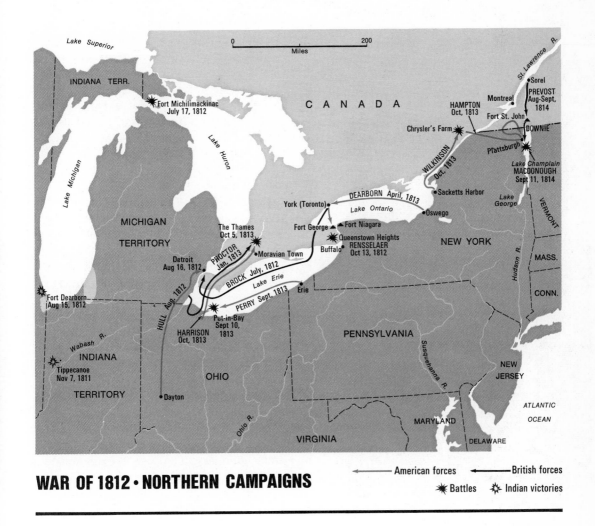

WAR OF 1812 · NORTHERN CAMPAIGNS

American forces — British forces
Battles — Indian victories

cans felt certain that the English, completely preoccupied with their struggles against Napoleon, could not spare a single regiment to protect Canada.

Unfortunately, the American Army was a faulty instrument. Congress expanded the Army to 35,000 soldiers, but this meager force was poorly commanded. As one bright young officer, Winfield Scott, commented: "The old officers had very generally slunk into either sloth, ignorance, or habits of intemperate drinking." Most of the new ones were either "coarse and ignorant," or, if educated, "swaggerers, dependents, decayed gentlemen and others unfit for anything else." The United States had potentially a much stronger land force in the state mili-

Captain Oliver Hazard Perry, the hero of Lake Erie, not only designed and built American warships, but he also successfully commanded them.

tias, which numbered some half million men. Many men enlisted in them, but a number refused to serve outside of their states' boundaries, and the best-trained were all in New England, which, as a section, strongly objected to participating in the war.

PLANS TO CONQUER CANADA

The War Hawks had looked forward, with a tinge of avarice, to conquering Canada. So much land, soon to be under the Stars and Stripes! To their chagrin, Canada's five thousand professional soldiers were well trained, and America's invasion turned into a fiasco. America's General William Hull, a Revolutionary veteran, marched from Detroit toward the British garrison at Malden. After trying to decide whether or not to ask for a naval contingent to back up his land forces, and unable to decide whether to attack Malden or Lake Erie first, Hull lamely opted to return to Detroit. There, on August 6, a clever British commander, General Isaac Brock, surrounded Hull and forced him to surrender. Brock was backed up by Tecumseh and several hundred braves. Tecumseh disliked the English, but he hated the Americans and had decided to throw his lot in with the lesser enemy to defeat the greater. Hull, paralyzed by fear and indecision, surrendered without ever firing a shot. The American public was outraged and Hull was sentenced to death for his cowardice, but Madison pardoned him because of his record in the Revolution.

Two other planned attacks on Canada were also ill fated. An invasion across the Niagara River ended in American defeat when New York's militia refused to cross its state boundary. The New Yorkers watched as their countrymen were mowed down by Canadians. Finally, a campaign was led by General Henry Dearborn along Lake Champlain toward Montreal. Dearborn's militia-men turned out to be equally unprepared to cross into Canada. They balked at the boundary line and the general was forced to march back to Plattsburg. Thus ended the American offensive of 1812. Jefferson's "a mere matter of marching" had fallen far short of defeating the British.

In 1813, America's poor war record was vindicated by a brilliant victory. Captain Oliver Hazard Perry, in ships he had de-signed and built, crippled a British squad-ron at Put in Bay on Lake Erie on Sep-tember 10, 1813. Perry secured American control over the Great Lakes and reported his victory in the terse, and now famous, phrase, "We have met the enemy and they are ours." A second American victory re-sulted from the Battle of the Thames on October 5, 1813. General William Henry Harrison, after receiving news of Perry's triumph, bore down on the English and

their Indian allies under Tecumseh, and with his rough Kentucky militiamen, com-pletely routed them. Tecumseh died mys-teriously; his body was never found, and with his death the last remnants of the Indian confederacy were demolished. De-spite these triumphs, the United States had not even begun to conquer her northern neighbor. Canada was still resolutely Brit-ish.

THE BRITISH ATTACK

In April, 1814, Napoleon abdicated and the war in Europe came to an end. Now the British turned to the task of chastising their troublesome former colonies. Some of Eng-land's best troops, many of them Welling-ton's men, were shipped to American or Canadian shores. Psychologically, one of the worst blows dealt by the English occurred when redcoats invaded Washington in Au-gust, 1814, and burned the Capitol, the White House, and other public buildings. Seeing the dependent militia routed by the enemy, Madison fled the city. The prestige

The nation's Capital at Washington was cap-tured and burned by the British on August 24, 1814, shortly after President Madison had fled.

WASHINGTON.

Reprefentation of the capture of the CITY of WASHINGTON, by the British Forces under the command of Major Gen.ᶦ Rofs and Rear Adm.ˡ Sᵗ I.Cockburn, August 24ᵗʰ 1814, wherein are shewn, the Fort and the Flotil.ᵗ

of the Presidency was never at a lower point in American history.

The sacking of Washington, however, was not Britain's main thrust. The English projected serious attacks at three strategic points—Niagara, Lake Champlain, and New Orleans. The British offensive at Niagara was quickly turned back by the able General Jacob Brown and his subordinate, Winfield Scott, in July, 1814. Two months later, Sir George Prevost attempted to capture Lake Champlain. Once that position had been secured, the English apparently planned to cut off the New England states and restore them to the British Empire, by this time a move that many Yankees would have welcomed. Decisive victory was won by the American fleet, however, under Captain Thomas Macdonough, in September at Plattsburg, which forced Prevost to retreat to Canada. This was the last battle before a treaty brought the war to a close.

Transatlantic, even transcontinental, communications were still maddeningly slow and the time lag permitted General Andrew Jackson of Tennessee to score the most spectacular victory of the war after the peace treaty was signed. Jackson, an able military man, had already defeated the Creek Indians at the Battle of Horseshoe Bend on March 27, 1814, thus acquiring twenty-three million acres or two-thirds of the tribe's lands in the Mississippi Territory. Jackson then captured and destroyed Pensacola in Spanish Florida to prevent its use by the British as a base. Next, Jackson marched his men through Mobile to New Orleans.

In a counter move, the British set sail from Jamaica and approached New Orleans from the Gulf of Mexico. On January 8, 1815, 8,000 British troops under Sir Edward Pakenham met Jackson's army, composed of local pirates, government forces, and the French-speaking militia. Pakenham assaulted Jackson's defenses and the Americans opened fire. In five minutes Jackson inflicted 2,036 casualties and sustained only

21. The crippled British army retreated in haste. The Battle of New Orleans made Andrew Jackson the most popular American hero since George Washington.

In summary, the historian Marshall Smelser has written: "Had not the United States crushed the Creeks, defended Mobile, seized Pensacola, and held New Orleans, all of the Louisiana Purchase could have been lost and part, perhaps, given to Spain. . . ."

THE NAVAL WAR

The *London Evening Star* had described the American fleet as a "few fir-built frigates, manned by a handful of bastards and outlaws," but in the first few months of the war the Americans scored a series of dazzling triumphs. Although there were too few American frigates, they were larger and better armed than their British counterparts. Two months after the war began, Captain Isaac Hull of the U.S.S. *Constitution* gunned the English *Guerrière* into submission in the middle of the Atlantic. In October, 1812, Stephen Decatur (who had previously demonstrated his bravery and prowess in the war against the Barbary pirates) pitted his ship, *United States,* against H.M.S. *Macedonian.* Decatur killed one hundred members of the English crew and hauled the battered enemy vessel into New London as a prize. Then the *Constitution* (nicknamed "Old Ironsides") engaged in conflict with the British frigate *Java* off Brazil, shot away *Java*'s mast, and reduced her to rubble.

Nevertheless, by 1813, most of the American men-of-war were bottled up in their home ports by the Royal Navy, and British squadrons roamed up and down the American coast. Still, American privateers continued to harass British shipping and captured about one thousand British vessels during the war.

The English blockade almost destroyed American shipping. Not only international commerce, but interstate trade suffered, since the United States had few roads and most shipments were still made along coastal waterways. Looking back, one New Englander described the blockade in this way: "Our harbors were blockaded; communications coastwise between our ports were cut off; our ships were rotting in every creek and cove where they could find a place of security; our immense annual products were mouldering in our warehouses; the sources of profitable labor were dried up."

An economic disaster of this sort (although exaggerated in the foregoing account) was what New England Federalists had feared and predicted. In the peak year of 1807, American imports and exports had totaled a quarter of a billion dollars. By 1814 the figure had declined to one tenth that figure and shipbuilding to one fifth. Federalists regarded Madison as a greater enemy than George III. The governors of Massachussetts and Connecticut refused to send their state militia to the aid of the national government. Daniel Webster, a young Federalist congressman from New Hampshire, asked, "Where is it written in the Constitution that you may take children from their parents, and parents from the children, and compel them to fight the battles of any war in which the folly or the wickedness of government may engage it?" The Jeffersonians temporarily lost ground throughout New England, and the Federalists gained almost total control over Connecticut. New England, the richest section of the country, subscribed to only a tiny fraction of the bonds issued by the government to pay war costs.

THE HARTFORD CONVENTION

Despite the blockade and their loud complaints, New Englanders actually made a great deal of money during the War of 1812. Convinced that an inept government was fighting an unnecessary war against the wrong enemy, they continued whenever possible to carry on their lucrative trade with the British. Massachusetts and Rhode Island, both friendly to England, were not blockaded through most of the war. As late as 1813 New England was shipping nearly a million bushels of grain a year to British armies.

The section used its war profits to build new factories. Between 1810 and 1814 the number of cotton spindles increased from 80,000 to 500,000 and there was a corresponding growth in the number of looms. Since New England banks refused to accept paper money during the war, they quadrupled their hoards of silver and gold, thereby draining the rest of the country of almost all specie.

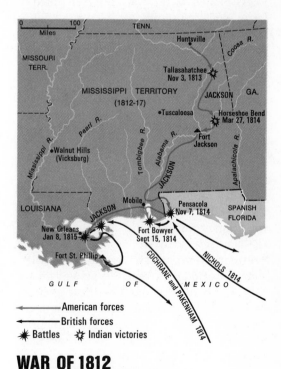

American forces
British forces
✳ **Battles** ✵ **Indian victories**

WAR OF 1812 SOUTHERN CAMPAIGNS

PEACE AND NATIONALISM

Prosperity, however, did not diminish political opposition to the war. In 1814 the Massachusetts legislature called for a convention to discuss a course of action. Some New Englanders hoped the convention would lead to a secession of the region from the Union. Others hoped to amend the Constitution. A few even expected the convention to sign a separate peace with England. While many Federalists did not support such a meeting, twenty-six delegates assembled on December 15, 1814, in Hartford, Connecticut. Following three weeks of debate the convention adopted a fairly moderate stand.

After condemning the "withering influence" of the Jefferson Republicans on the United States and specifically their "visionary and superficial theory in regard to commerce, accompanied by a real hatred but a feigned regard to its interests," the convention demanded a series of Constitutional amendments. All were designed to decrease the power of the central government, the influence of the South and the West and the importance of the Presidency, and to restore the dominance of New England and the commercial interests.

When representatives from the Hartford Convention arrived in Washington with their demands, they came like gloomy guests to a victory celebration. The war was over, Jackson had scored his great triumph at New Orleans, and a peace treaty with Britain had just been signed. The New Englanders, snubbed by Madison, beat a hasty retreat, but the authors of the ultimatum were regarded with ridicule and a suspicion of traitorous intent which never died out.

The War of 1812 was popularly considered a second war for independence that finally secured for the United States the international recognition which she had sought through the Revolution. Unlike most wars, however, negotiations for peace began soon after war was declared, actually one week later, on June 26, 1812. This first attempt to negotiate failed, as did the Czar of Russia's offer, the following fall, to mediate between England and America. Americans had made it very clear that they were fighting a war against the British practice of impressment. The English suspected that the Czar might not be objective in arbitrating this question. Russia, like the United States, had a small Navy and might take America's side against a big naval power. President Madison was optimistic enough about the Russian offer, however, to send Treasury Secretary Albert Gallatin and a moderate Federalist, James Bayard, to Moscow. There they joined America's ambassador to Russia, John Quincy Adams, son of the second President, to await diplomatic moves that failed to materialize.

THE TREATY OF GHENT

By August, 1814, Britain and the United States had settled down to direct peace negotiations in Ghent, Belgium. The British representatives were men of little stature, controlled by the British Foreign Minister, Lord Castlereagh, but the Americans were from among the ranks of her ablest politicians: John Quincy Adams, Albert Gallatin,

Henry Clay, and two minor figures, James A. Bayard, a former senator, and Jonathan Russell, minister to Sweden. However, Adams and Clay had very different personalities and represented conflicting political views, so that tempers often flared. Adams, a brilliant but aloof and introverted man, at first dined separately. He arose every morning at five A.M. to put in extra hours of work and was quite scandalized by the late hours of the Speaker of the House. Adams noted in his diary, "Just before rising I heard Mr. Clay's company retiring from his chamber. I had left him . . . at cards. They parted as I was about to rise." For his part, Clay was frequently exasperated with Adams. When Adams offered the British the right to navigate the Mississippi

in exchange for New England's right to fish off Newfoundland, Clay shouted, "The navigation principle is much too important to concede for the mere liberty of drying fish on a desert." Fortunately, the urbane, Swiss-born Gallatin was usually able to calm his high-strung colleagues.

The Peace of Ghent, signed on December 24, 1814, was more a truce than a treaty. It did little more than return things to their prewar standing. Nothing at all was said about the important issue over which the United States had gone to war—impressment. Nor did the treaty mention neutral rights, national boundaries, fisheries, or compensation to the United States for shipping losses. "Nothing was adjusted, nothing was settled," said Adams, "nothing in substance but an indefinite suspension of hostilities."

The treaty was unpopular in England with shippers and squires and the British

This cartoon by William Charles in 1815 symbolized the tough Yankee resistance to "John Bull" (Britain). The reference to the swamp refers to the Battle of New Orleans and the British defeat at the hands of Jackson.

press, although the great British industrialists were quite pleased. They could now resume trade with the United States, a vast market for their manufactured goods. In America, the treaty was greeted with jubilation. Suddenly all the ineptness of the war was forgotten, the lack of public support, the nasty infighting. Holidays were proclaimed, and cheering, shouting patriots embraced one another in happy celebrations. Americans had feared that the British, having conquered Napoleon, would turn revengefully on the United States. But no, "Not one inch of territory ceded or lost" was the slogan of the hour. Madison promptly submitted the treaty to the Senate, which ratified it unanimously the next day. As the historian Thomas A. Bailey has written, "The Treaty of Ghent certainly was the most popular peace pact with a major power ever concluded by the United States."

THE RISE OF NATIONALISM

As soon as the War of 1812 ended, most Americans turned their backs on Europe and returned to purely domestic concerns. The Russian *chargé* in Washington complained, "They pay no more attention to us and our business than if we were so many Chinamen." In terms of specific territorial gains, the War of 1812 accomplished nothing, but the conflict resulted in many other benefits for the United States. The Indian Confederacy under Tecumseh had been crushed and the British were gone, thus opening the area east of the Mississippi to rapid settlement by frontier farmers. The growth of American manufacturing made the country still more prosperous and much more self-sufficient. The most widely felt effect of the war was probably the rebirth of patriotism. Gallatin wrote: "The war has renewed and reinstated the national feel-

ings and character which the Revolution had given. . . . The people now have more general objects of attachment. . . . They are more Americans; they feel and act more as a nation." They forgot the humiliating moments of the war and made heroes out of Andrew Jackson and Oliver Hazard Perry. The country had not suffered very much financially except for the heavy losses incurred by the shipping industry. Most important, they felt they had "licked the British twice."

RELATIONS WITH BRITAIN

Given the gloating of Americans, it is not surprising that following the war a great deal of ill feeling prevailed between England and the United States. Fortunately, animosity did not deter the statesmen of the two countries from making several amicable settlements of ticklish issues. By the Rush-Bagot Agreement of 1817 each country promised to demilitarize its side of the Great Lakes. The following year, a convention successfully established the northern boundary of the Louisiana territory at the forty-ninth parallel, provided for a joint occupation of the Oregon territory for ten years, extended an 1815 agreement which banned all discriminatory duties on each other's commerce, and finally, provided for the re-opening of the Newfoundland fishery to Americans.

All these compromises signaled a new spirit of rationality on both sides. Particularly beneficial were the arrangements made concerning the Canadian border. Rather than waste money and risk conflict by building up large fleets on the Great Lakes or on Lake Champlain, each country confined itself to a few small armed vessels. Eventually the entire border between Canada and America was demilitarized, an unparalleled achievement.

ACQUISITION OF THE FLORIDAS AND RECOGNITION OF THE LATIN AMERICAN REPUBLICS

Ever since the Louisiana territory was acquired without the inclusion of East and West Florida, the United States had sought, for several reasons, to obtain these areas. In part, this desire was based simply on the widespread expansionist zeal of the American people. They also feared that these areas would be used as a base of operations for attacks on the United States, and that they might pass from Spain into the hands of Britain. In addition, it was felt that the Florida sections would consolidate American territory in that area by linking the Atlantic Coast to New Orleans and would provide new river transportation to the Gulf of Mexico through the numerous waterways flowing through them to the Gulf. American ambitions for control of the Floridas were partially satisfied by the end of the War of 1812. In 1813, a group of American settlers in Spanish Florida tore down the Spanish flag, declared the birth of "The Republic of West Florida" and a few days later petitioned to join the United States. After one month Madison granted the request. Although this illegal land grab embarrassed the usually scrupulous President, he faked the needed documents for posterity's sake. John Quincy Adams was embarrassed also when he had to explain the

event to the Czar of Russia. With a faint smile the Czar remarked urbanely, "Everyone always grows a little in this world."

Americans now began to eye East Florida greedily. Spain had no troops to maintain control over the peninsula, her soldiers were fighting to put down revolutions against Spanish authority in South America. Into the vacuum of East Florida had drifted escaped American slaves, white renegades, and hostile Indians who used Florida as a sanctuary for making raids on Georgia outposts.

Amid this turmoil, the new President, James Monroe, took steps quickly and peacefully to secure the rest of the Florida territory as well as to establish the western boundaries of the Louisiana territory with Spain. The President not only was interested in these territories, but he also wanted the United States to be the first country to recognize the independence of Spain's Latin American colonies. To be able to do this, the administration needed to settle its territorial problems amicably with Spain. Then, if the ultraconservative group of European powers known as the Holy Alliance did not intervene to help Spain retain her colonial possessions, the President would have his way. With this end in view, John Quincy

Adams, the new Secretary of State, began a negotiation of the territorial and boundary issues with the Spanish Minister in December 1817.

In the midst of the negotiation the President unintentionally created a provocation by giving Andrew Jackson a general authorization to cross over the American border into East Florida, if necessary, to chastise marauding Indians. General Jackson interpreted his orders quite liberally. Never a man to hesitate, Jackson seized a Spanish military outpost and replaced Spain's flag with that of the United States. He then executed two British subjects he suspected of inciting the Indians to attack American settlers. Within a few weeks, Jackson had captured every Spanish fort in East Florida except St. Augustine, deposed the Spanish governor and put an American in his place, and declared that henceforth the revenue laws of the United States would be in force in Florida. He later expressed the thought that he should have hanged the Spanish governor as well.

James Monroe, the fourth President of the United States.

When news of the execution of the two Englishmen reached London, public opinion was outraged. "We can hardly believe," one London journal wrote, "that any thing so offensive to public decorum could be admitted, *even in America!*" The British government, however, was cautious and made no protest. In the United States, Jackson's enemies in Congress initiated an investigation of his conduct. Every resolution condemning the popular general, however, was defeated. The American public erupted in long victory celebrations for the vindicated Jackson. The celebration in New York lasted five days and Jackson received the keys to the city.

The situation was also a temporary embarrassment to Adams' negotiation. Spain demanded an apology for Jackson's invasion, but the Secretary of State took the offensive. He pointed out that the Spanish, by their own admission, were powerless to govern Florida. He asserted that if Spain was unable to restrain further Indian attacks on Georgia, she should immediately cede the territory to the United States. Adams also proceeded to demand a westward line stretching to the Pacific for the Louisiana territory. After months of hard bargaining, Spain finally acceded to all American demands, except for the territory of Texas. She ceded East and West Florida to the United States and made great concessions on a firm boundary line between her southwestern possessions in North America and the Louisiana territory. Driving a hard bargain, Adams won from Spain a recognition of the Rocky Mountains as the western boundary of Louisiana. The Spanish also accepted the forty-second parallel as the northern boundary of their North American claims west of the Rockies. This provision excluded her from any further claim to the Oregon territory. The United States now had undisputed control of the territory to the Rocky Mountains and a joint window on the Pacific by virtue of her control of the Oregon territory with

Great Britain. For these remarkable gains in territory, the United States agreed to pay only five million dollars worth of claims held by Americans against the Spanish government.

Following the successful Adams-Onís, or Florida Treaty negotiation and in view of the absence of any overt European intervention on behalf of Spain to suppress the Latin American revolts, President Monroe was able to recognize the independence of the Latin-American colonies in 1822.

THE MONROE DOCTRINE

Having settled its major differences with the European powers by 1820, the United States began to turn her attention away from the European intrigues which had preoccupied her since the beginning days of the republic. Before she could do so with complete assurance, however, she had to face the possibility even after 1822 that the Holy Alliance would intervene in the Western Hemisphere to help Spain reconquer

UNITED STATES · 1822

·········· Natural Boundary of Louisiana country

New states admitted since 1790

her Latin American provinces. The question became of immediate concern to the Monroe administration when a dispatch was received from its minister to Great Britain, Richard Rush, in the fall of 1823, indicating that England was interested in issuing a joint statement with the United States. This paper would have denounced the transference of the Spanish colonies to any other power, denied that either of the two powers had any interest in controlling them, and recognized that their independence or negotiated return to Spanish control was to be left an open question. By October the British Foreign Office had lost interest in a joint statement, but the United States had begun to earnestly consider the project in Cabinet meetings. By then Britain was, in fact, securing France's promise not to intervene on behalf of Spain in Latin America and the United States gradually abandoned the idea of a joint declaration with England and decided to issue an independent statement.

In a generally worded message to Congress, open to various future interpretations and committing the nation to nothing specific when it was made, the President, on December 2, 1823, enunciated the Monroe Doctrine. The basic points of the doctrine were that the Western Hemisphere was no longer subject to colonization or military intervention by the European powers and that the United States would not intervene in the affairs of Europe. It was a statement which recognized the existence of spheres of influence in the world, and implicitly claimed the Western Hemisphere as the American area of dominance. It represented American belief in the superiority of her political system and her determination to prevent the "decadent" European powers from interfering with her national destiny or that of any other part of the hemisphere. It followed the tradition of isolation begun during the Federalist period and early years of the republic; the doctrine was directed against no nation in particular but against all those not in the Western Hemisphere.

Although the United States could not enforce its terms herself, she knew that for all practical purposes she had nothing to fear. European intervention in Latin America would interfere with British trade there, and because of this the British Navy would stand between Europe and the reconquest of these colonies by Spain or any other European power.

The debate by the Monroe Cabinet indicates clearly that John Quincy Adams was not afraid to reject the British offer of a joint statement in favor of an independent statement by the United States which would not limit her westward expansion. It was Adams who saw that the Russian attempt to settle the Alaskan panhandle might be the beginning of new European attempts at colonization which would be detrimental to American expansion and political dominance in North America. It was Adams who was astute enough to see that, because of the power of the British fleet, America was safe in making an independent statement.

The Monroe Doctrine drew little international attention when it was first issued. The Russian Czar retracted his threat against Americans entering Alaskan coastal waters even before Monroe spoke. France abandoned her rather vague plans to help restore Latin America to Spain, but the decision had been made nearly two months before Monroe's famous message and because England, not the United States, had disapproved of the project. European aristocrats considered the Monroe statement "haughty," "arrogant," and "blustering." Even the new Latin American republics regarded the Monroe Doctrine with indifference once they found that the United States had no intention of implementing it with specific commitments to Latin America. At the time, America was too small and too weak to put her foreign policy into practice. Nevertheless, the Monroe Doctrine did clearly establish the principle of "America for the Americans." Within a few decades the United States would have the resources to back up her words with power.

Readings

GENERAL WORKS

Adams, Henry, *History of the United States During the Administration of Jefferson and Madison*. Englewood Cliffs, N.J.: Prentice-Hall, 1963—Adams' classic history interpreted the Jeffersonian period in terms of an inevitable growth of democratic nationalism. His views on both Jefferson and Madison are critical. It is one of the great works of nineteenth-century American historical writing, combining careful research, brilliant writing, and theoretical speculation. (Abridged version available in paperback.)

Borden, Morton, *Parties and Politics in the Early Republic, 1789–1815*. New York: Crowell, 1967—This is a brief account of the formation of American political parties. Borden emphasizes that the early leaders were essentially practical men whose actions were motivated more by realism than by ideology.

Bowers, Claude G., *Jefferson in Power*. Boston: Houghton Mifflin, 1936—A history of Jefferson's two terms in office, the rise of the Democratic-Republicans, and decline of the Federalists. Bowers, a Democratic Party political activist himself, was a strong supporter of Jefferson.

Channing, Edward, *The Jeffersonian System*. New York: Harper and Brothers, 1906—Channing's history of Jefferson's and Madison's Presidencies through 1811 interprets the election of 1800 as a revolution in governing principles.

Cunliffe, Marcus, *The Nation Takes Shape: 1789–1837*. Chicago: University of Chicago Press, 1959—In 1789, Cunliffe asserts, the United States was an experimental venture begun by men who had recently led an armed revolution. By 1837, however, the nation had developed the particular qualities and character with which it is associated today.

Cunningham, Noble E., Jr., *The Jeffersonian Republicans in Power*. Chapel Hill, N.C.: University of North Carolina Press, 1963—Not a conventional history of the period from 1801 to 1809, it is a detailed study of how the Jeffersonian Republican party

structure operated on the state, regional, and national levels.

Fischer, David H., *The Revolution of American Conservatism*. New York: Harper & Row, 1965—The Federalist defeat in 1800, Fischer claims, forced a major revision in the party. Younger Federalists after 1800 were increasingly willing to use democratic rhetoric and organizational techniques to win popular support for their conservative policies.

Peterson, Merrill D., *The Jefferson Image in the American Mind*. New York: Oxford University Press, 1960—A history of what Americans have thought and felt about Thomas Jefferson from his own era to the present. Peterson says that the unresolved tensions in Jefferson's thought make it possible to interpret Jefferson's ideas in very different ways.

Smelser, Marshall, *The Democratic Republic, 1800–1815*. New York: Harper & Row, 1968—Smelser's new interpretation of Jeffersonian America rejects older historians' unfavorable appraisal of Jefferson and Madison but shows that Jefferson was not a crusader but a cautious moderate in office.

Wiltse, Charles M., *The Jeffersonian Tradition in American Democracy*. Chapel Hill, N.C.: University of North Carolina Press, 1935—Wiltse sees Jefferson's thought as a consistent defense of democracy and the right of informed citizens to participate in governing themselves. This creed has been the major strain in American political life.

Wiltse, Charles M., *The New Nation: 1800–1845*. New York: Hill and Wang, 1961—Wiltse's thesis states that between 1800 and 1845, social and economic forces had all but destroyed concepts of "states' rights" and had created a spirit which had made the United States one nation.

SPECIAL STUDIES

Abernethy, Thomas P., *The Burr Conspiracy*. New York: Oxford University Press, 1954—Although the Burr conspiracy is still a rather mysterious episode in our history,

289

Abernethy shows that it grew out of social problems in the West, including a motley population without clear governing authority and little nationalist sentiment. Although it failed dismally, the conspiracy did reveal serious problems for advocates of national unity.

Bemis, Samuel F., *John Quincy Adams and the Foundations of American Foreign Policy*. New York: Knopf, 1949—Bemis deals with Adams' service as diplomat and as Secretary of State under Monroe. He maintains that Adams spelled out the essence of United States foreign policy based on continental expansionism and opposition to European colonialism.

Brown, Roger H., *The Republic in Peril: 1812*. New York: Columbia University Press, 1964—A history of the coming of the War of 1812 which emphasizes domestic American politics as a cause of the war. In particular, Brown shows that many Americans thought that the disputes with Great Britain threatened our republican form of government.

Burt, A. L., *The United States, Great Britain and British North America*. New Haven, Conn.: Yale University Press, 1940—Many of the diplomatic and military conflicts between Great Britain and the United States from the Revolution through the War of 1812, centered around Canada. Burt discusses the changing forms of these disputes and their resolution after the War of 1812.

Coles, Harry L., *The War of 1812*. Chicago: University of Chicago, 1965—This is primarily a military history of the conflict. The author feels that both Western expansionism and violations of maritime rights were responsible for America's declaration of war.

Horsman, Reginald, *The Causes of the War of 1812*. New York: Octagon, 1970—Horsman maintains that the basic causes of the War of 1812 are to be found in Europe, not America and that the United States was for the most part reacting to British policy. This, in turn, was dictated by the course of Britain's war with France.

Perkins, Bradford, *Castlereagh and Adams*. Berkeley, Calif.: University of California Press, 1964—John Quincy Adams and Viscount Castlereagh were the main figures in British-American relations from the War of 1812 through the Monroe Doctrine. Perkins examines both the American and the British sides and concludes that social and economic forces as well as American nationalism influenced diplomatic relations.

Perkins, Bradford, *Prologue to War*. Berkeley, Calif.: University of California Press, 1963—Perkins' account of Anglo-American relations between 1805 and 1812 indicates that mistakes and political factionalism in Washington as well as British attacks on American honor were among the prime causes of the War of 1812.

Perkins, Dexter, *A History of the Monroe Doctrine*. Boston: Little, Brown, 1963—Perkins shows that the Monroe Doctrine had been misinterpreted by those who think it prescribes complete isolation from Europe or that it immediately established the United States as the protector of Latin American independence. The doctrine has undergone changes over time to match varying objectives of American foreign policy.

Pratt, Julius W., *Expansionists of 1812*. Gloucester, Mass.: Peter Smith, 1957—Pratt concentrates his attention on American sectional politics at the time of the War of 1812. He found strong pressure for expansion into Canada among Westerners and for annexation of Florida among Southern "War Hawks."

Whitaker, Arthur P., *The United States and the Independence of Latin America, 1800–1830*. New York: W. W. Norton, 1964—The emergence of United States Latin American policy is treated here as a merging of national self-interest and republican ideology. Whitaker believes the influence of Monroe and John Quincy Adams on that policy has been overrated.

PRIMARY SOURCES

DeVoto, Bernard, ed., *The Journals of Lewis and Clark*. Boston: Houghton Mifflin, 1953

—A modern edition of the journals of the two men whose expedition to the West enabled Americans to comprehend for the first time the vastness of the Louisiana Purchase.

Koch, Adrienne, and William Peden, eds., *The Life and Selected Writings of Thomas Jefferson.* New York: Random House, 1944 —A collection of Jefferson's letters and other writings including his public papers, *Autobiography,* and *Notes on Virginia.*

Padover, Saul, ed., *The Complete Madison.* New York: Harper and Brothers, 1953— Madison's writings, which include examples of his social and economic theories. Padover's introduction claims that Madison's belief that many competing interests in society can be brought together in a republic is at the core of his thinking.

BIOGRAPHIES

Brant, Irving, *James Madison: Commander-In-Chief.* Indianapolis, Ind.: Bobbs-Merrill, 1961—This is the sixth and final volume of Brant's biography of the fourth President. Brant credits Madison with much of the responsibility for leadership in the War of 1812 and also analyzes his post-presidential career.

Brant, Irving, *James Madison: The President.* Indianapolis, Ind.: Bobbs-Merrill, 1956—This is the fifth volume of Brant's biography of the fourth President. It covers the years from his first inauguration to the declaration of war in 1812. Brant defends Madison's conduct in diplomatic affairs.

Corwin, Edward, *John Marshall and the Constitution.* New Haven, Conn.: Yale University Press, 1919—Marshall's term as Chief Justice, from 1801 through 1835, was marked by a consistently nationalistic interpretation of the Constitution, establishment of the sanctity of contracts, and a growth of the Supreme Court's power and prestige. Corwin is a great admirer of Marshall, the architect of these developments.

Dangerfield, George, *Chancellor Robert R. Livingston of New York, 1746–1813.* New York: Harcourt, Brace & World, 1960—Although a great landholder and member of an aristocratic family, Livingston turned from Federalism to Jeffersonianism and helped to negotiate the Louisiana Purchase. Dangerfield attempts to explain this unusual conversion.

James, Marquis, *Andrew Jackson: Border Captain.* New York: Grosset & Dunlap, 1933—A biography of Jackson covering the period before 1819. James tries to avoid making Jackson into simply a romantic hero and stresses his military career.

Kirk, Russell, *Randolph of Roanoke: A Study in Conservative Thought.* Chicago: University of Chicago Press, 1951—This is an intellectual, not a political biography of the Virginian who was a consistent, even extreme, champion of states' rights, agrarianism, and a landed aristocracy.

Malone, Dumas, *Jefferson the President: First Term, 1801–1805.* Boston: Little, Brown, 1970—This is the fourth volume of Malone's biography of Jefferson. The author points out the tensions which are created when an idealist exercises real political power.

Tucker, Glenn, *Tecumseh: Vision of Glory.* Indianapolis, Ind.: Bobbs-Merrill, 1956— This is an admiring biography of the Shawnee chieftain. Tucker believes that Tecumseh's political and military achievements make him the most remarkable Indian in American history.

Schachner, Nathan, *Aaron Burr: A Biography.* Cranbury, N.J.: A. S. Barnes, 1961— This biography defends Burr against many charges leveled at him by his contemporaries and other historians. Schachner claims that Burr was not overly ambitious, was provoked by Hamilton to duel with him, and was not a traitor.

Schachner, Nathan, *Thomas Jefferson: A Biography,* Vols. I–II. New York: Appleton-Century-Crofts, 1951—A biography of Jefferson which concentrates on his personal rather than his political life or the significance of his ideas. Although Schachner finds Jefferson to have several personal weaknesses, he also admires his many accomplishments.

291

Locks on the Erie Canal. De Witt Clinton was the driving influence behind the building of the canal. Clinton convinced the state legislature that the 363-mile-long canal could be built, although at a cost of about $20,000 per mile of canal. The canal proved profitable. In seven years it paid back the original investment of 7 million dollars and went on to add 3 million dollars a year to the state treasury in profits. The canal made New York the leading industrial city in the East.

292

Nationalism and a Changing Economy

8

If any one proposition could command the universal assent of mankind, we might expect it would be this: that the government of the Union, though limited in its powers, is supreme within its sphere of action. This would seem to result necessarily from its nature. It is the government of all; its powers are delegated by all; it represents all, and acts for all. . . .

The government of the United States, then, though limited in its powers, is supreme; and its laws, when made in pursuance of the constitution, form the supreme law of the land, "anything in the constitution or laws of any State, to the contrary, notwithstanding."

—*John Marshall,*
McCulloch v. Maryland

In 1815, the ratification of the Treaty of Ghent ended the War of 1812, and a period of prosperity and apparent political harmony followed in the United States. The war itself may have been unnecessary and Madison's administration had certainly mismanaged it, yet in the aftermath the nation's economy flourished. In New England, shipping revived to a degree, but more important, new industries reaped handsome profits, and emphasis in the Northeast began shifting from commerce to manufacturing. In the South, cotton replaced tobacco and rice as the leading export and busy British and New England textile manufacturers bought increasing quantities of Southern cotton. At the same time, tobacco was again in demand in Europe, and because Europe had poor harvests in 1816 and 1817, demand for American grain increased. The West's population grew and by 1820 totaled 2,200,000, becoming greater than New England's. Western agricultural produce meanwhile found new markets in the Atlantic coastal states and in Europe as new transportation facilities (roads, steamboats, and canals) connected the West to the seaboard.

Politically the people of the United States were so much in accord that the years from 1816 to 1819 were called "The Era of Good Feelings." During this period, most of the nation's new political leaders were in agreement that the federal government should be given more power to control the American economy. Although the Democratic Republicans under Jefferson had espoused states' rights and rejected Hamilton's concept of a strong central government, now the leading spokesmen for the party, Henry Clay, John C. Calhoun, and John Quincy Adams, began to think so much like Hamilton that they created a political program based on a strong central government which came to be called "neo-Federalism."

American nationalism at this time went through a new phase destined to be of short duration. The bases of patriotism, or loyalty, in the United States were the beliefs that American political institutions were superior to all others, and that America offered unbounded economic opportunity. Until this time, most Americans had never associated American preeminence with the concept of a strong central government having broad powers over the political and economic life of the citizenry. Quite the contrary, most Americans associated the political and economic superiority of their nation with a federal government of limited power. In fact, early American nationalistic thought was based on the principle that political and economic freedom was not to be interfered with by government. This is why the Jeffersonians, not the Federalists, were the embodiment of the American spirit of nationalism. Yet in the aftermath of the War of 1812, when pride and confidence in America flowered, much of the leadership of the Jefferson coalition was converted for a short time to neo-Federalist policies, and for a few years these policies had wide, if not universal, support.

THE AMERICAN SYSTEM

The first important sign that neo-Federalism was the new mood of the nation came in Madison's seventh annual message to Congress on December 5, 1815. Before the War of 1812 the Jeffersonian Republicans were opposed to the establishment of a large army and navy because they believed that the country could not support them and that a military establishment was dangerous to the liberties of the people. The War of 1812, however, demonstrated the need to build national defenses and Madison urged Congress, in his 1815 address, to expand the navy, reorganize the militia, and enlarge the Military Academy at West Point which had been established in 1802.

Both Jefferson and Madison had fought on constitutional principles the chartering of the first Bank of the United States in 1791. The first Bank ceased to exist in 1811, when its renewal was defeated by a combination of agrarian interests and those new business interests which found the Bank's policies too restrictive. The management of the country's finances had been chaotic during the war, and now Madison suggested that "a national bank will merit consideration." As we have seen, Jefferson and his early supporters had envisioned America as an agrarian paradise. They had had little use for industry and had feared its effects on the American people. Jefferson himself, however, had modified his views over the years. In 1813 he wrote, "manufacturers are as necessary to our independence as to our comforts," and now Madison proposed to Congress that a federal tariff be instituted to protect native industries. Finally, the Jeffersonians had always feared that the federal government might overstep its powers and encroach on areas of activity best left to the states. Madison continued to agree with this position in principle, but for practical purposes he also believed that an amendment should be added to the Constitution giving the federal government the right to establish "throughout our country the roads and canals which can best be executed under national authority."

Many men following Madison's lead abandoned Jeffersonian Republicanism for a neo-Federalism. At a time when the Federalist party was virtually defunct, its principles were adopted by the opposition. Whereas the Jeffersonians had originally championed states' rights, a strict construction of the Constitution, and the agrarian way of life, now Madison pointed the way to a new role for his party, one that broadened the federal government's authority and took up industry's cause. Henry Clay, by now a dominant political figure, eventually labeled the nationalistic program that evolved, the "American System." Its purpose was to bind all sections of the country together through mutual economic interdependence.

This about-face by the Democratic Republicans resulted primarily from the war, which had revealed that it was important for the United States to have an adequate army and navy. The war had also demonstrated how vital it was for the nation to have a good inland system of transportation, after the British blockade of the Atlantic coast brought nearly all American interstate commerce to a halt. The war had furthermore exposed America's weakness as a nation with little industry. Before 1812 the United States had basically traded its raw materials for European manufactured goods, but during the war America had been cut off from these markets and was compelled to develop its own industries.

PROTECTIONISM

At the heart of the American System was the demand for higher tariffs to protect American manufacturing. After the war ended in February, 1816, British manufacturers proceeded to dump on American markets the surpluses they had been accumulating since 1812. Because British factories were large and highly efficient, they were able to produce at low prices. Cheap British goods easily outsold American commodities and threatened to destroy America's infant industries, located principally in New England. Here the need for tariff protection was deeply felt, but every other part of the country also had something to gain from protectionist measures. In the Carolinas, as

In Favor of the Tariff

———————————————————

" *Having called the attention of the Committee to the present adverse state of our country, and endeavored to point out the causes which have led to it; having shown that similar causes, wherever they exist in other countries, lead to the same adversity in their condition; and having shown that, wherever we could find opposite causes prevailing, a high and animating state of national prosperity exists, the Committe will agree with me in thinking that it is the solemn duty of Government to apply a remedy to the evils which afflict our country, if it can apply one. Is there no remedy within the reach of the Government? Are we doomed to behold our industry languish and decay yet more and more? But there is a remedy, and that remedy consists in modifying our foreign policy, and in adopting a genuine American system. We must naturalize the arts in our country, and we must naturalize them by the only means, which the wisdom of nations has yet discovered to be effectual—by adequate protection against the otherwise overwhelming influence of foreigners. This is only to be accomplished by the establishment of a tariff, to the consideration of which I am now brought.*

And what is this tariff? It seems to have been regarded as a sort of monster, huge and deformed; a wild beast, endowed with tremendous powers of destruction, about to be let loose among our people, if not to devour them, at least to consume their substance. But let us calm our passions, and deliberately survey this alarming, this terrific being. The sole object of the tariff is to tax the produce of foreign industry, with the view of promoting American industry. The tax is exclusively levelled at foreign industry. That is the avowed and the direct purpose of the tariff. If it subjects any part of American industry to burdens, that is an effect not intended, but is altogether incidental, and perfectly voluntary. "

—Henry Clay, Annals of Congress

Attacking the Tariff

———————————————————

" *The present revenue is not only sufficient to support the government, fortify the sea ports, and increase the navy, but to pay off the debt as fast as it becomes due. Sir, by the Constitution you can impose duties only for revenue. Examine the Constitution, line by line, sentence by sentence, and show, if you can, a clause which authorizes duties on imported articles, for purposes other than revenue. In my opinion, such grant of power cannot be found. . . .*

This sir, is my doctrine. Let the people encourage manufactures as much as they please—as circumstances shew they are necessary—manufactures are the creatures of necessity—the South, the North, East, and West will betake to them when indispensable. What I complain of, is this, that our laws oppress other branches of industry to sustain them. I hold it to be good policy to let labor, commerce, and enterprize, alone. Say to the citizen, make your living by tilling the earth, navigating the sea, or manufacturing, as you please, the government will guarantee to you the enjoyment of the fruits of your labor from molestation. And to the merchant and farmer, I would say, dispose of your produce where you can get the best price, and buy where you can get the article you want, the cheapest.

—Nathaniel H. Clairborne,
United States Congress,
Register of Debates

well as New England, there were new cotton mills that were staggering under the blows of English competition. In western Pennsylvania iron smelters had to compete with Scottish and Swedish iron. In Kentucky the manufacturers of hemp bags were endangered by Russian hemp and the Scottish bagging industry. In New York grain farmers, no longer permitted to sell to England, demanded sole rights to the American market. In Vermont and Ohio wool growers needed measures to protect them from the competition of English wool merchants.

In response to these needs, Congress passed the rather mild Tariff of 1816. Earlier federal tariffs had been established primarily to provide the government with revenue; this tariff, passed to protect America's industries, maintained the wartime rates of about 20 to 25 percent on imported goods. The vote in the House of Representatives revealed the diversity of economic interests in the country. New England, which had the most to gain, voted for the tariff, but only by a vote of seventeen to ten. The ten dissenting votes represented New England's shipping interests, who feared that higher duties might slow down foreign trade and thus cut into their profits. The South had almost no industry, and indeed the South voted against the bill by a vote of thirty-four to twenty-three. The twenty-three Southern Representatives who supported the measure did so out of patriotism, even though they believed it would serve to raise the prices of manufactured goods and thus penalize the Southern purchaser. Many Southerners voted for the tariff out of their nationalistic feeling that what was good for New England was good for the nation as a whole. Or, like John C. Calhoun, they believed that if another war broke out with England, the American army and navy would need American industries to manufacture goods. Moreover, many Southerners expected that soon the South would experience its own industrial boom. Only the Middle and Western states

gave their wholehearted support to the measure. Despite these regional differences, the relative harmony that prevailed during this period between the different parts of the country was remarkable. Unfortunately, it was only temporary.

REVIVAL OF THE BANK

After the first Bank of the United States expired in 1811, more than three hundred state and private banks were chartered, and these issued about a hundred million dollars' worth of paper money. There was no national currency and frequently paper money offered by a state or private bank was not negotiable in neighboring areas. Worse still, the various paper currencies were seldom able to command their face value. As in the days of the Continental Congress, the country was plagued by a host of different currencies, almost all of them devaluated. This devaluation took place because few state-chartered banks had adequate reserves of gold and silver. Only the banks of New England were able to back up their paper dollars with specie.

The absence of a national bank also caused other problems. The federal government no longer had a place to deposit its funds or reliable machinery for transferring them from one place to another. Neither did it have a financial institution through which to sell government bonds for revenue. These inconveniences, as well as the fiscal chaos created by the lack of a national currency, were described by Albert Gallatin, who wrote in December, 1815: "Public credit, heretofore supported simply by common honesty, declines at home and abroad; private capital placed on a still more uncertain basis; the value of property and the nature of every person's engagements equally uncertain; a baseless currency varying every fifty miles and fluctuating everywhere."

To correct this state of affairs, Henry Clay proposed the creation of a new national bank as the second point in his American System. He and his close political ally at that time, John C. Calhoun, pushed hard for such an institution, and a second Bank of the United States was chartered by Congress in 1816. Its structure was similar to the first Bank except for an increase in its capitalization from ten to thirty-five million dollars. As before, the federal government subscribed one-fifth of its stock (seven million dollars); however, this time, five of the twenty-five directors were appointed by the President with Senate approval.

A NATIONAL PROGRAM FOR IMPROVEMENTS

The nation had a pressing need for internal improvements. By 1816 only a hundred miles of canal had been dug. Rather efficient turnpikes had been created in Pennsylvania, New York, New Jersey, and New England, but users had to pay tolls, and the cost made transportation of most goods prohibitive. In general, American commerce moved in a clumsy pattern: on barges down the Mississippi, and on ships around Florida and up the Atlantic Coast. Eastern goods traveled west on wagons across wretched roads, many of which were only dirt paths, over the Alleghenies.

President Madison was willing to approve appropriations for the eventual extension of the existing National Road from Cumberland, Maryland, to Columbus, Ohio, and finally to Vandalia, Illinois. Congress first voted money for this project in 1806. Construction began in 1811. By 1818 the road had reached Wheeling, Virginia, on the Ohio River. Coaches, covered wagons, and livestock crowded this highway, the most significant road-building undertaking of the early Republic.

The President, however, strongly doubted the federal government's right to finance other internal improvements without a specific Constitutional amendment to empower

it to do so. In this regard, he was still a traditional Jeffersonian Republican, with a more limited concept of the government's role than many of his fellow party members. When Congress sent him a bill in 1817 to appropriate one-and-a-half million dollars for local internal improvements, Madison reluctantly vetoed it as one of his last Presidential acts. Because of Madison's veto, the financing of roads and canals continued to be primarily the responsibility of states and private companies. An essential element in the American System had been defeated at the outset.

THE ELECTION OF JAMES MONROE

James Monroe, who had served as Madison's Secretary of State, succeeded him as President. Madison supported his candidacy for President while old-line Republicans supported John Randolph's choice of William H. Crawford, a prominent Georgia lawyer, although Crawford himself did not oppose Monroe's nomination. Madison's will prevailed and Monroe was nominated in 1816. He won easily in the electoral college by a vote of 183 to 34 over his Federalist opponent, Rufus King. King, as a New Yorker, had been nominated in an effort to draw attention away from the sectional, New England character of the Federalists, but the strategy failed; King was the last Federalist candidate ever nominated for the Presidency. He carried only Massachusetts, Connecticut, and Delaware.

The new President had served the public for many years. He had been appointed Madison's Secretary of State in 1811 and was made Secretary of War, in addition, in 1814. His vigorous handling of the end of the war won him great popularity, and probably the election. He was the third Virginia Republican in a row to be President and critics grumbled about the so-called "Virginia dynasty." Third in line, he was also third in ability. He had neither Jefferson's remarkable idealism and encyclopedic interests nor Madison's fine, theoretical mind. What he had was a perfectly respectable record of service to the nation. He fought under Washington during the Revolution, served twice as the governor of Virginia, and later as a senator and Cabinet officer. His greatest distinction was won as a diplomat, serving at various times as the nation's representative in Paris, Madrid, and London.

Monroe's appearance was a reminder of the heroic days of the Revolution. Historian George Dangerfield has written of him: "On certain special occasions, his tall, raw-boned, venerable figure would appear in the faded uniform of a Revolutionary officer; otherwise he wore the plain dark coat, the knee-length pantaloons, the white-topped boots of an earlier day; his hair was powdered and tied in a cue at the back; his manners were mild, but constrained, awkward, formal and old-fashioned."

Monroe not only had his record and his stately appearance to aid him, he had the best Cabinet since the administration of George Washington. In it, John Quincy Adams was the Secretary of State. Adams, son of the second President, was well-prepared for his important office. He had served as America's ambassador to Russia,

Prussia, The Netherlands, and England. Madison's last Secretary of the Treasury, William H. Crawford, was retained by Monroe. One of the leading lawyers of the day, William Wirt, was made Attorney General, and John C. Calhoun was appointed Secretary of War. All these men were gifted and all possessed sound administrative abilities.

The historian Edward Channing has described Monroe as "one of those men of persistent mediocrity from whom useful and attractive Presidents have been made." The Monroe Doctrine, his administration's most important accomplishment in foreign policy, was formulated chiefly by John Quincy Adams. Most of the domestic policies carried out under Monroe had been worked out under Madison. Monroe was so popular and his first term so peaceful that when he was reelected for a second term in 1820, only one electoral vote was cast against him!

THE ERA OF GOOD FEELINGS

Monroe began his first term with a good-will tour of New England, formerly the center of Federalist opposition. The Republican President came upon the invitation of a Federalist newspaper, the *North American Review*. Everywhere Monroe went he was greeted by cheering crowds. He spent six stirring days in Boston, the Federalist stronghold, and when he addressed the Massachusetts legislature he embraced political opponents in these words: "I indulge a strong hope that our principal dangers and difficulties have passed, and that the character of our deliberations and the course of the government itself, will become more harmonious and happy than it has heretofore been." Another Federalist newspaper, the *Columbian Centinel,* was so friendly toward the new President and so delighted with the political harmony he seemed to leave in his wake, that it entitled an article about the new administration, "Era of Good Feelings."

The slogan caught on and historians who write of this era have continued to use it. Prosperity and domestic harmony were the dominant postwar trends. Symbolic of the new harmony experienced by the nation was the renewal of friendship between Thomas Jefferson, the nation's most famous Democratic Republican, and John Adams, the most famous living Federalist. In 1801, Adams had skulked angrily out of Washington without attending Jefferson's inauguration. The two men had not corresponded for years. Now, however, they were again exchanging voluminous letters and addressing one another as "My dear friend." Indeed, a new era had dawned. Unfortunately, it ended before long.

THE INDUSTRIAL REVOLUTION

The years 1808 to 1816 provided a great stimulus for American industry. The United States had been largely cut off from foreign commerce and a number of small Northeastern manufacturing establishments had arisen to fill the gap. Shipping and commercial interests did not regain their full prewar strength until the 1840s and 1850s.

Madison, and later Monroe, were passive Presidents and their lack of political leadership left a power vacuum in national politics. Into this void stepped the brilliant Speaker of the House, Henry Clay of Kentucky. As mentioned earlier, it was Clay who conceived the American System, which he regarded as a means of attaining a self-sufficient economy, one that would free the nation forever from its dependence upon Europe. Essential to Clay's program was the setting up of protective tariffs that would give New England's infant industries an economic advantage over foreign imports. Clay envisioned an America in which New England's products, primarily cotton and linen cloth, woolen cloth, paper, leather, and iron goods, would supply the South and West. In return, the West would ship its meat and bread products to the rest of the country and the South would provide cotton for the textile factories of New England. Such a concept was not merely the product of postwar nationalistic fervor or political ambition, it also resulted from a desire to channel the remarkable economic and technological changes taking place in the country toward constructive national purposes.

TECHNOLOGICAL ADVANCES

A number of important technological advances in the late eighteenth century planted the seeds of the industrial revolution which became a flourishing reality by the middle of the nineteenth century. In the Era of Good Feelings, America was by no means truly industrialized. Most manufactured goods were still made in private homes by craftsmen. Nevertheless, the process of industrialization, which would eventually make America the richest country in the world, had already begun. The typical American after the War of 1812 was still a farmer, living isolated from the city. Only 700,000 people out of a national population of 9,600,000 lived in urban centers of more than 2,500 persons. Indeed, most Americans were hardly aware that a revolution had started in their midst.

For a factory to undersell goods made in homes, it needed to be mechanized and specialized and to have a system for national distribution of its product. In an early form all three of these requirements had already been met by industry in 1820. In 1790, the first effective factory in America was set up in Pawtucket, Rhode Island to make cotton thread. English factories had had a monopoly on the cotton-spinning trade since the 1770s, through the technological genius of Richard Arkwright who had devised a rudimentary assembly line for producing cotton fabric. Using newly invented machines (the flying shuttle, spinning jenny, and water frame) which made production more efficient and cheaper by reducing the amount of human labor required, Arkwright turned out machine-spun cotton that was less expensive and more durable than hand-spun cotton.

Americans were eager to copy Arkwright's factory system, but the British inventions were closely guarded. No one was allowed to take the plans for these machines out of England and skilled textile workers were not permitted to travel abroad or emigrate.

THE FACTORY

The secret eventually leaked out, however, when a young Englishman, Samuel Slater, slipped out of Britain, came to Rhode Island, and reconstructed the machines from memory for the firm of Almy & Brown. The factory began operation early in 1791. Nine children, most of them from poor farming families, tended its seventy-two spindles and each earned less than a dollar a week. The only product was cotton thread; no cloth was made.

During the Napoleonic Wars, many more cotton mills opened. By 1815 there were 213 factories. Few survived the war, however, and most were forced out of business by tough British competition before the Tariff of 1816 could come to their rescue.

One factory opened its doors in 1816 and instead of going under, survived and prospered dramatically. The Boston Associates, led by the wealthy merchant Francis Cabot Lowell, built a new cotton mill at Waltham, Massachusetts. This factory was the first wholly integrated cotton-manufacturing plant in the world, a miracle of American ingenuity and efficiency. Under one roof raw cotton was unbaled, corded, and spun by efficient power looms; finally the finished cloth was dyed and printed.

Instead of employing children, the Boston Associates hired farm girls aged eighteen to twenty-two from respectable families. The Associates sheltered and fed them in company-built houses, educated them, and insisted on high standards of hygiene and religious instruction. This system proved so attractive that company morale remained high and turnover of employees was low.

In its first year of operation, the factory paid out a dividend of 12 percent to its stockholders. By 1822, the original investors had received back all monies invested, and were reaping handsome yearly dividends. Soon several other large factories were set up by the Boston Associates, the most important at Lowell, Massachusetts.

NEW INVENTIONS

While serving as Secretary of the Treasury under Washington, Alexander Hamilton noted that there existed "in the genius of the people of this country, a peculiar aptitude for mechanical improvements." Hamilton's observation was soon borne out in practice, and inventions were protected by the patent act Congress adopted as early as 1790 to protect inventors.

American manufacturers, almost more than their British counterparts, mechanized because of the high cost of labor. Labor was so expensive, with American workers earning as much as 50 percent more than wage-earners in Britain, that great savings were effected each time a machine replaced a human being.

Eli Whitney was an important inventor of the early Republic. In 1800 he devised a way of manufacturing rifles, using machinery with interchangeable parts, a highly significant advance toward the assembly-line method of production. Earlier, in 1793, Whitney invented the cotton gin. Before 1793 only cotton of the long-staple variety could be cleaned of seeds by hand at a reasonable cost. The process never was cheap, however, and long-staple cotton was a fragile plant that could be grown only under ideal weather conditions and only in certain types of soil. The gin made it economically feasible to clean short-staple cotton, which could be grown in almost any soil and was hardy enough to survive any weather, provided the growing season was sufficiently long.

The cotton gin revolutionized Southern agriculture, with far-reaching economic and political effects. Nearly as influential was the development of the steamboat. By 1790, John Fitch had constructed and was operating the world's first regularly scheduled steamboat service. When this vessel was eventually used to ply the Mississippi, it

reduced transportation costs and established regular trading routes between the West and the East. Since the steamboat could sail upstream, it also served to turn the Mississippi into a two-way highway.

A number of minor inventions and mechanical improvements after 1815 led to major changes in American industry. Better-designed water wheels, leather transmission belts, and metal gears made machines more durable and more efficient. Development of the rolling mill eliminated the need to hammer out sheet metal by hand. A new process for refining pig iron facilitated a switch from coal, which was expensive, to cheaper charcoal. The perfection of the cylinder process for making paper led to the mechanization of that industry. A new method for canning food in airtight containers proved highly useful for conserving perishable foods and transporting them from the country to the city.

DOMESTIC MANUFACTURING

Despite the strides taken toward industrialization, most nonagricultural workers in the years following the War of 1812 did not labor in factories but in their houses or in small shops. The Napoleonic Wars stimulated not only American industry but also domestic manufacturing. As late as 1823 most of the country's half million urban laborers were engaged in household manufacturing and at the same time produced most of their own food.

These craftsmen made everything from pianos and cigars to pencils and barrels. Even small, remote towns had their own ironworks, brickyards, flour mills, and lumberyards. In 1810, for example, the tiny town of Lebanon, Ohio (population 300) had three tanners, four shoemakers, two blacksmith shops, a hatter, a nail-maker, and two saddle shops. It should be pointed out, however, that few of these crafts were full-time occupations, but rather were side lines conducted in basements or spare rooms by farmers, shopkeepers, lawyers, and doctors.

Generally, these manufacturers turned out only small quantities of goods and sold only to the immediate neighborhood. Occasionally, however, domestic manufacturing would sell to a national market. For ex-

Samuel Slater began the first successful textile mill in America in 1791. Located at Pawtucket, Rhode Island, the mill employed nine children to work on seventy-two spindle machines that Slater reconstructed from memory of the English factory.

Eli Whitney's original, hand-cranked model of the cotton gin. The cotton is drawn into a cylinder in the middle of the machine through slits that are too small for the cotton seeds, thus separating the two. Because the machine worked on so simple a principle, Whitney was never able to enforce his patent.

ample, merchants in the Northeast bought shoe leather in wholesale quantities and distributed it to cobblers who worked in their homes. The finished shoes were collected, inspected for quality, and packaged in a central warehouse, from which they were shipped all over the country. Hat manufacturing in Danbury, Connecticut, also became a business with a national market.

THE RISE OF THE CORPORATION

Domestic manufacturing continued to flourish after the War of 1812, but its days were numbered. The factory system gradually pushed craftsmanship aside, and the business corporation became one of the nation's principal economic institutions, making possible the financing of large factories.

The English joint-stock companies which had paid for the colonization of some American colonies had been corporations, but the corporation had not played a significant part in the New World since colonial times. A corporation is an institution that acquires capital by issuing shares of stock to many individual investors. Its distinguishing feature is the principle of limited liability, which protects the stockholder by relieving him of the legal responsibility for the corporation's debts. Hence his personal assets under law are beyond the reach of its creditors and he is not held liable in the event of the corporation's bankruptcy or deep indebtedness. Since the company is owned by stockholders, its liability is limited and the individual stockholder's risk is limited to the depreciation or loss of only his investment.

In the late eighteenth and early nineteenth century, the device of incorporation was used by a number of private companies which built canals, bridges, and turnpikes. In 1813 the Boston Associates, which had built the cotton plant at Waltham, Massa-

chusetts, adapted the corporate form of organization to manufacturing. Previous corporations had backed specific public projects, such as founding a colony or building a turnpike, which would presumably reach a goal within a limited number of years; now the corporate form was made the organizational basis for a different kind of undertaking, the industry with a limitless future and possibilities for expansion.

The corporation provided safeguards to private investors that made it an ideal way to attract money to capitalize industry. With corporations it became possible to raise large sums of money to build factories by allowing many people to pool their accumulated savings for the needed amounts. The corporate form of enterprise had an additional advantage: stocks could easily be bought and sold without disturbing the financial structure of the business and without requiring quantities of paperwork or meetings of all stockholders. In a partnership, by contrast, each partner was fully responsible for the debts of the company and the election or retirement of a new partner caused great complications. Corporations were relieved not only of total liability but of certain kinds of internal red tape. Their activities were restricted, however, by external regulations. Throughout the early 1800s, corporations were supposed to obtain special charters granted by a state legislature to allow them to organize, and the number of rules governing the establishment of every new corporation discouraged many businessmen. Consequently,

A cotton loom in a New England factory. Women and children were paid about $1 to $3 for a 78-hour week. In this drawing, two women are running a loom, and two children are running a calico-printing machine. Over one-half of the labor force in the textile factories were children under sixteen.

most businesses remained unincorporated until the second half of the nineteenth century.

America's first successful implementation of the corporation system took place in the cotton-textile industry, notably in plants under the management of the Boston Associates. Like the great incorporated industries that dominate American manufacturing today, these early corporations were geared not to the individual craftsman but to the machine, they were financed by many investors and not one great capitalist, and they were managed not by the owners but by hired professional managers.

The incorporated Boston Associates was so successful with its first mill at Waltham

that between 1821 and 1835 it opened nine new companies in Massachusetts and New Hampshire, each specializing in a particular textile product on a large scale. Capital for these and similar ventures often came from private banks, and more often from the state banks that were increasing almost daily. From 1815 to 1819 state banks doubled in number from 204 to 400 active institutions.

LABOR

During the infancy of American industry, conditions in manufacturing establishments were not as oppressive for workers as they became a few decades later. True, the cot-

ton mill at Waltham, and later at Lowell, Massachusetts, which soon became the center of the Boston Associates' activity and the leading industrial city of the nation, hired young women at low wages, but at first these women were well treated. Usually, they were able to save about half of their weekly salary of three dollars. The English novelist, Charles Dickens, wrote of them: "They were all well dressed. They were healthy in appearance, many of them remarkably so, and had the manners and deportment of young women. . . . The rooms in which they worked were as well ordered as themselves." Even in this relatively benign period however, the women laborers worked long hours, thirteen hours in summer and from dawn to dusk in winter. Moreover, almost half of the labor force in New England's textile factories were children under sixteen.

These conditions are more startling to us than they were to people living in the early nineteenth century. After all, farmers and their families, even the very young children, toiled in the fields extremely long hours and farm workers made much less than millhands. However, working conditions in textile factories began to deteriorate steadily. The direction of the mills owned by the Boston Associates was turned over to hired managers. These professionals, striving to reap ever greater profits for their masters, lowered wages and turned factories into places of drudgery. In 1846 an observer described the Lowell factory routine in this way:

At half past four in the morning the factory bell rings, and at five girls must be in the mills. A clerk placed as a watch, observes those who are a few minutes behind the time, and effectual means are taken to stimulate punctuality. This is the morning commencement of the industrial discipline (should we not rather say industrial tyranny?) which is established in these Associations of this moral and Christian com-

munity. At seven the girls are allowed thirty minutes for breakfast, and at noon thirty minutes more for dinner, except during the first quarter of the year, when the time is extended to forty-five minutes.

As early as 1834 a thousand Lowell girls went out on strike in protest against a 15 percent wage cut. "One of the leaders," wrote a Boston newspaper, "mounted a stump, and made a flaming . . . speech on the rights of women and the inequities of the 'monied aristocracy' which produced a powerful effect on her auditors, and they determined to 'have their way, if they died for it.'" The strikers, however, were poorly organized. Striking was looked upon as a crime and they had no precedents for such protests. The leaders of the insurrection were fired and the young women went back to work at the reduced wages. All other strikes that broke out in New England during the 1830s ended similarly in failure.

STATE AID TO BUSINESS

Corporations, legally and financially the organizational form best adapted to the development of large industrial concerns, received some encouragement in the nineteenth century. When individual corporations were first formed, state legislatures issued charters for each company that applied for incorporation. The time required for each separate piece of legislation often delayed the founding of corporations for long periods and also consumed much of the legislators' time. In order to simplify and speed up the procedure, New York issued in 1811 the first general incorporation law, a blanket measure that set up rules whereby charters could be issued to corporations without specific legislative action in each case. Other states began to allow general incorporation by the late 1830s.

Tax benefits were also introduced to aid new businesses. For example, in 1817, New

York passed a law that exempted textile mills from taxation and in 1823 Ohio extended tax benefits to textile, iron, and glass companies. Enactment of the United States Patent Law also helped business not only by encouraging inventors of new industrial products and processes but by protecting the manufacturers who bought exclusive rights to these inventions.

THE SUPREME COURT UNDER JOHN MARSHALL

The Supreme Court after 1816 reflected a national mood that was both patriotic and sympathetic to the protection of business enterprise. Within a few years both attitudes had been modified by political and economic developments, but not until the 1830s did the Supreme Court begin to reflect the wishes of a majority of Americans for stronger emphasis on states' rights and less concern for the vested rights of private property.

The Supreme Court's lag behind public opinion in the first third of the nineteenth century can be explained by the great influence of the Chief Justice in those years.

The Court was headed for 34 years, from 1801 to 1835, by John Marshall, a Federalist who was appointed Chief Justice by President John Adams. Marshall was a thoroughgoing supporter of strong central government. He was also an ardent defender of private property and regarded businessmen as the group in the country most likely to defend the federal government against the encroaching power of state governments. He believed that "the business community was the agent of order and progress," and was determined to aid it in every way against restrictions by state legislation.

When Marshall retired he was eighty years old. He had seen the country progress from a collection of loosely knit states into a unified new nation. He had done everything he could to aid this trend by handing down a number of decisions that confirmed the supremacy of federal law and the federal courts over state legislatures and state courts.

John Marshall, Chief Justice of the Supreme Court, in a painting by Rembrandt Peale.

Marshall had fought in the Revolution, practiced as a lawyer in Virginia, his native state, and served as a Congressman. He had been John Adams' Secretary of State for a brief period, but his lasting fame came from his years on the Supreme Court. There he was a dominating figure, exerting influence even over the justices appointed by the Jeffersonian Republicans. In over 34 years he found himself a member of the minority opinion in only eight cases. Although Marshall was an unprententious man with simple tastes, he entertained a life-long suspicion of putting too much power in the hands of the common man, and most of his decisions reflected his defense of vested property rights rather than human rights and of the authority of a strong central government.

Marshall had established the right of judicial review in 1803, in the case of *Marbury v. Madison* (see Chapter 7). This right gave the Supreme Court the authority to decide whether a law passed by Congress and signed by the President was constitutional. The Constitution itself did not specify that the Supreme Court was to have this privilege, although most of the Founding Fathers probably expected the Court to review legislation. Marshall, an advocate of judicial review, asserted the Court's power to protect and interpret the Constitution.

Because Marshall was a nationalist, however, he did not wish to undermine the prestige of Congress but rather to enhance it. During the rest of his tenure he never again declared a federal law unconstitutional. He was eager to keep Congress and the Supreme Court in a position superior to state legislatures and state courts.

INTERSTATE COMMERCE

The Marshall Court declared state laws unconstitutional on thirteen occasions in a remarkable series of decisions of nation-

alistic character. In one of these cases, *Gibbons v. Ogden* (1824), Marshall ruled that Congress had virtually absolute power to regulate interstate commerce.

New York had granted Robert Fulton and Robert R. Livingston a monopoly over all steam navigation within the state. In 1815, Aaron Ogden, a former Governor of New Jersey, purchased from Fulton and Livingston the right to operate a ferry between Elizabeth Point, New Jersey, and New York City. Afterward, Thomas Gibbons, who held a federal license to operate a vessel along the Atlantic Coast, set up a rival ferry line. Ogden sued Gibbons, arguing that Gibbons had no right to enter waters on the New York side of the state line, since he, Ogden, had secured a monopoly over New York navigation.

When the case was appealed to the Supreme Court, Marshall decided in favor of Gibbons, thus destroying the New York monopoly. Marshall ruled that a state could regulate commerce or navigation within its own boundaries, but once either activity involved the crossing of state lines it became subject to regulation by Congress. The decision had two important legal consequences. First, Marshall firmly stated that an "act of Congress is supreme: and the law of the state . . . must yield to it." Second, the Constitution referred only to Congress's right to regulate interstate "commerce," but Marshall broadly interpreted "commerce" to also include "navigation." This broad construction of the word "commerce" enabled later Supreme Court Justices to grant Congress the right to regulate interstate electric power companies, radio and television transmission, and even factory conditions.

The effect of the decision at that time was to open up the steamboat business to any competitor. Unlike many of Marshall's decisions, this one was quite popular. Soon dozens of ferries were crossing New York waters. Even more important, *Gibbons v. Ogden* disallowed *all* interstate monopolies.

From now on steamboats could go wherever they pleased with only a federal coasting license. Freedom of use of the Mississippi and the Gulf of Mexico were assured and in a few years steamboats were shortening the distance between the West and the East. In a tribute to the importance of the steamboat, George Dangerfield wrote: "Having triumphed over monopoly, in 1824, with the aid of the Supreme Court, it proceeded on its own unsubsidized momentum to triumph over space and loneliness."

DEFENDING THE BANK

Marshall again promoted his two major interests of aiding business and establishing the federal government's authority in *McCulloch v. Maryland* (1819). The state of Maryland had sought to tax the Baltimore branch of the Bank of the United States, in fact, to tax it out of existence. The Constitution does not specifically grant Congress the right to charter a bank (see Chapter 6), but Marshall, following in Hamilton's footsteps, held that this authority was implied in the Constitution. "Let the end be legitimate," Marshall wrote, "let it be within the scope of the Constitution, and all means which are appropriate, which are plainly adapted to that end, which are not prohibited, but consistent with the letter and spirit of the constitution, are constitutional." By broadly interpreting the powers of Congress, Marshall extended its authority into finance. By defending the Bank of the United States against state regulations, Marshall aided business enterprise, for the Bank gave businessmen loans, provided them with a safe place for investments, and helped maintain a reliable national currency. Another significant aspect of the decision was Marshall's announcement that states did not have the power to "retard, impede, burden, or in any manner control" the operations of Constitutional laws passed by Congress.

Until the Civil War, a subject of constant debate was whether the state legislatures or the Supreme Court had the final authority on the constitutionality of federal laws. *McCulloch v. Maryland* and many other decisions handed down by Marshall sided with the power of the federal government over that of the states. The great defenders of states' rights argued that the United States was exactly what its name meant, a federation of states, and that the state governments had the final authority over the constitutionality of federal acts. Nationalists like Hamilton and Marshall, on the other hand, argued that the United States government under the Constitution was formed by the *people* of the country who had placed final authority over federal legislation under the jurisdiction of the Supreme Court. State governments, they insisted, had no right to interfere with enforcement of federal legislation. The decision in *McCulloch vs. Maryland* was very unpopular at the time it was handed down, but it was a landmark in American constitutional history.

SANCTITY OF CONTRACTS

Marshall made two more significant decisions in 1819 that were of great aid to the business community. The more important decision was handed down in *Dartmouth College v. Woodward*. Dartmouth had received a royal charter from King George III in 1769. This charter was later acknowledged by the New Hampshire legislature, but then ignored when the legislature, without Dartmouth's agreement, sought to turn the college from a private into a public institution. Dartmouth sued the state. The Chief Justice ruled in favor of the college on the grounds that such a charter could not be changed unilaterally. This decision defined charters granted to schools, or to businesses, as contracts that could be altered only with the consent of both parties. Under the decision, corporations licensed by states could not be regulated at all by states except under restrictions written into the original charter. The second case, *Sturges v. Crowninshield,* declared unconstitutional a New York law that relieved debtors of their obligations. Again Marshall upheld the sanctity of contracts, pointing to a constitutional provision that forbade all legislation that impaired contractual obligations.

REACTION TO MARSHALL'S DECISIONS

Marshall was applauded by the business community for upholding the sanctity of contracts and by nationalists for confirming the supremacy of federal legislation over the laws of the separate states. (As it turned out, Marshall's rather extreme stand in favor of the utter inviolability of contracts was modified by later Supreme Court decisions.) The long-range effect of his rulings was to: (1) establish the right of judicial review, an important factor in the balance of powers among the three branches of the federal government; (2) extend Congressional authority over interstate commerce; (3) set the Supreme Court and Congress above state legislatures and state courts; and (4) ally the Court with a broad and flexible interpretation of the Constitution.

Men such as Jefferson, who were suspicious of a concentration of power in the federal government and who wanted to ensure states' rights, greeted Marshall's decisions with alarm. Jefferson declared: "The Constitution is a mere thing of wax in the hands of the judiciary, which they may twist and shape into any form they please." But Marshall's desire to use the Constitution as a buttress and protection for the business community did not come to full flower until after the Civil War. Marshall's emphasis on a strong central government to help regulate the economy for the na-

tional welfare was not an acceptable development to the majority of Americans until the twentieth century.

Federal Supremacy

" The great question, whether a federal or a national system of government will best secure the liberty and happiness of the people, remains to be more fully considered. . . .

Liberty and power are adverse pleaders, and the arguments or temptations offered by both, have never failed to make proselytes. Between the tyranny of concentrated power, and of unbridled licentiousness, is a space filled with materials for computing the effects produced by controlling both extremes, and estimating the chances for promoting human liberty and happiness. It seems to be nature's law, that every species of concentrated sovereignty over extensive territories, whether monarchical, aristocratical, democratical, or mixed, must be despotick. In no case has a concentrated power over great territories been sustained, except by mercenary armies; and wherever power is thus sustained, despotism is the consequence. . . .

The geography of our country and the character of our people, unite to demonstrate that the ignorance and partiality of a concentrated form of government, can only be enforced by armies; and the peculiar ability of the states to resist, promises that resistance would be violent; so that a national government must either be precarious or despotick. By dividing power between the federal and state governments, local

AGRICULTURE AND TRANSPORTATION

partialities and oppressions, the common causes of revolution, are obliterated from our system. "

—*John Taylor,*
New Views of the Constitution
of the United States

Federal Supremacy

That the United States form, for many, and for most important purposes, a single nation, has not yet been denied. In war, we are one people. In making peace, we are one people. In all commercial regulations, we are one and the same people. In many other respects, the American people are one; and the government which is alone capable of controling and managing their interests in all these respects, is the government of the Union. . . . for all these purposes, her government is complete; to all these objects, it is competent. The people have declared, that in the exercise of all powers given for these objects, it is supreme. It can, then, in effecting these objects, legitimately control all individuals or governments within the American territory. The constitution and laws of a State, so far as they are repugnant to the constitution and laws of the United States, are absolutely void. These States are constituent parts of the United States. They are members of one great empire— for some purposes sovereign, for some purposes subordinate. "

—*John Marshall,* Cohens v. Virginia

While technological innovations were making possible the rise of a small manufacturing establishment in America in the early nineteenth century, they were also influencing the development of the nation's agriculture.

THE DOMINANCE OF COTTON

The change in the nature of the American economy after the War of 1812 owed much to the advent of cotton as a major cash crop. Eli Whitney's invention of the cotton gin made cotton the leading cash crop in the South. As pointed out earlier, before the invention, only the long-staple variety was profitable because its black seeds could be easily removed. This variety, however, could be grown only in humid, warm lands, for even the lightest frost killed it. The short-staple variety was much hardier. In fact, it was able to grow in any area that had about two hundred consecutive days without frost and a rainfall of about 24 inches. Almost all states south of the Mason-Dixon line offered these favorable climatic conditions. The green seeds of this short-staple variety, however, were extremely hard to remove. A person who worked all day cleaned only about a pound. As a result, only about three thousand bales of long- and short-staple cotton were produced in the United States in 1790.

The cotton gin changed all this. The ingenious device was based on an extremely simple principle. A cylinder armed with rows of wire teeth rotated within a metal sleeve. The teeth protruded through slits

311

The cotton gin, invented by Eli Whitney, revolutionized the cotton industry of the South. Before the gin, only long-staple cotton was grown because it was easy to clean by hand. This cotton gin was simply a large version of Whitney's hand-cranked model. One gin, such as this, could clean more than fifty pounds of cotton a day, compared to a worker who could clean only one pound per day. By 1820, the South supplied three-quarters of the world's supply of cotton.

in the sleeve and caught onto strands of cotton as the cylinder was revolved. The teeth would draw the cotton strands into the center of the hollow cylinder, but the slits in the sleeve were too narrow to allow the seeds to pass through. The design was so simple that Whitney was never able to enforce his patent; once a farmer saw the invention he was able to construct one of his own. With a gin, 50 pounds or more could be cleaned in a day and soon huge, horsedriven gins were cleaning thousands of pounds a week. By the 1820s annual production of cotton had soared to 400,000 bales, three-fourths of the world's supply.

SLAVERY AND COTTON

Slave labor was easily adapted to cotton farming. Whereas tobacco farming required a great deal of delicate planting and pruning, cotton farming could be done by unskilled workers. None of the operations was complex. Children and old people could be put to work picking cotton. The plant grew only waist high and overseers could keep track of as many as forty slaves at once. Furthermore, cotton grew all year round and provided constant employment to slaves, increasing the profitability of their use.

The foreign slave trade was made illegal on January 1, 1808, but it continued nevertheless. Slave ships smuggled some five thousand Africans into America almost every year. Residents of those states with surplus slaves—Virginia, Maryland, and Kentucky—sold them to plantation owners in states that were in short supply—Alabama and Mississippi, and to some extent Tennessee, Arkansas, and Florida. The interstate slave trade was big business and state laws were slowly being changed to accommodate it.

Cotton was first grown in South Carolina and Georgia, but by 1820 the land in these states was worn out and badly eroded. Cotton planters were forced to push west into the lands that General Jackson had recently opened up during the War of 1812.

Cotton aided, and to a surprising degree shaped, the national economy. Most American cotton was exported to the textile factories of Europe in general and to England in particular in exchange for European manufactured goods. Northern merchants became rich as the middlemen who arranged for the sale and transportation of Southern cotton crops. Cotton yielded such high profit that Southerners used every spare inch of land to grow it. As a consequence, the South came to depend on the Western states for foodstuffs and work animals. The South's specialization in cotton production complemented and abetted the West's specialization in grain, meat, and mules.

OVERLAND TRANSPORTATION

Improved overland transportation quickened trade between the West and the rest of the country. At first the West was quite isolated from the East and South. Western settlers, in fact, reverted to a style of life rather like the subsistence standards of the Pilgrims. In their first years on a farm, a settler and his family divided their time between clearing the land and building a log cabin, between planting crops and fashioning crude household articles. Nothing but dust paths connected one farmhouse with another, and for months at a time settlers might never see a stranger's face.

When Western farmers were finally able to grow surplus produce, they had difficulty finding a market for it. Farm products could be floated down the Mississippi on rafts and flatboats, but spring floods and summer droughts endangered such traffic.

Even under ideal conditions the trip from Pittsburgh to New Orleans required at least a month. Once a farmer reached the Gulf of Mexico, there was no easy way for him to ascend the river again.

ROADS AND BRIDGES

The flatboat voyage down the Mississippi was long and dangerous, and even if the trip went well, there was still the impossibility of making a trip upriver. As a result, the West was able to sell some of its produce to the East via the Mississippi River network, but the inland water system brought few products from the East to the West. These products had to come overland and roads were needed.

In the days before explosives and modern road machinery, blasting a road through a mountain range or leveling uneven ground was a slow, laborious, and expensive operation. One excellent road, complete with drainage ditches, firm foundations, and a gravel surface was built as early as 1794 in Pennsylvania, connecting Lancaster with Philadelphia. This was the Lancaster Turnpike, a road built by a private company, with its 62 miles costing 465 thousand dollars to complete. By 1825 private companies in the Northeast and in the Middle States had built about 10,000 miles of turnpike. These projects, financed by private companies but frequently aided by state or federal money, were costly to construct, averaging between five and ten thousand dollars a mile. Consequently, turnpike owners were forced to charge high tolls which in turn discouraged traffic so that in the 1830s, thousands of miles of turnpike were abandoned or handed over to the states to operate.

A few highways served the West: the National Road, connecting Maryland with Illinois; the Wilderness Road, which crossed on a diagonal down from the northern boundary of Virginia through the Cumberland gap into Kentucky; and the Natchez

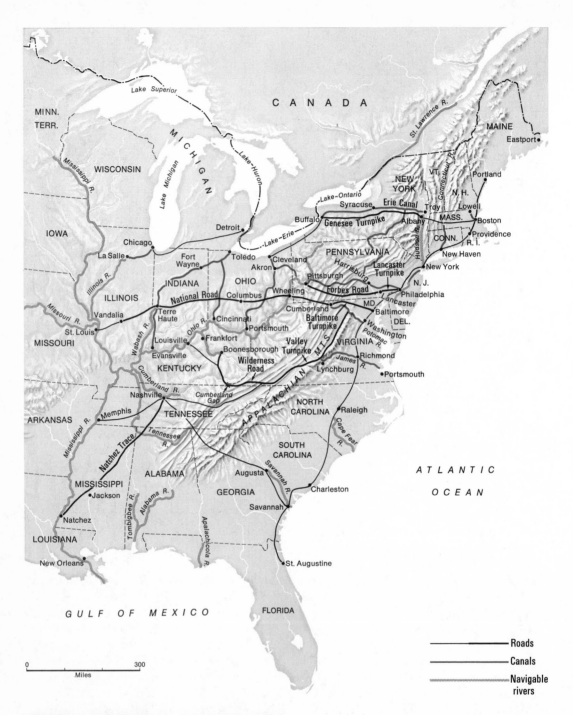

MINN.
TERR.

WISCONSIN

IOWA

Lake Superior

CANADA

MICHIGAN

Lake Michigan

Lake Huron

MAINE
• Eastport

VT.
N.H.
• Portland

St. Lawrence R.

Connecticut R.

Chicago

La Salle

Detroit

Lake Ontario

Syracuse

Buffalo

NEW
YORK

Erie Canal

Troy
Albany

• Lowell

MASS.

• Boston

Genesee Turnpike

CONN.

• Providence

R. I.

Hudson R.

Fort
Wayne

Toledo

Cleveland

PENNSYLVANIA

Harrisburg

Lancaster
Turnpike

• New Haven

• New York

ILLINOIS

INDIANA

OHIO

Akron

Pittsburgh

Columbus

Wheeling

Forbes Road

N. J.

Lancaster

• Philadelphia

Illinois R.

National Road

Vandalia

Terre
Haute

Ohio R.

• Cincinnati

Cumberland

MD.

DEL.

Baltimore

Missouri R.

Wabash R.

Louisville

Frankfort

• Portsmouth

Baltimore
Turnpike

Washington

Potomac R.

St. Louis

MISSOURI

Evansville

KENTUCKY

Boonesborough

Wilderness
Road

Valley
Turnpike

APPALACHIAN MTS.

VIRGINIA

James R.

• Richmond

Lynchburg

• Portsmouth

Cumberland R.

Nashville

*Cumberland
Gap*

ARKANSAS

Mississippi R.

Memphis

TENNESSEE

*Tennessee
R.*

NORTH
CAROLINA

• Raleigh

Cape Fear R.

SOUTH
CAROLINA

ALABAMA

Augusta

Savannah R.

ATLANTIC

OCEAN

MISSISSIPPI

Natchez Trace

• Jackson

GEORGIA

• Charleston

Tombigbee R.

Alabama R.

Savannah

• Natchez

LOUISIANA

Apalachicola R.

• New Orleans

GULF OF MEXICO

FLORIDA

St. Augustine

0   300
.Miles

——————— Roads

——————— Canals

~~~~~~~~ Navigable
rivers

CANALS AND ROADS · 1820 TO 1850

Trace, which lay between Nashville, Tennessee, and Natchez, Mississippi.

The two toll routes, the National Road and the Wilderness Road, provided feasible routes for settlers to migrate into the Western lands, but overland transport of goods on them was prohibitively expensive. Wagon freight rates, for instance, averaged about thirty cents a ton per mile in 1815, and the cost of long distance transportation at this rate pushed the price of common foodstuffs such as oats a great deal higher than the cost of oats grown nearby. To illustrate, the cost of transporting a ton of oats hauled from Buffalo to New York was twelve times greater than the value of the cargo.

The Frederick Road, west of Baltimore, was a stagecoach line, a cattle run, and an artery to the West. Construction of roads was expensive and financed most often by private companies who paid up to $10,000 per mile of road. The companies thus charged high tolls which in turn discouraged traffic. By 1830, thousands of miles of roads were turned over to the states to operate.

In addition to road building, sturdy stone bridges spanned creeks and even lakes (in 1800, a mile-long bridge was completed across Lake Cayuga in New York) and wooden bridges were built as early as the 1790s. These bridges, like most of the turnpikes, were found in the eastern sector of the country.

GOVERNMENT AID

The major highways, especially those that cost a great deal and traversed the mountains, could have been built by the federal government. Leading politicians in Washington had long recognized the need for such "internal improvements" as a national highway and canal system, if for no other reason than for military transport. In 1817 Calhoun had addressed a Congressional committee, saying:

Let it not be forgotten, let it be forever kept in mind, that the extent of the republic exposes us to the greatest of calamities—disunion. We are great, and rapidly—I was about to say fearfully—growing. This

is our pride and danger, our weakness and our strength. . . . We are under the most imperious obligations to counteract every tendency to disunion. . . . Whatever impedes the intercourse of the extremes with this, the centre of the republic, weakens the union. . . . Let us, then, bind the republic together with a perfect system of roads and canals. Let us conquer space.

A transportation bill passed both houses of Congress only after much debate. New England was opposed to a national system of roads; she already had good roads, and feared that an improved system might divert some of her trade to her rivals, Philadelphia, Baltimore, or New York. The South felt it had little to gain from what was essentially the establishment of communications and trade routes between the Northeast and the West. Nevertheless, the bill passed the House and the Senate, but President Madison vetoed it. Although Madison agreed with the necessity for national roads, as a strict constructionist he felt that the Constitution should first be amended to permit Congress to enter this area of jurisdiction.

When a transportation bill came up again in the 1820s, President Monroe also opposed the proposal on constitutional grounds. By this time sectional rivalries had also become more pronounced (see Chapter 9). People who lived in the West, in the state of Pennsylvania and in the Potomac Valley, favored a national road system, but those in New England, New York, and the old South opposed the project. Henry Clay, the most ardent champion of federally sponsored highways, exclaimed in irritation after he listened to objections on Constitutional grounds: "A new world has come into being since the Constitution was adopted. Are the narrow, limited necessities of the old thirteen states, of indeed, parts only of the old thirteen states, as they existed at the formation of the present Constitution forever to remain the rule of interpretations?"

The outcries of Clay and congressmen who agreed with him had little effect on the reluctance of the federal government to become involved in national highway building. The government at times subscribed to stock in private companies engaged in road building, but a real, long-range federal highway program was not begun until the twentieth century. Federally sponsored internal improvements, as a part of Clay's American System, were never put into effect in his time.

WATERWAYS

The expense of transporting goods on roads, and the lack of a federally financed road system, turned American attention to water travel. Two developments made inland water commerce highly successful, so much so that the entire nation was soon bound together in economic interdependence.

First came the perfection of the steamboat. In 1807 Robert Fulton made his famous voyage up the Hudson River in the *Clermont.* Four years later another Fulton steamboat, the *New Orleans,* sailed down the Mississippi from Pittsburgh to its namesake city. Fulton and his partners retained a monopoly over Mississippi River traffic until the *Gibbons v. Ogden* decision in 1824. Thereafter the river remained open to all competitors and by 1830 some two hundred steam-powered shallow draft vessels were sailing freely through Western waters.

Second, the Erie Canal opened, establishing a transportation link between Lake Erie and Albany. From Albany vessels could sail down the Hudson River to New York City. The Erie Canal turned New York City into a great trade center for Western livestock and grain. Before the canal was dug, farmers in Ohio or Illinois had to route their produce down the Mississippi River system to New Orleans, then around the tip of Florida to the East Coast.

The canal made this lengthy voyage unnecessary and redirected a large part of the business that used to flow through New Orleans to the harbor of New York City.

The perfection of the steamboat and the digging of the Erie Canal were crucial to the evolving American economy and both should be given close examination.

THE STEAMBOAT

Robert Fulton, a young American artist and engineer living in France, met Robert R. Livingston in Paris in 1802 when Livingston was the American Minister to France. Livingston and his wealthy brother-in-law, John Stevens, had obtained from the state of New York a monopoly over all steam navigation on New York waters. The problem was that no workable steamboats existed. Stevens had designed an improved steam boiler, but no one knew exactly how to make this boiler drive a vessel. Young Robert Fulton soon became interested in

the problem and in 1807, when he returned to New York, he constructed a ship 142 feet long that drew only 7 feet of water (such a shallow draft made the boat ideal for most river traffic). Fulton did not invent any startlingly new machinery, but he came up with a highly workable means of combining all the ship's elements, the engine, the paddlewheels, and the boiler.

Fulton's ship, the *Clermont*, confined its travels to the east coast, but it was in the West that the steamboat made its greatest contribution to the development of the American economy. Steamboats could travel downstream much faster than flatboats. More important, they could travel upstream. Light keel-boats poled along by strong men could carry freight upstream, but the trip

This Currier and Ives print shows a Mississippi steamboat "wooding up." By 1842, steamboat shipping cost only 25 cents per hundred pounds. In addition to the inexpensive shipping costs, steamboats offered a luxurious way of traveling.

was long and the rates high, as much as five dollars for every hundred pounds. Steamboats lowered this rate by 1820 to two dollars, and competition brought it still lower, to twenty-five cents per hundred pounds by 1842. Steamboats also offered a way to travel that was far more attractive than bumpy coaches careening over dusty roads. Luxury passenger vessels, with comfortable cabins decorated with carpets and mirrors, offering entertainment and floating restaurants, soon turned long-distance travel, always an agony in America, into an enjoyable experience.

THE ERIE CANAL

The steamboat, however, could not conquer all the problems of travel along the Mississippi. The river alternated between floods and droughts, and in many places snags consisting of trees and branches hazardous to navigation or shallow areas made the river and its tributaries difficult to use. Moreover, it still took a long time to send manufactured goods from Boston to Cincinnati by way of New Orleans, even on a steamboat.

The Erie Canal provided a direct route between the Northeast and the West. At one end the canal emptied into Lake Erie. As the Great Lakes were all connected with one another, and because a later canal connected Lake Erie with the Ohio River, an immense part of the West could now be reached by waterways. At its other end, the canal connected with the Hudson River and thus with New York City. From New York City ships could sail to all of the Eastern seaboard and even Europe.

Canals were not designed for the steamboat but rather for cheaply operated barges drawn by horses walking along towpaths on the banks. This method of transportation was vastly cheaper than moving goods over roads. Yet, if transportation was cheaper, construction was considerably more expensive. While roads cost five thousand dollars a mile to construct, canals cost

twenty thousand, and even a short canal took as long as 10 years to build. In 1816 there were only three canals in the country that were as long as 2 miles and only 100 miles of canal existed altogether in the United States.

The building of the Erie Canal owed nothing to the federal government and everything to the former mayor of New York City, De Witt Clinton. Long aware of the economic advantages of a canal from the Great Lakes to the Hudson, Clinton in 1816 renewed efforts to interest the state legislature in the project. Armed with a mass of technical information, Clinton approached the New York legislature and convinced even his political opponents of the wisdom of his plan for a canal between Albany and Buffalo. Clinton quite correctly predicted that with the canal "the whole island of Manhattan, covered with habitations and replenished with a dense population, will constitute one great city." The legislature appropriated seven million dollars for the enterprise, which was raised from such sources as land sales, taxes on salt, lotteries, and special appropriations.

The canal, 363 miles long and equipped with eighty-three locks, was completed in 1825. Although the engineers in charge had little experience constructing canals, they learned by trial and error and by studying British canals. The chief engineer, Benjamin Wright, was an excellent organizer and promoter of new talent. One of his protegés was Canvass White, who was sent to Britain to study the design of locks. Another of Wright's associates on the project was John B. Jervis, who went on to become the most famous American civil engineer of his generation. The builders devised a new kind of plow to cut the matted roots of trees. They were able to use the stone they dug up in construction after White discovered that American limestone could be turned into waterproof cement.

When the Erie Canal opened, it proved a sound financial venture. In its first nine years of operation, the canal paid back in tolls its original seven million dollar investment. Soon it was bringing three million dollars a year into the state treasury. For shippers, the canal was a great boon. The Erie reduced freight rates from Buffalo to Albany from one hundred to fifteen dollars a ton, and cut the trip from twenty to eight days. New York City, already the largest metropolis of the country, experienced rapid new growth, as Clinton predicted. In 1818, a regularly scheduled passenger and freight service opened between New York and the English port of Liverpool. Now most of the goods sent from Europe to the West passed through New

York rather than through New Orleans. The canal thus ensured New York's status as the country's leading city.

A CANAL BOOM

The success of the Erie Canal inspired other canal-building projects. New York State itself opened another canal, between Lake Champlain and the Hudson River, in 1823. In New England promoters considered digging a canal west from Boston, but the terrain was too hilly, and instead they dug short canals connecting Worcester and Northampton, Massachusetts, with the coast. In 1828 a canal running from northeastern Pennsylvania across New Jersey and New York to the Hudson was completed. It was used to carry Pennsylvania coal in barges to the eastern seaboard. Pennsylvania built a route that was part canal and part railroad between Philadelphia and Pitts-

The building of the Erie Canal was a great scientific achievement. The engineers of the canal developed a plow that would cut through tree roots and discovered that cement could be made from an American limestone.

burgh at a cost of ten million dollars. However, this canal never gave much competition to the Erie since its 177 locks and stretch of railroad tracking made the trip slow and cumbersome.

West of the mountains, canal building met with great popular enthusiasm. By 1837, Ohio had 750 miles of canals. The most important, the Ohio and Erie, connected Portsmouth on the Ohio River with Cleveland on Lake Erie. Another canal linked Toledo to Cincinnati. Indiana constructed the 450-mile Wabash and Erie Canal. By 1840 there were some 3,300 miles of canals in the United States, most of them in the Northeast and the West. The cost was high for those days, about 125 million dollars, but well worth it to the national economy. Only the Southern states had not invested heavily in roads and canals. With their excellent river systems Southerners did not feel the same urgency to improve public transportation as the rest of the country.

HAZARDS OF THE NEW ECONOMY

In the early nineteenth century the United States slowly started to change from an agrarian to an industrial economy, and the various self-sufficient localities gradually evolved into an interdependent system of mass markets. The change was brought on by industrialization in the Northeast, the advent of cotton as a major cash crop in the South, and the linking of the West to the East through improved transportation (the National Road, the steamboat, and the canal). Manufacturers and businessmen were assured protection by the decisions of the Marshall court, in particular by those supporting the sanctity of contracts and the defense of the country's main financial institution, the Bank of the United States.

The years of general economic prosperity immediately after the war were followed, however, by the country's first economic depression, the Panic of 1819. Between 1816 and 1819 the United States had experienced great economic expansion unregulated either by government policy or by the fiscal control of the second Bank. The American staples of corn, beef, pork, flour, cotton, and tobacco were bought in unprecedented quantities by Europeans who had been starved by the Napoleonic Wars and had suffered two bad harvests. Clothing had been scarce during the war years and at first American cotton was bought at extremely high prices, as much as thirty cents a pound, to feed the textile manufacturers of Britain. By 1818, however, Europe was recovering. Cheap cotton from India was imported into England and the demand for cotton and woolen textiles from the United States slackened. In addition, good harvests supplied Europe with most of the wheat it required. These conditions, along with overproduction of cotton in the United States, caused a great drop in cotton prices. The earlier boom in cotton for a short period after the War of 1812 left Americans unprepared for the general downward trend in world prices after 1815. This trend resulted from a decline in the amount of precious metals on the world market when mining in Mexico and Peru was disrupted during the Latin American revolts against Spain.

Unaware of international economic conditions, Americans had responded confidently to the general prosperity in the United States by speculating wildly in western lands. By 1819 Americans owed the government some twenty-two million dollars for western lands they had purchased on credit. Moreover, western farmers eager to buy plows and other heavy farm equipment, and additional land, had become heavily indebted to the Bank of the United States. That Bank, particularly its western branches, had pursued a foolishly generous policy in making loans on mortgages, renewing notes repeatedly, and issuing new loans without making certain that they could be repaid. When the European demand for American cotton and wheat declined, farmers made less money and became less able to pay for agricultural equipment or meet mortgage payments on their farms. A modern economic historian, Bray Hammond, has written: "Enterprise had placed such subtle instrumentalities as a credit, accounting, and the corporate forms of organization at the disposal of people unaccustomed to such things. . . . An economy in which barter had been important and financial transactions had been wholly subordinate to the exchange of goods was giving way to an economy concerned more and more with obligations, contracts, negotiable instruments, equities, and such invisible abstractions."

Not only were Americans confronted with a battery of unfamiliar, sophisticated financial arrangements, but the Bank of the United States itself was terribly mismanaged. Adequate supplies of gold and silver were never kept on hand and inflationary paper money was issued by the Bank in great quantities. The president of the branch in Baltimore absconded with bank funds, as did several of his subordinates. By July, 1818, the Bank had liabilities of twenty-two million dollars and only two million dollars worth of gold or silver on hand.

The situation was dangerous and the collapse of the Bank appeared imminent. Jefferson, writing to John Adams, blamed the panic on overissuance of paper money: "The paper bubble is then burst. That is what you and I, and every reasoning man, seduced by no obliquity of mind or interest, have long foreseen." The president of the Bank, William Jones, and his successor, Langdon Cheves, took drastic steps to curtail the inflated economy by calling in loans and exerting pressure on the state banks to redeem their notes in specie. After making the mistake of lending too much money too easily, the Bank blundered further by taking

a too stern attitude at a time when money was scarce.

In the depression that ensued, Americans everywhere called the Bank of the United States "The Monster." One after another, state banks closed their doors. Prices fell drastically—cotton to ten cents a pound. In Pittsburgh almost a third of the population abandoned the city and Pittsburgh's manufacturers of textiles, glass, and iron closed shop. The value of property in New York declined from 315 million dollars to 256 million dollars in one year! In Kentucky a civil war was imminent; two fiercely warring political parties were born out of a controversy over laws designed to aid penniless debtors. The Bank, calling in its debts, was suddenly the unwilling owner of hotels, stables, and stores in Cincinnati, those businesses that the owners were forced to give up when they were unable to pay their loans. One can easily see why Marshall's decision in *McCulloch v. Maryland* in 1819 defending the constitutionality of the Bank was highly unpopular!

In this economic crisis, far from acting with its recently acquired fervor for national planning, the federal government took only limited action to alleviate the nation's hardship. Because most Americans were still farmers and able to produce most of their own food, the government's attitude did not seem unduly callous nor did it create protest. Congress, however, did pass a new land act in 1820 whereby a settler could buy an 80-acre homestead for one hundred dollars. The following year Congress wrote another relief act to assist people whose credit had become shaky. The most drastic step taken by Congress was passage of the Tariff of 1824 when the country was already well out of its economic doldrums. Many farmers in the West and manufacturers in the East blamed the Panic of 1819 on the glut of cheap European goods which had been poured into the American market. The tariff was designed to place such a high duty on these foreign goods that they could no longer compete with their American counterparts. It raised the cost of pig iron from Scotland from fifty cents to fifty-six cents a hundred pounds; of hemp from fifteen dollars a ton to thirty-five dollars; and it increased the duty on cotton fabrics by 8 percent. The bill barely scraped through the Congress. Different, competing interests in the country had pressured Congress with opposing demands. For example, American wool growers wanted a high duty on imported wool, but the woolen manufacturers desired only an increased duty on imported woolen fabrics. Iron manufacturers called for a duty on pig iron from Scotland, but manufacturers who used Scottish pig iron for the casting of small mechanical parts had opposed this part of the tariff. Southerners had fought against a duty on hemp, since they far preferred Russian hemp baggings (used to bag raw cotton) to hemp from Kentucky. In general, the grain, wool, and manufacturing interests supported the Tariff of 1824; the planting, commercial, and fishing interests opposed it. The net effect of the tariff was to boost duties 30 to 37 percent of the value of imported, itemized goods.

By the middle of the 1820s prosperity returned to the United States. Nevertheless, the panic left deep scars and turned many Americans into permanent enemies of the Bank of the United States. The popular sentiment was expressed emotionally by Senator Thomas Hart Benton of Missouri as he declared that the Western cities were at the Bank's mercy: "They may be devoured by it at any moment. They are in the jaws of the monster! A lump of butter in the mouth of a dog! One gulp, one swallow, and all is gone!"

Western settlers saw the Bank as the darling of Eastern financiers; henceforth farmers in the West would be highly suspicious of Eastern business interests. After the Era of Good Feelings, rivalries were rising again in America. The development of the American economy had revived and intensified the fears of the advocates of a weak central government. It also fostered a gradual economic interdependence between the Northeastern states and the states of the Northwest, such as Ohio, Indiana, and Illinois. For a time, the new West continued to support positions taken by Southern politicians, but ultimately economic ties with the Northeast destroyed this alliance and the three easily identifiable geographic divisions of the country were reduced to two, the North and the South.

Readings

GENERAL WORKS

Bruchey, Stuart, *The Roots of American Economic Growth, 1607–1861*. New York: Harper & Row, 1965—A synthesis of historical research and theory on American economic development. Bruchey believes that institutional factors such as the role of government in providing the setting for growth and the importance of cultural factors such as education are important in understanding America's economic growth.

Burlingame, Roger, *The March of the Iron Men*. New York: Grosset & Dunlap, 1960—Burlingame's thesis is that American social history can be explained by a long series of inventions which shaped our economy, politics, and culture.

Dangerfield, George, *The Awakening of American Nationalism, 1815–1828*. New York: Harper & Row, 1965—A general history of the United States from the end of the War of 1812 to the inauguration of Andrew Jackson. Although nationalism was on the rise, there were conflicts between "economic" and "democratic" nationalists.

Dangerfield, George, *The Era of Good Feelings*. New York: Harcourt, Brace & World, 1962—A Pulitzer Prize-winning history of what Dangerfield calls the transition from Jeffersonian democracy to Jacksonian democracy. Dangerfield believes that "good feelings" were not dominant and that the Jacksonians were unable to forge a new political party until 1828.

Dorfman, Joseph, *The Economic Mind in American Civilization*, Vols. I–V. New York: Viking, 1946–1959—Dorfman's work is a broadly conceived history of American economic thought. He discusses not only professional economists' theories but also the ideas of public officials, businessmen, labor leaders, and the like.

Faulkner, Harold U., *American Economic History*. New York: Harper & Row, 1960—A standard textbook on American economic history.

Nagel, Paul C., *One Nation Indivisible: The Union in American Thought, 1776–1861*. New York: Oxford University Press, 1964—Through a broad sample of rhetoric about American "union," Nagel explores the changing meaning and ideals of American nationalism from the Declaration of Independence to the Civil War.

North, Douglass C., *The Economic Growth of the United States, 1790–1860*. Englewood Cliffs, N.J.: Prentice-Hall, 1961—An important example of the "new economic history" which uses the techniques of economic theory in historical analysis. North believes that regional specialization in production and the great demand for American cotton in Europe were among the main causes of economic growth before the Civil War.

Shannon, Fred A., *America's Economic Growth*. New York: Macmillan, 1951—A standard textbook on American economic history.

Taylor, George R., *The Transportation Rev-*

olution. New York: Harper & Row, 1968—A history of American economic development from 1815 to 1860. Taylor emphasizes canals, steamboats, and railroads as crucial factors in reducing costs and increasing levels of output.

SPECIAL STUDIES

Billington, Ray A., *Westward Expansion.* New York: Macmillan, 1967—A broad study of the history of the American West which deals with the economic, political, and social causes and consequences of expansion.

Cochran, Thomas C., and William Miller, *The Age of Enterprise.* New York: Macmillan, 1943—A history of American industrial growth which also deals with the impact of economic change on the political and social system.

Commons, John R., et al., *History of Labor in the United States,* Vols. I–IV. New York: Macmillan, 1918–1935—The standard work on American labor. Commons and his associates maintain that the presence of political democracy and cheap land caused American workers, while conscious of their class position, to be optimistic about working within the capitalistic system and that their unions reflected this by avoiding political radicalism.

Curti, Merle, *The Roots of American Loyalty.* New York: Columbia University Press, 1946—Curti traces the changing and conflicting ideas of nationalism and patriotism in America from colonial days through World War II. He analyzes patriotic literature, Fourth of July speeches, sermons, and songs.

Goodrich, Carter, *Government Promotion of Canals and Railroads, 1800–1890.* New York: Columbia University Press, 1960. Goodrich shows that government at all levels was active during the nineteenth century in providing capital and other assistance for internal improvements. He claims that this was a boon to American economic growth.

Gray, Lewis C., *History of Agriculture in the Southern United States to 1860,* Vols. I–II. New York: Kelley, 1969—Broader than the title implies, Gray's classic work analyzes the relations between Southern agriculture and the region's social structure, slavery, the position of poor whites, and of planters.

Havighurst, Walter, *Voices on the River: The Story of the Mississippi Water Ways.* New York: Macmillan, 1964—This history spans three centuries of transportation on the Mississippi, ranging from the canoes of early Indians through the paddle-wheel steamers to today's fleets of barges.

Miller, Nathan, *The Enterprise of a Free People.* Ithaca, N.Y.: Cornell University Press, 1962—Miller discusses the role of canals in the early development of New York State. He shows that in the early years of the Republic, Americans looked to the state as the main source of economic development. Gradually, opinion shifted from support for public enterprise to government aid to private initiatives.

Shaw, Ronald E., *Erie Water West: A History of the Erie Canal, 1792–1854.* Lexington, Ky.: University Press of Kentucky, 1966—In addition to its direct impact on the economy of New York and the nation, the Erie Canal had important social and

324

political impact, including the linking of the Old Northwest to the Northeast and the emergence of New York City as the nation's greatest metropolis.

Wade, Richard C., *The Urban Frontier*. Chicago: University of Chicago Press, 1959—Wade asserts that historians have forgotten that the West had many cities in its frontier days and that they had developed their own distinct life styles by the 1830s. The economic and intellectual features of Western cities were vital to the development of the region.

Warren, Charles, *The Supreme Court in United States History*, Vols. I–III. Boston: Little, Brown, 1923—A classic history of the Supreme Court which deals with both the legal aspects of the Court's ruling and the political context in which it has operated.

BIOGRAPHIES

Beveridge, Albert J., *The Life of John Marshall*, Vols. I–IV. Boston: Houghton Mifflin, 1916–1919—Beveridge was a Progressive Era Republican politician and also a biographer of Lincoln. He considers Marshall a great statesman who was in large measure responsible for the triumph of nationalism over sectionalism.

Corwin, Edwards, *John Marshall and the Constitution*. New Haven, Conn.: Yale University Press, 1919—Marshall's term as Chief Justice, from 1801 through 1835, was marked by a consistently nationalistic interpretation of the Constitution, establishment of the sanctity of contracts, and a growth of the Supreme Court's power and prestige. Corwin is a great admirer of Marshall, the architect of these developments.

Cresson, William P., *James Monroe*. Chapel Hill, N.C.: University of North Carolina Press, 1946—A sympathetic biography of the fifth President of the United States.

Dangerfield, George, *Chancellor Robert R. Livingston of New York, 1746–1813*. New York: Harcourt, Brace & World, 1960—Although a great land holder and member of an aristocratic family, Livingston turned from Federalism to Jeffersonianism and helped to negotiate the Louisiana Purchase. Dangerfield attempts to explain this unusual conversion.

Green, Constance M. L., *Eli Whitney and the Birth of American Technology*. Boston: Little, Brown, 1956—Although better known for his invention of the cotton gin, Whitney also was a pioneer in developing interchangeable parts in manufacturing. He combined good theoretical training with a great practical talent.

Nevins, Allan and Jeannette Mirsky, *The World of Eli Whitney*. New York: Macmillan, 1962—The authors discuss Whitney's technological advances, such as the cotton gin and interchangeable rifle parts, in the context of the scientific and intellectual life of the early years of the Republic.

Porter, Kenneth W., *John Jacob Astor*, Vols. I–II. New York: Russell & Russell, 1966—A detailed biography of the fur trader, land speculator, merchant, and investor who was the richest man in America during the early nineteenth century. The book contains many of Astor's letters and other documents.

The Emergence

# of Sectional Strains

9

. . . I have found the back-woodsmen to be such as I have described; a hardy, adventurous, hospitable, rough, but sincere and upright race of people. I have received so many kindnesses from them, that it becomes me always to preserve a grateful and affectionate remembrance of them. If we were to try them by the standard of New England customs and opinions, that is to say, the customs of a people under entirely different circumstances,

there would be many things in the picture, that would strike us offensively. They care little about ministers, and think less about paying them. They are averse to all, even the most necessary restraints. They are destitute of the forms and observances of society and religion; but they are sincere and kind without professions, and have a coarse, but substantial morality.

—*Timothy Flint*, Recollections of the Last Ten Years

Philadelphia's Second Street with Christ Church in the background. Philadelphia was one of the most progressive American cities of the day, and boasted of its well-paved streets, handsome houses, and water supply.

327

By 1820 the outburst of national unity that brought Americans together after the War of 1812 subsided and the country reverted to the sectional differences that had prevailed since colonial times. Different economies, manners, and even accents had long distinguished the various parts of America. Many Southerners and Northerners had long been suspicious of one another and pioneers in the back country had a well-defined distrust of their fellow citizens along the seaboard.

During the War of 1812, these differences were submerged as Americans united to fight their common enemy, Britain. The war cultivated a temporary unity, but it also implanted new seeds of divisiveness which bore fruit four years after the Peace of Ghent. As shown in Chapter 7, the British embargo encouraged American manufacturing in the Northern states. Previously, the Northeast had engaged primarily in commerce and shipping. After 1776, this section continued to trade America's natural resources and agricultural products for Britain's manufactured goods. Following the War of 1812, however, New England's factories began to compete with Britain's and many New Englanders began to consider the advantages of a closed national economy which would exclude foreign goods by high tariffs.

No similar change occurred in the South. Southerners continued to ship tobacco, rice, and indigo to Europe in exchange for factory-made commodities. Now cotton had become their primary product for export. The political and economic interests of the North were of little concern to Southerners for they had nothing to gain from a closed economy. Tariffs meant only that the Southern customer would be charged higher prices for imported goods to support Northern factories. The South was left with an essentially colonial economy and it remained as dependent as ever on England. Southerners knew that they could not rely on Northern mills to consume all the cotton they produced. The South's main customers were, and would long continue to be, the English textile factories of Lancashire.

The West was the third factor in the American economic equation. Before 1812, most settlers west of the Appalachian Mountains were Southerners. Most came from Virginia and North Carolina to Kentucky and Tennessee. Thus, the early West was by and large a relatively insignificant extension of the old South. After the war, however, large numbers of Northerners and small farmers from the South entered the Northwest and settled the Illinois and Indiana territories. These men and women detested slavery, sometimes for religious and moral reasons, sometimes because they feared that they would be unable to compete successfully with the owners of slave labor. By 1821, the new West was producing large quantities of corn, wheat, beef, and pork for the rest of the country. This section of the country also contained one-quarter of the nation's population, making it influential in national politics.

Conflicts of interest arose between the Northwest and the Southwest that compared with those on the Atlantic seaboard between Northern and Southern states. Yet the West was capable of showing a degree of political cohesiveness over specific Western issues such as internal improvements, Indian affairs, or government land policy. Regardless of their origins or views on the slavery question, all Westerners wanted better roads linking them to the East, protection against the Indians, and cheap farm land.

DIFFERENT WAYS OF LIFE

Political and economic differences among the three sections of the United States found expression in different occupations and attitudes. Cultural life, religious fervor, and standards of education varied greatly from section to section.

LIFE IN THE NORTH

The North had the largest population in the nation, but its population, particularly in New England, was not growing rapidly. All of New England, except parts of Maine and New Hampshire, was settled by 1800. In the 30 years before 1820, the population of Connecticut increased by only 10 percent, and the growth of Rhode Island and Massachusetts was similarly slow. Between 1815 and 1820 about one hundred thousand foreigners emigrated to the United States, but very few went to New England, choosing instead to settle in the Middle Atlantic states and the West. Not only did New England receive few immigrants, but many of its own young men and women left to go west.

The Middle Atlantic states in contrast, especially New York, experienced sharp increases in population. Throughout the eighteenth century New York's landlords had preferred to rent rather than sell farms and this restrictive land policy discouraged immigration. In the nineteenth century these restrictions were generally abandoned; moreover, western New York was opened up for settlement after the Iroquois, who formerly dominated this territory, were expelled. Consequently, New York, which was the fifth most populous state in 1790, had the largest population in 1820.

By 1820, New York City had become the largest American metropolis. In fact, all cities throughout the Northeast grew by leaps and bounds with the advent of industrialization. New York City and Philadelphia each had a population of more than 150,000 by 1830. In the preceding decade the number of American towns of more than 8,000 inhabitants had risen from eleven to twenty-four. Most of these towns were in the Northeast.

REPUBLICAN MANNERS

Urban life and the intense nationalism of the postwar years spawned a new kind of social behavior. Previously many Americans, uncertain about their manners, had self-consciously imitated those of Europeans. Etiquette books such as the *Complete Gentleman* and *A Pretty Little Pocket Book* taught American men how to talk to the rich and famous, and girls how to perform a proper curtsy. Now Old World etiquette was rejected as un-American. A popular magazine entreated Americans to "get rid of *imported superfluities* of etiquette," and one writer echoed the cry, saying, "We should all be glad to see a distinctively American school of good manners, in which all useless etiquettes were thrown aside."

CULTURAL LIFE

The approved mode of conduct was to be simple and natural but not lacking in culture. The Northeast, in fact, took pride in being the intellectual and artistic center of America. The United States had a swelling population, and much of it was literate. This growth in the reading public resulted in an increase in the number of libraries. There were twenty times more books in the libraries of New York, Boston, Philadelphia, and Baltimore in 1825 than in the entire nation at the turn of the century.

Ingersoll Defends Cultural Advances

" *The American mind has been called more to political, scientific, and mechanical, than to literary exertion: and our institutions, moreover, partaking of the nature of our government, have a levelling tendency. The average of intellect, and of intellectual power in the United States, surpasses that of any part of Europe. But the range is not, in general, so great, either above or below the horizontal line. In the literature of imagination, our standard is considerably below that of England, France, Germany and perhaps Italy. . . .*

. . . In the literature of fact, of education, of politics, and of perhaps even science, European pre-eminence is by no means so decided. The American schools, the church, the state, the bar, the medical profession, are, all but the last, largely, and all of them adequately, supplied by their own literature. Respectable histories are extant by American authors of the States of Kentucky, Georgia, North Carolina, South Carolina, Virginia, Maryland, Pennsylvania, New York, New Jersey, Vermont, Maine, Massachusetts, Connecticut, and New Hampshire; besides some general histories of New England, and several geographical and topographical works on Ohio, Indiana, Illinois, and Missouri, containing histories of their settlements. Our national histories, inferior in subordinate attractions to the romantic historical fictions of Europe, are composed of much more permanent and available materials. In biography, without equal means, have we not done as much since we began as our English masters? In the literature as well as the learning of the sciences, botany, mineralogy, metallurgy, entomology, ornithology, astronomy, and navigation, there is no reason to be ashamed of our proficiency. In mathematics and chemistry, our comparative deficiency is perhaps the most remarkable. In grammatical researches, particularly in the interesting elements of the Indian languages, American erudition has preceded that of Europe, where some of the most learned and celebrated of the German and French philologists have caught from American publications the spirit of similar inquiry. "

—Charles Jared Ingersoll,
A Discourse Concerning the Influence
of America on the Mind

Smith Attacks American Culture

" *In the four quarters of the globe, who reads an American book? or goes to an American play? or looks at an American picture or statue? What does the world yet owe to American physicians or surgeons? What new substances have their chemists discovered? or what old ones have they analyzed? What new constellations have been discovered by the telescopes of Americans?—what have they done in the mathematics? Who drinks out of American glasses? or eats from American plates? or wears American coats or gowns? or sleeps in American blankets?—Finally, under which of the old tyrannical governments of Europe is every sixth man a Slave, whom his fellow-creatures may buy and sell and torture?*

When these questions are fairly and favourably answered, their laudatory epithets may be allowed: But, till that can be done, we would seriously advise them to keep clear of superlatives.

—Rev. Sidney Smith, Edinburgh Review

More and more books were being published and their cost declined as materials became cheaper and publishing became more mechanized.

However, the books bought by Americans were, for the most part, works by foreign authors. Although American intellectuals called for a native literature, the reading public was more interested in English fiction. By 1810 Daniel Defoe's *Robinson Crusoe* had already run through nineteen editions in the United States and Samuel

Richardson's novels reached as many as forty editions. Sir Walter Scott's historical romances sold half a million copies in America before 1823. British authors never received one cent of profit from these huge sales, since American publishers did not observe British copyright law. The Reverend Sidney Smith, the British critic, commented acidly, "Why should the Americans write books when a six-weeks passage brings them in our own tongue, our sense, science, and genius, in bales and hogsheads?"

Before 1830, only two American writers were as popular in the United States as the aforementioned foreign rivals. James Fenimore Cooper produced a long series of best-selling novels that were highly romanticized versions of the confrontation between In-

Leatherstockings Meets the Law, *painted by John Quidor in 1832. Leatherstockings was a character created by James Fenimore Cooper, a prominent American author, who wrote of American and Indian confrontations in* The Pioneers.

dians and settlers: *The Pioneers* (1823) and *The Last of the Mohicans* (1826) were two of the most popular in this series. The prejudice against American novelists was so strong that Cooper pretended his first novel, *The Spy* (1821), was written by a "prominent Englishman." The other leading literary figure in America was Washington Irving, perhaps most famous for his tale, "Rip Van Winkle," published in *The Sketchbook* (1819). The cultural historian, Russell Nye, has written: "Washington Irving became the first American classic. He was the first to compel Europe to recognize an American author as a major literary figure—not as an imitator of a British author or style, but as an American artist with a mind and an art of his own. *The Sketchbook* was a swift, decisive answer to Sidney Smith's famous sneer of 1820, 'Who reads an American book?' "

AMERICAN PAINTERS

American painting, like American fiction of this period, coped with the problem of evolving a distinctively American tradition that borrowed from the British tradition but was not enslaved by it. The artistic movement sweeping Europe in the early nineteenth century was romanticism, characterized by flights of fancy rather than reason, by insights that were intuitive and personal rather than traditional and universal. American artists sought ways to express their own sensibilities within the context of the romantic movement.

The real solution to this problem was not found until the next generation, in the landscapes of the Hudson River school. These painters rendered mountains, streams, and meadows in imaginative, luminous compositions that were in the Romantic tradition yet faithful to the natural grandeur of America. However, the Hudson River school owed much to a gifted earlier painter, Washington Allston (1779–1843). Allston was the only American painter of his era to try to evolve original artistic

concepts. He restlessly shifted from portraiture to landscape and then to historical subjects. Allston stands as the most original artist of his time, pointing the way to a truly American style in painting.

CITY LIFE

While new creative energies were being released in the nation, a process of deterioration had begun in the cities. American cities of the eighteenth century had reflected the comfortable economic circumstances of the merchants and craftsmen who lived there, but in the first decades of the nineteenth century large slum areas began to appear in many cities. New York City

An illustration from Washington Irving's most well-known work, "The Return of Rip Van Winkle."

This drawing from Washington Irving's Sketchbook illustrates the fictitious figure of Ichabod Crane from the famous "Legend of Sleepy Hollow."

may have boasted of its literary groups, the Uranian and the Calliopean Societies, and its centers of intellectual life, such as Wiley's Bookshop, but it also had slums worse than those in London. Members of wealthy old Dutch families lived in stately yellow brick houses, but pigs were allowed to forage in the garbage that littered every public avenue. The city had the wealth of more than a mile of warehouses along the East River, but it also swarmed with thousands of penniless immigrants.

On the whole, American cities were a study in contrasts. Philadelphia was probably the most progressive American city of the day, with its well-planned, well-lit, well-paved streets, a good water supply, and handsome houses and public buildings; Boston also offered its citizens many similar improvements. On the other hand, American cities had almost no police protection and people out walking at night had to carry pistols. An average of one fire a night broke out in every large city and there were only volunteer fire companies, or firemen hired by insurance firms, to battle the flames. No city had an adequate sewerage system.

EDUCATION

The Northeast was not a land of pioneers; a young person could not hope to

make his fortune by carving a farm out of a wilderness that no longer existed. Yet, there were many opportunities for those who had acquired specialized knowledge through education. America had always been a land for people of ambition, but for the first time an individual's chance for advancement in certain lines of work in urban centers was linked to education. Equipped with a background in mathematics and technology, a young man could become an engineer, an architect, or a bridge or road builder.

The state school systems were slow to respond to the demand for specialized knowledge in these areas and for an adequate general education for all young people. Massachusetts opened public high schools in every town with more than five hundred families after 1824, but the training offered by these schools was generally poor and teachers were underpaid. Bronson Alcott, the writer-reformer, for example, made only 120 dollars in 1820 for teaching eighty students for four months. Many teachers, moreover, were of dubious character and poorly trained. A Massachusetts parent complained sourly in 1824: "If a young man can be moral enough to keep out of state prison, he will find no difficulty in getting application for a schoolmaster."

An anonymous painting of the "Schoolroom." Schools taught morals as well as reading, writing, and arithmetic. For discipline problems, the teachers used hickory sticks and birch rods.

To correct this situation, Massachusetts opened a teacher-training school in 1839. New York had the most advanced free school system, but even there, as late as 1828, twenty-five thousand children between the ages of five and fifteen were not in school.

Some American colleges had low standards, and all were poorly financed. Every year college presidents would conduct fund-raising drives. Yale received only three thousand dollars from its endowments in 1830. The faculty of Amherst had to go without salary for several weeks when money ran low. Princeton reduced its deficit in 1821 by cutting the salaries of two professors. The primary source of income of every college was tuition. To attract more students, many schools lowered admission standards and relaxed academic requirements in general, causing a severe deterioration in the quality of American higher education.

The curricula of most American colleges continued, as in the colonial period, to be based on the Greek and Latin classics, with the addition of a small measure of philosophy, mathematics, and theology. However, a few schools offered some courses of a more practical nature. Colleges began to offer history as a separate course, not merely as an adjunct to classical studies. Economics and political science were taught in several schools, as were German and French. Many colleges gave courses in the physical and natural sciences, but the subject was treated superficially. High academic standards were a rarity in the seventy-eight permanent colleges and universities that were founded in the United States by 1840.

LIFE IN THE SOUTH

Life in the pre-Civil War South was full of paradoxes. For example, while committed to the continued degradation of one segment of the population under the insti-

tution of slavery, Southerners carried the idealistic, sentimental worship of white womanhood to almost religious heights. During the celebration of Georgia's centennial, a toast that aroused the audience to cheers went: "Woman!!! The center and circumference, diameter and periphery, sine, tangent and secant of all our affections." It has been said that Southerners "took seriously only cotton, oratory, horses, and elections." Yet, no one could deny that the South had produced some of the finest minds of Revolutionary America—Washington, Jefferson, Madison, Monroe, and other outstanding statesmen.

All of these leaders were from Virginia, a state which lost its preeminence in the South after the invention of the cotton gin. Virginia was too far north to raise cotton profitably in competition with the lower South and its soil had been worn thin by the cultivation of tobacco. Planters could have put their money into manufacturing, but the spell that cotton cast over the South was too strong. As Virginia's influence waned, South Carolina's increased. South Carolina was the South's new center of cotton agriculture. Between 1790 and 1820 the state's population doubled, while the neighboring state of Georgia experienced even greater growth.

CULTURAL LIFE AND EDUCATION

There were other contrasts in Southern life. Charleston had a public library before Boston and the wealthier citizens of Richmond, Norfolk, and New Orleans customarily imported the latest books from England, as well as paintings and statues from various parts of Europe. Many towns had Shakespeare libraries and clubs. Yet the Southern rate of illiteracy for whites was higher than in any other section of the country.

Many of the very wealthy could not read and many of those who could owned only one book, the Bible. Although a few colleges existed, public grade schools and high schools were almost unheard of. Jefferson himself had proposed a rational scheme for promoting free education in Virginia, but he was unable to persuade the state to adopt it. He blamed his failure on "the vicious constitution of our county courts (to whom justice, the executive administration, the taxation, police, the military appointments of the county, and nearly all our daily lives are confided) self-appointed, self-continued, holding their authorities for lives."

Indeed, Southern local government was aristocratic and often corrupt and inefficient. In many states, officers held their positions for life, and usually they were not elected by the people but appointed by the legislature or the governor. In every Southern state, the planter class dominated po-

---

Defending Slavery and Its Expansion

" *Throughout all the Southern States, it was well known a very large portion of the population consisted of slaves, who, at the same time, stood towards the white population of the same States in the relation of property; although they were held as property, yet they were considered and treated as the most valuable, as the most favored property; their masters remembered that they were men, and although certainly degraded in the scale of society, by reason of their servitude, we felt for them those sympathies which bind one man to another, though that other may be our inferior. We are attached to them, too, by our prejudices, by our education and habits, in short, such were the feelings of the Southern people towards their slaves, that nothing scarcely but the necessity of the master, or the crime of the slave, would induce him to sell his slave. If the master emigrated, he would carry his slaves with him, not only for the various reasons which he had already stated, but because, going into a wilderness, where much labor was necessary to clear the country, they were, on that account, peculiarly necessary. Under these circumstances, a prohibition of the importation of slaves would, in almost every instance, be tantamount to a prohibition of the emigration of the Southern people to the State of Missouri. . . . He hoped from this view of the subject, the House would be struck with its monstrous injustice. . . .*

. . . the real question is, what disposition shall we make of those slaves who are already in the country? Shall they be perpetually confined on this side of the Mississippi, or shall we spread them over a much larger surface by permitting them to be carried beyond that river? . . . Now, sir, in relation to the physical force of the country, if ever the time shall come when we shall be engaged in war, and they should be excited to insurrection, it is obvious that there must be an immense subduction from the efficiency of the slave-holding section of our country; its actual efficiency would consist only, or nearly so, in the excess of the white beyond the black population; by spreading them over a more extended surface, you secure these advantages; first, by diminishing the proportion which the slaves bear in point of numbers to the whites, you diminish their motives to insurrection. Secondly, that if that event ever should occur, it would obviously be much more easily and certainly suppressed, because, upon the supposition which he had made, they would have a much smaller relative proportion of physical force.

—*Philip P. Barbour, United States Congress, Debates and Proceedings*

litical as well as cultural life on the state and local levels.

SLAVERY

Slavery had never been of economic importance to the North and by 1800 all states north of Maryland had abolished it or provided for its gradual demise. The institution also had been prohibited by law from the Northwest. In the South it became more widespread after the introduction of the cotton gin. Yet, many Southerners detested slavery. In fact, of 130 anti-slavery societies established in America before 1827, more than a hundred, representing four-fifths of the total membership, were in the South. Viriginia twice came close to abolishing slavery altogether.

After 1820 a tide of immigration brought a steady influx of settlers to the new South-

ttacking Slavery and Its Expansion

*have the fortune and the honor to stand
ere as the representative of freemen, . . .
know the will of my constituents, and,
egardless of consequences. I will avow it;
s their representative, I will proclaim
eir hatred to slavery in every shape; as
eir representative, here will I hold my
and, until this floor, with the Constitution
f my country which supports it, shall sink
eneath me. . . .
Sir, extend your view across the
Iississippi, over your newly acquired
rritory; . . . Look down the long vista
f futurity. . . . Behold this extended
npire, inhabited by the hardy sons of
merican freemen—knowing their rights,
nd inheriting the will to protect them—
vners of the soil on which they live, and
terested in the institutions which they
bor to defend—. . . . Compared to
urs, the Governments of Europe dwindle
to insignificance, and the whole world is
ithout a parallel. But, sir, reverse this
ene; people this fair dominion with the
aves of your planters; extend slavery—
is bane of man, this abomination of*

heaven—over your extended empire, and you prepare its dissolution; you turn its accumulated strength into positive weakeness; you cherish a canker in your breast; you put poison in your bosom; you place a vulture on your heart—nay, you whet the dagger and place it in the hands of a portion of your population, stimulated to use it, by every tie, human and divine. The envious contrast between your happiness and their misery, between your liberty and their slavery, must constantly prompt them to accomplish your destruction. Your enemies will learn the source and the cause of your weakness. . . . With this defect, your Government must crumble to pieces, and your people become the scoff of the world. . . .

Sir, if the Western country cannot be settled without slaves, gladly would I prevent its settlement till time shall be no more. If this class of arguments is to prevail, it sets all morals at defiance, and we are called to legislate on the subject, as a matter of mere personal interest. **"**

—*James Tallmadge, United States Congress,* **Debates and Proceedings**

337

western states of Alabama and Mississippi. The wealthiest of these settlers were cotton planters and wherever cotton was grown slavery came with it. In 1853 Joseph Glover Baldwin revealed the character of this migration in his book *The Flush Times:*

The country was just settling up. Marvellous reports had gone forth of the fertility of the virgin lands; and the productions of the soil were commanding a price remunerating to slave labor as it had never been remunerated before. Emigrants came flocking from all quarters of the Union, especially from the slave-holding states. . . . In the fullness of time, the new era had set in—the era of the second great experiment in independence; the era, namely, of credit without capital, and enterprise without honesty. . . . The condition of society may be imagined;—vulgarity—ignorance—fussy and arrogant pretension—unmitigated rowdyism —bulling insolence. . . .

Gradually, slavery exerted a widening influence over the whole of the Southern economy. States with surplus slaves, that is, the states too far north to grow cotton profitably, such as Virginia, Maryland, and Kentucky, acted as slave producers for the cotton kingdom. Licensed traders bought slaves at auctions in these states and sent them to the deep South. Slaves bought in eastern Virginia or Maryland were shipped to the Florida towns along the Gulf of Mexico. Those purchased in Kentucky and western Virginia were forced to march to the Mississippi River, where they were then

A North Carolina pioneer family emigrating West. By 1840, more than one-third of the population of the United States was drawn to the Western frontier.

floated on flatboats down to New Orleans. That city was the great slave emporium of the cotton kingdom; its streets were lined with slave showrooms, depots, and some two hundred slave auction marts. In the four decades preceding the Civil War, some 742,000 blacks were moved from the upper South to the cotton-growing states. Thus, the institution of slavery represented an enormous investment to Southerners.

LIFE IN THE WEST

"Old America seems to be breaking up and moving westward," an Englishman accurately observed in 1817, of the first great postwar shift of population across the Ap-

palachians. In 1810 only one-seventh of the American people lived west of the Appalachians. By 1840, more than a third of the population had crossed the mountains. In the decade 1810 to 1820 the population of Ohio doubled and by 1840 it had climbed from 230,760 to 1,519,467. Other states experienced an only slightly smaller influx of settlers.

INCENTIVES FOR MIGRATION

What was life like for Western settlers? What motivated so many of them to go West? A detailed description of the life awaiting the settler was offered by J. M. Peck in *A New Guide for Emigrants to the West,* published in Boston in 1837.

Generally, in all the western settlements, three classes, like the waves of the ocean, have rolled on after the other. First comes the pioneer, who depends for the subsis-

A Missouri pioneer family built a home on bottomland near a river. Lack of roads in the West forced families such as this to risk the threat of flooding in order to be near transportation for their produce.

tence of his family chiefly upon the natural growth of vegetation, called the "range," and the proceeds of hunting. His implements of agriculture are rude, chiefly of his own make, and his efforts directed mainly to a crop of corn, and a "truck patch." The last is a rude garden for growing cabbage, beans, corn for roasting ears, cucumbers and potatoes; a log cabin, and, occasionally, a stable and corn-crib, and a field of a dozen acres, the timber girdled or "deadened" and fenced, are enough for his occupancy. It is quite immaterial whether he ever becomes the owner of the soil.

The next class of emigrants purchase the lands, add field to field, clear out the roads, throw rough bridges over the streams, put up hewn log houses, with glass windows, and brick or stone chimneys, occasionally plant orchards, build mills, school houses, court houses, etc., and exhibit the picture and forms of plain, frugal, civilized life.

Another wave rolls on. The men of enterprise and capital come. The "settler" is ready to sell out and take the advantage of the rise of property—push farther into the interior, and become, himself, a man of capital and enterprise in turn. The small villages rise to spacious towns or cities; substantial edifices of brick, extensive fields, orchards, gardens, colleges and churches are seen. Broadcloths, silks, leghorns, crapes, and all the refinements, luxuries, elegancies, frivolities and fashions are in vogue. Thus wave after wave is rolling westward. . . .

Another observer, the Englishman William Cobbett, in considering the question of why settlers were willing to endure such a strenuous, primitive life, wrote in 1817: "To boil their pot in gipsy-fashion, to have a mere board to eat on, to drink whiskey or pure water, to sit and sleep under a shed far inferior to English cowpens, to have a mill at twenty miles' distance, an apothecary's shop at a hundred, and a doctor

nowhere." Why, he was asking, would anyone put up with such a life?

First, Americans were used to moving. Unlike most Europeans who seldom left their native villages, Americans were a restless people. Second, Americans not only believed in the principle of equal opportunity, but felt duty-bound to seize every chance to realize it. Life in the West represented this opportunity. Third, the West offered much richer soil than either New England or the old South. Land in the Northeast was rocky and had always been so. Once-fertile land in the old South had become barren from overcultivation. Finally, the proliferation of state banks which offered easy credit terms made it very simple for a man to borrow money for farmland. The price of land had dropped, for the federal government had introduced a land law in 1820 that allowed a man to buy an 80-acre farm for only one hundred dollars. The Indians east of the Mississippi were being removed and transportation, particularly the canal system, was improving rapidly.

RELIGION AND EDUCATION

The West had no highly developed culture to speak of, although most towns had subscription libraries, and Cincinnati had an important book publishing firm. While the Northwest Land Ordinance of 1785 contained provision for land colleges and a section of each district to be set aside for a school, little public education resulted.

In the area of popular culture, on the other hand, the West proved to be a fertile ground, the true genius of the region showing itself in evangelical religion. A second Great Awakening began in New England with Universalism, but it had its most profound effect on the West. Wandering evangelical preachers, such as the colorful James McGready, attracted thousands of converts.

Spain, the first colonizer of America, sent two kinds of visionaries to the Southwest in the sixteenth and seventeenth centuries—the soldier of fortune and the cleric. Sent north by the Spanish Crown from the conquered cities of Mexico, the adventurer, not finding the gold he sought, returned empty-handed. The Catholic missionary, on the other hand, remained, eager to make conversions for the glory of the Church. Another Spanish influence was the ranchero. He appeared in the later phases of colonization and his culture left a lasting mark on the American frontier.

The Spanish In the Southwest

*Chimney Rocks, painted by Paul Kane,
looks today much as it did when the
Spanish first came to the Southwest in the sixteenth century.*

In 1538, the Spanish Viceroy in Mexico, Mendoza, sent a priest, Fray Marcos, northward in search of the fabled seven Indian cities of splendor. In a letter, Mendoza instructed him, "You must explain to the natives of the land that there is only one God in heaven, and the emperor on earth to rule and govern it, whose subjects they must all become, and whom they must serve."

Fray Marcos walked three thousand miles and brought fanciful tales of treasure that encouraged Mendoza to outfit a massive expedition in 1540 headed by Francisco Vázquez de Coronado. Setting off with three hundred conquistadors, several Franciscans, hundreds of Indian scouts and servants, and herds of horses, sheep, cattle, and mules, Coronado spent two fruitless years searching for the gilded mansions of the so-called Seven Cities of Cíbola.

Another expedition was sent in 1598, led by Juan de Oñate. Again, the Spaniards found no riches, but the Franciscans remained and set up missions in New Mexico, Texas, Arizona, and California. Santa Fé, established in 1610, became the hub of their activity, and by the middle of the seventeenth century, the missionaries claimed one hundred thousand converts.

The Franciscans taught the Mohave Indians of California to farm, build missions, forge iron, tan leather, and shear sheep. Forced to work by the secular Spaniards, who beat them and plied them with liquor, the Indians frequently turned against their Franciscan overseers. Friction between the religious and secular authorities confused the Indians and further encouraged rebellion. In 1680, the Indians destroyed the missions of Santa Fé, killing a number of Franciscans. Santa Fé was recaptured by a military expedition led by Diego de Vargas in 1692, and the following year the Franciscans returned to begin rebuilding the missions.

In Arizona in the 1690s, a Jesuit, Eusebio Kiño, founded missions and towns, and mapped the territory. Thereafter, throughout the Southwest, writes Edwin Scott Gaustad, "Franciscans, Dominicans, Jesuits and other clergy from Spain raised a Christian cross wherever a Spanish flag unfurled."

In 1767, an edict by Carlos III expelled the Jesuits from the Spanish colonies. This move, coupled with the monarch's wish to keep Russia out of the Southwest, led to the assignment of an outstanding pioneer Franciscan to California. Junipero Serra founded nine missions from San Diego to San Francisco, and set up organizational procedures for the chain of twenty-one missions that were ultimately strung along California's El

Camino Real.

In 1833, Mexico confiscated funds used for the missions and turned their properties to secular use. By 1847, when California became a territory of the United States, both the clerics and the Indians had left the missions.

Through their indifference, Spanish colonials who had acquired huge cattle ranches contributed to the fall of the missions. These rancheros did little more than enjoy their wealth. Indians worked the land and served the hacienda as household servants. The proprietor watched bull and cock fights, gambled or entertained, but spent most of his time in the saddle. Spain made one of its greatest contributions to the West when it brought in the horse and splendid horsemanship of its colonials.

The Spaniards brought gaily adorned clothing, dancing, and fiestas wherever they settled in the New World. Their jewelry influenced Indian craftsmen who adapted the Spanish motifs to their own traditional designs. With their handsome, sprawling haciendas built around internal courtyards, and their adobe missions, the Spaniards left enduring architectural monuments. The westward migrations finally brought Spanish domination to a close, but their culture has remained a part of the American heritage.

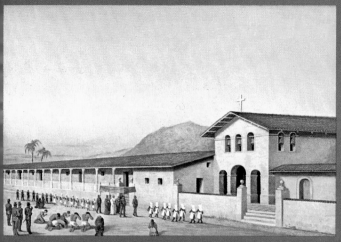

Mission San Luis Obispo de Tolosa by Oriana Day.

Mission San Francisco de Solano by Oriana Day.

Mission San Francisco de Asis by Oriana Day.

Many California Indians, here shown gambling, were converted by the missionaries.

*The Indian's road
to conversion from
an eighteenth-century
transcript by
Friar Pablo Beaumont.*

Third Station of the Cross by William Herbert. Original in Mission San Gabriel.

Saint Francis, bulto, *made in New Mexico in the late eighteenth or early nineteenth century.*

Indian basket made by
Anna Maria Marta, Mission of San Buenaventura,
California.

Indian wall painting, Mission San Fernando Rey de España.

Geoffrey Holt

Padre Junipero Serra.

Spanish adobe homes
were influenced by Indian pueblos such as this one
in Taos, New Mexico.

Costume worn by the child of a Spanish colonial.

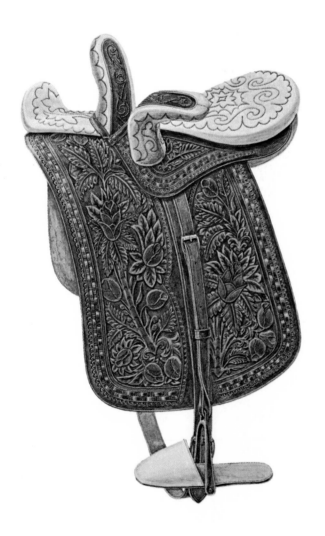

Sidesaddle made on Nipomo Ranch, San Luis Obispo County, California.

These itinerant ministers were mainly Presbyterians, Congregationalists, Baptists, or Methodists. Baptists and Methodists exerted the most compelling appeal, the Baptists because of their reliance on lay preachers and the Methodists because of their emphasis on the doctrine of universal salvation.

The revival meeting emerged again as the scene of emotional preaching and mass conversions. Such a gathering usually began on a Thursday and lasted until the following Tuesday. Members of the congregation brought their own bedding and food. Probably the largest revival took place in Cane Ridge, Kentucky, in 1801. Some fifteen thousand "sinners" listened to forty ministers for a week. At one point more than one hundred members of the congregation had passed out from exhaustion following outbursts of religious frenzy. The unconscious bodies were then thoughtfully laid out in neat rows on the ground. After listening to descriptions of all the horrors of hell: the lakes of fire, the yawning pits of brimstone, and other various torments awaiting sinners, people would bark like dogs, roll about on the ground, or shake violently in the "jerks." Describing a fit of the jerks, one minister said that the hands of the sufferers flew, "with wondrous quickness, from side to side in various directions, and their necks doubled like a flail in the hands of the thresher. Their faces were distorted and black, and their eyes seemed to flash horror and distraction. Numbers of them roared out in sounds the most wild and terrific."

When the evangelist moved on, he usually left in his wake an established church. To the satisfaction of the preachers, emotional release of a camp meeting was frequently followed by the formation of a congregation and the building of a house of worship. These churches became the cultural centers of frontier towns. As one contemporary put it, people went to church "almost as much to meet each other as to attend upon the means of grace." After the service, boys courted girls, farmers exchanged bits of farming wisdom, and adults mulled over current events. Churches not only served as information clearing centers and meeting houses for social visits, but as houses of moral regeneration. Pioneer life often degenerated into immorality and ignorance. Whiskey selling for a quarter a gallon encouraged heavy drinking. Eye-gouging matches were a familiar sport and gambling, swearing, and various forms of dishonesty and immorality were in evidence. After a few camp meetings, reprobates frequently changed their ways, as the Reverend David Rice was pleased to report that "drunkards, profane swearers, liars, quarrelsome persons, etc. are remarkably reformed. . . . Some neighborhoods, noted for their vicious and profligate manners are now as much noted for their piety and good order."

RELIGIOUS COLLEGES

The Second Great Awakening also nurtured several new denominational colleges in the West, schools that sprang up, said one man from Nashville, "like mushrooms on our luxuriant soil." Some of the most important included Allegheny, Centre, Kenyon, Western Reserve, Denison, and Oberlin. The Baptist Convention of 1820 adopted as its slogan "Every state its own Baptist college." Soon Wesleyan universities were opened by the Methodists in Ohio, Illinois, Dakota, Iowa, and Nebraska. The primary purpose of the church schools was expressed in the charter of Western Reserve, which aimed to train "an able, learned and pious ministry for the infant churches. . . ." Altogether thirty-five permanent new colleges were established in the United States between 1830 and 1840 and almost all were denominational schools.

SECTIONAL POLITICS

By 1820, the economic and political differences of the sections put strains on the leading American politicians not experienced by the founders of the nation. The greatest leaders of the Revolutionary era—Washington, Hamilton, Franklin, Jefferson, John Adams, and Madison—had strong ties to their native states, but usually they were able to free themselves and "think continentally," as Hamilton put it. These giants, however, were gone and a new era of sectional politics was emerging which hampered the effectiveness of such nationalists as Henry Clay of Kentucky and John Quincy Adams of Massachusetts. Others such as John C. Calhoun of South Carolina, Daniel Webster of Massachusetts, and Martin Van Buren of New York, while defenders of the supremacy of the Union, were equally devoted to the advancement of their own regions.

POLITICAL LEADERS

JOHN QUINCY ADAMS

The best-known Northern political figure was John Quincy Adams, son of the second President and destined himself soon to become President. The younger Adams was an able diplomat who had held various posts in Europe, served on the commission that forged the Peace of Ghent, and tenaciously negotiated the brilliant Treaty of 1819.

Adams had a strict Puritan upbringing that left him with the lifelong habit of examining his own character flaws microscopically, as well as those of everyone else. He entered the Presidency a bald, stout man with a tense and compulsive attitude toward work. Possessing a highly developed moral sense, he could be harsh and dogmatic. Intelligent and courageous, he was also suspicious and fearful of the future. His enemies accused him of being a monarchist, but he had the manner of a republican. An Englishman, seeing Adams at the Russian court, reported that the American sat "with cotton in his leathern ears . . . like a bulldog among spaniels." Introspective and vain, he regarded his voluminous diary as "next to the Holy Scriptures, the most precious book ever written by human hands."

In his political actions, Adams was as strong a nationalist as the great men of his father's generation. He subscribed enthusiastically to Henry Clay's "American System," supporting the protective tariff, the second Bank of the United States, and a federally financed program for constructing

John Quincy Adams *by George P. A. Healy Adams, a dominant political leader, was an economic nationalist who sought to serve the nation by rational planning and controlled expansion.*

internal improvements such as roads and canals. In fact, Adams went beyond Clay when in his first address to Congress as President he entreated Congress unsuccessfully to vote funds for a national university and national astronomical observatories.

Adams might be considered an economic nationalist rather than a democratic nationalist. Economic nationalists like Adams and Clay sought to serve the nation's interests by rational planning on the federal level and by controlled expansion. While they believed in a democratic suffrage, they thought the federal government and its policies could best be managed by an intellectual elite. Moreover, they clung to the old Federalist notion that the most trustworthy supporters of nationalism were the nation's merchant and manufacturing interests.

DANIEL WEBSTER

Another great exponent of economic nationalism was Daniel Webster, one of the young leaders of New England in the 1820s, who did not reach his prime as a political leader until the 1840s. Although intelligent and a famous orator and lawyer of imposing appearance, Webster did not have an independent mind. It has been said of him that he was "a perfect barometer of opinion among men of wealth." He was foremost a political reflection of the changing economic interests of New England. Like the New England merchants he so much admired, Webster opposed the War of 1812, and on the strength of his opposition he was elected to Congress. Always attuned to his well-to-do constituency, Webster opposed both a cheap land policy and internal improvements at federal expense, which he felt would benefit only the West. At first, he also opposed a protective tariff and the creation of a second national Bank, as did the New England merchants. However, by the 1820s Webster's views began to change as the manufacturing interests became of prime importance to the New England

Daniel Webster *by George P. A. Healy. Webster, well-known as a lawyer and brilliant orator, was also a successful congressman representing wealthy New Englanders in Washington.*

economy, turning him into a strong supporter of high tariffs and the second Bank of the United States. By the 1830s he was brilliantly defending the supremacy of the national government against the sectional interests of the South. Always a staunch defender of the Union, he never had wide enough political appeal to become President.

Ralph Waldo Emerson described Webster as follows:

He obeys his powerful animal nature;—and his finely developed understanding only works truly . . . when it stands for animal good; that is, for property. He believes, in so many words, that government exists for the protection of property. He looks at the Union as an estate, a large farm, and is excellent in the completeness of his defense of it. . . . Happily he was born late,— after independence had been declared, the

343

Union agreed to, and the Constitution set-
tled. What he finds already written, he will
defend. Luckily that so much had got well-
written when he came.

MARTIN VAN BUREN

Another bright young lawyer beginning to gain prominence in national politics by the 1820s was Martin Van Buren, described by one of his contemporaries a bit unfairly as "a first-rate second-rate man." He had made a name for himself as a practicing lawyer, and when he was thirty entered the New York State legislature. In 1820 he won a seat in the United States Senate.

He was a fence straddler on the major issues of the day. No one knew what he thought about slavery, although later in his career he became an outspoken opponent of the institution; his attitude toward the Bank of the United States was unclear; and he was equally vague about the protective tariff. Once he avoided casting a vote on a controversial issue simply by not showing up in the Senate. Later he casually explained that he had promised a friend to go on a walk through the Congressional Cemetery. His speaking style was so complex that, although he always sounded intelligent, it was frequently difficult to be sure on which side of an issue he was arguing. The shrewd John Randolph of Roanoke said maliciously of Van Buren that he "rowed to his objective with muffled oars."

"The Red Fox," as Van Buren was sometimes called, was a master of the art of politics. He was one of the first national politicians to try to break down the indistinct Jeffersonian Republican coalition which by the 1820s embraced politicians with such differing views as Clay and Calhoun. Van Buren actually was very much opposed to the economic nationalism represented by the American System. Not only did he believe this political philosophy to be contrary in certain of its aspects to the interests of his state of New York, but he

also felt that it was incompatible with the old Jeffersonian concept of a central government with limited powers and a laissez-faire economic system. As a result, in the 1820s Van Buren began to work assiduously for a revival of pure Jeffersonian Republicanism, a project which ultimately brought about a new national two-party system. The National Republican Party held aloft the banner of the economic nationalism of Clay and Adams. The Democratic Republicans, created by Van Buren with the aid of Calhoun and William H. Crawford and led by Andrew Jackson, stood for a reassertion of Jeffersonian or democratic nationalism, with stress on equal economic opportunity and political democracy unhindered by government direction.

SOUTHERN LEADERS

WILLIAM H. CRAWFORD

Perhaps the most prominent Southern politician was William H. Crawford, who was elected Senator from Georgia in 1807 and served after 1816 as Monroe's Secretary of the Treasury. The modern picture of Crawford is rather blurred, since his private papers have been lost and the historian must rely on documents generally written by his enemies. He was a crude, boisterous but good-natured man with an immense physique. Despite his rough manners, he was quite popular in Washington society. He was a smart politician, one of the first leaders to attempt to build a national machine. But there was little consistency in his political views. As a Jeffersonian Republican, he favored the states' rights position and as a conservative he defended the interests of Georgia's rich planters against its poor white farmers. Despite his conservatism and sectionalism, he also favored federal control of internal improvements and a mild protective tariff. As Secretary of the Treasury he also backed the second

Bank of the United States. Dismissed by many of his enemies as a cunning opportunist, Crawford nevertheless proved to be an excellent and even progressive administrator of the Treasury.

JOHN C. CALHOUN

John C. Calhoun was more brilliant, if less popular, than Crawford. He was born in South Carolina in 1782, graduated from Yale in 1804, and further educated at Tapping Reeve's law school in Litchfield, Connecticut. At an early age Calhoun displayed a logical and precise mind, one that later was always dazzling in argument, but not always adapted to practical politics. A Calvinist who had converted to Unitarianism, he combined the rigor and gloom of his first religion with the rational tone of his second. To one woman in 1830 he seemed a "cast-iron man who looks as if he had never been born."

His political career, like Webster's, reflected the changing temper of his native state. As a young Congressman, elected in 1811, Calhoun had persuaded South Carolina to stand behind the postwar nationalism of the "Era of Good Feelings." South Carolina, the dominant Southern state of the cotton kingdom, had gone so far as to support a moderate protective tariff. Such a tariff, far from helping the South, actually imposed a financial burden, but South Carolina, and Calhoun, were willing to sacrifice their own interests to strengthen the nation's economy. In 1817, Calhoun was made Secretary of War by Monroe and his experience in this office led the South Carolinian to endorse other parts of Clay's American System. Calhoun believed that America had to become stronger and more unified in the event of a future war; accordingly, he called for a well-trained army, a large navy, and a federally supported, unified system of roads and canals, all measures which would have had a defensive value. In addition, Calhoun supported a moderate tariff and the national Bank to make the United States more self-sufficient. "Our true system is to look to the country," Calhoun announced, "and to support such measures and such men, without regard to sections, as are best calculated to advance the general interest."

His attitude of disinterested nationalism did not last long. The Panic of 1819 brought a strong reaction from both South Carolina and Calhoun. During the panic, cotton prices dropped drastically. They soon leveled off, but for many years afterward prices for farm products remained depressed. Moreover, the soil in South Carolina was rapidly becoming depleted and the state was producing less and less cotton. In the decade of 1810 to 1820, when South Carolina had topped all other states in cotton production, the state was able to submit generously to the inconvenience of a pro-

John C. Calhoun *by Charles Bird King. A Southerner educated in the North, Calhoun represented South Carolina in Congress in 1811, and went on to become the nation's Secretary of War under Monroe.*

tective tariff. Now, however, the state was less prosperous and the newly settled cotton states of the lower South were becoming dangerously competitive. The tariff became a convenient scapegoat for all of South Carolina's woes and by 1826, Calhoun, reflecting his state's growing sectionalism, had become an eloquent champion of free trade. By 1829 he had become so firm a defender of states' rights for the South that he declared the protective tariff unconstitutional as well as objectionable. Unquestionably, Calhoun, and South Carolina, had abandoned nationalism for sectionalism.

WESTERN LEADERS

HENRY CLAY

The most intelligent and glamorous Western leader of the 1820s was Henry Clay of Kentucky. Gray-eyed, lean, and

Henry Clay *by George P. A. Healy. Clay represented Kentucky in Congress in 1810, and then served two terms as Speaker of the House.*

handsome, Clay as an orator was almost as persuasive and hypnotic as Daniel Webster. Little of his magic in debate can be deduced from the written records of his speeches, for they do not show what the historian George Dangerfield has described as "the strange posturings and glidings, the punctuating pinches of snuff, the pointed finger, the unforgettable smile, and all the music of that wonderful voice."

Clay was born in Virginia, but at twenty he moved to Kentucky, practiced law, and won a seat in Congress in 1810. Like Calhoun, he was one of the War Hawks, earning himself the epithet, "Glorious Harry of the West." He served as Speaker of the House from 1811 to 1820, and again from 1823 to 1825. He could be overly aggressive and subject to intense anger, but he always apologized for these outbursts afterward.

Clay is celebrated for his "American System," which he was formulating by the early 1820s. The system was a combination of federal aid for roads and canals to aid Western farmers in transporting their produce to the East, a tariff to protect Eastern manufacturers, and a national bank to facilitate national government operations and inter-regional financial transactions. The system was intended to benefit all parts of the country. Privileged Northeast industries would consume Southern cotton, Southern cotton growers and Northern town dwellers would consume Western farm produce, Western farmers would purchase Northern manufactured goods, and the Bank would make all these economic exchanges run smoothly. Everybody, in theory, would profit. Unfortunately, both in theory and in practice, the appeal of Clay's package was short-lived.

THOMAS HART BENTON

Other than Clay, Thomas Hart Benton of Missouri and Andrew Jackson of Tennessee were the most important Western politicians of the 1820s. Benton was a man of great vanity who could also be gracious and urbane. He was considered by some to be a man of learning and the best constitutional lawyer in the country. Benton's voting record was basically Jeffersonian and devoted to Western interests, although he supported parts of the American System. He backed the right of small farmers to free homesteads and opposed all banks, all paper money, and easy credit. He disliked Clay's proposed tariffs, but voted for them in order to obtain protection for Missouri's lead and furs. He also enthusiastically endorsed an extensive federal transportation network.

Benton served in Congress for 30 years, making speeches in a loud voice and colorful style. He was fond of affirming that he and the people were one: "Benton and democracy are one and the same, sir; synonymous terms, sir; synonymous terms, sir."

POLITICAL ISSUES

The great issues of the postwar period, the tariff, the second Bank, land policy, westward expansion, and slavery were caught up in the sectional animosities of the 1820s.

THE TARIFF QUESTION

Immediately after the War of 1812, many people throughout the country had favored a protective tariff. The North, where manufacturers had most to gain from excluding cheap European goods, was solidly in favor of the tariff (except for parts of New England, where shipowners feared a tariff might cut down on international commerce and thus diminish their business). Southerners still hoped that industry would spring up below the Mason-Dixon line. The West was convinced that the tariff would eventually provide a market in the North and South for its produce and livestock.

If the War of 1812 was most responsible for bringing about this state of national

harmony, several factors were important in undermining it. The Panic of 1819 was a major factor, as was the Tariff of 1816, which had set duties on itemized imported goods at about 25 percent of their value, a figure considered too low by Northeastern manufacturers who wished to protect their infant industries. They wanted duties raised still higher. However, the panic hurt not only Northern industry, but also Southern cotton growers by drastically lowering the price of cotton in a few short months from thirty-three cents to ten cents a pound, and industry was not developing in the South as had been expected in 1816. Now the South had no reason to support a higher tariff bill and every reason to defeat one, and indeed a proposed tariff bill was defeated in 1820 by Southern votes in Congress. Also, a bill in 1822 to provide money for the National Road was stopped by Southern Congressmen. The South's stand on these two issues caused hard feelings in the North and the West. Many Northern manufacturers and even many Western farmers believed that the depression would end only if protectionism shielded American industry against foreign competition and federally sponsored transportation bound the West to the East. The South's refusal to go along with these projects aroused strong animosity in the rest of the nation. Clay tried again to raise the tariff in 1824 and this time he was successful. The bill raised duties on such imports as wool and woolen goods, lead, glass, and iron from 30 to 36 percent. The commercial interests were against the bill but could not defeat it, even with the aid of the South and the Southwest. The Ohio Valley and Middle Atlantic states were strongly behind it.

THE BANKING QUESTION

The second Bank of the United States was authorized in April, 1816, and founded in 1817. At first the Bank offered easy loans, but during the Panic of 1819 it reversed its policies and began to tighten up on credit. Under a new director, Langdon Cheves, the Bank called in loans and foreclosed mortgages, thereby dispossessing thousands of Western farmers of their property. The Bank also began to gather up state bank notes and demand that the state banks redeem them in hard cash. Since most state banks had only very small cash reserves on hand, many of them closed.

When the Bank was authorized in 1816, its creation had not been a regional issue and indeed every section of the country had Congressmen who supported it. After the panic, however, the West and South, quite understandably, had strong feelings against the Bank for the stern measures it had enacted during the depression.

LAND POLICY

The three major regions of the United States also differed sharply over the government's land policy. The federal government still owned millions of acres in the West. Westerners wanted this land sold as cheaply as possible, whereas Northerners and Southerners regarded government-held lands as public assets that should be sold off for large sums in order to ease the rest of the nation's tax burdens. Moreover, Northern industrialists feared that if land were cheap, factory workers would abandon their jobs and head West. If such a migration occurred, it was foreseen that laborers who stayed behind would be able to command steep wages as factory owners competed for their services. Similarly, the cotton planters

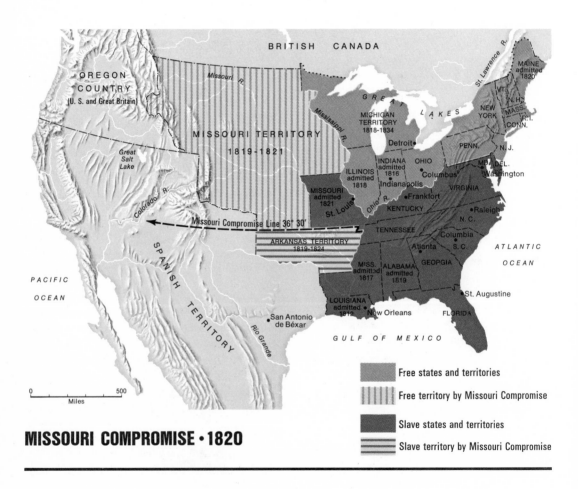

MISSOURI COMPROMISE · 1820

Free states and territories

Free territory by Missouri Compromise

Slave states and territories

Slave territory by Missouri Compromise

of South Carolina and Georgia feared that cheap land in the Southwest would turn that territory into a rival cotton-growing area, which, in fact, it did.

The Panic of 1819 affected land policy as it did all other key political questions. Over the years, government land policy had grown increasingly liberal, now it became still more so. The Land Act of 1800 specified that the smallest land parcel that could be purchased was 320 acres and the minimum price two dollars an acre. In 1804, the minimum size of a farm was reduced to 160 acres, but the price of two dollars an acre remained unchanged. A purchaser, however, could now pay for his farm in installments: eighty dollars down, the remaining two hundred and forty dollars to be paid off over the next 4 years. This attractive policy promoted huge land sales. The government sold one million acres in 1815 and five million in 1819. Then the panic struck. The land that farmers had purchased through bank loans was repossessed by the banks, in particular by the Bank of the United States. As one historian has described the depression, "Crops rotted in the field, trade stood still, and helpless farmers watched miserably as a numbing paralysis settled upon the section."

To relieve the distress of Western farmers, the government, despite the protests of many Northerners and Southerners, passed the Land Act of 1820. The minimum acreage for purchase was again reduced, this time to eighty acres, and the minimum price was cut to one dollar and twenty-five cents an acre. The sum of one hundred dollars for the eighty acres, however, had to be paid immediately, in cash, to the government. The installment plan, which had led to so many foreclosures during the panic, was abolished. Under each of these laws, however, the land was first offered at a government land auction and went to the highest bidder. Much of the land, particularly unusually rich land, therefore, went for much more than the minimum price. For example, land in some areas of Ala-

bama and Mississippi sold for as much as one hundred dollars an acre.

THE MISSOURI COMPROMISE

Probably the most emotion-laden issue of all was slavery expansion. Since the debates over ratification of the Constitution, slavery or its expansion had not been an issue in national politics. Slavery was considered the "peculiar institution" of the South. If Northerners discussed the issue at all, they deplored its existence, although not always with an easy conscience, as Illinois and New Jersey had forms of black servitude of their own. Northerners occasionally grumbled against the constitutional provision which allowed Southerners to count three-fifths of their slaves in determining how many Representatives they would have in Congress. Similarly, in the South some slaveowners protested against the federal law which closed the African slave trade on January 1, 1808, but their complaints had little substance since smugglers constantly broke the law.

THE TALLMADGE AMENDMENT

When Alabama entered the Union in 1819, an exact balance of power was achieved in the Senate where eleven free states were balanced by eleven slave-holding states. In the House of Representatives, the more populous North had many more Congressmen than the South, but because every bill had to be passed by both houses of Congress, the South felt secure in its power.

However, the nation's growing sectionalism was aggravated further by the months of debate that attended Missouri's application for statehood. When Louisiana became a state in 1812, the rest of the Louisiana Purchase was organized into the Missouri Territory. By 1820 this territory had a total population of 66,000, including 10,000 slaves. As early as 1817 the Missourians were petitioning Congress for admission into the Union.

Admitting a state to the Union had always been a routine matter, but Missouri's petition created a furor that was to occupy Congress from 1819 to 1821. Northerners opposed the petition, first because they disliked the practice of apportioning Representatives on the basis of three-fifths of the slave population, and they did not want to see this practice extended west of the Mississippi River. Second, the creation of a new slave state would give the South the advantage in the Senate. Third, abolitionist societies such as the Manumission Society of New York and Quaker organizations in Pennsylvania objected to the admission of another slave state on moral grounds.

Accordingly, when James Tallmadge, Jr., a New York Representative, proposed in February, 1819, to bar the further introduction of slavery into Missouri after it became a state, careful attention was given to the wording of the Tallmadge amendment since it was the first serious challenge to the extension of slavery in the United States:

Provided, That the further introduction of slavery or involuntary servitude be prohibited, except for the punishment of crimes whereof the party shall have been duly convicted: and that all children born within the said State after the admission thereof into the Union shall be free, but may be held to service until the age of twenty-five years.

The amendment passed the House of Representatives by a small majority, but was defeated in the Senate because a few Northern Senators felt that the government did not have the constitutional right to meddle with the internal affairs of a state. When the next Congress met in December, 1819, the Missouri issue was raised immediately. Now, however, the question had a new aspect, for the District of Maine, having separated itself from Massachusetts, was also applying for statehood. Henry Clay, the Speaker of the House, seeing an oppor-

tunity for compromise, said: "Equality is equality, and if it is just to make the restriction of slavery the condition of the admission of Missouri, it is equally just to make the admission of Missouri the condition of that of Maine."

Clay worked out a compromise in 1820 which earned him the nickname, "The Great Pacificator." Missouri entered the Union as a slave state and Maine as a free state. Senator Jesse B. Thomas of Illinois added another provision designed to prevent similar conflicts in the future: slavery was to be "forever prohibited" in all other parts of the Louisiana Purchase north of the 36 degree 30 minute line. In other words, slavery could be extended only into the present states of Arkansas and Oklahoma.

THE SECOND COMPROMISE

In 1820 Maine was duly admitted as a state, but Missouri was only authorized to write a constitution. When the constitution was presented for Congressional approval, it contained a clause forbidding free blacks or mulattoes from other states to enter Missouri "under any pretext whatever." This clause clearly violated that part of the federal Constitution that reads: "The Citizens of each State shall be entitled to all Privileges and Immunities of Citizens in the several States." Under the Missouri clause, a black citizen of New York, for example, would not be allowed to enter Missouri— a flagrant violation of national authority. Henry Clay again came up with a formula for peace, one that was utterly hollow: Missouri's constitution was accepted with the proviso that no law passed in Missouri should ever violate the United States Constitution. The Missouri constitution *already* was in clear violation of the federal Constitution, but Missouri was nevertheless admitted as a state in 1821.

IMPACT OF THE COMPROMISE

The Missouri Compromise had two major effects: it opened up the subject of slavery to national debate and it made sectional lines even tighter.

Slavery had been discussed by the Founding Fathers, but the entire subject had been conveniently buried for three decades. Now it was out in the open again and at a time when the South was more fiercely dedicated to preserving slavery than ever before. Jefferson wrote John Adams that the dispute, "like a fire bell in the night, awakened and filled me with terror," and Adams responded: "I take it for granted that the present question is a mere preamble—the title page to a great tragic volume."

The Missouri debates disrupted party unity and increased the trend toward sectionalism in the country. The Northwest, despite the large number of settlers from the South, voted generally with the Northeast; similarly, the Southwest went along with the Southeast. Thus, a political "North" and a political "South" began to develop.

Placed on the defensive by the debates, Southerners no longer argued for slavery as a necessary evil but defended it as a positive good. Senator Nathaniel Macon of North Carolina wished that Northern Congressmen could "go home with me, or with some other southern member, and see the glad faces and the hearty shaking of hands." Charles Pinckney of South Carolina went further, insisting: "Every slave has a comfortable house, is well fed, clothed, and taken care of; he has his family about him, and in sickness has the same medical aid as his master, and has a sure and comfortable retreat from old age. . . . During his whole life he is free from care, that canker of the human heart."

However, after the Missouri debates, a freedman named Denmark Vesey, mistakenly imagining that the North would support a slave revolt, immediately planned a massive uprising in Charleston. The plot was detected and the revolt aborted, but it caused Southern whites to become extremely fearful of future uprisings. Life became even more severely restricted for slaves and free blacks.

In the North also, the rights of free blacks received a setback. The compromise called attention to black people at a time when the country was not willing to accept the concept of racial equality. In 1821, for instance, the New Jersey Supreme Court proclaimed that "black men are *prima facie* slaves," i.e., black men were to be considered slaves unless proven otherwise. The elimination of slavery in that state proceeded at an even slower pace than formerly. Other states also limited or denied free blacks equal opportunities for education, economic advancement, and the right to vote.

THE ADAMS ADMINISTRATION

Jefferson had chosen Madison to succeed him in the Presidency and Madison had passed on the mantle to Monroe. Now Monroe, in the election of 1824, expected to choose his successor. He selected the Secretary of the Treasury, William H. Crawford, who was duly nominated by a Congressional caucus as the official Republican Party candidate.

The Jeffersonian Republican Party, how-

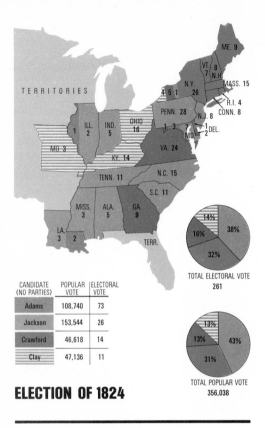

ELECTION OF 1824

CANDIDATE (NO PARTIES)	POPULAR VOTE	ELECTORAL VOTE
Adams	108,740	73
Jackson	153,544	26
Crawford	46,618	14
Clay	47,136	11

TOTAL ELECTORAL VOTE
261

TOTAL POPULAR VOTE
356,038

The choice was between Jackson and Adams. Clay, not on warm terms with Adams personally, nevertheless recognized that Adams was much more likely to support the American System than was Jackson, whose political views, in fact, had never been clearly stated. As Clay put it, "I cannot believe that killing 2,500 Englishmen at New Orleans qualifies him for the various difficult and complicated duties of the Chief Magistracy." Clay, ignoring instructions from his own state of Kentucky to vote for Jackson, met secretly with Adams and after announcing his choice persuaded several other states to follow his example. When the votes were counted, Adams received thirteen votes, Jackson seven and Crawford four.

One of President Adams' first acts was to appoint Clay Secretary of State. Jackson, furious, accused Clay and Adams of having made a corrupt bargain, and wrote to a friend, "So you see the Judas of the West has closed the contract and will receive the thirty pieces of silver. His end will be the same."

Throughout Adams' administration, the supposedly "corrupt" bargain between Clay and Adams was constantly revived by Jackson's supporters. Clay's decision to support Adams was justified in terms of national policy, but it was a political blunder of great magnitude.

ADAMS AS PRESIDENT

The breakup of the Jeffersonian Republican Party, the persistent name-calling of the Jacksonians, and the failure of foreign negotiations served to hurt Adams' prestige. Even in his first annual address to Congress, Adams was greeted with ridicule for his proposals, which in general were remarkably far-sighted but out of step with popular feelings in the country. After the Congressional election of 1826, Adams' enemies, the new Jacksonian coalition known as the

ever, was in shambles as a result of the sectional strife, and four candidates ran for President, all of them as Jeffersonians. Besides Crawford, there were John Quincy Adams, Henry Clay, and Andrew Jackson. After this disastrous splintering, the party never recovered.

Jackson had the highest popular vote and also was ahead in the electoral college with ninety-nine electoral votes; Adams received eighty-four votes, Crawford forty-one, and Clay thirty-seven. Jackson received a plurality, but not a majority. According to the Constitution, under such circumstances, the decision was left to the House of Representatives. Because under law the House could choose from only the three leading candidates, Clay was automatically eliminated. Crawford had become quite ill so that he was no longer regarded as a serious contender.

Democratic Republicans, gained control of both houses of the Congress and thereafter every move by the President was blocked by a hostile legislature.

ADAMS AND
THE AMERICAN SYSTEM

Adams was determined to extend Clay's American System. In fact, his desire for federally sponsored improvements went far beyond Clay's wildest dreams, to the dismay of his Cabinet. In particular, Clay begged Adams to drop his request for money for a national university, saying, "Let us not recommend anything so unpopular as is not likely to succeed." Adams, however, ignored these warnings and proceeded with the "perilous experiment" of his bold recommendations to Congress. He suggested that Congress pay for expeditions to explore the far West, establish a uniform standard of weights and measures, found a national university, and erect an astronomical observatory. More generally, he urged laws "promoting the improvement of agriculture, commerce, and manufactures, the cultivation and encouragement of the mechanic and of the elegant arts, the advancement of literature, and the progress of the sciences, ornamental and profound. . . ."

These recommendations were certain to appear far-fetched and absurd to a nation internally divided and basically devoted to the concept of a federal government of limited power. Furthermore, Adams also made the tactical error of comparing American progress in the sciences unfavorably with that of the Europeans. When he told Congressmen not to be "palsied by the will of our constituents," his words were taken as proof by his enemies that he held American democracy in contempt.

The President was heaped with ridicule and most of his other proposals were sidetracked. In passing he had referred to observatories as "lighthouses of the skies" and the phrase became a national joke. Only a few small parts of his grand design were ever enacted. Two and one-half million dollars were appropriated for the maintenance of the National Road and an additional sum of roughly two million was earmarked for investment by the government in private canal companies. Adams had wanted a Department of the Interior, but this plan too came to nothing. His comprehensive program for centralized economic development also went unrealized. He had envisioned a massive federal program for internal improvements, but aside from the appropriations just mentioned, this program was defeated. Twelve years later Adams wrote: "With this system in ten years from this day the surface of the whole Union would have been checkered over with railroads and canals. It may still be done half a century later and with the limping gait of State legislature and private adventure. I would have done it in the administration of the affairs of the nation."

THE TARIFF OF ABOMINATIONS

The most controversial legislation passed during Adams' administration was the Tariff of 1828. Adams and Clay had wanted a tariff that would help America achieve a centralized, independent economy. What they got instead was an assortment of piecemeal provisions, each representing a special interest group, none leading toward a truly rational system.

Manufacturers in the Northeast demanded higher duties on foreign factory-made goods and Senator Benton clamored for duties on fur and lead. Even a free-trader like Levi Woodbury of New Hampshire threw his principles to the wind and asked for a duty on manufactured silk to protect New Hampshire's silk mills. Similarly the hemp raisers in Kentucky, the wool growers of New York, and many other regional groups jumped on the bandwagon. With hard bargaining, the tariff was passed, supported by a massive majority of Western and Northern votes. Even New England, until now under the influence of free-trade merchants, changed its mind and instructed Webster, who was directing administration forces in the Senate, to vote for the tariff. It appears likely that Van Buren and other supporters of Andrew Jackson voted for the bill in the belief that the South was already behind Jackson and that passage of the tariff would attract Western and Northern voters to the Democratic Republicans. The bill, called by its enemies the "Tariff of Abominations," finally passed with the same alignment of votes as the 1824 tariff—the Northwest and Middle Atlantic states for it, the South and Southwest against it, and the Northeast divided. Solid Southern opposition to the ever-rising tariff, now as high as 60 percent on some items, was again frustrated. Within a few years this frustration was to produce ominous results.

INTERNATIONAL PROBLEMS

Even in the area of diplomacy, where President Adams had shown great skill as Monroe's Secretary of State, he suffered defeat and humiliation. In 1825, Simon Bolivar, the liberator of much of South America, called for a Pan-American Congress in Panama. Clay, eager to see Pan-American harmony established, obtained an invitation to the conference for the United States and persuaded Adams to send two delegates. Adams asked Congress for approval of the plan.

The President did not need Congressional approval and by asking for it stirred up a hornets' nest. Many Congressmen were isolationists opposed to participation in any international conference. Southerners in particular disapproved of the conference in Panama because they feared that Latin Americans might raise the question of slavery in the United States. On the other hand, commercial interests in the North thought the contacts with South American countries might be economically beneficial.

Finally, after four months of debate, Congress gave its reluctant approval. Ironically, one of the delegates died on his way to the conference and the other delayed his departure so long that the conference ended before he set out for it.

Adams also bungled negotiations with Britain over American access to the West Indian trade. The British had kept this lucrative trade closed to Americans, but in 1825 Parliament offered to open a part of it to the United States. Adams regarded British restrictions on the offer as distasteful and, after delaying a year, instructed his minister in London to demand better terms. Galled by Adams' stubbornness, the British once again slammed the door to the West Indies. The American public reacted by accusing Adams of mishandling the entire affair.

THE JACKSONIANS AWAIT THEIR TURN

The stern, puritanical, soul-searching Adams had been a failure as President. His aloof manner attracted little sympathy to his causes. His custodial approach to government, the attitude that an educated elite should shape the destiny of the nation for the benefit of the ordinary citizen, repelled the fiercely individualistic farmers of the West. His high-minded ideals prevented him from bestowing political plums on his supporters and made him all the more vulnerable to the Jacksonian Democrats who were formulating both the theory and practice of extensive political patronage. The Jacksonians, who already controlled Congress, kept up their attacks on the President for 4 years. In South Carolina, a toastmaster at a banquet raised his glass and speaking of "Adams, Clay and Company," proposed: "Would to God they were like Jonah in the whale's belly; the whale to the devil, the devil in hell, and the door locked, key lost, and not a son of Vulcan within a million miles to make another."

Readings

GENERAL WORKS

Abernethy, Thomas P., *The South in the New Nation*. Baton Rouge, La.: Louisiana State University Press, 1961—Covering the period from 1789 to 1819, the author stresses the importance of the expansion of Southern society in its western and southern frontier areas.

Brooks, Van Wyck, *The World of Washington Irving*. New York: Dutton, 1944—This is not a biography of Irving, but a literary and cultural history of the United States between 1800 and the 1840s. Brooks analyzes such authors as Cooper, Bryant, and William Gilmore Simms, as well as Irving.

Dangerfield, George, *The Awakening of American Nationalism, 1815–1828*. New York: Harper & Row, 1965—A general history of the United States from the end of the War of 1812 to the inauguration of Andrew Jackson. Although nationalism was on the rise, there were conflicts between "economic" and "democratic" nationalists.

Dangerfield, George, *The Era of Good Feelings*. New York: Harcourt, Brace & World, 1962—A Pulitzer Prize-winning history of what Dangerfield calls the transition from Jeffersonian democracy to Jacksonian democracy. Dangerfield believes that "good feelings" were not dominant and that the Jacksonians were unable to forge a new political party until 1828.

Eaton, Clement, *The Growth of Southern Civilization*. New York: Harper & Row, 1961—A history of the South from 1790 to 1860. Eaton stresses that there were several Southern cultures, not just one, and shows both consensus and conflict within the South.

Eaton, Clement, *The Mind of the Old South*. Baton Rouge, La.: Louisiana State University Press, 1964—Eaton's sketches of a variety of antebellum Southerns bring out the growing unity of Southern thought. As the Civil War approached, an extreme racist conservatism came to dominate the Southern mind.

Hammond, Bray, *Banks and Politics in America from the Revolution to the Civil War*. Princeton, N.J.: Princeton University Press, 1957—A monumental study of the interaction between economic and political developments. Hammond is a strong defender of the second Bank of the United States and feels that the Jacksonians who destroyed it put personal gain above the interests of the country.

Larkin, Oliver W., *Art and Life in America*. Rev. ed. New York: Holt, Rinehart and Winston, 1960—In this standard, well-illustrated history of American art, Larkin is more concerned with the cultural influences on American art, and its role in revealing American society, than in purely esthetic matters.

Nye, Russel B., *The Cultural Life of the New Nation*. New York: Harper, 1960—A cultural history of the United States from 1776 to 1830. Nye traces the emergence of nationalism, linked frequently to a democratic, reformist spirit, in all phases of American culture.

Wade, Richard C., *The Urban Frontier*. Chicago: University of Chicago Press, 1959—Cities and towns, Wade claims, were important aspects of the frontier. Towns provided outlets for the growth of Western agriculture and commerce, and themselves soon became centers of trade, industry, and culture.

Wish, Harvey, *Society and Thought in Early America*. Vols. I–II. 2nd ed. New York: David McKay, 1962—An account of American social and intellectual history emphasizing our European background and the lasting importance of religious and ethnic differences in American life.

Wright, Louis B., *Culture on the Moving Frontier*. Bloomington, Ind.: Indiana University Press, 1955—Six essays on American culture in frontier settings varying from the original colonies to gold-rush settlements. Wright detects underlying similarities in cultural patterns, based, in large part, on the importance of English cultural values in America.

SPECIAL STUDIES

Haines, Charles G., *The Role of the Supreme Court in American Government and Politics, 1789–1835*. Berkeley: University of California Press, 1944—This work deals with the Supreme Court from a political rather than a purely legal standpoint. Haines attempts to correct what he feels was a conservative-nationalist bias among most previous historians of the Supreme Court.

Livermore, Jr., Shaw, *The Twilight of Federalism*. Princeton, N.J.: Princeton University Press, 1962—Livermore argues that the Federalist Party did not dissolve after the War of 1812. It continued as a major political force in New England and the Middle States and many Federalist party leaders continued their ambitious search for political office throughout the 1820s.

Moore, Glover, *The Missouri Controversy*. Lexington: University of Kentucky Press, 1953—Moore maintains that the Missouri controversy resulted primarily from longstanding reactional economic disputes. He believed that the opposition in the Northeast to Missouri's admission was rather hypocritical, in that political, not moral,

considerations were uppermost in the Northerners' minds.

Mudge, Eugene T., *The Social Philosophy of John Taylor of Caroline*. New York: Columbia University Press, 1939—Taylor represented an extreme form of Jeffersonian agrarianism and individualism. Mudge gives a systematic outline of Taylor's social thought.

Rothband, Murray N., *The Panic of 1819*. New York: Columbia University Press, 1962—An economist's view of the Panic of 1819 which analyzes the theoretical explanations of the panic given at the time and discusses the possible responses which were considered.

Turner, Frederick J., *Rise of the New West*. New York: Collier, 1962—The only full length book which the great historian of the American frontier ever completed. This is a history not only of the growth and development of the West itself but also of the role of the West in sectional controversies between 1819 and 1929.

Weisberger, Bernard A., *They Gathered at the River*. Boston: Little, Brown, 1958—A study of the religious revivalism from the frontier days of the early 1800s through the 1920s. The author argues that revivalists must be taken seriously as religious leaders and are not just fanatics.

PRIMARY SOURCES

Benton, Thomas H., *Thirty Years View*. Vols. I–II. New York: Greenwood Press, 1968—Reminiscences of "Old Bullion Benton," one of the leading spokesmen for Western democratic sentiments. A valuable source for the political history of the nation in the Jacksonian era.

Nevins, Allan, ed., *The Diary of John Quincy Adams*. New York: Ungar, 1929—A one volume abridgement of a vitally important source for the study of early nineteenth-century politics. Adams reveals himself as a stern and stubborn individualist who was, nevertheless, a brilliant intellect and a man of high principle.

Van Buren, Martin, *Autobiography*. J. C. Fitzpatrick, ed. New York: Kelley, 1969—A valuable first-hand account of the development of the second American party written by the man who was probably most responsible for the formation of the Democratic Party. It does not, however, reveal much of Van Buren's personality.

BIOGRAPHIES

Bemis, Samuel F., *John Quincy Adams*. New York: Knopf, 1956—The first volume of this biography covers Adams' service as diplomat and Secretary of State. The second deals with his years in the White House and his long service in the House of Representatives after his Presidential term.

Chambers, William N., *Old Bullion Benton*. Boston: Little, Brown, 1956—Chambers' biography of the Democratic Senator from Missouri shows a man at the center of the democratic struggles in national politics. Immensely popular, Benton typified the ideals of the American West.

Current, Richard N., *Daniel Webster and the Rise of National Conservatism*. Boston: Little, Brown, 1955—This short biography of the Massachusetts Whig leader emphasizes his role as a spokesman for conservative business interests who was willing and able to use democratic rhetoric to appeal to the masses.

———, *John C. Calhoun*. New York: Washington Square Press, 1963—A rather critical biography of the South Carolina leader, which treats him as an exponent of a romantic, reactionary social philosophy.

Eaton, Clement, *Henry Clay and the Art of American Politics*. Boston: Little, Brown, 1957—Eaton pays high tribute to Clay's ability to bring opponents together and work out compromises. However, the growth of the two-party system made these talents less important and thwarted Clay's personal ambition to be President and his broader goal of keeping the Union intact.

Remini, Robert V., *Martin Van Buren and the Making of the Democratic Party*. New York: Columbia University Press, 1959—This study shows that the efforts of Van Buren and other ambitious politicians to form the Democratic Party were motivated by political, not economic or social aims.

Wiltse, Charles M., *John C. Calhoun: Nationalist*. Indianapolis: Bobbs-Merrill, 1944—The first of a three-volume biography of the South Carolina spokesman, covering the nationalist phase of his career up to the nullification controversy. Wiltse strongly admires Calhoun as a man of genius and principle.

FICTION

Melville, Herman, *Moby Dick*. New York: Modern Library, 1950—Considered by many to be the greatest American novel ever written, *Moby Dick* is both a remarkable adventure story and a philosophical investigation of man and fate.

Twain, Mark, *Life on the Mississippi*. New York: Signet New American Library, 1961—Twain spent 3 years on Mississippi river boats and gained much of his sense of adventure and of human character there. This book consists of a series of sketches of pre-Civil War river boating.

The Jacksonian 10 Era

There can be no doubt that . . . a representation would be all the better if the most ignorant, profligate, and vagabond part of the community were excluded from the right of voting. It is just as true that if all the rogues and corrupt politicians, even including those who read Latin and have well-lined pockets, could be refused the right of voting, honest men would fare all the better. But as it is very well-known that the latter are not, nor cannot well be, excluded from the right of suffrage anywhere except in a despotism, we have come to the conclusion that it is scarcely worthwhile to do so much violence to natural justice . . . as to disfranchise a man merely because he is poor. . . .

But the experience of the world goes to prove that there is a tendency to monopoly wherever power is reposed in the hands of a minority. Nothing is more likely to be true than that twenty wise men will unite in opinions in opposition to a hundred fools; but nothing is more certain than that, if placed in situations to control all the interests of their less gifted neighbors . . . , fifteen or sixteen of them would pervert their philosophy to selfishness. This was at least our political creed, and we therefore admitted a vast majority of the community to a right of voting. Since the hour of the Revolution, the habits, opinions, laws, and I may say principles of the Americans are getting daily to be more democratic.

—James Fenimore Cooper,
Notions of the Americans

John Vanderlyn's painting of Andrew Jackson portrays the brilliant militarist as tall, lean, and ruggedly handsome. Jackson was the epitome of heroism to the average American long before he became President.

JACKSON TAKES COMMAND

By the time Jackson became President, Americans believed not only that men were created equal but that every man was entitled to the same opportunities. The emphasis on political equalitarianism was an important difference between Jeffersonian and Jacksonian democracy. Jefferson had stood for the right of the "common man" to choose leaders from among those qualified to lead. Jackson, coming as he did into office with a limited understanding of the complexities of government, enabled the ordinary man to see himself as worthy of political office. Jacksonian democracy made Americans distrustful of social rank and proud to be one of the great mass of average Americans.

The Jeffersonians had urged citizens to vote, confident that they would elect the best man to govern them from those who were superior in wisdom, position, and education. The Jacksonians not only encouraged people to vote, but also to run for office. They insisted that social status and education were not a prerequisite for political leadership, that the average American was capable of managing his own government. Careers in politics were open to men of talent, no matter how simple their beginnings. Jackson himself was an example of this philosophy. He was the first American President to be born in a log cabin. He entered office as the "people's President" and his continued political strength rested on their solid support.

On March 4, 1829, the day of Jackson's inauguration, ten thousand people jammed into Washington, whose population was only eighteen thousand. When Jackson emerged on the Capitol portico, the crowd cheered wildly. He took the oath of office, pushed through the mobs, mounted a horse, and rode off to the White House. The crowd followed on horseback, on foot, and in wagons. Relentlessly they surged into the Executive Mansion and interrupted the official reception. Chaos resulted as well-wishers climbed up on delicate chairs, swarmed over valuable rugs with muddied boots, shouted, overturned furniture, broke glassware, and even pressed the President helplessly against the wall, all to express their approval and enthusiasm for their new Chief Executive. Naturally, their celebration evoked a variety of reactions. Some political observers expressed fear of an oncoming rule by "King Mob." Others saw the festivities as symbolic of the victory of the "common man." According to Daniel Webster: "People have come five hundred miles to see General Jackson, and they really seem to think that the country has been rescued from some dreadful danger."

THE DEMOCRATIZATION OF POLITICS

The Jacksonian era in American politics should not be regarded as the beginning of a movement to obtain political democracy. It was rather the result of forces that had made themselves felt long before his Presidency. In the newly settled West, men of disparate education and background were

Howard Pyle's drawing depicts Jackson speaking to crowds along the road to his inauguration as the seventh President of the United States.

prone to accept each other as equals and allies in a common struggle against the wilderness. In the cities of the East, middle-class reformers, small businessmen, and spokesmen for craft guilds were united in their demands for political practices that would match the concept of the rights of man embodied in the Declaration of Independence.

There was no reason for even the most aristocratic American landowner to feel threatened by popular democracy. The country had no mass poverty or sharp class lines and no ambitious man had to change the social structure to thrive in it. Reformers repeatedly stressed that no one's rights or privileges would be impaired if property qualifications for voting were eliminated. Recognizing the vote as the key to political power, they did not foresee changes in the class structure of society as a result of mass suffrage. "Will not our laws continue the same?" they asked. "Will not the administration of justice continue the same?"

Manhood suffrage, that is, the right of all men to vote, came to the country relatively easily. The American Revolution had provided the impetus for the first successful attempt to reduce the property qualification for voting. Uninhibited by any constitutional restrictions, when the new Western states drew up their constitutions during the first 20 years of the nineteenth century, they required only that a man be a taxpayer to vote or hold office. In the East, one state after another removed property qualifications until the last holdouts, Virginia and North Carolina, gave way in the 1850s, extending the right to vote to adult males everywhere in the country.

The nation, however, was not ready to grant suffrage to women. It would wait more than 100 years before an amendment to the Constitution gave women the right to vote. Nor did the suffrage include most free blacks. Before 1820, free blacks had voted legally in the Northeast, Tennessee, and South Carolina, but only as a result of omissions in the voting laws. Throughout the 1820s and 1830s, the laws were deliberately changed to exclude them. The black man's right to vote survived only in the

361

New England states, with the exception of Connecticut.

Although suffrage did not extend to these significant groups of the population, the liberalization of white male suffrage produced several swift and important political changes. Many state offices, even some judgeships, were soon filled by election rather than appointment and voters began to play a more direct role in the selection of the President. By 1832, all the states except South Carolina had transferred the choice of Presidential electors from the legislature to the voters, and party nominating conventions had replaced the secret Congressional caucus which, since Jefferson's time, had named Presidential candidates.

THE EFFECT OF MASS SUFFRAGE

Having the vote, however, was not the same as using it. Enlarging the suffrage had little impact on politics until the mass of voters took a personal interest in public policies, until, for example, small businessmen, skilled and unskilled workers, and large-scale farmers began to conceive of the vote as an instrument to effect economic legislation. Tariffs, internal improvements, banking laws, all could be altered or controlled by the weapon of the vote. The expanded use of the suffrage was also influenced by social forces at work in the country. Separation of church and state had been established in most states by the early nineteenth century, indicating a public dislike for special privilege of all kinds. Many state constitutions also had clauses forbidding the creation of monopolies. The free school movement had begun, more people were acquiring secondary education, and there was a glimmer of interest in adult education. Certainly, these were signs of the average man's eagerness to improve his knowledge. In addition, political affairs received more publicity than ever before as the number of newspapers rose and their prices declined. With their increased awareness and concern, men soon realized that they needed to take an active part in government.

Officeholders responded to the increasing political alertness of the average American by stressing that they were representatives as well as leaders and by more overtly and actively wooing voters. In the Presidential election of 1828, attendance at the polls doubled that of 1824. And in 1840, 78 percent of America's adult white male population voted.

As voting mushroomed, it became increasingly apparent that political parties would have to strengthen their organizational efforts to win members and gain offices. In the attempt to fashion a smooth-running, effective body, party leaders and workers often looked upon their jobs as ends in themselves. Workers who had proven their loyalty were frequently the recipients of public offices, a not unfair practice if those so rewarded were men best able to carry out the principles of the party and the desires of the voting constituency. This, however, was not always the case. Many began to view their government patronage jobs as a lucrative livelihood, rather than as an opportunity and obligation to serve the people and further the purposes of the democratic government. The "spoils system" ("To the victor belongs the spoils," said the New York politician, William L. Marcy) emerged with its connotation of plunder, as did the military term "campaign," for seeking out votes. Simultaneous with these practices and the promise of rich political rewards came a new breed of politicians, men dedicated to winning elections at almost any cost. Rather than address themselves to the issues, these office-seekers more frequently resorted to demagoguery and flattery to win votes. They played on popular fears and prejudices. Andrew Jackson, who was experienced in government service but whose views on national issues were hazy, was the first politician to be elected President as a result of a national campaign based on these techniques. It was largely his charisma, and not his position on controversial political questions, that gained him the White House.

Jackson's background was tailored to the demands of the new democratic politics. He was not only a Westerner, but a self-made man as well. Born in the backwoods of South Carolina, he was left without family and had fought in the Revolutionary War by the time he was 14. After a few years of carousing and becoming a self-taught lawyer, he moved to the Tennessee territory. There he practiced law, made friendships with influential men and married. He became a well-to-do planter and land speculator and held various political jobs in the new state of Tennessee. In 1804 he received

the coveted position of general of the Tennessee militia and subsequently led his troops to victory in the battle of Horseshoe Bend in the War of 1812. His greatest victory at New Orleans came after he had been made a general in the United States Army. He was a great hero to most Americans and his popular reputation was not diminished by his foray into Florida to chastise the Indians. He began to be mentioned by friends and politicians around the country as a Presidential possibility on the strength of his record as a military hero, Indian fighter, and as a symbol of the democratic forces of the West. This was the basis of his candidacy in 1824.

County election day was a festive affair for both candidate and voter. There is little evidence of piety at the polls in George Bingham's painting.

THE ELECTION OF 1828

By the middle of the 1820s Senator Martin Van Buren had conceived of a plan whereby the amorphous coalition of politicians backing Monroe could be split and a new political coalition created on pure Jeffersonian principles. He particularly wanted to purge the Jeffersonian coalition of men like Clay, Webster, and Adams, who, he believed, had infused national politics with neo-Federalist ideas. His plan was to bring those in the Northern states who adhered to the equalitarian and states' rights ideas of Jefferson together in a new coalition with the wealthy planters of the South behind the candidacy of the popular General Jackson. By 1827 his tireless efforts behind the scenes had produced a regrouping of political forces in the country into the Demo-cratic-Republicans (Democrats) led by Jackson and the National Republicans (later Whigs) led by Adams and Clay.

As early as 1826, when he lost his majority in Congress to Jackson's followers, Adams knew he had little chance of reelection. He tartly referred to the anti-administration group as "the base and profligate combination." These critics included not only those who did not like the nationalistic American System, but also those who disapproved of Adams' handling of both public affairs and public relations. In addition to Martin Van Buren, Jackson's other important supporters were all masters of the new party politics: Thomas Hart Benton of Missouri, John H. Eaton of Tennessee, William H. Crawford of Georgia, and John C. Calhoun of South Carolina who became Jackson's running mate in 1828, as well as newspapermen Amos Kendall and Francis P. Blair of Kentucky, and Isaac Hill of New Hampshire.

It was almost inevitable that the campaign of 1828, with its contest between the antagonists of 1824, would degenerate into a virulent personal clash, uncontrolled by any discussion of national issues. Jackson, continuing to believe he had been robbed of the election in 1824, devoted his full efforts to Presidential electioneering during the next 4 years. Although his previous career had shown little evidence that he was a devoted champion of the country's democratic aspirations, he almost instinctively associated himself with these goals after 1824. He came to believe that he was the leader of American democracy.

When the supporters of Jackson gained control of Congress in 1827, they used the full year before elections to try to undermine Adams' position still further in a series of unrelenting attacks on his conduct of the Presidency and his personal life. The Jackson camp also had almost unlimited funds to underwrite the first really expensive campaign in American history, costing one million dollars. As the campaign accel-

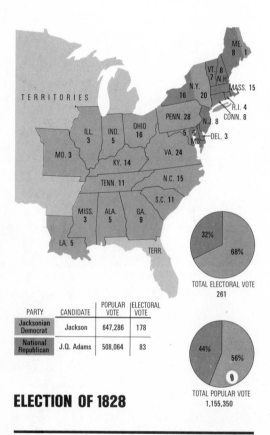

ELECTION OF 1828

TOTAL ELECTORAL VOTE
261

TOTAL POPULAR VOTE
1,155,350

PARTY	CANDIDATE	POPULAR VOTE	ELECTORAL VOTE
Jacksonian Democrat	Jackson	647,286	178
National Republican	J.Q. Adams	508,064	83

erated, the mud-slinging, misrepresentation, and name-calling increased on both sides. Among the epithets used against Jackson by Adams' men were "tyrant," "drunk," and "gambler." In addition, Jackson's ailing wife, Rachel, became a target for the opposition as a "convicted adulteress" because her divorce from a previous husband was discovered not to have been legally final when she married Jackson. Adams, on the other hand, was the recipient of a barrage of spurious charges of corruption: he was accused of paying for private possessions with public money, supplying the Russian Czar with a young American mistress, and pandering to private interests in the administering of public lands. The accusations from both sides rose to a feverish pitch and descended to the most degrading depths of any campaign in the nation's history to that time. Unaided by party platforms or pertinent exchanges on issues confronting the country, the voters followed their emotions and backed the man they were convinced would protect the interest of the people against special privilege. Jackson received 56 percent of the popular vote and in the electoral college he won with 178 votes to Adams' 83. The Jacksonians also controlled both houses of Congress.

THE PRESIDENT OF THE PEOPLE

Jackson came to the White House as the democratic hero of the common man. He "reigned" (as his enemies put it) there for two terms. The new type of politics that he introduced into national life permeated the American political scene in some measure from this time on. "Old Hickory" himself, while a man of intelligence and firm resolve, had few intellectual interests. His enemies thought of him as brutal, dictatorial, and vulgar. When the Whigs, in contempt, created the jackass as a symbol for the Democratic Party, basing their choice on the intellectual shortcomings of Jackson, the party not only embraced the symbol,

but kept it. There was, however, little that was common or vulgar about Jackson himself. A natural gentleman, independent-minded, easy in his manner, and gallant in deportment, his judgment, though based on instinct, was usually sound. Over 6 feet tall, with proud military bearing and an impressive shock of white hair, the hot-tempered general was a man characterized by James Parton as "not taking kindly to culture but able to achieve wonderful things without it." He had an iron will and an iron constitution, as witnessed by his ability to withstand a perennial siege of illnesses that plagued him throughout his years in the White House. Because he went

Jackson's adversaries attacked his position on the veto, the spoils system, and internal domestic improvements. Here they caricatured him as King Andrew I, a power-hungry monarch grinding the Constitution underfoot during his "reign."

KING ANDREW THE FIRST.

from lowly birth in a log cabin to wealth, military distinction, and, finally, to the nation's highest office, he became a symbol of what could be achieved under a democratic system of government. The key to his success in politics was the same as it had been in war: he was a natural leader, a personality that men followed instinctively. He drew support and admiration from every section of the country and social class. His convictions on public issues were virtually unknown when he became President. But this fact did not hamper his success with the voters since his own life was a testament to what could be achieved through equality of opportunity.

THE SPOILS SYSTEM

"Office is considered a species of property," observed President Jackson to Congress. The Jacksonian Democrats had constantly accused the previous administration of corruption. The guiding tenet of "reform" conveniently paved the way for a new reapportionment of this political "property." Jackson sincerely believed that offices should be democratically rotated regularly to root out or prevent corruption. As it turned out, however, there had been little previous corruption, certainly nothing to compare with the graft and inefficiency that took place once certain offices had been reassigned under the spoils system.

There was nothing new about firing opposition officeholders to give jobs to deserving partisans. It had long been the policy in New York and other Northern states and previous Presidents had removed men without creating much attention. But the fact that there had not been a real political shift for many years, since most men in government jobs had been appointed by Thomas Jefferson, made Jackson's attitude seem revolutionary.

In practice, President Jackson used the system with moderation. He wisely did not

fire experts in the Departments of the Army and Navy. Nor did he dismiss judges or high-ranking diplomats. In fact, he replaced only about 252 Presidential appointees out of 612, and only about 900 of the more than 10,000 officeholders on the government payroll. The Jackson appointees, however, created far more extensive scandals than did any of their similarly rewarded predecessors. A prime example was Samuel Swartwout who was given the collectorship of the Port of New York for his diligence in the 1828 campaign. In less than 10 years, Swartwout managed to steal over a million dollars from the government.

The concept of reward was not the real key to an understanding of the President's use of the spoils system, although it tended to strengthen party organization. Jackson's belief in rotation derived from his desire to increase opportunities for more widespread participation in government. The execution of this belief sometimes created corruption, and in a broader sense it represented a clash between the virtues of experience and the merits of equality of opportunity. Jackson tended to demean the importance of training and experience in political office. He felt that the duties connected with such offices were essentially simple, and that any man of intelligence could readily assume them. Holding the same office for a long time bred indifference, he felt, and this was far worse than any of the problems that might arise from the concept of periodic rotation in office.

KITCHEN CABINET

During the Presidential campaign, Jackson's opponents had maintained that the general was a simple soldier being manipulated by greedy politicians. His behavior in office, however, left little doubt that he was clearly his own master. Although he sought advice from his personal friends in his unofficial "Kitchen Cabinet," and had his speeches written for him, he ultimately made his own decisions. With the exception of Martin Van Buren, the Secretary of State, and John Eaton in the War Department, his official Cabinet consisted of men of essentially mediocre abilities. His "Kitchen Cabinet" consultants, Van Buren, William B. Lewis, Andrew Jackson Donelson (a nephew who functioned as his private secretary), Francis P. Blair, and Amos Kendall were important in advising Jackson, but never dictated to him.

CONCEPT OF PRESIDENCY

Unlike earlier Presidents, who had accepted the idea of an equal balance between the three branches of government, Jackson felt that the executive branch was supreme because the President alone was elected by the whole country. The people were always right, he said, and as President he was their spokesman. To exercise this supreme power given him by the people, Jackson did not hesitate to use the veto. Together, all of his predecessors had vetoed only nine bills and had done so on the grounds that they were unconstitutional. Jackson alone vetoed twelve, frequently his only objection being personal disapproval. He was also the first Chief Executive to employ the "pocket veto" —leaving a bill unsigned until Congress adjourned, which meant that it did not become law. However, his tendency to veto bills he thought granted powers to the federal government which had originally been given to the states by Congress belies to some extent his opponents' charge that he was a despot.

FOREIGN AFFAIRS UNDER JACKSON

In foreign affairs, Andrew Jackson was tenacious and extravagantly patriotic. These qualities often caused him to take unnecessary risks for petty victories, but they also helped him to straighten out several long-standing diplomatic tangles. In addition, a strongly nationalistic foreign policy greatly aided Jackson in strengthening loyalty and cohesion within the Democratic Party.

Seeking to open the British West Indies to American shipping, Jackson negotiated with patience and tact, although he told Secretary of State Van Buren that the United States would act "with the promptness and energy due our national character" if England continued to delay a settlement. By trading the admittance to the United States of British ships sailing from the West Indies for American entrance to these Caribbean ports, Jackson won a concession that the United States had been demanding since 1783.

Utilizing a tougher approach, the President also succeeded in working out treaties with foreign countries for settling damage claims that had been incurred during the Napoleonic Wars. France, for example, had agreed in 1831 to pay American claims against ships and cargoes damaged or destroyed in the wars. But in 1833, when the United States presented a bill for one million dollars for the first payment, the French Chamber of Deputies refused to provide the funds. Jackson was furious, especially since the government had to pay the Bank of the United States $170,041.18 for preparing the bill. When the French continued to delay, he sent a message to Congress calling for "a law authorizing reprisals upon French property." Although Jackson had a just claim, Congress refused to sanction his request on the basis that it presented too openly a threat of war. Jackson countered by breaking off diplomatic relations with France and ordering the Navy readied. Insulted, the French sent a fleet of their own to the West Indies. In 1835, France voted the money, but refused to pay until given "satisfactory explanations" of the language used by Jackson. "We will not permit France or any, or all European governments to dictate to the President what language he shall use," thundered Jackson, and the crisis mounted. War was averted, however, when Jackson's advisers managed to convince him to modify the tone of his comments and disclaim any intention to insult France. The quarrel was resolved and in 1836 the French payments began to flow regularly into the American treasury.

AN ERA OF CONTROVERSY

Even as he came into office in 1829, Jackson faced the problem of holding together the separate factions that had elected him. The Democratic Party of the time was a loosely organized coalition of men with different and often conflicting sectional interests. Northern Democrats wanted to keep the tariff high and Southern Democrats wanted it reduced. Western supporters wanted to reduce the price of federal lands; New Englanders wanted it to remain the same. The Democrats had a majority in the Congress, but they seldom voted as a unit. It was an almost impossible task for the President to reconcile and control various sectional interests. Moreover, if a Democratic Congressman disagreed with the President, it was not uncommon for him to leave the party and join the opposition. Some of the men, for example, who supported Jackson in 1828, turned to the anti-Jackson National Republicans and followed the leadership of Henry Clay of Kentucky. By the same token, others who originally opposed Jackson came into the Democratic Party when they found that they agreed with Jackson on a crucial issue.

INTERNAL IMPROVEMENTS, INDIANS, AND PUBLIC LANDS

One of the early issues that produced shifts in party affiliations concerned internal improvements. Democrats in the West liked this aspect of the American System and firmly supported federal financial backing for roads and canals. Democrats in the South and in New York and Pennsylvania were just as adamantly opposed to it. The latter two states had financed their own internal improvements and were not enthusiastic about Western competition. No matter what position he took, the President was certain to antagonize some elements of his party.

Jackson announced his position on internal improvements in 1830, when he vetoed a bill authorizing federal funds for the purchase of private corporate stocks to build a 60-mile road from Maysville to Lexington, Kentucky, part of a projected interstate system. In his veto message, Jackson indicated that he opposed as unconstitutional the use of federal monies for internal improvements within a state; he was not opposed if the

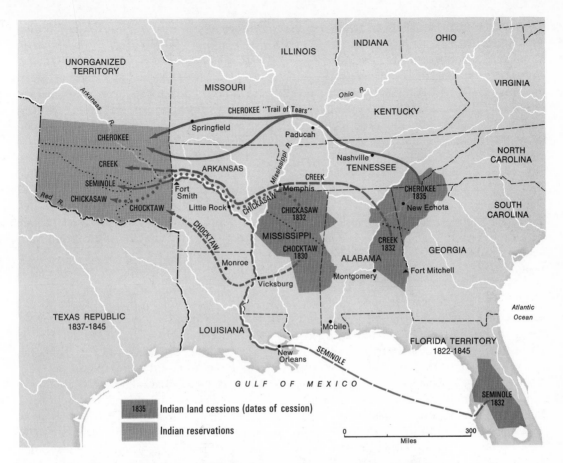

INDIAN LAND CESSIONS AND MIGRATIONS • 1820 TO 1840

projects were national in scope. He did hint, however, at Van Buren's suggestion, that all public programs at federal expense might be unconstitutional. The Maysville veto was a canny political move. Jackson's instincts were right. The majority of the people agreed with him that federal funds should be saved and used to pay off the public debt. Furthermore, the veto also enabled Jackson to strike a blow at Clay, who had fervently backed the Maysville Road for his home state. It did not affect many votes and showed the administration's regard for strict adherence to the Constitution and economy in government. For his part, Clay took up the issue with even

greater passion and exploited it particularly in the West, where the construction of improved transportation was often the only national issue of interest to voters.

The Maysville veto slowed the use of federal funds for internal improvements but it did not stop it entirely. Later, Jackson endorsed other internal improvement bills sent him by Congress, even some that gave financial support to local roads, canals, and harbor projects.

Jackson evolved an Indian policy that had few political repercussions, repelling only a minority of humanitarian critics in the Northeast, for the most part already on the side of the anti-Jacksonian National

369

Republicans. To the delight of Southerners and Westerners, and in particular land speculators who rapaciously eyed the fertile areas held by the Indians, the President introduced a plan to enforce vigorously the removal of all Indian tribes to reservations west of the Mississippi. Removal had been started by Jefferson, but it had not been carried out with dispatch and had slowed down considerably under the even-handed approach of Adams. Now Jackson, as a Westerner and old Indian fighter, revived the removal policy, not only because he professed to believe that Indians were unhappy living among white men, but also on the grounds that removal was the only way to save the tribes from extinction. "Doubtless it will be painful to leave the graves of their fathers," he acknowledged, but it was only necessary to "open the eyes of those children of the forest to their true condition" to make them realize the "humanity and justice" of the scheme.

During his military years, Jackson had negotiated several removal treaties and doubtless knew the hardship his policy would inflict. The plan was insensitive to the claims and traditions of the Indians and its execution was brutal. Tribes were given "evacuation treaties" and token payment for their lands, and then they were made to move west. Tribal chiefs were often tricked, coerced, or bribed into signing away their lands by federal agents. If these methods did not work, they were plied with liquor. Grasping white settlers often drove Indians off their property before preparations to migrate could be completed and the land to which the Indian was forced to go was rarely as fertile as that from which he was driven. The migrations themselves were poorly planned and entailed great suffering. For instance, Indians from the South, thinly dressed and without moccasins, went North in December, crossing the Mississippi in zero weather. During the journeys, measles took hundreds of lives and a cholera epidemic in 1832 further

thinned out the tribes. Alexis de Tocqueville, author of *Democracy in America,* watched as a group of Choctaw Indians began to cross the Mississippi River at Memphis. "Never will that solemn spectacle fade from my remembrance," he wrote. "No cry, no sob, was heard among the assembled crowd; all was silent. Their calamities were of ancient date, and they knew them to be irremediable." Later historians have called this western trek of the Indians a "trail of tears." Ralph Waldo Emerson protested that "such a dereliction of all faith and virtue, such a denial of justice, and such deafness to screams for mercy were never heard of in time of peace . . . since the earth was made."

The forced migration of Indians began soon after Jackson took office and went on for more than 10 years. Through the decade, only a few tribes resisted the policy and those who did were treated severely. In 1832, Chief Black Hawk led about one thousand Sac and Fox Indians back across the Mississippi to Illinois. He had hoped to find a hospitable prairie to plant a crop of corn for his starving people. The resistance, known as the Black Hawk War, was easily ended by militia and regular army troops. In the vastness of the Florida Everglades, however, the Seminoles were able to wage a more effective though futile fight. Led by Chief Osceola and supported by a great number of runaway slaves, the Seminoles managed to hold off the United States Army from 1835 to 1842. Their rebellion cost the United States about 40 million dollars and 2,000 lives. Most of the Seminoles were wiped out, and the Army only managed to capture Osceola himself by treacherously seizing him during a peace conference.

The Cherokees of Georgia, a tribe that had adopted many of the white man's ways, becoming farmers and cattle-raisers, building roads, houses, churches, and schools, fought for their cultivated lands with legal action. Convinced that literacy was the key to their survival, they developed a written language, printed Bibles, and published a weekly newspaper, the Cherokee *Phoenix*. In 1827, they drafted a constitution and formed a Cherokee state within the state of Georgia. The United States formally recognized the Cherokee nation, but the state of Georgia did not. In 1828, Georgia passed a law nullifying all Cherokee laws and claiming Cherokee lands as part of Georgia. Two years later, Georgia passed an additional law requiring all white men living in Cherokee country to swear allegiance to the state.

The Cherokees appealed to the Supreme Court. John Marshall, then Chief Justice, refused to issue any opinion on nullifica-

tion but did rule that the state of Georgia had no jurisdiction over Cherokee territory. When Georgia tried a Cherokee named Corn Tassel for murdering another Indian on Cherokee territory, the Indians again took the case to the Supreme Court to protest the trial of the accused in the Georgia court. Once more, the Supreme Court ruled in the Cherokees' favor, declaring that Georgia's action was unconstitutional and ordering the conviction to be set aside. Without legal support, but with the tacit approval of the White House, Georgia defied the Supreme Court, hanged Corn Tassel, and forced the evacuation of the Cherokee nation to Oklahoma.

The only Western statesman to denounce the shabby treatment of the Cherokees was Henry Clay. Although the Indians had no vote, and although his constituents in Kentucky had no interest in the matter, Clay made a fervent speech in the Senate in 1835

Robert Lindneux's painting typifies Indian suffering on the "Trail of Tears." Four thousand Cherokees died of starvation and disease during the move. Indians were removed from their lands and forced to relocate on government reservations during Jackson's tenure.

accusing Georgia of violating the most elementary principles of justice and decency,
and castigating Jackson. But Jackson remained firm, a Westerner forever unsympathetic to the Indians and convinced that
their removal was desirable and endorsed
by the majority. Yet, at the same time, his
tacit acceptance of Georgia's nullification of
the decisions of the Supreme Court strongly
indicated support of the idea of state nullification of laws or court decisions believed
to be unconstitutional.

Jackson also won the approval of the
West with his public land policy, agreeing with Westerners that the government
should encourage the settlement of public
land by selling it cheaply. The alternative,
which had been the policy of Adams, was
to support higher prices to bring as much
money as possible into the federal treasury.

There were several new plans proposed
to dispose of the public lands. One, originated by Senator Thomas Hart Benton of
Missouri, suggested that the government
lower the price of poor public land, first to
one dollar and a quarter per acre, then
to seventy-five cents, and then to fifty cents
an acre, finally giving away free to settlers whatever land remained unsold. This
scheme was called graduation. Another
plan, preemption, urged that "squatters"
already settled illegally on public land be
given options to buy the quarter sections of
160 acres where they had squatted as soon
as the government offered the land for sale.
These plans placed more importance on
opening up the country to settlement than
on financial gain for the treasury. Clearly in
favor of this policy, Jackson told Congress
in 1832 that "the public lands shall cease
as soon as practicable to be a source of
revenue." The President believed that settlers should be able to buy land in small
tracts for little more than it cost to survey
and clear away Indian titles. He also felt
that each new state should be given the
public lands that lay within its borders.
Moderate though these plans were, they
greatly displeased Easterners who viewed

western migration as a severe drain on their
sources of labor and thus a catalyst for
higher wage demands by those who remained. They attacked both the graduation
scheme and preemption, and proposed additional legislation to halt completely the
survey and sale of new lands in the West.
To resolve this conflict, Clay suggested that
instead of giving public lands to individual
Western states, they should be sold, with
10 percent of the proceeds going to the
Western states and the remaining revenue
distributed among all the states for public
works, education, or the reduction of state
taxes. Congress passed Clay's distribution
scheme in 1833, but Jackson vetoed it. Jackson never did settle the land question during his time in office.

THE NULLIFICATION
CONTROVERSY

The nullification controversy, which dealt
with whether a state had the right to set
aside laws of the federal government as unconstitutional if they were deemed detrimental to the interests of that state, grew
out of strong Southern opposition to protective tariffs. Southern cotton growers felt
these duties discriminated against them in
favor of Northern manufacturers. When he
first came to office, Jackson pleased protectionists by endorsing import duties on "all
products that may be found essential to our
national independence." As Southern objections increased, however, he saw that the
tariff was a divisive issue and shifted his
position by asking Congress for a revenue
tariff that would give only "temporary and,
generally, incidental protection," a position
more in line with traditional Jeffersonian
economic theory. The President's reversal
antagonized the protectionists but encouraged the South Carolina legislature to assume incorrectly that he would tolerate
direct state action against the tariff.

The protective tariff was not entirely a
sectional issue, but most sentiment for protection was in the industrial North and

Proclamation on South Carolina Ordinance

The ordinance is founded, not on the indefeasible right of resisting acts which are plainly unconstitutional and too oppressive to be endured, but on the strange position that any one State may not only declare an act of Congress void, but prohibit its execution; that they may do this consistently with the Constitution; that the true construction of that instrument permits a State to retain its place in the Union and yet be bound by no other of its laws than those it may choose to consider as constitutional . . . I consider,—the power to annul a law of the United States, assumed by one State, incompatible with the existence of the Union . . . *The people of the United States formed the Constitution, acting through the State legislatures in making the compact, to meet and discuss its provisions, and acting in separate conventions when they ratified those provisions; but the terms used in its construction show it to be a Government in which the people of all the States, collectively, are represented . . . It is a Government in which all the people are represented, which operates directly on the people individually, not upon the States . . . The laws of the United States must be executed. I have no discretionary power on the subject; my duty is emphatically pronounced in the Constitution. Those who told you that you might peaceably prevent their execution deceived you; they could not have been deceived themselves . . . Their object is disunion. But be not deceived by names. Disunion by armed force is treason. . . .*

—Andrew Jackson

Pro Nullification

" *Whereas, the Congress of the United States, by various acts, purporting to be acts laying duties and imposts on foreign imports, but in reality intended for the protection of domestic manufacturers . . . are unauthorized by the Constitution of the United States, and violate the true meaning and intent thereof, and are null, void and no law, nor binding upon this State, its officers, or citizens; . . . in no case of law or equity, decided in the Courts of this State, wherein shall be drawn in question the authority of this Ordinance, or the validity of such act or acts of the Legislature as may be passed for the purpose of giving effect thereto, or the validity of the aforesaid acts of Congress, imposing duties, shall any appeal be taken or allowed to the Supreme Court of the United States . . . we will not submit to the application of force, on the part of the Federal Government, to reduce this State to obedience; but that we will consider the passage, by Congress, of any act authorizing the employment of a military or naval force against the State of South Carolina . . . as inconsistent with the longer continuance of South Carolina in the Union; and that the People of this State will thenceforth hold themselves absolved from all further obligation to maintain or preserve their political connection with the people of the other States, and will forthwith proceed to organize a separate Government, and to do all other acts and things which sovereign and independent States may of right do.* "

—South Carolina Ordinance of Nullification, 1832

most free trade sentiment was in the South. By the 1820s, Southerners were already swarming to public meetings to protest that the tariff was unfair to farmers and planters because it gave manufacturers "undue influence and importance." The South had few factories and exported two-thirds of its crops to Europe. The money from these exports paid for a majority of the country's imports, and the federal government supported itself mostly by the tariff on foreign goods coming into the country. Because the tariff raised the price of everything they bought but protected nothing they sold, Southerners felt that they were paying too large a share of federal taxes. To make matters worse, a lot of the income from the tariff was going for internal improvements outside of the South.

Many Southerners naturally began to consider the tariff discriminatory, with the most vociferous outcries coming from South Carolina. The state was in economic and social trouble, and it pointed to the spirit of nationalism in the country in general and the tariff in particular as the causes of its ills. The state's plantation aristocracy was already uneasy over race relations and strongly feared that a powerful federal government might tamper with the institution of slavery. The number of slaves already outnumbered the rest of the population, and an unsettling threat had been posed to the state when Denmark Vesey, a free black man, had organized a massive, though unsuccessful, slave conspiracy in 1822 to capture the city of Charleston. By the late 1820s, the state had become hypersensitive to the faintest hint of criticism of its "peculiar institution" from any source. If the federal government already had the power to impose unfair taxation, might it not someday assume the power to impose emancipation?

Nervousness over slavery was a chronic condition, but South Carolina's acute economic difficulties in the 1820s sharpened it considerably. The days when the state flour-

ished and planters made huge fortunes cultivating rice and cotton had ended with the Panic of 1819. Cotton prices had dropped in the ensuing depression and had fallen even lower as the new states of Alabama and Mississippi increased the supply of cotton. South Carolina's profits fell disastrously as its wornout fields produced smaller yields at higher production costs. The state's population remained stagnant as ambitious farmers emigrated West looking for better land. The economic problems and the stresses created by slavery resulted in great political unrest and a strong states' rights stand from which there was little dissent in a state with a uniformity of economic interests in all areas. Unwilling to place the cause of their misery on soil exhaustion and competition from newer states, South Carolinians blamed the tariff and other federal encroachments as the real culprits.

The position of his state posed a dilemma for Vice-President Calhoun, South Carolina's leading politician. Since 1816, he had been both a nationalist and a protectionist. Now, he had to modify his views to satisfy his constituency, without at the same time offending friends in the North and the West whose support was necessary in furthering his ambition for the Presidency.

In 1828, Calhoun published an unsigned essay called the *South Carolina Exposition and Protest,* attacking the high tariff of that year. It was apparent from the document that he had abandoned much of his nationalism and had become a supporter, however expediently, of states' rights. In the document he proposed the doctrine of nullification as a method whereby a numerical minority, such as the South, could protect itself from offensive laws passed by the majority. "Nullification" rendered to a state legislature the right to decide whether or not a federal law was constitutional, and if it was not, to pass a state law preventing its intrastate enforcement. He argued that the consequences of the protective tariff, whereby one-third of the country was paying two-thirds of the expenses of the national government, showed that the federal government had exceeded its powers.

For his nullification doctrine, Calhoun had borrowed a line of reasoning from the 1798 Virginia and Kentucky Resolutions of Madison and Jefferson. Like them, he argued that the states had been completely sovereign before 1787 and had not surrendered their sovereignty when their representatives wrote and ratified the Constitution. They had only formed a "compact" and the federal government they had created served only as an "agent" to execute that compact. The agent had limited powers which were determined, not by the Supreme Court, but by the sovereign states. Unlike Jefferson and Madison, however, Calhoun did not say that a majority of the states was necessary to nullify a federal law. Each individual state had the right to judge when its "agent" had overstepped its authority. If Congress assumed more authority than a state had delegated, the state could interpose its own authority to stop the law's enactment. Procedurally, the doctrine stipulated that the people of a state would elect delegates to a state convention who, in turn, would vote upon the constitutionality of the Congressional law. If the delegates decided the law was unconstitutional, they would declare it null and void in that state. Congress could prevent nullification, but only by getting three-quarters of the states to ratify an amendment making the challenged legislation constitutional. If the federal government tried to coerce a state into accepting legislation, the state had the right to secede from the Union. Calhoun believed this scheme would protect the minority South and encourage Congress to pass only bills that would benefit the entire country.

Calhoun's doctrine had a full-scale review in the Senate in 1830, when a debate that began over the public land policy expanded to an examination of the nature of the federal Union. The chief orators were Robert Y. Hayne of South Carolina and Daniel Webster of Massachusetts. Calhoun, as Vice-President and presiding officer of the Senate, listened intently as Hayne, his spokesman, brilliantly explained and defended the concept of nullification, recited the South's grievances, and appealed to the West to adopt the doctrine as a means of preventing the enforcement of any policy to limit the sale of public lands.

The debate reached a peak on January 26, as Webster made a stirring response to Hayne in the most eloquent and fiery speech of his career. One of the most impressive men in the Senate, Webster held the Senate galleries spellbound for two days, asserting that the sovereignty of the states was limited by the Constitution. In a vibrant defense of the Union, he denied that the federal government was an agent of the states. "It is," he said, "the people's constitution, the people's government, made for the people, made by the people, and answerable to the people." If a state felt that it had not been justly treated, it could seek action in the courts, at the polls, or in the amending process. Otherwise, any disturbance of federal sovereignty by a state would be considered treasonable and could lead to civil war. He closed the speech with the memorable phrase, "Liberty and Union, now and forever, one and inseparable!"

Although a states' rights man, Jackson accepted without reservation the sovereignty of the federal government's powers under the Constitution, a position he made quite clear at a Democratic Party banquet celebrating Jefferson's birthday. The affair took place only a short time after the Webster-Hayne debate, and Calhoun and his followers attempted to use the occasion to gather support for their cause, proposing toast after toast, each subtly implying a connection between nullification and Democratic Party orthodoxy. Jackson sat patiently and silently until, after twenty-three toasts, he rose, raised his glass and said "Our Federal Union—It must be preserved."

Calhoun, his political career already in jeopardy, brought his relations with the President to the breaking point with his immediate and defiant countertoast: "The Union—next to our liberty, the most dear! May we all remember that it can only be preserved by respecting the rights of the states and distributing equally the benefits and burdens of the Union."

The rift between the President and the Vice-President was encouraged by Secretary of State Van Buren who hoped to take Calhoun's place as Jackson's heir to the Presidency. In addition to the occasion of the banquet encounter, Van Buren was aided by two other events. One was a social clash created by Administration wives when Secretary of War John Eaton married Peggy O'Neale, the attractive but morally suspect daughter of a tavernkeeper. Mrs. Calhoun's refusal to receive the "hussy" was quickly followed by that of the wives of other Cabinet members, Senators, and Congressmen. Always gallant about ladies and still passionately haunted by the memory of the slander against his wife before her death, Jackson was outraged by the incident and promptly pronounced Peggy Eaton "as chaste as a virgin." Van Buren, a widower, seized upon the event to go out of his way to pay Mrs. Eaton marked attention.

More important than the division caused by the "Eaton malaria," as gossips called it, William H. Crawford, an old political enemy of Calhoun, placed letters in the "right hands" to let the President know that in 1818, Calhoun, then Secretary of War, had criticized Jackson's invasion of Florida. Calhoun defended himself with a long, explanatory letter which Jackson immediately rejected as "full evidence of the duplicity and insincerity of the man." Both incidents sped Calhoun's downfall. In 1831, Jackson, at Van Buren's urging, reorganized his Cabinet, thus forcing Calhoun's friends out of the Administration. Shunted aside as a national leader, Calhoun found himself in the position of chief defender of the South.

The nullification controversy simmered for a few years as South Carolina waited for Congress to reduce the "tariff of abominations." But it flared out of control in 1832 when Congress passed the new tariff law, which, though it reduced tariffs to the 1824 levels of 30–36 percent, was considered by the South as adding insult to injury. The South Carolina state legislature, made up chiefly of nullifiers, now proceeded to adopt Calhoun's plan of action by calling for a convention to draw up an Ordinance of Nullification. The delegates declared both the Tariffs of 1828 and 1832 null and void, and forbade any collection of federal duties within the state. Furthermore, the state legislature voted funds to raise a volunteer army to defend the state from "invasion." The nullifiers also arranged for Hayne to become governor and for Calhoun to take Hayne's place in the Senate after resigning from the Vice-Presidency.

Interpreting South Carolina's actions as open defiance of the sovereignty of the Union, Jackson quickly reinforced the federal Army and naval units in Charleston. His intention was to bring military pressure to bear in order to force an essentially political and peaceful solution. He did not want war, and he rightly calculated that South Carolina felt the same way. He issued an official proclamation on December 10 declaring nullification treason, and nullifiers traitors. "I consider, then," stated the Proclamation, "the power to annul a law of the United States, assumed by one State, incompatible with the existence of the Union, contradicted expressly by the letter of the Constitution, unauthorized by its spirit, inconsistent with every principle on which it is founded, and destructive of the great object for which it was formed." Implicit in the final statement of the Proclamation was Jackson's warning to the people of South Carolina that the laws of the United States left him no alternative but to punish treason with force: "The laws of the United States must be executed. I have no discretionary power on the subject; my duty is emphatically pronounced in the Constitution."

In Congress, Jackson sought a two-pronged solution. He asked for passage of a Force Bill giving him the authority to use the Army and Navy, if necessary, to collect customs duties, and, as a concessionary measure, he called for a new tariff bill that would significantly lower duties. Calhoun unsuccessfully led the fight against the Force Bill as Webster again argued for the preeminence of the Constitution and the Union. Meanwhile, South Carolina was further weakened, not only by division within its own ranks, but by the fact that the support it had counted on from the other Southern states had not materialized. Virginia said that nullification was a caricature of her Resolutions of 1798, Georgia "abhorred the doctrine," and Alabama denounced it as "unsound in theory and dangerous in practice." South Carolina stood alone.

The state was forced into a dilemma. It was all too obvious that a military showdown would be virtually suicidal, and yet to concede defeat would mean a disastrous loss of prestige and the ruination of its political leaders. The state and Calhoun were saved by the intervention of the "Great Pacificator," Henry Clay, who devised a compromise scheme that would gradually lower tariff rates over a 10-year period to no higher than 20 percent. Calhoun endorsed the plan as a means of compromise. The tariff bill was passed, ironically, on the same day as the Force Bill. Webster held out against any concessions to the nullifiers, but Jackson signed both measures, satisfied that national harmony would now be restored.

The South Carolina convention reassembled and repealed its Ordinance of Nullification, but at the same time *nullified* the Force Bill, which had been already withdrawn. Since the tariff had actually been lowered as a result of the critical encounter, Calhoun and his followers claimed a victory. They continued to work for nullification by building Southern solidarity until that day when a united Southern front might effectively resist federal political and military power. Jackson, though he had not effected a permanent solution, nevertheless managed to relax national tensions on a crucial issue and avoid a military confrontation. The Calhoun group also worked more closely with Clay for the next few years in an effort to embarrass Jackson whenever possible.

THE BANK WAR

Jackson was easily reelected President in the fall of 1832 and a central issue in his campaign was his stand against the Bank of the United States. There was no doubt that his position was an extremely popular one, and like many of the old General's postures on national issues, highly combative. It was, nevertheless, more popular than prudent, based on instinct and prejudice rather than a sound comprehension of economics. Jackson had opposed the Bank before he became President, criticized it steadily during his first term, used it as the primary issue of his reelection campaign, and permitted his second term to be dominated by his personal obsession to destroy it. Considerable support for Jackson's position came from agrarian-minded Westerners and Southerners who instinctively distrusted any central bank that controlled state banks and placed enormous sums in the hands of a few rich and powerful men. Thomas Hart Benton of Missouri said that the Bank was "too great and powerful to be tolerated in a government of free and equal laws." It was, to Jackson's way of thinking, a monster to be slain, and he probably considered its destruction his greatest single accomplishment in office. However, the Bank had also been a stabilizing factor in the nation's economy, an important control on credit, whose removal allowed the country to plunge into frenzied speculation that was ultimately followed by its first serious depression.

Henry Clay, right, supported the Bank of the United States. Andrew Jackson, shown here with Van Buren, is losing the race on the back of a jackass. Jackson eventually won his battle against the Bank.

A POWERFUL INSTITUTION

The second Bank's largest single depositor was the federal government, yet in spite of this it managed to remain aloof from politics until Jackson's time, a conservative and responsibly administered business enterprise that provided the Treasury with a place to deposit its monies and the nation with a central and vital regulator of credit policy. In 1823, a sophisticated and brilliant banker, Nicholas Biddle, became its president. Biddle was an astute economist who realized that the Bank and its twenty-nine branches had the potential to regulate the growing American economy. The Bank bought and sold government bonds. As a source of credit, it advanced loans to the business community, and it issued bank notes that gave the country a sound and uniform paper currency. It also restrained state banks from reckless lending policies by forcing them to back their bank notes with gold and silver and repay loans from the Bank of the United States on demand. Such control over the flow and exchange of money gave Biddle's bank tremendous in-

fluence. However, since Biddle knew much more about banking than did his board of directors, the power of the Bank lay entirely in his hands.

Though Biddle's thinking was sound in principle and protected not only the Bank but the state banks and the nation's economy as well, it met with considerable opposition, much of it based on an inability to share the foresightedness of Biddle's policy. A distrust of paper money and bankers in general still lingered from the days of Adams and Jefferson. Jackson was among those hard-money men who wanted to have all transactions made in gold and silver. Many working men whose wages were paid in fluctuating paper also took this point of view. Resentment of the great power of the institution was increased by the fact that it ultimately acquired much of the coin that had been in the other banks. On the other hand, with the Bank's stringent control over the availability of money in the hands of the state banks, local businessmen found it more difficult to borrow. Most rising businessmen and state bankers resented the Bank of the United States because they considered its credit policies too tight—it did not allow enough paper to circulate. The state banker, discovering that he could not extend credit as liberally as he liked, resented the loss of potential profits from interest on loans.

There were several other criticisms of the Bank. Objections came from business and government officials who condemned the Bank as a monopoly that held 100 percent of federal funds but had no federal controls whatsoever. States' rights groups and working class groups opposed the Bank as not provided for in the Constitution. That Biddle was wealthy, charming, talented, and cultured, hardly mitigated their antagonism. New Yorkers were particularly hostile to the Bank, for it diverted the financial plum of customs revenues from the port of New York into the Bank's head office in Philadelphia. In political circles,

Jacksonians condemned the Bank on the basis that it had not supported Jackson in his 1828 campaign, although the Bank had, in fact, made loans to both parties and Biddle himself had worked for Jackson. He was frequently accused of corrupting politicians and editors with generous loans. There was the fact that Daniel Webster not only borrowed heavily but was on the Bank's payroll as a legal counselor. "I believe my retainer has not been renewed or *refreshed* as usual," he wrote Biddle on one occasion. "If it be wished that my relation to the Bank should be continued, it may be well to send me the usual retainer."

The supporters of the bank tried to outmaneuver Jackson. Biddle visited Jackson and assured him of the Bank's sound fiscal position. He appointed Democrats as directors of branches and told the President he would accept some restrictions on the Bank's power. However, Biddle was sure Jackson was hostile and he decided to work with Clay and Webster to get the Bank rechartered before the election of 1832, even though the charter would not expire for 4 years. Clay believed that the Bank would be rechartered by the Congress, thus putting the President in an embarrassing position. If Jackson signed the bill, he would show the nation he was a hypocrite. Furthermore, Clay did not believe Jackson would dare veto the bill since he believed the Bank was popular in the country. If it were vetoed, the President would have provided a winning issue for the National Republicans in the 1832 campaign. It did pass both houses with restrictions on its powers by July, 1832, and went to the White House for the President's signature.

THE BANK VETO

There are no necessary evils in the government. Its evils exist only in its abuses. If it would confine itself to equal protection, *and, as Heaven does its rains, shower its favors alike on the high and low, the rich and the poor, it would be an unqualified blessing. In the act before me (for rechartering the Bank of the United States) there seems to be a wide and unnecessary departure from these just principles . . .*

In his message, the President, by stressing emotional charges against the Bank, conveniently ignored the conflicting points of view of the hard-money men and those who were for an inflated paper currency. He attacked it, as had other opponents, as a monopoly with a stranglehold over the nation's economic development. In addition, much of its stock was not even in American hands but had been bought by foreigners. Next Jackson charged that it was unconstitutional since the Constitution had not specifically provided for the creation of a national bank. Finally, it was an invasion of the rights of the states and favored the economic development of the Eastern part of the country at the expense of the West.

Although the President's message revealed an ignorance of the positive economic functions of the Bank, it was a masterpiece of political propaganda. He clearly saw the political weaknesses of the Bank and exploited them for party advantage. While his definition of the Bank as a monopoly was technically incorrect (it made only 20 percent of the country's bank loans and issued 20 percent of the paper money), it was a powerful institution; Jackson's charge made him appear the champion of the common man and of economic equality. Even though the Supreme Court had ruled that the Bank was constitutional in *McCulloch v. Maryland* (1819), many people, including the President, did not accept the validity of the decision. Finally, the message was a dramatic appeal to American patriotism and to states' rights. The counterattack in the Senate by Clay and Webster based on the economic need for the Bank was weak in comparison.

Attacking the Constitutionality of the National Bank

❝ It is maintained by the advocates of the bank that its constitutionality in all its features ought to be considered as settled by precedent and by the decision of the Supreme Court. To this conclusion I can not assent. Mere precedent is a dangerous source of authority, and should not be regarded as deciding questions of constitutional power except where the acquiescence of the people and the States can be considered as well settled . . .

If the opinion of the Supreme Court covered the whole ground of this act, it ought not to control the coordinate authorities of this Government. The Congress, the Executive, and the Court must each for itself be guided by its own opinion of the Constitution. Each public officer who takes an oath to support the Constitution swears that he will support it as he understands it, and not as it is understood by others . . . The opinion of the judges has no more authority over Congress than the opinion of Congress has over the judges, and on that point the President is independent of both. The authority of the Supreme Court must not, therefore, be permitted to control the Congress or the Executive when acting in their legislative capacities, but to have only such influence as the force of their reasoning may deserve. ❞

—Andrew Jackson

THE ELECTION OF 1832

Swept in on the Bank issue, Clay was the overwhelming choice of the National Republicans, while Jackson, with Van Buren as his running mate, carried the banner for the Democratic Republicans. In addition, the campaign of 1832 introduced, for the first time, a third party—the Anti-Masons, led by William Wirt, a well-known Baltimore lawyer.

Defending the Constitutionality of the National Bank

❝ . . . I now proceed, Sir, to a few remarks upon the President's constitutional objections to the Bank; and I cannot forbear to say, in regard to them, that he appears to me to have assumed very extraordinary grounds of reasoning. He denies that the constitutionality of the bank is a settled question. If it be not, will it ever become so, or what disputed question ever can be settled?

. . . Hitherto it has been thought that the final decision of constitutional questions belonged to the supreme judicial tribunal. The very nature of free government, it has been supposed, enjoins this; and our Constitution, moreover, has been understood so to provide, clearly and expressly . . .

The President is as much bound by the law as any private citizen, and can no more contest its validity than any private citizen. He may refuse to obey the law, and so may a private citizen; but both do it at their own peril, and neither of them can settle the question of its validity. The President may say a law is unconstitutional, but he is not the judge. The judiciary alone possess this unquestionable and hitherto unquestioned right. . . .

—Daniel Webster

The new party actually had begun to take shape in 1826 after the disappearance of William Morgan, a New York bricklayer who planned to publish a book that presumably revealed the secrets of his Masonic lodge. Rumors that Morgan had been murdered by the Masons revived old prejudices against secret societies as undemocratic institutions. Many political leaders and judges were Masons, which created the suspicion among some people that Masonic secrecy somehow hid a widespread conspiracy against democratic values despite the fact that the great man of the people, Andrew

Jackson, was himself a Mason. The movement against the Masons grew large enough to attract such rising young politicians as William H. Seward and Thaddeus Stevens, who skillfully forged it into an anti-Jackson party, more extreme in its attitudes than the National Republicans. Because they did not have officeholders to form a caucus and name a candidate, the Anti-Masonic Party held a national nominating convention in Baltimore in September, 1831. This was the first national political convention of its kind and set the precedent followed to this day for a similar procedure in nominating all Presidential and Vice-Presidential candidates.

Although it was anti-Jackson, the entrance of the new third party into the campaign actually bolstered the President's chances for reelection. Wirt had accepted the Anti-Masonic Party's nomination be-cause he believed the same endorsement would soon be forthcoming from the National Republicans, also strongly against Jackson. The latter, however, nominated Clay and adopted the first party platform, which attacked Jackson for misuse of patronage and the veto power, and demanded the recharter of the Bank. To the Democrats, as they were now called, the convention was a mere formality and a platform seemed unnecessary. Jackson was at the peak of his popularity and the opposition was not strengthened by being split into two parties. It was a bitter campaign in which the parties denounced each other by means of cartoons, pamphlets, and speeches. A united front might conceivably have been effective, but the votes that went to Wirt merely drained support away from Clay, and Jackson won by the comfortable majority of 219 to 49 in the electoral college. The National Republicans also lost seats in the Congress and the Anti-Masons had 31 in the House. To the reelected President, the meaning of the victory was clear: the people had given him a mandate to fight and destroy the Bank of the United States.

DEATH OF THE BANK

Since the Bank's charter ran to 1836, Jackson could not deliver an immediate and lethal blow to the institution. He could, however, gradually weaken the Bank by refusing to use it for new federal deposits. Such a policy could legally only be performed by the Secretary of the Treasury, and when the incumbent Secretary refused to give the order, the President replaced him. When he also delayed, Jackson removed him and appointed a third Secretary, Roger B. Taney, a close friend who began the systematic removal process immediately. The government opened accounts with a group of state banks, made no new deposits in the Bank of the United States, and withdrew on its existing deposits to pay its bills. The federal reserves in the Bank

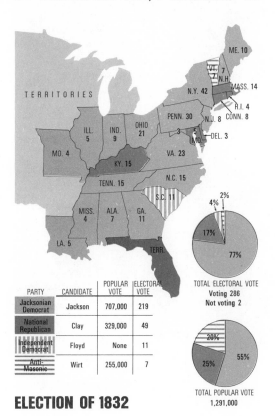

PARTY	CANDIDATE	POPULAR VOTE	ELECTORAL VOTE
Jacksonian Democrat	Jackson	707,000	219
National Republican	Clay	329,000	49
Independent Democrat	Floyd	None	11
Anti-Masonic	Wirt	255,000	7

TOTAL ELECTORAL VOTE
Voting 286
Not voting 2

TOTAL POPULAR VOTE
1,291,000

ELECTION OF 1832

of the United States dwindled rapidly, while those in the state or "pet" banks rose, although not without the criticism that these banks were too often chosen for their political affiliations rather than their financial soundness.

The Senate, already angry at Jackson's exertion of executive authority, now opened a virulent attack on him. Many Senators did not believe the President could remove a man from office without Senate consent after he had been appointed with its consent. In December of 1833 Clay pushed through resolutions censuring Jackson for removing a second Secretary of the Treasury and the Bank deposits without asking the Senate's agreement. Taney's appointment as Secretary also was rejected. Jackson fought back by declaring that as Chief Executive he inherently had the power to dismiss men who would not carry out his policies, a position later upheld by the Supreme Court. The censure resolutions were ultimately stricken from the official records in 1837 at the urging of Thomas Hart Benton.

Biddle, meanwhile, was not willing to stand by idly and watch the destruction of the Bank and national monetary planning without a fight. As the federal withdrawals from the Bank began to run into the millions, Biddle decided to call in loans made to the state banks and to raise appreciably the interest rates for borrowing money. By thus creating a credit shortage, he hoped to produce a business panic so widespread that the resultant depression would turn public pressure against Jackson and force him to return the deposits to the Bank of the United States and to call for its recharter. "Nothing but the evidence of suffering . . . will produce any effect," he asserted.

The suffering Biddle relied on as his weapon did indeed come about. During the winter of 1833 to 1834, interest rates almost tripled, businesses collapsed, and unemployment rose rapidly. The administration denied any responsibility and Biddle relent-

lessly and irresponsibly kept up the pressure on the economy. Soon even business leaders who sympathized with Biddle were urging him to give in. Finally, he did reverse himself, and began to grant credit at reasonable rates. The panic subsided, but it had, in actuality, failed to help the Bank. The charter expired in 1837 and with it, Biddle's restraining influence on state banks.

Jackson had ultimately won the war on the Bank, but the desirability of such a victory was a debatable question. The Bank of the United States was an extremely useful financial institution for controlling credit and preventing wild speculation. If Jackson had not been so prejudiced against banks in general, he might more wisely have chosen only to reduce the Bank's power. A bank that could control all credit to other banks in the country was too important and powerful to be left unchecked in the hands of a small group of men, even though some were appointed by the government. The Bank recharter bill in 1832 had provided for some needed restrictions on its operations, but the President and his advisers chose to ignore them. For his part, Biddle ruined any hope of recharter by his willingness to vindictively place the entire country in economic jeopardy with his retaliatory scheme against Jackson, showing that he would place personal power before the country's welfare.

With the National Bank's restraining influence removed, the many state banks began to lend vast sums regardless of their gold and silver reserves. In January, 1835, there were 83 million dollars in bank notes in circulation; by December, 1836, the amount had leaped to 120 million dollars. Prices rose, and with them the nation's economic optimism. Expansion increased, and without any sound national restraint, such as Biddle had provided, it soon began to get out of hand. The most serious manifestation was a speculative land boom. Buying land to sell in the future at even higher prices became the national mania. Chicago, for example, was only a village of some two or three thousand people, but speculators sold and resold small lots for 25 miles around, confident that the area would expand. Throughout the West, land speculation became especially feverish because the government put the vast public lands on the market at the same time that lending loosened and interest rates declined. An escalating spiral took place as many Western farmers mortgaged their own property to buy more government lands and then mortgaged these to buy still more.

The government itself contributed to the spiral by depositing money from land sales in "pet" banks that eagerly lent it out again. The land boom produced a demand for internal improvements and much of the borrowed money went to reckless canal, turnpike, and railroad projects, financed both privately and by the states.

Political leaders were divided in their reaction to the speculation and growing inflation. Many of them, in fact, had become speculators themselves. Senator Benton made the ominous prediction that this "bloat in the paper system" would only bring on another depression, and in 1836, Jackson, foreseeing the truth of Benton's warning, issued a specie circular which ordered all federal land offices to accept only gold and silver in payment for public lands. The result of the President's sudden announcement of a shift in government policy was a sharp curtailment of Western land sales, a desirable condition but one with disastrous side effects. The public's confidence in the state banks declined when the banks were no longer able to lend specie or even cover the loans they had already made with gold and silver. The hoarding of hard money was greatly encouraged and became an important factor in bringing on the Panic of 1837. Prices plunged. Speculators who could not sell their lands abandoned them to the banks who held their mortgages, but the foreclosed property could not make up for the banks' losses

on loans. By the time Jackson left office, in the spring of 1837, many banks in the country had been forced to close their doors. Booming prosperity disappeared and the United States sank into a depression from which she did not recover for six turbulent years.

THE RISE OF POLITICAL PARTIES

By Jackson's second term in office, a new two-party system had evolved out of the breakdown of the massive Jeffersonian coalition that had controlled political life for a decade after the War of 1812. The Democratic Republicans, led by Andrew Jackson, were now simply called the "Democrats," and were primarily distinguished, outside of being dominated by Jackson's personality, by their concern for the welfare of the average citizen and their distrust of the business and commercial interests and special privilege. The key Democratic Party politicians understood that policies should be geared to the new mass electorate and that in order to get out the vote the party should have strong local organization all over the country. Organization based on Jackson's popularity and the spoils system was the key to the party's success.

The National Republicans under Clay took the name of "Whigs" as a symbolic indication, borrowed from English history, of their defiance of "King Andrew," a position which was basically the cohesive element of that party. On questions of policy the Whig Party from 1832 to 1848 was the vehicle for the continued advocacy of Clay's American System.

THE JACKSONIAN DEMOCRATS

For 8 years it was essentially Jackson's forceful personality that dominated American politics and shaped a diverse coalition into a unified party. As the election of 1836 approached, the Democrats were still a diverse mixture of economic groups from all parts of the country: small farmers in the North and South, urban workers, middle-class businessmen and bankers, and wealthy slaveholders. Very conservative planters and extreme states' rights men had, however, left its ranks. Those groups that made up the coalition had come to be identified with the positions that Jackson had taken on issues during his administration, such as, freedom of economic opportunity with neither government nor private interference, universal white male suffrage, and the struggle for political power represented by the belief that an ordinary man could conduct public affairs. Jackson had warned that he would guard against "all encroachments upon the legitimate sphere of state sovereignty." His party, though dedicated to the supremacy of the federal government in the areas where it was specifically empowered to act by the Constitution, likewise committed itself to the support of states' rights. Perhaps the only issue that separated Jackson and the urban members of the Democratic Party was the General's idealization of an agrarian society. He felt that agricultural interests were "superior in importance" to any others and that farmers were the "best part" of the population. Though some Democrats hardly yearned for a return to the agrarian-minded Jeffersonian past, they followed the President both out of personal loyalty and a conviction that his popular philosophy had opened up a plethora of political opportunities.

Jackson's years in office also contributed to an expansion of the role of the Chief Executive. By his dramatic use of the office of President, Jackson made policy rather than merely carrying out the law. He announced policies, vetoed bills, and appointed and dismissed subordinates, all in the name of the people. This innovative concept of Presidential power enabled the Chief Executive to apply his strength in dealing with other government branches, Congress and the Supreme Court, friends or foes, and foreign governments. Jackson's determination to play a powerful role in the government contributed directly to the modern concept of the Presidency and ended an era of strong Congressional leadership.

Jackson's leadership was wedded to his popularity in the country. He had the great politician's feel for what the average citizen thought. He did not address himself to the issues or his enemies. He spoke over the heads of his foes directly to the people. Much of his appeal came from his uncanny talent for reducing the most complex matters to a simple clash between good and evil. His defense of the Union in the nullification crisis, his attack on the Bank, his support of the nominating convention as opposed to the undemocratic Congressional caucus made him a national hero. His vetoes, even his unprecedented use of the pocket veto, brought him praise from the populace. In a country of rugged individualists, Jackson loomed as the most impressive individual of them all.

The Jacksonian movement was representative of the deep dilemmas of the American democratic heritage. It was an unmistakable turning point in the meaning and development of democracy. Yet, with the new concept of the common man as a fit candidate for political office came the abuses of the spoils system. Jackson destroyed the Bank of the United States, an institution a majority of Americans thought of as a monopolistic monster, but in doing so the President set the stage for the depression that followed. The Jacksonian movement championed political and economic equality in theory but in practice this applied only to white men! The party, dominated to a great extent by Southern planters and Western farming interests, had no interest in the plight of the black man and the Indian in America. Moreover, the Jacksonian Democrats disassociated themselves from most of the reform movements of the times, such as abolitionism and women's rights.

Since the Jacksonian era, historians have seen the period and Jackson himself in varying ways. Throughout the nineteenth century most important historians admired the outlook of the Whigs. Authors such as James Parton and William G. Sumner criticized Jackson as spiteful, coarse, illiterate, and autocratic. The Jacksonian movement, by introducing the spoils system, had allowed the vulgar and uneducated to hold important government positions while men of worth were excluded from public life. They saw the debasement of political life in the late nineteenth century as the direct result of Jacksonian politics.

With the enunciation of the Turner thesis in 1890, a new trend toward admiration for the American frontier and its legacy of democracy emerged. The revival of faith in democratic reform at the beginning of the twentieth century brought a new respect for the emphasis on popular control of government in the Jacksonian era. This idea dominated the historiography of the Jacksonian period for several decades and was represented in Marquis James' popular biography of Jackson, Claude Bowers' *Party Battles of the Jacksonian Period,* and Arthur Schlesinger, Jr.'s *The Age of Jackson.* Other historians also stressed Jackson's development of the modern Presidency. However, T. P. Abernethy in *From Frontier to Plantation in Tennessee* and Charles M. Wiltse's biography of Calhoun continued the older, more critical view of the Jacksonians as not really reformers but wily politicians mainly concerned with obtaining the spoils of office.

Schlesinger not only stressed the importance of the upsurge of democracy in American life, but was the first historian to see that it was not just a geographic movement but a class movement as well. He stressed the importance of the hard times following the Panic of 1819 in bringing Eastern work-

"Old Hickory," in this famous painting by Thomas Sully, was a fist-pounding, violent-tempered man who often extemporized fury in order to win a point. His hatred and distrust of the Bank of the United States, was well established.

ingmen into the Jacksonian coalition. Bray Hammond's work on early American banking has challenged Schlesinger's emphasis on the class struggle by showing that many rising entrepreneurs were likewise drawn to the Jacksonian movement by its attacks on monopolistic power in the hands of a small number of wealthy men. Richard Hofstadter in *The American Political Tradition* also followed this line of interpretation in seeing Jacksonian democracy as not essentially a class-conscious movement but the manifestation of the forces in America determined on a laissez-faire economy untrammeled by government support of monopolistic privileges for a few. All these interpretations reflect the urban environment of twentieth-century America as opposed to the stress in Turner's work on the amorphous democratic forces of rural

America as the major ingredient of Jacksonian democracy.

More recently such historians as Marvin Meyers and John Ward have turned their attention to the intellectual and psychological aspects of the movement. In doing so, they have in part returned to Turner's stress on the influence of the frontier in Jacksonian democracy. Meyers has described the movement as an effort to preserve the virtues of a simple agrarian republic bequeathed to them by the Jeffersonian era. Uneasy with the rapid industrialization of the country, they struck out at the national Bank as the symbol of the corporate money power. Yet its destruction hastened the rapid development of an unregulated capitalist economy rather than preventing it.

Finally, historian Lee Benson has questioned whether the phrase "Jacksonian democracy" is even appropriate. Benson does not believe that there was any well-organized reform group centered around Jackson. The stress by the Jacksonians on states rights, strong executive leadership, and the idea of limited government power was not necessarily to be equated with democracy. The struggle between the parties was over means not ends, with both coalitions mainly interested in obtaining jobs, not in debating issues. He has suggested that the term "Jacksonian democracy" be replaced with the "Age of Egalitarianism."

THE WHIGS AND
THE ELECTION OF 1836

The Whigs included a variety of groups, who rarely agreed except in their opposition to Jackson: former National Republicans such as wealthy Southern planters, well-to-do Northern farmers, the business and commercial interests, and workers whose jobs were protected by the tariff; Anti-Masons; a scattering of Northern abolitionists; and a few former Democrats who had become disillusioned with Jackson. Be-

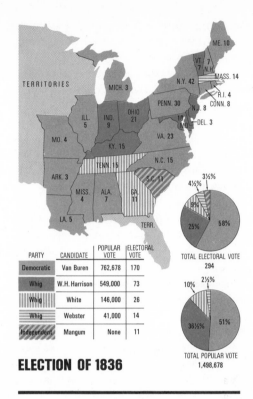

PARTY	CANDIDATE	POPULAR VOTE	ELECTORAL VOTE
Democratic	Van Buren	762,678	170
Whig	W.H. Harrison	549,000	73
Whig	White	146,000	26
Whig	Webster	41,000	14
Independent	Mangum	None	11

ELECTION OF 1836

TOTAL ELECTORAL VOTE
294

TOTAL POPULAR VOTE
1,498,678

cause of its extremely diverse nature, there were many conflicts within the party, even though a few political demands shaped a barely discernible rallying point. The Whigs essentially wanted federally sponsored internal improvements, high protective tariffs, and a national bank.

By 1836 the lack of unity among the Whigs was matched by the factionalism among the Democrats. Clay and Webster, the new party's leaders, managed the 1836 Whig campaign, adopting the tactic of "favorite son" candidates. They realized that the Whig Party itself had no leader who could successfully oppose the Democrats, so they chose to have popular Whig candidates run in each section of the country. They had no national nominating convention and issued no party platform. The "favorite sons," it was hoped, would draw local votes away from Jackson's chosen successor, Van Buren, and thereby prevent him from winning a majority in the electoral college and thus force the election into the House of Representatives. Daniel Webster ran for the Whigs in New England, Hugh Lawson White of Tennessee was chosen for his appeal to the West and the South, and General William Henry Harrison was expected to attract those in the Northwest who would support a military hero. The strategy failed. Martin Van Buren, the choice of Andrew Jackson, although not popular in the South, was elected with 170 electoral votes to 124 for his opponents combined. However, Van Buren had a very small popular majority and the House was dominated by a combination of Whigs and Southern Democrats opposed to the new President.

VAN BUREN'S TIME OF TROUBLE

Van Buren's Presidency coincided with the great Panic of 1837, resulting both from Jackson's specie circular and from a worldwide economic crisis. The specie circular, forcing banks to curtail lending, had spread doubt as to the soundness of banks in general. A depression in England also lessened the demand for American cotton. Construction projects were halted throughout the United States as British capitalists began calling in their loans. With construction down, thousands of laborers were left without any employment. Factories closed and the ranks of the unemployed swelled. Many Americans faced starvation as crop shortages turned the winter of 1837 to 1838 into an unforgettably grim experience. State banks folded and the depression spread rapidly. The United States entered a 7-year period of depression.

Van Buren had little responsibility for the depression that overwhelmed the country in 1837, and given his economic philosophy he took little responsibility for trying to alleviate it. As a true Jacksonian, Van Buren believed in a minimal amount of government interference in the economy. He felt the government had little responsibility in stabilizing the financial condition of the nation. According to Van Buren, the government should not concern itself with the plight of individual farmers, workers, and businessmen. "The less government interferes with private pursuits the better for the general prosperity," he said. His chief interest was to keep the federal treasury from going into the red in order to maintain confidence in the soundness of the economy which would encourage business to revive. Van Buren also recognized that banking procedures needed reform, but he was adamant in his belief that the government should remain entirely out of banking. He, therefore, proposed an independent treasury system to Congress. Under this scheme, all connections between the federal government and any bank or group of banks were to be cut. Vaults, or subtreasuries, were to be constructed in various cities to take in and pay out government funds strictly in gold and silver. The country's banking business would be carried on by private banks regulated by the states. The new President's scheme naturally aroused the opposition of the Whigs. Clay and Webster condemned it as sabotaging the country's present banking structure. It would, they admitted, protect the government from loss, but it would also keep gold and silver out of banks that needed it desperately to back their loans, thus curtailing credit. Those who had lost lifetime savings in the state banks favored Van Buren's proposal. It obviously reinforced their own suspicion of banks. Congress, however, did not immediately yield to public clamor. It did not pass the Independent Treasury Act until 1840, when Van Buren's term in the White House was virtually at an end.

THE ELECTION OF 1840

Van Buren, though tainted by the panic, was renominated for the Presidency by the

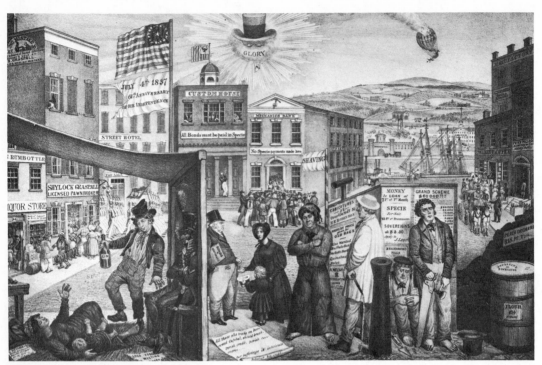

The Panic of 1837 and the ensuing depression coincided with Van Buren's tenure as President. Unemployment and poverty, as well as failing banks are characterized in the cartoon. Only the pawnbroker and the liquor store are open and active.

Democrats in 1840. The Whigs referred to him as Martin Van "Ruin," and for the Democrats not to have him run again would only have been to admit the validity of that epithet. Given the country's woeful circumstances, the Whigs scented victory. Drawing upon the lessons learned in Jackson's campaigns, they prevailed upon Clay not to seek the nomination and deliberately nominated a military hero—William H. Harrison of Ohio, a military chieftain who had achieved some notoriety in the battles of Tippecanoe (1811) and the Thames (1813), during the War of 1812. The Whigs used Harrison's robust military image as a direct contrast to that of Van Buren, a man who drank not cider but expensive French wines. The issues of the

campaign were the depression and the Independent Treasury, but it was an election based mostly on personalities and ballyhoo. Harrison lived in a log cabin and, in the Jacksonian tradition, was therefore pictured as a fit candidate to truly represent the people. Van Buren had no such background and was described by the Whigs as dining off imported gold plates. The fact that Harrison was not really low-born, or poverty-stricken, or an early resident of a log cabin did not seem to matter. His astute political backers knew what was needed to offset and ultimately defeat the aristocratic image of Van Buren. On the one hand there was the educated Harrison, whose father had been one of the signers of the Declaration of Independence, made out to be a rough-hewn frontiersman, and on the other hand there was the politically wily Van Buren, the son of a tavern keeper, now denounced as an aristocrat who wore corsets and ate French foods. The Whigs jeered

This cartoon characterized the Presidential campaigns of Harrison and Van Buren. The campaign turned out favorably for Harrison who was elected on the plank of his log cabin and hard cider platform.

that the party of Jackson was saddled with a supercilious dandy from the East. Taking a leaf from the pages of the Jacksonian Democrats, the Whigs now chanted or shouted such slogans as: "Two Dollars a Day and Roast Beef," and "With Tip and Tyler We'll Bust Van's Biler!" And of course there was the well-known:

Tippecanoe, and Tyler too.
And with them we'll beat little
  Van, Van, Van,
Oh! Van is a used-up man.

Almost two and one-half million voters turned out, basically perhaps in a vote against hard times. They swept Harrison

into office. The electoral college vote was a resounding 234 to 60. The Democrats had, in effect, been beaten by their own tactics, their appeals to emotions and prejudices.

THE SUPREME COURT UNDER TANEY

Although the Whigs now controlled the White House and the Congress, Jacksonians still held the third branch of the government, the Supreme Court. Jackson had named six new Associate Justices, and when Chief Justice Marshall died in 1835, he appointed Roger B. Taney to replace him. The nomination of Taney, a states' rights agrarian, was bitterly contested in the Senate. Webster and other nationalists feared the possibility of a too strict interpretation of the Constitution and reversals of the Court's earlier decisions.

Actually, the main body of the Marshall Court decisions survived almost intact. The only decisions modified by the Taney Court were some opinions on corporation rights and the sanctity of contracts. The Taney Court, however, was more inclined to give the states power to regulate corporations than was Marshall. For example, in the case of *Charles River v. Warren Bridge,* in 1837, the issue was the right of Massachusetts, which had chartered the Charles River Bridge Company to build and run a toll bridge over the Charles, to charter the Warren Company to build and run another bridge. The second bridge would compete directly with the first. Also at issue was Massachusetts' order to the Warren Company to return the bridge to state ownership after the company had collected its construction expenses in tolls. This meant that the second bridge, planned to be almost toll free, would lower if not end the value of the original and competing bridge. The Charles River Bridge Company held the state in breach of contract. The Taney Court disagreed, saying that the rights of corporations are less important than those of the community: "that the community also have rights, and that the happiness and well-being of every citizen depends on their faithful preservation."

As Chief Justice, Taney did not let his sympathy for states' rights undermine most of Marshall's precedents, but he made definite distinctions between those areas of government under federal law and those under state law. "The object and the end of all government," he said in one opinion, "is to promote the happiness and prosperity of the community by which it is established, and it can never be assumed that the government intended to diminish its power of accomplishing the end for which it was created." Here was a lesson in Jacksonian democracy.

TYLER BECOMES PRESIDENT

When Harrison entered office in the winter of 1841, it appeared to the leaders of his own party that he would be a puppet President, but the question still remained exactly whose puppet, Henry Clay's or Daniel Webster's. The question had not been settled before the election, and a rivalry developed for influence in the White House between Clay, who remained in the Senate, and Webster, who became Secretary of State. As they squabbled for control, Harrison was simultaneously besieged by Whig officeseekers looking for the same patronage that they had so vociferously condemned the Democrats for dispensing. Under the pressure, the President became gravely ill with pneumonia, and died on April 4, 1842, a month after his inauguration. John Tyler of Virginia, the states' rights man whose nomination for Vice-President had been engineered to balance the Whig ticket, became President, the first man to reach the office because of the death of his predecessor.

Receiving the bulk of his support from the South, Tyler ran almost immediately into a clash over policy with Clay and the Whig majority in Congress. The President went along with Clay on the repeal of the Independent Treasury. After two vetoes Tyler also accepted a revision of the tariff upward to 30–36 percent, thus reneging on the promise to the South in 1833 to reduce tariffs to 20 percent in 10 years. But he vetoed a bill that would have granted a charter to a third national Bank in an effort to wrest control of the Whigs from Clay. When Tyler vetoed a second bank measure pushed through by Clay, all the members of his Cabinet, with the exception of Webster, resigned in protest. Clay went further and called the Whig Congressmen into caucus, from which came a statement denouncing the President and reading him out of the Whig Party. As a Southerner and supporter of states' rights, the President's path was indeed a lonely one for the remainder of his term.

Spurned by the Northern and Western factions of the Whigs, and supported in the main by the lukewarm Southern Democrats, Tyler became, in effect, a President without a party. Though honest and conscientious, Tyler was virtually powerless without the backing of Cabinet and Congress. He had none of Jackson's combative strength, personal resolution, or national popularity. He was helpless as he faced the Whig movement for the reform of American government. With little alternative, Tyler was forced to court the Southerners. He gave Calhoun the opportunity to regain Southern leadership by appointing him Secretary of State. With renewed prestige, Calhoun devoted his efforts into making himself a national figure and making the South into a unified force.

Tyler's attempts to form a new party made up of states' rights men failed and he turned to the issue of an expansionist foreign policy in a last desperate effort to avoid political annihilation.

Readings

GENERAL WORKS

Benson, Lee, *The Concept of Jacksonian Democracy*. Princeton, N.J.: Princeton University Press, 1961—A reinterpretation of the meaning of Jacksonian democracy through an analysis of political party conflict in New York State. Benson argues that both Democrats and Whigs adopted the rhetoric of democracy and equality and that voting patterns were based more on ethnicity than on class.

Hammond, Bray, *Banks and Politics in America*. Princeton, N.J.: Princeton University Press, 1957—Hammond's book argues that the men around Jackson who convinced him to destroy the national Bank were ambitious capitalists with ties to New York financial circles, not opponents of privilege. The destruction of the Bank, he claims, did considerable harm to the American economy.

McCormick, Richard P., *The Second American Party System: Its Formation in the Jacksonian Era*. Chapel Hill, N.C.: University of North Carolina Press, 1966—Through a state-by-state survey of party organization and voting statistics, McCormick shows the emergence of organized Whig and Democratic parties. He suggests that Presidential elections and the emergence of groups of professional politicians helped spur the new political alignments.

Schlesinger, Arthur M., Jr., *The Age of Jackson*. Boston: Little, Brown, 1945—Schlesinger's influential study of Jacksonian democracy saw it as the forging of a coalition of small farmers and urban workmen around a program attacking vested interests and special privilege.

Syrett, Harold C., *Andrew Jackson: His Contribution to the American Tradition*. Indianapolis, Ind.: Bobbs-Merrill, 1953—A brief sketch of Jackson's political thought is followed by documents which outline the meaning of Jacksonian democracy.

Van Duesen, Glyndon G., *The Jacksonian Era*. New York: Harper & Row, 1963—A general history of the 1828 to 1848 period which concentrates on political developments. Van Deusen tends to doubt the claim that Jackson was an important democratic reformer and feels his main accomplishment was widening the powers of the President's office.

White, Leonard D., *The Jacksonians*. New York: Macmillan, 1954—An administrative history of the 1829 to 1861 period. White's figures show that Jackson's "spoils system" was not so revolutionary as either his admirers or attackers had often claimed.

Williamson, Chilton, *American Suffrage: From Property to Democracy*. Princeton, N.J.: Princeton University Press, 1960—Williamson's study of suffrage extension stresses the importance of state and local conditions in bringing about the reforms which led to universal white manhood suffrage before the Civil War.

Wiltse, Charles M., *The New Nation, 1800–1845*. New York: Hill and Wang, 1961—In this brief survey, Wiltse analyzes the contrasting trends of sectionalism and the growing power of and pride in a united American nation.

SPECIAL STUDIES

Foreman, Grant, *Indian Removal: The Emigration of the Five Civilized Tribes*. Norman, Okla.: University of Oklahoma Press, 1969—A history of the forced migration of five Southeastern Indian tribes from their homelands to the Oklahoma Indian Territory.

Freehling, William W., *Prelude to Civil War*. New York: Harper & Row, 1966—A history of the nullification controversy in South Carolina. Freehling argues that what might appear to be a controversy simply over tariffs was really a struggle of South Carolina slaveholders to defend a system and a way of life against internal and external challenges.

Hugins, Walter, *Jacksonian Democracy and the Working Class.* Stanford, Calif.: Stanford University Press, 1960—Through a study of working class organizations and politics in New York State, Hugins outlines the complicated history of the workingmen's associations and the Democratic Party. He shows also that the members of these movements were generally skilled workers.

McGrane, Reginald C., *The Panic of 1837.* Chicago: University of Chicago Press, 1924 —An older study of the conflict between Andrew Jackson and Nicholas Biddle which puts the blame for the economic setback of 1837 on the Jacksonians.

Meyers, Marvin, *The Jacksonian Persuasion.* Stanford, Calif.: Stanford University Press, 1957—An interpretation of the Jacksonians as torn between their desires to advance economically and their longing for an older, simpler, more stable society.

Miller, Douglas T., *Jacksonian Aristocracy: Class and Democracy in New York, 1830–1860.* New York: Oxford University Press, 1967—Miller's study of social structure in New York finds that great inequalities in wealth and status accompanied the rhetoric of political democracy. A new group of capitalists mixed with the older landed upper class while at the bottom, waves of immigrants became the urban proletariat.

Remini, Robert V., *Martin Van Buren and the Making of the Democratic Party.* New York: Columbia University Press, 1959— A study of Van Buren's role in organizing a national party following the "Era of Good Feelings." Remini insists that the origins of the Democratic Party are not to be found in economic and social conflict but in the struggle for national office.

Turner, Frederick J., *The Rise of the New West, 1819–1829.* New York: Macmillan, Collier Books, 1962—A major work by the originator of the frontier thesis. In this volume, Turner stresses the role of emerging sectional conflict during the so-called "Era of Good Feelings."

Ward, John W., *Andrew Jackson: Symbol for an Age.* New York: Oxford University Press, 1962—Ward shows that Andrew Jackson was used in popular songs, speeches, pamphlets, and cartoons to stand for the values which Americans believed in during the 1830s and 1840s.

PRIMARY SOURCES

Benton, Thomas H., *Thirty Years' View,* Vols. I–II. New York: Greenwood, 1968— Reminiscences by the Missouri Democrat who exemplified Western Jacksonianism. The work covers the political scene from 1820 to 1850, encompassing Benton's Senatorial career.

Cooper, James F., *The American Democrat.* Baltimore: Penguin Books, 1962—The famous novelist wrote this bitter political treatise to express his disgust at the greed and vulgarity he felt were associated with America's democratic values.

Grund, Francis J., *Aristocracy in America.* New York: Harper Torchbooks, 1959— Grund, a German, emigrated to the United States in 1827. His account of American society stresses the pretensions of upper-class Americans to aristocratic status and the desirability of increasing democracy.

Martineau, Harriet, *Retrospect of Western Travel.* New York: Johnson, 1970—A description of Miss Martineau's Western journeys in Jacksonian America. Although repelled by the crudities of Western life, she was impressed with its vitality.

Nevins, Allan, ed., *America Through British Eyes.* New York: Oxford University Press, 1948—A collection of British travelers' accounts of the United States from the Federalist era through World War II. Nevins points out the changing attitudes and purposes of the British visitors.

de Tocqueville, Alexis, *Democracy in America*, Philip Bradley, ed. New York: Vintage Books, 1945—This is the classic study of American political and social life before the Civil War. Written by a liberal French aristocrat, Tocqueville's interpretations of democracy are still important influences on scholars.

Trollope, Frances, *Domestic Manners of the Americans,* Donald Smalley, ed. New York: Vintage Books, 1960—Mrs. Trollope's impressions of the new nation, based on her stay in the United States in the late 1820s and early 1830s, were distinctly unfavorable. She found Americans boastful, ill-mannered, uncouth, and dirty.

Van Buren, M., and John C. Fitzpatrick, eds., *The Autobiography of Martin Van Buren.* New York: Plenum, 1969—Although not deeply revealing of his personality, Van Buren's autobiography is an important source for both New York and national political history.

BIOGRAPHIES

Chambers, William N., *Old Bullion Benton: Senator from the New West.* Boston: Little, Brown, Atlantic Monthly Press, 1956—The Senator from Missouri is pictured here as second only to Jackson as a symbol of democratic forces before the Civil War. His long public career put him in the center of many crucial political battles.

Coit, Margaret L., *John C. Calhoun: American Portrait.* Boston: Houghton Mifflin, 1950—A sympathetic biography of the South Carolina leader which views him as a courageous and brilliant spokesman for an embattled minority. Calhoun, Coit maintains, tried to hold the Union together on the basis of the principles of states' rights and individual liberties.

Current, Richard N., *Daniel Webster and the Rise of National Conservatism.* Boston: Little, Brown, 1955—A brief biography of the Massachusetts Senator. Current feels that Webster successfully masked a pro-business outlook with the rhetoric of democracy and formulated a position which was highly useful to later conservative spokesmen.

Goven, Thomas P., *Nicholas Biddle: Nationalist and Public Banker.* Chicago: University of Chicago Press, 1959—A biography of the president of the second Bank of the United States which defends Biddle against the charges of the Jacksonians and their historical supporters.

James, Marquis, *Andrew Jackson: Portrait of a President.* Indianapolis: Bobbs-Merrill, 1937—The second volume of James's Pulitzer Prize biography of Jackson. James concentrates on the Presidential years and gives a detailed account of Jackson's stormy personality.

Swisher, Carl B., *Roger B. Taney.* New York: Macmillan, 1935—A biography of the Chief Justice of the Supreme Court appointed by Jackson. Taney's Court began a trend toward laissez-faire rulings. In his most famous case, the Dred Scott decision, Taney's opinion upheld the pro-slavery position.

Wiltse, Charles M., *John C. Calhoun: Nullifier,* Vol. II. Indianapolis: Bobbs-Merrill, 1949—The second of a three-volume biography of Calhoun, covering the 1829 to 1839 period. Wiltse discusses Calhoun's break with the Jacksonians and his gradual return to the Democratic fold to fight for pro-Southern policies.

FICTION

Adams, Samuel H., *The Gorgeous Hussy.* Boston: Houghton Mifflin, 1934—An historical novel which revolves around the career of Peggy O'Neale, the woman whose stormy love life caused a political crisis in Andrew Jackson's administration.

3

NATIONALISM AND SECTIONALISM

The William Mason, *built in 1856, was known
for its beauty as well as its utility.*

The American Economy in the Antebellum Period

11

What indomitable enterprise marks the character of our people! What immense forests have disappeared, and given place to cultivated towns, thriving villages, and wealthy cities! Agriculture, and manufactures, and commerce, and schools, and public buildings, and houses of public worship; all these testify to our matchless enterprise. The rapidity of our progress throws all Eastern countries into the shade. We build steamboats for the Sultan of Turkey, and railroads for the Autocrat of Russia; and our enterprises extend to the icebergs of the poles—to India, China, and Japan.

—Orin Fowler

A huge surge in agricultural and industrial growth took place in the nation in the years before the Civil War and much of it arose out of the continuous westward sweep of America's population. In an irregular flow, for three centuries after the founding of Jamestown, Americans moved first from the towns of the Atlantic coast toward the interior regions, and then finally across the entire continent. The urge to expand seemed innately American. Hardly had a new state or territory been formed when further emigration took place. Much of this movement westward resulted after the War of 1812. New Englanders and New Yorkers began to settle in Ohio, Indiana, and Illinois. Settlement of Texas by Americans took place in the 1820s. Gold was discovered in California in 1848, and thousands made the trek across the continent to seek their fortune at the same time that large expansion occurred in the Kansas territory. Minnesota and Oregon entered the Union before the Civil War, attracting new inhabitants. Nearly forty thousand people sought riches in the mines around Denver, Colorado. The prairie enticed farmers and the rich virgin forests drew lumbermen. By 1870 over half of the country's population lived west of the Appalachian Mountains.

Americans believed in the economic potential of the continent and in their own individual powers to develop that potential. The West offered untapped resources and opportunities, a place where a free man could, almost without restrictions, stake out a claim and create a home for himself and his family, and eventually, perhaps, a prosperous farm or a thriving business. Historian Frederick Jackson Turner labeled the West "the richest free gift that was ever spread out before civilized man." With this "free gift" came opportunities for people to move upward on the economic and social scale. As the economy developed, the standard of living rose to the benefit of all Americans: farmers, skilled and unskilled laborers, manufacturers, and merchants.

THE WESTWARD MOVEMENT

GROWTH OF THE WEST

The new West gained its population from all states on the eastern seaboard. The South and its growing cotton culture too, contributed steadily to the westward migration. Established planters sold their Eastern lands and pushed into the West, as did those who wished to add to their Eastern holdings. Less prosperous planters saw in the new land an opportunity to escape the monopolistic control of the planter-aristocracy. These men laid the foundations for the states of Alabama and Mississippi. Many too poor to own slaves left the South for Indiana, Illinois, and Missouri. Kentucky and Tennessee frontiersmen began to feel crowded as a growing number of small farmers moved in from the back country of Virginia and the Carolinas and many of them settled further west in the Mississippi Valley. The Great Lakes region drew migrants from the New England and Middle Atlantic states.

The majority of Western settlers came from the lower middle class. They traveled by wagon, pushcarts, and pack horses, and on flatboats. Whatever the starting point, the Ohio River was for most of them the main route or "grand track."

SEVENTEENTH- TO NINETEENTH-CENTURY FRONTIER LINES

During the course of the seventeenth century the frontier had advanced along

Free states and territories by Missouri Compromise

Slave states and territories by Missouri Compromise

Decision left to the territories

UNITED STATES · 1854

the rivers flowing into the Atlantic Ocean. The "fall line" was the seventeenth-century frontier established by fur traders and trappers. These first frontiersmen of America gave guns to the Indians and ironically handed them the means to resist the further advancement of settlers. Indian resistance and the Allegheny Mountains formed the frontier barriers of the eighteenth century. Traders made their way to the Delaware and Shawnee Indians along the Ohio. Scotch-Irish and German immigrants pushed up the Shenandoah Valley into the western part of Virginia and along the Piedmont region into the Carolinas. During the early decades of the nineteenth century, the Mississippi River was the line that established the farming frontier. By the 1800s, farmers had moved across the Alleghenies into Kentucky, Tennessee, and

Ohio, and by the 1820s had advanced the frontier line to the Mississippi and Missouri rivers. Aided by the development of steamboats and canals, the frontiersmen settled Ohio, Indiana, Illinois, southeastern Missouri, and Louisiana. By the 1840s, while the Middle West and prairie lands were being settled, Americans crossed the Great Plains to claim the Utah, California, and Oregon territories as well.

OCCUPATIONAL AND SOCIAL MOBILITY

The West was the "land of opportunity." To anyone of courage and ambition, it offered the chance to improve social and economic position. To discover which field suited him best, the new settler often tried his hand at several occupations, from

399

An ad from Harper's Weekly, *1863, offering land for sale in Illinois.*

farmer to miner to lumberman to cowboy.

This was a heady environment for the restless and eager European, one completely different from his Old World background. Most Europeans lived for centuries rooted to the same village and those who settled in America made a radical break with this tradition. Once they became Western migrants, they tended to break other ties with the past. The structure of their European society had dictated that men inherit the occupations and social status of their fathers. The American West had no such rigidity, offering instead mobility in economic and social life. Individual drive and economic success determined one's future, not ancestral background and geographical birthplace.

AGRICULTURAL EXPANSION

Westward expansion to a great extent was the history of agricultural expansion. Farmers drove westward in search of new areas in which to raise wheat, corn, tobacco, cotton, cattle, and sheep. Stimulated by the gigantic growth of transportation facilities, Western farmers were soon able to become part of a widening national market economy. By the 1840s, roads, canals, and steamboats were being replaced by the railroad as

the most convenient means of getting farm products to market. Many farmers switched from self-sufficient farming to commercial agriculture. "Money crops" could now be produced for sale in the distant markets of the Eastern seaboard and Europe. As Western agricultural entrepreneurs, their profits could, in turn, be poured back into the economy as they became ready consumers of the manufactured goods of Europe and the Northeast.

LIFE ON THE FRONTIER

Pioneer life in the West was never easy. The propaganda literature of the land speculators seductively glossed over the facts. The truth was that it took tremendous courage to cultivate virgin land in an isolated wilderness. There were few trained doctors to combat disease and malnutrition. Homes were initially primitive shacks or floorless cabins. Diets seldom consisted of more than corn and salt pork. Most people on the frontier lived lives of drudgery and loneliness. Animals tended to be scrawny. Hogs were often so thin they were referred to as "wind splitters." The early Western migrant lived with almost no governmental authority in a world only partly civilized by Eastern standards. As pioneers moved into the prairie lands, log cabins gave way to houses made of sod that were smoky, damp, and vermin-ridden. Water often had to be hauled for miles in a barrel. Without forests, the first fuel was dried buffalo dung burned in primitive stoves. Farmers were also frequently confronted with dishonest land speculators who overcharged them or misrepresented the quality of the land.

There were social restraints but little formal law. A man was expected to defend his women, his reputation, and his property. Among capital legal offenses were cattle or horse stealing and "dry-gulching," or shooting an enemy in the back. Officers of the law all too frequently resembled "Old

Turner on the Frontier and Democracy

. . the most important effect of the frontier has been in the promotion of democracy here and in Europe. As has been indicated, the frontier is productive of individualism. Complex society is precipitated by the wilderness into a kind of primitive organization based on the family. The tendency is anti-social. It produces antipathy to control, and particularly to any direct control. The taxgatherer is viewed as a representative of oppression. . . . The frontier individualism has from the beginning promoted democracy.

The frontier States that came into the Union in the first quarter of a century of its existence came in with democratic suffrage provisions, and had reactive effects of the highest importance upon the older States whose peoples were being attracted there. An extension of the franchise became essential.

—*Frederick Jackson Turner,*
The Frontier in American History

A Midwestern pioneer family in their sod dug-out home. Sod was cut into "bricks," dried, and then used to repair the walls and roof of the dugout.

Wright on the West as Imitative

" In their choice of political institutions the men of this section were imitative, not creative. They were not interested in making experiments. Their constitutional, like their domestic, architecture was patterned after that of the communities from which they had moved westward. However different their life during the period of frontier existence may have been from that of the older communities, they showed no substantial desire to retain its primitive characteristics when they established laws and constitutions of their own choice. To be sure they ordinarily, although not invariably, adopted the more democratic practices where there was variation in the East, but even in this respect they never varied from some well-established seaboard model, unless it was in the case of the proportion of elected officials. And even in this instance, which came not directly from the pioneering period but after a considerable interval had elapsed, one can trace precedents and some tendencies in this direction in the older states. In short, the result of the developments in the newer section seems to have been somewhat to accelerate the rate of growth of the democratic movement, not to change its direction. "

—*Benjamine F. Wright,* **Sources of Culture in the Middle West**

Necessity," an elderly justice of the peace on the Texas Plains: he literally knew no law, but he kept a mail-order catalogue bound in sheepskin on his bench, so that it would look like an impressive law book. Once, when a man pleaded guilty, "Old Necessity" opened his book at random and said, "I fine you $4.98." The man jumped up in protest, but his attorney remonstrated, "Sit down. Be thankful he opened it at trousers instead of at pianos!"

401

Although frontier life was difficult at first, it became less harsh as schools and churches were built, as neighbors became less remote, as transportation improved, and as manufactured goods became cheaper.

THE INDIANS

American settlement of the West increased proportionately to the decline of the Indian tribes. After 1815 many tribes were rendered helpless by military action and the advancing frontiersmen.

One of the basic problems in Indian-white relations was that the white settlers came to occupy and exploit the land, and had no interest in preserving the Indians' way of life. Thus, the main contact with the tribes other than through trade was in open conflict over possession of the land. Most frontiersmen saw the Indian as an adversary in war, and a very brutal one at that. Between the two races, there were great cultural differences. The Indians had no concept of the Judeo-Christian religious tradition or of the political, economic, and social ideas that governed European civilization. Because the life style of the Indians was different from their own, the Europeans immediately judged them to be inferior. The white settlers knew little of the nature of Indian society, they did not understand the limited authority of tribal leaders and group use of land. Some early writers saw the Indians as innocent, child-like persons spending their time in the pursuit of pleasure—the romantic picture of the naturally free man. But the frontier conflicts with the tribes soon led most settlers to view the Indians as bloodthirsty savages. Only those settlers who lived far from the frontier developed a desire for justice for the Southern and Western tribes.

The United States government had no policy toward the Indian tribes, other than to provide for their removal westward by treaty or through military force. After 1800 the government moved to secure treaties with the tribes for their removal from areas east of the Mississippi River. The ceding of lands in the Old Northwest that opened up the Michigan and Illinois territories caused the tribes to form the *Indian Confederacy* under the Shawnee Chief, Tecumseh, to resist further white encroachments. The defeat of this confederacy at Tippecanoe and the subsequent departure of the British at the end of the War of 1812 left the Indians at the mercy of the Americans. The same treatment of the Indian tribes was carried on after 1815: treaties for Indian removals were reinforced by a new series of military forts in the West. Some tribes settled peacefully on reservations west of the Mississippi, but as already noted, the Seminoles in Florida offered tough resistance and tragedy befell the Cherokees and Creeks in their midwinter forced march to the trans-Mississippi area.

Under Jackson, several bills were passed providing permanent Indian homes on reservations, and the Indians were forced to sign treaties accepting these arrangements. Congress created a Bureau of Indian Affairs to oversee the new system. The Indians were to receive payment for the lands they relinquished and annual government support; no white man without a license was to enter Indian country.

In spite of the good intentions of some government officials, the pressure of the westward movement undermined all efforts to protect the tribes. Many traders insisted on payment of Indian debts before the tribes could be compensated for lands taken; consequently, many tribes received next to nothing for the massive territories they had relinquished. Moreover, after 1854 the Government Land Office began to sell Indian lands in spite of the law. In addition to geographical confinement, the tribes suffered other disasters in ensuing decades. Attempts were made to dissolve their social organization by creating internal dissension, and eventually warfare between the major tribes themselves. Massacres, diseases often transmitted by the white man, and

DEVELOPMENT OF NORTHERN AGRICULTURE

starvation helped to diminish the Indian population. Said one Oregon settler, "they [the Indians] came to be thought of as game to be shot or vermin to be destroyed." Many, like the Californian Indians and the tribes living in the area from the Mohave Desert to the Great Lakes, were exterminated when their food supply was wiped out. The relentless slaughtering of the buffalo, the introduction of smallpox, tuberculosis, venereal disease, and whiskey, killed more Indians than did warfare. By the outbreak of the Civil War, only the Plains Indians remained a significant obstacle to the westward march of the white settler.

RESULTS OF WESTWARD EXPANSION

The development of the West initially dealt a severe blow to sectionalism and strongly promoted a feeling of nationalism. Western expansion decreased America's economic and cultural dependence on England, and helped fuse the United States into a country with a single national identity. Economic growth created important urban centers West of the Appalachians which consumed the industrial products of the East. Gradually, however, the social and cultural growth of the West directly affected the sectional struggle over the expansion of slavery, thus hastening the clash between the North and South. Finally, the Western part of the country was also in the forefront of the movement to democratize American political life, to broaden the suffrage and to make more offices elective rather than appointive.

Farming remained the most important economic activity of the northern part of the United States in the years before the Civil War. Corn was the predominant crop, and the famous "corn belt" reached from Pittsburgh, Pennsylvania, to Iowa. Wheat, which ranked second to corn as an important commercial crop, was grown principally in eastern Ohio, western New York, and Pennsylvania. Other major crops were oats, barley, rye, and flax. Dairy farming developed as a significant business in New England and the Middle Atlantic States. Livestock provided milk and meat for farm families as well as an increasing commercial income. The improvements in transportation, which included the development of the refrigerator car, facilitated the shipping of hogs, cattle, and sheep from the Mississippi Valley to the seaboard cities, and enabled new industries related to agriculture to develop in the West. Cincinnati and Chicago became important meat-packing and flour-milling centers in the 1840s and 1850s.

From 1838 to 1858, the North grew extensively in the production of milk and fruits. Dairy farming became a thriving business by 1850. Fruit orchards which produced apples, melons, strawberries, blackberries, and peaches, abounded on the Northern soil. Their value and development further increased when an Englishman invented the tin can, providing an excellent method for packaging and storage of fruits and vegetables.

Corn became the North's principal commercial crop. It was eaten off the cob, baked into bread, and distilled into "likker." The national diet was mainly corn bread and corn-fed pork. Throughout the year corn was used to fatten hogs and in winter it was fed to cattle. By 1860 American corn production had reached a record 838 million bushels, an increase of over 40 percent in less than ten years.

Supported by a sizeable international market as well as by domestic consumption, wheat production, too, soared rapidly. Wheat had the distinct advantage of being less bulky than corn, making it cheaper to transport and therefore more profitable.

An important boost was given to Northern agriculture when new domestic markets began to open. As the nation's population and frontiers expanded, new consumers could be fed (by utilizing improved transportation facilities). Farmers found markets among the loggers of the northern woods, among the lead miners of Iowa and Wisconsin, and the gold miners of California. The frontier forts of the federal government also became significant customers.

FOREIGN CONSUMPTION OF AMERICAN FARM PRODUCE

Until the depression of 1837, much money was to be made in the marketing of agricultural produce. A series of international circumstances added to the growing demand for foodstuffs. Europe was beginning to industrialize, bringing about larger urban centers which depended on outside sources for food. Moreover, European tariffs and the currency exchange were being simplified and stabilized. Thus, the American farmer found himself the beneficiary of worldwide business expansion.

The depression of the late 1830s dealt American overseas trade in agricultural produce a hard blow, and it was not until the early 1840s that European economic recovery again created a demand for American farm products.

International trade went from a low of 125 million dollars in 1843 to 687 million dollars in 1860. In this great revitalization of America's foreign trade, wheat and flour were ahead of all other exports. Industrialized Europe needed American foodstuffs, and because the United States imported more than she exported during this period, agriculture was the chief factor in maintaining a reasonable balance of trade.

MECHANIZATION

By the early nineteenth century generations of Americans were still farming new land in the same way it had been cultivated for centuries. After he picked out his land and officially registered it, the farmer built a sod hut, or a one-room cabin out of rough logs, and a small barn. A patch of earth was set aside for a vegetable garden, which became his wife's responsibility. The farmer fenced in his main field, usually at a cost of $1.25 an acre. Because the ground was hard, his initial plowing usually had to be done by a hired team of professional "breakers." Steering huge plows drawn by a dozen oxen, these "breakers" would cut the first furrows in the land. Then the farmer would himself dig deeper holes into the furrows with an ax, and in these holes he would plant Indian corn, pumpkins and beans. After the first season with the ground sufficiently broken, the farmer and his family would themselves do all the plowing and planting.

Increased mechanization was a vital factor in the increased output of Northern farms. In 1800, farmers had only wooden plows and harrows, pulled by oxen and horses, and a few hand tools. Corn, for example, was planted, cultivated, and reaped by hand. Without benefit of mechanization, the most a farmer could cultivate was a little over an acre a day.

Though farmers tended to resist change, mechanization was essential for agriculture to grow into a commercial enterprise. The men most responsible for revolutionary advances in the development of farm machinery were John Deere, Cyrus McCormick, and Obed Hussey. Deere, an Illinois blacksmith, invented a steel plow in 1830. This plow was light enough for a single man to sling over his shoulders, and capable of cutting clean, deep furrows. Deere continued to make improvements in his original design, and by 1858 he was turning out 13,000 steel plows a year. McCormick of Virginia and Hussey of Ohio built reapers which greatly reduced the labor necessary for harvesting. With one of these steel-toothed, horse-drawn machines, it became possible for a single man to do the work of five men with scythes. The reapers did not achieve widespread use until McCormick moved his plant to Chicago in 1848 and sent salesmen with demonstration models to the frontier areas. Ten years later, McCormick was manufacturing 500 reapers a month and still could not keep up with the demand.

Further mechanization occurred in the 1850s with the invention of mechanical threshers, cultivators, hayrakes, mowers, and reapers which reduced the need for field hands.

The manufacture of farm machinery became an important national industry. Whereas in 1800 the average farmer rarely spent more than twenty dollars for his tools, by 1857 it was expected that a farmer with one hundred acres of land would need six hundred dollars' worth of machinery. By the time of the Civil War, it was estimated that a total of 250 million dollars was invested in farm implements and machines.

SHIFTS IN SPECIALIZATION

Because of developments in transportation, farm mechanization, and population, there were all sorts of shifts in the types of specialization characteristic of the particular geographical areas. Farmers in the

Cyrus Hall McCormick is shown with his agriculture inventions: the reaper and mower, the self-binding harvester, and the iron mower.

Northeast stopped producing wheat, corn, hogs, and sheep for sale and concentrated instead on growing fruits and vegetables, and on dairying. They poured their products into the cities of New York, Boston, and Philadelphia, where they had a distinct price advantage over competitors from other regions. The Northeast surpassed the West in truck gardening, with New York leading in apple production, and peaches becoming a principal product of Delaware and New Jersey. The production of certain products gradually moved westward. New York, Pennsylvania, and Virginia were eventually exceeded in the production of corn by Illinois, Missouri, and Ohio. In 1840 the leading wheat states were New York, Pennsylvania, and Ohio; in 1860 the lead was held by Illinois, Indiana, Wisconsin, and Michigan. These staples could no longer be produced profitably in the East in competition with the richer soils of the West. However, the East did keep its leadership in the production of oats, rye, and barley.

Competition from the West, spurred largely by a drop in the cost of shipping by canals and railroads, also drew meat producers from the New England and the Middle Atlantic states. In 1840, New York, Pennsylvania, and New England were the principal cattle-raising states. By 1850 they had been replaced by Illinois, Indiana, Iowa, and Texas. Ohio soon outranked New York in sheep production. Hog raising also moved westward with corn production.

COMMERCIALIZATION

The most significant change in agriculture before the Civil War was the swing from self-sufficient to commercial farming. When transportation improved, farmers were able to turn more and more of their land over to production of crops for sale rather than simply for home use. Commercial production was also stimulated by the mechanization of farm equipment. Investments in machinery forced farmers to grow more crops in order to pay for the machinery. Larger crops entailed the buying of more land, and increased acreage meant still more machines and still further production. By the 1850s large-scale commercial agriculture was firmly established as far west as Illinois and Wisconsin.

When world prices for agricultural goods collapsed in 1857, the event was a particularly devastating blow to American wheat farmers. As a protective measure they began to combine into associations and cooperatives. With little success, they called for state and federal regulation of railroads and other speculative industries responsible for increases in farming costs. Further, they demanded free land for homesteads and the establishment of agricultural colleges, to be financed by the federal government, where farm youths could learn the modern scientific principles of agriculture which were becoming fundamental to successful commercial farming. Not until the Presidency of Abraham Lincoln were some of these demands fulfilled.

SCIENTIFIC FARMING

Meanwhile, other attempts were made in the antebellum period to lessen the damage being done to America's landed heritage through unplanned cultivation of the soil. Because of the growing importance of agriculture to the nation's economy, attention was being turned to new methods for utilizing and preserving the land. Jesse Buel, a New York agricultural reformer, introduced basic concepts for a more scientific and farsighted approach to farming: "By draining, manuring, ploughing, harrowing, hoeing . . . we may preserve, unimpaired, the natural fertility of our soils." By 1830, some farmers were already aware of the necessity for soil conservation, the benefits to be gained from the rotation of crops, and the value of fertilizers for greatly enriching the soil.

County and state agricultural societies were organized to study the improved farming methods and promote their usage. Agricultural fairs, magazines, books and school courses multiplied in the 1840s and 1850s.

Planting sweet potatoes on a South Carolina plantation in 1862.

DEVELOPMENT OF SOUTHERN AGRICULTURE

In the years before the Civil War the South remained principally agricultural. Its chief staple crops for export were cotton, tobacco, sugar, rice, and hemp. Cotton was the leading crop. By the 1840s cotton was the major agricultural product of Mississippi, Alabama, South Carolina, Georgia, and Florida. In the steady expansion of production, cotton raising proceeded in a westerly direction, with over 1.3 of the total output of 4.3 million bales coming from west of the Mississippi by the time of the Civil War. In the upper South, Virginia remained a leading producer of tobacco, but by the 1850s the states of Kentucky, Tennessee, and Missouri were raising more than half of the nation's tobacco crop. As a result, older sections of the South, such as Maryland, Virginia, and North Carolina, shifted to some extent to diversified farming. Rice was still produced in the Carolinas and in Georgia. Rice growing reached overwhelming proportions until the 1850s when higher slave and land prices drew farmers to an increased production of cotton. Sugar-cane growing developed in Louisiana and along the Mississippi River north of New Orleans. Hemp became Kentucky's major export crop.

Many other crops were also produced in the South for home consumption. For example, corn, another important Southern crop, was raised by almost every farmer. In fact, it accounted for more acreage and had a greater value than cotton, rice, and tobacco combined. Corn farmers utilized their crop in corn bread, corn pone, hominy grits, whiskey, and fed corn to their livestock and poultry. In addition, yeoman farmers in the upper South grew wheat, oats, rye, and flax, and the Southern border states produced Irish and sweet potatoes.

Land and labor were expensive, as was modern machinery. The larger planters concentrated their efforts on producing a cash crop for the commercial market. Virginia sent its tobacco to the Northeast. Cotton growers sent crops to dealers in New Orleans, Mobile, Augusta, Charleston, and New England. New York merchants who were responsible for selling much of the South's cotton in turn imported most of the supplies needed by Southern planters. A Natchez newspaper commented in 1842 that "the large planters, for the most part, sell their cotton in Liverpool; buy their wines in London or Havre; their Negro clothing in Boston; their plantation implements and supplies in Cincinnati; and their groceries and fancy articles in New Orleans."

Many farmers in the upper South showed an early interest in the improvement of farming techniques and methods. In the days of George Washington and Thomas Jefferson, planters in Virginia had already experimented with fertilizers and with crop rotation. In the middle of the nineteenth century Edmund Ruffin introduced the use of marl to Virginia planters. Marl, an earth rich in calcium, helped to counteract the acidity of fields that had become worn out with the planting of tobacco. Land enriched by marl additives eventually doubled and tripled the output of corn and wheat. Other planters experimented with contour planting to keep erosion under control, and with new kinds of plows, agricultural machinery, and improved breeds of cattle.

407

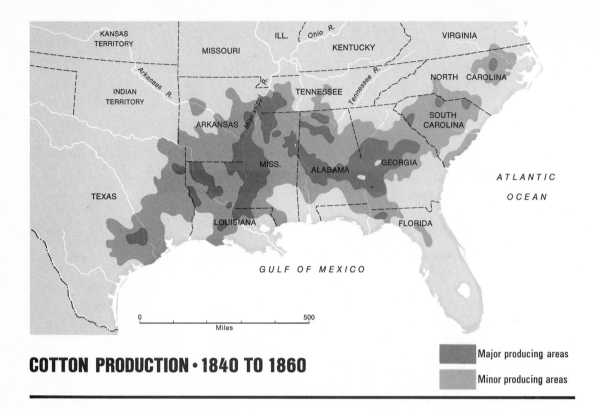

COTTON PRODUCTION · 1840 TO 1860

Major producing areas

Minor producing areas

COTTON

The South never became industrialized in the years before the Civil War. Her economy was based essentially on cotton raising. In the colonial period, cotton was produced mainly for home use, but before the beginning of the nineteenth century, a series of developments increased the commercial demand for the crop: Eli Whitney's cotton gin created a practical means for rapidly removing the seeds from raw cotton, Britain made important technological advances in her textile industry, and John Kay's flying shuttle greatly speeded up the processes of spinning and weaving. These processes were further modernized by Richard Arkwright's water frame, James Hargreaves' spinning jenny, and the power loom invented by Edmund Cartwright.

After 1815, cotton played a critical role in the developing market economy of the entire nation. It fed the Northern textile industry and provided consumer goods for every region in the country. It represented half of the exports of the United States, and paid for a major percentage of its imports. By 1860, the South had become the major cotton supplier for the world, with Mississippi the leading producer among the states.

The plantation system provided a capitalistic type of farm organization for the raising of cotton as well as other staple cash crops. Plantation owners made extremely heavy investments in land and slave labor. Some were as successful as Stephen Duncan of Natchez, Mississippi. In 1850 Duncan owned one thousand slaves and had an annual income from his cotton crop of about $170,000.

SLAVERY AND AGRICULTURE

After 1800 the use of slave labor increased rapidly in the South and unified

TABLE 11-1.   SLAVE POPULATION OF THE UNITED STATES*

States	1790	1800	1810	1820	1830	1840	1850
Alabama				41,879	117,549	253,532	342,844
Arkansas				1,617	4,576	19,935	47,100
California							
Connecticut	2,759	951	310	97	25	17	
Delaware	8,887	6,153	4,177	4,509	3,292	2,605	2,290
Florida					15,501	25,717	39,310
Georgia	29,264	59,404	105,218	149,654	217,531	280,944	381,682
Illinois			168	917	747	331	
Indiana		135	237	190	3	3	
Iowa						16	
Kentucky	11,830	40,343	80,561	126,732	165,213	182,258	210,981
Louisiana			34,660	69,064	109,588	168,452	244,809
Maine					2		
Maryland	103,036	105,635	111,502	107,397	102,994	89,737	90,368
Massachusetts					1		
Michigan			24		32		
Mississippi		3,489	17,088	32,814	65,659	195,211	309,878
Missouri			3,011	10,222	25,091	58,240	87,422
New Hampshire	158	8			3	1	
New Jersey	11,423	12,422	10,851	7,557	2,254	674	236
New York	21,324	20,343	15,017	10,088	75	4	
North Carolina	100,572	133,296	168,824	205,017	245,601	245,817	288,548
Ohio					6	3	
Pennsylvania	3,737	1,706	795	211	403	64	
Rhode Island	952	381	108	48	17	5	
South Carolina	107,094	146,151	196,365	238,475	315,401	327,038	384,984
Tennessee	3,417	13,584	44,535	80,107	141,603	183,059	239,459
Texas							58,161
Vermont	17						
Virginia	293,427	345,796	392,518	425,153	469,757	449,087	472,528
Wisconsin						11	
Territories							
D. of C.†		3,244	5,395	6,377	6,119	4,694	3,687
Minnesota							
New Mexico							
Oregon							
Utah							26
Aggregate	697,897	893,041	1,191,364	1,538,038‡	2,009,043	2,487,455	3,204,313

*The number of slaves in the United States in 1850 was 3,204,313. Of these, 2,957,657 were black or of unmixed African descent, and 246,656 were mulatto.

†The District of Columbia is technically a federal area governed by Congress, but has been placed with territories for the purpose of simplification.

‡Total less 87 deducted to make the aggregate, published incorrectly in 1820.

From: J. D. Debow, *Statistical View of the United States.* New York: Gordon & Breach, 1970, p. 82.

the section's interests, first economically and then politically.

By the early nineteenth century, the heavy demand for cheap labor in the almost exclusively agricultural South eliminated most sentiment in that section for ending the institution of slavery. Planters of cotton, rice, and sugar relied on unskilled workers for the simple, backbreaking tasks on their farms. Slaves—black men, women, and children—provided the easiest solution. When not at work in the fields, they could clear the owner's land, build his fences, and perform any of the many chores needed to maintain the plantation.

From the turn of the century to the beginning of the Civil War, the number of slaves swelled from 857,000 to 3,838,000. While most Southern farmers wanted to be slave holders, most slaves were owned by a very small proportion of the population. By 1860 there were about 12,240,000 people in the fifteen slave states: eight million whites, four million black slaves, and 240,000 free blacks. Of this population only about two million either owned or had some connection with the owning of slaves. To be a planter a man had to have thirty or more slaves—at least fifteen field hands and fifteen to carry out other tasks. A planter also employed an overseer to manage his laborers. There were about 25,000 men in the planter class in the entire Southern population. Though small in number, they were highly envied; and those in the so-called Southern gentry, men with ten to thirty slaves, dreamed of joining this exclusive group above them. Below the gentry were the bulk of the slave-owning whites who usually had five slaves or less and worked in the fields with them. The rest of the small farmers in the South, three-fourths of the population, owned no slaves at all but were usually trying to make enough money to buy a few. At the very bottom of the social and economic ladder

Slave quarters on a Southern plantation. In 1860 there were about four million blacks in slavery in the South.

were the poor whites and free blacks, living on the poorest land or in the towns, barely able to make a living.

AS ECONOMIC INSTITUTION

By 1815 the entire economy of the South was closely tied to the cultivation of cotton, and cotton was yoked to the use of slave labor. Whereas the overall size of farms was generally declining in the other parts of the nation, the trend in the South was distinctly toward larger agricultural units. The slave population was concentrated in the staple crop areas where the need for labor was constant.

Slaves were considered, and legally defined, as "property." They were sold at auction together with paintings, furniture, land, and other valuables. When the importation of slaves was abolished by the federal government in 1808, politically prominent Southerners saw the ruling as a direct attack on the constitutional right of private property. Planters had made enormous capital investments in slaves (some sold for as much as $1,800). Because of this deep financial commitment and because of the continuing need for more farm laborers, a thriving *internal* slave trade developed. Farmers in the upper South, who found that keeping a large number of slaves was no longer profitable, sold them to the lower South. Slave prices followed those of the staple crops, and many slave traders became wealthy. Between 1830 and 1860 about 700,000 slaves were transported from the border states to the deep South. Isaac Franklin and John Armfield collected slaves from Maryland and Virginia, deposited them at their "model jail" in Alexandria, and then shipped them to the huge slave depot at Natchez. Before their retirement, each of these traders had cleared over half a million dollars. Thus, slave trading was a big business.

Students of American history have always been interested in whether the use of slave labor was actually profitable to the South. After studying slave prices, hiring rates, the prices of cotton and land, interest rates, the natural increase of the slave population, and life expectancy and upkeep of the individual slave, several historians in recent years have come to the conclusion that the use of slave labor was extremely profitable to the planter class as a group. Yet slavery may actually have had a detrimental effect on the economic development of the South as a section. Slave labor made possible the South's continued emphasis on staple crop agriculture, but capital invested in slaves left little for investment in transportation and industry, and agricultural profits from the South often went to the North to pay for marketing. As a result, the South remained far behind the rest of the country in manufacturing and urbanization. Furthermore, the concentration of wealth in the hands of a few, and the presence of a large slave class and a growing populace of low-income whites, greatly limited the development of a consumer market within the South. Purchasing power was low and local markets for local goods were virtually nonexistent.

The stubbornness of the planter-aristocracy in clinging to the status derived from slave holding and to their rural way of life helped to create a rigid economic system that prevented change and diversification.

THE PLANTER CLASS

It was essentially the planter class, the smallest and wealthiest segment of the Southern population, that set the tone of Southern society. Despite its size in relation to the total population, this class was looked up to by all other groups and it dominated the economic, social, and political life of the South. Most Southerners wanted to become planters and thus, in spite of the great economic spread between the classes, there was no overt class conflict. The planters controlled society and politics.

The emphasis on white supremacy became the key technique of planter control.

For the planters, land was their birthright, and they were determined to protect and develop it. The sons of many wealthy planters of the Old South went to the Southwest to settle and hopefully, through toil and wise management, to build plantations of their own. Most of these prospective planters spent their early years in crude surroundings, creating agricultural estates in such states as Alabama, Mississippi, and Louisiana, without benefit of conveniences. As they made money, they often built beautiful mansions and allowed themselves more leisure.

On the whole the planters lived well, some lavishly. Their style of life was rustic, with hunting, horse-racing, and card playing as principal diversions. It was a society characterized by hospitality but not cultural attainments.

SLAVERY AS A LABOR SYSTEM

The system of slavery locked the black man into strict servitude from which he had no escape unless it was willed by his owner. Slaves were dressed shabbily and lived in flimsy cabins near the master's home. They ate mainly salt pork and corn meal. It was legal to beat slaves, but it was illegal to teach them to read or write. They were not permitted to own property or firearms or to assemble in public in groups over five. Marriages were not considered binding and slaves could not leave the plantation without a letter or a pass.

There were basically two approaches to the use of slave labor in the antebellum South: the gang system and the task system. The cultivation of cotton was ideal for the gang system which enabled one overseer to watch as many as forty slaves. Cotton was a hardy crop, not easily damaged by unskilled labor. Picking required no age limits, no mental effort, no health standards. Slaves worked from dawn until dusk with only short periods of rest for meals. Under the task system used in the cultivation of tobacco, rice, and sugar, the slave had to be trained carefully to care for the plants and harvest them. Each slave was also assigned a specific amount of work. Once he had completed his daily task, he was free to spend the rest of the day in his own garden or at some other job.

In addition to owning slaves, the Southern farmer or tradesman hired slaves. The hired slaves generally were offered better food and clothing, and sometimes even a weekly allowance. The hired slaves were usually found in the towns, where the master-slave relationship was not as strong as on the plantation. These slaves, who could hire their own time, were able to mingle with free blacks in church and social affairs.

Slaves who fared best in the agricultural regions of the South were the domestics—butlers, cooks, housemaids, personal maids, and coachmen. The labor of house slaves was lighter, and their food, clothing, and housing infinitely better than that of field hands. Some were even taught to read and write, and some traveled extensively with their owners as maids and valets.

Below the house slave in the occupational scale were the skilled workers and craftsmen. These were the trained carpenters and blacksmiths, and the shoemaker, and chair maker, or harness maker; these brought higher prices on the internal slave market and consequently received better treatment from their owners.

Commanding the highest price among plantation slaves was the foreman or "driver." He was the right-hand man of the plantation superintendent. He called the hands to work, laid out their specific chores, and checked individual quotas at the day's end. The "driver" was a valuable aide to the plantation owner. His food rations and his clothing were better than those of the other field hands, and occasionally he was awarded a bottle of rum.

Nat Turner's Plans for Rebellion

❝ . . . on the 12th of May, 1828, I heard a loud noise in the heavens, and the Spirit instantly appeared to me and said the Serpent was loosened, and Christ had laid down the yoke he had borne for the sins of men, and that I should take it on and fight against the Serpent, for the time was fast approaching when the first should be last and the last should be first. . . . And by signs in the heavens that it would make known to me when I should commence the great work—and until the first sign appeared, I should conceal it from the knowledge of men—And on the appearance of the sign, (the eclipse of the sun last February) I should arise and prepare myself, and slay my enemies with their own weapons. ❞

—The Confessions of Nat Turner

EXPLOITATION

In 1838 Calhoun told Congress: "We see it [slavery] now in its true light, and regard it as the most safe and stable basis for free institutions in the world." Calhoun's words were strongly contradicted by the New England historian Richard Hildreth, whose visit to the South left him convinced that slavery "is a far more deadly and disastrous thing, more fatal to all the hopes, the sentiments, the rights of humanity, than almost any other system of servitude which has existed in any other community."

The slaves themselves gave evidence of the dehumanizing nature of the system. Frederick Douglass, who fled from slavery in Maryland in 1838, wrote, "perpetual toil; no marriage; no husband, no wife, ignorance, brutality, licentiousness; whips, scourges, chains, auctions, jails and separations; an embodiment of all the woes the imagination can conceive." There was usually a fifteen-minute lunch break for cold

Thomas R. Gray Comments on Nat Turner

❝ He is a complete fanatic, or plays his part most admirably. On other subjects he possesses an uncommon share of intelligence with a mind capable of attaining any thing; but warped and perverted by the influence of early impressions. He is below the ordinary stature, though strong and active, having the true negro face, every feature of which is strongly marked. I shall not attempt to describe the effect of his narrative, as told and commented on by himself, in the condemned hole of the prison. The calm, deliberate composure with which he spoke of his late deeds and intentions, the expression of his fiend-like face when excited by enthusiasm, still bearing the stains of the blood of helpless innocence about him; clothed with rags and covered with chains; yet daring to raise his manacled hands to heaven, with a spirit soaring above the attributes of man; I looked on him my blood curdled in my veins.

I will not shock the feelings of humanity, nor wound afresh the bosoms of the disconsolate sufferers in this unparalleled and inhuman massacre, by detailing the deeds of their fiend-like barbarity. ❞

—The Confessions of Nat Turner

bacon rations. Each slave was assigned a weight of cotton he would be expected to pick. If he failed, he was whipped; if he succeeded, his assignment was increased. Once a week he was given a food allowance which generally consisted of bacon and corn. He lived in a dark cabin. He slept on a plank, a "foot wide and ten feet long." There was another stick of wood for a pillow, and occasionally some coarse burlap for a blanket.

ESCAPE FROM SLAVERY

The notion that slaves were essentially contented has little basis in documented fact. Many of the slaves tried, to little avail, to buy their freedom. Owners were in constant fear of conspiracies and revolts, a fear that kept most of the South on edge in the period before the Civil War. There were regular, though essentially unorganized uprisings, and with each of these the brutality of the reprisals increased. Runaways were tracked down with bloodhounds, and once caught, were beaten severely and frequently branded as troublemakers.

Perhaps the most successful method of escape from slavery was the "Underground Railroad" to the North. Most of the "conductors" on the railroad were former slaves who had successfully escaped from the South or blacks who had been born free in the North. Over three thousand of these railroad workers managed to assist many slaves in their journey to the North. However, the Underground Railroad, together with the famous Nat Turner rebellion of 1831, served to make treatment of the slave

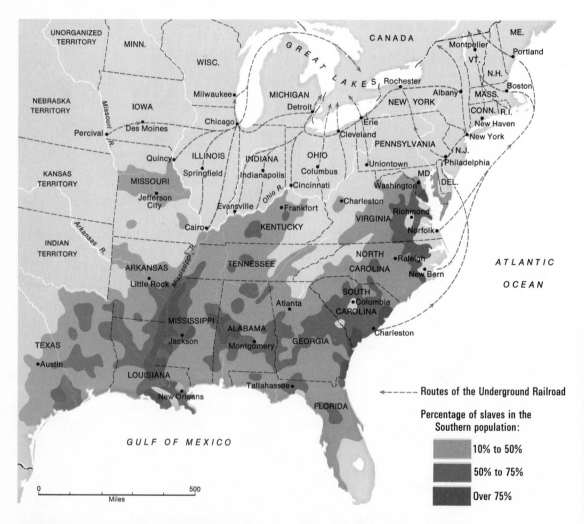

Routes of the Underground Railroad

Percentage of slaves in the Southern population:

10% to 50%

50% to 75%

Over 75%

SLAVERY AND THE UNDERGROUND RAILROAD · 1840 TO 1860

and free blacks in the South even more restrictive and harsh.

Nat Turner was a Virginia Negro preacher who led the most sensational of all the slave revolts, and certainly the one that had the greatest repercussions. His total band at first numbered no more than eight, but he believed that his plans were divinely inspired. On an August evening in 1831, Turner and his small squad killed Nat's master and his family. Then they pushed through the countryside, gathering additional recruits along the way until the avenging blacks numbered seventy. On the way they came upon sixty whites, whom they seized and murdered. Their rampage lasted for forty-eight hours, and during this time the terrified white population in the vicinity mobilized volunteer reprisal forces and called out the state militia. Before they were caught, Turner and his band managed to kill more than sixty white persons. After a brief imprisonment Turner was sent to the gallows, together with about 20 other blacks.

Turner's was the last of the organized slave revolts, but insurrection panics occurred many times between 1831 and 1860. Open revolts had little chance of success. Night patrols were on constant alert throughout the South. A great deal of money poured into the coffers of the local municipal and county police to pay for increased vigilance.

COMMERCE AND TRANSPORTATION

Increased trade created a demand for faster, cheaper transportation. As this demand was met by new means of land and water travel, the transportation improvements themselves spurred a new thrust forward by the economy. A growing volume of imports was being bought by Americans, and these added steadily to the already acute need for swift and reliable domestic transportation. Seaport cities on the coast had to have a dependable means for distributing goods to the interior. This was particularly true in the 1840s and 1850s when the country experienced a revitalization of foreign trade.

IMPORTS AND EXPORTS

For thirty years after 1830, United States imports and exports increased greatly. The country imported more than it exported. It remained basically an importer of manufactured goods and a supplier of raw materials to foreign buyers. The leading imported materials were textiles and iron products, while cotton held prominence as the major single export, bringing in 191 million dollars in 1860. For thirty years before the Civil War, American whalers sailed the oceans of the world, making the United States the leading exporter of whalebone and whale oil. After gold was discovered in California, it too gained immediate significance as an export.

Throughout this era, Great Britain was not only the leading foreign supplier of the United States but also its best customer. Trade with England rose as the West Indian market declined. The islands, once major consumers of American goods, accounted for only 20 percent of the country's exports in the 1820s, and then purchases fell sharply to a mere 7 percent in the years before the Civil War.

INTERNATIONAL TRADE

American shipowners, merchants, and manufacturers were hurt by the Panic of 1837 and the depression that followed. Within ten years, however, internal economic recovery and a series of favorable foreign developments gave a tremendous boost to overseas trade. In 1846, Britain repealed "The Corn Laws," which protected domestic agriculture, thereby opening up a large market for American wheat. That same year, America's passage of lower tariff rates attracted a greater flow of European manufactured goods to the United States. As a result, the combined value of American exports and imports increased from 222 million dollars in 1840 to 318 million dollars in 1850, and 687 million dollars in 1860.

Most of this commerce was with Europe— American wheat, flour and cotton were exchanged for the products of foreign factories—but trade inroads were being made in other parts of the world. Early nineteenth-century American merchant ships stopped in the Philippines, India, and Java. By the 1840s, the country had signed a trade agreement with Siam and American merchants were active in the China trade. At Canton, the central Chinese port, American furs were traded for tea and spices. By the treaties of 1842 through 1844, signed by China with the Western powers, including the United States, five Chinese ports were opened to trade. Specified customs duties and collectors were for the first time established, and all crimes committed in Chinese ports were placed under the jurisdiction of the country whose national was involved.

A significant development in international trade at this time was the first commercial contact between the United States and Japan, a nation isolated for two cen-

turies from the rest of the world. In an effort to pry open the islands, the United States government sent Commodore Matthew C. Perry and his fleet of steam warships to Japan in 1853. Though Perry had the strength of his warships to back up any claims or entreaties, his initial dealings

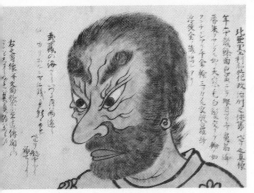

Two Japanese renditions of Commodore Perry. Perry was sent to Japan to end a 200-year "closed door" policy.

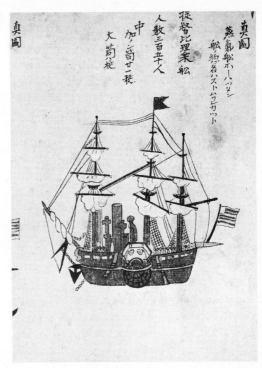

Japanese drawing of Commodore Perry's steam warship, the Powhatan.

with the Japanese government were exploratory and peaceful. He presented the Japanese emperor with letters from President Pierce and a gift consisting of an array of Western gadgetry. In 1854 he returned and found that Japanese officials, who in the meantime had apparently considered the alternative to a peaceful agreement, were eager to come to terms. After Perry secured the opening of two small ports to American trade, the United States Department of State sent diplomat Townsend Harris to Japan as its first American consul. Harris' charm and diplomatic abilities were even more persuasive than Perry's warships. He managed to convince the Japanese that the United States had no territorial ambitions in the Pacific, and obtained further commercial concessions in the 1858 agreement. In 1860 relations were firmly established by a visit of the first Japanese mission to the United States.

DOMESTIC TRADE

While American foreign trade grew to five times its previous level from 1843 to 1860, domestic trade outpaced it, expanding at twice that rate. The vitality of the international trade helped to spur domestic commerce, for the deposit of commodities for export at port cities created a great deal of business for home carriers.

Expansion of internal trade was also strongly aided by population increases and by regional tendencies toward specialization which created interdependency. As the various areas began to specialize in distinct commodities, the need for the exchange of goods grew. These exchanges were further served by the mining of gold in California, which produced a stable monetary basis for transactions. The invention of the telegraph and the development of railroads also made speedier transactions possible and greatly improved the collection of bill payments. With a rapid rise in the amount of money in circulation, the pace of domestic economic activity also quickened.

The country's excellent system of waterways was a great asset to growing domestic commercial traffic. Coastal vessels carried

417

Southern cotton to the cities of New York and New England. Steamboats plied the Mississippi River, hauling both freight and passengers, and controlling the flow of goods from farm to market until the elaborate canal network began to divert much of the business from the river to the Great Lakes. The heavy traffic on the Mississippi had accounted for the preeminence of New Orleans as the nation's principal trade center. Canals made it possible to ship the huge exports of the rapidly expanding West more easily to Eastern markets, and New York gradually replaced New Orleans as the commercial capital of the country.

The USS Constitution. *Clipper ships, sometimes averaging 433 miles in one day, were a vital link between the East and West Coasts in the 1850s, cutting the travel time around South America from five to three months.*

CLIPPER SHIPS

The construction of ocean-going vessels was considerably affected by the sharp increases in the value and volume of trade, and by the deposit of goods at the larger ports. The old three-masted packet ships were no longer fast enough to meet the needs of the day. Radical design changes in the packets produced the clipper ships, a fleet of sailing vessels that even today remain unmatched in their beauty. They were extremely swift and in a favorable wind could actually outsail the steamships that ultimately replaced them.

The launching in 1845 of the *Rainbow* ushered in the era of the famed clipper ships. Her hull was long and sleek, her

stern rounded, and her bow concave. Her tall, raking masts held an enormous spread of canvas that moved her 750 tons with ease through the water. Subsequently, clipper ships set records for speed that helped to give the United States a more prominent share of the international carrying trade than it had ever had before. The clippers of builder Donald McKay of Newburyport, Massachusetts, made naval history and established McKay as the most successful of the clipper-ship builders. His *Flying Cloud, Sovereign of the Seas,* and *Great Republic* held supremacy for speed. On a voyage from New York to San Francisco, the *Flying Cloud* averaged an incredible 433 miles a day.

Gold rushes in California and Australia provided an excellent opportunity for travelers to use clipper ships. Moreover, when the British Navigation Acts, which had restricted trade in the ports of the British empire to British ships, were repealed, the clippers carried the world's tea cargoes. Even though their major use was in trade with Europe and the Far East, their best performance was in the 1850s as a vital link between the Atlantic and Pacific coasts. The clipper ships took three months to make the voyage around the Horn of South America, whereas the older boats took over five months.

Until 1875 the clippers carried the fast freight and passenger traffic of the world, but years earlier their supremacy began to be threatened. The Panama Railroad deprived them of much of the California trade, and the appearance of the British iron steamships challenged their position on the oceans of the world.

STEAMSHIPS AND CANALS

The answer to the conquest of great masses of water seemed to be a boat driven by steam. As we have already seen, steamboats were being used successfully on domestic waterways by the end of the War of 1812. Now, it remained to construct them successfully for oceanic voyages.

Engineers of many nations were responsible for the successful utilization of steam in ocean travel. Two American steamships —the *Savannah* in 1819 and the *Great Western* in 1838—were prominent transatlantic carriers, but American steamship companies were hard pressed to compete with their British rivals, which had the advantage of being ironclad and driven by a huge screw propeller. America's carrying trade position declined, and not until World War I did she regain the mastery of the sea that she had achieved in the glorious days of the clippers.

Canals too were of crucial importance to domestic trade in the 1830s and 1840s. Transporting wheat from the interior was greatly eased by the canals. It was actually cheaper to ship New York flour from western New York to Charleston, South Carolina, than to bring it to that city from the lowlands of the same state. The Great Lakes region became the world's granary. Swiftly, the cities on the Great Lakes mushroomed in population, surpassing the cities on the rivers. In the 1830s, Chicago, for example, was an insignificant village. By 1860 it had a population of over 100,000.

Competitive cities began to follow New York's lead in canal building; Baltimore merchants constructed the Chesapeake and Ohio Canal along the Potomac River. Canal building, in fact, became a national craze. Some states, particularly in the West, overbuilt, only to be brought to a disillusioning halt by the Panic of 1837 and the ensuing depression. By the 1840s the shaky monetary structure had collapsed. Eight Western and Southern states defaulted on payments to investors in canals, with the result that public sentiment against state ownership, already strong, was considerably strengthened. All these events created public support for the construction of railroads by private financing.

RAILROADS

The many advantages of railroads were not immediately apparent. At first—with primitive locomotives and tracks—schedules were most irregular, there were constant breakdowns, and passengers were usually treated to a shower of sparks spurting on the open cars from the wood-burning locomotives. Soon, however, safety and efficiency were increased by the use of solid roadbeds and iron "T" rails, and by the substitution of coal for wood. The design of the locomotives and cars was improved, sleeping cars were added, and the invention of the telegraph made it easier to supervise railroad operations, by quickly relaying messages. As more refinements were introduced the railroads became the ideal solution to the country's transportation needs. They were fast, they could get through rough terrain to service the most remote markets, and they were dependable in winter when water in the canals often froze. During the 1850s, when railroad mileage was greatly expanded and small, independent lines were consolidated into trunk lines, they performed a valuable service by joining heretofore unconnected sections of the country.

The Memnon *as she appears today in the* B. & O. Museum. The locomotive was built in 1848.

"Americans," commented Emerson, "take to this little contrivance, the railroad, as if it were the cradle in which they were born." In the thirty years before the Civil War, railroad building boomed. Baltimore and Philadelphia employed the railroad as a way to compete with New York for the interior trade. The construction of the Baltimore and Ohio began in 1828, and by 1830 a 13-mile segment opened for business. New York answered with the Mohawk and Hudson, establishing regular service between Albany and Schenectady. Philadelphia, Boston, and South Carolina soon had railroads, with Charleston successfully diverting inland trade from Savannah. The Illinois Central gave Chicago a connection to Cairo in the southern part of the state. Lines ran East from Chicago to meet the Eastern trunk lines. By 1860 lines had penetrated into Iowa and Missouri.

Federal government support for the railroads came mostly through land grants. In 1850 Congress, in a grant to the Illinois Central, passed the first of the railroad land-grant bills. By 1860 twenty-eight million acres from the public land domain had been turned over to private companies for the construction of railroads which, by this time, had linked—in over 30,000 miles of tracks—most of the great cities east of the Mississippi and north of the Ohio.

INFLUENCE OF THE RAILROADS

Railroads and their transportation predecessors drew West and East together. With the coming of the railroads, settlers were attracted to the fertile lands of the trans-Mississippi prairie. Previously, the development of that area had been delayed partially because of its remoteness from navigable waters. Population now increased, and the production of wheat and corn flourished. Railroads stimulated the activity and interdependency of seaport cities as well as intermediate centers, such as Buffalo and Cincinnati. The railroads' consumption of large amounts of iron gave a new boost to the mining and smelting industries and to the creation of foundries that would turn out locomotives. Even the man on the edge of the frontier now became a businessman, for the cheaper transportation had increased production, raised the Westerner's income and standard of living, and almost erased the isolation of earlier days.

The ease of movement from section to section stimulated by the railroads, and the resulting economic integration of East and West, had a profound effect on the nation's politics. The South had not been active in building railroads. Southerners relied on the Mississippi and other rivers to carry their traffic. As a result, their share of the nation's trade declined sharply. Meanwhile, the sections of the country with railroads—the Northeast and Northwest—were drawn together economically and prospered. Economic ties encouraged social and cultural connections. These links stimulated nationalism in the North and nationalism became an important force in preserving the Union.

THE INDUSTRIAL REVOLUTION

In the thirty years after the Civil War, the United States moved from fourth to first place among the manufacturing nations of the world. This great acceleration had been indicated by pre-war trends. A firm base for a rising industrial economy had taken shape rapidly in the 1840s and 1850s in increased output of raw materials

and the development of speedy, inexpensive means for transporting them.

A number of factors contributed to the enormous industrial potential of the nation. There were massive quantities of natural resources available: coal, salt, lumber, oil, copper, lead, zinc, sulfur, limestone, and iron ore. New machinery was developed to tap these resources more efficiently, and innovations in production techniques turned them into salable commodities. Modern mass production methods—the use of machines with interchangeable parts, and the introduction of assembly lines and standardized procedures for labor—enabled factories to make the most efficient use of men and materials. The labor force, always in short supply until now, expanded rapidly with a growing population swelled also by a great influx of immigrants. An increase in workers meant an increase in consumers.

Industrial expansion was also bolstered by a generous flow of capital into the new enterprises, and by the emergence of business initiative and leadership. Using the corporation as the means for setting up and operating huge industrial, transportation, and mining enterprises, wealthy, and sometimes unscrupulous, individuals became the moving force in the development of the country's natural resources. Powerful businessmen gained control of the railroads, oil refining, banking, meat packing, and the manufacture of farm machinery.

The philosophical foundation for the Industrial Revolution rested upon America's belief that part of its destiny was the expansion of economic well-being. The desire for a higher standard of living was widespread. Individual accumulation of wealth was considered the standard of progress by most Americans.

INDUSTRIAL GROWTH

Industrial development was closely linked to the new products and markets created by technological developments. A rubber-goods industry sprang up after Charles Goodyear patented a method for "vulcanizing" rubber, making it resistant to heat. The iron and steel industry expanded with the consumption demands of the railroads and the farm machinery producers. (Between 1840 and 1860 the production of pig iron tripled.) The oil industry made huge profits selling to new markets created by the kerosene lamp and the internal combustion engine. Introduction of the new refrigerator car to the railroad proved a boon to the meat packers. And in 1851, Isaac Singer started an industry with far-reaching impact when he mass-produced the sewing machine, based on an invention patented five years earlier by Elias Howe. Thus, the United States came into an era of economic growth that was the direct result of the interaction of such forces as improved technology, higher income, and greater consumption.

GOVERNMENT ASSISTANCE

Government on all levels recognized the needs of big business and responded in a number of favorable ways, direct and indirect. Establishment of a stable banking system in most states benefited both the banks and general business. Railroads received direct assistance in the form of impressive land grants from the federal and state governments. Timber and mineral interests were able to take advantage of liberal government land policies to create monopolies over these natural resources. Fairly high tariffs, even after 1833, protected American industry from foreign competition. Indirectly, the failure of government on all levels to pass legislation to prevent the growth of monopolies and regulate business practices, made possible the unrestricted growth of business enterprises. At the same time, the states prevented labor from in any way hampering the unrestricted growth of business, by the use of troops and court injunctions to quell boycotts and strikes.

NATURAL RESOURCES

The basic material for the nation's industrialization came from its rich natural resources. Foremost among these was iron ore, with the largest deposits to be found in Pennsylvania and New Jersey and eventually in the Lake Superior region, for example, the great Mesabi Range in Minnesota. The nation possesed most of the basic resources needed by its industries. These were transformed from raw materials into manufactured goods, or—as in the case of coal and oil—they provided the necessary power to run manufacturing establishments and transportation facilities.

CAPITAL

By 1857, one billion dollars in private capital had been invested in the railroads and another billion had been channeled into manufacturing enterprises. Much of this money had come from speculative investments in corporate stocks and bonds. These securities were frequently purchased with minimal down payments supplemented with high interest loans from New York banks. Overspeculation was a primary factor in the crash of 1837, and helped to call attention to the need for creating restrictions on the availability of funds. The attraction of speculation did not cease, but many industrialists had learned the lesson of financial discipline.

INDUSTRY AND AGRICULTURE

In many respects the agricultural and manufacturing interests supported one another. As the industrial cities expanded, the landless people who lived and worked in them became dependent on the produce of farms. The number of farms increased and farm families became more affluent as their markets expanded. They could now afford the manufactured goods of the East and soon became major consumers of industrial products.

The availability of natural agricultural resources also made it possible for industry to develop in the West. Factories sprang up to make wood products from the extensive virgin forests and by 1860 lumber production was equal in value to cotton-textile production. Western cattle provided a sound basis for the meat packing and leather tanning industries. Grain was turned into flour and meal, liquor, and beer, by a growing number of mills and distilleries.

The farmer's own direct needs created one of the most important industries of the era: the development and manufacture of farm machinery.

MAJOR AMERICAN INDUSTRIES

The 1850 census showed that the value of the annual output of American manufacturing had recently passed one billion dollars, surpassing the figure for agricultural products by several million dollars. By 1860 the annual dollar value of manufactures had doubled. The commodities were varied. Leading the list were textiles, iron and steel, lumber and foodstuffs. Industries also had developed for the production of canned goods, tobacco, sugar, and whiskey.

The discovery of petroleum and a process for making steel from iron ore gave a tremendous boost to American industry and provided opportunities for industrial capitalists such as Andrew Carnegie and John D. Rockefeller after the Civil War. Steel was found to be a hard, durable, malleable, plentiful, and inexpensive structural metal, attributes that eventually made steel production a major industry. In 1859 Edwin L. Drake drilled the country's first oil well near Titusville, making way for the petroleum industry in western Pennsylvania. The chief product refined from crude oil was kerosene, widely used in lamps.

Only about 10 percent of the manufactured goods of the United States came from the South. Although some Southern planters invested a portion of their capital in Northern manufacturing, they saw to it that their own society remained essentially agrarian. Southern cotton planters flourished, but their economy relied on Northern textile mills, Northern transportation, and Northern brokers and bankers to finance cotton transactions. Some attempts were made at local manufacturing, notably by William Gregg of South Carolina, who established a textile mill in 1846. Gregg successfully employed over 300 workers in 1850, but his operation was insignificant when compared to the extensive Northern industry. The single town of Lowell, Massachusetts, had more spindles revolving in 1860 than did the entire South.

Local needs, however, brought about local manufacturing in some areas. Virginia became a center for processing chewing tobacco; Richmond, Virginia, contained the Tredegar Iron Works, a nationally famous foundry; iron and coal mines were operating in Virginia, Kentucky, and Tennessee; and small flour and lumber mills appeared in most areas of the South.

CORPORATIONS

In America the industrial entrepreneur and the corporate form of business organization were spreading rapidly and becoming an established fact of economic life. During the 1850s the nation's manufacturing corporations virtually doubled in number, their growth assisted by governmental policies that encouraged private enterprise on a grand scale. Industrial management and the building of railroads emerged as the principal means for achievement of wealth and power. Phelps, Dodge & Company of New York, and Amos and Abbot Lawrence of Boston were prime examples of firms that shifted their capital from mercantile enterprise to mining, manufacturing, and railroads.

THE AMERICAN WORKER

The rise of entrepreneurs and the development of a factory system may have contributed a great deal to American economic progress, but almost from the outset they also revealed a distinct tendency toward human exploitation. Even before Samuel Slater constructed his cotton plant in 1791, America had many "spinning houses" which employed the children of the poor, and, in most cases, abused them. The trend toward industrialization in the United States after 1800 created new problems for workers. In the East, deteriorating working and living conditions blighted factory towns. The workers were legally free, but the drudgery of their lives was not far removed from the dreary and arduous existence of the Southern slave. Immigrants, who came with hope to the new land, discovered too soon that they were expected to be satisfied with the leavings of the native populace. Workers who came from the farms to better their lot by working in factories found that life in the factory towns was bleak, that the work routine was oppressive, and that living was expensive in the boardinghouses operated by the companies. Eventually, out of common misery and human need, laborers began to organize to better their lot. They formed unions, but their strikes were prohibited by law and repressed by their employers.

LABOR RECRUITMENT

From its colonial beginnings America had been faced with a scarcity of labor. At the opening of the nineteenth century, 90 percent of Americans still lived and worked on farms. The workers in the cities were skilled artisans, not factory hands. However, in response to the increasing demands of new industries, a sizable class of wage earners took form. Its members came from the farms of the East and later from Britain and other European nations.

The accelerating economy used new machinery that required fewer specialized skills and less physical strength, making it possible to employ many women and children. By the early 1820s half the cotton textile workers in the factories were children under sixteen. Many argued that the employment was a blessing to children and young women. Factory work, it was argued, gave young girls an opportunity to escape the doldrums of the farm, to save for a trousseau, to meet new people, or to help educate a younger brother.

In the textile mills, basically two labor systems were used, the Family System and the Lowell System.

THE FAMILY SYSTEM

In certain sections of New England and the Middle Atlantic states, companies transported whole families from the farms to the mills. Parents and children, some only four or five years old, worked side by side tending looms in the factories. Though the employment of small children became offensive to later generations, its antebellum defenders argued that it helped to maintain family solidarity and provided a reasonable standard of living for the people involved. These family workers lived in factory towns provided by their employers and had little contact with the outside world.

THE LOWELL SYSTEM

This system, also known as the Waltham System, was developed by the Boston Associates for their mills in Lowell, Massachusetts. It enlisted young women in their late teens and early twenties. These were unmarried women who came from the farms to the factories, and returned after a few years to the farms. They did not form a permanent working class.

WORKING CONDITIONS

The working conditions of labor prior to the Civil War can be described from several perspectives. Laborers in American mills fared much better in terms of wages

The Lowell system enlisted unmarried farm girls, between 13 and 20 years-of-age, to work in factories. Working conditions were oppressive, and in 1834, the first strike took place when 1,000 girls walked out in protest. They soon resumed work, however, since they lacked organization and were threatened with unemployment.

and working conditions than their English counterparts. Wages were from one-half to one-third higher in the United States than in England. Even so, unskilled workers made only about one dollar a day, skilled workers from one to two dollars. Mill hands worked from 12 to 15 hours a day. Child labor seemed less debilitating and, according to a writer of the day, "entailed fewer evils in the United States where children remained under the control of their parents, than in England." Similarly, another contemporary observer tells us that "the lot of working women in mills like those of Lowell seem idyllic in contrast with the plight of the women who work in the British mills. . . . The Lowell girls lived in pleasant boarding houses (much like college dormitories) where their morals were carefully scrutinized." The mill girls placed flowering plants at the windows of the factories, attended lectures regularly, organ-

ized sewing circles, and edited their own literary periodicals.

The working conditions of the mill girls were hardly utopian, for in 1834 one thousand of them walked out in protest. They soon resumed work, however, for like mill hands in other parts of the country they lacked funds, leadership, and organization to pursue their demands. Virtually all such strikes ended in failure.

Perhaps even worse off than the mill hands were the unskilled laborers in construction gangs on railroads, turnpikes, and canals, who were unable to earn enough in a year to support a family.

By 1840 conditions in the factories deteriorated even further as employers shifted from regular daily wages to piece rate payments. The change, designed to speed up production, succeeded in further exploiting the laborer.

IMMIGRANTS AS WORKERS

The enormous influx of immigrants before the Civil War had important consequences for the nation's labor supply. Half a million entered the United States in the 1830s, a million and a half in the 1840s, and over two and one half million in the 1850s.

The immigrants came from various parts of Europe to the new land, driven by technological unemployment, religious persecution, and famine. They poured in from northern and western Europe, especially from Germany and southern Ireland in the 1840s and 1850s. Low transatlantic fares lured immigrants and the steamships that carried American cotton and lumber to Europe converted unoccupied space on their return trips into rough passenger quarters. An immigrant could travel in steerage on these cargo vessels from Liverpool to New York for under fifteen dollars. As might be expected, "steerage" conditions lacked the most elementary comforts. The food was bad and quarters were crowded and stuffy. Health hazards abounded and outbreaks of epidemics were common. On one crossing of the steamship *Lark,* for example, 158 out of 440 steerage passengers died of typhus.

Germans and some Scandinavians pushed into the Western regions of the country. The poorer immigrants, however, were unable to do this. They had no money to purchase farm land, and most, like the Irish, remained in the Eastern seaport cities. They were usually destitute, mainly unskilled, and eager for work of any kind. Swiftly, they were absorbed into the factories of the Northeastern states. Because they demanded less comfort, because, unlike the mill girls, they stayed on, providing the mills with a permanent working force, the mill owners gradually replaced the girls with Irish immigrants. By 1860 they accounted for over half of the labor force in the New England mills. Economic desperation forced them to accept lower wages and to further please their employers by shunning unionization.

The influx of immigrants was a major contributing factor to the rapid growth of the American economy in the antebellum period. The Welsh and some English worked the coal mines of Pennsylvania and the lead mines of Missouri and Wisconsin. The Germans and the English also increased the supply of skilled craftsmen. The Irish toiled in New England factories, built the nation's railroads, and dug her canals. Chinese immigrants were also an important source of labor for the Western mines and railroads.

LIVING CONDITIONS

The depressed wages of the immigrant were hardly sufficient to live on. The new arrivals were easy prey for swindlers who overcharged them for food, lodging, and transportation. Most lived in dire poverty in the larger Eastern seaboard cities, where, because they could afford only the cheapest housing, they occupied the slums and tenement districts of the larger cities. They were ideal prospects for greedy realtors who crowded their tenements with as many families as they could hold. The worst slums were in New York and Boston. A typical New York tenement housed as many as 4,000 people, most with nowhere else to go. These buildings had deplorable sanitary conditions, life expectancy was low, and the mortality rate high.

Though they were not as readily exploited as the other immigrants, the Scandinavians, Germans, Dutch, Czechs, and Finns who moved into the interior of the country also found hardships. Their new life was considerably unlike the one they had left behind. The soil was different here and they were unfamiliar with the crops in America. European village life differed radically from American frontier life. Unlike the Europeans, American farmers lived in houses that were widely separated from their neighbors. The loneliness and isolation that the European immigrant farmer experienced in the new country told heavily upon his family, particularly the women.

LABOR MOVEMENT

As a result of the working and living conditions of both native and immigrant workers, a number of efforts were made in the pre-Civil War period to organize labor unions. The labor movement was severely hampered in the United States by total lack of support from management and the state and federal governments. Labor combinations were regarded with prejudice and believed to be conspiracies to inspire revolt and violence. Their very existence was considered a menace to both employers and nonunion workers.

It was not until 1842, when Chief Justice Lemuel Shaw of the Supreme Court of Massachusetts ruled that labor unions were not illegal conspiracies unless they were planning a conspiratorial action, that unions had any official sanction to exist. The organization of labor was further discouraged by the traditional emphasis on individual effort to overcome obstacles; the use of women and children for unskilled jobs; and the social instability of American society brought about by the lure of the frontier and by the inflow of destitute immigrants.

UNIONS

Important and lasting organizations for the protection of American workers did not develop until after the Civil War, but there were important preparatory efforts in this era. Guild-style craft unions existed very early in the nation's history. They were composed of independent skilled artisans who employed journeymen and apprentices. By the beginning of the nineteenth century, these artisans had, because of expanded business, become "merchant capitalists." The competition among them grew and this factor forced them to cut their employees' wages. When their income dwindled and their status was threatened by mass production, these skilled laborers formed the country's first unions.

Initially, the trade unions took the form of city centrals, or societies of workers in urban areas. Shoemakers and printers organized in the large Eastern cities. The Mechanics' Union was formed in 1827. Agricultural workers combined into the New England Association of Farmers. Between 1834 and 1837, when the economy was booming, trade union membership rose from 26,000 to 300,000. By 1836, thirteen city centrals had been formed. Essentially, these were nonpolitical organizations, but in Philadelphia unions organized into the American Working Men's Party in order to more effectively seek a 10-hour day, and an end to licensed monopolies, equal property taxes, and a free education for their children. Led by Ely Moore, the local organizations were eventually amalgamated into the National Trades Union, which held a national convention in 1834.

The economic crash of 1837 dealt a staggering blow to the trade union movement. Some craft unions, such as the printers, managed to weather the worst years, but most of the crafts were unable to compete with the rising mass production techniques which broke down jobs into simpler tasks. These crafts, together with their unions, gradually disappeared.

By the 1840s labor union organization began to revive along with the economy. In earlier years, union organization had been somewhat hampered by too much cooperation with general reformers and not enough emphasis on the issues vital to the laboring population: better wages and working conditions, and shorter hours. By the 1850s many more workers were thinking of their status as workers, organizing unions, and pushing demands for specific improvements to raise their living standards. By the mid-1850s almost all skilled workers were organized.

STRIKES

Although threatened by criminal prosecution and the use of state troops, union members employed the strike as a means for achieving higher wages and improved working conditions. Between 1831 and 1840 there were 114 strikes in Pennsylvania alone. Collective bargaining machinery was nonexistent, and strikes were the only known weapon for securing basic demands from employers.

In addition to increased wages, labor's greatest cry was for the reduction of the working day to 10 hours. In 1834, the building trades unions were the first to gain this end. In 1840, President Van Buren established a 10-hour day for federal employees. Factory workers received a similar benefit after the organization of the New England Workingmen's Association and a series of strikes in the Pittsburgh area in 1845. The movement spread, and within 10 years, seven states had laws that insured the laborer a 10-hour working day.

Readings

GENERAL WORKS

Billington, Ray A., *America's Frontier Heritage*. New York: Holt, Rinehart & Winston, 1966—A history of the frontier which attempts to test Frederick Jackson Turner's hypotheses by modern historical research and social scientific theories. The author concludes that the frontier did affect American character, although not precisely in the ways Turner claimed it did.

Billington, Ray A., *Westward Expansion*. New York: Macmillan, 1967—A history of westward expansion as suggested by Frederick Jackson Turner's frontier thesis. Billington deals with successive frontiers from colonial times through the nineteenth century.

Clark, Thomas D., *Frontier America*. New York: Scribner's, 1969—A long, illustrated history of westward expansion from the middle of the eighteenth century through the end of the nineteenth.

Eaton, Clement, *The Growth of Southern Civilization*. New York: Harper & Row, 1961—Eaton emphasizes the diversity of the South between 1790 and 1860, but sees certain distinguishing features of the whole region, including a sense of pride and aggressiveness and an obsession with slavery.

Eaton, Clement, *A History of the Old South* New York: Macmillan, 1966—A general history of the South before the Civil War. Eaton shows how the society moved to increasingly repressive and intolerant policies to maintain itself in the face of moral and political opposition.

Gates, Paul W., *The Farmer's Age: Agriculture, 1815–1860*. New York: Holt, Rinehart & Winston, 1960—Although the 1815 through 1860 period was predominantly one of success for American farmers, Gates suggests that the coming of the Civil War and the growth of industry meant the beginning of the end of the "farmers' age."

Gray, Lewis C., *History of Agriculture in the Southern United States to 1860*, Vols. I–II. Washington, D.C.: Carnegie Institution, 1933—A massive history of Southern farming which relates changes in agricultural techniques to their social and economic causes and consequences.

Nevins, Allan, *Ordeal of the Union*, Vols. I–II. New York: Scribner's, 1947—The first two volumes of the major modern history of the Civil War era. Nevins, although stressing economic and social trends in America, feels that in the end, the Civil War was fought over the moral issue of slavery.

Riegel, Robert E., and Robert G. Athearn, *America Moves West*. New York: Holt, Rinehart & Winston, 1970—A history of the American West which discusses intellectual and cultural trends as well as political and economic developments.

Sydnor, Charles S., *The Development of Southern Sectionalism*. Baton Rouge, La.: Louisiana State University Press, 1948—A history of the South between 1819 and

1848. While tracing the growing consciousness of the South's uniqueness, Sydnor also shows that the region itself was marked by diversity.

SPECIAL STUDIES

Aptheker, Herbert, *American Negro Slave Revolts*. New York: Columbia University Press, 1943—Outlines the long history of slave rebelliousness, finding hundreds of reports of slave uprisings. The author demonstrates that white Southerners were continually afraid that the slaves' resentment would burst into open revolt.

Dick, Everett, *The Dixie Frontier*. New York: Knopf, 1948—An attempt at showing the daily lives of Southern frontiersmen and women before the Civil War. Dick adopts Frederick Jackson Turner's thesis in explaining the special characteristics of Southern frontier life.

Elkins, Stanley M., *Slavery*. Chicago: University of Chicago Press, 1968—A collection of four provocative essays which attempt to compare United States slavery with slavery in Brazil and with Hitler's concentration camps to discover the distinctive nature of the system and its effects on the slaves themselves.

Fogel, Robert W., *Railroads and American Economic Growth*. Baltimore: Johns Hopkins Press, 1964—A collection of essays in the "new economic history." The most controversial essay argues that the railroads contributed relatively little to United States growth and that the net saving they provided in transportation cost was slight.

Jones, Maldwyn A., *American Immigration*. Chicago: University of Chicago Press, 1960 —Jones attributes many national characteristics to the fact that the United States is a nation of immigrants. Successive waves of immigration provided a labor supply, led to partial substitution of ethnic for class conflict, and affected the practice of American politics.

Owsley, Frank L., *Plain Folk of the Old South*. Baton Rouge, La.: Louisiana State University Press, 1949—Owsley rejects the picture of Southern society which concentrates on the great slaveholding plantation owners. He discusses the poorer whites who, he claims, had achieved considerable power in the South before the Civil War.

Pelling, Henry, *American Labor*. Chicago: University of Chicago Press, 1960—A brief survey of American labor history by an English historian who feels that weak class consciousness, the possibility of social mobility, and the existence of a large middle class have made American labor more conservative than its European counterpart.

Smith, Henry N., *Virgin Land*. Cambridge, Mass.: Harvard University Press, 1950—An intellectual history of the significance of the West in American thought. Smith concentrates on the themes of a Northwest passage, the frontiersman as a social type, and the West as garden for the world.

Stampp, Kenneth M., *The Peculiar Institution*. New York: Knopf, 1956—A history of slavery in the American South which uses a wide variety of evidence to show the slave's view of the system. Slavery, Stampp maintains, was harsh and brutal and the slave's rebellion against it took many forms.

Wade, Richard C., *The Urban Frontier*. Chicago: University of Chicago Press, 1959 —Cities and towns, Wade claims, were important aspects of the frontier. Towns provided outlets for the growth of Western agriculture and commerce, and themselves soon became centers of trade, industry, and culture.

Ware, Norman J., *The Industrial Worker, 1840–1860*. Boston: Houghton Mifflin, 1924 —A study of working conditions and labor organizations during the early period of American industrialization. Ware argues that workers' living standards and conditions declined during these years.

PRIMARY SOURCES

Aptheker, Herbert, ed., *A Documentary History of the Negro People in the United States*. New York: Citadel Press, 1910— This collection deals with the history of blacks from the early seventeenth century through the middle of the twentieth, showing the parallel themes of integrationism and nationalism.

Goodrich, Carter, ed., *The Government and the Economy, 1783–1861*. Indianapolis: Bobbs-Merrill, 1966—An introductory essay and collection of documents on internal improvements, tariff policy, changes in corporate law, and regulation of labor which show that the period before the Civil War was not one of laissez-faire.

Olmsted, Frederick L., *The Cotton Kingdom*. Arthur M. Schlesinger, ed. New York: Knopf, 1953—Olmsted's accounts of his journeys through the South in the 1850s are brought together in this work. An antislavery Northerner, he nevertheless found many admirable aspects of Southern society.

Wish, Harvey, ed., *Slavery in the South*. New York: Farrar, Straus & Giroux, 1964—A collection of primary–source accounts of Southern slavery, from the point of view of slaves, slave owners, poor whites, and Northern and foreign observers.

BIOGRAPHIES

Craven, Avery O., *Edmund Ruffin, Southerner*. New York: Appleton, 1932—Ruffin was a Virginia agricultural reformer and extremist politician who continually agitated for secession. Craven attempts to link his concern for Southern agriculture to his political role.

Green, Constance M., *Eli Whitney and the Birth of American Technology*. Boston: Little, Brown, 1956—Whitney is best known for inventing the cotton gin, but Green also stresses his innovations with industrial machinery. By developing the principle of interchangeable parts Whitney helped pave the way for mass-production manufacturing.

Lane, Wheaton J., *Commodore Vanderbilt*. New York: Knopf, 1942—Vanderbilt was one of the leading nineteenth-century American businessmen, whose steamship and railroad empire made him a multi-millionaire. Lane's biography concentrates on his business activities rather than his flamboyant personality.

Mitchell, Broadus, *William Gregg, Factory Master of the Old South*. Chapel Hill, N.C.: University of North Carolina Press, 1928—Gregg was a leading Southern industrialist who developed Southern cotton manufacturing before the Civil War. Mitchell also shows Gregg as a humanitarian reformer concerned about the plight of poor whites in a slave society.

Neu, Irene D., *Erastus Corning, Merchant and Financier*. Ithaca, N.Y.: Cornell University Press, 1960—Corning was a nineteenth-century businessman whose activities spanned banking, land speculation, manufacturing, and railroad management. Neu's biography shows Corning as talented, but ruthless.

Camp meetings, such as this 1836 Methodist gathering, were important religious as well as social events for the isolated settlers.

The old and moth-eaten systems of Europe have had their day, and that evening of their existence which is nigh at hand will be the token of a glorious dawn for the down-trodden people. Here *we have planted the standard of freedom, and here we will test the capacities of men for self-government. We will see whether the law of happiness and preservation upon each individual, acting directly upon himself, be not a safer dependenc*

Religion, Romanticism, and Reform

12

...than musty charters and time-worn prerogatives of tyrants. Doctrines that even now are scarcely breathed, innovations which the most fearless hardly dare propose openly, systems of policy that men would speak of at the present day in the low tones of fear for very danger lest they might be scouted as worse than Robespierrian revolutionists— that hackneyed bug-bear theme which has never been presented in its fairness to the people of this Republic—will, in course of time, see the light here and meet the sanction of popular favor and go into practical play. Nor let us fear that this may result in harm. All that we enjoy of freedom was in the beginning but an experiment. We have been long enough frightened by the phantom of the past; let us dare to know that we are out of leading strings. . . .

—*Walt Whitman*, Brooklyn Daily Eagle

RELIGIOUS AND SOCIAL BACKGROUND

The generation of Americans that came to maturity before the Civil War felt the influence of several intellectual forces. The culture of this era was shaped by modifications of the religious and philosophical thought of the colonial period, as well as by new ideas from Europe.

One of the earliest influences on American thinking had been Calvinism, in the form of Puritanism. According to Puritanism, man was inherently evil and only a small number of people were predestined for salvation. God was a stern Father, who in his unfailing wisdom controlled the universe and meted out justice to sinners. By the early nineteenth century, Calvinist thought was under sharp attack and membership in the Calvinist churches was declining. Nevertheless, even though Puritan theology was losing ground, the Puritan habit of stern moral judgment remained, and the conviction persisted that the only life worth leading was one that was scrupulously and continuously reexamined. During this period, individuals not only submitted their own lives to a close, moralistic examination, but also the social institutions of the nation.

A second important influence on American character derived from the success ordinary men enjoyed in accomplishing their earthly goals. Pioneers were pushing back the frontier, wresting farmland out of dense forests; engineers were digging roads through mountains, laying bridges across rivers, and tying the country together through an intricate network of canals; conquest and diplomacy had expanded America's boundaries to the Pacific; immigrants from Europe were tilling their own land

within a few years after their arrival; inventors were patenting labor-saving devices almost every month. The confidence and optimism brought about by these successes served to shift interest from salvation in the next world to happiness and prosperity in this one. The philosophy of the Enlightenment of the eighteenth century had held human society to be rational and perfectible, and these ideas seemed just as applicable to America in the nineteenth century. By the patient application of reason and the scientific method to even morality and social problems, Americans believed they could cure all ills and establish an ideal society. The Garden of Eden and Adam's fall from innocence had been a favorite theme of the Puritans, but for the followers of eighteenth-century rationalism, the Eden of the past was replaced by the Utopia of the future.

A third persistent theme in American life was religious revivalism. America had gone through a Great Awakening in the early eighteenth century and a Second Awakening at the beginning of the nineteenth century. The evangelical religions, particularly the Baptists and the Methodists, had rejected what they considered to be both the gloomy, doom-ridden world view of the Puritans as well as the bland, slightly cold optimism of the philosophy of the Enlightenment. Unlike the Puritans, the evangelical religions did not believe that all human actions were unavailing, or that salvation or damnation had already been determined before an individual's birth. They held that even the most terrible sinner, through an exercise of his free will, could repent and find God through either a startling conversion or through the patient accumulation of good works. While the Puritans had believed that whether or not a man was to be saved in the world to come was not in his hands but had been predestined by God, the evangelists embraced the doctrine of free will. The fate of human beings was in their own power to shape, if they sought God's grace. In addition, the Methodists believed in universal salvation.

Finally, a fourth force that shaped American culture in this period was Romanticism. The Romantic movement had started in Germany in the last quarter of the eighteenth century and had steadily gained momentum until it came to dominate the arts and philosophy of all Europe. Romanticism was a vague term used more to describe a cluster of loosely related attitudes than a precise philosophy. Basic to the Romantic spirit was a rejection of the Enlightenment position that reason could solve all human problems. Romanticists, on the contrary, believed that rational examination was at best a limited tool and that instinct, or intuition, was the true guide to ultimate wisdom. Similarly, men of the Enlightenment had looked upon untamed nature with revulsion and something akin to dread. They wanted to think of nature as a perfect mechanism with every part serving its function and nothing out of order. The disorderliness of many natural phenomena struck them as appalling excesses. One figure of the Enlightenment, Casanova, had pulled down the shades of his coach when he drove through the Alps so that he would not have to gaze upon those misshapen and unruly formations. For Romanticists, however, nature's mysterious secrets were best revealed by lonely mountain peaks or wind-swept, unpeopled valleys, and the violence and unpredictability of tempests and volcanoes suggested the hidden depths of an unfathomable cosmic force. In short, where the Enlightenment had relished the normal, the rational, the ordered, and the familiar, the Romantic

Age searched out the bizarre, the instinctual, and disordered, and the exotic corners of experience. The Enlightenment had stressed the universality of all human characteristics, while Romanticism emphasized the uniqueness and genius of each individual and nationality. Yet another important distinction was the Enlightenment's interest in a smoothly working society and the Romantic Age's concern for the intensely committed individual. Whereas the Enlightenment had praised cool, far-seeing administrators of society, the Romanticists paid homage to the hero who patriotically led his nation against a corrupt society. Patriotism and the cult of the patriotic hero were salient aspects of the Romantic Age.

The Romantic glorification of nature and the stress on the genius of each nation had an instant appeal, although Americans, who had actually contemplated vast forests and combatted a hostile wilderness, were far less likely than Europeans to regard nature as sublime or picturesque. The Romantic's love of nature had extended to a love of the natural man, the untutored farmer, the noble savage, the humble peasant. Less intellectual and closer to his instincts, the natural man was considered more in touch with essentials than the city dweller or the overrefined aristocrat. This democratic aspect of Romantic thought concurred with American ideas. The stress on individualism, on bold men and patriotic heroes rising above humdrum circumstances, was also attractive to a nation of self-made men fiercely dedicated to their new country.

THE AMERICAN CHARACTER

The Calvinist emphasis on moral rectitude, the Enlightenment's faith in the perfectibility of human nature, the evangelists' doctrine of an emotional redemption

435

through grace and good works, and the Romantic emphasis on an emotional individualism all combined and sometimes came into conflict in shaping the intellectual life of the United States before the Civil War.

THE NOBILITY OF WORK

In Europe, working for a living had always been looked down on by the aristocracy as an open admission, in a society with rigid class lines, that one belonged to the inferior "laboring classes." In America, however, work, far from being considered menial, was thought to confer distinction on the worker. The man who performed manual labor frequently had no time for the niceties of etiquette or refinement of sentiment but there was social respect for his ability to get things done. Calvinism had stressed the dignity of hard work. In England in this same period many upper-class families were eking out an existence of "genteel poverty" rather than lose caste by soiling their hands. Their American counterparts who suffered a reversal were more likely to exert themselves in an effort to renew their fortunes.

BELIEF IN PROGRESS

America had made such amazing economic strides in its brief history that even such a critical foreigner as Charles Dickens, the English novelist, had to admit: "There is no other country on earth which in so short a time has accomplished so much."

Americans themselves were the first to recognize that they had made progress. Typical of this native pride was George Bancroft's massive *History of the United States,* begun in 1834, which set out to demonstrate in ten volumes that God had directed all human history to the ultimate perfection of the American experiment. The editor of the New York *Tribune,* Horace Greeley, voiced similar sentiments

when he advised his readers: "We could not retard the great forward movement of Humanity if we would, but each of us may decide for himself whether to share in the glory of promoting it or incur the shame of having looked coldly and indifferently on." Progress was not a mere abstraction or a dubious goal to Americans. Progress was a living, recognizable reality, and the special mission of every citizen was to nurture it. The democratic ideals of the American Revolution had already had their impact in France and were even now liberalizing British political institutions. The mania for improvement fired American scientists and inventors and encouraged the development of many reform movements.

So certain were Americans that they were on the path to perfection that they resented any outside criticism of their experiment. As the Frenchman Alexis de Tocqueville observed, Americans displayed an "irritable patriotism," and the visitor might not disparage "anything at all except, perhaps, the climate and the soil; and even then Americans will be found ready to defend both as if they had cooperated in producing them." The only self-doubt expressed by Americans was the admission that perhaps later generations of Americans might carry the banner of progress still further; as the New England minister and intellectual, Theodore Parker, wrote: "Progressive development does not end with us; we have seen only the beginning; the future triumphs of the race must be vastly greater than all accomplished yet."

FAITH IN EDUCATION

The progressive spirit slowly changed American educational philosophy in the years before the Civil War. Before the 1820s, most Americans had not considered free public education a duty of the state, and even in the following decades many traditionists continued to insist that people should not receive an education at public expense. As one North Carolina legislator shouted during a debate over tax-supported schools, "I hope you do not conceive it at all necessary that *everybody* should be able to read, write, and cipher."

A growing number of Americans, however, did think that every citizen should attain such a basic education. By the 1850s, most states in the North had some sort of public elementary school system. The South was also beginning to improve public education on lower levels. During the 1850s, school attendance increased by some fifty percent in the South, and public money spent on schools doubled. In Boston the first public high school had been built as early as 1821 and by 1860 there were 321 tax-supported high schools across the country, although more than half of them were in Massachusetts, New York, and Ohio. The state university system was also gaining ground. Supported by government land-grants, state universities were opened in Indiana, Michigan, Wisconsin, Virginia, Alabama, Tennessee, and Missouri. Despite this proliferation of public schools, however, nowhere in the United States was education compulsory.

For decades public schools were considered suitable only for paupers. This bias was slowly fading, but most people who could afford to send their children to private academies did so. Accordingly, the number of private academies, including a few co-educational institutions and quite a number for women only, had grown to some six thousand institutions, which enrolled more than 250,000 students. The curricula of these private academies were beginning to accommodate more practical subjects such as algebra, botany, American history, and geography.

The same practicality marked American colleges. For generations doctors and law-

In country schoolhouses, such as this one in Maine, children were taught the three R's from McGuffey's Readers *and* Webster's Spellers.

The title page of McGuffey's Second Eclectic Reader. *The first* Readers *contained stories and poems that stressed honesty and morality; the more advanced* Readers *contained masterpieces of literature and famous speeches.*

yers had learned their professions by apprenticing themselves to experienced men in the field. But in 1826 Harvard opened a law school, Baltimore founded the first dental college in 1839, and after 1862 the land-grant colleges began to teach agricultural and mechanical subjects.

An increase in books, newspapers, and lectures also served to inform the public. Publishing had become such a lucrative enterprise that by the time of the Civil War there were more than two thousand book-

sellers in the United States. Many of the books sold in America made a distinct appeal to self-improvement. Readers could buy how-to-do-it books on every subject from raising chickens to carving tombstones. Public lectures held in community cultural centers, called lyceums, attracted large audiences to consider problems ranging from the abolition of slavery to sculpture. Moreover, newspapers, which used to be relatively expensive, were now being published for only a penny a copy, enabling an ever-growing number of readers to keep abreast of foreign events, domestic politics, and the innovations of science and the arts.

PRACTICALITY

"Immediate practical results are more attractive for the American mind, although not exclusively, then the claims of the imagination," wrote one foreign visitor. Certainly Americans had little patience with "idle" speculation, and not until the end of the nineteenth century would the country produce a major philosopher, William James; and even he developed a philosophy that favored practical experience over abstract ideas. European critics, however, had been too quick to dismiss America's poor response to "the claims of the imagination." In the 1840s and 1850s, the United States witnessed an astounding burst of creativity in literature.

Practicality, of course, was more a virtue than a vice in a new country where so many things had to be accomplished. As the sympathetic yet analytical de Tocqueville remarked of Americans: "Their strictly Puritanical origin—their exclusively commercial habits—even the country they inhabit, which seems to divert their minds from the pursuit of science, literature and the arts—the proximity of Europe, which allows them to neglect these pursuits without relapsing into barbarism—a thousand special causes, of which I have only been able to point out the most important—have singularly concurred to fix the mind of the American upon purely practical objects."

THE RELIGIOUS BACKGROUND

The establishment of American independence from Great Britain had little effect on such churches as the Presbyterian, Baptist, and the newly formed Methodist denomination, but churches with European ties, such as the Anglican, Lutheran, and Roman Catholic found it necessary to reorganize.

The Anglican Church, the established church in all the Southern colonies, now was reorganized as the Episcopal Church, with an American hierarchy not directly connected with English church officialdom. While the church was out of favor for a time as a result of the Revolutionary struggle, it gradually reclaimed a number of its adherents. Virginians, particularly wealthy Virginians, were Episcopalians. As one Virginian put it: "No gentleman would choose any road to heaven but the episcopal." The new cotton aristocracy of South Carolina and Mississippi sometimes followed the religious example of the planters of Virginia, but more often they favored the more emotional religions that were having a great revival throughout the West.

The Lutherans now also broke their ties with Germany, established a new American organization, and began using the English rather than the German language in services. The small Roman Catholic Church, now freed from English jurisdiction, applied directly to Rome for an American bishop. The priest, John Carroll of Maryland, was so ordained in 1789, and Baltimore became the seat of the first American diocese. Both the Lutheran and Roman Catholic churches, small in number until about the 1840s, began to increase rapidly with the great influx of German and Irish immigrants during that decade. By 1846, there were twenty Roman Catholic bishoprics in the United States.

In New England, many Congregationalists deserted their church for Unitarianism. Unitarianism took a cheerful view of man and his potential for good, and interpreted God as a merciful, benign being. Unitarians, deeply influenced by the philosophy of the Enlightenment, preached tolerance of other faiths, urged individuals to come to their own, private understanding of the Scriptures and gave up as irrational the concept of the Trinity. The name Unitarian derives from their belief that God is a single being.

The Enlightenment philosopher Thomas Paine had declared in *The Age of Reason:* "I believe that religious duties consist in doing justice, loving mercy, and endeavoring to make our fellow creatures happy." The leading Unitarian thinker William Ellery Channing (1780–1842) reflected Paine's humanitarianism when he endorsed reform "because I have learned the essential equality of men before the common Father . . . because I see in him a great nature, the divine image, and vast capacities."

At Harvard, which had always been the stronghold of Puritan theology, a great struggle took place in the early nineteenth century between the defenders of orthodoxy and the proponents of Unitarianism. Despite strong resistance by the conservatives, the liberals took over Harvard and engineered one of their own men into the prestigious Chair of Divinity. Unitarianism won the day because it appealed to educated minds. As one Congregationalist lamented: "All the literary men of Massachusetts were Unitarians, all the trustees and professors of Harvard College were Unitarians. All the elite of wealth and fashion crowded Unitarian Churches." Whereas Unitarianism appealed to the elite, a watered-down version of the movement called Universalism attracted the less educated. The zealous, harrowing Puritanism that had so long held New England in

439

its grip had been weakened by the Enlightenment and was now seriously undermined by Unitarianism and Universalism.

EVANGELISM

While the Enlightenment, as embodied in Unitarianism, won converts in New England, the South and West were in the throes of yet another outburst of revivalism. Like the Puritans, the evangelical religions (primarily the Baptists and Methodists) believed in a literal hell and heaven, in the Trinity, and in the Bible as an infallible record of divine revelation. Unlike the Puritans, however, the evangelists believed that redemption could be earned. A man or woman, by freely confessing his sins and opening his heart to God, could be reborn. In the 1820s revivalism took on a new character under the leadership of the Reverend Charles G. Finney, who combined an interest in saving souls with a conviction that Christians must better society. According to Finney, "All sin consists in selfishness; and all holiness or virtue, in disinterested benevolence." Luther and Calvin, the two founders of Protestantism, had both doubted the effectiveness of good works. American revivalists such as Finney, however, reintroduced into Protestantism a belief in the saving grace earned by moral, benevolent behavior, particularly if it led to social reform. "And what is to reform mankind but the truth?" asked Finney. "And who shall present the truth if not the church and the ministry? Away with the idea that Christians can remain neutral and keep still, and yet enjoy the approbation and blessings of God."

The religious ferment in America before the Civil War also led to the creation of several new religious movements, many of them short-lived. One sect that survived was a denomination founded in 1832 called the "Disciples of Christ," now known as the Christian Church. Organized as an attempt to restore Christian unity and return all believers to a single, simple faith in the Gospels, the Disciples of Christ claimed 100,000 converts by 1850. Another new sect was the Seventh Day Adventist Church. In the 1830s, William Miller, a Baptist minister from Vermont, had preached that Christ's Second Coming, or Advent, would occur on March 21, 1843 (later the date was changed to October 22, 1844). As the judgment day approached, Miller's disciples sold their belongings, dressed in white, and assembled on hilltops, awaiting the coming of the Lord. When the prophecy failed to materialize, the faithful gave up the idea of an immediate Second Coming and in 1846 organized a formal denomination, the Seventh Day Adventist Church ("Seventh Day" because they contended that Saturday, rather than Sunday, had been God's day of rest and hence should be the sabbath).

TRANSCENDENTALISM

Transcendentalism was the American counterpart of the European Romantic movement with its emphasis on intuition and the importance of nature. Transcendentalism was also closely connected to the first flowering of American literary genius and with the important reform movements of the early nineteenth century. The Transcendentalists were mostly from New England, and a surprising number of them had attended Harvard and had served as Unitarian ministers. They never comprised a religious sect so much as a loosely knit group with similar philosophical attitudes. Starting as an informal discussion club in 1836, the Transcendentalists met and exchanged ideas in and around Concord, Massachusetts, for several years.

Just as the Unitarian faith had been the Enlightenment's rejection of Puritanism, so the Transcendentalists represented Romanticism's rejection of Unitarianism. The Transcendentalists dismissed Unitarianism as "corpse-cold," pallid, uninspiring, too impressed by human reason and too neglectful of the human spirit. One of the idols of the Enlightenment had been the English philosopher, John Locke, who had held that ideas do not rise spontaneously in the mind but only as a result of being implanted there by impressions from the external world, received through the senses. The Transcendentalists argued against this theory and contended that ordinary experience can never be a guide to ultimate reality, which can be reached only by "transcending" into intuitive, mystical perception. As a rather critical journalist, Orestes Brownson, remarked of the Transcendentalists: "They do not swear by Locke, and they recognize no authority in matters of opinion but the human. . . . Some of them . . . *ignore* all philosophy, plant themselves in their instincts and wait for the huge world to come round to them. . . . Some of them reason . . . others merely dream." Like other Romantics, the Transcendentalists celebrated nature because they believed that it was divine, the direct expression of God, whom they called "The Oversoul." The leading Transcendentalist, Ralph Waldo Emerson, exclaimed: "Standing on the bare ground . . . all mean egotism vanishes. I become a transparent eyeball; I am nothing; I see all; the currents of the Universal Being circulate through me; I am part and parcel of God."

Like the Unitarians, the Transcendentalists perceived no evil in the human mind, but unlike the Unitarians, they urged people to trust their intuition, not their reason. Fundamental to Transcendental belief was the conviction that each man had an inner spiritual conscience, similar to the Quaker "inner light." The movement was a blend of German Romanticism, Unitarianism, Quakerism, and Hindu pantheism. Emerson celebrated India's pantheism in a poem to the all-encompassing God called Brahma in these stanzas:

Far or forgot to me is near;
  Shadow and sunlight are the same;

The vanished gods to me appear;
  And one to me are shame and fame.

They reckon ill who leave me out;
  When me they fly, I am the wings;
I am the doubter and the doubt,
  And I the hymn the Brahmin sings.

LITERATURE

The decades before the Civil War witnessed a phenomenal burst of literary activity which produced six writers of genius: Emerson, Thoreau, Poe, Hawthorne, Melville, and Whitman. So great was their artistic achievement that Melville confidently declared, "Believe me, men not very much inferior to Shakespeare are this day being born on the banks of the Ohio."

Indeed, the decade before the Civil War represented a golden age in American literature. As the modern critic F. O. Matthiesen has written: "You may search all the rest of American literature without being able to collect a group of books equal to these in imaginative vitality." Between 1850 and 1855, the following masterpieces were published: Nathaniel Hawthorne's *The Scarlet Letter* and *The House of Seven Gables,* Herman Melville's *Moby Dick,* Henry David Thoreau's *Walden,* and Walt Whitman's *Leaves of Grass.*

RALPH WALDO EMERSON

The leading Transcendentalist and the most famous American author and thinker of his day was Ralph Waldo Emerson (1803–1882). Descended from a long line of New England preachers, Emerson studied at Harvard between 1817 and 1821, and then taught school, studied theology, and became a Unitarian minister. When he was thirty he decided that "to be a good minister one must leave the ministry," and he resigned from the Second Church of Boston where he was pastor. He immediately set out on the first of his three trips to Europe.

Ralph Waldo Emerson was a minister before becoming well-known as a writer, lecturer, and philosopher.

There he met the English poet William Wordsworth and the Scottish philosopher Thomas Carlyle, who became a lifelong friend. When he returned to America, Emerson settled in Concord, Massachusetts, and began to earn his living as an essayist and lecturer. He traveled far and wide giving talks on philosophical subjects, receiving as much as fifty dollars a talk. On the platform his manner was grave, his speaking voice so beautiful that one small-town observer said, "Our choir was a pretty good one, but its best was coarse and discordant after Emerson's voice."

In his first book, *Nature,* published in 1836, Emerson called for an original American response to philosophy. "There are new lands, new men, new thoughts," he wrote. "Let us demand our own works and laws and worship." In 1841 and again in 1844 he brought out books of *Essays,* which made him famous on both sides of the Atlantic.

Emerson was never a systematic philosopher, or even a coherent essayist. His ideas were more brilliant flashes of insight than integrated parts of a unified philosophical system. Nevertheless, these isolated flashes illuminated previously unnoticed parts of the American experience. Emerson was a great optimist and a believer in the perfectibility of man.

Opposed to organized religion, which he felt had lost its warmth and relevance, Emerson commented, "It is already beginning to indicate character and religion to withdraw from the religious meetings." But if he considered church-going superfluous, he regarded the pursuit of virtue as an activity of primary importance. "Virtue is the business of the universe," he wrote. Pursuing virtue, Emerson thought, "is divine and deifying. It is the beatitude of man. It makes him illimitable. Through it, the soul first knows itself." Knowing *oneself* was crucial, as well as relying on one's own inner strength. Like so many Americans, Emerson was a rugged individualist; one of his most famous essays was titled "Self-Reliance."

Another American attitude that Emerson embodied was the belief in equality. Though not an admirer of General Jackson, he was in tune with "Jacksonian democracy." A man "is equal to every other man. . . . Let a clear, apprehensive mind, such as every man knows among his friends, converse with the most commanding poetic genius, I think it would appear that there was no inequality such as men fancy, between them; that a perfect understanding, a like receiving, a like perceiving, abolished differences; and the poet would confess that his creative imagination gave him no deep advantage, but only the superficial one that he could express himself and the other could not; that his advantage was a knack, which might impose on indolent men but could not impose on lovers of truth. . . . I believe it is the conviction of the purest men that the net amount of man and man does not much vary."

Individual Reform

. . . Whoso would be a man, must be a nonconformist. He who would gather immortal palms must not be hindered by the name of goodness, but must explore if it be goodness. Nothing is at last sacred but the integrity of your own mind. . . . No law can be sacred to me but that of my nature. Good and bad are but names very readily transferable to that of this; the only right is what is after my constitution; the only wrong what is against it. . . . I am ashamed to think how easily we capitulate to badges and names, to large societies and dead institutions. Every decent and well-spoken individual affects and sways me more than is right. I ought to go upright and vital, and speak the rude truth in all ways. If malice and vanity wear the coat of philanthropy, shall that pass? If an angry bigot assumes this bountiful cause of Abolition, and comes to me with his last news from Barbadoes, why should I not say to him, 'Go love thy infant; love thy wood-chopper; be good-natured and modest; have that grace; and never varnish your hard, uncharitable ambition with this incredible tenderness for black folk a thousand miles off. Thy love afar is spite at home.' . . . I tell thee, thou foolish philanthropist, that I grudge the dollar, the dime, the cent I give to such men as do not belong to me and to whom I do not belong. . . .

. . . I do not wish to expiate, but to live. My life is for itself and not for a spectacle. . . . **"**

—*Ralph Waldo Emerson,*
"Self-Reliance"

The aspect of American life that Emerson and all the Transcendentalists disapproved of was its vulgar materialism. He felt that the acquisition of wealth must be matched by spiritual gain, and he was skep-

Communal Reform

" *The most prevailing fear about Association is on the score of that undefined thing, Individuality. The very vagueness of the term, as used, however, is proof that it covers more than is understood. False Individuality is a thing very well defined; but of true Individuality the scientific account is locked up in the future. Yet it shall soon be unlocked, since this new light has been thrown upon its complement, or true association. We are prepared to take the ground that there is not and never can be Individuality, so long as there is not Association. Without true union no part can be true. The members were made for the body; if the whole body be incoherent, every member of it will be developed falsely, will become shrunken or overgrown, distorted and weakened, since it will have either more or less than its share, both of duty and of sustenance. Variety itself is dull, if it lack unity; for unity is the beginning and end of variety. . . .* **"**

—*John S. Dwight,*
"Individuality in Association"

tical about the advantages of industrialization. Yet even materialism he considered simply an absence of higher ideals, rather than an expression of greed: "Men such as they are, very naturally seek money or power. . . . And why not? For they aspire to the highest, and this, in their sleepwalking, they dream is highest. Wake them, and they shall quit the false good and leap to the true, and leave governments to clerks and desks. This revolution is to be wrought by the gradual domestication of the idea of Culture. The main enterprise of the world for splendor, for extent, is the upbuilding of a man."

Greed was missing from Emerson's world and evil had no permanent existence. Un-

443

like the Puritans, who had believed sinfulness in men could never be eradicated, Emerson held that "Good is positive, Evil is merely privative, not absolute: it is like cold, which is the privation of heat. All evil is so much death and nonentity. Benevolence is absolute and real. So much benevolence as a man hath, so much life hath he." Not only were all men potentially good, but all were part of one great spiritual mind, the Oversoul: "There is one mind common to all individual men. Every man is an inlet to the same and to all of the same . . . Who hath access to this universal mind is a party to all that is or can be done, for this is the only and sovereign agent."

HENRY DAVID THOREAU

A close friend and former student of Emerson, Thoreau eventually equaled his master as a writer. Thoreau was born on July 12, 1817. He entered Harvard in 1833, where he studied literature. So outstanding was he as a student that he was asked to deliver a commencement address, in which he first expressed his unconventional views: "This curious world which we inhabit is more wonderful than it is convenient; more beautiful than it is useful; it is more to be admired and enjoyed than used." After graduation, he worked with members of his family in their meager, poorly paying home industry, making lead pencils. He taught school for a while in Concord but resigned when the directors insisted he dispense corporal punishment. In 1841 he went to stay with the Emersons for two years, serving them as a handyman. In March, 1845, he built a one-room cabin on the shore of Walden Pond, a mile and a half from the center of Concord. There he lived from July, 1845, to September, 1847, writing, hiking, and gardening or, as he put it, "making the earth say beans instead of grass." His first book, *A Week on the Concord and Merrimack Rivers,* was published

at his own expense in 1849; it sold only three hundred copies in his lifetime. *Walden,* his second, was his masterpiece.

Walden contained Thoreau's most insistent message. As a modern critic, Joseph Wood Krutch, has written: "The lesson he had taught himself, and which he tried to teach others, was summed up in the one word 'simplify.' That meant simplify the outward circumstances of your life, simplify your needs and your ambitions; learn to delight in the simple pleasures which the world of Nature affords. It meant also, scorn public opinion, refuse to accept the common definitions of success, refuse to be moved by the judgment of others."

Thoreau's life was indeed simple. As Emerson said in his movingly beautiful portrait of Thoreau: "He was bred to no profession; he never married; he lived alone; he never went to church; he never voted; he refused to pay a tax to the State; he ate no flesh, he drank no wine, he never knew the use of tobacco; and though a naturalist, he used neither trap nor gun. He chose, wisely no doubt for himself, to be the bachelor of thought and Nature." The only public issue that ever aroused his indignation was slavery. He was a passionate defender of even the most extreme abolitionists. To protest against the federal government, which he felt was condoning the spread of slavery, Thoreau refused to pay his Massachusetts poll tax. He was imprisoned for one day, until his tax was paid by a member of his household. In a famous essay, "Civil Disobedience," Thoreau argued that disobeying a law is preferable to disobeying one's own conscience. His doctrine of passive resistance against evil inspired the Russian novelist and social thinker, Leo Tolstoy, as well as the father of India's independence, Mahatma Gandhi. In the mid-twentieth century the civil rights movement and many student protests have invoked Thoreau's name.

Thoreau was a Romanticist in his love of nature and his defense of individual non-conformity. He was never a member of a formal religion; he found God in nature. On his deathbed, when a friend asked him if he had made his peace with God, he responded, "I am not aware that we ever quarrelled."

WALT WHITMAN

Emerson had called for a great national poet in 1842: "We have yet had no genius in America, with tyrannous eye, which knew the value of our incomparable materials, and saw, in the barbarism and materialism of the times, another carnival of the same gods whose picture he so admires in Homer. . . ."

The nation received a great native poet in the person of Walt Whitman (1818–1892). Born on Long Island, Whitman left

Walt Whitman as he appeared on the title page of Leaves of Grass.

school when he was only thirteen and worked as a printer and newspaperman. He absorbed the writings of Shakespeare, Carlyle, Sir Walter Scott; and of Emerson he remarked, "I was simmering, simmering, simmering. Emerson brought me to the boil."

His collection of poems, *Leaves of Grass,* first appeared in 1855, although he was to revise it many times over the course of his life. The poems were highly unusual both for their style and content. Instead of the familiar repetitious rhythm of conventional poetry, *Leaves of Grass* employed broad cadences, more typical of Biblical prose than of ordinary verse. The subject matter was also new, even shocking. Sex, work, and the common man were important themes; the poems partook "of the common idioms, manners, the earth, the rude visage of animals and trees, and what is vulgar," as Whitman remarked.

NATHANIEL HAWTHORNE

In a sense Emerson, Thoreau, and Whitman were all optimists. Each man criticized American culture to the extent of its conformity, inequalities, and materialism, but all felt that human beings were potentially good and American life could be progressively improved. Writing at the same time, however, were three figures of equal importance who did not espouse this generally hopeful view of life. Nathaniel Hawthorne, Herman Melville, and Edgar Allen Poe partook of the Romantic movement to the extent that they ardently studied nature, trusted the instincts more than the intellect and were fond of exotic places and faraway times. They did not, however, consider evil merely the absence of good. All three saw evil as an active, inescapable force in human affairs. In this respect they were part of the older Puritan tradition in American life. None of them was a philosopher, nor wanted to be. As artists, they did not formulate a clear-cut philosophy of life. Critics

445

have argued for years about their exact beliefs, but fundamentally all three were haunted by the notion of sin, of vice, and of pride.

Hawthorne (1804–1864) was born in Salem, Massachusetts, the son of a local shipmaster. After four conventional years at Bowdoin College, Hawthorne retired to Salem and hid himself. As he once said, he thought that not more than twenty people in the town knew of his existence. He wrote his old Bowdoin classmate, the poet Longfellow, saying: "Since we last met . . . I have secluded myself from society; and yet I never meant any such thing, nor dreamed what sort of life I was going to lead. I have made a captive of myself and put me into a dungeon, and now I cannot find the key to let myself out—and if the door were open, I should be almost afraid to come out."

Nathaniel Hawthorne in 1860. Hawthorne was best known for The Scarlet Letter, *a novel in which he explored Puritan preoccupation with the wrath of God.*

Hawthorne was still a boy when his father died, and his mother retired into such deep mourning that even her children seldom saw her. After graduation, Hawthorne's only amusements were long walks along the Salem seashore, reading and daydreaming. As the years went by, these daydreams became more and more morose. Like his Puritan ancestors, Hawthorne was obsessed with men's sinfulness which in his opinion was basically selfishness. He never attended church, but nevertheless brooded over religious concepts, watched churchgoers on Sunday from his bedroom window, and filled his notebooks with entries about possible tales that spoke of a stern faith.

Out of these broodings came many of Hawthorne's short stories, tales like "Young Goodman Brown," in which a village boy is commanded by the devil to "penetrate, in every bosom, the deep mystery of sin, the fountain of all wicked arts, and which inexhaustibly supplies more evil impulses than human power—than my power at its utmost—can make manifest in deeds." Yet Hawthorne did not become a truly productive writer until he fell in love with Sophia Peabody and married her in 1842. During his marriage he became less withdrawn and more ambitious. He attempted one year to live in the utopian community, Brook Farm, but left in disappointment. Over the next twenty years he wrote four major novels. *The Scarlet Letter* is considered by many to be his best work. The books were moderately successful, but not enough to support the Hawthornes. He held a variety of government civil service posts, from weigher and gauger in the Boston Custom House in 1839 to his most important, and highest paid, appointment as United States consul in Liverpool, England.

Although many critics recognized Hawthorne's mastery of prose, his tales, which were skeptical of progress, went against the American grain. His attitude toward science was expressed in "Rappacini's Daughter," the story of a mad scientist, who purely out of the love of experimentation, turned his beautiful daughter into a poisonous object whose very breath killed flowers and insects. Hawthorne's masterpiece, *The Scarlet Letter,* recounts the story of a Puritan woman who committed adultery with a minister. When she gave birth to a daughter, who served as her mother's "messenger of anguish," the adulteress was forced by the community to wear a scarlet letter *A* sewn to her dress. The minister only confessed his part in the sinful situation at the end of his life, when he opened his shirt to reveal an identical letter branded by God into his flesh. Hawthorne's preoccupation with this kind of tragic subject offended Americans caught up in the prevailing optimism of the mid-nineteenth century.

HERMAN MELVILLE

One of Hawthorne's few close friends was Herman Melville, the author of *Moby Dick.* Melville (1819–1891) was always fascinated by religious questions, although he himself lacked faith in God. His father, a bankrupt importer in New York City, died when Melville was thirteen. After working in a hat store in Albany and then teaching school, Melville went to sea on a whaling vessel. After three years in which he wandered about the Pacific and served in the United States Navy, Melville returned to Albany. His voyages provided him with the material for his first two books, *Typee* and *Omoo.* Both were best-sellers, dealing with exotic cultures that few Americans had seen. A third book, thought to be a strange allegorical novel about America, *Mardi,* was so confusing that it failed to sell at all.

Melville did not achieve his full stature until he wrote *Moby Dick.* In 1850 he and his wife had moved to a farm in Massachusetts, where Melville began to immerse himself in the writings of Shakespeare and Hawthorne. Shakespeare's work elevated

Portrait of Herman Melville *by Joseph Oriel Eaton.*

Melville's language and gave him a taste for heroic actions and noble themes. Hawthorne introduced Melville to the technique of symbolism. Under Hawthorne's influence, *Moby Dick* changed from simply the tale of a whaling expedition to a dark allegory of good and evil.

Precisely what Melville meant to convey by *Moby Dick* has been disputed since the early twentieth century when an interest in Melville's works began to grow. He is now regarded by many as America's greatest novelist. The book's plot concerns a Yankee skipper, Ahab, who had lost one leg in a struggle with the great white whale, Moby Dick. As a result Ahab became obsessed with a desire for revenge against the whale. He and his crew pursued the great animal from one end of the Pacific to the other, but failed to capture him. Finally the ship was attacked by the whale, who then killed Captain Ahab.

Some commentators have seen the whale as the representation of evil; others have judged Ahab to be the evil figure in the drama. The whale has been variously interpreted by some as the mysterious force of nature, as the subconscious hostility lurking in every creature, or as the cruelty of fate. Today many scholars hold still another view, that Melville regarded the whale, and all of nature, as impersonal, morally neutral. Ahab's madness was that he imagined the whale to be evil, and yet this folly was carried out on such a heroic scale that it ennobled him. Ahab's attempt to see meaning in the universe, even if it was a sinister one, amounted to a very real victory. According to these critics, Melville seems to be saying that in fact the world is as morally colorless as the white whale. Human beings cannot stand this chilling emptiness, however, and Ahab heroically created a determined, if unrealistic, moral crusade by imputing evil to Moby Dick.

Regardless of the interpretation of the book, *Moby Dick* is a superb adventure story, a mine of information about whaling, and a penetrating psychological study of obsession. Melville's descriptive powers are shown by this passage from the book, when Ahab's ship has floated into the midst of a school of nursing whales and their babies:

But far beneath this wondrous world upon the surface, another and still stranger world met our eyes as we gazed over the side. For suspended in those watery vaults, floated the forms of the nursing mothers of the whales, and those that by their enormous girth seemed shortly to become mothers. The lake, as I have hinted, was to a considerable depth exceedingly transparent; and as human infants while sucking will calmly and fixedly gaze away from the breast, as if leading two different lives at the time; and while yet drawing mortal nourishment, be still spiritually feasting upon some unearthly reminiscence;—even so did the young of these whales seem looking up towards us, but not at us, as if we were but a bit of Gulf-weed in their new-
born sight. Floating on their sides, the mothers also seemed quietly eyeing us.

EDGAR ALLAN POE

Like Hawthorne and Melville, Poe (1809–1849) did not accept the prevailing American belief that human nature was perfectible. He wrote in one letter: "I have no faith in human perfectibility. I think that human exertion will have no appreciable effect upon humanity. Man is now only more active—not more happy, nor more wise—than he was 6,000 years ago. The result will never vary—and to suppose that it will, is to suppose that the foregone man has lived in vain—that the foregone time is but the rudiment of the future—that the myriads who have perished have not been upon equal footing with ourselves—nor are we with our posterity. I cannot agree to lose sight of man the individual in man the mass. I have no belief in spirituality."

Poe was born in Boston, a city he later came to loathe, calling it "Frogpond." His parents were actors. When Poe was still an infant, his father deserted the family. The abandoned mother traveled with her three young children from city to city as an actress. She died in Richmond, Virginia, when Edgar was two. Poe was then adopted by a wealthy merchant, John Allan. After spending five years in England, he enrolled at the University of Virginia. There he drank and gambled so much that his adoptive father disowned him.

His life was short and passed in misery. He suffered from alcoholism and periodic bouts of insanity. Despite his brilliance, Poe was never able to earn more than three hundred dollars a year as a journalist, critic, editor, and writer. In 1836 he married his thirteen-year old cousin, Virginia, to whom he was passionately attached. When she became fatally ill, his lapses into insanity grew more frequent. As he described it to a friend, "I became insane, with long intervals of horrible sanity. During these fits of absolute unconsciousness, I drank—God only knows how often or how much. As a matter of course, my enemies referred the insanity to the drink, rather than the drink to the insanity. I had, indeed, nearly abandoned all hope of a permanent cure, when I found one in the *death* of my wife. . . . In the death of what was my life, then, I receive a new, but—Oh God! how melancholy an existence."

Despite his personal tragedies, Poe managed to turn out a truly impressive body of work. His literary criticism set new standards of taste and insight. His short stories, among them the first detective stories ever written, were amazingly tight dramatic structures in which every element contributed to a final, dazzling effect. His poetry was as formal as Whitman's was loose, and his experiments with a poetry of pure sound (that is, verse in which music took precedence over meaning) had great influence on French literature. Perhaps the best-known example of this type of verse is "The Bells":

> *Hear the mellow wedding bells*
> *Golden bells!*
> *What a world of happiness their*
> *harmony foretells!*
> *Through the balmy air of night*
> *How they ring out their delight!—*
> *From the molten-golden notes,*
> *And all in tune,*
> *What a liquid ditty floats*
> *To the turtle-dove that listens, while*
> *she gloats*
> *On the moon!*

THE VISUAL ARTS

While literature scaled new heights, American painting was not far behind, and the development of painting reflected the same blend of intellectual currents that had shaped literature: Puritanism, the Enlight-enment, Romanticism, and to a lesser extent, evangelism.

THE HUDSON RIVER SCHOOL

The founder of the Hudson River School of landscape painting was Thomas Cole (1801–1848), a poor English boy who had emmigrated to the United States when he was seventeen, and who only a few years later was regarded as America's leading painter.

Cole attained this fame by breaking with neoclassicism. An outgrowth of the Enlightenment, neoclassicism had been the ruling taste of the generation in America that preceded Cole. According to neoclassical standards, artists should ignore the bizarre and the emotional and celebrate the rational and the ideal. The artist's job was to eliminate all the accidents of nature and simplify every scene until the underlying perfect form was revealed. Thus, instead of showing real people neoclassical artists attempted to show idealized human beings, freed of all particularity. To avoid the temptation to paint what was merely of the moment, neoclassical artists concentrated on historical subjects. In the generation before Cole, the three leading American artists were all of the neoclassical school and all painted historical subjects. For example, Washington Allston (1779–1843) rendered scenes from the Bible; Samuel F. B. Morse (1791–1872) portrayed *The Dying Hercules;* John Vanderlyn (1775–1852) pictured *Marius Amid the Ruins of Carthage.*

Cole was infected with Romanticism's love of nature, and on his long rambles through the Catskills and along the Hudson, he made sketches which he later worked into full oil paintings. Cole believed that America, with its rugged mountains, large rivers, and gorgeous sunsets, offered rare possibilities to the landscape painter. His paintings, and those of the other landscape artists of the Hudson River

449

School, are distinguished by their luminous quality. Many of their canvases combine a lyrical tribute to the vastness and beauty of nature with a burnished, glass-like surface. They captured the quality of light and air at a specific moment in time. Nevertheless, Cole was troubled by the natural world. On the one hand, he embraced the Romantic view that whatever was natural was good, and that the contemplation of a landscape could lead the viewer into "religious musing." On the other hand, he sometimes assumed the old Puritan view that nature was frightening, sinful, diseased, and unbearably lonely. As he put it: "There was an awfulness in the utter solitude that was almost painful. Man may seek such scenes and find pleasure in the discovery, but there is a mysterious fear comes over him and hurries him away. The sublime features of nature are too severe for a lone man to look upon and be happy."

Kindred Spirits by Asher Durand portrays William Cullen Bryant and Thomas Cole on a walk through the Catskill Mountains. Cole was acknowledged as America's greatest landscape painter, a position Durand inherited when Cole died.

When Cole died, Asher Durand (1796–1886) was acknowledged as America's greatest living painter. A landscape painter, who would cheerfully allow his patrons to specify the species of tree (beech, oak, hemlock) they wanted portrayed, Durand and his followers in the Hudson River School entertained none of Cole's misgivings about nature. They promoted instead a purely Emersonian view of the natural world. Optimistic and convinced that God was in every mountain and stream, Durand regarded landscape as a perfect form of moral art, since "its wondrous structure and function that minister to our well-being is fraught with high and holy meaning, only surpassed by the light of Revelation." The theory that something could be learned from painting was vastly reassuring to practical Americans who, uncertain about the value of art, feared that paintings might only be useless baubles.

GENRE PAINTING

America, during this period, also produced two important painters of ordinary, everyday life. The first was William Sidney Mount (1807–1868), a self-taught artist who began work as a sign painter. Endeavoring to be entirely original, Mount declared: "I launched forth on my sea of adventure with the firm determination to avoid the style of any artist and to create a school of my own." His most popular canvases were of blacks at their daily activities on Mount's native Long Island. Unlike the neoclassicists, who had wanted to eliminate all topical or accidental details from their "pure" subjects, Mount tried to catch, as he said, "the unstudied circumstance of the moment." Traveling about in his portable, horse-drawn studio, Mount attempted to make his paintings seem like actual scenes from life. He had respect for human beings and presented their actions with simplicity and directness. So popular were his paintings of blacks, and so successfully did they appeal to Europeans' curiosity about American life, that engravings were made of ten of his canvases in Paris where they sold in large numbers.

The other great genre artist of the age was George Caleb Bingham (1811–1879), who also started out as a sign painter. After a brief formal study in Philadelphia and New York, Bingham worked unsuccessfully as a portrait painter in Washington, D.C. He then returned to his home in Columbia, Missouri. Remembering that the Apollo Gallery in New York had expressed interest in scenes of life along the Mississippi, Bingham began to turn out works with titles

The Jolly Flatboatmen *by George Caleb Bingham.*

like *The Jolly Flatboatmen.* His many river pictures show men playing cards, making music, dancing, or fishing on boats or docks. He also created many paintings capturing moments in Missouri political life, pictures of stump speakers or an election day scene such as one titled *Canvassing for a Vote.*

PAINTINGS OF INDIANS

In the 1830s George Catlin (1796–1872) and Alfred Jacob Miller (1810–1874) turned to the West for subjects. Catlin had been raised in the Wyoming Valley in Pennsyl-

vania and had seen Indians as a boy—seen them, feared them, and been fascinated by this "truly lofty and noble race," as he called them. As an adult he traveled across the Great Plains, furiously turning out hundreds of oil portraits of Indians. Espousing the Romanticist belief that "a state of primitive wilderness and rudeness" was a sure guide to ideal beauty, Catlin trekked through the wilds carrying on his back oil pigments and canvases and worked at breakneck speed. In just eighty-six days in 1832, for example, he managed to travel 1,500 miles and paint 135 canvases. He not only painted portraits, but scenes of warriors enduring ritual tortures or hunting buffalo, and of medicine men dancing in splendid plumage and masks. Lamenting the fact that the white man's civilization was destroying the red man's way of life, Catlin attempted to raise money and procure sympathy for the Indians by touring Europe with his paintings and a troupe of

The Chief of the Blackfeet was portrayed by George Catlin whose interest in the American Indian's way of life dominated his canvases.

451

Indian braves who performed war dances for awed spectators.

Miller was never as personally attached to the Indians as was Catlin. In fact, Alfred Jacob Miller, the son of a Baltimore grocer, probably would never have traveled to the West at all if an eccentric Scottish baron had not hired him to make the journey and record scenes of Indian life to decorate the baron's castle. During the one summer of 1837 Miller made scores of rapid, lively watercolors of Indians in the Rockies and on the Great Plains.

SCULPTURE
AND ARCHITECTURE

Before the Civil War, the United States did not present any important sculpture to the world. The taste of the day went toward sentimental subjects of children and their pets or mothers and their babies. Nude female figures, generally leathery, uninspired copies of ancient Greek and Roman sculpture, attracted many "connoisseurs," although the American people were still so prudish that one sculptor had to change the name of his voluptuous *Venus* to *Purity,* and finally by a sleight-of-hand, to *The Triumph of Chastity.*

From a visit to an American sculptor in Rome in 1858, Hawthorne left a revealing glimpse of the taste of the times:

A few days ago, my wife and I visited the studio of Mr. Mozier, an American, who seems to have a good deal of vogue as a sculptor. We found a figure of Pocahontas, which he has repeated several times; another which he calls the "Wept of Wishton-Wish"; a figure of a smiling girl playing with a cat and dog, and a school-boy mending a pen. These two last were the only ones that gave me any pleasure, or that really had any merit, for his cleverness and ingenuity appear in homely subjects, but are quite lost in attempts at a higher ideality. Nevertheless, he has a group of

the Prodigal Son, possessing more merit than I should have expected from Mr. Mozier; the son resting his hand on his father's breast, with an expression of utter weariness, at length finding perfect rest, while the father bends his benign visage over him, and seems to receive him calmly into himself. . . . Miss Lander tells me that Mr. Mozier has stolen—adapted we will rather say—the attitude and general idea of this group from one executed by a student from the French Academy, and to be seen there in plaster.

The Romantic movement, with its love of exotic, faraway times and places, had its inevitable effect on American architecture. Greek and Italian styles flourished, but the most popular style was the Gothic, with its towers and curlicued trimmings. The most important building in the Gothic tradition was the Smithsonian Institution in Washington, built in 1846. The huge, pink building had nine different types of towers, a sight which appealed to Americans with a fondness for the medieval castles described in Sir Walter Scott's popular novels.

SCIENCE

The Smithsonian Institution was founded after an Englishman bequeathed 500,000 dollars to the United States "for the increase and diffusion of knowledge." America's most famous scientist, the physicist Joseph Henry, became the first head of the institution. Henry, a science professor at Princeton, made important contributions in the early 1830s to the understanding of magnetic fields created by electrical currents. The modern unit of electromagnetic induction, the henry, is named after him.

DEMOCRACY AND SCIENCE

Henry was only one of several important scientists America was proud to acknowledge in the 1830s and 1840s. Others were Crawford W. Long, a Georgia doctor who discovered that ether could be used as an anesthetic, and two Harvard professors, Louis Agassiz and Asa Gray. Agassiz made significant discoveries in geology and zoology and Gray's studies of plant distribution greatly aided Charles Darwin in his formulation of the theory of evolution.

Almost all of the nation's top scientists saw a strong link between democracy and science. As a journalist wrote in 1840, "Democracy is the cradle of science and only an unfettered mind can expand to its utmost." When the first National Scientific Congress met in Washington in 1844, Senator Robert J. Walker confidently announced to the assembly that "the scientists could make this country the greatest and freest nation in the world."

AMERICAN INVENTIONS

More startling, more immediately useful, and more widely celebrated than America's theoretical scientific contributions were the many practical inventions she gave the world. In 1832, a New England painter, Samuel F. B. Morse, developed the idea of an electromagnetic telegraph. He had to wait eleven years, however, before he received a thirty-thousand-dollar appropriation from Congress to build an experimental telegraph line from Washington to Baltimore. Finally, on May 1, 1844, the first message was sent over the line. The invention was such a triumph that by 1850 thousands of miles of line had been installed across the United States east of the Mississippi. In 1858 a transatlantic cable was buried under the ocean and the United States was at last only seconds away from Europe. No longer would week-long lags in communication separate the New World from the Old.

Americans devised many other useful inventions in these years. The McCormick reaper, an improved harvesting machine, was patented in 1834. By 1860 twenty thousand reapers were being manufactured every year, greatly easing the burden of farming in a country hampered by a shortage of manpower. The sewing machine, patented by Elias Howe in 1846, permitted garment manufacturers to step up production; the sewing machine stitched the uniforms of thousands of Northern soldiers in the Civil War. Yet another American invention was the revolver. Samuel Colt, a sixteen-year-old boy from Connecticut, whiled away the long hours, as he traveled from Boston to Calcutta as a sailor, by whittling a wooden model of a pistol with a revolving cartridge. A few years later he patented his invention in both England and America and by 1838 a factory in New Jersey had begun to manufacture the new pistols. In 1836, another inventor from Connecticut, Charles Goodyear, learned how to vulcanize rubber by treating crude India rubber with sulfur and subjecting it to intense heat to make it more durable.

REFORM MOVEMENTS

"It may be said, without much exaggeration, that everything is done now by Societies," wrote William Ellery Channing. "You can scarcely name an object for which some institution has not been formed." From the 1820s until the Civil War, a host of reform movements flourished in the North, particularly in the Northeast. Schools, prisons, mental hospitals, factory conditions, alcoholism, war, the status of women, and above all slavery, became issues of concern to those who wanted to see social evils corrected. With the decline of Puritan theology and its gloomy assessment of human nature, a new spirit swept through the Protestant denominations. The adherents of Unitarianism and Universalism strove to reform society by awakening the principle of reason they believed every man possessed. They supported the widely held belief in human progress and preached the perfectibility of man through his own rational efforts, efforts which harmonized with the optimistic mood of early nineteenth-century America.

The revivalist movement was also committed to reforming society, though from different motives. The central figure in the reform movement in the evangelical churches, Charles G. Finney, maintained that "the church must take right ground on the subject of Temperance, and Moral Reform, and all the subjects of practical morality which come up for decision from time to time." Certain practices were sinful and must be rooted out of society. Many Presbyterians, Baptists, and Congregationalists responded enthusiastically to this call to support the reform of society.

MODEL COMMUNITIES

In an effort to end the degrading conditions of workers that accompanied the industrial and transportation revolutions, some reformers wanted not only to improve social conditions but to reorganize society into self-sufficient communal units. So bold and optimistic were many American reformers that they undertook to change the basic composition of society itself by establishing model communities, small experiments in cooperative living that they hoped would eventually work a deep, curative effect on the country at large. An early nonreligious experiment in what has been called utopian socialism was New Harmony, Indiana, a community organized by Robert

Owen, a successful British textile manufacturer and social philosopher. Founded in the 1820s, New Harmony was to function as a socialist venture, cooperatively owned by all the members of the village and governed by a democratically elected assembly. New Harmony sought to abolish poverty through shared labor and collective ownership. Owen believed men must be happy to work well. There was to be an eight-hour day and a variety of activities to interest the inhabitants. Most of the people who came to live there, however, were too individualistic to adjust to communal living. Moreover, Owen wanted to run the community himself and stamp it with his ideas, most of which were considered radical at the time. He was against organized religion, marriage, and the holding of private property. As a result, the project broke down and was abandoned after a few years.

Another short-lived utopian community was a project in Tennessee called Nashoba. It was started by an Englishwoman named Frances Wright who wanted to use it to train slaves and then give them their freedom. Her plan was for them to stay there five to ten years and then colonize them outside the country. A few slaves were placed at Nashoba and trained in a skill, but the project collapsed after two years because of popular opposition. The slaves were freed and sent to Haiti.

In the 1840s about forty American communities were set up on the principles of a French socialist, Charles Fourier. Quite unlike Owen, Fourier proposed that each community (called a "phalanx") should be like a joint-stock company. Profits from all enterprises of the association were to be divided, with one-third paid out as dividends to stockholders, and the remainder fed back into the community in the form of salaries and cash rewards for the members. All participants would live together and work for the community with each member allowed to choose his own occupation and change jobs eight times a day for variety.

As with Owen's project, each community was to be a self-sufficient, autonomous unit outside of organized society.

Brook Farm, a basically religious community opened in 1841 by twenty members, many of them Transcendentalists, became a Fourierist center in 1845. At one time or another many of New England's leading intellectuals lived at Brook Farm, which was only ten miles from Boston. The idea of its chief sponsor, George Ripley, was to combine the life of the thinker and worker outside competitive society—to develop the complete individual. Hawthorne, briefly a member, based one of his novels, *The Blithedale Romance,* on his experiences there.

The community managed to put out a brilliant weekly journal, the *Harbinger,* which contained some of the country's best prose by such authors as Charles A. Dana, James Russell Lowell, John Greenleaf Whittier, and Horace Greeley. Unfortunately, a disastrous fire destroyed much of Brook Farm in 1846 and the community disbanded as an economic failure.

One after another the other Fourierist phalanxes failed, although not always for economic reasons. In fact, in 1854 the total assets of the communities exceeded their debts. Exactly why they *did* disband is a matter of conjecture. Surely one reason is that many of the farmers were city-bred intellectuals who were not really cut out for rural life. Many of them also practiced ideas which were out of step with American life at the time.

On the other hand, a religious colony such as the Amana Society in Iowa was flourishing. Unlike the Fourierist experiments, it was composed of people who had a shared religious and cultural identity, were brought up to farm and were used to a simple village life.

One other religious community, the Perfectionist settlement of John Humphrey Noyes at Oneida, New York, lasted until the 1880s. Noyes, who had been expelled from the ministry, formed the Perfectionist Sect in 1846. Its members believed in complete release from sin by conversion to faith in God, faith healing, and complex marriage in which all men and women in the community were the husbands and wives of one another. As Noyes wrote: "Religious love is very near neighbor to sexual love, and they always get mixed up in the intimacies and social excitement of Revivals. Revivals lead to religious love; religious love excited the passions; the converts, finding themselves in theocratic liberty, begin to look about for their mates and their paradise. . . ." The community devoted itself to farming, logging, and the manufacture of fur traps. Yet, in spite of internal success, popular antagonism to its marital practices ultimately forced it into abandonment.

EDUCATIONAL REFORM

During the 1830s, large segments of the population began to demand state-supported primary education as a prerequisite for a democratic society and for the self-advancement of the poor. As in so many other struggles, Massachusetts led the way by establishing the first state board of education in 1837 and by appointing Horace Mann as its first secretary. Mann, like other educational reformers, recognized that more and more occupations required the ability to read, write, and do simple arithmetic. He also recognized that a true democracy could only work if all citizens were educated: "If we do not prepare children to become good citizens, if we do not enrich their minds with knowledge . . . then our republic must go down to destruction, as others have gone before it."

Mann analyzed the school systems of Europe and incorporated aspects of every advanced system he studied into his plan for Massachusetts. He lengthened the school year by one month to a full term of six months, organized a state association of teachers, and doubled teachers' salaries. In 1839 he helped create the country's first teacher-training college in Lexington, Massachusetts. Called a "normal" school after the École Normale of France, the college helped convince the public and the teachers themselves that education should be considered a profession.

By the 1850s, most states had agreed with Mann's position that education should be tax-supported and that public schools should not be thought of simply as an expedient for paupers. Several states passed laws requiring local communities to open public primary schools. For example, in 1835 Pennsylvania made state funds available for the education of *all* children, not merely paupers. In 1839, North Carolina, which led the public education movement in the South, provided for a system of free schools. The program, however, did not become a reality until 1852.

Like so many other reform movements, the public-education crusade sought to make the United States a land of greater equality. As Horace Mann expressed it, "Now surely nothing but universal education can counterwork this tendency to the domination of capital and the servility of labor. If one class possesses all the wealth and the education, while the residue of society is ignorant and poor, it matters not by what name the relation between them may be called: the latter, in fact and in truth, will be the servile dependents and subjects to the former."

Despite the reforms *in principle* that Mann effected before the Civil War, only one white child out of every six actually attended school in 1860 in the North, and only one out of every seven in the South. If the United States had a very high literacy rate despite the low level of school attendance, this was only because most children who could read had received rudimentary instruction in reading and writing at home.

THE LYCEUM MOVEMENT

Adult education was furthered by the lyceum movement, which started in Massachusetts in 1826 under the influence of Joseph Holbrook. A nationally organized system of public lectures on important topics, the lyceum brought famous thinkers such as Emerson, and major writers, such as the English novelist Charles Dickens, to hundreds of small communities. Abolitionists and temperance workers also frequently addressed lyceums. By 1860 about three thousand lyceums had been established, most of them in New England, New York, and the Northwest. Besides offering lectures, local lyceums assembled libraries and formed discussion groups to contemplate subjects as widely different as "wealth" and "electromagnetism."

PRISON REFORM

Humanitarians also turned their attention to improving the lot of convicts and struggled to change imprisonment from a means of punishing the guilty to a method for reforming the weak.

One of the most obvious faults of the American legal system was the practice of jailing debtors, often those indebted only for their inability to pay trifling sums. For example, in 1816 some two thousand debtors were imprisoned in New York jails, many of them for owing less than twenty-five dollars. Records reveal that in 1831 a large percentage of the one thousand debtors jailed in Baltimore owed less than ten dollars. In 1817 New York changed its laws so that no one could be imprisoned for owing less than twenty-five dollars. By 1848 nine states had abolished debtor prisons altogether.

Another practice that aroused indignation was the jailing of young first offenders in cells with hardened criminals—a practice that was considered likely to corrupt rather than reform the adolescents. In New York, the Society for the Prevention of Pauperism built a home for young offenders in 1825. By the late 1850s, many states had their own reform schools. New York, Pennsylvania, and Massachusetts also adopted the recommendation of penologists to separate people convicted of misdemeanors from those who had been sentenced for felonies. In the 1830s, several states did away with capital punishment altogether and several others decided to hold executions in private, replacing the previous practice of hanging convicts in public places, a custom believed to be "edifying" for spectators and a sure way to discourage crime.

Some of the prison "reforms" still seem very harsh to us today. Advanced penologists introduced a new system into the New York prison at Auburn in 1821. It consisted of solitary confinement by night and communal meals and work by day, although even during the day prisoners had to maintain absolute silence. Reformers believed this system would lead convicts to reflect at length on their wrongdoings. Pennsylvania subjected its prisoners to total isolation around the clock. Strangely enough, many visiting European penologists hailed this system as the most enlightened of all approaches.

MENTAL HOSPITALS

When a Boston schoolmistress named Dorothea Dix visited a women's prison in Boston to teach Sunday school in 1841, she was appalled to discover that the insane there were treated worse than criminals. In most states the insane were imprisoned rather than hospitalized. They huddled together in unheated cells, and, as Miss Dix reported to the Massachusetts legislature, were kept "in cages, closets, cellars, stalls,

pens! Chained, naked, beaten with rods, and lashed into obedience."

For the next forty-six years Dorothea Dix crusaded across the country for improved conditions for the mentally ill. By 1860 a dozen states had established hospitals for the insane, and by 1887, when she died, twenty-one more states had opened public asylums.

TEMPERANCE

Concern for the lot of workingmen, criminals, and the insane was related to the temperance movement, which commanded more attention than any other cause except the abolition of slavery. The heavy consumption of liquor was an old English custom imported into America, but whereas most Englishmen consumed nothing more potent than ale or wine, Americans took to much harder drinks such as home-distilled whiskey and hard cider. Drinking was almost universal among both sexes, and drunkenness usually was treated more as an occasion for jokes than condemnation or pity. American religious groups, far from frowning on liquor, often permitted ministers to make and sell it. Even the Puritans, whom legend has made into prudes, drank large quantities of alcohol.

The revivalist movement that began in the early nineteenth century, however, denounced drunkenness. Excessive drinking was condemned as a contributing factor to poverty, crime, and mental illness. As early as 1811, Presbyterian ministers spoke out against heavy drinking and in 1816 the Methodists took a small step by forbidding their preachers to sell liquor to their congregations. The movement led by Dr. Justin Edwards developed into a crusade after 1825. Soon many local temperance societies formed, and in 1833 the United States Temperance Union became a national organization, one that required members to pledge not just moderation but total abstinence from liquor. By the following year the Union had more than a million members. The movement sponsored the publication of many tracts that illustrated the ill effects of alcohol. Probably the most widely read novel propagandizing abstinence was Timothy Shay Arthur's, *Ten Nights in a Bar Room and What I Saw There,* which was soon adapted into a still more popular play. Temperance workers sang songs outside bars; these songs were strongly reminiscent of the revivalist hymns on which most of them had been brought up. A typical stanza:

> *Disease and death forever nigh,*
> *Stand ready at the door,*
> *And eager wait to hear the cry—*
> *"O give me one glass more!"*

In 1846 Maine passed a partial prohibition law and in the next ten years a dozen other Northern states tried to control the sale of liquor. During the Civil War most of these laws were repealed. Undaunted, temperance workers continued their efforts until they reached their ultimate goal in the twentieth century—a national prohibition law.

THE PEACE MOVEMENT

Another movement that enlisted many reformers, but that did not have as wide an appeal as the crusade against liquor, was the peace movement. One American denomination, the Quakers, had long held that war was evil and should be abolished. After the War of 1812, many Americans were ready to agree. Moreover, the revivalist religious sects argued that killing was patently inconsistent with the teachings of Christ. By 1819 more than a dozen local peace societies had sprung up, and in 1828 a Maine merchant named William Ladd coordinated the activities of the country's

pacifists by founding the American Peace Society. Ladd also proposed an early version of a world organization like the United Nations which would interpret and administer international law.

Early pacifists had generally argued only for an end to all wars of aggression. In 1838, however, the peace movement split apart when Henry Clark Wright and William Lloyd Garrison demanded an end to all wars, whether aggressive or defensive. Those who accepted this extreme position formed the Non-Resistance Society. The Civil War and its aftermath sidetracked the efforts of this movement, as well as several others, and both factions of the early peace movement evaporated.

WOMEN'S RIGHTS

Before the women's rights movement was formed, individual women began to fight for, and win, the right to a college education. In 1837, Oberlin in Ohio became the first co-educational college in America, but when Antoinette Brown sought to major in theology, the school did everything it could to stop her. She persisted and was among the graduates in the field, but her name was deleted from the class list. In 1837, the first women's college, Mount Holyoke in Massachusetts, was also established. By the 1850s Antioch College in Ohio and the University of Iowa were accepting young women as students. In 1850 the Women's Medical College of Pennsylvania opened its doors, establishing not only an educational but a professional breakthrough, since women had formerly been effectively excluded from practicing medicine.

Kate Millet, the author of *Sexual Politics,* has written, "It was the Abolitionist Movement which gave American women their first opportunity for political action and organization. In the United States, where the Women's Movement began and from whence it spread to other Western countries and beyond the Western world, it was the cause of eradicating slavery which provided the impetus for the emancipation of women."

America's four leading crusaders for women's rights, Lucretia Mott, Susan B. Anthony, Elizabeth Cady Stanton, and Frances Wright had first gained organizational experience in other reform movements: peace, temperance, and anti-slavery. When Lucretia Mott and Elizabeth Cady Stanton traveled to London in 1840 to attend the World Anti-Slavery Convention, they were excluded from the proceedings because they were women. The irony of discovering themselves treated as inferiors by a radical organization dedicated to the equality of all human beings, dramatized the plight of women in society. Accordingly, they banded together to hold the first

"The Age of Iron. Man as He Expects to Be" is an 1869 comment on Women's Liberation. Women's rights movements have been active since 1840, when they were begun by crusaders Lucretia Mott, Elizabeth Cady Stanton, and Frances Wright.

Women's Rights Convention in Seneca Falls, New York, in 1848.

The 250 women who attended the convention worked out a paraphrase of the Declaration of Independence that insisted "that all men and women are created equal," and went on to say: "The history of mankind is a history of repeated injuries and usurpations on the part of man toward woman, having in direct object the establishment of an absolute tyranny over her."

An examination of the laws of the day gives substance to this statement. Women could not vote or hold public office. As late as 1850, many states permitted husbands to beat their wives "with a reasonable instrument." Every cent a wife earned was legally her husband's. Women were denied custody of their children, and in divorce cases husbands were far more likely than wives to be given the children. Women could not manage their own property. They could not sign papers or be called as witnesses in trials, and married women could not hold property in their own names.

They could not sue or be sued. Even where a woman lived was determined solely by her husband. Except that they could legally hold property, single women enjoyed as few civil rights as married women. Legally, married women were the equivalents of children, the insane, and the mentally retarded.

Aside from such legal discrimination, women suffered from many social taboos. They were not allowed to speak before mixed audiences, deliver sermons, or enter any of the professions.

Before the Civil War, the women's rights movement did not win the crucial right to vote. Crusaders did, however, change the laws of several states so that married women could retain ownership of their own property. The new profession of teaching in elementary schools was opened everywhere to women. A few women were licensed to preach, and many more began to address audiences as lecturers, usually on the subject of abolition or women's rights. Several women did attain noteworthy stature in spite of the various legal limitations imposed upon them, such as Dr. Elizabeth Blackwell, who became famous as a doctor; Dorothea Dix, who earned distinction as a champion of reform in mental hospitals; Emma Willard and Catherine Beecher who made important contributions to progressive education; and Margaret Fuller, a Transcendentalist and friend of Emerson, who became the brilliant literary critic of the New York *Tribune,* editor of the Transcendentalist magazine *The Dial,* and the author of a controversial best-seller, *Women in the Nineteenth Century.*

THE ANTI-SLAVERY MOVEMENT AND THE DEFENSE OF SLAVERY

The use of slave labor was the most explosive social evil of the day to reformers. By 1804 all Northern states had arranged for immediate or gradual abolition of slavery. By 1808 Congress had banned all importation of slaves into the United States. At the end of the eighteenth century, optimists in both the North and South had imagined that slavery would soon die out, but expansion of the world cotton market made slavery grow rather than diminish in importance. As slavery became more economically significant in the South, it became more repellent to Northern reform leaders. A clash was inevitable.

FREE BLACKS

The anti-slavery issue often overshadowed the plight of free blacks in America before the Civil War. In 1790 there were only 59,000 free blacks, but by 1860 11 percent, or 488,000, of the nation's 4,441,000 black people were free. They were denied admittance to white schools and by 1860 only five Northern states had granted blacks equal voting rights. Railroads, theaters, and restaurants refused them admission. There were lynchings of blacks by mobs in many Northern cities. Most trades and almost all professions were closed to them. The federal government excluded blacks from the army and almost all jobs. A 1790 law also denied citizenship to nonwhite immigrants.

Despite these hardships, free blacks in both the North and South managed to achieve distinction. Thomy Lafon, a free black merchant in New Orleans, amassed a fortune of half a million dollars. James Forten of Philadelphia owned a major sailmaking business and employed forty black and white workers. Norbert Rillieux invented a revolutionary process for refining sugar. Most significant of all, free blacks in the North were a very important factor in the abolitionist movement. Frederick Douglass in eloquent lectures and books helped to raise support for anti-slavery in the North. As early as 1829 David Walker authored a widely circulated "Appeal" for an end to slavery. During the first years of publication of the leading abolitionist newspaper, *The Liberator,* three-fourths of the subscribers were blacks. Black women, such as Harriet Tubman and Sojourner Truth and men like William Still risked their lives venturing into the South and leading slaves to freedom in the North via the Underground Railroad.

THE AMERICAN COLONIZATION SOCIETY

One early attempt, fostered mainly by Southern whites, to find a solution to racial tensions was a plan to transport free blacks to Africa. In 1816, the Virginia legislature suggested that a territory in Africa, or elsewhere, be found for blacks. In the following year a group formed the American Colonization Society. Under its auspices the black republic of Liberia was founded on the west coast of Africa in 1822. The Society received private donations, federal aid, and appropriations from the legislatures of Virginia and Maryland.

The movement, however, proved unsuccessful. Northerners began to suspect that the Society, composed mainly of Southerners, was simply looking for a way to rid the United States of free blacks, who represented a threat to slavery. Most blacks themselves refused to leave the United States, feeling that America was now their country and that they should receive their full rights as citizens. Between 1821 and 1867, fewer than 15,000 of them left the United States. "The Colonizationists want us to go to Liberia if we will," one black declared; "if we won't go there, we may go to hell."

WILLIAM LLOYD GARRISON

The anti-slavery movement truly got underway in the North when William Lloyd Garrison began to publish his abolitionist periodical, *The Liberator,* in 1831. In the first issue of the publication, Garrison stated his purpose in no uncertain terms: "I am in earnest—I will not equivocate—I will not excuse—I will not retreat a single inch—and I WILL BE HEARD."

Born in Massachusetts, the son of a poor sailor and a deeply religious mother, Garrison had worked from age thirteen to twenty as an apprentice printer, and had then become involved with the temperance and peace movements. During the 1820s, one of the most active anti-slavery men in the country was a New Jersey Quaker, Benjamin Lundy, who published an anti-slavery newspaper, the *Genius of Universal Emancipation.* Garrison next worked for Lundy, but believing that he was too moderate, Garrison left his employ and went to Boston where he founded *The Liberator.* He called for the immediate abolition of slavery on moral and religious grounds. He opposed gradual emancipation as well as a much-discussed plan for state governments to compensate slaveowners for freeing their slaves. Garrison was also against the colonization experiment. What he wanted was total freedom for blacks, immediately. Since he was also a pacifist, he did not recommend armed coercion against the South. His only weapon against slavery was moral persuasion. He hoped the South would see the error of its ways and reform. To this end he founded the New England Anti-Slavery Society in 1832 and a year later the American Anti-Slavery Society.

Garrison considered not only slaveowners immoral, but also the federal government, since it was based on the Constitution, a document that specifically recognized the legality of the institution. He termed the Constitution "a covenant with death and an agreement with hell" and publicly burned a copy of it. As the abolition movement grew, Garrison's position seemed so extreme that he had little influence outside of New England. In 1839, he brought about a split in the abolitionist movement by his refusal to work through the political process to gradually undermine the foundations

461

of the institution of slavery, and by insisting that women had the right to participate fully in anti-slavery activities. Nevertheless, by 1840 the American Anti-Slavery Society numbered some 200,000 members, with many more sympathizers.

THEODORE DWIGHT WELD

The leading abolitionist of the West was Theodore Dwight Weld, who converted thousands to a stand against slavery by employing revivalist techniques. Weld had been converted by the evangelist, Charles Finney. Using Finney's methods, Weld held anti-slavery meetings that went on for days. As one witness reported, he "held increasing auidences at fever pitch, with his flashing eye, his clarion tones and marvelous

Ex-slave Frederick Douglass became famous as an editor, author, lecturer, and abolitionist.

eloquence, without manuscript or note, for sixteen successive evenings." In 1833, Weld led students at the Lane Theological Seminary in Ohio in a prolonged debate over the merits and faults of slavery. The debate converted many of these future ministers to abolitionism. In 1839, Weld compiled a highly effective pamphlet, *Slavery As It Is,* which exposed the evils of slavery simply by quoting verbatim from Southern newspapers and court records.

FREDERICK DOUGLASS

Douglass, the most eminent American black of the nineteenth century, had escaped from slavery in Maryland. He founded his own abolitionist newspaper, the *North Star,* in 1847. Through his cogent and beautifully written editorials and orations, Douglass· fanned the flames of antagonism against slavery in the North. He also protested ardently and effectively against racial discrimination in the North.

THE ABOLITIONIST MOVEMENT

At first abolitionists had hoped to end slavery through what they termed "moral suasion." When that failed, the more moderate group led by Weld pressured Congress to abolish slavery in Washington, D.C., to end the interstate slave trade, and to prevent further expansion of slavery into the West. They also aided runaway slaves to escape to freedom. These actions, which seemed extreme to many, made the abolitionists not only anathema in the South but also extremely unpopular in the North. Mobs threatened Garrison repeatedly and in 1837 at Alton, Illinois, an enraged group killed Elijah Lovejoy, the editor of an anti-slavery newspaper. By the late 1850s, however, more and more Northerners, probably a majority, had come to see slavery as an evil that could not be allowed to expand and that would gradually die out.

The abolitionist appeal to the small town and farming populations of the Northern states gradually widened after the middle of the 1830s. Slavery was thereafter not only associated with immorality, but also with the denial of civil rights. Southern Congressmen were so outraged by the flood of petitions to end the slave trade in the District of Columbia that they persuaded Congress to pass the Gag Rule in 1836 which provided that all such petitions should be tabled, that is, not read to the members. John Q. Adams, not an abolitionist but a great defender of free speech, fought the rule until it was repealed in 1844. In the case of *Prigg v. Pennsylvania* in 1842 the Supreme Court ruled that individual states could ignore the Fugitive Slave Act. This decision led many Northern states to pass "personal liberty" laws barring local officials from aiding in the capture of fugitives. In the minds of many Northerners, the anti-slavery crusade was now related to the protection of civil rights.

The abolitionist movement gained even wider popular appeal as it became associated in the 1840s and 1850s with the westward expansion of free men. The Liberty Party, a small party devoted to attacking slavery as a great moral evil, polled 7,000 votes in 1840 and 62,000 votes in 1844. Its successor, the Free Soil Party, with the added emphasis on "Free Soil, Free Speech, Free Labor, and Free Men," collected nearly 300,000 votes in 1848. Moreover, there was now a small but formidable group of political abolitionists sitting in the Congress who constantly attacked the expansion of the great evil of slavery into the new Western territories. This was a favorite theme in the speeches of such Senators as Charles Sumner of Massachusetts, William H. Seward of New York, and Salmon P. Chase of Ohio, and of Congressmen Joshua R. Giddings of Ohio and Charles Francis Adams of Massachusetts.

THE SOUTHERN RESPONSE

Many in the South no longer defended slavery as a necessary evil. John C. Calhoun described it as "a good—a positive good." His full statement said: "I hold that in the present state of civilization, where two races of different origin, and distinguished by color, and other physical differences, as well as intellectual, are brought together, the relation now existing in the slave-holding States between the two is, instead of an evil, a good—a positive good. . . . I hold then, that there never has yet existed a wealthy and civilized society in which one portion of the community did not, in point of fact, live on the labor of the other. . . . I may say with truth that in few countries so much is left to the share of the laborer, and so little exacted from him, or where there is more kind attention paid to him in sickness or infirmities of age."

Many of the pro-slavery arguments are expressed in Calhoun's 1837 argument. Champions of slavery contended that: (1) every advanced society needed slaves, whether called by that name or not; (2) Southern slaves enjoyed much more security and comfort than Northern industrial workers, the "wage slaves" of the factories; (3) slaves were private property, and no outsider had the right to interfere over the belongings of others; (4) slavery was justified by both the Bible and the ancient Greek and Roman philosophers; and (5) blacks were anthropologically inferior to whites and destined by nature to servitude.

THE MUD-SILL THEORY

The notion that all civilization depended on slavery was called the "mud-sill theory," deriving its name from a statement by James H. Hammond, Governor of South Carolina: "In all social systems there must be a class to do the menial duties, to perform the drudgery of life. . . . Such a class you must have or you would not have that other class which leads progress, civilization, and refinement. It constitutes the very mud-sill of society and of political government." The prevalence of this theory led many Southern intellectuals to renounce the principle of equality as advanced in the Declaration of Independence. As Professor Thomas Cooper of South Carolina wrote: "We talk a great deal of nonsense about the rights of man. We say that man is born free, and equal to every other man. Nothing can be more untrue: no human being ever was, nor is or ever will be born free."

Slavery's apologists also pictured the lot of blacks in the rosiest tints. George Fitzhugh, a Virginia lawyer, wrote in 1854: "A Southern farm is the beau ideal of Communism: it is a joint concern, in which the slave consumes more than the master, of the coarse products, and is far happier, because . . . he is always sure of a support." So moved was one poet by this image of black contentment that he wrote:

Secure they toil, uncursed their
   peaceful life,
With labor's hungry broils and
   wasteful strife,
No want to goad, no faction to deplore,
The slave escapes the perils of the
   poor.

One Virginia gentleman insisted, "A merrier being does not exist on the face of the globe, than the Negro slave of the United States."

In truth, the slave had watched his few pitiful advantages disappear every year as the South became increasingly anxious about slave revolts and abolitionism. Slaves were forbidden by law to read or write in every Southern state except Maryland, Kentucky, and Tennessee. Punishments became harsher, living and working conditions more deplorable, controls tighter as slave-

owners became more and more fearful of their chattels. Similarly, even the civil liberties of whites were more tightly restricted. Most states had made it illegal for postmasters to accept abolitionist literature. Southern education was carefully planned to exclude all mention of abolitionist ideas, books were censored, liberal teachers fired, and reform in general, for any cause whatsoever, became suspect. As the South fought to save slavery, it became the bastion of reaction.

The religious revival in the North had contributed support to abolitionism and other reform movements, but in the South religion was used to defend the status quo and slavery itself, as were the Enlightenment's appeals to reason. Finally, Romanticism, which in the North had led to a new respect for the natural man, in the South found expression in an enthusiasm for the aristocratic values and rigid class structure underlying Sir Walter Scott's novels. The South's greatest Romantic writer, Edgar Allan Poe, called democracy "the most odious and insupportable despotism . . . upon the face of the earth."

Readings

GENERAL WORKS

Brooks, Van Wyck, *The World of Washington Irving.* New York: Dutton, 1944—Not a biography of Irving but a literary and cultural history of the United States between 1800 and the 1840s. Brooks analyzes such authors as Cooper, Bryant, and William Gilmore Simms, as well as Irving.

Eaton, Clement, *The Growth of Southern Civilization.* New York: Harper & Row, 1961—A history of the South from 1790 to 1860. Eaton stresses that there were several Southern cultures, not just one, and shows both consensus and conflict within the South.

Eaton, Clement, *The Mind of the Old South.* Baton Rouge: Louisiana State University Press, 1964—Eaton's sketches illustrate the growing unity of Southern thought. As the Civil War approached, an extreme racist conservatism came to dominate the Southern mind.

Larkin, Oliver W., *Art and Life in America.* New York: Holt, Rinehart & Winston, 1960—In this standard, well-illustrated history of American art, Larkin is more concerned with the cultural influences on American art, and its role in revealing American society, than in purely esthetic matters.

Levin, David, *History as Romantic Art.* Stanford, Calif.: Stanford University Press, 1959—Deals with four major nineteenth-century American historians from the standpoint of their literary achievement. Levin claims that the four adapted stories of romantic heroes fit liberal, republican ideals.

Matthiessen, F. O., *American Renaissance.* London: Oxford University Press, 1941—A classic work in American literary criticism. Matthiessen analyzes the ideas of Emerson, Thoreau, Whitman, Hawthorne, and Melville on the purpose and nature of literature. He seeks to explain the burst of literary creativity in the early 1800s.

Nye, Russel B., *The Cultural Life of the New Nation.* New York: Harper, 1960—A cultural history of the United States from 1776 to 1830. Nye traces the emergence of nationalism, linked frequently to a democratic, reformist spirit, in all phases of American culture.

Parrington, Vernon L., *Main Currents in American Thought,* Vols. I–III. New York: Harcourt, Brace, 1927–1930—A classic interpretation of American culture. The author traces what he feels is a confirming struggle between democratic and oligarchic forces in America and argues that this tension is found throughout American literature.

Sweet, William W., *The Story of Religion in America.* New York: Harper, 1930—A detailed general history of American religions, which finds common patterns of faith beneath the surface of hundreds of conflicting denominations.

Wright, Louis B., *Culture on the Moving Frontier.* Bloomington, Ind.: Indiana University Press, 1955—Six essays on American culture in frontier settings varying from the original colonies to gold rush settlements. Wright detects underlying similarities in cultural patterns, based in large part on the importance of English cultural values in America.

SPECIAL STUDIES

Bartlett, Irving H., *The American Mind in the Mid-Nineteenth Century.* New York: Crowell, 1967—A brief account of American intellectual life in the mid-nineteenth century. Also contains an interpretive bibliographical essay.

Bestor, Arthur J., Jr., *Backwoods Utopias.* Philadelphia: University of Pennsylvania Press, 1950—A study of communitarian experiments in America before 1829. Bestor maintains that the communities were laboratories for experiments in new forms of social organization and religious models of the good life.

Brooks, Van Wyck, *The Flowering of New England.* Cleveland: World, 1936—A literary and intellectual history of New England from 1815 to 1865. Brooks believes that this was the high point of Boston cultural life, and that its decline was matched by the decline of New England in the political and economic life of the United States.

Cash, W. J., *The Mind of the South*. New York: Knopf, 1941—A classic essay on the Southern mentality which outlines the conflicts between the Southern ideologies of the romantic Old South and progressive New South, and the realities of racism and poverty.

Donald, David, *Lincoln Reconsidered*. New York: Knopf, 1956—A series of essays about Lincoln in which he is discussed both as an historical figure and as an American mythical hero. A controversial essay on the social origins of abolitionism is also included.

Duberman, Martin, ed., *The Antislavery Vanguard*. Princeton, N.J.: Princeton University Press, 1965—A collection of essays on abolitionists and their cause. Most of the essays defend abolitionism from the charges of fanaticism and extremism which have been directed against the movement. Some attempt is made to draw parallels to present-day racial developments.

Dumond, Dwight L., *Antislavery*. Ann Arbor, Mich.: University of Michigan Press, 1961 —A large, well-illustrated history of anti-slavery activity. Dumond maintains that the crusades against the great moral wrong of slavery brought on the Civil War.

Filler, Louis, *The Crusade Against Slavery*. New York: Harper, 1960—A general history of anti-slavery thought and action. Filler depicts the abolitionists as courageous and skillful propagandists engaged in the most important reform movement of their era.

Jenkins, Williams, *Pro-Slavery Thought in the Old South*. Chapel Hill, N.C.: University of North Carolina Press, 1935—Jenkins shows how Southern thought became increasingly obsessed with defending slavery as a positive good. He argues that the waste of intellectual talent defending an immoral institution was a tragedy.

Rudolph, Frederick, *The American College and University*. New York: Knopf, 1967—A survey of the history of American higher education that stresses, among other things, the close involvement of governmental bodies even with private colleges and universities.

Smith, Timothy L., *Revivalism and Social Reform in Mid-Nineteenth Century America*. New York: Abingdon Press, 1957—Smith shows how the perfectionist spirit of American religion influenced and encouraged reform movements, including abolitionism, and traces the growing importance of urban revivalism.

Taylor, William B., *Cavalier and Yankee*. New York: Braziller, 1961—An intellectual history of the images of North and South which developed before the Civil War. Analyzing literary and folklore material, Taylor characterizes the South as torn between imitating the North and retreating into a fantasy of medieval aristocracy.

Tyler, Alice F., *Freedom's Ferment*. Minneapolis: University of Minnesota Press, 1944 —This study of reform in America before the Civil War emphasizes the democratic, optimistic spirit of the nation, which made it easy for a wide variety of causes to gain followings.

PRIMARY SOURCES

Commager, Henry S., *The Age of Reform 1830–1860*. Princeton, N.J.: Van Nostrand, 1960—A brief introductory essay precedes excerpts from reformers ranging from Thomas Jefferson to Abraham Lincoln.

Commager discusses the economic, political, and social reforms of the era.

McKitrick Eric L., ed., *Slavery Defended.* Englewood Cliffs, N.J.: Prentice-Hall, 1963 —A collection of documents showing the varying forms of the defense of slavery. McKitrick suggests that the defenders of slavery were capable of occasional insights about nonslaveholding cultures.

Miller, Perry, ed., *Margaret Fuller: American Romantic.* Garden City, N.Y.: Doubleday Anchor, 1963—An anthology of the prose and poetry of Margaret Fuller, who personified many of the intellectual and social trends of antebellum New England, such as Transcendentalism and the women's rights movement.

Miller, Perry, ed., *The Transcendentalists.* Cambridge, Mass.: Harvard University Press, 1950—An anthology of Transcendentalist writings, not only by Emerson and Thoreau, but by lesser-known figures in the movement. Miller stresses the religious origins of Transcendentalist thought.

Thomas, John L., *Slavery Attacked.* Englewood Cliffs, N.J.: Prentice-Hall, 1965—A collection of abolitionist writings, showing the differing appeals of political abolitionists and the ways in which anti-slavery became a program with mass appeal.

de Tocqueville, Alexis, *Democracy in America,* Vols. I–II. Phillip Bradley, ed. New York: Viking, 1945—The classic traveler's account of the United States, written by a French aristocrat who toured the country to investigate American prison reforms.

BIOGRAPHIES

Arvin, Newton, *Herman Melville.* New York: William Sloane, 1950—A combination of biography and literary criticism. Arvin sees Melville as expressing a realization that good and evil are intertwined together and a belief that love, rather than intellect, should rule man.

Krutch, Joseph W., *Henry David Thoreau.* New York: William Sloane, 1948—A short biography of the famous essayist and naturalist, written by his twentieth-century admirer. Krutch, like Thoreau, was deeply involved with nature.

Marshall H. E., *Dorothea Dix: Forgotten Samaritan.* Chapel Hill, N.C.: University of North Carolina Press, 1937—A biography of the great champion of reform in the treatment of the mentally ill and of others who were confined to institutions.

Nye, Russel B., *William Lloyd Garrison and the Humanitarian Reformers.* Boston: Little, Brown, 1955—A short biography of Garrison which emphasizes his role as abolitionist leader but also discusses his involvement in other humanitarian reforms of his day, such as the peace and the women's rights movements.

Rusk, Ralph L., *The Life of Ralph Waldo Emerson.* New York: Scribner's, 1949—A long biography of Emerson, perhaps the most influential American literary figure of the early nineteenth century. Rusk claims that Emerson's greatness was far more complex than his contemporary admirers realized.

Thomas, Benjamin P., *Theodore Weld: Crusader for Freedom.* New Brunswick, N.J.: Rutgers University Press, 1950—A biography of one of the leading abolitionists of the 1830s. Weld represented a more politically oriented branch of the movement, based in the Midwest, than Garrison's New England radicalism.

Van Doren, Mark, *Nathaniel Hawthorne.* New York: William Sloane, 1949—Hawthorne is distinctive, says Van Doren, for rejecting many of the prevailing beliefs of American culture, such as a faith in progress and the perfectibility of man.

To St Louis. 350 Miles.
To California. 1700 Ms.

KELLOGGS & COMSTOCK 150 FULTON ST NEW YORK & 130 MAIN ST HARTFORD CONN   ENSIGN & THAYER 32 EXCHANGE ST BUFFALO

THE INDEPENDENT GOLD HUNTER ON HIS WAY TO CALIFORNIA

I NEITHER BORROW NOR LEND

Mid-Nineteenth Century Expansion: Manifest Destiny

13

. . . Why, were other reasoning wanting, in favor of now elevating this question of the reception of Texas into the Union, out of the lower region of our past party dissensions, up to its proper level of a high and broad nationality, it surely is to be found, found abundantly, in the manner in which other nations have undertaken to intrude themselves into it, between us and the proper parties to the case, in a spirit of hostile interference against us, for the avowed object of thwarting our policy and hampering our power, limiting our greatness and checking the fulfilment of our manifest destiny to overspread the continent allotted by Providence for the free development of our yearly multiplying millions. . . .

—John L. O'Sullivan

"The Independent Gold Hunter on His Way to California" is equipped with pick and shovel, a pan for mining, a scale for weighing, and other necessities for the adventure.

After announcing the Monroe Doctrine in 1823, American foreign policy over the next thirty years was concerned almost exclusively with the Western Hemisphere, particularly the acquisition of the territory between the Louisiana Purchase and the Pacific Ocean. From the beginning of the colonial period Americans had been constantly moving westward even when forbidden to do so by the British government. Both Jefferson and John Quincy Adams believed the United States would ultimately control the whole of the North American continent. The Louisiana Purchase, the objectives of the War of 1812, and the Adams-Onís Treaty of 1819 were manifestations of the country's expansionist tendencies. Even the Monroe Doctrine can be seen as an attempt to prevent European interference with what was considered an area designed for American control.

The movement to push the country's boundaries to the Pacific reached its peak during the 1840s. In ten years, the United States acquired 7,000 square miles of territory on the border of Maine and Canada, annexed the Republic of Texas, settled the Oregon boundary dispute with England, and fought a war with Mexico which resulted in the acquisition of the territories of New Mexico and California. This aggressive wave of expansion was dignified by the term "manifest destiny." The phrase was coined in the middle of the decade to describe the widely held belief that the people of the United States were predestined to possess all of North America to the Pacific Ocean. The term first appeared in an article by John L. O'Sullivan, the editor of the *Democratic Review* of New York. It is "our manifest destiny," O'Sullivan wrote in July, 1845, "to overspread the continent allotted by Providence for . . . our yearly multiplying millions." This pithy phrase, which identified the movement with a feeling of lofty inevitability, caught on quickly and became a part of the American vocabulary.

The phenomenon of expansion can be seen in varying ways. It might be regarded by some as a manifestation of American aggression against Indian tribes occupying the western part of the continent as well as against a weaker nation—Mexico. On the other hand, the mood of "manifest destiny" was in harmony with the spirit of adventure so characteristic of nineteenth-century America. Americans went West not only to satisfy their economic needs with new, fertile farmlands and new markets for trade, but also out of a pioneering instinct born of the original impetus to leave Europe and come to the New World. Henry David Thoreau spoke for his entire generation when he said, "I am leaving the city more and more and withdrawing into the wilderness . . . I must walk toward Oregon and not toward Europe."

While most Americans were quickly caught up in the fervor of expansionism, there was opposition to the trend expressed by many humanitarian reformers. They feared not expansionism itself but the aggressive attitude of many of its advocates. American ideals should be spread across the continent, but by example and not by force. The pacifists feared that expansion through force, which might make the United States an imperial power with colonies, could eventually lead to a military dictatorship in Washington. The abolitionists opposed all westward expansion which might ultimately lead to the addition of more slave states to the Union.

ORIGINS OF MANIFEST DESTINY

POPULATION GROWTH

The expansionist movement was touched off by the phenomenal growth of the American population. "Alien passengers," that is, immigrants, were flooding the older regions of the country. In the 1820s, only 129,000 immigrants entered the United States, in the 1830s, the number jumped to 540,000. In the 1840s, the figure tripled and by the 1850s it reached almost 3 million people. Farmers and cotton planters sought the border lands of Texas, California, and Oregon almost as much to get away from areas they considered too crowded as to fulfill their simple desire for new lands.

Some Americans began to concern themselves with population growth and to talk about and plan territorial expansion to accommodate later generations. The aforementioned John L. O'Sullivan estimated that the number of Americans would double every twenty-five years. In one hundred years, he wrote in August, 1845, the population would reach over 250 million and land had to be provided for them *now*. "We must extend our territory in latitude and longitude to the demand of the millions who are to follow us," said one official. The obsession with making room for future Americans was connected with the Biblical idea that a multiplying population was a sign of the favor of Divine Providence. In addition, many people believed literally that the fertility of Americans was a tribute to democracy.

POLITICAL MOTIVES

Strong political motives also lay behind the expansion of America westward. Pioneers already living in the border lands wanted to be part of the United States and they asked those they left behind to work for this goal. As one viewpoint of the time expressed it, people who moved westward felt that "the Government should follow them with the laws and instructions which they love and cherish and thereby add strength and permanent glory to the Republic."

The concept of "strength and permanent glory" varied according to local political interests. For example, in the South, planters wanted Texas to be admitted as a state because it was a slave territory and would give support to other slave states against the growing number of free states. Southern states' rights advocates felt that their economic security would increase with the number of states admitted to the Union. The South, already outnumbered in the House of Representatives, would still be able to protect what it considered its vital interests if there continued to be an equal number of slave states in the Union. An equal number of slave and free states would mean equality in the Senate, and no bill could become law without the approval of both houses of Congress. For similar reasons the Northern states wanted to add new territory out of which to carve free states. By increasing free-state influence in the Congress, Southern opposition to the tariff and other demands of the Northern business interests could be overcome.

COMMERCIAL INTERESTS

Another cause of the westward expansion was the increase of commerce with its promise of rich profits. The spread of "cotton culture" across the continent aroused the avarice of planters, textile manufacturers, and merchants who dreamed of an ever-expanding market for cotton products. In addition to Thomas Hart Benton's dream of developing America's inland waterways, there were also the superb natural harbors at Puget Sound, San Diego, and San Francisco to tempt shippers. The bay at San Diego, according to an American captain in the 1820s, was "as fine a bay for vessels under 300 tons as ever was formed by Nature in her most friendly mood to mariners."

San Francisco Bay was already an important port for the California hide trade. With such harbors as terminals for a planned transcontinental railroad, merchants dreamed of an American Pacific coast as the jumping-off place for extensive trade with the Orient.

FEAR OF EUROPE

In addition to the factors of population growth and commercial and political motives, an important impetus to expansion was fear of Europe. Americans did not want European influences on their borders. Foreign countries, especially England, with her vast experience in diplomacy and command of the seas, not only might compete with America commercially, but might also try to establish colonies on the west coast of North America. The fear of Europe that made Americans want to insure their safety by expanding their borders created a vicious circle, since Europe, in turn, tended to interest herself in North America, mostly out of fear of the political and economic ambitions of the United States. Americans believed that if European countries acquired a new foothold on the continent, they would threaten the existence of democracy and the American democratic mission.

MORAL IMPLICATIONS

Like many other Western countries in the nineteenth century, the United States was highly nationalistic. Americans thought their system of government was superior to all others and that they had the right, perhaps even the responsibility, to impose their way of life on peoples who were less enterprising or less successful than themselves. Who had made better use of the soil? Moreover, was not growth the law of nature and of nations? Most Americans believed it was divinely ordained that the country should expand to its natural limits. Yet, behind the arrogance of such a posture was a sincere and optimistic idealism. Americans generally believed that by taking lands on the continent from Indians and Mexicans, and from Spain and England, they were providing a haven and opportunity for freedom to the oppressed hordes of Europe. A politician of the day asked his listeners to rejoice over "state after state coming into this great temple of freedom, and burning their incense upon the altar consecrated to the enjoyment of civil and religious liberty." As one orator explained: "It is not good taste in individuals to indulge in boasting; but a nation is allowed to assume an elevated tone." Such comments accurately reflected the self-confidence of Americans who maintained that, by providing adequate space for her own economic and political development, the United States would undermine tyranny all over the world.

THE MAINE BOUNDARY DISPUTE

The decade which was to feel the explosive effect of expansionism in national life began modestly with the amicable agreement in 1842 between the United States and England over the Maine-Canada border dispute. The Webster-Ashburton Treaty, however, was not motivated by American desire to expand the territory of the United

States, it was intended only to adjust contested areas. Yet, it set the stage for manifest destiny because it put the American flag in a part of the continent that another country had claimed. The treaty set a precedent for additional adjustments which ultimately added significantly to the territorial size of the United States.

BRITISH ATTITUDE

Americans, English visitors regularly reported, were brash, dirty, money-mad, and boastful. Charles Dickens, who had made a lecture tour of the United States in 1842, had an American character in his novel *Martin Chuzzlewit* explain, "We are a model of wisdom, and an example to the world and the perfection of human reason." Canadians, to the English, were even more uncivilized; but although Canada itself seemed virtually hopeless as a profitable

possession, it had a strategic value. It was prized "above all," wrote a future British colonial secretary, E. G. Stanley, "in case of war with the United States (no improbable future contingency)." In a war, he continued, Canada "furnishes ample assistance in men, timber and harbours for carrying on the war, and that on the enemy's frontier." In fact, England prepared in part for her defense from the 1820s on by spending millions of pounds building an inland canal in case the St. Lawrence Waterway should ever be taken by American invaders.

THE *CAROLINE*

The possibility of war seemed strong indeed after the *Caroline* affair. In 1837, a group of Americans had supported a Canadian insurrection, hoping it would lead to American annexation of Canada. The British suppressed the rebellion easily, but

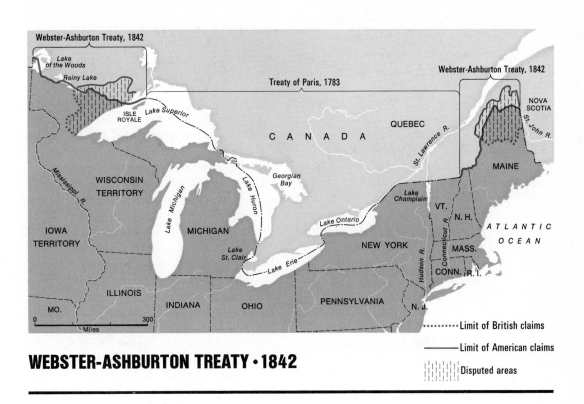

WEBSTER-ASHBURTON TREATY • 1842

.... Limit of British claims

——— Limit of American claims

Disputed areas

Americans at the border sheltered the rebel leaders and helped them slip back into Canada on regular raiding parties. One night, Canadian officials crossed the Niagara River, killed an American, and set fire to an American boat, the *Caroline,* which had been carrying supplies for the rebels.

The burning of the *Caroline,* even though the ship was used to bring in Canadian rebels from the American side, created an uproar along the border. The Rochester, New York, *Democrat* called for revenge "not by simpering diplomacy but by blood," and tens of thousands of American backwoodsmen from Vermont to Michigan banded together in organizations called "Hunters' Lodges," well-armed organizations whose members swore to "help destroy . . . every power, or authority of Royal origin upon this continent . . . So help me God!"

Fortunately, the excitement did not extend to Washington or London. Both President Van Buren and Prime Minister Palmerston recognized that the incident did not justify war. Van Buren asserted American sovereignty and demanded an apology and reparations from England. At the same time, he issued a proclamation asking Americans to maintain the laws of neutrality and sent a trouble shooter, General Winfield Scott, to the border to disband the "Hunters." The British, while not reimbursing the United States for the attack on the *Caroline,* showed restraint by neither defending the attack nor denying that they were responsible for it. Although Queen Victoria knighted the daring young man who had led the Canadian foray, both sides allowed the situation to simmer down.

AROOSTOOK WAR

A second near-clash occurred between America and England over timberlands in the Aroostook River valley, an area claimed by both the Canadian province of New Brunswick and the state of Maine. When

the British started to build a road from the Bay of Fundy in New Brunswick to Montreal and Quebec, they sent Canadian lumberjacks into the valley to obtain timber for shipbuilding. Because the lumberjacks cut down trees that were commercially valuable, Maine quickly assembled state militia to chase the "foreigners" out. The militia took over the area and established forts. This time war fever began to rise in Washington, where Congress voted 10 million dollars for defense and authorized Van Buren to call up 50,000 volunteers.

The provinces of Nova Scotia and New Brunswick also made hurried preparations for war. Once again, Van Buren called upon General Scott who persuaded the governor of Maine to withdraw his troops. The Canadians agreed to stay out of the area until the dispute was settled by a boundary commission. The Aroostook War had ended before it began.

THE WEBSTER-ASHBURTON TREATY

The frictions caused by the Aroostook situation, the attack on the *Caroline,* and several other irritants in Anglo-American relations ceased when the United States conceded 5,000 square miles of territory between Quebec and New Brunswick to Canada and kept 7,000 squares miles as part of Maine in the Webster-Ashburton Treaty. The boundary dispute had simmered since the end of the Revolutionary War. The wording of the Treaty of 1783 was so vague that it was impossible to determine the boundary line. Webster was friendly to England and Britain also wanted an amicable settlement. A compromise on the border line around northern New Hampshire and Lake Champlain was reached. A border line between Lake Superior and the Lake of the Woods was also decided upon, putting in United States possession the later-discovered rich iron ore deposits in northern Minnesota. The American gains were substantial but they did not satisfy people imbued with the rising spirit of manifest destiny. Daniel Webster was severely criticized by many of his countrymen for not obtaining all the disputed territory between Maine and Nova Scotia. "Selfish egotism is the only continuous thread I find running through the crooked life of this famous American," asserted the eminent clergyman Theodore Parker.

ANNEXATION OF TEXAS

The first area beyond the border of the United States to arouse the ardent spirit of manifest destiny was the warm, rich Southwestern land of Texas. Larger than France and blessed by a good climate and a large variety of natural resources, Texas was a likely but difficult prospect for annexation. It was desirable territory because its great plains offered vast fields for cotton to expansionist Southern planters, but it presented difficulties to the nation for the same reason: cotton meant a slave economy, and abolitionists forcefully objected to the spread of slavery. The strong sentiment against so large an area entering the United States as one or more slave states impelled three Presidents—Jackson, Van Buren, and Tyler—to sidestep the issue until 1843, when the national urge for more territory could no longer be resisted.

Annexation itself was the crowning accomplishment in the spectacular career of one of America's most picturesque heroes, Sam Houston. As a teenage boy, Houston

For Annexation of Texas

" *. . . The addition of new and adjacent regions to our dominion, instead of weakening, greatly strengthens the bonds of our Union. It augments the power against which the spirit of disunion must contend whenever it awakens. It multiplies counteracting interests, and lessens the danger of its influence. . . .*
. . . Why not rest where you now are, if patriotism dictates the cry of "the Union as it is," and not as its immortal founders intended it should be? Sir, away with this fettering system. Why wing the eagle in his bold ascent towards the sun? The sky was given for his dominion. Why strip him of his plumage, and fix him to the earth? Sir, you cannot, if you would, set bounds to the indomitable energy of our noble race. Where has the Creator raised mountains so high that we cannot scale them—ay, and subdue and cultivate them? or spread an ocean so broad and so deep that we cannot swim it, and whiten its bosom with our commerce? No, sir. To arrest our peaceful and onward march would be treason to the cause of human liberty. . . . "

—*Rep. Chesselden Ellis*

had lived as an Indian among the Cherokees. At 24, he was a government agent to the Cherokee chiefs; at 30, a Congressman from Tennessee; and at 34, the governor of the state. A favorite of President Jackson, he seemed on his way to the White House when, at 35, he married an 18-year-old Tennessee society beauty. Three months later, his young wife left him without explanation and Houston's career collapsed. Public rumors about his private life were so widespread that he was forced to resign as governor. He fled back to the Cherokees,

Against Texas Annexation

> " *. . . I observe, that the cause of Liberty, of free institutions, a cause more sacred than union, forbids the annexation of Texas. It is plain from the whole preceding discussion, that this measure will exert a disastrous influence on the moral sentiments and principles of this country, by sanctioning plunder, by inflaming cupidity, by encouraging lawless speculation, by bringing into the confederacy a community whose whole history and circumstances are adverse to moral order and wholesome restraint, by violating national faith, by proposing immoral and inhuman ends, by placing us as a people in opposition to the efforts of philanthropy, and the advancing movements of the civilized world. It will spread a moral corruption, already too rife among us, and, in so doing, it will shake the foundations of freedom at home, and bring reproach on it abroad. It will be treachery to the great cause which has been confided to this above all nations. . . .* "

—William Ellery Channing

who took him in and gave him an Indian wife. For the next few years, Houston drank heavily and thought up improbable schemes for leading the Indians on rampages into Mexico. One day, he said that an eagle had swooped near his head, then flown off, "lost in the rays of the setting sun." This he took as a sign that "a great destiny waited for me in the West." In 1832, he left for Texas where he quickly took the leading role in its stormy political life. By a skillful combination of persuasion, politicking, and threats, he led the fight which freed Texas from Mexico and brought it into the United States.

476

SETTLEMENT OF TEXAS

American settlement in the Mexican province of Texas began in 1823, when Mexico, two years independent of Spain, invited immigration by offering land grants at very reasonable prices to *empresarios,* American promoters, such as Stephen Austin, to bring in and colonize groups of families who would swear allegiance to Mexico. Probably the most important motive of the Mexican government for attracting foreigners was to develop the resources of the land, thus strengthening the economy and increasing Mexico's tax revenues. Possibly, too, the government thought that settlers would protect the area from Indian raids and even from American land hunger. This expectation failed and the experiment in hospitality resulted in the loss of Texas.

Thousands of Americans flocked into Texas, attracted by tales of rich soil. Many of the newcomers were law-abiding, but many more were rough adventurers, whose habits confirmed the comment once made by John Jay that American frontiersmen were more troublesome than Indians. By the fact of geography, most Texan settlers came into the territory from Louisiana and the Mississippi valley. In fact, throughout the Old Southwest the usual explanation for a missing person was "GTT"—"Gone to Texas." Southerners often brought their slaves with them, skirting Mexico's law forbidding slavery by claiming that the slaves were bonded servants. By 1834, some twenty thousand settlers with two thousand slaves had settled along the coastal plains of East Texas, outnumbering the Mexican population four to one.

GOVERNMENT BY MEXICO

Almost from the start, Americans clashed with their Mexican neighbors and the Mexican government. The underlying friction was cultural, a clash between the brash and dynamic Anglo-Saxon culture of the United States with the proud, ancient, and slower-paced Latin culture of Mexico. However, there were also specific troubles over land titles, taxes, and most of all, politics. Although there were many Americans in Texas, they formed only a tiny part of the Coahuila-Texas province and had almost no support or representation in the provincial legislature in Saltillo, the capital, 700 miles away. The settlers also resented the Mexican attacks on slavery and the government's failure to provide better marketing facilities for their agricultural products. In 1830, Mexico passed a law to prevent further immigration into Texas and proposed to garrison the province with convict soldiers to enforce Mexican law.

In 1832, Mexico had one of its periodic revolutions which ended with General Antonio Santa Anna at the head of the government. The Americans, calling themselves Texans, backed Santa Anna in return for the General's promise to separate Texas from Coahuila and make it into a Mexican state with self-rule. Three years later, Santa Anna became the dictator of Mexico and centralized the government. He not only failed in his promise to give Texas self-government but abolished all local powers in all the Mexican states. The Texans took Santa Anna's move as an act of aggression against them and rebelled against the new regime, proclaiming the Independent Republic of Texas. In November, 1835, a group of representatives met to set up a new government. They sent Stephen Austin to the United States to obtain support and placed Sam Houston at the head of their insurgent army.

THE ALAMO

The Texas War of Independence lasted six months and consisted of one defeat and one victory.

The first of the two conflicts took place shortly after several hastily organized companies of Texas volunteers drove the Mexican garrison from the town of San Antonio de Bexar and then departed for other towns, leaving as its own garrison only 145 men under the command of Lieutenant Colonel W. B. Travis. When Santa Anna crossed the Rio Grande and marched against San Antonio, Travis stubbornly declared, "I shall never surrender or retreat," and herded his small band of men into the old walled mission of the Alamo.

There, for ten days, the Texans held off four thousand Mexican troops. On March 6, 1836, Santa Anna signaled an attack and his troops scrambled over the walls to trumpets blazoning "no quarter." In the slaughter that followed every defender was killed, among them the famed Davy Crockett and Jim Bowie. Although the defense of the Alamo was a foolhardy military tactic, it gave Texas—and American history—one of its most dramatic legends of bravery.

BATTLE OF SAN JACINTO

After the Alamo, Sam Houston gathered the ragtail, stubborn companies of the Texas army and retreated, deftly avoiding the advancing Mexicans in order to give himself time to weld his unruly recruits into a disciplined army. Ahead of the troops were thousands of women and children refugees trying to escape either on foot or riding whatever animals and wagons they could find. In pursuit of the army rode Santa Anna and 1,500 men, burning towns and homesteads and slaughtering cattle as they advanced. For forty days during March and April, the refugees fled toward the Louisiana border of the United States with the two armies moving up behind them.

Then, on April 21, Houston decided his army was ready to take a stand. While the women and children trudged on ahead, he stopped to wait for the Mexicans in a grove of oak trees along the San Jacinto River near present-day Houston. Santa Anna pitched camp by the river and confidently retired to his tent for a siesta, the customary Mexican midday sleep. At that moment, Houston and his 800 men rushed over the Mexican defensive walls shouting, "Remember the Alamo!" In eighteen minutes of furious hand-to-hand fighting, 630 Mexicans lay dead and about 700 more, including Santa Anna, were taken prisoner. Texan casualties totaled only nine dead and thirty-four wounded.

The defeated Santa Anna signed a treaty recognizing the new Republic of Texas. Mexico refused to acknowledge the treaty, but it could do nothing about the fact that Texas was now independent. Houston was elected president and he promptly sent an envoy to Washington to ask for annexation to the United States or recognition of the Republic.

SENTIMENT FOR AND AGAINST ANNEXATION

With typical boastfulness, Americans at that time cheered the triumph of "the generous Anglo-Saxon blood" over the "blood-thirsty barbarians of Mexico." In calmer moments, they continued to believe that the Texas rebels had fought a war for humanity and democracy and deserved to be rewarded for their success. Hundreds of adventurers, stirred by the drama of the defense of the Alamo and by liberal offers of land, journeyed to Texas to join its army.

Although President Jackson did nothing to stop American citizens from offering support, the American government was officially neutral. Jackson did not want to invite a war with Mexico by American complicity in the revolt. Jackson, sensitive to the delicacy of the situation, refused to be more than diplomatically correct on the matter of recognition or annexation. The most he would commit himself to was the formal recognition of the Lone Star Republic, and he waited to do this until March 3, 1837, his last day in office.

THE SLAVERY QUESTION

Jackson's cautious sidestepping of "the Texas question" was primarily due to the fact that by the 1830s, the annexation of Texas to the United States, which the Lone Star Republic wanted, was not simply a matter of the addition of a new state to the Union, but raised the thorny question of slavery expansion.

Southerners saw in the huge area, which might come into the Union as one or several states, not only the opportunity to extend their slave-based cotton economy but also a chance for the balance of political power in the United States government to shift in their favor. Southern leaders were uneasily aware that, with the recent admission of Arkansas and Michigan, the Union now had thirteen free and thirteen slave states. Florida was the only slave territory left but there were three free territories, Wisconsin, Iowa, and Minnesota, which soon would be demanding statehood. "It needs but a glance at the map to satisfy the most superficial observer that an overbalance is produced by the extreme northeast, which as regards territory would be happily corrected and counterbalanced by the annexation of Texas," reported the Alabama legislature. The annexation of Texas would put additional Southern votes in the Senate and in the electoral college.

Among many Northerners, the annexation of Texas began to appear as a Southern plot to extend slavery and the political domination of slave states. In 1836 the Quaker abolitionist, Benjamin Lundy, published a pamphlet called "The War in Texas: A Crusade Against the Government Set on Foot by Slaveholders." Lundy claimed that the Texas revolution was plotted by a Southern pro-slavery conspiracy. Abolitionism was also beginning to have greater political influence as a growing number of Northerners openly denounced slavery in Congress and elsewhere, and expressed moral indignation over its possible extension. In 1837, for instance, the legislature in Vermont "solemnly protested" admitting any state "whose constitution tolerates domestic slavery." In an attempt to influence Northern attitudes, Sam Houston predicted an enormous future market for Northern manufactured goods in Texas, but to no avail.

AS A BRITISH BUFFER

Thwarted in his first attempts at annexation, Houston applied the strategy that had worked so well at San Jacinto: "concentrate, retreat and conquer." If the United States did not want to annex Texas, Texas would find "some other friend" to protect it. He approached the English about creating an enormous Southwestern country that would stretch to the Pacific and rival the United States in size and strength. England listened with great interest! An independent Texas, under British influence, would provide a buffer against American expansion and would break the American monopoly on cotton by providing British textile mills with a new source of supply and at the same time a big market for exports. Moreover, British abolitionists hoped they could convince Texas to end slavery and to show America that the labor of free men could also produce cotton profitably. In 1840, both England and France recognized Texas and arranged trade treaties. Houston made certain all the negotiations were well publicized. Hearing about them, Northern businessmen became alarmed at the possibility that Texas might link itself to English business interests, and Southern slaveholders, even more disturbed, began to fear that British pressure for abolition in Texas might encourage black insurrections within the slave states. As Houston had hoped, both Northerners and Southerners developed an irresistible desire for Texas. Well-pleased with his maneuver, he remarked, "If ladies are justified in making use of coquetry," surely he could be excused for "making use of the same means" to bring Texas into the Union.

ELECTION ISSUE

By election time in 1844, the country was dominated by the aggressive spirit of manifest destiny and the fever to annex Texas ran so high that it became the primary campaign issue. The Whig candidate, Henry Clay, yielded to anti-slavery sentiment in his party and hedged on the question, but the Democratic nominee, James K. Polk of Tennessee, ardently supported it. The voters elected Polk, telling him—and the incumbent President—just where they stood on the Texas question.

President Tyler, who had tried to push through annexation in February of that year, was determined to do the deed himself, before Polk took office in March, 1845. His earlier attempt had failed because of a blunder by Calhoun, his Secretary of State. After completing negotiations with Texas, Calhoun had sent a note to the British minister in Washington defending slavery and asserting that England's stand against it required that the United States annex Texas to protect the institution. When the note was made public, it looked like proof to the North that annexation would be the successful culmination of a pro-slavery plot, and an annexation treaty was defeated in the Senate 35 to 16, in June, 1844. After Polk's election, Tyler decided that if he could not annex Texas by treaty, which required the approval of two-thirds of the Senate, he would do so by a joint resolution which only needed approval by a simple majority in both houses of Congress.

The resolution Tyler offered gave Texas control over its public lands, allowed it to be divided into no more than five states, and protected slavery by including Texas in the provisions of the Missouri Compromise. The resolution passed the house by a comfortable margin and squeaked through the Senate by only two votes. Tyler signed it on February 28, 1845, and by the end of the year Texas accepted the invitation to become the twenty-eighth state of the Union.

ELECTION OF 1844

By 1844, the idea of manifest destiny unmistakably appealed to the majority of Americans, yet Clay, who expected the Whig nomination, and Martin Van Buren, who appeared to be the Democratic favorite, by mutual agreement tried to avoid the subject of annexation of Texas as an election issue. Because the question of Texas' entrance into the Union might intensify the sectional battle over the extension of slavery as well as provoke a possible war with Mexico, they decided that it was better to ignore the subject altogether.

To prevent losing either pro-slavery or anti-slavery votes and to preserve peace, by prearrangement they made separate public statements declaring that they opposed annexation without the consent of Mexico. This cautious action cost Van Buren the nomination and Clay the election.

Delegates to the 1844 Whig nominating convention evidently were not sufficiently aware of the appeal of expansionism because, although they nominated Clay unanimously, they wrote a party platform that discreetly omitted any mention of Texas. The Democrats, however, were more attuned to the temper of the country, for the expansionist delegates at the Democratic convention blocked Van Buren's nomination and instead named James K. Polk, a former governor of Tennessee who was a dedicated expansionist. Polk was the first Presidential "dark horse." To exploit the expansionist fever yet avoid charges of sectional favoritism, the Democrats produced a party platform that linked a firm demand for the annexation of slave-holding Texas with an equally forceful demand for the free territory of Oregon. "The re-occupation of Oregon and the re-annexation of Texas," said the platform, "at the earliest practicable period are great American measures, which this convention recommends to the cordial support of the Democracy of the Union." The implication that both areas had once been American, by the use of the words "re-occupation" and "re-annexation," was an attempt to make the proposed acquisition of land seem legal, even if without the consent of Mexico or Great Britain.

The campaign itself was one of slogans and personalities instead of a rational debate of issues facing the country. Clay claimed that he favored annexation if it could be accomplished by "just and fair terms" that would not bring on war with Mexico. To this, Southern Democrats shouted defiantly, "Re-annexation of Texas!" The sober Whigs suggested that the Oregon border, which the United States and England shared and which was an issue merely because it balanced the cry for Texas, might one day be settled at the forty-ninth parallel. In answer, Western Democrats called for "All of Oregon or none," with the slogan "Fifty-four forty or fight!" It was a close contest. Although in the electoral college vote Polk won 170 to 105, his lead in the popular vote was only 38,181 votes. Clay's loss of New York, where he had to compete not only with Polk but also with the Liberty Party, cost him the election. It was the final defeat of his Presidential aspirations.

POLK'S ADMINISTRATION

Because Polk was relatively unknown to the country at large when he ran for President, his opponents used the question "Who is James K. Polk?" as one of their campaign themes. The new President was, in fact, very well known in political circles. He had learned the craft of politics in Tennessee where he had been governor, and he had spent fourteen years in the House of Representatives, the last four as Speaker. Polk was thin, stiff, and angular, and at forty-nine already looked like an old man, although he was the youngest man to become President up to that time. He had

'ames Knox Polk, a dedicated expansionist, won the Presidency unexpectedly as the naion's first "dark horse."

sharp gray eyes set in a sad, lean face. He was also secretive, essentially humorless, unimaginative, and riddled with prejudice against all Whigs and abolitionists, many Democrats, and most Englishmen. However, he had an extremely good mind and approached the job he called "no bed of roses" with intense single-mindedness from his first day in office. In addition to being patient, Polk had tact, good judgment, a will of iron, and a strong sense of duty. Few Presidents before him had entered the White House with so clearly defined a program. Moreover, he accomplished all his aims in one term, all his health would allow him to serve. Three months after leaving office, he died.

Although Polk's concern with domestic policies was subordinate to his primary interest in geographical expansion, his administration reflected in all its aspects the growing power of the South in the Democratic Party. Polk was a Tennessee planter and slaveowner. He did not want to extend slavery, but otherwise his opinions on the subject reflected the Southern viewpoint. If slavery was abolished, he felt, "the dissolution of the Union . . . must speedily follow." On the question of protective tariffs, he also held Southern ideas. One of the goals he achieved was reduction of the tariff which Congress had raised in 1842. The Walker Tariff of 1846 produced important but not drastic reductions in duties. The average duties were about 25 percent. Only the manufacture of iron products was retarded, and the cheaper iron imported from abroad aided the construction of the railroads. The United States, by reducing its tariff wall, was also in line with the general European tendency at that time to lower tariffs, thereby facilitating world trade. The next few years saw the profitable sale abroad of big American surpluses of cotton

481

and wheat. Polk annoyed Westerners by vetoing internal improvement bills, in the Southern tradition of opposition to such measures. However, he pleased many Westerners as well as Southerners by reinstituting Van Buren's Independent Treasury which the Whigs had killed in their efforts to set up a new national banking system. All of this, plus settlement of the dispute over Oregon and the acquisition of a vast new territory west of Texas, was accomplished by dominating a Cabinet of highly capable men.

Polk was a President of ability and strength of purpose. He fully exerted his power to influence Congress and to use the veto against actions he opposed. He also was the first American President to act as a real Commander-in-Chief, directing all phases of the Mexican War.

GEOGRAPHICAL EXPANSION

Polk's main concern was westward expansion, in an era when frontiersmen were moving into Texas, Oregon, and California. At this time, Yankee skippers carried goods from California to Asian ports and even as far as Zanzibar and the Persian Gulf. Trade treaties were established with Latin America as well as England and France. The government sought trade with Japan, and America offered Spain 100 million dollars for Cuba to keep Spain from selling the Pearl of the Antilles to a foreign power. Polk pushed American influence all over the globe, but spent the most effort in acquiring a landed empire in North America. Although a Southern Democrat, Polk was very much impressed with the desire of the commercial interests for control of the Pacific Coast, hence his emphasis on the settlement of the Oregon boundary dispute and the acquisition of California from Mexico.

TEXAS AND OREGON

When Polk came into office, his predecessor, Tyler, had already carried out half of the Democratic Party's 1844 expansionist platform by annexing Texas. The new President immediately set out to fulfill the second half, which was the annexation of Oregon. The problem was how to make good that campaign slogan, "Fifty-four forty or fight!" For all its hunger for land, the United States had not previously claimed the entire Oregon territory. The question had always been whether the forty-ninth parallel, which was the northern border of the Louisiana territory, should be extended through the Oregon territory to the Pacific Ocean. Polk realized that to demand all of Oregon probably would mean war with England, a reckless move as long as war with Mexico over Texas threatened. In his inaugural address, de-

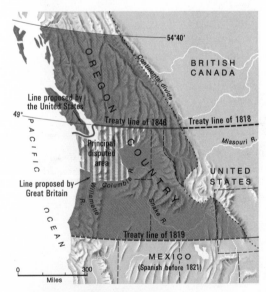

OREGON CONTROVERSY 1818 TO 1846

livered on a dark, rainy day to what John Quincy Adams described as "a large assemblage of umbrellas," Polk spoke of the "right of the United States to that portion of our territory which lies beyond the Rocky Mountains. Our title to the country of Oregon is clear and unquestionable, and already are our people preparing to perfect that title by occupying it with their wives and children." This was strong talk and the Oregon situation was explosive, but an amicable compromise on the boundary was reached because both England and the United States, in spite of the latter's aggressive posturing, wanted peace rather than war.

SETTLEMENT OF OREGON

Until the 1840s, England and the United States had jointly occupied Oregon because both had valid claims to the territory—America, on the basis of treaties, voyages, and explorations dating back to the discovery of the mouth of the Columbia River by Captain Robert Gray in 1792, and England, on the basis of her own agreements and explorations starting with the discovery of the Oregon coast by Sir Francis Drake in 1579. Through the years, the two countries had not been able to agree on a dividing line. The United States suggested the forty-ninth parallel to the Pacific, a direct extension westward of America's northern border. The British countered with the forty-ninth parallel to the mouth of the Columbia River, which would have left them in control of the fur trade in northwest Oregon and of the natural harbor of Puget Sound. Since neither side would yield, in 1818 they decided to postpone the decision by means of an agreement to leave all of Oregon to 54° 40′ free and open for ten years. Nine years later, they extended the agreement to run indefinitely or until one country gave the other country a year's notice that the agreement was to be canceled. The United States government was convinced that the Oregon territory was too distant from Great Britain to be of vital interest to her. Moreover, in the long run, the country would fill up with American farmers and agriculture would supersede the British fur trade.

THE HUDSON'S BAY COMPANY

Until infected with aggressive expansionism in the 1840s, the United States had little interest in the isolated Oregon wilderness beyond the Rockies, but England had built the area around Vancouver into a profitable fur-trading center. England's activities were run by the great Hudson's Bay Company, which had established Fort Vancouver as its trading "factory" in 1828. The Hudson's Bay Company factor, or manager, was a medical doctor named John McLoughlin who turned the settlement into an extraordinarily smooth-running operation. For more than twenty years, McLoughlin gave Oregon's traders, half-breeds, Indians, and English immigrants its only

483

government, which was efficient, effective, and scrupulously fair in dealing with the Indians.

One of McLoughlin's responsibilities to the Hudson's Bay Company was to keep American traders out of the region. "They must be opposed as much as we can," he said in 1826. However, in the 1830s, when a few American adventurers found their way to Oregon, neither he nor the Hudson's Bay Company felt threatened. Later, when settlers and missionaries began to arrive at Fort Vancouver after the long, exhausting trip from the East, he welcomed them cordially, lent them sufficient food to last them through the first harsh winter and offered valuable advice about their new country. McLoughlin was astounded, therefore, when, in 1843, the Americans in Oregon, now numbering about fifteen hundred, began demanding the "right" to the entire territory.

"OREGON FEVER"

Americans were infected with "Oregon fever" by the missionaries who were among the earliest settlers there. Methodists, Presbyterians, and Catholics had flocked to Oregon in the 1830s, lured by a false report that the Indians were eager to embrace Christianity. It was not their religious work but the publicity they gave Oregon that bore fruit. In letters and reports, they praised the area's rich soil and fine climate and the word was picked up by Eastern newspapers. Soon thousands of people in the Mississippi Valley, convinced that Oregon's Willamette Valley was a new Garden of Eden, were setting off in their "prairie schooners," the canvas-covered Conestoga wagons, for the new country 2,000 miles away.

OREGON TRAIL

The journey along the Oregon Trail was among the most difficult that Ameri-

cans made in their search for new lands in the West. Its jumping-off place was Independence, Missouri, where in May, 1843, parties of covered wagons gathered, appointed a captain, and hired an experienced mountain man as guide. Bugles blew, long whips cracked and the caravan, some one hundred wagons in length, started up the west bank of the Missouri River, then turned northwest to the Platte River. When they reached Fort Leavenworth, in the future state of Kansas, they were on the frontier of Indian country and no longer had United States government protection. Although the first migrations often lost their way because there was neither road nor trail to follow, by the middle of the 1840s wagon wheels had dug ruts into what became known as the Oregon Trail.

Every night in the Indian country, the wagons drew up in a circle around a campfire with horses and mules inside the enclosure and cattle grazing outside. As sentries stood guard and prairie wolves howled, the emigrants sustained their spirits by singing hymns and old ballads in the darkness. Around dawn, they put the horses and mules out to graze for a few hours. Then the men rounded up their oxen, hitched them to the wagons and, to the sound of the bugle, set off westward again.

In southern Wyoming, the trail became hilly, then mountainous as it approached the South Pass over the Rockies. Once through the pass, it became torturous. Over the arid stretches of Wyoming, grass was sparse for grazing and where water was found it was so salty as to be almost undrinkable. The caravans followed the twisting Snake River for 800 miles; sometimes the wagons were even floated down the river like rafts.

With good luck, a caravan might reach the Willamette Valley below the Columbia River by Thanksgiving. But it seldom reached Oregon with the same number of people it started out with, for only the heartiest survived. Some parties never arrived at all, either because they lost the trail and starved to death or were killed by Indians.

POLK'S NEGOTIATIONS

Although publicly Polk was committed to "Fifty-four forty or fight!", privately he was more than ready to compromise on the Oregon boundary. In July, 1845, four months after his inauguration, he informed the British minister in Washington that his government would accept the forty-ninth parallel as the dividing line in Oregon. The British envoy, without consulting his government, turned the offer down. Polk then went on the offensive, saying, "the only way to treat John Bull is to look him straight in the eye." In April, 1846, at Polk's urging Congress gave the one-year notice of the end of the joint occupation of Oregon. A crisis was in the making, but England, like the United States, did not want to go to war over Oregon, for already almost all of its settlers were Americans, and the fur trade, which had made Oregon valuable to Great Britain, was no longer of major importance. In the mid-nineteenth century, England was also more interested in free trade than more territorial acquisitions. The British, therefore, suggested that Oregon be divided at the forty-ninth parallel, turning Polk's proposal into their own. Polk blustered that the offer should be rejected, but he allowed his Cabinet to send it to the Senate for advice. With the decision in the hands of Congress, Polk was confident he could have the compromise agreement he wanted and still be politically uncompromised.

OREGON TREATY

The Senate advised acceptance of the compromise agreement in a vote that reflected annoyance with the extremist views on American expansionist policy. When the final treaty reached the Senate in June, 1846, the Mexican War had already begun, and it went through easily 41 to 14. The treaty divided the Oregon territory along the forty-ninth parellel to the Pacific, giving the United States control of the Columbia River Valley and the Puget Sound area and leaving Vancouver Island to the British. It was a compromise of a long-standing dispute agreeable to both countries.

FURTHER WESTWARD EXPANSION

While the main focus of American expansionist interest as late as 1844 was on Texas and Oregon, there was a general desire among most Americans to acquire all of the trans-Mississippi west to the Pacific Ocean. Not only did this idea fit in with the motives behind manifest destiny, but Americans could also point to the growing number of settlers in territory nominally under Mexican control—territories such as New Mexico, Utah, and California.

SANTA FE TRADE

At the time the question of Texas stirred the attention of the country, a band of enterprising small businessmen appealed to the American vision of manifest destiny to include the New Mexico territory in the Union as well. Santa Fe, the capital of New Mexico and its only town, lay on the upper Rio Grande in a country described as "marvels and enchantment, shimmering plains with no vegetation but strange cacti, mesas striped with ochre and vermilion, aboriginal cliff dwellings and the stupendous canyon of the Colorado River." To its boosters such land was clearly intended for Americans to own.

SANTA FE TRAIL

Starting in 1824, every spring for twenty years an armed caravan of American merchants had assembled pack mules and wagons at Independence, Missouri, to take the long journey through Osage and Comanche Indian country for trading with the lonely outpost. The hundred or so merchants who traveled the Santa Fe Trail always found a good market for their products and returned loaded with salable silver and furs. In 1844, however, Santa Anna banned all Americans from Santa Fe as an indication of Mexico's displeasure with the United

TRAILS TO THE FAR WEST

- - - - - Present-day state boundaries

States over the annexation of Texas. Mexico still felt that Texas was rightfully hers. The Mexican move came too late, however, for although only a few of the traders who regularly traveled the Santa Fe Trail had actually settled in the remote town, the yearly caravans had opened a route to the Far West. They proved that heavy wagons could cross the Western plains and had worked out a system of traveling that provided protection against the Indians.

THE MORMONS

Meanwhile, though vast numbers of Americans went west, as Polk put it, to "perfect" American rights to the continent, one group made the journey in order to escape from the United States. The group was the Mormons, who settled in the Utah territory.

The Mormon religion, or Church of Jesus Christ of Latter Day Saints, was founded by Joseph Smith, who grew up in Palmyra, in western New York, an area called the "burnt-over district" because it was the scene of fiery religious revivals in the early 1800s. Deeply influenced by the religious emotionalism of this area, in 1823, Smith claimed that angels led him to a place where "there was a book deposited written upon gold plates" which, translated by Smith with the aid of Divine Providence, became the Book of Mormon. Its text is based on stories of the settlement of America and a prophecy which said that the supposed lost tribes of Israel were the Indians of the Western Hemisphere whom Smith's followers were to convert from their pagan religion. In 1830, Smith organized his church and printed the Book of Mormon. Organizationally, the movement was a theocracy, with Smith, a shrewd and able Yankee, in complete charge as God's "prophet." An elaborate hierarchy below him gave opportunity for leadership to the talented among its members.

PERSECUTION

As the movement grew, Mormons aroused the annoyance of their neighbors by their close-knit communal social patterns, by their thriving self-sufficient economic life, and by their contempt for other religious sects. The anger of the "gentiles," the Mormon name for other Christians, forced the sect to move first to Ohio, then to Missouri, and then, in 1839, to Nauvoo, Illinois, where they prospered. In 1844, Smith claimed to have received a revelation approving the practice of polygamy. He took several wives, and many other Mormons followed their leader's example. Polygamy was an invitation to trouble in a land of religious orthodoxy. It led to a split in the Mormon Church and enraged non-Mormons. A wave of violence against the settlement reached its crest when Smith was arrested and then murdered by a mob before he could be brought to trial.

BRIGHAM YOUNG

Brigham Young, a brilliant and strong-willed follower of Joseph Smith, became the new "Lion of the Lord" of the Mormons. He resolved to lead them out of the land of the "gentiles" where, according to a Mormon writer, they had been "eternally mobbed, harassed, hunted, our best man murdered and every good man's life continually in danger." Young hoped to find the homeland Joseph Smith had envisioned. It would be "in the midst of the Rocky Mountains . . . where we can . . . build a city in a day and have a government of our own."

EXODUS TO SALT LAKE

In one of the most remarkable westward migrations in American history, Brigham Young organized several thousand Mormons and journeyed with them to Council Bluffs on the Missouri River and then southwest into the Utah territory, arriving at the Great Salt Lake basin in July, 1847. About them stretched the most inhospitable of lands: "a broad and barren plain . . . a seemingly interminable waste of sagebrush . . . the paradise of the lizard, the cricket, and the rattlesnake." In a year, five thousand Mormons settled in the desolate territory which belonged to Mexico, although the Mormons never asked the Mexican government for permission to live there. From Brigham Young, the provisional state acquired the name of Deseret, meaning "land of the honeybees." Within a decade, they transformed the grim landscape into a prosperous farming area.

A COMMUNITARIAN PROJECT

Unlike typical Western pioneers, the Mormons did not work as individuals in competition with one another. Under the forceful control of Brigham Young and the church organization, they functioned as a vast cooperative community. Young arranged for an irrigation system that channeled the rain and snow from the mountains and distributed water evenly throughout the settlement. For smaller units within the overall community, he and a committee of planners parceled out ninety-five plots of land. Governing through a complicated church hierarchy, Young regulated both the religious and civil affairs of the Mormons. With shrewdness, rough humor, and a firm system of justice, he created a large, flourishing enterprise, the most successful communitarian project America has ever known.

However, the Mormons were unable to remain apart from the United States. The war with Mexico pulled them into American territory when, in 1850, their remote Mexican region came under Union jurisdiction. Washington renamed Deseret the Utah territory, and although Brigham Young remained the leader and driving force in the area, now it was by appoint-

ment of the United States government and with the new title of territorial governor. Nevertheless, the Mormons gave up very little of their independence. They drove federal judges out of Utah when the judges ruled against Young's decisions, and when a new territorial governor was named in the late 1850s, Washington had to send federal troops to support him. The polygamous theocracy survived almost intact in the midst of a monogamous democracy until well after the Civil War.

CALIFORNIA

SPANISH SETTLEMENTS

California, the most distant Mexican province, the acquisition of which was one of Polk's major objectives, had been a Spanish possession from the middle of the eighteenth century. Spain had held it loosely by means of a chain of Franciscan missions established along the coast from San Diego to Sonoma. Protected by small garrisons, the missions served a twofold purpose: to convert Indians and to maintain Spanish control of the area. The Franciscan missionaries were highly successful in Christianizing thousands of Indians and teaching them farming. In fact, the friars trained and supervised the Indians so well that the missions became large-scale agricultural enterprises.

MEXICAN RULE

When Mexico freed itself from Spain by the early 1820s, officials and land speculators called for distribution of the mission property, for they had always resented religious ownership of such productive land. By 1834, the mission system had broken down; half the land was in private hands and most Indians were now forced to work for the new ranch owners. As Spain's religious administration gave way to a succession of inefficient and often corrupt Mexican governments, the territory of California fell into political chaos.

INCREASE OF AMERICANS

New England whaling and trading ships made the first American contacts with California when they stopped at the Pacific ports for supplies or touched along the coast to exchange a wide and colorful assortment of American products and foreign merchandise. From the 1820s on, occasional bands of Mountain Men from Oregon (hunters employed by the Rocky Mountain Company) wandered into the province on trapping expeditions and remained there. In the 1830s, a few merchants arrived to trade with the Indians and Mexicans. Jim Clyman, a master Mountain Man, commented about the Americans he met in California: "The Foreigners which have found their way to this country are mostly a poor discontented set of inhabitants and [have] but little education hunting for a place as they [want] to live easy . . . and I do not hear of but one man that has gone to the trouble and Expense to get his [land] title confirmed. . . ."

The Americans found in California a small scattered population of Spanish-Americans at the top of which were the aristocratic caballeros, the ranchers. "Half barbaric, half elegant," their law of life was hospitality and their goal of life was pleasure. Splendid and romantic-looking in their gay silk vests, velvet breeches, deerskin boots, jackets lavishly embroidered and sombreros heavy with gold and silver ornaments, the ranchers awed the plain pioneers.

Yet it was soon apparent to the vigorous new arrivals that the caballeros were defenseless. Clyman wrote that they were "a proud lazy, indolent people doing nothing but ride after herds from place to place without any apparent object." The drudgery was done by Indians. Such men as

Thomas O. Larkin, a merchant who arrived in Monterey in 1832 and built a flourishing trade, realized that Americans could take over the land from the ranchers, and tirelessly promoted immigration.

By the 1840s, many caravans of covered wagons were turning south off the Oregon Trail near the Snake River to follow the California Trail across the Nevada Desert, over the Sierra Nevada Mountains, and into the Sacramento River Valley. By 1845, California was home to at least seven hundred Americans, few of whom planned to give up their American citizenship or to stay for long under the jurisdiction of Mexico.

SUTTER'S FORT

Once in the Sacramento Valley, most emigrant caravans made their way to Sutter's Fort, the vast private domain of John Augustus Sutter, a Swiss-born merchant who

California miners digging for gold on the property of John Sutter. Sutter bought the land from Russians and started an independent state with himself as lord, granting passports to Americans to settle the Mexican land. When gold was discovered, miners overran Sutter's land, staking out their own claims without his knowledge or approval.

had become a Mexican citizen. However, he operated independently of the Mexican government to the point of issuing passports to people who wanted to go deeper into Mexican territory. Sutter provided supplies for Americans and helped them settle.

When the first American immigrants arrived, Sutter was well on his way toward expanding the fort into an independent state called New Helvetia, with himself as absolute overlord. The dream ended in 1848 when gold was discovered on his property. Sutter tried to keep the news secret, but hints appeared in newspapers, rumors passed from one traveler to another, and when a storekeeper in the fort flashed a quinine bottle filled with gold dust in the presence of a customer, the secret was out. In the gold rush that followed, miners overran Sutter's land and Sutter himself died penniless in Washington trying vainly to reclaim it.

JONES AT MONTEREY

So keen were Americans to have California that the town of Monterey was captured temporarily in 1842, four years before California was actually taken. The commander of the United States Pacific naval squadron, Commodore Thomas Catesby Jones, had picked up a rumor in Peru that British warships were moving toward the California coast. Convinced that hostilities between the United States and Mexico had started and that Britain was taking advantage of the conflict, Jones promptly sailed into Monterey Bay, forced the astonished Mexican government to surrender, hoisted the American flag, and announced that the United States had annexed California. The State Department awkwardly offered apologies to the Mexican government for the mistake. The premature "conquest" made Mexicans more certain than ever that North Americans were aggressive men who could not be trusted.

THE MEXICAN WAR

Although California was not a major issue in the 1844 Presidential campaign, soon after the election it began to be coupled in the public mind with Oregon. By the following summer, there was widespread talk about a great nation extending from the Atlantic to the Pacific, talk matched by the expansionist ambitions of the new President. California was being extravagantly praised as "the richest, the most beautiful and the healthiest country in the world," and while Polk appreciated giant forests, broad valleys for wheatfields, vast grazing grounds, and mountains rich in scenery and minerals, his eagerness to take over California arose more from the advantages of the ports, the whale fisheries, and the commercial opportunities he envisioned on both sides of the Pacific. California also would be the logical terminus for a projected transcontinental railroad. Thus, he wanted almost desperately to get these actual and potential riches into United States' possession before they fell to England or France. In fact, in his first annual message to Congress, Polk replied to the remarks of the French Foreign Office that it was necessary to maintain the balance of power in the New World by stating that the United States would not permit European countries to establish colonies in North America either by force or diplomacy. Nor could a European country keep an independent territory from coming into the Union. "The people of *this continent* alone have the right to determine their own destiny," he

War with Mexico: Right or Wrong?

... The strong desire to establish peace with Mexico on liberal and honorable terms, and the readiness of this government to regulate and adjust our boundary, and other causes of difference with that power, on such fair and equitable principles as would lead to permanent relations of the most friendly nature, induced me in September last to seek the reopening of diplomatic relations between the two countries. ... An envoy of the United States repaired to Mexico, with full powers to adjust every existing difference ... the Mexican government not only refused to receive him, or listen to his propositions, but, after a long continued series of menaces, have at last invaded our territory, and shed the blood of our fellow-citizens on our own soil. ... Our forbearance has gone to such an extreme as to be mistaken in its character. Had we acted with vigor in repelling the insults and redressing the injuries inflicted by Mexico at the commencement, we should doubtless have escaped all the difficulties in which we are now involved.

Instead of this, however, we have been exerting our best efforts to propitiate her good-will ... the cup of forbearance had been exhausted, even before the recent information from the frontier of the Del Norte. But now, after reiterated menaces, Mexico has passed the boundary of the United States, has invaded our territory, and shed American blood upon the American soil. She has proclaimed that hostilities have commenced, and that the two nations are now at war.

As war exists, and, notwithstanding all our efforts to avoid it, exists by the act of Mexico herself, we are called upon by every consideration of duty and patriotism to vindicate with decision the honor, the rights, and the interests of our country.

—*James K. Polk*

War with Mexico: Right or Wrong?

... I am now through the whole of the President's evidence; and it is a singular fact that if any one should declare the President sent the army into the midst of a settlement of Mexican people who had never submitted, by consent or by force, to the authority of Texas or of the United States, and that there and thereby the first blood of the war was shed, there is not one word in all the President has said which would either admit or deny the declaration. This strange omission it does seem to me could not have occurred but by design. My way of living leads me to be about the courts of justice; and there I have sometimes seen a good lawyer, struggling for his client's neck in a desperate case, employing every artifice to work round, befog, and cover up with many words some point arising in the case which he dared not admit and yet could not deny. Party bias may help to make it appear so, but with all the allowance I can make for such bias, it still does appear to me that just such, and from just such necessity, is the President's struggle in this case. ....

—*Abraham Lincoln*

said. The message was actually a restatement in specific terms of the Monroe Doctrine, which had been almost forgotten since 1823. It came to be known as the Polk Corollary to the Monroe Doctrine.

PRELUDE TO WAR

Given the American desire for California, war with Mexico was almost inevitable. However, hostilities between the two countries began over the boundary of Texas. Texas claimed the border line was at the Rio Grande River whereas Mexico insisted it was at the Nueces, a river 150 miles farther north. When Texas was invited to enter the Union, Mexico broke diplomatic

relations with the United States and moved troops into the area of the Rio Grande. In the fall of 1845, Polk countered by sending General Zachary Taylor into Texas to protect the border. Taylor crossed the Nueces into the disputed territory with some fifteen hundred men, stationing himself at Corpus Christi. He was under orders not to incite the Mexicans by marching to the Rio Grande but to take "appropriate action" if Mexico started hostilities or came over the river with a military force.

For a time Polk seems to have believed that by frontier pressure he would be able to badger Mexico into accepting the Rio Grande as the southern boundary of Texas and into giving up California without resorting to war. To this end he tried to get

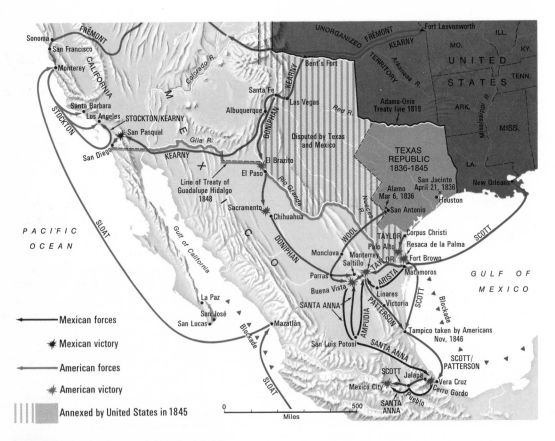

MEXICAN WAR · 1846 TO 1848

Texas to seize the disputed territory between the Rio Grande and Nueces. He believed this maneuver would prevent Mexico from recognizing the independence of Texas and bring the Lone Star Republic into the Union with the Rio Grande already as its southern boundary. With the failure of this intrigue, the President then sent John Slidell of Louisiana to Mexico in December, 1845, to negotiate directly with the Mexican government. He was to demand the Rio Grande as the southern boundary of Texas and offer as much as 30 million dollars for all of New Mexico and California. Before his arrival, the Mexican government got wind of the proposals to carve up their country and refused to see Slidell. He returned after six months, asserting testily that "nothing is to be done with these people until they have been chastised."

WAR DECLARED

When Polk heard of Mexico's treatment of Slidell, he ordered Taylor to advance to the Rio Grande. By March, Taylor was at Matamoras. He was ready to send his army of four thousand men into action when a Mexican force of sixteen hundred crossed the river and attacked one of Taylor's mounted patrols of sixty-three men. All were killed or captured. American blood had been shed "upon American soil," Polk announced to Congress. A state of war existed "notwithstanding all our efforts to avoid it," he said. Polk had already been preparing a war message before the attack, having reached the conclusion that only force would succeed in making America's expansionist dreams a reality. He now revised the address to blame Mexico directly for the hostilities. Both houses quickly voted for war and the President issued a declaration on May 13, 1846. However, many Whigs and some Northern Democrats only wanted to repel a Mexican invasion of Texas and were not thinking of either

an aggressive war to seize California or of the deep thrust into Mexico which ensued.

Polk's plan for war had two major components: first, to take possession of California and New Mexico; and second, to clear Mexicans out of Texas and by taking Mexico City compel the Mexican government to make peace on American terms.

KEARNY TAKES NEW MEXICO AND CALIFORNIA

California was easily taken by American forces. In June, 1846, an expedition of seventeen hundred men, led by Colonel Stephen W. Kearny, set out from Fort Leavenworth, Kansas, to march to the Pacific. The progress of this Army of the West had almost an epic quality, as the men tramped down the Santa Fe Trail past blazing fields of flowers and great herds of buffalo. After marching two months, Kearny and his men entered the adobe town—"Mud Town," they called it—of Santa Fe, which they captured without firing a shot. Kearny announced that New Mexico was now annexed by the United States, and, after his men rested Kearny led them on to California.

Most of their work had already been done for them by American settlers under the leadership of John C. Frémont who had taken most of the region without difficulty. Kearny, however, put down scattered resistance near Los Angeles and San Diego in Southern California. Thus by January, 1847, New Mexico and California were American possessions, and the first of Polk's goals had been reached.

CHANGE IN COMMAND

The most difficult part of Polk's plan was the campaign against Mexico itself, for Americans would have to cut themselves off from their home base and move south through hundreds of miles of rough country dotted with virtually impregnable defense points before they would see the mountains rimming Mexico's capital. Moreover, the job of an aggressive war in Mexico was complicated by Polk's desire to find a good general to take charge of the operation who was also a loyal Democrat. General Zachary Taylor, who had so ably started the war at the border of the Rio Grande, was a Whig, and also, to the President's distaste, an outspoken, self-made soldier who was becoming dangerously popular as a military hero in the Andrew Jackson mold. "Old Rough and Ready" began to be talked about for the White House shortly after the war began. Polk wanted a "small war, just large enough to require a treaty of peace, and not large enough to make military reputations dangerous for the presidency," in the words of Democratic Senator Thomas Hart Benton. To bypass Taylor, Polk planned to name Benton himself, now aged 64, lieutenant general and place him in nominal control of the army. Congress, however, voted down this choice as unsuitable. The President was then forced to turn to Major General Winfield Scott, also a Whig, who although politically astute, was also a pompous dandy not likely to attract widespread popularity.

TAYLOR
AT MONTERREY

Although Polk's attitude was partisan, it was also realistic. Taylor, though competent, courageous, and very popular with his troops, was not a brilliant soldier. He had limitations when it came to campaign tactics and was inclined to be overcautious. Both factors were evident at the Rio Grande, where he refused to move forward without reinforcements and additional supplies, and when he led six thousand men against the Mexican city of Monterrey in September, 1846. The city was like a natural stone fortress and the Americans had to storm it in

the face of blazing gunfire. After a three-day battle in the city streets, Taylor defeated the Mexican defenders. His popularity rose to new heights in the United States, but characteristically he let the Mexicans withdraw instead of surrender and agreed not to continue the offensive against them for eight weeks.

The battle at Monterrey betrayed Taylor's weaknesses as a commander, but it also showed the fighting quality of the Texas volunteers. Until now, the Texans had only shocked the American soldiers by their cruelty to the Mexican people, a result of years of border warfare. They were a tough, wild breed, of whom Taylor had commented that they were "too licentious to do much good." On the other hand, many were hard-fisted cowboys and, going to battle, they let out the wild, eerie cry of the cattle range. Years later, in the Civil War, men would again break and flee with terror at the sound of the "rebel yell."

THE BATTLE OF
BUENA VISTA

In February, 1847, another important battle took place at Buena Vista, south of Monterrey, where Taylor's army, greatly reduced, was under government orders to stay on the defensive and keep out of Mexican territory. Taylor, convinced that the orders were part of a plot to downgrade him politically, marched south anyway. Santa Anna, Mexico's commanding general and dictator, marched north to meet him with troops that outnumbered the Americans by four to one. The armies clashed inconclusively, neither side winning any permanent ground and both, at one time or another, retreating. On the second day, however, it became clear that the American line would not break, and Santa Anna, with his troops demoralized, retreated with two captured American flags and three American cannon as his only comfort in defeat.

SCOTT TAKES VERACRUZ

Polk's judgment was correct when he chose General Winfield Scott to lead the army into Mexico. According to one of his young officers, Lieutenant Ulysses S. Grant, Scott was "the finest specimen of manhood my eyes ever beheld." The son of an old Virginia family, he stood almost 6 feet, 6 inches tall and was an imposing figure in uniform. Although he tended to be particular and self-important, Scott was intelligent, even-tempered, and cultured, and as commanding general in Washington, he made a permanent contribution to the American army by modernizing military administration and strengthening the professional training of officers. His greatest achievement, however, was the brilliant strategy he planned and carried out for the entire Mexican campaign.

Scott decided to invade Mexico by sea, at the Gulf Coast, and march straight to the capital. The first step was to land his army near Veracruz. He did so by towing ten thousand men crowded into surfboats close to the shore and directing them to leap into the water holding their guns over their heads. By following this plan the Americans established their beachhead and besieged Veracruz. With a loss of only a handful of men, they captured the city in less than three weeks.

SCOTT MARCHES TO MEXICO CITY

From Veracruz, Scott marched inland to complete his campaign, one of the most daring and best managed in American military annals. With an army of never more than fourteen thousand men and sometimes not more than nine thousand, he advanced 260 miles through enemy country. Without losing a battle, he insured the safety of his forces and carried out his objectives. Keep-ing tight discipline so his men would not inflame the countryside, he moved over the rugged Mexican terrain toward Mexico City. When he found his way blocked at Cerro Gordo by artillery and a large army led by Santa Anna, he sent a force of men to the rear of the Mexican position and then stormed it, taking some three thousand prisoners and large quantities of equipment. After this battle, he met little resistance and advanced rapidly to the outskirts of the capital.

SCOTT DEFEATS SANTA ANNA

At the edge of the city, Santa Anna fought desperately, but Scott hammered him into defeat in two hard battles. The first, near Contreras, lasted seventeen minutes and ended in a rout of the Mexicans and a loss to them of about seven hundred men and their best cannon. During the second encounter, at Churubusco, Americans were riddled for hours by Mexican sharpshooters and a battalion of American deserters. On September 14, six months after landing at Veracruz, Scott and his American army overwhelmed the Mexican defenders, boy cadets of the Mexican military school, and entered and occupied the enemy capital. Santa Anna's government collapsed, but it took four months before a new government would recognize the fact of defeat and negotiate a treaty.

TRIST NEGOTIATES PEACE

Nicholas Trist, the chief clerk of the State Department, had accompanied Scott's army from Veracruz with instructions from Polk to "take advantage of circumstances as they might arise to negotiate a peace." He was to offer terms similar to those Slidell had carried to Mexico earlier. Because of the confusion that followed the fall of Mexico City, however, Trist could

495

STORMING OF THE CASTLE OF CHAPULTEPEC, BY THE AMERICAN ARMY UNDER GENERAL SCOTT, SEPT. 13, 1847.

General Winfield Scott storming the Castle of Chapultepec, the last of a series of battles which resulted in the fall of Mexico City.

not start peace talks with Mexican officials until January, 1848. Polk, from afar, wanted to demand more concessions from Mexico and ordered Trist home for further instructions just as negotiations finally began. Trist believed that Mexico would grant no more than the huge territorial concessions already being asked and feared that further demands would result in a deterioration of the military situation into a guerrilla war which would be to America's disadvantage. He decided to ignore the summons. On February 2, 1848, he signed the Treaty of Guadelupe Hidalgo, under whose terms the United States received California, the New Mexico territory, and the Rio Grande as the southern boundary of Texas for 15 million dollars—5 million dollars less than Trist was originally authorized to spend—and the United States assumed the claims of American citizens against Mexico. Polk was furious when he heard that Trist had acted against his orders. "Impudent and unqualified scoundrel," Polk called his peace commissioner, and fired him from the State Department as soon as he returned home.

Trist's act was insubordinate but courageous. It came at a time when opinion in the country was very much divided on the merits and continuance of the war. A number of expansionists were calling for all of Mexico. Such sentiment was strongest in the East where many in industry and commerce thought total absorption of the country would bring great profits. The belief that slavery would not flourish in Mexico brought Free-Soil expansionists in the West to the cause. Furthermore, American irri-

496

tation at Mexico's continued resistance and the capture of Mexico City helped convince many that the United States was obligated to take over the entire country and rule it—for the well-being of Mexicans, for the benefit of Americans, and for the advancement of world civilization. On the other hand, there were also many Whigs and Northern Democrats who had always been opposed to the invasion of Mexico, who disliked the expense of the conflict, and who still feared slavery expansion. Calhoun Democrats were also against the war, since they did not believe Mexico would be useful for agriculture. After 1846 the Whigs controlled the House of Representatives. Polk thus feared that he could not get needed funds to continue the war and decided in spite of his disappointment to submit the treaty Trist brought back to the Senate for ratification. It passed easily, 38 to 14.

What were the results of the Mexican War? The United States gained over 500,000 square miles of territory, outlets for trade on the Pacific Coast and in the Orient, and the soon-to-be-discovered gold mines in California. The losses in money and lives were small in comparison with future wars. However, the acquisition of this new territory intensified the growing sectional conflict over the expansion of slavery which ultimately split the Union. The war was also a manifestation of the tendency of mankind to rationalize aggressive deeds by cloaking them in idealistic statements. The war embittered Mexican-American relations for many years to come.

The problem of the expansion of slavery into the territories arose even before the end of the Mexican War, when David Wilmot, a Free-Soil Democrat from Pennsylvania, tacked an amendment called the Wilmot Proviso to an appropriation bill. The amendment proposed that "neither slavery nor involuntary servitude shall ever exist" in territory acquired from Mexico. The House voted for the amendment, but the Senate voted against it. Wilmot persistently added it to other bills in Congress, and through the country generally it was vigorously debated. Northerners were indignant that the "land of the free" should consider introducing slavery where it did not already exist, and Southerners felt that such a formal amendment was an insult to their way of life and discriminatory against the South.

ELECTION OF 1848

By 1848 the issue of expansion of slavery into new territories was agitating the whole country and dividing the leadership of the two major parties. Early in the year, Congress voted to bar slavery from Oregon, but this was hardly a test of the nation's acceptance of anti-slavery laws since there was no demand for slavery so far north, where cotton could not be cultivated. The election campaign could have provided a forum for a discussion of slavery expansion, but the political leaders refused to debate the issue.

DEMOCRATIC PLATFORM

Lewis Cass, whom the Democrats backed, was an expansionist who tried to placate the South. An early opponent of the Wilmot Proviso, he believed that the people in each new territory should decide for themselves whether or not to have slavery. His vague stand was politically disastrous. For example, he never made it clear whether a territory should decide the slav-

TAYLOR,

ery question before or after slaves were brought into a territory first occupied by free settlers. The failure of Cass to offer an answer to such questions made him a lackluster candidate. For their middle-of-the-road candidate, the Democrats wrote a platform that ignored slavery altogether.

WHIG PLATFORM

The Whigs, too, hoped to ignore slavery and direct attention from every election issue by nominating the popular "Hero of Buena Vista," General Taylor. Clay was alarmed at the abandonment of Whig principles but was overridden. The qualifications of "Old Rough and Ready" for the highest office in the land consisted of "sleeping forty years in the woods and cultivating moss on the calves of his legs," said one opponent. Taylor was completely lacking in political sophistication and refused to give his opinion on any current subject. He did, however, offer one naive, almost pathetic campaign comment: "I am a Whig," he said, *"but not an ultra Whig. If elected . . . I should feel bound to administer the government untrammeled by party schemes."* As befit their popular hero-candidate, the Whigs offered no party platform at all.

THE FREE-SOIL PARTY

The creed of the "regulars" in both political parties was "party harmony." However, in 1848, the Democratic regulars overlooked the "barnburners" in New York and New England, the determined anti-slavery faction which contained those who called for burning of the "barn" of the Democratic Party to get rid of the pro-slavery

"rats." Nor did the Whigs consider as significant the differences between their anti-slavery "conscience" and pro-slavery "cotton" elements. In each of these parties, anti-slavery factions bolted from their regular party conventions and combined to hold their own convention where they formed the Free-Soil Party. Its platform was a slogan: "Free soil, Free speech, Free labor, and Free men." Martin Van Buren of New York, an anti-slavery Democrat, was their Presidential candidate.

The electorate responded with very little enthusiasm to the election campaign. Neither major candidate had appeal to party workers, and Martin Van Buren, the third-party Free-Soil candidate, had no national political machine to work for him. Influential men backed one candidate or the other for negative reasons. For example, Horace Greeley supported Van Buren only because he thought the Democratic candidate, Lewis Cass, was a "pot bellied, mutton-headed cucumber," and Daniel Webster gave the Whig candidate, Zachary Taylor, a token endorsement after much obvious hesitation. Although Taylor won the election, the Free-Soilers turned out to be a very important factor in the outcome. They polled 10 percent of the vote, which split the Democratic vote in New York sharply enough to give the state to Taylor. In Ohio and Indiana they split the Whig vote sharply enough to give those states to Cass. In the House of Representatives the nine Free-Soilers held the balance of power. They had shown the disruptive effect of a party based on a strong issue. The Free-Soilers also had shown that the subject of slavery expansion could not be shunted aside and their emergence set the stage for a realignment of the political parties in the next decade.

CALIFORNIA, AND NEW MEXICO

GOLD RUSH

Slavery and all other sectional tensions relaxed for a while in 1848, when news spread that gold had been discovered in California. Numerous Americans of every class and occupation headed for the Pacific coast. Men from all over the world joined them: Englishmen, Frenchmen, Indians, Mexicans, Australians, and Chinese made the perilous voyage around Cape Horn, through the Isthmus of Panama, or across the Pacific to get to the gold. Many traveled overland, touching at Salt Lake City where the Mormons grew rich supplying miners at exorbitant prices. Within a year, California had a population of 100,000. San Francisco alone changed from a squalid village to a city of 20,000 inhabitants in a matter of months.

THE SLAVERY ISSUE

The government of California, although still theoretically military, was in fact demanding entrance into the Union as a free state without going through the territorial process. Taylor, well-intentioned but politically inexperienced, had to lead a deeply divided Congress in determining what to do about California and how the rest of the Mexican Cession should be organized. Northern opinion generally wanted these territories organized without slavery (the Wilmot Proviso) or through popular sovereignty by letting the people in the territory decide what they wanted. Some people from all parts of the country wanted to decide the issue of slavery expansion by

extending the Missouri Compromise line to the Pacific Coast. Most Southerners wanted to be able to take their slaves anywhere since they considered them property and thus protected by the Constitution. Taylor's decision was that California be admitted as a state without going through the intermediate step of becoming a territory. This would relieve Congress of making any decision on the slavery issue because, as a state, California could decide for itself whether or not it wanted slavery. Taylor also thought the New Mexico territory could follow a similar course.

Southerners were horrified by the prospect. California as a state was certain to be free, thereby destroying the Senatorial balance between free and slave states. Furthermore, to permit all the new lands to enter the Union as free states would surround the South by hostile states. They did not believe slavery could be sustained under such circumstances, even in the determined state of South Carolina. Taylor's move played directly into the hands of Southern extremists who were as early as 1850 declaring themselves strongly in favor of secession.

CLAY'S RESOLUTIONS

Of all the leaders, old and new, who understood the mounting crisis, the most perceptive was Henry Clay, now well past 70 and in ill health. Clay felt that the Union was close to dissolution. He realized that California had to be admitted as a free state but believed that the South was entitled to concessions; her mood was too desperate to ignore. Consulting with his

499

old Whig rival, Daniel Webster, Clay offered the Senate a proposal "founded upon mutual forbearance" which stated: 1) that California be admitted as a free state; 2) that the territorial governments to be set up in Utah and New Mexico should decide for themselves whether slavery should be permitted; 3) that the western boundary of Texas be fixed to exclude the eastern portion of New Mexico; 4) that in return for this concession, the United States would assume that portion of the public debt of Texas contracted before annexation; 5) that the slave trade be outlawed within the District of Columbia; 6) that slavery was not to be abolished in the District of Columbia except with the consent of its residents and those of Maryland, and with compensation to slaveowners; 7) that a stricter fugitive slave law be adopted; and 8) that Congress could not interfere with the interstate slave trade.

WEBSTER'S SPEECH

Clay's proposals brought on one of the most magnificent of all Senate debates, covering a period of seven months. Every important Senator took part. Clay himself, haggard and with faltering voice, appealed to the North for concessions and to the South for peace. His passionate devotion to the Union enthralled his audience. Calhoun, as much as Clay, realized the danger to the nation's unity; nevertheless, he reacted strongly to Clay's compromise proposals. Too ill to speak, he sat muffled in a cloak while Senator James M. Mason read his speech. In a bitter denunciation of the North, he called for an end to the crusade against slavery, reasserted the principle of states' rights, and demanded strict enforcement of the fugitive slave law. If his intention was to alarm his listeners to the danger threatening the nation's unity, he succeeded only in offering an argument for secession. If Northerners did not yield, he asserted, "let the states . . . agree to separate and part in peace."

On the third day of the debate, Webster rose for his last great speech. His voice was no longer powerful and he had to pause for breath, but he was still able to cast a spell on the Senate and galleries as he began: "I speak today for the preservation of the Union. Hear me for my cause." To the dismay of many Northern anti-slavery people, the great Yankee statesman used his eloquence to support Clay's proposals. The speech diminished his standing among the opponents of slavery, but it had the immediate effect of consolidating support for compromise. In both the North and the South, feeling for compromise grew in the months of debate that followed.

TAYLOR'S DEATH

Although in time the majority of the Senate came to the support of some form of compromise, President Taylor stubbornly opposed every proposal that conflicted with his own plan to take California and New Mexico into the Union unconditionally and without direction from Congress. However, Taylor died suddenly of a stomach disorder on July 9, 1850. Millard Fillmore, the Vice-President and a political moderate, succeeded him. Although Fillmore was a Free-Soiler, he nevertheless favored Clay's compromise and broke the deadlock between the White House and Congress.

THE COMPROMISE OF 1850

Each section of the compromise had to be voted on separately, otherwise too many Congressmen would have rejected the entire plan because they disliked certain sections of it. For example, Senator Benton would not accept the fugitive slave provision and objected to the Texas boundary settlement. Partisanship and economic interests got in the way of total compromise. Speculators became ardent compromisers only after they thought of the federal government paying

500

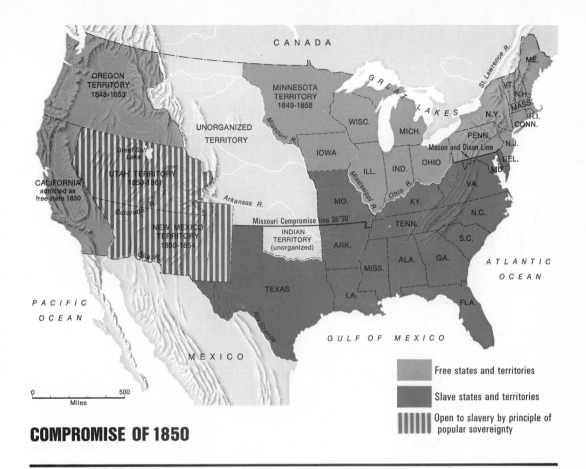

COMPROMISE OF 1850

Free states and territories

Slave states and territories

Open to slavery by principle of popular sovereignty

the debt of Texas. One by one, however, the individual measures were pushed through the Senate and then through the House by combinations of Southern and Northern Congressmen from opposing parties. Party lines wavered in the Senate as seventeen Democrats and fifteen Whigs voted to admit California as a free state. Sectional votes ran parallel when eleven Northern Senators and sixteen Southern Senators voted to create the New Mexico Territory. Great numbers of Congressmen were absent when the time came to vote on parts of the settlement that were unpopular in their home districts. Mississippi's Senator Jefferson Davis voted for the fugitive slave section, stayed silent on New Mexico, and voted against the balance of the compromise. At the same time, Senator William H. Seward of New York, a strong anti-slavery

politician, supported the admission of California and the abolition of the slave trade in the District of Columbia, stayed silent on the fugitive slave and New Mexico measures and voted against the rest of the bills.

Under the compromise finally passed, California entered the Union as a free state in 1850, and its eastern boundary was fixed at the 120th meridian. Texas received 10 million dollars in return for giving up all claims to New Mexico. Utah and New Mexico were formed as new territories, with the slavery question left for their voters to decide in their respective constitutions. The slave trade was outlawed in the District of Columbia and a more stringent fugitive slave law was passed. Despite the turmoil that arose from America's drive to the Pacific, through this compromise, the Union nevertheless remained intact.

501

Readings

GENERAL WORKS

Billington, Ray A., *The Far Western Frontier*. New York: Harper, 1965—A history of Western frontier development between 1830 and 1860 which attempts to show the impact of national and international politics on expansion and to test Frederick Jackson Turner's frontier thesis.

Graebner, Norman A., *Empire on the Pacific*. New York: Ronald Press, 1955—This is a controversial interpretation of American expansionism in the 1840s which claims that its fundamental motivation was to gain control of the Pacific Coast in order to further commerce with Asia.

Lavender, David S., *Westward Vision: The Story of the Oregon Trail*. New York: McGraw-Hill, 1963—Lavender describes the attraction of the Oregon Trail. Since the eighteenth century, the route to Oregon had been dreamed of as a shortcut to the Orient.

Merk, Frederick, *Manifest Destiny and Mission in American History*. New York: Knopf, 1963—A study of public opinion on expansionism during the 1840s which concludes that continental expansionism was not the true spirit of the American people, but a trap into which they were led by their sense of an American mission to spread her ideals throughout the world.

Nevins, Allan, *Ordeal of the Union*, Vols. I–II. New York: Scribner's, 1947—The first two volumes of Nevins' history of the Civil War era. These cover the period from the Mexican War through 1857. Nevins discusses the ways in which complex sectional tensions emerged around issues related to race and slavery.

Parkman, Francis, *The Oregon Trail*. New York: Holt, Rinehart & Winston, 1931—A classic history of pioneers, trappers, and Indians along the trail to the Oregon Territory in the 1840s, by the great nineteenth-century American historian.

Van Deusen, Glyndon G., *The Jacksonian Era*. New York: Harper, 1959—A history of the United States from 1828 to 1848 which concentrates on political developments.

Weinberg, Albert K., *Manifest Destiny*. Baltimore, Md.: The Johns Hopkins University Press, 1935—A history of the idea of manifest destiny through American history. The author concludes that while it was often a tool for policies of self-interest, manifest destiny also had an idealistic side.

SPECIAL STUDIES

Allen, Harry C., *Great Britain and the United States*. London: Odhams Press, 1954—A history of Anglo-American relations from the end of the Revolution to the present day.

Cleland, Robert G., *This Reckless Breed of Men*. New York: Knopf, 1950—A history of fur traders and trappers in the Southwest between 1820 and 1842. The book contains many old prints and maps.

DeVoto, Bernard, *The Year of Decision: 1846*. Boston: Little, Brown, 1943—An attempt to portray the personal and political impact of westward expansion, focusing on the year in which America took the irrevocable step toward continental empire.

Gunderson, Robert G., *The Log-Cabin Campaign*. Lexington, Ky.: University of Kentucky Press, 1957—A history of the election campaign of 1840 which attempts to put the new campaign strategies and techniques in the context of the development of mass-based political parties.

Hawgood, John A., *America's Western Frontiers*. New York: Knopf, 1967—A broad history of westward expansion in the nineteenth century which makes extensive use of firsthand accounts of pioneer life.

Merk, Frederick, *The Monroe Doctrine and American Expansionism, 1843–1849*. New York: Knopf, 1966—An attempt to describe the psychology of American expansionism under Tyler and Polk. Merk contends that Polk was an opportunistic expansionist and that American diplomatic objectives were closely tied to American war plans.

Morgan, Robert J., *A Whig Embattled*. Lincoln: University of Nebraska Press, 1954—Morgan rejects the view that John Tyler as President betrayed the Whig Party. He shows that Tyler was in principle a Jacksonian, who joined the Whigs to protest Andrew Jackson's use of excessive Presidential power, and that Tyler was loyal to his principles.

Seager, Robert, *And Tyler Too!* New York: McGraw-Hill, 1963—A long, detailed biography of John Tyler and his wife, both representatives of proud, upper-class American families.

Siegel, Stanley, *A Political History of the Texas Republic*. Austin: University of Texas Press, 1956—Texas' nine years of independence were marked, this study maintains, by political and social developments which made Texas very similar to the cotton-growing, slave-holding Southern states of the United States, both in ideals and in reality.

Singletary, Otis A., *The Mexican War*. Chicago: University of Chicago Press, 1960—This brief history of the Mexican War shows how petty military and political ambitions led the United States into a war of aggression against Mexico. Although the results of the war were a great success for the United States, the expansionist ambitions which caused it are no reason for national pride.

Stegner, Wallace, *The Gathering of Zion: The Story of the Mormon Trail*. New York: McGraw-Hill, 1964—A history of the Mormon migration from Missouri to the Great Salt Lake settlement in Utah. Stegner carries the Mormon story up to the completion of the transcontinental railroad in 1869.

PRIMARY SOURCES

Nevins, Allan, ed., *Polk: The Diary of a President*. London: Longmans, Green, 1929 —This edition of the daily record Polk kept of his four years in office reveals him to have been honest and conscientious, but also narrow-minded and stubborn in applying his Jacksonian and expansionist principles.

BIOGRAPHIES

Brodie, Fawn, *No Man Knows My History*. New York: Knopf, 1945—A biography of Joseph Smith, founder of the Mormon faith, which shows Smith both as a prophet who inspired his followers and as a human being with human virtues and faults.

Hamilton, Holman, *Zachary Taylor*, Vols. I–II. Indianapolis, Ind.: Bobbs-Merrill, 1941–1957—Vol. I of this biography deals with Taylor's long military career. The second covers his two years in the White House, defending his opposition to the Compromise of 1850.

James, Marquis, *The Raven*. Indianapolis, Ind.: Bobbs-Merrill, 1929—A biography of Sam Houston, tracing the heights and depths of Houston's career as military commander, President of the Texas Republic, Governor of two states, and United States Senator.

Morgan, Dale L., *Jedediah Smith and the Opening of the West*. Indianapolis, Ind.: Bobbs-Merrill, 1953—Smith, although he died at the age of 32, was one of the most important "Mountain Men" of the old Southwest. His biography is also a history of Southwestern pioneer life.

Nevins, Allan, *Frémont: Pathmarker of the West*, Vols. I–II. New York: Frederick Unger, 1955—A biography of the explorer whose exploits gained him widespread popularity. Frémont's political career and his military accomplishments are also covered in detail.

Nibley, Preston, *Brigham Young, the Man and His Work*. Salt Lake City, Utah: Deseret Books, 1936—An account of the life and works of this leader of Mormonism.

Sellers, Charles, *James K. Polk*, Vols. I–II. Princeton, N.J.: Princeton University Press, 1957–1966—The first two volumes of a modern biography of Polk. The first volume traces his Jacksonian philosophy. The second describes Polk's election and the beginning of the Mexican War.

CHARLESTON

MERCURY

EXTRA:

Passed unanimously at 1.15 o'clock, P. M., December 20th, 1860.

AN ORDINANCE

To dissolve the Union between the State of South Carolina and other States united with her under the compact entitled " The Constitution of the United States of America."

We, the People of the State of South Carolina, in Convention assembled, do declare and ordain, and it is hereby declared and ordained,

That the Ordinance adopted by us in Convention, on the twenty-third day of May, in the year of our Lord one thousand seven hundred and eighty-eight, whereby the Constitution of the United States of America was ratified, and also, all Acts and parts of Acts of the General Assembly of this State, ratifying amendments of the said Constitution, are hereby repealed; and that the union now subsisting between South Carolina and other States, under the name of "The United States of America," is hereby dissolved.

THE

UNION

IS

DISSOLVED!

The 1850s: The Gathering Storm

14

I believe this government cannot endure, permanently half slave and half free. I do not expect the Union to be dissolved—I do not expect the house to fall—but I do expect it will cease to be divided. It will become all one thing, or all the other. Either the opponents of slavery will arrest the further spread of it, and place it where the public mind shall rest in the belief that it is in the course of ultimate extinction; or its advocates will push it forward, till it shall become alike lawful in all the States, old as well as new—North as well as South.

—Abraham Lincoln, 1858

An 1860 poster hailing the secession of South Carolina from the Union. South Carolina had fired upon Union ships at Fort Sumter during Buchanan's last days in office, but the incident only resulted in a wait-and-see attitude for a country about to receive a new President, Abraham Lincoln.

ELECTION OF 1852

At the time of the election of 1852, the nation seemed generally eager to maintain the status quo and to enforce the Compromise of 1850. However, no section of the country was wholly satisfied with the Compromise. Southerners objected to California's admission as a free state, and many Northerners violently attacked the Fugitive Slave Law.

Nevertheless, the Compromise of 1850 held out the possibility of gradually lessening sectional strife. In the election of 1852 the Democratic candidate, Franklin Pierce, triumphed over his Whig opponent, General Winfield Scott, largely because Pierce endorsed the Compromise more energeti-

cally than Scott. Indeed, the Democrats had pledged their unreserved devotion to the Compromise and had promised to oppose attempts of "any shape or color" to open the slavery question to debate again. Despite their ease in reaching unanimity on this issue, the Democrats had a hard time selecting a candidate; forty-nine ballots were cast before they decided on Pierce, an obscure contender who practiced law in New Hampshire. Pierce won twenty-seven states, while Scott carried only four. The Free-Soil Party suffered a major setback with its candidate, John P. Hale, attracting only half as many votes as the party had received in 1848.

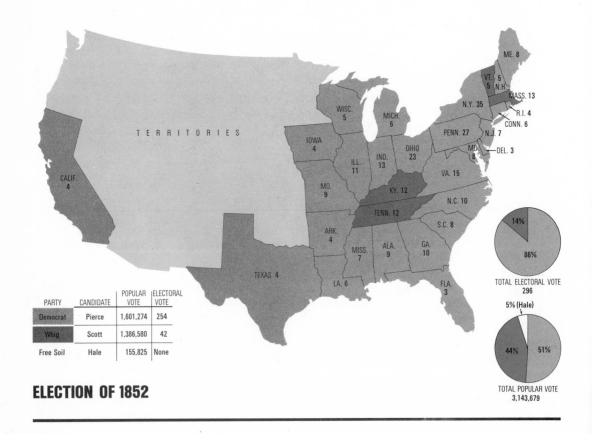

PARTY	CANDIDATE	POPULAR VOTE	ELECTORAL VOTE
Democrat	Pierce	1,601,274	254
Whig	Scott	1,386,580	42
Free Soil	Hale	155,825	None

TOTAL ELECTORAL VOTE
296

TOTAL POPULAR VOTE
3,143,679

ELECTION OF 1852

PARTY REALIGNMENTS

Every party, even the victorious Democrats, was torn by divisions and realignments. The Democrats embraced several factions, all on uneasy terms with one another: the small farmers of the West who were against the expansion of slavery into the territories, many planters and most small farmers in the South who defended slavery expansion, merchants of the East with business interests in the South, and many skilled and unskilled workers in the Northern towns who were not abolitionists but were against slavery. The Free-Soilers were seriously weakened because they were the only party to oppose the Compromise; moderate Northerners in the Free-Soil Party returned to the Democrats.

The election took its greatest toll of the Whigs, however, and never again would they run a candidate for the Presidency. In fact, within a few years the party would be extinct. Its Northern and Southern factions were hopelessly divided, so irreconcilably in fact that in their platform for 1852 the Whigs could only lamely agree to "acquiesce in" the Compromise, rather than endorse or repudiate it. Southerners were abandoning the Whig Party, largely because the Whigs had always stood for a strong central government, which in Northern hands the South feared would destroy slavery and with it the whole Southern way of life. The great Unionists in the Whig Party had been Webster and Clay, holding rival factions together in an alliance to preserve the nation. In 1852 both men died, but even before their deaths, the party was in a state of confusion.

CONTINUATION OF THE SLAVERY CONTROVERSY

When Franklin Pierce was sworn into office on March 4, 1853, he and most of the nation hoped that the Compromise of 1850 would be of lasting effect. However, beneath this surface calm, old attitudes and problems persisted. In the North, population was increasing and industry expanding. The Northwest and Northeast were more closely linked every day in economic and political interests by the railroad. The South had in fact become a financial colony of the North and Southerners saw no end to Northern demands for higher tariffs, federal support of internal improvements, and free public lands for yeoman farmers. The entire coastal trade was in Northern hands.

In addition to the economic problems underlying relations between the North and South, events in the early 1850s reopened the slavery controversy, thus undermining the Compromise. A few extreme abolitionists sought to keep the crusade against slavery alive by preventing enforcement of the law on fugitive slaves. Several Northern states, beginning with Vermont in 1850, enacted "personal liberty laws" in opposition to the new Fugitive Slave Act included in the Compromise. Fugitives received legal support and jury trials in the Northeast. Some abolitionists spirited fugitives over the border into Canada, beyond the reach of American laws. The black leader, Frederick Douglass, expressed a new militancy when he declared, "Every slavehunter who meets a bloody death in this infernal business, is an argument in favor of the manhood of our race."

Another important event that disturbed the national calm restored by the Compromise of 1850 was the publication of Harriet Beecher Stowe's *Uncle Tom's Cabin* in March, 1852, a novel that sold 300,000 copies within a year. The daughter of a New England clergyman, Mrs. Stowe wrote a compelling work that was careful to restrict its attack to the institution of slavery and did not attack the Southerners who perpetuated it. In fact, she made Simon Legree, the sadistically cruel overseer in *Uncle Tom's Cabin,* a Northerner. Mrs.

Stowe had never traveled in the South, but her writing was vivid; the melodramatic appeal of her book and its dramatization performed on stages across the country turned thousands against slavery.

THE KANSAS-NEBRASKA BILL

Franklin Pierce, the new President, was one of the handsomest Chief Executives ever to hold that office, and at forty-nine, the youngest thus far. Unfortunately, he did not have the inner resolve to match his stalwart outer appearance. He was dominated by strong men in his Cabinet, men such as Secretary of War Jefferson Davis from Mississippi and Secretary of State William L. Marcy of New York. Pierce was often paralyzed by indecision, and when circumstances forced him to take a stand, he allowed his Southern friends to dictate his action. His handling of the Kansas-Nebraska Bill is a case in point.

DOUGLAS INTRODUCES THE BILL

The area west of Missouri and Iowa was set aside in 1830 as an Indian Reserve, but by the 1850s farmers were eyeing the land greedily. Earlier, it had been thought that this area could not be farmed, but now land hunger, together with American possession of the entire continent to the Pacific Ocean, changed the minds of many. Projected plans to run a transcontinental railroad through this area also prompted the government to take another look at America's so-called permanent Indian reserve.

On January 4, 1854, Stephen A. Douglas, a Democrat from Illinois, submitted a bill to the Senate proposing to break the government's treaties with the Indians and to organize the land west of Missouri and Iowa into territories and eventually states. Few Congressmen objected to breaking the treaties, but the Douglas bill raised an issue that troubled them more: Could slaves be taken into the new territories? The Missouri Compromise of 1820 forbade slavery forever "in all territory ceded by France to the United States . . . which lies North of 36° 30'." Since the land under discussion (called the Nebraska country) lay within the Louisiana Purchase and north of the 36° 30' latitudinal line, the entire area was closed to slavery. Douglas, the foremost advocate of "popular sovereignty," ignored the Missouri Compromise and suggested that the people of Nebraska should be left free to decide for themselves whether they wanted slavery or not, in accordance with the plan recently worked out for the territories of New Mexico and Utah. Douglas believed that most of Nebraska was too far north for cotton agriculture and was therefore unlikely to become a slaveholding area, but he suggested self-determination for the territory in the hope of insuring Southern support for his proposal.

Before formal debate began, Douglas was pressured by Southern Congressmen to make three changes in the bill. According to the original wording of the measure, even if the people of the territory voted to legalize slavery under their state constitution, Congress would still be free to reject a pro-slavery constitution. The revised bill

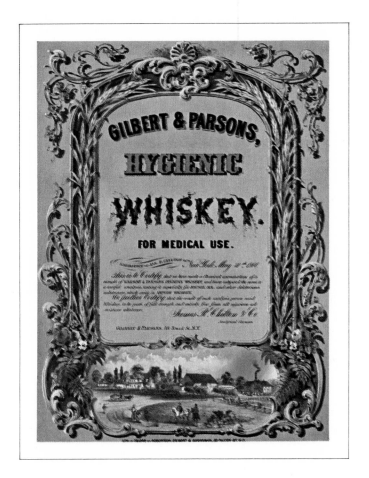

Poster advertises a nineteenth-century cure-all .

Nineteenth-Century Posters

*P*osters advertising patent medicines, beer, breakfast cereals, ladies' corsets, and other consumer products became popular in the nineteenth century. These, and the boldly illustrated posters of the theater companies, circuses, and Wild West shows, made up in drama or sentimentality what they lacked in truth and aesthetic value. For example, an 1899 poster for Dr. Jayne's Expectorant promised "a sure remedy for worms, colds, asthma or any lung or throat disease." Illustrated with an angelic, Madonna-like mother and child, in the style of Raphael, and the grossly over-sentimental tradition of nineteenth-century commercial art, the poster was designed to appeal to the most hardened of cynics. Such misleading advertising was made illegal by the Pure Food and Drug Act in 1906.

In the twentieth century, cultural enterprises and political causes became the chief purveyors of posters. In recent years, posters created purely for decorative purposes have been in demand. For the history student, however, the real interest of posters lies in the crude, wood-engraved posters that capture the flavor of the nineteenth century from covered-wagon days to the heyday of the horsecar, and remain as an authentic record of cultural change and national growth. They are of interest, too, as early examples of American advertising, which in time became a major enterprise, creating mass markets for mass production.

In the infancy of advertising, steamship and stage-coach posters lured adventurers westward after gold was discovered in the San Joaquin Valley in California in 1848. Steamship posters were also used in Europe to attract immigrants to the farms and factories of America, making possible the nation's phenomenal agricultural and industrial growth.

Throughout the West, posted notices offered rewards for train and stagecoach robbers, murderers, and horse thieves, such as Jesse and Frank James, the Dalton gang, Butch Cassidy, and Tom Nixon, the notorious Union Pacific robber. These were good years for Smith & Wesson and Winchester. In 1855 both companies issued posters advertising a popular item, the volcanic repeating pistol.

In the South, antebellum posters offered to buy slaves, described slaves for sale, offered rewards for runaway slaves, and announced slave auctions. At the same time, abolitionists in the North posted announcements of anti-slavery meetings and abolitionist propaganda.

During the Civil War, both the North and the South used posters for specific recruiting purposes. They called for sharpshooters, cavalry troops or foot soldiers, to fight in particular areas. Union posters appealed to black men to enlist, while the Confederacy urged enlistment to avoid conscription.

Throughout most of the nineteenth century, the poster served as a way to tell people about important events, and goods and services for sale. Farm machinery, fashion apparel, religious meetings, and horse mating services were advertised by posters as well as in the press. Most significantly, posters were used to influence the vote in Presidential campaigns, usually depicting the candidates, whatever their origins, as men of humble background. William Harrison, for example, owned a magnificent country estate in Ohio, but his campaign posters showed him with a farm implement in front of a log cabin. Image making, then as now, was a crucial strategy in the game of politics.

A number of American book publishers and theatrical producers commissioned the work of fine artists for store windows and wall posters. People hung these posters in their parlors and some were exhibited in art galleries. The names of such poster illustrators as Edward Penfield, William Bradley, and Ethel Reed became well known in America as well as in the cultural centers of Europe.

This dramatic appeal for pain relief was published during the Civil War.

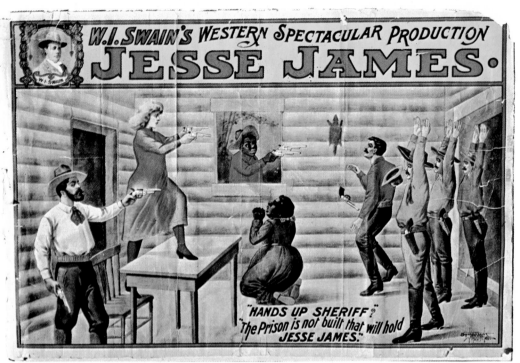

Jesse James receives help in holding the law at bay.

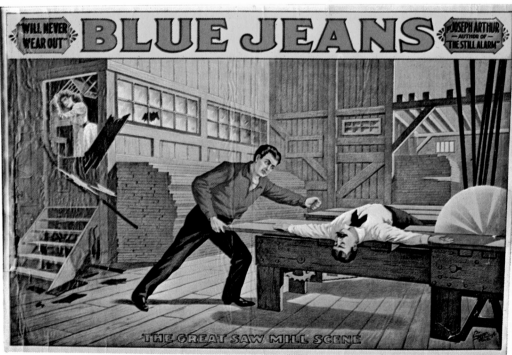

Poster published in 1890 advertises the play, Blue Jeans.

Poster advertises Uncle Tom's Cabin, *one of the best-selling books of the century.*

*This recruiting poster
was issued just after Fort Sumter fell.*

Poster advertises slave sale.

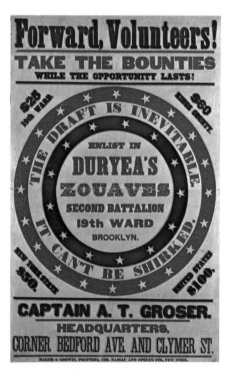

Civil War enlistment poster.

Galatea offered passage to California where gold had been discovered a decade earlier.

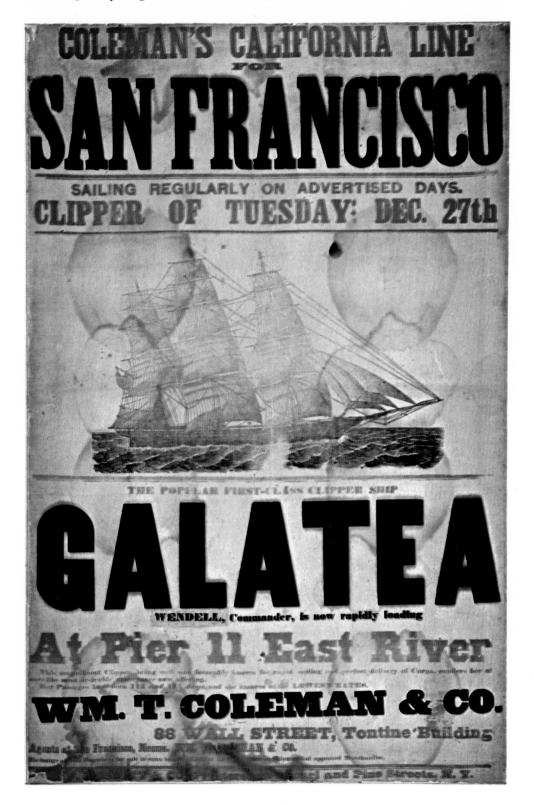

Ku Klux Klan broadside.

Nineteenth-century businesses used posters as a form of advertising.

Lincoln and Hamlin campaign poster.

Campaign poster of 1852 displays Pierce and running mate, King .

Scribner's *poster was designed for display by newsdealers.*

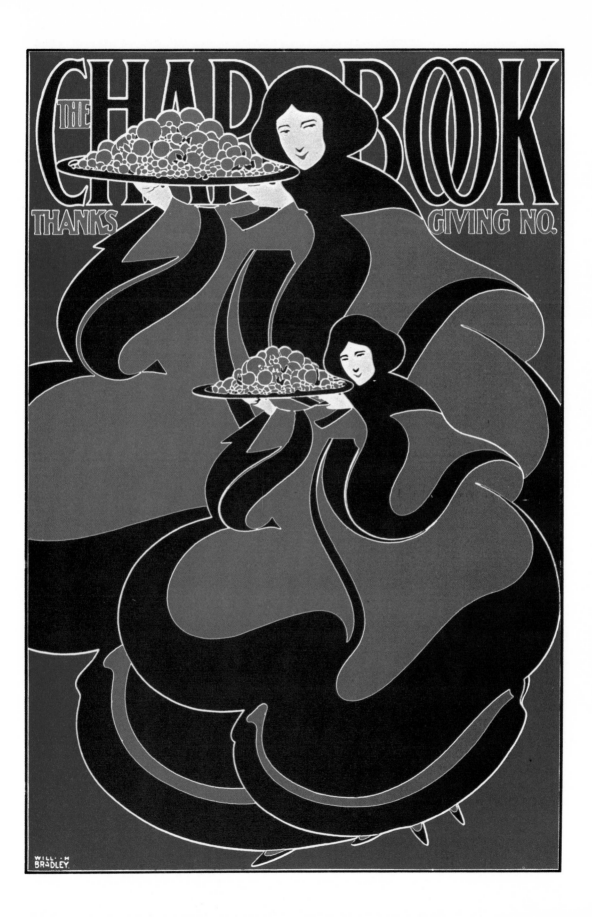

Poster by C. A. Cox advertises Bearings.

removed that power from Congress and left it solely with the people of Nebraska. Second, although Douglas' proposal contradicted the Missouri Compromise, it did not repudiate the Compromise in so many words. Now the revised bill stated that the Compromise was henceforth "inoperative and void"—a technical change that represented an important psychological victory for the South. Third, the revised bill specifically divided the land into two territories, the northern part to be called Nebraska, the southern, Kansas. This division made it much more likely that the southern part of the territory, Kansas, would become a slave state, particularly since it lay immediately to the west of the slave state of Missouri.

Douglas had made these changes in his bill simply to speed its passage through Congress. He had no deep personal feelings about the slavery question. He was, in fact, fond of saying, "I don't care whether slavery is voted up or down." Thus, it was natural that he failed to gauge the depth of the North's moral revulsion against slavery. Douglas thought that everyone would be pleased by his bill: Chicago, because it would be the western terminus of a proposed transcontinental railroad; Westerners in general, because they would now have free access to lands formerly reserved for the Indians; Southerners, because the principle of "popular sovereignty" over the slavery question would be extended to parts of the Louisiana Purchase that had been

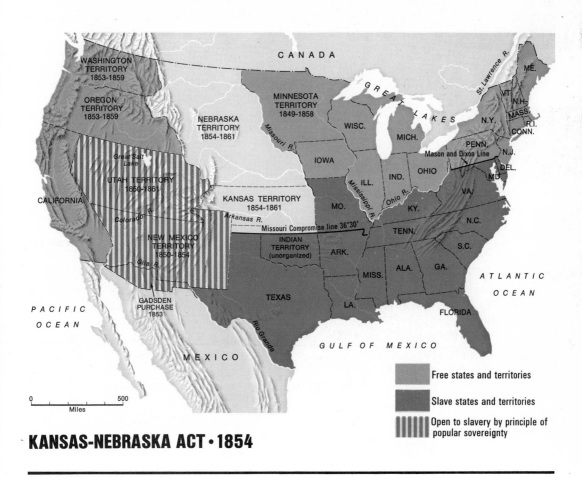

Free states and territories

Slave states and territories

Open to slavery by principle of popular sovereignty

KANSAS-NEBRASKA ACT • 1854

closed to slavery under the old Missouri Compromise; the nation as a whole, because he had cleverly avoided a new sectional controversy and preserved the Union. In fact, Douglas hoped to be elected President because of his success with the Kansas-Nebraska Bill.

As it turned out, the bill helped both to destroy Douglas' supreme position in the Democratic Party and to split the party irretrievably. Although the Senate passed the bill by a vote of 37 to 14, the more sharply divided House passed it by a vote of only 113 to 100. Despite its passage, the bill opened up the old wounds temporarily closed by the Compromise of 1850. Only 7 out of 42 Northern Democrats who voted for the Kansas-Nebraska Act were re-elected to office. Douglas was mobbed in his own state of Illinois by abolitionists, and ruefully said he could have traveled from Chicago to Boston by the light of his burning effigies. Rarely had an American public figure been so savagely attacked.

THE REPUBLICAN PARTY

The most important immediate result of the Kansas-Nebraska Act was the coming together of anti-slavery and Free-Soil factions from all parties in the North into a new political alignment, the Republican Party. At first, the party had only one plank in its platform, that of opposition to the Kansas-Nebraska bill and the spread of slavery in general. By the end of the summer of 1854, the Republicans had drawn together followers from several political factions: Northern Whigs, and many Northern Democrats; former Free-Soil Party members; abolitionists, and temperance advocates. Although each of these groups held a wide variety of opinion on other issues, they were solidly united against the Kansas-Nebraska bill. They were also all Northerners. In the past, parties had cut across sectional lines and had thereby been truly

national organizations; now a party was emerging that was purely sectional.

Moreover, the Republican Party grew rapidly and made impressive political gains. In the Congressional elections of 1854, the infant party scored a stunning victory. In the House of Representatives, Republicans won 108 seats, Democrats only 83, and another new party, the Know-Nothings, took the balance of 43.

THE SETTLEMENT OF KANSAS

The new territory of Kansas immediately became a battleground. Northern abolitionists, determined to make the territory a free state, financed the migration of about one thousand anti-slavery Yankees to Kansas. Southern champions of slavery from the neighboring state of Missouri, as well as from Alabama, Georgia, and South Carolina, also poured into the region.

When Kansas held its first territorial election on March 30, 1855, there were only two thousand men registered to vote, most of them from the North. But hordes of pro-slavery Missourians crossed the border into Kansas and illegally cast some four thousand additional ballots. When Andrew H. Reeder, appointed governor of Kansas by President Pierce, tried to disqualify eight of the thirty-one members of the territorial legislature on the grounds that they had been elected irregularly, Southern Congressmen put pressure on Pierce to veto this move since the disqualified legislators were all pro-slavery men. Pierce, giving in to their demands, agreed and refused to back up Reeder. The illegally elected Kansas legislators remained in office. When the pro-slavery Kansas legislature asked the President to remove Reeder from office, Pierce did so and made William Shannon of Ohio the new governor.

The Kansas legislature now passed a series of stringent laws designed to drive all anti-slavery factions out of Kansas. These included a death sentence for anyone who aided a fugitive slave, and a prison term for anyone who merely expressed the opinion that slavery should be outlawed in Kansas.

Anti-slavery Kansans, however, were not intimidated by these measures. They called a convention of their own, framed a state constitution that made slavery illegal in Kansas, conducted a new election, and announced that Charles Robinson would be their new governor. The Free-Soilers also sent the ousted former governor of Kansas, Andrew H. Reeder, as their territorial delegate to Washington.

An outbreak of violence in "Bleeding Kansas" between pro-slavery and abolitionist factions. Abolitionists were not as much opposed to slavery as they were to the cheap labor of free blacks that threatened their livelihood. Thus, when Kansas was made a state in 1861, both slavery and free blacks were excluded from the state.

THE OUTBREAK OF VIOLENCE

Kansas now had two governors and two legislatures, representing two sharply antagonistic factions. Pierce might have been able to pacify both sides at this point if he had called for a new, carefully monitored election, but he hesitated. In May, 1856, a small war broke out in Kansas; and before it was over, two hundred men had died.

First, a drunken United States marshal and an impromptu posse of pro-slavery men raided the Kansas town of Lawrence. The chief Free-Soil towns were Lawrence and Topeka, and the pro-slavery settlers were clustered in Atchison and Leavenworth. The posse attacked Lawrence, sacked it, and kidnapped several Free-Soil leaders. Seeking retribution, John Brown, a fanatical abolitionist, led a counterattack. Seeing himself as an avenging angel sent by the Lord to chastise slaveowners, Brown led a band of six followers into enemy territory and murdered five pro-slavery settlers.

SOUTHERN CHIVALRY _ ARGUMENT versus CLUB'S.

Violence resulting from the slavery controversy reached Congress itself. In 1856, Charles Sumner of Massachusetts delivered a speech to Congress in favor of a free Kansas. Sumner was attacked by a congressman from South Carolina, Preston Brooks. This illustration, a Northern cartoon of the attack, shows Sumner and Brooks in battle, while Southern congressmen look on in amusement.

In the meantime, Pierce had appointed yet another governor, John W. Geary. In order to maintain a semblance of peace in the explosive Kansas territory, Geary ordered out federal troops. Gradually the conflict simmered down, but although no more blood was shed, tempers were raised all over the country. "Bleeding Kansas" had witnessed the latest outbreak over the unyielding slavery question.

However, few of the Kansas Free-Soilers were true abolitionists. Most opposed slavery, not because they considered the practice a sin but because they feared that cheap slave labor would threaten their own livelihoods. Significantly, when Kansas finally became a state in 1861, its constitution forbade slavery but also excluded free blacks. Abolitionists in faraway New York and New England, however, did not see the economic side of the issue in 1856. They thought of Kansas as a battleground where divinely inspired abolitionists were fighting to crush the satanic forces of slavery.

BROOKS AND SUMNER

Violence over the slavery question even spread to the halls of Congress. Never be-fore had Senators and Representatives been forced to fear for their personal safety, but now legislators carried knives and pistols with them into the chambers. On May 19, 1856, Charles Sumner of Massachusetts delivered an impassioned speech in favor of a free Kansas. In the course of his oration, Sumner denounced slavery in general and in particular the pro-slavery Missourians who had participated illegally in the Kansas election. Sumner's spleen, however, was most sharply reserved for Senator Andrew P. Butler of South Carolina. Butler's nephew, Congressman Preston Brooks, was so enraged that the young man attacked Senator Sumner a few days later as he sat at his desk on the Senate floor. According to a newspaper account, Brooks said, "Mr. Sumner, I have read your speech against South Carolina, and have read it carefully, deliberately and dispassionately, in which you have libelled my State and slandered my white haired old relative, Senator Butler, who is absent, and I have come to punish you for it." Brooks then struck Sumner a dozen times with his cane, beating him so badly that he was an invalid for three years. News of the vicious attack was sped over telegraphic lines to all parts of the country. Cartoons in Northern newspapers showed the noble Sumner, quill in hand, falling before the merciless onslaught of "Bully" Brooks, while crude-looking Southern Congressmen stood aside and snickered in the background.

THE DECLINE
OF MANIFEST DESTINY

Undaunted by the rising sectional tempers over the slavery issue, Pierce planned to continue the expansionist foreign policy of his Democratic predecessor, James K. Polk. In his inaugural address, the President voiced the hope that America's territorial growth would not be held back by "any timid forebodings of evil." Yet, for most Northerners, expansionism under a President whom they considered the pawn of Southern pro-slavery forces inevitably raised "forebodings of evil" in the form of slavery expansion. In the past, the majority of Americans had been able to endorse virtually any act which would lead to the acquisition of new territory, but now the ever-present issue of slavery expansion entered into almost every consideration of foreign as well as domestic policy.

CUBA

Pierce's interest in acquiring Cuba confirmed the worst suspicions of Northerners opposed to slavery. Cuba and Brazil were the last strongholds of slavery in the Western world except for the United States. If Cuba became a possession of the United States, it would ultimately join the Union as a slave state.

As early as 1848 President Polk had offered Spain 100 million dollars for Cuba, but the Spanish foreign minister had replied that he would rather see the island sunk than sold.

Aside from objections raised over the expansion of slavery, there was sufficient reason for acquiring the island for its strategic advantage to the United States. The island commands the entrance to the Caribbean and American ownership would ensure the safety of her commerce in the Gulf of Mexico and of her interoceanic canal through Central America. There was the additional danger that Cuba could in foreign hands be used as a base for attacks on the United States.

Some Southerners were not easily dissuaded from the dream of acquiring the island, and many of them supported a Venezuelan adventurer named General Narciso López in his three attempts, between 1849 and 1851, to take Cuba by force. When López was captured and executed by the Spanish, disappointed Southern expansionists retaliated by destroying the Spanish consulate in New Orleans.

President Pierce made the acquisition of Cuba one of his prime objectives. Unfortunately, he appointed an ardent and indiscreet Senator from Louisiana, Pierre Soulé, as his minister to Spain and instructed him to use every method available to obtain Cuba. Soon after arriving in Spain, Soulé made several gross blunders. He challenged the French ambassador to a duel for a far-fetched reason and injured him for life. Then, early in 1854 an American ship, the *Black Warrior*, was seized in Havana for violating Spanish custom laws. In violation of his instructions, Soulé demanded not only an indemnity of 300,000 dollars from the Spanish government but also an apology within 48 hours. When Spain refused to comply, Soulé threatened war. Fortunately the Spanish foreign minister recognized that the envoy had exceeded his instructions and went over Soulé's head and settled the matter directly with Pierce's Secretary of State, William L. Marcy. As the New York *Herald* commented about Soulé: "We wanted an Ambassador there, we have sent a matador."

THE OSTEND MANIFESTO

In spite of these setbacks, Pierce did not give up the idea of buying Cuba. Secretary of State Marcy now instructed Soulé to confer on the subject with James Buchanan, the American minister in London, and John Y. Mason, the American minister in Paris. Marcy was not particularly interested in knowing if his ministers thought the United States should seize Cuba or not; he wanted to know how the European powers would respond if Americans should invade the island. The ministers, however, misunderstood their instructions and, instead of sounding out European opinion, sent Marcy a confidential dispatch from Ostend, Belgium, recommending that the United States offer Spain 120 million dollars for Cuba. If rejected, the United States "by every law, human and divine, shall be justified in wresting" Cuba from Spain "if we possess the power."

When this so-called Ostend Manifesto was made public in the United States, Southerners greeted it with enthusiasm, but Northern Free-Soilers immediately branded it as a plot to add another slave state to the Union. The New York *Tribune* called it a "Manifesto of Brigands," and Northern indignation became so intense that President Pierce was forced to repudiate the recommendations. Marcy sent a sharp rebuke to Soulé who, in anger and humiliation, resigned. The question of Cuba's fate was temporarily left unsettled.

CENTRAL AMERICA

After the acquisition of California, the United States seriously began to consider

digging a canal through Central America to shorten by several weeks the sea voyage from coast to coast. Several American diplomats considered the tiny republic of Nicaragua as the best possible site for an isthmian canal. Great Britain, however, did not want such a vital link between two oceans to be under the exclusive hands of the United States. To block American plans, Britain suddenly declared herself the protectorate of the Mosquito Indians on the eastern coast of Nicaragua, the very area where the proposed canal would connect with the Caribbean. When the United States learned of this move, she warned Great Britain that she would never permit the canal to become the exclusive property of England. The dispute was finally settled in 1850 with the signing of the Clayton-Bulwer Treaty, which provided that any canal built by either country would be open to ships of all nations and would be unfortified even during time of war, and that neither the United States nor Britain would attempt to gain political control over Central America. Congress ratified the treaty despite strong protests from American expansionists. The treaty was looked upon as a diplomatic defeat by those who wanted more territory or saw it as a violation of the Monroe Doctrine. However, it did prevent a showdown with Great Britain at a time when she was much more powerful than the United States, and it established the principle of a neutral, unfortified canal.

Ignoring their government's pledge not to interfere in Central American politics, a group of businessmen formed the Panama Railway Company and began to operate a railroad line across Panama in 1855. At the same time, the railroad promoter Commodore Vanderbilt backed an adventurer named William Walker who seized control of Nicaragua in 1855 and proclaimed himself President. Walker apparently planned to make himself dictator of all Central

ELECTION OF 1856

America and to open the area to slavery. Pierce recognized Walker's government in Nicaragua and the Democratic platform of 1856 praised him. At this point, however, Walker became involved in a controversy with Vanderbilt, who cut off his supplies. Then the neighboring republics forced him to flee Nicaragua. When he attempted to return to power in 1860, British naval officials arrested him and turned him over to Honduran authorities, who executed Walker immediately. During his short career Walker had stirred up Northern suspicions that he was working to bring Central America into the Union as a slave state. Such suspicions were even stronger when another adventurer, George W. L. Bickey, tried to organize an expedition to conquer Mexico. Bickey proposed to divide Mexico into a total of twenty-five slave states. Only one important Southern leader, the governor of Mississippi, offered him assistance.

THE GADSDEN PURCHASE

Despite all of Pierce's expansionist ambitions, only one small territory was added to the United States during his administration. In 1853, the War Department made a survey of possible routes for the first intercontinental railroad. The shortest southern route proposed by the surveyors would cross Mexican territory south of the Gila River. Fearing that Northerners would seize on this objection as a reason for building the railroad in the North, Pierce's Secretary of War, Jefferson Davis, persuaded the President to send James Gadsden, a Southern railroad promoter, to negotiate a treaty with Mexico. In 1853 Gadsden purchased 40,000 square miles of desert for ten million dollars.

The assault on Sumner, the violence in Kansas, and the controversies over Pierce's pro-Southern foreign policy were very much on the public mind during the election campaign of 1856. The Democrats cautiously endorsed the Kansas-Nebraska Act and took the position that whether a territory was to permit slavery or not should be decided by popular sovereignty. However, the Democrats realized that their two best-known defenders of popular sovereignty, Pierce and Douglas, were political liabilities. Therefore, the party ignored both the President and the leading contender and settled on James Buchanan, a stalwart party man who had offended no one, having passed the last few troubled years in Great Britain as America's minister. Four years earlier the Democrats had selected Pierce because he was a relatively unknown lawyer, a "dark horse" unlikely to arouse strong antipathies. Now the party chiefs were adopting the same strategy again by nominating the politically neutral Buchanan. At a time when strong leadership was needed, political expediency placed two inadequate men in the White House who were either indecisive or acted as spokesmen of the influential Southern leadership of the party.

The new Republican Party nominated General John C. Frémont, a glamorous explorer whose views on key issues were as much a mystery as Buchanan's and whose primary distinction was his military leadership in the annexation of California in 1846 during the war with Mexico. Like Andrew Jackson, William Henry Harrison, and Zachary Taylor before him, Frémont was a war hero drawn into politics, more respected for his victories than for his political views. The Republican Party itself, however, stood firmly in opposition to the Kansas-Nebraska Act. In addition, the party came out for a federally financed program of internal improvements which were opposed by Southerners. These two positions established still more clearly that the Republicans were a Northern-based party whose appeal could be only to that section.

The American, or Know-Nothing Party, formed in 1852, had done well in the Congressional elections of 1854. Its appeal was to the prejudices of native-born Americans, committed to keeping foreigners out of the country. The party derived its name from its candidates who were instructed to keep their inflammatory prejudices against foreigners secret and to answer when questioned that they "know nothing" about the matter. In its platform for 1856 the American Party urged "a change in the laws of naturalization, making a continued residence of twenty-one years, . . . an indispensable requisite for citizenship." Former Whigs, dissatisfied Democrats, native-born workingmen, and many Southerners had pledged their allegiance to the Know-Nothings.

Why were so many Americans opposed to immigration? Laborers were opposed because they feared the competition of cheap foreign labor; Southerners, because they realized that most Europeans were against slavery, and furthermore, would settle in the North, thereby increasing its advantage in population. Like the Whigs and the Democrats, however, the Know-Nothings split apart over the issue of slavery. Northern Free-Soilers joined the Republican Party and pro-slavery Southerners defected to the Democrats. The remaining Know-Nothings nominated former President Millard Fillmore whom the few surviving Whigs also endorsed.

Buchanan and the Democrats scored impressive majorities in the election; Buchanan won the Presidency with 174 electoral votes, while Frémont polled only 114 votes, and Fillmore only eight. Buchanan carried every Southern state, except Maryland, and five Northern states. The Republicans did not win a single Southern electoral vote. Obviously, while the Democratic Party was still a national, rather than a sectional organization, it owed its victory to the South. Just as clearly, the Republicans were an exclusively Northern party; yet if they had won only a few more popular votes in two more big Northern states, such as Pennsylvania and Illinois, Frémont would have been President. Considering that this new party was a recent phenomenon, it had made a remarkably good showing in the election.

BUCHANAN AS PRESIDENT

Like Pierce, Buchanan was an indecisive President. His long public career before his inauguration, however, had been favorably regarded. For 43 years Buchanan had been in government service. His most important appointments were as minister to Russia and to England under Jackson and Pierce, respectively, and as Secretary of State under Polk. Buchanan was 66, and the first bachelor to serve as President. His public experience had been so long and varied that many people expected him to steer the ship of state expertly out of troubled waters. As it

James Buchanan, the fifteenth President of the United States, supported the pro-slavery Supreme Court decision in the Dred Scott case. Buchanan's attempt to admit Kansas as a slave state was blocked by the House.

turned out, Buchanan was inclined to vacillate and to accept the views of his Southern advisers when decisive, independent action was needed to hold the republic together.

THE DRED SCOTT DECISION

Two days after Buchanan's inauguration, the Supreme Court announced its controversial decision in the case of Dred Scott, a black man seeking freedom from slavery. Dred Scott's owner, a Dr. John Emerson of St. Louis, Missouri, became an army surgeon in 1834. He was sent on duty to Rock Island, Illinois, and later transferred to Fort Snelling in the Wisconsin Territory. In 1838 he returned to Missouri. Through all these changes of residence Emerson had been accompanied by Dred Scott. After Emerson died, abolitionists persuaded Scott to sue for his freedom in the courts of Missouri on the grounds that his residence in

Illinois and the Wisconsin Territory had made him free, since slavery was prohibited in both areas. Scott lost his case in the Missouri Supreme Court, but in the meantime had become the property of a New Yorker, J. F. A. Sanford. Because Sanford lived in another state, Scott was now able to take his suit to the federal courts which had jurisdiction over all interstate matters.

Regardless of the final court decision, Scott would be freed since Sanford himself was an abolitionist. The proceedings, therefore, would have no immediate practical consequences but were being used by the abolitionists as a test of the laws. Before his inauguration, Buchanan urged one of the Supreme Court Justices, Robert C. Grier of Pennsylvania, to make the Court's decision as broad as possible. He wanted the Court to determine once and for all whether Congress had the power to outlaw slavery in the territories. By the time he gave his inaugural address, Buchanan already had been informed of the Court's pro-slavery decision and approved of it. He therefore requested the American people to abide by whatever the Supreme Court might decide.

The Supreme Court had handed down a 6-to-3 decision against Scott. Chief Justice Taney's opinion declared that blacks were not citizens of the United States and thus were not entitled to the rights of citizens. Of the five other Southern justices on the bench, only two of them shared Taney's opinion. The decision against Scott was actually based on the grounds that Dr. Emerson's temporary residence in Illinois and the Wisconsin Territory had not altered the fact that the Missouri slave laws still applied to Scott.

Beyond the immediate grounds for denying Scott his freedom, the Court needlessly went beyond Scott's case and laid down broad principles that created violent controversy across the nation. The majority of the justices declared that the Missouri Compromise was unconstitutional: neither Congress nor the legislatures of territories had

517

Dred Scott v. Sanford

❝ *It is very clear, therefore, that no State, can by any Act or law of its own, passed since the adoption of the Constitution, introduce a new member into the political community created by the Constitution of the United States. . . .*

The question then arises, whether the provisions of the Constitution, in relation to the personal rights and privileges to which the citizen of a State should be entitled, embraced the negro African race, at that time in this country, or who might afterwards be imported, who had then or should afterwards be made free in any State; and to put it in the power of a single State to make him a citizen of the United States, and endue him with the full rights of citizenship in every other State without their consent. Does the Constitution of the United States act upon him whenever he shall be made free under the laws of a State, and raised there to the rank of a citizen in every other State and in its own courts?

The court think the affirmative of these propositions cannot be maintained. And if it cannot, the plaintiff in error could not be a citizen of the State of Missouri, within the meaning of the Constitution of the United States, and consequently, was not entitled to sue in its courts. . . . ❞

—Chief Justice Taney

the right to outlaw slavery, they argued, since the Fifth Amendment expressly guaranteed every man protection of his property, and a slave was property. In a complicated, 240-page decision, the Court thus also flatly contradicted Douglas' doctrine of popular sovereignty. Douglas had assured the people of Kansas that they could ban slavery from their territory if they chose to

Dred Scott v. Sanford

❝ *. . . One mode of approaching this question is, to inquire who were citizens of the United States at the time of the adoption of the Constitution. . . .*

I can find nothing in the Constitution which, . . . deprives of their citizenship any class of persons who were citizens of the United States at the time of its adoption, or who should be native-born citizens of any State after its adoption; nor any power enabling Congress to disfranchise persons born on the soil of any State, and entitled to citizenship of such State by its constitution and laws. And my opinion, is, that, under the Constitution of the United States, every free person born on the soil of a State, who is a citizen of that State by force of its constitution or laws, is also a citizen of the United States. . . .

I dissent, therefore, from that part of the opinion of the majority of the court, in which it is held that a person of African descent cannot be a citizen of the United States. . . .

—Justice Curtis

do so, but now the Court had ruled that only a state, and not a territory, could make such a decision.

Two justices expressed dissenting opinions. One of them, Benjamin F. Curtis, a Free-Soil sympathizer, filed a 69-page decision in which he argued that not only were free blacks citizens of the United States but that Congress was constitutionally empowered to exclude slavery from the territories, since the constitutional right to create territories obviously included the right to govern them.

Southerners rejoiced over the Court's decision. Now they had reassurance from the highest tribunal of the land that Congress could not interfere with what henceforth had to be regarded purely as a local issue. Northern Free-Soilers were furious when the decision was announced. They pointed out that now slavery could be extended into the Minnesota Territory and even Oregon. The Republicans promised that when they were in power they would pack the Court with their own justices and bring about a reversal of the Dred Scott decision. Abolitionists jeered at the irony of the Court's defense of slavery in the name of the Bill of Rights. Typical of the Northern response was an editorial in the Chicago *Tribune* which stated: "That bench full of Southern lawyers which gentlemen of a political temperament call 'august tribunal' is that last entrenchment behind which despotism is sheltered, and until a national convention amends the Constitution so as to defend it against the usurpations of that body, or until the Court itself is reconstructed by the dropping off of a few of its members and the appointment of better men in their places, we have little to hope for by congressional action in the way of restricting slavery."

BUCHANAN AND KANSAS

Before the Dred Scott decision, Buchanan had secretly encouraged the Court to take away from Congress and from territorial legislatures the power to ban slavery. After the decision, in an effort to appease the Southern wing of the party even further, he tried to bring Kansas into the Union as a slave state, although most Kansans were Free-Soilers.

The President appointed Robert J. Walker territorial governor of Kansas. Although Walker, an able administrator, was from the slave state of Mississippi, he quickly recognized that most Kansans wanted to bar slavery from their state. Accordingly, Walker worked to help them turn their preference into law. The pro-slavery faction in Kansas, however, had already convened a constitutional convention of its own at the town of Lecompton and drafted a pro-slavery state constitution. The Lecompton constitution guaranteed the protection of slavery and was presented to the voters in such a way that they would not have the chance to vote on the issue at all. When this constitution was submitted for ratification, most of them stayed away from the polls.

Walker went to Washington to urge the President to reject the Lecompton constitution and to convene a new, more representative convention in Kansas. Buchanan, however, had been elected largely by Southern votes, and he was now completely under the influence of his Southern-dominated Cabinet. Terrified by numerous Southern threats of secession if the constitution were not accepted, Buchanan refused Walker's request and stated that the Lecompton constitution was valid. Even more important, Douglas came out in opposition to the pro-slavery document. Nevertheless, the Lecompton constitution was submitted to Congress for approval. It passed in the Senate, but in the House, Republicans and "Douglas Democrats" in favor of popular sovereignty forced the President to withdraw it and substitute the English bill which provided that if a new referendum in Kansas on the Lecompton constitution resulted in its acceptance, Kansas would receive a federal grant of about four million acres of land and immediate admission into the Union. If rejected, statehood and the land grant would be delayed for two years or until the territory had about 90,000 inhabitants. The bill passed both houses even though Douglas himself and many Republicans opposed it.

In the meantime a Kansas legislature, fairly elected, had been placed in office for the first time. This body called a referendum on the Lecompton constitution, and the electorate voted it down on January 4, 1858, by a vote of 10,226 to 162. Despite its overwhelming rejection, Buchanan stubbornly persisted in regarding the Lecompton constitution as a legitimate document. The United States Congress then called for another referendum, under the terms of the English bill. Nevertheless, Kansans again rejected the Lecompton constitution, by a vote of 11,812 to 1,926. When Kansas finally did enter the Union in 1861, it did so as a free state.

Buchanan's stubbornness had not only made his name hated throughout much of the North, but also had led to a deep split in the Democratic Party. Stephen A. Douglas was the most powerful Democrat in the country after the President, and Buchanan's rejection of Douglas' cherished theory of popular sovereignty had permanently estranged Douglas and his followers. Now the party was divided into Southern Democrats who backed the President and "Douglas Democrats" who flocked behind their hero. The country's last national party was rapidly losing its unity.

THE PANIC OF 1857

Sectional strains were further intensified by an economic depression in 1857 that mainly affected the North. New railroad lines had been built at a breakneck pace, but many of them extended into thinly settled areas in the Northwest where there was as yet little demand for railroad service. When this fact became clear, the value of railroad stocks tumbled. State banks had overextended credit to farmers in the Midwest and Northwest, and now the farmers began to default on their mortgages. Farmers also had been hurt by an event halfway around the world. The Crimean War had created a temporary demand for surplus American grain and meat, but when the conflict ended in 1856, the European market was glutted and food prices fell drastically.

Because the world demand for cotton remained high, the South was relatively unaffected by the depression. Southerners, smarting under recent Northern attacks on their way of life, now exulted and pointed to their economic invulnerability as proof of the superiority of their slave-based cotton economy.

Northerners, failing to understand the true causes of the panic to be the overextension of railroad building, land speculation, and the deflation of farm prices overseas, blamed it on the low Tariff of 1857, which had been pushed through Congress by the South. Now the Republican Party demanded a high protective tariff for Northern industry. The endorsement of a protective tariff by the Republicans gave Southerners still another reason for hating the new party.

THE LINCOLN-DOUGLAS DEBATES

The economic dislocation in the North together with ever heightening sectional tensions made the Democrats realize that they had a hard battle on their hands in the upcoming Congressional elections. The question of slavery expansion still overshadowed all other issues, and the most dramatic debate on the subject was conducted in Illinois, where Stephen A. Douglas, the colorful Democratic leader, sought re-election as Senator. He was opposed by Abraham Lincoln, the Republican candidate. The continuing contest between these two men soon attracted the national interest, and their views were reported in newspapers across the land.

The choice of Illinois' next Senator actually lay with the Illinois state legislature, because Senators at this time were not popularly elected. Nevertheless, a popular election was generally held to indicate the people's preference.

Lincoln challenged Douglas to seven debates, covering many topics, but on each occasion the focus was on slavery expansion into the territories. Douglas tried to depict Lincoln as an abolitionist in order to frighten moderates away from the Republican camp. Although Douglas personally was opposed to slavery, he insisted upon the right of people in each territory to decide whether they wanted slavery or not, the theory of popular sovereignty.

Lincoln carefully pointed out that he was not an abolitionist, that neither he nor the Republican Party had any intention of rooting slavery out of the Southern states where it already existed, at least not by force. In order to court the southern Illinois vote, Lincoln also made clear that he did not favor the destruction of all social distinctions between the two races. "I am not, nor ever have been, in favor of bringing about in any way the social and political equality of the white and black races."

Nevertheless, Lincoln staunchly condemned slavery itself as "a moral, social and political wrong," something Douglas carefully avoided doing. The expansion of slavery had to be stopped, Lincoln said, lest it become so divisive an issue as to create a civil war. If slavery could be restricted, it might even be abolished in the South some day, but without bloodshed. Lincoln is supposed to have remarked that so patent an evil as slavery was certain eventually to end.

The crucial moment in the debates came in Freeport, Illinois, when Lincoln asked Douglas how he could reconcile his doctrine of popular sovereignty with the Supreme Court's recent Dred Scott decision. No matter what Douglas said, he was bound to be in trouble. If, on the one hand, he rejected popular sovereignty, the Free-Soilers of Illinois would denounce him; if on the other hand, he rejected the Dred Scott decision, he would lose Southern support. Since Douglas had strong Presidential ambitions and the Democratic Party was still very much in the control of Southern politicians, he certainly did not wish to offend pro-slavery sentiments. Douglas tried to solve the dilemma posed by Lincoln by announcing what was thereafter called the "Freeport Doctrine." Douglas stated that no matter what the Supreme Court decided, the people of a territory had the lawful means to introduce slavery "or exclude it as they please, for the reason that slavery cannot exist a day or an hour anywhere, unless it is supported by local police regulations. Those police regulations can only be established by the local legislature; and if the people are opposed to slavery, they will elect representatives to that body who will by unfriendly legislation effectually prevent the introduction of it into their midst."

The Freeport Doctrine displeased many in the North because it glossed over the moral question of slavery and it horrified the South because it suggested a loophole whereby a territory could exclude the "peculiar institution." Douglas had already lost much Southern support by opposing Buchanan's endorsement of the Lecompton constitution. Now the rift between Northern "Douglas Democrats" and Southern pro-slavery Democrats became even wider.

THE 1858 CONGRESSIONAL ELECTIONS

When the popular election results were counted, Lincoln received a few more votes than Douglas. Nevertheless, the Democrats had won control of the Illinois legislature, and there they returned Douglas to his seat in Congress. The wedge Lincoln had driven between Douglas and Southern Democrats, however, hastened the break-up of the Democratic Party, a consequence which would doom Douglas' Presidential ambitions. Moreover, Lincoln had won prominence throughout the North as a sane, articulate, moderate spokesman of Republican ideals.

In the 1858 elections the Democrats lost ground in almost every state, including President Buchanan's own Pennsylvania. Democrats retained control of the Senate, but Republicans won a plurality in the House. Despite these gains, Republicans were unable to get any of their bills through Congress or the White House. Southern Congressmen and Presidential vetoes blocked such Republican measures as a higher protective tariff, a homestead bill, a transcontinental railroad, and federal land grants for the endowment of agricultural colleges.

JOHN BROWN AND HARPERS FERRY

While Republican gains in the elections of 1858 had alarmed Southerners, John Brown's raid on the federal arsenal at Harpers Ferry, Virginia, filled their hearts with terror. Brown, the "avenging angel" who had killed five supporters of slavery in Kansas, had shifted his abolitionist activities to the upper South. In his fanatical determination to uproot slavery, Brown conceived a wild scheme in which he planned to capture the federal arsenal at Harpers Ferry, arm his followers, and establish a black state in the mountains of Virginia. Once slaves heard about the state, they would turn on their masters, fight for their freedom, and join Brown. Gradually Brown's army of rebellious blacks would swell. Ultimately it would force the white South to its knees. Not for a moment did Brown doubt that blacks would rise up spontaneously. "When I strike," he said, "the bees will swarm."

Financed by Northern abolitionists, Brown and eighteen followers attacked Harpers Ferry on October 16, 1859. A few slaves joined Brown's army, but by the next morning a hastily assembled local militia counterattacked. Dangerfield Newby, a fugitive black fighting to liberate his wife and seven children from slavery, was the first of Brown's men to die. Buchanan heard alarming reports of the raid and ordered Colonel Robert E. Lee and Lieutenant J. E. B. Stuart to lead a detachment of marines to Harpers Ferry. The next day Stuart regained the arsenal, capturing Brown and five of his men. Ten of Brown's men had died in the exchange of fire.

Brown was tried for treason at Charles Town, convicted, and sentenced to hang. Governor Wise of Virginia ignored the pleas of Brown's relatives and friends to place him in an insane asylum. Wise, like thousands of other Southerners, was at once angry and afraid—angry because several Northern abolitionists had backed Brown, and fearful that Brown's raid would touch off a general slave insurrection throughout the South.

The majority of Northern moderates condemned Brown's violent tactics, but his behavior during his trial was so dignified and so moving that he was quickly elevated to the stature of a martyr for freedom. His last statement received great publicity:

Now, if it is deemed necessary that I should forfeit my life for the furtherance of the ends of justice, and mingle my blood further with the blood of my children and

John Brown (left) at his trial in Virginia. Brown led a raid on the arsenal at Harpers Ferry in 1858 with an army of ex-slaves. Although convicted and hanged, Brown's idealistic cause made him a martyr to the abolitionists.

with the blood of millions in this slave country whose rights are disregarded by wicked, cruel, and unjust enactments, I say, let it be done.

By hanging Brown, the South made him the hero of millions of Northerners. Thoreau observed that after his execution John Brown became "more alive than ever." As a result, Southern antipathy toward the North hardened further. One North Carolinian wrote, "I have always been a fervid Union man," but now "I am willing to take the chances of every probable evil that may arise from disunion, sooner than submit to Northern insolence and Northern outrage."

ELECTION OF 1860

Both Northerners and Southerners were apprehensive about the Presidential election of 1860. The North saw that the South had become more rigid than ever in its defense of slavery; the conflict over the fate of Kansas, the Dred Scott decision, and John Brown's raid had done much to fire Southern pride and anger. The South saw that the North had gained a pronounced political advantage with the admission of the free states of California, Minnesota, and Oregon.

The great issue of the election was once again the fate of slavery in the territories. The Republicans came out clearly against the expansion of slavery. The Democrats were split between their Southern wing that wanted a law guaranteeing federal protection of slavery in all territories, and the Northern wing, led by Stephen Douglas, that wanted to leave the question of slavery up to the people living in each territory.

THE DEMOCRATIC CONVENTION

The Democratic Party met in April, 1860, in Charleston, South Carolina, to nominate a Presidential candidate. Southern extremists were unhappy over Douglas' Freeport Doctrine, which had attempted to reconcile the Dred Scott decision with the theory of popular sovereignty. Southerners demanded a plank in the Democratic platform explicitly stating that it was the duty of the national government to protect the rights and property of persons in the territories, thus refuting the Freeport Doctrine.

Douglas could not accept such a plank. One of his spokesmen said of the theory of popular sovereignty, "We cannot recede from this doctrine without personal dishonor, and so help us God, we will never abandon this principle." Delegates from eight Southern states then withdrew from the convention and Douglas was unable to get the endorsement of the necessary two-thirds of the elected delegates. A new convention met in Baltimore on June 18, and when the Southern delegates bolted again, new men from the South favorable to Douglas replaced them. The party was now split irreconcilably. The Northern Democrats nominated Douglas on a popular sovereignty platform and the Southerners, meeting independently in Baltimore on June 28, chose John C. Breckinridge of Kentucky. Breckinridge, Buchanan's Vice President, was a moderate himself, but his wing of the Democratic Party adopted a platform calling for a federal code to protect slavery in the territories.

THE REPUBLICAN CONVENTION

On May 16, the Republicans met in Chicago in a convention that attracted more spectators than any previous political gathering in American history with more than ten thousand people attending each day. The leading contender for the Presidential nomination was William H. Seward of New York, who had been the dominant figure in the party from its inception. Nevertheless, there was strong opposition to his candidacy. He was considered a "political" abolitionist and had even incautiously spoken of a coming "irrepressible conflict" between the North and South. This phrase distressed the moderate faction of former Whigs among the Republicans who feared a civil war. Seward had also aroused dislike by his association with Thurlow Weed, the wily political boss of New York.

Only Lincoln, among all the other contenders for the nomination, was without important political enemies.

On the third ballot, the convention unanimously nominated Abraham Lincoln. A compromise candidate, Lincoln was an ardent enough opponent of slavery on moral grounds to satisfy abolitionists in the Northeast and yet a moderate enough spokesman for the peaceful, legal containment of slavery to win the confidence of former Whigs and other delegates from the Middle West.

At the time of his nomination, Lincoln described himself in the following wry terms: "It may be said I am, in height, six feet four inches, nearly; lean in flesh, weighing on average one hundred and eighty pounds; dark complexion, with coarse black hair and gray eyes. No other marks or brands recollected."

He was born in Kentucky in 1809, the son of an uneducated frontier farmer who, when Lincoln was seven, brought his family to Indiana, and then, in 1830, to southern Illinois. As a child, Lincoln received almost no formal schooling, but educated himself by reading widely. At twenty-three he won his first political post as a Whig member of the Illinois state legislature. He studied law and in 1836 was admitted to the Illinois bar. Lincoln became the leading Whig in Illinois, and in 1846 he was elected to serve

one term in the national House of Representatives. Between 1849 and 1858 he became one of the leading lawyers in Illinois, and after passage of the Kansas-Nebraska Act, Lincoln joined the new Republican Party. However, while his name was well known in Illinois, and he was certainly the Republicans' strongest man in that state, his national reputation was not made until his debates with Douglas in 1858.

The Republican platform contained a strong statement against the spread of slavery into the territories: "We deny the authority of Congress, or a territorial legislature, or of any individuals, to give legal existence to slavery in any territory of the United States." Unlike the Douglas Democrats, who were willing to leave the question up to the residents of each territory, the Republicans condemned the expansion of slavery even if the people of a territory wanted to legalize the institution.

The Republicans also broadened their appeal by coming out for several measures that they had tried in vain to push through Congress during the preceding session. These measures were the immediate entrance of Kansas into the Union; a protective tariff, designed to appeal to Eastern manufacturers and factory workers; a homestead law that would provide free land for settlers, to attract the votes of Western farmers; internal improvements and a transcontinental railroad, to win the allegiance of Californians and businessmen; and a plank attacking any abridgement of the right of citizenship, to win votes from recent immigrant arrivals.

All of these planks appealed to various economic interests in the North. Moreover, the ticket was well balanced. Lincoln himself was certain to draw support from voters in the Middle West while his running mate, Hannibal Hamlin of Maine, a former Democrat, would presumably win votes from disaffected members of that party and from people in the Northeast.

THE CONSTITUTIONAL UNION PARTY

The race for the Presidency was complicated by the entry of a fourth party. Composed of old-line Whigs, Know-Nothings, and dissident Democrats, the new Constitutional Union Party nominated John Bell of Tennessee and campaigned on one simple statement: "It is both the part of patriotism and of duty to recognize no political principle other than the Constitution of the country, the union of the states, and the enforcement of the laws." On the crucial question of the expansion of slavery into the territories, the Constitutional Union Party took no stand at all. Its appeal was limited and it won votes primarily in the border states along the Mason-Dixon line which had the most to lose in the event of a civil war, or so it seemed in 1860.

THE CAMPAIGN

The campaign was spirited. There were many parades for Douglas, and he spoke widely throughout the North. Lincoln made no speeches, in order to avoid misrepresentation of his opinions, but Republican orators led by Seward and Salmon B. Chase of Ohio covered the country. By election time about fifty thousand speeches, generally moderate in tone, had been made in behalf of the Republican ticket. The tremendous enthusiasm of the party, displayed in rallies and parades, distracted its supporters from thinking seriously about Southern threats of secession should Lincoln win. Lincoln himself thought the threats were a bluff.

Lincoln won the election by a decisive margin in the electoral college, 180 votes to 123 votes cast for all of his rivals combined. His popular vote of 1,865,593, however, was barely 40 percent of the national total. His opponents had among them almost a million more votes than Lincoln, with Douglas alone receiving 1,382,713 votes.

The contest had been a peculiar one, in reality two contests. In the South, Bell and Breckinridge had competed against one another, Breckinridge topping Bell by 250,000 votes. Lincoln had won only 26,000 votes in the South and in many states his name had not even appeared on the ballot. Douglas had broken with precedent by delivering many campaign speeches in the South. Douglas decided to campaign there actively, not to advance his own cause so much as to prevent the South from seceding following a Republican victory, which he regarded as inevitable. As he said, "Mr. Lincoln is the next President. We must try to save the Union. I will go South." Unfortunately, Douglas made almost no impression south of the Mason-Dixon line.

In the North, Lincoln's only competition was Douglas. The race was extremely close in some states. For example, Lincoln carried California by only 643 of that state's 119,000 votes and Oregon by only 264 out of a total of 13,000 votes.

An analysis of the returns shows that although Lincoln did not win by a clear majority, more than two-thirds of the country's voters, by casting ballots for Douglas and Lincoln, had expressed their determination to stop the expansion of slavery. Lincoln and Douglas received 69 percent of the total vote, and this constituted a strong Free-Soil mandate. Most Americans obviously were opposed to the spread of the "peculiar institution."

SECESSION

Southern reaction to the Republican victory was typically represented by an editorial from the New Orleans *Daily Crescent* on November 13, 1860: "They have robbed

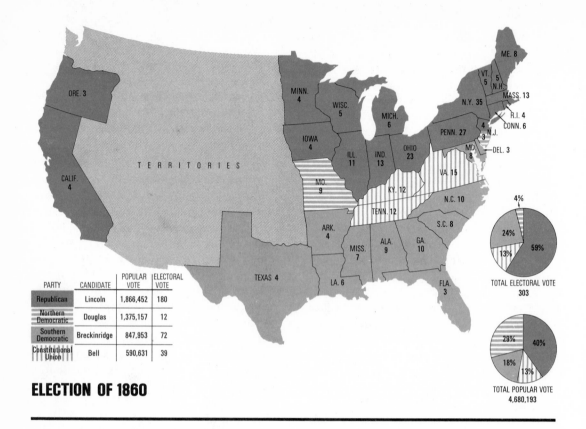

PARTY	CANDIDATE	POPULAR VOTE	ELECTORAL VOTE
Republican	Lincoln	1,866,452	180
Northern Democratic	Douglas	1,375,157	12
Southern Democratic	Breckinridge	847,953	72
Constitutional Union	Bell	590,631	39

TOTAL ELECTORAL VOTE
303

TOTAL POPULAR VOTE
4,680,193

ELECTION OF 1860

us of our property . . . they have set at naught the decrees of the Supreme Court, they have invaded our States and killed our citizens, they have declared their unalterable determination to exclude us altogether from the Territories, they have nullified the laws of Congress, and finally they have capped the mighty pyramid of unfraternal enormities by electing Abraham Lincoln . . . on a platform and by a system which indicates nothing but the subjugation of the South and the complete ruin of her social, political and industrial institutions."

SOUTH CAROLINA SECEDES

Throughout the fifteen slave states, people were angry and anxious over the election of Lincoln. For years Southerners had

been threatening secession. Certainly the most popular theory of the Union in the South held that it was a compact voluntarily formed by sovereign states, and that states could separate from the rest of the nation whenever they chose to do so. Although many Southerners continued to be Unionists after Lincoln's election, the secessionists were better organized, and they quickly went into action. South Carolina with its unified economic and social outlook had long been the center of Southern separatism. Even before the 1860 election the governor of South Carolina had warned that the victory of a Republican would "inevitably destroy our equality in the Union, and ultimately reduce the Southern states to mere provinces of a consolidated despotism, to be governed by a fixed majority in Congress hostile to our institutions and fatally bent upon our ruin." The South

Carolina legislature had remained in session over election day, and as soon as the returns were counted, it called for a convention to provide for the state's secession from the Union. While that convention met, President Buchanan gave a speech denying the right of states to secede from the Union. He admitted, however, that he did not think the federal government could constitutionally coerce states to remain in the Union. Ignoring the President's remarks, on December 20, 1860, the South Carolina convention voted unanimously to withdraw from the United States.

SECESSION SPREADS

Over the next month and a half, six more cotton-growing states of the deep South followed South Carolina's lead. Mississippi chose on January 9, 1861, to withdraw by a vote of 84 to 15; Florida on January 10 (62 to 7); Alabama on January 11 (61 to 39); Georgia on January 19 (208 to 89); Louisiana on January 26 (113 to 17); and Texas on February 1 (166 to 8).

None of the upper South and border states seceded at this point. From Virginia to Missouri, eight slave states remained in the Union. Even in the seceding states, the separatist urge was not as strong as the voting statistics cited above might indicate. A large group of moderates, called "cooperators," recommended a wait-and-see policy. They pointed out that Lincoln had promised not to abolish slavery where it already existed. They also underlined the fact that Southern Democrats still controlled the Senate and the Supreme Court. The small farmers in northern Georgia and Alabama who did not own slaves tried to persuade the rich plantation owners from the southern parts of their states to wait until a slave-state convention had presented its demands to the North. But when these cooperators saw that their cause was hopeless, they decided to cast their lot with the secessionists.

Governor Sam Houston of Texas was such a strong Unionist that he refused to call the legislature into session for fear that they would vote for secession. As Houston warned, "You may after the sacrifice of countless thousands of treasure and hundreds of thousands of precious lives, as a bare possibility, win Southern independence, if God is not against you; but I doubt it." Despite Houston's stand, the secessionists forced a public vote on the issue and the people, later backed by their legislatures, voted overwhelmingly to withdraw from the Union.

Thus, even before Lincoln assumed office, seven states had broken away from the Union. On February 4, 1861, they formed a new government at Montgomery, Alabama. The new nation was called the Confederate States of America and Jefferson Davis of Mississippi was chosen provisional President. A new Southern Congress began to draft a constitution and a new flag, the "Stars and Bars," was designed.

Secessionists expected nothing but good to come out of their action. The insults of Northerners would be silenced, tension created by conflicts over the fate of slavery in the territories was now broken, and Southerners would no longer have to pay high tariffs on manufactured goods. The world market for cotton remained sound and prices high, and adventurers backed by the Confederacy would soon bring Cuba, Mexico, and Central America into the Southern confederation. Most Southerners were confident a war would not be fought with the North. On the contrary, secession would allow the South to break its dependency on Northern manufacturing and to develop its own balanced, self-sufficient economy.

THE CRITTENDEN COMPROMISE

Meanwhile, in an effort to halt secession, Buchanan asked Congress to frame compro-

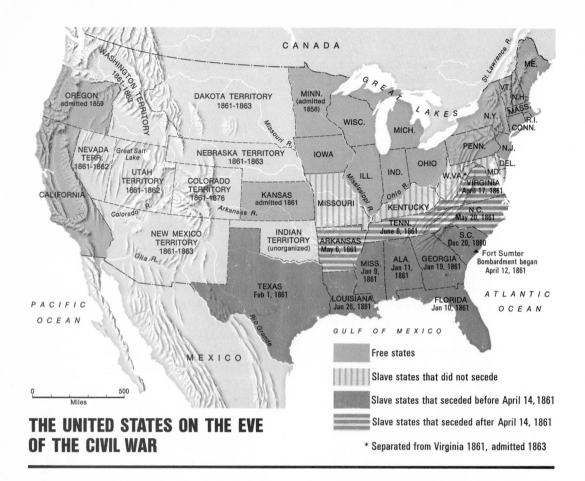

CANADA

WASHINGTON TERRITORY 1861-1863

OREGON
admitted 1859

DAKOTA TERRITORY
1861-1863

MINN.
(admitted 1858)

WISC.

MICH.

ME.

VT.

N.H.

MASS.

N.Y.

R.I.
CONN.

NEVADA TERR.
1861-1862

Great Salt Lake

UTAH TERRITORY
1861-1862

NEBRASKA TERRITORY
1861-1863

IOWA

PENN.

N.J.

CALIFORNIA

COLORADO TERRITORY
1861-1876

KANSAS
admitted 1861

OHIO

IND.

ILL.

W.VA.*

MD.

DEL.

VIRGINIA
April 17, 1861

Colorado R.

Arkansas R.

MISSOURI

KENTUCKY

N.C.
May 20, 1861

NEW MEXICO TERRITORY
1861-1863

Gila R.

INDIAN TERRITORY
(unorganized)

ARKANSAS
May 6, 1861

TENN.
June 8, 1861

S.C.
Dec 20, 1860

Fort Sumter
Bombardment began
April 12, 1861

MISS.
Jan 9, 1861

ALA.
Jan 11, 1861

GEORGIA
Jan 19, 1861

TEXAS
Feb 1, 1861

PACIFIC OCEAN

LOUISIANA
Jan 26, 1861

FLORIDA
Jan 10, 1861

ATLANTIC OCEAN

Rio Grande

GULF OF MEXICO

MEXICO

0   500
Miles

Free states

Slave states that did not secede

Slave states that seceded before April 14, 1861

Slave states that seceded after April 14, 1861

THE UNITED STATES ON THE EVE
OF THE CIVIL WAR

* Separated from Virginia 1861, admitted 1863

---

mise measures that would remove Southern fears. After deliberation, the House called for an amendment that would forever deny to Congress the power to abolish slavery in states where it already existed. Southern spokesmen, however, speedily rejected the proposed amendment because it said nothing about slavery in the territories. A Senate committee, headed by John J. Crittenden of Kentucky, then recommended a series of amendments which would guarantee the permanence of slavery in the states where it already existed, strengthen the fugitive slave code, prevent interference with the interstate slave trade, preserve slavery in the District of Columbia, and, most important, re-establish the old line of 36° 30' created by the Missouri Compromise. Below this line, all territory now

owned by the United States or acquired in the future, would be open to slavery. North of this line, slavery would be prohibited forever.

There was wide support throughout the country for the Crittenden Compromise, but few Northern and Southern leaders were for it. Moreover, when Lincoln was approached for his approval, he rejected the plan. He made it clear that he would never compromise in his determination to keep slavery from expanding into new territories. He also feared that it would encourage the South to embark on imperialistic wars in Latin America. As Lincoln suspected, Southerners had visions of turning parts of Mexico, Central America, and all of Cuba into slave states.

The legislature of Virginia also tried to

be a conciliator by inviting the other states to a peace conference in Washington, D.C. Delegates from twenty-one states attended, but the plan they devised for a reconciliation merely followed the broad outlines of Crittenden's scheme; furthermore, their proposal, made public in February, 1861, came too late.

Why did the spirit of compromise which had always prevailed in past national controversies fail this time? In the country as a whole and among the people of the border states, "Douglas Democrats," and conservative businessmen in particular, there was still a widely held hope for compromise. But the great initiators of past compromises to save the Union were gone. Men like Clay, Webster, and Calhoun had now been replaced by new leaders in both sections who were less willing to compromise, men like Seward, Chase, Sumner, Jefferson Davis, Alexander H. Stephens of Georgia, William B. Yancy of Alabama, and Robert Barnwell Rhett of South Carolina. Also, enmity between the sections had increased almost beyond hope of reconciliation. Lincoln insisted that any compromise had to exclude slavery expansion, yet there was not the slightest possibility that the South would accept any such compromise plan. Even as compromises were being proposed, sectional economic and political interests still governed the thinking of Northern and Southern political and business leaders. Finally, the move for secession had progressed so rapidly that by the time compromises were proposed, the seven states of the deep South had already left the Union.

BUCHANAN'S POLICY

Before giving up his office, Buchanan did stiffen his opposition to the whole separatist movement. He weeded secessionists out of his Cabinet and replaced them with reliable Union men. In his last message to Congress he also emphasized his duty as President to collect federal revenues and protect federal properties even in the South: "The Union must and shall be preserved by all constitutional means. . . . The present is no time for palliations. Action, prompt action, is required."

When the state of South Carolina sent commissioners to Washington to demand that Buchanan hand over federal property in the South, such as Fort Sumter in the harbor of Charleston, Buchanan refused. Since this fort was defended by only a small garrison, under Major Robert Anderson, Buchanan sent supplies and reinforcements to strengthen the fort. To avoid stirring up antagonisms in South Carolina, Buchanan dispatched an unarmed merchant ship, the *Star of the West,* instead of an armed naval vessel. When the ship steamed into the Charleston harbor, shore batteries fired on it, forcing it to turn around and return to New York. The South had fired on the Stars and Stripes, but Northerners did not react by demanding war. They were too bewildered by the event. Everyone waited to see what course Lincoln would pursue.

LINCOLN TAKES COMMAND

On April 4, 1861, when Lincoln gave his long-awaited Inaugural Address, seven states had already seceded, but in the upper South, Virginia, Maryland, North Carolina, and Delaware were still debating whether to stay in the Union. The same question was being argued in the remaining undecided slave states farther west, Tennessee, Kentucky, Arkansas, and Missouri.

Lincoln took a firm but cautious stance and entreated the states of the Confederacy to return to the Union. He reassured the South that he had no intention of abolishing slavery where it already existed and promised to support the Fugitive Slave Laws. He emphatically denied, however, the right of any state to secede from the Union: "I hold that, in contemplation of universal law and of the Constitution, the Union of these States is perpetual. . . . No State, upon its own mere motion, can lawfully get out of the Union." He pledged to protect federal property, collect federal revenues, and keep up federal services.

"My countrymen, one and all," Lincoln said, "think calmly and well upon this whole subject. Nothing valuable can be lost by taking time. If there be an object to hurry any of you in hot haste to a step which you would never take deliberately, that object will be frustrated by taking time; but no good object can be frustrated by it." The new President insisted that if war broke out, it would not be initiated by him: "In your hands, my dissatisfied fellow-countrymen, and not in mine, is the momentous issue of civil war. The Government will not assail you. You can have no conflict without being yourselves the aggressors. You have no oath registered in Heaven to destroy the Government, while I shall have the most solemn one to 'preserve, protect and defend it.' "

In a final eloquent paragraph, Lincoln appealed to the patriotic memories of Southerners:

I am loath to close. We are not enemies, but friends. We must not be enemies. Though passion may have strained, it must not break, our bonds of affection. The mystic chords of memory, stretching from every battlefield and patriot grave to every living heart and hearthstone all over this broad land, will yet swell the chorus of the Union, when again touched, as surely they will be, by the better angels of our nature.

Abraham Lincoln as a candidate for President of the United States.

FORT SUMTER:
THE WAR BEGINS

When Lincoln gave his inaugural address, he thought that Major Anderson had enough ammunition and food to hold Fort Sumter for many months. The very next day, however, he received a letter from Anderson warning the President that the fort could be held only if twenty thousand additional men were immediately sent, as well as a large naval force and ample provisions.

For about six weeks the President hesitated. He was determined to keep Fort Sumter and also Fort Pickens at Pensacola, Florida, but he still believed there was enough Union sentiment in the South to settle the matter without the use of force. He therefore proceeded to organize his administration and to tend to patronage problems. As weeks passed, however, the press and then the Northern population began to express impatience. By the time Lincoln fully decided on a policy of action, Northern public opinion was ready to back him in a strong move to save the Union.

Lincoln realized that if he sent an armed naval expedition to Fort Sumter, the Confederacy would consider the move an act of war. On the other hand, if Fort Sumter were allowed to fall into the hands of Confederate forces, Lincoln would seem to be recognizing the independence of the seceding states. Most of the members of his Cabinet advised him not to send food to Fort Sumter. Only two members, Secretary of the Treasury Salmon P. Chase and Postmaster General Montgomery Blair, favored aiding Anderson. The Secretary of State, William H. Seward, even proposed a scheme to instantly provoke a war between the United States and France or Spain over their designs on Mexico and Santo Domingo, respectively, in the hope that a major conflict would bring the seven states of the Confederacy back into the Union. Seward felt certain that even Southerners would want to present a united American front against a foreign enemy.

After listening to all opinions, Lincoln made up his own mind. He decided that he had to relieve Fort Sumter, but he chose to send only food in unarmed ships. "If such attempt be not resisted," Lincoln wrote the governor of South Carolina, "no effort to throw in men, arms, or ammunition will be made without further notice, or in case of an attack upon the Fort." Thus Lincoln forced the Confederacy to take the next step. If the South shelled a peaceful expedition bringing food to the beleaguered fort, then the Confederacy would be responsible for firing the first shot of a civil war.

The governor of South Carolina, Francis W. Pickens, sent Lincoln's message on to President Jefferson Davis in Montgomery. The Confederate President immediately sent back word ordering General Pierre G. T. Beauregard to request Major Anderson to evacuate Fort Sumter by 4 A.M. on April 12, 1861. When Anderson refused to leave, Beauregard opened fire at 4:30 A.M. The shelling continued for the next 34 hours. On the afternoon of April 13, Anderson lowered the Stars and Stripes. Lincoln's unarmed flotilla then approached the fort and, with Confederate permission, carried away Anderson's force. Miraculously, not a single soldier died on either side, but the war had begun.

Even at this point, however, many Americans still doubted that a real war would follow. Some radical abolitionists such as William Lloyd Garrison and the Quaker poet John Greenleaf Whittier recommended that Lincoln permit the Confederate states to depart from the Union in peace. Many prominent businessmen in the North, fearful that a war would interrupt commerce, reduce the value of government securities, and interfere with the collection of debts owed by Southerners, also wished for peace. Many Southerners also expected peace to follow. They were convinced that Northerners were too obsessed with making money to allow their economy to be disrupted by war.

Yet, in spite of initial Northern hesitation about fighting to save the Union, the aspiration to keep the nation together was a stronger force. The desire for continued use of the Mississippi River and unhampered access to the Southern market for Northern agricultural and manufactured goods certainly played a part in the decision. In addition, there were powerful ideas shaping Northern pro-Union sentiment. Some abolitionists wished to use the war as a means of destroying slavery, and Northerners in general believed in the concept of American nationalism with its ideal of the special mission of the United States to establish an enduring democratic society.

VIEWS ON THE CAUSES OF THE CIVIL WAR

Was the Civil War inevitable? If so, what forces had brought it about? Was slavery the decisive issue? Which section was guilty of causing the conflict—the North or the South? How important were the roles of opposing economic interests? Could war have been avoided if hotheads had not stirred up animosities and the nation's leaders had been wiser during the 1850s? These questions have been debated by historians ever since the Civil War ended, and each generation has interpreted the conflict in the light of its own experience.

Immediately after the war, Northern historians, many of whom participated in the struggle or lost relatives on the battlefield, argued that the South had plotted destruction of the Union so that the evil institution of slavery might be preserved. The North, they contended, took up arms in a crusade against an absolute moral wrong. The three volumes of Henry Wilson's *History of the Rise and Fall of the Slave Power in America* (1872–1877) embodied this viewpoint. On the other hand, Southern postwar historians denied the importance of slavery as a cause of the war and blamed Lincoln and the Republican Party's unconstitutional, overbearing actions in 1860 and 1861. A third point of view was expressed by others, such as former President Buchanan, who felt that extremists in both the North and South were at fault. Had Northern abolitionists and Southern advocates of slavery been more temperate, they believed, war might have been avoided.

In the 1890s, the first generation able to look at the Civil War from some distance began to publish accounts of the events. Writing in an era of intense economic nationalism, historians such as James Ford Rhodes regarded the conflict as a blessing in disguise. American growth had been hampered by sectionalism and slavery. The war had abolished both evils and permitted the United States to become a unified nation and a first-rate industrial power. Slavery, and the South, had been at fault, Rhodes wrote, but individual slaveowners were merely victims of impersonal economic forces. Southerners were not personally to blame, they deserved sympathy more than censure. The Civil War had been an "irrepressible conflict" between two eco-

Abolitionism as Cause of Civil War

*Because it combined in itself both
the moral and the democratic appeal,
and because it coincided with sectional
rivalry, the abolition movement gradually
swallowed up all other reforms. The
South became the great object of all
efforts to remake American society.
Against early indifference and later
persecution, a handful of deadly-in-earnest
men and women slowly built into a
section's consciousness the belief in a
Slave Power. To the normal strength of
sectional ignorance and distrust they
added all the force of Calvinistic morality
and American democracy and thereby
surrounded every Northern interest
and contention with holy sanction and
reduced all opposition to abject
depravity. When the politician, playing
his risky game, linked expansion and
slavery, Christian common folk by the
thousands, with no great personal urge
for reforming, accepted the Abolition
attitudes toward both the South and
Slavery. Civil war was then in the
making.* 99

—Avery O. Craven,
The Coming of the Civil War

nomic systems—the industrial wage system of the North and the agricultural slave system of the South.

Rhodes had an obvious bias in favor of the North, but Southern historians soon echoed his basic theory that the war had been waged between two different ways of life and two economies. Buoyed up by a return to prosperity in the South, they regarded the Civil War favorably. They too wrote critically of slavery and secession, not as moral wrongs, but as hindrances to economic progress in the South. Woodrow Wilson was one of those Southerners who felt

Abolitionism Defended

66 *... it is difficult for historians seriously to suppose that northerners could have denied themselves feelings of disapproval over slavery. To say that there "should" have been no abolitionists in America before the Civil War is about as sensible as to say that there "should" have been no anti-Nazis in the nineteen-thirties or that there "should" be no anti-Communists today. People who indulge in criticism of remote evils may not be so pure of heart as they imagine; but that fact does not affect their inevitability as part of the historic situation.*

Any theory, in short, which expects people to repress such spontaneous aversions is profoundly unhistorical. If revisionism has based itself on the conviction that things would have been different if only there had been no abolitionists, it has forgotten that abolitionism was as definite and irrevocable a factor in the historic situation as was slavery itself. And, just as abolitionism was inevitable, so too was the Southern reaction against it— a reaction which, ... steadily drove the free discussion of slavery out of the South. The extinction of free discussion meant, of course, the absolute extinction of any hope of abolition through internal reform. 99

—Arthur Schlesinger, Jr.,
*"The Causes of the Civil War:
A Note on Historical Sentimentalism"*

that the Civil War was an unfortunate but inevitable event that had a fortunate outcome. The fact that black Americans, while legally free, were not integrated into American society even after the Civil War did not disturb most of these historians. Like most

Slavery as Cause of Civil War

" *. . . The slavery question is not to be taken as an independent controversy in American politics. It was not a moral dispute. It was the mere incident of a sectional animosity, the causes of which lay far beyond the domain of morals. Slavery furnished a convenient line of battle between the disputants; it was the most prominent ground of distinction between the two sections; it was, therefore, naturally seized upon as a subject of controversy, became the dominant theatre of hostilities, and was at last so conspicuous and violent, that occasion was mistaken for cause, and what was merely an incident came to be regarded as the main subject of controversy. . . .* "

—*Edwin A. Pollard,* **The Lost Cause**

white Americans of their period, they considered blacks racially inferior and fated to a subordinate position in society.

The complacency and optimism of the nationalist school was sharply challenged in the early twentieth century by the Progressive historians. Perhaps the greatest work of this new movement was Charles and Mary Beard's *The Rise of American Civilization,* published in two volumes in 1927. Like the nationalist historians, the Beards believed that economic forces were at the bottom of the Civil War, but unlike the nationalists, the Beards did not see the results as an unmixed blessing. They saw the war as a "social cataclysm in which the capitalists, laborers, and farmers of the North and West drove from power in the national government the planting aristocracy of the South." Furthermore, in the postwar era, a small band of Northern capitalists had ruthlessly exploited the great mass of American workers. The Beards

Slavery Defended

" *. . . [The] new [Confederate] Constitution has put at rest forever all the agitating questions relating to our peculiar institution—African slavery as it exists among us—the proper status of the negro in our form of civilization.* This was the immediate cause of the late rupture and present revolution. *JEFFERSON, in his forecast, had anticipated this, as the "rock upon which the old Union would split." He was right. . . .* The prevailing ideas entertained by him and most of the leading statesmen at the time of the formation of the old Constitution were, that the enslavement of the African was in violation of the laws of nature; that it was wrong in principle, socially, morally and politically. . . . Those ideas, however, were fundamentally wrong. They rested upon the assumption of the equality of races. This was an error. . . .

Our new Government is founded upon exactly the opposite ideas; its foundations are laid, its cornerstone rests, upon the great truth that the negro is not equal to the white man; that slavery, subordination to the superior race, is his natural and moral condition. This, our new Government, is the first, in the history of the world, based upon this great physical, philosophical, and moral truth. . . .

The great objects of humanity are best attained, when conformed to his laws and degrees, in the formation of Governments as well as in all things else. Our Confederacy is founded upon principles in strict conformity with these laws. This stone which was rejected by the first builders "is become the chief stone of the corner" in our new edifice.

—*Alexander H. Stephens*

and other Progressives, eager to curb the power of big business in their own day, saw the postwar period as the beginning of the development of great social and economic inequities in American life.

Although the Progressives were influenced by the economic writings of Karl Marx, they were not orthodox Marxists. They did not want a revolution, but rather democratic reform. In the 1930s, however, a small group of American Marxist historians also began to analyze the Civil War, but, unlike the Beards, they did not deplore the outcome of the conflict. In classical Marxist terms, every economy must progress from feudalism to capitalism and then to socialism. Since the Civil War had brought an end to a slave economy, regarded as a form of feudalism, and strengthened American capitalism, the conflict had to be seen as an important step toward a socialist economy in the United States. As one Marxist, James Sallen, put it, "The destruction of the slave power was the basis for real national unity and the further development of capitalism, which would produce conditions most favorable for the growth of the labor movement."

During the Depression, two other schools of interpretation of the Civil War also arose. One was a movement of Southern nationalists who placed the blame for the conflict on the North. Typical of these was Frank L. Owsley, a professor at the University of Alabama. Not surprisingly, he attacked pre-Civil War Northerners for their rudeness—"an impatient generation who had no . . . understanding of the essence of national unit. The result was that urbanity, self-restraint, and courtesy—the ordinary amenities of civilized intercourse— were cast aside; and in their gracious place were substituted the crude, discourteous, and insulting language and conduct in intersectional relations. . . . It was the Missouri debates in which intersectional comity was first violated; and it was the political leaders of the East, particularly

the New Englanders and those of New England origin, who did it when they denounced in unmeasured terms slavery, the slaveholder, and southern society in general." Owsley refused to see slavery as a moral issue. Slavery had been merely a system of discipline necessary for social control.

The third and probably most important school of thought to arise in the 1930s was the revisionist movement. Having experienced profound disillusionment over the outcome of World War I, the revisionists regarded all wars as pointless and unavailing. Whereas the nationalists, the Progressives, and the Marxists had all considered the Civil War an inevitable outburst of violence, the revisionists thought that it might easily have been averted if the country's leaders had been more skillful during the 1850s. Historians like Avery Craven and James G. Randall insisted that the war had been a "repressible conflict" caused by "The Blundering Generation." Earlier historians had been influenced to varying degrees by Marx, but the revisionists were impressed by the ideas of Sigmund Freud. As Randall wrote on the eve of World War II: "War-making is too much dignified if it is told in terms of broad national urges, of great German motives, or of compelling Russian ambitions. When nations stumble into war, or when peoples rub their eyes and find they have been dragged into war, there is at some point a psychopathic case. Omit the element of abnormality, or of bogus leadership, or inordinate ambition for conquest, and diagnosis fails. . . . The writer doubts seriously whether a consensus of scholars who have competently studied the Civil War would accept either the cultural motive or the economic basis as the effective cause."

Craven emphasized, as well, the factor of abnormality as a cause of the war and charged that Americans had "permitted their shortsighted politicians, their over-zealous editors, and their pious reformers to emotionalize real and potential differences and to conjure up distorted impressions of those who dwelt in other parts of the nation. . . . In time a people came to believe that social security, constitutional government and the freedom of all men were at stake in their sectional differences; that the issues were between right and wrong; good and evil. Opponents became devils in human form. Good men had no choice but to kill and to be killed." The revisionist position was in essence a more sophisticated restatement of the old Buchanan thesis that the war had been caused by abolitionists and slavery advocates—extremists on both sides.

Since World War II, still another view of the Civil War has emerged. Historians such as Allan Nevins and Arthur M. Schlesinger, Jr., have returned to the theory that the war was fought over the moral issue of slavery and that the North was justified in prosecuting a war against the institution. Schlesinger also rejected what he characterized as the easy optimum of the revisionists concerning man's rationality. Having just endured a war against the Nazis, Schlesinger could write, "the experience of the twentieth century has made it clear that we gravely overrated man's capacity to solve the problems of existence within the terms of history. . . . Man generally is entangled in insoluble problems; history is consequently a tragedy in which we are all involved, whose keynote is anxiety and frustration, not progress and fulfillment." The revisionists had contended that slavery would have eventually disappeared without the Civil War since it was an "outmoded" institution. Schlesinger gravely doubted the validity of their arguments, given the emotional attachment of the South to the "peculiar institution."

Readings

GENERAL WORKS

Catton, Bruce, *The Coming Fury*. Garden City, N.Y.: Doubleday, 1961—In the first volume of Catton's 3-volume *Centennial History of the War,* the author emphasizes military preparations.

Craven, Avery O., *Civil War in the Making*. Baton Rouge: Louisiana State University Press, 1959—A brief summary of Craven's position on the origins of the Civil War. In this work, he has moved somewhat away from his extreme revisionism and recognized strong forces at work in the North and South that drove the nation into war.

Craven, Avery O., *The Growth of Southern Nationalism, 1848–1861*. Baton Rouge: Louisiana State University Press, 1953—A history of the South in the years before the Civil War by a leading revisionist historian. Craven stresses the irrationality and extremism of Northern abolitionists and Southern fire-eaters and argues that the majority in both regions were eager to reconcile their conflicts.

Dumond, Dwight L., *Anti-Slavery Origins of the Civil War*. Ann Arbor: University of Michigan Press, 1959—A brief work which argues that the Civil War was in large measure precipitated by the development of Free Soil and abolitionist sentiment in the North into a massive moral force.

Nevins, Allan, *The Emergence of Lincoln*, Vols. I–II. New York: Scribner's, 1950—A history of the pre-Civil War era. In these volumes, Nevins traces the increasing difficulties in reconciling sectional conflicts in the late 1850s and the coming to power of Lincoln, a politician representing the dominant outlook of the North.

Nevins, Allan, *Ordeal of the Union*, Vol. II. New York: Scribner's, 1947—Subtitled, "House Dividing," this volume of Nevins' appraisal of the Civil War era covers the years from 1852 through 1857.

Nichols, Roy F., *The Disruption of American Democracy*. New York: Macmillan, 1948—A political history of the 1850s that concentrates on the disruption of the older Whig and Democratic parties.

Simms, H. Henry, *A Decade of Sectional Controversy*. Chapel Hill: University of North Carolina Press, 1942—A history of sectional antagonisms in the 1850s which concentrates on political and social conditions in the South.

SPECIAL STUDIES

Crandall, Andrew W., *The Early History of the Republican Party, 1854–1856*. Boston: Badger, 1930—An older monograph describing the different groups that came together between 1854 and 1856 to form the Republican Party.

Current, Richard N., *Lincoln and the First Shot*. Philadelphia: Lippincott, 1964—An analysis of Lincoln's strategy during the crisis at Fort Sumter which argues that Lincoln felt that war was inevitable and wanted to maneuver the South into firing the first shot.

Fehrenbacher, Don E., *Prelude to Greatness, Lincoln in the 1850s.* Stamford, Calif.: Stamford University Press, 1962—A collection of essays on Lincoln's career before the 1860 election, putting Lincoln in the context of the Midwestern political scene of the times.

Hopkins, Vincent, *Dred Scott's Case.* New York: Atheneum, 1967—A careful analysis of the entire Dred Scott case, focusing on the legal aspects of the affair.

Isely, Jeter, A., *Horace Greeley and the Republican Party, 1853–1861.* New York: Octagon, 1965—As publisher of the New York *Tribune,* Horace Greeley was one of the leading public figures in the early Republican Party. Isely's study discusses the impact of journalism on politics at the time.

Jaffa, Harry V., *Crisis of the House Divided.* Garden City, N.Y.: Doubleday, 1959—Jaffa explores the political and moral philosophies of Lincoln and Douglas as expressed in their 1858 debates. He rejects the view that the two had similar positions and argues that Lincoln's philosophy, based on the concept of equality, sharply differed from Douglas' creed.

Luthin, Reinhold H., *The First Lincoln Campaign.* Cambridge, Mass.: Harvard University Press, 1944—After describing the background of the Republican Party, Luthin narrates the history of the 1860 Presidential race. He shows that the Lincoln campaign was in the American tradition of emotional appeals and self-interested political maneuvering.

Malin, James C., *John Brown and the Legend of Fifty-Six.* New York: Haskell, 1970—A history of John Brown's activities during the skirmishes in Kansas in 1856. Malin portrays Brown as a scoundrel more interested in shedding blood and stealing horses than in the anti-slavery cause.

Malin, James C., *The Nebraska Question, 1852–1854.* Gloucester, Mass.: Peter Smith, 1968—Part of the author's history of the "grasslands," this study recounts the development of the Kansas-Nebraska Act controversy.

Phillips, Ulrich B., *The Course of the South to Secession.* New York: Hill & Wang, 1964—Six lectures by a leading Southern historian of the earlier years of this century. Phillips maintains that the basic theme of Southern society was the way of life and thought created by plantation slavery.

Potter, David M., *Lincoln and His Party in the Secession Crisis.* New Haven, Conn.: Yale University Press, 1942—A study of Lincoln in the months between his election and his inauguration. Faced with conflicting pressures within the Republican Party, the President-elect maintained a silence which some have called evasive.

Stampp, Kenneth M., *And the War Came: The North and the Secession Crisis, 1860–1861*. Baton Rouge: Louisiana State University Press, 1960—A detailed analysis of Northern opinion during the winter of 1860 and 1861, showing the diverse motives of those who favored going to war.

PRIMARY SOURCES

Angle, Paul M., ed., *Created Equal*. Chicago: University of Chicago Press, 1958—The full texts of the famous Lincoln-Douglas debates from their senatorial campaign of 1858.

Johannsen, Robert W., ed., *The Letters of Stephen A. Douglas*. Urbana, Ill.: University of Illinois Press, 1961—A collection of the major correspondence of the Illinois Democrat who ran against Lincoln for both Senator and President.

McKitrick, Eric L., ed., *Slavery Defended*. Englewood Cliffs, N.J.: Prentice-Hall, 1963 —A collection of pro-slavery writings, showing the transition from the defense of slavery as a necessary evil to its advocacy as a positive good.

Nevins, Allan, and M. H. Thomas, eds., *The Diary of George Templeton Strong*, Vols. I–IV. New York: Macmillan, 1952—Strong was a wealthy conservative, New York businessman, and his detailed diary vigorously presents his reactions to the Civil War as it affected him and men of his position.

BIOGRAPHIES

Capers, Gerald M., *Stephen A. Douglas, Defender of the Union*. Boston: Little, Brown, 1959—A short biography of the Illinois Democratic politician which stresses Douglas' strong nationalist sentiments.

Donald, David, *Charles Sumner and the Coming of the Civil War*. New York: Knopf, 1960—A prize-winning biography of the Massachusetts abolitionist Senator, tracing his career up to the Civil War. Donald attempts to analyze Sumner's career and personality through psychoanalytic theory.

Klein, Philip S., *President James Buchanan*. University Park: Pennsylvania State University Press, 1962—A conventional biography of the last President before the Civil War. The history of Buchanan's Presidency is also the history of the break-up of the Democratic Party.

Swisher, Carl B., *Roger B. Taney*. New York: Macmillan, 1935—The standard biography of the Jacksonian Chief Justice of the Supreme Court who headed the Court at the time of the Dred Scott decision.

Thomas, Benjamin P., *Abraham Lincoln*. New York: Knopf, 1952—The standard single-volume biography of Lincoln.

FICTION

Stowe, Harriet Beecher, *Uncle Tom's Cabin*. New York: Macmillan, 1962—The classic anti-slavery novel which became a best-seller in the North and South.

The Civil War

15

. . . Longstreet suddenly commenced a heavy cannonade on the right. Ewell immediately took it up on the left. The enemy replied with at least equal fury, and in a few moments the firing along the whole line was as heavy as it is possible to conceive. A dense smoke arose for six miles, there was little wind to drive it away, and the air seemed full of shells. . . .

. . . After passing General Lee and his staff, I rode on through the woods in the direction in which I had left Longstreet. I soon began to meet many wounded men returning from the front; many of them asked in piteous tones the way to a doctor or an ambulance. The farther I got, the greater became the number of the wounded. At last I came to a perfect stream of them flocking through the woods in numbers as great as the crowd in Oxford Street in the middle of the day. Some were walking alone on crutches composed of two rifles, others supported by men less badly wounded than themselves, and others were carried on stretchers by the ambulance corps. . . .

—Arthur J. L. Fremantle

Charge of the Rebels on Cemetery Hill during the Battle of Gettysburg.

President Lincoln wrote to Horace Greeley on August 22, 1862, "I would save the Union. I would save it the shortest way under the Constitution. . . . If there be those who would not save the Union, unless they could at the same time save Slavery, I do not agree with them. My paramount object in this struggle is to save the Union, and is not either to save or destroy Slavery." With these words Lincoln made it unmistakably clear that for him as for most Northerners the preservation of the Union was the central issue of the conflict.

THE OPENING STAGES OF THE WAR

For its own part, the South was as firmly convinced of its own right of self-determination. Ironically, however, Southern nationalism was founded on the deeply entrenched belief in states' rights. The Confederate constitution explicitly recognized individual state sovereignty, denying to the central government any power to interfere with the management of a state, even though the actions of that state might run blatantly counter to the national interest. As it turned out, the "states' rights" philosophy, though the constitutional foundation of the Confederate cause, greatly handicapped the South's mobilization, and hampered its success in the war.

CALL TO ARMS

Early in 1861, the Union Army was made up of little more than sixteen thousand men, and this number was reduced by the secession of Southern states. After the attack on Fort Sumter, Lincoln issued a call to all the governors of the North for 75,000 volunteers to "put down" the rebellion. The call was answered quickly because of the intense concern Northerners felt for saving the Union. In the middle of May, the President asked for 42,000 more volunteers, these to serve for three years rather than ninety days, the previous term of enlistment.

A SHORTAGE OF TROOPS

The North's population was greater than the South's, but this was not at first reflected in the size of the Northern Army. The half million persons scattered from Dakota to California made no substantial contribution to Union strength. Furthermore, during the Civil War, many Union regiments were sent to serve in the West to counter Indian attacks. Also, many in the loyal border states and in southern Ohio, Indiana, and Illinois favored allowing the South to secede and would not fight in the Union Army. Massachusetts, Vermont, Michigan, and Wisconsin, in fact, furnished men for the Southern cause.

As a result, the Union resorted to various inducements to raise an adequate army. In 1861, the government gave 100 dollars to each volunteer. Later this amount was increased to 302 dollars for recruits and 402 dollars for veterans. States, cities, and counties added additional bonuses, and by 1864, a volunteer in New York City, for example, could receive 375 dollars in addition to his federal bonus. In Illinois, the grand total of all bonuses combined came to 1,056 dollars per volunteer. This system had its drawbacks, since men sometimes would enlist, pick up their bonuses, and desert. Some would even re-enlist under assumed names to collect additional revenue.

In March, 1863, the Union had to resort to conscription to enlarge its regular army and navy, the latter for an extensive blockade of the Confederate coast. About 50,000 men eventually were drafted amid much resistance and draft evasion. Not only were the laws unpopular in general, they were particularly disliked because they discriminated in favor of the well-to-do. The rich were either exempted or were able to pay someone to serve in their place. Such conscription practices resulted in rising opposition to the draft. In the bloody draft riot in New York City in July, 1863, for example, angry mobs unleashed their hostilities against the wealthy and the black laborers of the city.

In the South, Jefferson Davis at first called for one hundred thousand volunteers. By 1861, the Confederate Congress enacted several measures authorizing a volunteer army of four hundred thousand troops for three years. The number that enlisted, however, did not reach this figure, even though the initial response was an enthusiastic one. Although the South had far more volunteers than the North, more than were needed immediately, most joined for only 12 months. In April, 1862, the South had to institute a draft. Its First Conscription Act declared that all able-bodied white males between 18 and 35 were liable to military service and that men already in the army had to serve for three years from the date of their enlistment. The act, similar to one in the North, exempted professional men and those who owned more than twenty slaves. These provisions alienated many of the less privileged and aroused resistance to volunteering since they favored the educated and wealthy. To the average young Southern male it appeared to be "a rich man's war and a poor man's fight."

With resistance to volunteering and evasion of conscription on both sides, it was difficult at times to maintain military discipline. There are no reliable figures as to exactly how many men served on either side. Estimates tell us that probably two million men wore the Union blue and less than half that number wore the Confederate gray. Terms of enlistment varied from two weeks to the duration of the war.

PREPARATIONS FOR WAR

THE MILITARY

The South counted on several factors for victory. Southern leaders believed that cotton was so important to the English and French textile manufacturers that these industrialists would force their governments to grant the South diplomatic recognition. They were certain that eventually these European powers would enter the war on the side of the South because its independence would be economically profitable to them. The Confederacy also maintained that the North's need to defend national boundaries created a strategic advantage for the South. Furthermore, the Union Army had to conduct an offensive war against the South which would be infinitely more difficult militarily than the defensive war the Confederacy expected to wage. The North would need more men and equipment, as well as longer lines of communication, all of which needed defending, to bring about Southern defeat. Finally, the South began with an emotional advantage in that it believed that it was fighting for its liberty. The philosophy of states' rights aroused massive Southern loyalty.

The South also could claim superiority in the brilliance of its field commanders. For 20 years before the inauguration of Lincoln, a coterie of Southern commanders had directed the United States Army under the leadership of General Winfield Scott of Virginia. Under Scott's regime, many West Pointers from the North, including Sherman and Grant, found little opportunity for advancement and they left the army to pursue more lucrative civilian careers. The Southern officers advanced up the ladder of command and became well-trained, superior officers. When the war broke out, they embraced the Confederate cause. Robert E. Lee, Joseph E. Johnston, and Albert Sidney Johnston, the finest of the alumni of West Point, were relied upon to give the South the fighting edge in a war they expected to be brief and defensive.

On the other hand, such was the state of the Northern Army at the beginning of the war that its commander, General Scott, was one of only two officers in the entire Union service who had ever commanded troops large enough to be called an army. The other was John E. Wool, who was 77 years old—two years older than Scott himself. Though Scott was a Southerner, he remained loyal to the Union. He had, in his own words, "fought fifty years under the flag and would fight for it, and under it, till death."

The military officers who were available in the first stages of the conflict wasted any initial advantages they might have had. In time, men such as Grant, Sherman, Thomas, and Sheridan would emerge to become highly effective and memorable Union leaders, but their predecessors bumbled through a series of unsuccessful campaigns because they were frequently disorganized, slow-moving, and inadequately prepared for the great challenges that faced them.

In a short war, military superiority would have been decisive and numerical superiority would have meant relatively little. But as the actual conflict ground on, strength in numbers became both a psychological and a physical weapon in the hands of the North. At the outbreak of the war, the Union, with twenty-three states, had a population of approximately twenty-two million as opposed to the eleven-state Confederate population of a little over nine million, with more than a third slaves. Eventually, the armed forces of the North were double that of the South. As battles became more extensive and, hence, more fatiguing, the strength of the Confederate Army was sapped and reinforcements almost ceased. Its losses only weakened the general will to continue the conflict, while Northern armies, in spite of heavy casualties, seemed to grow more powerful with every engagement.

MANUFACTURING

The fact that the Civil War stretched over years instead of months also magnified another liability of the South, its agrarian-based economy. At the beginning of the war, there were nearly 110,000 manufacturing concerns in the North, turning out products valued in excess of one and one-half billion dollars annually, and employing over one million workers. The South's industrial growth, on the other hand, had been stunted by its attachment to an agricultural economy based mainly on the export of cotton. As a result, on the eve of the war there were only about 20,000 manufacturing concerns in the Confederacy employing 110,000 workers and producing annually about 155 million dollars' worth of goods.

During the course of the war, Southern troops lacked food, uniforms, supplies, and ammunition. Whatever resources the South had at the beginning of the conflict were quickly consumed by the war machine. Moreover, Southerners were unable to exchange their key staple, cotton, for the foreign manufactures they needed. In reduced circumstances, the South was compelled to turn most of its possessions into war material. Church bells were cast into cannons, carpets were made into clothes, and newspapers were printed on the back of wallpaper.

On the Northern homefront, the war acted as a stimulus to production, and its demands affected many areas of the economy. Industries that produced iron and steel, woolens, boots and shoes, arms and ammunition, railroad equipment, petroleum, prepared foods, coal, and lumber increased their output. With increased production came the remodeling of old factories and the building of new ones, all spurred by the war effort. Agricultural production also increased tremendously to meet the war needs and increased European demands for food following poor harvests abroad.

At the same time, however, the new boom brought out contractors and suppliers who overcharged the government and delivered inferior goods. The ethical conduct of business and commercial leaders was more questionable during the Civil War than during any previous period in the nation's history. Though not without critics, public graft and private profiteering flourished. All too frequently, public officials ignored the evidence of corruption or shared in the fraud. Some newspapers of the time protested, crying out that Washington was "reeling in the whirl of dissipation."

RAILROADS

The Civil War was the first war in which railroads were used extensively to transport men and supplies. Railroads gave the North a distinct advantage. The Union claimed nearly 21,000 miles of track, more than twice as much as there was in the Confederacy. More important, the Southern railroads were only short lines, with major gaps between vital points, which meant that supplies had to be detoured for long distances or transported between railroads by wagons. Also, the track gauge was less uniform in the South than in the North, which prevented the interchange of railroad cars on different lines. The through lines that existed in the South ran close to the sea and were easy targets for enemy bombardment. Finally, when equipment broke down in the South it could not be replaced, since railroad manufacturers were in the North. As the war lengthened, Southern troops suffered severely from the Confederacy's inability to transport supplies, clothing, and ammunition to them.

FINANCES

The South suffered from a lack of adequate banking facilities, and, contrary to its expectations, it was unable to obtain needed loans from Europe. These circumstances, together with a population hostile to taxation, forced the Confederacy to issue paper currency to help pay the cost of the war. All told, it issued one and one-half billion dollars in paper, more than three times the amount of Federal greenbacks in circulation. In addition, because of inadequate Confederate monetary backing, currency diminished much more rapidly in value and to a far greater extent than did currency issued by the Union.

The United States government also had difficulties in underwriting the conflict. However, it eventually obtained the necessary financial resources through the efforts of Lincoln's Secretary of the Treasury, Salmon P. Chase, in spite of personal conflicts Chase had with the North's banking community. When the war began, the Union government was operating with an empty treasury, and the uncertainty of the banking community over the outcome of the conflict led the banks to end all payments in gold and silver. Eventually, however, the administration was able to finance the war in the following ways:

1. *Tariffs.* By 1864, Congress had raised tariff rates to 47 percent, the highest to that date. These duties yielded over 300 million dollars for the Union during the war.
2. *Taxes.* It was difficult for individual Americans to recognize and face the fact that the war was costing over two million dollars a day. Even though rising industrial profits enabled businesses and Northerners in general to pay excise taxes, the revenue was still not enough to support the astronomical costs of the war. In 1861, Congress enacted for the first time an annual personal income tax of 3 percent. Later it was raised to 5 percent on incomes from 600 to 5,000 dollars, and 10 percent on incomes above 5,000 dollars. Together, the personal and excise taxes produced over 350 million dollars in wartime revenue, more taxes than Americans had ever paid before but hardly enough to finance the war effort.
3. *Printing Paper Money.* Congress authorized the printing of over 400 million dollars in paper currency, which was made

legal tender for payment of almost all debts, public and private. Although this currency depreciated because it was not backed by a gold reserve, it did not drop in value as radically as the Confederate currency. Union "greenbacks" dipped to 39 cents in the dark days of the war but had risen by the end of the war to 60 cents.

4. *Bonds.* To avoid too heavy taxation, Chase made Treasury bonds and notes bear the heaviest load of wartime financing covering over two billion dollars by the end of the war, three times the sum of the other sources. People came to look on them as a good investment as well as a way to show their patriotic support of the Northern cause. An important measure affecting the government and the business commu-

nity was the National Bank Act, enacted in 1863. This act created the National Banking System which enabled the government to market its bonds more economically and to aid the financing of the war by issuing still another type of currency, national bank notes. The bankers thought that the government should sell its bonds to them, and then permit them to resell them to the public at a profit. Secretary Chase's response was at first a firm negative, but in order to finance the war, both the government and business realized that they had to compromise. Chase accepted a high interest on some issues, sold bonds below par, and allowed long-term loans. In return, the bankers advanced the huge sums needed by the government.

TWO GOVERNMENTS IN WARTIME

THE CONFEDERATE CONSTITUTION

In February, 1861, shortly before the war began, the delegates to the first convention of the seceding states met in Montgomery, Alabama, to draft a form of government for the new Southern republic. As it turned out, their document did not depart greatly from the federal Constitution, except on a few crucial points. Slavery was specifically protected from government control and the government was empowered to acquire new territories but forbidden to interfere with slavery there too. The Confederate Constitution also declared that it was established by the "people of the Confederate states, each state acting in its sovereign and

independent character." Thus it was clear that the secessionist states were a confederation of sovereign states, not a federation of united ones.

Although the new Constitution protected the sovereignty of the states it denied to the central government any authority to impose tariffs and finance internal improvements. However, nothing was stipulated in the new document about the right of secession. In fact, the new government was described as "permanent."

The structure of government under the Confederate Constitution was very similar to that defined by the United States Constitution. However, the framers did make the following change: the President's term was extended to six years, and he was not permitted re-election. This provision tended to undermine the little political leverage he had in the Congress. However, he did have the power to veto single items in appropriation bills and he could plan a yearly budget. There was also to be a Supreme Court, but none was ever set up.

The Montgomery Constitutional Convention named Jefferson Davis of Mississippi provisional President and Alexander H. Stephens of Georgia provisional Vice-President. Though neither man sought nor really wanted the job, the voters confirmed the convention's choices in the first Confederate election. While Lincoln's task was to preserve a nation, Davis' was to make one.

THE CONFEDERATE PRESIDENT

A native of Kentucky, Jefferson Davis grew up in Mississippi, was graduated from West Point, and served as Franklin Pierce's Secretary of War. Then as a Senator he made a reputation as the spokesman for Southern interests in the Senate. Honest, energetic, and devoted to duty, he could also be unyielding and petty. He constantly changed his mind and his personnel. His slight executive experience and lack of forcefulness made him inadequate for the task of drawing the Confederacy together. Although he made many speeches, they were essentially unemotional and scholarly. Even among those who worked closest to him, he was unable to foster loyalty and he could not bind them into a smoothly functioning governmental organization. He meddled constantly in other officials' responsibilities and, insensitive to public opinion, allowed friends to remain in posts after they could no longer claim public confidence. He played favorites and often switched personnel out of whim or impatience. His military judgment was highly erratic, and he rigidly refused to accept counter advice from his commanders. His energies were largely spent in quarrels with his staff, including the Vice-President, Alexander H. Stephens.

ALEXANDER H. STEPHENS

Stephens was a thorn in Davis' side, even though he remained at his home in Georgia during most of the war. His election to the Vice-Presidency was a gesture designed to induce Southerners undecided about secession to support the Southern cause. He was a scholar who yearned for the solitude of study. Stephens was fanatical about states' rights, but opposed the draft and wartime measures necessary for achieving victory. Most important, he detested President Davis, forever complaining, whenever Davis exercised Presidential power, that he was becoming a despot. From the outset, Stephens was convinced that the Confederacy could never succeed and his pessimism increased during the course of the war.

Jefferson Davis, the Confederate President.

DAVIS' CABINET

Throughout the war, Davis' Cabinet continued to squabble and shift its position on issues with irritating regularity. At best, its members displayed only an average ability. This could be blamed largely on the fact that initially Davis filled each Cabinet post on a geographical basis. As a result, men were named for one post even though they might be better qualified for another. For example, the first Confederate Secretary of State, Robert Toombs, did not have the temperament for diplomacy; he did, however, have great financial expertise, and might have been an excellent Secretary of the Treasury. During the life of the Confederacy, no less than fourteen men filled the six Cabinet posts. There were three Secretaries of State, two Secretaries of the Treasury, four Attorney Generals, and five Secretaries of War. This turnover alone was a critical factor in the Cabinet's lack of effectiveness.

Perhaps the ablest of all Davis' Cabinet members was Judah P. Benjamin, a lawyer from New Orleans who served through the entire war. He was first named Attorney General, then Secretary of War, and finally Secretary of State. He was intelligent and far-sighted, and endeavored in vain to get the Confederacy to face its financial, economic, and diplomatic shortcomings. However, his informed opinions and earnest concern ran counter to popular opinion and only earned for him ceaseless criticism from Southern newspapers and legislators.

THE CONFEDERATE CONGRESS

The Congress was more stable in its membership than the Cabinet, but it was no more responsible. Three distinct Congresses held office for the duration of the Confederacy, and many men served in all three. With each military setback, the Congress became more opposed to wartime legislation and to Davis' program for mobilizing

men and resources. They also became more open in their dislike for each other. In addition to the traditional horsewhips and canes that members of Congress brandished to cut short an unpleasant harangue by a colleague, many now wore guns and bowie knives to the sessions. They were prepared to use them if a member taxed the limits of their patience.

THE UNION PRESIDENT

The times called for a President of sensitivity and strength, a man who would not crumble under the grueling pressures of his office, a military strategist, and a bold head of state. To a great extent Lincoln fulfilled these qualifications. The President was greatly supported by his own belief in the righteousness of the Union cause. He never doubted his mission. Unlike Davis, Lincoln was tolerant, flexible, and politically shrewd. It was said of him, "He had a genius for giving men enough rope to hang themselves." He was a superb conciliator and an accomplished tactician because he understood the foibles of men. Lincoln proved to be infinitely superior to Davis as a war leader, even though the Confederate President was a professional soldier.

LINCOLN AS "DICTATOR"

One of the most controversial aspects of Lincoln's leadership was his extensive use of executive power to bring the war to a satisfactory conclusion. Though he had permitted several months to pass before he acknowledged that the rift between the North and South could only be mended by war, Lincoln lost no time in implementing the decision once it had been made. From April through July, 1861, Congress was not in session, so Lincoln acted on his own as Commander-in-Chief and thereby earned the epithets "despot," "tyrant," and "dictator" for his actions. Until Congress reconvened he made all the decisions alone, stretching executive power further than any other President before him. On April 19, he proclaimed a maritime blockade of the South. Then, on May 3, without any precedent, he issued a call for forty regiments of three-year United States volunteers to supplement the state militia he had called out in April. He further usurped Congressional power by expanding the Navy. He ordered two million dollars for military expenditures, although the Constitution states: "No money shall be drawn from the Treasury, but in consequence of appropriations made by law." Ultimately, however, Congress sanctioned these actions.

More widely opposed than these military and monetary decisions was Lincoln's seeming disregard for the constitutionally protected personal rights of citizens throughout the war. Mail was examined as the federal government pried into private letters and telegrams. It detained anyone whose passport was questionable in any respect. Lincoln gave his military commanders the power to make summary arrests without warrants and, in Lincoln's words, "in extreme necessity," to suspend habeas corpus. Lincoln was known for his clemency, but in September, 1862, a Presidential proclamation attributed insurrection to those who discouraged enlistments, resisted the draft, or committed other disloyal acts. Those accused were to be tried by military court-martial. Under this order, at least fifteen thousand Americans were jailed, and many remained there until the end of the war without ever knowing who their accusers were or what the charges were against them. As Lincoln took firm hold of the reins of government, his use of force increased. When the Sixth Massachusetts Infantry Division passed through Baltimore on its way to Washington, it opened fire on mobs of anti-Union demonstrators, killing both soldiers and civilians. Lincoln sanctioned the act by sending, eight days later, a garrison of federal troops to occupy the city

and arrest all suspects. Many were subsequently tried by military courts.

UNDECIDED BORDER STATES

One of the most pressing problems Lincoln faced after the firing on Fort Sumter was how to keep certain border states within the Union. When the President had called for 75,000 troops on April 15, Virginia, North Carolina, Tennessee, and Arkansas immediately joined the Confederacy. Of all the slave states, only Delaware was openly loyal to the Union cause. Kentucky, Maryland, Missouri, and West Virginia remained undecided. Their leaders were essentially pro-Confederate, their populace was divided, and they refused to furnish troops to the Union Army.

MARYLAND

The people of Maryland were divided in sentiment, but their governor was pro-Union. As a compromise, the governor agreed to send men to defend Washington but not to fight directly in the South.

MISSOURI

Here Union sentiment prevailed even though the governor was a secessionist. When the governor called the state militia into a camp on the edge of St. Louis with the intention of seizing the federal arsenal there, Lincoln authorized a Missouri Congressman to gather together a "home guard" pledged to federal service. The home guard attacked the governor's militia and forced its surrender. As the federal troops marched away, they clashed in a riot with St. Louis civilians, killing many of them. Guerrilla warfare followed in Missouri, and lasted until federal troops achieved a firm victory. The governor and his supporters then proclaimed an independent Missouri government which seceded and operated as a

549

government-in-exile in Texas. Ultimately, about thirty thousand Missourians fought for the South. But more than three times that number enlisted for service with the Union Army.

KENTUCKY

The governor of Kentucky was pro-Confederate, his legislature was Unionist, and the state remained neutral for several months. When the Union Army under Grant took Paducah, Lincoln's patience with the state was rewarded. The Kentucky legislature authorized a military force to drive out a Confederate Army which had taken the town of Columbus. With this state on the side of the North, the Union had secured an additional area through which to transport military supplies.

WEST VIRGINIA

Many West Virginians strongly resented the plantation interests in eastern Virginia and Lincoln capitalized on their anti-Confederate feelings. In June, he ordered twenty thousand volunteers into western Virginia. The presence of these soldiers encouraged the separatist tendencies of the people. In November, the western counties split away and formed the new state of West Virginia, which Congress admitted into the Union in 1863.

With the holding of the border states, the Union secured a major transportation link between the East and the Ohio Valley. West Virginia's Baltimore and Ohio Railroad line became invaluable in mobilizing troops and transporting them and supplies to where they were needed. The transportation superiority thus acquired by the North provided an important military edge.

OPPOSITION TO LINCOLN

The outstanding spokesman for the Democratic Party after the death of Douglas was Horatio Seymour, who won the governorship of New York in 1862 with the slogan "The Constitution as it is and the Union as it was." The Democrats were loyal to the Union and they supported the war, but they strongly objected to both Republican economic policies and, in their view, the autocratic authority with which Lincoln had denied habeas corpus in Maryland and tried civilians under military law. They strove to keep their party organization strong and active in the hope of regaining power in the next election.

COPPERHEADS

There was a faction in the Democratic Party, however, the "Peace Democrats" or Copperheads, who were not in favor of the war. They endeavored to secure a negotiated peace with the South and opposed all war measures, especially if they were connected with anti-slavery proposals. They also feared that the popularity of the Republican prosecution of the war would undermine the Democratic Party. They were led by Ohio Congressman C. L. Vallandigham, and their strength lay primarily in the Middle West. In 1863 they tried, but failed, to elect Vallandigham governor of Ohio. Many of them joined secret peace societies.

As the Confederacy's chances for victory clearly grew dimmer, the Copperheads became more insistent in their demands for a compromise, ignoring the fact that the South was not interested in making concessions. They encouraged Northerners to fight for the South and actively engaged in campaigns to retard Union enlistments.

THE RADICALS

The President also faced criticism from within his own party. Though Lincoln's emphasis on the preservation of the Union as the central issue of the war initially won the support of most Republicans, the

Radicals or abolitionist wing worked to make the end of slavery the main aim of the conflict. They launched an attack on anyone who wanted to restore the Union as it was when the war began. To them, the South had to be subjugated. They also urged the admission of free blacks to the armed forces. Boasting formidable strength in both houses of Congress, their efforts helped to stress the idealism of the Union cause. Their principal spokesmen were Senators Benjamin F. Wade of Ohio, Charles Sumner of Massachusetts, Zachariah Chandler of Michigan, and Representative Thaddeus Stevens of Pennsylvania. Chairman of the powerful Ways and Means Committee, Stevens was the most influential and vindictive of the Radicals. Early in his career he denounced slavery as "a curse, a sham, and a crime." Moreover, he demanded that blacks as well as whites be given suffrage, and he used all his talents unsparingly to exert pressure on the President, who needed the Radicals' vote for re-election.

The Radicals wanted to take control of military policy and to formulate a plan for emancipation of the slaves. To this end they created in December, 1861, the Congressional Committee on the Conduct of the War. Its representatives went so far as to cross-examine military commanders about their battle strategies and to challenge Lincoln's choice of military commanders. The Committee succeeded, however, in uncovering scandals and inefficiency in the military. General McClellan was the chief target of their charge that the war was not prosecuted vigorously enough. Moreover, they attacked him because he was a Democrat. The Committee and its reports had a powerful effect on Northern public opinion.

In addition, the Radicals pushed through Congress a series of confiscation acts which provided for seizure of all property of the enemies of the Union. For example, slaves were to be liberated and used in the North-ern armies. The acts had little effect, but their passage showed the hardening of Northern feeling against slavery. The Radicals were harsh and abusive in their manner but their ideas were basically sound.

CAMPAIGNS

Time was an important factor in Union strategy. If the North was to put an end to the Confederacy, it had to take the offensive and move fast. General Winfield Scott, Supreme Commander of the Union Army, offered a plan to Lincoln designed to blockade the South along its sea and land frontiers. This tactic of containment, called the Anaconda Plan, ultimately might have been effective, but its operation would have been far too slow to bring a swift end to the war and the Confederacy. The people of the North wanted quick and decisive action and the Anaconda plan was hardly the answer.

BULL RUN

Throughout the war the capture of the rival capitals by the opposing armies was a major objective. In preparation for an assault on Richmond, General George B. McClellan cleared western Virginia of Confederate soldiers. In retaliation, General P. G. T. Beauregard brought a Confederate force as far as Manassas, 20 miles from Washington.

Urged on by popular sentiment, thirty-five thousand Union troops under Brigadier General Irvin McDowell were ordered to begin an overland advance against the Confederate position. On July 21, they met twenty-five thousand Confederate troops

MAJOR BATTLES OF THE CIVIL WAR • 1861 TO 1865

under Brigadier General Beauregard at Manassas Junction (Bull Run). The soldiers of both the North and the South were raw recruits who had never seen battle before. Approximately 30 miles from Washington, they faced each other in the first large-scale battle of the war. The Union might have had the advantage had not Confederate General Joseph E. Johnston and his men slipped away from Union troops in the Shenandoah Valley and come to the aid of Beauregard and his men. Against these combined forces, the Union attack failed. Moreover, as McDowell retreated, his army began to fall apart in a wild retreat to Washington. The Confederate troops might have created greater havoc had they been able to pursue McDowell, but their armies, too, had become disorganized.

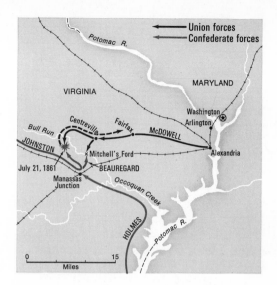

FIRST BATTLE OF BULL RUN

FEDERAL VICTORIES ALONG CONFEDERATE COASTS

Bull Run was a terrible shock to Northern leaders; it helped to convince them that this war was not going to be won by calling out the militia for 90 days. The short-term regiments were sent home. McClellan replaced McDowell as the commander of a new force of three thousand volunteers. McClellan was a good military man and a very patient one. Until the spring of 1862 he devoted his efforts to creating a real fighting force out of "a mere collection of regiments . . . perfectly raw, others dispirited by the recent defeat." When Scott retired in the fall, McClellan was made General-in-Chief of all the Union armies.

While McClellan was training a professional army, the Union in the fall of 1861 launched a land and naval expedition to seal off the Confederate coastline along the Atlantic. These forces took two Confederate forts at Hatteras Inlet, North Carolina.

During the winter, similar amphibian expeditions captured Roanoke Island, which sealed off the North Carolina coastline completely. Subsequently, Union forces moved further down the coastline and occupied Port Royal, South Carolina—a victory that gave them a secure base for their blockading operations. Another expedition that same winter seized Fort Pulaski at the mouth of the Savannah River in Georgia. An important result of the federal victories along the Southern coastline was that they forced the Confederate government at Richmond to disperse some of its troops to the sea frontier to guard against invasion there.

WESTERN CAMPAIGNS

In the West, Union forces tried to secure control of the Mississippi River Valley. Thus, the fighting in 1862 saw the United States Navy playing an important role not only in the operations along the southern coast, but also on the western rivers. While the Union Navy attempted to seal in the

553

Confederacy along the seacoast, in the West it tried to open a path through the Confederacy.

The Union Army in the West was also active. It was commanded by General John C. Frémont, who by the autumn of 1861 had built up a Union base at Cairo, Illinois, and placed Brigadier General Grant in charge. General Henry Wager Halleck replaced Frémont shortly before the Confederate commander of the Mississippi area, Major General Leonidas Polk, occupied Columbus, Kentucky. Grant countered Polk's victory by taking Paducah. The Union troops now occupied northern Kentucky, while the Confederates took the southern

part of the state. In November and December the two lines faced each other. Jefferson Davis sent General A. S. Johnston to take command, but he neglected to give him enough soldiers and Johnston was outnumbered two to one as he faced Grant and General Don Carlos Buell. Meanwhile, General Halleck was at St. Louis clearing Missouri of its Confederate armies.

SEIZURE OF FORTS HENRY AND DONELSON

In the beginning of 1862, Buell's Union forces defeated the Confederates under Crittenden at Mill Springs, Kentucky. Early in February, fifteen thousand Union troops went up the Tennessee River with a flotilla of gunboats under the command of Grant and captured Fort Henry, the Confederate bastion south of the Kentucky-Tennessee line. This victory wiped out Johnston's

WESTERN CAMPAIGNS · 1862

Confederate war strategy was planned by Generals "Stonewall" Jackson (left), A. S. Johnston (center), and Robert E. Lee (right).

access to transportation, and he was forced to retreat to Fort Donelson, Tennessee, on the Cumberland River. Halleck brought his troops to meet those of Grant and the combined forces seized Fort Donelson on February 16, capturing twelve thousand Confederate prisoners.

The Union occupation of Forts Henry and Donelson was a decisive step in the war. The seizures destroyed Johnston's entire defensive line and he was left no choice but to abandon his stronghold at Columbus and regroup his army in northern Mississippi.

THE BATTLE
OF SHILOH CHURCH

Halleck, after the Union successes at Forts Henry and Donelson, persuaded the Administration that he was responsible for them and was rewarded with the combined command of the West, over Grant and Buell. There was no mistaking that the Confederates were now thrown off balance, and Lincoln was extremely anxious to capitalize on that advantage. He sought to move Union troops into eastern Tennessee as soon as possible. Together with McClellan, the President urged Buell to occupy Knoxville, but Buell protested that the terrain was not serviceable enough to keep his army sufficiently supplied. Halleck sided with Buell and their hesitancy cost the Union precious time which the Confederate Generals Johnston and Beauregard utilized quickly to revitalize their forces at Corinth, Mississippi. When Halleck finally did send Grant up the Tennessee River, the Confederates were prepared. Grant, with forty thousand men, established himself at Pittsburg Landing, Tennessee. While he waited there for Buell to join him with twenty-five thousand more men, Johnston advanced with forty-five thousand men, and on April 6 and 7, in the woodlands and pastures near a country meetinghouse known as Shiloh Church, he and Grant fought the most extensive battle to take place on the

Ulysses S. Grant, the temperamental and aggressive Union general.

North American continent up to that time. On the first day Grant was nearly driven into the river because Buell's forces did not arrive in time to counter the first Confederate attack. Not until 24 hours later did Grant receive reinforcements, and only then was he capable of challenging the Confederate forces. The armies battled on for another full day—the South now without the leadership of the courageous Johnston who had died of a leg injury. Finally overwhelmed by Union numbers, the battered Confederate Army under Beauregard was forced to retreat back to Corinth, Mississippi.

In a tactical sense, the Northern victory at Shiloh Church was an extremely narrow one. Both sides suffered severely, with over ten thousand Confederate and over thirteen thousand Union casualties. Strategically, however, the North had gained a decisive advantage and its forces were now in possession of much of Tennessee and

Kentucky. The South had failed in its attempt to prevent a concentration of federal troops in the South, and its own forces were left in a vulnerable defensive position in Tennessee.

FARRAGUT ON THE MISSISSIPPI RIVER

After the battle of Shiloh Church, a powerful Union fleet under Flag Officer David Glasgow Farragut entered the Mississippi River from the Gulf. A native Tennessean, Farragut had spend almost 50 years in the American Navy. He was a brilliant sailor and a determined commander. Under heavy firing from Forts St. Philip and Jackson which had been built to protect the approach to New Orleans, Farragut and his fleet managed to "run the forts." On April 25, 1862, he took possession of New Orleans, the largest city in the Confederacy and its principal seaport. Confederate troops were forced to withdraw and the city was placed under the control of General Benjamin F. Butler, whose army had accompanied Farragut. Butler's occupation of New Orleans was harsh and controversial. He even issued an order stating that any female caught insulting a Union soldier would "be regarded and held liable to be treated as a woman of the town plying her trade." This was considered an unforgivable insult by Southerners, and the act inflamed the entire South.

GAINS ALONG THE MISSISSIPPI TO MEMPHIS

Thus, by the spring of 1862, the Confederacy appeared to be near defeat. Most of the South's Atlantic coast had been sealed off by a Union naval blockade, and Halleck was in northern Mississippi. Following his possession of New Orleans, Butler moved

up the river and seized Baton Rouge. In June, a federal fleet of gunboats annihilated a Confederate fleet at Memphis and the Union was thereby able to take that city and open up all of the upper Mississippi. Halleck came down to Pittsburg Landing, joined his forces with those of Grant, Buell, and General John Pope, and with unflagging persistency finally drove Beauregard out of Corinth, Mississippi. In Virginia, McClellan was preparing to advance against Richmond. The administration was so confident that the war was about to end that it halted all further troop recruitments.

This confidence proved to be premature, however. Federal progress was impeded by a critical lack of centralization in the military command, and the different theaters of the war were not coordinated. McClellan had been removed as Chief of Command and made head of the Army of the Potomac. As his drive on Richmond began, there was no comparable offensive in the West. Just when the Union offensive in the West might have proved decisive, that theater of the war became inactive.

MONITOR v. MERRIMACK

Another major blow to the Union's hopes for a quick victory was the startling introduction of an ironclad warship by the Confederacy. In 1861, the steam frigate *Merrimack* had been scuttled by the Union. The Confederates recovered and rebuilt the vessel in their naval yard at Norfolk, Virginia. They added several innovations to the original ship, including an iron-plate citadel amidship, powerful guns behind it, and an enormous iron ram at the bow. The vessel, now rechristened *Virginia,* was slow and clumsy, but its iron plating made it invulnerable to gunfire. When it first engaged Union warships, it caused a near panic in the North. It sank the Union frigate *Cumberland,* brought the Union *Congress* to surrender, grounded the steamer *Minnesota,* and loomed as a threat of destruction to the entire Union fleet around McClellan's bastion of Fort Monroe on the Virginia coast.

The Union, however, soon countered with an iron-clad vessel of its own—the *Monitor.* It was completed in time to be sent down to Hampton Roads, Virginia, to challenge the *Merrimack* in a wearying battle in March, 1862, which sank neither ship but won a distinct advantage for the Union by ending the fear that the *Merrimack* would be able to take control of Chesapeake Bay. The *Merrimack* remained on the lower James River, however, barring that waterway to federal shipping and preventing McClellan from making greater advances up the peninsula. Eventually, when the Confederates were forced to evacuate Norfolk, they burned the *Merrimack* to keep it from falling into the hands of the North.

Although the battle between the *Monitor* and the *Merrimack* was a stalemate in terms of the progress of the Civil War, it demonstrated to the world that wooden battleships were now worthless in naval warfare and ushered in the modern era of military seamanship. It spurred a race among the naval powers of the Western world to bring their outmoded ships up to date.

McCLELLAN'S PENINSULAR CAMPAIGN

In mid-March of 1862 McClellan moved down the Potomac River and then by steamboat down Chesapeake Bay to the tip of the Virginia peninsula where he took a position at Fort Monroe. McClellan dug in for a siege, gradually and methodically moving up heavy artillery for the anticipated shattering bombardment of the Confederate capital, and by the latter part of May, his forces were less than ten miles from Richmond.

STONEWALL JACKSON IN THE SHENANDOAH VALLEY

McClellan had nearly one hundred thousand men with him in northern Virginia, and he waited there for several thousand more troops, moving overland, to join him. In the interim, however, the South had placed fifteen thousand soldiers in the Shenandoah Valley under the wily military genius, General Thomas J. Jackson, nicknamed "Stonewall" for his unyielding stand at Bull Run. Jackson, with comparatively few troops but shrewd military tactics, began a series of brilliant offensive maneuvers in the Shenandoah Valley. His feints managed to convince the Union Army and the Lincoln administration that he had a much larger force than was actually the case, and he let it be known that with this force he intended no less than the capture of Washington. Alarmed, the President sent a great number of men, forces which McClellan was depending upon for his siege of Richmond, to the Shenandoah Valley to drive out Jackson. The Union forces numbered forty-five thousand, three times those under the Confederate general's command. But in a series of dazzling military tactics, Jackson eluded his pursuers, defeated them in several engagements, and rejoined Lee in the defense of Richmond. The Union Army was left totally confused regarding Jackson's strength, location, and plans.

Meanwhile, General Johnston, who held a defensive position at Yorktown, waited until McClellan had completed his preparations for the siege of Richmond. Then he evacuated Yorktown, and withdrew from the peninsula, pausing only long enough to fight a brutal but inconclusive rear-guard action at Williamsburg on May 5.

When McClellan was practically at the gates of the Confederate capital, Johnston attacked him on May 31 at Seven Pines and Fair Oaks Station. It was a bloody battle for both sides and an indecisive one. Johnston was critically wounded and President

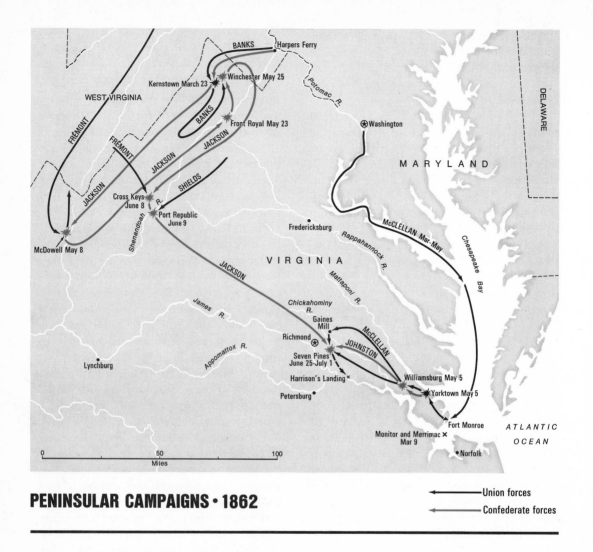

PENINSULAR CAMPAIGNS · 1862

Union forces ←
Confederate forces ←

Davis now appointed Robert E. Lee to command the Army of North Virginia. McClellan held his position, and settled down to await reinforcements and make preparations in his methodical fashion for another siege.

Like the Administration, McClellan had been completely confused by General Jackson, and it was this bewilderment that caused McClellan to change his plans, a move that resulted in the disastrous Seven Days' Battle. To counter Jackson, McClellan positioned twenty-five thousand of his troops north of the Chickahominy River.

Meanwhile, Lee brought Jackson and his men down from the Shenandoah Valley, and by the last week in June Lee had gathered together eighty thousand men. He left 25 percent of his army to confront McClellan's main force and he took the rest north of the Chickahominy to attack a smaller unit of the Union Army. He made another savage assault on the Union the next day at Gaines' Mill, forcing McClellan to retreat. As McClellan fell back, Lee pursued him in a relentless attempt to destroy the Union Army. Brutal engagements were fought during the course of McClellan's retreat, at Savage Station, Glendale, and Malverne Hill. Lee, with Jackson's aid, had seized the initiative for the South and poured on a heavy offensive lasting from June 25 to July 1. By the end of the week, McClellan had withdrawn to a defensive stance at Harrison's Landing on the James River. Though Lee lost twenty thousand men to McClellan's fifteen thousand, the Southern Commander had thwarted the Union's attempt to take Richmond.

MC CLELLAN RECALLED BY LINCOLN

Finally, out of patience with McClellan's finicky and indecisive maneuvers, Lincoln brought Halleck back to Washington as General-in-Chief. He also put Pope in command of a new army composed of the remnants of the Union forces that had tried to destroy Jackson in the Shenandoah Valley.

SECOND BATTLE OF BULL RUN

In the late summer of 1862 Pope led his Union men down the line of the Orange & Alexandria Railroad, intending to catch Lee at Richmond. Pope counted on the assistance of McClellan in this battle, but the Union commanders were unable to work in harmony. McClellan stolidly refused to move on Richmond and at last Halleck was impelled to issue firm orders to him to return his forces to Washington by boat in order to join Pope. As the Union forces were busy regrouping, Lee once more took advantage of the enemy's delay. He detached Stonewall Jackson to meet Pope, while he remained with a contingent of men to watch McClellan. Jackson moved north and pushed Pope into a retreat, finally forcing him to take a stand along the upper Rappahannock River. Then Lee divided his army and took twenty-five thousand men to join Jackson at the rear of Pope's position. On August 28 and 29, Lee battled Pope on the old field of Bull Run.

Spectacularly outfought by Lee, Pope was driven back to his fortifications near Washington. The battle discredited the Northern general, and he too was soon relieved of his command. McClellan was reinstated as commander of the troops around Washington and given the specific assignment of saving the Union capital.

LEE AND JACKSON

Because of the genius of commanders such as Lee and Jackson, the Confederacy, which had been weakening in the spring of 1862, was on the offensive again by autumn.

Born in 1807, the son of General "Light-Horse Harry" Lee of Revolutionary War fame, Lee was the supreme military genius of the South. He was graduated from West Point with an outstanding record, only to begin a rather uneventful career in the

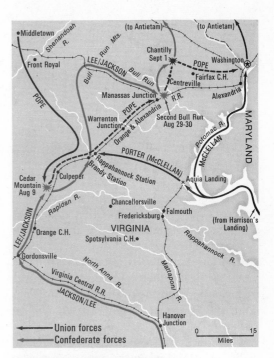

EASTERN CAMPAIGNS: SECOND BATTLE OF BULL RUN

United States Army with the exception of serving as Scott's right-hand man during the Mexican War. When the South seceded, Lee dutifully heeded the call of his native state of Virginia. Duty, in fact, was the ultimate motivating force in Lee's life. He himself said it was "all the pleasure, all the comfort, all the glory we can enjoy in this world."

Physically, Lee was an impressive figure. His jet-black hair had turned completely white by the time of the war, and he had a statuesque military bearing. Lee became a legend in his own time, both because of his personal qualities and his military intelligence and courage. His war accomplishments were formidable, particularly since he was usually outnumbered and undersupplied in battle. He had the capacity for building his army while he fought, and he was bold in forming and carrying out plans.

If anything, his shortcoming was a stubborn tenacity in hopeless situations. A major asset was his keen judgment of character—of the enemy as well as his own men and officers—which served him well in making strategic decisions.

While Robert E. Lee represented the aristocratic cavalier, General Thomas Jonathan Jackson exemplified the Puritan zealot. Stonewall Jackson proved a humble servant to Lee, even though his own talents on the battlefield were equal to those of his chief. Jackson, born in 1824, was a grave and simple man imbued with evangelical piety and a profound belief in the righteousness of the cause for which he fought. His skill in military maneuvers caused the Union many a surprising setback, even though he modestly deprecated his feats out of his supreme devotion and subservience to Lee.

THE TURNING POINT

INFLUENCES ON EUROPEAN POWERS

The blockade of the Southern coast was a recognition on the part of the North that a Southern state existed, even if not independent. The response of the European powers, under international law, to this move by the United States government was to proclaim their neutrality. Led by England, the major powers of Europe did so rather quickly.

The South was convinced that the neutrality of the European nations was the prelude to recognition of the independence of the Confederacy. But Southern hopes of active support from the European powers

were doomed to disappointment. Confederate leaders made the mistake of thinking cotton was more important to the European economy than it actually was. A Southern embargo and then curtailment of the cotton crop to influence British and French policy was a failure. In 1862, when Britain, especially, began to run so low in her cotton supply that men were put out of work, she turned to India and Egypt for replenishment.

Moreover, purchase of wheat and other agricultural products from the North were important to the English economy. Since merchants could continue their trade unimpeded with the North and gradually build up a profitable trade in munitions as well, there was a strong economic reason not to interfere in the conflict. Finally, until the battle of Antietam in the fall of 1862, England thought the South could win on her own; but Northern victories by 1863 ended any prospect that England, or any of the other European powers, would intervene on behalf of the South.

SEIZURE OF MASON AND SLIDELL

The Northern blockade of the South provided the background for an incident that brought the Union to the verge of war with England. In 1861, Jefferson Davis sent two commissioners abroad to plead the Confederate cause in England and France. The representatives, James Mason and John Slidell, were aboard the British steamer *Trent* when it was detained and boarded by a Union officer, Captain Charles Wilkes, commander of the warship *San Jacinto*. Wilkes removed Mason and Slidell from the *Trent* and transported them to the United States, where they were placed in prison. Although Wilkes's act was very popular with the Northern public, he was denounced in London, where the British retaliated by sending troops into Canada. With English forces poised for invasion, the British Foreign Secretary, Lord Russell, sent a caustic note to the United States demanding the release of the prisoners and a public apology. Certainly, Lincoln did not want a war with England but neither did he wish to back down in the face of British threats. Seward composed a clever if not totally logical diplomatic note to London in which he did not admit that the United States was wrong in seizing the men, but provided for their release on technical grounds. Lincoln then released the prisoners and permitted them to complete their journey. The end of the incident, however, did not see any relaxation of tension between the two governments.

FLORIDA AND ALABAMA

Though Britain did not intervene directly in the war, she was a constant irritant to the North by her willingness to build sea raiders for the Confederacy. British law permitted the building of ships in England for belligerents but it forbade these vessels from being "equipped, fitted out, or armed for fighting purposes." British shipbuilders got around these legal restrictions by allowing unarmed ships to leave England for an island port such as Nassau, where they were provided with guns and ammunition which had also been transported there from the British Isles. Several of these "brigands of the sea" plied the Atlantic and preyed on Northern shipping. The most famous and successful of these raiders were the *Alabama* and the *Florida,* built for the Confederacy in Liverpool in 1862. Lincoln protested strongly against this practice through his minister Charles Francis Adams and by threatening to unleash a "flood of privateers" against British sea trade. Finally, the *Florida* and *Alabama* were captured by the Union Navy, but not before they had destroyed over fifteen million dollars in Northern commerce. The British government finally interceded in the spring of 1863 to stop the building of ships with the obvious purpose of destructive attacks on a friendly power. Two heavy ironclad ships, to be equipped with deadly battering rams, were being built for the South. They were seized by the British government under threat of war by the United States.

EMANCIPATION OF THE SLAVES

As the tide of battle turned against him, Lincoln needed the support of the abolitionists to fire his dispirited army with their own ardor for the cause of anti-slavery. He had to turn the war into more than a struggle for the preservation of the Union. He

The meeting of President Lincoln and General McClellan at Antietam in 1862.

had to make it a fight for human freedom, a fight against slavery. If the North was to win, it needed a lofty cause to rally a new wave of support. Moreover, the President was also fearful that without the North's moral commitment to the anti-slavery cause, Europe might throw its power on the side of the South. Lincoln maneuvered cautiously until he believed most areas of Northern opinion would support such a policy. In April the Congress abolished slavery in the District of Columbia and in June it abolished it in the territories. Earlier, Lincoln had urged compensation for owners of freed slaves in the border states. In July, 1862, he informed Congress that he would issue a general proclamation of emancipation. This, in effect, would then commit the federal government to a total policy of emancipation. Seward, however, urged Lincoln not to issue the proclamation until the North had achieved a military victory. The President agreed to wait, and soon after, victory came.

BATTLE OF ANTIETAM

In September of 1862, a few weeks after the second Battle of Bull Run, Robert E. Lee led his army toward Pennsylvania for an invasion. He crossed the Potomac River, reached Frederick, Maryland, and halted. He knew that McClellan and the Army of the Potomac were coming up from Washington. But close by there was a garrison of ten thousand federal troops at Harpers Ferry. With his usual boldness, Lee divided his forces. He occupied Hagerstown, Maryland, and the South Mountain passes with half his men, and he sent the other half under Stonewall Jackson to take Harpers Ferry. The plan might have worked except that a copy of Lee's orders was lost and fell into the hands of McClellan who, by now, was flanked by the two halves of Lee's army. He moved quickly to force Lee into combat, but not in time to save Harpers

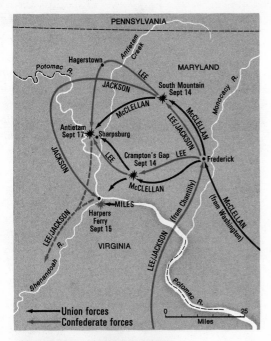

EASTERN CAMPAIGNS: BATTLE OF ANTIETAM

Ferry, which was captured with its entire garrison by Stonewall Jackson. Meanwhile, McClellan met Lee on September 17 on the high ground above Antietam Creek near Sharpsburg, Maryland, in what was perhaps the bloodiest single day's battle of the entire war. McClellan had almost eighty-seven thousand men, and he lost nearly thirteen thousand. Lee lost at least 25 percent of his forty thousand troops. The fight was a draw tactically, but strategically a Confederate defeat. Lee's plans to invade the North were shattered and he was forced to withdraw back into Virginia.

EMANCIPATION PROCLAMATION

With the Battle of Antietam, Lincoln had the victory he needed. Acting within his war powers, Lincoln issued a prelimi-

nary emancipation proclamation on September 22, 1862, together with the announcement that a final proclamation would be forthcoming on January 1, 1863, "unless the Confederacy surrendered."

The initial significance of the proclamation was limited. Lincoln demanded that all the seceded states return to the Union by January, 1863, or face the following consequences: ". . . And by the virtue of the power and for the purpose aforesaid, I do order and declare that all persons held as slaves within said designated States and parts of States are, and henceforward shall be, free; and that the Executive Government of the United States, including the military and naval authorities hereof, will recognize and maintain the freedom of said persons . . ." With these words the President asserted freedom for slaves in areas not under the control of the federal government. However, nothing was said about emancipation of slaves in those border states remaining in the Union. The proclamation was foremost a military measure to undermine the Confederacy. It was in line with the Confiscation Acts of Congress and the War Department directive of August, 1862, instructing the federal military governor of the South Carolina Sea Islands to raise five regiments of black troops. Its larger implications also were inescapable. At last the Administration was fighting both to preserve and restore the Union and to abolish slave labor.

Following the Emancipation Proclamation, the United States armed forces began to use freed blacks with the President's encouragement. A May, 1863, directive from the War Department called for the raising of black troops all over the country. Soon there were fourteen such regiments in the field and by the fall of 1864, 150,000 blacks were in the Union forces, most of them from the South. Many Northern black men hesitated to join the army since they were barred from becoming officers and kept segregated, but some agreed with Frederick

Emancipation Proclamation Defended

" *Thank God for what is already done, and let us all take heart as we go forward to uphold this great edict! For myself, I accept the Proclamation without note or comment. It is enough for me, that, in the exercise of the War Power, it strikes at the origin and mainspring of this Rebellion; for I have never concealed the conviction that it matters little where we strike Slavery, provided only that we strike sincerely and in earnest. So is it all connected, that the whole must suffer with every part, . . .* "

—*Charles Sumner*

An 1865 photograph of "Company E, Fourth U. S. Colored Infantry." About one hundred-fifty thousand blacks served in the Union Army during the Civil War.

Emancipation Proclamation Attacked

" *. . . The President has at last weakly yielded to the "pressure" put upon him about which he has so bitterly complained, and issued his proclamation of negro emancipation . . . he has no constitutional power to issue this proclamation—none whatever. . . .*

Nobody need argue with us that he has the power under military law. Military law does not destroy the fundamental civil law. In war, as in peace, the Constitution is "the supreme law of the land."

The government, then, by the act of the President, is in rebellion and the war is reduced to a contest for subjugation. . . .

—**The Chicago Times**

Douglass, who argued that wearing the American uniform was a step toward real citizenship.

The Confederacy had passed its high water mark. After the Battle of Antietam and the Emancipation Proclamation, the Southern tide began to recede in the West as well as the East. From then on, it remained on the defensive, and would never again come as close to victory as it had at the beginning of the autumn of 1862.

As long as reunification remained the single issue, there existed the possibility of a negotiated peace between the North and the South. Antietam and the Emancipation Proclamation, however, made it inevitable that the war would have to be fought to a finish. The South would not negotiate the end of slavery; as a result the country was committed to an exhausting all-out war.

LINCOLN REPLACES COMMANDERS

As the first step toward the final defeat of the South, Lincoln made several changes in military commanders. Disgusted by McClellan's sluggishness and his failure to exploit his victories, Lincoln replaced him with Major General Ambrose E. Burnside, who, ironically, had refused the post twice before on the grounds that he was unqualified. McClellan was also in disfavor with many in the North because of his opposition to the Emancipation Proclamation. Lincoln also removed two of McClellan's favorite aides, Major General Porter, who commanded the Fifth Army Corps, and Major General Buell, a friend of McClellan's who shared his sentiments about slavery. Buell was replaced in the West by Major General William S. Rosecrans.

LEE REPULSES BURNSIDE

Lincoln expected his new commanders to gain a victory without delay, but circum-

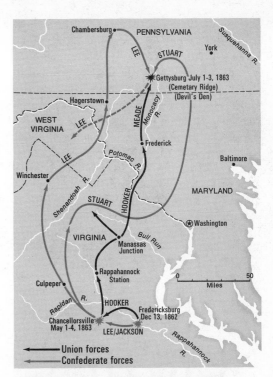

BATTLES AT FREDERICKSBURG, CHANCELLORSVILLE, GETTYSBURG

stances worked against an immediate success. For example, Burnside decided to undertake an unprecedented winter campaign, and he crossed the Rappahannock River on December 13, 1862, to advance on Richmond by way of Fredericksburg, Virginia. He met Lee and flung his armies at him in a series of hopeless, bloody attacks. Lee repulsed him with ease, inflicting twelve thousand Union casualties in the process. Lincoln then replaced Burnside, at the General's own request, with "Fighting Joe" Hooker, a favorite of the Radicals.

WESTERN CAMPAIGNS IN 1863

In the West, too, Union victories were delayed. In Tennessee, Rosecrans advanced against Confederate General Bragg, and from December 30 to January 2 their armies fought ferociously around Stones River, 30 miles southeast of Nashville. Bragg was forced to retreat, but he left Rosecrans' army so mangled and disorganized that it could not resume an offensive for several months. Grant, too, was stymied in his attempt to capture Vicksburg, Mississippi. Marching south from the Corinth area to Oxford, Mississippi, he planned to attack Vicksburg from the east, while a subsidiary army under Major General William T. Sherman went down the Mississippi River with a convoy of gunboats and at-

tacked the Confederate defenses south of the Yazoo River, just north of Vicksburg. Union strategy was to trap Confederate General John C. Pemberton between two military forces. The plan was upset when Confederate forces under General Van Dorn slipped behind Grant's lines and captured his base of supplies at Holly Springs. In addition, a Confederate cavalry detachment under Major General Nathan B. Forrest joined Van Dorn's troops to immobilize Grant. Finally, Sherman reached the mouth of the Yazoo and attacked, but Pemberton swiftly drove him off. For the moment, the campaign against Vicksburg was stalled.

THE NORTHERN VICTORY

In January, 1863, Grant reorganized his men on the Mississippi River just above Vicksburg and prepared to launch a new campaign. Rosecrans, meanwhile, was busy refitting his army at Murfreesboro, and Hooker made ready for a new offensive in the East with his Army of the Potomac.

JACKSON v. HOOKER

Hooker planned to attack Lee from the rear by taking the Union army across the Rappahannock and Rapidan rivers a few miles above Fredericksburg. He moved against Lee at the end of April, with twice as many men under his command as the Confederate general. Leaving some of his men to hold a position on the river bank opposite Fredericksburg, he took the rest upstream toward Lee's left and rear at Chancellorsville. He sent his cavalry on a

long sweep to slice Lee's supply lines, believing that this plan would certainly compel the Confederate general to draw back. Instead, Lee attacked and ordered Stonewall Jackson and his men to take Hooker's right flank. The first three days of May saw savage engagements at Chancellorsville and Fredericksburg that totally defeated Hooker, a spectacular victory for the Confederacy, dimmed only by the death of Stonewall Jackson.

LEE AND MEADE AT GETTYSBURG

Heartened by the success of Chancellorsville, Davis and Lee decided on one more attempt to invade the North, mindful that a victory in Pennsylvania would put the major cities of Philadelphia and Washington in direct peril. Also, Lee's army badly needed the food in the barns and warehouses of Pennsylvania. Finally, he needed to capture a Northern city to counter what he believed would be the inevitable fall of Vicksburg; it was hoped that such a victory might also tip sentiment toward peace among Northerners weary of war.

Early in June, Lee crossed the Blue Ridge and headed for the Potomac. Hooker followed him, constantly maneuvering to keep between the capital and Lee. On June 28, Lee's entire army was in Pennsylvania and the Army of the Potomac was positioned near Frederick, Maryland. At this crucial hour, Hooker requested additional men and supplies from the Administration, but Lincoln denied them because Hooker's actions at Chancellorsville had shown that he did not know how to use his resources. Angered and in disfavor, Hooker resigned, and his place was taken by General George Gordon Meade. On July 1, 1863, Lee and Meade clashed at Gettysburg, Pennsylvania, beginning the largest battle of the war.

For three days the Confederate Army piled assault after assault on Union forces. Losses on both sides were enormous. Although the Union Army was on the brink of defeat, Lee's mutilated army no longer had the strength to deliver the final blow. The climax came on the third day when Lee rammed against the Union center column with fifteen thousand men under Major General George Pickett. The Union was able to repel the attack, destroying Lee's capacity for further offensive action. The next day, the Confederates began their retreat to Virginia and by the middle of July they were back in the lower part of the Shenandoah Valley.

In the Battle of Gettysburg, more than seven thousand men were killed on both sides—more than 25 percent of all the men engaged in combat. Although Meade was unable to pursue Lee and make military capital of the opportunity presented to him, his encounter with Lee showed decisively that the South had insufficient resources to strike an effective counterblow. With this battle, the final Confederate gamble to invade the North had failed. News of the rout, which arrived in the North the same time as a bulletin announcing Grant's capture of Vicksburg, provided a tremendous lift to Union morale.

GRANT TAKES VICKSBURG

Unable to attack Vicksburg from the river, Grant marched his army down the western bank and crossed the Mississippi about 30 miles below Vicksburg. Confederate forces were on their way to rescue Pemberton, but at the state capital at Jackson, Grant drove them off in a battle at Champion's Hill. Then the Union general drove Pemberton and his men into the lines of Vicksburg, cutting him off from the rest of the Confederacy. By the end of May, Grant had Vicksburg in his grip, and by July 4, 1863, he had captured both the fortress and its defending armies.

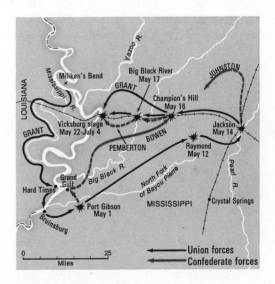

GRANT'S VICKSBURG CAMPAIGN

Grant's capture of Vicksburg was even more significant than the Union victory at Gettysburg. Pemberton was forced to surrender his thirty thousand men, and the federal government now had control of the Mississippi River all the way to the Gulf. The Southern states west of the Mississippi River were also detached from the rest of the Confederacy. The effect of the successes at Vicksburg and Gettysburg was to reduce the South to defensive warfare.

ROSECRANS AND BRAGG AT CHICKAMAUGA

After the fall of Vicksburg, General Rosecrans moved his Army of the Cumberland against Braxton Bragg's Army of Tennessee. He forced Bragg to retreat to northern Georgia, but there Bragg regrouped and delivered a counterattack against Rosecrans at Chickamauga on September 19 and 20. The Army of the Cumberland was routed and had to withdraw to Chattanooga where General Rosecrans was replaced by Major General George H. Thomas. For his part, Bragg entrenched himself near the Cumberland forces, believing that lack of supplies would ultimately force General Thomas to surrender.

GRANT BECOMES SUPREME COMMANDER

Events moved quickly. On November 24 and 25, in the twin battles of Lookout Mountain and Mississippi Ridge, Grant drove Bragg's army back into Georgia, and assumed firm federal control of Tennessee. In March, 1864, the President appointed Grant as supreme commander of all the Union Armies, with Halleck as chief-of-staff, and sent him to Chattanooga with reinforcements.

The selection of Grant at this time was an appropriate and popular choice, for the

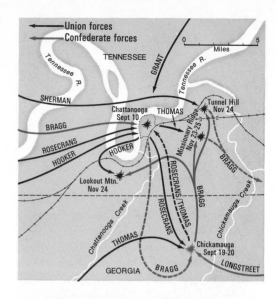

FIGHTING AROUND CHATTANOOGA

General had demonstrated at Vicksburg that Northern resources, applied relentlessly, would bring victory. Almost recklessly, Grant plowed through the kind of obstacles that had stopped the more cautious McClellan. He was a solidifying force, both militarily and politically. With Grant, the President had found a general who would bring the war to a finish in one year.

GRANT AND HIS GENERALS

Unlike Robert E. Lee, his Confederate counterpart, Ulysses S. Grant did not possess a long and distinguished military career. He was born in 1822 in Ohio, the son of a tanner. He was a poor student at West Point. Though he had served capably under Scott and Taylor in the Mexican War, he was a Northerner, and Scott rarely favored with advancement any military officer not from the South. In addition to resenting his failure to be promoted, Grant was bored by the inactivity of the peacetime army. When he took to drink and received a reprimand for it, he simply presented his resignation. He then earned a precarious living in a variety of civilian occupations. At the outset of the war, he was working in his family's leather store at Galena, Illinois. In June, 1861, he entered the Illinois militia as a colonel. Several months later he was raised to the rank of brigadier general.

Grant was short, bearded, squarely built, and often slovenly in appearance. Temperamentally, he was shy, with sluggish movements, and a somewhat forlorn look. One first-hand observer said of him, "He habitually wears an expression as if he had determined to drive his head through a brick wall." Grant might have been careless in his military etiquette and appearance, but there was no mistaking his courage and his eagerness to take responsibility. He would plunge into battle fearlessly and demand the same of his men. He was so zealous that he was sometimes accused of having a callous disregard for human life. But his enormous determination and aggressiveness helped to fire the Union armies and eventually led them to victory after a series of defeats. He was not well schooled in the art of war as carried on in earlier eras. Careful maneuvering for position, a strategy which aided the South in the early phases of the war, gave way before Grant's use of the North's superior weapons, numbers, and transportation facilities. With ferocity he struck the enemy, using all the military power available to him.

Grant's chief of staff was John A. Rawlins. Rawlins was not a West Point graduate but a lawyer from Galena, Illinois. He was intelligent and supplied the ambition and political polish that Grant lacked. He was indeed Grant's closest military associate. Said one commentator: "If you hit Rawlins on the head, you knock out Grant's brains."

The greatest of all Grant's generals was William Tecumseh Sherman of Ohio. Sherman was tall and gaunt, with an impressive military bearing enhanced by tousled red hair and piercing eyes. He had a reputation for eccentricity, but actually he was cool and quick-thinking, and a tough fighter. If Sherman lacked anything, it was strong ambition. He had little interest in army political intrigues, and when he was asked to run on the 1884 political ticket he replied, "I will not accept if nominated and will not serve if elected."

Grant also obtained excellent support from his other generals, Philip A. Sheridan, a clever fighter and an aggressive leader, the magnetic James B. McPherson, and the rather phlegmatic and slow-moving George H. Thomas.

FINAL OFFENSIVES

Grant was a commander willing to pay any price for a victory which might spare the country another year of war. In his final offensives he battered the enemy relentlessly and without mercy.

GRANT AND LEE NEAR RAPIDAN RIVER

Grant's objective was the defeat of the two major Confederate forces: the Army of Northern Virginia under Lee and the Army of Tennessee under General Joseph E. Johnston. Setting up his headquarters with Meade's Army of the Potomac, Grant led them across the Rapidan River on May 4 to strike at Lee.

The armies of Grant and Lee fought without a halt for more than a month near the Rapidan River. Their engagements, among the hardest fought in American history, included the battles of the Wilderness, Spotsylvania Court House, and Cold Harbor. Grant seemed to be alone in his conviction that a general assault against the Confederate line at Cold Harbor was feasible; his subordinates felt it would be almost hopeless. Quietly, before battle, they pinned on their blouses scraps of paper bearing their names, and then they charged the enemy. In less than ten minutes five thousand Union troops were dead. Doggedly, Grant refused to ask for a temporary truce in order to care for the wounded. They lay suffering for days until they finally died where they had fallen. In his campaign, Grant had lost fifty-five thousand men, and the repercussions were widespread in the North. Politicians and newspapers assailed the commander as "Butcher" Grant.

At the same time, Major General William T. Sherman, now in charge of the Union forces in the West, led a strong force against Johnston in the vicinity of Dalton, Georgia. Sherman took Dalton, but also with tremendous casualties.

SHERMAN'S MARCH TO SAVANNAH

After the re-election of Lincoln in 1864, Sherman was ordered to march across Georgia to Savannah. Leaving Dalton, he took Resaca and Kennesaw Mountain. In July, Davis replaced Johnston with General Hood, and after six weeks of battle against Hood, Sherman took Atlanta. As he moved across the state toward Savannah, Sherman devastated everything that lay in his path. His harsh measures caused widespread civilian misery and contributed to the buildup of a lasting hatred for Sherman and the North. Savannah fell on December 20, and

by the beginning of 1865 the Confederacy consisted of little more than the Carolinas and the southern half of Virginia.

In February of 1865, Sherman moved across the Carolinas. Confederate resources were so low by this time that General Johnston remarked: "I can do no more than annoy him." Union forces moved into North Carolina and by the end of March were in Goldsboro, 160 miles south of Richmond.

THE WAR ENDS

The days of the Confederacy were numbered. From Tennessee, a Union cavalry corps moved down, captured Montgomery and destroyed the munitions works at Selma, Alabama, on April 2, 1865. An am-

General William T. Sherman devastated everything in his path in his "March of Death" through Georgia.

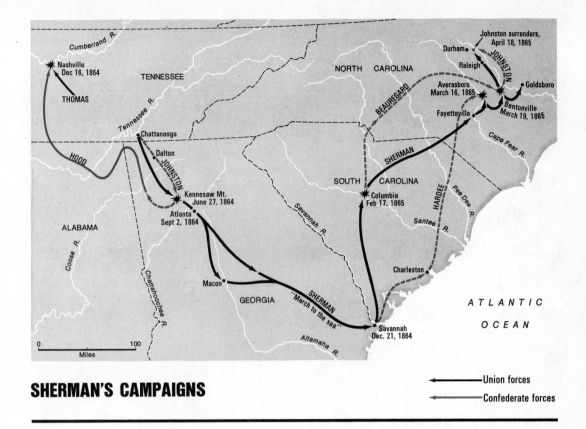

SHERMAN'S CAMPAIGNS

Union forces
Confederate forces

phibious expedition sealed off Wilmington, North Carolina, the last seaport held by the South. In desperation, Lee attacked Grant's position at Petersburg to disable his opponent so that his own forces could break away and consolidate with those of Johnston. But on April 1, 1865, Grant's troops fragmented Lee's right flank in a battle at Five Forks, and Lee had no choice but to evacuate Petersburg and Richmond.

With the occupation of Richmond by the North, the final hour for the South had come. Most Southerners no longer cared to continue the struggle. The price was too high for a lost cause. Loyalty to Robert E. Lee seemed to be the only unifying force left in the Confederacy. One of Lee's staff is said to have remarked. "Country be damned! There is no Country. There has been no Country, general, for a year or more. You are the Country for these men.

They have fought for you. If you demand the sacrifice, there are still thousands of us who would die for you." Lee did not demand the sacrifice.

On April 9, in the McLean farmhouse at Appomattox Court House in southern Virginia, General Lee surrendered his Army to Grant, and the war virtually ended. The two generals arranged the terms of surrender: Confederate soldiers were to be paroled, public property and war materials surrendered, officers were allowed to keep their side arms, and all men who owned a horse or a mule could "keep them to work their little farms."

Johnston surrendered to Sherman a few days later. By early June, Davis and a few Confederate officials had been arrested in Georgia and imprisoned in Fort Monroe. The remaining vestiges of Southern resistance had been obliterated.

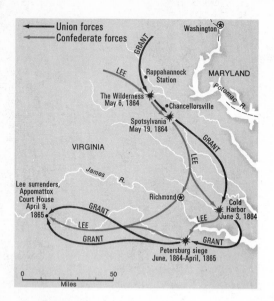

Union forces
Confederate forces

Washington

MARYLAND

Rappahannock
Station

The Wilderness
May 6, 1864

Chancellorsville

Spotsylvania
May 19, 1864

VIRGINIA

James R.

Lee surrenders,
Appomattox
Court House
April 9,
1865

Richmond

Cold
Harbor
June 3, 1864

Petersburg siege
June, 1864-April, 1865

0   50
      Miles

APPOMATTOX • 1865

ELECTION OF 1864

As the conflict came to a close, Northern politics reflected the tensions that had built up during the war. In the war-weary Union, Lincoln was able to please hardly anyone. He had offended the Radicals by his discharge of their favorite, General Frémont, and moderates by the Emancipation Proclamation. Union war casualties had upset everyone.

The nation's economy was in a boom period, stimulated by government purchases of war materials. Crops were good, prices were high, and there was a general shortage of labor. The General Price Index had risen 79 percent since 1860. However, the boom carried with it several drawbacks. The Northern economy had been industrialized before the war began and would probably have progressed without it. The stepped-up pace brought on by war tended to disturb the normal flow of investments and prevent certain desirable innovations in industry. There was much war profiteering and speculation, highly resented by many businessmen and all farmers. A manpower shortage on the farms impeded agricultural growth, causing a rise in food costs for the industrial workers that was not equaled by increased wages. Thousands looked for solutions to their problems in the peace movements, whose strength was growing. On the other hand, many antislavery Republicans were adamantly against any suggestion of compromise with the South.

REPUBLICAN PLATFORM

By 1864, the Republicans had adopted the name "Union" Party. Though there were certainly members who balked, Lincoln managed to control his party. He had doubts that he would be reelected, but did not doubt that he was the best-qualified person to meet the current crises. Coolly and shrewdly he devoted himself to obtaining the nomination, using as his primary weapon skillful control of the patronage.

He won renomination unanimously at the regular convention in Baltimore in June. His control of the convention and the elimination of Radical influence was insured by the nomination of Andrew Johnson, of Tennessee, a member of the pro-war faction of the Democratic Party. The platform of the Union Party denounced slavery and declared it a cause of the war, issued a call for a united front in the pursuit of the war, promised protection for black soldiers, and encouraged immigration.

572

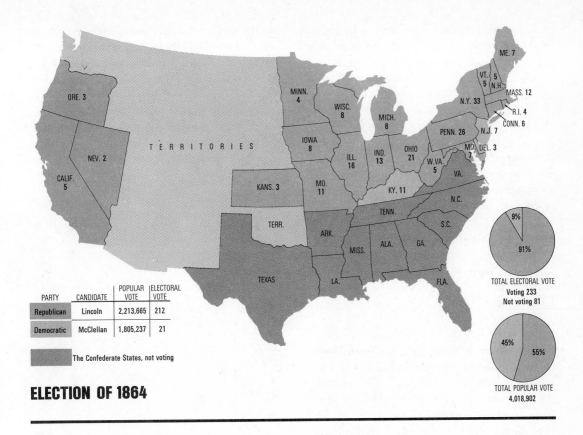

ORE. 3

NEV. 2

CALIF. 5

T E R R I T O R I E S

MINN. 4

WISC. 8

IOWA 8

ILL. 16

MICH. 8

IND. 13

OHIO 21

PENN. 26

ME. 7

VT. 5 / N.H. 5

MASS. 12

N.Y. 33

R.I. 4

CONN. 6

N.J. 7

DEL. 3

MO. 7

W.VA. 5

VA.

KANS. 3

MO. 11

KY. 11

N.C.

TERR.

ARK.

TENN.

S.C.

TEXAS

MISS.

ALA.

GA.

LA.

FLA.

PARTY	CANDIDATE	POPULAR VOTE	ELECTORAL VOTE
Republican	Lincoln	2,213,665	212
Democratic	McClellan	1,805,237	21

The Confederate States, not voting

9%

91%

TOTAL ELECTORAL VOTE
Voting 233
Not voting 81

45%

55%

TOTAL POPULAR VOTE
4,018,902

ELECTION OF 1864

DEMOCRATIC PLATFORM

Sentiment for peace in the country was becoming so pronounced that the Democrats put off their convention during the summer of 1864 while C. L. Vallandigham led demonstrations for peace in the Middle West. It soon became apparent, however, that only through force would the South accept a peace based on the abolition of slavery as well as the restoration of the Union. To please the regular Democrats, the party nominated General McClellan, the popular war hero, in their August convention. To appease the peace faction, it adopted a platform which condemned the war as a failure and called for an armistice that would permit peace negotiations based on a restored Union of all the states. The

Democratic platform excluded emancipation as a condition for peace and assumed that peace would be easily negotiable. McClellan repudiated the platform, however, and ran as a war leader, attacking the Lincoln administration for inefficiency and charging that it failed to prosecute the war successfully.

LINCOLN WINS

"This morning as for some days past, it seems probable that this Administration will not be re-elected." These words were uttered by President Lincoln on August 23. Although the peace movement had no real champion and the Radicals no effective candidate, his view was pessimistic. With characteristic firmness, Lincoln had no intention, however, of withdrawing from the race, and his prospects soon looked brighter. With the victory of General Sherman over General Hood and the occupation of Atlanta, spirits in the North were raised, and the tide began to turn toward the Republicans. The Radicals now joined with the President. In November Lincoln won, polling 52 percent of the popular vote of the dismembered Union and carrying the electoral college by 212 to 21. Congress also went again to the Republicans. Lincoln's re-election assured that the war would not end until the Union was restored and slavery was abolished.

THE ASSASSINATION OF LINCOLN

On April 9, 1865, with the surrender of Lee to Grant at Appomattox Court House in Virginia, the restoration of the Union was no longer in doubt. But the triumph for the North was shadowed by the tragedy that struck on Good Friday, April 14. On that night, while attending a performance of *Our American Cousin* at Ford's Theatre in Washington, Lincoln was shot by the actor John Wilkes Booth, a pro-slavery fanatic. Booth entered the Presidential box crying *"Sic Semper Tyrannis! The South is avenged!"* and shot Lincoln through the head. He then sprang from the box to the stage of the theater and escaped. Lincoln was quickly carried across the street from the theater to a private home where he died the next morning at seven-thirty. A few days later, Booth was overtaken and shot in a barn in Virginia.

Lincoln's assassination greatly diminished hopes for a true reconciliation of the North with the South. It not only deprived the nation of a great leader, but took from the South a compassionate friend. His instructions to Grant had been to arrange surrender "on the most liberal and honorable terms." In his Second Inaugural Address, he had called on the North to act "with malice towards none, with charity for all." General Robert E. Lee expressed his own feelings for Lincoln and sense of loss when hit by the impact of the assassination. At first unable to believe the news, Lee sorrowfully told a visitor several days after that tragic Good Friday that he had "surrendered as much to Lincoln's goodness as to Grant's artillery."

Readings

GENERAL WORKS

Catton, Bruce, *Centennial History of the War*, Vols. I–III. Garden City, N.Y.: Doubleday, 1961–1965—The three volumes are: *The Coming Fury, Terrible Swift Sword,* and *Never Call Retreat.* Catton emphasizes the military aspects of the Civil War.

Cole, Arthur C., *The Irrepressible Conflict 1860–1865.* New York: Reprint House International, 1960—An older history of the Civil War period, written in the Beardian tradition stressing economic and social conflict between North and South.

Donald, David, ed., *Why the North Won the Civil War.* New York: Macmillan, 1960—A collection of five brief essays on different aspects of the Civil War comparing Northern and Southern positions on such matters as military ability, economic strength, and public spirit.

Eaton, Clement, *A History of the Southern Confederacy.* New York: Macmillan, 1954 —A narrative history of the Confederacy which includes material on Southern life during the Civil War as well as on the Confederate government.

Kirwan, Albert D., ed., *The Confederacy.* New York: Meridian, 1959—A history of the Confederacy which uses government documents as well as other material to tell the story.

Leech, Margaret, *Reveille in Washington, 1860–1865.* New York: Grosset & Dunlap, 1941—A history of life in Washington, D.C., during the Civil War, when the city was frequently on the fringe of heavy fighting.

Nevins, Allan, *The War for the Union*, Vols. I–III. New York: Scribner's, 1959–1970— The newest and most comprehensive history of the Civil War by a leading contemporary historian. The three volumes include: *The Improvised War 1861–1862, War Becomes Revolution 1862–1863,* and *The Organized War to Victory 1864–1865.*

Nichols, Roy F., *The Stakes of Power.* New York: Hill & Wang, 1961—A brief history of the United States from 1845 to 1877.

Randall, James G., and David Donald, *The Civil War and Reconstruction.* Boston: Heath, 1961—A standard history of the period, written from a basically revisionist standpoint, sympathetic to the compromisers and hostile to the abolitionists and radical reconstructionists.

Roland, Charles P., *The Confederacy.* Chicago: University of Chicago Press, 1960— A short description of the Confederacy's efforts to win independence and uphold the values and institutions of an agricultural, slaveholding society.

Williams, Kenneth P., *Lincoln Finds a General: A Military History of the Civil War*, Vols. I–IV. New York: Macmillan, 1949— Fundamentally a study in military leadership, this work centers on the inability of Lincoln to find a successful general before Ulysses S. Grant.

SPECIAL STUDIES

Andreano, Ralph, ed., *The Economic Impact of the American Civil War.* Cambridge, Mass.: Schenkman, 1967—A collection of articles and comments relevant to the controversy over whether the Civil War helped or hindered industrial development in the United States.

Current, Richard N., *The Lincoln Nobody Knows.* New York: McGraw-Hill, 1958— Essays on several aspects of Lincoln's life and career, such as his family life, his ability as a military leader, and speculations on what he might have done had he not been assassinated.

Donald, David, *Lincoln Reconsidered.* New York: Random House, 1956—A collection of essays on Lincoln and the political structure of the Civil War era which attempts to apply social science techniques to a variety of historical questions.

Franklin, John H., *The Emancipation Proclamation*. Garden City, N.Y.: Doubleday, 1963—Franklin sets the Emancipation Proclamation in the context of struggles within the Republican Party and Lincoln's Cabinet and of the complex diplomatic situation of 1862 to 1863.

Frederickson, George M., *The Inner Civil War: Northern Intellectuals and the Crisis of the Union*. New York: Harper & Row, 1965—Frederickson argues that, with the exception of Nathaniel Hawthorne, the leading intellectual figures of the North rallied wholeheartedly to the Union cause, either because they viewed the war as a battle to perfect American democracy or because they hoped that wartime discipline would put order into a disorderly society.

McPherson, James M., *The Struggle for Equality: Abolitionists and the Negro in the Civil War and Reconstruction*. Princeton, N.J.: Princeton University Press, 1964—McPherson defends the abolitionists against the charge that they forgot the black people after Emancipation and shows active cooperation between many abolitionists and black groups in the struggle for civil rights.

Owsley, Frank L., *King Cotton Diplomacy*. Chicago: University of Chicago Press, 1959—A detailed history of the Confederacy's efforts to win diplomatic support and recognition from Europe. Owsley interprets the British refusal to recognize the Confederacy in economic terms.

Randall, James G., *Constitutional Problems under Lincoln*. Urbana: University of Illinois Press, 1964—A classic treatment of the legal and constitutional issues which arose from Lincoln's conduct of the Civil War. Randall discusses such issues as the suspension of writs of habeas corpus, relations with Congress, and the constitutional theories of reconstruction.

Wiley, Bell I., *The Life of Johnny Reb*. Indianapolis, Ind.: Bobbs-Merrill, 1943—Through exploration of diaries, letters, and other documentation, Wiley describes the difficult life of the Confederate soldier.

Wiley, Bell I., *The Life of Billy Yank*. Indianapolis, Ind.: Bobbs-Merrill, 1952—Complementing his book on Southern soldiers' life, Wiley describes the activities and feelings of Union soldiers during the Civil War.

Williams, T. Harry., *Lincoln and the Radicals*. Madison: University of Wisconsin Press, 1941—Williams contends that Lincoln was continually harassed by a small faction of Republican Radicals who were responsible after Lincoln's death for the harsh reign of Congressional Reconstruction.

PRIMARY SOURCES

Chestnut, Mary B., *A Diary from Dixie*. Boston: Houghton Mifflin, 1949—A diary of a Southern plantation owner's wife which reveals hatred of the slave system combined with deep racism, and contempt for the Northern way of life. A graphic account of the Civil War's devastation.

Commager, Henry S., ed., *The Blue and the Gray: The Story of the Civil War as Told by Participants*, Vols. I–II. Indianapolis, Ind.: Bobbs-Merrill, 1950—Incorporating approximately 450 narratives, Commager has compiled a history of the Civil War as seen from the perspective of the men who fought it.

Grant, Ulysses S., *The Personal Memoirs of U. S. Grant*. New York: Grosset & Dunlap, 1962—A valuable source for the study of political and military life during the Civil War.

McPherson, James M. ed., *The Negro's Civil War*. New York: Pantheon, 1965—A documentary history of the Civil War as seen by black people, revealing the important political and military roles blacks achieved despite racism in the North and South.

Melville, Herman, *Battle-Pieces and Other Aspects of the War*. New York: T. Yoseloff, 1963—A collection of poems, mostly reflecting on the Civil War and what Melville felt were its effects on American life and character.

Stephens, Alexander H., *Recollections*. New York: Doubleday, 1910—Stephens, essentially a Southern moderate, found himself serving as Vice-President of the Confederacy. His memoirs are a valuable source for understanding the Confederate government.

BIOGRAPHIES

Dowdey, Clifford, *Lee*. Boston: Little, Brown, 1965—A one-volume biography of the Confederate general which emphasizes his spiritual and intellectual life more than his military career.

Duberman, Martin, *Charles Francis Adams*. Boston: Houghton Mifflin, 1961—A sympathetic biography of the abolitionist son of John Quincy Adams who served as Minister in London for the United States during the Civil War.

Randall, James G., *Lincoln, the President: Springfield to Gettysburg*, Vols. I–IV. New York: Dodd, Mead, 1946–1955—In this massive work, Randall praises Lincoln for his qualities of moderate and well-balanced liberalism.

Sandburg, Carl, *Abraham Lincoln: The War Years*, Vols. I–IV. New York: Harcourt, Brace, 1939—An impressionistic literary biography of Lincoln by one of America's most famous poets.

Strode, Hudson, *Jefferson Davis*, Vols. I–IV. New York: Harcourt, Brace, 1955–1966—An enthusiastically favorable biography of the Mississippi politician who became the President of the Confederacy.

FICTION

Cable, George W., *Dr. Sevier*. Upper Saddle River, N.J.: Gregg, 1970—A romantic novel of life in New Orleans during the Civil War by an author who became a leading Southern advocate of equal rights for blacks.

DeForest, John, *Miss Ravenal's Conversion*. New York: Holt, Rinehart & Winston, 1955—Probably the first realistic novel to portray life in the South during the Civil War. DeForest drew on his own experiences.

Lancaster, Bruce, *For Us The Living*. New York: Stokes, 1940—An historical novel based on the early life of Abraham Lincoln and on pioneer life in Kentucky and Indiana.

4

EMERGENCE OF INDUSTRIAL AMERICA

16

Reconstructing the Union

Under the pressure of federal bayonets, urged on by the misdirected sympathies of the world in behalf of the enslaved African, the people of Mississippi have abolished the institution of slavery. . . . We must now meet the question as it is, and not as we would like to have it. . . . The negro is free, whether we

like it or not. . . . To be free, however, does not make him a citizen, or entitle him to social or political equality with the white man. But the constitution and justice do entitle him to protection and security in his person and property, both real and personal.

—The Black Code of Mississippi

Richmond, Virginia, after the Civil War. Richmond was demolished by Robert E. Lee's Confederate troops before they were forced to evacuate the city by a threatening Union Army.

The Civil War had a number of far-reaching results. It prevented the destruction of the Union and vindicated American nationalistic pride, and it laid to rest in all but theory the old concepts of nullification and secession. As a nation founded on popular rule, the United States had survived a great trial, a fact which gave encouragement to those who were working for democratic reforms abroad, especially in England. The war abolished the institution of slavery, and in so doing caused drastic political and economic changes in the South. At the same time the dominant influence in the national government of the Southern planter aristocracy was decisively removed. It was replaced by the Republican Party, dominated by Northern agricultural and business interests. These groups immediately used their power to enact higher tariffs, a national banking system, free homestead legislation, and federal support for a transcontinental railroad.

In the aftermath of four years of conflict, the nation was beset by many severe problems and a host of lingering animosities. The most obvious conflict arose out of the determination of a vengeful North to punish an unrepentant South. Less apparent was the struggle that followed between the triumphant Republican Party and the slowly reviving Democratic Party in the South. Much of the legislation of the period which appeared to be punishment meted out by a Northern Congress was in fact part of a deliberate attempt by the Republicans to maintain their control over the federal government by disenfranchising Southern Democrats. Finally, a major battle also was waged between the Executive and Legislative branches in Washington over control of national policy. During the Civil War, Abraham Lincoln had greatly strengthened the Presidency by his assertion of prerogatives in carrying out wartime measures without Congressional consent. After his assassination, Congress was determined to restore its control of the government. The Reconstruction period ushered in an era of Congressional supremacy reminiscent of the days of Madison and Monroe, an era which lasted until the early twentieth century.

In all these power moves—between North and South, Republicans and Democrats, and the President and Congress—poor Southerners, and blacks in particular, were the pawns. The black man, after being politically exploited for more than a decade after the war, was ultimately abandoned by his protectors in the North. Left to itself, the new South built a society based on segregation of the races along social, economic, and political lines.

THE ISSUE OF RECONSTRUCTION

When the Civil War ended, the South was in ruins. Entire sections of Charleston, Atlanta, Mobile, Vicksburg, and Galveston, lay in ashes. One Northern traveler who visited Columbia, South Carolina, in September, 1865, described it as "a wilderness of ruins. . . . Not a store, office, or shop escaped; and for a distance of three-fourths

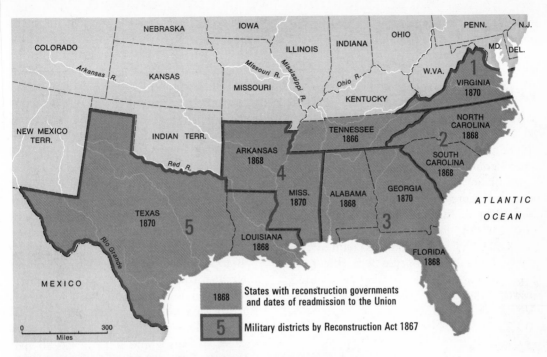

RECONSTRUCTION OF THE SOUTH · 1865 TO 1877

The devastation of Columbia, South Carolina by Sherman's troops.

of a mile on each of twelve streets there was not a building left." A returned Atlantan said, when he saw the destruction to his home town, "Hell has laid her egg, and right here it hatched."

The countryside often was hurt as severely as the cities. Sherman's armies, marching through Georgia and South Carolina, left behind a charred wasteland. The Tennessee and Shenandoah valleys were both devastated. War had made seed scarce and during the strife two-thirds of the livestock had run away or been butchered.

Transportation had always been inadequate in the South; now it was in a shambles. Sherman's armies had heated rails along major train lines and twisted them around trees like corkscrews. Five tracks once led into Columbia; now the nearest functioning line was almost 30 miles away. Many roads were impassable, but aside from this, travel was impeded by burned bridges and the scarcity of mules, horses, and wagons. River transportation was also slowed to a standstill. Wharves had been torn up or burned, and channels had filled up with

583

mud and become unnavigable. Few steamboats survived undamaged. In some areas, highwaymen made cross-country travel dangerous.

EFFECTS OF EMANCIPATION

The South's greatest economic loss resulted from the freeing of the slaves. Emancipation destroyed a 2.5 billion dollar investment represented by some 3.5 million blacks. In addition there was also a loss of one billion dollars in capital. All Southern banks had closed and the credit system was paralyzed. So hopeless were the prospects that thousands of cotton planters moved to the Far West or emigrated to Mexico or Brazil.

Many former slaves crowded into shack towns built by the Union armies. These shack towns, called "contraband camps," were so unhealthy that in 1865 alone an estimated hundred thousand blacks died from starvation and disease. Conditions became so bad that in the summer of that year twenty thousand freedmen drifted into Washington, D.C., demanding food and shelter. The Freedmen's Bureau, founded on March 3, 1865, and administered under the War Department, tried to bring relief by distributing food rations in the South between 1865 and 1869, most of them to starving black people.

Blacks hoped to receive farm land of their own from Union officers, and rumors circulated among them that the Freedmen's Bureau was planning to confiscate all land over 200 acres belonging to white property owners and distribute it to blacks in parcels of 40 acres. "Forty acres and a mule" became a popular slogan among ex-slaves,

Ex-slaves arriving at a " contraband camp." The camps served as homes for 3.5 million blacks.

but nothing came of the plan. The federal government's failure to provide blacks with farms of their own ultimately undercut the political program of the Republican-dominated Congress and had far-reaching economic effects in the South. The idea of confiscating private property belonging to one group and distributing it to another had a momentary emotional appeal in the North, but the centuries-old American belief that a man's property was almost as valuable as his life and liberty prevented widespread acceptance of such a program as a means of reorganizing the Southern economy.

Congress, however, did open some 46 million acres of federal lands in the South to black homesteaders, but the land for the most part was so undesirable that few took advantage of the offer.

After the war, many ex-slaves rebelled against working for their former masters. As a consequence, the old plantations suffered a serious manpower shortage. Southern attempts to promote the settlement of Northern farm laborers, European immigrants, and even Chinese coolies, all failed.

LINCOLN'S PLAN

Even before the war's end, Lincoln tried to plan for an orderly reconstruction of the Union. He and his successor, Andrew Johnson, each drew up plans for Reconstruction which were much more lenient than those eventually put into effect by Congress.

On December 8, 1863, as Arkansas was on the verge of capitulating to Union forces, Lincoln issued his "Proclamation of Amnesty and Reconstruction" which came to be known as the "10 percent plan." The plan stipulated that:

1. All top officers of the Confederacy and civil officials would be permanently excluded from politics as punishment for their disloyalty to the Union.

2. When the citizens of a rebellious state had sworn to obey all acts of Congress and all Presidential proclamations abolishing slavery, they would be granted amnesty and would be given back all of their property except, of course, their slaves.
3. When 10 percent of a state's *electorate* (not population) had taken this oath and sworn allegiance to the Union, that state could write a new constitution, elect new state officers and Congressmen, and return to its accustomed position in the Union.

Lincoln's plan was magnanimous in that it reflected his genuine desire to restore harmony. It was also a deliberate effort to lure states from the Confederacy and back into the Union. Since approval by only 10 percent of the electorate was required to effect such a move, each state needed only a relatively small group of Unionists to start a new state government.

OPPOSITION TO RADICALS

The Radicals, a highly vocal and influential minority of the Republican Party in Congress, had many objections to Lincoln's plan. First, they thought Lincoln was far too lenient toward the South. The leader of the Radicals in the House, Thaddeus Stevens of Pennsylvania, felt that the South had to be punished. A long-time advocate of racial equality, he asserted that "the whole fabric of southern society *must* be changed and never can it be done if this opportunity is lost."

Stevens and other Radicals wanted a Reconstruction plan that would be under Congressional rather than Presidential control, treat Southern states as "conquered provinces" devoid of all Constitutional rights rather than as rebellious states that had remained legally within the Union, ensure the continuing freedom of ex-slaves and turn blacks into property owners and voters, and confiscate all large Southern plantations and sell the land. It was pro-

585

posed that profits from the land sale would reduce the Union debt; pay pensions to Union soldiers, and their widows and children; and compensate Northern property owners for the losses they had incurred during the war. Some of the confiscated lands would go to the freedmen.

Even moderate Republicans in Congress agreed that Reconstruction should be a Congressional rather than a Presidential responsibility. The President had assumed certain extraordinary powers during the Civil War, but now it was time for Congress to reassert itself. Certainly, they felt, the President should play some role in readmitting the rebel states; for instance, he would have the power to pardon Confederate soldiers and civilians for their treasonous actions against the Union. Otherwise, most Congressmen believed the President's role should be minimal.

A second point on which the Radicals disagreed with Lincoln was whether to treat Southern states as conquered provinces or as merely rebellious governments that had never legally left the Union. Both Lincoln and Andrew Johnson argued that Southern states had never technically left the Union, for the Union could not be dissolved by the states. The Radicals contended that the Confederate states had indeed seceded and had thereby committed legal suicide. The South was no longer a part of the United States, and Congress could determine the conditions under which the former states would re-enter the Union as if they were new territories petitioning for statehood. Lincoln regarded their viewpoint as "a merely pernicious abstraction" and said: "Let us all join in doing the acts necessary to restoring the proper practical relations between these states and the Union; and each forever after innocently indulge his own opinion whether, in doing the acts, he brought the states from without into the Union, or only gave them proper assistance, they never having been out of it."

The third, and perhaps major, point of disagreement between the Radicals and Lincoln concerned the status of black people. Lincoln had never been an ardent abolitionist, for although he freed the slaves, he doubted whether blacks and whites could ever live peacefully side by side on equal terms.

Unlike Lincoln, the Radicals believed that the main purpose of the Civil War had been to free black people and to elevate their status. Real freedom, the Radicals believed, included the freedom to vote and hold property. Their insistence upon giving blacks the vote was not entirely disinterested. Now that the slaves were freed, the black population would be counted as equal to the white population in terms of representation. The Constitution had provided that five slaves would be counted as equal to three white men in determining how many Representatives each state would have in Congress; however, now that slavery was ended, each black adult male could be counted. Accordingly, Southern states would have more Representatives in the House than ever before, and therefore more power in the federal government. If blacks were denied the vote, most of the new Southern Representatives would undoubtedly be Democrats; on the other hand, if blacks were allowed to vote, many, perhaps the majority, of the Southern Representatives would be Republicans. In order to preserve their control over Congress, the Radical Republicans believed that the freedmen had to become voters.

The final point of disagreement between the President and the Radicals concerned the holding of property. Lincoln simply wanted to return all farms and plantations seized by Union forces to their prewar owners. As noted, radicals like Stevens and Senator Charles Sumner of Massachusetts, however, wanted to carve up all large estates into small farms and either give them to blacks, sell them in order to reduce the national debt, or sell them and give the profits as pensions or reparations to Northern citizens. As Stevens said, "The Southern States have been despotisms, not governments of the people. It is impossible that any practical equality of rights can exist where a few thousand men monopolize the whole landed property. The larger the number of small proprietors the more safe and stable the government. . . . This [confiscation] must be done even though it drive her nobility into exile. If they go, all the better. . . . It is far easier and more beneficial to exile 70,000 proud, bloated, and defiant rebels, than to expatriate four millions of laborers, native to the soil and loyal to the Government. . . ."

THE WADE-DAVIS BILL

The Radicals offered their own alternative to Lincoln's Reconstruction plan on July 4, 1864, the last day of the Congressional session. Called the Wade-Davis bill, this Congressional plan demanded that a majority of each state's citizens swear that they would always be loyal to the Union and it limited political participation to those who always had been loyal to the Union. The Wade-Davis bill also demanded that the new state constitutions, worked out by delegates chosen by those eligible to vote, recognize the abolition of slavery, repudiate all debts contracted by the Confederacy, and deny the vote to all ex-Confederate officials. The South understandably preferred Lincoln's plan since the Wade-Davis bill would have made reconstruction of the South by Southerners impossible. Lincoln let this bill, which was passed by both houses, die by a pocket veto. The Radical leaders were so angry over Lincoln's action that they issued the Wade-Davis Manifesto in August, 1864: "The President, by preventing this bill from becoming a law, holds the electoral votes of the Rebel States at the dictation of his personal ambition. . . . A more studied outrage on the legislative authority of the people has never been perpetrated." This emotional outburst clearly underlined the growing conflict between the Congress and the President.

In February, 1865, Congress refused to admit members from Louisiana, which had completed reconstruction under Lincoln's plan. The next month it passed the Thirteenth Amendment to the United States Constitution, declaring an end to slavery forever in the United States. Many Radicals feared that if Southern states gained control of Congress they would reinstate slavery; thus, instead of a law, they preferred an amendment to the Constitution because it would be harder to revoke. Also, an amendment would prevent the possibility of a Supreme Court decision declaring the abolition of slavery unconstitutional. Lincoln was careful to assure the South when he proposed his 10 percent plan that the national government would not interfere with state control of the freedmen, that Congress could repeal its antislavery measures, and that the Supreme Court could nullify the Emancipation Proclamation. The Radicals maintained that should slavery be reinstated, the war would have been fought in vain. The Thirteenth Amendment was designed, therefore, to exclude this possibility; and, regardless of personal reservations, when it came up for a vote in Congress, Lincoln used his influence to see that it was passed.

ANDREW JOHNSON AND RECONSTRUCTION

Lincoln's assassination on April 15, 1865, brought Andrew Johnson to the Presidency. At first the Radicals were misled into thinking that Johnson would be an ally. "Johnson, we have faith in you," said Ben Wade, one of the Radical authors of the Wade-Davis bill. "By the gods, there will be no trouble now in running this government."

Johnson seemed to sympathize with the Radicals because he also detested the rich planters of the South and wanted to punish them severely for their "crimes" against the Union. The origin of Johnson's dislike, however, was quite different from that of

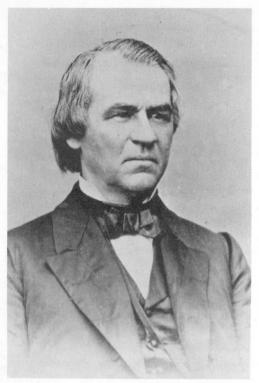

Andrew Johnson served as President for three stormy years following Lincoln's assassination. Johnson, a Southern Democrat and a staunch Unionist, was at odds with the Radical Republicans who held an overwhelming majority in both the House and the Senate.

Thaddeus Stevens and the rest of the Radical leadership. The Radicals were Northerners and abolitionists who had had little personal contact with Southerners. Their hostility was based on their hatred of slavery and the economic and political attitudes of the South. For years Southern Democrats had blocked legislation in Congress that favored Northern industry. Such legislation, including a high protective tariff, a national banking system, and government subsidies for building a transcontinental railroad, was passed only after secession had removed Southern Congressmen from the federal government.

Johnson, on the other hand, was a Southerner himself, but his poverty-stricken back-

ground was the basis of his hatred of the rich slaveowner. His rage against the planters made him sound like a Radical, but in fact he had little in common with the Radical Republicans. Johnson wasted no love on the black man and had no interest in promoting racial equality. Nor was Johnson willing, like the Radicals, to let Congress dictate the terms on which Southern states could return to the Union. Johnson, like most other Southerners, firmly believed in states' rights. In his opinion, Congress did not possess the Constitutional right to interfere with the domestic problems of the states, such as the status of ex-slaves. Congress stood for the triumphant doctrine of national supremacy while Johnson was still championing the declining cause of states' rights.

JOHNSON'S BACKGROUND

Johnson was born in Raleigh, North Carolina, in 1808, of humbler beginnings than those of any preceding President. At the age of ten he was apprenticed to a tailor. He never attended school, although he did teach himself to read. Years later, his wife instructed him in writing and simple arithmetic. At sixteen, he moved to Tennessee where he eventually served in the Tennessee legislature as a Jacksonian Democrat, in 1835. In 1843 he was sent by Tennessee to the House of Representatives. After 10 years as a Representative and two terms as the Governor of Tennessee, he was elected to the Senate in 1857. In December, 1860, he avowed his support of the Union and continued to sit in the Senate even after his state had seceded. In 1862, when Tennessee fell to Union troops, Lincoln made Johnson military governor of that state.

Johnson was among those members of his party, known as War Democrats, who remained loyal to the Union. In 1864 he was rewarded for his loyalty by being named as Lincoln's running mate. Lincoln's Union Party felt that a War Democrat would bring in more votes than a Republican candidate. A month after Lincoln's Inauguration Johnson became President of the United States.

Johnson was deeply at odds with the Union Party leadership in Congress. He was a Democrat; they were Republicans. He represented the interests of the small farmer; they represented the interests of Northern industry. He was a champion of states' rights; they were nationalists. Whereas the Radicals were intensely interested in elevating the freedmen, Johnson had once declared: "I wish to God every head of a farm in the United States had one slave to take the drudgery and menial service off his family."

THE PROCLAMATION OF AMNESTY

In the spring of 1865 Congress was not in session, nor would it be until the following December. Johnson, quickly altering his friendly attitude toward the harsh Radical outlook, hoped to take advantage of the Congressional recess to push through his own plan of Reconstruction, one much like Lincoln's.

First, Johnson recognized the new state governments established by Lincoln, under the 10 percent plan, in Louisiana, Arkansas, Tennessee, and Virginia. Then, to the remaining Southern states Johnson issued a Proclamation of Amnesty on May 29, 1865. Under its provisions, the citizens of each state, presumably a majority, would have

to take a loyalty oath to the Union. State constitutional conventions were directed to repeal their ordinances of secession, abolish slavery, and repudiate all Confederate war debts. Johnson hoped that educated blacks would be given the vote, but he left the question entirely up to the individual states. He excluded from the general pardon a larger number of former Confederates than Lincoln had specified. For example, he specifically refused pardon to all property owners who owned more than twenty thousand dollars' worth of land and goods. This provision singled out Johnson's old enemies—the big plantation owners. They could regain their full rights and privileges as American citizens only by petitioning the President himself. Scores of planters did in fact come to the White House and beg for forgiveness, and seeing these once-proud aristocrats humbled, Johnson promptly pardoned most of them.

By December, 1865, when Congress reconvened, every Confederate state except Texas had organized new state governments, accepted the Thirteenth Amendment abolishing slavery, and elected new Senators and Representatives. Johnson recommended these new state governments to Congress, not realizing that he was laying the groundwork for a titanic battle, not just over the reconstruction of the South but for control of all federal government policy by the Congress rather than the President.

CONGRESSIONAL RECONSTRUCTION

The Radicals were angered by the Southern choice of Congressmen, because among the Southern contingent were many top-ranking former Confederate officials. There

was also evidence that the South was not only reluctant to reincorporate itself emotionally into the Union but had some reluctance to repudiate the ordinances of

589

secession and the Confederate debt. Disturbed Republican Congressional leaders were also alarmed by Johnson's actions because they hampered their plans for reconstructing the South in a way that would insure Republican control of the area.

Many of the new Southern Congressmen, including Alexander H. Stephens, had actually opposed secession and only reluctantly sided with the Confederacy. Radicals were in no mood, however, to make careful distinctions. They feared their own loss of power in Congress, and it distressed them to think that their loss would be the gain of unrepentant rebels. A song was circulating in the South against the Union: "I'm glad I fought against her, I only wish we'd won; And I ain't asked any pardon for anything I've done; And I don't want no pardon for what I was or am; I won't be reconstructed and I don't give a damn." This song struck Northerners as the arrogant outcry of a still defiant South.

THE BLACK CODES

Radicals protested not only against the election of Southern Confederates to Congress, but also against mounting evidence that the South was determined to keep the freedmen in a position of social, economic, and political inferiority. Under the so-called Black Codes, harsh regulations were compiled by Southern states to regulate the labor and restrict the freedom of movement of black people. These laws were frequently based on parts of former slave codes, prewar vagrancy laws, and laws regulating the status of free blacks before 1860.

Blacks were prohibited in most states from jobs in which they might compete with white craftsmen, merchants, or factory workers. Thus, almost everywhere, blacks were forced by economic circumstances to return to farm labor. In South Carolina a black was prohibited from any work other than as a farm laborer or a servant. In

Mississippi, he could farm only for a white, since the law forbade blacks to own or rent land except in a town. Mississippi's laws prompted the Chicago *Tribune* to editorialize: "We tell the white men of Mississippi that the men of the North will convert the state of Mississippi into a frog pond before they will allow any such laws to disgrace one foot of soil in which the bones of our soldiers sleep and over which the flag of freedom waves." In one Louisiana parish, black workers could not leave the premises of their employer without a written permit after ten o'clock, nor could blacks sell, barter, or exchange any merchandise. Frequently black workers had to sign a contract at the beginning of the year to work until the following January for one employer, and if such an employee left his job, he was not paid his back wages. Legally, the Black Codes conferred some privileges upon blacks: now they could own property under certain conditions, make contracts, sue or be sued, and marry. But they could not vote, hold office, testify against a white man in court, serve on juries, or bear arms. They could be educated, but only in segregated schools. In many states public transportation and theaters were also segregated. While much of Northern public opinion was outraged by the unrepentant attitude of the South as exemplified by these regulations, the North conveniently overlooked the fact that in only five Northern states could blacks vote, and between 1865 and 1868 eight Northern states had rejected extending the franchise to black people.

The most oppressive measures were the vagrancy laws. In Georgia, unemployed blacks were rounded up and set to work on state chain gangs or hired out to white farmers. The 1865 Mississippi Vagrancy Statute read: "All freemen, free negroes and mulattoes in this State, over the age of eighteen years, found on the second Monday in January, 1866 or thereafter, with no lawful employment or business, or found unlawfully assembling themselves together, either in the day or night time, and all white persons so assembling themselves with freedmen, free negroes or mulattoes . . . on terms of equality, or living in adultery or fornication with a freed woman, free negro or mulatto, shall be deemed vagrants." As in Georgia, such "vagrants" could be hired out to white employers, their wages going to pay their fines. As the Radical Republican Carl Schurz observed, Southerners thought that "the blacks at large belong to the whites at large."

THE FREEDMEN'S BUREAU

As its first step in subduing the unrepentant South, Congress refused to seat the newly elected Southern delegations. A Joint Committee of Fifteen, six Senators and nine Representatives, checked the qualifications of the Southern delegates and rejected them. By turning down the South's new Senators and Representatives, Congress rejected both Lincoln's and Johnson's plans for Reconstruction. Now the entire planning process had to begin again, but this time it would be executed under stern Congressional observation and direction.

In early 1866 Congress also passed a bill to continue the Freedmen's Bureau, broadening its powers so that, besides dispensing relief to starving ex-slaves, it would also supervise labor relations and contracts. Whenever blacks felt they were being cheated or mistreated by employers, they could appeal to the Freedmen's Bureau and arrange to have any dispute reviewed in an administrative court.

Although the bill to renew the Freedmen's Bureau passed both houses of Congress, Johnson vetoed it on February, 1866, on the grounds that to continue the agency in peacetime would be to invade the right of Southern states to supervise their own internal affairs. Congress was not immediately able to muster the necessary two-thirds vote to override the President's veto.

Balked in their first attempt to protect black people, Radicals now drew up a civil rights bill, a measure that would guarantee citizenship to all blacks, and prohibit states from legally discriminating against citizens on the grounds of color or race. Johnson vetoed this bill as well. Not content with merely overturning the civil rights bill, the President unwisely embarked upon a campaign of crude insults aimed at the Radical leadership. Now even the Republican moderates in Congress, who had formerly opposed many Radical measures, realized that they had to present a united Congressional front in order to protect their prerogatives against "Sir Veto," as they called the President. This new solidarity in Congress permitted the civil rights bill to be passed over the President's veto by the necessary two-thirds vote. A few months later, in July, 1866, the Freedmen's Bureau bill was revived and passed over a second Presidential veto.

THE FOURTEENTH AMENDMENT

In order to secure the principles of the civil rights bill by making them part of the Constitution—thus guarding them against future Congressional revocation or annulment by the Supreme Court—the Radicals now drew up the Fourteenth Amendment. More than any other measure, this amendment embodied the Congressional plan for Reconstruction. First, it held that anyone born or naturalized in the United States was a citizen of the nation, the first time that United States citizenship had ever been clearly defined. Second, the amendment stipulated that no state could deny to any person within its jurisdiction the equal protection of the laws or abridge his privileges and immunities or deprive any person of life, liberty or property, without due process of law. The amendment did *not* confer the vote on every citizen, but it attempted to force states to do so by establishing that if a state denied suffrage to any part of its citizens, that state's representation would be proportionally reduced in the House of Representatives and in the electoral college.

In order to prevent Southern states from electing Confederate officials to Congress, the amendment disqualified from federal office all people who had once pledged loyalty to the Constitution and then later served under the Confederacy. These men could hold office only if pardoned by two-thirds of each house of Congress. Finally, the amendment invalidated the Confederacy's war debts.

While the amendment was being framed, Susan B. Anthony and other agitators for women's rights fought to have the indirect suffrage provisions extended not only to black male adults but also to adult women. Radical leaders turned a deaf ear to these demands. Even those Radicals who sympathized with the women's suffrage campaign felt that the chances of getting the amendment ratified would be greatly lessened if a clause relating to women were added.

JOHNSON'S OPPOSITION

Congress had rejected Johnson's almost painless plan of Reconstruction and now demanded that the South accept the Fourteenth Amendment to regain representation in Congress. However, the Fourteenth Amendment was still a fairly lenient arrangement. Most of the Confederate leaders would be barred from public office under the amendment, but it did not force the South to give the vote to blacks even though such an omission would theoretically reduce Southern representation. It also made no provision for the economic independence of the individual freedman. Johnson, had he been wise, would have recommended the amendment to the South; under its terms the Southern states would finally have been reconstructed. The President, however, was adamant against any compromise with the Radicals.

Before the Congressional elections of 1866, he made a campaign tour stumping for opponents of the amendment. The President made a fool of himself personally and demeaned his high office with his intemperate remarks and blustering language. Radical hecklers called Johnson "Judas" and accused him unjustly of heavy drinking. Forced to choose between the President and the Radicals, the American public decided to "stand by Congress." After the elections 42 Republicans and only 11 Democrats sat in the Senate. In the House, 143 Republicans overwhelmingly outnumbered 49 Democrats. Now the Radicals had the necessary two-thirds majority in both houses to allow them to pass any legislation they proposed over a Presidential veto. The President's "Swing Around the Circle," as he had called his speaking tour, had been a failure, and his reputation was further damaged when violent race riots broke out in Memphis and New Orleans. The riots in fact occurred when Radicals sought to register literate blacks as voters, but blame was placed on Johnson's failure to support the Fourteenth Amendment.

When the Fourteenth Amendment was submitted for ratification, Johnson, undaunted, encouraged the South to reject it. There were eleven former Confederate states, and rejection by ten would be sufficient to defeat the amendment. Although many far-sighted Southern leaders entreated their states to ratify, only Tennessee actually did so, and was thereupon readmitted into the Union. The other ten Southern states rejected the amendment, as did Kentucky and Delaware. Rather than disqualify the former leaders of the Confederacy from holding office, the South was willing to risk arousing the vengeance of a solidly Republican Congress.

THE 1867–1868 RECONSTRUCTION ACTS

Southern stubbornness was answered by a militant policy. Congress was ready to demonstrate its mood for vengeance. As Ohio Congressman James A. Garfield declared in February, 1867: "The last one of the sinful ten has at last with contempt and scorn flung back into our teeth the magnanimous offer of a generous nation. It is now our turn to act."

First, Congress declared all the existing state governments in the South illegal. The First Reconstruction Act, passed over the President's veto on March 2, 1867, organized the ten Southern states into five military districts. A major general governed each district with the aid of the armed forces. Each general registered all the voters in his district, black and white. Exact figures are not known, but about 150,000 whites were probably disenfranchised for having served under the Confederacy. The result of the registration was that in the five military districts, about 703,000 blacks to 627,000 whites were given the franchise.

One of the chief goals of military Reconstruction was government-supervised voter registration. Under the Constitution, Congress could not interfere with state voting procedures, but it could interfere in "conquered provinces." Only by treating the ten former Confederate states as enemy territory could Congress exclude former Confederate officials from voting rolls and include blacks. However, only the three Southern states of Louisiana, Alabama, and Arkansas actually enforced disenfranchisement of whites for very long, and in May, 1872, an Amnesty Act returned voting and office-holding rights to all but 750 white Southerners.

Once each major general determined the voting lists, the electorate chose members of constitutional conventions and new state governments. Each new state constitution had to provide for black suffrage and each new state government had to ratify the Fourteenth Amendment. Once the amendment was ratified by the requisite number of states, Congress would accept their new constitutions and readmit them into the Union. Military rule ended more or less

at the same time the state was readmitted. By June, 1868, all states except Mississippi, Texas, and Virginia had fulfilled the terms of reconstruction and were able to participate in the Presidential election that year.

THE IMPEACHMENT TRIAL

Military reconstruction of the South was an extreme measure on the part of Congress, and the Radicals, realizing this, feared that either the Supreme Court or the President might try to overturn it. In 1866 the Supreme Court in *Ex parte Milligan* ruled that if military rule "is continued *after* the courts are reinstated, it is a gross usurpation of power." Since civil courts had already reopened in the South before military reconstruction was imposed, a case challenging the constitutionality of the First Reconstruction Act soon appeared on the Supreme Court docket. The Supreme Court justices, however, feared the Radical leadership in Congress, and anxious to avoid a battle, refused to review the constitutionality of the controversial measures after the Congress passed a law over Presidential veto repealing Supreme Court jurisdiction in such cases.

Having thoroughly intimidated the Supreme Court, Congress next set about to reduce the President's powers. In March, 1867, Congress passed two measures that took away two Presidential prerogatives—the right to remove his own Cabinet members and the right to remove army officers under his command. The Tenure of Office Act forbade the President to remove without Senate approval any federal official, including Cabinet members, originally appointed with the consent of the Senate. This act was specifically designed to protect the job of the only remaining Radical in Johnson's Cabinet, Secretary of War Edwin M. Stanton. The Command of the Army Act forbade the President to issue orders to the Army except through General Grant.

593

The Act further provided that Grant was to live in Washington and could not be fired or ordered to move elsewhere except by consent of the Senate.

To test the constitutionality of the Tenure of Office Act, Johnson removed Stanton from office on February 21, 1868. He thus walked into the trap the Radicals had prepared and gave them the opportunity to try to remove him from office. A few days later the House voted to impeach the President. A special committee drew up eleven charges, nine of them relating to infractions of the Tenure of Office Act, and the remaining two accusing Johnson of delivering "inflammatory and scandalous harangues" designed to bring public contempt upon Congress.

As provided by the Constitution, the Senate, presided over by Chief Justice Chase, conducted the trial, proceedings never before instituted against a President of the United States. During the proceedings, which lasted more than two months, wild charges were hurled at the President, including one that implied that Johnson had conspired in the assassination of Lincoln. Nevertheless, the President behaved with dignity. His lawyer pointed out that none of the eleven charges against Johnson qualified as "high crimes and misdemeanors," the only Constitutional grounds for removing a President from office. Moreover, he charged that the Tenure of Office Act did not even apply to the dismissal of Stanton, since the Act's wording related only to federal officials appointed by the incumbent President, and Stanton had been appointed by Lincoln.

Johnson was acquitted—but only by one vote. The seven Republicans who sided with him did so out of a sense of decency and respect for the office of President, as well as a clear knowledge that Johnson, though inept, was no criminal. For their courageous action, all seven Congressmen were mercilessly attacked by their colleagues and the Republican press, and most were hounded out of public life. Congress had gained control of the federal government.

THE ELECTION OF 1868

While Johnson was still on trial, the Republicans held their national convention in Chicago and nominated General Ulysses S. Grant as their Presidential candidate. Grant was a war hero who had few announced political views. He was known to have voted for two Democrats, Buchanan and Douglas, so the Democrats tried to lure him to their party; but Grant had already been drawn into the Republican camp by the flattery of the Radicals. At one time Grant was on friendly terms with Johnson, but after military reconstruction began, the General became increasingly annoyed with what he considered to be the President's misconception of conditions in the South.

While insisting upon universal suffrage in the South, the Republicans were careful to assure the North that each Union state could determine for itself whether or not to enfranchise black people. This hypocrisy led Southerners to make up a derisive jingle:

> To every Southern river
> Shall Negro suffrage come;
> But not to fair New England,
> For that's too close to hum.

The other planks in the Republican platform were realistically chosen to please the various Northern economic interests and allay their fears. Powerful manufacturers in the Northeast wanted the Republicans to continue their endorsement of the high protective tariff; the party tacitly gave their promise to do so, but did not put a tariff plank in their platform for fear of alienating Western farmers, who disliked the measure. A pledge to encourage immigration was designed to please manufacturers, since

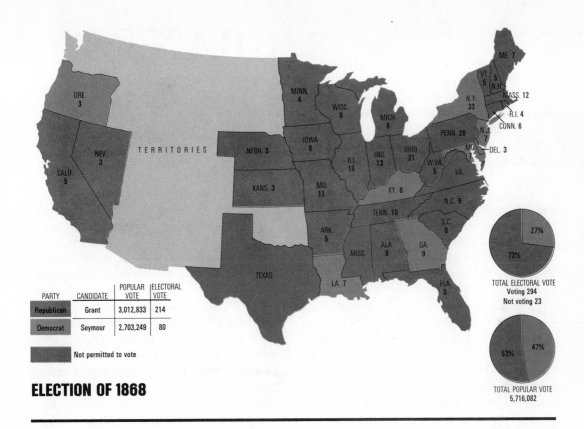

PARTY	CANDIDATE	POPULAR VOTE	ELECTORAL VOTE
Republican	Grant	3,012,833	214
Democrat	Seymour	2,703,249	80

Not permitted to vote

TOTAL ELECTORAL VOTE
Voting 294
Not voting 23

27%
73%

47%
53%

TOTAL POPULAR VOTE
5,716,082

ELECTION OF 1868

foreign labor was invariably cheap labor.

Johnson sought the Democratic nomination, but he was rejected in favor of a less controversial figure, Horatio Seymour, a former governor of New York. Seymour was popular with Southern whites because he had opposed the Emancipation Proclamation and because he now denounced Radical Reconstruction as unconstitutional and an embodiment of "military despotism and Negro supremacy."

Democrats made money a campaign issue, one that they hoped would draw in votes from Western farmers and other indebted portions of the population. During the war Congress had issued about half a million dollars' worth of paper money that was not redeemable in gold. Between 1866 and 1868 Congress gradually began to retire these greenbacks. By the time of the elections about 100,000 dollars had already been

withdrawn from circulation. Since greenbacks were not redeemable in gold, the public had less confidence in them than in ordinary money and their value was accordingly less. Western bankers and farmers, as well as railroad promoters, all favored greenbacks. These groups were generally debtors, and greenbacks allowed them to pay back their loans in "cheap" money, that is, in money worth less than ordinary dollars. Eastern bankers and financiers, on the other hand, urged the government to retire all the greenbacks, since they were usually creditors and wanted to receive full value on every dollar they had loaned.

During the campaign, the Republicans resorted, as they had in 1866, to a practice that came to be known as "waving the bloody shirt." They pictured themselves as the party that had saved the Union and the Democrats as the party of rebellion. In typical bloody-shirt oratory, the Radical governor of Indiana called the Democratic Party "a common sewer and loathsome receptacle, into which is emptied every element of treason North and South, and every element of inhumanity and barbarism which has dishonored the age."

By using such emotional rhetoric and by running the popular Grant, the Republicans won, but the vote was surprisingly close. The electoral vote of 214 for Grant and 80 for Seymour was deceptive. In the popular vote, Grant had a mere 306,000 edge over his opponent. In the end Grant owed his victory to the 700,000 ballots cast for him by Southern blacks.

THE FIFTEENTH AMENDMENT

Analyzing the election returns, the Republicans quickly realized the importance of the black vote, and set about to protect it through a new amendment to the Constitution. The Fourteenth Amendment had indirectly encouraged Southern states to enfranchise the freedmen by threatening to reduce their Congressional representation if they refused to allow black residents to vote. The Fifteenth Amendment went still further and stated that the right of citizens to vote "shall not be denied or abridged by the United States or by any State on account of race, color, or previous condition of servitude." Unfortunately, the wording of the Fifteenth Amendment was not as strong as many Radicals had hoped. It did not *give* the vote to blacks, but merely prohibited states from denying it on the basis of color. This loophole allowed Southern states later to exclude blacks without appearing to do so because of race.

In March, 1870, the Amendment was ratified by the necessary number of states. After ratifying the Fourteenth and Fifteenth Amendments, the three Southern states that were still under military rule—Virginia, Mississippi, and Texas—were readmitted to the Union.

GRANT'S PRESIDENCY

THE SOUTH DURING RECONSTRUCTION

Among historians this era is one of the most controversial in American history. Historians who have deplored the harsh measures of the Radicals have charged that: (1) honest Southern whites were excluded from holding office or voting, while most state governments were controlled by "carpetbaggers," "scalawags," and ignorant blacks; (2) these governments plunged the South into enormous debt in order to fill their own purses; and (3) none of these corrupt practices benefited the great mass of black people, but instead created undying enmity between the races.

What is the evidence for these charges? Certainly many white people were disenfranchised and forbidden to hold office, but this number never exceeded 150,000, and by 1872 it had been reduced to 750. Seven states never even bothered to enforce the restrictions against white voting. Yet the fact remains that Northerners did play a surprisingly large part in Southern politics. In 1868, for example, four Southern states had Northern governors. The records of seven Southern states for the same year show that ten of their fourteen Senators and twenty of their thirty-five Representatives were from the North. Throughout the entire Reconstruction period, nineteen Northerners represented the South in the Senate. Called "carpetbaggers," they have been pictured as immoral scoundrels who came to the South simply to plunder it. Many of these Northerners undoubtedly were interested in obtaining power and enriching themselves through their political influence. However, many were idealists genuinely dedicated to securing a solid position for the freedmen in the new South. Similarly, the term "scalawags" was applied to Southerners regarded as unscrupulous collaborators, willing to sell out in order to advance their own interests. This view has neglected the fact that many of the so-called scalawags were Southern Unionists and Whigs who had opposed secession from the very beginning and were now only implementing the policies they had always promoted. Other scalawags were poor whites who hoped to break up the great plantations and distribute the lands among the landless. Still other whites who cooperated with the Radicals were Southern businessmen eager to link their region to the financial and manufacturing economy of the North.

The facts also indicate that the freedmen played a less decisive role in Reconstruction politics than was formerly believed. In no Southern state did blacks ever control both houses of the legislature, and only in South Carolina and Louisiana were black legislators in the majority. There were no black governors, although in South Carolina, Mississippi, and Louisiana, blacks became lieutenant governors. One black man, Jonathan Jasper Wright, was named to the Supreme Court of South Carolina. Between 1868 and 1875 twenty-eight black men served in the Senate and in the House of Representatives. Since black citizens outnumbered whites in Louisiana, South Carolina, and Mississippi, it was not surprising that they held as many positions of importance as they did. An examination of the records reveal that most black office-holders served only on the local level in posts such as county supervisor of schools or justice of the peace. Some historians have asserted that Radicals manipulated voter registration figures in order to overrepresent blacks, but only in Alabama was the number of black registrants actually above the potential number of adult black male voters as counted in the federal census.

A second criticism of Congressional Reconstruction has been that the Radical legislatures plunged the South into debt and corruption. It is a fact that state debts and taxation did skyrocket in the South after the war, and many instances of corruption can be cited. For example, in Florida the cost of printing government publications in 1869 was higher than the cost of running the entire government had been in 1860. In South Carolina the legislature voted to award one thousand dollars to one member after he lost the same amount betting on the horses. The same state appropriated 75,000 dollars to take the state census in 1869, even though the legislature knew that the federal government would be conducting its own census the following year. In Louisiana, a yearly session of the legislature had cost the taxpayers only an average of 100,000 dollars, but under Radical rule the cost rose to one million dollars a year, half of which went to pay the salaries and expenses of the members of the legislature and their clerks. Public funds were spent on furniture, homes, jewelry, and liquor among other luxuries.

On the other hand, after the Civil War corruption was widespread throughout the United States, North as well as South. Grant's administration was riddled with intrigue and corruption. In New York, the state government was in collusion with criminals who absconded with millions of dollars of public funds. In the South itself, after the period of Reconstruction ended, new depths of political corruption were reached. As historian Carl N. Degler has pointed out: "The fraudulent dealings of the Radical regimes appear less exceptional and noteworthy if they are placed within the context of the times. For instance, it is instructive to realize that after the end of Reconstruction, each of the conservative Democratic governments in Georgia, Alabama, Virginia, Mississippi, Louisiana, and Tennessee had treasurers or other officials who absconded with or embezzled state funds, the individual defalcations often running to half a million dollars."

The Reconstruction governments also allocated large sums of money for social reform. Before the Civil War, the South had had very little public education for its white population and none for blacks. As provided for in the new state constitutions, the Radical regimes set up a free school system for both races. By 1877, 700,000 blacks were in school. Every region damaged by the war had to spend a great deal of money for repairs and part of the public funding helped rebuild destroyed cities. Most of the state debts incurred went toward subsidizing badly needed railroads. Money was also spent setting up insane asylums, poorhouses, and courts. Before the war, slaves were not tried in court, but simply were punished by their masters. Now a large part of the population was subject to the official legal system, and new courts had to be built and staffed to handle the extra load of cases.

The black man's plight after the war is depicted in this 1870 engraving of a black family surrounded by the Ku Klux Klan and the White League.

To pay for the extravagance of these regimes as well as their legitimate reforms, new taxes were required. The heaviest levies fell on the planter class. Business and personal taxes remained low. The Southern state governments also raised some revenue by selling bonds in the North. Southern credit was so low, however, that bonds frequently sold at as much as a 75 percent discount.

A final charge against the Reconstruction process has been that the Radical governments did not really help black people but instead bred enmity between the races. The Reconstruction years did indeed witness several terrible race riots. For instance, a hundred blacks died in riots in Jackson County, Florida, and in Alabama a small war broke out when black Republicans tried to keep a member of their own race from voting for the Democrats.

THE KU KLUX KLAN

Of greater significance in intensifying racial enmity were secret societies in the South. To combat carpetbag rule and the black vote, thousands of white Southerners banded together in secret organizations, such as the White Brotherhood, the Knights of the White Camellia, and the best-known, the Ku Klux Klan. Particularly strong in the upper South, the Klan was dedicated to driving blacks out of politics, ending Reconstruction, and restoring white supremacy. Between 1867 and 1869 members of the Klan cloaked themselves in sheets, pretending they were the ghosts of dead Confederate soldiers, and roamed the countryside at night, speaking in muffled voices and terrorizing blacks. Burning crosses and beating or killing its victims, the Klan divided its hatred between "uppity" blacks and white members of Union Leagues (these Leagues were Republican organizations devoted to enrolling black voters). The nature of the Klan was well defined in one of its own boastful statements:

Niggers and Leaguers, get out of the way,
We're born of the night and we vanish by
*   day.*
No rations have we, but the flesh of man—
And love niggers best—the Ku Klux Klan;
We catch 'em alive and roast 'em whole,
Then hand 'em around with a sharpened
*   pole.*
Whole Leagues have been eaten, not
*   leaving a man,*
And went away hungry—the Ku Klux Klan.

Klan behavior became so outrageous that its own leader denounced it and officially disbanded the organization in 1869. It had attracted to its ranks criminals and outlaws who used it as a front for murder and robbery. Meanwhile, Congress struck at the Klan through three Enforcement Acts. Elections were placed under federal jurisdiction and fines and sentences were imposed on persons convicted of interfering with any qualified citizen's right to vote. As most of the presiding judges in the South were white, however, of the 7,300 persons indicted under the Enforcement Acts only about 1,250 were convicted. President Grant went so far as to send federal troops to nine South Carolina counties, under the 1871 law, to quell rebellion against Radical Reconstruction.

RETURN TO HOME RULE

The historian Albert B. Moore has defined the racial implications of Reconstruction as follows: "Race friction and prejudice were engendered by Reconstruction, which was an unfortunate thing for both races and especially for the Negroes. It caused greater discriminations against the Negroes in politics and education, and in other ways. The Negroes had been so pampered and led as to arouse false notions and hopes among them and to make them for many years lame factors in the rebuilding of the South. The Negro after Reconstruction, and in large degree because of it,

continued and continues to be a source of division between the North and South. The North either could not or would not understand the necessity of race segregation, and the idea that the Negro must have a definite place in the scheme of life was obnoxious. . . . The North freed the Negro from slavery but by repressing and exploiting the South it has contributed much to conditions that have deprived him of some of the opportunities that a free man should have."

From another vantage point, many institutions and reforms that were undertaken during Reconstruction have endured as a legacy of the period. New schools, courts, and a railroad system were all built under Reconstruction legislation. The state constitutions written by Radical legislatures were so superior to earlier constitutions, that even after Reconstruction collapsed these new constitutions were generally retained or only slightly modified. The constitutions eliminated property qualifications for voting and office-holding. They also abolished debtors' prisons.

As extreme as Radical Reconstruction appeared to most Southerners at the time, it actually did not go far enough in economic terms to change the basic structure of Southern life. The Freedmen's Bureau attempted to confiscate the lands of the great plantations and distribute them among landless blacks, but, as noted earlier, the attempt was not successful. Because blacks could not achieve economic independence, they were unable to retain their newly found political equality after Northerners pulled out of the South. Similarly, the Radicals failed to set up lasting machinery that would protect the black man's right to vote. The enduring legacy of Radical Reconstruction remained in two great statements—the Fourteenth and Fifteenth amendments to the Constitution.

The remnants of Radical Reconstruction lasted a decade, but in fact its measures endured only three years in Virginia and

North Carolina and remained as long as ten years only in South Carolina, Florida, and Louisiana.

Radical governments collapsed as Northern troops pulled out, but Radical rule was also gradually weakened by associations of white Southerners, who no longer banded together secretly but now acted in open racist leagues. A number of such movements sprang up in 1874. The Mississippi redshirts publicly whipped militant blacks. Other organizations like the Rifle Clubs and the White Leagues armed their members and used force, if necessary, to win elections. They also coerced the white population to vote Democratic. By overt violence and covert economic pressure, blacks were kept away from the polls and whites were welded into the solidly Democratic South.

This activity among Southern whites was matched by a corresponding passivity among the Northern population. The Civil War was fading into memory and Northerners were no longer interested in defending the rights of black people. The expense of maintaining an army in the South seemed unnecessary, as long as blacks were not actually enslaved again. In addition, the sectional hatred between the North and South was declining with a new birth of nationalism.

Meanwhile, the Radicals in Congress were losing their influence. By 1872, they were willing to pass an Amnesty Act restoring voting and office-holding privileges to almost all white Southerners. That same year the Freedmen's Bureau expired. The Radical program in the South was now seen as a failure on both political and economic grounds. With the election of 1872 coming up, Republicans wanted to divest themselves of a political liability. Moreover, they were beginning to realize that the party could win elections by carrying the populous Northern and Western states. The black vote in the South no longer seemed indispensable to them.

CORRUPTION IN WASHINGTON

During Grant's two terms as President, the word "politician" became synonymous with double-talking and self-serving. The corruption in Washington, and elsewhere in the country, was the result of a lowering in the moral tone of the nation during and after the Civil War. Immense fortunes in industry had been made during the war. Wealth was worshipped, and material display became a passion. Few politicians could resist the bribes for favors which businessmen dispensed freely. Grant was not responsible for this general moral laxity, but by his infatuation with business success and his negligence in office he allowed it to flourish. The early idealism of the Republican Party was smothered in this atmosphere of materialism. In fact, both major parties became agencies for obtaining and dispensing the spoils of office.

In this 1876 cartoon, "Uncle Sam" is trying to open Grant's eyes to the corruption in his administration.

GRANT'S VIEW OF THE PRESIDENCY

His military triumphs did nothing to prepare Grant for the Presidency. He was probably the least experienced and most naive citizen ever to hold that position. Grant chose his advisers for their personal loyalty rather than administrative ability. He had only a limited understanding of the complicated postwar economic situation. He did not know how to maneuver politically, was an easy mark for self-seeking

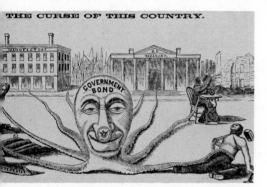

THE CURSE OF THIS COUNTRY.

An 1870 pro-greenback cartoon showing a gold-nosed government octopus strangling labor, farmers, and small businessmen.

politicians, and never clearly understood the positive functions of the office of President. Going back to the pre-Jacksonian era, Grant believed that Congress, as the body that most directly represented the people's will, should make all the decisions. The President, Grant thought, should simply execute the will of Congress. He did not grasp the potential of the great office which had been bestowed on him, and gladly acquiesed in the doctrine of Congressional supremacy announced by Senator John Sherman of Ohio: "The President should obey and enforce the laws, leaving to the people the duty of correcting any errors committed by their representatives in Congress."

One of the few private acts of initiative undertaken by Grant was the appointment of his Cabinet officers, and his choices were generally disastrous. For example, he made Elihu B. Washburne of Illinois Secretary of State, even though Washburne was totally unqualified and planned to give up the post a few days after assuming it. Washburne simply wanted to be able to brag that he had held the Secretaryship when he went to France as America's minister. The Secretary of the Navy had no distinctions other than his wealth. The Secretary of War was simply one of the President's old army cronies. The President's White House staff was also dominated by old army friends who had no political experience. This "Kitchen Cabinet" controlled federal patronage appointments and awarded jobs to friends and relatives, arousing the anger of leading Republican Senators. An outstanding exception to the mediocrity of Grant's appointments was the able and steady Hamilton Fish. Fish was Grant's Secretary of State for eight stormy years.

MONEY PROBLEMS

One of the central domestic issues facing Grant was the question of what to do with greenbacks. When Grant entered the White House, 387 million dollars of the Civil War notes were still in circulation. The President wished to please the East Coast financiers, since they were big contributors to the Republican campaign chest, but he also feared that retiring all greenbacks would alienate Western farmers and lose their votes. Consequently, the President favored a compromise—keeping the greenbacks in currency, but making them redeemable in gold. Two weeks after Grant took office, Congress enacted this compromise.

Although the money compromise was not particularly favored by the population at large, another move, Grant's decision to abolish the wartime income tax, proved highly popular. On the recommendation of the President and his special tax commissioner, the economist David A. Wells, Congress eliminated the income tax and most of the wartime excise duties.

TARIFFS

If the Republicans had been consistent in wanting compromises on economic matters they also would have lowered the high protective tariff enacted during the war, presumably as an emergency measure. The business community, however, strongly favored the retention of high tariffs. Organized lobbies representing businessmen convinced Congress and Grant that high tariffs were necessary to preserve America's industries. Grant's own economic adviser, the aforementioned David A. Wells, argued against the tariffs, pointing out that they tended to foster monopolies and penalized such consumers as the Western farmers solely to enrich East Coast factory owners. Grant ignored Wells's arguments, however, and soon dropped him from the government. The President and Congress not only backed retention of high tariffs but actually raised them on many items in 1870. However, as the election of 1872 approached, Grant became fearful that criticism of the high tariff wall might hurt the Republicans. He ordered an across-the-board slash of 10 percent from all duties. These cuts were restored three years later.

THE FISK-GOULD SCANDAL

A large scandal erupted in Grant's first term arising from the attempt of two bold speculators, Jay Gould and Jim Fisk, to corner the nation's gold supply. These men schemed to buy all available gold, hold it until its price soared, and then dump it suddenly on the market to reap huge profits. The entire plot depended upon the cooperation of the government, since it could succeed only if the government with-

held from sale its ordinary supplies of gold. Working through the President's unsuspecting brother-in-law, Gould sought to convince Grant that by holding back the normal supply of gold the government could raise the price of bullion and thereby indirectly raise the price of American farm commodities in Europe. The President did not understand Gould's reasoning, but awed by his wealth, he vaguely assented to the proposal. Meanwhile Fisk and Gould began to buy or borrow all available gold, telling speculators that they had the President's word that the government would cooperate. On September 24, 1869, the price of gold soared so high that there was a panic at the stock exchange, when not enough gold could be obtained for ordinary trading purposes, and many businesses were seriously affected. Shortly after this "Black Friday," the President released four million dollars' worth of bullion to stabilize the market. Gould and Fisk, by simply refusing to repay the money they had borrowed, were untouched by the debacle.

GRANT'S SECOND ELECTION

Toward the end of Grant's first term, a large group of disillusioned Republicans formed a new political party, the Liberal Republicans. Gaining strength in 1871, the new party was supported by an impressive list of reformers: Carl Schurz; B. Gratz Brown of Missouri; Charles Francis Adams, son of John Quincy Adams; Salmon P. Chase, Chief Justice of the Supreme Court; Senator Charles Sumner; and several prominent newspaper editors, including Horace Greeley of the New York *Tribune*. Grant and Grantism were targets of the new coalition. Unfortunately, the members of the new party could agree on nothing except their dislike of Grant. Some were against Grant's uncompromising prosecution of military reconstruction; they wanted the troops called home and a universal amnesty declared. Others attacked the political corruption under Grant and called for civil service reform. There were Northern Democrats who recognized that their party's name struck many voters as the symbol of Southern rebellion; these Democrats became Liberal Republicans simply because they wanted a new, innocuous party label. Some men favored the withdrawal of all tariffs and the introduction of free trade; others were ardent protectionists. In general, economic questions became sources of insurmountable party division. One segment of the party wanted more greenbacks, another wanted none at all. The new party was so divided over the issue of hard or soft money that the convention finally evaded the matter altogether.

The party's platform reflected this clash of viewpoints. It called for removal of all federal troops from the South and an amnesty for former Confederates, but it also approved Congressional Reconstruction. It called for an end to railroad land grants, civil service reform, and resumption of specie payments. The platform avoided any stand on the tariff.

The new party insured its doom when it nominated Horace Greeley, perhaps the most famous newspaper editor in America. Greeley was much respected for his years of crusading against slavery, but he was regarded as an eccentric—a perilous reputation in politics. Erratic and enthusiastic, Greeley affected strange white chin whiskers and had taken up every fad of the last few decades, including vegetarianism and spiritualism. He was a poor judge of men, and was so ridiculed during his campaign that he observed in bewilderment that he did not know whether he was running for the White House or the penitentiary.

The Democrats endorsed Greeley as their only hope in unseating Grant, but many Democrats remembered Greeley's flinty attacks against the South and stayed home on election day. The Republicans were astounded and overjoyed to learn of Greeley's nomination. One Republican boss said he could not believe that any gathering "outside a lunatic asylum" could have nominated the eccentric newspaperman.

In contrast to the Liberal Republican confusion, the regular Republican Party took a strong stand behind its record of high tariffs and Radical Reconstruction. Industrialists and bankers poured large sums into Grant's campaign. Grant won the 1872 election with a bigger margin than he had received in 1868—286 electoral votes to Greeley's 62. Greeley carried only two Southern states and four border states. He was in such despair over his defeat, the recent death of his wife, and the threatened loss of his job on the *Tribune,* that three weeks after the election he collapsed and died.

NEW SCANDALS

Grant's second term was blighted with so much evidence of corruption that qualified, honest men began to turn away from politics to other careers. One of the worst scandals developed from shady deals made before Grant came into office, but many of the members of Grant's administration were implicated, including his first-term Vice President, Schuyler Colfax. In 1867 the Crédit Mobilier, a construction company that helped build the transcontinental Union Pacific Railroad, virtually gave away some of its stocks to Congressmen and other high government officials. These bribes were offered in order to keep Congress from investigating the business dealings of the company. The Crédit Mobilier had good reason to fear an investigation, since it had defrauded the Union Pacific, which was heavily subsidized by the government, of millions of dollars.

These dealings were kept from the public until the New York *Sun* published an exposé during the campaign of 1872. A subsequent Congressional investigation revealed that Congressman Oakes Ames of Massachusetts had distributed Crédit Mobilier shares to Congressmen during the session of 1867 and 1868. Not only was Grant's first Vice President, Schuyler Colfax, implicated, but also his second Vice President, Henry Wilson. So low were the ethics of the day that one Congressman accused of having accepted stocks voiced regret that the bribe "was no larger in amount."

Sensational scandals continued to unfold upon a public growing accustomed to corruption. The most famous was the "Whiskey Ring" conspiracy, involving hundreds of distillers who bribed government officials to file false reports that cheated the government of millions of dollars in excise taxes. Grant's able Secretary of the Treasury, Benjamin H. Bristow, discovered that

Grant's own private secretary, General Orville E. Babcock, was one of the conspirators. In a move that served to discourage any honesty among public officials, Grant defended Babcock and insured his acquittal by serving as a character witness for him during the trial. Soon after, Grant rewarded Bristow for his revelations by firing him. Graft was also rampant in lower levels of government. The most notorious example in this era was the Tweed Ring in New York City, although similar examples were to be found in several other large cities. Led by the Democratic boss of Tammany Hall, William Tweed, the machine regularly received bribes for favors and in 1869 bribed the state legislature to issue a new charter for the city that entrenched the machine in power. The use of fraud made election victories easy. Graft was obtained

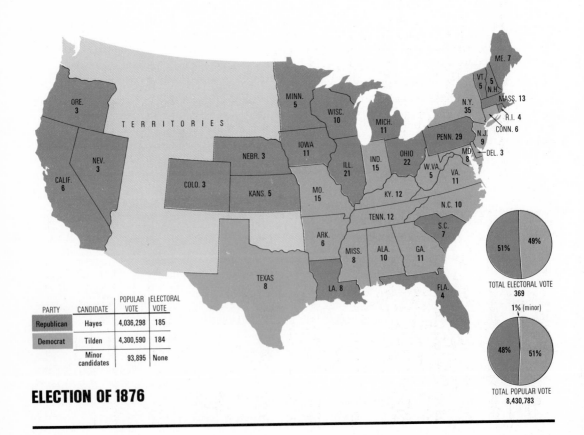

PARTY	CANDIDATE	POPULAR VOTE	ELECTORAL VOTE
Republican	Hayes	4,036,298	185
Democrat	Tilden	4,300,590	184
	Minor candidates	93,895	None

TOTAL ELECTORAL VOTE
369

51% 49%

1% (minor)

48% 51%

TOTAL POPULAR VOTE
8,430,783

ELECTION OF 1876

from bills padded up to 85 percent. The ring was finally broken in 1871 by public-spirited and incorruptible newspapermen and citizens. Many members of the ring, including Tweed, were subsequently sent to prison.

THE PANIC OF 1873

Racked by scandals, the nation was also subjected to a disastrous economic decline during Grant's second administration. Since 1850, except for short intervals, the economy in the North and the West had enjoyed unparalleled prosperity. By 1871, however, the structure began to totter, and two years later it collapsed. During the boom years, thousands of new businesses had opened and railroad lines had rapidly spread across the continent. America was building at such a rapid pace that it was importing far more than it was exporting. An unfavorable balance of payments drained about 130 million dollars' worth of gold out of the United States every year.

The founding of too many new businesses and the building of too many railroads without immediate prospects of profit, overextended the economy, already weak from the constant drain of specie out of the country to pay for foreign imports. Demand for Western agricultural products had also fallen off since the war. Credit was extended unwisely to too many borrowers. Fluctuations in the value of greenbacks both reflected and caused new rents in the economic fabric. By 1872 there were over four thousand business failures. Finally, in September, 1873, the foremost banking firm in the country, Jay Cooke and Company, collapsed in bankruptcy. The announcement set off a chain reaction of business failures and the nation was hurled into a serious depression. By the end of 1873 more than five thousand commercial firms had failed and eighty-nine railroads had gone under. Soon half a million railroad workers were out of jobs. The hard times that began in 1873 did not end until six years later.

AN ELECTION AND A COMPROMISE

THE ELECTION OF 1876

Corruption, popularly called "Grantism," and the depression had hurt the President's reputation, but the professional hard core of the party close to Grant, known as the "Stalwarts," wanted to renominate him anyway. Another faction—the "Halfbreeds"—who claimed to be reformers, although they had not broken with the party in 1872, worked for the nomination of Representative James G. Blaine of Maine. In a speech

proposing Blaine's name at the convention, a prominent Republican, Robert G. Ingersoll, extravagantly described him as "the man who has snatched the mask of Democracy from the hideous face of rebellion; for this man who, like an intellectual athlete, has stood in the arena of debate and challenged all comers, and who is still a total stranger to defeat. Like an armed warrior, like a plumed knight, James G. Blaine marched down the halls of the American Congress and threw his shining lance full and fair against the brazen foreheads of the defamers of his country and the maligners of her honor."

This flowery rhetoric won Blaine the epithet "the plumed knight," but it could not hide the fact that he had been accused of corruptly using his office of Speaker of the House to dispense favors to several railroad companies, including the Union Pacific. To avoid all taint of scandal, the party instead nominated the untarnished but innocuous Rutherford B. Hayes, three times governor of Ohio.

The Democrats nominated Governor Samuel J. Tilden of New York, famed as a reformer. He had been instrumental in breaking the power of Boss Tweed's racketeers in New York. Later Tilden exposed another fraud, the New York State Canal Ring. However, Tilden was not interested in social reform. He was a conservative corporation lawyer and millionaire who wanted only an end to governmental fraud and scandals. Accordingly, the Democrats called for civil service examinations, a system that would fill important offices with qualified professionals. The Democrats also wanted an end to Reconstruction, still in force in three Southern states.

No clear issues emerged out of the campaign. Both candidates were in favor of civil service reform, both hedged on the tariff question, and both promised to end Reconstruction. To disguise the lack of substantial points of debate, the Republicans again "waved the bloody shirt." The eloquent Ingersoll told an assembly of Union veterans: "Soldiers, every scar you have on your heroic bodies was given you by a Democrat." The Democrats in turn painted the Republican Party as an organization sunk in filth and corruption.

THE ELECTION RETURNS

On the morning after election day Tilden seemed to have won. He had 248,000 more popular votes than Hayes and had carried four Northern states as well as the solid South. The outcome, however, was undecided since returns from Florida, South Carolina, and Louisiana were still in dispute, as well as one electoral vote from Oregon.

Tilden needed only one more electoral vote to win. Hayes needed twenty. There were exactly twenty votes in dispute. The chairman of the Republican national committee sent telegrams to Republican leaders in the three crucial Southern states: "Hayes is elected if we have carried South Carolina, Florida, and Louisiana. Can you hold your State? Answer immediately."

No one will ever know exactly which way the voters in these states had decided, but Tilden probably won in Florida and thus deserved to go to the White House. Republican and Democratic supervisors of election returns, however, filed their own fraudulent returns. In December, 1876, Congress received two sets of returns from each of the disputed states.

To solve a dilemma for which there was no remedy provided by the Constitution, Congress appointed an electoral commission. By an elaborate procedure seven Republicans, seven Democrats, and an independent Republican were chosen to investigate the returns and award them to the rightful winner. However the "independent" member was disqualified at the last moment and an organization Republican took his place. In a straight party vote the eight Republicans gave the Presidency to Hayes.

THE COMPROMISE OF 1877

Why was the Democratic Party willing to accept this decision which deprived them of their first opportunity to control the White House since 1856? The intricacies of a consummate piece of political horse trading only came to the surface in the middle of the twentieth century. In his superb book *Reunion and Reaction,* C. Vann Woodward has clearly outlined the reasons for the Democratic Party's acquiescence in the decision of the Electoral Commission.

Republicans feared that Northern Democrats would stage a filibuster in the Senate that would prevent the Electoral Commission from reporting its decision. A filibuster could prevent Hayes from gaining clear title to the White House. To prevent such a deadlock, the Republicans made a deal with Southern Democrats who favored the industrialization of the South. Republicans were interested in forming such an alliance for long-term as well as immediate reasons. They knew that when the last Reconstruction governments fell the party would no longer be able to control the black vote in the South. If Southern whites were drawn into the party, Republicans had a chance to maintain their strength below the Mason-Dixon line. In response, some prominent Southern Democrats agreed to defect to the Republican camp in return for certain important concessions.

In January, 1877, Republicans made four concessions to Southern Democrats: (1) Hayes if elected would appoint at least one Southerner to his Cabinet; (2) the South would gain control of federal patronage within its own section of the country; (3) the government would promise internal improvements and aid to the Texas and Pacific Railroad (the first Southern transcontinental line); and (4) all troops would be withdrawn. In return, Southern Democrats would insure Hayes' victory and elect a Republican Speaker of the House, even though the chamber was now controlled by a Democratic majority.

After this set of agreements was made, a conference at the Wormley Hotel in Washington, D.C., reconfirmed the arrangements to remove federal troops from the South in return for guarantees that Southern Senators would not filibuster against Hayes.

Republican Rutherford B. Hayes succeeded Grant in 1876 in an election that was decided by a Republican-dominated committee. In a compromise between the two political parties, the Democrats would allow Hayes to be President if control of the South would be given back to the Southern states, thus ending Reconstruction.

As so often happens, each side delivered only part of its promise. Hayes obtained the Presidency, but the new Speaker was a Democrat, not the expected Republican. For his part, Hayes appointed a Southerner to one Cabinet post, allowed Southerners to dispense their share of federal offices, as agreed, and recalled all troops by the end of April, 1877. As President, he did not come up with the promised railroad appropriations, however. The coalition between the Republicans and the Southern Democrats expired. Had it succeeded, the South would not have become the one-party section it remained until recent times.

SEGREGATION

As Reconstruction ended, so did a national policy for promoting social, economic, and political equality for black Americans. State governments in the South fell into the hands of the old planter aristocracy and the new business classes, a group so conservative they were known as "Bourbons," after the old royal house of France. This did not mean an immediate loss of the right to vote by blacks. Actually, voting rights were not taken away until the 1890s. Until that time black voters were too useful to the Bourbon Democrats who courted their vote and played them off against the poor white population. Although blacks temporarily retained the franchise, they were quickly deprived of the legal right to use integrated facilities. In 1875, Congress had passed a Civil Rights Act guaranteeing all citizens "full and equal enjoyment of . . . inns, public conveyances . . . theatres and other places of amusement." This act was declared unconstitutional by the Supreme Court in 1883. The Court decreed that Congress had no jurisdiction over discrimination by private organizations and private citizens. In 1896, the Court further declared, in the case of *Plessy v. Ferguson,* that railroad cars could be segregated as long as blacks were pro-

Plessy v. Ferguson

66 *This case turns upon the constitutionality of an act of the General Assembly of the State of Louisiana, passed in 1890, providing for separate railway carriages for the white and colored races. . . .*

A statute which implies merely a legal distinction between the white and colored races—a distinction which is founded in the color of the two races, and which must always exist so long as white men are distinguished from the other race by color

—has no tendency to destroy the legal equality of the two races, or reestablish a state of involuntary servitude. . . .

. . . Laws permitting, and even requiring, their separation in places where they are liable to be brought into contact do not necessarily imply the inferiority of either race to the other, and have been generally, if not universally, recognized as within the competency of the state legislatures in the exercise of their police power. The most common instance of this is connected with the establishment of separate schools for white and colored children, which has been held to be a valid exercise of the legislative power even by courts of states where the political rights of the colored race have been longest and most earnestly enforced. . . .

We consider the underlying fallacy of the plaintiff's argument to consist in the assumption that the enforced separation of the two races stamps the colored race with a badge of inferiority. If this be so, it is not by reason of anything found in the act, but solely because the colored race chooses to put that construction upon it. . . . The argument also assumes that social prejudices may be overcome by legislation, and that equal rights cannot be secured to the Negro except by an enforced commingling of the two races. We cannot accept this proposition. If the two races are to meet upon terms of social equality, it must be the result of natural affinities, a mutual appreciation of each other's merits and a voluntary consent of individuals. . . . Legislation is powerless to eradicate racial instincts or to abolish distinctions based upon physical differences, and the attempt to do so can only result in accentuating the difficulties of the present situation. . . . If one race be inferior to the other socially, the Constitution of the United States cannot put them upon the same plane. . . .

—*The United States Supreme Court*

Plessy v. Ferguson: *Dissenting Opinion*

. . . I deny that any legislative body or judicial tribunal may have regard to the race of citizens when the civil rights of those citizens are involved. Indeed, such legislation, as that here in question, is inconsistent not only with that equality of rights which pertains to citizenship, National and State, but with the personal liberty enjoyed by every one within the United States. . . .

. . . . Every one knows that the statute in question had its origin in the purpose, not so much to exclude white persons from railroad cars occupied by blacks, as to exclude colored people from coaches occupied by or assigned to white persons. . . . The thing to accomplish was, under the guise of giving equal accommodation for whites and blacks, to compel the latter to keep to themselves while travelling in railroad passenger coaches. No one would be so wanting in candor as to assert the contrary. The fundamental objection, therefore, to the statute is that it interferes with the personal freedom of citizens. . . . If a white man and a black man choose to occupy the same public conveyance on a public highway, it is their right to do so, and no government, proceeding alone on grounds of race, can prevent it without infringing the personal liberty of each. . . .

The white race deems itself to be the dominant race in this country. And so it is, in prestige, in achievements, in education, in wealth and in power. . . . But in the view of the Constitution, in the eye of the law, there is in this country no superior, dominant, ruling class of citizens. There is no caste here. Our Constitution is color-blind, and neither knows nor tolerates classes among citizens. In respect of civil rights, all citizens are equal before the law. The humblest is the peer of the most powerful. The law regards man as man, and takes no account of his surroundings or of his color when his civil rights as guaranteed by the supreme law of the land are involved. . . .

"

—*Justice John Marshall Harlan*

vided with "separate but equal" facilities. In 1899, the Court upheld the right of Southern communities to establish "separate but equal" schools.

Blacks were deserted by all their former allies. Most of the Radicals were old or out of office. The Freedmen's Bureau had expired in 1872. Federal troops had been recalled and the Bourbon Democrats assumed control of politics in the Southern states.

In the late 1880s and 1890s a severe agricultural depression struck the South. In 1894 cotton prices fell to four and one-half cents a bale. Suddenly a new political movement began to stir. Poor whites recognized that they and poor blacks were suffering from the same depression under the economic tyranny of the Bourbons. A new bi-racial Populist Party developed throughout the South with enough power to win control of the North Carolina legislature in 1894.

Conservative white Democrats throughout the South were deeply alarmed by this development. They began to cry for the unity of the white race against the black, and made white Populists several attractive offers. Many poor, illiterate whites had been denied the vote because of literacy or property-holding requirements which were reinstated after the end of Reconstruction. The Bourbons now enacted the "grandfather clauses" that gave the vote to any man whose ancestors had been enfranchised before the Civil War. The Supreme Court upheld these laws as well as a host of other technical disqualifications designed to deny blacks the vote, in *Williams v. Mississippi* in 1898, on the grounds that, since they "did not on their face discriminate between

609

the races," they were in accordance with the Fifteenth Amendment.

The Populist movement dissolved, poor whites joined the Bourbons, and blacks were kept away from the polls. Poor whites, however, did not for the most part play an important role in the new South. The grandfather clauses were operative for an individual only if he registered within a limited amount of time; if he failed to do so, he had to meet certain property or education qualifications, which was often impossible. Or he might have to pay a poll tax, which was cumulative year by year. In the end, blacks and large numbers of poor whites stopped voting. Conservative Democratic cliques had gained a voting monopoly in the South that would decide the outcome of elections for many years to come.

THE ATLANTA COMPROMISE

During Reconstruction, capital was in extremely short supply in the South. Southerners hoped to sell the cotton they accumulated during the war in return for much-needed cash, but Union agents illegally confiscated most of the cotton. Since few had money in the South, planters could not pay wages to their newly freed slaves. Blacks and poor whites therefore became tenants on small plots on the old plantations. The planters paid no wages and the

workers paid no rent—each party agreed to share the profits derived from the forthcoming crop. The tenants were called sharecroppers. The planter provided food, seed, tools, and animals for the tenants in return for which he usually received two-thirds of each tenant's crop.

In cases where the planters could not provide the sharecroppers with the needed tools and seeds, the landowner turned to the local merchant for help. Merchants advanced supplies to the planters in return for a lien on the tenants' share of next year's crop. This system, called the crop-lien system, made planters and sharecroppers debtors of local merchants who usually insisted that the dependable crop of cotton be planted. These merchants in turn were usually indebted to Northern suppliers. The system revived Southern agriculture, but the crop-lien system based on the cheap labor of landless tenants retarded the technological improvement of Southern agriculture. Thousands of white and black farmers were kept in a submarginal economic status. The South as a whole continued as it had been before 1860, chained to a one-crop economy and to Northern creditors.

Black sharecroppers, only slightly better off than in slave days, barely eked out a living. The profit of their labor went to local merchants and planters. Seventy-five

H. R. Revels of Mississippi (far left) became the first black Senator in 1872. Shown with him in this Currier and Ives print are the first black Representatives elected to the House. From left to right, Benjamine S. Turner of Alabama, Robert C. DeLarge of South Carolina, Josiah T. Walls of Florida, Jefferson H. Long of Georgia, Joseph H. Rainy of South Carolina, and R. Brown Elliot of South Carolina.

percent of all blacks in the South were tenant farmers, and as late as 1890 only 121,000 blacks owned their own farms.

It was apparent that the black man was not achieving equality in the new South. One distinguished black educator, Booker T. Washington, in a speech at the Atlanta Exposition in 1895, therefore proposed that for the time being blacks should give up their desire for political rights and strive simply for the achievement of economic security. Known as the Atlanta Compromise, Washington's concept was summed up in his statement: "The wisest among my race understand that the agitation of questions of social equality is the extremest folly. . . . It is important and right that all privileges of the law be ours, but it is vastly more important that we be prepared for the exercises of these privileges. The oppor-

tunity to earn a dollar in a factory just now is worth infinitely more than the opportunity to spend a dollar in an opera-house."

Upper-class whites looked with favor upon Washington's words, as did many blacks of his own day. As early as 1903, however, W. E. B. Du Bois asked, "Are we going to induce the best class of Negroes to take less and less interest in government, and to give up their right to take such an interest, without a protest? . . . Daily the Negro is coming more and more to look upon law and justice, not as protecting safeguards, but as sources of humiliation and oppression." A famous black classical scholar, William Scarborough, also rejected the Atlanta Compromise on the grounds that Washington's emphasis on menial work ignored the necessity of furthering higher education among black people.

INTERPRETING RECONSTRUCTION

Between 1890 and 1930, the first important group of Reconstruction historians, under the leadership of William A. Dunning of Columbia University, represented the period as one during which vengeful Northerners cruelly punished a defeated South and threw it to the mercy of Radical governments made up of ignorant freedmen and unscrupulous scalawags and carpetbaggers.

In his book, *Reconstruction, Political and Economic,* Dunning contended that the South should have been restored to the Union immediately after the war. Moreover, Northerners should not have tried to give blacks the vote. Because of Dunning's

assumption that the black race was biologically inferior, a theory in vogue during his lifetime, he and his followers painted the entire period as one in which the Southern white population was subjected to mental torture. One member of the Dunning school, Albert B. Moore, went so far as to blame the sharecropper and crop-lien systems on Northern vandals and to insist that all of the South's twentieth-century ills were the result of Reconstruction mistakes.

In the 1920s another school of historians emerged who rejected many of these opinions. While acknowledging that Dunning had amassed much valuable factual information about the postwar era, the new his-

Readings

torians attempted to demonstrate that "Black Reconstruction" was neither so black racially nor so depraved morally as the Dunning school had suggested. Francis B. Simkins and Robert Woody, Southern historians, pointed out that blacks never controlled both houses of any state legislature. They further maintained that most white Southerners had lived quietly and peacefully between 1865 and 1877. Corruption was less prevalent among Radical regimes than it was under the Bourbons who followed them in office. The new historians stressed the economic factors motivating Radicals. They claimed Radicals represented the business and financial interests of the North against the old agrarian interests of the South. The new historians, influenced by the progressive movement for reform of their own day, also contended that blacks deserved the vote. The Dunning school had not understood this necessity because it had been permeated with racist ideas.

Historian C. Vann Woodward concluded that the Compromise of 1877 "did not restore the old order in the South, nor did it restore the South to parity with other sections. It did assure the dominant white population political autonomy, nonintervention by the North on the question of racial equality and promised them a share in the blessings of the new economic order. In return, the South became, in effect, a satellite of the dominant region."

After 1950 a third school of Reconstruction historians emerged, called the neo-revisionists. Men like R. P. Sharkey, E. L. McKitrick, LaWanda and John Cox, and K. M. Stampp emphasized the moral issue of racial equality as the central theme of the Reconstruction era. The Dunning school had seen the Radicals as amoral, corrupt, and power-mad; the revisionists emphasized the economic motives behind the actions of the Radicals; now the neo-revisionists claimed that many Radicals had been sincere idealists concerned about the role of black people in American society.

GENERAL WORKS

Brock, William R., *An American Crisis.* New York: St. Martin's, 1963—An English historian's analysis of Reconstruction from 1865 through 1867. Brock suggests that perhaps the federal system and weaknesses in Presidential-Congressional relations hindered the solution of the problems of Reconstruction.

Buck, Paul H., *The Road to Reunion, 1865–1900.* Boston: Little, Brown, 1937—A history of sectional relations in the 35 years after the Civil War which focuses on and praises those whose aim it was to reunite North and South.

Cash, Wilbur J., *The Mind of the South.* New York: Knopf, 1960—An impressionistic and influential essay on Southern history and the Southern way of life and thought. Cash viewed Reconstruction at a time when a rising business elite in the South adopted many of the worst features of Northern industrialism.

Cruden, Robert, *The Negro in Reconstruction.* Englewood Cliffs, N.J.: Prentice-Hall, 1969—Cruden shows that the role of blacks in demanding and, in many cases, obtaining power during Reconstruction has frequently been ignored.

Donald, David, *The Politics of Reconstruction.* Baton Rouge: Louisiana State University Press, 1965—An attempt to apply quantitative techniques of political science to the political situation of Reconstruction. Donald relates Republican extremism on Reconstruction issues to the needs of Congressmen to win elections in their home districts.

Du Bois, William E. B., *Black Reconstruction in America 1860–1880.* New York: Atheneum, 1969—A pioneering work in black history, one of the first works to reject the pro-Southern, white interpretation of Reconstruction. Du Bois argues that Reconstruction was an unfulfilled revolutionary period because Congressional Republicans were unwilling to combine economic reforms with their political programs.

Dunning, W. A., *Reconstruction, Political and Economic, 1865–1877*. New York: Harper & Row, 1968—Dunning was one of the leading historians of an older school of thought which viewed Reconstruction from the standpoint of Southern whites, and opposed the racial and political policies of the Radical Republicans in Congress.

Franklin, John H., *Reconstruction After the Civil War*. Chicago: University of Chicago Press, 1961—A short history of Reconstruction which pays particular attention to the role of blacks in Southern state governments. Franklin refutes the myth that blacks and carpetbaggers dominated the states during Reconstruction.

Josephson, Matthew, *The Politicos, 1865–1896*. New York: Harcourt, Brace, 1938—A lively political history of the Gilded Age which emphasizes the business orientation of the political leaders of the era.

Patrick, Rembert W., *The Reconstruction of the Nation*. New York: Oxford University Press, 1967—A survey of Reconstruction history which attempts to reconcile revisionist scholarship with older interpretations.

Randall, James G., and David Donald, *The Civil War and Reconstruction*. Boston: Heath, 1961—A standard history of the period, written from a basically revisionist standpoint, sympathetic to the compromisers and hostile to the abolitionists and Radical Reconstructionists.

Stampp, Kenneth M., *The Era of Reconstruction 1865–1877*. New York: Knopf, 1965—An introductory survey of the Re-

construction period which rejects the idea that the Radicals were fanatics who imposed harsh rule on a compliant South.

SPECIAL STUDIES

Bentley, G. R., *A History of the Freedmen's Bureau*. New York: Octagon, 1970—The Freedmen's Bureau, before its liquidation in 1872, was a continuing political football in its sometimes halfhearted efforts to assist former slaves. Bentley connects political maneuverings in Washington to the Bureau's operations in the field.

Cox, La Wanda, and John H. Cox, *Politics, Principle and Prejudice, 1865–66*. New York: Free Press, 1963—An analysis of President Andrew Johnson's policies in the first year of Reconstruction which argues that among his main goals was the rebuilding of the Democratic Party in the North as a party standing for opposition to Congressional Radical policies.

De Santis, Vincent P., *Republicans Face the Southern Question—The New Departure Years, 1877–1897*. Westport, Conn.: Negro Universities Press, 1959—During the years following Reconstruction, the Republican Party was plagued with the problem of gaining a base of support in the South. Alternative strategies of building a base on black votes or on the backing of Southern industrialists were debated and tried.

Gillette, William, *The Right to Vote, Politics and the Passage of the Fifteenth Amendment*. Baltimore: Johns Hopkins Press, 1965—Gillette argues that Republicans, in pressing for the Fifteenth Amendment, were willing to write off the Southern black vote but hoped to win the black vote in the Northern and border states.

James, Joseph B., *The Framing of the Fourteenth Amendment*. Urbana, Ill.: University of Illinois Press, 1956—A legal and political study of the motives of those who drafted the Fourteenth Amendment. James argues that Charles Beard was wrong in contending that the framers intended the amendment to protect corporations against state economic legislation. Moral and political considerations predominated.

Logan, Rayford W., *The Negro in American Life and Thought, The Nadir 1877–1901*. New York: Macmillan, 1965—During the quarter of a century following the end of Reconstruction, whites in both the North and the South consistently refused to commit themselves to advancing the rights of black people. Logan analyzes the opportunistic betrayal and its dismal consequences.

McKitrick, Eric L., *Andrew Johnson and Reconstruction*. Chicago: University of Chicago Press, 1960—In discussing relations between the President and Congress, McKitrick finds Johnson stubborn and rigid, unable to comprehend the workings of the American political party system which called for communication and compromise. Johnson, in his eagerness to exercise great authority, managed to let his true power slip away.

McPherson, James M., *The Struggle for Equality, Abolitionists and the Negro in the Civil War and Reconstruction*. Princeton, N.J.: Princeton University Press, 1964 —The author defends the abolitionists against the charge that they forgot the black people after Emancipation. McPherson discusses the active cooperation between abolitionists and black groups in the struggle for civil rights.

Wharton, Vernon L., *The Negro in Mississippi, 1865–1869*. New York: Harper & Row, 1965—Wharton shows how the legal freedom granted blacks in Mississippi allowed them briefly during Reconstruction to achieve significant gains, but restoration of Democratic rule led to the creation of formal and informal codes which seriously restricted their personal freedom.

Williamson, Joel, *After Slavery, the Negro in South Carolina During Reconstruction, 1861–1877*. Chapel Hill, N.C.: University of North Carolina Press, 1965—A revisionist analysis of Reconstruction which stresses the initiative and progress of South Carolina blacks. However, Williamson maintains, the return of the Democrats to power erased the gains and imposed racial segregation.

Woodward, C. Vann, *Reunion and Reaction: The Compromise of 1877 and the End of Reconstruction*. Boston: Little, Brown, 1966—An analysis of the bargain that elected Rutherford B. Hayes President, and led to withdrawal of the last occupying troops from the South. Woodward discusses the influence of railroad lobbyists and the impact of the North's lack of interest in assisting black people in the South.

Woodward, C. Vann, *The Strange Career of Jim Crow*. New York: Oxford University Press, 1966—An important study of the origins of racial segregation in the South. Woodward maintains that segregation and disenfranchisement of blacks were not introduced until the conservative Bourbon Democrats needed to exploit racial divisions among the poor to stop the growth of Populist strength.

PRIMARY SOURCES

Current, Richard N., ed., *Reconstruction, 1865–1877*. Englewood Cliffs, N.J.: Prentice-Hall, 1965—A collection of documents relating to the Reconstruction years.

Meier, August, *Negro Thought in America, 1880–1915*. Ann Arbor, Mich.: University of Michigan Press, 1963—The reactions of black spokesmen to the all-pervasive racism of the period forms the theme of Meier's study.

Reid, Whitelaw, *After the War, A Tour of the Southern States, 1865–1866*. New York: Harper & Row, 1965—Reid, a Northern newspaperman and Republican, visited the former Confederate states shortly after the war, and his account emphasizes the devastation the war had brought to the South.

Shenton, James P., *The Reconstruction, A Documentary History: 1865–1877*. New York: Putnam, 1963—A history of Reconstruction from documents. The collection stresses social and economic developments as well as political events.

Turner, Arlin, ed., *The Negro Question, A Selection of the Writings on Civil Rights in the South by George W. Cable*. Garden City, N.Y.: Doubleday, 1958—Cable was a white Southern liberal who, in the later years of the nineteenth century, espoused granting of civil rights to Southern blacks. Cable warned that society would be torn apart unless civil rights were achieved for all.

Washington, Booker T., *Up from Slavery*. New York: Bantam, 1970—The classic autobiography of the former slave who became founder and President of Tuskegee Institute, and was the leading black advocate of moderation and compromise on the racial question.

BIOGRAPHIES

Brodie, Fawn M., *Thaddeus Stevens, Scourge of the South*. New York: Norton, 1959—A sympathetic biography of Stevens, the Pennsylvania Republican who was the leading spokesman for Congressional Radicals during Reconstruction.

Hesseltine, William B., *Ulysses S. Grant: Politician*. New York: Ungar, 1957—The standard account of the troubled Presidency of General Grant.

Lomask, Milton, *Andrew Johnson: President on Trial*. New York: Farrar, Straus & Giroux, 1960—A sympathetic biography of the man who succeeded Lincoln which portrays him as an honest man victimized by Congressional fanatics.

Nevins, Allan, *Hamilton Fish: The Inner History of the Grant Administration*, Vols. I–II. New York: Ungar, 1957—Fish was Secretary of State under both Grant and Hayes. Nevins discusses the details of foreign policy during these years as well as the political scandals of the Grant administration.

Van Deusen, Glyndon, *Horace Greeley: Nineteenth-Century Crusader*. Philadelphia: University of Pennsylvania Press, 1953—A full-length study of the mid-nineteenth century editor of the *New York Tribune,* who was also a leading Republican Party activist and champion of many reform movements.

FICTION

Faulkner, William, *Go Down, Moses*. New York: Random House, 1942—A collection of short stories which describe, directly or indirectly, the fate of one Mississippi family.

Faulkner, William, *The Hamlet*. New York: Random House, 1940—One of Faulkner's series of novels about life in a rural Mississippi county. This book recounts the destruction of the hamlet of Frenchmen's Bend by the Snopes family.

A farmer and his family in Nebraska. Sod homes were common on the Plains where lumber was scarce.

17

The Conquest of the Far West

Every year's advance of our frontier takes in a territory as large as some of the kingdoms of Europe. We are richer by hundreds of millions, the Indian is poorer by a large part of the little that he has. This growth is bringing imperial greatness to the nation; to the Indian it brings wretchedness, destitution, beggary.

—*General Francis A. Walker,*
Commissioner of Indian Affairs

At the end of the Civil War, very few white men lived in the area that stretched westward from Kansas to California and was bounded on the north by the Canadian border and extended south to Texas. By 1890, however, this entire domain had been carved into states and territories and filled with settlers as a result of the most rapid migration in American history.

After 1865, gold and silver miners were the first to come into the territory. Next, cattle breeders and sheepherders entered the Great Plains. Finally, farmers took over the land and learned to farm an area that had little rainfall, few trees, and violent extremes of heat and cold. The settlement of this vast region was made possible by two developments: the building of the first transcontinental railroad and the suppression of the Indians.

617

The Great Plains and the Rocky Mountains were the last part of America to be settled. West of the Rockies were deserts and plateaus with an average yearly rainfall of only 5 inches. The Rockies themselves were towering, nearly impassable mountains. The Great Plains between the Rockies and the Mississippi were so uninviting that they were called "The Great American Desert" by early travelers. This part of the country has an average rainfall of only 20 inches a year. Drought-resistant grasses were the most prevalent vegetation. The wildlife of the plains included antelopes, jack rabbits, coyotes, wolves, prairie dogs, and, most important, buffalo. In 1865 some fifteen million buffalo, called American bison, roamed the grasslands.

White men at first regarded the Great West as a forbidding wasteland, habitable only by Indians and buffalo. Nevertheless, the population of the area surged from over 6 million in 1870 to over 16 million in 1890 as settlers came to dig precious metals from the earth and raise cattle, and later, to farm.

THE PLAINS INDIANS

The Great Plains were inhabited by the most warlike Indians in North America. Even with superior numbers and technology, prospective settlers found that wresting the land from the Indians was no easy matter. Post-Civil War expansion took place with the assistance of the United States Army. Between 1869 and 1876, two hundred pitched battles were fought between soldiers and Indians. Three wars in the 1860s alone cost the American government more than 100 million dollars, or about one thousand dollars for each Indian killed in battle.

NOMADIC HUNTERS

Two innovations introduced to the Indians by Europeans changed the traditional forms of Indian hunting. One was the horse, introduced by the Spanish, and the other was the gun, which they received from the British and the French in the Northeast. By the eighteenth century, guns and horses enabled the Indians to hunt buffalo over wider ranges. The Plains Indians became nomads on horseback. They sometimes had semi-permanent villages where women planted a few crops, but for most of the year the tribes were on the move, living in easily transportable tepees.

The buffalo provided the main source of food and a host of other resources. Buffalo skins were dressed and sometimes tanned. They were used to make tepees as well as clothes, moccasins, blankets, and robes. Buffalo lungs were used for water bags and dried buffalo manure was the chief fuel. Tendons became bowstrings and strips of hide served as lariats. Buffalo bones were shaped into knives. The horns and hoofs were boiled into glue. An oily mixture of buffalo brains was used in dressing hides. Leather made from buffalo hides was turned into pouches, workbags, and cosmetics kits. The buffalo has been aptly described as "a galloping supermarket."

INDIAN CULTURE

The Indians of the Plains had distinctly different languages, which can be grouped into six major families. This diversity of tongues did not, however, prevent communication among the tribes. They had a

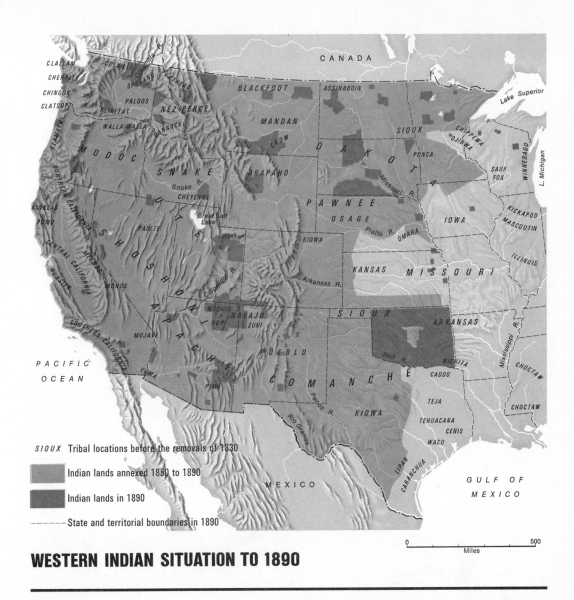

SIOUX Tribal locations before the removals of 1830

Indian lands annexed 1850 to 1890

Indian lands in 1890

-------- State and territorial boundaries in 1890

0 ———————————————— 500
Miles

WESTERN INDIAN SITUATION TO 1890

highly developed shared sign language which permitted them to tell long stories, exchange ideas, and give precise, detailed warnings or advice to one another.

The principal tribes of the Plains were: the Sioux in the Dakotas, the Blackfeet of Idaho and western Montana, the Crow of southern Montana, the Cheyenne and Arapaho of the central Plains, the Pawnee in western Nebraska, the Osage in western Kansas, and the Apaches and Comanches of

Arizona and New Mexico. The Hopi and Zuñi Indians of the Southwest lived in adobe cities in communal fashion and were primarily farmers and herders. To the west were the California seed-gatherers, a group of Indians who dwelled together in very primitive bands, existing on seeds and roots dug from the ground.

Among the Plains Indians, bravery was a much-stressed ideal, and in many tribes young boys were taught that it was more glorious to be killed in battle as a youth than to die as a peaceful old man.

However, the Plains Indians did not indulge in prolonged periods of warfare. The primary motives for entering battle were the seeking of revenge against another tribe or the capture of its horses.

An important way to gain distinction in Indian society was through generosity. The liberal bestowal of gifts on friends and relatives was as significant as bravery in battle. The Indians reserved their highest praise for two classes of tribesmen—those who "had given to the poor on many occasions, and had invited guests to many feasts" and those who "had killed several of the foe and had brought home many horses."

A tribe was never large. The average number of members in the tribes of the 1850s was about three or four thousand. In general the men hunted and the women farmed, if the tribe was semi-nomadic, or collected berries and roots, if the tribe was exclusively nomadic. This sexual division of labor was so strong that when white men tried to force Indian males to farm, they at first had little success. Males who did till the soil were taunted by the other braves. Moreover, the ethic of generosity worked against a successful agricultural way of life since a farmer would have felt obliged to give away large amounts of his crops and profits.

The Plains Indians did little weaving, but the women were quite skillful in porcupine-quill embroidery. Beadwork, painting on skins, and rawhide decoration were also prized crafts. Colors extracted from the earth were organized into geometric designs with symbolic meanings.

An 1891 photograph of a Sioux Indian camp. The white man's introduction of guns and horses, his inane massacre of the buffalo—the chief source of Indian food and clothing—and his greed for the Indian land all but destroyed the highly developed culture of the Plains Indians.

SUPERVISION OF THE INDIANS

Before the 1860s there had been no serious conflicts with the Plains Indians because whites had not lingered but simply passed through the Plains on their way to Oregon and California. The United States government had pledged that the Indians could own "forever" the land west of a line extending from the Wisconsin territory in the North to the western borders of Missouri and Arkansas in the South.

CONCENTRATION

In 1851 the government took the first step toward breaking its word by calling a council of ten thousand Indians in Wyoming. Ostensibly the purpose of the meeting was to encourage the Indians to set definite limits to each tribe's hunting grounds in order to avoid intertribal wars, but actually the objective was to enable the government to deal with each tribe separately. Earlier in the century, when the Indian tribes east of the Mississippi banded together under Tecumseh, they posed a serious threat to settlers. The government was determined that no new Indian nation should emerge again. The Plains Indians were promised gifts and payments in return for agreeing to draw clear boundaries between each tribe's hunting grounds. The government called this policy "concentration," but it could have been called "divide and conquer."

THE INDIAN BUREAU

Two government agencies dealt with the Indians of the Plains—the Army, which acted when war broke out and to enforce the signing of unfavorable treaties, and the Bureau of Indian Affairs (transferred from the War Department to the Department of the Interior in 1849). The Indian Bureau was riddled with corruption. Federal agents distributed motheaten blankets and spoiled beef to the Indians and pocketed most of the funds appropriated by the government for these goods. One agent, for example, earned a salary of 1,500 dollars a year, but after four years he was able to retire with 50,000 dollars. Another agent owned a mine and consistently diverted supplies intended for the Indians to his own mining operations. When an inspector was sent to investigate the fraud, he was bought off with shares in the mine.

THE SAND CREEK MASSACRE

Corruption and incompetence in the Indian Bureau were only minor ills compared to the pressure put on the Indians by miners. The Cheyenne and Arapaho had been guaranteed their lands in Colorado, but the discovery of gold in that area in 1858 attracted thousands of prospectors. To avoid a head-on collision, the government purchased most of Colorado in 1861 from the Indians—barely 10 years after the land was pledged to them "forever." The tribes were removed to a barren territory near Sand Creek in southeastern Colorado. However, in 1864 Colonel J. M. Chivington ordered his seven hundred soldiers to attack the Cheyenne without warning. Chivington agreed heartily when one of his aides said:

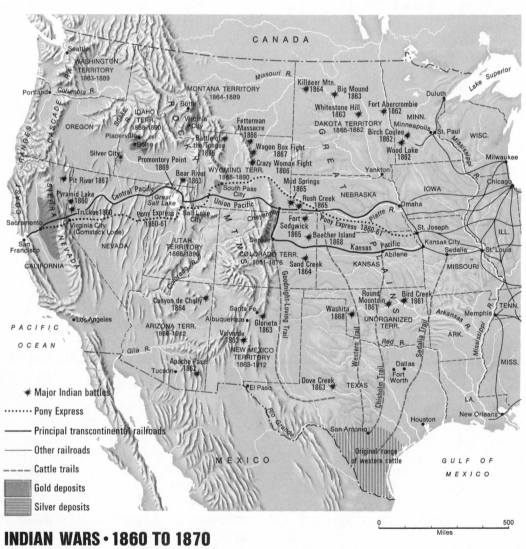

Major Indian battles

······· Pony Express

—— Principal transcontinental railroads

—— Other railroads

----- Cattle trails

Gold deposits

Silver deposits

INDIAN WARS · 1860 TO 1870

Map labels:

CANADA

Seattle
WASHINGTON TERRITORY 1863-1889
Portland
Columbia R.
OREGON
MONTANA TERRITORY 1864-1889
Missouri R.
Killdeer Mtn. 1864
Big Mound 1863
Fort Abercrombie 1862
Duluth
Lake Superior
MINN.
Minneapolis
St. Paul
WISC.
Whitestone Hill 1863
DAKOTA TERRITORY 1868-1882
Birch Coulee 1862
Milwaukee
Butte
Virginia City
IDAHO TERR. 1863-1890
Fetterman Massacre 1866
Wood Lake 1862
Mississippi R.
Chicago
Silver City
Placerville
Boise
Battle of the Tongue 1865
Wagon Box Fight 1867
GREAT
Promontory Point 1869
Bear River 1863
WYOMING TERR. 1868-1890
Crazy Woman Fight 1866
Yankton
IOWA
Pyramid Lake 1860
Central Pacific
Great Salt Lake
South Pass City
Mud Springs 1865
Rush Creek 1865
NEBRASKA
Omaha
Truckee 1860
Pony Express 1860-61
Salt Lake City
Union Pacific
Cheyenne
Pony Express 1860-61
Platte R.
St. Joseph
ILL.
Sacramento
Virginia City (Comstock Lode)
NEVADA
UTAH TERRITORY 1868-1896
Denver
Fort Sedgwick 1865
Beecher Island 1868
Kansas Pacific
Abilene
Kansas City
Sedalia
St. Louis
San Francisco
CALIFORNIA
Colorado R.
COLORADO TERR. 1861-1876
Sand Creek 1864
KANSAS
MISSOURI
PACIFIC OCEAN
Los Angeles
Canyon de Chelly 1864
Santa Fe
Washita 1868
Round Mountain 1861
Bird Creek 1861
Arkansas R.
Memphis
TENN.
Albuquerque
Glorieta 1863
UNORGANIZED TERR.
ARIZONA TERR. 1866-1912
Valverde 1863
NEW MEXICO TERRITORY 1863-1912
Goodnight-Loving Trail
Western Trail
Red R.
Chisholm Trail
Sedalia Trail
ARK.
Mississippi R.
MISS.
Gila R.
Apache Pass 1862
Tucson
El Paso
Dove Creek 1863
TEXAS
Dallas
Fort Worth
LA.
New Orleans
Rio Grande
San Antonio
Houston
MEXICO
Original range of western cattle
GULF OF MEXICO

0   500   Miles

622

"I think and earnestly believe the Indians to be an obstacle to civilization, and should be exterminated." Nearly all of the Cheyenne were murdered in cold blood, despite all efforts of their chief to halt the massacre.

The massacre of Sand Creek. After relocating Indians from another reservation in Colorado, the United States government moved troops to Sand Creek, and proceeded to exterminate the relocated Indians.

One of the officers in Chivington's militia described the event in these chilling terms:

We arrived at the Indian village about daylight . . . Colonel Chivington moved his regiment to the front, the Indians retreating up the creek, and hiding under the banks . . . White Antelope ran toward our columns unarmed, and with both arms raised, but was killed. Several other of the warriors

INDIAN WARS · 1870 TO 1890

were killed in like manner. The women and children were huddled together, and most of our fire was concentrated on them. . . . The Indian warriors, about one hundred in number, fought desperately; there were about five hundred all told. I estimated the loss of the Indians to be from one hundred and twenty-five to one hundred and seventy-five killed; no wounded fell into our hands and all the dead were scalped. The Indian who was pointed out as White Antelope had his fingers cut off. Our force was so large there was no necessity of firing on the Indians. They did not return the fire until after our troops had fired several rounds. . . . I told Colonel Chivington . . . that it would be murder, in every sense of the word, if he attacked those Indians. His reply was, to bring his fist down close to my face, "Damn any man who sympathizes with Indians" . . . he had come to kill Indians and believed it to be honorable to kill Indians under any and all circumstances.

After the massacre, the Cheyenne and other tribes abandoned the Sand Creek reservation and again were forced to relocate, betrayed once more by the government. Although miners in the West congratulated Chivington on his "brave" action in establishing peace and security in the area, many Easterners condemned him. The Commissioner of Indian Affairs denounced the massacre as outright murder. Old Indian scouts, such as Kit Carson and Jim Bridger, expressed outrage. Humanitarian indignation over the entire history of Indian dealings finally found eloquent expression in an influential book, *A Century of Dishonor*, by Helen Hunt Jackson. Recounting the long record of broken treaties and rank injustice, the author demanded a change in government policy, and sent a copy of her book to every member of Congress. No one, however, was ever punished for the Sand Creek massacre, though the murdered Indians were theoretically "wards" of the federal government.

A SIOUX UPRISING

Another slaughter took place a few years later in Montana, this time with white men as the victims. Gold was discovered in Montana in the early 1860s, and miners flocked into the territory, ignoring Indian treaty rights. To provide transportation to and from the mines near Bozeman, miners began to construct the Powder River Road from Wyoming through southern Montana, directly through the Sioux hunting grounds. Reacting to this invasion, more than two thousand Sioux rose up under their great chief, Red Cloud, and ambushed and destroyed an eighty-one-man force under Colonel William J. Fetterman.

Up to this point Indians had relied on bows and arrows, but paradoxically, despite the ambush of Fetterman (December 21, 1866), the Bureau of Indian Affairs began to issue rifles and ammunition in return for Indian treaty signatures. Their intimate knowledge of the terrain, coupled with good marksmanship and incomparable horsemanship, now made small bands of Indians extremely dangerous foes, even when vastly outnumbered by government soldiers. According to General Sherman, fifty Indians could checkmate five thousand soldiers. Eventually the Army won the advantage because of its troop strength and because it had the railroad and the telegraph at its disposal. Information sent via telegraph enabled the Army to keep close watch on Indian movements, and when reinforcements were needed they could be sent immediately by train.

THE PEACE COMMISSION

It became obvious that the "concentration" policy was not working, primarily because gold continued to lure prospectors into Indian territory, and their contacts with the Indians invariably led to violence. These outbreaks led to Congressional joint committee investigation in 1867. Its report indicted the miners and blamed their encroachment on tribal lands for the disturbances. At the same time, a Peace Commission studied ways to end the conflict. In a day when there was little understanding of the differences between the two cultures, the commission's recommendations were naive and ineffective. The commission proposed that the Indians should be confined to two small reservations, a northern one in the Black Hills of the Dakota Territory, and one to the south, in the Oklahoma Territory. In two great conferences the leading chiefs agreed to the government's plan. Henceforth, they were to give up their life as nomads and become sedentary, peaceful farmers.

The "small reservations" policy did not work either. The Army would herd Indians into one of the two reservations, but as soon as it left, the Indians would drift back into the open countryside. They did not want to give up hunting buffalo, and when the herds moved to their summer feeding grounds, the tribes followed them. The government promised liberal supplies if the Indians would cooperate, but these promises too went unfulfilled. Finally, the American government had a mistaken notion of the chief's role, since he could not sign away lands without consulting his men. Moreover, the Indians had difficulty in understanding the idea of private property, and hence found little meaning in treaties that handed over land from one party to another. General Philip Sheridan, after visiting the Indians, reported, "Many of the young men were bitterly opposed to what had been done, and claimed that most of the signatures had been obtained by misrepresentation and through offers of arms and ammunition to be issued in the spring of 1868."

THE SIOUX WAR

Feelings were intensified when Indian agents systematically stole funds and food intended for the reservations. Red Cloud, the Sioux chief, asked a visiting Yale professor to take samples of the moldy flour and beef that agents had given the tribe, to show to President Grant. The professor agreed, but Grant, though shocked, did nothing about the situation. Indians who lived near army camps fared no better. For example, one quartermaster in New Mexico sold for his personal profit twelve thousand pounds of corn intended for the hungry Apaches.

Mistreatment of the Indians was both cruel and illegal. Radicals in Congress had pushed through the Thirteenth Amendment in 1868 which forbade slavery, but Indians were frequently forced into "involuntary servitude." The Fourteenth Amendment passed in 1870 made citizens of "all persons born or naturalized in the United States" and assured all citizens equal rights. Nevertheless, as a modern authority on Indian history has written, the federal and state governments "denied Native Americans basic civil rights, even going so far as to forcibly suppress their religions, customs, social organization, and languages. . . . Of course, the government considered most Native Americans 'wards' of the United States. However, the Constitution does not extend to the government the authority to declare residents of the United States 'wards,' . . . It would appear, then, that all of the coercive policies adopted by the federal government from 1870 to 1928 were strictly illegal. . . ."

Abusive and illegal government policies brought further bloodshed. In 1874 miners discovered gold in the Black Hills region of South Dakota, part of the Sioux reservation. Thousands of prospectors swarmed into the region. The Army tried for a season to keep them out, but then gave up and overlooked the invasion. Angered by the presence of the prospectors as well as the approach of crews building the Northern Pacific Railroad, the Sioux again went on the warpath. The Sioux and other tribes were concentrated along the Big Horn River in southern Montana Territory. The government ordered them to return to their reservation, but the Indians ignored the command and won several small victories over the Army. By the summer of 1876, three columns of troops were in pursuit of the Sioux, who were led by Chief Crazy Horse and their powerful medicine man, Sitting Bull.

A young officer, Colonel George A. Custer, was particularly eager to gain fame as an Indian fighter. Because he had recently exposed corruption in the War Department, he was on President Grant's blacklist. Eager to regain favor through a great exploit, Custer recklessly ignored orders and followed the Sioux into a trap. At the Little Big Horn River in Montana, Custer and 264 cavalrymen were killed by the Sioux on June 26, 1876.

The following year the more peaceful Nez Percé Indians of Oregon and Idaho were finally routed by the Army as they were fleeing to Canada. Chief Joseph voiced the feeling of many Indians when he said, "I am tired of fighting . . . My heart is sick and sad. From where the sun now stands, I will fight no more forever." The remnants of the tribe were put on a reservation.

DESTRUCTION OF TRIBAL LIFE

The Indians did not give up fighting, and they were never successfully defeated by the Army. It was the disappearance of the buffalo, their chief resource, that sapped their strength and ended their nomadic way of life. After the Civil War as many as fifteen million buffalo roamed the plains, but by 1875 fewer than a thousand survived. The animals had become the prey of white hunters. One hunter, William F. Cody, better known as Buffalo Bill, had killed 4,280 buffalo in eighteen months. He had been hired by the railroad to provide on-the-

The White Man's Attack

" . . . *The American public does not know the meaning of the phrase, Indian atrocity —not its true meaning. For their sakes I am glad they do not, but for the sake of the small but not insignificant number of Americans whose homes are darkened through their knowledge of it, I wish the American public did know it.*

The whites on our frontier are suffering the tyranny of a democracy. The Indian question is a local question, and the treatment of it by representatives of the people at large is naturally careless and defective. The people of Arizona and New Mexico are not allowed to settle their Indian troubles themselves, and the national government will not settle them for them.

It was a mistake ever to remove westward the Indians that had settled on reservations east of the Mississippi. If they had remained there, we should now have samples of Indian life and character, and more or less interest in Indian legislation in every section of the country. The Indian question, if there still were such a question, would be national in fact as well as in name, and its final answer not far off. As it is, people in the East can not know the horrible particulars of Indian murder, torture, and outrage. There is no public organ to give them utterance. Their revolting indecency often excludes them from every respectable paper and the lowest publication of sensations and horrors would reject them on the very eminence of their qualification for admission; for the most morbidly-depraved imagination would be sickened by them. . . .

—John Bigelow, Jr.

Geronimo's Defense

". . . I want to talk first of the causes which led me to leave the reservation. I was living quietly and contented, doing and thinking of no harm, . . . I was living peaceably and satisfied when people began to speak bad of me. I should be glad to know who started those stories. I was living peaceably with my family, having plenty to eat, sleeping well, taking care of my people, and perfectly contented. I don't know where those bad stories first came from. There we were doing well and my people well. I was behaving well. I hadn't killed a horse or a man, American or Indian. I don't know what was the matter with the people in charge of us. They knew this to be so, and yet they said I was a bad man and the worst man there; but what harm had I done? I was living peaceably and well, but I did not leave on my own accord. Had I so left it would have been right to blame me; but as it is, blame those men who started this talk about me. Some time before I left an Indian named Wodiskay had a talk with me. He said, "they are going to arrest you," but I paid no attention to him, knowing that I had done no wrong; and the wife of Mangus, "Huera," told me that they were going to seize me and put me and Mangus in the guard-house, and I learned from the American and Apache soldiers, from Chato, and Mickey Free, that the Americans were going to arrest me and hang me, and so I left. I would like to know now who it was that gave the order to arrest me and hang me. I was living peaceably there with my family under the shade of the trees, doing just what General Crook had told me I must do and trying to follow his advice. . . . I was praying to the light and to the darkness, to God and to the sun, to let me live quietly there with my family. . . .

"I have several times asked for peace, but trouble has come from the agents and interpreters. I don't want what has passed to happen again. Now, I am going to tell you something else. The Earth-Mother is listening to me and I hope that all may be so arranged that from now on there shall be no trouble and that we shall always have peace. . . ."

"

—*Britton Davis*

spot food for the hundreds of workers laying track. Many hunters, including the Grand Duke Alexis of Russia, third son of the Tsar, came to the Plains for the sport. Hunters often shot at the animals from train windows and cut out only the tongue as a trophy, leaving the body to the vultures. Buffalo robes became a fad in the East; thousands of hides were shipped across the Mississippi. Buffalo meat also proved tasty and popular, and buffalo bones were ground up and used as fertilizer. In two years the railroads shipped East a million and a half hides, almost seven million pounds of meat, and thirty-two million pounds of bones.

Yet even after the destruction of the buffalo, there were still the same Indians who had to be forced to accept the white man's authority. The Apaches, under their chief Geronimo, carried on the struggle until 1886, when their leader was captured and exiled to Florida. The Sioux, bewildered and humiliated by the dissolution of their cultural identity, espoused a new religion that taught that a messiah was coming who would deliver their people from bondage. When federal troops tried to enforce a government ban against this cult and its "ghost dancing," hundreds of Indians were killed in battle at Wounded Knee, South Dakota, on December 29, 1890. The next month the last of the Sioux surrendered. One of the Sioux holy men, Black Elk, spoke out: "Once we were happy in our own country and we were seldom hungry, for then the two-leggeds and the four-

627

leggeds lived together like relatives, and there was plenty for them and for us. But then the white men came, and they have made little islands for us and other little islands for the four-leggeds, and always these islands are becoming smaller, for around them surges the gnawing flood of the white man; and it is dirty with lies and greed."

New government policies further destroyed Indian culture. In 1884 the Department of the Interior adopted a criminal code that forbade and penalized certain Indian religious practices. In 1887 the Dawes Severalty Act openly set out to destroy tribal independence and unity. During the period of "concentration," the government had dealt with each tribe as a unit. Now the Dawes Act proposed to ignore the unity of the tribe and to divide the tribal reservation lands among individual Indians.

It gave the President power to dissolve the tribes and divide the reservation lands into 160-acre farms for each family and lesser acreages for unmarried adults, orphans, and dependent children. Of the 137 million acres in the reservations only 47 million were needed to make the farm allotments to the Indians. The remaining 90 million acres were made available to new settlers. Revenue from the sale of this land was then used to educate the Indians. To make sure the Indians were not tricked out of their property, the Dawes Act stipulated that Indians could not sell the land for 25 years. Nevertheless, by the 1930s more than half the land given to Indians under the Dawes Act had passed out of their hands through various manipulations of the law. Indians were also made citizens of the United States by the act, but this provision was not fully implemented until 1924.

Burying the dead after the Battle of Wounded Knee, S.D. –1890.

The philosophy behind the Dawes Act assumed the desirability of assimilating the Indians into the predominant white culture. Yet, while some Indians did adopt the mores of white society, most wanted to keep their tribal structure and retain communal landholding. In the twentieth century, many sociologists and anthropologists began to stress the value of cultural diversity in American society, and this point of view is gradually replacing the older concept of assimilation.

GOLD FEVER

Invasion of Indian lands invariably followed the discovery of gold. The heyday of mining was between 1860 and 1880. Individual prospectors used picks, shovels, and pans to remove gold from deposits of sand, gravel, or earth. Since gold was heavier than soil, the prospector would jiggle a panful of sediment in flowing water, and everything but the gold would float away. This method, called "placer" mining, quickly exhausted the surface gold. The remaining ore was locked in quartz crystals beneath the surface of the earth, and expensive equipment was required to extract it. Only large companies could afford such equip-

One of the last battles between the Indians and the white man took place at Wounded Knee in 1890. The battle resulted from the white man's attempt to outlaw the Indian's religion. This photograph shows a burial trench for the Indians killed at Wounded Knee.

ment. They moved in, dug mines, and crushed tons of quartz, drawing out the gold through a complex refining process. The original prospectors either stayed and worked for wages or drifted off in search of new sites of surface gold. Finally, when even the gold below the earth was exhausted, many of the company's workers turned to farming or ranching. Small towns had risen near the mines and they attracted farmers and ranchers from other parts of the country or Europe.

Many of the first prospectors came from California. These men were generally experienced at pan and placer prospecting and had already searched for gold in California. Only a few of them found the fortunes they were seeking. More than 500 million dollars' worth of ore came out of the West between 1848 and 1858, and most of the profits went into the pockets of East Coast financiers who backed the big mining companies.

In July, 1858, gold was found along Dry Creek, near present-day Denver. The following spring about one hundred thousand gold seekers started out for Colorado from the Missouri River towns. A new lode was discovered in the mountains west of Denver near Central City. Later, silver mining at Leadville and Aspen added to Colorado's wealth, as did a gold strike at Cripple Creek in the 1890s. By the turn of the century, however, Colorado had exhausted most of its resources of precious metals and farming and ranching became the mainstays of its economy.

THE COMSTOCK LODE

In 1859 the famous Comstock Lode, rich in both gold and silver, was discovered in western Nevada. The most fabulous strike in the West, the Comstock Lode was soon being panned and mined by thousands of prospectors, most of them from California. Ten thousand inhabitants settled Virginia City by 1860, where a year before there was

629

only sand and coyotes. Soon Nevada was producing more gold and silver than all the other states combined. Between 1860 and 1880, 306 million dollars was earned from the Comstock.

In 1864 pay dirt was struck at Last Chance Gulch in Montana, but gold soon became less important to Montana miners than copper, which was in demand as an essential component of newly invented electrical equipment. In Arizona the biggest boom town was Tombstone, which produced millions of dollars' worth of silver between 1880 and 1900. The last gold rush occurred in the Sioux Reservation territory in the Black Hills country of South Dakota in 1874. It was this miners' invasion of the Indian preserve that had led to the Battle of Little Big Horn.

MINING TOWNS

Perched above the Comstock Lode was Virginia City, which Mark Twain described in *Roughing It:*

Joy sat on every countenance, and there was a glad, almost fierce, intensity in every eye, that told of the money-getting schemes that held sway in every heart. Money was as plenty as dust; every individual considered himself wealthy, and a melancholy

countenance was nowhere to be seen. There were military companies, fire companies, brass-bands, banks, hotels, theaters, "hurdy-gurdy houses," wide-open gambling palaces, political pow-wows, civic processions, street-fights, murders, inquests, riots, a whiskey-mill every fifteen steps . . . a dozen breweries, and half a dozen jails and station-houses in full operation, and some talk of building a church. The "flush times" were in magnificent flower.

A mining town in Montana. Towns like this came into being almost overnight if ore were discovered nearby. The towns were deserted just as quickly when the ore ran out.

Towns like Virginia City, Deadwood, South Dakota, and Tombstone, Arizona, were crowded with gamblers and outlaws. Virginia City had twenty-five saloons before its population reached four thousand. Deadwood was the home of such free-wheeling characters as "Wild Bill" Hickok, "Deadwood Dick," "California Jack," "Poker Alice," and "Calamity Jane." Even some sheriffs were notorious gunmen, such as Wyatt Earp, the marshal of Tombstone, and Henry Plummer of Montana, an outlaw in his spare time, whose gang killed more than a hundred men.

The mining property itself was governed in every town by a miners' association, which established the size of claims, the number of claims each person could hold, and arbitrated water and gulch rights and questions relating to absentee ownership and land tenure. Eventually, as each community grew in population, vigilance committees to keep order and miners' associations gave way to more traditional forms of governmental organization.

The mining towns were connected to the outside world by horse-drawn coaches and ox-drawn freight wagons. Before railroad lines ran to the mining centers, stage-

A mining community in Colorado. The discovery of gold and silver drew thousands of people to the West Coast where makeshift accommodations were set up for the miners.

coach companies performed an important and profitable function. After 1866 the biggest such enterprise was Wells, Fargo & Company. Travelers were carried in specially constructed Concord coaches, designed to stand up under the shock of rough roads. To carry gold out of the West, the company owned six thousand wagons and seventy-five thousand oxen. In one boom year the miners paid Wells, Fargo three million dollars in freight bills.

Beginning April 3, 1860, the Pony Express carried mail from San Francisco through the Great Plains to St. Joseph, Missouri. Nearly two hundred stations were strung out across the country and riders would change mounts every 15 miles or so. The mail sometimes reached San Francisco from St. Joseph after only eight days—an amazing record for swiftness on horseback through dangerous country. The special charge was five dollars per half ounce, later reduced to a dollar.

The transcontinental telegraph began to operate on October 24, 1861, ending the brief, colorful career of the Pony Express. Similarly, in 1869 the completion of the transcontinental railroad ended Wells, Fargo & Company's long-distance hauling, although animal-drawn vehicles did continue to serve small communities in the West for decades to come.

CATTLE FEVER

For 20 years after 1865 the West was dominated by a great cattle kingdom that stretched across the plains from Texas to the Canadian border and from the Rockies on the west to Kansas on the east.

This kingdom was built upon a revolution in the meat-packing industry. Before 1860 beef could not be transported long distances unless it was pickled. There was no form of refrigeration to keep the meat from spoiling. After the Civil War, however, the railroad network and the invention of the refrigerated railroad car permitted beef to be transported from the slaughterhouses of Chicago or Kansas City to the great industrial cities of the Middle West and East, where an ever-growing urban population provided a huge market for fresh meat.

There were five million beef cattle roaming the plains of Texas in 1865, but up to this point they had been sold primarily for their hides and were worth only a few dollars a head. Texas ranchers knew that a steer would bring as much as fifty dollars in the North, but they had not figured a way to transport cattle there. After the Civil War the nearest railroad terminals were still hundreds of miles away.

THE LONG DRIVE

In 1866 and 1867 Texans opened the era of the "long drive." Cattlemen discovered that steers could be driven slowly from Texas to a shipping point in Kansas, Nebraska, or Wyoming, and that instead of losing weight during the journey the cattle would actually fatten up on the nourishing grasses of the Plains. Few farmers had yet settled in the Great Plains, and the Indians, after 1867, were being confined more and more effectively to reservations. Every year there were fewer buffalo to compete for the herbage of the Plains. Thus the cattlemen were able to feed their animals on millions of acres of free pasturage. Between 1866 and 1888, some ten million steers were driven to market, and cattlemen earned a yearly profit of as much as 40 percent on their investment. Cattle-raising became such a big business that in just one year twenty corporations were chartered in Wyoming alone, with a combined capital of twelve million dollars. These companies controlled millions of acres of ranch lands.

LIFE ON THE RANGE

The American imagination was stirred by the image of a new folk hero, the cowboy. He wore chaps over his jeans, high-heeled boots, and a ten-gallon Stetson hat, sat in a 40-pound "Western" saddle, and roped calves with an 18-foot lasso. His life, which seemed independent and adventurous, was at the same time lonely and never well paid (wages ranged from twenty-five to forty dollars a month). In addition to guarding the herds on the long drive, cowboys broke wild horses and repaired equipment.

Every spring the cowboys would round up the new calves and brand them with the distinctive insignia of their employer. "Mavericks," stray, unbranded cattle, were divided up equally among the several possible owners. Mature three- and four-year-olds were combined into herds of two to five thousand steer. A herd of this size needed only about twelve or fifteen cowboys to supervise it, and five or six extra horses for each man. The cattle traveled about 15 miles a day. They were stopped for an hour or two every morning and again at noon to graze. Cowboys had to stay ever alert. A sudden roll of thunder, a strange animal cry, or even some very small disturbance might frighten the cattle and send them on an uncontrollable stampede. Eventually, after traversing 1,200 to 1,500 miles, the herd would be halted at a "cow town" such as Abilene, Kansas, from where it was shipped to the East. In 1871 the Santa Fe extended its tracks to Dodge City, Kansas, while the Union Pacific established a railhead at Ogallala, Nebraska, and these cities also became shipping centers.

The long drive depended on open range. As long as few inhabitants lived on the Great Plains, the cattle were free to roam unimpeded all the way from Texas to Canada. The Indians seldom objected to groups passing through the territory; in fact, the Cherokee even issued grazing licenses for a small fee.

DOOM OF THE OPEN RANGE

Between 1878 and 1885 the open-range cattle business reached its peak. Large operators, no longer satisfied to share the open range, claimed exclusive rights to grazing lands. In order to bring some order to the cutthroat competition for control of the land, stock growers' associations were formed. They worked out rules for governing the range which had the force of law in some Western territories. These regulations also restricted competition in the cattle business by keeping out newcomers, but they were never completely effective in preventing new entrepreneurs from entering this lucrative enterprise.

By 1885 the cattle-boom years were coming to a close as grazing became more limited. Homesteading farmers were surrounding their property with the same kind of barbed wire that ranchers used to fence their ranges. Barbed wire was an important commodity in a treeless country where rail fences could not be built. In 1874 Joseph F. Glidden started manufacturing the wire, and by 1883 the American Steel and Wire Company was turning out 600 miles of it

a day. Also, sheepmen were grazing their animals across the Plains, and cattle would not eat where sheep had grazed, since the sheep ate the grass down to the root, leaving nothing for the cattle. The sheep owners and cattlemen became involved in many hundreds of small, bitter skirmishes. In addition, Texas fever (caused by a parasite and transmitted by a tick) to which the Texas longhorns had long since become immune, infected newly introduced breeds of cattle and caused them to die by the thousands.

Overproduction drove the price of beef down at the same time that cattle-raising expenses rose. Then, in the summer of 1886, drought struck the Great Plains. The herds, feeding on a diminished range sparse in vegetation, were in weak condition when winter set in—and the winter of 1886 to 1887 was the worst in memory. When spring finally came, nine out of every ten cattle on the range were dead.

After this disaster, many small cattlemen sold out to big corporations. Cattle breeding, like mining before it, ceased to be a spirited, individualistic enterprise and became an efficiently managed business. The remaining open range gave way to enclosed ranches. Like the farmers, the cattlemen fenced in their land and laid up supplies of hay and feed in barns to see the herd through the winter. The railroads were now building lines down into the Southwest, so there was no longer any need to drive cattle hundreds of miles to a railroad terminal. The trains brought in much of the feed for the cattle and caried away thousands of pounds of dressed beef every week. Blooded bulls were introduced into the herds and scientific hybrid breeding began. The Texas longhorns were hardy but sinewy animals descended from Spanish runaway bulls. The horns of some of them had an 8-foot span. These durable but not very tender animals were now bred with less sturdy but fleshier breeds. The relative frailty of the new hybrids was another reason cattlemen could no longer entrust their herds to the perils of the long drive, even if barbed wire had not closed off that possibility. In 1887 an English reporter, writing about the amazingly quick conversion of the open range to fenced-in ranches, observed:

No doubt there is money in cattle yet, but the halcyon days of enormous fortunes rapidly made are past. Well watered and adequately sheltered grazing lands have now become difficult to find. Year by year the acreage over which cattle can range decreases. The granger with his spade and plough drives before him the cattleman, who himself in former years drove out the aboriginal Indian.

FARMING IN THE WEST

After the miners came the cattlemen, who were followed by the farmers. Neither mining nor cattle-breeding brought large numbers of people to the great West, but farming caused the population to almost triple from 1870 to 1890.

Farmers, however, did not have an easy time adapting to this new frontier. In fact, farmers who tried to conquer the arid plains had a tougher battle than did earlier American farmers anywhere in the nation. Many farming families, exhausted after a few years of living in sod houses, tilling dusty fields, carting water from the nearest well miles away, gave up in despair and went back to their former homes. At all times

farming on the Great Plains was an expensive and risky proposition. In the winter, blizzards sixty and seventy degrees below zero would sweep across the country. In the summer, droughts often destroyed crops, tornadoes struck unexpectedly, and in the summer of 1874, a grasshopper plague attacked the vegetation. Furthermore, farmers had to use the railway lines to receive supplies from the East and ship their harvests back at charges that were often disastrously high.

THE HOMESTEAD ACT

The Homestead Act of 1862 had provided that any settler could have a 160-acre farm free if he lived on it for 5 years, improved it, and paid a fee of ten dollars. This act was carefully designed as an aid to those of limited economic means. Presumably, hordes of landless tenant farmers and jobless urban dwellers would rush across the Mississippi in response to the offer to set up their own homesteads, so that America would again be composed of small, independent property-holders.

Subsequent events did not fit into this idealistic scheme. First, few truly poor Americans could afford the cost of transporting their families and farm machinery to the Great Plains (about a thousand dollars at a minimum). Second, soil and weather conditions were utterly foreign to anything in the typical farmer's experience, and only the brave or foolhardy attempted to till the dry, windswept land. A serious flaw in the Homestead Act, however, was its provision of 160 acres, an area not practical for Western farming. This number had been determined by middle western standards, where 160 acres was considered generous. But in the West a farmer had to irrigate his land, in which case 160 acres was too large an area to work, or, more frequently, he had to practice dry farming, a technique that required expensive farm equipment. If a farmer spent a great deal on farm machinery, he could recoup his investment only by owning a huge farm, extending over thousands of acres.

Corruption also blighted the Homestead Act. Wealthy land speculators bribed poor people to file claim for homesteads and hand them the property rights. As the historians Charles and Mary Beard wrote:

Millions of acres of valuable timber, mineral, and grazing lands were literally stolen under the eyes of dishonest or negligent officials in the federal land office; and other millions were wrested from the government by chicanery of one kind or another. In the history of political corruption, seldom if ever, had there been transactions on a scale so prodigious or conducted with more brazen effrontery. Thousands of great fortunes in the East as well as in the West were built out of resources wrung from the government for a pittance or for a bribe to its officials, if not actually stolen. . . . In the lavish parceling out of the national domain, some acreage went directly to men and women who entered lands under the Homestead Act. Relatively speaking, however, it was small in size.

LAND POLICY ADJUSTMENTS

To adapt the Homestead Act to the special climate and soil conditions of the Great West, Congress passed a number of supplementary land laws. The Timber Culture Act of 1873 provided that a homesteader could obtain an additional 160 acres if he planted trees on at least 40 acres. This piece of legislation was impractical, since growing trees in an arid region was impossible. The Desert Land Act of 1877 awarded temporary title to 640 acres for 160 dollars. After three years the farmer could have permanent title by paying an additional 640 dollars and by proving that at least one-eighth of his tract had been irrigated. Few farmers, however, could af-

ford to irrigate in desert areas and generally only wealthy cattle ranchers benefited from this act. The third government "remedy" was the Timber and Stone Act of 1878. This measure offered for sale to each individual 160-acre tracts of valuable forest land at the low cost of two and a half dollars an acre. Again few small farmers benefited, while the poorly drawn act permitted a few great lumber companies to destroy many of the forests covering the Rocky and the Sierra Mountains. Once again corporations hired dummy entrymen to file claims. The commissioner of the General Land Office complained in 1901: "In many instances whole townships have been entered under this law in the interest of one person or firm, to whom the lands have been conveyed as soon as receipts for the purchase price were issued."

THE RAILROADS AND WESTERN SETTLEMENT

The railroad was the crucial instrument in enabling the great Plains to become agricultural. Not only did the miles of track link the prairie states to the East, but railroad companies actively encouraged immigration. The Northern Pacific Railroad at one point had one thousand paid agents handing out leaflets in Europe, which glowed with descriptions of the fertile Eden that lay west of the Mississippi. The Union Pacific described its holdings as "a flowery meadow . . . watered by numerous streams." Steamship lines, eager to transport European settlers, joined in the selling campaign. Altogether the railroads owned 183 million acres, granted to them by the federal and state governments as subsidies. Some railroads tried to hold out for the highest possible prices for their land, but in general they sold it at low rates, from one to ten dollars an acre, because every farmer who settled along the track was another potential freight customer. Indeed, until the end of the nineteenth century far more land was sold to settlers by the train companies than was settled under the Homestead Act.

Despite land-grabbing by corrupt speculators and the terrible hardships of farming on the Plains, many parts of the West were quickly populated during the quarter-century from 1865 to 1890. Hordes of land-hungry farmers from Scandinavia poured into the Northwest after 1860. Irish, Scottish, English, German, and Russian immigrants also made up a significant proportion of the population that settled the Great Plains in the 1870s. Some of these Europeans came to escape military duty, others were lured by the bright promises of railroad agents, and some fled Europe because of the poor wheat-growing years of the 1870s. Most settlers, however, were poor American farmers from the South and the Old West. One homesteader who settled in Greer County, western Oklahoma, inspired a famous folk song:

> Hurrah for Greer County! The land of the free,
> The land of the bedbug, grasshopper, and flea;
> I'll sing of its praises, I'll tell of its fame,
> While starving to death on my government claim.

NEW STATES

Kansas became the first new state west of the Mississippi in 1861. Three years later, Nevada was admitted into the Union. After the admission of Nebraska in 1867 and Colorado in 1876, no new states were created until 1889 when North Dakota, South Dakota, Montana, and Washington were all hastily admitted by a Republican Congress that hoped to build up party strength in these areas. For the same reason Wyoming and Idaho were added to the list of

states in the next year. Utah was accepted into the Union in 1896, after abandoning the practice of polygamy. The federal government also opened part of the Indian reservation of Oklahoma to settlement in 1889, and its rich land and the discovery of oil attracted 60,000 people within ten months. In 1907 Oklahoma became a state, with a population of half a million. New Mexico and Arizona were admitted to statehood in 1912. Except for the addition of Alaska and Hawaii, the American Union was now complete.

SOLUTIONS TO THE FARMER'S PLIGHT

The settlement of the Great Plains came about as a growing number of inventions enabled farmers to cope with their unusual environment. The use of barbed wire has already been mentioned. Water shortage was a persistent problem. In the East, a well might be 15 or 20 feet deep at the most, but in the West wells had to be dug 300, even 500 feet below the surface of the ground. Windmills were required to draw water up from such great depths. They were introduced to the West in the 1870s, but were not cheap enough to be generally available until the 1890s. By the turn of the century almost every farm on the Plains had its own windmill and well.

Even with the aid of windmills, water was not plentiful. Not until the government sponsored dam projects in the twentieth century did large-scale irrigation of the desert begin. Formerly, the federal government had handed the problem to the states, and the states were too poor to tackle such ambitious projects. Special farming techniques, known as "dry farming," also compensated in arid areas for the lack of water. First used by the Mormons, this method required tilling the land in a manner that would create a blanket of finely compacted soil particles which would retard evapora-

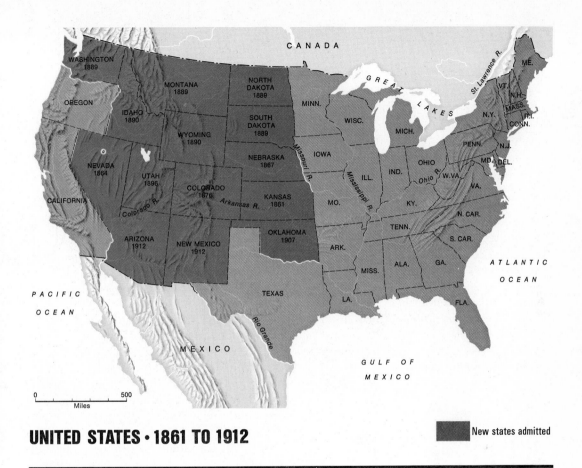

UNITED STATES • 1861 TO 1912

New states admitted

tion of rainwater held in the soil bed immediately below the growing crops. Additional ways to compensate for the lack of moisture in the plains were by the use of a strain of cold- and drought-resistant wheat introduced from Russia and the practice of allowing each section of land to stand uncultivated every other year.

New equipment was devised to meet special problems. The hard soil resisted ordinary plows, but in 1869 James Oliver of South Bend, Indiana, solved this problem by inventing an unusually sturdy chilled-iron plow. In the 1870s John F. Appleby invented a twine binder, which greatly simplified wheat harvesting. In the 1880s big farms began to use the "combine," a combined reaper and thresher. Pulled by twenty

to forty horses, the combine reaped and bagged grain in several furrows at once. Similarly, several chilled-iron plowshares were mounted on a single sulky, so that one farmer could cut several furrows at once.

All this equipment was expensive. To make such an investment profitable, farms had to be very large. Bonanza wheat farms in Minnesota and North Dakota were as large as 1,500 acres by 1890—so vast, in fact, that telephone instructions were generally used to coordinate the activities of scattered teams of workers.

In the interest of large profits, the farmer increasingly converted to a single crop, either corn or wheat. He was no longer able to live off the produce of his own

637

property. Now to survive he had to ship his grain to market and compete with other wheat growers, not only in America but also in Russia, Argentina, and elsewhere. In the 1890s, overproduction led to falling prices and a serious depression. The price of wheat fell from one dollar a bushel in 1885 to fifty cents in 1890. In the latter year more than 100,000 farms in Nebraska alone were heavily mortgaged with ruinous rates of interest—some as high as 40 percent. As the last chapter showed, a drop in cotton prices in the 1890s also undermined the Southern economy. The concept of an America of comfortable, independent farmers—Jefferson's agricultural paradise—was largely a myth. (In fact, as early as 1880, tenants worked one-fourth of all American farms.) The farmer protests which grew out of these conditions contributed greatly to the social, economic, and political unrest of the late nineteenth century.

THE END OF THE FRONTIER

In 1890 the Superintendent of the Census announced that for the first time in American history there was no longer a discernible frontier line. Millions of acres still remained open to homesteading until the 1930s, but most of this acreage was desert or grazing lands of marginal value.

Three years after the frontier line was consigned to history by the Census Superintendent, a young professor from the University of Wisconsin, Frederick Jackson Turner, read a provocative paper to the American Historical Association meeting in Chicago on "The Significance of the Frontier in American History." Turner presented the bold thesis that the frontier, and not the country's European heritage, had shaped the national character. Nationalism, democracy, and individualism were all determined by the tough, heroic settlers who for decades had slowly moved westward. "Now, four centuries from the discovery of America," he concluded, "at the end of a hundred years of life under the Constitution, the frontier has gone, and with its going has closed the first period of American history."

Several of the ideas expressed by Turner in his address have continued to be debated by historians. These include: (1) The existence of cheap and easily available land along the frontier had made it possible for settlers to move time after time from complex to simple forms of civilization, and thereby they refreshed and reshaped the national spirit through a series of new beginnings; (2) the frontier had served as a "safety valve of discontent" which permitted disgruntled factory workers of the East to pull up stakes and seek their fortunes in the West, thereby relieving social and economic discontent in older parts of the country; (3) the frontier had allowed democratic ideas and institutions to grow and had nurtured the principle of rugged individualism in America; (4) the frontier had served as a melting pot, a place where recent European immigrants could shed their national customs and adopt those of their new country; and (5) the frontier had produced a people of unique characteristics.

Turner himself was born in 1861 of pioneer parents in Portage, Wisconsin. At the University of Wisconsin he came into contact with Darwin's theory of evolution and the ideas of the Social Darwinists, who believed that human institutions, like animal species, evolve from simple to complex forms in progressive continuity. When

Turner did graduate work at Johns Hopkins University in Baltimore he studied under Herbert Baxter Adams, who also viewed human development in evolutionary terms, but ascribed no importance to the factor of geography. To Adams, America's democratic institutions ultimately were to be traced far back into European history, to the medieval Teutonic tribes of the forests of Germany.

When Turner returned to his native state, he began to doubt Adams' ideas. If the source of American civilization lay in the German forests, then Wisconsin and the West in general were simply offshoots of European culture; yet the frontier had surely helped to shape the American character, Turner thought. By 1893 he came to believe that the wilderness had been ill-adapted to the habits, institutions, and culture of Europe. Settlers had discarded old forms and sunk back into a primitive society, devoid of complex governmental institutions, class distinctions, and cultural refinements. Gradually, as an increasing number of settlers arrived, the frontier caught up with the times; in its development it represented the evolution of human history from simple to complex forms. However, the developing frontier towns did not reclaim all the European heritage, but remained free of the class system and the autocratic forms of European government as well as the etiquette and prejudices of the Old World. The frontier bred such distinctively American traits as mobility, optimism, a ready acceptance of new ways; and, on the negative side, materialism and an exploitive wastefulness of natural resources. The desire for America's vast natural riches produced in frontiersmen a dislike of government intervention, and particularly of economic control. The leveling influence of frontier conditions and the need to solve their common problems as a group also produced in frontiersmen a respect for majority rule. In this way, the frontier was the seedbed of democracy.

DISCUSSION OF THE TURNER HYPOTHESIS

Turner's frontier hypothesis, one recent commentator has written, "was the most widely influential idea conceived by any American historian." A brilliant and persuasive teacher, Turner attracted many disciples, and although he himself published little before his death in 1932, his ideas were disseminated widely by his followers. His theory was perfectly adapted to the spirit of early twentieth-century America, stressing as it did the strong sense of patriotism and optimism and emphasizing the success of the individual through his own efforts.

After Turner's death in 1932, hitherto unexpressed criticisms of his thesis came into the open. The United States was in the middle of its worst depression, and the optimism of the Turner thesis struck historians as an inadequate explanation for American development. Writers with Marxist leanings stressed the influence of class conflict on American character rather than the geographic forces emphasized by Turner. The importance Turner gave to the individualism that grew out of the frontier experience conflicted in the 1930s with the trend toward the use of more collective action and governmental regulation to solve the country's problems. American life seemed too complex to be explained by a single factor. An urban, industrialized nation looked to sources other than the agricultural frontier for explanations of its development and character.

Professor Robert Riegel, in a 1952 article, while admitting that the frontier may well have influenced the shape of American history, nevertheless expressed certain doubts about Turner's thesis. In a summary of the major attacks on the thesis over the last few decades, Riegel questioned Turner's emphasis on the importance of free land. "Certainly farmers wanted cheap land, but they took surprisingly little advantage of the free land provided under the Homestead Act of 1862," Riegel wrote. He also noted that Turner had overlooked that much of the free land had not passed into the hands of poor farmers, but became instead the property of land speculators. The comparison of frontier development with the concept of evolution was itself called into question by Riegel, who said, "Most present authorities feel that Turner's point of view led him to oversimplify the whole frontier process and to place undue emphasis on physical environment and on uniformity of result."

Riegel and many other modern historians also have disagreed with that part of the frontier thesis which deals with the "safety valve of discontent." Turner suggested that hard times had caused factory workers to migrate to the West, but Riegel countered, "The greatest movements to the West were in periods of prosperity, and relatively few of the migrants came from the more industrialized parts of the East. The concept of an unemployed and penniless mill worker moving to take up a job or a farm in the West is difficult even to imagine." To support his objection, Riegel pointed out that a great deal of capital was needed to move West, to buy farm equipment and to live until the first crop was harvested. Industrial workers were unlikely to possess much money at any time, and few people were likely to have extra cash in times of depression.

The third point made by Turner, that the frontier was the seedbed of democracy and of many political innovations, has also been doubted. Riegel conceded that in the early Western settlement, pioneers were all equally poor, but that the absence of social and economic distinctions did not last long. Moreover, the West was divided over most political issues. For example, the Northwest opposed slavery, whereas the Southwest favored it. It was significant that Jacksonian democracy won no more support in the West than in the East. "Popular Presidents such as Jefferson, Jackson and Lincoln, noted for their love of the common man, were elected more by eastern than by western votes." In addition, "Considerable interest has been given to the western support in the years around 1900 of such democratic measures as the direct primary, popular election of Senators, votes for women, the initiative, referendum and recall. In every case, however, the idea came from Europe, while the support was largely eastern, with the West itself divided."

In regard to Turner's point that the frontier served to Americanize European immigrants, Riegel contended that "Turner's feeling that each new frontiersman shed his old customs, started anew and became a real American appears to have been more a hope than a fact. Several historians have demonstrated very clearly the extent to which national characteristics were retained in western settlements."

Several historians have also challenged the Turner view that the frontier environment in America produced a people with unique characteristics. Studies on frontier expansion in such diverse areas and periods of history as the periphery of ancient Rome, Spanish America, and the Russian penetration of Siberia have shown that settlers in these areas developed attitudes and approaches to problems similar to those of America's Western pioneers. In each instance, frontiersmen were crude, tough, individualistic, and inventive. The Hispanic American frontier probably did not produce a more democratic society because there was no strong Spanish heritage of self-government to transmit to the New World. This would tend to indicate that freedom for experimentation on the American frontier resulted in an expansion of the English heritage of representative government but the frontier environment did not of itself create a democratic political system.

A DEFENSE OF TURNER

Another modern historian, Ray Allen Billington, while conceding that Turner's hypothesis was wrong in many details and oversimplified in general, nevertheless insisted that the frontier theory pointed to an essential truth:

The recurring rebirth of society in the United States over a period of three hundred years did endow the people with characteristics and institutions that distinguished them from the inhabitants of other nations. It is obviously untrue that the frontier experience alone accounts for the unique features of American civilization; that civilization can be understood only as the product of the interplay of the Old World heritage and New World conditions. But among those conditions none has bulked larger than the operation of the frontier process.

To support this generalization, Billington contended that the frontier, while it did not invent democratic theory and institutions, "tended to make them, in practice, even more democratic." Billington credited two factors with strengthening democratic attitudes—the widespread ownership of land and the absence of any prior leadership structure. The first factor gave each member a stake in the community; the second meant that the community did not simply inherit leaders, but had to choose them. Moreover, in every new territory along the frontier, pioneers had to write a new constitution in which "constitution-makers adopted the most liberal features of older frames of government with which they were familiar."

Billington also attributed two other aspects of the American character to the frontier, anti-intellectualism and materialism. The strenuous life on the outskirts of civilization made the sensitive or artistic person an unwelcome member of society, while the struggle for survival was extended in good times into competitive overesteem for wealth. In summation, even if the Turner thesis was flawed in many particulars, Billington regarded as unassailable his general contention that "frontiersmen did develop unique traits and that these, perpetuated, form the principal distinguishing characteristics of the American people today."

Readings

GENERAL WORKS

Billington, Ray A., *America's Frontier Heritage*. New York: Holt, Rinehart and Winston, 1966—An analysis of the significance of the frontier in American life. Billington, with modifications, accepts much of Frederick Jackson Turner's thesis on the subject.

Billington, Ray A., *Westward Expansion*. New York: Macmillan, 1967—A detailed, standard history of the American West and of Americans' desires to settle it.

Brown, Dee, *Bury My Heart at Wounded Knee*. New York: Holt, Rinehart and Winston, 1971—A graphic history of relations between Indians and whites told from the Indian point of view. The title of the book refers to the massacre at Wounded Knee.

Clark, Thomas D., *Frontier America: The Story of the Westward Movement*. New York: Scribner's, 1969—A history of the American West that for the most part rejects the Turner thesis on the role of the American frontier.

Smith, Henry N., *Virgin Land*. Cambridge, Mass.: Harvard University Press, 1950—An exploration of the symbolic uses of the West in American literature and popular culture. The author discusses such themes as the continuing dream of a Northwest passage to China and the faith in the virtues of frontier man.

Taft, Robert, *Artists and Illustrators of the Old West 1850–1900*. New York: Scribner's, 1953—During the latter half of the nineteenth century, many American artists were drawn to Western themes. Taft explores the background of their work.

Turner, Frederick J., *The Frontier in American History*. New York: Holt, Rinehart and Winston, 1963—A collection of essays by the great historian of the American West, including his famous "The Significance of the Frontier in American History," first presented to the American Historical Association in 1893.

Webb, Walter P., *The Great Frontier*. Austin: University of Texas Press, 1964—An attempt to generalize Turner's frontier thesis to a worldwide scale. Webb argues that the existence of a frontier in America has profoundly influenced European history since the age of discovery.

Webb, Walter P., *The Great Plains*. New York: Grosset & Dunlap, 1957—A history of the Great Plains in the context of its role in America's westward expansion.

Webb emphasizes the importance of the physical characteristics of the Plains region.

SPECIAL STUDIES

Atherton, Lewis, *The Cattle Kings.* Bloomington, Ind.: University of Indiana Press, 1961—A history of Western cattlemen which maintains that the importance of the cattle kings has been slighted in favor of nostalgic but inaccurate cowboy stories.

Choate, Julian E., and Joe B. Frantz, *The American Cowboy: The Myth and the Reality.* Norman: University of Oklahoma Press, 1955—After tracing the role of the cowboy in the development of the West, the authors compare the legends with the reality of cowboy life.

Dick, Everett, *The Sod-House Frontier, 1854–1890.* Lincoln, Neb.: Johnsen, 1954—A social history of the prairie frontier from the Kansas-Nebraska Act controversy through the admission of the Dakotas as states.

Fite, Gilbert C., *The Farmer's Frontier, 1865–1900.* New York: Holt, Rinehart and Winston, 1966—A survey of the role of the farmer in America's last continental fron-

tier. Fite maintains that farmers played a stabilizing and civilizing role in the Far West.

Fritz, Henry E., *The Movement for Indian Assimilation, 1860–1890.* Philadelphia: University of Pennsylvania Press, 1963—A study of Grant's "Peace Policy" toward Indians which argues that Protestant churchmen had a large influence in shaping this and subsequent Indian policies.

Gard, Wayne, *The Great Buffalo Hunt.* Lincoln: University of Nebraska Press, 1959—An illustrated history of the 1871 to 1883 era when buffaloes were hunted and virtually exterminated on the Great Plains.

Greever, W. S., *The Bonanza West: The Story of the Western Mining Rushes, 1848–1900.* Norman: University of Oklahoma Press, 1963—A history of mining rushes from Colorado to Alaska, which recounts many vivid anecdotes of the bonanza periods.

Osgood, E. S., *The Day of the Cattleman.* Chicago: University of Chicago Press, 1957—A history of the era of the cattle kingdom in the West which stresses the economic and organizational skills of cattle barons rather than the sensational exploits of cowboys.

Paul, Rodman W., *Mining Frontiers of the Far West 1848–1880*. New York: Holt, Rinehart and Winston, 1963—A history of Far Western mining which emphasizes the importance of mining technology and explores the economic consequences of the mining activities.

Roe, Frank G., *The Indians and the Horse*. Norman: University of Oklahoma Press, 1955—Roe argues that the horse did not revolutionize the Indians' life style, but that its introduction did alter migration patterns and methods of warfare.

Shannon, Fred A., *The Farmer's Last Frontier: Agriculture 1860–1897*. New York: Holt, Rinehart & Winston, 1945—A history of Western farming in the later years of the nineteenth century which investigates such factors as settlement patterns, technological changes, and land speculation.

Utley, Robert M., *Last Days of the Sioux Nation*. New Haven, Conn.: Yale University Press, 1963—The tragic outbreak that led to the massacre of the Sioux at Wounded Knee in 1890 was brought about by the inability of the Sioux to cope with the life style forced upon them by white men. Utley describes the resulting breakdown of Sioux society.

PRIMARY SOURCES

Adams, Andy, *Log of a Cowboy*. Lincoln: University of Nebraska Press, 1964—Memoirs of a Western cowboy which describe both the hardships and the excitement of life in the cattle kingdom. Adams is not romantic about cowboy life and remains a valuable source for those interested in Western history.

DeQuille, Dan, *History of the Big Bonanza*. New York: Apollo, 1969—A colorful account of mining and society in Virginia City, Nev., during the mining boom at the Comstock Lode.

Dunn, J. P., *Massacres of the Mountain*. New York: Putnam, 1969—A detailed contemporary account of Indian wars of the mountain regions, covering the years from 1815 through 1875.

Jackson, Helen H., *A Century of Dishonor*. New York: Harper & Row, 1960—A classic attack on government policy towards American Indians which brands that policy as dishonest and brutal.

Twain, Mark. *Roughing It*. New York: New

644

American Library, 1962—Twain's famous first-hand account of life in Nevada during its earliest mining days.

BIOGRAPHIES

McCracken, Harold, *George Catlin and the Old Frontier*. New York: Dial, 1959—A biography of one of the leading American frontier artists.

Sandoz, Mari, *Old Jules*. Lincoln: University of Nebraska Press, 1962—A biography of the author's father, a Swiss settler in western Nebraska in 1884. The author pictures her father as embodying the virtues and vices of frontier society.

Stegner, Wallace, *Beyond the Hundredth Meridian: John Wesley Powell and the Second Opening of the West*. Boston: Houghton Mifflin, 1954—A biography of the military engineer and geologist who directed the United States Geological Survey and began the scientific and social planning necessary for the setting of the "Great American Desert" west of the 100th meridian.

Stewart, E. I., *Custer's Luck*. Norman: University of Oklahoma Press, 1955—A biography of General Custer which attempts to provide a complete and accurate account of what actually happened at Custer's "Last Stand" at Little Big Horn.

Wilkins, Thurman, *Clarence King*. New York: Macmillan, 1958—Clarence King, founder of the United States Geological Survey, was an accomplished explorer and scientist who was also at home with intellectuals and literary figures. This biography explores his public career and his troubled personal life.

FICTION

Cather, Willa, *My Antonia*. Boston: Houghton Mifflin, 1918—A novel of the life of a Bohemian girl whose family had migrated to the prairie in the late nineteenth century.

Cather, Willa, *O Pioneers!* Boston: Houghton Mifflin, 1913—A novel of pioneer farming life by a great Nebraska author, Miss Cather describes the impact of the land and climate on her characters' lives.

Rolvaag, Ole, *Giants in the Earth*. New York: Harper & Row, 1927—A novel of Scandinavian pioneers in the upper Great Plains during the later years of the nineteenth century.

18

Becoming a Great Industrial Power

This, then, is held to be the duty of the man of wealth: To set an example of modest, unostentatious living, shunning display or extravagance; to provide moderately for the legitimate wants of those dependent upon him; and, after doing so, to consider all surplus revenues which come to him simply as trust funds, which he is called upon to administer, and strictly bound as a matter of duty to administer in the manner which, in his judgment, is best calculated to produce the most beneficial results for the community—the man of wealth thus becoming the mere trustee and agent for his poorer brethren, bringing to their service his superior wisdom, experience, and ability to administer, doing for them better than they would or could do for themselves.

—Andrew Carnegie

Carnegie, after arriving in America as a poor Scottish immigrant, had risen to great wealth and influence. He approved wholeheartedly of an economic system that allowed men to lift themselves above their humble beginnings by hard work and shrewd investments of capital.

Homestead, Pennsylvania, the company town built by Andrew Carnegie for his steel workers.

647

AN ERA OF EXPLOITATION AND MATERIALISM

In the pre-Civil War years the nation had been mainly agricultural, lagging far behind England in industrial production. The typical American was a farmer who worked his own land, grew most of his own food, and did without the conveniences offered by the city. The United States still resembled Jefferson's ideal of an agrarian society living close to nature and the soil, away from the corruptions of urban life.

The Civil War shifted the emphasis in the American economy toward rapid industrialization. The industrial momentum begun in the 1850s now speeded up considerably, although the steel and oil industries, not dependent on the war for expansion, may have been retarded somewhat by the conflict. Northern armies needed supplies, and war-related industries were created to meet the demand. At the same time, the South, by seceding from the Union, surrendered its influence on national politics long before its armies surrendered in the field. Northern businessmen were now unimpeded in their efforts to obtain federal support for policies and projects they had long desired. The slave states had held up construction of a transcontinental railroad, fearing a northern route would strengthen the free states. Relieved of Southern pressure, Congress in 1862 passed the Pacific Railroad Act, which provided a northern route to the West Coast. During the war, Northern business interests were also successful in obtaining a higher tariff and currency stabilization through the National Banking Act. The process of rapid indus-

trialization begun during the Civil War continued in the period that followed. Wartime businesses found an expanded peacetime market for goods. New England mills turned out civilian clothing instead of uniforms. New York bankers lent less money to the government, more to homesteaders in the West. Countless other businesses flourished because of this transformation of the American economy. The change in the size of the gross national product over the next several decades reflected the shift in the national economy from agriculture to industry. Goods and services produced in 1869 were worth 6.7 billion dollars. By 1914 the total had zoomed to 40 billion dollars.

There are various explanations for this phenomenal growth. America possessed the natural resources required for an industrial base, including waterpower, timber, and minerals. Coal and oil were near at hand in Pennsylvania, iron in the vast Mesabi Range near Lake Superior. Also, an expanding population provided a market for increasing production of goods. The influx of immigrants that helped swell the population created cheap labor pools in cities from Boston to Chicago. Meanwhile, tariffs protected American businessmen from foreign competition, while the courts and sometimes government troops helped protect them from employees who attempted to defy their power by striking. Another boon to economic expansion came from increased European investment in American industry. Due to European scientific advances, the United States also achieved important technological gains. For example, after Michael Faraday, an Englishman, produced an explanation for electromagnetism, Thomas Alva Edison, an American, was able to perfect the electrical storage battery. "Yankee know-how" was applauded as a national characteristic as Americans received nearly half a million patents between 1860 and 1890. Christopher Sholes invented the typewriter, Alexander Graham Bell the telephone, and William S. Burroughs the adding machine. Edison, the "Wizard of Menlo Park," was the most productive inventor of them all, holding more than a thousand patents on such items as the electric light bulb, the phonograph, and the motion-picture camera.

A belief in progress based on material well-being infused the spirit of the times. Americans were aware that gadgets, inventions, and production methods were improving. The standard of living was rising steadily. Money and the display of material wealth were the hallmarks of success, and most Americans approved of the aggressive business practices that made such achievement possible.

RAILROAD EXPANSION

The period from 1865 to 1914 could aptly be named "The Railroad Era." The railroad was not yet fully integrated into national life at the end of the Civil War, since it scarcely crossed the Mississippi, and it was doomed after the First World War by competition from the motor vehicle. In the intervening years, however, the railroad dominated transportation. Many Americans

had a romantic view of the Iron Horse on "ribbons of steel." Whole towns listened for the sound of the locomotive whistle before the train came into view around the bend. Millions sang or whistled "I've Been Working on the Railroad."

IMPORTANCE OF THE RAILROAD

The locomotive did as much to change human life in the nineteenth century as the sailing ship did in ancient times. Americans became even more mobile than in the earlier decades. Travel time was shortened to hours instead of days, and days instead of weeks or even months. For the first time, farmers could easily make trips to the big cities, too long or arduous to undertake with horses. Factory workers could return to see their families on the farm on weekends or holidays.

A NEW MASS MARKET

The railroad affected not only life styles but the development of business. The railroads in themselves constituted an industry. Wherever they went, they brought jobs for the men who laid the rails and handled the switches. Local stores in towns along the lines profited from trade brought in by the trains, and giant industries such as steel and coal flourished from the production of rails and fuel for the locomotives. George Pullman founded a new business to produce sleeping cars. New bridges needed to be built, strong enough to carry the weight of the trains, and this led to a revolution in civil engineering crowned by John Roebling's remarkable Brooklyn Bridge and James Eads's span across the Mississippi at St. Louis. Use of the telegraph expanded with the railroad. The telegrapher wearing his green nightshade, tapping out messages along the line, became a familiar figure in American life.

Railroad advertisement offering a special excursion trip to New York for the opening of the Brooklyn Bridge in 1883.

The vast reach of the railroads gave an impetus to mass production. Sales were no longer limited to local markets. Manufacturers on the Eastern seaboard were now able to offer their products for sale in the West. Wisconsin lumber rolled on freight cars to Eastern markets. Perishable goods from rural areas reached Philadelphia, New York, and Boston in good condition. Mass consumption absorbed the output of mass production. As unfamiliar items appeared on store shelves—Arkansas pork in Cleveland, Milwaukee beer in Denver—new purchasing habits resulted, which, in turn, stimulated production.

The railroads helped build new markets by moving people to new localities to settle, even encouraging European immigrants to cross the Atlantic. Scandinavians came by train to Minnesota, Germans to St. Louis, Slavs and the Irish to Chicago. Were it not for the Iron Horse, many of the open expanses in the West would not have filled up so quickly.

A UNIFIED NATION

To Americans of the period, the railroad tracks seemed like steel bands holding the nation together. Many a locality remained isolated in the hinterlands until a trunk line came its way. Distant points enjoyed interdependent prosperity based on a single enterprise, with the railroad as the axis between buyer and seller. For example, Pittsburgh relied on Mesabi iron for use by its steel mills, and Minnesota depended on the Pittsburgh mills to buy its Mesabi iron. Whole areas rich in natural resources, such as the Rocky Mountains with their metals, could not have been exploited without the carrying power of the railroads. The number of Texas cattle shipped to Chicago increased from a trickle to an abundant flow in direct ratio to the extension of lines into the Lone Star State.

The railroad also helped to reduce the barriers of time. A new and vastly improved mail service was a unifying factor made possible by the railroads. Previously, letters had moved over long distances so slowly that they often arrived too late to serve their purpose. The speedy mail cars made it easier for relatives and friends to keep in touch, and for businessmen to fill orders promptly. The four time zones in the continental United States were created out of the need for nationwide train schedules, a list virtually impossible to establish in the old welter of local time zones.

BUILDING THE RAILROADS

When the Civil War began, the United States had only a little over 30,000 miles of track. By 1880 this distance had grown to more than 93,000 miles; a decade later, to over 166,000 miles; and when the First World War broke out, the country had more railroad track mileage than all of Europe, including Russia.

FINANCING

Railroad building consumed money greedily. In 1890 the railroads were worth more than 8 billion dollars, owed an accumulated debt of over 5 billion dollars, and took in revenue exceeding 1 billion dollars. To fund such a monumental enterprise, shares were purchased by private individuals and institutions, many of them overseas investors who put their money to work in the United States through large banking houses. Banks invested in the railroads, generally with good results, but with occasional disastrous failures. Jay Cooke, the well-known Civil War financier, backed the Northern Pacific in 1870. Three years later the financial strain proved too great, and he went bankrupt.

State and local governments gave money and land in return for railroad lines connecting them with the major rail arteries. The principal source of revenue, however, was the United States government. Millions of dollars were lent from the federal treasury. Even more important, the government made land grants of 10 square miles in alternate sections on each side of the tracks where tracks were to be laid. The Illinois Central received the first grant in 1850. Federal land was no longer given to the railroads after 1871, but by that date 130 million acres had been handed out. The owners were able not only to extend their lines across land for which they did not have to pay but also were able to realize additional profits by selling excess acreage and cutting timber.

ROUTES

Everywhere in the nation, people were fascinated by the great transcontinental railroad systems, and most of all by the pioneering effort of the Union Pacific and the Central Pacific to link up west of the Rockies. The federal government wanted this transcontinental line badly enough to offer the companies 30-year loans and 20 square miles of land in alternate sections, in the usual checkerboard pattern, for every mile of track laid along the right-of-way. This offer amounted to 60 million dollars and 20 million acres of land.

Sidney Dillon and Thomas C. Durant headed the Union Pacific, whose crews laid the rails westward from Omaha; and Collis P. Huntington and Leland Stanford were

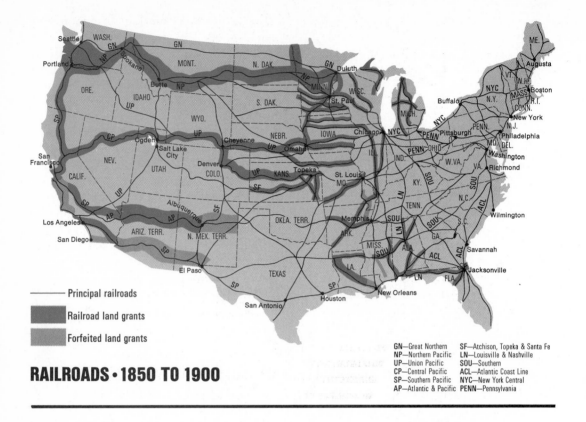

- Principal railroads
Railroad land grants
Forfeited land grants

RAILROADS · 1850 TO 1900

GN—Great Northern   SF—Atchison, Topeka & Santa Fe
NP—Northern Pacific   LN—Louisville & Nashville
UP—Union Pacific   SOU—Southern
CP—Central Pacific   ACL—Atlantic Coast Line
SP—Southern Pacific   NYC—New York Central
AP—Atlantic & Pacific   PENN—Pennsylvania

the major figures behind the Central Pacific, which constructed the line eastward from San Francisco. The work crews of the two lines were driven on by a spirit of competition. Irish immigrants working for the Union Pacific and Chinese laborers imported by the Central Pacific engaged in a race to the meeting point. Honor fell to both sides when they joined the rails at Promontory Point, Utah, on May 10, 1869, and Stanford drove a golden spike to observe the linkup. Railroad workers and directors alike cheered and waved their hats in the most dramatic scene in the history of American railroading.

Other transcontinental lines followed. The directors of the Central Pacific established the Southern Pacific, which began at San Francisco and ended at New Orleans. Another group, working from the opposite direction, brought the Atchison, Topeka and Santa Fe from Atchison, Kansas, to San Diego, California.

Meanwhile, Jay Cooke had failed with the Northern Pacific. Five years later Henry Villard shouldered the burden of reorganizing this line because he had railroad and shipping interests in Oregon and wanted to have rail access to the Great Lakes region. He reached his goal in 1883 when the Northern Pacific began carrying passengers and freight between the Twin Cities of Minneapolis-St. Paul and Portland, Oregon.

The Northern Pacific was rivaled by the Great Northern, under the control of James J. Hill. A remarkable exception among the railroad builders, he did without government aid and instead raised loans from bankers. He used the money well and in 1893 had the satisfaction of seeing the Great Northern extend into Seattle after crossing the continent from Duluth, Minnesota.

RAILROAD BARONS

Regarding the post-Civil War decades, historian Allan Nevins wrote: "The next generation after Lincoln was to produce no great statesmen, few novelists and poets of stature, and but two or three artists of world eminence; but produced more business genius than any country in the world had yet seen."

The energy of enterprising men was channeled into the development of business. Industrial opportunities existed, and men of immense ability came forward to exploit them. Nowhere was this more evident than in the railroad industry with its competing lines, billions of dollars of investment, government support, and opportunity for national renown. Fame and fortune awaited those who succeeded, and. they formed a varied gallery of human types. Most were builders, a few were wreckers, and all knew how to wield power.

Collis P. Huntington of Connecticut made the trek across the continent during the Gold Rush. He failed to make a fortune panning for gold in California; but he met three other ambitious men, Leland Stanford, Charles Crocker, and Mark Hopkins, and together they succeeded in acquiring wealth and power. They formed an alliance, and became the Big Four of the Central Pacific Railroad. Crocker's specialty was construction, Hopkins' bookkeeping. Stanford, the company spokesman, fended off political investigations and legal suits. Huntington, a formidable figure, standing more than 6 feet and weighing more than 200 pounds, achieved his greatest triumph when he secured government backing to enable the Central Pacific to push east beyond California to the famed meeting with the Union Pacific.

Thomas A. Scott rose to prominence during the Civil War when Secretary of War Simon Cameron appointed him to manage the railroads for the war effort. The appointment helped further Scott's career with the Pennsylvania Railroad, which connected Philadelphia to Pittsburgh. After the war, Scott expanded the Pennsylvania into the big cities beyond the Keystone State—New York, Washington, Chicago, St. Louis—until his railroad vied with Vanderbilt's New York Central for the place of number one line in the East. However, he was ruthlessly outmaneuvered by Huntington in his efforts to build a line in the Southwest between California and Texas.

Jay Gould was a railroad man only insofar as he was a wrecker of railroads. He went into railroading, as into other enterprises, solely for the sake of making money, and he stooped to the lowest chicanery to get it. Competitors underestimated Gould, a small figure with a humble manner, and hence were often outwitted before they suspected his motives. He was outsmarted by Commodore Vanderbilt, who failed to acquire the Erie Railroad from Gould and his two piratical partners, the slovenly Daniel Drew and the flashy Jim Fisk. Gould, Drew, and Fisk manipulated Erie stock to prevent Vanderbilt's takeover of the line. They were aided by the New York State legislature, which prohibited a merger of the Erie with Vanderbilt's New York Central after Gould gave legislators substantial bribes. While in control of the Erie, Gould systematically cheated the line of millions of dollars.

Later he used one of his choice techniques against the Union Pacific, the acquisition of a property simply for its nuisance value. The Kansas Pacific Railroad competed with the Union Pacific. Gould, therefore, bought into the Kansas Pacific, improved the line, announced his intention to keep it, and then cannily allowed himself to be persuaded to sell the line to the Union Pacific for a huge profit.

"Uncle Dan'l" Drew said of Gould: "His touch is death." The words may have been intended as a compliment. "Jubilee Jim" Fisk, their other partner, uttered the classic self-criticism when he and Gould came under fire: "Nothing is lost save honor." Eventually he and Gould ousted Drew from the partnership. Fisk later was killed by a jealous rival for the favors of his mistress. Only Gould remained to enjoy the fruits of their conspiracies. When he died in 1892, he left his heirs a colossal fortune.

James J. Hill, in contrast to Gould, was probably the best example of the public-spirited railroad builder. He too made a fortune, but not at the expense of the line he headed. Hill, who had come from Canada to find a career in the tier of states along the border, not only extended his Great Northern Railroad from Minnesota to the West Coast, but took personal pride in its performance. He even directed his work gangs as they laid the tracks. Once, when aboard a train stopped by a snowdrift, he jumped out of his car and wielded a shovel along with his hired hands. Concerned for the welfare of the people along the Great Northern route, he lent money to farmers, imported British bulls to improve cattle herds, and paid experts to give free demonstrations of farming methods.

Along with his integrity and public spirit, Hill had courage. Challenged by Edward E. Harriman over the right to run tracks along the Columbia River, Hill ordered his lawyers and workmen to resist. Real battles erupted on the banks of the Columbia, wild melees fought with picks, shovels, and crowbars. Violent confrontations ended only after the courts decided in Hill's favor. An observer said of him: "Mr. Hill's judgment has never been seriously at fault in any of his undertakings." It should be added that Harriman's judgment too was rarely at fault. He rivaled Hill as a constructive railroad builder.

DISORDERS AND DISCRIMINATION

The struggle between Hill and Harriman typified one of the chief problems of the Railroad Era—the railroad war. The country offered a vast amount of space in which to built railroads, and conflicts inevitably broke out between those determined to control the same area. Too many railroads were built. As a result, various lines competed for the same trade. Overexpansion ended in bankruptcies that shook more than the railroad industry. During the 1870s no less than 450 failures occurred, spreading economic disaster not only among railroad owners and investors but also railroad workers thrown out of jobs, and businessmen, farmers, and others dependent on these lines to carry their products to market.

Struggling desperately to survive, railroad directors resorted to discriminatory practices. The most notorious was the use of the rebate. Where a single large industry paid a substantial amount in freight charges, it could often wangle a secret deal with a particular railroad whereby it would pay less for shipment than its competitors by arranging to have a portion of its shipping costs returned by the railroad. In return, the railroad line would receive all the industry's freight business. In 1869 the Lake Shore Railroad agreed, in such a deal, to give John D. Rockefeller rebates on his shipments of oil into Cleveland. The Lake Shore line promptly began to prosper, while the Cleveland refineries competing with Rockefeller dropped in number from thirty to ten. This pattern was repeated over and over throughout the country by other industries.

Yet, where a railroad had no nearby rival line, it would charge as much as the traffic would bear. Hence the "long and short haul abuse": a short journey where no competition existed would cost more than a long one where two or more lines competed for the same business.

Railroad men opposed to the lawlessness of the system tried to regulate their industry by forming pools in which a number of companies agreed to share the market in a fair and aboveboard way. The pool device failed because the agreements had no binding force. Too often a member would be tempted to make a quick profit regardless of what the rest thought. Such an action undermined their agreement and caused a return to the old cutthroat competition.

The public began to lose patience with such practices. Shippers attacked the discriminatory charges and rebates. Farmers resented their helplessness against abuses of the railroad operators when there was only one line near them. Accidents often occurred on poorly run lines. Plunder seekers like Gould brought the whole system into disrepute, especially when bribery of judges and legislators by railroad men came to light. Resentful of growing public criticism of railroad management, Vanderbilt demanded: "Can't I do what I like with my own?" His son William, when asked about responsibility to the public, retorted, "The public be damned."

During the 1870s, farmers, protesting against the lines, organized to form the Patrons of Husbandry, or the Grange. This organization called upon the state governments to regulate the railroads. To secure their demands, the Grangers turned out in large numbers on election days and put officials in office who were favorable to their cause. Several states began to appoint commissions to look into railroad practices. Illinois, Wisconsin, Minnesota, and Iowa passed legislation to protect the public interest. The railroads counterattacked by challenging this state regulatory legislation in the courts, with several cases reaching the Supreme Court.

THE INTERSTATE COMMERCE ACT

The most important of the Granger cases came before the Supreme Court in 1877, when a plaintiff appealed against an Illinois law which put a ceiling on warehouse rates for grain storage. The court ruled, in *Munn v. Illinois,* that the law was a constitutional exercise of the state police power to regulate because the business in question involved "a public interest." However, within a decade the court reversed itself and supported the railroads in *Wabash, St. Louis and Pacific Railroad v. Illinois.* It ruled that a state could not prohibit the long and short haul abuse, since only the federal government had the right to regulate interstate commerce. The Supreme Court was now dominated by justices who believed, as did businessmen, in a laissez-faire economy. The earlier success of the Grangers was in conflict with the prevailing idea that government controls over business hampered the proper functioning of the unchangeable laws of economics.

Over the next few years the Supreme Court handed down other rulings which further hampered state regulation of business. It extended the Fourteenth Amendment to cover corporations by declaring that a corporation was a "person" and could not be deprived of its property without due process of law. Thus, state regulations pertaining to corporations would require review by the courts when they involved the question of denial of property under the Fourteenth Amendment; the state legislatures could not decide such a matter alone. The Court contended that state regulatory legislation might so discriminate against a business or railroad as to be unreasonable, and in such cases, due process would have been denied. The phrase "the due process of law" underwent change from its traditional meaning, provision by the government of proper judicial procedures, to a new idea: the courts could consider that a person, or corporation, had been denied due process of law, even if granted the proper judicial procedures, if the provisions of a law which affected him were found to be unduly discriminatory in depriving him of his property. This concept became known as "substantive due process."

The Congress, under pressure for national control of railroad lines, began to investigate the problem. In 1887 it passed the Interstate Commerce Act, under which trains crossing state lines were prohibited from giving rebates or charging higher fares for short hauls than for long ones. Pools also were declared to be illegal. Power to enforce the act was given to the Interstate Commerce Commission. Although much litigation resulted, the courts offered little support for the Commission's demands for rate regulations until the Hepburn Act of 1906 gave the Commission power to fix rates and inspect company books.

CONTROL BY BANKERS

While Congress and the states moved gradually toward greater control of the railroads, the "lords of the rails" looked for ways to deal with their problems. They wanted to safeguard their interests and at

J. P. Morgan turned the railroad industry into an efficient and highly profitable organization.

the same time to silence the clamor raised by their critics. Increasingly disgusted by unethical practices in their industry, they looked for some way to end the overexpansion followed by bankruptcy of lines that were unable to meet competition. An answer to this dilemma was provided by America's most powerful banker, J. P. Morgan.

THE MORGAN INFLUENCE

At the outbreak of the Civil War, the House of Morgan was already a leader in the international money market. Junius S. Morgan had made a fortune in London handling funds for businessmen who needed an astute banker in what was then the financial capital of the world. His son, John Pierpont, soon showed he had inherited his father's ability to make money grow. He understood credit, the dollar exchange, and the technicalities of the banking business. He was so proficient at mathematics that he once considered teaching the subject. Instead, Morgan became the master of high finance. Ultimately he dominated not only banking but a number of other businesses.

He invaded the railroad business by degrees after he forced Jay Gould to surrender the Albany and Susquehanna in 1869. Eleven years later he picked up several small lines after they had suffered a shattering bankruptcy and joined them to form the Long Island Railroad. Subsequently, William H. Vanderbilt, whose Grand Central was under fire in the Albany legislature, turned to Morgan for help. Vanderbilt's lawyers had advised him to ease the pressure from legislators by giving up a large block of Grand Central stock. He needed to do this without disturbing Wall Street, and Morgan solved the problem for him by secretly distributing the Vanderbilt stock in Europe. Later Morgan stopped a feud between the Grand Central and the

Pennsylvania by persuading each to sell the other a subordinate competing line. Such arrangements made him known as the "Doctor of Wall Street" to a sick industry.

Finally Morgan decided to stop tinkering with railroad finance and begin a systematic and general reorganization of the railroads. He proposed to end the ruinous competition in the industry, and with this in view, on January 8, 1889, he summoned a group of railroad magnates to the Morgan mansion in New York. With Morgan presiding, they formed a committee to regulate their dealings with one another. Any line that defied committee decisions would find that it could not get bank loans. Bankers, as well as railroad men, would have a hand in running the railroads. Thus, the Morgan Group came into existence.

The Morgan Group did not take over the industry, but its members controlled enough lines to bring stability to the system as a whole. Unfair practices were curbed wherever their influence extended. Management improved because the bankers who moved into the boards of directors aimed to make the lines profitable, and as professional money men they saw to it that sound financial methods were followed. Passengers found higher standards of service when they rode the trains. Shippers could now depend on promised routes and schedules. Efficiency became the watchword under Morgan's direction.

THE SECOND INDUSTRIAL REVOLUTION

The first Industrial Revolution, beginning in the eighteenth century and accelerating in the nineteenth, was based largely on the steam engine and made Great Britain known as the "workshop of the world." The second Industrial Revolution, taking place in the late nineteenth century, raised the United States to leadership among the manufacturing nations, and it too followed from the invention of new machinery and techniques of production.

STEEL

TECHNIQUES OF PRODUCTION

The replacement of iron by steel, which was a stronger and more resilient metal, depended on the discovery of a method to purify iron ore. As early as the 1850s, an American, William Kelly, found a solution to the problem at his Suwanee Iron Works at Eddyville, Kentucky. Noticing that molten iron lost its impurities along the surface where the air touched it, he forced air into the heated mass and purification of the ore resulted. Kelly correctly guessed that the oxygen in the air combined with the metallic impurities and carried them away. Unfortunately, Kelly could not obtain the public support for this new process. His iron works failed because his clients demanded a product turned out "in the regular way."

Shortly after Kelly's discovery, an Englishman named Henry Bessemer repeated the experiment. Using a converter of his own design, he produced a fine steel which, following an enthusiastic reception from

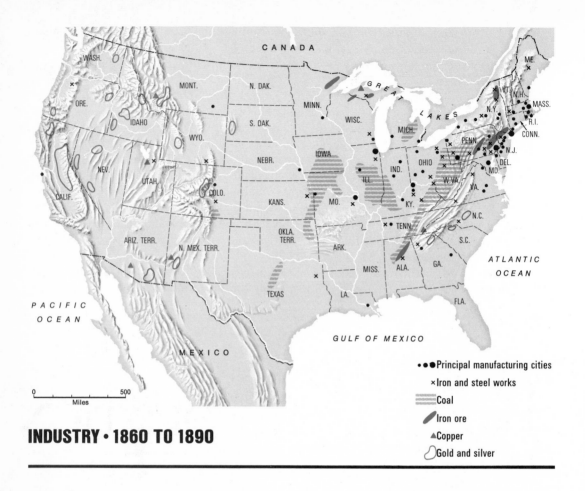

INDUSTRY • 1860 TO 1890

Legend:
●●● Principal manufacturing cities
× Iron and steel works
Coal
Iron ore
▲ Copper
Gold and silver

British industry, was brought across the Atlantic to an eager market. The railroad owners wanted steel for their tracks and bought large quantities of the British product. Kelly challenged Bessemer's patent in the United States, and eventually both men received recognition, but the name Bessemer remains associated with the process and the product, while his American predecessor is remembered chiefly by historians of the steel industry.

RAW MATERIALS

For Americans to build a native steel industry of international importance, they needed access to large amounts of iron ore. The rich Mesabi Range in northern Minnesota was discovered at precisely the right moment. Leonidas Merritt discovered the ore deposits in 1887 and for six years successfully marketed the raw material. The Mesabi ore deposits then came under the control of John D. Rockefeller, who saw that the iron was both plentiful and accessible. Deposited in broad horizontal layers, it could be removed by the open-pit method. Shovels would lift millions of tons of iron onto railroad cars for shipment to Duluth, Minnesota, where Great Lakes steamers would be waiting to take it to Chicago. Transshipment from the Windy City would speed the ore on its way to the steel mills. Carnegie also became an investor in these rich deposits after Henry

Oliver, the holder of Rockefeller's leases at Mesabi, came to Henry C. Frick, Carnegie's general manager, for financial support.

ANDREW CARNEGIE

The road to the top had been a steep one for the man whose name came to stand for the American steel industry. Carnegie, born in Dunfermline, Scotland, in 1835, was thirteen when his parents brought him to America. They settled in Pennsylvania, where the youth was employed as a telegraph messenger boy. He rose to telegraph operator and subsequently became the private secretary of Thomas A. Scott of the Pennsylvania Railroad. He invested his wages wisely, became superintendent of the railroad at twenty-eight, and then gained control of the Union Iron Mills. Foregoing a career in railroading, he shifted his investments to the steel industry.

In his early thirties, Carnegie was making 50,000 dollars a year. Most of his contemporaries would have regarded his income as sufficient proof of success. But as the years passed and money continued to pour into his bank accounts, Carnegie never lost his conviction that money was essentially worthless unless put to work in behalf of humanity. This outlook made him the foremost public benefactor of his time. He used his enormous wealth so wisely that to this day, his name is identified with some of the most useful public institutions in America and abroad—the Carnegie Libraries, the Carnegie Endowment for International Peace, the Carnegie Endowment for the Advancement of Education, and the Carnegie Institute of Technology (now known as the Carnegie-Mellon University).

Carnegie had a genius for selecting able subordinates, to whom he gave a free hand. One of his managers, Captain William Jones, had the wisdom to see that the exploitation of workers was counterproductive. When men were driven too hard, their work became inefficient and accidents were

more frequent. Jones therefore replaced the 12-hour day in his plant with the 8-hour shift and production increased dramati-

Andrew Carnegie, the mastermind of the steel industry.

cally. Jones remained in control until he was killed in an explosion at one of the furnaces. He was replaced by Charles Schwab, whose ability made him another trusted Carnegie lieutenant. Finally, Henry Frick joined Carnegie as general manager and right-hand man after he merged his coke business with Carnegie's interests. Interestingly enough, both Schwab and Frick reinstituted the 12-hour day, which remained the norm until the 1920s. With an able team and ample working funds, Carnegie added steel mills until he commanded the largest and wealthiest concern in the business, the Carnegie Steel Company.

THE UNITED STATES
STEEL CORPORATION

In 1898, J. P. Morgan organized the Federal Steel Company according to his familiar formula, adding one company to another to form a network with himself at the center. Federal Steel included various businesses connected with the steel industry, among them the American Bridge Company and the National Tube Company.

Morgan and his associates in Federal Steel posed a problem for Carnegie, now planning to retire. Carnegie had a formidable competitor, but his battling days were over. Besides, his colleagues opposed a fight with Morgan. Frick, still young enough to be ambitious, was more interested in branching out into new enterprises and new combinations, and Schwab felt the same way. Yet, Carnegie refused to let himself be coerced by Morgan's methods. He boldly challenged the Morgan men by threatening to compete with them on their own ground, building factories and turning out the same products. When he said he would manufacture tubing, the directors of the National Tube Company knew he meant it. He disturbed others in the Morgan Group by declaring he would build Great Lakes steamers and railroads to carry Mesabi ore to his mills without middlemen.

As a result, many investors connected with Federal Steel appealed to Morgan to make a deal with Carnegie, which was exactly what Carnegie had in mind.

Morgan always moved to buy out a competitor who could not be destroyed. He opened negotiations with Carnegie, who expressed a willingness to sell, given a satisfactory price of 447 million dollars. Morgan paid it, and proceeded to incorporate the Carnegie Steel Company into the mighty United States Steel Corporation, an organization that included the Federal Steel Company and numerous banking and railroad interests. United States Steel was then worth over one billion dollars, and controlled some 70 percent of the industry in the country. With Carnegie out of the way, Morgan dominated Wall Street, and through it, the business life of the United

John D. Rockefeller, the founder of Standard Oil.

States, as no one had ever done before. According to a joke then current, God created the world in 4004 B.C. and J. P. Morgan reorganized it in 1901.

OIL

Petroleum had been known and used from antiquity. Medicines and lacquers were made from it, and in the form of naphtha it formed the ingredient of the "Greek fire" that set aflame many an enemy warship outside of Constantinople. When the nineteenth century opened, Americans used petroleum to grease squeaky door hinges and the screeching axles of heavily laden wagons. However, attempts to refine it amounted to little until a professor of chemistry at Yale, Benjamin Silliman, Jr., revealed that petroleum is a mixture of hydrocarbons which could be separated by a distilling process. This process produced a refined oil, highly inflammable, easily handled and controlled, and therefore highly suitable as a fuel for lamps and heaters. The by-products made good lubricants. In a report, Silliman described the many different practical uses for petroleum. When drilling in Pennsylvania struck the first gusher in 1859, thousands of men rushed to the petroleum-bearing regions of the state to strike it rich.

JOHN D. ROCKEFELLER

John D. Rockefeller in his youth showed little indication of the driving, ruthless tycoon he would become. He had a low voice and a mild disposition. Shy and serious, he followed his mother's example and became devoutly religious. A life-long pillar of the Baptist Church, he frequently spoke to its Sunday school classes on the ideals of a virtuous life. However, when still a boy, he lent a neighbor fifty dollars at 7 percent interest. The return impressed him, as he himself testified: "From that time onward, I determined to make money work for me." At the same time, Rockefeller stuck to his religious convictions. His first job paid him a salary of three and a half dollars a week, and he dutifully turned 10 percent over to the local Baptist Church. Throughout his life he continued to contribute this percentage to his church. People often expressed amazement that a man who drove so many helpless competitors to the wall should at the same time be so faithful a son of the church. Rockefeller saw no conflict. Failure by the weak seemed to him inevitable. "There has been nothing in my life," he said confidently, "that will not bear the utmost scrutiny." As criticism of his business tactics grew in the late nineteenth century, he was puzzled; he considered it unjustified and he never understood why he was termed by some "the most unpopular man in the United States."

However, his son, John D., Jr., saw the need for refurbishing the Rockefeller image. The publicist Ivy Lee was brought in to think up ideas; none was more effective than the well-known picture of the venerable oil king, who lived to be nearly a hundred years old, handing out shiny new dimes to lucky boys and girls.

STANDARD OIL

The man who did the most to develop the petroleum business never prospected for oil himself, but he knew how to exploit the work of those who did. Rockefeller, born in 1839 and twenty years old at the time of the first Pennsylvania gusher, went into the oil fields to see whether the find was worth exploiting commercially. He returned to his Cleveland home convinced that here was a splendid new business opportunity. Persuading his two partners in a produce business to add their capital to his own modest sum, he started an oil refinery. The move was made as a result of faith in Rockefeller's judgment, for the industry had not yet become stable. Some observers predicted that the fields would suddenly run dry. Others predicted that

661

Rockefeller as Innovator

> ... The life of Rockefeller, we can say again, is not one which invites swift and dogmatic judgments. The lessons which men draw from it will vary according to the preconceptions with which they approach the subject. Some will give a heavier weight to the debit items in the ledger than others. But it can safely be said that the prime significance of Rockefeller's career lies in the fact, that he was a bold innovator in both industry and philanthropy; that he brought to the first a great unifying idea, which he insisted should be thoroughly tested, and to the second a stronger, more expert, and more enduring type of organization. It can be said also that by virtue of his organizing genius, his tenacity of purpose, his keenness of mind, and his firmness of character, he looms up as one of the most impressive figures of the century which his lifetime spanned. His fame went around the world, and it will be long before the world forgets it.

—*Allan Nevins*, John D. Rockefeller

A Pennsylvania oil field. At first, oil was an unstable industry with fields running dry or being bought out and closed.

Rockefeller as Robber Baron

. . . Very often people who admit the facts, who are willing to see that Mr. Rockefeller has employed force and fraud to secure his ends, justify him by declaring, "It's business." That is, "it's business" has come to be a legitimate excuse for hard dealing, sly tricks, special privileges. . . . Now if the Standard Oil Company were the only concern in the country guilty of the practices which have given it monopolistic power, this story never would have been written. . . . But it is simply the most conspicuous type of what can be done by these practices. The methods it employs with such acumen, persistency, and secrecy are employed by all sorts of business men, from corner grocers up to bankers. If exposed, they are excused on the ground that this is business. . . .

. . . Canonise "business success," and men who make a success like that of the Standard Oil Trust become national heroes! The history of its organization is studied as a practical lesson in money-making. It is the most startling feature of the case to one who would like to feel that it is possible to be a commercial people and yet a race of gentlemen. Of course such practices exclude men by all the codes from the rank of gentlemen, just as such practices would exclude men from the sporting world or athletic field. There is no gaming table in the world where loaded dice are tolerated, no athletic field where men must not start fair. Yet, Mr. Rockefeller has systematically played with loaded dice, and it is doubtful if there has ever been a time since 1872 when he has run a race with a competitor and started fair. Business played in this way loses all its sportsmanlike qualities. . . .

—Ida M. Tarbell, **The History of the Standard Oil Company**

many refineries would be wiped out by competition. Banks took a skeptical view of loan applications from oil men.

Convinced by geological reports of immense underground reservoirs of oil, Rockefeller determined to outmaneuver competition by maintaining money reserves to use whenever an oil company wanted to sell its wells. Moreover, careful never to be at the mercy of the banks, he made himself and his partners their own bankers, able to act instantly in financing their undertakings.

These policies paid off to an astonishing degree. The partners founded Standard Oil of Ohio in 1870. The oil continued to gush, and Rockefeller's refineries in Cleveland continued to refine it. When the Panic of 1873 forced other oil men into bankruptcy, Standard Oil, with cash-in-hand provided by Rockefeller's foresight, bought them out.

Many competitors who struggled to survive were forced out of business by Rockefeller's tactics. He raised the rebate system to a fine art, starting with the Lake Shore Railroad, which he compelled to carry crude oil to his refineries at a much lower rate than to anyone else. All the oil business in the Cleveland area was taken over by Standard Oil, to be followed in time by massive sections of the oil industry elsewhere. Rockefeller then founded the South Improvement Company as an instrument of expansion. He boldly succeeded, not only in making the railroads rig prices against his remaining competitors, but in obtaining from them their documents relating to shipments and clients. With this information, he was able to outmaneuver many a rival company. Another of his ideas was to gain control of everything his business depended on, including pipelines. Thus, as historian John Moody pointed out, "In 1879, the Standard Oil interests were the only bonafide buyers, the only gatherers, and the only refiners of all but ten percent of the petroleum of the country."

Rockefeller put the capstone on his financial structure by forming the Standard Oil

Trust in 1882; with this move, he controlled 95 percent of the country's oil-refining business. The stockholders in subordinate companies turned over their stocks to a board of trustees in exchange for certificates that paid dividends. The trustees were in this way handed the powers to vote all the stock and, thereby, to direct the entire oil empire. Needless to say, John D. Rockefeller was one of the trustees. He thus achieved his ideal, the eradication of competition, which he regarded as wasteful, inefficient, and tending to create high prices. He replaced conflicting interests with a stable monopoly. He was, in fact, successful in his drive to increase efficiency in the marketing of oil and cut production costs. He also provided a pension system for his employees. However, Standard Oil made no improvements in petroleum production before the turn of the century.

TRUSTS

GROWTH OF MONOPOLY

The Rockefeller logic had a fundamental flaw, which his critics were quick to point out. When he termed monopoly a force for good, he meant his monopoly. When he defended the right of the strong to destroy the weak, he saw himself as one of the strong. It never occurred to him that he might be hurt by somebody else's monopoly, or destroyed by a more powerful or more cunning adversary. Had he been less powerful in the oil business, he might have held a different business philosophy. His competitors had ample reason for complaint, as did the consumers who bought his oil. As the only oil producer for many localities, he could arbitrarily raise prices without fear of competition or consideration for the buyers. Moreover, his example was spreading; other industrialists saw the advantages of monopoly. Other trusts were formed, such as sugar, beef, flour, and tobacco.

THE SHERMAN ANTITRUST ACT

The creation of monopolies, which ended competition and often meant higher prices to consumers, caused widespread public protest. As a result, the federal government became concerned because state laws to prevent monopolies were proving unsuccessful. Finally, in 1890, under popular pressure, Congress passed the Sherman Antitrust Act, which declared: "Every contract, combination in the form of trust or otherwise, or conspiracy, in restraint of trade or commerce among the several states, or with foreign nations, is hereby declared to be illegal."

The act was too vaguely worded and ambiguous to be effective. Corporation lawyers made use of the phrase, "restraint of trade." As a result, the courts crippled the Sherman Antitrust Act as they had done to the Interstate Commerce Commission. In 1895, the Supreme Court went so far as to rule in *United States v. E. C. Knight Company* that although the Sugar Trust controlled virtually the entire production of that commodity, production could not be construed as restraining trade. In other words, since the Knight Company did not have a monopoly over interstate commerce, but only over the manufacture of sugar, the company could not be controlled by the federal government. The Supreme Court refused to recognize a connection between manufacturing and commerce—a recognition that would have allowed the federal government to control a monopoly over production by means of the interstate commerce clause of the Constitution.

As a result of the Knight case, monopolistic practices in business went on unhampered. United States Steel was founded without regard to the existence of the Sherman Antitrust Act. As for Standard Oil, Rockefeller transformed the trust into a holding company, a new form of monopolistic control with a method of operation to get around the law. The holding company could rightly deny that it exercised direct control over subordinate companies. By owning sufficient stock in them rather than holding all their stock, it was able to guide the decisions of their executive boards and to see to it that those decisions were agreeable to Rockefeller. "The day of combination is here to stay," the oil king commented. "Individualism has gone, never to return." Between 1897 and 1903, 234 new business monopolies were formed.

TECHNOLOGY

The phenomenal expansion of business created a demand for improved technology. An inventors' market came into existence. Every man with a new or superior gadget hoped to patent it and become wealthy. But not every successful inventor found it easy to market his product. Christopher Sholes spent six years trying to sell his typewriter, and then sold the rights to the Remington Arms Company.

Every inventor was faced with the possibility of a lawsuit over his patent. Alexander Graham Bell, for example, was challenged by Western Union over the rights to his invention, the telephone. The case was settled out of court, and Bell and his associates, in 1885, organized the American Telephone and Telegraph Company. By 1900, the American Telephone and Telegraph Company was the holding company for its segment of the communications industry. The telephone, by providing instant communication between distant offices, became known as the "little mother of the trusts."

Thomas A. Edison suffered from lawsuits more than any other inventor, probably because he had more inventions of immediate practical use. In 1882 he founded the Edison Illuminating Company, based on his carbon filament incandescent light, and then fought in the courts against competitors, such as Westinghouse, to maintain his rights. Toward the end of his life he protested: "My electric light inventions have

Alexander Graham Bell, the inventor of the telephone and the founder of the American Telephone and Telegraph Company, is shown here making the first telephone call between New York and Chicago.

brought me no profits, only forty years of litigation."

Edison's direct-current motor had a limited range and low voltage, however, and George Westinghouse soon came along with a superior system of transmitting electricity. Nikola Tesla, an immigrant from Hungary, developed the alternating-current motor of high voltage and indefinite range, and Westinghouse in conjunction with Tesla exploited the invention commercially. With it they lit Chicago's Columbian Exposition in 1893. The introduction of alternating current led to the development of one of America's foremost twentieth-century enterprises, the electrical industry.

Such new inventions revolutionized American business between the Civil War and the First World War. They also transformed American life in a way undreamed of by men and women of the antebellum period.

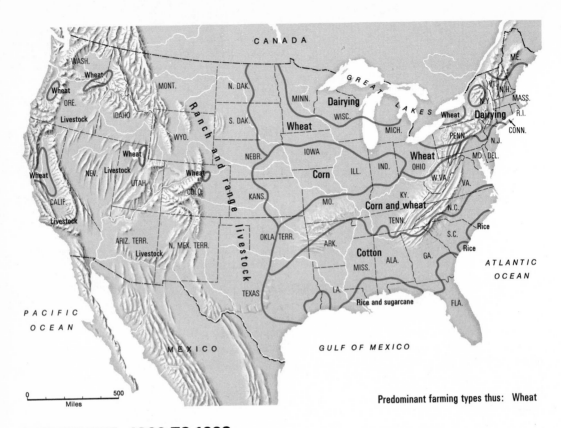

CANADA

GREAT LAKES

WASH.
Wheat
Wheat
ORE.
Livestock
IDAHO
MONT.
N. DAK.
MINN.
Dairying
WISC.
S. DAK.
Wheat
MICH.
Wheat
Dairying
ME.
VT. N.H.
N.Y.
MASS.
R.I.
CONN.
PENN.
N.J.
WYO.
NEBR.
IOWA
ILL.
IND.
OHIO
Wheat
MD. DEL.
Wheat
NEV.
Livestock
Corn
W. VA.
VA.
UTAH
Wheat
COLO.
KANS.
MO.
KY.
Corn and wheat
N.C.
Wheat
CALIF.
Livestock
TENN.
S.C.
Rice
ARIZ. TERR.
N. MEX. TERR.
Livestock
OKLA. TERR.
ARK.
Cotton
MISS.
ALA.
GA.
Rice
ATLANTIC
OCEAN
TEXAS
LA.
Rice and sugarcane
FLA.
PACIFIC
OCEAN
MEXICO
GULF OF MEXICO

Ranch and range
livestock

0   500
Miles

Predominant farming types thus: Wheat

AGRICULTURE · 1860 TO 1890

THE NEW
SOUTHERN ECONOMY

The South possessed an abundance of raw materials that had never been properly developed. The possibilities of a big logging industry in the Great Smokies, or of factories drawing their power from the rivers of Tennessee and the Carolinas began to be realized. Geologists noted seams of coal and iron in the Appalachians, and saw the prospect of a revised economy based on these resources. The antebellum plantation owners did not want change, fearing it would disrupt their way of life, but the Southerners who came into power after them felt otherwise. Henry Grady, publisher of the Atlanta *Constitution* and one of the most eloquent spokesmen for the

New South, commented: "We have established thrift in the city and country. We have fallen in love with work." State leaders now often talked of railroad mileage, plant production, and the application of the latest technology to industry.

INDUSTRIALIZATION

The South, like the rest of the nation, suffered through the depression of 1873. Industry began slowly to revive and gained momentum as the Reconstruction armies were removed. Enterprises based on the land were the first to climb back to the level they had occupied before the war. Cotton might no longer be the absolute monarch of the South's economy, but the cotton fields were flourishing and by 1880 production surpassed that of 1860. Cotton continued to climb to a record ten million bales in the mid-1890s. Cotton seed, once thrown away, was discovered to have marketable value in the form of oil and fertilizer. Moreover, between 1870 and 1880 cotton spindles nearly doubled in the South, and during the next decade cotton mills multiplied. Northern investments in cotton were seven times as great in 1890 as in 1880.

Tobacco also developed in a spectacular manner under the leadership of James B. Duke of Durham, North Carolina, who in 1890 organized the American Tobacco Company. Duke not only gained control of the tobacco crop but also opened an office in New York City to channel his cigarettes, cigars, pipe tobacco, and chewing tobacco into the Northern market. He understood thoroughly the trust concept worked out by Rockefeller and Morgan, and followed their example so closely that in 1911, the federal government brought an antitrust suit against his American Tobacco Company, compelling it to restore independence to two subordinates, Reynolds and Lorillard.

Other crops and industries led to the formation of flourishing new enterprises. The peanut crop in Georgia and citrus fruits from Florida found an expanding market. The famous pine forests of the South provided timber and turpentine. South Carolina restored its thriving textile industry. The raw materials and water power were still there. Impoverished people were desperately seeking work, and entire families came into the mill towns. The men would take the heavy duties, such as lifting bales onto wagons; the women would run the looms, and the children would do whatever odd jobs were available for as little as a dime a day. To many such people, a 70-hour week, however brutalizing, came as a welcome relief from the grinding poverty of unemployment. As activity increased, New England textile manufacturers became more worried by the challenge from the Southern mills.

Appalachian coal and iron did not remain undisturbed for long. Fifteen years after Appomattox, coal was being taken from over four hundred Southern mines, reaching approximately one-eighth of the nation's production. Iron worth 25 million dollars was produced yearly by two hundred foundries. The Tredegar Iron Works rose from ashes to spur the growth of Virginia's economy. Birmingham, Alabama, no more than empty land in 1870, became the "Pittsburgh of the South" within two decades.

As in the North, the railroads were fundamental to the entire pattern of industrial development. Alabama iron production could never have developed so astonishingly were it not for the Louisville and Nashville Railroad and other lines. The revival of Georgia cotton production depended upon the rebuilding of the rail network ruined by General Sherman. Business interests were often interlocking, in the South as in the North, as indicated by such a name as the Tennessee Coal, Iron and Railroad Company. Most of the capital for railroad activity came from Northern bankers, and in 1893, following the bankruptcy

667

of a group of lines, J. P. Morgan reorganized them and formed the Southern Railway, centered in Richmond with lines to New Orleans and St. Louis. Another railway, the Atlantic Coast line, for long held a monopoly of rail traffic from Virginia to Florida. The railroad mileage of the New South doubled between 1865 and 1880, and then doubled again before the turn of the century.

WEAKNESSES

Success came at a high price. Of all the home-grown evils that beset the New South, perhaps the sharecropping system of working the land was the most damaging to the quality of human life. Once the debtor farmer's crops were mortgaged in advance, the system tended to perpetuate itself from one season to the next. He saw little chance of ever paying his debts and saving money for his own farm. Always working the fields for a creditor, he took scant pride in his work. This large body of poverty-stricken farmers provided a poor market for a high-powered industrial economy.

Another legacy of the Civil War could not be undone. The national economic policies passed by Congress during the war years remained on the books. The high protective tariff, the national banking system, the Homestead Act providing free land in the West, and the transcontinental railroad along the Northern route, proposals opposed by the South before the war as dangerous to its economy, had become established national policy, and the South had to accept them. Business leaders of the New South, however, now favored tariff protection for their new industries.

Northern money played a vital role in boosting the Southern economy. Factories, mills, warehouses, mines, railroads, and ships had to be paid for, and the bill was far too large for the Southern states to finance themselves following the havoc of war. Investors on the lookout for speculative opportunities found an underdeveloped area of enormous potential below the Mason-Dixon line. Bankers and brokers encouraged investment by predicting a steady stream of profits. The North had money to invest and the South desperately needed capital. The former antagonists now came together in numerous enterprises undertaken for mutual benefit.

Nevertheless, Northern investment created a serious psychological problem for the South. Businesses in Boston, New York, Philadelphia, Cleveland, and Chicago had made rapid progress since the Civil War. Those in Richmond, Charleston, Mobile, and New Orleans had to begin all over again. An Alabama steel man could hardly hope to make a real dent in the national market controlled by Carnegie. A Louisiana banker could not realistically hope to ever become another J. P. Morgan. To their credit, Southern businessmen were undaunted by this challenge, although they knew that they were cast for a subordinate role in the country's industrial life for some time to come.

There were other advantages for the Northern economy. Federal lands in the South were sold to Northerners in large tracts during Reconstruction, and whole areas remained the property of absentee owners more interested in earning profits than in improving conditions for the local population. Northern businessmen also applied pressures to limit Southern business activity to the handling of raw materials or the initial stages of processing, so that the final steps in the manufacturing process could take place in the North. Many Southerners thus found that if they tried to produce finished goods, the bankers became difficult to deal with. Bankers even compelled Alabama steel mills to charge higher prices than those set by the mills of Pittsburgh. Nevertheless, an uneasy Carnegie complained, "The South is Pennsylvania's most formidable industrial enemy."

Southern railroads could not adopt a systematic policy to aid their own geographic section because they depended on Northern funds and took their orders from Northern directors. Freight differentials were sometimes openly discriminatory against the South. Shippers of raw materials received favorable rates, but those with manufactured goods to sell paid more to ship them than their competitors in the North. Northern business interests used Rockefeller's tactics to sidetrack their Southern competitors. Small wonder that the per capita income of the New South remained only about half the national average as late as 1914.

ACHIEVEMENTS

As late as 1900 the Southern states were still essentially agrarian, their urban population amounting to less than 10 percent of the whole. Yet cities had been built and rebuilt and hundreds of settled localities had expanded under the pressure of economic need. Earlier, Southern businessmen had cried urgently, "Bring the mills to the cotton!" Now the mills were a reality, with

an investment of nearly one billion dollars. Wealth poured into Southern treasuries, not as rapidly as in the North, and restricted to too few owners, but still proof that the South was back on its feet.

Northerners had been coming South to put their abilities to work. A few Southerners, in turn, migrated to the financial capital of the country, New York. John H. Inman of Tennessee, a former Confederate soldier, came out of the New South to penetrate the inner circle of Wall Street. He was "at thirty-six worth a million and a half," according to Henry Grady, the Southern journalist. Inman's success symbolized the growing economic reunification of the nation following the political reunification imposed on the South during Reconstruction. Southerners began to reenter the life of the nation as full-fledged partners capable of making their weight felt, and much of the credit for this transformation belonged to the farsighted business leaders of the New South.

THE IMPACT OF INDUSTRIALIZATION ON AMERICAN THOUGHT

During the 1890s the term "American millionaire" became familiar at home and abroad. More than four thousand Americans estimated their wealth in at least seven figures. Most of them, moreover, were recent millionaires who had emerged from the post-Civil War economic boom with their pockets full of gold. They made fortunes in industry, trade, railroads, banking, and in general wherever a commodity or

service responded to an extensive public demand. Never before in world history was so much money made so quickly by so many individuals.

THE ROBBER BARONS

The pioneers of big business in the late nineteenth century were alike in many ways. Most came from small-town or rural environments, started to work while quite young, had great inborn commercial ability and received no higher education. They were different from the former business elite, who usually came from more prosperous families and were better educated. The innovators, in addition, were not bound by the traditional business practices of this elite, and they found a receptive new climate in government for their operations. These new businessmen thought on a continental scale and usually in terms of speculation as well as business monopoly and personal power. Only Hill, Harriman, and Rockefeller were noted for sound financing of their enterprises.

The American millionaires were not universally admired. They were often regarded as ruthless exploiters whose methods would not bear examination. Although many Americans invested in business and railroads, they distrusted the operators, who were compared to the lawless nobles of the Middle Ages, and the epithet Robber Barons has stuck to them. Many a historian has used it in discussing the development of American capitalism in the late nineteenth century. Theodore Roosevelt later denounced these industrialists as "malefactors of great wealth."

The millionaires rejected this judgment; according to their own view of men and society, their business ethics were justified and the leadership they demonstrated made them worthy of their fortunes. Many of them sincerely believed in a philosophy that emphasized individualism and personal initiative, unrestrained by outside regulations. They were motivated not by simple greed but by the hunger to achieve and to impose their wills on a specific environment. Big business was the great game of the late nineteenth century. A few men dominated the game while continuing to talk in terms of an era of open and equal competition long since past. Moreover, many believed it was the will of Divine Providence that made the enterprising man

successful. Rockefeller meant it when he said: "The good Lord gave me my wealth." Carnegie provided a title for the philosophy in the name he gave his essay, "The Gospel of Wealth."

THE GOSPEL OF WEALTH

The Manchester School of British economists had described man's conduct in terms of the way he made his living. Carnegie accepted this, although he allowed wide scope for the noneconomic side of life. His essay attempted to justify vast wealth by identifying it with traditional American moral values. From his viewpoint, the democratic process was acceptable because it was based on the concept of limited government responsibility for the development of the American economy. Political democracy and laissez-faire economics were thus regarded by Carnegie as inseparable. Liberty meant particularly the right to an unlimited accumulation of private property through thrift and hard work. However, wealthy businessmen who defended this view saw no inconsistency in demanding high protective tariffs, free land grants, and government loans to further their own prosperity. Equality to Carnegie meant equal opportunity for gain, but his inclination was to oppose any effort made by the state to ensure equality of opportunity by curtailing monopolies. To him, the idea of progress implied economic development which led to the creation of more goods and more wealth—hence his emphasis on ever-increasing production.

While Carnegie recognized the economic gulf between the wealthy few and the rest of society, he praised corporate enterprise for raising the economic well-being of the whole nation. Furthermore, the successful businessman's accumulation of wealth gave him obligations to society. He had to set an example of modest living, to provide for those dependent on him, and to use his wealth to better the community.

The Gospel of Wealth was generally in line with traditional American ideals and was accepted by most businessmen, big or small. It also induced much private charity in Carnegie's era and in the times that followed—resulting in such contributions as universities, art galleries, and private foundations for medical and social research.

SOCIAL DARWINISM

In advocating a minimum role for the government in the social sphere, business leaders also believed that they were in harmony with the best scientific thinking of their time. The great name in science in the 1890s was Charles Darwin, whose *On the Origin of Species* had established the theory of evolution. According to Darwin, animals adapted to their environment through natural selection, a sifting process that enabled stronger species to survive and caused weaker ones to disappear.

Philosopher Herbert Spencer called natural selection "the survival of the fittest." Nature had put countless individuals on the earth. An intense struggle had developed among them for survival, and those best adapted to survive had passed on genes to their offspring. Spencer concluded that competition was the social expression of the concept of "the survival of the fittest." Consequently, he maintained that state activity to protect or guide society was a violation of the law of nature.

Professor William Graham Sumner of Yale studied the theories of Darwin and Spencer, and became America's foremost exponent of what was called Social Darwinism. Sumner roundly condemned any effort to save the weak from the consequences of their weakness and even went so far as to oppose factory legislation and child labor laws on the ground that they were artificial, "against the constitution of nature."

Big businessmen, without considering that support from the government helped them prosper, gratefully accepted the theory of Social Darwinism, finding that it validated their most deeply cherished convictions. Rockefeller spoke with deep conviction when he told his Sunday school class: "The growth of a large business is merely a survival of the fittest. . . . The American Beauty rose can be produced in the splendor and fragrance which bring cheer to its beholder only by sacrificing the early buds which grow up around it. This is not an evil tendency in business. It is merely the working out of a law of nature and a law of God."

A cartoonist made one of the memorable drawings of the time when he pictured Rockefeller as a gardener holding a plant in one hand and a pair of shears in the other. The plant was labeled "Standard Oil," and all around lay the "buds" (small businesses) the "gardener" had sheared off.

THE HORATIO ALGER STORY

A fictional counterpart of the theory of Social Darwinism appeared for children in a literature explaining how to grow up and get along in a society. The most successful creator of this kind of story was Horatio Alger, whose formula in books such as *Luck and Pluck* became a commonplace. The hero of an Alger tale rose from humble origins by working hard, being thrifty, and seizing "the main chance." Virtue was invariably rewarded. The old lady he helped cross the street would turn out to be a wealthy widow who, recognizing his sterling merit, would send him to college. Or the infant he saved from toppling off a cliff would turn out to be the son of the local banker, and the Alger hero would promptly be given a job at the bank, with the chance to be the banker one day. The moral was that the boy who got ahead was one of the "fit," a wealthy survivor in the process of natural selection. He did not accept the "artificial" help of the state, or rely on politicians who, after all, were not the most fit by any "natural" criterion.

Alger, however, informed his juvenile audience that the rich might properly help the poor, and in this he echoed a sentiment expressed by both Carnegie and Rockefeller, who felt that they would be judged for the good deeds they performed with their wealth. But Alger also taught a generation of youngsters not to consider social welfare legislation a state or national government responsibility—an idea that was acceptable because it basically upheld the traditional American belief that the less fortunate in society were properly the responsibility of their families or of private and local government charity.

Readings

GENERAL WORKS

Cochran, Thomas C., and William Miller, *The Age of Enterprise*. New York: Macmillan, 1942—An economic and social history of industrial America which emphasizes the growth and dominance of big business before the New Deal.

Fine, Sidney, *Laissez-Faire and the General Welfare State*. Ann Arbor: University of Michigan Press, 1964—American thought on economic and social policy was torn, Fine argues, between ideas of the sanctity of property derived from John Locke, and ideals of Christian brotherhood and commonwealth derived from dominant religious beliefs. The study covers the period between 1865 and 1901.

Hayes, Samuel P., *The Response to Industrialism: 1885–1914*. Chicago: University of Chicago Press, 1957—A study of the impact of industrialization on American life and thought. Hayes maintains that social con-

flict was brought about by the wide variety of reactions to industrial society, not simply by the emergence of sharp class distinctions.

Hofstadter, Richard, *Social Darwinism in American Thought*. Boston: Beacon, 1955 —A study of the use of Darwinian evolutionary theory applied to social issues. At first, Hofstadter shows that the main proponents of Social Darwinism used it to justify laissez-faire, but later on, modifications of the doctrines were adopted by more liberal social reformers.

Holbrook, Stewart H., *The Age of the Moguls*. Garden City, N.Y.: Doubleday, 1953 —A series of sketches of the business careers of some thirty tycoons of the late nineteenth and early twentieth centuries.

Josephson, Matthew, *The Robber Barons*. New York: Harcourt, Brace, 1934—A spirited account of the careers and per-

SPECIAL STUDIES

sonalities of many of those who made it to the top of the economic ladder during the late nineteenth century. Josephson sharply attacks their methods.

Kirkland, Edward C., *Dream and Thought in the American Business Community, 1860–1900.* Ithaca, N.Y.: Cornell University Press, 1956—Kirkland shows how businessmen unconsciously shaped an ideology which justified their wealth and power out of older American religious, political, and economic ideals.

Kirkland, Edward C., *Industry Comes of Age. Business, Labor, and Public Policy, 1860–1897.* New York: Holt, Rinehart & Winston, 1961—An economic history of the later years of the nineteenth century. While admitting the materialism and injustices of the age, Kirkland praises the energy and initiative of business leadership.

Mitchell, Broadus, and G. S. Mitchell, *The Industrial Revolution in the South.* Westport, Conn.: Greenwood, 1968—A collection of articles on Southern industrialization, with particular reference to the cotton textile industry.

Wiebe, Robert H., *The Search for Order, 1877–1920.* New York: Hill & Wang, 1968 —An interpretive survey of the era of industrialization which finds the major theme of the times to have been a search for new institutions of social control to replace those damaged by industrialization and urbanization.

Woodward, C. Vann, *The Origins of the New South.* Baton Rouge: Louisana State University Press, 1951—An important study of Southern history in the years after Reconstruction. Woodward argues that the "New South" Democratic leadership adopted the dominant materialistic business values of the Gilded Age and attempted, with some success, to implant them in Southern society.

Benson, Lee, *Merchants, Farmers and Railroads.* Cambridge, Mass.: Harvard University Press, 1955—A study of the role played by special interest groups in obtaining New York State railroad legislation between 1850 and 1887. Benson maintains that economic pressure groups, not reform ideology, determined regulatory practice.

Cochran, Thomas C., *Railroad Leaders, 1845–1890: The Business Mind in Action.* New York: Russell, 1966—An analysis of railroad leaders' letters using quantitative social science techniques. Cochran finds that the preferred role for a railroad leader was to be industrious, honest, and to further the best interests of leading stockholders.

Grodinsky, Julius, *Transcontinental Railway Strategy.* Philadelphia: University of Pennsylvania Press, 1962—This analysis of the construction of railways in the West concludes that the public got a good bargain from relatively low-priced and efficient transportation, with little profit for most of the railroad entrepreneurs.

Hidy, Ralph W., and Muriel E. Hidy, *Pioneering in Big Business.* New York: Harper & Row, 1965—The first volume of the authors' *History of the Standard Oil Company (New Jersey).* They discuss Rockefeller's creation of the great Standard Oil trust.

Hurst, James W., *Law and the Conditions of Freedom in the Nineteenth-Century United States.* Madison: University of Wisconsin Press, 1956—Three lectures on the purpose and nature of American law in the nineteenth century. Hurst maintains that law was to be used to release individual energies, help men master nature, and control competing interest groups.

Kolko, Gabriel, *Railroads and Regulations, 1877–1916.* Princeton, N.J.: Princeton University Press, 1965—Kolko maintains that the major pressures for federal railroad regulation came from railroad leaders themselves who hoped to use federal regulation to rationalize an unprofitably over-competitive system.

Lewis, Oscar, *The Big Four*. New York: Knopf, 1938—The story of the building of the Central Pacific Railroad, as shown in sketches of Collis P. Huntington and the other tycoons who planned and executed it.

McCloskey, Robert G., *American Conservatism in Age of Enterprise*. Cambridge, Mass.: Harvard University Press, 1951—Through studies of such conservatives as William Graham Sumner and Justice Stephen Field, McCloskey discusses how conservatives adopted American symbols and ideals and altered them to serve the power of big business.

Moody, John, *The Truth About the Trusts*. Westport, Conn.: Greenwood, 1960—A classic first-hand study of the economic results of the formation of great corporate trusts.

Stover, J. F., *American Railroads*. Chicago: University of Chicago Press, 1961—A short description of the railroads' role in the changing American economy. Stover points out that in the United States, as opposed to Europe, railroads often preceded, rather than followed, the creation of communities.

Weiss, Richard, *The American Myth of Success*. New York: Basic Books, 1969—From the boys' novels of Horatio Alger to Norman Vincent Peale's linking of success and religion, Weiss finds a tendency for success literature to recommend cultivating new mental or spiritual powers.

Williamson, Harold F., and Arnold M. Daum, *The American Petroleum Industry: Age of Illumination, 1859–1899*. Evanston, Ill.: Northwestern University Press, 1959—The first volume of a major history of the petroleum industry. Williamson and his co-author accept neither the sharp attacks on John D. Rockefeller nor Allan Nevins' defense of his tactics.

PRIMARY SOURCES

Adams, Charles F., Jr., and Henry Adams, *Chapters of Erie*. Ithaca, N.Y.: Cornell University Press, 1956—Three articles by the grandsons of John Q. Adams analyzing the financial machinations of Jim Fisk and Jay Gould concerning the Erie Railroad and the 1869 attempt to corner the New York gold market.

Chandler, Alfred D., Jr., ed., *The American Railroads*. New York: Harcourt, Brace, 1965—Chandler's anthology centers on the railroads as America's first "big business." He shows how business conditions led railroads to adopt new forms of management and control.

Diamond, Sigmund, ed., *The Nation Transformed: The Creation of Industrial Society*. New York: Braziller, 1963—An anthology of primary source material which illustrates the motives and the social effect of American industrialization.

Kirkland, Edward P., ed., *The Gospel of Wealth and Other Timely Essays by Andrew Carnegie*. Cambridge, Mass.: Harvard University Press, 1962—Carnegie, the great steel magnate and philanthropist, strongly felt the need to explain and justify his fortune in moral terms. In these essays he sets forth a social philosophy in which great fortunes were justified by their power to do good for society.

Lloyd, Henry D., *Wealth Against Common*

wealth. Englewood Cliffs, N.J.: Prentice-Hall, 1963—A classic statement of the Populist creed, attacking the concentration of great economic power and wealth as a threat to American democracy.

Twain, Mark, and C. D. Warner, *The Gilded Age*. Indianapolis, Ind.: Bobbs-Merrill, 1970—A book of sharp social comment which gave the Gilded Age its title. To Twain and Warner, a grasping materialism and vulgarity dominated the era.

BIOGRAPHIES

Allen, Frederick Z., *The Great Pierpont Morgan*. New York: Harper & Row, 1949 —A popular biography of the financier who controlled a good share of American industry and whose activities led to the rapid growth and concentration of industrial wealth and power.

Josephson, Matthew, *Edison*. New York: McGraw-Hill, 1959—A long biography of the famous inventor which argues that his fundamental aim was to bring about the progress of industry and commerce.

Lane, W. J., *Commodore Vanderbilt*. New York: Knopf, 1942—A biography of one of the first American multimillionaires. The man who reputedly said, "The public be damned." Vanderbilt's activities in shipping, railroads, and real estate revealed his business talent.

Nevins, Allan, *Study in Power: John D. Rockefeller, Industrialist and Philanthropist*, Vols. I-II. New York: Scribner's, 1953 —A revision of Nevins' 1940 biography of the founder of Standard Oil. Nevins devotes much attention to Rockefeller's abilities and impact as an organizer and executive for mass-production industry.

Nixon, Raymond B., *Henry W. Grady*. New York: Russell, 1969—A biography of the Atlanta publisher who was probably the most influential spokesman for the "New South" creed.

FICTION

Dreiser, Theodore, *The Financier*. New York: New American Library, 1967—A study of the rise of Frank Cowperwood to the role of great financier. Dreiser, the famous American exponent of naturalism, views American society here in Darwinian terms as a struggle for existence.

Dreiser, Theodore, *The Titan*. New York: New American Library, 1968—Another study of the corruption of American big business as seen in the career of Frank Cowperwood by the author of *The Financier*.

Hay, John, *The Breadwinners*. Upper Saddle River, N.J.: Gregg, 1967—Although better known for his service as Secretary of State, Hay was also a poet, novelist, and historian. This anti-union novel was inspired by the railroad strikes of 1877.

Howells, William D., *The Rise of Silas Lapham*. New York: Macmillan, 1962—A novel about the career of a businessman, and the effect of success on his character. Howells, one of the most prominent literary figures of his day, was a moderate social reformer.

James, Henry, *The American*. New York: Dell, 1960—An early novel by the American author who spent most of his life in England and whose novels reflected his cosmopolitan, upper-class background. In *The American*, James's hero comes in contact with European society and shows his moral superiority to it. In the end, however, he rejects his earlier business career.

675

The Social and Economic Response to Industrialism

19

Give me your tired, your poor,
Your huddled masses yearning to
  breathe free,
The wretched refuse of your
  teeming shore,
Send these, the homeless,
  tempest-tost to me,
I lift my lamp beside the golden
  door!

—Emma Lazarus, Inscription
on the Statue of Liberty

Italian immigrants working in the United States.

These welcoming words, inscribed on the base of the Statue of Liberty, a gift to the United States from the people of France in 1886, did not reflect the attitude of all Americans toward new arrivals to their country. Only four years before they were written, the United States Congress passed its first immigration restriction legislation, excluding the Chinese completely and certain "undesirable" groups of other nationalities. At that time, many immigrants were accused of exploiting the United States by coming to make a "fortune" which they intended to take back with them to the Old Country. It was true that of the twenty million immigrants who arrived from 1820

677

to 1900, about five million did return to their native lands. However, not many returned with fortunes. Actually, most aliens were exploited by the industrial economy into which they were absorbed. Generally, they encountered harsh living conditions, prejudice, and the hostility of native industrial workers who resented the immigrants'

usual willingness to work for low wages. The nation, however, owed much to these immigrants. Their physical and intellectual strength, their passionate desire to improve their lot, their diverse backgrounds all helped to shape the country's cultural uniqueness and enabled it to take important steps toward industrial leadership.

THE NEW IMMIGRATION

The flow of immigration that began to increase in the 1860s created both assets and liabilities for the United States. Unquestionably, the influx provided the labor and talent needed for an accelerating industrial economy. At the same time it was a source of serious problems for workers, the newcomers as well as those born in America. During the late nineteenth and early twentieth centuries, millions of workers competed for jobs in mining, manufacturing, and transportation at subsistence wage levels.

In the early 1880s, the national character of immigration began to change. Penniless, desperate streams poured in from Italy, Austria-Hungary, Russia, and Finland. Aliens arrived from the Balkan states, Turkey, Greece, and Portugal. Essentially destitute, they were eager to work at almost any wage. The competition for jobs was greatly sharpened and it was the rare employer who did not take advantage of the situation.

From 1860 to 1890 the United States population more than doubled, leaping from 31 million to nearly 76 million. Much of this rapid growth came from immigration. In the 30 years after 1860 almost 14 million aliens came to America. A single year high

was reached in 1882 when 788,922 immigrants entered the country—an average of over 2,100 a day. By 1910, the ranks of the foreign-born had reached 23 million, with almost 9 million having come in between 1900 and 1910. The peak year was 1907 when 1.3 million foreigners arrived.

SOURCE OF IMMIGRANTS

In the 1860s, almost 90 percent of all immigrants came from central and northern Europe, and only a comparative trickle arrived from southern and eastern Europe. By the 1890s the situation had reversed, with the bulk of emigration from the countries of southern and eastern Europe. Prior to 1890 most immigrants were from Great Britain, Germany, Ireland, and the Scandinavian countries. Many were attracted by the cheap land available in the West. Scandinavians settled on Midwestern farms and in cities such as Milwaukee, Chicago, and Cincinnati. Many Germans pushed even farther west, whereas the Irish and British tended to settle largely in the cities of the Eastern seaboard. Because the South had fewer agricultural and industrial opportunities, it attracted few immigrants.

678

By and large, the immigrants who came in the early nineteenth century were easy to assimilate because they had backgrounds similar to those already in America. Most were accustomed to a constitutional type of government; fair-skinned Anglo-Saxon or Teutonic types, they were usually Protestant and literate. Before the 1880s ended, however, a new wave of immigrants began to arrive who found it far more difficult to be accepted. The "new immigration" included a multitude of Catholics, Jews, and Orientals, who frequently experienced resistance to their presence. Nevertheless they came in a constant stream from Russia, Greece, Poland, Italy, Syria, Austria-Hungary, and Japan.

DISTRIBUTION OF IMMIGRANTS

Earlier immigrants usually had had some choice of where to live as they dispersed across the nation. The Irish had congregated on the Atlantic coast, seeking work in the industrial cities of the East, the Germans and Scandinavians still found land available to them in the Middle West or the Great Plains where they put their farming experience to work. The "new wave," on the other hand, was faced by two obstacles immediately upon arrival. Most of these later immigrants had no private capital and therefore had to find employment instantly. (Some were hired in Europe by

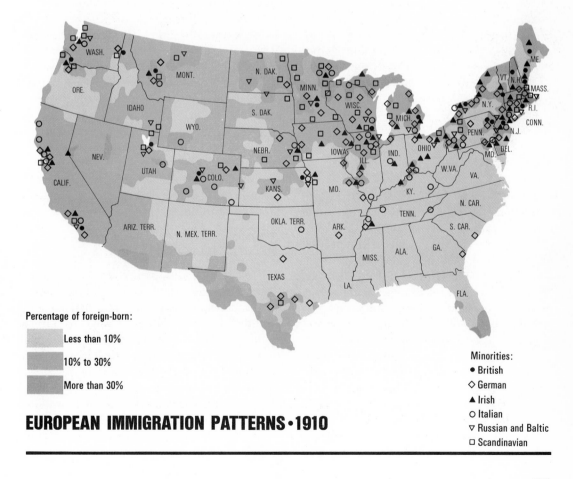

Percentage of foreign-born:

Less than 10%

10% to 30%

More than 30%

Minorities:
● British
◇ German
▲ Irish
○ Italian
▽ Russian and Baltic
□ Scandinavian

EUROPEAN IMMIGRATION PATTERNS • 1910

American companies and provided with passage fares that the immigrant agreed to pay off over a course of years as an employee of the company.) Although the majority of the new aliens came from rural areas, their desperate financial condition forced them to take low-paying jobs quickly offered them by the meat packers, the railroads, and the coal, iron, and steel producers who needed cheap labor. The basic need to survive, and the fact that cheap land was no longer available, served to herd the new arrivals into the industrial centers of the East. They became, in effect, city dwellers. Italians, Russians, Poles, Austrians, Hungarians, Croatians, and Bohemians were a ready supply of inexpensive manpower for America's industrial revolution. Except for the Russians, the majority of whom settled in Nebraska, Kansas, and the Dakotas, the new immigrants, by the early twentieth century, had taken over most of the jobs in the textile mills, the mines, and the manufacturing plants. With the coming of these immigrants and the internal movement of Americans from the farm to the city, the United States developed into an urban nation.

INCENTIVES

As can be said for the earlier migratory movements to America, the immigrants came basically to escape unfavorable conditions in their native lands. Perhaps the most common motive for leaving Europe was poverty. The United States with its "golden door" seemed to offer a chance for improved economic opportunity. It appeared as a land of hope and equality where people of all backgrounds, from any social level, could begin a new life and reach a higher station in life through hard work and personal ambition. This was the immigrant's expectation, all too frequently a fantasy fed by American relatives and more often by American companies whose advertisements in Europe for cheap labor lured

the innocent with exaggerated promises of widespread opportunities for newcomers.

The factors leading to this mass emigration were varied. Poverty led farmers and farm laborers in England, Ireland, the Scandinavian countries, and Germany to America after repeated crop failures, low prices, and depressed times. Economic changes in the Austro-Hungarian Empire and parts of Italy also created hardships for rural peasants and agricultural laborers. Italy was plagued with poor soil, an absence of coal, and a scarcity of manufacturing. Taxes were high, there was little education, and many farmers did not own the land they worked. Like the Italians, the Slavic peoples of the Austro-Hungarian Empire and Russia faced problems of poverty and illiteracy. Many emigrants also were driven out of Russia and eastern Europe by persecution for religious or political beliefs. Russian Mennonites were discriminated against, and the 1880s saw the beginning of pogroms and restrictive laws, extending into the early twentieth century, under which Russian Jews were often forced to flee their burning homes in violent anti-Semitic campaigns. Some immigrants were paupers and some were criminals, while others were seeking to avoid compulsory military service. But the greatest force in the vast emigration was the desire to escape squalor and persecution.

ADVERTISING CAMPAIGNS

Not only conditions in Europe, but also forces in America encouraged immigration. Before 1860, the United States had an unfulfilled need for labor to work its farmlands, dig its mines, and man its factories, a need which increased after 1860. Railroads had large landholdings they wished to dispose of, both for monetary gain and to encourage settlement of areas that would then require their service. Manufacturers, immigration bureaus of Western states, and railroad companies embarked on advertising campaigns in Europe designed to create an enticing picture of the United States. American representatives toured Europe painting glowing pictures of a "paradise" of opportunity. They were abetted by American steamship lines eager for human cargo to fill their holds on return trips. Travel in steerage was unquestionably an ordeal, but the low cost of this method of transoceanic travel greatly stimulated European emigration.

CONTRACT LABOR

In their need for cheap labor, growing industries adopted practices that, if profitable, were not necessarily humane. Companies often contracted for labor in Europe and imported it under the labor contract law. They advanced passage money to the emigrant, and once he was at work in America, collected it in small installments from his weekly paycheck. Usually, this indebtedness bound the immigrant to the company for a considerable length of time at subsistence wages. Not until passage of the Foran Act in 1885 was this practice officially outlawed.

In addition, immigrants were often profitably manipulated by their own compatriots in America, as typified by the *padrone* system of securing immigrant labor among the Italians and Greeks. The *padrone* was generally an ethnic leader. He organized "immigrant banks," or groups of workers, in the Old Country, arranged transportation, supplied these gangs of unskilled workers to the railroads and other companies for a handsome commission, and provided housing for his fellow countrymen, enriching himself by each activity. As a rule, he recruited immigrants unfamiliar with American wage levels, so that his rates for "sale" to the companies would reap maximum profits for himself.

Hester Street on New York's lower East Side was home to many newly-arrived immigrants.

PROBLEMS OF IMMIGRANTS

The immigrant who felt threatened by conditions in his native land frequently found that his dignity fared no better in his new environment. The living conditions, exploitation in employment, and prejudice did not improve the wretched existence of the new arrivals.

LIVING CONDITIONS

After interrogation and cursory physical and psychological examinations at an immigration station such as Ellis Island, the immigrant—if he was not placed under detention—was ferried to the mainland. There he usually had to settle in New York City's lower East Side, an overcrowded slum, packed with immigrants clustered in various ethnic groups. In its dingy tenements, the new aliens huddled together in poverty, unable to afford adequate housing. Said one observer of the Italian section in New York: "Here, the mud, dirt and filth, the

stinking humidity, the incumbrances, the disorder of the streets are beyond description." Many were never able to get out of the slums of New York and other large cities along the Atlantic seaboard, to which they had been relegated. They had no money to leave the cities; so their only alternative was to try to better themselves within it.

The new jobs created by America's expanding economy were located in the cities. The crowded urban areas also provided immigrants with their only source of education and companionship, through their churches, fraternal organizations, and newspapers. Moreover, lack of skills and inability to speak English were less of a problem for the alien employed in a factory than for one who attempted to strike out on his own as a farm worker. However, the average unskilled worker in manufacturing found little chance for advancement. Yet, some were able to start small businesses to serve, and sometimes exploit, their community of countrymen.

Most of the immigrants who arrived in the late nineteenth century rarely got beyond the cities and mining areas of the Eastern seaboard. Those who did, however, had to work for years before they had enough money to purchase a farm. "The difficulty," according to historian Oscar Handlin, "was that a man could live years in an American city without coming to understand the mainsprings of its economy." Some men left their families in the cities and joined construction gangs building railroads. Here, hoping to earn enough eventually to transport their relatives from the city, they lived in dilapidated shanties and broken-down freight cars. Too often, the money they hoped to save was spent for necessities at inflated prices at the company store, "In the country and city," added Handlin, "from 1830 to 1930, the Irish, the Bohemians, the Slovaks, the Hungarians, the Italians . . . took up for a period the service of the pick and shovel." Their wages went for the essentials needed to survive, and after their jobs were ended, most laborers still had as few assets as when they started.

PREJUDICE

In stark contrast to Emma Lazarus' invitation on the base of the Statue of Liberty, is the following excerpt from a bitter poem written in 1890 by Thomas Bailey Aldrich:

> *Wide open and unguarded stand*
> *   our gates,*
> *And through them presses a wild*
> *   motley throng . . .*
> *Flying the Old World's poverty and*
> *   scorn;*
> *These bringing with them unknown*
> *   gods and rites,*
> *Those, tiger passions, here to stretch*
> *   their claws.*

The idea of immigration itself did not arouse as much hostility as did the type of immigrants that arrived in the new wave. These arrivals provoked far more fear than earlier immigrants and, consequently, more prejudice and demands for some form of restriction. The hordes of poor and uneducated southern and eastern Europeans brought with them, together with their poverty, alien languages and customs. By the late 1880s American nativists were labeling as undesirable this influx of Italians, Slavs, Jews, and others. Racial and ethnic prejudices, manifested in housing discrimination and public attitudes, were particularly strong in the cities and directed most sharply against Orientals, the Irish, and southern Europeans.

A number of charges were leveled against these new arrivals. The new immigrants, unlike the earlier predominantly Protestant wave, were in large number Roman Catholic. In a basically Protestant country, their mere presence seemed an intolerable threat. Different in religious heritage, the new immigrants were generally illiterate and poor, and they tended to crowd together in their own communities. The "little Italys" and "little Polands" of New York and Chicago were typical examples. The new immigrants had, further, a high birth rate. All of this quickly led to outcries by some Americans that the country's original Anglo-Saxon stock would soon be outbred and outvoted, or even worse, mongrelized by "inferior" blood. As evidence, the defenders of America's purity pointed to the slums, which they accused the immigrants of creating. In addition, they charged that the new immigrant was dirty, immoral, and had brought with him from the Old Country such radical ideologies as socialism, communism, and anarchy which would undermine American democracy. Laborers, now fighting desperately for higher wages, also reacted with hostility to the new immigrant. Unfamiliar with the country and desperate for work, the newcomer saw no alternative but to work for whatever wages his employers offered. This made him a distinct counterforce to the efforts made by organized labor to increase its living standard. To his misfortune, the new immigrant had arrived at a time of profound economic change in the United States and was caught in the middle of the economic struggle between the industrialists and the workers. However, by the 1880s immigrants were increasingly joining labor unions.

Prejudice and fear of aliens led to the formation in 1881 of the American Protective Association. Claiming a membership of one million strong, it was organized to try to halt the flow of Catholic immigrants but also worked heatedly to curb the entrance of all foreigners. The APA's self-affirmed goals were nationalistic, its efforts directed particularly at excluding immigrants from southern and eastern Europe who, it was charged, were clannish, unable to assimilate, and racially inferior. Organized labor threw its weight behind the Association as it moved to stem the tide of incoming foreigners.

Fear of foreign radicalism and subversion also contributed heavily to prejudice against the new immigrants. Because they had emigrated from countries without representative governments, it was felt by many Americans that they could not readily be absorbed into American society, and that many were probably radical, subversive, and unsympathetic to a capitalistic economy. However, most immigrants did not attack American economic institutions but were passively exploited by them. They were even used by factory owners as strikebreakers. Labor union leaders discovered that immigrants were difficult to organize because they did not speak English and were made mistrustful by the strangeness of their new surroundings. However, by the late 1880s, many employers were becoming alarmed about the presumed radicalism of the immigrants, especially following a riot in Haymarket Square in Chicago that drew wide attention to a handful of foreign-born anarchists who participated in it. The riot unleashed a flood of wild charges that "anarchists and communists" had infiltrated the labor movement and were, in fact, dominating it.

RACISM

By the early years of the twentieth century anti-foreignism had veered toward racism. Many Americans expressed fear that the Nordic "races" would be polluted by the new ethnic strains introduced by the influx of Italians, Jews, Slavs, Bulgarians, Turks, and Greeks. Madison Grant in his book *The Passing of the Great Race* maintained that mixing the "races" would lead to a reversion to a lower type of civilization. This prejudice also was supported by certain social scientists. Said Henry Pratt Fairchild in his publication, *The Melting Pot Mistake:*

What such a country really needs to concern itself about is the effects of race mixture. . . . If we can imagine the mating of two persons of absolutely pure stock of different races, each of the offspring would receive half of its determiners from the germ plasm of one race and the other half from the germ plasm of the other race. In other words, they would be strictly half-breeds. . . . The plant or animal breeder knows that the indiscriminate mixing of a large number of varieties can be expected to produce just one result—the mongrel.

The fact that some social scientists and writers had asserted that different races had different national characteristics, and that some of these characteristics—and therefore nationalities—were undesirable, made prejudiced persons regard their bias as evidence of clear, scientific thinking. They agreed with Fairchild that the new arrivals belonged to races "in a more primitive stage of evolution," and approved when he declared, "The figure of the melting pot should really be replaced by the figure of the village pound."

Japanese immigration to the United States, which had begun in 1885, presented the country with a particularly difficult challenge after 1900. By 1910, although only 72,000 Japanese lived in the United States, most were concentrated in the Pacific Coast states, and Americans in that area were determined to prevent more from entering. The Japanese were charged with working for lower wages than American laborers and were resented for their success in farming. Because they were thrifty, they were able to buy some of the richest farm lands on the West Coast. Although this ownership amounted to only 1.6 percent of the land in that area, the Japanese farmers dominated the production of tomatoes, spinach, strawberries, celery, onions, and cantaloupes. They were also disliked for refusing to give up their Japanese citizenship. A Japanese Exclusion League, the labor unions, and the Hearst press on the West Coast took advantage of the unrest caused by an earthquake and fire in San Francisco

in 1906 to demand an end to the admittance of Japanese laborers and segregation of Japanese children in the schools. President Theodore Roosevelt, realizing that Japan was a proud nation gaining in world power, sidestepped the issue by working out the Gentlemen's Agreement with the Japanese government in 1908, whereby Japan voluntarily restricted the immigration of Japanese laborers to the United States. This device worked fairly well, but their enemies on the West Coast continued to attack the Japanese as an economic threat and to insist that they were racially unassimilable. By 1920 they were prevented from either leasing or buying land in California.

The rising tide of feeling in the United States against all immigrants prompted Congress to appoint a commission, created under the 1907 Immigration Act, to investigate demands for immigration restriction. The resulting Dillingham Commission Report of 1907 included the long list of existing complaints against the "new immigration." The fallacies on which they were based have only been brought to light with the perspective of time and with more objective investigations of the subject. The charge that the immigrants were congregating in little clans in the cities was not false, but it overlooked the fact that some immigrants became farmers and that prejudice and discrimination in jobs and housing prevented many immigrants from moving out of ghettos as they would have done under more encouraging circumstances. The assertion that many were unskilled could also have been said of most of the earlier immigrant groups, especially the Irish. Moreover, the charge of unassimilability into American political life has not been borne out by the facts of American history. Beginning in the 1870s the Irish, Germans, and Scandinavians became active in American politics and challenged its dominance by those of Anglo-Saxon ancestry. Subsequently, the Italians, Polish, and Jews have taken their place in political life with equal effectiveness.

According to Oscar Handlin:

It is therefore no longer possible to speak of meaningful distinctions between settlers and immigrants or between old and new immigrants. Englishmen, Germans, Italians, and Poles spoke different languages, had different languages and were accustomed to different forms of behavior. But the kinds of Englishmen who came to the United States in the seventeenth and eighteenth centuries were very much like the kinds of Irish, Germans, and Scandinavians who came in the middle of the nineteenth, and these in turn were very much like the Italians, Jews, and Poles who came later.

BEGINNINGS OF RESTRICTIONS

Given these complaints, even though the United States was a nation built by immigrants for immigrants, demands continued for the restriction of immigration. The first restrictive legislation was passed in the 1880s. A campaign by Dennis Kearney and his laborer followers in the late 1870s resulted in passage of the Chinese Exclusion Act of 1882. This act cut off Chinese immigration completely and created a good deal of Chinese resentment. In spite of this, the provisions were made permanent in 1902. In the same year Congress also forbade the entrance of "undesirables"—"lunatics, convicts, idiots, and those who might readily become public charges." These categories were expanded with later legislation. In addition, the 1882 law placed a head tax of fifty cents on every person admitted to further discourage the influx of immigration. In 1891 the administration of immigration legislation, which had been under the states was placed entirely under federal control. These measures did not keep out a great number of aliens, and certainly did not fulfill the purposes of the extreme

exclusionists, who then focused on obtaining a literacy test that would, they hoped, exclude further immigration from eastern and southern Europe.

LITERACY TEST

In 1897, Congress passed a measure sponsored by Senator Henry Cabot Lodge of Massachusetts which required all immigrants to take a literacy test. President

Emigration From Poland

" *. . . Praised by Jesus Christus. . . . I inform you that I intend to emigrate to America where I have many friends, for the most part relatives, who write that I can come to them and they will find work for me. . . . I know only one handicraft, carpenter's. I practiced with a country carpenter, but at the present time it is very difficult to find material, and therefore difficult to earn.*

We have little land, and I have a sister and two brothers. I am 18 years old; so if I can go to America and get work, as I have the intention of doing, before the call to the army I could earn still more money. . . . I know how to read and I read many books and papers, Gios Ludu, Lud Bozy and others [popular religious papers]. I also know something about writing, as you can see from this letter. I have been to some monthly agricultural courses in Lublin, where I learned a little about the science of agriculture and model farming. . . . I hope if I live to try with all my strength to organize a model farm but now, because of lack of money and because my father has still a debt, it is difficult to make practical improvements in any way or to buy agricultural machines, which are very dear. "

—*Thomas and Zuanieki,* **The Polish Peasant in Europe and America**

66 *Thus it is proved, first, that immigration to this country is increasing, and, second, that it is making its greatest relative increase from races most alien to the body of the American people and from the lowest and most illiterate classes among those races. In other words, it is apparent that, while our immigration is increasing, it is showing at the same time a marked tendency to deteriorate in character. . . .*

In a word, the continued introduction into the labor market of four hundred thousand persons annually, half of whom have no occupation and most of whom represent the rudest form of labor, has a very great effect in reducing the rates of wages and disturbing the labor market. This, of course, is too obvious to need comment, and this tendency to constantly lower wages by the competition of an increasing and deteriorating immigration is a danger to the people of the United States the gravity of which can hardly be overestimated. Moreover, the shifting of the sources of the immigration is unfavorable, and is bringing to the country people whom it is very difficult to assimilate and who do not promise well for the standard of civilization in the United States—a matter as serious as the effect on the labor market.

The question, therefore, arises,—and there is no more important question before the American people,—What shall be done to protect our labor against this undue competition, and to guard our citizenship against an infusion which seems to threaten deterioration? We have the power, of course, to prohibit all immigration, or to limit the number of persons to be admitted to the country annually, or—which would have the same effect—to impose upon immigrants a heavy capitation tax. Such rough and stringent measures are certainly neither necessary nor desirable if we can overcome the difficulties and dangers of the situation by more moderate legislation. These methods, moreover, are indiscriminate; and what is to be desired, if possible, is restriction which shall at the same time discriminate. . . . 99

—*Henry Cabot Lodge*

McKinley, however, vetoed the measure which, he felt, challenged the concept of America as a land of opportunity and set up a test that was not a true measure of a person's character. But from this time on the pressures for restrictions intensified. By 1917, Congress was able to pass a law, over President Wilson's veto, which denied admittance to aliens over sixteen who were unable to read in any language. This law was the first major step toward large-scale restriction.

THE CONDITIONS OF LABOR

Early in the nineteenth century, most of the country's workers were in agriculture. By the end of the nineteenth century, only a third of the labor force remained on the farms. The nation's economy became increasingly industrial, and as labor became industrialized, individual workers lost much of their self-sufficiency.

Once laborers resigned themselves to the fact that their place in the factory was permanent, they began to take steps to improve their lot as industrial workers. Men who had believed that their stay in the factory was temporary until they could accumulate enough money to become self-employed farmers or entrepreneurs, now turned their efforts to securing better working conditions. They struggled to adjust to the factory system and to discover how eventually to win a larger share of its financial rewards. As corporations grew larger and more mechanized, however, labor's desire for increased wages, shorter hours, and more humane working conditions became more difficult to attain. In the smaller businesses, the relationship between employer and employee tended to be a more personal one, and each was generally aware of the other's needs. With the growth of such giant corporations as Standard Oil and the New York Central Railroad, this kind of relationship virtually disappeared. The laborer's individual negotiating position was all but destroyed. Laborers were forced to look to each other for assistance. Though reluctant at first, they soon began to form unions to strengthen their position through solidarity. Ultimately they challenged powerful employers not only with strikes and boycotts but with pressure upon legislators for improved labor laws. The road was a stormy one, but by the early twentieth century labor's position, though still far from ideal, was considerably improved. As a Philadelphia newspaper put it in 1887: "Capital cannot consistently advocate combination among the employers, and at the same time denounce it among the employed."

DISCONTENT AMONG WORKERS

The widespread attitude of management toward labor in the "Age of Big Business" was typified by a remark made by a textile manufacturer of the time: "I regard my

Child labor in a Carolina cotton mill.

work people just as I regard my machinery!" A managerial view of labor as a commodity to be bought at the cheapest possible price, and maintained at minimal expense, was probably the strongest spur toward unified action by workers. This outlook on the part of corporations made them indifferent to the needs of labor. This attitude also helped prevent workers from rising within the ranks to become executives themselves. The Illinois Bureau of Labor Statistics reported in 1886: "The tendency in all industries is toward centralization and aggregation, and this involves a separation of the people into classes, and the permanently subordinate status of large numbers of them." Seeing the workingman's needs neglected by profit-minded employers, and deprived of advancement as a goal, labor concentrated on its immediate ills—wages too low to meet the cost of living, the long work day, and unsafe working conditions.

At first, the workingman's day lasted throughout the hours of daylight. In 1860, the average day's work was almost 12 hours. By 1880, only 25 percent of the country's labor force worked more than 10 hours, and even then some labor leaders were discussing the possibility of an 8-hour day. In the 1890s, the average work week for industrial workers was approximately 58 hours. By 1910, this had dropped to less than 55 hours, a national average offset by the fact that workers in many industries still had unusually long hours. Iron and steel workers, for example, had an average work week of over 70 hours.

The workers' discontent over wages grew out of the difference between their earnings and the cost of living. Wages continued to rise, but not at the same rate as the rising

In support of labor, this cartoon shows the plight of the "little guy" in a world of big business. Journalistic muckraking like this forced America to take a look at itself.

THE ROAD TO DIVIDENDS.

cost of living. Real wages had risen almost 50 percent between 1860 and 1890. In 1890, the average wage rate for industrial workers was 21 cents an hour, and by 1910, most industrial workers received 28 cents an hour. Yet, at the same time, the growth of immigration held back the growth of wages for industrial employees somewhat. Women received less than half as much as men, and workers in city sweatshops were pitifully underpaid. However, although wages in general were rising, prices too were increasing. The high standard of living supposedly enjoyed by the industrial worker in the city did not, in fact, exist. A Chicago laborer put it succinctly: "Land of opportunity you say. You know damn well my children will be where I am—that is, if I can keep them out of the gutter." Further, with the cost of living running ahead of wages, the laborer had little opportunity to save any money. During times of economic depression when he was unemployed, his personal hardships were excruciating. Pensions for retired workers did exist, but they were a rarity. Some companies were known, in fact, to discharge employees a few weeks before they became eligible for retirement on a pension.

Though safety precautions and safety laws were on the books, they were rarely enforced. The new machinery in an age of vast mechanization constantly threatened the laborer's safety. Accident compensation existed, but, as with the pensions, shrewd lawyers usually found ways for their powerful corporate clients to keep from paying this form of worker insurance. Power was on the side of the wealthy, and the injured laborer rarely found himself with legal recourse.

THE NEED FOR LABOR UNIONS

Unquestionably, labor had grievances, and these were not likely to be redressed by corporate management interested only in profits. To achieve results, labor had no alternative but to take matters into its own hands, but even this was not easily achieved. Unions were too often hindered by a lack of unity within their own ranks. The leaders and the rank and file members quarreled, not only about objectives, but about the methods for achieving them. As before the Civil War, some laborers looked to outside political reform for help. Some wanted nothing more than higher wages and shorter hours, and some regarded the unions as another obstacle to the fulfillment of their dreams of self-employment and self-sufficiency. The concept of a laissez-faire economy was still alive in the mind of many a laborer. However he might be held down at the moment, he could continue to dream that he, or at least, his son, would some day become a successful capitalist.

Yet as many workers became aware of class distinctions, they became convinced that solidarity provided the only effective way to deal with the big corporations, and they began to join unions. The public's reaction to unionization, based on ignorance and fear, was antagonistic. The public, in effect, approved of corporations, but it did not apparently approve of a similar incorporation of employees. Unions traditionally had been thought of as a conspiracy in restraint of trade. Moreover, the nation's populace had always favored a laissez-faire economy and unionizing attempts appeared as a formidable interference with individual initiative, capitalism, and the natural processes of the country's economic growth. Farmers and agricultural workers in particular looked upon the unions as national parasites only slightly less evil than capitalistic monopoly. When unions began to employ the weapon of the strike, the public in general became extremely fearful of disorder and backed the business community. There was widespread fear that radicals controlled the labor movement, and that they were attempting to undermine the economic and political stability of the entire country. The public also tended to believe that joblessness was a personal failing of the shiftless, that if a man could not find a job it was only because he did not really want to work, and that sloth was an unalterable characteristic of certain nationalities. Because feeling against unions ran high, whenever courts and employers placed obstacles in the way of the unions, even harsh and discriminatory ones, they generally had strong public support. In addition, the sympathies of state and federal governments were pro-corporation, another hindrance to union activity.

ATTEMPTS TO ESTABLISH UNIONS

After 1865, the growth of national craft unions accelerated, affecting such artisans as iron molders, printers, and cigar makers. By the early 1870s, about 300,000 workers belonged to craft unions, and others, such as railroad workers, had begun to unionize. Organization of the National Labor Union in 1866 was the first attempt to form a federation of craft unions, or a truly national union of workers in industry.

Throughout its short existence, the National Labor Union strove for two major objectives: the 8-hour day and measures to combat the evils of inflation. Its leader, Ira Seward, was a Boston machinist. Unfortunately, Seward, like the other leaders of the NLU, had lost sight of the practical needs of its membership. They tended to oppose anything that increased the worker's awareness of himself as a member of the working class. In 1868, William Sylvis became president of the NLU, and under his leadership the organization tried a system of work cooperatives whose profits would be divided among the laborers who operated them. Union workers attempted to set up cooperative stores, foundries and mines, but they ran into formidable obstacles. They were unable to obtain sufficient

" *... The schemes for improving the condition of the working classes interfere in the competition of workmen with each other. The beneficiaries are selected by favoritism, and are apt to be those who have recommended themselves to the friends of humanity by language or conduct which does not betoken independence and energy. Those who suffer a corresponding depression by the interference are the independent and self-reliant, who once more are forgotten or passed over; and the friends of humanity once more appear, in their zeal to help somebody, to be trampling on those who are trying to help themselves.*

Trades-unions adopt various devices for raising wages, and those who give their time to philanthropy are interested in these devices, and wish them success. They fix their minds entirely on the workmen for the time being in the trade, and do not take note of any other workmen as interested in the matter. It is supposed that the fight is between the workmen and their employers, and it is believed that one can give sympathy in that contest to the workmen without feeling responsibility for anything farther. It is soon seen, however, that the employer adds the trades-union and strike risk to the other risks of his business, and settles down to it philosophically. ... he has passed the loss along on the public. It then appears that the public wealth has been diminished, and that the danger of a trade war, like the danger of a revolution, is a constant reduction of the well-being of all. ...

A trades-union raises wages ... by restricting the number of apprentices who may be taken into the trade. Those who are in have, therefore, made a monopoly, and constituted themselves a privileged class on a basis exactly analogous to that of the old privileged aristocracies. But

whatever is gained by this arrangement for those who are in is won at a greater loss to those who are kept out. Hence it is not upon the masters nor upon the public that trades-unions exert the pressure by which they raise wages; it is upon other persons of the labor class who want to get into the trades, but, not being able to do so, are pushed down into the unskilled labor class. . . .

99

—*William G. Sumner*

The Need for Labor Unions

66 *. . . If you wish to improve the condition of the people, you must improve their habits and customs. The reduction of the hours of labor reaches the very root of society. It gives the workingmen better conditions and better opportunities, and makes of him what has been too long neglected—a consumer instead of a mere producer. . . .*

. . . The trades unions are not what too many men have been led to believe they are, importations from Europe. . . . Modern industry evolves these organizations out of the existing conditions where there are two classes in society, one incessantly striving to obtain the labor of the other class for as little as possible . . . ; and the members of the other class being, as individuals, utterly helpless in a contest with their employers, naturally resort to combinations to improve their condition, and, in fact, they are forced by the conditions which surround them to organize for self-protection. Hence trade unions. . . .

. . . I believe that the existence of the trades-union movement, more especially where the unionists are better organized, has evoked a spirit and a demand for reform, but has held in check the more radical elements in society. . . .

99

—*Samuel Gompers*

capital and credit, and the federal government refused to aid them. Lacking a solid economic footing, the cooperatives were doomed to failure. In a last-ditch effort, the NLU became involved in politics in 1872 as the National Labor Reform Party. When its political efforts on behalf of civil service reform and money inflation proved unsuccessful, the NLU collapsed and vanished from the public scene.

EFFECT OF DEPRESSION, 1873–1878

The depression of the 1870s, brought on by overexpansion and wild speculation, created widespread unemployment for immigrants without skills. For them, idleness lasted longer than for other workers. Even for those workers who managed to find jobs, the competition for work forced down the rate of pay. The workers hit first and hardest were those in the smaller mill and mining towns. Where a town had only one large industry, its closing had an immediate and catastrophic effect. An entire community would be thrown out of work, without job alternatives. In the cities, the diversity of occupations helped delay widespread unemployment. However, before long the laborer in the city as well knew that a harsh depression was upon him.

Signs of enforced idleness could be seen everywhere. Men lingered in groups on the streets during the day. Children came to the police stations for the daily dole of a pail of soup. Entire families scrounged for work in order to survive. Young boys drifted into such street occupations as bootblacking or hawking newspapers. Young girls went into sweatshops where they did men's work for children's wages. Mothers sought domestic service. This period put great strain on the American worker and his family. It also testified to his powers of endurance.

691

THE STRIKES OF 1877

The depression caused railroad workers to take action against abuses of management in a series of bitter strikes. The first of the great railroad strikes was instigated against the Baltimore and Ohio at Martinsburg, West Virginia. The workers there had suffered a 10 percent wage cut, and they refused to permit the movement of trains until that cut was restored. The strikes spread to other areas, including Pittsburgh, where federal troops were ordered in to clear the tracks. The workers refused to move out of their way and violence, rioting, burning, and looting followed. Twenty-six people died and there was five million dollars' worth of damage in the area. The railroad strike continued to spread, pushing into the West, until about two-thirds of the country's railroad mileage was shut down. Workers put yards to the torch, and

frightened businessmen organized militia companies to patrol the streets of the cities where the working people lived. The public became increasingly alarmed. Associating the strikes with political revolution, many people denounced the strikers as communists and radicals. With the hearty approval of their congregations, ministers railed against the strikers from the pulpits.

A certain amount of violence also took place within the ranks of labor, most of it directed against the Chinese. In 1877, Dennis Kearney was elected president of the Workingmen's Party with a platform that advocated not only unity and the destruction of monopolies, but active opposition to the presence of the Chinese in the American working force. Workers in

Violence erupted in 1877 when federal troops fired upon railroad workers during the strike against the B.&O. Railroad in Martinsburg, West Virginia.

California were the first to agitate militantly against Orientals, charging them with taking jobs from native Americans by their willingness to work for extremely low wages. Violent demonstrations erupted in San Francisco against the Chinese, and within several days the angry workers destroyed over 100,000 dollars' worth of property.

The violence of the 1877 strikes was unprecedented in American history. Pressured by the citizenry as well as business leaders, governors of the affected states appealed to the federal government for assistance. Finally, President Hayes responded by dispatching federal troops to the trouble areas to restore order. Faced with federal power, the strikes collapsed.

NOBLE ORDER OF THE KNIGHTS OF LABOR

With the return of prosperity in the 1880s, workers began to join unions again. The Knights of Labor, which flourished in that decade, was of more significance to the progress of American labor than any previous union. At its high point, the organization claimed membership of well over one half million. Yet, its opposition to strikes and strong emphasis on economic betterment of laborers through the establishment of workers' cooperatives, among other factors, eventually resulted in its extinction.

FORMATION

A secret organization designed to draw together all workers into one large union, the Knights of Labor was formed in Philadelphia in 1869 by a group of local garment workers led by Uriah S. Stephens. Its earliest members were skilled trade unionists, but the Knights were open to the semiskilled and unskilled as well; in effect, to anyone who worked for wages "without regard to sex, color, race, or position."

The Knights were not interested in a class struggle, and they strongly opposed any attempts to jeopardize the nation's system of free enterprise. Their cover of secrecy was merely intended to prevent management from learning of the union's plans.

Stephens stressed the necessity for organizing labor as the only effective way to protect labor's welfare. The growth of his union was slow, hampered particularly by the severe times of the 1873 depression and by the opposition of employers who repeatedly used blacklisting, lockouts, and the courts against union members. In an uphill struggle, the Knights of Labor gathered only 9,287 members by 1878.

The purposes of the Knights of Labor were set forth in its "first principles." The organization dedicated itself to working to create a favorable climate of public opinion in which a united labor movement could flourish without suspicion and reprisals. The new union also called for legislative programs for workingmen, and strongly supported the concepts of cooperatives and mutual benefit societies to improve the welfare of the wage earner. When Terence V. Powderly replaced Uriah Stephens as the head of the Knights of Labor, he reaffirmed the organization's faith in the potential of workers' cooperatives. "There is no reason why labor cannot, through cooperation, own and operate mines, factories, and railroads," said Powderly. At the First National Assembly of the Knights of Labor in 1878, the union restated its belief in cooperatives and public education and expanded its platform to include the abolition of the contract labor system, the enforcement of the 8-hour day, the establishment of a federal bureau of labor statistics, and the federal dispensation of public lands to those who wished to settle on farms.

When Powderly stepped into Stephens' place as "Grand Master Workman" in 1879, the Knights of Labor entered a new and more aggressive phase of their history, characterized by the use of more forceful methods to achieve their ends. Temporarily suspending their opposition to the weapon of the strike, the Knights used both the strike and the boycott against the railroads. In 1884, they staged successful strikes against the Union Pacific and Wabash Lines. Their strikes against the Missouri Pacific Railroad in 1885 secured the restoration of wage cuts and brought the union a flood of new members, increasing its ranks sixfold within one year.

In March of 1886, however, a strike by the Knights of Labor against Jay Gould's Southwestern railroads proved dramatically that management still wielded the greater power. Gould refused to negotiate with the workers, and brought in strikebreakers to put down the "insurrection" by force. As food shortages spread across the country, the public turned against the strikers. It was only a matter of time before the employees had to give up their fight and return to work. It was a major setback for the union and made the use of the strike appear costly, dangerous, and futile.

The organization's aggressive activities did not divert Powderly and other leaders from their interest in establishing workingmen's cooperatives. Between 1884 and 1887, workers managed to start many cooperative enterprises, including mines and foundries. But these experiments were short-lived. The major problems were lack of capital and lack of managerial experience. The businesses were forced to remain small, and as such were easily squeezed out by larger and more experienced private operations. After their extinction there were no further commitments by American labor to make cooperatives a major union objective.

Between 1885 and 1890, the membership of the Knights of Labor dropped to less than one hundred thousand. The failure of the cooperatives and the organization's early opposition to strikes were major factors leading to its downfall, but there were also other reasons. From the beginning the union had suffered from a lack of solidarity.

Skilled workers throughout the nation did not lend support to the Knights, and with the violence of the Haymarket riot in Chicago in May, 1886, public antipathy to all labor movements flared to a new, angry high.

THE HAYMARKET RIOT

In May, 1886, several hundred thousand laborers were on strike in various parts of the country in support of an 8-hour day. One of the primary centers of the 8-hour movement was Chicago where eighty thousand workers rallied to the cause. A small group of anarchists sought to exploit the situation to incite radical feelings. When a striker was accidentally killed in a scuffle at the McCormick Harvesting Machine Company, the anarchists lost no time in calling a protest meeting on May 4 at Haymarket Square. The police stepped in to break up the meeting, and some unknown person hurled a bomb into their ranks. Seven policemen were killed and many others injured in the ensuing melee. Public response to the outrage bordered on hysteria. Although a connection between the Knights of Labor and the bombing was never legally established, the union and the movement for an 8-hour day were stamped with the stigma of violence and subversion.

Before passing from the scene, the Knights, nevertheless, did succeed in effecting some measure of progress for labor. Largely through their efforts, Congress passed legislation outlawing contract labor in 1885, and a federal Bureau of Labor Statistics was set up in 1884.

AMERICAN FEDERATION OF LABOR

As the Knights of Labor declined, a new kind of national movement emerged, distinguished from its predecessor largely by its stress on the self-governing craft union as the basic structural unit within a national labor organization. In the late 1870s and 1880s, trade unions experienced a revival. Their leaders, notably Samuel Gompers and Adolph Strasser, leaders in the Cigarmakers Union, were strongly opposed to the political orientation of the National Labor Union and to the indiscriminate admission of workers to the Knights of Labor. Gompers and Strasser advanced the belief that labor's hopes for the future depended upon the consolidation of strong, independent trade unions. Gompers and Strasser rejected cooperatives or any other reforms of a socialistic nature designed to replace the wage system. To them, unionization was not a steppingstone to self-employment but a means of enlarging the worker's bargaining power within the capitalistic framework. By strengthening the trade unions, they believed, labor would be able to bargain more effectively.

In December, 1886, delegates who represented 300,000 trade union members convened in Columbus, Ohio, to form the American Federation of Labor. Gompers was elected its first president, and until his death in 1924 he remained the indomitable driving force behind the organization. Under his leadership, the American Federation of Labor fathered the modern labor movement. The AF of L was to be the most important representative of the workers of the United States for the next fifty years.

"We have," said Adolph Strasser, "no ultimate ends. We are going from day to day. We are fighting for immediate objectives." Emphasizing the workers' basic need for higher wages, shorter hours, and improved working conditions, the American Federation of Labor established the strike as labor's most potent weapon. If collective bargaining with employers failed, the union felt it could legitimately resort to strikes and boycotts to exert economic pressure on management. The new organization did not hesitate to use strikes, not only to win concessions from employers, but to attract new union recruits as well. Although it rejected alliances with political parties, the Federation did not reject the weapon of pressure on politicians. Labor legislation was important, and through its large membership, the AF of L clearly sought to make its voice heard at the polls by influencing workers to reward labor's "friends" and punish its enemies through the ballot.

Although it desired more members, the AF of L controlled entry into its ranks—and, consequently, the national supply of skilled workers—by a guild style apprenticeship system and by requiring high dues which discouraged some potential members. Although the dues restricted membership, they provided the Federation with the backlog of funds needed to support union strikes and other services for AF of L members.

SAMUEL GOMPERS

The founder and policy maker of the American Federation of Labor was its first president, a short, stocky cigarmaker of Jewish ancestry. Born in London, he was raised in New York among German and Hungarian workers. Among them he received an education that became the basis for his later thinking and accomplishments. His fellow workers hired men to read to them, while they worked, the philosophical and economic books and articles of the day. Eventually, Gompers, a brilliant administrator, organized the International Cigar Makers Union, shaping it into a model of efficiency and mutual aid for the large union to come. A friendly, earthy man and a hard worker, Samuel Gompers' approach to the problems of labor and their solutions was deceptively simple. "I have my own philosophy," he said, "and my own dreams, but first and foremost I want to increase the workingman's welfare year by year. . . ." When asked what the objective of the AF of L was, he answered succinctly: "More!" His emphasis on immediate needs and their achievement, through bargaining powers enhanced by strong trade unions, strikes, and a discriminate use of the ballot, produced continuous growth for the AF of L. Unions with approximately 150,000 members formed the basis of the Federation in 1886. By 1892, membership reached 250,000, and shortly after the turn of the century it passed the million mark. Union efforts were also instrumental in the creation of bureaus of labor statistics in several states and in the establishment of the Department of Commerce and Labor by Congress in 1903.

THE HOMESTEAD STRIKE

This steady growth of organized labor was not without opposition. The 1890s witnessed several great clashes between labor and management that heightened public feeling against labor. Increased mechanization of the steel industry brought on the great Homestead Strike of 1892. The steel men contended that the workers were preventing progress by resisting technological changes, while the workers insisted that if these advances increased profits, it was only fair that labor should share the gains. Homestead, Andrew Carnegie's steel plant near Pittsburgh, Pennsylvania, was managed by Henry Clay Frick, a tough and unyielding enemy of unions who was determined to crush them regardless of the cost. Frick brought in strikebreakers and over three hundred private Pinkerton guards to protect them when the employees of Homestead struck. After five months, the strikers attacked the guards, killed several

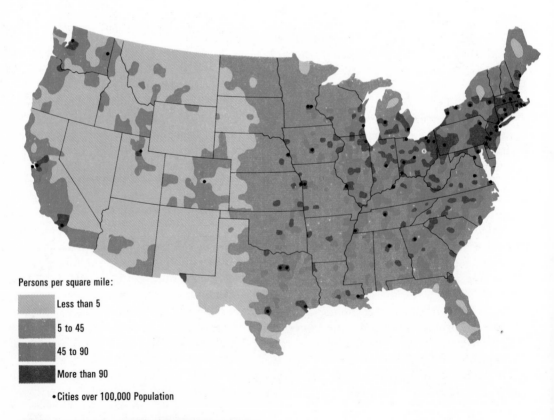

Persons per square mile:

Less than 5

5 to 45

45 to 90

More than 90

•Cities over 100,000 Population

POPULATION DISTRIBUTION • 1920

of them, and forced the rest to surrender and disperse. Simultaneously, an anarchist, Andrew Berkman, broke into Frick's private office and attempted to assassinate him. Frick was wounded only slightly, but as in the Haymarket riot, the bitterness of the strike—and especially the anarchist's attack—turned public sympathy away from the strikers. The state militia restored order and the strike was broken on company terms.

THE PULLMAN STRIKE

Two years later in the Pullman strike of 1894, labor lost another important encounter. Because of the depression the Pullman company cut wages. When the company refused to negotiate with its employees, the local unions voted to strike. The company responded by locking out the union members. The American Railway Union, under Eugene V. Debs, urged arbitration between the management and its employees. Pullman ignored the suggestion and the union voted to stop handling Pull-

man cars. Pullman workers were fired and entire train crews quit in sympathy. Within a month, train tie-ups affected most Midwestern lines. The General Managers' Association, which represented the railroads, called in strikebreakers and was able to have three thousand of them deputized as federal marshals. After two days of violent struggle, the railroad officials succeeded in obtaining a federal district court injunction against the strikers, on the basis that they were interfering with delivery of the mails and interstate commerce. President Cleveland sent in federal troops, a move which completely crushed the strike. Debs was indicted and sentenced to six months in jail.

One of the most significant developments of the Pullman Strike was the court's action in issuing an injunction against the union, a move that in itself labeled the strike as illegal. The courts based their decision on the Sherman Antitrust Act, declaring that the American Railway Union was "a combination in restraint of trade," and therefore engaged in illegal actions.

THE UNITED STATES BECOMES AN URBAN NATION

The giant technological strides made by the nation between the Civil War and World War I greatly facilitated settlement of the remaining land frontiers and hastened the rise of America to a position of leadership among the world's industrial powers. The growth of industry was aided by increased immigration and challenged

by unionization of the labor force. All these developments speeded the nation's change from a rural to an urban society by the beginning of the twentieth century.

Settlement in urban areas by the vast majority of the new wave of immigrants furthered the growth of the cities. Change also took place through the movement of earlier settlers in a pattern described by one historian as a shift "from the country-side to the nearest hamlet, from the hamlet to the town, and from the town to the city."

INCREASE IN URBAN POPULATION

In 1790, when the first census was taken, a little more than 3 percent of the population of the United States lived in towns of eight thousand or more. In 1800, only six cities had more than eight thousand inhabitants. After 1820, the trend was toward urbanization as cities began to grow faster than the nation as a whole, even though in 1860 the country was still predominantly rural with 80 percent of its population living on farms or in small villages and engaged in agricultural work. By 1890, however, there were 448 cities with a population above eight thousand, and twenty-six of these cities had more than one hundred thousand inhabitants. New York had more than one million and continued to grow at an unprecedented rate. Other cities that doubled, tripled, and quadrupled their population between 1880 and 1910 were Buffalo, Detroit, Milwaukee, Chicago, St. Paul, Minneapolis, and Denver.

Urbanization and, consequently, depopulation of the countryside did not take place at a uniform rate throughout the United States. The move to the cities was strongest in the Middle West and the North Atlantic states. The three West Coast states of Oregon, Washington, and California also experienced rapid urbanization. The South lagged behind the rest of the country with only 20 percent of its population in cities by 1910.

CAUSES OF INCREASED URBANIZATION

The movement to the cities was accelerated by the creation of jobs by new ma-chines, higher wages, and the growing monotony and loneliness of farm life. The cities were an irresistible attraction, their excitement represented by networks of telephone lines and bright lights, especially after electricity replaced gaslight. The city offered, too, improvements in central heating and indoor plumbing, and public water and transportation systems. New industries sprang up in the cities. As early as 1890 the number of industrial workers almost equaled the total number of farm owners, farm tenants, and farm laborers.

Many observers point to the influx of immigration as another primary cause of the growth of cities. Particularly among aliens in the new wave of immigration who had an immediate need for income, settlement in the cities became almost unavoidable. Few immigrants became wealthy, but their chances for earning adequate wages upon arrival was considerably greater in cities than in farm areas. By 1890, 25 percent of the population of Philadelphia and one-third of that of Chicago and Boston were foreign-born. In New York City alone, four out of five residents were either of foreign birth or of parents born outside of the United States.

Another strong factor in urbanization was the movement of native-born Americans from farm to factory. In the last two decades of the nineteenth-century agriculture was in a state of severe depression. Because crops were poor and debts were high, farmers found it increasingly difficult to meet mortgage payments. The farm had few weapons to fight the lure of the city life. Perhaps the most drastic abandonment of farms took place in New England. One Vermonter commented of his newly deserted village: "The church was abandoned, the academy dismantled, the villager lived on one side of the broad street, and he who owned the farm on the south lived on the other, and they were the only inhabitants."

ATTRACTION OF THE CITY

Hundreds of thousands of country and small-town boys followed the roads and highways to the cities. Among the basic attractions held by cities were those of culture, education, and entertainment. The city was a reservoir of new ideas and held promise not only of economic stability, but of great financial success. The young men from the villages had heard of the Rocke-fellers, the Vanderbilts, and the Carnegies. Stories of sudden rise to fame and fortune were part of the popular literature of the time and many arrived with a dream to fulfill.

Then, too, the city had conveniences that made the rural areas appear backward by comparison. Candles and kerosene lamps might have sufficed for rural living, but more efficient illumination was needed for the congested city. Gaslights served the cities well into the 1880s. However, in 1879, the arc lamp was introduced in Cleveland by Charles Brush, and a year later, Thomas A. Edison patented his incandescent light for indoor use. Companies emerged to build power stations. By 1884, for example, the entire city of Chicago was served by electric lighting supplied by almost a dozen power companies. Improved lighting not only made cities safer at night but permitted factories and schools to stay open longer and theaters to operate with much less danger of fire.

Alexander Graham Bell's invention of the telephone in 1876 was immediately in-corporated into city life. The first commer-cial switchboard was set up in New Haven, Connecticut, in 1878 and by the end of that decade, eighty-five cities throughout the United States had telephone exchanges. The first intercity connection was made between Boston and New York, and before the end of the century, the entire country was laced with connecting lines.

With thousands of people moving to and from work at about the same time, cities were pressed to seek better modes of trans-portation than the horse and buggy and the horse-drawn car. Before the Civil War, there had been some experimentation with street railway systems operated by corpora-tions. These horsecar lines appeared in most metropolitan centers, but they were too slow. They were followed by faster, steam-driven cars that were too dirty and noisy. A solution appeared when Frank Sprague invented the electric trolley car, and it was introduced in Richmond, Vir-ginia, in 1887. Its use spread rapidly to other cities and in time led to other means of transit such as overhead railways and subways.

URBAN PROBLEMS

Many new city dwellers soon discovered, however, that there were also disadvantages to metropolitan life. There was, in particu-lar, a general lack of adequate public serv-ices—specifically running water and proper sanitation. As late as the 1870s, hogs ran loose in many city streets. Sewage was dumped either in a large ditch within the city limits or in the closest river. A single outlet often supplied several families with their water supply. Because these conditions led to disease, particularly in the slums, cities ultimately were forced to take correc-tive measures. Central water systems were constructed, owned and operated by the cities themselves; garbage was burned and filter treatment plants were introduced. Sewage remained a problem, however, pol-luting lakes and rivers. Out of these prob-lems of the urban environment grew the need for boards of health to oversee the regular collection and disposal of garbage, the building of reservoirs, and the imple-mentation of water purification programs.

Most cities grew very quickly and hap-hazardly, without design or even rudimen-

699

Two glimpses of urban family life during the 1890s and the 1900s. In one photograph, a family spends the evening enjoying violin and piano duets while the smaller children play with their many toys. The adjacent illustration shows a tenement flat where only a few basic necessities of life are found.

tary planning. Housing was usually inadequate, except for people with means. The poor were compelled to crowd together, forming the city slum that grew as swiftly as the cities that contained them. Residents, largely alien newcomers, clustered in cramped tenements. Built in large numbers after the 1880s and designed to yield maximum financial return to landlords, tenements were generally four to six stories high. Each floor held several family units and each unit contained two to four poorly ventilated, dingy rooms. In his book, *How the Other Half Lives,* Jacob Riis, a New York reporter, exposed the grim facts of tenement life.

. . . the hall is dark and you might stumble over the children pitching pennies back

The hero of Franz Kafka's **Amerika,** *arriving in the United States full of optimism and expectation, beheld the Statue of Liberty in "a sudden burst of sunshine." The upraised arm, oddly enough, held not a torch but a sword, "as if newly stretched aloft," and "around the figure blew the free winds of heaven." Kafka, who had never been to America, created a land out of his imagination, surrealistic in detail, yet as full of promise to his hero as to any immigrant who landed on American shores.*

A Land of Immigrants

COMING TO AMERICA.

RETURNING FOR A VISIT.

*Leaving Ireland for America as a pauper,
an Irishman could return to his homeland as a wealthy man.*

Typically, the turn-of-the-century immigrant made the Atlantic crossing in the crowded, unventilated, and infested steerage section of the ship. As an alien worker in the city, he was exploited by employers and rebuffed at every turn. "If I had known it would be so bitter for me here, I wouldn't have come. I didn't come here for a fortune, but where is bread?" an immigrant wrote the editor of the Jewish Daily Forward *in 1908.*

This is the most familiar aspect of immigration to the United States, but there were many variations. From the days of the first landing in Virginia in 1607, Europeans with dreams of freedom and prosperity came to America to escape intolerable conditions elsewhere. They fled religious discrimination and political oppression but most often they came to escape poverty. What they found was not much of an improvement. Sometimes, however, America gave them a chance to improve their lot—but not without a struggle.

The English and the Dutch settled America first, followed by German Mennonites in 1663. French Huguenots, persecuted in Catholic France for their Protestant faith, came as refugees in 1697. At that time, the slave trade, which began in 1619, expanded, bringing shiploads of chained black men and women as involuntary migrants from Africa. A Scotch migration included indentured servants, artisans, and merchants.

The English sent criminals and debtors released from jails in 1717, and soon after, land abuses in the British Isles sent Scotch and Irish from the mother country. In the next decades, many Europeans, chiefly Scotch-Irish, voyaged to the colonies to get away from political upheaval, economic depression, and rural blight. Political refugees from revolution-torn France arrived at the end of the century.

Immigration virtually died out in the aftermath of the American Revolution and during the War of 1812,

Broadside of the Des Moines Navigation Company describes America to Germans.

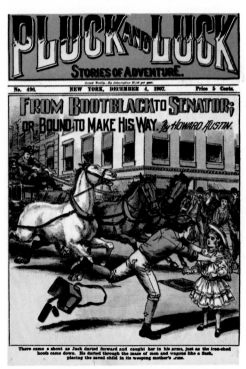

The rags to riches myth enticed many immigrants to America.

but the Treaty of Ghent started a dramatic revival.
Five million newcomers settled in America from 1815
to 1860. First were the Irish, British, Germans, and
Norwegians, unable to earn a living as farmers in their
native lands. Refugees from the revolution in Poland
came in 1830. Scandinavian immigration reached a peak
in 1842, helping to populate the midwest. Tens of
thousands of poor immigrants arrived following the
Irish potato famine of 1846 and 1847 and German and
Dutch crop failures. By 1860, the Irish alone accounted
for over one million immigrants. Crowding into the
cities, they were to provide the United States with
laborers, poets, and politicians. The Irish also helped to
lay the railroad lines and dig the mines, as did the Slavs
and Chinese.

However, the financial panic of 1837 set off anti-alien
feeling and American workers showed their hostility to
foreigners willing to work for low wages. Nativist pressures led, in 1882, to passage of the Chinese Exclusion
Act and a law barring entry of convicts and the mentally
unfit. From 1894 to 1896 massacres of Christians by
Moslems drove Armenians to America for safety. Systematic pogroms in Russia had already brought thou-

An immigrant-crowded steamship on its way to America.

Many immigrants slept on deck and had little to eat as they crossed the Atlantic.

sands of Jews to America. In flight from anti-Semitism and poverty, more than one and a half million more European Jews arrived from 1899 to 1914, the largest ethnic group to come in this period, outside of the Italians. "Ghetto life was grueling," says Harry Golden, recalling New York's old Lower East Side, but, "if nothing else, we had an atmosphere of vitality and excitement."

While immigrants manned assembly lines and built cities, feelings against foreigners grew, inflamed by cultural differences and the Immigration Restriction League. In the West, violence broke out against Orientals. The quota immigration system, introduced in 1921, sharply limited entry from Southern and Eastern Europe. The National Origins Act of 1924 established discriminatory national racial quotas.

America gave asylum to refugees from Nazism in the thirties, but gave less consideration during World War II to Japanese-Americans, who were ruthlessly herded into detention camps. After the war, Congress passed legislation to accept dislocated Europeans and later, to admit Hungarian refugees. While America gave with one hand, it took away with the other: The McCarran-Walter Nationality Act of 1952 tightened immigration laws and the quota system.

Tagging immigrants in railroad waiting room, Ellis Island, 1926.

Between 1840 and 1968, 7,144,000 immigrants came to the United States. Since 1945, poverty has sent a steady stream of Puerto Ricans to the mainland, and clashes in political ideology are today the wellspring of emigrés from Cuba, Hong Kong, Greece, Spain, and the Iron Curtain countries. They are drawn to the ethnic ghettos, where the vestiges of the old migrations resist the melting pot—the Latin enclaves, the China-towns, the Slavic neighborhoods of the cities.

Immigrants who failed their physical or psychological examinations had to return to Europe. The men in this photo are being given intelligence tests.

Immigrants were submitted to a medical examination upon arriving at Ellis Island.

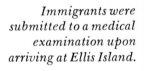

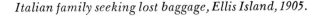

Italian family seeking lost baggage, Ellis Island, 1905.

New York's lower East Side housed many newly arriving immigrants.

The migration of blacks to Northern cities from the South increased just after World War I.

The Janssonists were farmers who immigrated to America from Sweden.

Scandinavian immigrants worked as lumbermen in the Pacific Northwest, 1906.

Welsh and Poles came to America in the nineteenth century to work in the coal mines of Pennsylvania.

Albert Einstein takes the Oath of Allegiance to the United States in Trenton, New Jersey.

The Amish or "the plain people" still follow the traditional customs of their forefathers.

The variety
of nationalities in America
is reflected in the Honor Roll
of this
World War I poster.

there. Not that it would hurt them; kicks and cuffs are their daily diet. . . . All the fresh air that ever enters these stairs comes from the hall door that is forever slamming, and from the windows of dark bedrooms. . . . The sinks are in the hallway, that all tenants may have access—and all be poisoned alike by their summer stenches. . . . The gap between dingy brick walls is the yard. That strip of smoke-colored sky up there is the heaven of these people.

Riis published his chilling book with photographs in 1890, drawing public attention to the economic, social, and political problems created by slum conditions.

By the end of the nineteenth century, there were 43,000 tenements in New York City alone. They housed a million and a half people, and were appropriately called such names as "Bandit's Roost," "Misery Row," and "Murderer's Alley."

The cities were also plagued by corrupt politicians, who leaned strongly on the slums for support. The political machine dominated city politics, and the boss dominated the machine. Said Andrew D. White, president of Cornell University in the latter part of the nineteenth century: "The city governments of the United States are the worst in Christendom—the most expensive, the most inefficient, and the most corrupt." As urbanization spread, good government seemed to decline. Scandalous political conditions prevailed, marked by dishonest elections, political graft, and payoffs to dishonest policemen. Vested business interests, faulty city charters, and the immigrant vote were vital factors behind the power of the machine and the bosses. Business interests that wanted public-utility franchises gave financial support to political machines. The political bosses also sought out newly arrived immigrants, strangers in need of help who were unfamiliar for the most part with the operation of representative government. They became easy prey for the ward boss who could get them a job, coal, or groceries

in exchange for a vote. As already noted, one of the most infamous examples of corrupt machine politics was the Tweed ring in New York City. Boss Tweed, an unscrupulous fireman who rose to the presidency of the Board of Supervisors of New York City, was worth twelve million dollars by 1870, the fruits of graft. His counterparts in other cities included men like Christopher Magee of Pittsburgh, "King" James McManes of Philadelphia, and "Czar" Martin Lomasney of Boston.

CONSPICUOUS CONSUMPTION

Although the United States was basically a middle-class country, by the next to the last decade of the nineteenth century the differences in the social classes were strikingly apparent in the large cities. In his book *The Theory of the Leisure Class,* economist Thorstein Veblen spoke of the era's conspicuous consumption as contrasted to its conspicuous poverty. The rich made a lavish display of their wealth with ostentatious houses, liveried servants, and gala parties. The city poor, on the other hand, lived in great squalor. In the 1890s, for example, when the nation was in the depths of a depression and thousands of unemployed roamed the streets, Marshall Field earned almost eleven hundred dollars an hour and Andrew Carnegie's annual personal income was almost twenty-three million dollars. Those who were employed rarely earned over four hundred dollars a year.

URBAN REFORM

The social, economic, and physical ills of the cities did not remain unchallenged. For example, in 1879, Henry George, a journalist who was angered by inequality, published *Progress and Poverty,* a great popular success and a source of inspiration to those interested in reform. The book, in essence, asked why poverty should be so prevalent in a society where industrial ad-

701

vances had created so much wealth. Other reformers soon began to organize civic federations and municipal leagues that sought to institute competitive civil service exams to curtail the appointment of unqualified persons.

THE CHURCHES AND URBAN AMERICA

The Protestant churches gradually began to take an interest in urban problems in the late nineteenth century by joining private agencies and philanthropic organizations in an effort to improve city life. The churches were able to do this, however, only after they had overcome their basically middle-class bias against any interference with individualism and a laissez-faire economy. Traditionally, they had taught that there would always be poverty and that only God could ameliorate the sufferings of the poor. However, once clergymen saw that the working people were drifting away from their churches, they began to challenge the old assumptions. A group of Protestant clergymen began to fashion a reinterpretation of Christianity known in later years as the Social Gospel. This approach emphasized the social and practical application of the Christian ethic, stressing good works and social reform over questions of doctrine. One of the movement's most influential leaders was Washington Gladden, a Congregational minister, who published a guidebook on the movement called *Applied Christianity*. The Social Gospel influenced most American Protestant denominations by the 1890s. The Episcopal Church formed the Christian Social Union to aid labor. A further step toward social awareness was taken by several denominations in 1908 with the formation of the Federal Council of Churches of Christ in America.

Most of the urban working class was Roman Catholic, however, and looked to its own religious heritage for support. The Catholic clergy were thus more aware and more sympathetic to the needs of the poor.

The Church founded philanthropic institutions and schools among the immigrant poor to give them religious training and to introduce them to American life and traditions. Cardinal Gibbons, the archbishop of Baltimore, supported the trade-union movement, and in 1891 Pope Leo XIII issued the encyclical *De Rerum Novarum* recognizing labor unions and social legislation as ways to ameliorate conditions of the poor.

The practical implications and obligations of the Christian ethic were particularly prominent in the activities of two new movements formed in the late nineteenth century, the Salvation Army and the Christian Science Church. The Salvation Army, founded in London by William Booth, reached the United States in 1879 under the leadership of George Railton. Its primary aim was to assist the poor in the cities and to do so it used revivalist methods, uniforms, and brass bands to attract crowds. Soon its recruiters supplemented sermons that preached repentance with practical social service to the poor. Slum brigades were sent into the tenement areas to bring them not only the gospel but food and clothing.

The Christian Science movement founded by Mary Baker Eddy in 1879 also appealed primarily to city dwellers. Clearly American in its origins, it was closely linked to Transcendentalist thought in its stress on the omnipotence and omnipresence of God and to the philosophy of pragmatism in its emphasis on the idea that theology must be practical to be true. A distinctive factor in Christian Science is its healing of physical disease and other problems that face mankind by absolute trust in divine power.

SOCIAL WORK MOVEMENT

Other individuals and groups concerned themselves with improving the living standards of the city poor, particularly the immigrants. These groups worked together with private philanthropists and in conjunction with city governments. They collected money for parks and playgrounds for the slums and many began to learn first-hand about slum life. The young social workers who visited the slums, the sweatshops, and the tenements acted as an important connection between the working class and the middle class. The concept of the settlement house also evolved as a new approach to social service, where social workers, from an established center in the slums, gave direction, encouragement, and physical assistance to the poor. After 1890, over fifty settlement houses were established in American cities. The houses often provided nurseries, playgrounds, libraries, and classes in a variety of subjects. They not only helped the poor but provided an excellent education for the social workers themselves.

The model for settlement houses was Toynbee Hall, founded in London in the early 1880s. Its American counterpart was the Neighborhood Guild which opened in 1886 on New York's lower East Side. Jane Addams, after visiting Toynbee Hall in the slums of London, was inspired to set up Hull House on Chicago's Halstead Street in 1889 to deal with slum life at its source. She wished, she said, "to make social service express the spirit of Christ." Her establishment also offered classes in music and art, developed a theatrical group, and provided a gymnasium and a day nursery. In addition, Jane Addams worked politically for improved public service and social legislation, even getting herself appointed garbage inspector of her ward so that she might pressure landlords and garbage contractors more effectively for regular collection service. The first two administrative heads of the new federal Children's Bureau came from Jane Addams' Hull House.

Equal in fame to Chicago's Hull House was New York City's Henry Street Settlement, founded by Lillian Wald, a nurse by training and the first social service worker to propose a federal Children's Bureau. She wrote, concerning the aims of her settlement house staff "... We were to live in the neighborhood ... identify ourselves with it socially, and, in brief, contribute to it our citizenship."

A settlement house on New York's lower East Side.

Readings

GENERAL WORKS

Commons, John R., and others, *History of Labor in the United States*, Vols. I-II. New York: Macmillan, 1918–1935—The classic history of American labor. The authors see the labor movement in America as fundamentally an attempt to better conditions within the context of a capitalist society.

Green, Constance M., *American Cities in the Building of the Nation*. Tuckahoe, N.Y.: De Graff, 1957—Using several different cities as case studies of urban development, the author describes the role of cities in American history.

Green, Constance M., *The Rise of Urban America*. New York: Harper & Row, 1965 —A general survey of American urban history.

Jones, Maldwyn A., *American Immigration*. Chicago: University of Chicago Press, 1960 —A short survey of the history of immigration and of the reaction of Americans to it.

McKelvey, Blake, *The Urbanization of America*. New Brunswick, N.J.: Rutgers University Press, 1962—A general history of the growth of American cities between the Civil War and World War I.

Mumford, Lewis, *The Culture of Cities*. New York: Harcourt, Brace, 1938—A history of the rise of cities since the Middle Ages in which Mumford advances a plea for social planning for urban life and suggests reforms for the future.

Schlesinger, Arthur M., *The Rise of the City 1878–1898*. New York: Macmillan, 1933— An overview of American urbanization in the last decades of the nineteenth century. Schlesinger's work led to a growing understanding of the importance of cities in shaping American life.

Taft, Philip, *Organized Labor in America*. New York: Harper & Row, 1964—A survey of the history of the American trade union movement.

Weber, Max, *The City*. New York: Macmillan, 1958—A pioneering work on the economic and social functions of cities by the great German sociologist.

Wittke, Carl, *We Who Built America*. Cleveland: Press of Case Western Reserve, 1964 —A general history of immigrant life in the United States.

SPECIAL STUDIES

Abell, Aaron I., *American Catholicism and Social Action*. Notre Dame, Ind.: University of Notre Dame Press, 1960—A history of reform currents in American Catholicism since the mid-nineteenth century. Abell shows that the Church concentrated more on social welfare than on political or economic reforms.

Bremner, Robert H., *From the Depths: The Discovery of Poverty in the United States*. New York: New York University Press, 1956—Around the turn of the century, reformers and intellectuals began to recognize poverty as a social problem. Bremner discusses the background which led to this realization and the ways in which people attempted to solve the problem.

David, Henry, *History of the Haymarket Affair*. New York: Macmillan, 1964—A detailed account of the Haymarket incident of 1886 in which a bomb exploded after a rally, killing seven policemen and leading to an hysterical campaign against radicals.

Erickson, Charlotte, *American Industry and the European Immigrant 1860–1885*. New York: Russell, 1967—During the quarter-century Erickson studies, American industries were able to import laborers under contract to work in United States factories. Erickson argues that the actual use of contract labor was rather rare.

Handlin, Oscar, *The Uprooted*. Boston:

PRIMARY SOURCES

Little, Brown, 1951—An important impressionistic study of the experience of immigrating to America which emphasizes the hardships and the social and psychological disorientation of immigrants.

Higham, John, *Strangers in the Land: Patterns of American Nativism 1860–1925*. New York: Atheneum, 1963—Higham traces the changing attitudes of different American groups to immigration. He relates nativist sentiment to social strains within American life.

Hopkins, C. H., *The Rise of the Social Gospel in American Protestantism, 1865–1915*. New Haven, Conn.: Yale University Press, 1940—Hopkins relates the growing concern for social applications of the Gospel in the 1865 to 1915 period to concern about industrial life and interest in scientific development.

May, Henry, *Protestant Churches and Industrial America*. New York: Octagon, 1963—A study of five Protestant denominations and their shifts from staunch conservatism on social issues to more liberal positions as the problems of industrial society grew.

Solomon, Barbara, *Ancestors and Immigrants*. Cambridge, Mass.: Harvard University Press, 1956—A study of the reactions of New England's Protestant elite to the influx of immigrants. Solomon finds that when immigrants threatened their political power and social standing, the elite turned to nativism.

Taft, Philip, *The A.F. of L. in the Time of Gompers*. New York: Octagon, 1970—The first volume in Taft's history of the American Federation of Labor, covering the long reign of Gompers as president. Taft admires Gompers as a man of moderation and realism.

Wolff, Leon, *Lockout*. New York: Harper & Row, 1965—An account of the Homestead strike against the Carnegie Steel Company. Wolff describes the company's campaign, led by Henry Clay Frick, to destroy the workers' union.

Diamond, Sigmund, ed., *The Nation Transformed: The Creation of Industrial Society*. New York: Braziller, 1963—An anthology of primary source material which demonstrates the motives and the social effects of American industrialization.

Gompers, Samuel, *Seventy Years of Life and Labor*, Vols. I-II. New York: Kelley, 1925—The autobiography of the early leader of the AF of L. Written when Gompers was old, the book reveals him at his most conservative and portrays him as a firm foe of radicalism and a strong American patriot.

Handlin, Oscar, ed., *Immigration as a Factor in American History*. Englewood Cliffs, N.J.: Prentice-Hall, 1959—A collection of documents on immigration to America from colonial times through the immigration restriction of the 1920s.

Powderly, Terence U., *Thirty Years of Labor*. New York: Kelley, 1962—Powderly, the leader of the Knights of Labor in its heyday, shows himself in his autobiography to be something of a utopian reformer advocating temperance and the formation of cooperatives as policies for workers to adopt.

Riis, Jacob, *How the Other Half Lives*. New York: Dover, 1970—A Danish immigrant who became a leading social reformer in New York, Riis shocked many with his accounts and photographs of poverty and slums in the city.

BIOGRAPHIES

Hibben, Paxton, *Henry Ward Beecher, An American Portrait*. New York: Doran, 1927—A sarcastic biography of the Brooklyn minister whose sermons set the moral tone for many middle-class Americans during the Gilded Age.

Peel, Robert, *Mary Baker Eddy*. New York: Holt, Rinehart and Winston, 1966—A biography of the founder of the Christian Science movement. Mary Baker Eddy's life is described up to 1875, when she first published *Science and Health*.

PICTORIAL ALPHABET.

A   AX   E  ELK

a   ax   e elk

B   BOX   F  FAN

b   box   f fan

C   CAT   G  GIRL

c   cat   g girl

D   DOG   H  HEN

d   dog   h hen

The Intellectual Response to Industrial America

20

With the laying of the Union Pacific rails in the late sixties the destiny of America as a self-sufficient economic unity was fixed. Henceforth for an indeterminate period the drift of tendency would be from the outlying frontiers to industrial centers, and with that drift would come far-reaching changes in the daily routine of life. The machine would reach into the remotest villages to disrupt the traditional domestic economy, and the division of labor would substitute for the versatile frontiersman the specialized factory-hand. . . . A new urban psychology would displace the older agrarian, and with the new psychology would come other philosophies in response to the changing realities.

—*Vernon Lewis Parrington*

torial alphabet from McGuffey's
ng-Book.

The social and economic evils that accompanied America's rapid industrialization could not be successfully attacked as long as the belief in the survival of the fittest prevailed in America. Thus, protests continued to come from workers who lost their jobs and employers who lost their businesses. Consumers continued to denounce rigged prices and people everywhere recoiled from reports that judges and politicians had been bribed by powerful industrialists to insure protection of their interests. In order to curb the inequities of American life, the assumptions of the laissez-faire economists, led by William Graham Sumner, had to be disproved. The only way to undermine this position was to attack the premise of Social Darwinism. Philosophical reformers in their quest for greater social justice denied that Sumner and his allies were really being scientific and rejected any so-called "natural law of free and untrammeled competition."

SOCIAL DARWINISM ATTACKED

HENRY GEORGE

An important critic of the theory of Social Darwinism was Henry George. He was not antagonistic to the idea of a competitive economy but to the fatalism of a philosophy that denied man a role in ordering the direction of his society. George expounded his solution in *Progress and Poverty,* one

of the few texts on economics to become a best seller. Neither a trained economist nor college-educated, George based his observations on his broad experience rather than on academic learning. He had been to sea before the Civil War, tried printing and journalism in California, and traveled across the continent from San Francisco to New York. The dreadful condition of the poor in the East made an indelible impression on him and the sight of huge tracts of land granted to the Central Pacific Railroad raised questions in his mind about land distribution. How was it possible for so much national economic progress to be accompanied by so much grinding personal poverty? Why did "The House of Have" and "The House of Want" stand side by side? He concluded that, given the existing system of land ownership, the two naturally went together. His theory started from the premise that all material progress depended on the productive use of land, which fluctuated in value. For example, when a new town was settled or a railroad built, land values increased. A report of coming improvements would send speculators running to snap up the choicest sites. In this way the available land in America had fallen into the hands of a small number of landlords who charged rent to the rest of the population who used it. This meant all land, coal mines and oil fields as well as urban developments, produced rent as unearned income. If a highway was built past a man's land, for example, the worth of his property might multiply several times over, and yet he himself had performed none of the labor that produced the increased value. He had not earned the additional dollars he put into his pocket.

What about the people whose toil made land values go up? They slipped collectively down the economic ladder since, with too many workers for too few jobs, wages fell and unemployment rose. At the same time, those who paid rent continued to hand over what they earned to those who had done no work to earn it. Hence the paradox of progress for the (useless) landlord and poverty for the (useful) tenant. "From this fundamental injustice," George argued, "flow all the injustices which distort and endanger modern development, which condemn the producer of wealth to poverty and pamper the nonproducer in luxury, which rear the tenement house with the palace, plant the brothel behind the church, and compel us to build prisons as we open new schools."

THE SINGLE TAX

According to George, if rent was the root cause of social ills, then getting rid of rent would eradicate those ills. The landlords must no longer be permitted to live off the public. He proposed to accomplish his reform in one stroke—taxing the land to its full value, thus bringing into the public coffers the wealth earned by the people that was now in the hands of a wealthy few. All rents would be paid to the government as the collective landlord. No other taxes would be necessary because the government would be able to pay its way from tax returns on land. The taxpayer would benefit because this would be the only tax laid on him, and would be less than the amount demanded by the present owners. He wanted the government to own the land, but in no other way did he attack private property. George thus reduced taxation to a single tax, the tax on land.

Each man would then profit only to the extent of his labor, and "when everyone gets what he fairly earns, no one can get more than he fairly earns," George maintained. Labor and management would have the same stake in this plan. Both produced value through work, and both were exploited economically by the landowners who were the parasites of society. If land exploitation was eliminated then the social evils accompanying it would also be eliminated.

CONTRIBUTIONS TO THE REFORM MOVEMENT

Henry George's theory of the single tax helped to undermine solid support for Social Darwinism by setting forth an alternative theory of the laws of nature. He argued that because nature had given the land a decisive influence on human society, a genuinely scientific sociology demanded public enjoyment of the wealth of the land, not the unbridled laissez-faire competition defended by Sumner.

George offered the public more than scientific analysis in support of his ideas. He defended a theory of social justice which he believed would establish a better world. He traveled through the United States and Europe to spread his theory of the single tax. Single-tax societies sprang up, single-tax communities were formed, and the single tax was tried as far away as New Zealand. Bernard Shaw confessed that hearing George speak in London gave a decisive turn to his own economic thinking. New Yorkers thought enough of George to nominate him for mayor, and although he lost the election of 1886, he was ahead of Theodore Roosevelt, who was also a candidate that year. He ran for the same office a second time in 1897, but died before the election.

George's idea failed in the long run. He had neglected to consider other factors present in the economy of an industrialized state. The economy of the United States was too complex for a single-tax solution. Economists have pointed out that taxing rent out of existence would apply not only to a few landlords but to a large number of small investors in land enterprises. Yet George's influence continued into the twentieth century, modified according to place and circumstance. Many tax structures, giving a special emphasis to the tax on land, reflect the single-tax theory put forward in *Progress and Poverty*.

EDWARD BELLAMY

While Henry George was preoccupied with the subject of land ownership, Edward Bellamy examined the broader question of the implications of unrestricted capitalism. Both wrote best-selling books, although Bellamy's *Looking Backward, 2000–1887*, published nine years after *Progress and Poverty*, was not a text in economics but a romantic novel. Both enjoyed enormous followings in their own time, but only George's ideas had any real influence on public policy in the twentieth century.

Bellamy's ideas were the product of his family background and early experiences. His father was a Baptist preacher in Chicopee Falls, Massachusetts. As a young man he went to Germany to study for a year in what was then the center of European learning. Many Americans discovered the intellectual heritage of Germany at about the same time, but Bellamy was one of the few who became concerned about the hard life of the lower classes there. His uneasiness about the social order grew after his return home and ultimately prompted him to write the book that captured the attention of the world.

LOOKING BACKWARD

As the son of a clergyman, Bellamy took an essentially religious view of man and society. Terming unrestricted capitalism "the brutal law of the survival of the strongest and the most cunning," he added: "The principle of the Brotherhood of Humanity is one of the eternal truths that govern the world's progress on lines which distinguish human nature from brute nature." Bellamy was adding his voice to the growing criticism of Social Darwinism. He saw in the theories of Spencer and Sumner an attempt to force man down to a sub-human level where the strong, "red in tooth and claw," destroyed the weak. He regarded such an attempt as unnatural and unscien-

tific since he believed that nature taught man a very different system of ethics.

In *Looking Backward,* Bellamy argued for a reformation of society and the state on a moral basis. He rejected the philosophy of socialism because of its "talk about burning, sacking, and blowing people up," and the manner in which its advocates appealed to "the red flag with an abusive tone about God and religion." He urged all classes to join in a general uplifting of society for the good of all, and he thought they would do so in due time because human beings were naturally good. The evil circumstances in which they were trapped derived from the unnatural system of competition that dominated American economic life. According to the narrator of the novel, "The labor of men, I explained, was the fertilizing stream which alone rendered earth habitable. . . . Let but the famine-stricken nation assume the function it had neglected, and regulate for the common good the course of the life-giving stream, and the earth would bloom like one garden, and none of its children lack any good thing." Regulated rather than competitive labor was his formula for healing the economic and social ills of the day.

UTOPIA

The ideal state founded on Bellamy's theories was projected by him into the year 2000. Countless thinkers since Plato have imagined utopias, and Bellamy's was among the more interesting. The hero of the novel fell asleep in 1887, awakened in 2000, and looked around at the society of the twenty-first century. He was astounded at the transformation. Regulated labor was universal, cooperation supplanting competition. As a result, no citizens were rich, none were poor, and all had whatever they required for a decent existence. Money had been replaced by credit cards on which each person could draw up to a certain amount. The profit motive had been removed from the social order, and man's incentive was not money but the honor to be earned by serving the state. Individuals labored in the industrial army of the state until the age of forty-five. Then they retired to enjoy themselves in any way they saw fit. In Bellamy's utopia the role of the government was limited. Fewer elected officials were needed and these were elected from those already retired from the industrial force. Removing competition allowed the naturally good human instincts to lead men to lead good lives. The behavior that made police forces and armies necesary was therefore outmoded, a thing of the past. "All these wonders, it was explained, had very simply come about as the results of replacing private capitalism by public capitalism, and organizing the machinery of production and distribution, like the political government, as business of general concern to be carried on for the public benefit instead of private gain."

THE NATIONALIST CLUBS

Bellamy supported his utopian novel with a mass of direct social criticism of the American scene, and his book *Equality,* published in 1897, achieved a popularity of its own with its promise of equality for all. He called his theory "Nationalism," an attractive title for those who wanted to be reformers without giving up loyalty to the nation. His insistence that industry be collectivized appealed to those who felt injured by the private interests then in power, and to idealists who believed he had propounded the only workable theory of equality that could be achieved without bloodshed. His followers founded Nationalist clubs across the country, pressing for implementation of his theories. However, popularity of Bellamy's ideas did not persist into the twentieth century. Although his work was appealing to read, it had no immediate practical application to America's industrial problems. Most Americans,

even if they wanted removal of the abuses created by industrialization, were strongly attached to the capitalistic system. A socialistic economy had no wide following in the United States in the late nineteenth century.

THE PHILOSOPHY OF PRAGMATISM

Henry George and Edward Bellamy were not philosophers in the full sense. Concerned about social policy, they paid little attention to the metaphysical foundations on which an effective social philosophy was based. Each appealed to the concept of natural law without providing a reasoned analysis of its meaning.

THE COMMON SENSE SCHOOL

The Civil War created a great watershed in American philosophy as well as in American life. The intuitive and emotional response to nature and to understanding man was too fragile to survive this conflict and the materialism of American life in the late nineteenth century. The "safe" metaphysics of the time that had migrated across the Atlantic from Scotland in the late eighteenth century seemed more applicable to the American environment. Its chief tenet was that common sense could be used as a weapon against skepticism. When the skeptic asked how one knew the world outside the mind existed, Thomas Reid, its chief exponent, replied that one knew through common sense. From this concept he developed an entire philosophy of existence. John Witherspoon, a New Jersey revolutionary patriot, brought the common sense philosophy to America. By becoming president of Princeton, he gave this philosophy the prestige of academic support, a trend of thinking that continued through a succession of Princeton professors until after the Civil War. Another president of the university, James McCosh, represented the common sense school during the 1880s. He taught philosophy students to believe that Divine Providence ruled the world, that man's soul was immortal, and pointed out the rightness of ethics guided by theology—all as a matter of common sense. Herbert W. Schneider, in *A History of American Philosophy,* has commented on the philosophy of McCosh: "The safe and sane system of Scottish realism . . . was an ideal pattern for preventing youth from indulging in speculative extremes."

THE ST. LOUIS HEGELIANS

To a number of thinkers the common sense philosophy seemed inadequate to explain the nature of the universe and man's place in it. While McCosh published his bland books, a band of thinkers in St. Louis were subjecting the universe and man to a more rigorous metaphysical analysis.

St. Louis was wealthy, cosmopolitan, and proud of its culture. French and German were heard almost as often as English. Ideas from Britain and the Continent received a ready welcome. Not surprisingly, St. Louis attracted remarkable individuals, and two of them, Henry C. Brokmeyer and William Torrey Harris, had a gift for philosophical speculation. Brokmeyer, a German, introduced Hegel's system to Harris and others who met to discuss philosophy. They adopted Hegelianism, translated Hegel's works, wrote explanations of his thought, and tried to apply his theories to practical politics.

Hegelianism provided a plausible explanation for some of the crucial events in American history. Hegel had spoken of history as moving by a logical progression involving groups of three elements or triads: a thesis, an antithesis, and a resulting synthesis. The St. Louis Hegelians applied the triadic pattern to such an event as the Civil War: the North (thesis) had collided with the South (antithesis), and from the collision had resulted the reunited nation (synthesis).

THE EVOLUTIONARY PHILOSOPHY

In spite of the systematic explanation of historical events provided by Hegel's philosophy, its proponents failed to win over most American philosophers. Although the Harvard exponent of Hegelian idealism, Josiah Royce, believed in more freedom of choice for the individual, most interpreters of his philosophy talked in terms of absolutes, insisting that the universe operated in an unchanging pattern, according to divine purpose. However, the denial of any unchanging pattern appeared implicit in Darwinian biology. If species came into being and disappeared, might not the same be said of everything else? Herbert Spencer had thought so and applied the theory of evolution to all the problems of philosophy, explaining whatever existed in society by the concept of the survival of the fittest. One of Spencer's leading followers in America was John Fiske, author of *Outlines of Cosmic Philosophy,* a volume so popular it ran through more than ten editions in twenty years. To Spencer's argument, Fiske added a few insights of his own. He spoke of "an Unknowable Reality, of which all phenomena whatever are the knowable manifestations," and declared "a continuous redistribution of matter and motion" to be fundamental in the operation of the universe. In his view, the theory of evolution explained human development, moral codes, political actions, and social mores as well as everything else which man experienced.

Although Fiske thought he was explaining everything on the basis of change, his critics pointed out that the result was in fact a philosophy of determinism that saw man's acts as resulting from natural law. The law of evolution he postulated governed all things. If evolution gave rise to man and society, did it not control both? This gave rise to the question of what place remained for individual initiative. Belief in such an evolutionary philosophy led logically to fatalism. Many metaphysicians objected to this view and rejected the cosmic law described by Fiske, finding it stifling. They were as anxious to show the fallacy in his evolutionary philosophy as the social philosophers were to expose the flaws in Spencer's concept of Social Darwinism.

THE ORIGINS OF PRAGMATISM

The American thinkers who overturned Spencer's philosophy never dreamed of denying evolution. Setting aside the grandiose structure erected by Spencer on the original concept, they went back to Darwin, who had proposed evolution simply as a scientific theory. They then developed the philosophy of pragmatism, which began in the Metaphysical Club where professors from Harvard and elsewhere gathered to discuss problems of life and mind.

Chauncey Wright, considered the best speaker there, propounded his theory of "cosmic weather," which held that man is only able to detect short-term patterns in the universe, not universal laws, evolutionary or otherwise. Charles Sanders Peirce formulated the basic tenet of pragmatism in his article "How to Make Our Ideas Clear," with this definition: "Consider what effects, that might conceivably have practical bearings, we conceive the object of our conception to have. Then, our conception of these effects is the whole of our conception of the object." Thus, Peirce defined an object as the sum of its consequences insofar as man was able to know it. The famous pragmatic test of truth—"what works" —was the next logical step. There were no fixed systems of belief. All ideas were to be judged by their consequences.

This theory caught on in a country that thought in terms of what was practical, in a nation of builders. Peirce belonged to the mainstream of American life and thought. Although generally regarded as having the most penetrating mind in the history of American philosophy, he wrote in too technical a style to become popular. One of his colleagues, William James, and a younger contemporary, John Dewey, reached a wider audience.

WILLIAM JAMES

The James family produced two of the greatest intellects in America in the late nineteenth century, William James, the philosopher, and Henry James, the novelist. William was educated at home and in Europe, studied art, and then psychology and philosophy. Suffering from a neurosis that made him a semi-invalid for long periods, he sought an interpretation of life that would bring him personal stability, and he decided that "[his] first act of free will shall be to believe in free will." He became a teacher and was a distinguished member of the Harvard faculty when he published his first great book, *The Principles of Psychology,* in 1890. Then he turned his attention to philosophy and religion, and wrote another masterpiece, *The Varieties of Religious Experience.* An artist in prose and a brilliant speaker, he held large audiences spellbound with his writings and his platform appearances. His renown was world-wide when he died in 1910.

PRAGMATISM

In elaborating his version of pragmatic philosophy, James coined the phrase "cash value" to describe the test of truth. A proposition had "cash value" when it worked—when it produced results. Pragmatism was not properly to be defined as a philosophic system but as a method of finding the truth. How was the truth to be determined in a given case? To James the truth was more than just observable facts; it also comprised the beliefs about those facts. He introduced the concept of the will to believe, which he thought had a decisive effect on events: "Often enough our faith beforehand in an uncertified result is the only thing that makes the result come true." In other words, a person's belief affected the outcome of events; one increased the effectiveness of an idea by belief in the possibility that it would work. Doubt was, conversely, likely to produce failure, because one who doubted that an event would occur helped to prevent it from happening.

James also accepted the idea that if belief in God gave meaning to a man's life it was true for him—a concept congenial to the tendency of twentieth-century thought to move away from absolute values to an individual choice of moral standards. Ideas or beliefs did not have to be provable by the scientific method to have reality in man's mind. By thus stressing free will and belief in the test of truth, James thought he had refuted the Spencerians and others holding to the concept of universal, unbreakable law. With this philosophy, James also broke with the common sense school in its unquestioning acceptance of un-changeable moral values and with the skeptics who believed that the only reality was one which could be proved through scientific experiments.

THE BLOCK UNIVERSE

By the same token, James disposed of arguments for what he termed "the block universe," an idea associated primarily with Hegelianism. Hegel, in James's view, was a rationalist who believed he could tidy up all the loose ends of philosophy by means of one consistent, all-embracing description of the way the universe operated. James, as an empiricist, believed that knowledge came from experience and he therefore accepted the concept of an open universe. He also chose to believe in a universe characterized by spontaneity, the sudden unpredictable chance event that upset prophecies based on so-called natural laws. The modern theory of the random behavior of subatomic particles is in line with his thinking, as is the existentialist theory of pure freedom in human acts.

JOHN DEWEY

John Dewey, an important follower of James, made contributions to pragmatic thought in his own right. When Dewey began teaching philosophy at the University of Minnesota, he was strongly influenced by Hegelianism, but further travels and studies, plus the example of William James, converted him to pragmatism. He taught in China, and at the request of the Turkish government wrote a guide for the modernization of Turkish education based on an experimental school he had created at the University of Chicago. His later career took him to Columbia University. Dewey was a prolific writer and most of his books and many of his articles have had a lasting influence on the philosophic thought of the twentieth century.

THE MEANING OF EXPERIENCE

Dewey accepted James's concept of an open universe which had no fixed, unchangeable laws and values. He made experience the basis of reality for each individual. Experience he defined as the organism reacting to its environment, arguing that man found himself in the midst of a universe in flux, with everything in the process of change and movement from second to second. Therefore, man had to deal with the course of events here and now, no simple thing to do, for the world was "a scene of risk; it is uncertain, unstable, uncannily unstable." Man's mind, too, was in a state of evolution and the interplay between his mind and his environment shaped the goals and movement of society. Through education, life's experiences, and natural science he was able to deal with a fluid universe. Finally, through philosophy he could reflect back on experience, make fundamental value judgments, and choose from the options open to him. Dewey had an optimistic belief in progress, based not on tradition or authority but on man transforming his environment to please himself while at the same time he is being subtly shaped by the universe around him. Understandably, Dewey had been called "the philosopher of freedom."

INSTRUMENTALISM

Dewey was more technical and less intuitive than James. In his form of pragmatism, ideas were instruments for dealing with practical problems. Their chief function was to explore social issues, using "social" in the broad sense to cover science in addition to all other human enterprises. It was the duty of philosophers, therefore, to guide experience toward sound and humane ends. Ideas were "plans of action" rather than merely reflections of external reality. Having also termed ideas "instruments," Dewey called his philosophy "instrumentalism." It was the most fully articulated theory of pragmatism.

EDUCATION

Dewey believed that adults had to make choices from the alternatives presented to them by their experience, and to do so wisely they had to be properly trained. Education was all-important to Dewey's instrumentalism. He achieved his widest fame as an educator, and his *School and Society,* published in 1899, was adopted as a textbook from America to Turkey and China. The experimental school he ran became celebrated for its method of progressive education where children learned by doing, instead of having information drilled into them by their teachers. Accused of being too permissive, he retorted that he was training his pupils to be citizens of a democratic social order, to make choices that would prevent economic anarchy and political despotism.

Over the years the nature of pragmatic thought has been strongly admired as well as criticized. Some have seen pragmatism as the natural extension of the emphasis, in the philosophy of the enlightenment, on experimentation to insure social progress. Thus, it was regarded as a liberalizing and creative outlook. Some also have applauded its stress on optimism and change as being in harmony with similar characteristics of American life generally. On the other hand, pragmatism has been criticized as a manifestation of less desirable characteristics of American life such as vulgarity and materialism. Moreover, its critics have said that as philosophy pragmatism is shallow. Stressing the idea that what is true is what works elevates means over ends. It demands no search for absolute values but is only concerned with techniques. Critics have asked, can man get along without fixed values? Without faith in unchanging religious principles or in natural law, how can man defend a concept of natural rights and basic order in society? A concept of reality based on the idea of an open universe with no fixed laws cannot prove that democracy is the best form of government; such an assurance can only be obtained from an accepted body of philosophical concepts. Finally, some critics of pragmatism have attacked it, especially Dewey's analysis, for neglecting the spiritual dimension of man's being.

THE REVOLT AGAINST FORMALISM

Pragmatic philosophy, in its insistence on experience and verification, gave a strong impetus to what Professor Morton White has labeled "the revolt against formalism." An open universe with limitless present possibilities for change replaced timeless categories and immutable laws, pragmatism provided room for reformers to circumvent traditional beliefs seen as barriers to improving society. Social scientists adopted the idea of a fluid human condition as a useful tool for social reform.

LESTER FRANK WARD

The founder of American sociology, Lester Frank Ward, was born in Joliet, Illinois, in 1841, when life on the frontier was still rugged. He grew up wondering whether the sufferings he saw and endured were really

a necessary part of the social order. After serving in the Civil War and later working for a while as a government scientist, he joined the faculty of Brown University, where he served until his death in 1913. While influenced primarily by the philosophy of pragmatism, Ward also absorbed the ideas of several older thinkers, especially those of the French philosopher Auguste Comte, who founded the science of sociology. Comte's writings convinced Ward that humanity was moving by stages toward a better life. He incorporated ideas from Darwin, Hegel, and Schopenhauer in his most important works, *Dynamic Sociology* and *Applied Sociology*.

REFORM DARWINISM

The Social Darwinists thought of society in terms of unending competition and institutions outside of man's control. They also pictured folk customs as relatively stable because the rate of evolutionary change was so slow. Ward took an opposite view, insisting that nature presented numerous examples of cooperation as well as competition, and that man had no need to wait for the natural law to produce movement in society. Man's will could intervene to speed up the process of change without violating any natural law, since he was a part of nature and human development. The key, then, was not structure, a rigid element, but function, a mobile element. Like Dewey, he argued that it was man's duty to choose correctly from the options he found in the flux of experience. If he could make society function properly, the right structure would evolve. For example, if man ensured democracy in practice, new democratic institutions would appear as the need for them was felt.

SOCIOCRACY

Ward favored "artificial means of accelerating the spontaneous processes of nature," by which he meant using intelligence, and above all scientific intelligence, to give direction to human life. Again, like Dewey, he saw education as fundamental to social change, but where Dewey stressed the education of children, Ward placed reliance on the training of sociologists and their employment by the government at every level. He proposed a social science institute in Washington, so that professionals would be near at hand whenever the President or Congress needed advice. Such social planning would produce a "sociocracy," to use Ward's term, a society moving toward worthwhile goals scientifically selected. Man would thereby ensure his own progress.

THORSTEIN VEBLEN

While Ward and the pragmatists were developing general theories of social behavior, Thorstein Veblen was concentrating on economic questions—specifically, the behavior of wealthy industrialists. The son of Norwegian immigrants, born on a Minnesota farm in 1857, Veblen never overcame the effects of the isolation of the frontier. His most successful years were spent at the University of Chicago, where he published *The Theory of the Leisure Class* in 1899 and *The Theory of Business Enterprise* in 1904. But his uncouth manners offended the head of the university, William Rainey Harper, and Veblen was forced to leave. He went from one institution to another, a restless wanderer full of satirical thoughts about the ways of his fellow men. Had he lived a few months longer, he would have seen the crash of the stock market in 1929, a catastrophe that confirmed his sardonic view of the ways of the business community.

THE THEORY OF THE LEISURE CLASS

Veblen had a first-hand look at the leisure class in Chicago, focus of a gigantic railroad system, center of the meat-packing industry, and a metropolis where the immensely rich lived off the laboring poor. Observing these people, he saw how they distinguished between dignified and undignified labor. According to Veblen, if a man worked little for much money, his labor was dignified; if a man worked hard for little money, his labor was undignified. Pure work was no longer considered honorable. Wealth was admired and poverty despised. To display their wealth, persons with means indulged in "conspicuous consumption." The tycoons of Chicago built mansions along the shore of Lake Michigan, drove handsome carriages, wore expensive clothes from Paris and London, and flaunted their jewelry. This ostentation was not required for their comfort, but by conspicuous consumption they were able to show the world that they belonged to the leisure class. It gained them the admiration of all the other classes, for even the poorest spent money, if they could, to enhance their dignity. The desire to emulate the rich bound society together in spite of class distinctions. Veblen acknowledged that the leisure class did confer some benefits on society by founding libraries, hospitals, and art galleries, but he hoped for a society that would someday confer these benefits without at the same time making money a badge of social distinction.

TECHNOCRACY

When Veblen sought the remedy for conditions brought about by the concentration of wealth and power in the hands of the unproductive, he drew a distinction between industry and business, contrasting the smooth functioning of machines under those trained to handle them (industry) with the periodic crises caused by the accumulators of wealth (business). As he saw it, businessmen and technicians were rivals, not partners. The recent past had shown too many examples of businessmen who lacked genuine concern for the industries they dominated. Jay Gould's ownership and destruction of the Erie Railroad for his own profit was the most notorious case. According to Veblen's theory, the Erie should have been placed under the control of engineers who would have taken pride in running it well. Generalizing from specific examples, he outlined a system of technocracy in which the technicians, mechanics, and engineers would oust the businessmen and take over the direction of industry for the good of society. He thus challenged the public's admiration of businessmen and the classical economists' view that an unmanaged, laissez-faire economy was based on natural law.

Veblen confessed that he was not optimistic about his suggested reform: "There is nothing in the situation that should reasonably flutter the sensibilities of the Guardians or of that massive body of well-to-do citizens who make up the rank-and-file of absentee owners, just yet."

CHANGING HISTORICAL VIEWPOINTS

The would-be reformers of America constantly referred to the past to show how present conditions evolved over a long period of time, but their historical knowledge was often limited. They needed help from professional historians, some of whom were deep in a re-examination of the historical process.

INSTITUTIONAL EVOLUTION

The ideas of some historians were closer to Social Darwinism than to its challengers. John Fiske, turning from philosophy to history, and utilizing concepts from German and English writers, traced American political institutions from the councils of the Germanic tribes that had overthrown the Roman Empire. He offered what was known as the "germ theory" of history, according to which the "seeds" planted by these Teutonic tribes flowered into free institutions, first in England and then in the United States. In its fullest statement it combined the concepts of biological evolution with the development of political institutions. Professor Herbert Baxter Adams offered a more comprehensive formulation of the germ theory, declaring that the Anglo-Saxon peoples had a natural inclination toward freedom and against tyranny, so that the institutions of freedom resulted wherever their influence was felt from the Rhine to the Pacific. This concept was used to justify both British and American imperialism in the 1890s.

On the other hand, Frederick Jackson Turner, whose frontier thesis was examined earlier, challenged the germ theory. He wrote: "Too exclusive attention has been paid by institutional students to the Germanic origins, too little to the American factors. The frontier is the line of most rapid and effective Americanization. The wilderness masters the colonist. . . . Little by little he transforms the wilderness, but the outcome is not the old Europe. . . . The fact is, that here is a new product that is American." For Turner, it was the evolutionary process on the American frontier that provided the most accurate explanation for the development of American mores and institutions.

THE NEW HISTORY

Shortly after the turn of the century, James Harvey Robinson of Columbia urged an overhauling of the historical profession. He criticized his colleagues for their narrow view of history as essentially political and proposed that they broaden their scope by including the study of nonpolitical subjects such as the history of science. Moreover, he held that their primary consideration should be the meaning in events, not the mere rehearsal of facts. Turning to Darwin's theory of evolution for support, he viewed the path followed by humanity in evolutionary terms, with different classes struggling for survival. However, as a Reform Darwinist he believed that since the struggle was still going on, man could see history as a weapon to effect changes in society. Robinson himself chose to help the lower classes by emphasizing their role in the historical drama instead of confining himself to discussions about kings, statesmen, and generals.

Two twentieth-century historians, Charles A. Beard and Carl L. Becker, also saw the study of history as relative to man's contemporary needs. Beard, in particular, supported Robinson's view of history as a tool in man's efforts for social reform. For example, in his book *An Economic Interpretation of the Constitution,* he took an irreverent view of the framing of that document. He believed he had proof that many of the Founding Fathers favored adoption of the Constitution because it would be advantageous to them financially, whereas earlier writers had viewed the delegates to the convention as public-spirited men whose sole aim was to improve the political system. While Beard's thesis on the origins of the Constitution has been largely discredited in recent years by more thorough research, when the book was published in 1913 it was used by progressive reformers in trying to curb the influence of wealthy business interests on government. His work remained influential in historical and political circles until after World War II.

Becker was more preoccupied with the pragmatists' concept that man and nature influenced one another and were each in constant evolution. From this premise he concluded that there were no absolute values in the universe and that man had no way to determine beyond question the truth about the past. Thus, the historian's interpretation of past events could never be objective but would always be influenced by his view of the present.

EVOLUTION AND THE LAW

Oliver Wendell Holmes, Jr. applied the theory of evolution and man's role in the evolutionary process to the study of the law. He interpreted the law and the court system as living adjuncts to the social and economic life of the country. Applying the pragmatic philosophy, he viewed legal changes as responses to practical needs, and believed a given principle could be judged according to whether or not it worked. "The life of the law has not been logic: it has been experience," he wrote in *The Common Law.* Similarly, he saw the Constitution as a living instrument whose meaning depended on interpretation by judges. In particular, he believed that it embodied no fixed, unchangeable economic theory. As we have seen, the American judiciary in the late nineteenth century came to believe that it was its duty to protect business against government regulation whenever possible. Many years passed before the judiciary accepted Holmes's view that a government regulation of the economy should not be overruled by the courts unless it was incompatible with a specific clause of the Constitution.

EDUCATION

In this era, education in the United States became more democratic and experimental. The Civil War heightened awareness of the need for an educated citizenry capable of understanding America's democratic heritage. Since only a minority of parents could pay to have their children educated, school attendance would have to be free and compulsory for the mass of America's children.

THE PUBLIC SCHOOL SYSTEM

The opponents of public schools pointed to the cost and contended that it was unconstitutional to use tax dollars for education. In dealing with this issue, the decision in the Kalamazoo Case of 1874 was a landmark. The case concerned the city's right to erect a high school, and when the Michigan Supreme Court ruled in its favor, Chief Justice Thomas M. Cooley delivered a sweeping defense of free public education from kindergarten to college. Other states referred to this decisive ruling when they established their own public school systems. By the turn of the century, the nation had more than six thousand high schools compared to but a few hundred when the Civil War ended. The number of pupils had jumped from under one hundred thousand to over one-half million. This addition of high schools to the established primary school system meant that boys and girls in greater numbers and more localities received an education lasting into their late teens. Much of this growth also resulted from the expectation in the growing cities that the public schools would take over many of the functions of parents, police, and ministers, and would, as well, "Ameri-canize" the immigrant. By 1900, over 250 million dollars went into school budgets annually, and all but two states outside of the South had compulsory education laws. There were fifteen million in the public schools at the turn of the century, and the illiteracy rate had dropped to a little over 10 percent.

METHODS OF INSTRUCTION

The "little red schoolhouse" presided over by a "schoolmarm" teaching the "three R's" was the stereotype of American education. Stories, poems, and autobiographies told of the one-room schoolhouse with each class chanting a lesson in unison. However, by the late nineteenth century advanced methods were being introduced by teachers informed about the latest European techniques. Some were interested in the ideas of Germany's Johann Herbart who maintained that education must be made a science. His system emphasized instruction of the child in terms relevant to his natural interests. Herbartians stressed effective presentation of lessons and more experimentation. In time the study of the classics began to be overshadowed by the sciences and practical subjects. Courses in sewing, cooking, and manual training were introduced. The system of "object teaching" used by Johann Pestalozzi, a Swiss educator, was widely adopted by advanced schools. In this method the use of books and writing was subordinated to physical activity. Mathematics, for example, was taught by giving children objects to handle instead of making them write numbers on a slate. William Torrey Harris, first as Superintendent of Schools in St. Louis and then as United States Commissioner of Education, held the older view that education should transmit the culture of the past. Increasingly, however, older methods gave way to those closer to Dewey's theory of progressive education with its insistence that learning by doing came before memorizing and drilling in traditional subjects.

THE STATUS OF TEACHERS

The rapid growth of schools created a demand for teachers that in many localities outran the supply. The best trained tended to stay in the cities where they could count on better buildings and facilities, and higher salaries. The rural schools generally had poorer teachers. A lack of well-trained teachers became less of a problem as teachers' colleges and institutes began to turn out graduates explicitly trained for entry into the teaching profession. Parents ceased to joke about those who taught their children and showed them the respect accorded the other learned professions.

HIGHER EDUCATION

Even in the darkest days of the Civil War, education was considered important enough to justify the effort spent on passage of a bill setting up land-grant colleges, the Morrill Act of 1862. Sixteen thousand square miles of public land were earmarked for institutions that would emphasize the teaching of better methods of agriculture and allied vocational subjects. The states quickly took advantage of the Morrill Act, and under its provisions some of America's finest state universities came into existence. The private university flourished, too, the University of Chicago, Cornell, Vanderbilt, Stanford, Johns Hopkins, and Carnegie Institute, to name a few of those founded by wealthy businessmen.

CURRICULUM

The land-grant colleges, geared to the practical demands of farming, contributed to the decline of classical studies. In their curriculums, the study of soil erosion and crop cultivation came before Latin and Greek. However, the older institutions and some new private schools were also caught in the drift toward a different curriculum. President Charles W. Eliot of Harvard was influenced by the experimental, pragmatic outlook then taking hold in higher education. In 1869 Eliot came to Harvard and soon introduced the elective system which allowed students to choose a certain number of the subjects they wished to study. Eventually even some Harvard scholars believed Eliot had gone too far, but experimentation within the framework of traditional disciplines has remained a trait of the educational process in the United States.

GRADUATE SCHOOLS

Until after the Civil War, Americans in search of advanced scholarship went to Europe to study, especially to Germany, a land of great universities and scholars. Americans brought back from Heidelberg and Jena the concept of higher learning using seminar sessions in which professors met their students in small groups. Seminars were designed to encourage students to engage in independent research. The first American graduate school, Johns Hopkins in Baltimore, took its direction from Daniel Coit Gilman, who adapted German ideas to the university's curriculum. His example spread through the American university system. Differences over the establishment of a Graduate College at Princeton provoked a clash between President Woodrow Wilson and Dean Andrew West that caused Wilson to resign and go into politics. By that time the quality of American scholarship had risen to the point that it compared favorably with the best in Europe.

BLACK EDUCATION

Following the Civil War, a number of privately financed vocational and normal schools for black youths were created. Many Southerners believed education was unnecessary for the freedman since he was expected to continue doing menial tasks. As Reconstruction ended, many of these schools closed or were forced to limit themselves to vocational training. In 1900, only 8,000 blacks attended public high schools throughout the South.

The mounting repression of black people in the South after 1876 caused the outstanding black educator, Booker T. Washington, to accept an "accommodationist" outlook. In setting up Tuskeegee Institute in 1881 he stressed that for the present it was important for black people to learn agricultural skills or a trade. In order to survive in a hostile society, they needed to be usefully employed and to keep out of trouble. He wrote concerning the South: "The agitation of questions of social equality is the extremest folly." Within a few decades his willingness to accept an inferior status for blacks in America came under sharp attack by more militant black leaders.

THE ARTS

The Civil War cut across every segment of American life, bringing about a new phase in the arts after 1865. The demands of the self-made man for self-improvement inaugurated an era of popular culture. There arose a mass market for books and lectures for the average reader.

The rise in the sale of books was partly attributable to the growth of public libraries committed to mass self-improvement through reading. The American Library Association was founded in 1876. Five years later the Carnegie Libraries began, and in 1893, the first state laws were passed to create local libraries. In the 1930s, three of the world's most splendid public libraries opened, in Boston and New York and the Library of Congress in Washington, D.C.

When the new century opened, nine thousand public libraries served Americans, offering more than forty-five million volumes. By World War I, the United States had some two thousand public libraries, each containing at least five thousand volumes.

A most remarkable institution for mass self-improvement began in 1874 at Chautauqua Lake in western New York. Lewis Miller, an Ohio businessman, and Bishop John Vincent of the Methodist Church set up a summer program to train Sunday school teachers. In response to a demand for broader intellectual investigation, new studies were continually added so that after the institute began, visitors were able to hear lectures and take reading courses in a variety of subjects from poetry to astronomy. This manner of spreading knowledge encouraged millions of Americans to read more widely in an era of limited educational opportunities for small-town Americans.

MASS JOURNALISM

In attracting readers and influencing them, no other printed matter could compare with the newspapers of this era. As early as 1871 a British observer commented in the *Quarterly Review:* "America is the classic soil of newspapers; everybody is reading; literature is permeating everywhere; publicity is sought for every interest and every order; no political party, no religious sect, no theological school, no literary or benevolent association is without its particular organ; there is a universality of print." A rough count of the more successful papers by decades would be: 1870 (4,500), 1880 (7,000), 1890 (12,000), 1900 (15,000). Circulation of the giants among them zoomed astronomically.

An example of "yellow journalism" from an 1898 copy of William Randolph Hearst's New York Journal.

Mechanical improvements in the craft of printing assisted the growth of the press: The attached folder was invented to gather, cut, and fold each copy of an edition, and presses evolved into giant drums able to stamp out several pages at a single turn. Wood pulp replaced the more expensive rag sheet. The crowning achievement was

---

NIGHT SPECIAL.

ZOLA'S "WIFE BEATERS"----READ IT TO-DAY.

NEW YORK EVENING JOURNAL

NIGHT SPEC

NO. 5,566—P. M.　　　　NEW YORK, FRIDAY, FEBRUARY 11, 1898.　　　　PRICE O

EXTRA

BABIES KILLED BY SCORE

Twenty Bodies Have Been Recently Found in the Streets of Harlem.

POLICE AFTER SLAYERS.

Direct Attention to Midwives and Already One Arrest Has Been Made.

SHE IS HELD WITHOUT BAIL.

Harlem is to-day confronted with such another gruesome mystery of dead babies as recently aroused the Hoboken police.

Hardly a day in the last thirty has gone by that a dead baby has not been found in some doorway or alley.

Ever since the appalling accusations of wholesale baby murder were made against Mrs. Augusta Nack, the ex-slayer of Wm. Guldensuppe, by her husband, Herman Nack, the police have been suspicious of the practice of midwives.

An Important Arrest.

They consider as highly important the arrest and arraignment to-day of Mrs. Eva Gogand, a midwife of No. 245 East One Hundred and Tenth street, who was held, without bail, to await the result of injuries to Mrs. Mary Ethel Gardner, upon whom she operated three weeks ago. Mrs. Gardner is dying at her home, No. 325 West Thirty-seventh street. A consultation of physicians has been held, and at their instance Coroner Zucci has taken the woman's ante-mortem statement. She has

---

ALLOWS $605,237 FOR THE TEACHERS.

Board of Estimate Fixes the Amount for Salaries and Other Expenses for January.

The Board of Estimate and Apportionment this afternoon allowed $605,237 for the Board of Education, covering expenses and salaries for January.

The Board heard Colonel Kearny on a proposition to renovate the brownstone building in City Hall Park for the use of the City Court. He agreed to put in new flooring and elevators and to make other improvements for $15,000.

The bid was accepted.

THE DE LOME QUESTION

Washington, Feb. 11. — Will Hale sail?

BELIEVED TO BE TROLLEY ROBBERS.

Four Men Arrested on Suspicion of Having Murdered a Philadelphia Motorman.

Detectives Cronin and Brown this after-

THE POLICE KEEP BRINGING THEM IN.

LIGHT ON DREYFUS PLOTTING

Colonel Picquart Tells of Disregarded Evidence Against Esterhazy.

HANDWRITING RECOGNIZED

Zola Feelingly Replies to a Reflection of General Pellieux Amid Great Excitement.

WHAT M. BERTILLON DISCOVERED.

Paris, Feb. 11.—Colonel Picquart, while waiting in the corridor of the Assizes to-day to be called as a witness in the trial of Emil Zola, created an immense sensation by declaring that he had decided to disclose the whole Dreyfus mystery in the witness box, regardless of consequences to himself.

Pellieux's Shaft at Zola.

General Pellieux, who was the first witness of the day, testified that General

---

THIGH OF THE BODY FOUND.

NEW CLEW TO THE EAST RIVER MYSTERY.

$1,000 REWARD FOR SOLU

Evening Journal Will Pay This for the Clearing Up of the Crime.

Questions to be answered and detective clews up to date:

WHO WAS HE?

Jean Lancret?	George Farrelll?
C. Swartchild?	Peter Smith?
T. Abrahamson?	—?
Wm. McGarigle?	

WHY WAS HE SLAIN?

For Money?	By a Woman?
For Revenge?	In a Quarrel?
For Jealousy?	By a Maniac?

WHO KILLED HIM?

Nothing Known of the Identity of the Murderer.

HOW WAS HE KILLED?

Choked? Crushed?
Shot? Dismembered?

WHERE WAS HE KILLED?

Not more than a week ago. No one knows, but somewhere in the limits of New York.

A man's thigh was found floating in the East River at the foot of Pacific street, Brooklyn to-day.

Careful measurements taken by the Evening Journal showed at once that the limb was a part of the body of the murdered man whose trunk was at the Morgue.

These measurements were confirmed by Coroner's Physician Donlin and other experts when the thigh was brought to the Morgue this afternoon.

About thirty contusions were found, proving beyond doubt that the murdered man had engaged in a fierce struggle.

The body had apparently been disjointed by the use of a hatchet, pounded with a hammer.

The bone in the thigh was complete. The joints were disarticulated. The flesh was hacked. Then the joints were twisted and torn from the sockets.

The finding of the thigh has added a new and thrilling interest to the great murder mystery. For information

Portion Originally Found

Portion To Day

---

leading to its solution the Evening Journal will pay $1,000 reward.

The right thigh of the murdered man whose trunk floated into the Roosevelt street ferry slip last Monday was found in the East River, at the foot of Pacific street, Brooklyn, to-day.

The thigh reached the Morgue at 1:30 o'clock. It was brought from Brooklyn in a baby's coffin and wrapped in a canvas covering.

It was placed in a closet in the dissecting room to await an examination by Coroner's Physician Donlin. No effort was made to do the task upon the body until Dr. Donlin had arrived.

DISCOVERY DRE WA CROWD.

At 7:30 o'clock this morning Joseph Morgan, a boatman, living at No. 73 Pacific street, saw an object bobbing up and down on the water near the shore. He drew it in with a boathook and found it was a man's thigh well preserved.

Morgan notified Policeman Ross.

The thigh was taken to the Fifteenth Precinct police station, at Emmett and Amity streets, Captain Michael Campbell at once notified Police Headquarters in the city, and detectives were sent over to confirm the suspicion that the thigh was a part of the body kept at the Morgue.

PARTS FIT PERFECTLY.

Dr. Donlin arrived at the Morgue at 2 o'clock.

He at once began taking the measurements of the thigh. When he had finished he said:

"This is undoubtedly the leg of the trunk."

The scars, Dr. Donlin said, were post-mortem marks.

EXTR

(BY WIRE TO THE EVENING JOURNAL FRE

DANGER OF RIOT IN PA

PARIS, Feb. 11.—At 4 o'clock the crowd outside the blocked all the neighboring streets, extending to the Po closed by the police.

It became evident that a serious demonstration close of the session, and a large force of troops was barracks. After the interruption of the sitting Colonel P testimony. "The interests of my chiefs," he said, "redd I was sent away on a secret official mission. This was in pursuing the investigation despite the discouragement attitude of my superiors."

Then there followed several genuinely French incide Picquart was confronted with several previous witnesses did not agree with him in certain points, each reaffirmed th dience giving loud expression to its sympathies on both si

REDMOND AMENDMENT OVERWHELMINGL

LONDON, Feb. 11.—In the House of Commons this a debate this evening, Mr. Redmond taunted Mr. Dillon, lodge, with not having moved a similar amendment. Nationalist cause was sacrificed to the maintainance of

Mr. James O'Kelly, Parnellite, member for North ended Redmond's motion. Sir William Harcourt, the L that Mr. Redmond had asked the Liberals to repudiate home rule bills with the consent of the Irish party. No effort was ment was rejected by a vote of 223 to 65.

EDGEMONT SMELTING COMPANY GON

TRENTON, Feb. 11.—A receiver was appointed to mont and Union Hill Smelting Company, a South Dakota ated in New Jersey with a capital of $6,000,000. This is on in which Cashier Quinlan is said to have invested the fun Bank, of New York. The receiver is Savery Bradley, of Ph

MR. ASTOR GETS HIS TAXES RED

John Jacob Astor got his personal taxes reduced in th to-day from $2,000,000 to $250,000. Mr. Astor admitted own million dollars' worth of property, but said that he was $250,000 worth on hishotel.

MORE MEN WALKED THE PLAN

Thirty-six employes of the Brooklyn Bureau of build were dismissed this afternoon.

WANTS TO RENT PIER

The New York and Monmouth Transportation Comp Dock Board to-day for the lease of Pier 1 for ten years The pier is now rented to the Iron Steamboat Company.

FOUND IN LONELY PLACES.

THEY ARE ABANDONED IN THE RAILROAD YARDS.

AND DISCOVERED IN DARK DOORWAYS.

Twenty Murdered Babies Found in Harlem Streets.

The Harlem police are convinced that a baby farm is in operation within their district. Twenty bodies of slaughtered babes have been found within the last month in doorways, alleys and secluded spots. A mysterious woman was seen at Park avenue and Ninety-eighth street carrying a small wooden box, which she threw under the "L" road. A policeman picked up the box and found it contained the body of an infant two days old. The scene in the sketch show some of the discoveries of dead babies by the police.

told of the treatment she received at the hands of Mrs. Gogand, and if she dies the case will go to the Coroner's office and the midwife will be charged with murder.

Detectives on the Case

Detectives have been assigned to the case, and no efforts are to be spared to investigate it to its bottom.

Mrs. Gardner sought the services of

noon arrested four men in a Bowery lodging house who are believed by the police to be the highwaymen who on December 26 held up a trolley car near Philadelphia, shot the motorman and robbed the passengers.

The prisoners were taken to the Centre Street Court and were remanded. Philadelphia police will come to identify the linotype machine, the invention of Ottmar Mergenthaler, a German immigrant. As its name implies, Mergenthaler's machine allowed lines of type to be cast in a single operation, replacing the laborious business of casting each piece of type by hand. One man at a keyboard could now handle masses of type rapidly. The linotype machine bore a resemblance to the typewriter, which had come into use a few years earlier. More than any other industry, journalism depended on the speediness of the typewriter and the telephone. Advertising mushroomed, affecting newspaper income and the make-up of pages. It also caused editors to think twice before running news stories unfavorable to advertisers.

PRESS LORDS

Horace Greeley of the New York *Tribune* and James Gordon Bennett of the New York *Herald* both died in 1872, ending a newspaper era. A new era began with Joseph Pulitzer, a Hungarian immigrant who, after building the St. Louis *Post-Dispatch* into a great paper, took over the New York *World* in 1882. Pledging to "expose all fraud and sham, fight all public evils and abuses," Pulitzer revolutionized American journalism. He used human-interest stories, hard-hitting editorials, crusades, many illustrations, and the colored comic strip. As one of his stunts he sent "Nellie Bly" (Elizabeth Cockran) around the world; she succeeded in making a trip in better time than the hero of Jules Verne's novel *Around the World in Eighty Days.* By 1898 daily sales of the *World* passed one million.

In 1895 William Randolph Hearst invaded New York from California, took over the *Journal,* and challenged Pulitzer in a circulation war. Hearst ran a freewheeling paper often criticized for taking the low road of sensationalism, with headlines that screamed of disasters, crimes, and divorce scandals. The term "yellow press" came to

mean Hearst-style journalism, no matter who practiced it. By 1901, Pulitzer's *World* had abandoned yellow journalism, seeing that the sober *New York Times* did not need to use such sensational techniques to be successful.

MAGAZINES

The periodical press developed enormously within a few decades after the Civil War. Two well-established monthlies, *Harper's* and the *Atlantic Monthly,* spanned the Civil War era and gained another generation of devoted readers. *Scribner's Monthly* rivaled them at the time. There were also special women's magazines such as the *Ladies' Home Journal* under Cyrus Eaton, Philadelphia's leading publisher. Other magazines that obtained a mass circulation were *Good Housekeeping, Collier's,* and *Cosmopolitan.*

Magazines became vehicles for crusaders. One of the most influential journals was the *Nation,* which exposed the laxity of the Grant administration and the corruption of the Gilded Age. Under the editorship of Edwin L. Godkin, it published contributions from the best writers and scholars of the era. In 1880, Henry Demarest Lloyd began his caustic exposés of Standard Oil in the *Atlantic Monthly* and then made them the basis of his famous book *Wealth against Commonwealth.* Lloyd startled and enraged the public with the ruthlessness and dishonesty of some of the leading businessmen in America. These examples prompted similar exposés in other magazines of corruption and dishonesty after the turn of the century.

LITERATURE

The great literature published between the Civil War and World War I was a mirror of the times. Early nineteenth-century romanticism as practiced by Poe and Cooper died out. Emerson, the Sage of Concord, lived until 1882, but he ceased to be the dominant influence he had been in the full tide of the Transcendentalist movement. Walt Whitman, the "good gray poet," tended the wounded from 1862 to 1865, and wrote moving verse about Lincoln and the Civil War; but his major work, *Leaves of Grass,* dated from before the conflict. With old forms disappearing, new writers with new themes appeared on the American literary scene. In 1880, a former Civil War general and territorial governor, Lew Wallace, published a massive Biblical novel entitled *Ben Hur,* which became the first best seller of the post-Civil War period. Wallace's sales figures proved that Americans were eager for popularized literature on religion. Anthony Hope's *The Prisoner of Zenda* revealed their leaning toward escapism. The British novelist wrote a romance about a place called Ruritania, replete with royalty, dungeons, and flashing swords, and it became a best seller and pacesetter for other so-called Ruritanic novels. Lesser writers tried to capitalize on the popularity of Wallace and Hope, but these authors were the only two whose books found a lasting place in American libraries.

THE REGIONALIST SCHOOL

Unification of the continent, symbolized by the linking of the Union Pacific and Central Pacific railroads in 1869, brought an upsurge of interest in the regions between the Rockies and the West Coast. Two writers in particular had a genius for depicting American regional life.

Bret Harte found his best ideas for stories in his native California. After a rather turbulent youth in which he tried teaching, gold mining, and printing, he became editor of the *Overland Monthly* in 1868. His best work appeared in this periodical, which attracted readers everywhere as copies circulated around the country. His eye for local color, his ear for the dialect of mining camps and waterfronts, his ability to write

dramatic and humorous scenes, explain his popularity. Of the many memorable characters he created, probably the best known was the typical Western gambler, John Oakhurst of "The Outcasts of Poker Flat." Harte's comic light verse, "Plain Language from Truthful James" is still a favorite of anthologists.

The other regionalist connected with the West, Mark Twain, has been called America's greatest writer. Samuel Langhorne Clemens used the pen name of Mark Twain, and he made his boyhood in Hannibal, Missouri, part of American folklore.

One of America's greatest writers, Samuel Langhorne Clemens, or "Mark Twain," wrote humorous tales of life on the Mississippi and in the West. Clemens' realistic portrait of human relationships, his common language, and natural humor have made his works American classics.

He often watched the riverboats curving into port to the cry, "Mark twain," a seaman's term to indicate the depth of the water, and the Mississippi haunted his imagination. Later he himself worked on the riverboats. Subsequently he became a printer and went West to Virginia City and San Francisco. His pungent prose style was admirably suited to the colorful and frequently rowdy settings he chose for such works as *Life on the Mississippi, Tom Sawyer,* and *A Connecticut Yankee at King Arthur's Court.* However, *Huckleberry Finn* is considered his masterpiece. Both humorous and profound, it is a study of the "natural man" cut off from the trappings of society, as well as an attack on social hypocrisy and the philistinism of a society based on the power of money. His use of common speech rather than formal literary language in the novel also began a revolution in American prose style.

REALISM

William Dean Howells, who was the editor of the *Atlantic* in Boston for ten years, was the close friend of Mark Twain and an outstanding novelist in his own right. Howells contributed a brand of realism to American letters by his penetrating observations on American manners and morals. *A Traveler from Altruria,* which contrasted the year 1850 with 1890 in American life, was actually a utopian romance somewhat along the lines of Edward Bellamy's *Looking Backward.* His most widely read novel was *The Rise of Silas Lapham,* published in 1884, the story of a self-made man who attempted to make himself acceptable to the snobbish society of Boston. When Howells left Boston for New York in 1889, he helped shift the center of America's literary life to Manhattan. A generation of writers measured success in terms of a favorable review from his pen, yet he himself never attained the stature accorded to his friends Mark Twain and Henry James by the critics of American letters.

Henry James took society for his province, and eventually found his ideal subject in British society with its sharp class distinctions. James, brother of the philosopher William James, moved to London in 1875 and remained there permanently. He became a British subject just before his death in 1916. Writing with subtlety, he based his work on a realistic understanding of human psychology, but only as he saw human problems revealed in the behavior of ladies and gentlemen of social standing. He looked for the moral dilemmas in the world of the upper class. The naive American confronting sophisticated Europeans was a theme he returned to again and again. His characters were often cultured individuals who judged one another by the standards of a fastidious etiquette. They felt emotions without rais-

William Dean Howells, a close friend of Mark Twain, was a famous novelist and newspaper editor during the latter part of the nineteenth century. His novel, The Rise of Silas Lapham, *is now an American classic.*

ing their voices. Henry James's novels thus amounted to a dissection of the classes he knew.

NATURALISM

Other novelists sought to show a different kind of realism. They turned their attention from refined society to what has been termed naturalism, emphasizing the violence, vice, crime, and degradation of life. Stephen Crane brought home to his readers the evils bred by poverty in *Maggie, A Girl of the Streets.* He showed the horrors of war in *The Red Badge of Courage,* a powerful study of how men react in battle. Frank Norris of Chicago attacked force and fraud in business, a subject he knew well. His "Epic of Wheat" went as far as two volumes —*The Octopus* and *The Pit*—before he died in his early thirties.

Theodore Dreiser, foremost of the naturalistic writers, did not publish his most important book, *An American Tragedy,* until 1925. His earlier novel, *Sister Carrie,* had been denounced as immoral, an accusation Dreiser faced many times before his works were accepted by the reading public. In *The Financier,* a book strongly influenced by the doctrines of Social Darwinism, and the first of his major works on subjects based on American business, he sketched in acid prose the portrait of a banker.

Jack London was a true adventurer who made the trek to the Klondike along the Trail of Ninety-eight, and put his experiences into a number of dramatic short stories. Primitive violence, whether displayed by nature, animals, or men, attracted him. He could exult in a boxing match or a storm at sea. His interest in brute ferocity led him to write such tales as *The Call of the Wild,* about a sled dog that chose to revert to the wilderness rather than remain with man. London's best novel was probably *The Sea Wolf,* published in 1904, because of his superb characterization of the central figure, the volcanic sea captain, Wolf Larsen.

ART

The fine arts went through a transformation comparable to the one that took place in literature. Painting, too, felt the impact of the Civil War, so that what had gone before seemed tame and ineffectual compared to the realities of the postwar era. Like Henry James, two of the era's most talented American painters went to Europe for inspiration. James McNeil Whistler chose London where he turned out a series of important paintings in which he subordinated subject matter to "an arrangement of light, form, and color." Mary Cassatt chose Paris, where she became associated with the Impressionist movement. Absorbed in subject matter as well as color, Cassatt painted many sensitive studies of mothers with their children. Other American artists studied abroad, but most returned to America to pursue their careers.

SYMBOLISM

The painter most affected by pre-Civil War attitudes was Albert Pinkham Ryder, whose work on canvas may be compared to the prose of Edgar Allen Poe. He was moved by darkness, moonlight, spectral figures, and symbols of tragic or uncanny events. A characteristic painting was *The Flying Dutchman,* inspired by Wagner's doomed operatic hero. Ryder, however, was too much a man of his time to evade realism, or to remain untouched by actual events. He fused symbolism and realism in *Death on a Pale Horse,* a theme which came to him when he heard of a man who committed suicide after losing his money on a horse race. Ryder showed Death as a ghostly apparition galloping, scythe in hand, around a race track.

REGIONALISM

The outstanding regionalist among American artists was Winslow Homer, who painted scenes from his native New England, particularly the rocky shores and pounding surf of the coast. During the Civil War, Homer drew illustrations for *Harper's Weekly,* developing skills of observation and technique, as well as training in realism, qualities evident in the New England scenes he painted after the war. A poet and dramatist of the sea, he put high color and a sense of movement into paintings with such descriptive titles as *The Hurricane* and *Breaking Storm.* His *Crack the Whip* caught the joy of children at play.

NATURALISM

Thomas Eakins, often considered America's most outstanding painter, pursued artistic naturalism. Thus, as with naturalism in literature, many were dismayed to see his portrait of President Hayes at work in his shirt sleeves, and a concert singer painted with the muscles in her throat distinctly visible. Determined to show life as it was, Eakins gained entrance to hospitals and medical schools, sketched what he saw,

and painted two magnificent group studies, *The Surgical Clinic of Professor Gross* and *The Clinic of Professor Agnew.* However, Eakins' stark realism did not totally represent his great artistry. His *The Swimming Hole* and *Boating on the Schuylkill,* for example, were infused with a romantic feeling for the natural world.

Eakins' naturalism was followed by a more extreme realism, as exemplified in the Ashcan School. John Sloan is the best remembered of the artists in this group. Their style received its name from an attraction

The Surgical Clinic of Professor Gross *by Thomas Eakins. In an attempt to portray hospitals and medical schools realistically, Eakins' paintings were long considered too "indelicate" for the public, and he was barred from exhibiting.*

The Gulf Stream *by Winslow Homer. An advocate of realism, Homer's paintings of his native New England displayed a flair for color and movement.*

to sordid scenes, usually taken from life in the big cities—scenes of asphalt underfoot and machines and ashcans at the curb. Their work paralleled the literary themes of Crane and Dreiser. The Ashcan School dominated the art scene until 1913, when the Armory Show in New York opened a new era in the history of American art.

POLITICAL CARTOONISTS

Joseph Keppler helped make *Puck* the best satirical publication of the late nineteenth century by drawing political cartoons which the magazine ran in vivid color. An outstanding cartoon was one in which he portrayed the new President, Chester A. Arthur, rejecting his old mentor, Senator Roscoe Conkling of New York. Keppler saw this as the scene from Shakespeare in which Henry V, newly crowned, rejected his old mentor, Falstaff. It was the most effective comment in any medium on the national situation immediately follow-ing the assassination of President Garfield.

The most famous political cartoonist of the Gilded Age, however, was Thomas Nast of *Harper's*. The scourge of the Tweed Ring, he once drew Boss Tweed and his cronies as harpies with beaks and talons, and called the caricature *Let Us Prey*. Nast had a genius for inventing symbols. Three of these symbols remain familiar to all voters, long after Nast's time, the Donkey for the Democratic Party, the Elephant for the Republicans, and the Tiger for Tammany Hall in New York City.

ARCHITECTURE

One of the most quoted statements about modern architecture, "Form follows function," was made by the American architect,

The famous Kaufmann or "falling water" house in Bear Run, Pennsylvania, designed and built by Frank Lloyd Wright in 1936.

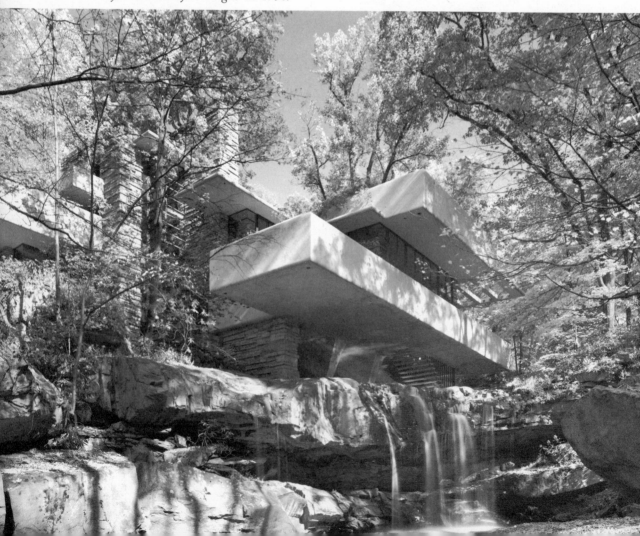

Louis Sullivan. He offered it as his prescription for rescuing architecture from the pretentious pseudo-Gothic and French provincial styles of the Gilded Age. He maintained that an architect should first consider the use to which a building would be put, and then decide on its form. A house called for one type of architecture, an office for another, a store for yet another. In line with his concept, Sullivan designed the skyscraper, a form of building which embodied the spirit of American enterprise. He designed monumental buildings in Chicago, St. Louis, and elsewhere, and a number of small banks and warehouses in the Midwest. His use of vertical steel frames and an abundance of windows can be seen in the Wainwright Building in St. Louis and the Auditorium Building in Chicago.

To Frank Lloyd Wright, Sullivan was "The Master." Yet during his career of over sixty years he was able to leave a deeper imprint than any other American on his field. Born in 1869, Wright was still influencing the direction of architecture at the time of his death in 1959. His creations hold a prominent place among the great buildings of the past century. The "Falling Water" house near Pittsburgh, the Larkin Building in Buffalo, the Imperial Hotel in Tokyo, and the Guggenheim Museum in New York, to name only a few of his buildings, represent Wright's highly original contribution to American architecture.

Wright called his style "organic architecture." His buildings seemed to grow out of the landscape around them. Both he and Sullivan developed their theories in the years before World War I, when so many thinkers were turning from form to function and applying the metaphor of "organism." Wright's organic architecture broke with past traditions, as did contemporary thought in philosophy, law, sociology, economics, and history. His work stands as an example of how a climate of opinion can infuse men in different fields with similar ideas during a given era.

Readings

GENERAL WORKS

Aaron, Daniel, *Men of Good Hope*. New York: Oxford University Press, 1951—A study of progressive intellectuals which stresses their optimistic tone and their faith in reform.

Bellot, H. H., *American History and American Historians*. Norman: University of Oklahoma Press, 1952—An analysis of American historiographic trends from about 1890 through 1940. Bellot considers this era to be dominated by nationalism in historical writing.

Commager, Henry S., *The American Mind*. New Haven, Conn.: Yale University Press, 1950—Commager's survey of American intellectual history since the 1880s is based on the idea that during this period a particularly American way of thought appeared.

Cubberly, Ellsworth P., *Public Education in the United States*. Boston: Houghton Mifflin, 1919—An introductory work on the subject by a pioneer in the history of American education. Cubberly tends to identify public education as both a product and determinant of American democracy.

Hofstadter, Richard, and Walter P. Metzger, *The Development of Academic Freedom in the United States*, Vol. II. New York: Columbia University Press, 1955—The second volume, by Metzger, traces the history of academic freedom at a time when large universities were forming and growing. Metzger maintains that academic freedom grew when an increasingly professional faculty reacted against control by churches or business forces.

Kazin, Alfred, *On Native Grounds*. New York: Harcourt, Brace, 1942—A cultural history of American literature since 1890, tracing divergent tendencies and calling for more searching criticism of American writers' works.

Larkin, Oliver W., *Art and Life in America*: New York: Holt, Rinehart and Winston, 1960—In this standard, well-illustrated history of American art, Larkin is more concerned with the cultural influences on American art, and their role in revealing American society, than in purely esthetic matters.

Martin, Jay, *Harvest of Change: American Literature 1865–1914*. Englewood Cliffs, N.J.: Prentice-Hall, 1967—A general history of American literature which concentrates on the works themselves while putting them into an historical context.

White, Morton G., *Social Thought in Amer-*

ica. Boston: Beacon, 1957—In the years around the turn of the century, White maintains, social theorists ranging from Oliver Wendell Holmes in law to Thorstein Veblen in economics to Charles Beard in history formulated new ways of looking at society that rejected abstract, formal theorizing for a greater realism.

Wish, Harvey, *Society and Thought in Modern America*, Vol. II. New York: David McKay, 1962—An account of American social and intellectual history emphasizing our European background and the lasting importance of religious and ethnic differences in American life.

SPECIAL STUDIES

Andrews, Wayne, *Architecture, Ambition and Americans*. New York: Free Press, 1964—A social history of American architecture since colonial times. Andrews concentrates on architecture as an art form, rather than as a social instrument.

Bleyer, Willard G., *Main Currents in the History of American Journalism*. New York: Plenun, 1969—A survey of the development of the American newspaper since colonial times.

Burchard, John E., and Albert Bush-Brown, *The Architecture of America*. Boston: Little, Brown, 1961—A history of American architecture in its social context. The authors emphasize the European background of most trends in American architecture.

Carter, Everett, *Howells and the Age of Realism*. Hamden, Conn.: Shoestring Press, 1954—Carter argues that Howells typified the career and craft of American authors of the late nineteenth century, an age dominated by literary realism.

Case, Robert O., and Victoria Case, *We Called It Culture: The Story of Chautauqua*. Garden City, N.Y.: Doubleday, 1948—As a form of mass adult education and entertainment, the Chautauqua movement was an important cultural influence on some thirty million Americans. Yet, the Cases point out, Chautauqua reached its peak before the inroads of radio, movies, and other electronic media.

Cremin, Lawrence A., *The Transformation of the School: Progressivism in American Education, 1876–1957*. New York: Knopf, 1961—Cremin traces the intellectual origins of progressive education, the influence of progressivism on the teaching profession itself, and the gradual splitting and decline of the progressive education movement.

Mott, Frank L., *A History of American Magazines 1885–1905*. Cambridge, Mass.: Harvard University Press, 1957—During the decades Mott discusses, magazines gained mass circulation, began extensive advertising, and, in some cases, started to criticize the operation of American institutions in muckraking journalism.

Rudolph, Frederick, *The American College and University, A History*. New York: Knopf, 1962—A general survey of higher education in America.

Tunnard, Christopher, and Henry H. Reed, *American Skyline: The Growth and Form of our Cities and Towns*. New York: New American Library, 1956—A history of the growth of urban society from the perspective of architecture and city planning.

Veysey, Laurence R., *The Emergence of the American University*. Chicago, 1965: University of Chicago Press—Veysey concentrates on disputes about universities' intellectual and moral purposes which took place largely before 1890 and the struggles for control of the new universities between approximately 1890 and 1910.

PRIMARY SOURCES

Hofstadter, Richard, and Wilson Smith, eds., *American Higher Education, A Documentary History*, Vols. I–II. Chicago: University of Chicago Press, 1961—A collection of documents on American colleges and universities which combines evidence about educational administrations with reflections about the nature and purpose of higher education.

Lerner, Max, ed., *The Mind and Faith of Justice Holmes*. New York: Random House, 1954—A collection of Justice Holmes's essays, speeches, letters, and judicial opinions revealing both Holmes's character, and his social and legal philosophy.

Miller, Perry, *American Thought: Civil War to World War I*. New York: Holt, Rinehart and Winston, 1954—An anthology which also includes an analytical introduction by Miller, one of America's foremost intellectual historians.

Veblen, Thorstein, *The Theory of the Leisure Class*. New York: New American Library, 1964—Veblen's sarcastic attack on the life styles of upper class Americans. Veblen claims that waste and ostentation were the main characteristics produced by the American business system.

BIOGRAPHIES

Barker, Charles A., *Henry George*. New York: Oxford University Press, 1955—A biography of the originator of the single tax plan which argues that George was fundamentally a backward-looking thinker whose theory was suitable for a society in which land, rather than capital, was the basic form of wealth.

Edel, Leon, *Henry James*. Minneapolis: University of Minnesota Press, 1960—A brief study of the famous American novelist who did most of his work in Britain. Edel is also the author of a definitive multivolume biography of James.

Hook, Sidney, *John Dewey*. New York: John Day, 1939—A short biographical sketch of John Dewey's life followed by an analysis and commentary on Dewey's social and philosophical doctrines. Hook defends Dewey's theories from radical and conservative critics.

Kaplan, Justin, *Mr. Clemens and Mark Twain*. New York: Simon & Schuster, 1966—Kaplan's biography of Twain portrays the author as a rugged, independent man who allowed himself to be cast into a genteel literary mold by the same Gilded Age forces which he attacked so powerfully.

Morgan, Arthur E., *Edward Bellamy*. Yellow Springs, Ohio: Community Service, 1944—A biography of the late nineteenth-century utopian novelist and social reformer which devotes considerable attention to the ideas Bellamy advanced in *Looking Backward*.

Perry, Ralph B., *The Thought and Character of William James*. Cambridge, Mass.: Harvard University Press, 1948—A biography of the great pragmatic philosopher, emphasizing James's search for "usable truth" and the reconciliation of faith and experience.

THE "BRAINS"

THAT ACHIEVED THE TAMMANY VICTORY AT THE ROCHESTER DEMOCRATIC CONVENTION.

21

Politics in the Gilded Age

The man who is employed for wages is as much a business man as his employer; the attorney in a country town is as much a business man as the corporation counsel in a great metropolis; the merchant at the cross-roads is as much a business man as the merchant of New York; the farmer who goes forth in the morning and toils all day—who begins in the spring and toils all summer—and who by the application of brain and muscle to the natural resources of the country creates wealth, is as much a business man as the man who goes upon the board of trade and bets upon the price of grain. . . .

—William Jennings Bryan

A Thomas Nast cartoon of "Boss Tweed," the ruler of New York's Tammany Hall.

From 1877 to 1896 the United States was in the process of becoming fully industrialized, but neither the government nor the political parties dealt effectively with the new social and economic conditions produced by industrialization. They took for granted the necessity for a laissez-faire economy and a hands-off attitude toward government regulation of business. In a time of growing railroad monopolies; oil monopolies; and sugar, iron, and steel trusts, this gave business interests a freedom they tended to abuse. Vital social and economic issues were avoided by politicians whose careers depended on the support of business interests, and few men in office were willing to risk their careers to promote timely and original legislation.

POLITICS IN THE LATE NINETEENTH CENTURY

Both parties depended for funds on captains of enterprise, who contributed large sums to both the Republicans and the Democrats. By the 1880s, the politics of business had begun to replace such Senate party bosses as Zachariah Chandler of Michigan and John A. "Black Jack" Logan of Illinois with men who had earned fortunes in business and now sought political power. These spoilsmen had control over the distribution of a tremendous number of federal, state, and local jobs to the party faithful, regardless of qualifications. As a result, the public service was riddled with inefficiency and corruption.

The era was dominated by Republican Party officeholders, but a basic balance of power existed between the parties. Grover Cleveland, the only Democratic President in the period, was elected partly because he reassured businessmen that the Democratic Party was no more of a threat to them than the Republican Party. "No harm shall come to any business interest as the result of administrative policy so long as I am President," he said, adding that "a transfer of executive control from one party to another does not mean any serious disturbance of existing conditions." Extremely close elections between 1876 and 1892 resulted in an avoidance of issues by both parties.

Cleveland's campaign remarks emphasized the continued stability of government regardless of which of the two parties was in power. He was the embodiment of the conservative view that the role of government was to promote economy and efficiency. It was to be the arbiter between equal and contending interests. This was an unrealistic attitude, considering the great power of private enterprise. To other groups in the country, farmers and laborers especially, the lack of difference between the two major parties proved that both were dominated by the same Eastern industrial interests. In its platform of 1892, the newly formed Populist Party looked back at the age and said: "We have witnessed for more than a quarter of a century the struggles of the two great political parties, while grievous wrongs have been inflicted upon the suffering people. We charge that the controlling influences dominating both these parties have permitted the existing dreadful conditions to develop without serious effort to prevent or restrain them."

Historians have generally agreed with this judgment of American political life in the late nineteenth century. Minor issues and power squabbles between and within the two parties took the center of the stage. Republicans continued to wave "the bloody shirt," reminding voters that the Democrats were the party of rebellion and that the Republicans had saved the Union. As late as the campaign of 1888, Benjamin Harrison was still using this technique in his bid for the Presidency. Within the Republican Party, Roscoe Conkling, of the "Stalwart" faction, fought with James G. Blaine, a "Half-breed." There were similar factions within the Democratic Party. The names were colorful, but the battle was largely for power, not over issues.

Even if politicians had understood that industrial growth called for new ideas of government responsibility, they would have been hampered by the traditional attitude that the government should not interfere in the nation's economic and social life. Moreover, the Civil War was still recent enough for them to want to avoid real issues that might renew bloodshed. It was an interim period during which tensions grew over specific issues that would eventually lead to reforms. Two major problems, the need for civil service reform in an expanding government and the need for aid to the farmer finally reached the critical point. In the final analysis, however, party politics determined the way these problems would be resolved.

THE REPUBLICAN PARTY

The Republican Party drew most of its support from the industrialized Northeast and the Middle West. Though these areas had conflicting interests, they were held together by a lingering party loyalty and memories of their common effort to preserve the Union. The farming community of the Midwest, more settled and prosperous than the Far West, was especially solid.

This regional alliance was joined by two other groups which became reliably Republican after the Civil War: Union army veterans and blacks.

"Vote as you fought!" still had political appeal. The Grand Army of the Republic was a powerful pressure group in this period. With patriotic talk, the party supported high veterans' pensions, generosity to the men who had fought for the Union being a point of honor. Although the pensions were given out carelessly and in huge amounts so that they became a bonanza for the greedy, the issue was not a completely bogus one. Maimed soldiers forced to beg for a livelihood were a common sight in parts of Europe. Blacks in the North and the South consistently voted Republican even though the party's concern for voting rights was more a matter of politics than of principles. Southern Democrats had committed themselves firmly to white supremacy, leaving black people little choice.

The Republican Party was thus a coalition of groups not really related to each other by interests or issues. When issues did arise, there were breaches in party unity. The most dangerous rift occurred between Eastern businessmen and Western grain growers. The businessmen favored a high tariff, a gold standard for the currency backed by gold in the Treasury, and legislation that fattened the profits of the railroads and other industrial giants. Though there were some farmers who supported the gold standard and a high tariff, most objected that these policies held down the money supply and raised the price of manufactured goods. Virtually all farmers disliked the railroads' high freight rates and widespread influence in politics.

THE DEMOCRATIC PARTY

The two great strongholds of the Democratic Party were the South and the machine-dominated cities of the Northeast. The Bourbon leadership in the South, playing on racial fears that had heightened since Reconstruction, was certain of support by most whites, including those who were poor and uneducated. Even when poor white farmers saw their own interests defeated by the entrenched order, they did not join any third party for fear that such action might weaken the Democrats enough to return the Republicans and their black allies to power.

In contrast to the Southern bloc, there was the predominantly Catholic, immigrant, industrial worker block of votes in the Northeastern cities. The cities themselves were run by political opportunists like Boss Tweed. Tweed himself was ousted in the early 1870s, but Tammany Hall and its machine bosses remained, as did the inheritors of the Gas Ring of Philadelphia.

There was also a small, conservative business wing in the Democratic Party consisting of merchants and bankers in the East who supported the Democrats because they wanted a lower tariff and favored sound money. Democratic leaders in the Middle West were also business-oriented conservatives, and their leadership was resented by the farmers, workers, and small businessmen in the party.

PRESIDENT V. CONGRESS

In the ongoing power struggle between the executive and legislative branches, Congress clearly had the upper hand from 1877 to 1896. No President, during this period, saw his party in control of both houses throughout his tenure of office. Republicans usually dominated the staid Senate, and Democrats the smokier, noisier House of Representatives. The President had neither the staff nor the funds to play a leading executive role.

There were other reasons for the weakness of the executive branch. Impeachment proceedings against Andrew Johnson strengthened the hand of Congress and showed its aggressive determination to dominate the government. Following Johnson, Grant had exerted little executive authority. His lax administration gave free reign to the assumption of more power by spoilsmen and political bosses. When Hayes took over and tried to exert moral authority from the White House, he met with opposition and derision from party bosses and lost any chance he had of being reelected.

In an isolationist era the Presidency offered a limited scope for action in world affairs. The office was left with little to make it appear glamorous or heroic. One President after another complained that he had to spend endless hours doling out minor political jobs. The Chief Executive became almost a figurehead to put the seal of approval on patronage appointments, while the party bosses ruled behind the scenes.

The patronage system—one of the hallmarks of the age—was as evident in the capital as bossism was in machine-dominated states and cities. Mark Twain noted, "every individual you encounter in Washington almost—and certainly every separate and distinct individual in the public employment, from the highest bureau chief, clear down to the maid who scrubs Department Halls . . . represents Political Influence."

The Pendleton Act, or Civil Service Reform Act, was the first permanent legislative action taken against the patronage system. More than a decade of protest by reformers had failed to inspire the public to pressure Congress for reform, but in the wake of President Garfield's assassination by a disappointed office-seeker, demands for reform swept the Congress. The effect of Garfield's death was more powerful than pleas for reform from a living President might have been. The Reform Act, passed in 1883, created a Civil Service Commission to oversee a new merit system for public office. The Commission's function was to give examinations, and to ensure that parties did not extort contributions from

Virtues of Civil Service Reform

66 *The perversion of the Civil Service to a mere party machine is pitilessly cruel. Lately there was an officer in one of the departments, faithful, industrious, valuable. Misfortune fell upon his home, and from his lean salary he scraped a shred to buy comfort for a sick daughter. One day he was politically assessed, but he honestly stated his utter inability to pay. He was reported and condemned. To remove him was impracticable because of the influence that appointed him—so he was "cut down." Against this inhuman blow he struggled as he could, seeking extra work at night, fighting to keep*

*himself and his family honestly alive.
The struggle was too severe. He had been
indeed "cut down," and he died. By the
charity of his fellow-clerks he was
decently buried and his family were
helped to their Western friends. That
man was our officer, doing our duty,
doing it well. And how many lives are
hanging at this moment in agony of
terror by that single thread of patronage.
It is unspeakable cruelty. I do not hold
the immediate appointing power
responsible for this tragedy. It is the
crime of the system. . . .*

*The Civil-Service Reform therefore
begins with the assertion that there is no
reason in the nature of things or of our
form of government that the United
States should not manage its affairs with
the same economy, ability, and honesty
that the best private business is managed;
and that to do this it must take the most
obvious means not incompatible with the
Constitution, with a popular government,
with experience and common-sense. It
therefore proposes a system of
examinations and probations open to all
citizens; the appointments to the
subordinate offices to be made from those
proved to be best qualified. . . .*

*. . . it will be a day of thanksgiving in
America when the mere party politician
in Congress shall no longer quarter his
bottle-holders and runners upon the
purses of the American people.*

*The objections which are urged against
this imperative reform show rather a
desire to oppose than any reason in
opposition. . . .* "

—*George W. Curtis*

Evils of Civil Service Reform

" *This Civil Service Law is the biggest fraud
of the age. It is the curse of the nation.*

*There can't be no real patriotism while it
acts. How are you goin' to interest our
young men in their country if you have
no offices to give them when they work
for their party? Just look at things in this
city to-day. There are ten thousand good
offices, but we can't get at more than a
few hundred of them. How are we goin'
to provide for the thousands of men who
worked for the Tammany ticket? It can't
be done. These men were full of
patriotism a short time ago. They
expected to be servin' their city, but
when we tell them that we can't place
them, do you think their patriotism is
goin' to last? Not much. They say:
"What's the use of workin' for your
country anyhow? There's nothin' in the
game." And what can they do? I don't
know, but I'll tell you what I do know. I
know more than one young man in past
years who worked for the ticket and was
just overflowin' with patriotism, but when
he was knocked out by the civil service
humbug he got to hate his country and
became an Anarchist.*

*This ain't no exaggeration. I have good
reason for sayin' that most of the
Anarchists in this city to-day are men who
ran up against civil service examinations.
Isn't it enough to make a man sour on his
country when he wants to serve it and
won't be allowed unless he answers a lot
of fool questions about the number of
cubic inches of water in the Atlantic and
the quality of sand in the Sahara
desert? . . .*

*When the people elected Tammany,
they knew just what they were doin'. We
didn't put up any false pretences. We
didn't go in for humbug civil service and
all that rot. We stood as we have always
stood, for rewardin' the men that won the
victory. They call that the spoils system.
All right; Tammany is for the spoils
system, and when we go in we fire every
anti-Tammany man from office that can
be fired under the law.* "

—*George W. Plunkitt*

public officials or discharge qualified office-holders for political reasons. At first only about 10 percent of the total offices came under the Commission's jurisdiction. However, Presidents were empowered to enlarge the list of offices on the merit system, and in the next sixty years they repeatedly did so. By 1950 about 90 percent of federal employees were under the merit system.

Yet reform of the civil service did not reform the governmental processes. Bosses of city machines, national party bosses, and Senators representing business interests continued to have more real power than the President. These "desk politicians" worked closely with lobbyists and business leaders to obtain funds once received from grateful officeholders. Less in evidence to the public than earlier party bosses, these men aided the railroads, or Standard Oil, or the sugar trust, behind the scenes for a price. The historian Henry Adams sneered, "Great leaders, like Sumner and Conkling, could not be burlesqued; they were more grotesque than ridicule could make them." Nevertheless, their power went unchallenged, and they steered through Congress legislation desired by private enterprise.

POLITICAL REFORM

To fight corruption and careless political power, several groups favoring reform appeared in different sections of the country, but they were unable to unite to build an effective coalition. There were conservative reformers of high social position who were opposed to the spoils system and patronage appointments but who continued to adhere to a belief in government based on traditional concepts of laissez-faire economics. Men such as George W. Curtis, the editor of *Harper's Weekly*, and Carl Schurz could never reconcile themselves to cooperation with agrarian, working-class, or socialist reformers who were trying to build an America in which business interests would be carefully restricted by government controls. Though both groups opposed the spread of business influence on government policy, their criticisms arose from different assumptions. There was a large, unbridgeable gap between men like Henry Adams, grandson of John Quincy Adams, and Eugene V. Debs, union organizer and socialist, or William Jennings Bryan, spokesman for the interests of the farmers.

Adams belonged to a relatively small group within the Republican Party, nicknamed "Mugwumps," made up of intelligent, critical men who could not stand manipulators like Conkling. They also advocated lowering the tariff to bring American industry into competition with the rest of the world. Although this view was in accord with prevailing laissez-faire economic theory and although scholars tried to show that American manufacturers no longer needed such protection, the high tariff persisted. Revenues from the tariff brought large amounts of money into the Treasury, and the party bosses used the Treasury surplus for their payoffs, log-rolling bills, veterans' pensions, and other politically profitable expenditures. They scoffed at the Republican reformers as impractical, nonpolitical theorizers.

Described as "sober, thoughtful, middle-class men," the Mugwumps did not speak the same language as the farmers. Their name was apt; it came from an Indian word meaning "great chief," which also had the connotation of assumed superiority to others.

The Mugwumps had an aristocratic disdain for the masses and a distinct fear of radicalism. A good example was Carl Schurz, Secretary of the Interior during the Hayes administration and a leading reformer. He and a few others led the group that deserted the Republican Party in 1884 when James G. Blaine, boss of the Half-breeds, was nominated for the Presidency. Schurz was a German immigrant, well-educated, and with a better knowledge of the pressures of industrialization than most men of his day. However, he had fears of insurrection in America, and his main concern during the Great Strike of 1877 during Hayes's administration was its revolutionary overtones. At one point he also docked by 20 percent the pay of workers who, under a new federal law, were required to work only an 8-hour day. It was evident that the reforms envisioned by Mugwumps were very different from reforms called for by labor.

The sectional divisions that troubled the nation as a whole and endangered the major parties also divided the reformers. Disagreements between Northern and Southern farmers over the issue of white supremacy made it difficult for them to unite. Within the South itself, poor black farmers found it impossible to organize with poor white farmers. Pro-reform Democrats did not mingle easily with pro-reform Republicans. Conservative reformers in the East were separated from groups elsewhere that wanted economic changes regarded as too radical by the Easterners. Thus, it was fairly remarkable that bipartisan legislation such as the Civil Service Reform Act could be enacted at all, and a truly national drive against political corruption and monopolies did not get under way until the 1890s.

CONSERVATIVE CONTROL

HAYES AS PRESIDENT

When Rutherford B. Hayes took office in 1877, the nation was in the middle of a worsening depression, the spoils system inherited from the Grant administration dominated American politics, and there was no thought of reform legislation. Hayes, a conservative politician who had helped found the Republican Party in Ohio, had been a general in the Civil War and governor of Ohio for three terms. Generally respected for his integrity, he tried hard to govern according to his principles. There was an aura of small-town morality about him and his family. His wife earned the nickname "Lemonade Lucy" for banning alcohol from White House affairs.

As President, Hayes planned to continue the policies of efficient administration and reform of the civil service that had earned him respect in Ohio. However, these ideas were not popular with the bosses of his party, and he further diminished his authority as a party leader by announcing that he would serve only one term. In addition, it was remembered that he had been nominated only as a compromise candidate when the party men failed to agree on another choice; and the results of his election contest with Tilden were also in dispute. Roscoe Conkling, the New York boss, derided him as "His Fraudulency," and Conkling's opinion that he had no real right to the office was shared by many others.

HAYES AND REFORM

The new President took immediate action to create a reform administration. Selecting a Cabinet on the basis of talent, he risked the displeasure of party leaders. The new Secretary of State, William M. Evarts, had developed a dislike for Conkling and the corrupt Customs House of New York. The new Treasurer, John Sherman of Ohio, was another advocate of reform. Carl Schurz was appointed Secretary of the Interior, because Hayes believed he would bring an honesty and efficiency to his department which would serve as a model for the rest of the government. When Hayes appointed Donald Key, a former Confederate, to head the Post Office, the patience of the party bosses finally ran out. Under their leadership, the Senate broke with the tradition of accepting the President's Cabinet nominations and sent Hayes's nominations into committee for more consideration. There was so strong a public reaction against this purely political maneuver, however, that within a few days the committee accepted the appointments and all were passed.

After this minor victory, Hayes spoke repeatedly about the need for reform, and

President and Mrs. Rutherford B. Hayes. A former Civil War general and three-time governor of Ohio, Hayes was a conservative who helped reform the corrupt government he inherited from Grant.

his cabinet continued its housecleaning. But reforms within the administration, when accomplished, resulted from the personal initiative of the President; there was no legislative action. The spoils system was so deeply entrenched that only in the Interior Department was the merit system effectively introduced. Hayes's crusade climaxed in a long struggle with Conkling over the New York Customs House. Two thirds of the nation's revenue came through that port, and a bevy of corrupt officials drew profits from it. The Customs House was a Republican plum and Conkling's special territory. "It is my wish that the collection of the revenues shall be free from partisan control," Hayes wrote to the Secretary of the Treasury. It remained a wish, however. No attention was paid to his directives, and he finally had to ask for the resignation of two Conkling appointments, Collector of the Port Chester A. Arthur and Naval Officer Alonzo B. Cornell. Conkling fought the dismissals in the Senate, but Hayes revealed records exposing the extent of graft at the port, and won his case. Yet there was no wholesale housecleaning of the spoils system, and when Hayes left the Presidency, most of the initiative for reform left with him.

HAYES AND LABOR

The depression that began in 1873 worsened after Hayes took office, particularly in the cities. *The New York Times* noted in 1877 that it expected a summer death toll of a thousand infants each week in the city. Large numbers of men were unemployed, and the power of the unions fell close to zero, since it was easy to break any strike with fresh supplies of workers.

Railroad workers felt keenly how weak their lack of organization made them in face of the power of the large railroads. In July, 1877, partly in protest against a 10 percent wage cut, the "Great Strike" against the railroads began. At the request of the state governors, Hayes sent federal troops into West Virginia, Pennsylvania, Maryland, and Illinois, thus setting a precedent used by later Presidents. With federal intervention the strikes were broken, but Hayes noted in his diary: "The strikes have been put down by *force,* but now for the *real* remedy. Can't something be done by education of the strikers, by judicious control of the capitalists, by wise general policy to end or diminish the evil? The railroad strikers, as a rule are good men sober intelligent and industrious." While Schurz worried about possible revolution, Hayes felt concern for the workers' welfare. He wanted a solution to the problem of labor unrest but had no specific proposals for dealing with the mass suffering of industrial workers.

Hayes further antagonized labor on the issue of Chinese immigration. A treaty with China in 1868 allowed for free immigration of Chinese laborers to the United States, and employers welcomed the treaty, but laborers, particularly on the West Coast, were soon protesting heatedly against cheap Chinese labor in the job market. This sentiment led Congress to pass a bill in 1879 restricting immigration. Hayes, true to form, vetoed the bill as a matter of principle. "I suspect that this bill is inconsistent with our treaty obligations," he wrote in his diary, although he realized that Chinese immigration was a problem. "If it violates the national faith I must decline to approve it." In keeping with his idea of good faith he immediately negotiated a new treaty with China, permitting the United States to restrict immigration. In this way he avoided breaking a treaty and also accomplished what the workers wanted. However, Hayes's popularity had been marred by his veto.

MONETARY POLICIES

Before Hayes came to office, Congress had passed the Specie Resumption Act of 1875, calling for the government to make all currency redeemable in gold by 1879. This act had been largely engineered by John Sherman, who was now Hayes's Secretary of the Treasury. On taking office, Sherman set out to fill the Treasury with gold and improve the reputation of the dollar.

At the same time that the Hayes administration was working to make the dollar more sound, a different credo was becoming popular among farmers and some workers. They believed that the government's "sound money" policy made the depression worse by raising the value of the dollar. Instead of hoarding money in the Treasury, they thought the government needed to increase the amount in circulation—a move that would inflate the currency.

There were two prominent proposals for increasing the money supply. The Greenback Party, which received over a million votes in the 1878 elections, believed in inflating the currency by keeping the greenbacks issued during the Civil War in circulation, even if they were not completely backed with gold. Others wanted to inflate the money supply by free and unlimited coinage of silver in addition to gold. Silver had been eliminated as a monetary standard in 1873 but at about the same time enormous new deposits of the precious metal were found in the West. As a result, silver became cheaper and farmers began to demand its free and unlimited coinage. Pressure from the "silverites" and opposition from monetary conservatives led to the passage of the Bland-Allison Act of 1878. It was a compromise measure that did not give the silverites "free and unlimited" coinage of silver, but provided that the Treasury would buy between two and four million dollars' worth of silver every month, and coin it at the ratio of sixteen times as much silver in a silver dollar as there was gold in a gold dollar. Hayes used his veto on the Bland-Allison Act also, but Congress overrode it.

The money question, like the other issues of Hayes's administration, was not resolved. The silverites still pressed for unlimited coinage of silver, and Sherman continued to balance silver coinage with gold coinage, thus preventing an inflated currency. But with the return of prosperity by 1880, there was not a sufficient money supply to match the expansion of the economy.

Hayes's efforts for reform in government had illuminated the conflict between reformers and spoilsmen, but nothing permanent was achieved except that Hayes made himself unpopular with party bosses and voters. Hayes later regained some public respect at the end of his administration, however, since the depression had lifted, unemployment had decreased, and farm prices had risen. The 1880s were to be fairly prosperous times for most Americans.

HANCOCK-GARFIELD CAMPAIGN

With Hayes out of the running, the two major factions of the Republican Party, the Stalwarts and the Half-breeds, engaged in a bitter struggle to obtain the nomination for one of their own supporters. The Stalwarts, dominated by Roscoe Conkling, set out to bring Grant and the spoils system back. They convinced the old man to seek the Presidency again, but the Half-breeds, more moderate and less committed to dispensing patronage on a grand scale, succeeded in blocking Grant's nomination. After thirty-five ballots the deadlock remained unbroken. On the thirty-sixth ballot, James Garfield, a burly politician from Ohio, finally won the nomination. Garfield leaned toward the Half-breeds, and made an effort to heal the split in the party. Chester A. Arthur, the Conkling appointee dismissed from the Collectorship of the Port of New York by Hayes, was nominated for the Vice Presidency to balance the ticket.

The Democrats nominated Union General Winfield Scott Hancock for the Presidency, in an effort to give their party a sure argument against any Republican attempt to again wave "the bloody shirt." They also renewed the charge of fraud in the Tilden-Hayes election, and claimed that the Democratic Party showed patriotic restraint when it allowed Hayes to become President with a minority vote. They also pointed to the Crédit Mobilier scandal of the early years of the decade, when large sums of money, supposedly for railroad construction, had gone into individual pockets. Garfield had been implicated and then cleared, but memory of the scandal remained. A forged letter that indicated his support of the importation of cheap Chinese labor cost him the California electoral vote. With prosperity on their side, the Republicans eventually won, but Garfield's margin of victory was extremely small, only 39,213 in the popular vote. The Republicans also gained control of both houses of Congress.

GARFIELD AS PRESIDENT

Garfield was a flesh-and-blood example of the popular myth of the poor boy who had made good. He had worked his way up from an orphaned childhood to become a major general in the army, and had served a number of years in the House of Representatives. In the White House, he showed independence in making appointments, but his term was too brief to allow him to accomplish much.

The major conflict of his four-month term, and the one linked to his assassination, was his attack on the Stalwart faction. He wanted to make it clear that the President was not just a "registering clerk of the Senate," and he showed it by appointing James G. Blaine as Secretary of State. Garfield further snubbed Conkling by appointing a Half-breed to the key office of Collector of the Port of New York. It appeared that the reform battle started by Hayes was being continued by Garfield, but, in fact, it is not clear whether Garfield wanted reform, or simply to give his own Half-breed faction of the party a solid organizational strength. Whatever the real motive, he succeeded in raising the prestige of his office in the process.

In protest against Garfield's raid on his political territory, Conkling staged a melodramatic resignation from the Senate. The junior Senator from New York, Thomas Platt, resigned with Conkling, thereby gaining the nickname, "Me, too" Platt. The resignations were intended only as a gesture. Conkling was not interested in martyrdom, and it was quite out of character for him to give up an office, but both he and Platt felt certain that the New York

President James A. Garfield with his daughter. Garfield was assassinated after only four months in office.

State legislature would come to their support by automatically voting to reseat them in the Senate. His reinstatement would be a slap at Garfield and would confirm Conkling's power in New York. Unexpectedly, the state senate refused Conkling's appeal and seated two other men. Conkling's political career was at an end.

During this power struggle, pro-Conkling journals were full of hysterical charges against Garfield, further increasing political tension in the party. On July 2, 1881, Charles J. Guiteau, who was turned down for an ambassadorship by Blaine, shot Garfield in the Washington Railroad Station. When he was seized he declared, "I am a Stalwart and Arthur is President now!" To Americans used to the operation of the democratic process in political struggles, the affair had overtones of a despotic struggle for a throne: Only a short time earlier, the Russian Czar had been assassinated. Now the assassination of Garfield, coming so soon after Lincoln's death, created a new public mood for reform.

ARTHUR AS PRESIDENT

Chester A. Arthur's public image was virtually the opposite of Garfield's. Arthur was a worldly, handsome man, six feet two inches tall, who loved good food and expensive clothing. Although he had been an abolitionist, after the war he seemed to be interested only in the spoils of office. Except for the Vice Presidency, he had never been elected to a public office. During the Conkling-Garfield feud, he had openly worked for Conkling against the President. Now, as Guiteau had gleefully announced, he was the President. "Chet Arthur! President of the United States!" was usually exclaimed in horror.

Arthur did reinstate the Stalwarts, up to a point. Blaine left the Cabinet. Senator Sherman, Half-breed leader in Ohio, found his position threatened by Stalwarts there and traced the move to President Arthur.

747

Arthur filled the Cabinet with friends of Grant and Conkling, mostly mediocre men. Playing politics in the politically critical state of New York, he tried to seize control of the old Conkling machine by running his own man for governor. But his candidate lost, making it clear that the public was still wary of the Stalwart intrigues.

Regardless of these maneuvers, the Stalwarts were at first dismayed and then shocked as Arthur's overall approach to running his office became clear. Arthur was not the simple party hack they had hoped for. He refused to throw all the Half-breeds out of office. He had been stunned by the assassination and seemed to have awakened to the importance and potential independence of the Presidency. He followed up Garfield's prosecution of the "Star Route" mail delivery frauds, a Post Office scandal embarrassing to the party. Worst of all for the Stalwarts, in his first annual message to the Congress, Arthur advocated civil service reform and called for an investigation of the tariff.

The Civil Service Reform Act of 1883, which passed with Arthur's backing, was the most lasting achievement of his administration. Arthur had encouraged popular indignation over the Garfield assassination and the agitation for reform that followed it. A National Civil Service Reform League was created, its cause publicized by such liberal journalists as E. L. Godkin of *The Nation*.

THE TREASURY SURPLUS

Arthur also centered his attention on the issue of the Treasury surplus. The high tariff duties poured in new revenues even faster than the Congressmen could spend them. Revenues often exceeded expenditures by 100 million dollars or more annually. Many people were critical of such a large surplus not only because it was regarded as a cause of tight money, but also because some of it remained in the Treasury and did not circulate in the economy.

Arthur resolved to reduce the surplus in two ways. First, he hoped to lower the tariff. With the approval of Congress, he created a commission to study the customs rates. Though the members of the study group were all solidly protectionist, after honest investigation they concluded that the rates needed to be reduced on the average by about 20 percent. Although this mild proposal left substantial import duties, it failed to get through Congress. In fact, lobbyists immediately flocked to Washington to put pressure for this or that industry on the Congress, and they were supported by Eastern politicians from both parties. The new tariff, called a "mongrel" by its detractors, was no different from the old one by the time all the extra favors to business were added. In fact, it raised the duties on a substantial number of commodities. It was only reluctantly signed by the President. Nevertheless, his commission had made its point. Men long committed to protection had been compelled to admit that such a high tariff was unnecessary.

Arthur's second technique for reducing the surplus, through increased government spending, was more successful. The United States naval fleet was in a shambles, far below the par of modern European iron-and-steel fleets. Arthur encouraged a hesitant Congress to appropriate funds for construction of several steel cruisers later christened *Chicago*, *Atlanta*, and *Boston*. Thus, he set the precedent for improvements that were to make the United States the third naval power in the world by the turn of the century.

THE 1884 PRESIDENTIAL NOMINATIONS

Arthur had failed to make himself acceptable to the party bosses and was passed over by his party for renomination. Since Roscoe Conkling's career had been destroyed, there was only one man left to take the Republican nomination in 1884, James G. Blaine, who had sought it twice before.

Blaine's supporters adored him. "The plumed knight" was a flashy, quick-witted man who seemed less corrupt than Conkling, and who frequently spoke with passion of the Republican Party as the fount of American progress. His style earned him the most enthusiastic and loyal following of any politician of the age. But some Republicans, especially those in the Eastern reform wing of the party, were not so adoring. Blaine had close ties with business interests and had never been completely cleared of charges of graft in the Crédit Mobilier scandal. Carl Schurz led a desertion of the Mugwumps from the Republican Party after Blaine was nominated. He observed that Blaine had "wallowed in spoils like a rhinoceros in an African pool."

In 1884, the Democrats appeared to have a strong chance of winning the Presidency for the first time since before the Civil War. The division in the Republican Party and an economic depression in farm areas and cities that resulted from a brief but devastating decline in the prosperity of the 1880s, accompanied by widespread unemployment, raised Democratic hopes for a return to power. The party selected Grover Cleveland, a stubborn and honest man, short and heavy of build, with a fairly good reputation with business interests as well as the American people generally.

Cleveland first attracted attention as mayor of Buffalo, where he had weeded out graft in municipal sewage and street-cleaning projects and thereby saved the city large sums of money. Later, even the Democratic machine in New York City, Tammany Hall, reluctantly supported the nomination of Cleveland for governor of the state. In this new post, Cleveland further enhanced his reputation for absolute public integrity. "We love him for the enemies he has made," said General E. S. Bragg, nominating him for the Presidency. As gov-

ernor of New York, Cleveland had not, in fact, succeeded in pushing through much reform legislation. After a bitter fight with Tammany Hall, he tried to clean up the government in much the same way Hayes had, through personal effort rather than legislation. He had even vetoed some reform legislation on the grounds that it was carelessly written.

Other acts by Cleveland as governor also convinced business interests that he was a genuine conservative. For example, when the legislature passed a bill limiting the fare on the elevated railroads in New York City to five cents at all hours, Cleveland vetoed the bill on the grounds that it was a breach of contract with the builders and owners of the railroads. He was a perfect combination—conservatives trusted him and the public saw him as a beer-drinking, middle-class, tough-minded, if unimaginative, reformer.

THE CAMPAIGN OF 1884

The year 1884 brought one of the most high-spirited, if meaningless, campaigns in American history. The Democrats, knowing that their hopes lay in obtaining votes from disenchanted Republicans as well as their own normal constituency, straddled the fence on the only issue then being discussed—the tariff. When Republicans, trying to lure them into debate, charged them with wanting to lower the tariff, the Democrats generally kept silent.

Instead of political issues, the campaign revolved around charges of moral lapses brought against each of the candidates. It was discovered that Cleveland, a bachelor until his second year in the White House, had accepted the responsibility for an illegitimate child. The Republicans eagerly tried to make political capital from the gossip. It was not clear, however, that Cleveland was the father, but he had granted the possibility, and agreed to support the child. Horrified Democrats rushed

749

to Cleveland. He allegedly said, "Tell the truth." This directness and honesty was publicized and won Cleveland applause. In revenge, some Democrats tried to spread slander about Blaine's marriage, but Cleveland put a stop to it. Blaine had enough scandal attached to his name already. The Credit Mobilier issue was being rehashed, and incriminating new evidence was brought to light, including a letter that Blaine had written that proved his corrupt dealings with the railroads, which ended with the phrase, "Burn this letter." Exuberant crowds marched, chanting either, "Ma, Ma, Where's My Pa?" or "Burn this Letter!"—each according to its political persuasion. Henry Adams, dismayed as usual, wrote in a letter, "the press is engaged in a most amusing dispute whether Mr. Cleveland had an illegitimate child, or did or did not live with more than one mistress; whether Mr. Blaine got paid in railway bonds for his service as Speaker . . . when I am not angry, I can do nothing but laugh."

Toward the last days of the campaign, when no one knew which party had the advantage, Blaine made two mistakes that cost him one ethnic bloc and possibly some votes of the poor. Tammany Hall, which controlled the Irish-American vote in New York, was hostile to Cleveland and liked Blaine because of his sympathy for Irish independence from Britain. But the Irish vote fell to Cleveland when a Protestant minister and supporter of Blaine called the Democrats the party of "rum, Romanism, and rebellion." Blaine failed to repudiate the remark. Blaine's second mistake was to attend a huge, extravagant banquet of wealthy businessmen in New York, in an effort to collect enough funds for last-minute campaigning. Joseph Pulitzer headlined the event the next day in the New York *World:* "The Royal Feast of Belshazzar Blaine and the Money Kings." In case anybody failed to understand the biblical allusion, the cartoon beneath made

the meaning quite clear. It showed fat rich men at their table while a tattered, starving citizen and his family held out their hands for a crumb. The irony of the whole affair was that the "Money Kings" did not care for Blaine, having no fear of Cleveland. Blaine, meanwhile, collected very little from them while acquiring a lot of negative publicity. Nevertheless, the election was close. Cleveland won by only 29,000 votes and had an electoral margin of 219 to 182. He faced a divided Congress with the Republicans still in control of the Senate.

CLEVELAND AS PRESIDENT

The first Democratic President since Buchanan, Cleveland came to office with a number of special problems to solve. Though moderately in favor of civil service reform, he could hardly refuse the patronage starved Democrats the new offices that came with their victory, so he dismissed about forty thousand Republican postmasters from office. Cleveland also removed other officials but not enough to satisfy his party. At the same time, the fact that he had made any concessions at all to the patronage system disappointed the Mugwumps who had supported him in the election. His attempt to steer a middle course on patronage was a failure.

Cleveland was also caught in a dilemma because of the unbreakable tie between the Democratic Party and the states of the old Confederacy. He, in fact, wanted to reintegrate the South fully into national affairs. But when he appointed two men who had been Confederate officers to his cabinet, old Union soldiers throughout the country were enraged. There was an even greater uproar when he began to return Confederate flags to the Southern states as a symbolic gesture.

Then, in 1887, Cleveland riled Civil War veterans again when he vetoed the Depend-

In 1884, Grover Cleveland became the first Democrat to serve as President after the Civil War. Issues of his administration included tariff and civil service reform.

ent Pension bill passed by Congress, the newest in a long series of congressional acts handing out exorbitant sums to veterans from the surplus in the Treasury. The bill provided support for disabled veterans whether or not they were disabled in Civil War battles. Any man who had fought for the Union and was unable to work was covered. Cleveland's veto, along with his rejection of several hundred out of the fifteen hundred claims that passed through his office, was seen as another act sympathetic to the South. Though Cleveland approved more private claims than any President before him, his rejection of a few hundred clearly fraudulent ones earned him passionate denunciations from the Grand Army of the Republic (GAR) which represented Union soldiers.

In spite of his campaign promise of "no harm" to business interests, several of his

actions reveal that he had a clearer understanding of the threat from the trusts than most men in his era. He forced investigations of the practices of railroads, lumber companies, and cattle interests. After their massive land-grabbing operations were exposed, about eighty million acres of public land were returned to the status of public property.

The most dramatic action of Cleveland's first term was taken against the tariff. Like his predecessors, he was confronted with a Treasury surplus. After some study, he concluded that the high tariff, traditional since the Civil War when revenues were needed to pay off the cost of the war, was no longer needed. But when he pushed quietly for tariff revision, no response came from either Democrats or Republicans in the Congress. Finally, he disregarded the advice of fellow Democrats, and in an extraordinary move devoted his entire annual message of 1887 to the tariff question. In the message, he called the tariff an "illogical source of unnecessary taxation." It raised prices of goods at home, imposing a special "burden upon those with moderate means and the poor, the employed and unemployed . . ." Appealing to conservative fears, he warned that if something were not done, these burdened masses might "insist upon a radical and sweeping rectification of their wrongs."

This speech, unusual for its timing and for the way it asserted Presidential authority against the advice of party men intent on re-election, was hailed in Mugwump quarters as an act of great courage and intelligence. Others derided what they thought was a "free trade" message. Actually Cleveland was not for "free trade" but for a lowering of the tariff rates to a more moderate level. Accordingly, Representative Roger Q. Mills of Texas introduced a tariff bill that lowered some duties and opened up the market entirely on other goods. In the Senate, the Republicans forced the bill into a deadlock with demands for continued high rates, and the stage was set for the major issue of the coming election.

THE ELECTION OF 1888

There was some grumbling by Eastern party men over Cleveland's low tariff policy, but he was renominated by acclamation in 1888. The Republicans chose Benjamin Harrison from the important but doubtful state of Indiana, a Union Army veteran and the grandson of President William Henry Harrison. He strongly favored a high tariff, and his nomination pleased the old soldiers. However, in contrast to Cleveland, who was outgoing and aggressive, Harrison was a cold and pious man whose small physical stature was made fun of by the Democrats. He was not an important politician but had served one term in the Senate and was personally honest, dignified, and competent. Firmly committed to "the bloody shirt" approach, he attacked Cleveland's veto of the Dependent Pension bill by saying that "it was no time to be weighing the claims of old soldiers with apothecary's scales."

Disregarding Harrison's thrust, Cleveland went ahead with his campaign centered on the tariff question. "Unnecessary taxation is unjust taxation," he wrote in his letter accepting the nomination. The tariff became the key plank in each party's platform. Protectionists who clustered around Harrison contributed the unprecedented sum of four million dollars to his campaign, some of which was used to buy votes on election day in key states. Meanwhile, the GAR continued to denounce Cleveland and organized extensively to defeat him. In New York, Cleveland's old enemy, Tammany Hall, also worked undercover against his campaign. Finally, near the last days of the campaign, Cleveland lost the Irish vote by a turn of events seemingly as inconsequential as the one that had given him that bloc four years earlier. The British Minister to the United

States wrote a letter to a naturalized citizen saying that he favored Cleveland. The Republicans obtained and exposed the letter to an American public that was still strongly anti-British as an example of foreign meddling in American domestic politics. Cleveland ousted the minister, but the damage was done.

Cleveland's popular majority was about ninety thousand votes. But he lost the electoral vote 233 to 168 because of slim leads by the Republicans in the key states of New York and Indiana, where he lost the Irish and veterans votes and was also the victim of election frauds. He accepted his defeat with dignity, satisfied that he had fought for an important and difficult issue.

HARRISON AS PRESIDENT

With Harrison's election the Republicans returned to Washington to reclaim the spoils they had lost four years before. Blaine became Secretary of State for the second time and wielded considerable power in the administration. Two men in Congress, Speaker of the House Thomas B. Reed, a man of quick wit and parliamentary skill, and Senator Nelson Aldrich, also influenced the politics of Harrison's term of office. Although Theodore Roosevelt, an active civil service reformer, was appointed to the Civil Service Commission, he could accomplish little and soon became frustrated with Harrison's administration. It became clear that the President's election statements in favor of this reform were mainly lip-service.

The new administration paid more serious attention to its election debts to protectionists and veterans. The McKinley Tariff, with average rates of 48.5 percent, the highest peacetime tariff in the nation's history, was pushed through Congress in 1890. Frankly favoring the principle of protection, the new act not only shielded active industries from competition with the outside world, but offered high tariffs to industries that did not yet exist in America, in order to encourage their formation. Strong sentiment against the bill, especially among farmers and workers, forced Eastern Republicans to make a deal with the party's Western wing to get it passed. The Westerners, now a bigger bloc in the Senate since the admission of six new Western states, represented farm interests. The new tariff, therefore, included high rates on products like potatoes and corn. As it turned out, prices on agricultural goods continued to fall and the tariff was of no help to the farmer.

In exchange for pro-tariff votes from Western politicians, Eastern Republicans also agreed to vote for the Sherman Silver Purchase Act. The so-called "silver craze" was picking up steam in the West. Farmers and others in debt were more convinced than ever that the way out of depression and debt was through inflation of the currency by free coinage of silver. The new silver miners were also lobbying for it. Eastern Republicans held fast to the gold standard, but they wanted Western support for the high tariff and, also, to keep the Western mining interests in the Republican Party. They therefore agreed to support the Sherman Act. Under the act, the Treasury was to purchase 4½ million ounces of silver each month, paying with Treasury notes redeemable in gold or silver coin. But the bill did not at the same time

provide for free and unlimited coinage of silver. Consequently, as long as Treasury certificates remained redeemable in gold, there was little expansion of the currency in circulation. As a result, silverites and Western debtor farmers continued to be unhappy with the act, correctly persuaded that its administration would not inflate the currency.

Keeping their promise to the veterans, the Republicans also passed the Dependent Pension Act of 1890, essentially the same act that Cleveland had vetoed. Hailed by the GAR as "the most liberal pension measure ever passed by any legislative body in the world," it handed out about 160 million dollars per year. The "Billion Dollar Congress" was attacked by some for wastefulness and defended by others as the generous legislature of a powerful nation.

The congressional elections of 1890 brought startling defeats for the Republicans. "People's Parties" formed all over the West and South, opposing the high tariff and monopolies, and demanding increased coinage of silver. After the election the Democrats had 235 seats in the House and the Republicans only 88. There were also nine Congressmen from the farmers' parties. The usually solid Republican majority in the Senate was now dangerously small. A new decade was beginning that would witness depression and great farmer unrest.

THE PLIGHT
OF AGRICULTURE

The industrialization during and after the Civil War that brought a revolution in communication and transportation opened

up a worldwide market for American farm products. Advanced machinery, sometimes baffling to the farmer and always costly, was put to work in a movement toward "scientific agriculture" to increase productivity. Though it was now possible for him to sell his goods in larger quantity and in the world market, the American farmer did not immediately benefit financially. With overproduction, the price of crops tended to fall, and political and economic power in the nation lay in the hands of industrial interests that had gained wealth at the expense of farmers. As a result, a number of organizations were formed for the purpose of uniting farmers, inflating the currency, and wresting power from monopolies like the railroads. But the scales in the new interdependence of city and country remained weighted on the side of the urban areas.

INCREASED PRODUCTIVITY

All over the world, farmers in what had been isolated regions—not only in Western United States but in Russia, Australia, Canada, and India—now could send their crops to industrial centers by using railways and steamships. Europe and the Eastern cities of the United States demanded more agricultural goods to feed large numbers of factory workers. The self-sufficient American farmer began to disappear. Many more farmers harvested for the domestic and foreign market than for subsistence. The old, Jeffersonian image of the self-reliant farmer who lived off the land and was less easily corrupted than city folk, whether or not it had ever been accurate, was now irrevocably altered by the times.

The farmer needed machinery. During the Civil War, the mechanization that had already changed the cities accelerated in agricultural areas. Farm laborers became soldiers, and machines took their place. By the last quarter of the century "combines" were coming into use—giant machines that performed the tasks of harvesting, threshing, and bagging all in one operation, al-

though they were extremely expensive and somewhat difficult to manage. Even the plow, the husker, and the mower were mechanized, along with an additional array of newly patented devices.

The machines saved labor and increased productivity. The time required to perform some operations was reduced to a tenth or a twentieth of what it had been previously. With the settling of the West, which doubled the amount of land tilled in the United States, the new mechanization meant that by 1900 triple the amount of wheat was produced as at the outbreak of the Civil War. Cotton and corn production increased similarly.

THE UNPROTECTED FARMER

It was expected that the world markets would absorb the increased production of crops. This, however, did not take into account the appearance of new suppliers other than the American farmer, who also benefited from the new mechanization and transport. The American farmer found himself selling his goods abroad on an open market in competition with farmers of other nations, while he bought his machinery in a highly protected market at home. He had the worst of both worlds. The price of his produce was unprotected even at home, where it tended to stay on a par with prices in the world market. In a year when European crops failed, the American farmer would do a little better, but more often the world market was glutted with agricultural produce, and farmers elsewhere in the world had the advantage of cheaper machinery. With high charges for his capital and low prices for his goods, the farmer was caught in an impossible squeeze.

A Department of Agriculture report during the period gives us a glimpse at the decline of agricultural prices. The price of wheat declined an estimated ninety-five cents a bushel from 1884 to 1887 to about sixty-three cents a bushel from 1894 to 1897 —about a 30 percent decrease. The price of corn fell at about the same rate and cotton, even more. In depression years farmers burned corn for fuel because the cost of shipping corn when its price was very low made it pointless to market the crop. When farmers did go to market, they often got less for the crops than it cost them to produce it.

This economic squeeze left large numbers of farmers in poverty and resulted in an increase in mortgaged farms and a sharp rise in tenancy in the Midwest and Great Plains states. In the South, tenant farming was more common than independent farming. Southerners who did own their own farms, like their Western counterparts, were more often than not in debt. They had trouble meeting the year's expenses, let alone freeing themselves from the mortgage. By 1900 about 35 percent of all farmers were tenants. "The most pressing want of the farmer is to get rid of debts for which his home is mortgaged," "Whiskers" Peffer, the Populist Senator from Kansas, wrote. He estimated "the aggregate debts resting upon the people's homes" at 3.75 billion dollars, two-thirds of it on farms.

FARMERS VICTIMIZED

During the last quarter of the century the railroads were the most visible monopoly in the nation. Endowed with public lands by acts of Congress and state legislatures—lands estimated at 129 million acres —the railroads looked for settlers to populate their new Western routes. They conducted advertising campaigns designed to make the West attractive. Though settlers were at first reluctant to come because of the popular notion that the area west of the Missouri River was a desert that no one could cultivate, it soon became known

that the lands were fertile. The railroads offered easy, long-term credit to men who had little money. By 1877 a large number of farmers had settled the West, but they were dependent on the railroads, in debt to them for the land itself, and forced by their monopoly of transportation to pay high freight rates.

The railroads also engaged in other abuses. Even if there happened to be two roads available to a farmer, they did not compete with each other to lower rates. In addition, railroads were frequently charged with "stock-watering": selling stock in excess of the actual value of the company. They then claimed that they had to raise freight rates in order to pay high dividends to Eastern stockholders.

The farmer, who fed the nation, saw himself as the victim of an economy controlled by railroads and other interests. Freight rates in the East, for example, were lower than those in the West. The railroad argument that it cost more to carry goods in the sparsely populated West seemed to farmers an unconvincing argument. As far as they were concerned, they were victims of discrimination. The railroads were profiting and the farmers were being crushed. They could easily identify with a cartoon of the period which showed the public lying underneath the rails like wooden planks, with the train—the railroad monopoly—coming around the bend to crush the public man by man.

The collection of government revenues also hurt the farmer. Both the tariff and internal taxes worked against him. The tariff protected manufacturers but not farmers, and the farmer paid a land tax that he could not avoid in any way. Underhanded practices of railroads, businesses, and stockholders, designed to conceal their properties and so reduce taxes, were common. The farmer, however, had no way of hiding his land. In addition, the mortgage on his farm prevented the farmer from evading full payment of the tax. He paid for the whole value of the mortgaged property. Actually he paid the tax for the owner —the railroad, for example—to whom he remained indebted. In fact, since the federal government in the late nineteenth century got its internal revenues from excise taxes on consumer goods, and not from an income tax, low income people always paid higher federal taxes in proportion to their means.

FARMERS' ORGANIZATIONS

THE GRANGE

No longer isolated from the outside world, farmers now found it necessary to end their isolation from each other, and to organize for their "mutual protection and advancement," as the National Grange *Declaration of Purpose* said in 1874. The

Grange had been founded in the 1860s to educate poor farm people and strengthen their sense of community. Admitting women on an equal basis with men, it held rallies, outings, discussions, distributed farmers' journals, and circulated books.

In the early 1870s, the interests of the Grange took a more political turn as crop prices fell and membership skyrocketed. Grangers argued among themselves about taking direct action in partisan politics; but by the election year of 1876, with the country in the depths of depression, the Grangers were making demands for low interest and freight rates and the regulation of monopolies.

On the state level, with its membership concentrated in the Midwest and receiving strong support in the South, the Grangers had already pushed through regulatory legislation. Illinois had set maximum rates on charges by railroads, grain elevators, and

warehouses. When the state supreme court held the new rates unconstitutional, the farmers promptly responded by voting out the judge in the next election and voting in their own man.

The most innovative tactic of the Granger fight against monopolies was the formation of cooperatives. The Grange, like some labor unions in this period, bought directly from wholesalers and distributed manufactured goods at low cost to its members. This method by-passed local merchants, who sometimes had connections with the railroads and to whom farmers were often heavily indebted. However, an overly ambitious Granger plan to set up a cooperative which would manufacture farm machinery failed because the farmers did not have the experience to run it or the capital to back it.

The Granger movement faded in the late 1870s. Failure of their cooperatives in competition with merchants hurt the Grange, but the main reason for failure was probably that farmers, who had joined the movement quickly during bad times, left it just as quickly during the good times that began in the late 1870s and lasted till 1887. Yet the new awareness of their economic situation promoted by the Grange remained. It expressed itself when farmers spontaneously formed small local groups to help themelves.

THE SOUTHERN FARMERS' ALLIANCE

In 1874 an organization known as the Texas Alliance began as a local group trying to ward off horse thieves. By 1878 it

A meeting of the Illinois National Grange in 1873. The Grange was a social, political, and economic organization for farmers. Originally founded to educate poor farmers, the Grange went on to become a strong political interest-group supporting legislation in favor of the farmer.

had worked out its own *Declaration of Purpose* echoing that of the Grangers. The Texas Alliance began spreading through the Southwest. Blacks, excluded from it, formed their own Colored Farmers Alliance and then affiliated with the white organization which became the Southern Alliance in 1888.

The Southern Alliance had the same general objectives and activities as the Grange, and it also tended to weaken when it tried to take political action. White farmers feared racial equality even more than monopolies and the "Bourbon" leadership of the Democratic Party. In order to obtain control from the ruling powers in the Democratic regime, they would have had to organize politically with the blacks, an idea they would not accept. Bidding for the black vote by various white groups, it was feared, might upset the Southern racial balance. As a result, the Southern Alliance occupied itself more with cooperatives and educational and mutual aid activities. The racism of its members caused it to lose black votes the few times it did put up candidates. Consequently, it turned more and more to working through the Democratic Party to get men elected who represented its views.

THE NORTHERN FARMERS' ALLIANCE

Starting in 1880, a Northern Alliance was created by Milton George, editor of the farm journal *Western Rural,* specifically to achieve the political aims of the Granger movement. Their 1880 constitution stated that the Alliance planned to "unite the farmers of the United States for their protection against class legislation and the encroachments of concentrated capital and the tyranny of monopoly." The demands were specific: a fair taxation of property including deductions for mortgages, an income tax fair to poorer people, reforms in government hiring, government regulation of interstate commerce, and government ownership of the railroads. It also favored tariff reduction, currency inflation, and an improved credit system. Unlike the Southern Alliance, the Northern Alliance planned to create a third party to carry out its platform.

The plans of the Northern Alliance were aided by the economy and the forces of nature. After 1887 the farmers' prosperity came to an end. Their revived optimism had encouraged unwise borrowing and speculation. In 1887 commodity prices went into a slump, on top of a freezing winter and terrible drought in the South and the Great Plains. For the next ten years bad weather brought poor crop yields but prices did not rebound, and thousands of farmers deserted the Plains states. Midwestern farmers with diversified crops were better off, but Western and Southern farmers, in desperation, were ready for new and even radical solutions to their problems.

As a result, the third party strategy succeeded in the Plains states in the elections of 1890. South Dakota and Kansas sent Alliance Senators to Washington. Many Alliance candidates in other states drew off enough votes from the Republican tickets to allow Democratic victories. In an important showing, fifty Congressmen and five Senators in all had been elected with Alliance backing, although in the South many of the victors in state and national elections were only giving lip-service to the farmer organization and still owed their real allegiance to the Democratic Party.

THE POPULIST PARTY

The Alliance candidates often belonged to what were called "People's Parties," each state having it own organization. Attempts to combine the Alliances into one political force consistently met with the obstacle of Southern allegiance to the Democratic Party. However, led by the People's Party of Kansas in February of 1892 pressure for combination succeeded in forming "The People's Party of the United States of America," which included members of both the Northern and Southern Alliances. It held its nominating convention a half year later in Omaha, choosing James B. Weaver of Iowa as the party's candidate for President. The Democratic and Republican conventions that year were staid and unenthusiastic, but the Populist convention was noisy, tumultuous, full of biblical eloquence and the excitement of a new party in rebellion.

The platform for the party was written largely by Ignatius Donnelly. Called "The Sage of Nininger," Donnelly was a brilliant journalist who believed that human rights took precedence over corporate power. In 1891 he published *Caesar's Column*, a nightmarish portrait of the future United States as a despotic nation with masses of miserably poor people in the towns and the country. He thought such an "absolute despotism," as he called it in the platform, was the probable result of the spreading power of huge corporate interests.

The Populist platform was full of emotionally charged language. Mary Ellen Lease, "The Kansas Pythoness," had been speaking around the country during this period urging farmers to "raise less corn and more hell!" She typified the new spirit of militancy among farmers. The platform described the government as breeding "two great classes—tramps and millionaires." The tramps were the masses of unemployed men and farmers thrown off their lands. The nation was on the verge of "moral, political, and material ruin." The formation of the new party was justified on the grounds that the two major parties were dominated by big interests that avoided the issues. "They have agreed to ignore, in the coming campaign, every issue but one. They propose to drown the outcries of a plundered people," the platform charged, "with the uproar of a sham battle over the tariff . . . They propose to sacrifice our homes, lives, and children on the altar of mammon . . ."

Specific proposals in the platform anticipated many of the demands for reform that would be made in decades to come. Among the planks were demands for an inflated currency and free coinage of silver at the rate of 16 to 1; a flexible national currency controlled by the federal government instead of private banks; restrictions on immigration to protect American workers from competition with "the pauper and criminal classes of the world," which, the platform asserted, were flocking to America; government ownership of railroads, telegraph, and telephone; postal savings banks; a graduated income tax; and shorter working hours. It also called for the following political reforms: the secret ballot, the initiative and referendum, direct election of Senators, and a one-term Presidency.

The most important point in the platform, and the most shocking to economic conservatives, was the statement that the federal government was responsible for social well-being. "We believe," it said, "that the power of government—in other words, of the people—should be expanded . . . to the end that oppression, injustice, and poverty shall eventually cease in the land." "The Civil War is over," the platform declared emphatically, "and . . . every passion and resentment which grew out of it must die with it." Key words for the Populists were "brotherhood" and "rights." They wanted to bridge the gap between farmers and industrial workers and to break down other class and regional barriers. Southern Populists even tried to overcome the racist thinking among Southern white farmers but this only hurt their cause. The Populists also saw their attack on corporations as constructive. "The people do not want to tear up the railroads," a Nebraska paper declared. They merely wanted to end their abuses and the continual financial drain on the poor.

DEPRESSION AND THE ISSUE OF FREE SILVER

CLEVELAND REELECTED

In the election campaign of 1892, the Democrats again nominated Grover Cleveland to run against Harrison. The contest between the two men was similar to the one of 1888, although quieter. Cleveland won by a landslide in both the popular and electoral vote. He returned to office in 1893, the only President to serve two nonconsecutive terms. Over the past four years his thinking had become more conservative, and he had allowed pro-business Democrats to persuade him to run again. They were afraid of the massive agitation for free silver that was beginning to snowball, and wanted to keep silverites in the Democratic Party from seizing control. Harrison, with little personal appeal, had made concessions to the silverites but had not satisfied them when he signed the Sherman Act. He had also earned the hatred of workers by making repressive moves against strikers. Cleveland was still personally popular, and believed firmly that the nation had to adhere to the gold standard. As a result, voters, both conservatives and working people, deserted the Republicans again as they had done in 1884, and Cleveland won by the decisive vote of 271 to 115 in the electoral college. He carried the South and the important doubtful state of New York as well as Harrison's home state of Indiana.

Weaver polled more than a million popular votes and received twenty-two electoral votes for the Populists. Five Senators and ten Congressmen also went to Washington for the new party. Yet in all the Northern states east of the Mississippi where the Granger movement had been strong, Populism was a negligible factor. Southern Populists still worked mainly through the Democratic Party and the People's Party failed to attract labor and middle class support. Their influence was limited to one area of agricultural discontent, the Plains states.

Looking back, the Populists appear more like rural middle class reformers than the radical firebrands many Americans considered them at the time. Conservatives believed that the movement, if it obtained power nationally, would overthrow the capitalistic system. No less susceptible to unreasonable fears, the Populists believed a conspiratorial money power was bent on victimizing rural America. The humane reform proposals they advanced were quickly taken over by other reformers as the movement declined, and most of their ideas were ultimately adopted in the United States over the next fifty years. While there was a nativist strain in the movement which emphasized fear of blacks and the new immigrants from Eastern Europe, its contributions to the solutions of the problems of an urban America were of much greater importance.

Cleveland's victory was a paradox. Popular demands for change had thrown the election to the Democrats, yet Cleveland himself was more conservative than he had been when in office before. In his inaugural address he strongly supported the gold standard, disappointing the silverites. He also put together a strongly conservative Cabinet.

THE DEPRESSION OF THE 1890s

Only a few months after Cleveland took office, general and vague economic uneasiness turned into the Panic of 1893. It was the beginning of the worst depression in the nation's history to that time, and its effects lingered on until 1897. It had multiple causes. Since 1887, there had been a depression in agriculture that was responsible for the Populist and free silver movements and also for a declining purchasing power among farmers. In the early 1890s, depressions rocked Europe and Australia, inevitably affecting American trade which relied to some extent on foreign markets. At home, strikes like the Homestead Strike, reflecting the low wages and discontent of the workers, had hurt the economy directly by stalling production, and indirectly, by lowering public confidence. Also, the railroads were greatly overextended, and the passage of the Sherman Silver Purchase Act under Harrison had made European investors uneasy, causing many to sell their American stocks.

FAILURE OF THE RAILROADS

Although the National Cordage Company was the first big company to fail, leading to the panic in May, the full impact of the depression was still to come in the summer as one railroad after another went into bankruptcy. The Reading, the Northern Pacific, the Union Pacific, the Erie, and the Sante Fe were bankrupt. By the end of 1895, more than 160 railroads had collapsed, tens of thousands of businesses went with them, and banks were either failing completely or inflicting a great burden on debtors by recalling loans. The network of boom time credit extending outward from railroads with their watered stock was now shattered and it brought the whole economy down with it. "Men died like flies under the strain," Henry Adams wrote, referring to businessmen ruined by the panic.

CLEVELAND'S EXPLANATION

Cleveland was convinced that the Sherman Silver Purchase Act had caused the depression. He thought that when the amount of gold in the Treasury had begun to decline, the result could only be a downward spiral in the economy. The Silver Purchase Act had depleted the Treasury of gold by calling for the purchase of 50 million dollars' worth of silver per year. The spending of the "Billion Dollar Congress" had only made matters worse. By the time Cleveland came to office the gold reserve was endangered, and in April, it fell below the 100-million-dollar mark, setting the stage for the panic.

The remedy, according to Cleveland, was to repeal the Silver Purchase Act and maintain the gold standard in any way possible. Because the Treasury had to be filled up again with gold, Cleveland called a special session of Congress to repeal the Sherman Act. A heated debate crossed party lines, and silverites, like William Jennings Bryan of Nebraska, were worked up to a fever pitch against repeal. Though they presented their case passionately, they lost as the President succeeded in driving the repeal through by means of political deals and threats. However, it was a costly victory since it split the Democratic Party.

The McKinley Tariff rates were so high that they had kept enough foreign goods out of the country to bring about a decrease in customs collections. The former Treasury surplus had been turned into a deficit of 60 million dollars by 1894. With the Democratic Party now badly divided, however, the President was not sure he had the votes to carry out his campaign promise to reduce the tariff. The House did pass a bill, introduced by Representative William Wilson of West Virginia, which provided mild reductions after agrarian interests succeeded in incorporating a clause for a 2 percent income tax on all salaries over four thousand dollars. In the Senate the bill was mangled by the protectionists. The final version of the Wilson-Gorman tariff reduced duties from 49 percent to 41 percent. Cleveland was chagrined at the high rates the conservative members of his party had put through and was equally unhappy with the income tax provision. Yet, he let it become law. The Supreme Court invalidated the income tax clause the following year on the ground that the federal government did not have the power to impose a direct tax. It was plain from the decision that the Court considered the tax an attack on private property.

THE UNEMPLOYED

During the depression years of this era the number of unemployed is estimated to have been between two and a half and four million, perhaps as much as 25 percent of the work force. Men wandered across the country looking for work in city after city, literally grabbing free rides on moving freight trains. Now it was often difficult to tell the difference between "professional hoboes," and workingmen who had to adopt their tactics of begging, stealing, and free-riding to stay alive during the crisis.

Charity and public projects on a small scale did not make much headway against mass suffering. The New York *World* distributed a million or more loaves of bread, the *Herald* gave clothing, and cities paid subsistence wages to men who swept streets or worked on other improvement projects. But many politicians still advocated the principle that it was "not the province of government to support the people," as expressed by the New York governor when he vetoed a public works project. "Never within my memory have so many people literally starved to death as in the past few months," declared a New York clergyman.

During 1893 many men out of work began to organize themselves into small "armies of the unemployed." Their purpose was not plunder but to find employment, and they kept together to force railroads to give them free rides, and distributed among themselves what they got by begging. Because they were orderly, many of these armies were respected by the public and occasionally they received praise in the newspapers.

COXEY'S ARMY

The movement reached a peak with the formation of Coxey's Army. Jacob S. Coxey of Massillon, Ohio, an old Greenbacker and a wealthy man who was a worker before he amassed his fortune, formulated a program of public work projects for the relief of the unemployed. His Good Roads bill, introduced in Congress in 1892, proposed that 500 million dollars be spent on road construction. All workers would be accepted and paid no less than a dollar and a half for an 8-hour day. In Coxey's view the proposed bill solved several problems at once. The roads were needed; the money would inflate the currency; the 8-hour day, a reform demanded by workers, was in need of more support through federal action; and the wages would keep people alive.

Modest and somewhat reserved, Coxey joined with Carl Browne, an outgoing and outspoken man, to send "an army of the unemployed" to Washington. The wandering armies would be given a direction. Their march across the nation could popularize the Coxey bill and be "a petition with boots on."

The men who joined the march knew what they wanted, legislation to provide work. In the spring of 1894, Coxey started from Massillon with his family, including his infant son named Legal Tender, and a large following. Coxey's group of five hundred, and twelve hundred other marchers, finally reached Washington. But he was stopped by federal troops and police who arrested the leaders and charged them with trespassing on Capitol grounds. The

"army" was dispersed, having gained nothing but public attention. Conservatives denounced Coxey's theory of public projects as a means of curing the depression, and it was not until the 1930s that similar projects actually came into being.

THE SILVERITES

The argument between sound money men and silverites, the most critical domestic dispute of the decade, involved monetary theories about which historians and economists still disagree.

Economic conservatives believed that the amount of gold actually in the Treasury determined the value and stability of the dollar. If the Treasury were full of gold, the currency would be sound, that is, respected at home and abroad. Accordingly, it was believed the government should print only as much paper money as it could back with its gold reserves. To print more would be to discredit the dollar. Silver, previously a rare metal, had been used along with gold to back up the dollar until 1873. Because there had been so little of it before that time, it did not threaten the gold standard. The gold standard was internationally accepted, another reason for conservative support of it.

The silverites saw money in radically different terms. To them, money should represent not the amount of gold in the Treasury but mainly the amount of goods in the society relative to the population. They saw it as a form of credit. The amount of money in circulation needed to be regulated by the government in the best interests of the people. It should keep up with expanding population and productivity. In fact, however, the amount of money per capita had barely increased in recent decades, in spite of the large increases in productivity. The Eastern business and banking interests were obviously keeping the nation chained to a gold stand-

A cartoon of the silver controversy. Uncle Sam is blinded by the silver coins on his eyes and pleads for someone to see him through the silver trouble.

position, became extremely popular and helped spread the "silver craze," although it never became as popular among workers as it did among farmers. In it Professor "Coin" explained the importance that silver had once had, and he hoped would have again:

It was the most favored as money by the people. It was scattered among all the people. Men having a design to injure business by making money scarce, could not so easily get hold of all the silver and hide it away, as they could gold. . . . It was so much handled by the people and preferred by them, that it was called the people's money. . . . Gold was considered the money of the rich. It was owned principally by that class of people, and the poor people seldom handled it, and the very poor people seldom ever saw any of it.

BOND SALES

Cleveland had singled out the Sherman Act as the cause of the panic, but its repeal did not produce the results he expected. The gold reserve continued to drop lower. More and more greenbacks and silver certificates were being redeemed in gold. Government policy prescribed that all these redemptions be honored, to uphold the credit of the currency. By January, 1894, the Treasury reserves had fallen below 70 million dollars.

The mood of panic was spreading to the White House itself. Cleveland, convinced that further depletion would force the nation onto a silver standard, decided that government bond sales might draw in enough gold to restore confidence. However, a bond issue floated in January of 1894, showed the low point of public confidence: Less than five million of the fifty million bonds were bought by the public. The administration was desperate until Secretary of the Treasury Carlisle at last persuaded New York bankers to take the issue.

ard, profiting from deflation and tight money. To debtors and the poor, money was not just a token of the amount of gold in the Treasury. It was functional, a medium of exchange used to buy goods and pay wages. If there was more of it, they reasoned, there would be better times.

The free and unlimited coinage of silver at the old ratio of 16 to 1, the silverites argued, would increase the amount of currency in circulation without making it necessary to issue merely paper money. By resuming the old policy of "bimetallism," coining silver and gold together, the country could inflate the currency but still retain a metal backing for its paper. The sound money men objected that since silver was now being mined in amounts unheard of during the earlier period, and since it was actually cheaper than its old value of 16 to 1, it would be coined without restraint, dangerously inflate the currency, and discredit the dollar on the world market.

Coin's Financial School, a tract by William Harvey that explained the silverite

Silverites immediately damned the sale to the bankers as proof of the government's dependence on Wall Street. The maintenance of the gold reserve had been strongly favored by business from the start. Now that it had failed, these same business interests, or so it seemed to the silverites, were underwriting a very desperate government. Moreover, the first bond sale did not achieve any permanent results. Many of the bankers later redeemed their own Treasury certificates in order to pay for the bond issue—creating a vicious circle. But Cleveland stood his ground and floated several other bond issues, each of which gave the reserve a temporary spurt.

Yet by February, 1895, the reserve was down to 41 million dollars. At this point, instead of conducting a public sale of bonds, the government negotiated with the house of J. P. Morgan, who agreed to supply gold and a guarantee that a run on the Treasury would not follow. The complex deal finally succeeded in stabilizing the reserves above the 100-million-dollar mark. But farmers and other silverites pointed to the enormous profits, estimated between 1.5 and 7 million dollars, gleaned by Morgan from the transaction. The silverites still believed, and some economic historians agree, that the Treasury could have adopted the policy of coining silver and healed the panic, without discrediting itself.

"THE CROSS OF GOLD"

The long-standing identification of each of the two major parties on fiscal policy was being shattered. Cleveland had made himself unpopular with laborers by breaking the Pullman strike and with farmers over the silver issue. The Populists were gaining strength. It seemed likely that mass desertions would destroy the Democratic Party if it insisted on supporting Cleveland's economic policies in the next campaign. Silverite Democrats had warned

Cleveland that the silver issue was enough to provoke a walkout. Either the Democrats would make enough concessions to keep the silver wing in the party and, perhaps, even allow fusion with the Populists, or silverites would bolt the party and join the Populists. Silverite Senators worked long and hard for two years to redirect the Democratic Party, and by the convention of 1896, they had won. Eastern Democrats came to Chicago to find that the noisy, colorful convention was already committed in spirit and numbers to free silver. The policies of the Cleveland administration were openly condemned.

William Jennings Bryan of Nebraska was selected the party's nominee, partly as a result of the "Cross of Gold" speech he delivered at the close of the debate over the silver plank in the platform. Later known as "The Great Commoner," Bryan was a fiery 36-year-old Congressman from Nebraska, whose need to speak for the "cause of humanity" arose as much from his religious fervor as from his politics. Steeped in the Bible, Bryan said, "I am interested in the science of government, but I am more interested in religion. . . . I would rather speak on religion than on politics." In his "Cross of Gold" speech, he seemed to be speaking on both subjects at once. Beginning humbly and without attacking Cleveland, the speech described the silverite position and the dignity of the poorer classes in inspired, vibrant tones. Without emphasizing hate or sectionalism, Bryan declared, "the gold standard has slain its tens of thousands."

In the last few minutes of the speech, "The Boy Orator of the Platte" addressed himself to the problems of his own times with the zeal of an ancient prophet. Speaking of the conflict between manufacturing cities and agricultural regions, he said, "Burn down your cities and leave our farms, and your cities will spring up again as if by magic; but destroy our farms and the grass will grow in the streets of every

The 1900 Democratic Presidential nomination went to William Jennings Bryan, whose campaign poster is shown here.

city in the country." Bryan's claim that "the great cities rest upon our broad and fertile plains" may have appeared naive in an era when the United States had become a great industrial power. It may also have been a remnant of the myth of an agrarian America inherited from Jefferson and Jackson. His main point, however, was that agriculture still had a vital role to play in the country despite the advances of industrialization.

Bryan ended the speech by comparing the struggle over the free coinage of silver to the American Revolution and vowing to fight for it. "Having behind us the producing masses of this nation and the world, supported by the commercial interests, the laboring interests, and the toilers everywhere, we will answer their demand for a gold standard by saying to them: You shall not press down upon the brow of labor this crown of thorns, you shall not crucify mankind upon a cross of gold." There was a brief silence, and then havoc—a fanatical silverite demonstration that led conservatives to compare the whole affair to the French Revolution and to call Bryan a demagogue or worse. Many bolted the party and many silverite Republicans ultimately voted for Bryan.

The Populists were now in a dilemma. The Democratic platform contained some of their reforms, including free silver. Those in the party who wanted to make free silver the key issue of the campaign called for fusion with the Democrats. Donnelly and the more radical agrarians wanted to remain separate in order to push a thoroughgoing reform of all American society. At their convention in St. Louis the fusionists won out, and the Populists nominated Bryan for President. Many old reformers left the convention feeling that the Populist Party had been ruined.

Bryan's Republican opponent was William McKinley of Ohio, sponsor of the McKinley Tariff. He earned the nomination largely through the efforts of Marcus Alonzo Hanna, wealthy businessman and a Republican Party boss in Ohio. Hanna, more than expert at discovering and manipulating the sources of political power, had risen to unprecedented influence in American politics. Although with close ties to the business interests, he was moderate enough to have criticized the Pullman Company for refusing to arbitrate the dispute with its workers during the bitter strike of 1894. He seemed to have had a genuine feeling of friendship for McKinley whose views on politics and economics were similar to his own. However, he also knew that McKinley would make an attractive candidate. McKinley had never taken a strong stand on the money question, and so there was hope that his nomination would prevent a desertion by Western Republicans.

Hanna engineered the convention in a way that left the gold standard as much in the background as possible. When the issue finally came to the fore, and a gold-standard plank was included by the Eastern wing of the party, Hanna and McKinley accepted it, thus gaining business support. However, twenty-three silverites walked out, among them Senator Henry M. Teller of Colorado, who had been present at the founding of the Republican Party.

The election campaign of 1896 was one of contrasts. Bryan, young and gifted with almost unbounded energy, traveled by railroad around the nation. He had visited twenty-seven states and covered almost 20,000 miles by the end of the campaign. He spoke to grassroots Americans in the moral and optimistic terms they understood and believed. McKinley conducted a careful

"front-porch" campaign. Hanna's strategy included prearranged exchanges with audiences around the porch which allowed McKinley to deliver his remarks so that they seemed spontaneous. Bryan did not make a successful appeal to workers, while McKinley assured them that a silver standard would inflate the economy and destroy the real value of their wages. "McKinley and the Full Dinner Pail" became the Republican slogan.

Perhaps the most critical difference between the parties was not in their candidates but in their campaign funds. Acknowledging 7 million dollars against Bryan's 300,000 dollars, the Republicans were astounded that Bryan, with so little financial backing, was still able to gather enormous popular support for his crusade. Some sources claimed that Republican campaign spending went as high as 16 million dollars. Hanna launched a fund-raising crusade, calling on businessmen for large contributions since he knew they were genuinely afraid of the possibility of Bryan's election. While McKinley spoke from the front porch, Hanna inaugurated a giant effort directly before the election to convince the people that Bryan's candidacy represented the forces of anarchy and sedition.

"Men, vote as you please, but if Bryan is elected tomorrow the whistle will not blow Wednesday morning," one manufacturer reportedly told his employees. The Democrats charged that many such threats were being made. It was not surprising, considering the hysteria of the campaign. While farmers saw the gold standard men as betrayers of America, there were rumors that the East would secede from the Union if Bryan won. A conservative clergyman asserted that Bryan's platform was "made in hell."

The Presidential campaign poster of McKinley and Hanna. The Republican slogan of the campaign was "McKinley and the Full Dinner Pail."

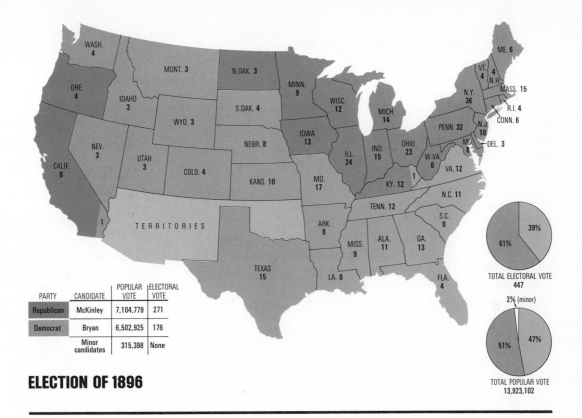

PARTY	CANDIDATE	POPULAR VOTE	ELECTORAL VOTE
Republican	McKinley	7,104,779	271
Democrat	Bryan	6,502,925	176
	Minor candidates	315,398	None

ELECTION OF 1896

TOTAL ELECTORAL VOTE
447

TOTAL POPULAR VOTE
13,923,102

The election results made it plain that Bryan's appeal was too sectional to win him the Presidency, and that the business interests knew how to effectively organize a winning campaign. McKinley had a plurality of 600,000 votes and defeated Bryan in the electoral college, 271 to 176. Bryan won all the states of the deep South, and all the states of the far West—except Oregon and California. McKinley won in the more populous regions, the Northeast and the Middle West. The Republicans had succeeded in persuading many laborers that coinage of silver would reduce the purchasing power of their wages. Midwestern farmers drew closer to McKinley when crop prices rose sharply in the late summer and the fall. This last group might have given Bryan the Presidency if times has been less prosperous.

Democrats pointed out that with the backing of the business interests, large sums

of money, and fear of economic anarchy all working to defeat Bryan, added to the reputation that Cleveland's Democratic administration had among farmers and silverites, it was surprising that Bryan won as many votes as he did. McKinley's victory made one important point clear: Agrarian interests alone could not hope to control national politics in an industrialized America. The defeated Democrats had appeared to represent regional and class interests in the campaign.

A RETURN
TO PROSPERITY

The final blow to agrarian politics came in 1897 with the return of prosperity. The economic upturn killed whatever was left of the Populist crusade. By 1900, European markets demanded about twice as much

767

wheat from America as in previous years, and wheat prices climbed for the first time in a generation. The free-silver issue virtually disappeared when sources of gold were discovered in the Klondike and elsewhere in the world. New supplies of gold had the same effect that free silver would have had. They inflated the currency, and brought the benefits of easier credit that the farmers had been pleading for. When the Gold Standard Act was passed in 1900, resolving the issue in favor of gold monometallism, there was relatively little protest. The myth that the independent farmer was the backbone of America had lost its force. Bryan had inadvertently acknowledged this fact when he characterized the farmer as a businessman.

Readings

GENERAL WORKS

Faulkner, Harold U., *Politics, Reform and Expansion*. New York: Harper & Row, 1959—A general history of the United States in the 1890s which emphasizes the interrelations between domestic political and economic developments and the expansionist impulse.

Garraty, John A., *The New Commonwealth 1877–1900*. New York: Harper & Row, 1968—A survey of American society during a period of rapid industrialization. Garraty feels the central theme of the era was the development of large-scale institutions to replace the smaller, more personal groups of an earlier time.

Goldman, Eric F., *Rendezvous with Destiny*. New York: Random House, 1956—A lively history of American liberal and reform movements from the post-Civil War period to modern times.

Grantham, Dewey, *The Democratic South*. Athens: University of Georgia Press, 1963 —A series of lectures which attempts to revise the view that Southern history has been dominated by an elite aristocracy. Grantham argues that democracy has long been a strong theme in the region's political life.

Hofstadter, Richard, *The Age of Reform*. New York: Random House, 1955—A major reinterpretation of the American reform spirit, focusing on Populism and Progressivism. Hofstadter finds that beneath the rhetoric of economic grievances and demands, reformers were expressing anxieties about their social status in a time of rapid change.

Josephson, Matthew, *The Politicos*. New York: Harcourt, Brace, 1938—A lively political history of the Gilded Age which emphasizes the business orientation of the political leaders of the era.

Merrill, Horace S., *Bourbon Democracy of the Midde West*. Seattle: University of Washington Press, 1969—From the Civil War until 1896, the Democratic Party was dominated by Eastern and Midwestern conservatives. Merrill studies the ideologies and policies of the Midwestern conservative Democrats.

Morgan, H. Wayne, ed., *The Gilded Age*. Syracuse, N.Y.: Syracuse University Press, 1963—A collection of essays on various aspects of late nineteenth-century America. Most of the contributors find that the picture of the era as completely dominated by vulgar, greedy business tycoons has been overdrawn.

Morgan, H. Wayne, *From Hayes to McKinley*. Syracuse, N.Y.: Syracuse University Press, 1969—A detailed account of party politics between 1877 and 1896. Morgan finds much to admire in the methods of Gilded Age politicians.

Rothman, David J., *Politics and Power, the United States Senate 1869–1901*. Cambridge, Mass.: Harvard University Press, 1966—A detailed study of the Senate as an institution which showed an increasing self-consciousness, a growing moral code, and strong tendencies to professionalization.

White, Leonard D., *The Republican Era*. New York: Macmillan, 1958—An administrative history of the federal government in the latter part of the nineteenth century. White deals with such topics as civil service reform and the growth of bureaucracies.

SPECIAL STUDIES

Darden, Robert F., *The Climax of Populism*. Lexington: University of Kentucky Press, 1965—A narrative of the election of 1896 which emphasizes the role of the Populist Party and explores some of the divisions within it.

Glad, Paul W., *McKinley, Bryan and the People*. Philadelphia: Lippincott, 1964—A description of the political battles of the 1890s which focusses on the Presidential election of 1896.

Hicks, John D., *The Populist Revolt*. Lincoln: University of Nebraska Press, 1961—A basic study of the Populist movement. Hicks emphasizes the importance of the agricultural problems of the Great Plains in shaping Populist policies.

Hirshson, Stanley P., *Farewell to the Bloody Shirt*. Bloomington: Indiana University Press, 1962—A history of the Republican Party's policies toward Southern blacks from 1877 through 1893. During this period, one Republican faction hoped to exploit the black vote while another wished to ignore blacks entirely and appeal to Southern businessmen.

Hollingsworth, J. Rogers, *The Whirligig of Politics*. Chicago: University of Chicago Press, 1963—Concentrating on the conflicts between Grover Cleveland and William Jennings Bryan, Hollingsworth describes the tensions in the Democratic Party from 1893 to 1904 between rural and urban forces.

Hoogenboom, Ari, *Outlawing the Spoils*. Urbana: University of Illinois Press, 1961—The author finds complex motivations in the effort to institute civil service reform during the Gilded Age.

Jones, Stanley L., *The Presidential Election of 1896*. Madison: University of Wisconsin Press, 1964—Jones emphasizes the importance of McKinley's party organization and of Bryan's failure to win the urban working-class vote as decisive factors in the 1896 Republican victory.

Keller, Morton, *The Art and Politics of Thomas Nast*. New York: Oxford University Press, 1968—Keller examines the work of Nast, the political cartoonist best known for his attacks on the Tweed Ring in New York City. The author places Nast within the Gilded Age reform tradition. It is well illustrated with Nast's works.

Nugent, Walter T. K., *The Tolerant Populists*. Chicago: University of Chicago Press, 1963—Examining the state of Kansas, Nugent finds Populists there to be less paranoid, anti-Semitic, and irrational than other groups in America in the 1890s. On the whole, Kansas Populists were tolerant and open-minded.

Pollack, Norman, *The Populist Response to Industrial America*. Cambridge, Mass.: Harvard University Press, 1962—In contrast to Hofstadter, Pollack argues from his study of Populist writings that the Populist movement was economically motivated and that its policies were rational and radical responses to capitalist industrialism.

Salontos, Theodore, *Farmer Movements in the South*. Lincoln: University of Nebraska Press, 1964—A study of Grangerism, the Farmers' Alliance, Populism, and other Southern protest and reform movements from the Civil War to the New Deal.

Unger, Irwin, *The Greenback Era*. Princeton, N.J.: Princeton University Press, 1964—A Pulitzer Prize-winning history of the money question after the Civil War. Unger shows that the simple identification of big business with hard money and farmers with inflation is untrue. Political ties and complex economic and ideological motivations determined positions on monetary issues.

PRIMARY SOURCES

Bryan, William J., *The First Battle*. Chicago: W. B. Conkey, 1896—A campaign statement representing the policies and aspirations of Bryan as leader of the free-silver Democrats.

Bryce, James, *The American Commonwealth*, Vols. I–II. Louis Hacker, ed. New York: Putnam, 1959—A classic study of American politics by a sympathetic but observant critic from Great Britain.

Harvey, William H., *Coin's Financial School*. Richard Hofstadter, ed. Cambridge, Mass.: Harvard University Press, 1966—Harvey's statement of the case for free silver quickly became a widely read Populist tract. In his introduction to this modern edition, Hofstadter analyzes some of the hidden themes in Harvey's book and in Populist rhetoric in general.

Tindall, George B., ed., *A Populist Reader*. New York: Harper & Row, 1966—A collection of party statements, speeches, and pamphlets, illustrating the Populists' grievances, policies, and spirit.

BIOGRAPHIES

Barnard, Harry, *Rutherford B. Hayes and His America*. New York: Russell & Russell, 1967—A long, detailed account of Hayes's career that attempts to revise the common portrayal of him as an ineffective President.

Coletta, Paolo E., *William Jennings Bryan*, Vols. I–III. Lincoln: University of Nebraska Press, 1964–1969—The most definitive biography yet of the "Great Com-

moner," exploring and explaining Bryan's long and varied career.

Morgan, H. Wayne, *William McKinley and His America*. Syracuse, N.Y.: Syracuse University Press, 1963—A sympathetic biography of the Republican President, which describes him as a resolute, if uninspired, nationalist who aimed to unify the nation.

Nevins, Allan, *Grover Cleveland*. New York: Dodd, Mead, 1932—A sympathetic biography of Cleveland, that portrays the President as an honest and capable man at a time of widespread corruption in politics.

Ridge, Martin, *Ignatius Donnelly: Portrait of a Politician*. Chicago: University of Chicago Press, 1962—A biography of the fiery late nineteenth-century reformer and politician. Donnelly did much to publicize and popularize the issues around which Populists united.

Woodward, C. Vann, *Tom Watson: Agrarian Rebel*. New York: Macmillan, 1938—A biography of the leading Southern Populist, dramatically showing the eventual failure of an attempt to build a movement in the South of poor people, based on class instead of race.

FICTION

Donnelly, Ignatius, *Caesar's Column*. Cambridge, Mass.: Harvard University Press, 1960—A novel of a future utopia by a leading Populist writer. The book has been interpreted as showing both the forward-looking and the reactionary sides of Populism.

Garland, Hamlin, *Main-Travelled Roads*. Columbus, Ohio: C. E. Merrill, 1970—Six stories of rural life in the Mississippi Valley by one of the leading realist writers of his time in America.

5

WORLD POWER AND DOMESTIC REFORM

American soldiers stationed at a street barricade in the Philippines. Pitted against Filipino insurrectos who fought guerrilla warfare with wooden spears and knives, the Americans made no headway in the war for more than two years.

22

Becoming a World Power

The United States is practically sovereign on this continent. . . . It is not because of the pure friendship or good will felt for it. It is not simply by reason of its high character as a civilized state, nor because wisdom and justice and equity are the invariable characteristics of the dealings of the United States. It is because . . . its infinite resources combined with its isolated position render it master of the situation and practically invulnerable as against any or all other power.

—Secretary of State Richard Olney

The boundaries of the United States had never remained static. By 1860 Americans had driven their way across the continent bringing the entire area between the Pacific and Atlantic oceans under their control. Although this national growth had involved the conquest and destruction of Indians and conflict with Mexico, Americans usually thought of the conquest of each new Western frontier as the inevitable march of progress.

By the end of the nineteenth century, when Turner wrote of the significance of the landed frontier in American historical development, there was no new frontier left on the American continent. At the same time the growing economy demanded new markets. Andrew Carnegie pointed out that the American population was still extremely sparse and urged that internal economic development was the best outlet for American energies. But many farmers and businessmen noticed that the depressions started by panics in 1873 and 1893 lifted with increases in the export trade. They drew the inevitable conclusion that expanded world markets would solve economic problems at home. Bryan's followers and the Populists argued that free silver, rather than aggressive acquisition of new territories, would secure these new markets. "A silver standard . . . ," said Bryan in 1893, "would make us the trading center of all the silver-using countries of the world, and these countries contain far more than one-half of the world's population." He was talking about non-European nations. Free silver would inflate the currency and reduce the price of American goods, and these goods would become salable to the poorer peoples of the world. But this theory was never tested. In the last years of the century the Spanish-American War erupted in part as a result of pressure for the acquisition of new territory to insure new world markets. The conflict with Spain brought the United States not only new territory but also a new influence and responsibilities in the Caribbean and the Far East. Moreover, the economic and physical expansion of the United States by the beginning of the twentieth century was the result of an aggressive foreign policy that had widespread support from the American people.

THE LATE NINETEENTH CENTURY

ISOLATIONISM

It would be inaccurate to term the foreign policy of the United States before 1900 "isolationism" without an explanation of the meaning of the word. Though the United States was expanding on the American continent, for strategic and cultural reasons she chose to isolate herself from political ties to Europe. Moreover, the high tariff was mainly to protect American industry from the competition of European manufactured goods. However, Europe was a highly developed market for American agricultural products, American traders were active in the Far East, and the United States was at least nominally committed to the security of the entire Western Hemisphere.

Latin America and the Orient both offered potentially vast markets for American agricultural products. Much of the expansionist energy after the Civil War went toward settling the West, which harnessed a huge new labor force for farming and railroad construction, and many felt that increased involvement in the Caribbean and the Far East would follow the settlement of the Pacific coast. A trade pact had been drawn up with China as early as 1844, and nine years later Commodore Perry penetrated the economic isolation of Japan. In 1846 William H. Seward predicted that "Our population is destined to . . . encounter Oriental civilization on the shores of the Pacific," and in 1889 Secretary of State James H. Blaine made the first significant move to solidify Pan-American relations and trade. These early policies in the Pacific and the Western Hemisphere were the first signs of the full expansionism of the 1890s.

Toward Europe the United States was more cautious in her relations. From the early days of the republic it had been the policy of the United States to avoid political entanglements with the monarchical powers of Europe. Great Britain was still disliked as the former mother country, and the memory of the Napoleonic Wars meshed with the notion that European power rivalries had brought unnecessary hardship to America. Later, during the Civil War, much of the British upper class had supported the South and the government had indirectly aided the Confederacy in spite of Britain's declared neutrality. At the same time the French had tried to set up a monarchy in Mexico contrary to the Monroe Doctrine. These actions further convinced Americans that the Western Hemisphere should quarantine itself from European politics to avoid infection.

CONFLICTS WITH GREAT BRITAIN

Hatred of England was a popular rallying cry for politicians and the American press until the end of the century. An Englishman stationed in Washington remarked during the Venezuelan crisis of 1895 to 1896 that it would be "a comfort to go to a country where one can read the news without finding in every paper an article accusing one's country of every conceivable crime." Silverites sometimes accused the supporters of the gold standard and big industrialists of having suspicious ties with England, the center of support for the gold standard and the world's leading banking power.

The diversity of ethnic backgrounds in America undoubtedly aided the perpetuation of anti-British sentiment. For example,

Populist dislike of the English may have been the result of the German, Scandinavian, and Dutch ancestry of most farmers. The English were disliked by the rest of the nations of Europe, and so it was likely that they would suffer the dislike of American immigrants from these countries. The Irish, a large and crucial voting block, were particularly anti-British. The Fenians, a group of Irish-Americans who supported Irish independence from Great Britain, even attempted small raids on Canada in 1866 and 1871. In their moments of greatest expectations the band hoped to conquer Canada and hold it hostage until the liberation of Ireland from oppressive British rule. They also hoped the raids would at least provoke British-American conflict and help the Irish indirectly. But Washington put a stop to the raids by a proclamation enforcing the neutrality laws.

Ironically, despite the anti-British feeling in America, the British were becoming more friendly toward the United States. Behind the shift was Britain's growing awareness by the late 1860s that American neutrality—if not friendship—might be vital to British security in the event of conflict with other European powers. An impending clash between France and Prussia could result in a powerful new enemy of England in Europe. Again, if Britain and Russia should go to war over the presence of Russian ships in the eastern Mediterranean, the United States might sell Russia ships such as Britain had sold the South during the Civil War.

As a result, in 1869, Great Britain agreed to submit to arbitration her disputes with the United States growing out of the Civil War years. But the Senate rejected the first agreement, on the grounds that it made no reference to the American demand that Britain admit her guilt in prolonging the war by having supplied for the Confederacy the cruisers *Alabama, Shenandoah,* and *Florida*. Such an admission would have meant huge payments to the United States for indirect war damages. Before the agreement had been worked out, Senator Charles Sumner, Chairman of the Senate Foreign Relations Committee, had made an unnecessarily violent anti-British speech. He calculated that British support had prolonged the Civil War by two years, and consequently that Britain owed the United States over 2 billion dollars. This absurd claim had some popular appeal at home. Nevertheless, two years after Sumner's speech, on May 8, 1871, the Treaty of Washington was drawn up. It was the result of the patient and astute diplomacy of Grant's Secretary of State, Hamilton Fish. In the treaty the British apologized for the escape of the *Alabama* and agreed to submit the claims resulting from it to arbitration at Geneva. The final decision awarded the United States over 15 million dollars for all Civil War losses, as well as the disputed San Juan Islands south of British Columbia. On the debit side, the United States had to pay Great Britain almost 2 million dollars for attacks on British ships during the Civil War, and over 5 million dollars more for fishing rights in the Canadian fisheries worked out under the treaty. Both countries also agreed that neutral countries would not build nor arm vessels for any country if there was reasonable ground to believe that they could be used against a friendly power, nor would they allow their ports to be used against a friendly power. The treaty established a valuable precedent for arbitration and foreshadowed a new era of American importance in world politics. The peaceful resolution of these Anglo-American disputes was an outstanding achievement of the Grant administration.

NAPOLEON III
AND MEXICO

During the Civil War, Napoleon III of France took advantage of American weakness and staged an invasion of Mexico,

presumably in order to collect unpaid debts. It soon became clear, however, that the French did not intend to leave. Napoleon III occupied the country and offered the throne to Ferdinand Maximilian of Austria in an effort to placate antagonism to his rule in France and Austria of conservative Catholic forces there. The young man was ambitious and naive enough to accept it, along with Napoleon's promise of military support for three years.

Secretary of State Seward made no formal protest since French neutrality was important during the war. However, the United States did not recognize Maximilian but the Mexican leader, Benito Juarez, as the legitimate ruler of the country. The war over, Seward began to push diplomatically for a French withdrawal, but the French were vague in their replies. In 1866 Seward at last made a blunt demand for a definition "of the time when French military operations may be expected to cease in Mexico." The French were aware that the American public was ready for war and that the United States had a large, well-trained army at its disposal. Faced also with Prussian hostilities in Europe, they backed down and abandoned the hapless Maximilian. Maximilian remained in Mexico and met death before a firing squad in 1867.

EARLY EXPANSIONISM:
SEWARD AND GRANT

William Henry Seward of New York became convinced during the Panic of 1837 that worldwide markets were needed. In the two decades before the Civil War he pleaded for economic and territorial expansion on the grounds that it was in the interest of both business and agriculture. Then in 1861 he became Secretary of State and held the office until 1869. His vision was essentially the same as that of later expansionists—the desire to control the Caribbean and to spread American influence across the Pacific.

Seward's greatest success was the purchase of Alaska from Russia. The huge territory called Russian America, though it had a fur trade, fishers, and even, it was rumored, gold, was at the time a burden to the Czar. It cost too much to oversee, and there was some likelihood that in the future the United States might seize the territory. Further, it was in the interest of both the United States and Russia "to cage the British Lion," their common competitor. The British had fishing interests in the area, and her further intrusion into that part of the world could be forestalled by American possession of Alaska. Accordingly, the Russian ambassador indicated that the territory might be bought.

Seward was so eager to close the deal that he negotiated a treaty late one night, agreeing to pay over 7 million dollars for Alaska. When news of the treaty was made public, there was widespread astonishment about the projected purchase of the "hy-

perborean territory," or "Icebox." The New York *Herald* mockingly suggested that Seward arrange to buy Patagonia, the southern-most part of the Southern Hemisphere, "to make both ends meet." The icy, spectral land mass in the north, "non-contiguous" with the rest of the states, seemed worthless at first to most Americans. But Seward conducted a successful campaign stressing Russo-American friendship, the potential value of Alaskan resources, and the strategic and commercial importance of the territory for Far Eastern trade and as a barrier to further British penetration of North America. He finally won the support of the influential Senator Sumner. The treaty was passed in the Senate and the House reluctantly agreed to appropriate funds for the purchase.

Among Seward's other projects were the annexation of the Midway Islands northwest of Hawaii which was successfully completed in 1867 and negotiations with both Nicaragua and Colombia preparatory to construction of an isthmian canal. Seward also had visions of acquiring Hawaii and even parts of Canada. In the Caribbean, he negotiated a treaty with Denmark for acquisition of the Danish West Indies, now called the Virgin Islands. The inhabitants of the islands voted for annexation, but Seward's plan was unpopular with many Congressmen who believed that his scheme to establish a naval base there was too expensive and unnecessary. Grant, taking office in 1869, hearing of hurricanes in the islands, also opposed the purchase and the treaty died in the Senate.

Grant was no anti-imperialist, however. Acting without the advice of Secretary Fish, he was persuaded that the United States ought to annex Santo Domingo for its commercial and strategic value. During the Civil War the Spanish had made advances toward their old colony, maneuvering an official request for recolonization from pro-Spanish forces on the revolution-torn island. Seward protested, but it was a combination

----- Line claimed by U.S.

·········· Line claimed by Great Britain

———— Line awarded by Alaskan Boundary Tribunal 1903

ALASKA BOUNDARY SETTLEMENT

of the Dominican revolt and yellow fever that ousted the Spaniards in 1865. Now, under a scheme supported by Grant, at the instigation of a small group of American investors in the economy of the island, a treaty of annexation was worked out. But Sumner opposed annexation and succeeded in defeating it in the Senate. The Grant-Sumner feud that followed resulted in the removal of Sumner from the Chairmanship of the Committee on Foreign Relations.

Seward's and Grant's interest in securing wider markets in the Western Hemisphere continued during subsequent administrations. However, only in the late 1880s was this desire combined with an effort to improve the country's relations with Latin America. Harrison's Secretary of State, James G. Blaine, wanted very much to increase both foreign trade and good will. As a result, in 1889, he planned a seventeen-nation conference of the American republics which would include a 6,000-mile tour of the United States. The Pan-American Union, an agency for the exchange of information among the republics, grew out of this conference.

THE IMPERIALISM OF THE 1890s

EXPANDING MARKETS

Bryan had called the new farmers businessmen whose market position made them expansionist even earlier than manufacturers. While industrialists sold their goods mainly at home, in a protected market, farmers needed foreign outlets to survive. "The most striking fact . . ." Populist Tom Watson said in 1894, "is that the number of our people today wholly dependent on foreign markets is larger than the number of

Pro-Imperialism

" *. . . in this campaign, the question is larger than a party question. It is an American question. It is a world question. Shall the American people continue their march towards the commercial supremacy of the world? Shall free institutions broaden their blessed reign as the children of liberty wax in strength, until the empire of our principles is established over the hearts of all mankind?*

Have we no mission to perform, no duty to discharge to our fellow-man? Has God endowed us with gifts beyond our deserts and marked us as the people of His peculiar favor, merely to rot in our own selfishness, as men and nations must, who take cowardice for their companion and self for their deity—as China has, as India has, as Egypt has? . . .

The ocean does not separate us from lands of our duty and desire—the oceans join us, rivers never to be dredged, canals never to be repaired. Steam joins us; electricity joins us—the very elements are in league with our destiny. Cuba not contiguous! Porto Rico not contiguous! Hawaii and the Philippines not contiguous! The oceans make them contiguous. And our navy will make them contiguous. . . .

We cannot fly from our world duties; it is ours to execute the purpose of a fate that has driven us to be greater than our small intentions. We can not retreat from any soil where Providence has unfurled our banner; it is ours to save that soil for liberty and civilization.

—*Albert J. Beveridge*

those employed in protected industries." The United States, with forty-five million people in rural areas, compared to thirty million in urban areas, was still demographically an agricultural nation in 1900, and the Populists were echoing earlier de-

Anti-Imperialism

66 *. . . What is our title to the Philippine Islands? Do we hold them by treaty or by conquest? Did we buy them or did we take them? Did we purchase the people? If not, how did we secure title to them? Were they thrown in with the land? . . . If governments derive their just powers from the consent of the governed, it is impossible to secure title to people, either by force or by purchase. . . .*

There can be no doubt that we accepted and utilized the services of the Filipinos, and that when we did so we had full knowledge that they were fighting for their own independence, and I submit that history furnishes no example of turpitude baser than ours if we now substitute our yoke for the Spanish yoke . . .

It is said that we have assumed before the world obligations which make it necessary for us to permanently maintain a government in the Philippine Islands. I reply that the highest obligation of this nation is to be true to itself. No obligation to any particular nation, or to all the nations combined, can require the abandonment of our theory of government, and the substitution of doctrines against which our whole national life has been a protest. . . .

Destiny is the subterfuge of the invertebrate, who, lacking the courage to oppose error, seeks some plausible excuse for supporting it. Washington said that the destiny of the republican form of

mands for expanded markets for agricultural products. Senator Breeze of Illinois had insisted in 1846 that "Ten counties of the state could supply all the home market. We want a foreign market for our produce, which is now rotting in our granaries." In 1880 the *American Agriculturist* dramatized the role of exports when it estimated that over one and a half million wagons would be needed to haul the grain that left New York Harbor; lined up, the wagons would stretch 15,000 miles. Statistics like these explain why, when McKinley toured the West during the debate over the Philippines, he found that farmers favored annexation. The pressure of agricultural surpluses drove American farmers to look for outside markets and to support aggressive policies that would provide those markets.

Though rural people were in the majority, they had a small political voice. Expansionism could not have succeeded without business support. After the Panic of 1893, businessmen noted that the depression had started six years earlier among farmers. There was a clear relation between outlets for the farm surplus and national economic health. Even more significant, statistics for the period of 1870 to 1900 show the increasing involvement of industry in the export trade. Total exports increased from 392 million to 1,394 million dollars over the 30-year period. But exports of

government was deeply, if not finally, staked on the experiment intrusted to the American people. How different Washington's definition of destiny from the Republican definition. The Republicans say that this nation is in the hands of destiny. Washington believed that not only the destiny of our own nation, but the destiny of the republican form of government throughout the world, was intrusted to American hands. The destiny of this republic is in the hands of its own people. 99

—*William J. Bryan*

manufactured goods increased even more rapidly, from 21 million to 805 million dollars. In the beginning of the period, agricultural goods accounted for more than two-thirds of the export. By 1900, manufactured goods had taken the lead, accounting for over half of the total. The statistics show both the skyrocketing of American world trade, and the reason why the business community was ready, after some hesitancy, to come out in support of imperialism in 1898.

INTELLECTUAL CURRENTS

Yet demands by farmers and businessmen for a more aggressive attitude on the part of the federal government in searching out new overseas markets which had begun as early as the 1870s cannot in themselves explain the phenomenon of American imperialism in the 1890s. The farmers and businessmen never asked for the acquisition of new territory or even complete economic and political hegemony over foreign areas in an effort to secure these wider markets. However, the acquisition of new territory or at least exclusive influence over a certain foreign area were the essence of late nineteenth-century imperialism. Where then did the ideas originate which led the United States down the same imperialist road as the major European powers, and why were Americans susceptible to these ideas in the 1890s when they had shown very little interest in overseas expansion in the 25-year period following the Civil War?

The historian Richard Hofstadter has suggested that, more than any decade following the Civil War, the 1890s was one of upheaval and uneasiness for the American people. The depression which began in 1893, the rise of Populism, concern about the development of trusts, the decline of the ideal of a competitive economy, the end of the American frontier, strikes, and even the influx of masses of new immigrants

all produced a state of anxiety in America. Domestically this crisis in American life led to new reform movements. In her foreign policy, it led to an aggressive nationalism.

Many of the ingredients of imperialist thinking in the 1890s were the same as those of the Manifest Destiny movement in the 1840s. But there was one powerful new factor based on the pseudo-scientific thought of the era drawn from Darwin's theory of natural selection. Writers of the period applied Darwin's ideas to the development of nations as Herbert Spencer had previously applied them to individuals in society.

The popular writer John Fiske turned Darwin's biological theory of evolution into a theory of history, and predicted that the Anglo-Saxon race would turn out to be the fittest. "Four-fifths of the human race," he said, "will trace its pedigree to English forefathers." A few notes by Darwin himself, pointing to the way civilized nations tended to supplant the "barbarous," seemed to lend support to these arguments, especially when he had used American development as an example of the process of natural selection. Picking up where Fiske left off, the Reverend Josiah Strong wrote the extremely popular *Our Country* in which he envisioned a "final competition of races." The victory would go to the Anglo-Saxon race, which "represented" the twin virtues of civil liberty and spiritual Christianity. His book encouraged demands for territorial expansion by both Protestant and Catholic clergymen who saw such expansion as opening up new areas for making converts to Christianity.

These attitudes became known as "the imperialism of righteousness." Many men more learned than the popularizers, such as the historian John W. Burgess, came to conclusions that were similar. "There is no human right to the status of barbarism," Burgess argued, after studying a variety of political systems. He held that it was the obligation of civilized nations to "force organization" on the uncivilized. His arguments, however, proved to be largely theoretical. In the following years Burgess denounced the expansionist policies his arguments had encouraged.

More sophisticated assessments of the place of the United States in the international competition for possessions supplemented these popular and crusading theories. By far the most important was Captain Alfred Thayer Mahan's work, *The Influence of Sea Power upon History, 1660–1783*. The publication of the first volume in 1890 heartened men like Theodore Roosevelt who believed quite early that the United States should take a central position in world affairs. Mahan rallied popular

Admiral Alfred Thayer Mahan, whose book The Influence of Sea Power upon History, 1660-1783 *affected America's position in world affairs.*

support for a strong navy, tracing the path of history from the seventeenth century onward to show that sea power had been the decisive factor in commercial and military ventures. He thought the Caribbean would be the heart of American sea power, but lamented that we were still "woefully unready" there. However, through the projected isthmian canal, the United States might spread its fleets over both oceans without splitting up its navy into two uncoordinated units. In addition to a strong navy the country needed an improved merchant marine, naval bases, and colonial possessions. The outstanding feature of Mahan's work was that it combined the concepts of Anglo-Saxon superiority and a moral mission to uplift the less fortunate with a clear statement of America's self-interest in a competitive world, the need of a strong naval force, and an understanding of power politics.

Mahan's work popularizing the need for a larger navy was the culmination of a decade of successful efforts in Congress to expand American naval power. The foundations of the American naval power in the 1890s were laid in the 1880s. Both politicians and the Navy Department supported appropriations for a Naval War College and the construction of vessels. By 1889, thirty-four new ships had been built and in 1890 three battleships were authorized by Congress.

These popularizers of the new Manifest Destiny gradually won converts among a small but influential group of politicians and publicists. In this group were politicians such as Theodore Roosevelt, Henry Cabot Lodge, Albert J. Beveridge, and John Hay; publishers Whitlaw Reid and Walter H. Page; and the writers Henry and Brooks Adams. Disdainful of and bored with economics and the money grubbing of the new business elite, they called for a new and broader horizon for the United States. They asked for a return to noble ideals, heroism, and courage, and a defense of American honor among nations. They followed Mahan in asking for a stronger navy, as the precursor to the acquisition of new markets, territorial possessions, and growth of American prestige among the powers of the world. American preeminence in world politics was more important in their thinking than the benefits of such a policy to the American economy.

THE PACIFIC

SAMOA

American interest in Samoa illustrates the quickening American interest in overseas possessions by the 1890s. The first real threat of war with a European power during the last years of the century came in 1889 over the Samoan archipelago. Mahan looked back on the incident and remarked that it was "eminently suggestive of European ambitions. America . . . roused from sleep." The islands, 3,000 miles south of Hawaii in the mid-Pacific, had long been a coaling and repairing station for American ships en route to the Far East. In 1878 the United States had won special rights to use Pago Pago Harbor as a naval station in exchange for a guarantee of diplomatic action should Samoa become involved in any dispute with another power. This guarantee was vague, but offered Samoa protection without setting up a protectorate. Some Americans welcomed it as a simple trade treaty; others warned that it might bring troublesome commitments in the future.

Soon after the American treaty was signed, Britain and Germany, the two other powers involved in Samoa, made similar treaties confirming their own spheres of influence. Germany was the dominant commercial power in the islands, but American involvement was deep enough for agent George H. Bates to write to the Secretary of State in 1886 that "citizens of the U.S. have acquired in Samoa substantial prop-

erty interests," and that "a very large proportion of imports into the country consists of American goods."

Between 1887 and 1888 tensions grew when the Germans disposed of the Samoan king and set up a puppet ruler friendly to their commercial interests. The natives rebelled and the Germans established martial law in their part of the islands. While American, German, and British warships confronted each other in Apia Harbor, ready for battle, arrangements were made for a conference in Berlin. Then in March a hurricane struck the harbor and all six German and American warships went down. The mutual tragedy encouraged negotiations, making the squabble seem trivial. A three-way protectorate was set up, even though President Cleveland was opposed to any such commitment.

In 1899, after American victory in the Spanish-American War and the acquisition of the Philippines, the need for the Samoan naval base seemed more urgent. New negotiations divided the archipelago between the United States and Germany, while Britain was compensated with the Gilbert and Solomon islands in the South Pacific. Senator Pettigrew of South Dakota, an anti-imperialist, was unhappy. "We blot out, then," he said, "a sovereign nation, a people with whom we have treaty obligations, and divide the spoils."

A BUSINESSMEN'S
REVOLUTION: HAWAII

Even more important to the United States for strategic and economic reasons were the Hawaiian islands in the Central Pacific. American missionaries had been active there since the early nineteenth century and in 1849 the United States had recognized the independence of the islands. By an 1875 treaty Hawaiian sugar came in to the United States duty free. When the treaty was renewed in 1887, the United States gained the added advantage of the exclusive use of Pearl Harbor. By 1890 Americans exerted the dominant influence in the Hawaiian Islands, as investors in the sugar industry, as landowners, and as residents. Three-fourths of the imports to the islands came from the United States, which in turn bought virtually all the islands' exports. Trade thrived until the McKinley Tariff of 1890 ended the duty on sugar and gave a two-cents-per-bushel bounty to American growers. Unable to share in the bounty, and afraid of depression in their single-crop economy, American planters and investors in Hawaiian sugar refineries began to agitate for annexation. Their will carried great weight. In 1887 they and other businessmen of European background had already forced King Kalakaua to accept a constitution that provided for protection for private property, personal liberty, and a legislature under their control. Now they wanted something more drastic. Harrison's administration was openly sympathetic to the annexationist movement.

King Kalakaua died in 1891, and his sister, Queen Liliuokalani, ascended the throne. Her slogan was "Hawaii for the Hawaiians." She wanted to erase the constitution and restore the full rights of the monarchy. Her chief opponent was John L. Stevens, the United States minister in Honolulu, a fervid annexationist. In January, 1893, as soon as the Queen had made her move to abolish the constitution, the planters planned their coup and enlisted Stevens' support. He summoned 160 marines from the U.S.S. *Boston* anchored in Honolulu Harbor. His excuse was the danger to American lives and property, but the marines took their posts at points calculated to strangle the authority of the Queen, not to guard Americans.

The coup was successful because of his own military intervention, and Stevens immediately conferred recognition on the new regime and proclaimed it a protectorate of the United States. Harrison, not displeased, did nothing to disavow these unauthorized actions nor did he attempt to restore the Queen.

A sketchy treaty of annexation was drawn up and sent to the Senate, but the islands were not to become American territory until 1898. Republicans on the whole favored the proposed annexation and saw Hawaii as a key to the Far East. They also feared Japanese control of the islands if the United States did not take them first. Democrats tended to be anti-imperialist, partly in opposition to ruling lands and people not actually assimilated into the republic and partly to oppose the Republicans in power. Cleveland, a confirmed anti-imperialist, had the treaty withdrawn when he became President again, and appointed James H. Blount his special commissioner to Hawaii to discover the sentiment of the Hawaiian people. On arrival Blount ordered the marines back to the *Boston* and to the horror of imperialists lowered the United States flag. He decided that the natives were loyal to the Queen and opposed annexation. But the Queen refused to accept any compromise with the revolutionaries, and Cleveland felt he could not ignore the American interests there. So the status quo prevailed and Hawaii proclaimed herself an independent republic on July 4, 1894. When expansionist sentiment in the United States reached its peak in 1898, Congress annexed the islands at the request of McKinley, who had always favored acquisition and wanted to prevent Japan from securing the islands.

LATIN AMERICA

CHILE

Other examples of a new aggressiveness in American foreign policy can be found in her relations with Latin America. Relations with Chile had been strained for some time because of American friendship with Peru, Chile's long-standing enemy. They deteriorated further when, during a revolt in

1891, United States authorities detained a rebel steamer, the *Itata,* with a cargo of arms. In addition, the American minister granted asylum to men fleeing the revolutionaries and showed sympathy to the government in power. The revolution was successful and Chilean public sentiment became heatedly anti-Yankee.

President Harrison, during whose administration these events occurred, was a staunch supporter of soldiers' causes and American naval expansion. His sentiments brought American-Chilean relations to the brink of war when Chilean rioters killed two American sailors on shore leave in Valparaiso from the U.S.S. *Baltimore.* After heavy drinking there had been a general brawl between the sailors and the Chileans. Besides the two dead, some twenty United States citizens were also injured. Harrison was enraged by the attack. He believed the incident was "an insult to the uniform of the United States sailors," and demanded both an apology and reparations to support the families of the dead. At first Chile assumed a warlike posture and demanded that the American ambassador be recalled. Both nations made preparations for war. Chile finally backed away from a direct confrontation, however, and paid the United States government a 70,000-dollar indemnity.

VENEZUELA AND
THE MONROE DOCTRINE

By 1895 popular sentiment for expansion was increasing and anti-British sentiment in the country was still strong. This combination of factors forced Grover Cleveland to make a sharp reassertion of the Monroe Doctrine in 1895. The boundary between Venezuela and British Guiana had been in dispute since the 1840s, but when gold was discovered around the disputed border Venezuela sought United States intervention and invoked the Monroe Doctrine. The American minister to Venezuela wrote a pro-Venezuela pamphlet which cir-

culated widely in the United States and resulted in a Congressional Resolution in February, 1895, calling for an arbitration of the dispute. Cleveland was caught between peace advocates and anti-British spokesmen, such as Henry Cabot Lodge, the silverites, and the Irish bloc in his own party. They claimed that the Monroe Doctrine was being tested by outrageous British demands.

Seizing the opportunity to forge popular support for himself, Cleveland decided to take a strong stand against Britain. The President evidently sincerely believed a threat to the Monroe Doctrine also was involved. In addition, he may have thought that he was acting as a true anti-imperialist advocate of free trade and arbitration of disputes when he finally demanded that the British submit to United States arbitration of the border question.

After four months of delay, Lord Salisbury, the Prime Minister, finally replied to a pugnacious note from Secretary of State Olney. He claimed that the Monroe Doctrine was not applicable in the situation and was not internationally accepted anyway. This was a diplomatic error. Cleveland was enraged at the snub and sent a message to Congress proposing that he be authorized to appoint a commission that would determine the boundary. It was implicit that the United States would go as far as war to back its findings. Historian Nelson M. Blake has called Cleveland's message "among the most crudely assertive ever issued by responsible American statesmen."

The British were unprepared for the uproar in America and for the first time realized the seriousness of the dispute. Unwilling to become further embroiled with the United States, they submitted to arbitration and in the end won 90 percent of their original land claim. The imperialists, forgetting their earlier assertion that the British claim was outrageous, were satisfied that the Monroe Doctrine had been upheld, while actually it had been reinterpreted to mean that the United States could interfere in almost any crisis involving territorial disputes in the Western Hemisphere. While Anglo-American relations improved after the arbitration, the assertion of American power in the Chile and Venezuela episodes frightened Latin Americans.

THE SPANISH-AMERICAN WAR

CUBA LIBRE

The movement called "Cuba Libre" (free Cuba) came into full maturity in the last years of the nineteenth century. Between 1868 and 1878 Cuban insurgents had fought a bloody 10-year war for independence, but the United States, preoccupied with internal problems and economic development, took little notice of the events. Spain put down the insurgents and added Cuba to the rankling problems of its dwindling empire. A rebel government-in-exile set up headquarters in New York, and Cuban journalists began publicizing their cause among sympathetic Americans.

Meanwhile, Cuban-American trade grew until Cuban tobacco and sugar crops imported into the United States became the bulwark of the island's economy. When depression struck in the United States in

1893, and Congress passed the Wilson-Gorman Tariff putting a high duty on sugar and withdrawing the special sugar agreement with Cuba, the island was plunged into economic depression. Between 1889 and 1897 Cuban sales to the United States dropped from 89 million dollars to 56 million dollars. Cuban businessmen, believing that Spanish-American competition was one of the reasons for the tariff cut-off, at last came over wholeheartedly to the poor people's cause of Cuba Libre.

Both Cuban and American business interests with Cuban connections, suffered when a revolution against Spain broke out in February 1895. The "scorched earth" tactics of the insurgents were designed to destroy any economic benefits Spain might squeeze from the colony and also to bring United States intervention to protect its economic interests there. Business interests in Cuba wanted any action that would end the conflict and restore the order that made profits possible.

The Spanish countered Cuban terrorism with the policy of *reconcentrado*. General Valeriano Weyler arrived in Cuba in 1896 and began a drive to isolate the populace from the insurgents. He set up camps of "reconcentration." Virtually the whole island was spotted with these camps of dislocated civilians, now supposedly prevented from making contact with revolutionaries and aiding them. The strategy, intended to "pacify" the island and starve out the resistance movement, instead starved the people in the camps. About fifty thousand Cubans, mostly women and children, died in the Havana province alone.

DEBATE AT HOME

Given the temper of the country by the mid-1890s, the Cuban situation inevitably created immediate interest among politicians and the general public. Cleveland did his best to isolate the United States from the uprising by proclaiming American neutrality in 1895. But everything about the crisis in Cuba made it a subject of intense interest to the American people. Cuba was geographically very close to the United States and the oppressions of the Spanish monarchy in the island offended United States democratic idealism. Thus what happened in Cuba was important to the American people for economic, strategic, and moral reasons. By 1896, the Congress adopted a joint resolution recognizing Cuban belligerency and Secretary Olney offered American mediation of the conflict. Moreover, the elections of 1896 returned the Republicans to power, and although McKinley himself was no imperialist, hopes for a more assertive American foreign policy and overseas expansion centered in the Republican Party.

The sensationalist press, William Randolph Hearst's New York *Journal* and Joseph Pulitzer's New York *World* elaborated on the atrocities of Spanish rule and advocated intervention by the United States. Weyler was called a "butcher," with some accuracy. Hearst allegedly told one of his illustrators to furnish atrocity pictures even if things looked quiet, and added, "I'll furnish the war." Sexual crimes by Weyler and his army were dramatized or invented. The style of the yellow press turned the genuine atrocities of Weyler's *reconcentrado* into a source of newspaper sales.

The business journals of the day reveal the practical disagreements among businessmen about the issue of intervention. The National Association of Manufacturers showed sympathy for intervening in Cuba, but most businessmen saw intervention as a threat to the new and fragile prosperity enjoyed by the nation after the panic earlier in the decade. When in 1895 the United States had been on the brink of war with Britain due to the Venezuela crisis, the stock market had fallen drastically. During the current crisis, every time war with Spain seemed to come closer, the market fell.

The strongest motive for the temporary business opposition to war may have been the silver question. During the Civil War, greenbacks had been introduced, and wars in general seemed to inflate currencies. As a group, the silverites sympathized with the Cuban rebels and hoped that war would bring free coinage of silver.

By the end of 1897 it appeared that the Spanish had almost crushed the rebellion. They had made two concessions to Cuba: they had promised self-government and they removed General Weyler. Moreover, the American public had shifted its interest to domestic problems. But two episodes in February, 1898, once more aroused public support for intervention to a fever pitch. One incident involved a letter written by the Spanish minister in Washington, Dupuy de Lôme, which was stolen from the mails and delivered to Hearst. In it, de Lôme called McKinley "weak and a bidder for the admiration of the crowd . . . who tries to leave a door open behind himself while keeping on good terms with the jingoes of his party." The Spanish government apologized for the incident, but McKinley's quiet efforts to prevent public demands for American intervention had been undermined, and the American people felt insulted by the remarks.

Prior to the de Lôme affair, the American battleship *Maine* had been stationed in the Havana Harbor on a "friendly" mission, to protect American interests during the insurrection. McKinley had sent the *Maine* in January, 1898, even though Mark Hanna complained that it was "waving a match in an oil well for fun." The Spanish, eager to avoid conflict, received the ship as diplomatically as possible. Hanna's metaphor became appropriate when the *Maine* sank on February 15 after "a terrible and mysterious explosion," as Hearst's New York *Journal* called it. Two hundred and sixty men died, and the yellow press rose to unprecedented hysteria. The *Journal* contradicted its own word "mysterious" with a sub-headline claiming that "the first belief is that a hidden Spanish mine annihilated her." It did not matter that on the same page the captain of the *Maine* urged against any such accusations. In his first dispatch he said, "Public opinion should be suspended till further report. All officers believed to be saved. . . . Many Spanish officers . . . now with me and express sympathy." His words put no damper on the popular conviction that Spain was responsible.

Public opinion was aroused further when on March 17, the respected Senator Proctor of Vermont returned from Cuba, spoke of Weyler's atrocities, and convinced moderate men that the sensationalist press did not reach the dire situation on the island. Of the people in the camps, he said, ". . . one-half died and . . . one quarter of the living are so diseased that they cannot be saved . . ." Mass meetings around the country called for war.

Business sentiment shifted in the early spring of 1898. Until March the main business support for a war in the Caribbean came from those directly connected to the Cuban economy. At this point, given renewed violence in Cuba, many businessmen apparently began to think that a protracted threat of war was as damaging to prosperity as the war itself might be. It was time to "get it over with." An adviser in New York telegraphed McKinley: "Big corporations here now believe we will have war. Believe all would welcome it as a relief to suspense." There had always been certain key industries that would profit from a war— mining interests, the steel industry, and the railways, and agricultural prices would be likely to soar during wartime. Western journals were now largely pro-war. As early as March 24, Easterners such as J. P. Morgan, John Jacob Astor, and John D. Rockefeller were found "to be feeling militant."

Pressures on McKinley for a declaration of war were mounting. Behind the scenes, the President continued to put pressure on

Spain for concessions to Cuba so that an open clash could be avoided. Theodore Roosevelt allegedly complained that Mc-Kinley's peaceable inclinations revealed the man had "no more backbone than a chocolate eclair." By April 9, Spain had capitulated to the American demand for an armistice in the island and an end to the *reconcentrado* policy. But they would not accept the demand that the United States be allowed to arbitrate all other questions between Spain and Cuba with the ultimate goal of Cuban independence.

At the same time, the United States ignored a joint note of the European powers asking for Spanish-American friendship. The administration knew that the European powers were too afraid of antagonizing each other to take a strong stand either for or against Spain. The British navy would have been a real threat if used to support Spain, but Britain far from wanting a quarrel with America was trying to cultivate her friendship. Isolated from the new alliances recently formed on the European continent and fearful of rising German power, England looked on an increase in United States power in the Caribbean as a means of lessening her own responsibilities in that area.

On April 11 McKinley asked Congress for authority to use armed force in Cuba to end hostilities. There is no way to know which of the many factors in this complex situation finally convinced the President that war was the only alternative left to the United States. The yellow press had stirred up public opinion to aggressive heights, but McKinley did not appear to be much influenced by its stories. Two months elapsed after the sinking of the *Maine* before he asked for armed intervention in the island. The President was close to the business interests and their influence on his policy by mid-March was no doubt considerable. Moreover, McKinley was an astute politician. As much as he wanted to prevent war, he knew that if he could not secure Spain's complete removal from Cuba, the American people were demanding American action to force her out. Refusal to heed public opinion and the wishes of the majority of Republicans in the Congress would not only spell defeat for his party in the fall elections, but might bring to power a Congress dominated by silverites which he felt would endanger the American economy. Even when he had almost given up hope of preventing an armed clash, McKinley successfully kept the timing of events pretty much in his own hands. Only when Congress had appropriated money for a war and he was convinced that Spanish concessions were too limited to gain popular acceptance in the United States did he ask for American intervention to free Cuba.

CONGRESS DECLARES WAR

Congress reinforced McKinley's reluctant request. Caught up in the war fever, and amid scenes described by foreign correspondents as hysterical, Congress passed a resolution equivalent to a declaration of war. The resolution declared Cuba independent and demanded that Spain withdraw completely. The President was to employ the army and navy to oust Spain if necessary. However, there was one note of apparent restraint. The proximity of Cuba to the United States had made it clear early in the history of the republic that the island was of strategic importance. John Quincy Adams had once remarked that the annexation of Cuba might in the future become "indispensable to the continuance and integrity of the union." The Teller Amendment, now added to the Congressional resolution, vowed that the United States had no interest in annexing the island. This was to be a war to liberate Cuba, not to gain territory. In the language of the amendment, the United States at the close of the war might station troops on

the "said Island," only so long as they were necessary for "pacification."

THE ACTUAL CONFLICT

Good spirits and popular support marked the extraordinarily brief war with Spain that followed. Soldiers went off with an adventurous, romantic attitude toward battle. The popular notion that it was a war of liberation invested the campaign with heroic purpose, and while bands played, what John Hay would remember as "a splendid little war" began.

The first and most significant victory of the war took place not in Cuba, not even in the Caribbean, but halfway across the world in the Spanish Philippines. The American people may have gone to war for the humanitarian purpose of freeing Cuba, but the small coterie of imperialists in strategic places in the government had much more specific goals in mind. Several

SPANISH-AMERICAN WAR PACIFIC THEATRE

months before the war began, then Assistant Secretary of the Navy, Theodore Roosevelt, had instructed Commodore Dewey in Hong Kong to "keep full of coal." As soon as war began, Dewey was to head south and attack Spanish ships in the Philippines. Roosevelt

sent the instructions surreptitiously one day while the Secretary of the Navy was out. The order was discovered, and Roosevelt

Dewey's defeat of the Spanish in Manila Bay, as announced in the May 2, 1898, edition of The World.

DEWEY SMASHES SPAIN'S FLEET

VICE-ADMIRAL MONTOJO.

The Defeated Commander of the Spanish Fleet.

Great Naval Battle Between Asiatic Squadron and Spanish Warships Off Manila.

THREE OF THE BEST SPANISH VESSELS WIPED OUT, OTHERS SUNK.

The Damage Done to the American Boats Engaged Only Nominal---Hundreds of the Enemy Slain in the Encounter.

COMMODORE DEWEY.

Winner of First Great Victory for New American Navy.

LISBON, Portugal, May 1, 11 P. M.----The Spanish fleet was completely defeated off Cavite, Philippine Islands, according to trustworthy advices received here.

WASHINGTON, May 1, Midnight.---President McKinley expresses entire satisfaction over the reported battle between Commodore Dewey's squadron and the Spanish fleet He accepts the news as true, but believes it is worse for the Spanish than they will admit. There has been no official confirmation of the news. Nothing official is expected for forty-eight hours.

THE THREE SPANISH CRUISERS COMPLETELY DESTROYED.

CASTILLA.

DON JUAN DE AUSTRIA.

SPANISH FLAG SHIP
"REINA MARIA CRISTINA."

FLYING SQUADRON STRENGTHENED.

FORT MONROE, May 1.---The reconcentrated South Boston is aboard of Lieut.-Commander Marix, joined the Flying Squadron in Hampton Roads at 7 P. M. to-day after a quick trip from New York. The bourgeon's arrival practically prepared Commodore Schley, as the despatches, while strong in heavy fighting ships, is weak in swift, lightdraught vessels.

Chaplain Jones, the "fighting parson" of the Texas, preached a red-hot war sermon to-day to the officers and men of the battleship. He took his text from the thirty-second chapter of Deuteronomy, reading from the eighteenth to the forty-third verse, inclusive.

He said that if these verses had been written in order to an admonition to Spain, their appropriateness could not be more emphatic, especially these:

"He said I will hide my face from them. I will see what their end shall be, for they are a very forward generation, children in whom is no faith.

"They shall be burnt with hunger and devoured with burning heat and with bitter destruction.

"The sword from without, and the terror within shall destroy both the young man and the virgin, the suckling also with the man of gray hairs.

"I said, I would scatter them into corners, I would make the remembrance of them to cease from among men.

"Were it not that I feared the wrath of the enemy, lest their adversaries should behave themselves strangely, and lest they should say, Our hand is high, and the Lord hath not done all this."

Nothing is known as to which the work of laying mines and torpedoes in the harbor continued all day.

Pennsylvania Railroad Annexations

ADMIRAL MONTOJO ADMITS HIS UTTER ROUT.

In His Report to Spain He Says Many Ships Were Burned and Sunk and the Losses in Officers and Men "Numerous."

MADRID (via Paris), May 2.—The time of the retreat of the American squadron behind the merchantmen was 11.30 A. M. The American squadron forced the port before daybreak and appeared off Cavite. Night was completely dark.

The Naval Bureau at Manila sends the following report, signed "Montojo, Admiral:"

"In the middle of the night the American squadron forced the forts, and before daybreak appeared off Cavite. The night was completely dark. At 7.30 the bow of the Reina Christina took fire, and soon after the poop also was burned.

"At eight o'clock, with my staff, I went on board the Isla de Cuba. The Reina Maria Christina and the Castilla were then entirely enveloped in flames.

"The other ships having been damaged retired into Baker Bay. Some had to be sunk to prevent their falling into the hands of the enemy. The losses are numerous, notably Capt. Cadarso, a priest, and nine other persons."

The Spaniards fought splendidly, the sailors refusing to leave the burning and sinking Don Juan de Austria. There is the greatest anxiety for further details.

MADRID'S FORLORN HOPE.

LONDON, May 2.—The Madrid correspondent of the Financial News, telegraphing this morning, says:

"The Spanish Ministry of Marine claims a victory for Spain because the Americans were forced to retire behind the merchantmen. Capt. Cadalso (or Cadarso), in command of the Reina Maria Christina, went down with the ship.

MADRID OFFICIAL REPORT ADMITS DISASTROUS DEFEAT

(Despatch Sanctioned by Spanish Government and Passed by the Censor.)

MADRID, May 1, 8 P. M.—The following is the text of the official despatch from the Governor-General of the Philippine Islands to the Minister of War, Lieut.-Gen. Correa, regarding the engagement off Manila:

"Last night, April 30, the batteries at the entrance to the fort announced the arrival of the enemy's squadron, forcing a passage under the obscurity of the night.

"At daybreak the enemy took up positions, opening with a strong fire against Fort Cavite and the arsenal.

"Our fleet engaged the enemy in a brilliant combat, protecte

(Continued on Second Page.)

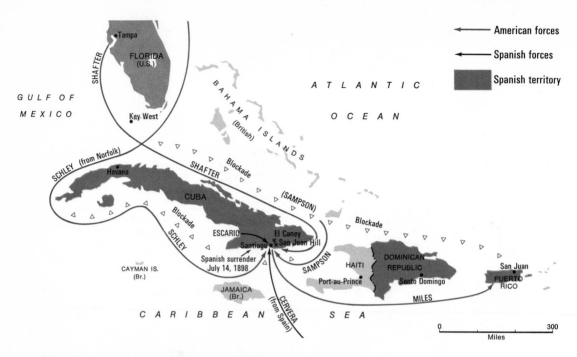

SPANISH-AMERICAN WAR · CARIBBEAN THEATRE

was mildly reprimanded for his act, but the strategy was kept.

Dewey's battle in Manila Bay to cripple the Spanish Navy was a total victory. All ten Spanish ships went down, and 381 Spanish sailors died. Four months later, ground troops from the United States arrived in the Philippines to join the Nationalist forces of Filipino leader Emilio Aguinaldo in overthrowing Spanish rule. After an attack on Manila, Spain's forces surrendered. The United States then officially declared her military occupation of the Philippines.

The war in Cuba was not carried out as efficiently. Long out of practice and run by bureaucrats, the American army was undersupplied and disorganized. Because no lightweight uniforms were available, many soldiers wore hot winter uniforms to fight in the semitropical island in spring and summer. They ate what they called "embalmed beef," and often had no rifles, blan-

kets, tents, or camping equipment. Luckily they confronted a Spanish army with extremely low morale, and only four hundred men were lost in actual battle. However, because of the poor sanitation and provision, another five thousand men died of diseases such as dysentery and malaria.

The war was centered around the town of Santiago. In April, panic spread at the news that the Spanish Admiral, Cervera, was on his way from the Cape Verde Islands, 400 miles west of Africa. Cervera evaded American patrols and finally entered Santiago harbor. American ships blockaded the harbor but did not commence battle. Meanwhile, the American army had embarked from the South for Santiago, taking along with it volunteer cavalry units including Theodore Roosevelt's Rough Riders. Near-sighted but aggressive, Roosevelt had pushed his way into the cavalry and became the real leader of the band of cowboys, polo-players, and ex-convicts. Convoys going to Cuba were so overcrowded that the Rough Riders had to leave their horses home; even then some of the men found it difficult to find transportation.

About seventeen thousand poorly trained men arrived in Santiago to confront a Spanish army even more disorganized, although the hills surrounding Santiago offered the Spanish a natural fortress. The Americans also suffered from archaic artillery, which smoked and betrayed positions. Roosevelt, hungry for honor, joined his cavalry-without-horses in a wild and dangerous charge up San Juan Hill. They were assisting better organized regular divisions in the attack. Newspapermen, annoyed by the generals' failure to give them much attention, rallied around Roosevelt, a conspicuous and willing hero. General Lawton, who like other military men was critical of Roosevelt, reportedly snapped that "this is no political campaign, but a military campaign." The traditional soldiers also called the uphill scramble of the Rough Riders a "school boys' charge." But there was no doubt that their sheer bravado added to Spanish be-

wilderment and won San Juan Hill. (Roosevelt himself, who in his youth had worked his way up from a sickly weakling to a solid fighter, was thrilled to shoot his first Spaniard and see him crumple, although he must have been fairly close to see him at all; he brought eight pairs of glasses along to Cuba.)

It was naval not land battles however, that determined the outcome of the war. Cervera's fleet, trapped in the harbor, had a choice between surrender and attempted escape. Cervera decided on the latter course and lost all his ships in the ensuing battle on July 3. The Spanish surrendered formally two weeks later. On July 25, the yearnings of American annexationists bore more fruit. An American expeditionary force landed in Puerto Rico, a territory not covered by the Teller Amendment, and claimed the island.

Colonel Theodore Roosevelt and his Rough Riders, the horseless cavalry unit that charged San Juan Hill on foot and took it from the Spanish.

ACQUISITION
OF THE PHILIPPINES

A NEW DEBATE

Spanish defeat after a 10-week campaign brought both Spain and the United States to the conference table in Paris in October. McKinley sent a five man commission, most of whom were expansionists. The Spanish negotiators quickly ceded Cuba, Puerto Rico, and Guam in the western Pacific. American superiority in the Caribbean, part of the program for an isthmian canal, was now assured. But Captain Mahan's

vision of the United States as master of both oceans, with the canal as a connecting link between them, had taken hold of the expansionist imagination.

The war had given the United States the Philippine Islands. Should she keep them? Few Americans had any idea of the intensity and seriousness of Filipino nationalism. After his almost magical victory, Dewey had linked arms with Emilio Aguinaldo, leader of the Filipino *insurrectos* in what Aguinaldo believed was a guarantee of Filipino

The signing of the Peace Protocol that ended the war with Spain. Secretary of State William R. Day signs the document while President McKinley looks on from the right.

sovereignty. Dewey, however, denied having made any such promise.

While the United States negotiating team was at work in Paris, and McKinley brooded over the question of acquisition, the Filipinos had already made up their minds. They saw little difference between one imperial rule and another. Aguinaldo organized his armies in the expectation that the archipelago might be ceded to the United States. Nationalist posters advertising the Filipino position all over the islands should have been sufficient to warn Washington that acquisition was no simple matter. However, Washington's men in the area failed to perceive, or to communicate, the extent of Filipino opposition. Up to the time that Congress agreed to annexation, McKinley apparently still believed that native opposition was mild and scattered, and that the good will of American administrators would soon pacify the inhabitants.

Debate over acquisition grew rapidly, and each side had its moral as well as practical justification. A year after the acquisition of the Philippines, McKinley described his decision as a religious crisis. He told members of the General Missionary Committee of the Methodist Episcopal Church that night after agonizing night, he "prayed Almighty God for light and guidance . . . And one night it came to me this way— I don't know how it was, but it came . . . that there was nothing left for us to do but to take them all . . . and Christianize them. . . . And then I went to bed, and went to sleep, and slept soundly, and the next morning I sent for the chief engineer of the War Department (our map-maker) and I told him to put the Philippines on the map of the United States."

The religious motive for extending the American map halfway across the globe was a little suspect. Most of the Filipinos had converted long ago, albeit to Catholicism. One historian, pointing to the trading interests of the United States in the area, has noted that McKinley's policy comes down to "God directs us—perhaps it will pay." Businessmen reluctant to acquire new territory before the war, were now encouraged by the stunning victory to support acquisition and hoped that the Philippines would become a base for American trade in the Far East. Commercial journals began to speak openly of America's economic destiny and need for markets. At the 1900 Republican convention, Henry Cabot Lodge defended acquisition with these words: "We make no hypocritical pretense of being interested in the Philippines solely on account of others . . . we regard the welfare of the American people first . . . we believe in trade expansion."

The belief in the superiority of Anglo-Saxon institutions played a part in some expansionist propaganda. Rudyard Kipling's poem containing the phrase "Take up the white man's burden" was used to urge the United States to take on the responsibilities of empire. The poem, one critic said, "circled the earth in a day and by repetition became hackneyed within a week." Senator Beveridge, a vocal imperialist, spoke more bluntly. "They are not capable of self-government," he said. "How could they be? They are Orientals, Malays, instructed by Spaniards . . ."

Against these arguments ranged the anti-imperialists, among them distinguished men like Cleveland, Andrew Carnegie, Carl Schurz, William James, and Mark Twain. They even formed an Anti-Imperialist League to further their cause. They argued that it was not necessary to hold colonies for American trade to expand. Moreover, the Philippine Islands were not contiguous and would be difficult to defend. Finally, the anti-imperialists argued that it was contrary to the spirit of the Declaration of Independence for the United States to acquire sovereignty over another country and keep it in a subordinate role. No matter how good her intentions, the arrangement could only be oppressive and might even endanger democracy in America.

But on October 26, McKinley, having convinced himself that the public wanted acquisition, instructed the Paris conference that "cession must be of the whole archipelago or none." Even the American negotiators were stunned. The Spaniards resisted, but in the end Spain was forced to accept payment of 20 million dollars in return for the Philippines. The Filipinos however, continued mobilization in the hope that the future would bring anti-imperialists to power.

FILIPINO RESISTANCE

When the treaty came up for ratification, William Jennings Bryan, though strongly opposed to acquisition, unexpectedly told his colleagues in Washington to approve it. He had developed the erroneous belief that it would be better to fight imperialism in the elections a year and half later, rather than in the Senate. Bryan's move guaranteed ratification. Even while the vote was being taken, on February 5, 1899, the news came that a Filipino insurrection against the United States had begun. The next day the Senate approved the treaty 57 to 27. The country did not yet understand the extent of Filipino resistance. The United States, caught up in the emotional fervor of the time had voted to take on new responsibilities for which she was ill-prepared. Blinded by the ease with which American power had vanquished Spain, she assumed without analysis that the superiority of American institutions and the ideals of American life would secure her position of leadership in the world without further troublesome commitments and responsibilities.

WAR IN THE PHILIPPINES

The United States began efforts to put down the insurrection under the impression that the *insurrectos* were a small and barbaric minority. Aguinaldo, in fact, had an army of about 80,000 men, used to fighting at night because of the tropical heat. The American armies, well-equipped, shocked the Filipinos with their own barbarism, fighting during the day against an enemy which had no guns and used bolo knives and wooden spears.

Major General Ewell Otis was in charge of the American forces. Otis conducted a conservative campaign, and by the time of the first summer rains, the United States still had not crushed the resistance to American rule. Otis called on Washington for more troops, modestly labeled "effectives" to ease the blow. Early in 1900, there were 65,000 "effectives" on the islands, including two black regiments. As the war dragged on, one of Otis' subordinates, General Lawton, let it be known that he thought 100,000 troops were needed.

During the first two years of war, Otis' strategy did succeed in breaking the organization of the *insurrectos*. The Filipinos reverted to their strategy of guerrilla warfare, merging into the civilian population. The bitterness of guerrilla war also spurred racial hatred between the armies. American soldiers, finding their buddies mutilated by bolo knives, would proceed to slaughter an entire village, men, women, and children. The American public began to hear of atrocities committed by the army, even the use of concentration camp methods similar to those previously used by General Weyler in Cuba. Reports also arrived that Americans used water torture and rope torture to extract information Filipinos were unwilling to give. Ironically, the United States had conquered the Philippines in part because of her outrage at the Spanish tactics in Cuba.

American trench warfare in the Philippines.

General Otis' strategy of "capturing" villages had ignored the fact that enemy soldiers were rarely caught during such a capture—they vanished into the jungle and returned to the villages as soon as the American force departed. Soon he was replaced by General Arthur MacArthur, who soon informed Washington that the situation required drastic methods. Tactics grew harsher and finally in March, 1901, Emilio Aguinaldo was captured. To save his men, he took an oath of allegiance to the United States, and the war ended, although there were sporadic outbursts of guerrilla activity for four years. Deaths from the conflict totaled about five thousand Americans from war and disease, and at least twenty thousand Filipinos.

At home, the war had again become a major issue by the election of 1900. Bryan, the Democratic candidate, claimed that the "paramount" issue was imperialism, and the Republicans, though denying this during the campaign, later saw a mandate for the Philippine policy in McKinley's sweeping victory. McKinley had been genuinely disturbed by the bloodshed on the islands and sent several commissions there after

1899 to try to assure the Filipinos that the United States wanted to aid them economically and politically. The commissioners concluded that the Filipinos needed a civilian government that would both respect their culture and Americanize them politically. As a result, the United States built schools, roads, and transportation facilities, and prepared the Filipinos for self-government.

THE PANAMA CANAL

With the acquisition of the Philippines, the United States had two-ocean interests and a one-ocean navy. Thus, the aftermath of the Spanish-American War brought with it renewed interest in construction of the long-planned isthmian canal. However, there were several obstacles, political and financial, to construction.

First, it was necessary to abrogate the old Clayton-Bulwer Treaty. After an unsuccessful negotiation with Great Britain, in 1901 the Hay-Pauncefote Treaty was ratified by the Senate, giving the United States a free reign to build an isthmian canal. It stipulated only that the canal be used internationally, open on an equal basis to all shipping.

The second obstacle was more serious. Congress had not yet decided between the alternative routes for the canal, one through Nicaragua, and one through Panama. Each route had its own complications. The Nicaraguan was much longer and yet much easier to build. An American company had begun construction there and failed, and now offered its assets to the United States. Around the same time Ferdinand de Lesseps, a French builder, had begun a canal across Panama; his firm, the New Panama Canal Company, had also failed and was offering to sell its assets to the United States.

The Nicaraguan route at first seemed preferable, because the government was amenable to the plan, and because it was believed that it would cost less to construct it there. However, the New Panama Canal Company spent a great deal of money on propaganda for its route, and an American lawyer for the firm lobbyed assiduously with Republican politicians to gain their support for the measure. Then, in May, 1902, thirty thousand people died in an eruption of Mt. Pelé in Martinique, and the Panama lobby in Congress encouraged a panic about volcanic danger in Nicaragua. When the Nicaraguan government denied there would be any problem, Panamanians produced a Nicaraguan postage stamp portraying a picturesque eruption. This stamp changed history. Congress enacted legislation to pay de Lesseps' company 40 million dollars and negotiated with Colombia for a land strip in Panama. Six months later, in January, 1903, the United States and Colombia prepared a treaty under which the Canal Zone would be leased for 100 years, at a rental of 250,000 dollars per year, with a lump sum of 10,000 dollars for Colombia. Colombia, like the United States, had a legislature free to ratify or defeat treaties. Reacting in part to the low price, the Colombians refused ratification.

Theodore Roosevelt, who had become President in 1901 after the assassination of McKinley, had changed none of his imperialist viewpoints. Moreover, he favored the Panama route and was impatient for construction of the canal to begin. In later years, justifying his policies, he explained that "The Canal was for the benefit of the entire world. Should the blackmailing greed of the Bogota ring stand in the way of civilization? . . . I determined that I would do what ought to be done without regard to them." They were not only standing in "the way of civilization," but also in the way of Roosevelt's political ambitions. He wanted to be re-elected in his own right in 1904 and believed the canal would dramatize the success of his Presidency.

The Panama business elite met with American army officers in New York in July, 1903, and though unpublicized and unofficial, it was clear that the plan was unopposed by the administration. Panama had rebelled against Colombia before, without American involvement; now the time was ripe for new resistance. The revolution took place on November 3, 1903, one day after the U.S.S. *Nashville* had arrived on the scene and United States troops had seized the Panama railroads to bar Colombian troops from the isthmus. The United States conferred recognition on the new regime after a few days, only to meet with widespread indignation in the world press for her obvious maneuver. Latin Americans saw it as the perfect expression of "Yankee imperialism." The United States worked out a new treaty with Panama which was ratified in February, 1904, giving the United States a permanent lease on an area 10 miles wide. Panama was given a guarantee of her independence. Roosevelt defended his action, insisting that if he had used "traditional, conservative methods," the canal would never have been built. "I took the Canal Zone," he said, "and let Congress debate; and while the debate goes on, the Canal does also."

CARIBBEAN POLICY

Between 1898 and 1916, the United States turned the Caribbean into an American lake. Puerto Rico became a territorial possession in 1898 and the Virgin Islands were acquired from Denmark in 1916 for 16 million dollars. Between these two dates Cuba, Santo Domingo, Haiti, and Nicaragua became American protectorates. The reasons for this extension of influence are not hard to find. Economic expansion should not be overlooked, but the primary concern of American policy makers was the strategic necessity of protecting the entrance to the Panama Canal.

PUERTO RICO

The Teller Amendment to the declaration of war in 1898 had guaranteed Cuban sovereignty once the island was liberated from Spanish rule; but there was no provision in it forbidding annexation of other former colonies of Spain in the Caribbean. Expansionists like Lodge and Roosevelt sought to insure that Puerto Rico would be retained. Many businessmen were now for territorial expansion and had a lively curiosity about the island. They urged that the "garden spot" of Puerto Rico was crucial as a port en route to the proposed canal. In addition, missionaries, caught up in the enthusiasm, spoke of Christianizing the island's population.

After the well-received American occupation, there was no real question about the cession of Puerto Rico. Chaired by Joseph B. Foraker, a Senate committee on Puerto Rico drew up a plan for governance. The Foraker Act was approved by Congress in 1900. Under its provisions, Americans dominated the government through a powerful Executive Council, an upper house appointed by the President of the United

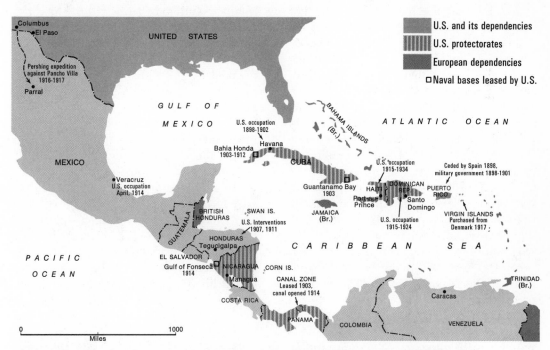

THE UNITED STATES IN CENTRAL AMERICA AND THE CARIBBEAN 1898 TO 1947

States. Puerto Ricans had more voice in the selection of the lower House of Delegates, roughly approximating a representative assembly; but this lower branch had no power to legislate without the Council's consent.

The Foraker Act provided a limited amount of self-government for Puerto Ricans. It was a special arrangement, midway between statehood and colonial status, but closer to the latter; and Puerto Ricans agitated for more power. In 1917 their status moved closer to statehood. They won United States citizenship, and gained their own elective upper house, replacing the Council. In 1952, Puerto Rico became a self-governing commonwealth, electing all her own officials.

CUBA

Though some expansionists regretted the fact, the Teller Amendment could not be erased. Even so, the United States did not withdraw immediately from Cuba, but instead set up a military government to pacify the island and restore order. Cuban nationalists protested that this was a betrayal. But Washington reasoned that it had no right to abandon the island, with its economy and political organization ruined by years of warfare. The land had been ravaged by the "scorched earth" policy of Spain and the rebels. Bandits overran the roads; cattle, numbering about three million before the war, had been almost entirely annihilated; and people were starving. The Spanish government had provided the last traces of bureaucratic order, and promptly, perhaps spitefully, pulled out and left the island in chaos. The military occupation of the United States between 1898 and 1902 established a rural police, public schools, government finance, and a public health program. The outstanding success of the occupation came when Dr. Walter Reed and co-workers isolated the carrier of yellow fever during a particularly

harsh epidemic, and proceeded to eradicate the stegomyia mosquito, saving thousands of Cuban lives and cutting the death rate in half. The United States also freed political prisoners, distributed food, and arranged for the import of inexpensive cattle to restock the land.

Nevertheless, the tensions of occupation marred this constructive record. Most of the Cuban population wanted independence, although there were some landowners, as in the Philippines, who feared their local poor more than foreigners and wanted annexation. To some Europeans and Americans, the military occupation seemed only a prelude to a longer occupation that would betray the promise of Cuban sovereignty.

There was some amazement among cynics when, in 1900, under orders from Washington, an elected Cuban assembly was asked to draft a constitution to take effect when American troops were withdrawn. The United States, however, unhappy with the complete autonomy suggested by the constitution the Cubans drafted, insisted that they accept the Platt Amendment. This rider, to be added to the constitution, was deeply resented by the Cubans. It limited Cuba's range in making treaties, giving the United States a veto over commercial and diplomatic agreements that might impair its independence. The amendment also guaranteed the United States the right to buy or lease "naval stations" on the island, and, in the most significant section, the Cubans were forced to agree that "the United States may exercise the right to intervene for the preservation of Cuban independence, the maintenance of a government adequate for the protection of life, property, and individual liberty, and for discharging the obligations with respect to Cuba imposed by the Treaty of Paris on the United States." Cuba reluctantly accepted the provisions in 1903.

The intervention clause was not only symbolic. The United States had intervened three times in Cuba by 1917. In 1906, acceding to a request from Cuban President Estrada Palma, Roosevelt ordered Secretary of War William Howard Taft to oversee the island torn by insurrection. Roosevelt warned the Cubans against their "insurrectionary habit," and promised that if it persisted Cuba would not remain independent. In 1912 a threat to American commercial interests brought another brief intervention, and later Woodrow Wilson, in spite of his renunciation of the policy of intervention, also used the American strongarm to keep order and protect commerce.

THE ROOSEVELT COROLLARY

The United States policy of intervention in Caribbean affairs, begun by the Platt Amendment, ripened into maturity during the Presidency of Theodore Roosevelt. Roosevelt faced a genuine difficulty in the Caribbean. The small republics there were unstable and often in debt to European powers. Failure to pay debts sometimes brought European intervention. For example, in 1902, Venezuela's dictator, Cipriano Castro, reneged on government debts to banking houses in Great Britain, Germany, and Italy. The European powers resorted to blockade, bombardment, and seizure of customs houses. Though Roosevelt despised Castro, American popular sentiment saw the European military action as a violation of the Monroe Doctrine. Faced with Roosevelt's dispatch of a naval force under Admiral Dewey to the Caribbean, Germany and Great Britain agreed to international arbitration of the dispute.

In 1904, the possibility of new European interventions brought Roosevelt to declare that "chronic wrong-doing or an impotence which results in a general loosening of the ties of civilized society . . . may force the United States . . . to the exercise of an international police power." In 1905, during a debt crisis in Santo Domingo, Roosevelt

clarified his meaning. The island was indebted to both Europeans and Americans and asked for United States assistance. Roosevelt set up the Santo Domingo Improvement Company to oversee Dominican revenues from customs and to make sure that 55 percent went to the island's creditors. The principle was clear. To prevent

Roosevelt's Policy Toward Latin America

❝ *It has for some time been obvious that those who profit by the Monroe doctrine must accept certain responsibilities along with the rights which it confers; and that the same statement applies to those who uphold the doctrine. It can not be too often and too emphatically asserted that the United States has not the slightest desire for territorial aggrandizement at the expense of any of its southern neighbors, and will not treat the Monroe doctrine as an excuse for such aggrandizement on its part. We do not propose to take any part of Santo Domingo, or exercise any other control over the island save what is necessary to its financial rehabilitation in connection with the collection of revenue, part of which will be turned over to the government to meet the necessary expense of running it, and part of which will be distributed pro rata among creditors of the Republic upon a basis of absolute equity. The justification for the United States taking this burden and incurring this responsibility is to be found in the fact that it is incompatible with international equity for the United States to refuse to allow other powers to take the only means at their disposal of satisfying the claims of their creditors and yet to refuse, itself, to take any such steps.*

—*Theodore Roosevelt*

Wilson's Policy Toward Latin America

66 *We must prove ourselves their friends, and champions upon terms of equality and honor. You cannot be friends upon any other terms of equality. You cannot be friends at all except upon the terms of honor. We must show ourselves friends by comprehending their interest whether it squares with our own interest or not. It is a very perilous thing to determine the foreign policy of a nation in the terms of material interest. It not only is unfair to those with whom you are dealing, but it is degrading as regards your own actions.*

Human rights, national integrity, and opportunity as against material interests—that, ladies and gentlemen, is the issue which we now have to face. I want to take this occasion to say that the United States will never again seek one additional foot of territory by conquest. She will devote herself to showing that she knows how to make honorable and fruitful use of the territory she has, and she must regard it as one of the duties of friendship to see that from no quarter are material interests made superior to human liberty and national opportunity. 99

—*Woodrow Wilson*

European intervention, the United States would use her "international police power" and intervene in these countries herself to maintain order and fiscal responsibility. The policy worked well in Santo Domingo, keeping Europeans out and restoring the republic to financial health. New interventions to stabilize the island's economic and political life occurred in 1914 and from 1916 to 1924. But Congress would never ratify a treaty legalizing these actions.

Roosevelt and Wilson acted alone, boldly asserting executive authority.

TAFT'S DOLLAR DIPLOMACY

Roosevelt's successor, William Howard Taft, sought to carry on Roosevelt's Caribbean policies. Yet, Roosevelt's primary concern in enunciating the "Roosevelt Corollary" had been to protect America's strategic interest in the canal by preventing a strong European presence in the Caribbean. Whereas, Taft's interests were more closely connected to American economic expansion there.

In 1909, Nicaragua's dictator, Jose Santos Zelaya, was beset by a revolution, which was partly inspired by American mining interests. Taft sent the marines, and in the aftermath prepared a treaty with the new regime. It provided an arrangement similar to Roosevelt's earlier one with Santo Domingo. The United States would take charge of Nicaragua's finances, and supply the forces that would guarantee economic and political stability, putting down revolution if necessary. Congress balked, as it had before at Roosevelt's operations in Santo Domingo. Enemies of the administration called Taft's policy "dollar diplomacy." Though Congress did not sanction it, dollar diplomacy and the realities of Caribbean economics persisted. In 1911, American bankers were supervising Nicaraguan finances, and in 1912 the marines again arrived to break an incipient revolution.

WILSON AND MEXICO

Relations between the United States and Latin America had deteriorated to a very low point when Wilson became President. The United States had participated in three Pan-American conferences under his predecessors, but her actions in the Caribbean belied her words of friendship at these international gatherings. By 1914, Latin American hostility to what they considered the sinister nature of American foreign policy was rampant in the press and among students and intellectuals.

Wilson had undertaken a very unpopular and short-lived intervention in Mexico to try to force the authoritarian regime of General Victoriano Huerta to submit to free elections before the United States would recognize his government as legitimate. Under Huerta an oppressive and dictatorial regime like the one overthrown in the revolution of 1911 had returned to power. However, the government was still opposed by the revolutionists under Venustiano Carranza who controlled much of the country. Reports Wilson received from agents in Mexico encouraged the President to believe he could force Huerta to comply with his wishes. But in October, 1913, Huerta, backed by British oil interests, made himself dictator. Since Britain was now at war in Europe, and wanted American friendship, she withdrew her recognition of Huerta. Wilson also lifted an embargo on the sale of American arms to Mexico in order to supply the Carranza forces. Then in an effort to reach a quick showdown with Huerta, Wilson ordered the seizure of Veracruz on the east coast of Mexico in April, 1914, on the pretext that the Mexican regime had not properly apologized for the arrest of some American sailors in Tampico. Not only did the seizure of Veracruz cost American lives, but both Huerta and Carranza protested the violation of Mexican sovereignty. Wilson, seeing he had gone too far, accepted the offer of Argentina, Brazil, and Chile (ABC powers) to mediate the dispute. The conference established nothing except American withdrawal, but Huerta, now under heavy attack, abdicated in July and Carranza took power. Violence continued in Mexico, but Wilson recognized the Carranza government in October, 1915.

WILSON'S CARIBBEAN POLICY

In spite of these actions Wilson was much more popular in Latin America than Roosevelt or Taft had been. In 1913, Wilson delivered a speech at Mobile in which he assured Latin America that the United States sought no territorial conquests in the Western Hemisphere. He added that his country wanted to work with Latin American nations as a partner, on terms of equality and independence. Wilson also made it clear that his interventions were not based on the concept of dollar diplomacy but in an effort to aid the Caribbean regimes to develop methods of self-government. Wilson's missionary zeal tended to blind him to the realities of corruption and militarism in this area and his sense of the moral superiority of American institutions led him to try to impose his concept of democracy on them. Nevertheless, Latin Americans perceived to a certain extent that Wilson's motives were benevolent and not exploitive.

In 1914 Wilson signed a treaty with Colombia in which the United States expressed regret for the Panama affair and agreed to pay Colombia 25 million dollars. The Republicans in the Senate shelved the treaty (it passed in 1921 after Roosevelt died), but the sentiment was plain. In addition, Wilson not only accepted the mediation of the ABC powers over the Veracruz episode but also called for a new Pan-American League to further inter-American good will.

In some respects Wilson's Caribbean policy was no different from that of Roosevelt and Taft. He sent troops to Santo Domingo in 1916 to keep order, and they remained there until 1924. He continued the American presence in Nicaragua and in 1916 the Senate ratified a treaty giving the United States the right to build naval bases there. Due to unrest in Haiti, American troops occupied that island in 1914 and remained there under a 1916 treaty in control of the customs, the army, and the island's foreign policy until 1934.

THE OPEN DOOR POLICY

Acquisition of the Philippines committed the United States to a role in the Far East and especially focused attention on American interests in China. As a result of defeat in the Sino-Japanese War of 1895, China had been gravely weakened and forced to concede territory to Japan. The traditional "buffer" state of Korea fell under Japanese sway, and in the next few years the European powers—Russia, Italy, France, Great Britain, and Germany—consolidated territorial and economic concessions inside the Chinese mainland, and in her ports setting up so-called "spheres of influence." As foreign influence became more and more entrenched, with the Russians established in Manchuria, the Germans in the Shantung Peninsula, the British in numerous ports and in control of the Yangtse valley, and the French in South China, the United States began to fear that the old empire would actually be partitioned and closed off to free American trade.

BRITISH INTEREST IN ALLIANCE

Although it used to be thought that British pressure for support against the competition of the other European powers in China was the leading factor in the issuance of the Open Door notes, it is now generally believed that domestic pressures were the leading influences on Hay and McKinley in 1899. Great Britain, without allies in Europe, now looked to the United States, landless in China, as an ally against partition. In March, 1898, the British approached the United States to suggest the formation of such an alliance. This move was one harbinger of the improvement of Anglo-American relations in the coming

century. The British implied that they were willing to acknowledge United States sovereignty in the Americas in exchange for a cooperative alliance in the Far East. Secretary of State John Hay rejected the British advance, although he was personally attracted to it, since such an open alliance would still have been extremely unpopular in the United States. Although American investment and trade in China was still relatively slight, acquisition of Hawaii and the Philippines encouraged an interest in trade in the Orient.

UNITED STATES INTERESTS IN "OPEN DOOR POLICY"

COMMERCIAL

A glance at two American industries gives an idea of some of the commercial motives for what was to be called the "Open Door Policy." The America-China Development Company numbered among its shareholders Carnegie Steel, Senator Thomas Platt of New York, and Jacob Schiff. The company had plans for railroad construction in China and partition would make such plans impractical. Perhaps more important was the growth of American cotton export to China. Though Britain still did a larger trade in cotton with China, American exports had grown by 120 percent in the preceding decade, while British exports had actually declined. Manchuria was the center of the cotton trade. When Russia took Port Arthur, there was a chance that she might close off American trade. The American minister in China wrote that "Partition would tend to destroy our markets . . . In these countries we are destined to find our best customers for manufactured, as well as natural, and agricultural products." He was not a lone prophet. The Cotton Spinners' Association was also active in supporting a policy that would keep the China trade open. Supporting these efforts was the American Asiatic Association created in 1898 and backed by many important corporations and industrialists. Thus, while American trade in China was slight at the time, there was widespread, if naive, optimism about its future dimensions.

RELIGIOUS AND IMPERIALISTIC

As in the case of the acquisition of the Philippines, the policy of keeping the door open in China was strongly backed by American missionaries and the ardent imperialists in the United States government. There were 1,500 American missionaries in China in 1899, and they and their denominational leaders in America saw China as a vast area for converts. The imperialist element also felt that the United States as a great power had to play a decisive role in the economic future of China. Hay was greatly influenced by a close friend and former minister to China, William W. Rockhill. Rockhill loved China and wanted to see her reunited and strong enough to drive out the Western powers.

THE OPEN DOOR NOTES

McKinley, under pressure from all these groups, was finally convinced to take a stand when an agent he had sent to investigate conditions in the Philippines returned in August, 1899, and told the press that the great issue in the Far East was how to keep China open. As the partition of China by the European powers and Japan seemed imminent, McKinley strove to preserve equal industrial and commercial rights there. Secretary of State John Hay sent Open Door notes to the major powers involved to ensure these privileges.

The first Open Door note had three sections, each of which countered the tendency toward partition. The first required that treaty ports within spheres of influence or leased territories be kept open to all trading nations. This meant essentially that no imperialist power could bar international traders like the United States. Russia, for example, could not seal off Port Arthur. Second, the statement required that the Chinese tariff remain as it stood, and that Chinese officials continue collecting it. Third, port and railway rates were to be equal for all traders in spite of spheres of influence.

The American military presence in the Philippines gave some authority to Hay's notes, though the United States was by no means prepared to back them up with force. The great powers agreed with the notes in principle but took exception to references to matters that affected their interests directly. Despite this lack of a clearcut answer, Hay within a short time, and with bland bravado, declared that all the interested parties had given their "final and definitive" consent.

THE BOXER REBELLION

A few months after the announcement of Hay's first notes, the Boxer Rebellion brought a new crisis in China. The Boxers, their name derived from the Chinese *I Ho Ch'üan*, meaning "righteous, harmonious fists," were a militant nationalist group that could not endure either the "foreign devils" that devoured their country or the weak Chinese government that permitted them to. In May, 1900, the Boxers launched a fanatical war on foreigners and Christian Chinese, looting and murdering hundreds. In June, they laid siege to Peking and its foreign embassies and put the capital out of contact with the Western world for a month.

Responding to the rebellion, Japan, Russia, Britain, France, Germany, and the United States sent a combined force of 18,000 men to redeem the besieged city. Concerted international action of this sort once more endangered what was left of China's sovereignty. The presence of the international force was no mere police action. Though the Peking siege was lifted in August, the rebellion was likely to ignite new attempts by the foreign interests to demand concessions in China and perhaps even to partition her.

THE SECOND OPEN DOOR NOTE

With this danger in mind, and while the combined force was still in China, Hay in July, 1900, formulated the second Open Door note, to "preserve Chinese territorial and industrial entity . . . and safeguard for the world the principle of equal and impartial trade with all parts of the Chinese Empire." More sweeping and clearer than its predecessor, it included all parts of China, not only the spheres of influence, and emphasized the principle of "Chinese entity" or sovereign wholeness.

Alone, the United States would have been unable to force acceptance of the principle and prevent partition. American policy was guided by the knowledge that the European powers feared each other more than they wanted new concessions. Excessive competition in the Orient might upset the balance of power in Europe and lead to a general war. The Open Door notes, though they denied the imperialists the right to seize more, also had the aura of guaranteeing the status quo. Acceptance of them might avert costly international war as a result of a scramble for Chinese territory. Though without much enthusiasm, the other powers accepted the new principle and an extended invasion was avoided. Instead of territory, the powers took giant indemnities from the

Chinese people, totaling some 333 million dollars. The United States eventually realized that its own share, 25 million dollars, was exorbitant, and about 18 million dollars went to fund the education of Chinese students in American colleges and universities.

As far as the American people were concerned, as soon as the notes were issued they forgot about them just as they quickly forgot about the American commitment in the Philippines. Interest in imperialism declined rapidly in the United States after 1900.

THE RUSSO-JAPANESE WAR

Roosevelt undertood that it was impossible to carry out the Open Door policy and hoped that American influence could help maintain access to China by keeping the powers evenly matched in Asia. For example, believing that Russia was stronger than Japan, he followed an overtly friendly policy toward Japan in case there should be a conflict between them.

Russia and Japan, more locally involved in Asia than the European powers and more reluctant about the Open Door notes than any of them, did go to war in 1904 as a result of rivalry over Manchuria. Most sentiment in the United States was pro-Japanese. It was not yet understood how important a rival Japan might become. Czarist rule in Russia was considered oppressive, and, Russian rule over Manchuria threatened the trade interests of the United States. On the other hand, Roosevelt understood quite well that a clearcut Japanese victory, which was not expected, would upset the balance of power in Asia.

Despite Japanese victories over the Russian navy, American hopes for a stalemate still were realized when Japan, economically depleted, requested that Roosevelt mediate a truce. Russian and Japanese delegates met in New Hampshire, and Roosevelt used his influence behind the scenes to insure that the Japanese recognize the Open Door in Manchuria and disclaim any future interest in the Philippines. The Treaty of Portsmouth gave Japan the southern half of the Russian island of Sakhalin in the Sea of Okhotsk, great influence in the southern half of Manchuria, and recognition of Japanese dominion in Korea, first acquired in 1895 during the Sino-Japanese War.

The President won the Nobel Peace Prize in 1906 partly for his role in mediating the conflict. The treaty was a recognition of Japan's new influence in Asia and increased Japanese-American tensions. Roosevelt as mediator had thwarted the Japanese demand for an indemnity from Russia. In reaction, many Japanese took to the streets to riot against Roosevelt and their own negotiators. Furthermore, the American public began to feel less friendly to Japan as a result of the war and the demonstrations.

JAPANESE-AMERICAN RELATIONS

There were additional factors already present on the West Coast which precipitated these ill-feelings. While remaining outwardly friendly to Japan, Roosevelt now gave more thought to keeping her aware of American power and presence in the Pacific. In 1908, he sent the American fleet around the world, and it stopped at Japanese ports to show them American naval might. Roosevelt also made an executive agreement with Japan the same year in which both nations agreed to maintain the status quo in the Far East.

Roosevelt had acquiesced in Japanese dominance in Manchuria, but his successor hoped to use American pressure to arrest that influence. As in the Caribbean, President Taft favored a policy of dollar diplomacy in the Far East. With State Department backing, he encouraged American businessmen to invest more heavily in railroads in Manchuria to weaken the influence of Japan. American railroad men and bankers were unfavorable to the idea, however, especially since there was no commitment by the government to protect such a venture.

Wilson, antagonistic to American economic influence in the Far East, as well as in the Caribbean, repudiated Taft's policy. At the same time, he called for maintenance of the Open Door in China. The President naively believed that the overthrow of the Manchu Dynasty in 1912 was the precursor to the development of democracy there, and consequently recognized the new regime in 1913.

During World War I, Japan openly defied American pleas to maintain the Open Door in China. She took over the German concessions in North China, and in May, 1915, presented the Chinese government with Twenty-one Demands. They included Japanese dominance not only of Manchuria and North China but all of the China coast, and the right to develop the interior of the country. The United States made two protests, but preoccupation with the war in Europe prevented any further action. In 1917, in the Lansing-Ishii agreement, the United States reluctantly recognized Japan's "special interests" in China in return for a vaguely worded recognition of the Open Door policy by Japan.

Readings

GENERAL WORKS

Bemis, Samuel F., *The Latin American Policy of the United States.* New York: Norton, 1967—A general history of American diplomatic relations with Latin America which, for the most part, supports United States policies.

Dulles, Foster R., *The Imperial Years.* New York: Apollo, 1960—A survey of American imperialism between 1885 and 1909. The author believes that the United States fulfilled the idealistic claims it made for its rule over colonial peoples.

Griswold, A. Whitney, *The Far Eastern Policy of the United States.* New Haven: Yale University Press, 1938—A study which begins with the annexation of the Philippines and continues through the pre-World War II tensions between the United States and Japan.

Kennan, George R., *American Diplomacy: 1900–1950.* New York: New American Library, 1952—A critique of United States foreign policy in the twentieth century by a leading diplomat, which finds American policy to be insufficiently realistic and overly moralistic.

LaFeber, Walter, *The New Empire.* Ithaca, N.Y.: Cornell University Press, 1963—A history of expansionist pressures from the Civil War through the Spanish-American War. At the heart of growing imperialist desires, LaFeber finds consistent business pressure for overseas markets.

Munro, Dana G., *Intervention and Dollar Diplomacy for the Caribbean: 1900–1921.* Princeton, N.J.: Princeton University Press, 1964—American policymakers in the Caribbean, Munro claims, were guided more by political than by economic considerations, in particular by a fear of European influences in the Western Hemisphere.

Perkins, Dexter, *The Monroe Doctrine, 1867–1907.* Gloucester, Mass.: Peter Smith, 1966—Perkins considers the Monroe Doctrine to be flexible, changing with the purposes and needs of American foreign policy. During the period studied in this volume, the Doctrine took on new meanings under Cleveland, McKinley, and Theodore Roosevelt.

Pratt, Julius W., *America's Colonial Experiment.* Gloucester, Mass.: Peter Smith, 1964 —A territory-by-territory study of the lands which the United States has colonized, with particular attention to the varying forms of colonial rule.

Pratt, Julius W., *Expansionists of 1898.* Chicago: Quadrangle, 1964—A study of the American acquisition of Hawaii, the Philippines, Puerto Rico, and the virtual colonization of Cuba. Pratt focuses on the intellectual background and public opinion at home which supported expansionism.

Sprout, Harold, and Margaret Sprout, *The Rise of American Naval Power*. Princeton, N.J.: Princeton University Press, 1943—A history of naval policy from the American Revolution to the twentieth century, tracing the connections between naval developments and political considerations.

Young, George B., and John A. Grenville, *Politics, Strategy, and American Diplomacy*. New Haven, Conn.: Yale University Press, 1966—A collection of eleven essays on late nineteenth-century American foreign policy. The authors reject economic interpretations of the policies and emphasize strategic factors.

SPECIAL STUDIES

Beale, Howard K., *Theodore Roosevelt and the Rise of America to World Power*. Baltimore: Johns Hopkins Press, 1956—A detailed appraisal of Roosevelt's role in foreign affairs. While praising Roosevelt for having a broad view of international politics, Beale criticizes his enthusiasm for military action in foreign relations.

Beisner, Robert L., *Twelve Against Empire*. New York: McGraw-Hill, 1968—Sketches of a dozen anti-imperialists in the Mugwump reform tradition. Beisner shows that the anti-imperialists shared many assumptions about world affairs with the pro-imperialists in power.

Campbell, Charles S., Jr., *Anglo-American Understanding, 1898–1903*. Baltimore: Johns Hopkins Press, 1957—During the years Campbell studies, solutions to the remaining major problems of British-American relations were found and the two nations embarked on a period of close diplomatic cooperation.

Campbell, Charles S., Jr., *Special Business Interests and the Open Door Policy*. Hamden, Conn.: Shoestring Press, 1968—A study of the formation of China policy at the turn of the century, emphasizing the desire of American businessmen for the China market as a cure for the danger of overproduction.

Freidel, Frank, *The Splendid Little War*. Boston: Little, Brown, 1958—A well-illustrated description of the Spanish-American War. The phrase "splendid little war" comes from a letter by John Hay, but Freidel makes it clear that it was far from splendid for those who fought in it.

Healy, David F., *The United States in Cuba: 1898–1902*. Madison: University of Wisconsin Press, 1963—Healy maintains that the United States used Cuba between 1898 and 1902 as a laboratory for testing different methods of imperial control. When annexation of the island proved impractical, the United States settled on a policy of indirect rule, which it applied throughout Latin America for the next thirty years.

May, Ernest R., *Imperial Democracy*. New York: Harcourt, Brace, 1961—A study of American imperialism between 1893 and 1898. May analyzes both American and foreign records and concludes that popular pressures brought about and sustained American imperialism.

Millis, Walter, *The Martial Spirit*. Boston: Houghton Mifflin, 1931—An older study of militarism and nationalism which focuses on the Spanish-American War and is critical of imperialist policy.

Morgan, H. Wayne, *America's Road to Em-* *pire*. New York: Wiley, 1965—A brief account of the diplomatic developments leading to the Spanish-American War. Morgan feels that McKinley's legitimate efforts to get Spain out of Cuba by peaceful means failed because of the incompetence of Spanish rulers and the presence of Cuban guerrillas.

Pletcher, David M., *The Awkward Years*. Columbia: University of Missouri Press, 1962—During the Garfield and Arthur administrations, Pletcher shows that Republican leaders such as Blaine were edging toward an interventionist foreign policy. However, the political and diplomatic situation did not permit expansionism to develop fully.

Wolff, Leon, *Little Brown Brother*. Garden City, N.Y.: Doubleday, 1961—An account of the pacification of the Philippine rebels after the Spanish-American War. Wolff describes the sordid history of this little-remembered Asian war.

PRIMARY SOURCES

Gardner, Lloyd, ed., *A Different Frontier*. Chicago: Quadrangle, 1966—A collection of documents illustrating economic forces in the United States which pushed for imperial efforts as a substitute for Western expansion after the closing of the Western frontier.

Mahan, Alfred T., *The Influence of Sea Power Upon History*. New York: Hill & Wang, 1957—An influential late nineteenth-century plea for naval strength. Admiral Mahan's concepts were widely read and admired by such men as Theodore Roosevelt.

Roosevelt, Theodore, *The Rough Riders*. New York: New American Library, 1961—A jingoistic account of military heroism by the future President.

Strong, Josiah, *Our Country*. Cambridge, Mass.: Harvard University Press, 1963—A strongly nationalistic treatise by a clergyman and social reformer. Strong called for the spread of Christianity by American missionaries.

BIOGRAPHIES

Dennett, Tyler, *John Hay*. Port Washington, N.Y.: Kennikat Press, 1963—A biography of the Republican Secretary of State who wrote the Open Door Notes, which traces his development from a minor literary figure to a major political one.

James, Henry, *Richard Olney*. New York: Da Capo Press, 1969—As Attorney-General and Secretary of State under Grover Cleveland, Olney played important roles in both domestic and foreign policy. This is a sympathetic older biography of the conservative Democrat.

Leech, Margaret, *In the Days of McKinley*. New York: Harper & Row, 1959—A sympathetic but somewhat critical study of McKinley as President. Leech considers McKinley to exemplify the American spirit in the late 1890s.

Nevins, Allan, *Hamilton Fish*, Vols. I–II. New York: Ungar, 1957—Fish kept a diary as Secretary of State under Grant, and the diary is now a major source for the study of the Republican administration. Nevins draws heavily on it for his account of Fish's public life.

Swanberg, W. A., *Citizen Hearst*. New York: Scribner's, 1961—A popular biography of the publishing tycoon, portraying both his occasional warmth and generosity and the ruthless ambition and cruelty that made him one of the most hated men in America. The author believes Hearst was a decisive influence in bringing on the Spanish-American War.

Theodore Roosevelt speaking at Grant's tomb in 1911, while the press, in the front row, takes notes. Roosevelt, McKinley's Vice President, succeeded to the Presidency when McKinley was assassinated in 1901.

812

The Progressive Era 23

Suppose we look into one, No. ___ Cherry Street. Be a little careful, please! The hall is dark, and you might stumble over the children pitching pennies back there. Not that it would hurt them; kicks and cuffs are their daily diet. . . . You can feel your way if you cannot see it. . . . That was a woman filling her pail by the hydrant you just bumped against . . . . Here is a door. Listen! That short, hacking cough, that tiny helpless wail—what do they mean? . . . The child is dying with measles. With half a chance it might have lived, but it had none. That dark bedroom killed it.

—Jacob Riis

Jacob Riis wrote the above passage on tenement conditions in New York City in 1890. After coming to America from Denmark, he became a reporter for the New York *Tribune* and later for the New York *Evening Sun,* investigated conditions of squalor in this teeming, booming metropolis, and put his outraged feelings into a moving social document of the period, *How the Other Half Lives.* Riis touched the consciences of many New Yorkers, and Americans generally who were beginning to realize that similar brutalities were the lot of unfortunate city dwellers across the country. The book title became a popular phrase. He helped to stir to action hitherto unaware or unconcerned people who lived in fashionable urban districts and never saw the rancid slums where "the other half" lived amid poverty, vice, disease, and despair.

WHAT WAS THE PROGRESSIVE MOVEMENT?

Riis alone did not create the drive toward reform that became known as the progressive movement. Other writers were at the same time attacking America's social, political, and economic evils from various points of view. Politicians, clergymen, judges, businessmen, and social workers contributed their share to the indictment. The progressives were committed individuals who, while they did not agree on every solution, at least did agree that some problems were so serious they had to be solved if the nation was to live up to its ideals. It was a movement that grew out of the hope for a better America.

THE PROGRESSIVE PROFILE

The progressive movement for reform at the turn of the century had its roots in the protests and programs of the Populist revolt. The progressives attacked rule by the wealthy, brutal competition, and political corruption. They summoned men and women of good will to help transform political and economic life in America. They wanted, not cheap money, but government regulations to promote social and economic justice and eliminate corruption from political life. The essential ingredient of progressivism was the moral regeneration of American life. Unlike the Populist movement, which was overwhelmingly agrarian in make-up, the progressives were essentially middle-class, urban reformers. Most of the

estimated six million people associated with the movement lived in comfortable circumstances. Most were in their thirties and forties and of Anglo-Saxon descent. Most were Protestants strongly motivated by the old Puritan desire to rid the world of evil. The commentator Elmer Davis called the movement a political "carnival of purity." Progressives were willing to go to great lengths in behalf of the underprivileged to whom they had committed themselves in the social struggle.

The movement attracted many women motivated by the desire to bring moral reform to the country. The General Federation of Women's Clubs had a million members by the First World War, staunch fighters for social justice who were always prepared to send a spokesman to City Hall when the need for milk for babies or homes for wayward girls were placed on the agenda. For example, Jane Addams, a gently reared, well-educated, cultured and sensitive woman, boldly invaded the slums of Chicago in 1889. She founded Hull House, a haven of support for the immigrants and poor of Chicago's Nineteenth Ward. Famous men, from Mackenzie King, former Prime Minister of Canada, to Benny Goodman, have testified to the influence of Jane Addams and Hull House on their lives.

THE TRIANGLE SHIRTWAIST FIRE

Jane Addams led a crusade against unsafe working conditions in Chicago. A terrible accident in New York provided tragic support for her cause. The Triangle Shirtwaist Company employed about two hundred young women at sewing machines. On March 25, 1911, a fire broke out in the building where they worked. Flaring upward, the flames raced through the building. Some of those inside were burned to death, others were suffocated by smoke or killed when, panic-stricken, they jumped from the windows. The toll came to 146 dead. No one could pretend any longer that factory conditions in America were not in need of improvement.

THE MUCKRAKERS

The muckrakers, men and women who exposed the political and economic evils of the day in articles and books, received their name from Theodore Roosevelt. He took the unflattering epithet from *Pilgrim's Progress,* where John Bunyan speaks of the "man with the muckrake" who "would neither look up nor regard the crown he was offered, but continued to rake the filth on the floor." He feared that the written exposés of scandals in business and politics might cause revolutionary unrest in the country. Yet Roosevelt lived to hear himself called "the leader of the muckrakers" when he took up the cause of eradicating the worst evils they exposed.

The literature of exposure appeared in such magazines of the day as *McClure's, Collier's* and *Cosmopolitan.* In 1902, two of the most famous muckraking series began in *McClure's,* Ida Tarbell's reports on the Standard Oil Trust and Lincoln Steffens' articles on municipal corruption. For the next several years the magazines were full of exposés on a wide variety of social, economic, and political problems. The public read the magazines avidly, and many went on to books, such as Herbert Croly's *The Promise of American Life,* which influenced Roosevelt, and one by a rising young journalist named Walter Lippmann, *Drift and*

Mastery, a philosophical analysis that offered solutions to the problems created by laissez-faire capitalism.

The progressives, to a great extent, were trying to adjust to life in a country that had become 50 percent urban. They wanted to improve America's future without giving up traditional values. The basic religious and economic background of those in the movement made them resent the new concentration and consolidation of power in business, labor, ethnic groups, and city machines. They thought in terms of the free individual able to make his way in life by his own ability and not because he was part of a particular power bloc. Thus, although they were reformers, their ideals were conservative—to preserve the individualism they associated with the country's past. Most progressives were Republicans and supported McKinley in 1896.

While their primary emphasis was moralistic, rather than economic, the progressives wanted economic regulations instituted by government to curb the waste, discrimination, and high prices which they believed were caused primarily by the trusts and the labor unions. As small businessmen and professional people, they were angered at being victimized economically and psychologically by the power and the materialism of the new industrial order. They believed themselves morally superior to the men of great wealth, yet they resented the class-consciousness so evident in the developing labor movement.

Finally, most progressives were middle-class professionals, but there were other reformers in the era who did not fit this description. These included reform politicians from Roman Catholic and new immigrant backgrounds in the legislatures of New York and Massachusetts who mainly demanded economic reforms. They called for regulation of big business and factory legislation to protect workers. There were also some business leaders who actively worked for certain types of reform of benefit to them-

815

selves. For example, many rising young businessmen who distrusted the crusading spirit of the average progressive nevertheless supported local housing and health codes, sought an end to political corruption, and wanted federal regulation of business to make the capitalist system operate more equitably. To this end, they favored a stronger Interstate Commerce Commission, a federal trade commission, a government-run national banking system, and a curb on illegal corporate practices.

THE PROGRESSIVE MOVEMENT IN CITIES AND STATES

The appearance of *The American Commonwealth* in 1888 was a milestone in the study of democratic ideas and institutions. The author, James Bryce, was a clear-sighted Englishman who took a basically friendly attitude toward America. He was well aware of urban conditions when he wrote: "The government of cities is the one conspicuous failure of the United States."

CITY REFORM

Americans aware of the low level of urban politics were beginning to say much the same thing, and within a few years criticism had risen to a peak of protest and denunciation. Going beyond mere talk, an outraged public swept reform mayors into office in one city after another. The Municipal Voters' League of Chicago, founded in 1895, was largely responsible for the success of Mayor Edward F. Dunne, who won election despite the hostility of the ward bosses. Hazen S. Pingree won in Detroit on a reform platform. So did Tom Johnson in Cleveland, which he made, according to muckraker Lincoln Steffens, "the best governed city in America." The most famous of these reform mayors was Samuel L. Jones of Toledo. Announcing that he intended to run an administration guided by the Golden Rule of the Gospels which earned him the nickname "Golden Rule" Jones, he attacked political corruption, attended juvenile courts to see how youngsters in trouble with the law were being judged, and even changed the park signs from KEEP OFF THE GRASS to CITIZENS, PROTECT YOUR PROPERTY.

Each city politician who took office with reform on his mind worked from a general pattern. Here or there one issue might be especially pressing; for example, Chicago, but not New York, had a meat-packing problem. But social services were in demand everywhere, employees needed protection from exploitive employers, administrative corruption had to be curtailed, political bosses and ward heelers had to be stopped from rigging elections.

STATE REFORM

The most important figure in bringing reform on the state level was Robert La Follette, who came from the small town of Primrose, Wisconsin. He was intense, vastly self-assured, and an orator of high style. Greatly admired, he was honest and uncompromising, but a man with little humor and few friends. "Fighting Bob" entered politics as a Republican, put together a coalition of farmers and workers, and after several tries captured the governorship of Wisconsin over the opposition of most of the party leaders who were controlled by the railroad and lumber interests. He held the office from 1901 to 1906, when he was elected to the United States Senate. During those years he formulated and implemented what came to be called the "Wisconsin Idea," which included state regulation of railroads and industries, new banking laws, workmen's compensation, and conservation of natural resources. On every level he was a methodical planner. He tapped the best brains at the University of Wisconsin, bringing in renowned professors like sociologists Richard T. Ely and Edward A. Ross to advise him, thereby putting into effect something approaching Lester Ward's plan for an academy of specialists to assist politicians in making decisions and evaluating proposed legislation.

La Follette explained his reason for hiring experts in his autobiography: "They would have to match wits with the highly skilled, highly paid agents of the railroads, and they would have to make their work pass the critical consideration of the courts." This procedure resulted in efficiency as well as profits: "How has it been possible that both the people of Wisconsin and the investors in public utilities have been so greatly benefited by this regulation? *Simply because the regulation is scientific.*"

LABOR LEGISLATION

The protection of America's workers, of course, preoccupied the progressives. The principle of workmen's compensation, part of the Wisconsin Idea, was so quickly imitated that most states had such laws on the books before the end of the First World War. These laws took the burden of proof off the injured man or woman who sought to collect compensation. The employer could no longer evade the issue while his lawyer argued in court against his responsibility for the "negligence" (which often meant simply fatigue) of those who minded his machines. Child labor laws barring factory labor by children under fourteen were also adopted in many states through progressive pressure. There were gains in the drive for minimum wage and maximum hour legislation, and for improved factory conditions. The wage victories, however, were not lasting because of fluctuations in the value of money. More money in pay envelopes did not necessarily mean greater purchasing power.

In addition, state legislation to regulate hours and working conditions was challenged in the courts. The Supreme Court wavered between 1900 and 1937 on whether to end all regulatory legislation and the practical circumstances in individual cases which showed that the judges' theories were outmoded. Several state laws of this type had been voided before the famous case of *Lochner v. New York* in 1905. In this case, the Supreme Court ruled by a narrow 5 to 4 margin that a New York law which limited to ten the hours that bakers might work each day was unconstitutional because it was an arbitrary use of the state police power. It was unreasonable, said the Court, for the state to interfere with the freedom of bakers to make whatever contract they wished, a freedom protected by the Fourteenth Amendment. Justice Holmes, writing one of his famous dissents, argued that the Court had no right to interfere with the lawmaking process unless a piece of legislation specifically conflicted with a clause of the Constitution. He pointed out that the Court was reading into the Constitution its own economic interpretation, when this was a matter for the elected representatives of the people to decide. Three years later in *Muller v. Oregon* the Court reversed itself and upheld a 10-hour day for women workers in factories. The lawyer for Oregon, Louis Brandeis, swung the Court to his side with overwhelming data on the social and economic need for legislative protection of working women.

"RETURNING THE GOVERNMENT TO THE PEOPLE"

Two items in the Wisconsin Idea proved especially popular—a state income tax and the direct primary method of choosing political candidates. Until La Follette's tenure of office, party bosses had been the controlling factor in the process that produced men to run for office. Now the bosses had less control of elections since a man could hope to become a political success by winning enough votes in open competition with his party rivals. The ballot box replaced the notorious caucus of a few men who reached agreement through log-rolling and the exchange of favors.

Other states followed the Wisconsin example. On the West Coast, Oregon added its share to the reforming trend by adopting the initiative, by which the people could propose legislation, and the referendum, by which they could pass judgment on election day on issues of personal consequence to them. These practices spread to California, Missouri, Iowa, and other states. The business of "returning the government to the people" became a program as well as a watchword.

THE SEVENTEENTH AMENDMENT

The election of United States Senators by state legislatures, as provided in the Constitution, also seemed out of tune with truly democratic government. State legislatures were criticized as too vulnerable to political pressure to send the best men to Washington, too ready to vote for those who made it worth their while. Contributions to a particular party by a wealthy individual too often looked like a bribe if he were subsequently appointed to the Senate. As a result, a number of states decided to allow the public to show its preferences. The feeling grew that all states should do the same, and Congress submitted an amendment to the states for direct election of Senators. This was adopted in 1913 as the Seventeenth Amendment to the Constitution.

PROHIBITION

The drive against the sale of hard liquor, begun in the early nineteenth century, received new life in the progressive era. To many, the problem of drunkenness still seemed a matter for exhortation, not law. Many clergymen inveighed against it from the pulpit as a prominent cause of disease, crime, and broken homes. Prohibitionists arose to challenge the evil; one of the most notable was Carrie Nation, the victim of a drunken husband. Filled with anger, she would carry a small hatchet, barge into places that sold liquor, and proceed to smash bottles, hack at bars, and depart, leaving saloonkeepers fuming amid the wreckage. Carrie Nation was flamboyant, but only locally effective. However much the papers might play up her forays or photograph her with upraised hatchet, she could not make a noticeable change in national liquor consumption.

The churches, therefore, became more active with the formation of the Women's Christian Temperance Union. Then the Anti-Saloon League came forward in 1893 to join the cause. Their leader was Frances Willard, no hatchet wielder, but a militant woman who led her cohorts into saloons to set a good example by conducting prayers, singing hymns, and handing out temperance tracts. Some professional sociologists also argued for the social desirability of temperance enforced by law. Politicians found this a potent issue and various states and localities adopted prohibition before the First World War.

THE EIGHTEENTH AMENDMENT

During World War I, hard liquor was removed from the market for the duration as an economy measure. Patriotic Americans accepted this type of self-denial with good grace, and the temperance people saw

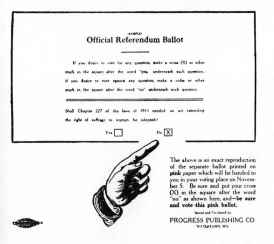

The militant faction of the women's equal rights movement had to overcome male hostility as well as female apathy before the Nineteenth Amendment could be ratified. This sample ballot instructs voters (men only) to vote "no" to the "menace" of woman suffrage.

their chance to extend the wartime situation and make prohibition a federal law. They campaigned vigorously for an amendment to the Constitution that would outlaw intoxicants permanently, except for carefully limited purposes such as medicinal use. Success came right after the war ended. The Eighteenth Amendment, prohibiting the manufacture, transportation, and sale of alcoholic beverages, was ratified at the beginning of 1919 and went into effect the following year. The United States had adopted the "noble experiment" with the high expectations of many people, but they were doomed to disappointment. The drinkers did not stop drinking but simply obtained their liquor illegally in speakeasies instead of in the old saloons. The Eighteenth Amendment and the Volstead Act, which enforced it, spawned the rumrunning gangster era that lasted until prohibition was repealed by the Twenty-first Amendment in 1933.

WOMEN'S SUFFRAGE

When Russian envoys came to Washington in 1917, they were met by two demonstrators carrying a sign with the words: "We, the women of America, tell you that America is not a democracy. Twenty million American women are denied the right to vote." The two demonstrators were suffragettes, representatives of a campaign for equality going back to 1848 when the first women's rights convention met in Seneca Falls, New York. Susan B. Anthony, the most prominent figure in the movement, helped found the National Woman Suffrage Association in 1869, and from then on these women gave the men of America no hope that they would accept anything less than equal power at the ballot box. These militant women had to overcome the apathy of their own sex as well. Carrie Chapman Catt, who followed Susan B. Anthony in leadership, spoke bitterly of the anti-suffrage woman who, appearing before an all-male legislative committee, would smile winningly and say: "Gentlemen, we trust you to take care of us and the government."

THE NINETEENTH AMENDMENT

The suffragettes, as in pre-Civil War days, stuck to their guns through ridicule, practical jokes, frequent barrages of overripe fruit, and occasionally more serious violence. Gradually men joined their cause. Victory came in the form of the "Anthony Amendment," which the great suffragette herself did not live to see. Susan B. Anthony died in 1906. The Nineteenth Amendment to the Constitution was ratified in 1920. It stated: "The right of citizens of the United States to vote shall not be denied or abridged by the United States or by any state on account of sex." By the 1920s, women were not only voting but running for and winning public office throughout the nation.

BLACK AMERICANS

The movement for racial equality also gained supporters in the progressive era, although most progressives had little interest in the subject. It is noteworthy that some of the most vehement opponents of racism came from Anglo-Saxon backgrounds. Jane Addams was particularly distressed by anti-black prejudice: "No group in our country has been more successful in overcoming all these difficulties than have the Negroes through three generations." Addams joined a group, which included William Dean Howells and John Dewey, that associated itself with W. E. B. Du Bois in founding the National Association for the Advancement of Colored People in 1909. Rejecting Booker T. Washington's willingness to accept an inferior economic and social status for his race in the United States, Du Bois was incensed by racial discrimination. A black man educated at Fisk and Harvard, he had taught at Atlanta University. He believed that black people should have the opportunity to go to college and enter the professions, and that they should have full political rights.

The NAACP grew in numbers and expanded its operations. Beginning with a campaign against lynching, it brought its cases to the courts. It pushed for the integration of all races in American society and became the most effective instrument in the efforts of black Americans to gain full equality with the rest of the population. By 1921 it had four hundred branches throughout the country, and had been joined by the Urban League, an organization devoted primarily to helping blacks find jobs and adjust to life in the cities.

PROGRESSIVISM ON THE NATIONAL LEVEL

By 1900, the progressives were looking beyond the efforts of local and state governments for reform to the possibility of obtaining their goals on a national scale. The federal government lagged far behind state leaders and state legislatures in reform efforts. When the state leader happened to be "Fighting Bob" La Follette, and the state legislature sat in Madison, Wisconsin, the contrast was extraordinary. Yet the Wisconsin Idea was an exception among the states; most had no intention of going that far in the direction of social justice, and many refused to move forward at all. The federal government, therefore, remained the hope of the progressives for nationwide economic and political reform. Their ideal was a President committed to progressive principles.

THEODORE ROOSEVELT

The answer to the progressives' prayer should, by all political odds, never have made it to the White House. Theodore Roosevelt, a political maverick, received the

In this 1905 cartoon, Roosevelt, dressed in his famous Rough Riders' outfit, is accompanied by Uncle Sam as they are barred from the Senate by the "tariff wall."

NO ADMITTANCE

Vice Presidential nomination on the McKinley ticket in order to remove him from the New York political scene and keep him from troubling the party councils with his "unsound and unreliable" ideas about society, politics, business, and economics. The Vice Presidency was not at that time considered a springboard to the Presidency, but rather "the graveyard of political ambition." Candidates for President came generally from Congress or the state governorships. The Vice President, by contrast, served out his years in Washington performing little more than ceremonial duties and then dropped back into some lesser office if not into private life. Mark Hanna, McKinley's campaign manager, termed Roosevelt "that damn cowboy," and hoped to see the classical pattern repeated in the new administration. So did the rest of the Republican Old Guard.

PERSONALITY

For a Vice President, Roosevelt was very well known to the public. He had gained fame as the Rough Rider from San Juan Hill, and was a cartoonist's delight with his sturdy build, square jaw, determined mouth, and challenging gaze through the pince-nez that made up for his nearsightedness. He was America's "Dutch Uncle," a reference to the fact that his ancestors came to America from Holland in the seventeenth century, and to his habit of reading stern lectures to those who opposed his principles and programs. Determination also came to him from his mother, who was, he says in his *Autobiography,* "a sweet, gracious, beautiful Southern woman" who remained "entirely 'unreconstructed' to the day of her death."

He had overcome asthma as a boy by taking special exercises, and, after being roughed up by a couple of bullies, he entered a boxing class and became its champion before leaving. At Harvard he continued to box, rode horseback, became

821

proficient with rifle and pistol, and culti-vated an abiding love for nature. Some of his happiest post-college days were spent in Montana on the Little Missouri, where he became a ranchman in partnership with three professionals. Some of his happiest post-Presidential days were spent exploring the Amazon and hunting big game in Africa. The Museum of Natural History in New York City is a monument to his interest in nature and conservation.

GOVERNMENT SERVICE

Theodore Roosevelt came from a rather well-to-do merchant family of culture and learning. He studied law at Harvard, but he sidestepped a legal career to go into politics. He found the Republican Party an exclusive club. "As a friend of mine picturesquely phrased it, I 'had to break into the organization with a jimmy.'" He worked hard on the precinct level, won election to the legislature in Albany, and quickly discovered the strong connections between members of the legislature and businessmen. "Even at that date I had nei-ther sympathy nor admiration for the man who was merely a money king, and I did not regard the 'money touch,' when di-vorced from other qualities, as entitling a man to either respect or consideration." Moreover, Roosevelt would not conceal his opinions or enter into deals with the vested interests.

He began to capture attention beyond his state in 1895 when the mayor appointed him president of the New York City Police Board, an assignment he accepted only after being assured a free hand in whatever ef-forts he made to clean up the city, without regard to persons or politics. One reason for Theodore Roosevelt's later attitudes can be found in this sentence from his *Auto-biography:* "The man who was closest to me throughout my two years in the Police Department was Jacob Riis." City evils that Roosevelt might never have seen were

brought to his attention by the author. Indeed, Roosevelt asked Riis to be his guide, and the pair often toured New York's worst districts by night, looking into gam-bling dens, houses of prostitution, and the places where payoffs were made to corrupt members of the Police Department. The Police Commissioner raised a ruckus that could be heard across the country. At the same time, he was a hero to the men on the force because he raised salaries and im-proved the conditions of their hazardous occupation.

Roosevelt's subsequent rise in national politics was meteoric. He left New York for Washington, where he became Assistant Secretary of the Navy in McKinley's first administration, just before the beginning of the Spanish-American War. After the charge up San Juan Hill, he came home an even more illustrious public figure and won the governorship of New York. While governor, he was able to secure from the legislature heavier taxes on railroads and utilities, money for the renovation of tene-ments in New York City, conservation leg-islation, trust regulations, and an 8-hour day for state employees. The desire of the political bosses in New York to get rid of this independent reformer set the stage for his nomination as Vice President in 1900.

CAMPAIGN OF 1900

Roosevelt threw himself into the cam-paign with his customary vigor, making a good foil for the staid McKinley, but in truth his aid was little needed. The Demo-crats again nominated William Jennings Bryan, who was determined to make im-perialism the issue of the campaign. A ma-jority in the country favored the acquisition of the Philippines; and free silver, although still popular in the West, had little appeal for the rest of the country, a point played up by the Republicans. The election re-turns revealed a wide gap between the two contestants. McKinley rode triumphantly back into the White House with the greatest popular majority since the landslide for Grant in 1872. Six months later he was dead, felled by an assassin's bullet in Buffalo, New York. His Vice President took the oath of office as America's twenty-sixth President on September 14, 1901.

ROOSEVELT AS PRESIDENT

The new Chief Executive came to office well schooled on the state of the nation, the depth of its problems, the possible remedies, and the nature of the men with whom he would certainly have to deal as Chief Executive. A tough-minded idealist with no patience for ineffective do-gooders, he was also impulsive, vigorous, fearless, and frequently self-righteous. He was an idealistic man with a social conscience yet an astute politician capable of leading public opinion and able to work with the party bosses while in power. Deeply religious and concerned for the downtrodden, he also loved power and believed in Anglo-Saxon superiority. Unreservedly committed to the ends he pursued, he sometimes did not care about the means he used to achieve them.

As President, Roosevelt meant to lead, to prod Congress, and to put men on the Court who would follow his ideas. He saw the Constitution not as a straitjacket, but an instrument by which to bring a better life to the nation. He believed the President could do anything not specifically forbidden by the document, and that he was entrusted with the welfare and destiny of the American people.

The Congress, however, was dominated by conservatives, so Roosevelt was cautious at first and kept McKinley's Cabinet. In fact, until his last two years in office, he was able to maintain fairly good relations with the Republican Old Guard which ran the Congress. The progressive Republicans,

led by La Follette, became powerful enough to challenge the party leadership only after Roosevelt left office. The Democrats were still deeply divided between the Bryan and Cleveland wings and caused Roosevelt little concern.

ROOSEVELT AND TRUSTS

Roosevelt preferred the soldier to the businessman, the man of action to the man of money. That was one reason for his unyielding hostility to the trusts. Another was derived from the memories left by his terms of office in the New York State Legislature and the New York City Police Department, where he had seen the public exploited by ruthless tycoons. The Presidency enlightened him further. He felt that not only social justice, but reason itself called for support of strikers even when they were bitterly assailed by employers and newspapers alike. On a White House conference during the coal strike of 1902 he wrote: "The representatives of the miners included as their head and spokesman John Mitchell, who kept his temper admirably. . . . The representatives of the operators, on the contrary, came down in a most insolent frame of mind, refused to talk of arbitration or other accommodation of any kind, and used language that was insulting to the miners and offensive to me."

THE NORTHERN SECURITIES CASE

The phrase "Trust Buster" is associated with Roosevelt. He attacked the trusts and stock speculators in his first message to Congress and the government soon began the prosecution of the Northern Securities Company, a combination resulting from a titanic struggle between James J. Hill and Edward H. Harriman for control of the nation's railroad lines. Hill, with the Great Northern and the Northern Pacific already in his hands, went after control of the

People wait to buy baskets of coal during the coal strike of 1902. Similar situations existed in every major American city and added to the desolation of the city-dweller.

Chicago, Burlington and Quincy. Harriman also wanted this railroad so that he would have a Chicago branch for his own system, headed by the Union Pacific. Hill seemed to have won by buying up sufficient stock in the railroad, but Harriman countered by buying the stock of the Great Northern. When Hill learned that his prize railroad was in danger of being wrested from him, he too used every means he could command to obtain additional shares of Great Northern stock. The stock, as a result, zoomed in price, creating pandemonium on Wall Street. Consequently, the two contestants decided to call off their economic warfare

and instead worked out a compromise, an agreement establishing the Northern Securities Company, with representatives of both Hill and Harriman on the board of directors.

To the President, this looked suspiciously like a monopoly. He ordered his Attorney General to begin proceedings against the Northern Securities Company on grounds that this holding company controlled "practically the entire railway system in the

Northwest—possibly as the first step toward controlling the entire railway system of the country." The company lawyers fought back, dragging the case through the courts for two years. In 1904, the Supreme Court ordered the Northern Securities Company to be dissolved under the Sherman Antitrust Act. The President had won his first big battle with the trusts.

OTHER CASES

In spite of the flamboyant victory, Roosevelt's record on breaking up giant conglomerations of economic power was not spectacular. He had never felt that all trusts were bad and believed that their right to exist should depend on their activities. He did secure the creation of the Department of Commerce and Labor in 1903 with the inclusion of a Bureau of Corporations to research the activities of the big industries. In 1905, in *Swift and Co. v. United States,* the federal government won its second big antitrust case, this time against the meatpacking industry. In all, Roosevelt called for action against forty companies and the Justice Department secured twenty-five indictments, but there were no more big antitrust victories until the Taft administration.

Roosevelt, generally sympathetic to the demands of labor for better working conditions, hoped labor would support the Republican Party. During the coal strike of 1902 he came to believe that the mine operators were not negotiating with their workers in good faith over higher wages and less hours of work. The country faced a major crisis if coal was not to be had that winter, and for this reason too, the President could not let the talks drag on indefinitely. He would, he disclosed in his *Autobiography,* have asked for government control of the mines if the magnates had not given way. They did not want binding arbitration, but J. P. Morgan forced them to accept it. The workers got half the wage increase they had asked for and a 9-hour day, but no recognition of their union. This was the first time the government had intervened to protect the public.

Roosevelt was a friend of labor but also wished to prevent a more radical move by the workers toward socialism. The President opposed the closed shop, violent tactics, and plans that called for the government to take over business. He firmly supported legislation to protect women and children in industry, and employers' liability laws for workers on interstate railroads.

THE 1904 CAMPAIGN

When Roosevelt ran for President in 1904, he characterized his administration as the Square Deal, taking his metaphor from playing cards. He explained himself to mean that he, the "dealer," intended to see that every "player" was dealt an honest "hand" in the "game." Anyone caught "with an ace up his sleeve" or slipping one "from the bottom of the deck," would be summarily punished. In terms of practical politics this meant preventing the rich and powerful from exploiting the poor and weak. Social justice was the equivalent of a fair card game, and his determination to enforce a square deal applied to any group attempting to take unfair advantage of any other group. Behind the scenes, he had also been working diligently to secure the support of both wings of the Republican Party. He used the patronage to secure positions for men he favored rather than friends of Republican boss Mark Hanna. Most of his appointments were youthful men of superior ability, as well as acceptable to most of the Old Guard. After several important conservatives came out for Roosevelt, he also appointed one of their friends, George Cortelyou, national chairman of the party.

Roosevelt was nominated easily and won the election by more than two million more votes than the Democratic candidate, the conservative Alton B. Parker. Even big business stood solidly behind him and contributed almost two million dollars to his campaign. The Rough Rider returned to the White House as an elected President and with large Republican majorities in both houses of Congress.

ROOSEVELT'S SECOND TERM

RAILROAD REGULATION

Roosevelt returned to the White House determined to get more far-reaching reform legislation, and public opinion was behind him. At the turn of the century the nation had well over a million men employed by the railroads. Unrest among these employees over poor working conditions had at times flared into strikes. Moreover, the public resented the lack of uniform standards for establishing fares and freight rates. Reformist newspapers condemned the system of free passes used by the railroads to reward politicians and others who did favors for them. Finally, the Northern Securities Company case brought the whole railroad problem under the President's scrutiny. He asked Congress to pass a law with teeth in it, which it did in 1906 with the Hepburn Act. Roosevelt showed his skill as a politician in steering the bill through a largely hostile Senate. The Old Guard, led by Nelson Aldrich of Rhode Island who was at first against it, ultimately voted for its passage when the President succeeded in making them believe that he was supporting a more drastic measure sponsored by the progressive bloc. The new act raised from five to seven the members on the Interstate Commerce Commission (ICC) and extended its jurisdiction over express and sleeping car companies and railroad terminals. The ICC was also given the right to fix maximum rates, nullify rates it found unreasonable, stop rebates, curtail free passes, and evaluate the conditions under which perishable goods were transported. When railroad cases came to court, the Commission did not have to prove the law was being violated; the railroads in question had to prove that they were obeying the law.

PURE FOOD AND DRUGS

In 1906, Upton Sinclair's *The Jungle* was published, a muckraking novel about the meat-packing industry which described the filthy conditions that prevailed in the slaughterhouses. Sinclair numbered among his readers the President of the United States, who ordered an investigation of the beef trust. The report that reached his desk revealed, he charged, "scandalous abuses" that needed to be "remedied at once" by action on Capitol Hill. After much pressure by the President, Congress passed the Meat Inspection Act in 1906, laying down binding rules for sanitary meat packing and government inspection of meat products crossing state lines. The Pure Food and Drug Act, passed at the same time, met a need long recognized by the Department of Agriculture and the American Medical Association. The new regulations forbade the manufacture or sale of mislabeled or adulterated food or drugs in interstate commerce. Among other enterprises, the time-honored patent-medicine business was jolted, and the "snake oil" peddler who hawked his powders and potions from state to state began to disappear.

CONSERVATION

The protection of America's lands, forests, rivers, and wildlife had great appeal for Roosevelt, the naturalist. He protested against the misuse and pollution of the nation's natural resources, demanded an end to the abuse, and suggested methods of undoing the harm already done. As President, he was fortunate to have at his right hand Gifford Pinchot, as head of the Forestry Service, whose ideas he largely supported on the removal of timber lands from public sale in order to preserve them to help prevent soil erosion and floods. The Newlands Act of 1902 pleased Roosevelt as much as any bill passed while he was in the White House. It provided for the irrigation of parched federal lands in the West through the building of federal dams. The Inland Waterways Commission was established in 1907 and a Conservation Conference the following year supported the President's demands for protection of waterways, forests, and coal, oil, and natural gas lands. However, not until 1920 did a law provide for the government to hold lands containing coal, oil, and natural gas.

EVALUATION OF ROOSEVELT AS PRESIDENT

Despite Roosevelt's accomplishments, his administration did not end on a positive

Theodore Roosevelt traveled to the West to dedicate the Grand Canyon National Park. During his Presidency, Roosevelt created five national parks and fifty-one wildlife refuges.

note. He was blamed for a brief business panic in 1907 on the grounds that he was anti-business and had caused businessmen to lose confidence in the economy. On the other hand, the advanced progressives in Congress were angry because he did not openly fight the conservatives in the party in an effort to lower the tariff. Even an outspoken message to Congress in 1908, in which he proposed all the reforms later set forth in the 1912 campaign, did not attract progressive support since he had pledged not to seek the Presidency again in 1908.

Nevertheless, historians are virtually unanimous in calling Roosevelt one of the greatest Presidents in American history. He was effective in his own time, and he set precedents for his successors. He instituted an attack on the trusts that was carried forward after he left the White House. He was aware of the problem of conservation and called for protection of America's natural resources long before the nation's ecology became a national issue. He enlarged the role of the Presidency, overshadowed by Congressional power in the late nineteenth century, and showed that it could be used as a platform for the moral leadership of the nation. His White House conferences accustomed both labor and management, and social action groups in general, to think of the Executive Mansion in Washington as a place for settling disputes and deciding momentous issues. His essential greatness lay in his ability to formulate and gain acceptance of progressive legislation on the national level.

THE 1908 CAMPAIGN

Theodore Roosevelt decided not to run again in 1908, but he wanted to have a hand-picked successor follow him into the Presidency. His choice fell on his colleague, Secretary of War William Howard Taft of Ohio, a massive figure of a man, devoid of spectacular popular appeal, conservative and unambitious, but a good administrator with a number of distinguished offices behind him. From a prominent Ohio family, Taft had made a particularly good impression as governor of the Philippines. Roosevelt believed Taft would continue "my policies" and his support assured Taft of the nomination and victory in the general election. Taft ran against Bryan, nominated by the Democrats for the third time. The Democratic platform was somewhat more progressive than the Republican, especially on curbing the trusts and protecting labor. However, even though the Democrats gained much labor support, Bryan lost by over one million popular votes and by a vote of 321 to 162 in the electoral college.

TAFT AS PRESIDENT

The new Chief Executive faced a special problem. "My coming into office was exactly as if Roosevelt had succeeded himself," he later explained. Everyone knew he owed the office to his predecessor. Roosevelt's partisans expected Taft to walk strictly in his predecessor's footsteps. Some of Taft's actions, in fact, followed the Roosevelt pattern, notably the initiative he took in bringing action in antitrust cases to the courts through his Attorney General. But ultimately the new President had to decide issues as he saw them, and he could not always see them through Roosevelt's eyes.

Taft was basically a retiring man who saw no reason to assert aggressive Presidential leadership. He even tended to act against his own inclinations in the interest of maintaining party harmony. Yet leadership of a special quality was needed at that time, for the elections had returned more progressives to Congress, making an open clash with the conservative leadership almost inevitable. The political trend in the country was toward progressivism in both parties, yet Taft did not see it and was in fact opposed to much of the progressive program.

THE PAYNE-ALDRICH TARIFF

Taft's inability to lead became evident as early as 1909 when a new tariff bill came up. The progressives were for lower rates because they would make imported goods cheaper on the American market. Roosevelt had been clever enough not to become bogged down in a tariff fight within his own party. But the progressive bloc was stronger now. Taft had appeased them during the campaign by calling for a revision of the tariff, and they confidently expected him to veto the Payne-Aldrich Tariff, a highly protective measure that provoked accusations of connivance between big business and the men who voted for the bill. The President had made little effort to influence its terms except to press for inclusion

When Roosevelt decided not to run for a second term of office, he picked Taft for the nomination. This cartoon shows Roosevelt "branding" Taft with the initials "TR."

THE BRANDING SEASON

of an income tax amendment to the Constitution. Although he said he had reservations about the bill, he signed it. Afterward Taft made the situation worse by stating in a political speech, "this is the best tariff bill that the Republican party has ever passed. . . ." The progressives considered Taft's conduct a betrayal, and the President, at the outset of his administration, responded by developing a dislike for the progressive bloc.

CANNONISM

When Taft became President, the Speaker of the House was Joseph Gurney Cannon, a crude and vulgar man, but popular with some of his colleagues. He had entrenched himself through a system popularly called "Cannonism," the shrewd use of dictatorial power to make himself virtual master of the House. In 1910, a coalition of progressives, angered by his ability to block consideration of reform legislation, rose against "Uncle Joe" and gained enough support to strip him of his power to appoint the Committee on Rules, which determined the bills that would reach the floor for debate, made its membership elective, and barred the Speaker from sitting on it. They thus dealt a death blow to Cannonism (although Cannon remained as Speaker), to the applause of progressives across the country who thought of it as a significant move to democratize national politics. Only the power of the Speaker was significantly reduced, however, and not the power of the Rules Committee. Taft failed to ingratiate himself with the progressives when he remained uninvolved during this fracas on Capitol Hill. Later he lamented: "I thought of encouraging a movement to beat Cannon, but I found that he was so strongly entrenched . . . it was impossible." In fact, Taft allied himself more closely with the conservatives in the party after this and cut the patronage of such progressive Republicans as La Follette and George Norris of Nebraska.

PROGRESSIVE MEASURES

Demands continued for further regulation of the railroads. Taft pleased the public in 1910 by signing the Mann-Elkins Act, which gave the Interstate Commerce Commission the right to suspend fare increases pending an investigation. The hand of the ICC was also strengthened in regard to the "long and short haul" abuse which continued despite previous laws. The new legislation stipulated that all shipping charges had to be based on the same rates. In 1913, the Physical Valuation Act gave the ICC the right to estimate railroad properties in order to establish a proper relationship between the value of those properties and charges made by the railroads. As a consequence, the ICC emerged as the most powerful administrative agency in Washington with broad authority over communications.

Taft's administration had other progressive triumphs to its credit. Many more antitrust cases were brought to court than under Roosevelt, notably suits against Standard Oil, American Tobacco, and United States Steel. However, when Standard Oil and the American Tobacco Company were dissolved by the Supreme Court, they simply reorganized themselves on different lines and continued operation. The Mann Act (1910) provided stringent penalties for those engaged in organized prostitution crossing state lines. That same year the Publicity Act forced candidates for Congress to reveal campaign contributions, a blow at businessmen in the habit of buying political favors during elections. Still another measure authorized post offices to hold small savings accounts for those who feared the banks because of bank failures in hard times.

Taft threw his support behind two measures of supreme importance to the progressives. One was the income tax, long demanded by those with low earnings, who felt it unfair that taxation should hit them as hard as it hit the rich. Progressives be-

Oregon Adopts Direct Democracy

66 *The legislative authority of the State shall be vested in a legislative assembly, consisting of a Senate and House of Representatives, but the people reserve to themselves power to propose laws and amendments to the Constitution and to enact or reject the same at the polls, independent of the legislative assembly, and also reserve power at their own option to approve or reject at the polls any act of the legislative assembly. The first power reserved by the people is the initiative, and not more than eight percent of the legal voters shall be required to propose any measure by such petition, and every such petition shall include the full text of the measure so proposed. . . . The second power is the referendum, and it may be ordered (except as to laws necessary for the immediate preservation of the public peace, health, or safety), either by the petition signed by five percent of the legal voters, or by the legislative assembly, as other bills are enacted. . . .* 99

—Constitution of Oregon

Taft Attacks
Direct Democratic Procedures

66 *. . . The initiative, the referendum and the recall have been urged and in many states adopted, as a machine which no boss or corrupt politician can prevent from producing honest, effective political results. They are expected to reform everything and those who doubt their wisdom are, for the time being, in the minds of many enthusiasts, public enemies.*

The representative system, on the contrary, recognizes that government, in the actual execution of governmental measures, and in the actual detailed preparation of governmental measures, is an expert matter. To attempt to devise and adopt detailed legislative measures to accomplish the general purpose of the people through a mass vote at a popular election is just as absurd as it would be for all those present at a town meeting to say, "We will all of us now go out and build a bridge, or we will use a theodolite." Thus to say that by injecting more democracy you can cure the defects of our present democracy is to express one of those epigrams that, like many of its kind, is either not true at all or is only partly true and is even more deceptive than if it were wholly untrue. . . .

—William Howard Taft

lieved a graduated income tax would provide the answer. Taft agreed, and had the satisfaction of seeing the Sixteenth Amendment—the "Income Tax Amendment"—ratified while he was still in the White House.

Direct election of Senators provided by the Seventeenth Amendment was ratified in the first term of Taft's successor, becoming law on May 31, 1913. The new President, however, had been in office only a matter of weeks; Taft had put his authority behind the measure long before, and the credit belonged to him.

THE
BALLINGER-PINCHOT AFFAIR

In spite of Taft's support for a number of progressive measures, he never seemed dynamic enough to please the insurgents in Congress and appeared too friendly with the Republican Old Guard. A good example is the Ballinger-Pinchot Affair. Secretary of the Interior Richard A. Ballinger came under fire in 1909 in an article in *Collier's* charging: "The Alaska Coal Lands Are in Danger in Ballinger's Hands." Gifford Pinchot, still heading the Forestry Service, accused Ballinger of dereliction of duty in failing to keep mineral and water power sites out of private hands and made clear his opinion that Roosevelt's conservation policies were being undermined. The Secretary of the Interior was also charged with allowing private developers to get control of coal and timber lands in Alaska. Both Ballinger and Taft believed that Roosevelt had gone beyond his legal authority in withdrawing federal lands from public sale. A Congressional committee found Ballinger not guilty of selling out public lands to private interests over the angry protests of the progressives, and Taft dismissed the head of the Forestry Service after asking plaintively: "Will Pinchot remain the St. George and Ballinger the dragon?" Still under fire, Ballinger also left the government.

One individual who replied with a thundering affirmative to Taft's question was Teddy Roosevelt, back from a trip abroad, primed with tales of the administration's misdemeanors, and deeply antagonized by the treatment of his old friend Pinchot. It was the culminating point of his rapidly growing disillusionment with Taft, who, he believed, had not only deserted his program but failed to hold the party together.

ROOSEVELT'S NEW NATIONALISM

The President was overwhelmed with problems a year before he had to face re-election. Angered by the higher tariff and demanding social reforms, the public had again put the House in the hands of the Democrats in the Congressional elections of 1910, and had greatly reduced the Republican majority in the Senate. Taft had proved to be too rigid in his adherence to the letter of the law, and politically inept. He was stubborn under fire but could not capture popular support and was not progressive enough for the times. In short, he was not Roosevelt.

When Roosevelt reached home in 1910, he was already being mentioned as a possible candidate for President in 1912. Many people were calling themselves "Roosevelt Republicans" to distinguish themselves from the party workers who stood by Taft. After listening to Pinchot speak of the President's "betrayal" of the Square Deal, Roosevelt resolved to go all-out to wrest the Republican nomination from his former protégé. Using as his rallying cry, "The New Nationalism," he demanded that the Presidential power be strengthened to defend the people against the "malefactors of great wealth," called for reform of the courts because they had too often ruled in favor of monopolists, and emphatically upheld human rights against property rights.

In the meantime, progressives in the Republican Party had become so alienated from Taft that they formed the National Progressive Republican League (Progressive Party) in January, 1911, to oppose his renomination. La Follette was its recognized leader and candidate. He spoke widely around the country, but lost support as progressives began moving toward Roosevelt as the stronger candidate. When La Follette had a physical breakdown in early 1912, the movement to Roosevelt accelerated. The former President had by this time decided to run again, believing that the people wanted him and that La Follette could not win. La Follette, not surprisingly, felt that the progressives had double-crossed him.

Taft, wielding the powers of the Presidency, and angered and bewildered by what he considered Roosevelt's radical statements, proved too strong even for Roosevelt. The Republican convention renominated the President after refusing to seat any of the disputed delegates pledged to

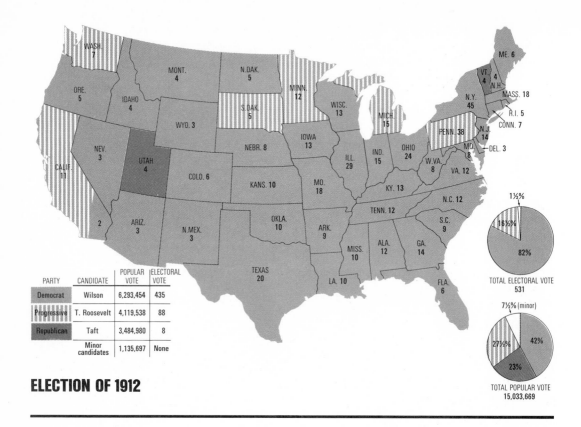

PARTY	CANDIDATE	POPULAR VOTE	ELECTORAL VOTE
Democrat	Wilson	6,293,454	435
Progressive	T. Roosevelt	4,119,538	88
Republican	Taft	3,484,980	8
Minor candidates		1,135,697	None

TOTAL ELECTORAL VOTE
531

TOTAL POPULAR VOTE
15,033,669

ELECTION OF 1912

Roosevelt. Roosevelt thereupon bolted the party, accepted nomination by the Progressive Party, and declared himself "fit as a bull moose," giving his adopted party its enduring nickname. Its platform stated its basic demands for reform under the heading, "A Contract with the People." Some clauses of the "Contract" were: workmen's compensation, minimum wage standards, prohibition of child labor, political primaries, direct election of Senators, women's suffrage, recall of judicial decisions, control of the trusts, and lower tariffs. Roosevelt accepted the progressive platform, and ran on it.

THE PROGRESSIVE PARTY

Emergence of the Progressive Party created a three-way race for the Presidency.

Taft had the loyal support of the more conservative Republicans, who denounced Roosevelt as a "traitor to the party." They preferred what they considered sound conservative politics to flamboyant candidates and novel measures. Roosevelt had the support of most progressive Republicans, except La Follette. They cheered loudly when Roosevelt shouted: "We stand at Armageddon, and we battle for the Lord!" The noise, the singing, the confident attitude, and the general hoopla of the progressive convention reflected their feeling that they represented the wave of the future.

The Democratic challenger of Taft and Roosevelt was Woodrow Wilson, governor of New Jersey. Wilson was not as well known as his rivals, and on the early ballots at the Democratic convention he ran behind an old party warhorse, Champ Clark of Missouri. William Jennings Bryan held the key to the nomination. Convinced that Clark was Tammany Hall's candidate, and realizing that he himself could not win a fourth nomination, Bryan switched to Wilson, helping to ensure the governor's victory on the forty-sixth ballot.

THE 1912 CAMPAIGN

The President had an insignificant personal impact on the campaign. Well-meaning but colorless, and lacking intensity, Taft fell far behind in the competition for public attention. Roosevelt toured the country, drawing crowds and creating enthusiasm with his eloquence. Decades later, many an American recalled with delight the memory of Roosevelt leaning forward belligerently, his arm outthrust, his fist clenched, his teeth bared in the grimace so dear to the cartoonists. When Roosevelt was shot and wounded by a would-be assassin, he paused only for medical treatment and returned to the campaign trail with all of his old gusto. The country loved it.

Wilson, meanwhile, took a middle path between Taft and Roosevelt. Neither colorless nor flamboyant, he knew how to convince crowds, he knew his own mind, and he had this advantage over the other two: people came out to hear him because they believed they were listening to the next President of the United States. The divided Republicans appeared bent on committing political suicide, and it was the general opinion that they would succeed.

THE TRUST ISSUE

As far as principles went, the three candidates were not as far apart as the campaign speeches made them appear. Their differences were sometimes more a matter of emphasis and strategy than of substance. They all, for instance, agreed on the danger of the trusts. Roosevelt considered this his

pet issue. Taft also could claim a good record, although his conservative followers winced as he listed the number of antitrust cases tried under his administration. Wilson, too, presented a case against the trusts. He spoke of an "invisible empire of special interest," declared the trusts an enemy of free enterprise, and vowed to keep them in line if and when he reached the White House.

NEW NATIONALISM AND NEW FREEDOM

Roosevelt called his program "New Nationalism" and Wilson described his as the "New Freedom." The similarity of titles suggested a similarity of content. Roosevelt placed more emphasis on conservation and Wilson more on tariff reform. Yet, whole areas of their thinking coincided to such an extent that Wilson as President supported measures, such as labor legislation, enunciated in the progressive platform. The real difference between the two programs came from the temperament and outlook of the two men. The New Nationalism was formulated by Eastern urban reformers, while the New Freedom came out of an agrarian heritage. Both leaders attacked the trusts, but from different viewpoints. Roosevelt thought combinations could be rendered socially useful by a watchdog government which saw to it that they did not step out of bounds. In other words, there were good trusts and bad trusts. Wilson approached this problem from the outlook of the small proprietor whose liberty and prosperity, he judged, were endangered by big business. Ideally, Roosevelt would allow the trusts to exist if they were not destructive of social justice, whereas Wilson would destroy them. Wilson therefore could rightly deny being an echo of his opponent when he summoned the federal government to "cheer and inspirit our people with the sure prospects of social justice and due rewards, with the vision of the open gates of opportunity for all." It was an echo of

William Howard Taft served as Secretary of War under Roosevelt and became President in 1908. He is shown here campaigning before the election.

Bryan and the traditions of Jacksonian Democracy.

THE SOCIALIST PARTY

The Socialist Party ran better in 1912 than in any subsequent election. Eugene V. Debs gained 900,000 votes, or 6 percent of the total. The party had been founded in 1901 and grew steadily over the next decade, claiming as adherents Upton Sinclair and Edward Bellamy, many Populists and some labor unions, and most important, Eugene V. Debs. Unlike the Socialist Labor Party led by Daniel De Leon, it was not a rigidly Marxist organization and did not call for seizure of the state by the working class. The Socialist Party's platform called for government ownership of the means of production and distribution, and other social and political reforms; but it pledged itself to strive for power through the democratic process. The revolution would be gradual, not violent.

Yet, the Socialists had fleeting support and declined rapidly after 1912. To most Americans, the idea of state control of the economy conflicted with their belief in the close association of political liberty with capitalist economy. Fundamentally religious and patriotic, they also detested the Socialist attack on religion and all national loyalty. To the Socialists, the class struggle was more important than allegiance to any state. But class divisions in the United States were not as sharp or as deeply rooted as those in Europe upon which Karl Marx had based his theory. Samuel Gompers told the Socialists in 1903: "Economically, you are unsound; socially, you are wrong; industrially, you are impossible." In 1909, Roosevelt had voiced what was probably a general point of view: "The immorality and absurdity of the doctrines of Socialism as propounded by these advanced advocates are quite as great as those of the advocates, if such there be, of absolute individualism."

WOODROW WILSON

As expected, Taft and Roosevelt nullified each other's chances in the election. Together they polled half the popular vote; 27 percent for Roosevelt, 23 percent for Taft. Roosevelt got just over 4 million votes, Taft well over 3 million. But Wilson obtained 41 percent with over 6 million votes. The electoral vote was crushing; 434 for Wilson, 88 for Roosevelt, 8 for Taft. Nevertheless, although he had a Democratic Congress behind him, Woodrow Wilson was a minority President when he entered the White House in 1913.

BACKGROUND AND PERSONALITY

Wilson had been a professor of political science and president of Princeton University before he became the successful reform governor of New Jersey. A devout member of the Presbyterian Church, he had a commitment to moral duty, believing one had an obligation to do the best one could, wherever directed by Providence. Once convinced he was right—a conviction that came easily to him—he rarely budged from his position. As he himself said: "I am not the kind that considers compromise when I once take my position." He could also allow a difference over issues to become a personal quarrel. A man of integrity, he nevertheless could "graze the truth" when he thought candor would harm a cause or person he believed in. He could be dictatorial and stubborn, when faced with political opposition. But, in his first term, when he had wide popular support for his domestic measures, and notable success in dealing with Congress, such a position was unnecessary.

Woodrow Wilson, who won the election of 1912 with 41 percent of the popular vote. The balance of the vote had been split between Roosevelt and Taft.

WILSON'S REFORM LEGISLATION

Wilson once said of the Presidency in his book, *Congressional Government:* "His office is anything he has the sagacity and force to make it." That principle, carefully thought out by a man who had written and lectured on the theory of government, guided him from the moment of his inaugural address. He immediately took up the task of making his New Freedom a reality by formulating a program and even going to Capitol Hill to address a special session of Congress instead of communicating his wishes in writing after the fashion of his predecessors. During his first term in office he was successful in using appeals to the public, meetings with politicians, and patronage to get his program passed.

THE TARIFF

Wilson made good his campaign promise to obtain a lower tariff. He worked closely with his manager in the House, Oscar Underwood of Alabama, against factions within his party that wanted to keep duties high to protect their own industries—textiles in the Carolinas, sugar in Louisiana, shoes in Massachusetts. Wilson, the defender of a competitive economy, called on American businessmen to understand that high tariffs at home could lead to retaliation abroad. The President used his personal influence to overcome pressure by lobbyists and publicly asked the American people to support the bill. He got what he wanted in the Underwood Tariff, which reduced many rates on foreign goods while removing tariffs completely from others. The passage of this bill showed Wilson at his best as an effective political leader who knew how to use a strong hand in dealing with Congress.

THE FEDERAL RESERVE SYSTEM

Another aim of the New Freedom was fundamental reform of the control of banking and currency in the United States. On the subject of banking, Wilson said: "Control must be public, not private, must be vested in the government itself, so that the banks may be the instruments, not the masters, of business and of industrial enterprises and initiative." There was no central banking system in the country, although national bank notes were in circulation. The currency was inelastic, which meant that it was difficult to obtain credit for investment purposes. Conservative businessmen and politicians, such as Nelson Aldrich, wanted the reinstitution of a strong central banking system under private control, similar to Hamilton's earlier concept. Some Senators led by Carter Glass of Virginia wanted a decentralized system of twenty independent banks under private control. Bryan and many progressives wanted a decentralized system of banks under strong federal government jurisdiction, and they finally won Wilson to their point of view.

The result was the Federal Reserve Act, which established the Federal Reserve system, with twelve regional districts across the country, each with a Federal Reserve Bank owned by its member banks and serving as their fiscal agent. The system was supervised by a central Federal Reserve Board of eight men, with the Secretary of the Treasury as a member. Federal Reserve notes provided an elastic currency, backed as they were by the amount of commercial paper in circulation at any one time. Thus, this act centralized the banking system, stabilized conditions in the Western and Southern states by allowing the Reserve Banks to borrow money within the system when necessary, and made the government in Washington responsible for helping to control financial ventures.

AID TO AGRICULTURE

While the Federal Reserve Act was passed with the idea of stabilizing com-

merce and banking, the Federal Farm Loan Act was to serve the same purpose in the field of agriculture. High mortgages to be paid with short term loans had plagued American farmers. Now they could get long term loans at lower rates of interest from twelve Farm Loan Banks using stored crops as security for loans. Other Wilson measures provided more federal aid to the states to train agricultural experts; and sums to match state allocations of money for commercial, industrial, and domestic science programs in high schools, and for the building of rural roads.

ANTITRUST ACTIVITY

Wilson was bound, by his integrity and his commitment, to launch a direct assault on the trusts. Lawyers still found loopholes through which corporations could carry on monopolistic control under different names and in different guises. To have let these practices continue without government intervention would have been an abandonment of the New Freedom, and the President had made up his mind before taking office that he would try to do something to deter them. He at once ordered his Attorney General to take action, and he prodded the men on Capitol Hill until they produced bills giving the federal government more regulatory powers over big business.

The Federal Trade Commission Act reflected Wilson's logic and made him a champion of the small businessman against powerful and ruthless competitors. The act sought to break up the trusts but at the same time it extended the government's regulatory powers in a way that Roosevelt would have approved. The five members of the Federal Trade Commission (FTC) were appointed by the President. After a particular investigation revealed a violation of the act, the Commissioners were required to "transmit to the Attorney General a report embodying its findings and recommendations" so that appropriate action might be taken.

Acting on a broader front, Wilson moved to supplement the Sherman Antitrust Act with the Clayton Antitrust Act in 1914. The Clayton Act contained specific references to price discrimination, corporations buying stock in other corporations, and interlocking directorates involving two or more businesses or banks. All were outlawed when employed to diminish fair competition or create a commercial monopoly. Notably, labor unions were exempted because "the labor of a human being is not a commodity or an article of commerce." They could strike, picket, and carry out boycotts. At the same time, the use of restraining orders and injunctions in labor disputes was carefully defined to make them applicable only when irreparable damage to property was involved. The request for one had to be "in writing and sworn to by the applicant or by his agent or attorney." No longer could employers obtain court orders against their employees by simply insisting that their factories or utilities were in danger from strikers. The unions called the Clayton Antitrust Act "Labor's Magna Carta."

EVALUATION OF WILSON'S FIRST TERM

Wilson, like Roosevelt, used the Presidency as a "moral office" from which to lead the nation toward humanitarian goals. He believed in an expanded role for the executive. By the end of his first term, he was clearly the leader of American progressivism, having combined many of the points of the New Freedom with those of the New Nationalism in his legislative program.

After the tariff, the new banking system, and laws regulating business and labor were passed, Wilson evidently felt that the aims of the progressive program had been reached. Subsequently, the FTC did issue a number of orders to businesses against certain practices and a few big combinations were dissolved. But as it turned out, the Commission's sympathies were with business and it preferred to advise rather than to order. The Federal Reserve Board, too, was under business control. It was not until 1916 that Wilson began to revise his views to accept the idea of more government regulation of the economy, and to abandon the traditional concept of laissez faire. The labor and agricultural wings of the party wanted more progressive legislation; and to keep the Democrats in power, the President began to adopt their views. He then supported such ideas as agricultural banks, child labor legislation, and workmen's compensation for federal employees.

Wilson's domestic triumphs in his first term indicate what he might have achieved if the First World War had not interrupted his program. The conflict diverted his attention from the home front to foreign policy, and the major issues of his second administration were international rather than domestic. In addition, some of his achievements in the years from 1913 to 1916 were hurt by the struggle in Europe. The Underwood Tariff was a casualty of the war, and federal regulation of business was also sidetracked during the war years. Yet these laws were there for future use.

PROGRESSIVISM IN PERSPECTIVE

Many of the progressive demands were enacted by the beginning of Wilson's second term and any further efforts at domestic reform were ended by the war years which followed. Moreover, some of the most ardent progressives lost public support because they opposed the American war effort as an interference with domestic reform. After the conflict ended, the mood of the American people was not congenial to reform legislation and there was no important expression of the spirit of progressivism until the 1930s.

The progressive movement, as distinguished from the Progressive Party, encompassed persons of various party affiliations. Roosevelt, a Republican, was an adherent of progressive ideals, as was Wilson, a Democrat. Progressivism was a humanitarian crusade in which even the rank and file felt themselves the instruments of destiny. It was often raucous, sometimes self-righteous, on occasion wrong-headed, but always exciting. Those who participated, who regarded political speeches of progressivism as sermons, its political songs as hymns, and its political leaders as prophets, basked in the involvement in a great moral drive to elevate the economic and political life of the nation. Yet, many progressives, unlike Roosevelt, did not fully understand the economic trends toward business consolidation and clung to the ideal of a smaller scale economy in which the trusts would not exist and competition among innumerable small entrepreneurs would regulate the economy. The movement had another significant failing. While it tended to be overly moralistic, it had no effective program for aiding black Americans. Roosevelt met with Booker T. Washington and made a few black political appointments in the South, but Wilson had a marked lack of interest in the welfare of black people, and maintained segregation in federal government departments. Finally, the progressives believed that an expansion of political democracy would automatically end corruption and lift the tone of American life. The problem of corruption in government did not end with the removal of certain political machines from power, or because the initiative and referendum were instituted.

Nevertheless, the movement had an important impact on American political and economic life through progressive laws and Constitutional amendments. The principle of government regulation of railroads, businesses, and banks would never be repudiated. The Federal Reserve System, with modifications, proved an effective system of fiscal control. The income tax remained in force, and was eventually extended. Federal protection of natural resources came to be expected by all Americans.

Readings

GENERAL WORKS

Goldman, Eric F., *Rendezvous with Destiny*. New York: Random House, 1956—A lively history of American reform movements from the post-Civil War period through modern times.

Hays, Samuel P., *The Response to Industrialism*. Chicago: University of Chicago Press, 1957—A study of the impact of industrialization on American life and thought. Hays maintains that social conflict was brought about by the wide variety of reactions to industrial society, and not simply by the emergence of sharp class distinctions.

Hofstadter, Richard, *The Age of Reform*. New York: Random House, 1955—A major reinterpretation of the American reform spirit, focusing on Populism and progressivism. Hofstadter finds that beneath the rhetoric of economic grievances and demands, reformers were expressing anxieties about their social status in a time of rapid change.

Kolko, Gabriel, *The Triumph of Conservatism*. New York: Macmillan, 1963—A study of progressive regulatory legislation. Kolko's thesis is that leading businessmen saw federal regulation as a desirable weapon to use against smaller competitors and as a shield against disruptive state legislation.

Lasch, Christopher, *The New Radicalism in America*. New York: Knopf, 1965—Essays on leading American reformers which suggest that psychological problems and the uneasy role of intellectuals in American society may have shaped their thought and activities.

Link, Arthur S., *Woodrow Wilson and the Progressive Era*. New York: Harper & Row, 1954—A political and social history of the period from Woodrow Wilson's election to America's entry into World War I. Link is the author of the definitive multi-volume biography of Wilson.

Mowry, George, *The Era of Theodore Roosevelt*. New York: Harper & Row, 1958—A standard general account of American politics and society from 1900 through 1912.

Newby, Idus A., *Jim Crow's Defense: Anti-Negro Thought in America, 1900–1930*. Baton Rouge: Louisiana State University Press, 1965—Newby points out that anti-black thought was common in the North as well as the South. He analyzes racist writers and theorists to find the intellectual and social foundations of their ideas.

Nye, Russel B., *Midwestern Progressive Politics*. East Lansing: Michigan State University Press, 1959—A study of progressive traditions in Midwestern politics from 1870 to 1958. Nye considers Midwestern progressivism to be a unique brand of social protest.

Shannon, David A., *The Socialist Party of America*. Chicago: Quadrangle, 1967—Shannon maintains that the Socialist Party's downfall began soon after the election of 1912 and was caused fundamentally by the lack of class consciousness among American workers.

Wiebe, Robert H., *Businessmen and Reform*. Cambridge, Mass.: Harvard University Press, 1962—In studying the relations of progressive-era businessmen to reform activity, Wiebe demonstrates that the business community was frequently split along lines of geographic location, size, or nature of the industry.

SPECIAL STUDIES

Aaron, Daniel, *Men of Good Hope.* New York: Oxford University Press, 1951—A study of progressive intellectuals which stresses their optimistic tone and their faith in reform within the system.

Blum, John M., *The Republican Roosevelt.* Cambridge, Mass.: Harvard University Press, 1954—A brief study of Theodore Roosevelt as a political leader. Blum finds Roosevelt to be particularly talented at conserving and amassing executive power through bargaining and compromise.

Chalmers, David M., *The Social and Political Ideas of the Muckrakers.* New York: Citadel Press, 1964—Chalmers claims that muckrakers were more than simply disillusioned critics of corruption. He argues that many of them had a broader concept of the failure of traditional ways of operation and had plans for positive reforms.

Forcey, Charles B., *The Crossroads of Liberalism.* New York: Oxford University Press, 1961—An analysis of the policies of the founders of the *New Republic*—Herbert Croly, Walter Lippmann, and Walter Weyl —which interprets their support for American entry into World War I as a betrayal of the more humane strains of American liberalism.

Grimes, Alan P., *The Puritan Ethic and Woman's Suffrage.* New York: Oxford University Press, 1967—Grimes finds in his analysis of the women's suffrage movement a link between that issue and fundamentally conservative causes such as prohibition and immigration restriction. Some advocates of votes for women claimed that women would guard the values associated

with the Protestant ethic.

Lubove, Roy, *The Progressives and the Slums.* Pittsburgh: University of Pittsburgh Press, 1963—Lubove traces the rise of concern among progressives in New York City on the issue of slum housing and the private and public efforts at reform and regulation.

Mann, Arthur, *Yankee Reformers in the Urban Age.* New York: Harper & Row, 1966—A study of reforms current in Boston after the Civil War. Mann feels the Boston reformer espoused a fundamentally liberal and humanitarian philosophy.

Manners, William, *TR and Will.* New York: Harcourt, Brace, 1969—A study of the relationship, personal and political, between Theodore Roosevelt and William Howard Taft, explaining Taft's role first as protégé and then as opponent of Roosevelt.

Maxwell, Robert S., *La Follette and the Rise of the Progressives in Wisconsin.* Madison: State Historical Society of Wisconsin, 1956 —Maxwell attributes La Follette's success to his political skills more than to his idealism. He devotes considerable attention to problems of party organization and control.

Mowry, George E., *The California Progressives.* Chicago: Quadrangle, 1963—Mowry finds California progressives to be, for the most part, middle-class, upwardly mobile, small businessmen or professional men with a strongly moralistic approach to political activity.

Noble, David W., *The Paradox of Progressive Thought.* Minneapolis: University of Minnesota Press, 1958—A study of the ideas of nine progressive-era intellectuals and social reformers. Noble finds them eager to redefine the meaning of civilization so it would become a method of freeing man from the burdens of traditional institutions.

PRIMARY SOURCES

Addams, Jane, *Forty Years at Hull House.* New York: Garrett Press, 1970—Memoirs of social work among Chicago's immigrants by the famous founder of Hull House. Addams also played a large role in many of the political and intellectual debates of the progressive era.

Croly, Herbert, *The Promise of American Life.* New York: Bobbs-Merrill, 1965—A statement of purpose from a progressive intellectual that was to influence Theodore Roosevelt, among others. Croly called for a nationalistic reform program to unify the nation and end divisions of class.

Lippmann, Walter, *Drift and Mastery.* Englewood Cliffs, N.J.: Prentice-Hall, 1961—At the time a young editor of the *New Republic,* Lippmann called in *Drift and Mastery* for a strong national program of reform, stressing the need for powerful leadership.

Resek, Carl, ed., *The Progressives.* New York: Bobbs-Merrill, 1966—An anthology of progressive thought and policies, showing the diversity within the progressive movement.

Weinberg, Arthur, and Leila Weinberg, eds., *The Muckrakers.* New York: Putnam, 1964 —An anthology of muckrakers' writings. The Weinbergs view muckrakers as courageous men and women who wanted the United States to fulfill its democratic promises.

Wilson, Woodrow, *The New Freedom.* Englewood Cliffs, N.J.: Prentice-Hall, 1961—A statement of Wilson's campaign theme. The New Freedom was to entail an attempt to guide the economy back to the competitive conditions which had prevailed before the era of the trusts.

BIOGRAPHIES

Harbaugh, William H., *Power and Responsibility.* New York: Macmillan, 1963—A general reader's biography of Theodore Roosevelt. Harbaugh views Roosevelt as a leader of heroic dimensions, combining conservatism and progressivism.

Hoover, Herbert, *The Ordeal of Woodrow Wilson.* New York: McGraw-Hill, 1958—A study of Wilson's peacemaking efforts which draws on Hoover's own experience in administering post-war relief in Europe. Hoover praises Wilson highly for taking a principled stand for old-style liberalism.

Leopold, Richard, *Elihu Root and the Conservative Tradition.* Boston: Little, Brown, 1954—Root was a leading Republican conservative whose service as Secretary of War, Secretary of State, and Senator helped to shape a tradition of legalistic, pro-business foreign policy.

Pringle, Henry, *The Life and Times of William Howard Taft.* Hamden, Conn.: Shoestring, 1965—A detailed biography of President Taft. Pringle admires Taft as a man of humane principles and political integrity.

Pringle, Henry, *Theodore Roosevelt.* New York: Harcourt, Brace, 1956—A biography of the President which finds him to be essentially a conservative, despite his ability to employ liberal rhetoric.

National Guard recruits begin training in New York's Central Park in 1917.

World War I and the League of Nations

24

The right is more precious than peace, and we shall fight for the things which we have always carried nearest our hearts—for democracy, . . . for the rights and liberties of small nations, for a universal dominion of right by such a concert of free peoples as shall bring peace and safety to all nations and make the world itself at last free.

—Woodrow Wilson

Tensions between the European powers had increased rapidly after 1900. Added to the centuries-old desire of each nation to protect its territory and to add to it wherever possible was fear of the powerful new German Empire in central Europe. For her part, Germany was apprehensive of being surrounded militarily by hostile powers on both east and west. It was for each nation's protection and to maintain the balance of power in Europe that a new arms race developed and a new system of alliances was formed in the late nineteenth century. Germany formed the Triple Alliance with Austria-Hungary and Italy in 1882 which was countered by an alliance between France and Russia in 1894. Isolated from the European continent and alarmed by the rise of German naval power, Britain worked out military agreements with France in 1904 and Russia in 1907.

Prior to 1914 there had been minor conflicts in Europe caused by the unstable political and emotional situation in the Balkans. Both Russia and Austria-Hungary wanted to dominate the area which was torn by internal warfare between 1912 and 1913. The strongest Balkan state, Serbia, was seething with anti-Austrian feelings due to the latter's control of the neighboring province of Bosnia. A secret society in Serbia plotted the assassination of Archduke Francis-Ferdinand of Austria during his planned visit to Sarajevo, the capital of Bosnia, in June, 1914. When a young Serbian nationalist carried out the plot and assassinated the Austrian Archduke, it set in motion a series of events which plunged Europe into a devastating conflict. In one week, from July 28 to August 3, 1914, Austria-Hungary declared war on Serbia, and Germany came to Austria's support. Russia mobilized to help Serbia, her Slavic neighbor. Germany declared war on Russia and on France, Russia's ally. Finally, England, France's ally, declared war on Germany.

America's first reaction was to stay out of the struggle. Physically isolated from Europe and free of "entangling alliances," Americans felt smug and secure. "We never

appreciated so keenly as now the foresight exercised by our forefathers in emigrating from Europe," said one newspaper. Let Europe "stew in its own juice" was a common sentiment. Wilson favored strict neutrality and promptly issued a neutrality proclamation. It was not America's war.

Emotionally, however, most Americans favored the Allies. Franco-American friendship had dated from the eighteenth century, and the virulent hatred of England gradually was being replaced by a greater appreciation of the similar political and cultural heritage of the two nations. Moreover, alarmed by the rise of German power in the late nineteenth century, Great Britain had made significant diplomatic concessions to the United States after 1895 in the Caribbean and the Pacific. At the same time, the traditionally warm feeling in the United States for Germany had begun to decline. With the rise of the German Empire in the 1870s, Germany seemed to many Americans aggressive, militaristic, and a dangerous competitor for world markets.

DECISION FOR WAR

GERMANY'S INVASION OF BELGIUM

American suspicion of Germany deepened when, in the first move of the war, Germany overran neutral Belgium. Frightened by Russia's mobilization, the Germans wanted to outflank France and defeat her quickly in order to concentrate on repelling the Czar's armies. But to carry out the plan, they not only violated an international treaty to respect Belgian neutrality, but made it seem even worse by later explain-

ing that neutrality was "just a word" and that the treaty was only "a scrap of paper." England and France then shrewdly exploited America's justifiable sympathy for Belgium by publishing propaganda about German atrocities against Belgian civilians, some of it true but much of it blatantly false. However, such stories spread and Americans believed them.

In the first years of the war British propaganda in the United States was most effective. The news received in the United States about the war came from the London

For United States Entry Into War

A little common sense goes a long way, my friends. The common sense of this situation is that a man who is talking about "Congress bringing on war" has not ordinary intelligence. The war is here, and Congress has not brought it on, and the President has not brought it on, and the American people have not brought it on. The Junkerthum and the Kaiserthum of Germany have brought it on in contempt for you and me. . . .

I tell you, moreover, that if Germany does win that fight upon the Continent of Europe, with Belgium already a vassal State, Holland to become one, France by defeat one, with all their forts and naval stations and shipyards open as well as her own, she will begin to get ready to whip us unless England's fleet prevents it.

Now, Great Britain can, by sea power, defend herself almost indefinitely, defend herself long enough for us to get ready to help her to defend us. You can put it in your pipe and smoke it, the fact that you must choose whether you are going to fight Germany now with assistance or whether you are going to fight her later; you have got to fight her. . . .

—Senator John Sharp Williams

bureaus of the news services. Over and over the books, articles, movies, and speakers sent over by England concentrated on German atrocities and German war guilt.

THE PROBLEM OF NEUTRAL RIGHTS

Despite the effective propaganda, the American people had no desire to enter the conflict. "At the bottom," reported the British Ambassador, "the people desire to stay out of the European struggle and will do so if they possibly can." The United

Against United States Entry Into War

There are a great many American citizens who feel that we owe it as a duty to humanity to take part in this war. Many instances of cruelty and inhumanity can be found on both sides. Men are often biased in their judgment on account of their sympathy and their interests. To my mind, what we ought to have maintained from the beginning was the strictest neutrality. . . . We have loaned many hundreds of millions of dollars to the allies in this controversy. While such action was legal and countenanced by international law, there is no doubt in my mind but the enormous amount of money loaned to the allies in this country has been instrumental in bringing about a public sentiment in favor of our country taking a course that would make every bond worth a hundred cents on the dollar and making the payment of every debt certain and sure. . . .

. . . It is now demanded that the American citizens shall be used as insurance policies to guarantee the safe delivery of munitions of war to belligerent nations. The enormous profits of munition manufacturers, stockbrokers, and bond dealers must be still further increased by our entrance into the war. . . .

We are taking a step today that is fraught with untold danger. We are going into war upon the command of gold. . . .

—Senator George W. Norris

States was the richest neutral country and the largest neutral trans-ocean shipping country. Under the traditional rules of international law, neutrals could trade with other neutrals and with any belligerents not under blockade. Americans wanted to do so. The problem in the first stages of the war was to make England, with her command of the seas, acknowledge America's rights as a neutral carrier.

845

From the start of the war, England used her vastly superior sea power to cut Germany off from foreign supplies by means of a paper blockade. Blockading traditionally meant to close enemy ports by surrounding them with warships just outside the 3-mile limit, but because long-range guns and submarines made such techniques risky, British warships roamed the high seas, intercepting neutral ships sailing to Germany and forcing them into Allied ports to search for contraband. By British definition, almost everything, including food, was contraband.

Dominating the entire North Atlantic, England was able not only to keep supplies from going directly to Germany but also to control imports to such neutral countries as Holland, Denmark, and Sweden which were close enough to Germany to easily supply her.

American shippers vigorously protested when their cargoes were seized, sometimes without payment. Although British naval tactics exasperated Wilson, the immense growth of American commerce made it impossible for him to stop American ships from trading with England. Trade with Germany declined to a trickle but with the Allies it jumped from 825 million dollars in 1914 to more than 3.2 billion dollars in 1916. To try to limit the trade would have challenged the traditional position the United States maintained as a neutral carrier and threatened the stability of the American economy. Munitions makers and other businessmen were profiting from the war because the Allies were not as well supplied with munitions factories as Germany. The Americans wanted to continue their profit-making without interference. When the war began, the United States had been in a business recession. The boom in war supplies reversed this economic picture. A sudden halt in Allied buying probably would have plunged the country back into a depression.

Within a few months, however, it was clear that the Allies were running out of cash and would have to borrow from the United States to pay for their enormous orders. On the advice of Secretary of State Bryan, Wilson had banned loans to belligerents on the basis of America's official neutrality. "Money is the worst of all contrabands," Bryan warned, "because it commands everything else." But, facing the growing pro-Allied feelings in the country, Wilson relaxed the restrictions. In October, 1914, he allowed bankers to float a 500-million-dollar loan in the form of French and British bonds. Over the next year and a half, the Allies borrowed 1.7 billion dollars more. Before the United States entered the war, private American bankers had loaned the Allies some 2.5 billion dollars.

GERMAN U-BOATS

During the first months of the war, Germany, having a powerful army, was not particularly troubled about neutral rights, American trade, or even the blockade. But when their first thrust across the continent was stopped short at the Marne River in northeast France, the land war sank into a stalemate and Germany started to look for ways to counteract British naval strength. With time against them, they had to obtain food and supplies and prevent similar shipments to England. They turned to the submarine, better known as the U-boat.

A frail and vulnerable craft, the U-boat was a powerful fighter because it could get within torpedo range of big surface vessels, discharge its torpedoes before the enemy knew it was there, then turn and run for safety.

The very ability to hit and run, however, made the U-boat unable to operate by the customary rules of naval warfare. Historically, a raiding ship was required to stop and examine its prey, give crew and passengers time to lower lifeboats before sinking the ship, and hover nearby to see to the safety and welfare of survivors. The U-boat could do none of these things. If it surfaced near a warship or armed merchant ship, it was a defenseless target for deck guns. Once stopped, it could even be sunk by ramming. Inside the slim vessel, crammed with officers and crew, there was no room for rescued survivors. According to maritime tradition, Germany's most useful naval weapon was as illegal as it was effective.

In February, 1915, Germany announced that she intended to establish a war zone surrounding Britain and that U-boats would sink without warning any ship sailing into the area. The world was shocked. Although England had violated the rules of the sea with her paper blockade, no citizen of a neutral state had been killed as a result. Announcing the war zone, Germany told the American government specifically that the German government could not guarantee the safety of people or cargoes of neutrals. Wilson immediately informed Germany that the United States would hold her to "strict accountability" if American ships, goods, or citizens were endangered.

THE *LUSITANIA*

On May 1, 1915, the English Cunard steamship line advertised the sailing of her passenger liner, the *Lusitania,* in American newspapers. The Germans published a warning in the same papers that "travellers sailing in the war zone on ships of Great Britain do so at their own risk." The passengers and crew of the *Lusitania* discussed the unusual German notice, but the ship sailed as scheduled. A week later, it was proceeding slowly along the coast of Ireland, carrying 4,200 cases of small arms, ammunition, and other munitions. The commander of a submarine on patrol saw the large ship and fired a torpedo. Almost instantly, the ship leaned to one side too sharply for lifeboats to be launched. Moments later its bow went high in the air and for the first time, the U-boat commander

The German U-boat was too small to carry survivors from torpedoed enemy vessels. The submarine's ability to hit and run made it illegal according to maritime tradition.

read the name *Lusitania*. In 18 minutes the ship sank, taking with it the lives of 1,198 men, women, and children, including 128 Americans.

The American public reeled with shock at the sinking of the *Lusitania*. "It is a colossal sin against God and it is premeditated murder," declared a prominent clergyman. "Damnable! Damnable! Absolutely hellish," cried the evangelist Billy Sunday. Some men, including Theodore Roosevelt, clamored for war and many newspapers concurred. "The Germans shall no longer make war like savages drunk with blood," insisted *The New York Times*. Wilson, however, correctly judging that the American public, while emotionally upset, did not want war, chose to react with words rather than action. He demanded that Germany deny connection with the sinking, make reparations, and take immediate steps to make sure passenger ships were not attacked again. When the German government quibbled, he sent a second, sharper note. The diplomatic correspondence continued for a year, but finally Germany issued secret orders to naval officers not to attack passenger liners. Roosevelt sneered that Wilson's last letter was "No. 11,765 on the subject." Yet, Germany finally apologized and offered reparations for the *Lusitania* in February, 1916.

Meanwhile, in spite of the desire of the German government not to alienate the United States, the British liner *Arabic* was sunk on August 19 with the loss of two American lives. The German government immediately apologized and offered an indemnity. She also extended another pledge to the United States that no unarmed passenger ship would be sunk without warning unless the ship resisted.

By 1915, American production was becoming the pivotal factor in the European struggle. The Allies would have been helpless without American munitions and food. At the same time, Germany was trying to respect America's neutral rights in order to keep her from entering the war. As a neutral, the United States aided the Allies, but as a belligerent, the American contribution could be disastrous for the Central Powers. Wilson knew, though, that Germany would surely disregard America's neutral rights in desperation if defeat seemed imminent. He understood that the only way to keep the United States neutral was for the war to end quickly.

Early in the year, he sent his close friend, Colonel Edward M. House, on a secret mission to England, France, and Germany. He hoped House could persuade each of the warring powers to let the United States mediate the conflict. House was rebuffed in London and Paris because the Allies were sure they would break the German lines in a spring offensive. In Berlin, the Germans also turned him down flatly since they too believed they were one step away from a clear-cut victory.

By this time, Secretary of State Bryan had become unpopular in Washington and much of the rest of the country because he took the official policy of neutrality with the seriousness of a pacifist. At the time of the *Lusitania* sinking, he reminded Wilson that the President had not objected to the German sinkings when American citizens were not involved. It was essential, he said, to keep Americans out of the war zone. Like Wilson, Bryan saw the situation in terms of American lives, not commerce. But unlike Wilson, he did not feel that the United States should set herself up as the special protector of international law and morality. As a matter of principle rather than necessity, Wilson refused to keep Americans at home or to stop opposing German submarine practices. Since Wilson ignored Bryan's advice, Bryan resigned. As his successor, Wilson named Robert Lansing, a lawyer in the State Department who was already extremely pro-British. Lansing wholeheartedly backed the President in his moral—and strictly legal—stand against Germany.

THE *SUSSEX*

The United States Congress, not satisfied that the President's defense of neutral rights would keep the country out of war, introduced the Gore-McLemore Resolution in February. It declared that American citizens would henceforth travel on armed belligerent ships at their own risk. Wilson regarded the resolution as an admission that the United States was giving up her defense of neutral rights and succeeded in having it defeated.

Given the President's attitude, new submarine warfare brought a confrontation between Germany and the United States. On March 1 Germany announced that she would sink armed merchant ships without warning. A U-boat sank an unarmed French liner, the *Sussex,* on March 24, injuring several Americans. Another such incident, warned Wilson, and the United States would break off relations with Germany. The alarmed Berlin government sent solemn declarations that they would spare all lives on not only neutral merchant ships but on all belligerent merchant ships before an attack by U-boats. In return, they asked Wilson to force the British to ease its blockade. Wilson ignored the demand but the exchange of notes had the effect of easing America's tense relations with Germany. Britain showed no interest in Lansing's proposal that all merchant vessels be unarmed. Wilson's *Sussex* ultimatum had totally committed America's honor and prestige to making Germany responsible for American lives and property lost from German submarine attack. If Germany renewed submarine warfare, the United States would be on the brink of war.

ADVOCATES OF PREPAREDNESS

Although Americans were relieved by the *Sussex* pledge, they were growing increas-ingly frightened by Germany's war policies. Skillful Allied propaganda fed their original anti-German prejudices, intrigues in Mexico and sabotage at home made them nervous, lurid novels and movies offered visions of invasions of the United States and other terrible acts by a Germany still bloodthirsty after defeating all of Europe. Finally, there was the crisis over submarines. The country still did not want to go to war, but it had reached the point of approving national defense measures. Peace groups which had maintained that increased armaments would lead to war were losing support.

From the beginning of the war, military men, largely ignored in peacetime, attracted followers as they pleaded for increases in the armed forces. Admirals warned that the United States faced catastrophe if the British fleet collapsed. Two of the most vehement apostles of rearming, General Leonard Wood, recently Chief of Staff, and his comrade from Rough Rider days, Colonel Theodore Roosevelt, constantly made headlines calling for a larger army. Wood even set up voluntary training camps. While the Navy was already the third largest in the world, the Army, numbering less than 100,000 men, shared fifteenth place among world armies with that of Persia. In 1913, the quartermaster corps was thinking about using trucks to supplement horse-drawn supply wagons but had not yet started to test them seriously. The air force, a part of the army signal corps, had seventeen planes and a yearly appropriation of 125,000 dollars. At one time in 1915, the Army had only a two-day supply of ammunition for artillery, and the artillery was largely obsolete.

Wilson opposed new armaments at first; like most Americans he believed there was no threat to the United States from the European conflict. But the submarine menace turned him gradually toward active preparedness. A preparedness group, the National Security League, claimed twenty-

*Advocates of peace felt that increased arma-
ments would lead America to war.*

two governors among its members by the
middle of 1915. In November, 1915, fifteen
months after the war began in Europe,
Wilson asked Congress for massive appropriations to enlarge the Navy and build the
Army to 400,000 men. Although Wilson
made a series of speeches for his program
throughout the country, Congress, reflecting
the pacifist West and the progressive element in the South, refused the request.
Wilson then substituted a compromise program which was passed. Among its proposals was the National Defense Act of
1916, authorizing a 175,000-man Army, a
National Guard of 400,000 and an officers'
reserve corps. For the Navy, Congress authorized 500 million dollars for a three-year
building program for new ships.

New revenue had to be found to finance
the preparedness program. Conservatives
wanted to issue bonds. Wilson, however,
suggested heavier taxes. Most progressives
were against preparedness in general, fearing that it was the forerunner of intervention which would end domestic reform and
only enrich business and banking interests.
Southern and Western progressive Democrats objected to Wilson's proposed taxes,
saying that they would burden the people
in the middle and low income brackets.
The progressives fought for a tax that
was frankly aimed at the rich who, they
claimed, had brought on the need for preparedness by selling munitions and loaning
money to the warring powers. Their tax
proposals passed. The new income and inheritance taxes established by the Revenue
Act of 1916 fell heavily on the rich for the
first time in American history.

THE 1916 CAMPAIGN

In 1916, Wilson faced not only the foreign crisis but also the domestic turmoil of an election campaign. Theodore Roosevelt was so enraged at Wilson's refusal to enter the war on the side of the Allies that he was ready to back the regular Republican candidate if such support guaranteed Wilson's defeat. The Republicans chose Charles Evans Hughes, a dignified Supreme Court Justice who earlier had made an excellent record as governor of New York and was a mild progressive. As soon as he was named, Roosevelt, who had been nominated by the remnant of the Progressive Party, promptly led his supporters back to the Republican fold. The party's platform was strong on preparedness.

At the Democratic convention, it was obvious that many Americans approved of Wilson's opposing German policy with notes instead of bullets. Although Wilson had planned to emphasize his now whole-hearted support of preparedness as a campaign theme, whenever speakers mentioned his success in keeping America out of the war, the convention cheered. Wilson responded by changing his approach. "He kept us out of war" became the Democratic slogan. Yet Wilson did not pledge to preserve United States neutrality at any cost. "I can't keep the country out of war," he said to a Cabinet member. "Any little German lieutenant can put us into war at any time by some calculated outrage."

Hughes proved to be an unexciting candidate and his campaign was badly managed in some parts of the country. Such phrases as "America first and America efficient" sounded so cautious that some wits said he had left the bench for the fence. Roosevelt, goading from the sidelines for strong pro-war statements, complained to newspapermen that instead of taking advice, Hughes just "withdraws into his whiskers." As Hughes reluctantly gave in to such pressure, he began to sound like a war candidate, which frightened many voters. Hughes was also hurt by his managers' blunder in not scheduling a meeting between him and the progressive Republican leader of California, Hiram Johnson. As a result, he lost most of the progressive vote there. He also alienated organized labor in California by speaking only to business groups. Still, on election night the returns indicated that he had won. In fact, he went to bed thinking he was to be the next President. Although Wilson had been cultivating the progressives and warning that a Republican victory would mean war in Europe, returns from the East and Middle West indicated a near landslide for Hughes. However, late returns from California turned the tide. Hughes awoke the next morning to learn that Wilson had received 9.1 million popular votes to his 8.5 million votes. The narrow margin for Wilson in the electoral college was 277 to 254.

A NEW GERMAN OFFENSIVE

Bolstered by reelection, Wilson made a final attempt to end the war. In December, 1916, he sent identical notes to all the warring countries asking for a clear statement of their war goals. But it was a useless query. The question disturbed the Allies deeply because the new approach seemed too genuinely neutral. Both sides felt they had fought too long to compromise their terms for peace, although the Allies told Wilson privately that they were willing to enter peace talks if Germany would be reasonable. Germany, believing she could win the war, made sweeping demands, calling for direct negotiations between the powers. Britain and France were not interested.

In early 1917, Wilson was feeling more neutral than at possibly any other time during the war. Even though his efforts to negotiate an end to the conflict had been rebuffed, the Germans had stopped sinking merchant ships without warning and the English had been increasingly irritating, searching United States mail for correspondence with Germany and blacklisting United States and South American firms which they claimed employed Germans.

Yet Germany chose this moment to embark on an all-out war for victory. She had over 100 U-boats and well-trained submarine crews by early 1917 and decided to use them to starve England before England's blockade starved them—and before full American power could be rallied against them. Therefore, on February 1, a week after Wilson's plea for "peace among equals," Germany declared that submarines would be unleashed against *all* ships sailing toward Allied ports. One brightly painted American liner would be allowed through to the English port of Portsmouth once a week provided it carried no contraband. As far as other ships were concerned, Germany was returning to unrestricted submarine warfare. "I guarantee that for its part the U-boat war will lead to victory," said Germany's Admiral Franz von Holtzendorff.

THE ZIMMERMAN NOTE

Keeping to his *Sussex* threat, Wilson broke diplomatic ties with Germany three days later, and Secretary of State Lansing handed German Ambassador Count von Bernstorff his passport. Nevertheless, the President still hoped to resist the pressures which relentlessly seemed to be pulling the United States into the conflict. The hope faded on February 24, 1917, when the British delivered to the United States government a German dispatch to Mexico which they had intercepted. The telegram, known as the "Zimmerman Note" after Alfred Zimmerman, the German Foreign Secretary, proposed a secret alliance between Germany and Mexico if and when America joined the Allies. In return for attacking the United States, Mexico would recover

her lost provinces of Texas, New Mexico, and Arizona. When the note was released to the press, it created a great furor throughout the country. The West and the Southwest, previously the most antiwar sections of the country, now became much more warlike in their thinking.

AMERICA GOES TO WAR

After the disclosures of the Zimmerman Note, American entry into the war seemed inevitable. Wilson asked Congress to vote to arm American merchant ships, and when a filibuster in the Senate prevented it, the President began arming American vessels on his own. In March, German submarines sank an unarmed American ship, the *Algonquin,* without warning, and within days, sank three other American vessels. Also in March, the autocratic Czarist regime in Russia was overthrown and a more representative provisional government was set up. Now even many Americans who had been hesitant called for war. On April 2, Wilson addressed an extraordinary session of Congress. War already existed, he said, because of acts by the German government. The United States had no honorable choice except to fight, not to conquer but for "peace and justice." He made a sharp distinction between the German government, which had thrown away "all scruples of humanity" and the German people, for whom he expressed sympathy and friendship. For them, and others, he said, "The world must be made safe for democracy." The Senate voted 82 to 6 and the House 373 to 50 to declare war on Germany on April 6, 1917.

Some historians, such as Walter Millis and Charles C. Tansill, later disillusioned with American participation in World War I, argued that the United States should never have become involved in the conflict. Basically, they blamed Wilson. They claimed that he always wanted to enter the war on the Allied side and to this end allowed the British complete freedom in spreading their propaganda and in no way interfered with the expansion of trade and loans to the Allies. They believed that the German submarine attacks were used as a pretext to cover a policy Wilson wished to pursue as soon as American public opinion was ready to support it.

Others, such as Charles Seymour, Arthur Link, and E. R. May, have argued that Wilson had no wish to have the country enter the conflict. He was a legalist and moralist who was determined to protect America's rights as a neutral in wartime. He would much have preferred to have the country remain neutral so that he could act as a mediator of the conflict. These historians believe Wilson made every effort to maintain American neutrality until German submarine warfare made such a position untenable. Germany's gamble on complete victory brought America in. Then Wilson was ready to enter the conflict to save American honor, create a peaceful and orderly world in the future, and prevent a threat to the Western Hemisphere that would follow a German victory in Europe.

THE HOMEFRONT IN WARTIME

When the United States entered the war, the Germans were close to defeating both France and Britain. The Allies were not winning the land war, and at sea German submarines were sinking as many as nine merchant ships a day. By April, 1917, Eng-

land had only enough food left for six weeks. For an Allied victory, America had to send supplies as well as men immediately into battle. "It is not an army we must train for war," Wilson said. "It is a nation."

The gigantic job of changing a civilian country into a massive war machine fell to independent federal agencies acting under the general guidance of a seven-man Advisory Committee of the Council of National Defense directly under the President. Several of the agencies were new, requested by Wilson and authorized by Congress especially to meet the wartime emergency quickly and effectively. They included the Food and Fuel Administrations, a War Industries Board, a Railroad Administration, a National Labor Board, and a War Labor Policies Board, whose directors were known as Wilson's War Cabinet. The unique quality of the agencies was that they gave the government almost total control over areas of the economy that seldom if ever had been touched by federal regulations. Congress delegated almost unrestrained power to Wilson for the duration of the crisis. Not since Lincoln's Presidency had any Chief Executive exercised such vast authority to organize the nation's resources. Under the Overman Act of 1918 the Congress gave Wilson responsibility to enforce wartime acts and reorganize the government for greater efficiency. They specified only the most general guidelines for carrying out these powers. At the same time, an attempt by some Congressmen to limit Presidential authority by a Joint Congressional Committee on Conduct of the War was sidetracked at Wilson's insistence.

FOOD CONTROL PROGRAM

Increased food production was one of the pressing problems of the war. The United States not only had to feed herself but produce enough extra food to supply her allies. Although food exports to Europe had jumped from 7 million tons in 1914 to more than 12 million tons from 1917 to 1918, lack of government regulations had produced steep price increases. The government took charge of the program to increase food production and distribution on a fair and effective basis.

The Lever Act of 1917 established the country's first Food Administration with power to fix food prices, license food distributors, coordinate food purchases, oversee food exports, act against hoarding and profiteering, and encourage farmers to grow more crops. The bill was hotly contested in Congress before it was passed. To many people, tampering with the freedom of farmers to produce the amount of crops they wanted was un-American.

The man selected to head the Food Administration was one of the civilian heroes of the war, Herbert C. Hoover, a Quaker humanitarian who was already famous for supervising food relief in Belgium.

To increase production, Hoover priced wheat, the most important agricultural product, at $2.20 a bushel, less than farmers might have received on the open market but enough to spur them to produce higher yields. He organized the supplying and buying of meat and managed to buy up the entire American and Cuban sugar crops which he then assigned to American and English refiners.

Hoover's greatest accomplishment, though, was to persuade the American people to economize on food voluntarily, or, as the slogans put it, to observe the "gospel of the clean plate," to practice "the patriotism of the lean garbage pail," and when eating apples, to be "patriotic to the core." They also abided by his request for wheatless Mondays and Wednesdays, meatless Tuesdays, and porkless Thursdays and Saturdays. As substitutes, they experimented with such items as wheatless "Victory bread," sugarless candy, vegetable lamb chops, whale meat and horsemeat. To hold back on food be-

came "to Hooverize," and so successful was the policy that by 1918, America exported to the hard-pressed Allied countries three times the prewar amounts of wheat products, meat, and sugar.

WAR INDUSTRIES BOARD

In contrast, the mobilization of America's giant industries got off to a fumbling start. In July, 1917, a War Industries Board was created but it had so little power to regulate the country's manufacture of munitions and other war goods that its first two chairmen resigned in despair. But in March, 1918, Wilson appointed Bernard Baruch, a Wall Street broker, to the task and gave him sweeping authority. Gathering about a hundred businessmen and military officers as his lieutenants, Baruch located, allocated, set priorities on and fixed prices of some 30,000 different items. He also initiated a standardization program to end the duplication of products and the unnecessary use of vital materials. For example, to free steel for guns he decreased the variety of sizes and styles of plows from 376 to 76, cut 232 different kinds of buggy wheels to four, and saved 8,000 tons of steel by banning its use as stays in women's corsets. Such standardization, conceived and put into effect by the war emergency, became a permanent feature of postwar industrial practice.

FUEL ADMINISTRATION

The Lever Act which created the Food Administration also created a Fuel Administration primarily concerned with mining more—and, at home, using less—coal. Directed by Harry A. Garfield, the president of Williams College and a son of President Garfield, the Fuel Administration encouraged the mining of unused marginal coal fields by offering high prices for the fuel.

People patriotically observed "heatless Mondays," "lightless nights," and, in the case of motorists, "gasless Sundays." In fact, domestic consumption was cut back so far that in the winter some nonessential factories shut down for lack of fuel and in New York at one period chilly public schools were closed. One measure that Garfield introduced to conserve fuel subsequently became a permanent feature of American life: daylight saving time.

UNITED STATES RAILWAY ADMINISTRATION

Railroads were essential to the war because freight trains fed the transatlantic "bridge of ships" that supplied the Allies. But, unsupervised, the more than thirty different privately owned rail systems operated at such cross purposes that raw materials were not getting to Eastern factories and munitions were not getting to ports. In December, 1917, Wilson placed the whole railroad network under a government Railway Administration directed by Secretary of the Treasury William G. McAdoo, Wilson's son-in-law. Price was no object if the railroads ran well, so McAdoo operated them at a loss, charging low rates but guaranteeing that the government would give the owners high returns. The final deficit was 862 million dollars, but McAdoo untangled the railroad snarl so successfully that a 1917 shortage of 150,000 freight cars became a surplus of 300,000 in 1918.

FINANCING THE WAR

Among the enormous problems Wilson faced was how to finance the war. In the last days of the war, the cost was 44 million dollars a day. Some of the necessary funds came from increased taxes on such items as individual and corporate incomes, taxes on excess profits, and higher luxury taxes on such items as theater tickets and tobacco.

The bulk of the money, about two-thirds of the total, however, was raised by selling bonds. Unlike Civil War loans, which were made by private, profit-making banking houses, the government borrowed directly from the American people. Liberty and Victory bonds were issued in amounts as low as fifty dollars, and for twenty-five cents children could buy their own Thrift Stamps. In four massive Liberty Loan drives and, in a 1919 Victory Loan drive, citizens loaned the government over 21 billion dollars.

SELLING THE WAR

To mobilize traditionally isolationist America behind the war, Wilson set up the Committee on Public Information and placed in charge George Creel, an outspoken and imaginative journalist.

Creel's approach was to "sell" the war as a crusade of good against evil—the forces of freedom and democracy against autocracy and militarism. For his campaign, he enlisted more than 150,000 artists, writers, lecturers, poets, historians, actors, educators, photographers, and ministers. The committee flooded the country with posters, cartoons, editorials, pamphlets, and movies. The committee's propaganda glorified America's war aims and portrayed the Germans as depraved, barbarian "Huns."

So effective was Creel's campaign that soon the country was in a state of virtual hysteria, and enthusiasm for the war became a cry for the suppression of all dissent. From the beginning, there had been opposition to United States participation in the conflict. Many Americans of German and Irish extraction were against intervention because they were anti-British, but many other critics of the war were pacifists, progressives, and socialists, who opposed the war on moral grounds. Now the government began to feel that wartime "patriotism" was more important to the country than the right of such citizens to speak or even hold these opinions. Elihu Root, a distinguished statesman who had won the 1912 Nobel Peace Prize, raised cheers in New York when he said, "There are men walking the streets of this city tonight who ought to be taken out at sunrise tomorrow and shot for treason."

As the Creel Committee promoted conformity and intolerance, vigilante groups started to appear around the country. Among them were the American Protective League and the National Security League. These groups broke up pacifist and socialist meetings, lynched an organizer for the radical Industrial Workers of the World, and even denounced and hung in effigy the eminent progressive, Senator Robert M. La Follette, in his home state of Wisconsin. They also attacked all things German. People with German names were mercilessly hounded. The orgy of hate against Germany forced schools to drop the teaching of the German language, threw German books out of libraries, barred German music and musicians from public performance, renamed sauerkraut "liberty cabbage," and hamburger "liberty sausage."

GOVERNMENT RESTRICTIONS

Although Wilson had said that the Bill of Rights was not to be suspended, he also indicated that its guarantees were limited in wartime if the government believed there was a conflict with military necessity. Wilson was willing to compromise civil liberties for his dream of leading the world to lasting peace.

The federal government's first official act to curb civil liberties in wartime was the Espionage Act of June, 1917. The act placed penalties of up to 20 years in prison and a 10,000-dollar fine on anyone who willfully helped the enemy, obstructed the draft, or encouraged insubordination or mutiny in the armed forces. The act also allowed the Postmaster General to ban from the mails anything written or printed which he considered helpful to the enemy or which seemed to call for action against the government.

Censorship increased four months later, when Congress passed the Trading-with-the-Enemy Act of October, 1917. The primary purpose of the law was to prevent American supplies from reaching Germany by licensing imports and exports and blacklisting companies suspected of trading with the enemy through neutral countries. However, one of its provisions restricted the publication of foreign language newspapers and magazines which had the effect of shutting down major outlets of "patriotic" as well as possibly protesting voices.

Since both of these laws failed to stop the antiwar activities of radical and pacifist groups, Congress passed the Sedition Act of May, 1918. Under this act it became a crime punishable by fine and imprisonment to discourage the sale of war bonds. Equally criminal was to "utter, print, write or publish any disloyal, profane, scurrilous or abusive language about the form of government of the United States, or the Constitution . . . or the flag . . . or the uniform of the Army or Navy."

Simple criticism became an invitation to arrest and imprisonment. Over fifteen hundred persons were arrested by the Justice Department for disloyal speech and ten for sabotage. Economic radicals were the chief victims. Small socialist magazines and newspapers were suppressed. Eugene V. Debs defended the right of free speech by publicly preaching socialism as he had always done and arguing against American participation in the war. He was indicted for inciting resistance to the government and sentenced to 10 years in a federal penitentiary. (He received a Christmas pardon from President Harding two years later.)

Of great importance for the history of civil liberties in the United States were two

856

court cases testing the constitutionality of the wartime restrictions. In the case of *Schenck v. the United States* a man had been arrested for distributing anti-draft leaflets under the Espionage Act. Justice Holmes wrote the opinion for the Court which held that the Espionage Act was constitutional since the right of free speech was not absolute at any time. "Free speech would not protect a man in falsely shouting fire in a theatre, and causing a panic." But Holmes also added that the act did not as a matter of course supersede the First Amendment. A man's speech could only be suppressed if there was a "clear and present danger" that it would bring about the evils Congress had a right to prevent. It was a question of determining the relationship between words and subsequent illegal acts.

In the same year, in *Abrams v. the United States,* the Court upheld the conviction of a man under the Sedition Act for publishing pamphlets attacking the sending of an expeditionary force to Russia, and calling for a general strike. This time Holmes and Brandeis dissented, arguing that these actions presented no direct attack on the government and created no direct danger to the war effort.

THE MILITARY FRONT

Three weeks after the American declaration of war, French and British missions arrived in Washington to tell a startled Wilson and his equally unprepared advisers that American troops would be needed to help fight the war. The administration had not even thought about sending American men into battle. They assumed that America's contribution would be in money, shipping, and supplies. Neither the Army nor the Navy had worked out any plans to raise, train, equip, and transport a mass army to Europe. Although the armed forces quickly plunged into the enormously complex task, well over a year passed before an American force went into battle and became a significant factor in the war effort.

THE SELECTIVE SERVICE ACT

The Allied plea for men resulted in a draft law at the beginning of the war. The American tradition of depending on volunteers aroused opposition to conscription. In Congress, Champ Clark, the Speaker of the House, declared that he saw "little difference between a conscript and a convict." Many people associated a military draft with autocratic European governments like that of Germany. Others recalled the Civil War draft which had allowed the well-to-do to buy or hire their way out of military service. Still, to Wilson, Congress, and finally, the whole country, nationwide conscription seemed the disagreeable but only way to raise a large army at the necessary speed.

The Selective Service Act passed in 1917 required all men between the ages of 18 and 45 to register at local civilian draft boards. They were placed in any one of five classes of eligibility and called up by numbers chosen through a countrywide lottery. To raise the morale of draftees, Congress provided allowances for their dependents as well as War Risk Insurance that paid up to 10,000 dollars in case of death. The first registration day was like a patriotic holiday. Flag-wavers led gala parades to registration centers which were fittingly

U.S.A.
1917

NORWAY
Oslo

FINLAND
Indep. July, 1917
Helsinki

Lake
Ladoga

Petrograd

SWEDEN
Stockholm

ESTONIA
Indep.
Feb, 1918

NORTH
SEA

BALTIC
SEA

LATVIA
Indep. Riga
Nov, 1918

RUSSIA
1914

Riga offensive
Sept, 1917

Battle of Jutland
May-June, 1916

Edinburgh

DENMARK

Memel

LITHUANIA
Indep. Feb, 1918

Smolensk

Königsberg

Vilna

GREAT
BRITAIN
1914

Copenhagen

Kiel

Danzig

Masurian Lakes
Sept, 1914

Minsk

Hamburg

Tannenberg
Aug, 1914

London

Amsterdam

NETH.

Berlin

POLAND
Indep. Nov, 1918

Pinsk

Cologne

GERMANY
1914

Warsaw

Brest-Litovsk

Brussels
BELG.
1914

Leipzig

Dresden

Lublin

Kiev

GERMAN INVASION
AUG-SEPT, 1914

LUX.

Prague

Cracow

Lemberg

Kerensky offensive
July, 1917

Mainz

GALICIA

Paris

Metz

Rhine R.

Danube R.

Galicia offensives
Aug, 1914

Brusilov offensive
June, 1916

Strasbourg

BAVARIA

Berne

SWITZ.

Munich

Vienna

Pressburg

UKRAINE

FRANCE
1914

Vittorio-Veneto
Oct-Nov, 1918

Graz

Budapest

AUSTRIA-HUNGARY
1914

Odessa

Milan

Piave June, 1918

Venice

Trieste

Genoa

Invasion of Serbia
1914

RUMANIA
1916

Bucharest

Danube R.

BLACK
SEA

Marseilles

ITALY
1915

BOSNIA

Belgrade

SPAIN

CORSICA

Withdrew from
Triple Alliance 1914

Sarajevo

MONTENEGRO
1915

SERBIA
1914

Sofia

BULGARIA
1915

Rome

Constantinople

SARDINIA

Naples

ALBANIA

OTTOMAN EMPIRE
1914

PORTUGAL
1916

Salonika

Gallipoli

MEDITERRANEAN

GREECE
1916

Dardanelles campaign
1915-1916

Smyrna

SICILY

SEA

Athens

CRETE

1916 Date of entry into the war

——— Maximum advance of the Central Powers

------- Maximum Russian advance

·········· Line of the Brest-Litovsk Treaty Mar, 1918

——— Armistice lines

0   500
        Miles

Central Powers

Allied Powers

Neutral nations

WORLD WAR I • 1914 TO 1918

decorated with red, white, and blue bunting. However, Theodore Roosevelt's argument that volunteers were always more enthusiastic than drafted soldiers also proved to be correct. Twenty-four million men were enrolled in the draft and 2.8 million were selected but some 2 million more men volunteered for service.

PERSHING MADE HEAD OF THE AEF

The commanding general of the American Expeditionary Force, the AEF, was John J. Pershing, an officer with a driving personality and a talent for organization. Pershing was one of the few American generals with fighting experience. He had commanded the troops in 1916 which chased

Two million Americans volunteered for service in World War I.

the bandit Pancho Villa back into Mexico after he had invaded the United States. Within a few months after the war began, the President sent Pershing to Paris to set up his headquarters and start planning for the use of one million men. Soon after, the vanguard of that number, some 12,000 troops, arrived in France.

John J. Pershing, the commanding general of the American Expeditionary Force, arriving in France.

From the beginning, "Black Jack" Pershing wanted the AEF to operate as a separate unit. The Allied generals had hoped to use American soldiers simply as reinforcements for the war-weary French and English troops. Pershing stubbornly refused their request except during a few crucial months of intensive German attack in 1918. Instead, he demanded and received his own section of the front, the 45 miles between Verdun and Switzerland. Pershing's attitude reflected his country's continuing tendency toward isolationism and suspicion of Europeans. It was part of an overall American policy to stay away from full membership in the Allied cause. Wilson always called the other countries fighting Germany "associates." He never used the term "Allies."

The AEF of 1917 and 1918 was an army of great dash and reckless fighting spirit that surprised both the enemy and the Allied powers. With perhaps eight months of training in thirty hastily put-together American army camps, they were seldom ready for combat when they arrived in France. But from the first their presence lifted Allied morale. At Pershing's direction, the American forces were eager for attack. The AEF training was to stress taking the offensive, Pershing said, "until it becomes a settled habit of thought." Many American soldiers finished their training hurriedly, in camps near the fighting front, but their exuberance and zestful spirit made up for the hasty instruction.

TRENCH WARFARE

For four years the Germans and the Allies had carried on debilitating and deadly trench warfare. The Germans had not been able to push farther into France and the Allies, despite repeated attempts, had not been able to force the Germans back more than a few miles. Both sides "dug themselves in." Between the two lines of trenches was a "no man's land." An attack started with days of cannon fire. Then thousands of infantrymen, with shallow steel helmets their only armor, went "over the top" to try to overrun the enemy's trenches. "Bullets, millions of them, flying like raindrops," an American soldier wrote in his diary. "Rockets and flares in all directions. Shrapnel bursting the air and sending down its deadly iron. . . . Every minute looking to be gone . . . to the great beyond. A mad dash for 50 feet and then look for cover."

GERMAN OFFENSIVES

Two events in the second half of 1917 changed the course of the war for the AEF by changing the conditions of battle on the western front, the line between the French and Germans that extended from the North Sea to the border of Switzerland. The first event took place in October, when an Austrian drive broke through the Italian lines on the front between Italy and Austria. Italy, a prewar partner of Germany and Austria-Hungary, had proclaimed her neutrality at the start of the war and then joined the Allies. For two years, the Italians had been able to hold back the Austrians. Now their defeat and rout at Caporetto forced the Allies to send the Italians reinforcements from the western front.

The second event was the Russian Revolution, the most important nonmilitary occurrence of World War I, which took place in November and paved the way for Russian withdrawal from the war. By the beginning of 1917, the Czarist armies fighting the Germans on the eastern front had reached the point of collapse. In March, the Czar had been deposed by the Duma, the representative body elected by the people, and Russia had become a republic. While the harried new leaders tried to reorganize the country and keep public order, the Russian armies fell into a state of almost total disarray—part still loyal to the Czar, part loyal to the Duma and all infiltrated by both German and communist agitators. In an effort to encourage these chaotic conditions and undermine the republican government in Russia, the German government gathered all the leading Russian communists in exile, including V. I. Lenin, put them in a sealed train and sent them to Petrograd, the Russian capital. The Bolsheviks, the most radical minority in the Communist Party, overthrew the liberal provisional government which wanted to continue the war. The new government immediately approached Germany for a peace treaty. The negotiations took place at Brest-Litovsk where Lenin in March, 1918, in exchange for giving up Russia's claims to Finland, Poland, the Ukraine, and the Baltic states, agreed to take Russia out of the war. Having neutralized Russia, seasoned German troops were now free to fight on the western front.

WESTERN FRONT

With British and French forces weakened by transfers to the Italian-Austrian front and new German troops pouring in from the east, there was soon explosive action on the previously stalemated western front. The Germans were now determined to crash through the Allied line, overrun Paris, and completely defeat the Allies. The time had arrived when Americans, in rapidly increasing numbers, would engage in major battles. In fact, the AEF fought for about two hundred days between April and November, 1918.

The first important American assignment came at the end of May, when the Germans, in a powerful spring offensive, reached the west bank of the Marne River near the town of Château-Thierry which was only 50 miles from Paris. About 27,000 American troops halted the Germans and, in a fierce four-day battle, drove them back across the Marne bridges to the east bank of the river.

Beginning on June 6, American marines forced experienced German troops to retreat from a square mile section of the forest of Belleau Wood near the highway to Paris, a crucial stronghold. Although the fighting took several weeks and American losses were heavy, the action astounded the Germans who had been dismissing American soldiers as "a rabble of amateurs." To

After fierce fighting and heavy losses in the Argonne Forest, the Allies broke the Hindenburg Line, Germany's major defense on the western front.

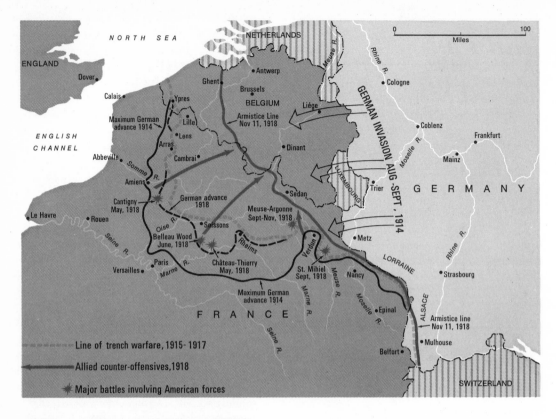

NORTH SEA

ENGLAND
Dover•

ENGLISH
CHANNEL

NETHERLANDS

•Antwerp

Ghent•   •Brussels
Ypres•   BELGIUM   Liége•
Calais•   •Cologne
Maximum German   Armistice Line
advance 1914   •Lille   Nov 11, 1918
Arras• •Lens   •Coblenz
Abbeville•   Cambrai•   •Dinant   Frankfurt•
Somme R.   •Mainz
Amiens•   •Sedan   Trier•   G E R M A N Y
Cantigny   German advance   Meuse-Argonne
May, 1918   1918   Sept-Nov, 1918
Oise R. •Soissons   Verdun•   •Metz   LORRAINE
Belleau Wood   Rheims   •Strasbourg
June, 1918   St. Mihiel   •Nancy
Le Havre•   •Rouen   Sept, 1918
Paris•   Marne R. Château-Thierry   ALSACE
Versailles•   May, 1918   Armistice line
Seine R.   Maximum German   Nov 11, 1918
advance 1914   •Mulhouse
F R A N C E   Belfort•   SWITZERLAND
Seine R.

GERMAN INVASION AUG.-SEPT., 1914

Rhine R.
Moselle R.
LUXEMBOURG
Meuse R.
Moselle R.
Rhine R.
•Epinal

0   100
Miles

•••• Line of trench warfare, 1915-1917

➤ Allied counter-offensives, 1918

✳ Major battles involving American forces

WORLD WAR I • WESTERN FRONT

honor American heroism, the French renamed the spot Bois de Marins, the Marine Woods.

Still undaunted on July 15, the Germans made a desperate lunge toward Paris. It was their last great offensive of the war. In the Champagne region of France between the towns of Rheims and Soissons, they met the stubborn resistance of 85,000 American troops. "We well-nigh reached the objectives prescribed for our shock divisions," wrote the German general, ". . . with the exception of the one division on our right wing. This encountered American units." Three days later, 270,000 Americans in a counterattack with French and English troops "turned the tide of the war," as Pershing put it. On July 15, Ger-

many was confidently expecting peace overtures from the Allies. "On the 18th," the German Chancellor wrote later, "even the most optimistic among us knew that all was lost. The history of the world was played out in three days."

After the impressive American showing under fire with Allied units at Rheims and Soissons, French Marshal Foch, who was the supreme commander of all Allied forces, finally approved Pershing's plan for a separate American army. Its first assignment was to assault and wipe out the enemy salient, the trench fortifications at St. Mihiel, a vital railroad junction which the Germans had held since early in the war. The Germans, knowing they could not hold it against a determined assault, planned to withdraw when, on September 12, in a heavy fog, an Allied force of 550,000 attacked. The fortification fell in two days, and the Americans took 16,000 prisoners and 443 guns. Their own casualties were considered light—about 8,000 men.

Pershing wanted the powerful American offensive to roll on eastward, toward Metz, Germany's important communications center, but Foch, still supreme commander, insisted that the Americans help the Allies break the German lines to the north.

A gigantic Allied offensive along a 200-mile front began on September 26 and was one of the most savage ever fought by American troops. Over one million Americans in a 24-mile line drove forward into the Argonne Forest. Pershing described the region as a "vast network of uncut barbed wire, the deep ravines, dense woods, myriads of shell craters and a heavy fog." The Americans inched through the Argonne. Units got hopelessly entangled and faced heavy fire from German artillery beyond the forest. Though slowed by heavy rains small American platoons and companies independently took German gun emplacements. After 47 days of bloody battle, the Allied army regrouped, passed through the Argonne and broke the Hindenburg line, the main German defense on the western front. On November 7, it reached the outskirts of Sedan, the goal of the long battle, and threw bridges across the Meuse River thereby cutting Germany's most essential supply railroad. On November 11, with the French and British armies advancing just as relentlessly along the rest of the front, Germany signed the Armistice that ended the fighting.

THE AIR WAR

Both the American Army and the Navy had had air units in the war. The Army's Bombardment Squadron had been formed in 1913. The Army had 55 planes at the start of the war and the number had increased to 3,227 by the war's end. Sailing for France in 1917, the squadron joined the American volunteer Lafayette Escadrille and began combat duties with French planes in March, 1918. During the Argonne Forest fighting, the squadron had grown to three groups which were used to reconnoiter enemy territory. The American "ace" of the war was Lieutenant Eddie Rickenbacker, who shot down twenty-six enemy planes. It was from the Army Air Force operations that Colonel William Mitchell developed his idea of the importance of air power to national defense. Meeting opposition to his ideas, he became more heated in his defense of them, which brought his demotion, subsequent court-martial, and forced his retirement from the service.

The naval air units that went to France used mainly foreign-built airplanes in the beginning. One outfit was supplied with the "flying coffin" seaplane, a reject from the French navy. Another used Italian models. Flying these planes back to air bases in the north was often more dangerous than flying in combat. Eventually the naval aviation units had American float planes, using five hundred from twenty-seven different bases in Europe. These planes helped protect Allied shipping by spotting U-boats. Some of them were converted to bombers and, with the army air force, made air raids on German installations.

THE WAR AT SEA

The Navy had been quicker to enter combat than the Army. By the summer of 1917, it had placed itself on a war footing and was playing a decisive part in beating back U-boat attacks. Six American destroyers had reached the British naval base at Queenstown, Ireland, as early as May 6. By the close of the war, 834 American naval vessels were in service in European waters; most were destroyers and submarine chasers.

Although the British navy made the largest contribution to the antisubmarine war, American help was vital in reducing losses from U-boat attacks to about one-third of the peak period of early 1917. Another important antisubmarine measure suggested by the Americans was to lay some 70,000 mines in the waters of the North Sea between Scotland and Norway. The mines had new antenna-firing mechanisms which made them extremely effective in ending the submarine threat.

Perhaps the most vital American antisubmarine technique was the use of a system of convoys to protect Allied shipping. The British technique had been to scatter merchant ships at sea while patrols near the British Isles scouted for U-boats. The system was not successful, in large part because the British did not have enough patrol ships. However, the British Admiralty objected to the convoy plan on the grounds that merchant ships could not keep in formation and the slowest ship in the convoy would set the speed of the whole group. But when Secretary of the Navy Josephus Daniels and American Admiral William S. Sims overruled British resistance, the results were encouraging. With the convoy system in operation, the submarine menace was, for all practical purposes, brought under control. The successful drive against the U-boat permitted British and American ships to transport some two million American troops in a period of less than seven months in 1918, without the loss of a troopship.

WAR CASUALTIES

In the chapel of St. Cyr, the West Point of France, there is a memorial tablet honoring the dead of the First World War. Among the names is a plaque that simply reads "The Class of 1914." Every man in the class had been killed in battle. For all the European armies, the war had been a massive slaughter. Over a four-year period,

battle deaths amounted to one out of every twenty-eight people in the population of France, one out of every thirty-two of Germany, one out of every fifty-seven of England and one out of every 107 of Russia, a total of some 6.4 million men. For the United States, too, the casualties had been enormous. In just six months of intensive fighting in 1918, losses numbered some 321,000—more than 50,000 killed in action, almost 63,000 dead from disease, 2,900 listed missing in action, and about 206,000 wounded.

POSTWAR DIPLOMACY

WILSON'S FOURTEEN POINTS

Wilson set forth a blueprint for the postwar world in a speech to a joint session of Congress on January 8, 1918. Calling it the "only possible program" for permanent peace, Wilson proposed Fourteen Points. Summarized, they were: (1) "Open covenants of peace, openly arrived at . . ."—that is, no secret agreements during the negotiations for peace; (2) freedom of the seas, in war as in peacetime; (3) no barriers to trade between countries; (4) disarmament; (5) adjustment of colonial claims—that is, respect for the just interests of native peoples in the British, German and other empires; (6) withdrawal from captured Russian territory and Russia's freedom to decide its own policies and politics; (7) withdrawal from Belgium; (8) withdrawal from captured French territory and the return to France of the province of Alsace-Lorraine; (9) readjustment of the

Italian frontiers; (10) self-government for parts of the Austrian Empire; (11) freedom for the Balkan countries, with access to the sea for Greater Serbia (Yugoslavia); (12) an independent Poland, with access to the sea; (13) freedom and self-government for Turkish peoples and countries formerly ruled by the Ottoman Empire; (14) a League of Nations to guarantee political independence and territorial integrity to all states.

Coming at a time when all the warring countries were weary of conflict, the Fourteen Points seemed a message of hope that lasting peace would follow the war. The Creel Committee spread the Fourteen Points by means of millions of pamphlets and booklets dropped behind enemy lines. People all over the world hailed Wilson's ideas. Peasants pinned his picture on their cabin walls next to images of patron saints. Even many Germans, facing their country's defeat, praised him because they saw his first five points as a promise that a democratic Germany would be able to return to the community of nations as an equal. With the war going against them by the fall of 1918, the German Kaiser abdicated on November 9 and a republican government was organized. Two days later it signed an armistice which included the Fourteen Points. The German government had to accept them as the basis of the peace settlement before the Allies would sign the agreement. The Allies themselves were not happy to have to agree to the Fourteen Points. But they accepted them reluctantly, although Britain would not go along with the concept of freedom of the seas and both Britain and France were determined to force harsh postwar reparations on Germany.

THE VERSAILLES TREATY

WILSON'S BLUNDERS

Because of the Fourteen Points, Wilson was a hero to the rest of the world when the war ended. Yet, by the time he went to Europe to negotiate a peace settlement, his prestige in the United States had begun to crumble as a result of his own actions.

First, he prematurely ended the truce in domestic politics he had called for during the war. When the United States declared war, Wilson had announced that "politics is adjourned" until peace returned. Yet in October, before the 1918 Congressional elections, he appealed to people to vote for Democrats as a sign of support for his leadership. Republicans who had supported him in his war policies even more ardently than some Democrats were furious. Such leading Republicans as Roosevelt urged the Senate to reject the Fourteen Points because Wilson had insulted the patriotic honor of Republicans. The influential Senator Henry Cabot Lodge of Massachusetts reversed his earlier support of an international organization to enforce the peace. When the Republicans won the House, 237 to 190, and carried the Senate by a two-vote majority, the result was interpreted by some politicians as a sign that both Wilson and the ideals of the Fourteen Points had been rejected by the country.

Wilson's next blunder was to announce that he personally would head the United States delegation to the peace conference in Paris. Apparently he thought he had a moral obligation to be physically present in order to have his peace program accepted. Again Republicans protested. No previous President had ever left America while in office. So sacred was the custom that Taft, while he was President, did not even take vacations at his summer house in Canada. Even such friends as Colonel House wanted him to change his mind, but Wilson was a stubborn man.

Wilson also seriously miscalculated in his choice of the Peace Commissioners to go with him. He did not choose a single Senator, although the Senate, with its Republican majority, would have to ratify any treaty he brought back. Nor did he include any of the powerful and capable Republicans in the country—Nobel Peace Prize winner Elihu Root, former President Taft, or Justice Hughes, who strongly favored Wilson's cherished idea of a League of Nations. They could have created bipartisan support in the United States for the President's proposals. The only Republican in the delegation was a nonpolitical career diplomat, Henry White, who had been out of the government for nearly 10 years. Other Commissioners included Colonel House, Secretary of State Lansing, and a military adviser, General Tasker H. Bliss.

CONFERENCE PARTICIPANTS

Twenty-seven large and small victorious powers had representatives in Paris. But from the beginning, decision-making rested with Wilson; England's dynamic Prime Minister David Lloyd George; Italy's genial Premier Vittorio Orlando; and the "tiger of France," Premier Georges Clemenceau. Although their people welcomed Wilson, the three Old World realists were only moderately attracted to the American's visionary schemes. They had every intention of carving up the territorial spoils of victory, as they had arranged beforehand in

Prime Minister Lloyd George, Premier Orlando, Premier Clemenceau, and President Wilson at the Versailles Conference in Paris.

secret treaties. They also planned to insure their own national security and to exact revenge on Germany. Wilson faced these masters of power politics with idealistic dedication to the spirit of the Fourteen Points and a vast capacity for work. He had the advantage of seeking no territorial gains for the United States. He also had the extra strength of speaking for the only country to come out of the war richer and more powerful than it had been in 1914. But this combination of unselfishness, idealism, and power encouraged his natural tendency to be unyielding. Wilson found it difficult to compromise, especially when he believed a question of morality was involved. Once, to soften an argument, a professor at Princeton had said, "Well, Doctor Wilson, there are two sides to every question." "Yes," Wilson had snapped back, "a right side and a wrong side." When he felt, as he did in Paris, that the fate of all humanity depended on his actions, his inflexibility became even more noticeable. Convinced that his Fourteen Points would make the world "fit and safe to live in," he ignored the possibility that they all might not be practical or that there might be conflicts among them. Clemenceau murmured a reminder that men could not keep all of God's Commandments and there were only ten of those. Yet, in the end, against all disadvantages, Wilson got a Peace Treaty which, if not what he ideally wanted, was at least less vindictive than the Allies would have written without him.

WILSON'S GOALS IN PARIS

POLITICAL SELF-DETERMINATION

High on Wilson's list of important goals was to assure the right of peoples to govern themselves. Never again, he felt, should Slavs have to live under the rule of Austrians, nor should Moroccans, for that matter, be ruled by Turks. On the surface, it would seem that independent countries, each representing a national group, could have been established fairly easily from the German and Austrian empires in eastern Europe. In fact, the treaty granted self-determination to several such national groups. It created the countries of Poland, Yugoslavia, and Czechoslovakia and, therefore, in part accomplished Wilson's objective. But complete self-determination was impossible to obtain because of the many regions of mixed population in Europe and the skill of the leading European diplomats in securing territorial gains for their own countries. Italy received the Brenner Pass region of the Alps where 200,000 Austrians lived, Yugoslavia acquired the Italian-speaking port of Fiume, and Czechoslovakia received the Sudetenland area where there were millions of Germans.

FREE TRADE

Another of Wilson's hopes was that the treaty would provide freedom of trade between countries, the third of the Fourteen Points, on the grounds that trade restrictions created troublesome barriers between nations. From the first, however, he was frustrated in gaining this point. Many Americans strongly opposed the idea of removing tariff barriers. The subject was not even mentioned in the final treaty.

THE LEAGUE OF NATIONS

The one issue that outweighed everything else in Wilson's mind was the establishment of the League of Nations. He cherished a vision of an organization of countries that would eventually help create a world of peaceful international order. He wanted to replace Europe's reliance on power politics with a world-wide alliance against war and the use of force. He insisted that the League become an inseparable part of the treaty, and he worked long and hard in designing the details of its structure. All his stubbornness went into his fight for the League of Nations because he thought that through it and it alone the whole world could avoid future wars.

CONFLICTS AMONG THE ALLIES

Among the Allied representatives, the dominant figure was Clemenceau who, as head of the host country, France, was the presiding officer of the Peace Conference. At 78, Clemenceau had few illusions about politics—he had seen America's Civil War and had been through the Franco-Prussian War. His main concern was the security of France and, from his point of view, it was logical and reasonable that all the Allies should have the same goal. For centuries, France had led the continent of Europe politically and culturally and, as one historian put it, "like all Frenchmen, Clemenceau was quite innocently unable to see how civilization could survive unless this position was maintained." To Clemenceau, security meant the traditional device of keeping Germany so financially weak that she could not become a threat again. He was, for a time, unyielding on the French demand for large areas of rich German land as a buffer zone. France was awarded Alsace-Lorraine and occupation of the Saar territory on the German border for fifteen years. However, he gave up French demands for control of the Rhineland area in return for its demilitarization and security treaties with both England and the United States stating that the two countries would defend France in case of a future German attack. The security treaty was not even considered by the United States Senate. Similarly, England's Lloyd George was most interested in punishing Germany and dividing the spoils of war to his country's best advantage; and Orlando, also a nationalist, was being goaded by extremists at home to acquire every possible territorial advantage for Italy. When Fiume was given to Yugoslavia instead of Italy, Orlando was so furious that he left the Conference permanently.

COLONIES AND MANDATE SYSTEM

Following old customs, the Allies had signed secret treaties at the beginning of the war providing for territorial gains. For example, in return for joining the conflict, England had promised Japan the German rights to the Chinese peninsula of Shantung and the German Empire's Pacific Islands. Wilson strongly opposed giving Japan control of some thirty million Chinese, but he gave way when England insisted the promises be honored. He did, however, persuade Japan to agree to return the strategic peninsula to China at a later date, an agreement Japan kept in 1923. He also had a degree of success when the Allies began to distribute the other German colonies in Africa and the Far East as well as the remains of the empire of Turkey, a wartime member of the Central Powers. He devised the so-called "mandate" system under which the Allies would hold certain colonies and territories on a basis of trusteeship under the League of Nations. The trustees would give annual accounts of their supervision to the League and prepare the colonial populations for independence. Although the mandate system was not exactly self-determination, as Wilson wanted, it was not the outright possession of lands and peoples envisioned by the Allies.

GERMAN REPARATIONS

The Allies wrote into the treaty clauses that made Germany accept full responsibility for causing the war. It was an act of sheer revenge as well as a senseless oversimplification of a complex sequence of events. Even more humiliating to Germany, the victors also demanded that she sign a "blank check" to cover all expenses of the war. Germany was to pay not only for damage to civilian property but also for such indirect costs of the war as future pensions to Allied veterans. She was presented with an immediate bill for 5 billion dollars. A later bill, worked out by a special commission, came to about 33 billion dollars. Germany could not possibly pay such amounts in cash and the strain of paying drained her economically. Germans had to hand over coal, livestock, and other goods to England, France, and Belgium. German merchant ships, those existing and those constructed in the future, also went to the Allies to make up for Allied shipping losses by Germany. German spokesmen blaming Wilson said that he had reduced their country to economic slavery by betraying his promises. "President Wilson is a hypocrite," they charged.

TREATY DEMANDS ON GERMANY

On June 28, 1919, Germany signed the Versailles Treaty. As a conquered country she could do nothing else. The British blockade, which continued all through the 10 months of peace negotiations, had reduced economic conditions within Germany even more than the war itself. The Kaiser had been dethroned earlier, as the Allies had wished, but the new republican government had not been permitted any voice at the peace table. In addition to the war debt and the admission of war guilt put on Germany, the treaty imposed strict reductions of the army and navy and stripped her of all her colonies.

There have been many assessments of the Versailles Treaty. Some writers have seen it as embodying the triumph of self-determination for many nationalities, while others have looked upon it as the instrument of Allied vengeance against Germany which carried the seeds of a new war in the future. Some believed the treaty's two

EUROPE AFTER VERSAILLES · 1919

New independent nations   Plebiscite areas   Allied occupation zone

worst features were the indefinite war costs, which kept Germany financially unsteady, and the disarmament clauses which made her incapable of defending herself. Political rather than economic considerations dominated the treaty's provisions. However, few people outside of Germany criticized either of these clauses at the time. In addition, France and Britain had little sympathy with Wilson's views on self-determination and the importance of a League of Nations. It has also been argued that the breakup of Austria-Hungary into small nations created a power vacuum in eastern Europe into which both Germany and Russia could move in the future.

THE LEAGUE OF NATIONS

For Wilson, the most satisfying outcome of the conference was his success in making the Allies accept the League of Nations as part of the Versailles Treaty. "A living thing is born," he said. As he saw it, after the passions and prejudices of the war had simmered down, the League would correct all the imperfections of the Treaty.

The League was a remarkable innovation in international politics. It had no supreme authority, no armies, not even a way of forcing members to pay their financial dues. It was an international forum whose power depended entirely on the conscience of mankind. By the creation of the League, men of many nations finally began to see that war and the acts that lead to war were everybody's responsibility. The League gave countries a world organization to which they could bring their problems for debate. It also offered a hope that the force of habit, a growing number of successful actions, and the common interests of the members would give the organization lasting strength.

ORGANIZATION

The Covenant, or constitution, of the League of Nations called for an Assembly, a Council, and a permanent Secretariat headed by a Secretary-General with headquarters in Geneva, Switzerland. With the exception of the defeated Central Powers and communist Russia, all countries and self-governing members of the British Commonwealth such as Canada were eligible to join the League. Each member nation had one vote and equal representation in the Assembly. The nine-country Council was to be made up of five permanent representatives from the victorious countries—the United States, Britain, France, Italy, and Japan, and four temporary members chosen by the Assembly. The Assembly was to directly control most of the internal

Wilson and the League of Nations

66 *The United States entered the war upon a different footing from every other nation except our associates on this side of the sea. We entered it, not because our material interests were directly threatened or because any special treaty obligations to which we were parties had been violated, but only because we saw the supremacy and even the validity of right everywhere put in jeopardy and free government likely to be everywhere imperiled by the intolerable aggression of a power which respected neither right nor obligation and whose very system of government flouted the rights of the citizen as against the autocratic authority of his governors. And in the settlements of the peace we have sought no special reparation for ourselves, but only the restoration of right and the assurance of liberty everywhere that the effects of the settlement were to be felt. We entered the war as the disinterested champion of right and we entered in the terms of peace in no other capacity . . .*

A league of free nations had become a practical necessity. Examine the treaty of peace and you will find that everywhere throughout its manifold provisions its framers have felt obliged to turn to the League of Nations as an indispensable instrumentality for the maintenance of the new order it has been their purpose to set up in the works,—the world of civilized men. . . .

—*President Woodrow Wilson*

operations of the League itself but as far as international affairs were concerned, it could only investigate and advise. The more powerful Council carried out League recommendations. The League Covenant also established a Permanent Court of International Justice, the World Court, set up at The Hague in The Netherlands.

Lodge Speaks Against League of Nations

. . . I object in the strongest possible way to having the United States agree, directly or indirectly, to be controlled by a league which may at any time, and perfectly lawfully and in accordance with the terms of the covenant, be drawn in to deal with internal conflicts in other countries, no matter what those conflicts may be. We should never permit the United States to be involved in any internal conflict in another country, except by the will of her people expressed through the Congress which represents them. . . .

. . . We may set aside all this empty talk about isolation. Nobody expects to isolate the United States or to make it a hermit Nation, which is a sheer absurdity. But there is a wide difference between taking a suitable part and bearing a due responsibility in world affairs and plunging the United States into every controversy and conflict on the face of the globe. By meddling in all the differences which may arise among any portion or fragment of humankind we simply fritter away our influence and injure ourselves to no good purpose. We shall be of far more value to the world and its peace by occupying, so far as possible, the situation which we have occupied for the last 20 years and by adhering to the policy of Washington and Hamilton, of Jefferson and Monroe, under which we have risen to our present greatness and prosperity. . . . 99

—Senator Henry Cabot Lodge

PURPOSE

The chief purpose of the League of Nations was to keep world peace. Article X, which Wilson called "the heart of the Covenant," pledged the member nations "to respect and preserve against external aggression the territorial integrity and existing political independence" of all members of the League. If any country, in or outside of the League, threatened any other with aggressive action, the Council of the League would be informed and confer on what measures to take. The members agreed to submit their disputes with each other to arbitration. It would also investigate any outside interference with the independence and self-government of the small nations. If nations violated their pledge to the League by going to war to settle an argument, the League Council could call on member nations to use economic, financial and, if necessary, joint military and naval pressure to stop the aggressor. To keep the peace, the League also supervised the mandates over former German and Turkish colonies and directed an International Labor Office, which looked after labor conditions, world health, and the international traffic in women, children, drugs, arms, and munitions.

PARTISAN ATTACKS ON THE TREATY

Wilson's earlier partisan attack on the Republicans began to cause him trouble when, in June, 1919, he left Paris for Washington to win his country's approval of the treaty. Although a large majority of Americans favored a League of Nations, difficulties in securing its passage were accumulating. Conservatives and nationalists said the terms of the treaty were too soft on Germany and the Covenant of the League a dangerous threat to the tradition of isolationism and to American sovereignty. Liberals said the terms were too harsh, a "hell's brew" that would lead to a second world war. They also contended that it perpetuated the status quo of prewar power rivalries. While the treaty was still being drawn up, German-Americans sharply protested that its severity toward Germany showed a gross betrayal. "It is a very severe

871

settlement with Germany," Wilson agreed, "but there is nothing in it she did not earn." Irish-Americans hissed and booed Wilson's name because he did not include the question of Irish independence in his negotiations. Italian-Americans were almost as angry as Orlando had been because Wilson refused to give Fiume to Italy. Too, many people were just no longer interested and others were preoccupied with domestic problems. Finally, the Senate, dominated by the Republicans, was in a hostile mood.

As early as March, 1919, thirty-seven Republican Senators had shown their open opposition to the League by signing a "round robin" warning that they would not approve a peace treaty containing the League Covenant as it was written. Answering them, Wilson had gotten the Allies to agree to changes that would prevent the Covenant from interfering with the Monroe Doctrine. He also obtained other revisions that the Senate wanted: that member countries could withdraw from the League after two years' notice and that the League would not concern itself with immigration or other internal affairs of its members. However, many Republicans saw these concessions as minor. Wilson's feeling for the Senate was disdainful because he was sure that public pressure for the League would force them to accept it. When a reporter asked him whether he would accept reservations—that is, limitations on some parts of the Covenant that the Senate might request—Wilson answered, "I do not think hypothetic questions are concerned." In private, he commented on the "pigmy minds" of some Senators. In June, the stage was set for a titanic battle between a Democratic President and the Republican majority in the Senate.

SENATE DIVISIONS

While Democratic Senators stood behind the President, Wilson's Republican opponents divided roughly into three groups,

motivated both by principle and by partisanship. One group of about a dozen Republican Senators were known as the "irreconcilables." They were totally against any treaty that included an international organization in any form. Their chief spokesman was Senator William E. Borah of Idaho, an able, kindly man inclined toward progressive ideas but also an extreme and uncompromising isolationist. His followers had the same convictions. At the other end of the opposition stood "mild" reservationists, again about a dozen Senators. They approved the League in principle but wanted to change it in minor ways because it would be good politics to do so. In the middle was a group that wanted "strong" reservations added to the treaty. They would go along with the League only if American interests were fully protected by their standards and only if it was made perfectly clear that Republicans had played a major part in creating the final version of the Covenant. The strategist for all these opponents of the treaty was Senator Henry Cabot Lodge, Chairman of the Senate Foreign Relations Committee.

ROLE OF LODGE

Historians still are not in agreement as to why Lodge was so determined to defeat the League of Nations in the form Wilson had presented it to Congress. Part of the reason was surely political since both Irish and Italian voters were important in his state and to be enthusiastic about the League and treaty would have alienated their support. Lodge was not against the idea of a league, and had advocated such an organization during the war. Yet, he was also attached to the traditional belief in American self-sufficiency and isolationism in world affairs. Lodge had been an ardent imperialist in the 1890s, but he had never favored political alliances with other countries. Perhaps the most important element in his opposition was his personal animosity toward the President. Lodge was first and foremost a Republican politician, not an idealist. His opposition to Wilson was at first political but gradually became personal as the war progressed and their differences in outlook became more obvious. He had disliked Wilson's legislative program and what he considered his autocratic manner, and he was angry at the personal rebuff he suffered at not being invited to be a member of the Peace Commission. "I never expected to hate anyone in politics with the hatred I feel towards Wilson," he said.

Lodge was ready to use every tactic his great intelligence and full knowledge of parliamentary procedure could devise in order to change or delay acceptance of the treaty. He knew that there was wide backing for the treaty in the country, so his first step was to use delaying tactics in the debate on its provisions until the people became bored and turned to other interests. He also wanted to give himself time to rally the necessary votes against it. Then he proposed limitations on the obligation of the United States to support the League, emphasizing that only the Congress could decide when to honor these obligations. If the treaty did pass the Senate, he wanted to be sure that it had the stamp of the Republican Party on it and that the Republicans got the credit for it.

There were fourteen Lodge reservations to match Wilson's Fourteen Points. Some were quibbles. For example, a Lodge reservation kept the League from ruling on the Monroe Doctrine, a point that already was in the Covenant. Another said that the United States would not approve Japan's taking Chinese territory, a point that was made simply to embarrass Wilson by stressing the compromises he had made in Paris. The most important and substantial reservation, however, struck at Article X which Wilson had called "the heart of the Covenant." It attacked the idea of America's protecting the political independence and territory of all members of the League. The United States would honor this article in a "particular case" only if Congress passed an act or resolution permitting it. It can be argued that this would have been the case, even if Article X had been accepted as originally presented.

Wilson tried to win Republican Senators to the moral, rather than legal, importance of Article X, but the Senators were not impressed. Most Americans, while supporting the general concept of a world organization, were not prepared to commit themselves to Article X as it was presented to the Senate by the President. Moreover, sincere friends of the League could accept the reservations without giving up their principles. They suggested that Wilson would have to agree to some reservations if he wanted the treaty and the League ratified. Senator Hitchcock, a Nebraska Democrat, was willing to sponsor reservations for the sake of getting Senate passage. But Wilson's answer was, "Never! Never!"

Wilson's inability to compromise showed up in its most extreme manifestation over the ratification of the Versailles Treaty. He was determined that the treaty would not be tampered with, especially by the Republicans. He had always distrusted Congress and now with Lodge, whom he despised, leading the opposition, Wilson was willing and eager for a showdown rather than budge an inch. He had made many compromises in Paris, but would make none at home and seemed incapable of realizing that his political position within the country was precarious.

WILSON'S SPEAKING TOUR

When after two months the treaty was still buried in Lodge's committee, Wilson set out on a cross-country speaking tour to appeal to the people to support the League. The trip was made despite stern warnings from his doctor. The President's health had never been good, and six years of constant crisis had taxed his physical strength. At 63, he was pale, trembling, and exhausted as he traveled more than 8,000 miles in twenty-two days, making thirty-six hour-long speeches. Although some of the speeches were brilliant, they did not sway the Senate and the strain proved to be too much for Wilson. On September 25, he collapsed after a speech at Pueblo, Colorado, and was hurried back to Washington. A few days later, he had a severe stroke which paralyzed his left side. For two weeks he was near death. During the following six weeks his mind was clear, but he was so seriously ill that he only attended to the carefully selected business his wife and doctor decided would not upset or tire him. For more than seven months, he lived in seclusion, cut off from affairs of state, screened from contact with Cabinet members and Congressmen while Lodge maneuvered the fourteen reservations through the Senate.

DEFEAT OF THE LEAGUE

A combination of Democrats and moderate Republicans could have passed the treaty easily. That it was voted down was as much Wilson's fault as the Republicans'. When it was time for the final roll call, on November 19, Wilson, who was bitter and emotionally upset, ordered the Democrats to vote only for the treaty without the Lodge reservations. "Better a thousand times to go down fighting than to dip your colors to dishonorable compromise," he said to his wife when even she urged him to change his mind. When the vote came, the thirteen "irreconcilables" were joined by forty-two Democrats and the treaty with the reservations was defeated.

Lodge then allowed the treaty without reservations, the original version Wilson had brought home, to come to a vote. Thirty-eight Senators, all Democrats but one, voted for it but there were fifty-five votes against it and again the treaty was defeated.

Dismayed friends of the League of Nations, both Democrats and Republicans, forced another vote for the treaty with reservations in March, 1920. Even at this last chance for the success of the most cherished work of his life, Wilson refused to change his stand against compromise, and Lodge saw no reason to budge from his position. Although directed by the President to vote against ratification, half the Democrats in the Senate ignored him and voted for it. At the final count, though, Lodge's forces had a seven-vote margin, 49 to 35, and for the final time the United States refused to approve the Treaty of Versailles and the League of Nations. The war with the Central Powers ended formally in July, 1921, by a joint resolution of Congress. In August, 1921, Washington signed separate treaties with Germany, Austria, and Hungary.

The effect of American rejection of the treaty was one of shock in Europe. Britain and France felt let down by America and lost confidence in any dependence on her in the future. Contrary to Wilson's belief, both nations would have accepted the Lodge reservations to have had the United States in the League. Unrestrained, they now proceeded to deal harshly with Germany on war reparations which further embittered European politics in the postwar years. The League was organized but had little effectiveness without the influence and power of the United States.

Readings

GENERAL WORKS

Baldwin, Hanson W., *World War I*. New York: Harper & Row, 1962—A brief military history of the First World War, outlining the politics and personalities behind military developments.

Link, Arthur S., *Wilson the Diplomatist*. Baltimore: Johns Hopkins Press, 1957—A collection of lectures on aspects of Wilson's diplomacy. Link finds Wilson to have closely guarded Presidential control of foreign affairs, which led to a highly individualistic style of diplomacy.

Marshall, S. L. A., *The American Heritage History of World War I*. New York: American Heritage, 1964—A military history of the First World War by a general and expert on strategy. Marshall's volume contains some 300 photographs and maps.

May, Ernest R., *The World War and American Isolation*. Cambridge, Mass.: Harvard University Press, 1959—A study of World War I diplomacy that makes use of European as well as American archives. May concludes that by entering World War I, the United States reversed many years of isolation from European affairs.

Millis, Walter, *The Road to War*. New York: Fertig, 1969—An attack on Wilson and those around him who took an interventionist course and led the nation into World War I. Millis suggests that an irresponsible press, munitions makers and conspiratorial Presidential advisers caused United States entry into the war.

Notter, Harley, *The Origins of the Foreign Policy of Woodrow Wilson*. New York: Russell, 1965—An analysis of Wilson's foreign policy which finds the origins of his plans for collective peacekeeping in his pre-war thought.

Paxson, Frederick L., *American Democracy and the World War*, Vols. I–IV. New York: Cooper Square Publishers, 1966—A study of the response of American political and social institutions to World War I. Paxson believes that American democracy showed its strength and flexibility by meeting the challenges of war.

Seymour, Charles, *American Neutrality*. Hamden, Conn.: Shoestring, 1967—A collection of essays on the period of neutrality from 1914 to 1917. Seymour attributes American entry to the German submarine campaign and points out the difficulties which modern warfare presents for those who would remain neutral.

Stallings, Laurence, *The Doughboys*. New York: Harper & Row, 1963—A history of the American Expeditionary Force in World War I. The author was a veteran of the European campaign. Well illustrated.

Tansill, Charles C., *America Goes to War*. Boston: Little, Brown, 1938—A detailed account of American diplomacy before entering World War I. Tansill attributes the decision to go to war to political influence from Secretary of State Lansing and Colonel House, not the economic pressures of munitions makers.

Tuchman, Barbara, *The Guns of August*. New York: Macmillan, 1962—A best-selling account of the origins of World War I, analyzing diplomatic and social factors in European politics.

SPECIAL STUDIES

Bailey, Thomas A., *Wilson and the Peacemakers*. Chicago: Quadrangle, 1963—Bailey in this volume combines two studies, one on Wilson and Versailles, the other on the domestic aftermath. Bailey criticizes Wilson as inflexible and unwilling to face political reality.

Birdsall, Paul, *Versailles Twenty Years After*. Hamden, Conn.: Shoestring Press, 1962—A study of post-World War I diplomacy written on the eve of United States entry into World War II. Birdsall defends Wilsonian internationalism as both realistic and courageous and attacks European nationalists.

Fleming, D. F., *The United States and the League of Nations*. New York: Russell, 1968—A detailed study of the struggle between Wilson and the Senate over ratification of the League Covenant. Fleming admires the President's principles.

Kennan, George F., *The Decision to Inter-*

vene. Princeton, N.J.: Princeton University Press, 1958—A study of Allied intervention in the Russian Civil War. Kennan, an influential former diplomat, argues that American intervention was motivated by fear that Russia's separate peace would hurt the United States war effort against Germany

Kennan, George F., *Russia Leaves the War*. Princeton, N.J.: Princeton University Press, 1956—This first volume of Kennan's study, *Soviet-American Relations, 1917-1920*, deals with the diplomatic and military consequences of the Russian Revolution, in particular her conclusion of a separate peace with Germany.

Levin, N. Gordon, *Woodrow Wilson and World Politics*. New York: Oxford University Press, 1968—According to Levin, Wilson's actions during and after the war were dominated by a desire to spread American concepts of liberal capitalist democracy throughout the world. For this reason, Wilson viewed Bolshevism as a major threat to his plans.

Livermore, Seward W., *Politics is Adjourned*. Middletown, Conn.: Wesleyan University Press, 1966—A study of Congress during World War I. Although bipartisanship was shakily established during the war, Wilson was unable to maintain full Congressional support for his peace plans.

Mock, James R., and Cedric Larson, *Words That Won the War*. Princeton, N.J.: Princeton University Press, 1939—A history of the Committee on Public Information, the Washington agency, under George Creel's direction, that conducted an expensive campaign of home-front propaganda during World War I.

Parrini, Carl P., *Heir to Empire: U.S. Economic Diplomacy 1916–1923*. Pittsburgh, Pa.: University of Pittsburgh Press, 1969—According to Parrini, American businessmen after World War I had a world-view of peace which would be maintained through open-door free trade under benevolent American leadership.

PRIMARY SOURCES

Baruch, Bernard M., *American Industry in War*. New York: Prentice-Hall, 1941—This volume reprints Baruch's 1921 report on the operation of the War Industries Board, which he headed. It is a statement of the power of government over the economy in wartime.

Creel, George, *How We Advertised America*. New York: Harper, 1920—Creel was in charge of mobilizing pro-war sentiment among the American people. His description of this massive undertaking reveals one of the striking features of modern war, the role of mass support at home.

Keynes, John M., *The Economic Consequences of the Peace*. New York: Harcourt, Brace, 1920—A blistering attack on the Versailles Treaty by the famous British economist. Keynes maintained that the settlement would ruin Germany economically and fail to restore the balance of power in Europe.

Lodge, Henry C., *The Senate and the League of Nations*. New York: Scribner's, 1925—As leader of the Republican opposition to American participation in the League of Nations, Lodge sharply attacks Wilson's entire diplomatic position.

Pershing, John J., *My Experiences in the World War*, Vols. I–II. New York: Stokes, 1931—The memoirs of Pershing's activities as commander of the American Expeditionary Force in World War I.

Sullivan, Mark, *Our Times*, Vols. I–VI. New York: Reprint House International, 1960 —A social history of American life. The final three volumes cover the years from World War I through 1925 and are a valuable source for studying the popular culture of the era.

BIOGRAPHIES

Blum, John, *Woodrow Wilson and the Politics of Morality*. Boston: Little, Brown, 1956—A brief study of Wilson as political leader, focusing on the postwar peace settlements. Blum is critical of Wilson's stubbornness over the League of Nations issue.

Garraty, John A., *Henry Cabot Lodge*. New York: Knopf, 1953—A biography of the Republican Senator from Massachusetts who led the Congressional opposition to the League of Nations Covenant.

The Ziegfeld Follies were popular entertainers during this "Era of Wonderful Nonsense."

The 1920s: The End of an Era

25

The positive values of the 1920s may perhaps best be suggested in the phrase "useful innocence." In the decade two generations collaborated in an exhaustive review of America's past greatness and present status. The old generation . . . surveyed the weaknesses of a tradition that culminated in a war and an uneasy peace. The other generation . . . assumed the task of reviewing that culture, of making it over according to new principles . . .

—*Frederick J. Hoffman*

As soon as the war ended, Americans were eager to resume life as they remembered it before the conflict. They had had enough regimentation, and the terms of the Versailles Treaty and the fight over the League had disillusioned them and discredited the idea that their country should assume world responsibilities. There was disillusionment with both war and idealism.

THE POSTWAR TRANSITION

DEMOBILIZATION

The government, reverting to the older tradition of a hands-off policy, provided no machinery for orderly demobilization. The nation simply scrapped wartime programs as quickly as possible. Of the approximately four million men in the armed forces in Europe, almost all were returned to the United States and discharged by January, 1920. The government lifted the economic controls it had imposed during the war and ended the operations of the War Industries Board with such haste in January, 1919, that many of its employees were left stranded in Washington. Certain that private industry would be able to switch easily to a peacetime economy, the government canceled all its war contracts without making any provision for reconversion. As a result, many businessmen and workers were left without work. Although government operations were expanded during the war, when it was over, the government issued no grants to employ people on public works. A plan for the government to reclaim land for farms for veterans was defeated in Congress, and the Vocational Training Act for disabled veterans had limited use. Many of these ideas were, however, tried successfully by state and private welfare agencies and their use ultimately aided about one million people.

The war itself had benefited American business. Technological advances and increased productivity which met the nation's military needs had created for most Americans a new faith in private enterprise. Wartime prosperity, resulting from business expansion, had raised the living standards of factory workers and even provided a temporary bonanza for the farmer. The respect for science and technology which had developed during the war continued unabated during the next decade. Business leaders in the great industries became the heroes of the twenties, and they reached positions of national leadership in an unprecedented number.

Businessmen were given credit for the wartime upswing in living standards, and they promised to raise standards even higher in the years ahead if the government would assist and protect them without interfering with their operations. As long as the country was prosperous, there was broad popular support for this outlook and the government followed a modified laissez-faire policy toward business as the nation entered a new business age.

One development in the immediate postwar period was an inflated economy. People who had savings now spent them to buy the things which had been in short supply during the war. However, the sudden dropping of government controls permitted prices to soar. During 1919, the cost of living jumped to 77 percent above the prewar level, and during 1920, it rose another 20 percent. Rising costs not only hurt the public economically but turned white-collar workers and the middle class in general against factory workers who were attempting to meet rising costs by striking for higher earnings.

After the war, both government and management were anxious to settle the problem of the nation's railroads, which were taken over by the government during the war. The railroad companies wanted them under private control, but railway workers believed it more to their advantage to have the railroads under public control. The attorney for the railway unions, Glenn E. Plumb, proposed a plan to nationalize the railroads, but it was unacceptable to Wilson, who said he would return them to private hands unless Congress could devise a better solution. In the Esch-Cummins Transportation Act of 1920, Congress provided a compromise that returned the railroads to their private owners but called for increased government supervision. The plan gave the Interstate Commerce Commission control over the financial operation of the railroads, including issuance of securities and establishment of rates. It also grouped the lines into a limited number of systems and provided financial assistance for the weaker roads. Yet the act had its critics. It disappointed labor because it left the railroads under private control and a compulsory Railway Labor Board proved ineffective. Further, it made no provision for the regulation of trucks or airplanes.

LABOR PROBLEMS

For most workers, conditions had improved during the war. Business began to be less antagonistic towards labor, and wages in general rose. Management's attitude was to a great extent based on the realization that increased wages deterred workers from joining unions and were also a means for expanding the market for consumer goods. Consequently, further labor unionization suffered a setback in the 1920s. During the recession that hit the country from mid-1920 to mid-1922, the labor union movement which had grown to five million in 1920 declined to three and one-half million as a result of unemployment. Government policy during the twenties also favored management over labor. Organized labor was threatened by federal injunctions or even the use of troops if it sought to redress grievances by strikes or boycotts. Federal courts consistently stood behind management's enforcement of anti-union or "yellow dog" contracts and often prevented boycotts and picketing.

During the decade, many businesses adopted an approach to their workers known as welfare capitalism. Besides granting better wages, many companies lowered working hours, provided vacations with pay, recreation halls, cafeterias, and more equitable hiring and firing procedures. Workers were encouraged to buy company stock. Some businessmen even established company unions from which workers were elected to confer with management. But these unions, under company control, had no independence, and their support by management depended on economic prosperity.

Immediately following the war, a great wave of strikes by unions spread throughout the nation. In 1919, they involved some four million workers. Some were successful, such as those in the textile, telegraph, and telephone industries. But the unions faced great hostility, for the public had begun to associate strikes with subversion after a general strike in Seattle in February, 1919, was branded as communist-inspired by the mayor, Ole Hansen. A public saturated with wartime propaganda warning against spies and sabotage, and adrift without national leadership in 1919, easily succumbed to such an allegation.

Several unsuccessful major strikes took place in 1919. Steelworkers, putting in a 12-hour day for subsistence wages, called a strike in September. The union called for an 8-hour day, 6-day week, decent wages, and recognition as the collective bargaining agent for the workers. Even with 365,000 workers out, the United States Steel Company refused to deal with the union. There were disorders at Gary, Indiana, which company heads decried as fomented by communists. The company, largely supported by the public, and employing thousands of strikebreakers protected by state and federal troops, forced the workers to capitulate by January, 1920. While President Harding persuaded the company to grant an 8-hour day in 1923, the union was not recognized.

Under the leadership of John L. Lewis, almost 400,000 coal miners walked out in November, 1919, demanding a 60 percent wage increase, a 6-hour day, and a 5-day week. The Attorney General, A. Mitchell Palmer, with the President's approval, obtained an injunction against the union, and faced with the full force of federal power, Lewis called off the strike. The miners refused to return to work, however, and the government finally ordered the mining companies to grant a 14 percent increase in pay immediately with an additional 27 percent to follow.

Even more damaging to the cause of organized labor was the Boston police strike of 1919. When the Boston police commissioner refused to allow the police to affiliate with the AF of L, the mayor of Boston appointed a citizens' committee to negotiate with rank-and-file representatives. The committee gave in to most of the policemen's demands, but it rejected their desire to affiliate with the national union. When the police protested, the police commissioner fired many of the policemen involved, and policemen went out on strike. The press increased public frenzy with false reports that the walkout was incited by communists. With the help of volunteers and some of the state militia, the mayor was able to restore order in about three days. Finally, Governor Calvin Coolidge sent out the rest of the state militia. He rebuked Samuel Gompers' attempt to unionize the police in a telegram which brought him nationwide fame: "There is no right to strike against the public safety by anybody, anywhere, any time."

THE RED SCARE

Strikes had alienated most of the public, which feared disorder. They backed man-agement and the government, accepting the industry's argument that the inflationary spiral was the result of the rise in wages. Management emphasized that "individualism" and not unionization was "the American way." They warned the public—with great success—that union demands were influenced by foreign radicals in labor's ranks.

The campaign by management also succeeded because, following the Russian Revolution of 1917, proletarian strikes and uprisings had swept over Europe. Pronouncements of Bolshevik leaders at the establishment of the Third, or Communist, International at Moscow in March, 1919, had stressed hopes for communist victories all over the world, especially in the industrial countries of the West. Fearful and on the defensive, many Americans became intolerant of all "isms," distrusting not only foreign nations but also the foreign-born in the United States. Protestant America feared anew that the country's "older stock" was threatened by arrivals from Asia and eastern Europe. When the Boston police strike left the city open to looters, belief in the radicalism of organized labor swelled to a new high.

As hysteria over radicalism continued to mount, schoolteachers had to sign loyalty oaths, professors under suspicion were dismissed, textbooks were censored, and workers who voiced unconventional economic ideas were harassed or fired. Thirty-two states enacted antiradical laws, and twenty-eight states made it punishable to display the "Red" flag.

Yet, within the United States the Communist Party was essentially feeble. Organized in September, 1919, at the instigation of Nikolai Lenin, then the Soviet premier, it had barely more than fifty thousand members. Unlike the earlier socialist movement led by Americans, such as Eugene V. Debs, who wanted peaceful conversion to a socialist economy, this new party preached violent overthrow of the capitalist system.

It united with the old Communist Labor Party in 1920, and was dominated by foreign, non-English-speaking radicals who knew little about the American political system. The American labor movement was generally antagonistic to communism and the Communist Party wanted no cooperation with such a group as the AF of L. Only the radical and violent Industrial Workers of the World, or Wobblies, founded in 1905, joined with the communists. From its inception, the IWW was based on class hatred and had its strongest support among Western miners and migratory workers, and unskilled immigrants in Eastern mill towns. Its use of violence and sabotage alienated most American workers.

The nervous public reacted strongly when bombs were mailed in April to the mayor of Seattle and thirty-six other eminent citizens, including John D. Rockefeller and Justice Holmes. The Post Office intercepted all the bombs except the one to the mayor, which wounded his maid. In September, 1920, there was a large blast on Wall Street killing thirty-eight and causing two million dollars' damage. The public was not capable of differentiating between radical anarchists or communists and labor unions. Moreover, they saw radicalism in everything foreign and endorsed the witch hunts soon initiated by state governments and by the federal government under Attorney General A. Mitchell Palmer.

Palmer had been a progressive Democrat, who had worked for women's suffrage and the League of Nations, but once he took office in March, 1919, he threw himself into a campaign against aliens and radicals. He claimed that he and the FBI, created in August, 1919, with J. Edgar Hoover as its head, were averting revolution: "Like a prairie-fire, the blaze of revolution was sweeping over every American institution . . ."

On his own, Palmer ordered a series of raids on radical meetings, beginning in November, 1919. On the first raid, his agents arrested and beat 250 members of the Union of Russian Workers. In December, Palmer and the Department of Labor authorized the deportation of 249 aliens to Russia. In January, 1920, his nationwide raid led to the arrest of six thousand citizens who were taken without warrants from their homes and herded into jails. Ultimately, 556 people were deported from the United States under government order. Although the raids revealed no evidence of a grand plot, Palmer persisted in ordering them. When he predicted a communist outbreak on May Day, 1920, which did not materialize, the Attorney General appeared ridiculous even to the most prejudiced of the public. Communism had not taken over Europe and conservative forces were firmly in control in the United States. The Communist Party had declined to eight thousand members by 1927.

Although the Red scare waned in 1920, intolerance of those associated with radical ideologies continued unabated throughout the 1920s. An outstanding example of public hatred of aliens and radicals was the case of Sacco and Vanzetti. Nicola Sacco and Bartolomeo Vanzetti were arrested, tried, and convicted for murdering two employees of a shoe company in South Braintree, Massachusetts, during a payroll robbery in 1920. Despite their pleas of innocence and with no conclusive evidence produced against them, they were convicted, apparently, because of the widespread belief that they were anarchists. Even the judge at their trial referred to them as "those anarchist bastards." The cause attracted liberal sympathies around the world, but in 1927 Sacco and Vanzetti were electrocuted although new evidence had come to light indicating they were not guilty.

Nativism also manifested itself in further restrictions on immigration. In February, 1921, Congress passed the Emergency Quota Act aimed at cutting immigration from southern and eastern Europe. It limited the number of immigrants in any year to 3 percent of the foreign-born of each national group that had been living in the United States in 1910. Immigration was reduced even further in 1924 when Congress passed the National Origins Act which based annual quotas on 2 percent of each nationality resident in the United States in 1890. The Japanese were excluded from admission altogether, a severe affront to their national pride.

RACIAL PROBLEMS

Postwar intolerance also produced a new wave of racist attacks on black Americans. The war had given blacks a chance to break away from the narrow caste structure of the South. Almost half a million blacks served in the Army during the war, more than half of these in Europe. Largely because of the war, many black people had moved from the South to the industrial centers of the North. They suffered less overt racism in the North, but even there discrimination forced them to live in slums and take jobs with low pay. They also endured the hatred of white workers who saw them as competitors for jobs.

Black communities developed in such major metropolitan areas as New York, Buffalo, Cleveland, Chicago, and Detroit. Educated by city experiences, military service, and by the "democratic ideal" preached in the war they had helped fight, black people began to demand the rights long denied them. They wanted higher wages, the same protection under the law as white people, and an equal opportunity to vote and hold political office. But these demands for racial equality came at a time of heightened racial fears among white Americans. White supremacists throughout the country often played on the nation's fear of radicalism in general and communism in particular to prevent black people from gaining their demands. Southern political leaders frequently warned the nation that black demands were inspired by communists. In

1919, the nation witnessed the most severe race riots in its history. Especially tragic were those in Washington, D.C., and in Chicago where mobs of whites rampaged through black slums for thirteen days. Before 1919 ended, over twenty-five race riots caused hundreds of deaths and injuries and millions of dollars in property damage.

The long inactive Ku Klux Klan re-emerged in full force during the 1920s. The Klan, as in Reconstruction days, was built on prejudice, racism, and fear. It claimed to protect the country's pioneer stock and heritage from the threat of blacks, radicals, and the new immigrants. Revived in Georgia in 1915, and claiming a membership of nearly five million by 1925, the Klan's creed was relentless persecution of the enemy. In 1919 alone, Klan lynch mobs murdered over seventy blacks. The Klan used floggings, kidnappings, cross-burnings, arson, and homicide to terrorize entire communities of blacks and Roman Catholics. In politics, the Klan held the balance of power in several Southern states. It also had great strength among the lower middle class in the small towns of the Middle West, Southwest and Far West. Its influence did not begin to fade until after 1925 when, to the evidence of its violence, was added the disclosure of the personal immorality of its leadership in Indiana. By the end of the 1920s it had only nine thousand members.

The NAACP urged black people to resist their attackers, as well as to achieve civil rights through legislation. In 1919, together with other organizations, the NAACP began a campaign that resulted, two years later, in passage of the first anti-lynching bill by the House of Representatives. The measure, however, was killed in the Senate by a Southern filibuster.

Another and more extreme organization, the Universal Negro Improvement Association, also was organized in the 1920s and claimed a membership of half a million in 1923. It was created by a Jamaican nationalist, Marcus Garvey, and it planned to build a new empire in Africa with Garvey as its leader. W.E.B. Du Bois called Garvey's plan "bombastic and impractical" and the idea eventually collapsed. Although the plan instilled pride in their heritage, most had little interest in returning to Africa. In 1923, Garvey was sent to prison, convicted of having used the mails to defraud. His words to his people at that time have a contemporary ring: "To be a Negro is no disgrace," he said, "but an honor. . . . We do not want to become white. . . . We are proud and honorable. We love our race. . . ."

FUNDAMENTALISM

Traditionalism and fear of change made many people apprehensive about modern scientific discoveries. People in rural areas, in particular, seized upon modern science as the archenemy of the Protestant faith. These "fundamentalists" insisted that the Bible must be accepted literally, and sixty years after the publication of Darwin's

The Origin of Species they still rejected biological evolution and attacked those who taught it. Under pressure from William Jennings Bryan, who led the battle to prevent faith in biblical truths from being undermined in the schools, the Tennessee legislature in 1925 made it illegal to teach any theory counter to that of creation as recorded in Genesis. When the American Civil Liberties Union offered counsel to any Tennessee teacher who would test the law, John T. Scopes, a 24-year-old high school biology teacher, stepped forward, more in amusement than anger. He lectured from Darwin's work in his classroom in Dayton, Tennessee, and was subsequently arrested and brought to trial.

Two famous lawyers, Clarence Darrow and Arthur Garfield Hays, agreed to defend Scopes. The World's Christian Fundamen-

The Ku Klux Klan marches down Pennsylvania Avenue in Washington, D.C. By 1925, the Klan claimed a membership of 5 million Americans.

tal Association retained Bryan for the prosecution. The "monkey trial," as it was called, caused a great stir throughout the nation. It reached its climax when Darrow pressed his examination of Bryan, who had taken the stand as an expert on the Bible, until he revealed Bryan's great ignorance of modern learning. Scopes was convicted for violating the law, but the state Supreme Court reversed the decision, and the law's constitutionality was left untested. Exhausted by the strain of testifying and by the circus atmosphere of the trial, Bryan died soon afterward.

PROHIBITION

In October, 1919, over the veto of President Wilson, Congress passed the Volstead Act which implemented the new prohibition amendment to the Constitution. It prohibited the sale of all liquors containing

The Volstead Act was passed in 1919, thus giving rise to the famous "speakeasies" of the twenties.

more than one-half of one percent of alcohol. The enforcing agency, the Prohibition Commission, depended on a small force of agents who were often third-rate political appointees unable to resist bribes, and the act only succeeded in encouraging illegal traffic in alcohol. Smugglers brought whiskey across the Canadian border, from the Caribbean, or from European vessels hovering off the long coastline of the United States. In addition to the rumrunners, there were thousands of domestic distillers of illegal whiskey. "Speakeasies" did business in every major city, frequently under the protection of the local police. Thus, prohibition made it necessary to buy drinks at outrageous prices in private establishments and enabled traffic in bootlegging to provide a rich source of income and influence for the growing underworld of organized crime. City governments came under the control of gangsters who did not hesitate to resort to murder in the battle for "territory." In 1920, the most notorious gangland chief, "Scarface" Al Capone, moved to Chicago. Here, in seven years, he established a 60-million-dollar enterprise in whiskey, drugs, gambling, and prostitution. With a private army of about one thousand gangsters, he was so powerful that not a single murderer was convicted when Capone's gang slaughtered his competitors during 1926 and 1927. Prohibition did not create organized crime, but unquestionably it gave gangland a vast new area to exploit.

THE ELECTION OF 1920

The election of 1920 occurred in the aftermath of postwar demobilization and disillusionment with American participation in the conflict. It ushered in a decade in which public policy was dedicated primarily to protecting the business interests.

The Republicans convened in Chicago, and the contestants for the nomination were General Leonard Wood, an independent personality who stood for nationalism and antiradicalism, Governor Frank O. Lowden of Illinois, an experienced executive with special appeal to farmers and businessmen in the Middle West, and Hiram Johnson of California, a progressive and an isolationist. However, the professionals of the party, sensing victory in November, were determined to name a candidate that they could easily manage. On the tenth ballot, the convention chose Warren G. Harding of Ohio after the party bosses, meeting in the now famous "smoke-filled room," had decided on him as the most acceptable man. Calvin Coolidge was chosen by the convention to be his running mate.

Harding's most striking feature was his looks. Many claimed that he looked like a President, or at the least, like a Roman senator. Beneath this façade, he was little more than a small-town politician with an undisciplined taste for women, liquor and cards. But he did have an abiding faith in and loyalty to the Republican Party. His voting record was basically conservative. He could be counted on to allow the reassertion of party and Congressional control of national politics. His manner was genial. He epitomized the small-town America of his day. Folksy, unpretentious, and easygoing, he was always eager to win and please friends.

Harding followed the advice of his managers, making few speeches and taking few positions on the issues of the day. His platform promised lower taxes, higher tariffs, restriction of immigration, and assistance to farmers. It condemned the League of Nations but called vaguely for an agreement among nations to preserve the peace.

The Democratic Party, by contrast, was in a state of confusion. Attorney General Palmer, highly favored for the top office, had lost much popularity with the decline of the Red scare. William G. McAdoo was an able candidate, but he was Wilson's son-in-law, and the Democratic bosses did not

Warren G. Harding brought the Republican party to victory in 1920 by winning 61 percent of the popular vote.

want a candidate who could be identified with the Wilson administration. The party leaders wanted James M. Cox of Ohio, a proven vote-getter and an opponent of prohibition. Palmer and McAdoo ran neck and neck for almost forty ballots, but neither one could muster the two-thirds majority necessary to secure the nomination. Finally, on the forty-fourth ballot, the convention nominated Cox and chose as his running mate the Assistant Secretary of the Navy, Franklin D. Roosevelt. The party's platform favored the League, tax reductions, and Philippine independence, but remained noncommittal on prohibition.

In most campaigns, Harding would have been an insignificant candidate. In 1920, he had only to sit back and wait for the landslide against Wilson and the Democratic Party. Moreover, the Republicans were still the majority party in the country, so it appeared certain that the Democrats had little chance of winning. The once progressive middle class was resentful of high taxes and labor strikes. Most Americans, even in the cities, were now hostile to Wilson's policies, and most were infected with the fear of communism.

887

These factors combined to produce a great Republican victory in 1920. Harding received 61 percent of the popular vote, and led Cox, 404 to 127, in the electoral college. The Republicans had big majorities in both houses of Congress. The voters had repudiated internationalism and voted for a return to what Harding called "normalcy."

REPUBLICAN ASCENDANCY

HARDING ADMINISTRATION

Harding's campaign slogan had been "less government in business and more business in government."

The President, aware of his own limitations as a leader, turned over the formulation of most policy to his Cabinet and Congress. Though not known as a judge of character, Harding had promised to recruit "the best minds" in the country to serve in his administration. Many of his Cabinet appointments were men of proven abilities, but some of them were merely old cronies who, as it turned out, used their political influence for personal profit. Andrew Mellon, chosen as Secretary of the Treasury, was a multimillionaire from Pittsburgh whose family holdings and connections had permitted him to acquire the aluminum monopoly. Harding appointed the brilliant Charles Evans Hughes Secretary of State, and he made Henry C. Wallace, a spokesman for the farmers of the Midwest, the Secretary of Agriculture. For Secretary of Commerce, Harding chose Herbert Hoover, who had so successfully managed the food program during the war. On the other hand, he placed his old friend, Albert B. Fall, in charge of the Department of the Interior, despite the fact that Fall was a staunch anti-conservationist, and Harry M. Daugherty, a long-time Harding backer, became Attorney General.

TREASURY POLICIES

Harding turned over a great deal of the management of the domestic economy to the Secretary of the Treasury, and Mellon exercised that power for the benefit of the business interests. He believed that the government was a business to be run according to strict principles of business efficiency. He dedicated himself and his department to slashing government spending by shifting the burden of the nation's taxes to the lower-income groups, insisting that taxing the wealthy only inhibited the growth of business prosperity. Mellon was widely hailed by businessmen for his service under both Harding and Coolidge; some even called him the greatest Secretary of the Treasury since Alexander Hamilton.

TAX AND TARIFF PROGRAMS

Mellon sponsored the tax programs desired by the nation's business community. In 1921, he urged Congress to repeal the excess-profits tax and reduce the surtax on personal incomes from a maximum of 65 percent to 32 percent for 1921, and 25 percent thereafter. With the House of Representatives calling for tax cuts for low-income groups and Mellon wanting them for the wealthy, the Secretary was in a constant battle from 1921 to 1925. The Congress did reduce taxes on lower income brackets in 1924, but by 1926, Mellon had his way and millionaires paid less than one-third of the taxes that they had paid the year before. Mellon himself saved over 800,000 dollars in taxes. During the course of the 1920s, the government managed to refund to the wealthy almost 4 billion dollars.

The administration and Republican leaders in Congress also set out to restore the protective tariff rates that existed before 1913. They advocated a self-sufficient economy, overlooking the need of European powers to sell goods in the United States in order to be able to earn money to pay their war debts. They were aided this time by the South, which had become more industrialized, and by the farmers who felt that higher tariff rates would assure them greater profit. During the spring of 1921, Midwestern Congressional leaders met in the offices of the Farm Bureau Federation and organized the "Farm Bloc." Their purpose was to force upon the administration desperately needed farm legislation. They opposed Mellon's tax bill but helped push through his tariff protection program. The Farm Bloc joined with business leaders to promote passage of the Emergency Tariff Act of 1921, which placed prohibitive duties on twenty-eight agricultural commodities. The Farm Bloc in Congress had won a victory but Congress had failed to understand the basic difficulties of agriculture. Farmers were besieged by high interest charges on mortgages and by heavy taxes on their land. Enormous crop surpluses were created because war demands had ceased, the American diet had changed, and great advances had taken place in technology. In the 1920s, some segments of the agricultural community were impoverished. The new tariff protection, in spite of ear-

nest support from the Farm Bloc, only succeeded in creating more crop surpluses and thus impaired, rather than assisted, the farmer in his plight.

The Revenue Act of 1921 was, in effect, a compromise measure by which Mellon satisfied a group of Western Republicans and Democrats. The act did eliminate the excess profits tax, but it held the maximum surtax on personal income at 50 percent. It further granted some tax relief to lower- and middle-income groups by raising the exemptions for heads of families and their dependents.

The following year, Congress passed the Fordney-McCumber Act. This act continued the high tariff rates, empowered a Tariff Commission to help the President determine the differences in production costs between the United States and other nations, and granted the President the power to raise or lower any rate by 50 percent. This measure protected American business against competition and encouraged its consolidation, but it greatly damaged foreign trade. By making it almost impossible for Europeans to sell their goods in the United States, it also made it impossible for them to buy American products —especially agricultural surpluses.

Mellon also advocated measures to increase the efficiency of the federal government. In 1921, Harding signed the Budget and Accounting Act which streamlined government budgeting methods. A Director of the Budget was appointed to assist the President in preparing an annual, overall budget, and a Comptroller General was selected to audit all executive accounts. However, the Bureau of the Budget, although it promoted greater efficiency, could not eliminate Congressional squabbles over appropriations.

Following the lead of the Treasury Department, the government bureaucracy in general was solidly pro-business during the 1920s. Government agencies such as the ICC, the FTC, and the Tariff Commission were dominated by men with business backgrounds. They considered their roles on these commissions as basically to advise and aid business rather than to regulate it. The Commerce Department under Hoover also acted as a clearing house for information and advice to business on more efficient methods of operation. Hoover was particularly interested in helping the voluntary trade association movement among small businessmen. His department sponsored conferences and issued statistical information to help businesses restrict production and hold down prices.

The prevailing economic outlook of the 1920s was a new form of conservatism. Most business and government leaders thought of conservatism as dynamic and forward looking. The emphasis was on material prosperity, based on increased production, business efficiency, and cooperation between government and business to keep prices stable, avoid strikes, and keep up wages. Many recognized that the laissez-faire capitalism of the late nineteenth century was a thing of the past.

HARDING SCANDALS

Harding's placement of political cronies in high government offices proved to be his undoing. However, when government scandals came to light in which some of these men were implicated, the moral climate in the country was such that neither the press nor the public voiced significant protest. Since Harding knew little about the operations of the federal government, and did not know whom to trust, he turned to the same companions with whom he had associated in his hometown of Marion, Ohio. The "Ohio Gang" came to Washington. "Ed" Scobey from Marion was made Director of the Mint by Harding. "Doc" Sawyer became White House physician with the rank of brigadier general. Charles R. Forbes, whom Harding had met by chance on a vacation in Hawaii, was chosen to

head the Veterans Bureau. As noted, Albert B. Fall had become Secretary of the Interior, and the new Attorney General, Harry M. Daugherty, was an Ohioan who had helped promote Harding's career.

FORBES SCANDAL

As head of the Veterans Bureau, Forbes personally pocketed a large portion of the 250 million dollars annually allotted his agency. When Daugherty informed Harding in 1923 of the rumors he had heard about Forbes, Harding permitted Forbes to resign and go abroad. When a Senate Committee began investigations of the Veterans Bureau, the Bureau's attorney committed suicide. This was followed by a second suicide, that of Jesse Smith, an old friend of Harding who was suspected of selling his influence at the Justice Department to lawbreakers. Ultimately, Forbes himself was tried and sent to prison.

DAUGHERTY SCANDAL

One of Jesse Smith's ventures had involved Thomas Miller, Harding's Custodian of Alien Property. Miller had agreed to the return of American Metal Company bonds to German owners for a large bribe. The attorney in the transaction was John T. King, Republican national committeeman. King received a fee of almost a half million dollars in bonds. Fifty thousand dollars' worth of these went to Miller and 200,000 dollars' worth to Smith, which was deposited in an account which the Attorney General managed. Miller eventually was tried and imprisoned, but two juries in 1926 acquitted Daugherty.

THE TEAPOT DOME SCANDAL

In 1921, Albert Fall persuaded Harding to transfer control of the naval oil reserves at Elks Hill, California, and Teapot Dome, Wyoming, to the Department of the Interior. After it was done, Fall secretly leased both reserves to oil companies, one to the company of Edward L. Doheny and the other to Harry Sinclair. In 1923, the Senate investigated the leases and discovered that Doheny had "loaned" Fall 100,000 dollars and that Sinclair had given him a herd of cattle together with 330,000 dollars in cash and bonds. By 1927, the government was able to cancel the leases. Sinclair was convicted of tampering with a jury. Fall was convicted of bribery, fined, and sentenced to a year in jail. He was the first Cabinet officer to go to prison.

The scandals weighed heavily on Harding. By mid-1923, he had grown distraught and nervous. To take his mind off conditions in Washington, he decided on a speaking tour through the Western states. While on the trip he learned of new disclosures of corruption. In July, while in Seattle, on the way home from Alaska, he suffered an acute attack of what was thought to be indigestion. On August 2, in a room at the Palace Hotel in San Francisco, Harding died, the victim of a cerebral thrombosis.

COOLIDGE BECOMES PRESIDENT

The new President, Calvin Coolidge, combined a devotion to conservative politics with respectability. Coolidge was a man of impeccable integrity and a strong believer in efficient and frugal government. The son of a Vermont storekeeper, he had worked his way through college, studied law in Northampton, Massachusetts, and entered politics there. He served in innumerable political offices in his patient climb to the top from city councilman to governor of the state. Massachusetts Republicans valued his integrity, his patience, and his reluctance to accept change. In 1919, twenty years after he first won public office, he achieved national prominence when, as governor, he dispatched troops to put down

the Boston police strike. This act prompted his selection as his party's Vice Presidential candidate in 1920.

Coolidge believed that if a man worked hard, practiced thrift, respected authority, and minded his own business, he would be a success. Coolidge himself fulfilled these requirements. He had a somewhat dour personality, which led Alice Roosevelt Longworth, Theodore Roosevelt's daughter, to remark that he must have been "weaned on a dill pickle," but his folksy virtues of patience and shrewdness won praise from the press. The *Literary Digest* called him the "High Priest of Stability" and most of the nation chanted the slogan, "Keeping cool with Coolidge." The President promised to scrub the government clean of the taint of corruption, but in most other areas he left the national government unaltered. His outlook was similar to Harding's: "The business of America is business. . . . The man who builds a factory builds a temple. . . . The man who works there worships there." In his first message to Congress, he called for the continuation of conservative Republican domestic and foreign policies, more tax cuts, very limited aid for agriculture, and asserted that the League of Nations should be shunned. To combat the Harding scandals, he chose two prosecuting attorneys with reputations for absolute integrity to clean out corrupt officeholders. When mounting evidence forced Attorney General Daugherty to retire in March, 1924, Coolidge replaced him with Harlan Fiske Stone, the eminent former dean of the Columbia Law School.

Coolidge exercised the powers of executive office only negatively by vetoing measures out of tune with his conservative philosophy. Harding had tried to work with Congress, but Coolidge made little effort to do so. He preferred to gain control of the party by giving businessmen important party positions, rather than by relying as Harding had on Congressional leaders. Since the country was prosperous, however,

Coolidge continued to rely on Mellon's economic policies.

The average money wage of industrial workers was twice what it had been in 1914, and it continued to advance through 1928. Profits, at an all-time high, invited further investments in new plants and equipment. Productivity increased as management mastered new ways to use machinery and men more efficiently. Coolidge was in awe of Mellon. In the shadow of the Secretary of the Treasury, Coolidge asserted that the federal establishment justified itself only in so far as it served business. He saw the prosperity that mantled the country as proof of the accuracy of this doctrine.

THE ELECTION OF 1924

As the nominating convention approached, Coolidge's only serious competition came from Henry Ford, who had run as a Democrat in the Senate race from Michigan in 1918 and lost. However, Coolidge had carefully brought the machinery of the party under his control and the convention gave him the nomination on the first ballot. Some Republicans organized a new Progressive Party in opposition to Coolidge which put forth a platform attacking monopolies and promising reforms for farmers and laborers, and nominated the old progressive, Robert La Follette.

The Democratic convention contest reflected the deep party split between its rural Southern wing and its Northern urban contingent. William G. McAdoo, an ardent supporter of prohibition, and Alfred E. Smith, the governor of New York, an opponent of the measure, battled for nine days for the nomination but finally withdrew when neither could get the support of two-thirds of the delegates. On the 103rd ballot, the Democrats finally nominated John W. Davis, a wealthy businessman, for President.

The campaign was issueless and uninteresting. Coolidge, with efficiency and prosperity in his favor, polled 54 percent of the popular vote to Davis' 29 percent. Coolidge won in the electoral college with 382 votes to Davis' 136 and La Follette's 13.

The sources of party support in the mid-1920s did not differ greatly from those in the late nineteenth century. The Republicans, riding the crest of the nation's prosperity, had the support of many different groups throughout the country, some of whom would desert their ranks in the next decade. In addition to being the party of the business and propertied people, it was the party of most farmers outside the South and of many workers and black people. The Democrats, while drawing some business backing, found that their base of support was still lodged in the solid South and among the working population of the large urban centers in the North.

ERA OF PROSPERITY

Perhaps one of the greatest delusions of the twenties was that it was easy to get rich quick. Most of the nation seemed to believe that the value of goods and property would increase indefinitely, and that the individual who bought something today could sell it tomorrow at a profit. For several years there was ready proof for such a belief, and speculation in stocks became a widespread pastime of the decade. Not only did the wealthy buy stocks, but barbers, stenographers, and elevator boys rushed to take advantage of the opportunity to make money in an expanding economy by buying on "margin," that is, with a small down payment.

INDUSTRIAL PROSPERITY

The nation's industrial output doubled between 1921 and 1929. The productivity of labor rose 50 percent. Technological advances had greatly helped this jump in output by creating improved systems of manufacturing. Productivity was also boosted considerably by industrial engineers, an emerging profession, who provided mass production or assembly-line techniques and time-motion studies of workers and machinery. Perfection of manufacturing techniques to the highest point of efficiency was the order of the day. It was believed this would not only increase output, but raise wages and lower consumer prices, thereby increasing buying incentive which would, in turn, create more demand for output. This "cult of productivity" was a national outlook, as Americans praised the rising number of goods and consumed them avidly. Instead of applying foresight to control the boom, public officials openly spurred it on. In his inaugural address on March 4, 1925, Coolidge declared that the nation had achieved "a state of contentment, seldom before seen."

INCREASE IN REAL INCOME

When the country moved out of its brief economic slump in 1921, unemployment became almost negligible—except in such industries as textiles and coal, which were in a slump throughout the twenties. By 1923, the average industrial worker was earning twice the wages he had earned in 1914, and his income continued to grow through 1928. By 1928, real income was over a third more than fourteen years earlier. As noted earlier, two factors primarily accounted for this increase. First, employers realized that higher wages lessened the workers' incentive for joining unions. Second, higher

wages gave the workers more purchasing power which, consequently, expanded the market for industrial products. Wages increased even further as certain prices fell, particularly prices of food and goods manufactured by improved production methods.

With more money in the consumer's pocket, and more goods more readily available, a mass market developed for cars, radios, phonographs, refrigerators, and vacuum cleaners. The average workingman bought luxury items he could not afford before. Easy credit and installment-plan buying made such things as appliances and furniture more accessible to the majority of Americans. More people than ever bought their own homes through monthly payments. The combination of material resources, streamlined productivity, higher wages, and easy credit, made possible the saturation of the nation with many kinds of goods and necessities, as well as modern conveniences and luxuries.

Among the phenomena associated with business in the 1920s was the amazing rise of advertising and public relations. Agencies in these fields were dedicated to making profitable businesses even more profitable. Thus, much of the business boom relied on illusions spread by the growing number of agencies in ads that urged the American people to buy commodities such as the latest cars and cosmetics to make them happier.

NEW INDUSTRIES

Many new industries in the twenties were created or brought to maturity by the war. Airplanes used in battle ushered in the era of commercial aviation, which eventually became big business after the solo flight of Charles A. Lindbergh from New York to Paris in May, 1927. The First World War also gave an enormous boost to the American chemical industry. By 1929, the Allied Chemical, Union Carbide, and DuPont companies had outdistanced all foreign chemical firms in the production of new plastics, alloys, and allied products. Together with electricity, chemicals helped revolutionize a number of other industries. Power costs were lowered by developments in the production of electricity itself. This enabled the American factory to operate its machinery at less expense. The petroleum industry was spurred by new electrical and chemical processes, as were the steel industry and the manufacture of such commodities as lamps, phonographs, refrigerators, and washing machines. Electricity also increased the efficiency of the moving assembly line, so vital in mass production.

Much of the decade's industrial growth was related to the automobile. Auto production jumped from 1.5 million in 1921 to 4.75 million in 1929. Also, by 1929, automobiles were directly or indirectly responsible for the employment of over three million people. The automobile had become a cornerstone of a dynamic business economy.

Automobile production created new demands for efficiency in manufacturing. It employed "systematized shop management," a term made prominent by Frederick W. Taylor, the formulator of "scientific management." His ideas were based on the use of a continuous machine process in which raw materials entered a plant to emerge, after innumerable operations, a finished product. In 1911, Henry Ford opened an automobile manufacturing plant at Highland Park, Michigan, where he adapted Taylor's principles to his own needs. As a result, Ford and his associates began turning out automobiles at an unheard-of rate. They led the way in "scientific management"—creating specialized tasks for men and machines and improving the technique of continuous motion with such devices as conveyor belts, monorails, and gravity slides. Ford, who had long dreamed of manufacturing a good low-cost family car, began doing so in Detroit as early as 1893. By 1914, he had produced half a

million of his famous Model Ts. The Model T was not an attractive or comfortable car, and other manufacturers soon began to offer competition with more luxurious models. General Motors, headed by William Durant, achieved prominence in the industry by catering to luxury and fashion. But Ford held first position in the small-car field for a long time, and he did not change his basic model for the more attractive Model A until 1927. By 1925, Ford became—in a title conferred by Upton Sinclair—"The Flivver King."

Ford was unique among automobile manufacturers in that he continued to own and operate his own company, refusing to reduce his control by selling stock to outsiders. As his market grew, he shrewdly lowered prices and raised wages. While he paid higher wages than most businessmen in the 1920s, he took the typical management attitude toward labor. He demanded the unstinting loyalty of his employees and was intolerant of labor unions.

By 1925, the average American family owned an automobile. The car affected the American way of life, its mores, society, and economy. The growth of the auto industry brought prosperity to manufacturers of iron and steel, fabrics, glass, and tires. It created new business establishments for sales and service. It was a major factor in the growth of the oil industry, and its wages and profits became supports for a building boom.

INCREASE IN CONSTRUCTION

The building boom extended from the modest houses of American workers to the towering skyscrapers that provided the offices for business leaders of industry. The key to the economic health of the nation was the prosperity of private construction. In the 1920s, houses were being built at a record rate, as were industrial buildings and railroad facilities.

During the decade, a new item began to appear in local, state, and federal budgets: enormous expenditures for building paved roads. Government spending for street and highway construction exceeded the capital outlay for most private industries. Here was a hidden subsidy, not only to the auto industry, but to the entire economy. Road building was another barometer of the country's economic health. Thus, when private investment in road construction slowed down in the late twenties, it was an important indicator of weakness in the economy.

ECONOMIC PROBLEMS

In spite of nationwide prosperity, economic problems did exist for which there were no easy solutions. During the 1920s there was a strong tendency towards consolidation in industry, and this trend continued to accelerate. Major industrial firms with heavy fixed costs had long known the value of administered, noncompetitive pric-

ing, and had resorted to consolidation to achieve industrial stability. With consolidation, administrators found it easier to control costs, prices, and output. In the 1920s, over eight thousand mining and manufacturing companies were absorbed into combinations. By 1929, over 25 percent of the nation's food, apparel, and general merchandise was being sold by chain stores. One-half of all the corporate wealth and 22 percent of the national wealth was owned by only two hundred corporations.

The consolidation of larger companies forced small businessmen to seek solutions among themselves in order to survive. One solution was the sponsorship of voluntary trade associations, and some two thousand were in operation by 1921. The associations tried to develop cooperation among businessmen toward such goals as regulation of

A Model T assembly line where the body of the car is being dropped onto its chassis. "Scientific management" enabled Ford to produce low-cost automobiles in large numbers.

operations, control of abuses, codes of ethics, standardization of production, and improvement of general efficiency. They strove to eliminate competition by setting fixed price schedules, thus assuring high profits. However, the trade associations, though they were free from government regulations, were often persecuted by the courts, thus forcing many members to drop out of the associations and merge their operations with larger firms. Further, many members failed to abide by the rules of their association since it was voluntary.

Andrew Mellon's fiscal policies intensified the trend toward a concentration of wealth and maldistribution of income. Stock dividends were rising much more rapidly than wages. Corporate leaders continued to boast confidently about the broad ownership of stocks, despite the fact that only one-third of 1 percent of the population received 78 percent of the dividends. The five hundred people with the highest incomes were receiving as much money as the total wages of over a half million auto workers. Only the well-to-do were able to save much money. The 2.3 percent of families with incomes of 100,000 dollars or more per year accounted for 66.6 percent of all personal savings, and those with incomes of under 2,000 dollars, only 1.6 percent. Corporations accounted for 40 percent of total savings.

AGRICULTURE

A major exception to the prosperity of the 1920s was the country's staple farmer. While the income of most Americans rose in the decade, that of the farming population dropped. After the war, the European market contracted, and unfortunately for farmers, this occurred almost simultaneously with the loss of wartime price supports. During the war there had been a large demand for food, wheat, and cotton. Responding to that demand, farmers had stepped up their output. They had bought more acreage and more machinery. Many went heavily into debt to buy land, livestock, and equipment at inflated prices. When the demand slowed, the farmers were left with huge crop surpluses. At the same time, a change in the American diet during the decade reduced purchases of bread and beef, and stimulated a demand for vegetables, fruits, and poultry. The cotton market was sharply curtailed by the fashion for shorter dresses and the increasing use of rayon and silk. The staple farmer suffered so badly as the victim of costly mechanization, overproduction, and changing markets, that in the five years that followed 1919, over 13 million acres of farm land were abandoned. Between 1921 and 1928, the agricultural population dropped by three million. Forty-two percent of the farmers were tenants in 1930 and 42 percent of landowners had mortgaged property. The Revenue Act of 1921 and the Fordney-McCumber Tariff, though they sought to aid farmers, were essentially ineffective, since the farmer's problem was not one of foreign competition.

Congress passed an Intermediate Credit Act in 1923 which established twelve new farm banks under the Federal Farm Loan Board. They were empowered to make short-term loans to producing and marketing cooperatives, with farm produce as collateral. The act extended government action on behalf of agriculture but it did not provide a solution to the farmer's chronic problem of low prices for agricultural products.

A new plan was proposed by George N. Peek, president of the Moline Plow Company, and General Hugh S. Johnson, an attorney for that company, both former administrators of the War Industries Board. Their "two price plan" was published in a pamphlet called *Equality for Agriculture*, and suggested that the protected price for crops should be raised to a "fair exchange value" based on the price of the crop during the ten years before the war as compared to the general average of all prices during the same period. The means for obtaining this price concept, or parity, would be a government corporation or farm board which would buy up the surpluses at the American price and sell them abroad at whatever they would bring on the world market. Then, to make up in part for any loss, the American farmers would be charged an equalization fee or tax on their entire crop.

Between 1924 and 1928, Senator Charles L. McNary of Oregon and Representative Gilbert Haugen of Iowa promoted this plan in Congress. Covering only grain, the McNary-Haugen bill was defeated in the House in 1924. But in 1926, when coverage for cotton, tobacco, and rice was added, it received Southern support and was passed by Congress. Revived again in 1927 and 1928, it was consistently vetoed by President Coolidge because he did not believe that it was the responsibility of the government to underwrite the prosperity of one segment of the economy. He also felt that such a measure would only encourage farmers to overproduce, because it did not set forth acreage restrictions at the same time. With costs extremely high, and prices very low, the staple farmer remained outside of the general prosperity of the twenties.

THE JAZZ AGE

"The Jazz Age," a term coined by the writer, F. Scott Fitzgerald, connoted a new way of life alarming to the older generation because it rejected traditional American values. It involved a movement by the younger generation away from the Puritan ethic of hard work, frugality, and conventional morality. Many of the young saw themselves as a generation that had survived a disillusioning war, to which they had been condemned by their elders, and the traditional values of those elders were now highly suspect. Many Americans turned from the idealism of the war years to an excessive preoccupation with material success and material comfort. They rejected traditional religion with its strict code of personal morality for the ideas of Darwin and Freud. They rejected rural patterns of living for an urban, mechanized, and standardized way of life.

Though often misquoted and seldom read first-hand, Sigmund Freud's theories greatly influenced the rebellious thinking of the twenties. In that decade, even the non-rebellious began to understand the significance of sex in human behavior. Unquestionably, the most important contributions in this area came from the writings and research of Sigmund Freud, whose work had first been introduced to America in the years before the war. As a national fad, Freudian psychology often took simplistic, unscientific, and distorted forms. Freud's emphasis on the importance of the sexual drive, which earlier generations had been loath to admit, was misread by many to mean that a free expression of sexual energy promoted mental health.

There were, however, dissenters from the success-oriented materialism of American life. New ideas and modes of living were distasteful to the traditionalism and fundamentalism of small-town America symbolized by Coolidge. Small businessmen, farmers, laborers, and minority groups had economic and social reasons for discontent with the dominant trends in the United States.

There was also widespread spiritual and psychological discontent among American intellectuals. They were repelled by both the narrowness and intolerance of traditional American life and the widespread

897

materialism and emptiness of the postwar business-oriented popular culture. Characteristic of the literary intellectuals was the attitude expressed by Sinclair Lewis in his novel *Main Street*, describing the cultural void and dullness of life in a small Midwestern town:

. . . It is an unimaginatively standardized background, a sluggishness of speech and manners, a rigid ruling of the spirit by the desire to appear respectable. It is contentment . . . the contentment of the quiet dead, who are scornful of the living for their restless walking. It is negation canonized as the one positive virtue. It is the prohibition of happiness. It is slavery self-sought and self-defended. It is dullness made God. . . .

In the words of H. L. Mencken, American society was dominated by the "boob-oisie." Believing they lived in a nihilistic world, many sought to live only for the pleasure of the moment and for the thrills of immediate self-indulgence. In 1920, F. Scott Fitzgerald spoke in his novel, *This Side of Paradise,* of the "sad young men" whose idealistic dreams were shattered by the Jazz Age and who now lived in an endless search for narcissistic pleasure.

This sense of emptiness and disillusionment dominated the works of many writers, both in Europe and the United States. Sinclair Lewis used biting satire to attack the narrowness and spiritual emptiness of the small Midwestern American town and metropolis. Theodore Dreiser, in his *An American Tragedy,* told how the materialism of the time drove a young man to the murder of his mistress. Willa Cather, in *My Antonia,* chronicled the struggles of the immigrants and their offspring to fit into the "American mold."

Charles A. Lindberg was given a hero's welcome when he returned from his New York to Paris flight in 1927.

JAZZ AS A SYMBOL OF PROTEST

The popular music of the twenties was in keeping with the new mood of rebellion against tradition, and the emphasis on spontaneity and sensuality. Jazz was not genteel; it was uninhibited. Arising from the improvisations of the black and white bands in New Orleans after the Civil War, the new music spread as the musicians went from New Orleans to Chicago, New York, and Paris. Great jazz musicians, such as W. C. Handy, Joe "King" Oliver, "Jelly Roll" Morton, Bix Beiderbecke, and Louis Armstrong became the craze of the nation's youth who danced to the lively rhythms. In its time, jazz was widely denounced as degenerate; but soon it found its way into musical comedy, and composers such as Aaron Copland, Roy Harris, and George Gershwin began incorporating jazz into symphonic forms. Eventually, jazz came to be universally recognized as a significant American contribution to twentieth-century culture.

IMPACT OF URBAN LIFE

Urbanization grew very rapidly in the 1920s, with profound effect on American life. By the end of the decade, less than 25 percent of the country's population lived on farms. The cities not only produced most of the nation's wealth but set its style in clothing, music, literature, and popular entertainment. Prosperity brought more leisure time, and this led to a craving for diversions. Crossword puzzles, contract bridge, spectator sports, beauty contests, dance marathons, and flagpole sitting developed out of the search for leisure-time activity. Radio networks broadcast from the city and motion-picture houses sprang up in metropolitan areas. Approximately fifty million people a week went to see Rudolph Valentino, the great screen lover, Clara

Bow, the "It" girl, and the comedy of Charlie Chaplin. Important to the silent movies of the twenties were the Mack Sennett comedies and the innovative works of D. W. Griffith, who began his film career a decade earlier with *The Birth of a Nation*. Louis B. Mayer organized his huge studio, Metro-Goldwyn-Mayer, and in 1927 with *The Jazz Singer,* starring Al Jolson, the era of talking pictures began.

The number of city tabloids increased, with their emphasis on sensational photographs and serialized comic strips. *Time,* the first of the news magazines, was founded. All these city-based influences tended to standardize the thinking and actions of most of the country. Mass journalism was able to create for the first time national heroes, such as Babe Ruth and Jack Dempsey. The most spectacular hero of the decade, however, was Charles A. Lindbergh, who alone in his tiny plane, *The Spirit of St. Louis,* flew from New York to Paris in May, 1927. He was acclaimed throughout the world. As F. L. Allen wrote in *Only Yesterday:*

> *A disillusioned nation fed on cheap heroics and scandal and crime was revolting against the low estimate of human nature which it had allowed itself to entertain. . . . Something that people needed, if they were to live at peace with themselves and with the world, was missing from their lives. And all at once Lindbergh provided it. Romance, chivalry, self-dedication—here they were, embodied in a modern Galahad for a generation which had forsworn Galahads.*

Because many of the old social restrictions first were set aside in the cities, urban life was to a great extent responsible for altering family living. The family of the city and the suburb existed in a world radically different from that of the family in rural America. In rural areas, families tended to grow and remain together. Parents, grandparents, aunts, uncles, and cous-

The Thrill and Joy of New York Style
With Every Assurance of Quality

14 G 312
All Silk
De Luxe
Crepe Satin
$14.98

14 G 300
Quality
All Silk
Flat Crepe
$9.98

14 G 306
All Silk
Crepe
Romaine
$14.95

10 G 326
Thibetine
Scarf
$7.98

14 G 318
All Silk
De Luxe
Crepe Satin
$14.98

14 G 324
All Silk
De Luxe
Crepe Satin
$14.98

10 G 330
Genuine
Red Fox
$12.98

14 G 336
All Silk
De Luxe
Flat Crepe
$13.98

14 G 330
All Silk
De Luxe
Crepe Satin
$13.98

14 G 342
All Wool
Poiret
Sheen
$12.98

14 G 346
All Silk
De Luxe
Crepe Satin
$14.95

These Dresses are
also Furnished in
Each of the Colors
Described on
Opposite Page

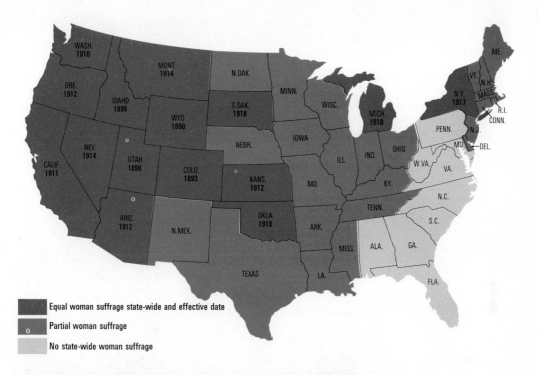

WASH.
1910

MONT.
1914

N.DAK.

ME.

ORE.
1912

IDAHO
1896

MINN.

VT.

N.H.

WYO.
1890

S.DAK.
1918

WISC.

MASS.

N.Y.
1917

R.I.

CONN.

NEV.
1914

CALIF.
1911

UTAH
1896

NEBR.

IOWA

MICH.
1918

PENN.

N.J.

COLO.
1893

OHIO

IND.

ILL.

MD.

DEL.

ARIZ.
1912

N.MEX.

KANS.
1912

MO.

KY.

W.VA.

VA.

N.C.

OKLA.
1918

ARK.

TENN.

S.C.

MISS.

ALA.

GA.

TEXAS

LA.

FLA.

- Equal woman suffrage state-wide and effective date
- Partial woman suffrage
- No state-wide woman suffrage

WOMAN SUFFRAGE BEFORE THE NINETEENTH AMENDMENT

ins provided support, discipline, and a sense of continuity in life. Community, and not isolation, was the most outstanding characteristic of rural family living. City living, on the other hand, proved to be more impersonal and the attractions of city life weakened the closeness of the family. Adolescents in the cities, often with their own cars, were freer to live more uninhibited lives than their country counterparts.

With the growth of urban life, feminism entered a new phase. Women had won the vote, but their entry into politics had been limited. However, many did demand the right to equal jobs and income, and to social and sexual freedom. The once modest, long-haired maiden shortened her dresses

Bobbed hair and shorter skirts were the hall-mark of the Jazz-Age woman as illustrated in this Montgomery Ward catalog.

to above her knees, bobbed her hair, and blossomed forth as the "flapper." The flapper painted her lips, rouged her cheeks, discarded heavy corsets and petticoats for much lighter garments, and wore beads and bangles. The flapper also smoked cigarettes and enjoyed bootleg gin, and danced the black bottom, the Charleston, and the Lindy. The flapper "costume" which had first caused so much alarm among elders became the standard of feminine fashion by 1929.

LITERATURE

For the most part, writers of the twenties turned their backs on material progress, economic prosperity, Wall Street, small-town America, and politics. Their cynicism was typified by the remark about politics of drama critic George Jean Nathan: "I de-

901

In the early 1900s, the Ashcan School, led by John Sloan and George Bellows, became known for realistic and sometimes exuberant paintings of the less attractive aspects of city life. In the twenties and thirties, two introspective painters, Charles Burchfield and Edward Hopper, saw less joy and more grimness in American life. Hopper's Early Sunday Morning is shown below.

Influenced by European cubism and futurism, such painters as Charles Sheeler, Stuart Davis, and Joseph Stella in The Bridge (right) distilled in their work the mechanistic and structural aspects of the American scene.

The depression years fostered a mood of nationalism, reflected in the popularity of Thomas Benton and Grant Wood, who glorified regional America. In the same era, the Social Realists, such as Ben Shahn and Jack Levine, illustrated social injustice in America.

Influenced by several major artists who came to America to escape European fascism, America in mid-twentieth century soon led the Abstract Expressionist movement with such innovators as Robert Motherwell, Jackson Pollock, and Mark Rothko.

cline to pollute my mind with such obscenities," and H. L. Mencken: "If I am convinced of anything, it is that doing good is in bad taste." Most writers abhorred the business culture. Many fled to Europe or Greenwich Village, the center of bohemian life in New York City. They despised American civilization above all, not for its inequities but for its superficial achievements. Edmund Wilson has remarked that writers in this generation attacked their own culture more consistently than in any other era of history. Frederick Hoffman, in his book *The Twenties,* concurred, asserting: "The aim was to invert the scale of decorum, to exalt vulgarity and explode convention . . ."

There were those critics who felt that in their negative outlook the writers of the 1920s presented a false image of life in that period. Bernard De Voto, for example, in his *The Literary Fallacy,* condemned such writers as Sinclair Lewis, H. L. Mencken, F. Scott Fitzgerald, and Ernest Hemingway for what he considered very biased and shallow viewpoints. "The rationale existed beforehand as a chart," asserted De Voto, "and when literature inquired what American life was like, it knew in advance that American life would turn out to be shallow, trivial, and mediocre. It is a short step from mediocrity to contemptibility . . ." De Voto further asserted, "What this generation had to say about life, it was generally agreed, found final expression in Mr. Eliot's poem *The Waste Land.* Here the modern world is rendered as a cheap inanity, love as a vulgar ritual without feeling, and mankind too unimportant to justify . . ." De Voto made an exception of such writers as Willa Cather, Stephen Vincent Benét, Carl Sandburg, E. A. Robinson, and Robert Frost, believing that their work upheld the belief that "human experience has dignity."

The Era of Wonderful Nonsense, The Jazz Age, The Lost Generation, names given to the period, were reinforced by the image created by the writers of the twenties. F. Scott Fitzgerald was in the vanguard of those who developed this image. In his first novel, *This Side of Paradise,* his hero Amory Blaine, a young man who had gone to war from the Princeton campus, spoke for the bohemianism and pathos of the lost young men of the postwar era. Writers like Fitzgerald and Hemingway became strongly identified with the characters and behavior that they created in their novels. Gertrude Stein, the American writer who befriended them in Paris, called these young writers "a lost generation." They had been schooled for a world other than the one that existed after the war. When their idealism confronted the prevailing materialism, they became disillusioned. Sinclair Lewis looked at the Middle West and saw only confused men and women trapped by their own materialism, stifled and unhappy. Lewis' *Main Street* and *Babbitt* created satirical symbols of average American life in the twenties. In *The Sun Also Rises* and *A Farewell to Arms,* Hemingway looked at nineteenth-century standards of conduct and the idealization of war and expressed his deep antipathy to both. John Dos Passos expressed his revulsion against war in *Three Soldiers,* published in 1921. His masterpiece was *U.S.A.,* a trilogy about American life in the twentieth century, the story of a spiritually empty, mass society. Armed with Freudian insights, William Faulkner examined small-town Southern life and exposed the tensions that he saw between the individual and society. T. S. Eliot looked at the twenties and painted a definitive portrait of despair in *The Waste Land* and other poems. The poet Ezra Pound, whose pre-war poetry had inspired many of the young writers of the twenties, left America for Italy and developed a sympathy for fascism. Writers like H. L. Mencken observed American democracy in the twenties, with its business cult as the democratic ideal and railed against a system that they believed produced a vulgar, selfish civiliza-

---ation

tion. Mencken labeled democracy "government by Orgy."

As writers who came to prominence in the twenties moved into the next decade, some looked back with regret, perhaps none more poignantly than F. Scott Fitzgerald. In the 1930s Fitzgerald wrote extensively about his "wasted youth." Novels such as *Tender Is the Night,* published in 1934, are filled with recriminations over the waste and the triviality of pursuits in the twenties.

The upsurge of artistic creativity among black Americans in the 1920s, known as the Harlem Renaissance, produced a different type of rebellion. The writers celebrated their cultural heritage from Africa with fierce vigor. The poet Claude McKay used his gift to protest racial bigotry, and Langston Hughes and Countee Cullen interpreted the black cultural experience in America. Just as Richard Wright, who pursued the same theme a decade later, they sought freedom of expression rather than social acceptability.

The decade produced writers who were to raise the nation's literary reputation. Most of these artists broke with past literary conventions, and this break seemed to free their creative abilities, permitting them to experiment with new ideas and forms.

ELECTION OF 1928

As the election of 1928 approached, Coolidge announced that he "did not choose to run." There was a chance that Coolidge might have accepted a draft, but the Republicans quickly swept aside that possibility by nominating Herbert Hoover on the first ballot. Senator Charles Curtis of Kansas was given the Vice Presidential nomination, as a Republican concession to the farm vote. Hoover did not have the backing of farmers nor the enthusiastic support of the professional politicians, but big business stood solidly behind him. At their convention, the Democrats nominated Alfred E. Smith for President on the first ballot and chose Senator Joseph T. Robinson of Arkansas as his running mate.

HOOVER AND SMITH

The Republican and Democratic platforms did not seem to offer the voters much alternative, but Hoover and Smith certainly cut strikingly different images. Hoover epitomized the self-made businessman. In a book, *American Individualism,* he set forth his personal credo. Denouncing both radicals and reactionaries, he extolled the virtues of enlightened capitalism. According to Hoover, the American system of economic freedom provided equal opportunity to its citizenry to succeed by individual merit. With personal achievement there should be in turn a rising sense of responsibility and service to the community. Hoover was living proof of his creed. While still a young man, he had made a fortune as an engineer and then turned his talents to public service. From the latter he never took a cent for his personal use, and he sincerely hoped that his own record of voluntary public service would inspire and become standard practice in the business community. However, he believed this would happen only if government cooperated with business to prevent economic injustice without placing arbitrary restric-

904

tions on its operations. Limited power in the federal government and more decentralized local responsibility would prevent a trend toward the evils of socialism that, Hoover felt, would destroy political freedom and economic initiative and opportunity.

With his impressive personal successes, Hoover enjoyed a reputation for efficiency and humanity. He stood on a platform that pledged the continuation of the high protective tariff, enforcement of the prohibition amendment, refusal to affiliate with the League of Nations, and the promotion of cooperative marketing as a method of controlling farm surpluses. Both Hoover and the Republican platform pointed to the success of the party's policies in creating an era of unparalleled prosperity. These were policies, Hoover emphasized in his campaign speeches, that had virtually conquered poverty in America. Now, he asserted, "the slogan of progress is changing from the full dinner pail to the full garage."

The Democratic platform likewise catered to the conservative spirit of the time. Progressive issues were avoided in the light of current prosperity. The platform deferred to the business community. It was vague on farm relief and silent on American entry into the League. Its only forthright plank was a call for more stringent federal regulations over hydroelectric power. It virtually forced Smith to avoid any outright declarations on other issues.

As governor of New York, Smith had a record for efficiency just as impressive as Hoover's. He had reordered both the state's finances and the workings of its administration. He had promoted public health and recreation, workmen's compensation, and civil liberties. His promotion of social legislation and his courageous stand during the Red scare damaged his standing with the nation's conservatives in his own party. He unquestionably tempered his own liberalism during the campaign in response to the mood of the times. He accepted the protective tariff, and even though he was against national prohibition and favored the control of liquor sales through state outlets, he opposed the return of the saloon. He even chose as his campaign manager John J. Raskob, a Republican industrialist who was strongly identified with both DuPont and General Motors.

Smith, however, hardly represented the traditional Presidential candidate. In fact, he symbolized the breakthrough in national politics of urban forces that had been gathering momentum for several decades. He was the grandson of Irish immigrants and a Roman Catholic, the first member of his faith to be nominated for the Presidency by a national party. He grew up on the lower East Side of Manhattan, and very proudly he identified himself with "the sidewalks of New York." To many voters in villages and small towns, Smith epitomized the alien influences endangering rural, Anglo-Saxon, Protestant America. He quickly became the target of criticism by prohibitionists and religious attacks by the KKK and others who circulated rumors that Smith's election would mean papal dominance of the White House.

SIGNIFICANCE OF ELECTION

In the final analysis it was economic prosperity that defeated Al Smith. Hoover had only to point to the Republican record of business prosperity and the nation's high standard of living. Predictably, the election was one-sided. Smith received only 87 electoral votes to Hoover's 444. Hoover captured 58 percent of the popular vote to Smith's 41 percent.

On the surface, the nation had voted to continue the policies that had brought a record-shattering and apparently endless prosperity. A closer examination of the election results, however, shows other significant political trends in the country. Smith had polled twice as many votes as Davis, the Democratic candidate for President in 1924, and former supporters of the Progressive Party had gone over to the Democrats. Undeniably, the Democrats were gathering long-range strength. The country was only 44 percent rural now and Smith carried the twelve largest cities in the nation. Apparently, he had managed to break the Republican hold on the country's industrial centers. The Republicans had won these easily in 1924. Support for Smith also cut sharply into the traditionally Republican agricultural vote in the West. Smith was the first Democratic candidate to carry the state of Massachusetts. Regardless of prosperity and religious prejudice, he had succeeded in splitting the "Republican North."

Readings

GENERAL WORKS

Allen, Frederick L., *Only Yesterday*. New York: Harper, 1931—A popular history of the twenties, written by an experienced journalist at the depths of the Depression and emphasizing how transitory and shaky the prosperity was.

Divine, Robert A., *American Immigration Policy, 1924–1952*. New Haven, Conn.: Yale University Press, 1957—A study of immigration policies after the passage of the restrictionist legislation of 1924. Divine shows considerable sympathy for the pro-exclusion argument.

Faulkner, Harold, *From Versailles to the New Deal*. New York: U.S. Publishers' Association, 1963—A survey of United States political, social, and economic history from 1919 to 1933. Faulkner devotes the majority of his attention to the administrations of Harding and Coolidge.

Hicks, John D., *Republican Ascendency*. New York: Harper & Row, 1960—A standard account of the twenties, stressing political developments. The book covers the administrations of Harding, Coolidge, and Hoover.

Hicks, John D., and Theodore Saloutos, *Twentieth Century Populism: Agricultural Discontent in the Middle West, 1900–1939*. Lincoln: University of Nebraska Press, 1964—The impulses of Populism were, the authors argue, the force behind a wide variety of farm-based movements in the Middle West. Yet farmers' individualism and their complex economic situation invited a broad spectrum of remedies and platforms.

Hoffman, Frederick J., *The Twenties*. New York: Viking, 1955—A literary history of the decade in which many of America's most talented authors rejected mainstream American culture, choosing to live bohemian lives at home or abroad.

Leuchtenburg, William E., *The Perils of Prosperity, 1914–1932*. Chicago: University of Chicago Press, 1958—A lively general account of the years during and after World War I up to the election of Roosevelt. Leuchtenburg points out the social strains that lurked beneath the façade of normalcy.

Schlesinger, Arthur M., Jr., *The Crisis of the Old Order*. Boston: Houghton Mifflin, 1957—The first volume of Schlesinger's study of the "Age of Roosevelt." This book deals with the 1920s, a time when, Schlesinger believes, business-oriented conservatives failed the test of ruling the nation.

Schriftgiesser, Karl, *This Was Normalcy*. Boston: Little, Brown, 1948—An attack on the Republican administrations of 1921 to 1933 for their conservative economic policies and their isolationist diplomacy. Schriftgiesser compares the Republican Presidents unfavorably with FDR.

Soule, George, *Prosperity Decade: From War to Depression*. New York: Harper & Row, 1968—An economic history of the 1920s. Soule is critical of the irresponsibly pro-business policies he believes the Republican administrations followed.

SPECIAL STUDIES

Bagby, Wesley, *The Road to Normalcy*. Baltimore, Md.: Johns Hopkins Press, 1962—A study of the campaign and election of 1920. Bagby claims that underlying trends made the Republican sweep inevitable.

Bernstein, Irving, *The Lean Years*. Boston: Houghton Mifflin, 1960—A study of American workers in the 1920s. A specialist in industrial relations, Bernstein provides much information on emerging patterns of labor-management relations during the decade as well as evidence concerning workers' life styles and attitudes.

Chafee, Zechariah, *Free Speech in the United States*. Cambridge, Mass.: Harvard University Press, 1941—A legal and political study of the ups and downs of freedom of speech from 1920 to 1941.

Chalmers, David M., *Hooded Americanism: The History of the KKK*. Garden City, N.Y.: Doubleday, 1965—The author has studied the Klan in its three periods of growth and power. He points out that the authoritarian racism it represented was not only a Southern phenomenon.

Ginger, Ray, *Six Days or Forever?* Chicago: Quadrangle, 1969—An account of the famous Scopes "monkey trial" in Dayton, Tennessee, in 1925, in which William Jennings Bryan was the spokesman for a fading fundamentalist creed in opposition to the attorney Clarence Darrow who upheld the validity of evolutionary doctrines and the scientific approach.

Johnson, Donald, *The Challenge to American Freedoms*. Lexington: University of Kentucky Press, 1963—A history of the origins of the American Civil Liberties Union in the civil liberties struggles that followed World War I.

Joughin, Louis, and Edmund M. Morgan, *The Legacy of Sacco and Vanzetti*. Chicago: Quadrangle, 1964—Less an analysis of the famous case itself than of its impact on the legal system. The intellectual response and popular opinion are discussed.

Lynd, Robert S., and Helen M. Lynd, *Middletown*. New York: Harcourt, Brace, 1929—A classic sociological study of a small Midwestern city. The Lynds found that sharp class distinctions and the existence of an elite power structure were masked by an ideology of democracy and equality.

Murray, Robert K., *The Harding Era*. Minneapolis: University of Minneapolis Press, 1969—An analysis of Harding's Presidency that to some extent saves him from charges of corruption and incompetence. Murray considers Harding a decent if uninspired leader, and points to significant administrative and diplomatic developments during his years in office.

Murray, Robert K., *The Red Scare*. Minneapolis: University of Minnesota Press, 1955—After World War I, governmental and private groups embarked on numerous antiradical campaigns. Murray shows the influences of such factors as political ambition, anti-union sentiment, and hostility to ethnic and national minorities on the development of the witch hunting era.

Osofsky, Gilbert, *Harlem: The Making of a Ghetto*. New York: Harper & Row, 1966—Shortly before World War I, a middle-class white neighborhood in northern Manhattan was converted by real estate speculators into a black ghetto. Osofsky analyzes this process and also discusses the social, cultural, political, and economic institutions in Harlem which made it a distinctively black community.

Sinclair, Andrew, *Prohibition: The Era of Excess*. Boston: Little, Brown, 1962—A study of the social effects of the prohibition amendment. Sinclair pictures the prohibitionists as representatives of an earlier era in American history; rural, conservative in religion, strict in morality, while the "wets" represented newer, more liberal forces.

Swain, D. C., *Federal Conservation Policy 1921–1933*. Berkeley: University of California Press, 1963—Swain argues that the impetus which Theodore Roosevelt gave to conservation carried through the administrations of Harding, Coolidge, and Hoover. He credits the latter with valuable innovations in the field of conservation.

PRIMARY SOURCES

Gatewood, Willard B., Jr., ed., *Controversy in the Twenties: Fundamentalism, Modernism and Evolution*. Nashville, Tenn.: Vanderbilt University Press, 1969—A documentary account of the struggles within American Protestantism during the 1920s, and their impact on politics, science, and society.

Leighton, Isabel, ed., *The Aspirin Age*. New York: Simon & Schuster, 1949—A collection of articles and interpretations of life in the twenties and thirties. The emphasis is on popular culture: prohibition, Lindbergh's flight, and boxing are among the subjects covered.

Mowry, George, ed., *The Twenties: Fords, Flappers and Fanatics*. Englewood Cliffs, N.J.: Prentice-Hall, 1963—An anthology of social and cultural trends of the decade.

Quint, Howard H., and Robert H. Ferrell, eds., *The Talkative President: The Off-the-Record Press Conferences of Calvin Coolidge*. Amherst: University of Massachusetts Press, 1964—Frequently called "Silent Cal," Coolidge in private could be witty and gregarious. The transcripts of his off-the-record press conferences reveal a more human side to Coolidge's personality.

BIOGRAPHIES

Cronon, E. D., *Black Moses*. Madison: University of Wisconsin Press, 1955—In the early 1920s, Garvey's Universal Negro Improvement Association had some 500,000 adherents. Cronon emphasizes that, although Garvey himself was not a leader of high caliber, the Garveyite movement contained many constructive impulses and was also the forerunner of later black nationalist activity.

Handlin, Oscar, *Al Smith and His America*. Boston: Little, Brown, 1958—Handlin interprets Smith as a representative of growing power and self-consciousness of urban and immigrant groups in American politics, and attributes his defeat in 1928 to his immigrant origins and religious beliefs.

Josephson, Matthew, and Hannah Josephson, *Al Smith: Hero of the Cities*. Boston: Houghton Mifflin, 1969—A detailed biography of the New York Democrat. Much of the documentation comes from the papers of Frances Perkins who worked under him in New York State government before becoming FDR's Secretary of Labor.

Mann, Arthur, *La Guardia: A Fighter Against His Times*. Chicago: University of Chicago Press, 1969—A biography of the New York Progressive Republican. This volume covers his career up to his election as mayor of New York. Mann shows him as a "marginal man," who had several different cultural identities.

McCoy, Donald R., *Calvin Coolidge, the Quiet President*. New York: Macmillan, 1967—A biography of the Republican President. McCoy maintains that Coolidge was an able representative of the conservative temper of the American people.

Russell, Francis, *The Shadow of Blooming Grove*. New York: McGraw-Hill, 1968—A popular biography of President Harding, arguing that Harding never outgrew his provincial Ohio political background.

26

The Depression and the New Deal

*The community is interested in
economic results. It must be
protected from economic as well
as moral wrongs. We must find
practical controls over blind
economic forces . . .*

—*Franklin Delano Roosevelt*

*With almost 11 million people out of work in
1932, many resorted to selling apples for a
livelihood.*

When he came to office in 1929, Herbert
Hoover enhanced the general mood of optimism by declaring in his inaugural address that "in no nation are the fruits of
accomplishment more secure." However, a
few cautious men noticed the warning sig-
nals: agrarian depression, unstable trading
conditions with Europe, and a vast overextension of credit in the country.

THE ORDEAL
OF HERBERT HOOVER

THE CRASH AND
ITS CAUSES

Trade between the United States and Europe had been shaky since the end of the First World War. The United States enjoyed an advantage in the amount of her exports to Europe and, in addition, European governments were indebted to the United States as a result of wartime loans. Gold accumulated in the United States, and Wall Street became the center of international finance. Germany was indebted to Britain and France and Britain and France were indebted to the United States and to the Wall Street banking houses which had helped finance the war. But because the balance of gold already lay in the United States, Germany needed to borrow money from America in order to repay Britain and France, which nations in turn could repay the United States. Capital tended to glut nonproductively in New York's banking houses. The presence of so much capital led to irresponsible investment. The Wall Streeters needed outlets for their capital, and when they turned to the American economy they found that the new boom industries, particularly automobiles and steel, had learned to do without them and to finance expansion through profits. As a result there was much speculation in the stocks of less stable and less important industries.

Speculation was for a long time encouraged rather than moderated by the Federal Reserve Board, which lowered interest rates, thus extending credit. The Board tried to retrench, too late to discourage the buying spree. "Buying on margin" became popular with thousands on a limited income, because a buyer only had to put up a part of the supposed high price of the stock. As long as the market was continuing to go up, everyone who could wanted to get in on the profits. Without an increase in productivity, stocks were inflated since they were priced above the earning power of corporations in whose name they were issued. New companies were set up on top of established firms which issued stocks but produced nothing themselves, a new version of the holding company and a manifestation of the underlying weakness of the "bull" market. A few wise businessmen knew that the boom was founded on overextension of credit and that capital was being poured into the speculative market, not into production or purchases of goods. Capital poured into stocks was effectively withdrawn from productive circulation in the economy. This meant that the boom was built on thin air. It was only the stock market, not the distribution of goods, that was booming. In fact, in 1928 sales had waned. Construction had fallen off dramatically. Manufacturers found themselves saddled with huge inventories. Yet the market went up and up during 1929.

THE DEPRESSION BEGINS

Thus the rise in the market after 1927 was unnatural. Ironically, Hoover warned both Coolidge and Mellon that the economy was inflated and should be curbed. However, neither man would listen to him. When he became President, Hoover, while stating that the economy was basically sound, did get the Federal Reserve Board to raise the rediscount rate to banks twice in 1929. But it was too late. In September the stock market showed its first signs of decline. It fluctuated for over a month and then, on October 24, "Black Thursday," the market fell disastrously. There was a breathing space of a few days. It ended the following Tuesday, October 29, when, as *The New York Times* reported, "Groups of men, and here and there a woman, stood about inverted glass bowls . . . watching spools of ticker tape unwind" till two hours past closing time. Over sixteen million shares of stock had been dumped on the market, many still unsold even at the lowest prices. The market had fallen 40 points since September. The life savings of many were gone.

Both Hoover and Secretary of the Treasury Mellon understood that the Wall Street boom was not a good index of the nation's economic health. Mellon disliked wild speculation and believed in sound business practice. As a result, when the crash came both men at first thought it would bring a positive readjustment of the economy. Investors would understand that stock speculation was risky. They would start putting capital into sounder and more productive enterprises, where profits were less flashy but more reliable. This theory, however, did not take into account the problem of maldistribution of wealth. Poorer families, already in debt for their new cars and other

Crowds on Wall Street in front of the Sub-Treasury Building during the stock market crash in 1929.

items, did not have the money to buy the products of those theoretically sounder industries. As soon as the market fell, a decline in buying power produced more unemployment. More unemployment in turn meant even less buying power. The downward spiral of the economy was gathering momentum. The austere Mellon, realizing this, still advised Hoover to allow the economy to suffer all the necessary pangs of readjustment. The market recovered briefly between January and June, 1930, and then turned down again.

The crash initiated the greatest depression of modern times. Wealthy interests such as the House of Morgan had immediately rushed in to purchase stocks in an effort to stabilize the market, and in fact managed to lend it some semblance of security. Hoover limited government action at first to a tax cut, a series of optimistic statements to rally the nation, and meetings with business leaders to discuss the distressing conditions. He believed the current situation was merely a "crisis of confidence," and reasoned that confidence might be restored by a show of good spirits. More concretely, he urged businessmen not to fire their workers—to reduce wages and hours if necessary, but to keep as many people as possible employed.

The voluntary restraint of businessmen did not prove to be an adequate policy. The period from 1929 to 1932 showed a steady decline in all major areas of economic life. In 1930 unemployment rose to about 4 million, and in 1932, though there are no exact statistics, about 12 million people, or roughly 25 percent of the employable population, were out of work. According to the September, 1932, issue of *Fortune* magazine, this meant that by a conservative estimate "next winter's relief is a problem of caring for approximately 25,000,000 souls."

Among the causes of unemployment were a decline in corporate profits averaging about 50 percent and resulting in mass layoffs; the failure of thousands of small businesses and banks; and the continuing decline of the stock market through 1932, with more and more stocks and other capital investments being liquidated. Between 1929 and 1932 national income dropped from 87 billion dollars to 42 billion dollars and production dropped proportionately. Bread lines, soup kitchens, and apple vendors became a familiar sight as workers were laid off in massive numbers by the end of 1931.

HOOVER'S ECONOMIC PHILOSOPHY

Looking back on the Great Depression in his *Memoirs,* Hoover called it "a product of some misdeeds of our own, but in the main the penalty of a great war and its impact upon Europe." He was convinced that the depression resulted from economic failures across the Atlantic that spread to the United States, rather than from internal problems in the American system itself. Until the end of his life he believed that in 1931, when the economy was shaken by European failures, it had been on the road to recovery. He also thought that "the wounds of the Depression opened our flesh deeply to collectivist infections from Europe," a reference to the New Deal, which gave the federal government an unprecedented role in directing the country's economy.

Hoover also held fast to his conviction that the federal government's policy during a depression was to wait out the crisis until stability returned. It had only a limited responsibility in guiding the economy beyond restoring business confidence by balancing the federal budget and efficient administration of its responsibilities. Too much federal intervention would create a permanent dependence on the government and undermine freedom and self-reliance. But men who recalled Republican rhetoric about prosperity became distrustful of

Hoover's economic vision. "Any party which takes credit for the rain must not be surprised if its opponents blame it for the drought," Dwight W. Morrow said in 1930.

Hoover had taken some credit for the rain. In his campaign he had claimed that "We in America are nearer to the final triumph over poverty than ever before in the history of any land . . ." While this grand assertion seemed ironic, by 1930 many critics were more irritated by what they considered Hoover's lack of effective action in the crisis at hand. Hoover, shy and stiff in public, reacted privately to criticism with resentment. He wrote in his *Memoirs* that "any organization by citizens for their own welfare is preferable to the same action by government." He also wrote that "you cannot extend the mastery of government over the daily working life of a people without at the same time making it the master of the people's souls and thoughts." Not inclined or sympathetic to political maneuvering, he thought that criticism of his policies was often spiced with more than a trace of demagoguery.

Hoover's personal history, a story of self-reliance and upward struggle, sheds some light on these deeply held convictions. Orphaned when he was ten, he lived for a few years with an uncle, and then attended Stanford University where he earned a degree in engineering. His brilliant mining career gave him the epithet "The Great Engineer." In an age of industrial and technological expertise, an engineer President seemed appropriate. He was widely traveled and had earned still another epithet, "The Great Humanitarian," as a result of his work in supervising wartime relief in Belgium and managing the Food Administration during World War I. With a reputation as a humanitarian and expert administrator, he went on to new public recognition as Secretary of Commerce under Harding and Coolidge. But Hoover was not a party politician and had little idea of how to deal with Congress. He came to

the Presidency with no specific legislative program and a deep-seated fear of strong executive power.

Gilbert Seldes gave Hoover his last and tragic title, "The Great Victim." Hoover received much of the blame for a crisis he did not cause. He held office at a turning point in history. The dominance of the business interests and the philosophy of laissez faire were under attack and losing their control in Washington. "The things Hoover believed in," historian Richard Hofstadter wrote, ". . . were all in the dominant American tradition. . . . In the language of Jefferson, Jackson and Lincoln these ideas had been fresh and invigorating; in the language of Herbert Hoover they sounded stale and oppressive." In the desperate economic conditions that accompanied the depression, the old American ideal of a purely individual struggle to overcome obstacles seemed to have lost much of its meaning.

HOOVER'S FARM PROGRAM

Farmers had not shared in the prosperity of the 1920s. Agrarian depression always had been an omen that the American economy was not sound, partly because the reduced buying power of farmers eventually hurt the business interests. Statistics show that the so-called boom of the twenties hid much actual poverty. The combined earnings of 36,000 wealthy families in the top brackets were almost equal to the combined earnings of 12 million families at the bottom of the economy. Five percent of the population had 30 percent of the country's wealth. A large proportion of the poor were farmers, many being tenants and sharecroppers. The 12 million poor families, about 40 percent of the total population, lived below the theoretical subsistence level of 1,500 dollars a year. The wealthy spent a great deal of their money on luxury items, nonconsumables, and speculation. Even many of the less well-to-do were able to spend part of their money on items like automobiles, not food. But the farmer was largely left out of the boom in consumer goods.

To deal with the ever-present farm problem, Hoover called a special session of Congress on April 15, about half a year before the stock-market crash and little more than a month after he took office. The program he offered was more conservative and, as a result, acceptable than the plan for subsidized prices advocated by the rejected McNary-Haugen bill. On June 15 Congress passed the Agricultural Marketing Act. It created a Federal Farm Board. The Board was to use its 500 million dollars to support farm cooperatives with loans and buy up surpluses when fair prices for farm produce were threatened. The plan was only a partial success. By 1932 the Board had used up its resources, lending about 165 million dollars to cooperatives, and buying up 330 million bushels of wheat and 1.3 million bales of cotton. Still, prices fell during the three-year period, and a comparison between prices in 1932 and 1920 shows the extent of the agricultural depression. In 1920 the price of wheat had been $1.82 per bushel. It dropped to 38 cents in 1932. Cotton during the same period fell from 16 cents to 6 cents a pound. The price of oats was slashed by about 75 percent; the price of corn by about 50 percent. In addition, the government had a tremendous surplus of farm produce on its hands and still no answer to the problem of overproduction.

Another effort by Hoover to aid the farmer was also unsuccessful. During the special session of Congress he proposed a new tariff, hoping to raise the price of foodstuffs at home. This would be a traditional way of meeting the objectives of the McNary-Haugen bill. But a deluge of lobbyists caused a disastrous revision of Hoover's original proposal. The highest protective tariff in peacetime history, the Hawley-Smoot bill of June, 1930, raised duties to an average of over 55 percent.

Exporters were appalled, and economists, aware of the consequences on European trade, petitioned Hoover to veto the bill. However, after some deliberation, the President decided that the measure would do more good than harm. In addition to his hope that the farmer would be helped, Hoover was influenced by pressures within his party, and also perhaps by his belief that American economic ties with postwar Europe actually had caused the depression. An economic quarantine of the United States would be one way of combating further economic decline.

Yet when it was finally passed, more than six months after the stock market crash, the Hawley-Smoot Tariff only made matters worse. The farmer now paid higher prices for manufactured goods, such as textiles. A number of industries relying on export trade were forced to leave the country. Some twenty-five foreign countries enacted retaliatory tariffs. The Hawley-Smoot Tariff added new dimensions to a growing international calamity.

LOCAL RELIEF EFFORTS

It soon became apparent that more concrete government policies were needed. Hoover initiated a program that involved more federal action than had been taken in any previous economic crisis in the nation's history, but he still clung to the belief that relief for the needy was a local responsibility.

In 1931 Senator George W. Norris again introduced a proposal for federal development of Muscle Shoals, and Congress approved. A dam had been begun there in 1916 under Wilson but was not completed until 1925. It was run by the Army and sold power to private companies. Coolidge wanted to sell it to private interests, but

Norris and his supporters in Congress blocked all such plans. Hoover vetoed the plan which was a forerunner of the TVA. "I am firmly opposed," he said, "to the Government entering into any business the major purpose of which is competition with our citizens. . . . Muscle Shoals can only be administered by the people upon the ground, responsible to their own communities, directing them solely for the benefit of their communities and not for purposes of pursuit of social theories or national politics. Any other course deprives them of liberty . . ."

As far as the immediate needs of masses of Americans were concerned, the principle of local relief proved inadequate. As late as the winter of 1931 to 1932 there were families in New York drawing total weekly support of $2.39. The city of Toledo, Ohio, had only enough funds to offer its poverty-stricken workers a little more than two cents a day for food. Black Americans were among the hardest hit. They were often laid off first because so many worked in households and at service jobs. "Even in starvation there was discrimination," the historian John Hope Franklin wrote, pointing to differences in the amounts of relief offered to blacks and whites in many local communities throughout the country.

Hoover was forced to take steps to supplement local relief programs and to foster employment. He asked Congress in 1930 for standby funds up to 150 million dollars for public works projects in addition to about 500 million dollars already appropriated, although he hoped he would not have to use them. In October of the same year he created the Emergency Committee for Employment, with Colonel Arthur Woods, a man experienced in relief work, as its director. Woods advocated public works projects, including slum clearance, but Hoover declined all his suggestions and instructed him to operate along already established lines of local supervision. Frustrated, Woods resigned in April, 1931.

HOOVER'S LEGISLATION

The Congressional elections of 1930 left the Senate evenly matched between Republicans and Democrats. During the session, however, twelve progressive Republicans usually joined with the Democrats in calling for more government action to meet the economic crisis. The Democrats controlled the House. Thus, when the President decided to offer a broadened legislative plan to meet the crisis at the end of 1931, many of his proposals foundered. Not only was there honest opposition to his proposals, but there were also Congressmen who emphasized porkbarrel legislation over national welfare, even during such desperate times. Many Democrats also were reluctant to help Hoover in any way since they expected victory in the coming election. Hoover's supporters charged them with thwarting worthwhile legislation in order to capitalize on the popular notion of the President's inactivity in meeting the nation's hardships.

Most of the legislation enacted during the Hoover administration was aimed at aiding industries rather than individuals. Critics charged that the new laws were helping those at the top of the economic pyramid in the hope that eventually the benefits would filter down to the real sufferers but the record indicates that some of Hoover's proposals were broader than that. The Home Loan Bank Act, with the object of decreasing the number of foreclosures, created special banks to extend emergency credit to those who held mortgages on private homes. It also had provisions that encouraged residential construction. Still another act expanded the lending powers of the Federal Land Banks by 125 million dollars.

The most important creation of Hoover's administration was the Reconstruction Finance Corporation (RFC). The agency came into being in January, 1932, as the result of pressure on Hoover from economists.

Federal Relief: The Position of the Unemployed

" *In Washington Township there are more than 1,350 families on the county unemployed fund, and the heads of those families have been unemployed anywhere from eight months to more than a year. The principal industry with us is coal mining. . . .*

This miners' relief has reached the end of its resources. In other words, the funds are about completely exhausted. In our community we have 50 or 60 families, it being a mining town, and those families are facing utter despair. There is no prospect whatsoever of getting anything for them. Our farmers have nothing. Our small merchants have gone bankrupt in trying to carry us. The banks have gone under, and there are only a few general stores.

I have heard the miners say, including myself, if it comes to the point where we must do it, we are going together and take over those general stores and take things we need to eat. We can not let our families starve. Our county is practically broke. It has nothing to give us by way of relief. They have been giving some families as low as $8 whether the family consists of two or say, nine. . . . the children are the principal sufferers. I have known several cases where children collapsed in school, and that is the only time they would get relief from the county—when the child would collapse in school from hunger. . . .

In our community we have a soup kitchen, as I have said, and the soup kitchen was maintained primarily by the donation from the miners' relief. . . .

I want to tell you gentlemen what we serve at the soup kitchen—bread and black coffee, and just enough sugar to make it palatable, and dry bread. That is served to the children who go to school. At dinner time they get the same thing, bread and black coffee. *At night time the principal things they eat are soup and bread. The soup contains rice, barley, and a little potatoes when we can get them. . . .*

The county has not given us a cent. The county is, as I have said, broke. "

—Joseph Rade, Fayette
County, Pennsylvania

Federal Relief: Hoover's Position

" *The proposals of our opponents will endanger or destroy our system. . . . I especially emphasize that promise to promote "employment for all surplus labor at all times." At first I could not believe that anyone would be so cruel as to hold out a hope so absolutely impossible of realization to these 10,000,000 who are unemployed. And I protest against such frivolous promises being held out to a suffering people. It is easily demonstrable that no such employment can be found. But the point I wish to make here and now is the mental attitude and spirit of the Democratic Party to attempt it. It is another mark of the character of the new deal and the destructive changes which mean the total abandonment of every principle upon which this government and the American system is founded. If it were possible to give this employment to 10,000,000 people by the Government, it would cost upwards of $9,000,000,000 a year. . . . It would pull down the employment of those who are still at work by the high taxes and the demoralization of credit upon which their employment is dependent. . . .* "

—Herbert Hoover

Starting with a capital of 500 million dollars and the power to incur debts of 1.5 billion dollars, it was essentially a loan agency for banks, trust companies, building and loan associations, insurance companies, agricultural and livestock credit associations, and railroads. Hoarding of gold, withdrawals by European investors, and cutbacks in trade had made it harder to get credit. Banks no longer had the collateral to get Federal Reserve loans. The agency's powers were extended until it had lent a total of 3 billion dollars. It was the most successful measure that had yet been tried. Though it could not satisfy all the needs of its recipients, it alleviated the decline of business and forestalled many bankruptcies. There is no doubt that the depression would have been even more grave without its activities.

One of the President's last proposals, the Glass-Steagall Act of February, 1932, increased credit to borrowers from the Federal Reserve System by diversifying the types of collateral that could be used. The effect was to inflate the currency, protect the gold standard, and to extend credit for investment and commercial loans.

AMERICANS DESPERATE

The desperation of farmers and workers occasionally erupted into episodes of violence. For example, the Farmers' Holiday Association tried to blockade Sioux City, Iowa, to prevent foreclosures on farms until prices rose. The attempt was a failure. The motivation was simple: prices were so low that burning corn for warmth was cheaper than trying to ship it and sell it. "The pur-

Hooverville, a village of the unemployed, near Seattle's waterfront.

Homes of the unemployed in New York City in 1932.

pose," Gilbert Seldes reported, "was simply to put up the price of farm produce to the point where it reached what farmers called the cost of production . . ." Farmers blockaded roads and punctured casks of milk. At the same time they lifted the blockade for food en route to hospitals and gave milk to the jobless. However, it was another poor people's movement doomed to failure due to lack of organization and planning.

In urban areas the depression produced apple vendors, shoeshiners, purveyors of all kinds of odds and ends, and clusters of shanties for the down-and-out, bitterly called "Hoovervilles." Americans, accustomed to the myth that their economy was somehow different from that in other parts of the world and exempt from such spectacles of starvation, were shocked by soup kitchens, endless breadlines, and news reports of people starving sometimes because they were too proud to take charity.

Veterans demanding legislation that would give them bonuses not originally due until 1945, staged the Bonus March on Washington, D.C., in 1932. About 12,000 men arrived in the capital from all over the country to lobby for passage of the Patman bill. When the bill met defeat in the Senate, the veterans were offered their fares home, with the amount of the fares to be deducted from their bonuses. Many accepted these terms, but about five thousand refused to leave and stayed on in shanties near the capital and in deserted federal buildings. Their presence was a continual embarrassment to the Hoover administration, especially in an election year. Hoover finally called in the Army and the police to clear them out. In an early skirmish two men were fatally wounded by police bullets. Then the Army under General Douglas MacArthur dispersed the remnants of the Bonus Army with bayonets, tear gas, and tanks. The administration charged that the Bonus Army was communist-infiltrated (an allegation with no apparent substance) and that the rest of the men constituted "a polyglot mob of tramps and hoodlums." Many Americans felt that Hoover's reaction to the protest had been excessive.

THE ELECTION OF 1932 AND THE FIRST NEW DEAL

THE ELECTION OF 1932

The Democrats met in an exuberant mood and produced a platform that promised both a balanced budget and extensive new federal and state relief programs. They nominated Franklin D. Roosevelt, the governor of New York, on the fourth ballot over Al Smith. FDR, effervescent and self-confident, took a plane to Chicago as soon as he had been nominated, without waiting for the traditional notification from the convention, and pledged himself to a "new deal for the American people." On the other hand, Hoover was unable to summon the confidence for his own campaign which he previously had called for from the public. Nominated without much enthusiasm by his party, he warned that Roosevelt's "New Deal" would be a departure from tradition, would wreck the economy, and would put an end to political liberty.

Roosevelt was deliberately vague on many issues in an effort not to alienate any important group in the country. What the country needed and demanded, he said, was "bold, persistent experimentation." In contrast to Hoover's caution and apparent pessimism, Roosevelt's mood seemed confident and practical.

This contrast between caution and experimentation was rooted in different interpretations of the causes of the depression. Hoover insisted on emphasizing that the election was "a contest between two philosophies of government," and warned that "true liberalism is not found in striving to spread bureaucracy, but in striving to set bounds to it." Roosevelt blamed maldistribution of wealth for the depression, not Europe. He asserted that there was "endless plenty" in the United States that was unused, and that the problem was one of "distributing wealth and products more equitably, of adapting existing economic organization to the service of the people." In short, the depression was the result of bad organization. Roosevelt offered his undefined New Deal as a humanitarian program that would help to avert revolution. Roosevelt echoed critics of the RFC when he demanded relief policies that "build from the bottom up not from the top down, that put their faith once more in the forgotten man at the bottom of the economic pyramid." Yet Roosevelt did not outline any bold plans for the future, causing the commentator, Walter Lippmann, to write: "He is no enemy of entrenched privilege. He is a pleasant man who, without any important qualifications for the office, would very much like to be President."

Though a superb natural politician, Roosevelt was not overly familiar with the intricacies of economics. To compensate for this lack he gathered around him a group of professorial advisers. Roosevelt called it the "privy council" at first, but the group had its permanent christening from a writer on *The New York Times* who called it the "Brain Trust." These advisers helped Roosevelt throughout the campaign. Raymond Moley, the central figure in the original Brain Trust, remarked in his book *The First New Deal* that the 1932 campaign revolved almost entirely around national economic issues. International depression had created a world of pocketed, self-involved nations, and the United States was no exception.

The result of the election was a Democratic landslide. FDR won by a margin of seven million votes in the popular vote, and 472 to 59 in the electoral college, carrying all states but six. The effectiveness of the new mandate was doubled by the election of an overwhelmingly Democratic Congress. At least one significant shift in voting patterns was evident in 1932. Many Northern blacks deserted the Republican fold and voted for Roosevelt. Economic suffering in the depression, and Republican failures to make an effort to end discrimination were two factors causing the shift. Hard times had also produced new support for the Socialist and Communist parties. Norman Thomas, the Socialist candidate, polled almost 900,000 votes, and William Z. Foster, the Communist candidate, over 100,000.

FDR TAKES OFFICE

Franklin D. Roosevelt shared with his distant cousin, Theodore Roosevelt, a conservative, upper-class social background. He was educated at a private prep school, Harvard, and Columbia Law School, and traveled widely as a young man. In 1910 Roosevelt entered politics by successfully running for the New York legislature on the Democratic ticket against a Tammany Hall candidate. He was rewarded for support of Wilson in 1912 with the post of Under Secretary of the Navy. In 1920 he was Cox's running mate. Then in 1921, he was struck down with infantile paralysis. While regaining strength over the next few years he learned to be more patient. He also maintained and expanded his political contacts. In 1928, he was elected governor of New York and made a strong record as a reformer during the next four years.

Like many public figures, Roosevelt's character was enigmatic. He had many strengths as a politician. He was a man of sunny disposition—outgoing, buoyant, self-confident, and good-humored. He had a keen understanding of human behavior; he was pragmatic and flexible in his approach to problems. He was intelligent but not overly intellectual. He was also crafty and opportunistic. The new President was a shrewd politician who frequently subordinated his colleagues and even the Democratic Party to his own ambition to stay in office. He loved being President and was adroit in managing the office. He usually knew when to talk to Congressional leaders and when to apply pressure on them

Roosevelt waves to the crowd on the way to his inauguration in 1933. Hoover, sitting beside him, seems almost somber.

through using the patronage, the veto, press releases, or appeals to the people. He made the Presidency into the dynamic center of ideas and government policies which it has remained in succeeding decades.

On March 4, 1933, delivering his inaugural address, FDR pointed the accusing finger at "unscrupulous money changers," whose "outworn tradition" had failed to restore confidence and prosperity. "They know only the ideas of a generation of self-seekers," he said. "They have no vision, and when there is no vision the people perish." Roosevelt sketched a new vision emphasizing creativity and achievement over the old and false "standard of success," material wealth. "The measure of the restoration," he predicted, "lies in the extent to which we can apply social values more noble than mere monetary profit."

Yet, the precise meaning of Roosevelt's new social vision was still not clear. While governor of New York, he had exercised the most original state leadership in the country, setting up public works projects and intensive relief programs. On the other hand, he was fairly unfamiliar with urban problems, having grown up in an upper-class, country atmosphere. He reportedly felt uncomfortable with city politicians and his battles with New York City's Tammany Hall revealed some of his distaste for urban machine politics. Yet he was the first national leader ever to integrate farmer and labor groups into a solid coalition. That alliance had been an old Populist dream, and only a dream. Labor leaders congratulated him on his governorship; farmers, more wary, still hoped that they might find a commitment to their interests. FDR seemed to have a genuine interest in getting what he considered a fairer "deal" for the poor and a dislike for the indifference of the wealthy to the effects of poverty.

His vague statements about crisis leadership as a moral and experimental endeavor were supplemented by other statements that indicated his future intentions a little more clearly. He believed especially in a strong executive. "The Great Presidents," he said, "were leaders of thought at times when certain historic ideas in the life of the nation had to be clarified."

Roosevelt, taking the reins of the new administration, expected a spirited debate over the limits of his executive authority. "It is to be hoped," he said in his inaugural speech, "that the normal balance of executive and legislative authority may be wholly adequate to meet the unprecedented task before us. But it may be that an unprecedented demand and need for undelayed action may call for temporary departure from that normal balance of public procedure"

The President's economic thought, influenced by economists in the Brain Trust, centered on the idea that the trend toward economic concentration had rendered obsolescent a hands-off policy by the federal government. They pointed out that the trusts tended to raise prices to a point where demand naturally fell. Concentration of industrial power had destroyed the supply-demand cycle which was the theoretical virtue of a laissez-faire economy. Adolf A. Berle emphasized the "moral bankruptcy" of concentrated, noncompetitive businesses as part and parcel of their "financial bankruptcy." It was implicit that concentrated business power called for a more concentrated federal effort to counteract it. According to these men, a free, competitive economy had died when modern corporations had ceased to be competitive.

THE "HUNDRED DAYS" BEGINS

Before Roosevelt assumed office, he and Moley met with Hoover to discuss the economy. Hoover wanted a commitment to a balanced budget, no inflation of the currency, and a scaling down of international debts owed to the United States. However, the President-elect would not commit himself to a specific policy until he had the reins of power, and he actually did not agree with Hoover's analysis of the causes of and remedies for the depression. The "unprecedented demand and need for undelayed action" was no mere rhetorical phrase. On the day Roosevelt took office, the economy was at its lowest point, with a new bank panic well under way. During the election, arguments over whether or not the RFC was working had brought demands for a public airing of its records. When the names of the banks supported by the RFC were exposed, all the good the agency was supposed to do them evaporated. Depositors began runs on the very banks the RFC had been designed to protect. Panic also spread as a result of uncertainty about Roosevelt's intentions, and Hoover claimed that the new panic was due to business fear of future Democratic policies.

By the eve of the inauguration, March 3, banking in the United States was on the verge of total ruin. A mass run on the banks was expected the next morning. Neither Roosevelt nor Hoover was willing in the interim hours to take the responsibility for declaring a bank holiday on March 4. Hoover did not think he had the legal power, and Roosevelt was unwilling to announce a policy until he was officially President. Earlier in the year, such holidays had already been imposed by state governors in Nevada, Michigan, and some Midwestern states. At four in the morning of March 4, Governor Lehman finally broke the spell and ordered that all New York banks be closed for two days. The governors of eighteen other states soon followed suit. As a result, when Roosevelt offered his assurance that "the only thing we have to fear is fear itself," he was talking in part about the psychological panic that darkened his first inauguration.

In the first hours of his Presidency, Roosevelt decided to use an old law, the Trading

With the Enemy Act of 1917, to try to stabilize temporarily the nation's banking problems. It gave the President authority to declare a national bank holiday and to put an embargo on gold exports. On March 6, Roosevelt proclaimed the holiday.

Congress convened on March 9, for a session that was to last till June 19 and which deluged the nation with new legislation. An atmosphere of improvisational frenzy prevailed during this Congressional session that came to be called the "Hundred Days." Because of the panic, Roosevelt had virtually a free hand with the legislators. The Banking Relief Act of March 9 was passed in a few hours. It approved Roosevelt's "holiday" declaration, extended the supportive powers of the RFC, ended hoarding by calling all gold and gold certificates into the Treasury, provided for the inspection of banks and the reopening of those that were solvent, and authorized "the twelve Federal Reserve banks to issue additional currency on good assets," thus inflating the currency.

"The new currency is being sent out by the Bureau of Engraving and Printing in large volume to every part of the country," he told the country over the radio in his first "fireside chat" on March 12. "It is sound money because it is backed by actual, good assets." The talk was calculated to explain to the average man the meaning of the intricate financial crisis, and more significantly, to reassure him that things would be all right. Roosevelt's dazzling impromptu style in the emergency worked superbly. The banks were quickly inspected, with the majority of them declared solvent and reopened on March 15. The panic did not return. "In one week," Walter Lippmann declared, "the nation, which had lost confidence in everything and everybody, has regained confidence in the government and in itself."

The first crisis past, Roosevelt had to turn his attention to the main tasks of relief and re-employment. At the same time, still suspicious of the theory that deficit spending was not only permissible but necessary in times of depression, he took steps to keep the budget balanced. The Economy Act of March 20 slashed salaries of government workers by 15 percent, slimmed down overgrown government agencies, and reduced veterans' pensions and allowances. This last clause brought a new expedition of the Bonus Army to Washington. This time the President offered the people meals and coffee, and medical aid. There was even a visit from the First Lady. These efforts had the beneficial effect of defusing the protest.

Roosevelt also moved quickly toward repeal of prohibition, hoping to increase government revenues with liquor taxes. On March 13, he asked Congress for "immediate modification of the Volstead Act, in order to legalize the manufacture and sale of beer and other beverages of such alcoholic content as is permissible under the Constitution; and to provide through such manufacture and sale, by substantial taxes, a proper and much needed source of revenue for the Government." Repeal had been a campaign promise. The ending of prohibition on December 5, with passage of the Twenty-first Amendment, brought in some revenue. But such small attempts at economy actually had little effect in the wake of the extensive relief legislation that was to be enacted during the "Hundred Days."

GOING OFF THE GOLD STANDARD

With the advent of depression, old silverite demands for inflation of the currency revived. Great Britain was forced off the gold standard in 1931, and international negotiations began for the purpose of re-establishing it. However, Roosevelt believed that high prices in the United States would be a critical factor in ending the depression. As a result, he threw a wrench into efforts being made at the London Economic Conference to revive the gold standard when he decried the "old fetishes of so-called international bankers," and made it clear that the United States would coin silver if necessary. "The sound internal economic system of a nation is a greater factor," he insisted, "than the price of its currency in changing terms of the currencies of other nations." It was the old Bryanite argument in slightly more sophisticated language. What counted to the President was the distribution of wealth inside the country not the theoretical value of the dollar vis-à-vis the pound or the franc. If an inflated currency would raise prices within the country and ease internal suffering, then that was the best policy to follow.

On January 30, 1934, the United States officially went off the gold standard and devalued the dollar. The price of gold was set at a new rate of 35 dollars an ounce, and each dollar was worth approximately 60 percent of what it had been under the gold standard. The move was motivated in part by a desire to appease farmers and avoid agrarian revolt. Farmers in debt profited from the cheaper dollar. With more money in circulation, it was easier to pay off creditors. At the same time, however, the government began to purchase silver to back the dollar, which had the effect of producing only a mildly inflated currency and had the support of leading bankers.

While the New Deal was trying to increase the public's buying power, it was also concerned with protecting the public's money once it was invested. In June, 1933, Congress passed the Glass-Steagall Act. It increased the powers of the Federal Reserve Board over expansion of credit by member banks and established the Federal Deposit Insurance Corporation (FDIC) which guaranteed individual bank accounts and could reorganize insured banks that failed. Deposits were at first guaranteed up to 2,500 dollars. By 1970 they were guaranteed to 20,000 dollars. The Banking Act of 1935 reorganized the Federal Reserve Board and gave it more authority over rediscount rates and market operations of member banks. Thus, the government now had more control over monetary policy and the volume of credit available.

The investigations of the Senate Banking and Currency Committee between 1932 and 1934 also exposed the extent of corrupt manipulations on the stock exchange. The result was new legislation to protect the public from fraud and misrepresentation in the sale of securities. All stocks for sale in interstate commerce had to be listed with the Federal Trade Commission, and the Securities Exchange Act of June, 1934, set up a five-man Securities and Exchange Commission to license stock exchanges, to prevent pools and price manipulation, and require registration of securities listed on the exchange. Though long-time Wall Street operators disliked the SEC, some younger men noted that it helped restore confidence in the market. The first SEC chairman was Joseph P. Kennedy, father of the future President. Though a Roosevelt supporter, Kennedy was a successful businessman, whose presence reassured Wall Street that the government was not trying to destroy capitalism.

THE AAA

At a press conference on March 13, Roosevelt told newsmen that the first three measures—rescue, the economy bill, and the beer tax—"shall still have done nothing on the constructive side" once they were enacted, "unless," he joked, "you consider the beer bill partly constructive." He indicated that he was in the process of formulating some genuinely constructive plans, the first of which was "a definite effort to put people to work," and the second "an effort to increase the value of farm products."

The presence of a huge farm surplus was perhaps the greatest irony of the depression. While millions in urban areas could not get enough to eat, farmers were impoverished because they produced too much and were unable to market it. The process of distri-

bution had collapsed. "It remained for us," Norman Thomas said in 1934, "to invent 'bread-lines knee-deep in wheat.'" Voluntary crop reduction had proved to be unworkable, given the farmer's fear that he would starve if he did not successfully compete for what market there was.

Dispute flourished in the first months of the New Deal over the type of program best suited to raise prices on agricultural goods. George Peek, who had been a sponsor of the McNary-Haugen bill, advocated the old plan of high prices at home and dumping the surplus abroad at the cheaper world market price. Roosevelt's Secretary of Agriculture, Henry A. Wallace, much preferred a plan whereby farmers would be paid to curtail production. He believed planned scarcity would bring prices up. Peek's plan was popular among smaller, poorer farmers, who would not be helped as much by curtailment as they would by sales at higher prices. Large farmers producing staple crops were more favorable to the Wallace plan.

During the debate, agricultural discontent again spilled over into violence. Farmers organized against foreclosures on farms nearly lynched an Iowa judge. There was talk of an agrarian revolt. The Farmers' Holiday Association prepared to strike unless the federal government offered direct relief to threatened farmers. The proposed crop reduction seemed to them too market-oriented, not people-oriented. In June, the Farm Credit Act met their demands part way, consolidating earlier farm boards and setting up an extensive system of loans for mortgages, production and marketing, and for buying back property.

The Agricultural Adjustment Act of May, 1933, with elements of compromise, was essentially the Wallace plan. The aim was "parity," or price levels that would restore the real buying power of the farmer until it was roughly equivalent to that of 1909 to 1914, years when farmers earned a reasonably high fraction of the gross national income. The method to be used was to buy and hold surpluses and to pay farmers to destroy excess crops. Agreements by farmers to reduce their acreages under cultivation would make the system work. The original list of products which included cotton, wheat, corn, tobacco, rice, hogs, and milk was later expanded. Faced by an imminent bumper crop of cotton, AAA agents worked hard to get compliance from Southern farmers. Those who agreed to reduce production were paid between 6 dollars and 20 dollars per nonproductive acre. Money for the payments came from taxes on food processors, so that consumers ended up paying the cost of destroying crops.

The nation's hog surplus was dealt with in a similar way. Hundreds of thousands of hogs were slaughtered, and some of the meat was distributed to relief rolls. But public indignation was aroused against the technique. It seemed absurd and unnatural to destroy food surpluses in a nation where hunger was still a problem, merely to preserve the marketability of food. Leftists in particular pointed to the solution as an example of capitalist madness. The Farmers' Holiday Association, enraged at the waste, the continuing hunger, and the failure of the AAA to aid the small farmer, threatened another strike.

Yet in the next three years farm income started to rise. To try to end continuing overproduction by farmers using new fertilizers, new legislation laid down mandatory quotas and penalties for overproduction of agricultural produce sold in interstate commerce. The AAA policy was helped along by the "dust bowl" tragedy of widespread drought in the Plains states in 1934. Wheat output dropped by about 300 million bushels during the period 1933 to 1935. Livestock perished. The disaster, though destructive of the livelihood of many people, had the positive effect of raising the income of those farmers who survived it. By 1936 farm income had risen to near parity.

INDUSTRIAL PLANNING

In Roosevelt's public papers there is the following note. "I think it can be safely said that there was not a major industry in the United States in April of 1933 that was not suffering either from overproduction, or its counterpart, underconsumption, or destructive competition or unfair practices or lack of any comprehensive planning. This was the low point in industrial activity. National income of $80 billion in 1929 had dropped to $38 billion in 1932 . . . Employment had decreased 40 percent and payrolls 60 percent." The President then went on to discuss his solutions. Rational planning, shorter hours, a minimum wage to boost consumption and relieve misery, and the expenditure of about 3.3 billion dollars on public works would all be key factors in national recovery.

During the First World War and throughout the 1920s business and government had allied successfully to increase production. Some of Roosevelt's advisers such as Rexford Tugwell thought that a similar but government-directed alliance would meet the new crisis. In keeping with the theory that competition was outmoded, and that creative national planning ought to be the hallmark of the new administration, the Brain Trust recommended that antitrust laws be discarded. Instead each industry would have its own production quotas and prices worked out in the public interest. The experiment also would include modernized labor codes which all the producers within any industry would agree to. The only reason for the prevalence of such brutal practices as child labor, sweatshops, long hours, and low wages was that they saved money. There were still women working in sweatshops who earned less than 2 dollars for a 60-hour week. Across-the-board wage increases would alleviate such misery.

The bill offered to Congress by the administration provided for the "organization

Cover of the sheet music inspired by the National Recovery Administration.

of industry for the purpose of co-operative action among trade groups." Another section of the bill appropriated 3.3 billion dollars for a Public Works Administration (PWA), which would provide jobs by putting people to work building large public facilities such as dams, highways, post offices, courthouses, naval vessels, army camps, hospitals, schools, and parks.

The National Industrial Recovery Act (NRA) was passed on June 16, 1933. It was a double-barreled effort to stimulate industry and at the same time institute social reform. The controversial section 7a of Title I guaranteed laborers the right to collective bargaining, shorter hours, and minimum wages. When the companies in any industry or trade association had worked out a code of fair competition which standardized behavior in that industry, they could then display the NRA sym-

bol, the Blue Eagle. Ninety-five percent of American business was ultimately involved but only tremendous pressure by the NRA brought about codes for labor which provided for a 35-hour week, a minimum wage of 30 cents an hour, no child labor, and the right of labor to bargain collectively. In the following months, the effort to create a government partnership with business ran into difficulties. There were numerous charges that the NRA under General Hugh Johnson's direction encouraged monopolies and price-fixing, its antitrust provisions allowing industries to police themselves. Although the purpose of the law was to increase purchasing power, appeals for moderate prices did not seem to work. Prices began to climb immediately. Moreover, the large corporations had many strategies for evading the collective bargaining guarantee. The National Labor Relations Board, set up to mediate labor disputes, showed little interest in collective bargaining. Encouraged by passage of section 7a, but enraged by corporate efforts to find loopholes in it, union organizers redoubled their calls for strikes in 1933.

The legacy of the NRA was a mixed one. Some called it the National Run Around. Its theory of cooperation among government, business, and labor was popular with some of Roosevelt's economists like Rexford Tugwell who believed in a planned economy. It was national planning with some industrial self-regulation. But in practice it led to monopoly in some industries and increased animosity between business and labor. Everyone resented its controls, and consumers thought it raised prices. Johnson did not prove to be a strong administrator and government crackdown on violators was weak. Yet it did help stop deflation and put the government behind minimum wages, maximum hours, an end to child labor, and the right of labor to organize. It also helped industry speed up production and increased purchasing power in the country.

RELIEF AND CONSERVATION

The most popular moves of the first New Deal were those designed to give direct relief to people, and to institute some federal ownership of public utilities. The Home Owners' Loan Act saved more than a million families from eviction by refinancing home mortgages. The Federal Emergency Relief Act of May, 1933, directed by Harry Hopkins, provided extensive federal aid for state relief programs. It was a compromise between the old principle of local control and the obvious need for federal revenue by giving one dollar of federal money for every three provided by local funds. It poured more than a half billion dollars into local relief efforts.

More extensive and newsworthy than these acts were the Civilian Conservation Corps (CCC) and the Tennessee Valley Authority (TVA). With these operations the federal government was able to merge two ideas of the New Deal: federal responsibility for economic development and conservation, and federal responsibility to offer people work in depression times.

CIVILIAN CONSERVATION CORPS

The CCC provided work for some of the millions of jobless young men, though it was not a major factor in reducing unemployment. Men usually between the ages of 17 and 25 were hired on a temporary basis to work on forestation and park projects between 1933 and 1942. They helped add over 17 million acres of new forest to the American landscape during the decade (especially important in the Middle West and Plains states swept by dust storms and drought in 1934), and worked also to prevent fires, blight, soil erosion, and to improve fisheries and reservoirs. Most of what they earned was sent back to their families. The CCC was especially popular with those who feared an increase in juvenile delinquency because of the depression.

FDR himself heralded the program as a means of preserving the moral and physical fiber of the youth of the nation.

TENNESSEE VALLEY AUTHORITY

The creation of the Tennessee Valley Authority was more controversial because it was a long range reform project, not just a relief measure. The Tennessee Valley, extending into seven states, became the site of the New Deal's major experiment in regional planning. The economy of the area had been chronically depressed since the Civil War. Under the TVA the government ultimately built new dams in a seven-state area and supplied electrical power, at rates lower than those charged by private utilities. Between 1934 and 1940 the number of farms in the area receiving electricity more than quadrupled. But both the utility interests and conservative theorists denounced the TVA as socialistic, unfair competition with private producers, and a violation of the Constitution. However, in a test case in 1936, the Supreme Court ruled that the federal government was operating within constitutional limits. Although the TVA became one of the largest utilities in the nation by 1950, it never accounted for more than a fraction of the entire industry, the rest of which still lay in private hands.

The TVA was much more than a project to produce electricity. It also included flood control, inland navigation, resettlement projects, advice on scientific farming, reforestation projects, industrial diversification, public health projects, and even some attempts to promote culture and recreation. It was also a breakthrough in government policy, insofar as it represented public control of public utilities, and an attempt to improve the lives of people by rational planning that transcended state boundaries. When Roosevelt proposed similar projects for six other regions in 1937, Congress refused to act. However, such individual projects as the Hoover Dam on the Colorado River and the Grand Coulee Dam on the Columbia River were completed at government expense. The TVA exemplified one of those "historic ideas in the life of the nation" of which Roosevelt had spoken earlier. It was a forerunner of other government reforms that would become part of New Deal policy from 1935 onward.

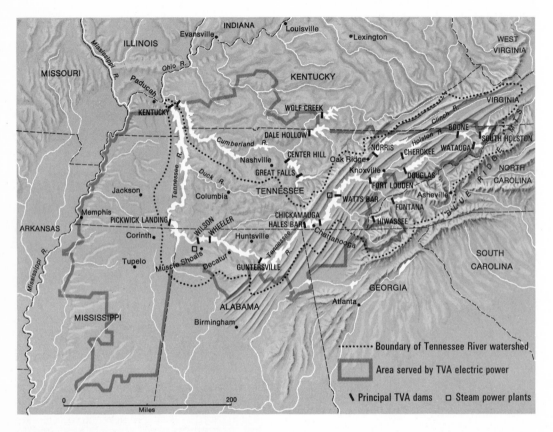

THE TENNESSEE VALLEY AUTHORITY

THE NEW DEAL TURNS LEFT

THE NEW SECURITY

The immediate success of the early months of the New Deal had made Roosevelt a national hero. Bankers and business-men, terrified by what seemed like their "day of judgment," had allowed Roosevelt a free hand during the panic. And the President, despite his early attacks on the "money-changers," was in practice still trying to halt the depression only by expanding traditional methods of stimulating industry and offering public relief projects. It was emergency legislation, not permanent reform.

By 1935, however, continued unemployment and the pressure of labor for reform, widespread hatred of Roosevelt among businessmen, agrarian unrest, the rise of popular demagogic movements, and attacks on New Deal legislation by the Supreme Court led Roosevelt to try to reinforce his popularity with the majority of Americans by adopting a more comprehensive approach to reform. What has come to be known as the Second New Deal was more far-reaching and permanent in its results than most of Roosevelt's earlier policies. The landmarks of the new reform were (1) passage of permanent welfare legislation, in the form of the Social Security Act; (2) more effective guarantees of the right of laborers to bargain collectively, which was followed by the subsequent growth and respectability of unionism; (3) heavier taxes on corporations and on the wealthy; (4) further curbs on trusts and holding companies; (5) continued public projects making the federal government the bulwark of the economy and the employer of millions; (6) open acceptance of the policy of deficit spending, which was necessary to finance the new federal activities.

Washington, with all the new agencies with their abbreviated names—the AAA, CCC, NRA, PWA, and TVA—was overflowing its limited facilities. As the number of government agencies increased, so did criticism of the New Deal by businessmen and economic conservatives generally. Al Smith called it "alphabet soup." Although Roosevelt's ally in former years, he felt cheated out of the Presidency in 1932 and became one of the New Deal's most bitter critics. While former President Hoover called the NRA "pure fascism," Al Smith joined with big businessmen like Du Pont to foster the American Liberty League,

which denounced Roosevelt's "radicalism." Whether the label was radical or fascist, the criticism was essentially the same: Roosevelt was turning the United States government into a bureaucratic maze, his centralizing policies threatened the freedom of Americans to run their own lives, and the New Deal would turn the American people into a breed of spongers and government employees.

Roosevelt seems to have accepted business antipathy as a fact of his political life; indeed, the contempt was mutual. Clarence Darrow, who had investigated and reported on the NRA, charged that with the erasure of the old antitrust laws the business world had been delivered "into the hands of its greatest and most ruthless units." Roosevelt did not accept Darrow's hysteria but soon realized that the NRA protected neither workers nor small business men, and came to believe that the myopia of the business community made a creative business-government partnership impossible. "I get more and more convinced that most of them can't see farther than the next dividend," he said privately.

Brain Trusters like Raymond Moley and Rexford Tugwell who had worked on the partnership with business gradually disappeared from Roosevelt's bevy of counselors. Hugh Johnson and George Peek also left. As they departed, a new group of advisers came into prominence dedicated to reforming American economic life. Thomas Corcoran, Benjamin Cohen, Marriner Eccles, and Harry Hopkins became central figures in New Deal planning. Hopkins was a social worker dedicated to the theory that simple handouts were degrading, that the dignity and health of the people should be kept up by work on public projects.

DEMAGOGUES IN OPPOSITION

The disaffection of businessmen combined with the mounting tide of demands

931

for more economic reform to persuade Roosevelt he had to act to stay in office. Three popular movements seem to have had special influence on FDR's decision. The first was led by Huey Long, who had forged a powerful and dictatorial political machine in Louisiana. Roosevelt considered him the most dangerous man in the country. Long demanded programs that went under the slogans "Share the wealth," and "Soak the rich." He called for old-age pensions, free education, and a minimum income of five thousand dollars a year per family. Under his authoritarian rule, Louisiana had been modernized; hospitals, schools, and other public facilities were constructed, and to some extent he did attack the big corporations. Long was popular around the country. A combination Robin Hood and petty dictator, he ran Louisiana according to personal whim. Only his assassination in 1935 prevented a struggle with Roosevelt for control of the Democratic Party, particularly its Southern wing. Had Long lived to run on a third-party ticket, he might have drawn millions of votes and even deprived Roosevelt of reelection. His influence, at least, would have been felt in the White House. Roosevelt's reform legislation, though by no means a simple concession to Long, had the political value of defusing the threat of his popularity.

There were other American demagogues at the time whose programs had fascist overtones. Father Coughlin, a Roman Catholic priest and ally of Huey Long, spread his proto-fascist and racist ideas by radio, earning the title "the radio priest." At first Coughlin had supported Roosevelt enthusiastically but by 1935 was denouncing capitalism, the New Deal, Wall Street, Jews, and communists as the causes of American economic troubles. He was sympathetic to Italian fascism and favored the nationalization of some industries and a minimum wage. He, like Long, had a large following among the lower middle class of old immigrant stock.

Another important challenger of New Deal policies was Dr. Francis E. Townsend, more benign and generous by nature than either Long or Coughlin. He won support among the elderly when he proposed a pension plan that would give every citizen over the age of sixty 200 dollars a month, provided that every penny was spent. Years later, Townsend reflected on the American ideal of struggling individualism, and said with more than a trace of pathos, ". . . there comes a time when people can't hustle any more"—a retrospective comment not only on the elderly, but on the entire era. People were tired of a competitive fervor that had ended in economic disaster and wanted more security. At first Townsend was thought of as a joke, but he soon rallied millions of supporters, and the resulting political pressure encouraged the administration toward passage of the Social Security Act in 1935.

CONSERVATIVE OPPOSITION: THE SUPREME COURT

Economic misery fueled the extreme demands of Coughlin, Townsend, and Long. Unemployment was still high, and small businessmen and tenant farmers were in desperate straits. The upturn in the economy had mainly helped large companies. Farmers of the Great Plains were particularly victimized by the dust storms, and families died or moved en masse. "The wind increases its velocity until it is blowing at forty or fifty miles an hour," wrote a Kansas wheat farmer, Lawrence Svoboda. "Soon everything is moving, the land is blowing . . . The fine dirt is sweeping along at express-train speed."

In 1935, the same year that radical demands and economic misery reached a new and dangerous peak, the Supreme Court, dominated by economic conservatives, began to dispose of some of Roosevelt's earliest programs, trying to turn back the tide of federal concentration and intervention. The majority of the judges were opposed to the New Deal social philosophy and the increase of federal power at the expense of the states. They thought they were trying to save the country from itself. One of the most significant series of judgments came in May, 1935. The Court overturned the NRA in *Schechter v. United States,* or the so-called "sick chicken" case. The Schechter brothers of Brooklyn had challenged the right of the NRA to enforce the Live Poultry Code, which regulated the wages and hours of their employees and prohibited the distribution of chickens allegedly diseased and unfit for consumption. The Court arrived at its decision on the grounds that a federal agency like the NRA could have no jurisdiction over intrastate commerce and that Congress had made an illegal delegation of power to a federal agency because they had failed to provide it with proper guidelines for operation. On the same day, the Court rebuked Roosevelt for illegally exercising his power of removal in the dismissal of a member of the Federal Trade Commission. It also held that creditors were unconstitutionally deprived of their property rights by the Frazier-Lemke Act of 1934, which had been designed to prevent foreclosures on farms.

LEGISLATION OF THE SECOND NEW DEAL

The Congressional elections of 1934 gave FDR the mandate he wanted. In the Senate, the Democrats gained nine seats and in the House their majority rose from 313 to 322. The GOP was at the lowest point in its history with only seven governors and twenty-five Senators.

The great legislative output of the Second New Deal began in 1935. In April Congress appropriated 1.4 billion dollars for the Works Progress Administration (later renamed the Works Projects Administration) to be run by Harry Hopkins.

Debate between Hopkins and Harold Ickes, the head of the Public Works Administration, over welfare policy ended in diverse approaches being followed by their two agencies. Ickes believed in careful and slow consideration of proposed projects, even if it meant delay and reduced employment, and he followed this approach with the PWA. Hopkins, on the other hand, saw the WPA as essentially a dignified form of relief and gave employment priority over architectural perfection. Most WPA funds were spent on wages, not equipment. For the remainder of the decade the WPA employed millions on small-scale projects such as road building, flood control dams, parks and playgrounds, schools, and libraries. It also included adult education classes, provided free lunches for children, and sponsored medical and dental clinics. Its most controversial activities were projects in the arts, giving writers, photographers, theater

Drought and high winds created the Dust Bowl and forced many farmers who were already poor to leave the Plains states.

groups, and others a chance to do work in the middle of an era of depression and recovery.

Two other offshoots of the relief program also came into being the same year. The Resettlement Administration under Rexford Tugwell operated for two years to try to aid tenant farmers, sharecroppers, and migrant laborers. It extended credit to poor farm families and resettled them on better land. It also sold farms on easy terms. It helped a few poor farmers but not nearly the number it had hoped to provide for. More successful was the Rural Electrification Administration which provided low interest loans and relief labor for spreading electrical power to farm homes not served by private utilities. By the 1950s, nine out of every ten American farms had electricity, mainly the result of REA support.

Two bills which passed in 1935 were a direct reflection of antimonopoly sentiment among Roosevelt's advisers. The Public Utility Holding Company Act restricted the concentration of economic power in a few hands in the electric and gas companies. Samuel Insull's holding pyramid in electric utilities had collapsed in 1932 and contributed to the panic later that year. The new act gave the government the power to dissolve inefficient holding companies and put financial practices of holding companies under the SEC. A Federal Power Commission regulated the interstate transmission of electricity. The Wealth Tax Act was a modified effort by the Roosevelt administration to tax the rich for social purposes. In addition to a graduated corporation income tax, there was an excess profits

Farmers fleeing the Dust Bowl from Oklahoma and other Plains states were forced to live in such places as this California migrant camp.

tax, and higher income and estate taxes on the wealthy.

The Social Security Act, signed by Roosevelt on August 14, 1935, was the landmark of the period. It provided a system of pensions for the retired, unemployment insurance, and care for the dependent and disabled. To provide pensions, employers matched small deductions from workers' wages with equal payment. Unemployment insurance came from funds from a federal tax on employers' payrolls. Federal grants were also made to the states to match state support for the dependent and disabled. The small original benefits were boosted over the years as were the categories of people to be covered. But the principle of government responsibility for the welfare of the aged and the jobless was now permanently institutionalized.

Opposition to the Social Security Act came from several quarters. Followers of Townsend criticized it for providing extremely skimpy pensions. In the 1936 campaign, the Republicans tried unsuccessfully to capitalize on the resentments and fears of workers at the hardship of even the small deductions in depression times. Since the act provided that money then being deducted would not be repaid until future joblessness or old age, some workers were suspicious that they might never be paid back at all, if unstable times brought still more changes in government policy.

The death of the NRA in the Supreme Court left a gap in protecting the unions that New Deal planners believed had to be filled. The Wagner Labor Relations Act of 1935, stalled for a year in Congress, finally won approval. It reinstituted section 7a, assuring strong government protection of the exclusive right to collective bargaining by labor unions. The act also forbade management to interfere with unionizing and outlawed company unions. A National Labor Relations Board (NLRB) was set up to hear complaints and could issue cease-and-desist orders enforceable in federal courts. Many union organizers regarded it as a turning point in American labor union history.

GROWTH OF ORGANIZED LABOR

Union organizers had found encouragement from New Deal legislation, especially the Wagner Act, and union membership grew to about 8.5 million by 1940. However, this new wave of activity was not without conflicts within the labor movement itself. Until the 1930s, the American Federation of Labor had dominated the movement. Under the leadership of William Green, who became president at Gompers' death in 1924, it continued to operate on the fundamental premises of trade and craft unionism. As a result, large numbers of workers in industries such as the automobile, steel, and textiles, and on mass-production lines in factories all over the country, still had no union organization.

A new movement seemed inevitable, and John L. Lewis of the United Mine Workers led an attack on the AF of L when its conservative leadership refused to accept a drive toward industrial unionism.

The Committee for Industrial Organization (CIO) was then organized in November, 1935. The AF of L was against the new group and expelled all the industrial unions in 1937. Now calling itself the Congress of Industrial Organizations, it maintained a separate labor movement until 1955.

Lewis represented a more leftward impulse in American unionism, and accepted the support of communist organizers when it was practical to do so. In the next few years a whole series of unions left the AF of L for the new organization while millions of workers previously unorganized joined the CIO. Intellectuals and professionals tended to prefer the industrial, mass-movement approach of the CIO, and some formed professional unions which were affiliated with it.

A recession during 1937 and 1938 found Lewis leading an unprecedented number of strikes in an effort to force giant corporations, particularly those in the automobile and steel industries, to recognize the union as bargaining agent for their workers. Among the tactics that were used was the sit-down strike, earlier introduced to the United States by the IWW. There was a dramatic air of sabotage to the new method. Instead of leaving the plant, workers stopped working and remained where they were, immobilizing everything, making the hiring of scabs more difficult, and sometimes defying attempts at ouster. The United Automobile Workers (UAW) won recognition from Chrysler and General Motors in 1937. But Henry Ford was recalcitrant and fought the UAW with all possible devices, such as the use of spies and hired thugs. However, he was finally forced to capitulate in 1941 and accept the union as the bargaining agent for his workers.

However, it was the steel industry that suffered the worst labor crisis in the late 1930s. Less centralized into giant corporations than the automotive industry, steel was divided into two groups: "Big Steel," or United States Steel, and "Little Steel," such as Republic and Bethlehem. Competition between these two groups had destructive side-effects. When U.S. Steel signed a contract with the Steel Workers' Organizing Committee in March, 1937, "Little Steel" unexpectedly balked at following suit. Bitter and violent strikes followed with the police killing ten strikers outside Republic Steel's South Chicago plant. In spite of reports decrying police brutality, a large segment of the public blamed the CIO's radical tactics for the violence. It was not until 1941 that Little Steel signed contracts with the union.

THE PHILOSOPHY OF THE SECOND NEW DEAL

"The cat is out of the bag," Rexford Tugwell had said in 1933. "There is no invisible hand. There never was. If the depression has not taught us that, we are incapable of education. . . . We must now supply a real and visible guiding hand to do the task which that mythical, nonexistent, invisible agency was supposed to perform, but never did."

The fundamental premise of this statement was that the federal government had to become the rational force regulating supply and demand to meet the public's needs. According to laissez-faire economic theory, supply and demand had regulated themselves, in a way beneficial to the community. That supply and demand would adjust to each other in the activities of the market place was considered a natural law that ruled the relationship between productivity and needs. To interfere with it would upset the natural order. The fundamental premise of the first New Deal had been that when a decline in private spending brought depression, it was the obligation of the government to increase public spending. The emphasis had been on relief and recovery. During the second New Deal, this premise was extended. Government spending became a more or less permanent fixture of the economy, though it would vary with the business cycle. Government spending was to be used to reform the economy. People were to be guaranteed minimal economic security permanently.

Though most New Deal laws were made intuitively and not according to any carefully reasoned theory, historians later saw a connection with the ideas of the economist John Maynard Keynes. Keynes wished to preserve economic freedom and at the same time eliminate the boom and bust of the business cycle. He regarded socialist control of the economy as oppressive and laissez-faire capitalism as unrealistic and dangerous. The middle way was a flexible government response to fluctuations in the business cycle. When necessary, the government would increase spending, pouring in money and providing work until the crises lifted. Government spending would safeguard democracy by relieving misery. Some New Dealers embraced Keynesian economics as a defense of their policies after the fact, but the ideas of the British economist had little direct effect on New Deal planning.

While the second New Deal extended the concept of government spending, there was also a movement away from the dream of Moley and Tugwell of total national economic planning as manifested in the NRA and AAA. Roosevelt's new advisers were less interested in national planning to end destructive competition than using the power of the federal government to extend social welfare while at the same time attacking economic monopoly. In theory, they would have liked to return the United States to a completely competitive economy. While this desire was economically naive by the 1930s, it did provide the framework for tougher reform legislation.

THE CLIMAX OF THE NEW DEAL

THE ELECTION OF 1936

Congressional elections in 1934 had brought more Democratic victories and given Roosevelt even more command over the legislature. But the reaction from the Supreme Court in 1935, in declaring some of the major legislation of the first New Deal unconstitutional, clarified and focused opposing outlooks in the country. The lines

of battle were drawn for the next campaign. Roosevelt abandoned his early effort to build a fully national coalition of farmers, laborers, and businessmen. "I welcome their hatred," he said about businessmen in the campaign. "I should like to have it said of my second administration that in it these forces met their master."

The Republicans could rely on a small but solid conservative vote marked by hatred of big government, the new unionism, and higher taxes. In spite of the fact that corporate taxes had not increased too dramatically since the aim of the New Deal was to encourage investment and circulation of capital, the rich had suffered extreme increases in personal income taxes. A typical cartoon of the period showed a wealthy old man, apoplectically rising from his chair, while his children reminded him of the doctor's warning not to talk about FDR.

The Republicans accordingly began a vast and well-funded attack on the New Deal. The Republican National Committee described the election as a chance for the voters to prevent the growth of "a socialistic state honeycombed with waste and extravagance and ruled by a dictatorship that mocks the rights of the States and the Liberty of the citizen." "America is in peril," the party platform warned.

The Republicans needed more than the support of the wealthy to win the election. Though they spent large sums in an effort to arouse popular unrest against the New Deal and enjoyed the support of the majority of newspapers in the country, the Democrats, too, had an organization able to collect equally vast sums. Although lacking strong support among businessmen and economic conservatives in both parties, Roosevelt's policies had secured for the Democrats a new and formidable coalition by 1936. Substantial prosperity had returned even with seven million still unemployed. Roosevelt could now count on widespread support from organized labor, farmers, black Americans, young business and professional people, intellectuals, and urban groups of new immigrant background. Roosevelt also had the traditional support of the Democratic machines north and south, support not always personally to his taste but politically welcome. The CIO alone contributed 770,000 dollars to the campaign.

The Republicans chose Alfred M. Landon of Kansas, a man whose Midwestern, "folksy" aura they hoped would bring in the farm bloc. Landon was a conservative with a reputation for balancing the Kansas budget during his governorship. However, the balanced budget was in part the result of 400 million dollars in federal money acquired under New Deal programs.

The Democrats quickly renominated Roosevelt and discarded the tradition of the two-thirds majority needed to nominate a candidate. This break with tradition effectively ended the stranglehold of Southern delegates on the party during future conventions. In their platform, the Democrats endorsed the New Deal and answered Republican charges by arguing that local governments were inadequate to meet the national crisis.

Roosevelt put on a magnificent campaign. He toured the country, gathering record numbers wherever he went. Landon turned out to be a disappointingly poor campaigner with little political glamour. He had the support of about 70 percent of the press, Hearst included, and there was so much publicity for him that some believed the *Literary Digest* straw poll predicting his victory. But Roosevelt, with Huey Long out of the way, and Socialist and Communist candidates taking much less of the vote than in 1932, won every state but two. Roosevelt had a margin of more than eleven million in the popular vote and a vote of 523 to 8 in the electoral college. It was the greatest landslide in American history to that time. The Democrats had become the majority party for the first time since 1860.

THE SUPREME COURT FIGHT

The federal government was now deeply split ideologically. On one side was a reformist administration backed by an unprecedented popular mandate, and on the other a conservative Supreme Court, most of whose members were economic conservatives. In 1936 the Court had further threatened the New Deal by overturning the AAA. In *United States v. Butler,* it held that the government had improperly used the taxing power to regulate agriculture and not just to gain revenue. It was a tax for a special group and not for the general welfare. The Court also held a coal conservative act unconstitutional and overruled a New York State minimum wage law for women.

In his inaugural address of January 20, FDR reminded the nation that poverty persisted in spite of the business upturn. "I see one-third of a nation ill-housed, ill-clad, ill-nourished," he said. Hoping to complete the New Deal with additional legislation that would eradicate these conditions, he saw the Supreme Court as the only stumbling block. On February 5 he took the first step of his new administration. It was not a new piece of welfare legislation but a proposal to push older Justices into retirement.

Of the nine Justices in the 1937 Supreme Court, seven had been Republican appointees. Four of the nine had voted consistently to restrict government regulation of business, three had consistently supported it, and two, known as "swing men," had no consistent voting pattern and thus often determined the majority ruling. Six of the current Justices were over 70, and FDR had as yet appointed no one to the Court. As a means of changing the composition of the Court, Roosevelt proposed that each time a Justice over 70 failed to retire, the President might appoint a new man, thus increasing the size of the Court to as many as fifteen. While the size of the Court had been changed six times in the past, according to changing needs, the new proposal was clumsy and inefficient. The number of Justices might keep shifting. A man reaching the age of 70 would find himself under pressure to retire albeit on full salary. If he remained on the Court he might look self-willed. Moreover, in spite of the fact that Brandeis and Holmes had supported New Deal legislation, they were well past the proposed retirement age.

It was clear that FDR's scheme was a calculated political maneuver to change the ideological complexion of the Court and perhaps a threat to balanced government as established under the Constitution. A long national debate began on the measure. Republican charges that Roosevelt had a flair for dictatorship were given new life and he was accused of trying to "pack" the Court and destroy the Constitution. Many liberals joined the critics, and by the summer of 1937, when the bill died in the Senate Judiciary Committee, public opinion had turned against the proposal.

Though FDR, perhaps intoxicated by his landslide, had brought on himself the only major defeat of his political career, the Supreme Court also had changed direction during the months prior to the bill's annihilation. Justice Van Devanter, an arch foe of the New Deal, retired, and Justice Roberts, formerly a New Deal critic, now began upholding administration laws, inspiring the gibe, "A switch in time saves nine." During the coming years further retirements allowed Roosevelt to appoint new members more to his liking. He appointed, among others, Hugo Black of Alabama, who had won recognition for antitrust activities; Felix Frankfurter, a Harvard professor and earlier a consultant on New Deal legislation; and William O. Douglas, a Yale law professor who had served on the Securities and Exchange Commission. During the judicial crisis of 1937, and prior to these appointments, the Court had also

begun to change its attitude on New Deal legislation. It had reversed an earlier decision against the Wagner Act, holding in the *NLRB v. Jones and Laughlin Corp.* case that the government could regulate a manufacturing establishment whose products entered or affected interstate commerce. The Court also proved sympathetic to Social Security and minimum wage legislation, and allowed the federal government a free hand in such projects as TVA. In the case of *West Coast Hotel v. Parrish,* a Washington State minimum wage law was upheld as a valid use of the state police power.

Ironically, although the Court gave new sanction to the kind of legislation offered by the New Deal, the New Deal itself was losing support. The Supreme Court fight marked a turning point in Roosevelt's relations with Congress. He was now regarded more suspiciously and many of his proposals were turned down. The great period of creative legislation had ended.

THE END OF THE NEW DEAL

Roosevelt's legislative program floundered after passage in 1937 of a farm tenancy law and the first act ever passed by the federal government to provide slum clearance and low-income housing. Further attempts at legislation were blocked by the revival of political conservatism in Congress. Some Southern Democrats detested Roosevelt both for his statements against racism and for his expansion of federal government power. Their legislative alliance with Northern Republicans was a reflection of the changing national mood.

At the same time, the apparent recovery of 1935 and 1936 was suddenly checked by the 1937 recession. A business slump was compounded by Roosevelt's failure to continue earlier policies. In 1937 he suddenly decided to try to balance the budget again, by spending more than a billion dollars less on welfare and reform. At the same time taxes had increased, so that a substantial amount of money was withdrawn from circulation. Business confidence was low. The stock market declined again, and unemployment soared from six million back to ten million by 1938, near the level of the worst months of the earlier panic.

Debate within the administration caused indecision as to what course to follow. Some advisers, led by Secretary of the Treasury Henry Morgenthau, Jr., told Roosevelt that the new depression was the result of businessmen's fears that deficit spending would lead to inflation and new taxes. As a result, they had cut back investment and production, thus arriving at a self-fulfilling prophecy. Opposition to this view came from Harry Hopkins and Marriner Eccles, Chairman of the Board of Governors of the Federal Reserve System. They insisted that the 1937 lapse in spending was the cause of the decline in the economy and that a resumption of deficit spending would reverse the trend.

What appeared to be Roosevelt's resolution of the debate was to experiment with both strategies. After waiting for a while to see whether his budget-balancing policy would revive business confidence, he finally requested from Congress 5 billion dollars for new public works projects. After a year, the recession had ended and unemployment was down, but genuine prosperity did not return until the Second World War brought full employment. In 1940, there were still ten million people unemployed.

The last New Deal legislation came in 1938. FDR was finally able to secure a Fair Labor Standards Act which provided a minimum wage of 40 cents an hour and a 40-hour week by 1940, no child labor under 16, and time and a half for overtime work for laborers. In the same year a new AAA provided for a permanent soil conservation program and retained the concept of national acreage allotments in major staple crops with subsidies to farmers who

accepted production controls to keep their income at the parity level of 1909 to 1914. The government also provided for taking any surplus off the market and storing it for emergencies. The New Deal ended with a broad antitrust campaign. Congress authorized a Temporary National Economic Committee which lasted three years. The Committee's final report urged strengthening antitrust laws. Meanwhile the Justice Department instituted ninety-two antitrust suits. Only the Second World War ended the drive on monopolies.

The Democrats met with severe reversals in the Congressional elections of 1938 because of Roosevelt's ill-conceived plan to intervene in local contests to get rid of conservative Democrats. The party still controlled Congress after the elections, but the Republicans had made important gains and the conservative coalition of Northern Republicans and Southern Democrats had gained new strength.

THE SIGNIFICANCE OF THE NEW DEAL

The New Deal's response to the question of how to meet the greatest economic upheaval in the nation's history was a combination of traditional concepts and new innovations. New Deal planners were not of one mind as to how to solve the depression, and Roosevelt's experimental temperament allowed a flexible and sometimes disorganized approach to issues.

Much of the New Deal legislation had the flavor of the American past. It had the traditional American optimism and restored the faith of millions that the country could solve its economic problems. In purpose it echoed the Jeffersonian dream of government sympathy for all the people, not one special group. Some of it also reflected the Jacksonian philosophy of restoring equality. Yet, the New Deal was closer to the late nineteenth-century social gospel which stressed that ethics had to be based on concern for society and the Populist drive for monetary inflation and control of the stock market.

The New Deal also drew heavily on the sometimes conflicting concepts of the progressivism movement. However, unlike this early twentieth-century movement, the New Deal was more concerned with social and economic rather than moral reform. It followed Theodore Roosevelt's devotion to conservation in the TVA, soil, and reforestation programs. It followed his concept of the New Nationalism, the need to control bigness by government regulation, in the first New Deal programs of the NRA and AAA. These programs were also closely related to the close relationship between government and business during World War I and the welfare conservatism of the 1920s. The second New Deal was much closer to Wilson's concept of the New Freedom, an updated version of the Jacksonian dream of breaking up all monopolies. The Wagner Act, heavy taxes on high incomes, strengthening the Federal Reserve System, and antitrust suits were evidence of this tendency.

Yet, with all its relevance to past approaches to reform in America, the New Deal was at the same time a break with the past. It did not try to socialize the country as many of its critics charged, but it did superimpose a welfare state on a capitalist economy. No previous administra-

tion had ever accepted so much responsibility for the daily needs of millions of the citizenry. Such agencies as FERA, CCC, PWA, and WPA put the government on record as taking on the obligation to feed, clothe, and employ Americans if there was no other way for them to acquire subsistence. Social security introduced a permanent government support for the aged, unemployed, and disabled which countries such as Germany and Great Britain had instituted in the late nineteenth and early twentieth centuries. It was the recognition on the part of the government and the majority of the American people that the United States was a mature industrial society and no longer a nation of self-sufficient farmers and artisans. The greatest innovation of the New Deal was the introduction of welfare capitalism, and its major legislative accomplishments remained and have been expanded by subsequent administrations.

THE NEW DEAL IN HISTORICAL PERSPECTIVE

Given the innovative features of the New Deal, it is not surprising that historians have seen the 1930s from differing perspectives. Roosevelt as a person also aroused intense feelings. A discussion of the merits of the New Deal did not wait for the period to pass into history. As this chapter has shown, FDR and the New Deal were being praised or were under attack throughout most of the 1930s.

Subsequently, historians of the progressive tradition, such as Henry Steele Commager, Arthur M. Schlesinger, Jr., and Frank Freidel have seen the New Deal as an extension of earlier conflicts in American life between economic conservatives and economic liberals. It was a continuation of the struggle against monopoly and special interests. Schlesinger saw the New Deal as more than a response to the depression. It was a phase of the liberal response to conservatism which had marked all of American history. He saw the New Deal as pragmatic and activist, a movement which combined adherence to a modified capitalist system with personal freedom. These men saw the New Deal as the only means of saving the capitalistic system which was at the same time clearly within the American political tradition.

Other writers, however, saw the New Deal as a great assault on individual freedom and competition. It was a rejection of the best of the American tradition. Following this line of hostile attack was John T. Flynn. In *The Roosevelt Myth,* he criticized the New Deal legislation as the product of crisis planning which had had the effect of weakening the free enterprise system. State governments and Congress also had been undermined by FDR's drive for power.

Richard Hofstadter, too, saw the New Deal as a break with the past. He believed that past reform movements had been based on the concept that the government was a negative force useful for destroying privilege but having no positive function in itself. The New Deal, however, saw American society as needing changes that could only be brought about by federal action. There was no effort to restore government to the people as in past reform movements. New Dealers were not interested in abstract moral positions as were the progressives, but in positive government programs. The New Deal was piecemeal and nonideological. It contained no rational government planning for the future.

Some neo-conservative writers also took the same view as Hofstadter that American history could not be correctly interpreted as the result of class conflict and ideological differences. To them domestic struggles were over means not ends. The New Deal was not the product of a specific ideology. It was the manifestation of the nation's maturity in solving problems through politics and not through violence. American insti-

tutions were stable as the New Deal proved. It represented the pragmatism of American thought.

A partial synthesis of several of these views of the New Deal was advanced by William E. Leuchtenberg in *Franklin D. Roosevelt and the New Deal, 1932–40.* He saw the era as more than a period of improvisation. New Dealers were practical men, but on the basis of the belief that human life could be improved by men who controlled their own destiny and were not the playthings of immutable natural laws.

Readings

GENERAL WORKS

Allen, Frederick L., *Since Yesterday*. New York: Harper & Row, 1940—An informal history of the depression and the New Deal which devotes much attention to popular trends and culture.

Draper, Theodore, *The Roots of American Communism*. New York: Viking, 1957—A history of the Communist Party in America from 1919 through 1922. Draper feels that the American Communist Party has always been a tool of Soviet foreign policy interests.

Hicks, John D., *Republican Ascendancy*. New York: Harper & Row, 1960—Covering the administrations of Harding, Coolidge, and Hoover, the book, a standard account of the twenties, stresses political developments.

Leuchtenburg, William E., *Franklin D. Roosevelt and the New Deal, 1932–1940*. New York: Harper & Row, 1963—A general history of the New Deal between 1933 and 1940. While sympathetic to President Roosevelt, the author also points out New Deal shortcomings and shows that Roosevelt was frequently reacting to pressures rather than initiating policy ideas.

Mitchell, Broadus, *Depression Decade*. New York: Holt, Rinehart & Winston, 1947—An economic history of the depression that is frequently critical of the New Deal for its failure to do more to effect economic recovery.

Perkins, Dexter, *The New Age of Franklin Roosevelt*. Chicago: University of Chicago Press, 1957—A generally sympathetic overall history of the New Deal and of Roosevelt's political activity.

Phillips, Cabel, *From the Crash to the Blitz: 1929–1939*. New York: Macmillan, 1969—A journalistic account of the depression years. Phillips considers the period to have produced a genuine social revolution under the auspices of the New Deal.

Rauch, Basil, *The History of the New Deal*. New York: Putnam, 1963—A history of Roosevelt's New Deal policies, written in wartime when the continuation or renewal of New Deal policies was uncertain.

Robinson, Edgar E., *The Roosevelt Leadership*. Philadelphia: Lippincott, 1955—An attack on Roosevelt and the New Deal by a conservative historian and political scientist who believes that the New Deal was an almost dictatorial betrayal of American liberties.

Schlesinger, Arthur M., Jr., *The Age of Roosevelt*, Vols. I–III. Boston: Houghton Mifflin, 1957–1960—A massive study of Roosevelt and his political life. The volumes thus far cover the years up to 1936. Schlesinger admires Roosevelt's pragmatism.

Tindall, George B., *The Emergence of the New South: 1913–1945*. Baton Rouge: Louisiana State University Press, 1967—A detailed history of the South which argues that Southerners finally shed their older agrarian values and adopted an outlook similar to that of other Americans.

Wecter, Dixon, *The Age of the Great Depression*. New York: Macmillan, 1948—Wecter discusses the New Deal as a peaceful revolution.

SPECIAL STUDIES

Aaron, Daniel, *Writers on the Left*. New York: Avon, 1969—A study of the relationship between literary intellectuals and left-wing politics in America. Aaron devotes considerable attention to the impact of the depression on writers' political ideas.

Corwin, Edward S., *Constitutional Revolution, Ltd.* Claremont, Calif.: Claremont College, 1941—A noted legal scholar's interpretation of the constitutional changes wrought by the New Deal. Corwin points to a new emphasis on federal and executive power, new roles for government, and new government moves to promote equality.

Fusfeld, Daniel, *The Economic Thought of Franklin D. Roosevelt and the Origins of the New Deal*. New York: AMS Press, 1970 —A study of the influences of Roosevelt's view of the economic situation which argues that even before Keynes, the President and many of his advisers recognized the crucial necessity of raising effective demand for goods and services.

Galbraith, John K., *The Great Crash*. Boston: Houghton Mifflin, 1965—A well-known economist's analysis of the causes of the stock market collapse of 1929 that ushered in the great depression. Galbraith attributes the crash to the shaky foundations of the prosperity of the 1920s.

Hawley, Ellis W., *The New Deal and the Problem of Monopoly*. Princeton, N.J.: Princeton University Press, 1969—Hawley maintains that the New Deal was a complex mixture of three different theories about the relations between business and government and the nature of private enterprise. The New Freedom and New Nationalism, when mixed with newer doctrines of government planning, created tensions among New Deal policymakers trying to work out an economic program.

Jackson, Robert H., *The Struggle for Judicial Supremacy*. New York: Random House, 1941—An essay on the proper role of the Supreme Court and a defense of Roosevelt's "Court-packing" plan by the New Deal Attorney General and Supreme Court Justice.

McCoy, Donald R., *Angry Voices: Left-of-Center Politics in the New Deal Era*. Lawrence: University of Kansas Press, 1958—A study of several third-party and other left-wing movements during the New Deal era. McCoy argues that these groups began with high hopes but were a political failure because of their delusions of power.

Millis, Henry A., and Emily C. Brown, *From the Wagner Act to Taft-Hartley*. Chicago: University of Chicago Press, 1950—A detailed study of federal labor law and policy which advocates a limited government role in labor relations and endorses collective bargaining.

Moley, Raymond, *The First New Deal*. New York: Harcourt, Brace, 1966—An analysis of the early days of the New Deal by an influential member of Roosevelt's "Brain Trust" who gradually broke with the President and became more conservative.

Romasco, Albert U., *The Poverty of Abundance: Hoover, the Nation, the Depression*. New York: Oxford University Press, 1965—The author of this study argues that Hoover and his advisers did try to put together a recovery program for the nation during the depression but were unsuccessful because of their outmoded ideas and ineffectual political activity.

Warren, Harris G., *Herbert Hoover and the Great Depression*. New York: Oxford University Press, 1959—A balanced account of Hoover's Presidential policies. Warren defends Hoover against charges of doing nothing to combat the depression.

Wolfskill, George, *The Revolt of the Conservatives*. Boston: Houghton Mifflin, 1962 —A history of the American Liberty League, a conservative group whose members such as Al Smith, sharply attacked the New Deal as too radical.

PRIMARY SOURCES

Arnold, Thurman, *The Folklore of Capitalism*. New Haven, Conn.: Yale University Press, 1937—An attempt to puncture myths about the working of the American economy and to provide a rationale for an active governmental role in regulating and supervising business. Arnold became the head of the Anti-Trust Division of the Justice Department during the later years of the New Deal.

Freidel, Frank, ed., *The New Deal and the American People*. Englewood Cliffs, N.J.: Prentice-Hall, 1964—A documentary history of the depression years and of New Deal policies.

Hoover, Herbert, *Memoirs: The Great Depression*. New York: Macmillan, 1915–1952 —Hoover's memoirs, published in his later years, reveal that he still held to his creed of individualism and his belief that federal activity would weaken American democracy even as the economy collapsed.

Ickes, Harold L., *The Secret Diary of Harold L. Ickes*, Vols. I–III. New York: Simon & Schuster, 1953–1954—As Roosevelt's Secretary of the Interior, Ickes was at the center of many political battles and was a sharp critic of the many men who displeased him. His diaries are full of valuable inside glimpses of the New Deal leadership.

Roosevelt, Eleanor, *This I Remember*. New York: Harper & Row, 1949—The second volume of Mrs. Roosevelt's autobiography, this book covers the period from Roosevelt's first term as governor of New York through his death in 1945.

Shannon, David A., *The Great Depression*. Englewood Cliffs, N.J.: Prentice-Hall, 1960 —An anthology of materials from the depression era.

BIOGRAPHIES

Burns, James M., *Roosevelt: The Lion and the Fox*. New York: Harcourt, Brace, 1956 —A political biography of Roosevelt during the New Deal years. Burns considers the President to be torn between strong executive leadership and wily political maneuvering.

Freidel, Frank, *Franklin D. Roosevelt*, Vols. I–III. Boston: Little, Brown, 1952–1956— The first three in a multi-volume biography of F.D.R., Freidel's books cover the period up to Roosevelt's first election.

Huthmacher, Joseph J., *Senator Robert F. Wagner and the Rise of Urban Liberalism*. New York: Atheneum, 1968—A biography of the New Deal Democratic Senator from New York. Huthmacher maintains that Wagner represented the liberals whose commitments were to the big cities and their mixed populations.

Pusey, Merlo J., *Charles Evans Hughes*, Vols. I–III. New York: Columbia University Press, 1951—A detailed biography of the moderate New York Republican. Considerable attention is devoted to Hughes's long service as Chief Justice of the Supreme Court and his position in the "Court-packing" controversy.

Sherwood, Robert E., *Roosevelt and Hopkins*. New York: Harper & Row, 1950—A detailed account of the relationship between the President and Harry Hopkins both in peacetime relief planning and in wartime strategy making and diplomacy. Sherwood, a speechwriter for Roosevelt, gives an intimate picture of the two men.

Williams, T. Harry, *Huey Long*. New York: Knopf, 1969—A massive biography of the Louisiana governor and Senator who some feared as an American fascist and others hailed as a poor man's champion. Williams considers Long to be a genuine populist who, however, was willing to resort to undemocratic means to achieve his ends.

6

THE CHALLENGES OF MATURITY

From Isolation to Intervention

27

. . . the broad masses of a nation are always more easily corrupted in the deeper strata of their emotional nature than consciously or voluntarily, and thus in the primitive simplicity of their minds they more readily fall victims to the big lie than the small lie, since they themselves often tell small lies in little matters, but would be ashamed to resort to large-scale falsehoods. It would never come into their heads to fabricate colossal untruths and they would not believe that others have the impudence to distort the truth so infamously. . . .

—*Adolf Hitler,* Mein Kampf

In the first years after World War I, American foreign policy had three major issues to confront: the question of membership in the League of Nations and the World Court; disarmament; and the war debt owed the United States by European nations. Sickened by the results of a war that had been oversold to them and yearning for the old ideal of an America isolated from and untainted by European conflicts, the American people chose to turn their backs on international political commitments. Americans believed that Europe and Asia could take care of themselves, not realizing that German militancy had not died and that China was very weak. The United States deluded herself into believing that moral force and world public opinion would prevent war. It was not simply peace that was desired, but peace through non-involvement.

Picasso expressed the horrors of war in Guernica. *The painting was named for a town destroyed during the Spanish Civil War.*

THE RETREAT FROM RESPONSIBILITY

THE LEAGUE OF NATIONS AND THE WORLD COURT

As World War I came to an end, the reaction against Wilson, war, and internationalism began to solidify. Harding, though he had remained ambiguous on the League question during his campaign, interpreted his landslide victory as a public repudiation of League membership. He declared in his inaugural address that the United States would "seek no part in directing the destinies of the Old World," and added, "We will accept no responsibility, except as our conscience and judgment may determine." At first, Harding even went so far as to shut down all communications with the League. Dispatches went unanswered and American ambassadors were embarrassed to be seen in the vicinity of the League's headquarters in Geneva. Eventually, however, Harding began to send unofficial observers to League meetings on issues that would not involve the United States in any commitments.

Membership in the World Court was another matter. Though the Court was attached to the League, its planners specified that nations outside the League could participate in the Court on an equal basis. The Court's function was to hear disputes involving international law when the parties involved agreed, and to present its decisions to the League. The Court had no power other than the respect that might be felt for its recommendations. It was thus more in tune with the philosophy of an isolationist America than the League of Nations. Its work might be thought of as "legal," rather than diplomatic or political, and so it was less associated with the taint of power politics.

Accordingly, in 1923 Harding proposed American membership in the World Court to the Senate. Several qualifying clauses were attached to his proposal, with the purpose of insuring unquestioned United States control of its own affairs and of making it doubly clear that membership in the Court would not imply any commitment to the League. Even so, the Senate was extremely slow to act and only consented to membership in 1926. The World Court found itself unable to compromise on the American demand that the Court never consider any question "in which the United States has an interest or claim" without the consent of the United States. As a result, membership was defeated. In 1935, when Roosevelt tried to prod the Senate into action, membership was again defeated.

DISARMAMENT AND PROMISES OF PEACE

The Treaty of Versailles had disarmed the defeated nations. The problem that remained was how to disarm the victors. The United States wanted to combine disarmament with a method of curbing Japan's aggressive intentions toward China. With these ideas in mind, Secretary of State Hughes called for an international conference in Washington toward the end of 1921. He then dramatically offered to halt current construction of battleships for ten years, which meant the United States would scrap fifteen then under construction, and otherwise reduce the United States Navy by destroying over sixty large ships, if the other powers—particularly Great Britain, Japan, Italy, and France—would make similar gestures.

To a war-sick world these proposals seemed bold and imaginative. The Japanese, though unwillingly, consented to partial disarmament, and even drew back some of their forces from eastern Siberia. In the Four Power Treaty, signed in December 1921, Britain, the United States, Japan, and France agreed to respect each other's rights in the Pacific and to consult with each other if there was a threat to those rights by another power. As a result, Britain and Japan agreed to give up an alliance which had been in effect since 1901. The Five Power Treaty, signed February 6, 1922, made firm commitments on ship building. It set the ratio of heavy warships such as battleships and aircraft carriers at 5:5:3:1.67:1.67 for the United States, Britain, Japan, France, and Italy, respectively. The Nine Power Treaty signed the same day seemed to further stabilize the power balance in Asia, eliciting solemn promises to respect the Open Door Policy in China.

When these agreements were signed, there was great optimism about their impact on the future of international peace, but the long-range significance of the Washington Conference in preventing aggression was limited. Right-wing military factions in Japan, already challenging the legitimacy of the liberal government in power, resented the fact that Japan did not obtain a status of parity in naval vessels with the United States and Great Britain. She did not allow these international agreements to prevent her from rearming her home islands. For her part, the United States had voluntarily abdicated her naval superiority, a naive if inspiring move, but historically a factor that helped encourage German and Japanese aggression in the 1930s. American policy was the result of her belief that disarmament would bring international security. Yet, just as she would not commit herself to any international security system, she also would not join in any plan to require international inspection of the progress of disarmament. Finally, disarmament was a failure because it was not total. Barred from the production of heavy warships, the major nations entered an arms race over lighter craft such as submarines. Responding to this, in 1930 the United States, Great Britain, and Japan met in London and agreed to set limits on the lighter warships also. The conference stipulated, however, that if a nation's security was endangered, the quotas could be exceeded.

The most inspiring but meaningless treaty of the whole era was the famous Pact of Paris, or Kellogg-Briand Pact of 1928. When the French foreign minister, Aristide Briand, wrote to Coolidge's Secretary of State, Frank B. Kellogg, proposing a bilateral pact permanently renouncing war between the two nations, Kellogg was inclined to reject it as a pipe dream. However, responding to isolationist and pacifist agitation at home led by Senator Borah of Idaho, he suggested to Briand that the treaty be made multilateral and in effect open to all signers. Antiwar sentiment in France propelled Briand to accept Kellogg's counteroffer, even though he thought a multilateral treaty would be meaningless. The final pact renounced war and called for a peaceful settlement of disputes. It was a sentimental declaration and no more, entailing no actual restraints and no actual commitments. Over sixty nations signed the pact.

DEBTS AND REPARATIONS

The United States was called "Uncle Shylock" by Europeans disgusted with American insistence that war debts of 12.5 billion dollars be repaid. The European victors economically battered by the war found it very difficult to repay the United States, now the major international creditor and the most prosperous nation in the world. They argued that the debts should be written off as part of the cost of the war for the United States, which had suffered far less damage than her European allies. But the United States stuck to her demand, thinking that repayment would prevent rearmament. The Allies, prevented from exporting large amounts of merchandise to the United States because of her high tariff policy, hoped that German reparations payments would supply most of the needed capital.

The payment of 35 billion dollars in reparations was one of the results of the war most loathed by Germany. It victimized an economy already unstable and inflated, and German default on payments as early as 1923 produced an invasion of the Ruhr area by French troops. Adolf Hitler, still largely unknown, staged an unsuccessful putsch in Munich in 1923, hoping to capitalize on spreading resentment in Germany against the whole postwar settlement. He was arrested, convicted, and spent a brief period in jail, where he began his famous book, *Mein Kampf*. John Maynard Keynes, the British economist, wrote a vigorous protest against the postwar exploitation of Germany, but it went unheeded. Recognizing the pressures on Germany, the United States at last offered the Dawes Plan in 1924, scaling down reparations to the level of Germany's economic productivity and providing loans for the defeated nation. But the United States was not willing then or later to recognize the important connection between repayment of the war debts and German reparations payments.

Five years of relative world prosperity ended in 1929 with the stock market crash. The German economy, crippled by an end to American investment, fell apart. The Young Plan furthered scaled-down German reparations in 1930, and in 1931 Hoover announced that all war debt payments would be suspended for a year. Amid the New Deal's general policy of economic nationalism there was one important effort to encourage international cooperation through trade in the 1934 Reciprocal Trade Agreements Act. But the United States never canceled the war debts.

THE GOOD NEIGHBOR POLICY

LATIN AMERICA

The spirit of noninvolvement brought a few positive changes in American foreign policy in the period between the wars. Foremost of these was the "Good Neighbor Policy" in Latin America, named and initiated by Herbert Hoover but made popular by Franklin Roosevelt. The repudiation of dollar diplomacy that Wilson had longed for was finally adopted in the 1920s. Since Europe was weak, Latin America now seemed secure.

The first major test of the changing American attitude toward Latin America grew out of two Mexican laws which threatened to nationalize American oil and mining investments. In 1927, the quarrel between Mexico and the United States came to a head. Secretary Kellogg blustered and even suggested there was communist influence at work in Mexico. The Senate, how-

> *I come to pay a call of friendship. In a sense I represent on this occasion the people of the United States extending a fellow greeting to our fellow democracies on the American continent. I would wish to symbolize the friendly visit of one good neighbor to another. In our daily life, good neighbors call upon each other as the evidence of solicitude for the common welfare and to learn of the circumstances and point of view of each, so that there may come both understanding and respect which are the cementing forces of all enduring society. This should be equally true amongst nations. We have a desire to maintain not only the cordial relations of governments with each other but the relations of good neighbors. Through greater understanding that comes with more contact we may build up that common respect and service which is the only enduring basis of international friendship. . . .*

—*Herbert Hoover, Address at Amapala, Honduras*

> *1. That the American Nations, true to their republican institutions, proclaim their absolute juridical liberty, their unqualified respect for their respective sovereignties and the existence of a common democracy throughout America; 2. That every act susceptible of disturbing the peace of America affects each and every one of them, and justifies the initiation of the procedure of consultation provided for in the Convention for the Maintenance, Preservation and Reestablishment of Peace, signed at this Conference; and 3. That the following principles are accepted by the American community of nations: (a) Proscription of territorial conquest and that, in consequence, no acquisition made through violence shall be recognized; (b) Intervention by one State in the internal or external affairs of another State is condemned; (c) Forcible collection of pecuniary debts is illegal; and (d) Any difference or dispute between the American nations, whatever its nature or origin, shall be settled by the methods of conciliation, or unrestricted arbitration, or through operation of international justice.*

—*Inter-American Conference for the Maintenance of Peace*

ever, holding fast to its noninterventionist stance, voted for mandatory arbitration of the disputed claims. Coolidge and Kellogg retreated. The President now made his friendly intentions clear by appointing Dwight D. Morrow, a man known to be sympathetic to the ideal of nonintervention in Latin American affairs, ambassador to Mexico. The appointment turned out to have more than symbolic value. Morrow worked brilliantly and tactfully toward better relations. While the social revolution in Mexico continued, the United States was able to salvage many of its oil interests there as well as modify Mexico's anticlerical laws so offensive to Roman Catholics in the United States.

Herbert Hoover was the first chief executive to evolve a sturdy and consistent vision of nonintervention in Latin America. After his election Hoover spent ten weeks touring Latin America. He spoke of a reorientation of American policy to one of being "a good neighbor." The new President also refrained from all interventions in Latin America while in office, although there were twenty revolts during that four-year period. Under his direction, Secretary of State Henry L. Stimson in 1931 withdrew the Marines from Nicaragua. Stimson also began the withdrawal of troops from Haiti, completed under Roosevelt in 1934.

The State Department offered its most important statement of the new policy in the unofficial Clark Memorandum of 1930. It indicated that intervention in Latin America was now considered justified only in those cases where national "self-preservation" was at stake. At the same time, it specifically repudiated the Roosevelt Corollary of the Monroe Doctrine. Many Latin Americans thought the Clark Memorandum only a slight clarification of the Monroe Doctrine, not a herald of great progress. However, for the State Department it was a major shift in United States foreign policy toward the rest of the Western Hemisphere.

When Franklin D. Roosevelt assumed office he adopted Hoover's catch-phrase, and in his first inaugural address promised to respect the sanctity of "agreements in and with a world of neighbors." At a Conference of American States in Montevideo in 1933, the United States accepted the principle that it had no right to intervene in Latin American affairs. Roosevelt demonstrated that he meant to abide by his vows when revolution broke out in Cuba shortly thereafter. American Marines did not intervene in a Cuban crisis for the first time in the twentieth century. In 1934, the Platt Amendment, the technical excuse for American interventions in Cuba since 1903, was officially abrogated. In addition, the United States withdrew all troops from Santo Domingo, and only protested and asked for payment of American claims when Mexico expropriated all foreign held oil property in the late 1930s.

When Roosevelt made a personal appearance at the Inter-American Conference at Buenos Aires in 1936, he was greeted with much enthusiasm. Already fearful of fascist aggression, the President called for a permanent committee to consult on dangers to the Western Hemisphere. Unable to secure this multilateralization of the Monroe Doctrine, the United States nevertheless stated unequivocally that it would not intervene in Latin America under any circumstances.

As war clouds gathered over Europe, the Latin American countries, with the exception of Argentina which had a large population of German extraction, agreed in 1938 that any country could call a special meeting if it feared a threat to the hemisphere. Roosevelt called such a meeting for September, 1939, in Panama. Meeting in the wake of the Nazi attack on Poland, the American republics announced a 300 mile safety zone around the Western Hemisphere to keep the area isolated and neutral in the European conflict. Roosevelt's fears were justified since there was strong pro-German sentiment in Uruguay as well as Argentina. Moreover, Hitler had made plans to use the merchant fleets of the defeated western European powers to take over Latin American trade as a prelude to setting up a series of Nazi states there.

In 1940, the Act of Havana ratified a United States plan to take over French and Dutch colonies in the Western Hemisphere rather than allow them to fall into German hands. The meeting also declared that an attack on one nation was an attack on all. The Monroe Doctrine had finally become multilateral.

During the war the United States had military missions in several Latin American countries and used bases there for the war effort. Eighteen of the twenty republics joined the United States against the Axis by January, 1942. Chile joined in 1943 but Argentina only entered the war on the side of the Allies in 1945 at the end of the conflict.

THE PHILIPPINES

American economic contributions to the well-being of the Filipinos did not put an end to their demands for political independence. Congress finally passed the Jones Act in 1916, setting up a democratic legislature elected by the Filipinos, and providing for eventual independence. During

Wilson's administration there was economic and political progress in the islands, and the President decided that the people were ready for self-rule. But his prompt action on the independence clause was rejected by Congress, and it was not until the Tydings-McDuffie Act of 1934 that the United States guaranteed that independence would at last be granted on July 4, 1946.

Relations between the two countries were complicated by a web of economic and military interests. American businessmen had discovered quite early that the Philippines were not the commercial gold-mine they had wished for. However, the islands were of strategic importance to the United States in the Far East. Filipinos themselves also had mixed feelings. They treasured independence and hated colonialism but also feared the loss of their trade advantages with the United States. In the 1930s, they also began to fear Japan. In 1935 President Quezon of the Philippines arranged with Roosevelt for the military leadership of General Douglas MacArthur on the islands. President Quezon hoped that this, combined with assurances of naval defense, would ward off a Japanese invasion.

RECOGNITION OF THE SOVIET UNION

After the Revolution of 1917 the United States, fearing the spread of communism throughout the world, had refused to recognize the Soviet regime in Russia. This policy prevailed throughout the years of Republican ascendancy in Washington. When Roosevelt came to office in 1933, he acted promptly to seek improved relations with the Soviet Union. There were a number of reasons for the shift. First, the rise of Japanese power in Asia had upset the traditional balance there, and a Russo-American bond might curb Japan's aggressive foreign policy. Also, the prospect of

commerce with Russia was alluring to businessmen. Finally, Josef Stalin apparently had put aside the internationalist dreams of the earlier Bolsheviks, sealed the Soviet Union off from the world, and adopted a Russia-first policy emphasizing nationalism and modernization of her economy.

Roosevelt arranged for talks between representatives of the two countries. Maxim Litvinov, the Soviet Foreign Minister, arrived in Washington in October, 1933. The United States accorded recognition in exchange for a series of verbal guarantees that the Soviet Union would not cause left-wing unrest in the United States, directly or indirectly, and would protect American lives and religious freedom within the Soviet Union. Soviet-American relations, though still strained, now had official sanction.

THE CHALLENGE OF FASCISM

THE RISING SUN

Japanese-American relations, strained since the turn of the century, deteriorated further during the 1920s. Following the disappointment of the Washington Conference, the American Immigration Act of 1924 had closed the door to Japanese immigration to the United States. This insult, however, was only a minor factor compared to the rise of militarism within Japan itself. Undergoing the economic crisis of the depression, which included high tariff barriers by the United States against Japanese goods,

Japan came more and more under the sway of its military faction. F. P. Walters, former Deputy Secretary-General of the League of Nations, has noted that just as in Germany, poverty in Japan "played into the hands of the party of violence." The United States, unaware of the internal situation in Japan, thought of her as a Western-oriented democracy. It was true that Japanese businessmen accepted this outlook, but the rising military group wanted no conciliation of the Western Powers or of China. The military believed that Japanese prosperity and prestige in the world could be attained only through force. The Japanese blueprint for conquest outlined in the Tanaka Memorial in 1927 called for taking Manchuria, China, and Southeast Asia, thereby driving the Western Powers out of the Orient.

In the meantime, China was gaining a degree of cohesiveness and stability after the overthrow of the Manchus in 1912. Led first by Sun Yat-sen and then Chiang Kai-shek, the Kuomintang Party was able to overthrow a number of local warlords and unite about half of China under its rule. Breaking with the communists, Chiang worked closely with the business interests in China. Further, he petitioned the Western Powers to end the unequal treaties of the 1840s. In 1928 the United States signed a treaty with China accepting her control over her own tariff policy and recognized Chiang Kai-shek's government in 1929.

The militarists in Japan, frustrated by what they considered the discriminatory treatment of their country at international conferences and the corrupt and unpatriotic policies of their own government, decided to take matters into their own hands. In September, 1931, the Japanese army invaded Manchuria, nominally a part of China but 40 percent Japanese, jolting the world and its own moderate civilian government. The pretext was a railway bomb explosion in Manchuria staged by its own men. Victorious, the Japanese generals forced the government to accept the new

territory by threatening Emperor Hirohito with assassination. In 1932 Manchuria was renamed Manchukuo and given a puppet ruler. In addition, Shanghai was bombed in retaliation for a Chinese boycott of Japanese goods.

The American response to this turning point in world history was uncertain and ineffective. Secretary of State Stimson and President Hoover disagreed about the best course to follow. Both favored a policy of nonrecognition of Manchukuo, on the grounds that the invasion was in open violation of the Kellogg-Briand Pact, and of the Nine Power Treaty guaranteeing the Open Door Policy. But nonrecognition, like those treaties themselves, was a moralistic statement rather than an effective political act, and Stimson thought it was insufficient. He advocated economic sanctions against Japan in the hope of thereby forcing her out of Manchuria. Hoover, aware of American public opinion against such a policy, refused to make any such provocative move, convinced that economic sanctions "are the roads to war." The resulting policy of nonrecognition announced in a note to Japan in January, 1932, combined with verbal expressions of indignation at aggression came to be known, ironically, as the Stimson Doctrine. The United States censured Japan before the rest of the world but did nothing to stop the aggression.

Stimson himself continued to think that the American reaction was too limited. In 1932, in a letter to Senator Borah, Chairman of the Senate Foreign Relations Committee, Stimson pointed out that the provisions of the Nine Power and Five Power treaties and of the Kellogg-Briand Pact were "interrelated and interdependent." This meant, he implied, that if Japan violated the provisions condemning war, the United States would be forced to undertake naval rearmament. Meanwhile, in that same year, China appealed to the League of Nations for help. Early in 1933 the League's Assembly adopted a statement confirming Chinese sovereignty in Manchuria, asserting that the will of the inhabitants there opposed the existence of "Manchukuo" and calling for nonrecognition of the puppet regime. The Japanese ambassador walked out of the Assembly. In 1934 Japan abrogated the Washington treaties and in 1935 officially withdrew from the League of Nations.

ISOLATIONISM AND EUROPEAN DICTATORSHIPS

Isolationism required, among other things, that the United States keep the European and Asian theaters of foreign policy distinct. American involvement in Asia always had been easier for isolationists to accept than American involvement in Europe. This may have been partly because isolationism had a strong agrarian base, and American farmers tended to distrust Europe, particularly Great Britain, and to see Asia as a potential market. The continuation of the Open Door Policy, backed by the Nine Power Treaty, and the country's commitments in the Philippines testified to American interest in the balance of power in Asia. By the 1930s the attempt to see events in Asia and Europe as separate from each other was nullified by the movement of events in world politics: The two supposedly distinct regions of the world merged with a tripartite alliance among Germany, Italy, and Japan.

The rise of militarism in Japan was accompanied by a series of political upheavals in continental Europe. Following the death of Lenin in 1924, a titanic struggle for leadership ensued in the Soviet Union. Stalin outmaneuvered his arch-rival, Leon Trotsky, had him exiled, and instituted a rapid and forced program of industrialization. Under consecutive five-year plans in the late 1920s and the 1930s the central government expanded heavy indus-

try without foreign capital and forced the collectivization of Soviet agriculture at the expense of untold numbers of Russian lives. By 1938, Russia was second to the United States in Gross National Product. At the same time, Stalin also instituted massive purges within the Communist Party to destroy any challenge to his own leadership. Russia had been turned into an industrialized police state.

In Italy a movement known as fascism arose under the leadership of Benito Mussolini, a journalist and political agitator. Fascist ideology called for a state in which both business and labor would work together for the good of the nation. Ownership of private property and a capitalistic economic system would continue under tight government regulation. Politically, the fascist state was totalitarian with only one party and no opposition allowed.

Mussolini entered the Italian power vacuum in 1922, promising to bring order out of turmoil. The government was forced to resign and Mussolini assumed leadership and then made himself dictator, instituting a new system of government based on close cooperation with industry. Mussolini had dreams of a new Roman Empire and adopted the *fasces,* the old Roman symbol of authority, as his own.

In Germany, Adolf Hitler and the National Socialist Party which he had helped found in 1920 copied Mussolini's fascist style and its use of a symbol. With the onset of the depression, political weakness and division in the German leftist parties gave Hitler his chance to come to power. He was supported by anticommunist industrialists and the middle class who were disillusioned with their economic condition but fearful of communism. Given this crucial backing, the enthusiasm of the German army, and weak opposition, Hitler was appointed Chancellor on January 31, 1933. After new elections in which the Nazis won only 44 percent of the vote, Hitler nevertheless demanded dictatorial powers. Due to the national emergency, the Reichstag (the German Parliament) gave in to his demands. In the two years after he became Chancellor, Hitler solidified his dictatorship through a reign of terror. Having brought about internal order and conformity, he was ready to embark on a program of German territorial expansion in Europe. In 1935 he announced that Germany was building an air force and organizing a large army, both of which were in violation of the Treaty of Versailles.

These events abroad initiated a new debate on foreign policy within the United States. Since the end of the First World War books had been written attacking the business interests with their desire for prof-

its, as the cause of American participation in the conflict. Many Americans had accepted these arguments and they seemed to be reconfirmed in the years 1934 to 1936 by the reports of the Nye Committee in the Senate. The Committee undertook to examine Congressional records, and records of industrial profit, and produced evidence to support the notion that the so-called "merchants of death" had dragged the President and the Congress into the European conflict.

The results of the Nye Committee investigation further convinced most Americans that the nation should follow a policy of isolation. Although uneasy about events in Europe, they wanted no involvement. Senator Nye proposed neutrality legislation to prevent a recurrence of an unnecessary war. The Neutrality Act of 1935 prohibited trading with belligerents, a simple device that would make American war profiteering impossible. Roosevelt was hesitant about the bill. Although in 1935 he certainly

Adolf Hitler addresses over 160,000 storm troopers in Nuremberg at a celebration of the founding of the Nazi party. Hitler's dictatorship began when he was appointed Chancellor of the German National Socialist Party in 1933.

nursed a sharp dislike for businessmen and for what he felt was their narrow interest in profits, he favored legislation that would prohibit trading only with the aggressor nations. Additional legislation in 1936 and 1937 prohibited Americans from traveling on belligerent ships except at their own risk, and from making loans, selling munitions, or arming belligerent merchant ships. As the world crisis intensified, this legislation was modified between 1937 and 1939 to allow belligerents to buy materials and arms from the United States if they took full responsibility for their transport. The neutrality laws were an abandonment of America's traditional policy of freedom of the seas and soon proved to aid aggressor nations.

When Roosevelt signed the 1935 bill Italy had already invaded Ethiopia. Roosevelt hoped that the arms embargo called for by the Neutrality Act would deter Italy. In fact, it hurt Ethiopia more, since she was an agricultural country and could not manufacture her own weapons. Moreover, private traders from all the Western countries continued to supply Italy with rubber and oil despite sanctions voted against her by the League. Roosevelt then called for a "moral embargo" on other trade relations with Italy, but Italy had already succeeded in conquering the poorly armed Ethiopians.

Meanwhile, negotiations between Italy and Germany in 1936 resulted in secret agreements for military cooperation, and shortly afterward Mussolini called the relationship between Germany and Italy an "Axis," around which Europe would revolve (Japan and other nations would eventually join the Axis). This new alliance had its first test of effectiveness when civil war erupted in Spain. The fascist forces of General Francisco Franco were attempting to overthrow the weak Republican government, which thus far had made an effort to remain democratic. Hitler and Mussolini sent supplies and forces to aid Franco. All the democratic powers, including the United States, remained neutral and embargoed arms; only the Soviet Union aided the Republicans. In spite of worldwide sympathy and enlistments of private individuals in the Republican cause, without real aid they had no chance. It was a perfect testing ground for Germany's new military machine.

In July, 1937, there was also new aggression in the Far East. The Japanese invaded north China. American sympathy was with the Chinese, and Roosevelt, taking advantage of the fact that the Japanese had not declared war, refused to recognize that a state of war existed. This allowed him to continue shipments of munitions to China under the Neutrality Act. Previously Roosevelt had said little about the international situation fearing loss of support for New Deal programs. But speaking in Chicago that October, Roosevelt made an ill-timed effort to counteract intense isolationism. He declared that "the very foundations of civilization are seriously threatened" by "international lawlessness," and warned that the United States was inevitably involved since peaceful nations had to uphold law and order. It became known as the "quarantine the aggressor" speech, because Roosevelt compared fascist aggression to a disease and implied that economic ties with the diseased nations ought to be cut.

When the British responded favorably to the speech, convening an international conference to invoke sanctions against Japan, Roosevelt could give no guarantee of American military support. The conference collapsed. Roosevelt was at a low point in his popularity at home because of the 1937 recession. Moreover, the strength of antiwar sentiment at home brought near passage of the Ludlow amendment to the Constitution, which would have required a plebiscite for any declaration of war, except after invasion. It was not until 1940 that the Committee to Defend America by Aiding the Allies was formed under William Allen White.

THE ROAD TO WAR

APPEASEMENT FAILS

With isolationist sentiment at its peak America was in no way ready to take the strong actions necessary to stop further aggression. The Japanese in their invasion of China had already committed atrocities against the Chinese and attacked English and American residents and businesses. Further, on December 12, 1937, the situation became even more serious when an American gunboat, the *Panay,* sank under bombardment. It looked like a deliberate act, yet American anger was easily cooled by Japan's apologies and reparations. This kind of incident made it clear to the Japanese and the Axis powers just how reluctant Americans were to play a decisive role in world politics.

In the next two years Hitler played on the even greater timidity of Great Britain and France to make territorial gains in Europe. Hitler had evolved a step-by-step plan to bring all of central Europe under Nazi rule. He planned to relocate or otherwise dispose of non-German inhabitants, turning them into a labor force, and to use the new territory both as lebensraum for the Germans, and as a military and industrial base for projected world conquest.

Both Hitler's racism and his strategy of conquest were founded, in part, on the fact that ethnic and national boundaries in much of Middle Europe were unclear. The Versailles Treaty had provided for an independent and demilitarized area west of the Rhine River. In 1936, German troops marched into the Rhineland and reclaimed it unopposed. A separate Germanic Austrian nation also had been one of the innovations of the Treaty of Versailles. Hitler, himself an Austrian, considered the innovation an atrocity and believed in the reunification of all Germans under one government. In addition, he was supported by pro-Nazi fascist movements in many European nations, even France, which came to be known as "fifth columns." They thought of Germany as a bulwark against communism. In March, 1938, when Hitler overthrew the Austrian government and annexed Austria to Germany, opposition within the experimental nation was not fierce. The Western Powers rationalized the occurrence by saying that Austria had always been part of the German community.

Hitler's next territorial demand was made in September. Czechoslovakia, whose Serbian population Hitler despised, also included under the hated Versailles Treaty the area of the Sudetenland, which was populated mainly by Germans. Hitler demanded cession of the Sudetenland to Germany, and he had the support of a large number of Sudeten Germans. Panicked at the thought of war, Prime Minister Neville Chamberlain of Great Britain and Prime Minister Edouard Daladier of France held several conferences with Hitler over the projected annexation. Roosevelt sent Chamberlain telegrams urging him to stand firm. But at Munich the two Ministers agreed that Czechoslovakia had to give in. Czechoslovakia was not consulted, even though she had an alliance with Britain and France. Several months later, in March, 1939, Hitler took the rest of Czechoslovakia by military force, and the appeasers were finally stunned by the recognition of the results of their policy. It was now clear that Hitler's designs were not limited to Germans. The next invasion was by Italy, on April 7, 1938, with Albania the victim. Time was running short for the war preparations that the Western Powers knew had to be made.

CRISIS OVER POLAND

Great Britain and France had begun last-minute attempts at rearmament and mobilization when Hitler, early in 1939, demanded Danzig, a German-speaking port that had been declared a free city under the Treaty of Versailles. Poland, whose territory surrounded the city, refused the German demand.

A new invasion was clearly imminent. It also seemed that if Hitler's European aggression was to be stopped, Great Britain, France, and Russia would have to form some kind of alliance. Long-standing conflicts between the three powers were the first obstacle to such an alliance. The second was their state of unpreparedness, which made each of them hesitant to take any action that might precipitate war too soon. In March, the French and British came to terms and promised aid to Poland, Romania, and Greece in the event of attack. President Roosevelt meanwhile sent a message to the Axis in April, calling for a guarantee that over twenty nations, specified by name, would not be invaded. Hitler's reply was derisive and noncommittal.

Since the new crisis centered on Poland, Russian participation in the Anglo-French alliance would have been a logical step. Poland, bordering Russia and Germany, had traditional disputes with both large powers, yet was also a buffer between them. Much of Hitler's rhetoric was anticommunist. This natural enmity had been acted out when the two nations took different sides in the Spanish Civil War. Consequently, the world was stunned when, even while the British were in Moscow trying to forge an alliance, a Russo-German nonaggression pact was announced at the end of August, 1939.

The new agreement not only prohibited war between the two powers, but even provided for an exchange of raw materials and manufactured goods. The pact included an agreement that Russia and Germany would divide Poland in the coming weeks. Problems of timing seem to have prompted both Stalin and Hitler to make the pact. Stalin was aware that a nonaggression pact with Hitler was worthless in the long run. Germany had made a similar agreement with Poland only a few years earlier when it was convenient. However, the new pact gave Stalin time to prepare for war with Germany, which he suspected was inevitable. It also gave him time, after the invasion of Poland, to seize the Baltic nations Latvia, Lithuania, and Estonia, which would act as another buffer if and when Hitler turned on Russia. Hitler for his part was also playing for time. The Soviet Union was on the schedule of conquest, but for his immediate purpose the agreement enabled him to appropriate two-thirds of Poland, rich in labor, agricultural goods, resources, and ports, and then to attack western Europe without fear of interference from the east.

Following shortly on the heels of a British guarantee of Polish security, on September 1, 1939, German troops marched into Poland and the German *Luftwaffe* began its first great aerial bombardment. Stunned by the series of events, Great Britain and France had no alternative but to declare war on Germany on September 3. That same day Roosevelt spoke to the American people over the radio, promising that the United States would try to stay out of war, but adding that he could not "ask that every American remain neutral in thought." The United States proclaimed her neutrality on September 5.

WAR BEGINS

There was little fighting during the winter of 1939 to 1940, and people were talking about the "phony war." The only major action was the Soviet drive toward the Baltic coast, and a subsequent invasion of Finland. American sympathy for the doomed

961

Allied nations

Axis nations

Neutral nations

JAPAN→

WORLD WAR II · ALLIANCES

Finnish resistance was more wholehearted than it had been for any other victim of aggression in the thirties.

In the spring of 1940 those who had sneered at the "phony war" had a chance to witness the real thing. In a blitzkrieg Hitler systematically invaded and defeated Denmark, Norway, Belgium, Holland, Luxembourg, and France, rounding out the map of the Third Reich by acquiring virtually all of western Europe. During a surprise attack on Norway, the British effort to provide assistance failed, and Winston Churchill, who had earlier spoken out against the appeasement of Hitler and called for British mobilization, replaced Chamberlain as Prime Minister.

In May, 1940, after Germany had overcome Holland, Belgium, and Luxembourg, the assault on France began. The invading German army trapped over 300,000 Allied soldiers on the northern coast of France around Dunkirk. This enormous force was vulnerable, and their slaughter might have spelled British defeat. But in one of the greatest retreats in history, a motley cluster of small ships and commercial boats enlisted for the emergency managed with air cover from the RAF to evacuate most of the army.

But France was falling and the French regarded Dunkirk as a desertion. Hitler's modernized army had pierced the Maginot Line, France's supposedly invulnerable wall of fortifications on Germany's western frontier. Mussolini seized the opportunity, declared war, and marched into southern France. On June 10, Premier Paul Reynaud cablegrammed Roosevelt to inform him that he was evacuating Paris, and that "another dictatorship has stabbed France in the back." "I beseech you," the cable continued, "to declare publicly that the United States will give the Allies aid and material support by all means short of an expeditionary force. I beseech you to do this before it is too late." But Roosevelt had no power to fulfill such a request, and he sent only a note professing his admiration for French bravery and his "utmost sympathy." At the end of the note he said simply, "I know that you will understand that these statements carry with them no implication of military commitments. Only the Congress can make such commitments." On June 22, France and Germany signed an armistice, but a French resistance movement was immediately established in London under General Charles de Gaulle.

Hitler was convinced that his defeat of France would now force the British to accept his terms. When Churchill refused, Hitler was shocked and still imagined that the refusal was a bluff. Many Germans, accustomed to appeasement by the Western Powers, believed that the war was over with Germany victorious. But Hitler had to face the fact that appeasement had ended and that Britain would fight for her life. He began to formulate a plan for the conquest of England, called "Operation Sea Lion."

First, the *Luftwaffe* was to bombard England and destroy the RAF. Afterward German forces would conduct a cross-channel invasion of the British Isles.

While Churchill rallied his people with fervent and dramatic oratory, British bombers, with the aid of radar, kept up their attack of the *Luftwaffe*. Night after night the English in industrial centers awoke and retreated into shelters. The blitz, although it caused enormous strain, did not succeed in breaking the English spirit or in destroying the RAF. Hitler was forced to abandon his plan to invade England in 1940.

Part of Churchill's oratory was a continuing appeal for aid from the United States. Roosevelt for his part had long corresponded with Churchill and liked him. The Nazi conquest of continental Europe made it clear to a growing number of Americans that Roosevelt's earlier warnings had been prophetic, but the great debate between isolationists and interventionists continued. The interventionists, however, were beginning to win out. The Burke-Wadsworth bill of September, 1940, instituted a peacetime draft for the first time in American history. By 1941, there was a standing army of 1.6 million. Roosevelt responded to Churchill's specific appeal for fifty World War I destroyers, by offering to exchange them for naval bases in Bermuda, Newfoundland, and the Caribbean. By doing so he prevented isolationist criticism, since he was able to demonstrate that he had merely traded fifty archaic warships for a network of bases in the Atlantic that would be invaluable in case of attack.

DEBATE AND THE ELECTION OF 1940

The Democrats broke the third-term tradition and again nominated Roosevelt. The President wanted the nomination and manipulated the party machinery to ensure it, as well as the nomination of Henry Wallace as his running mate.

The Republicans nominated Wendell Willkie, an appealing and personable man whose popularity had soared suddenly during the preconvention scramble. The Republican platform concentrated on an attack on the New Deal and Roosevelt's try for a third term. Although isolationists tended to cluster around the Republican ticket, Willkie himself refused to take an isolationist line. He did charge that Roosevelt was leading the country into war, but at the same time agreed with the President in advocating aid to the Allies and a tough posture toward fascism.

Behind the contest between these two engaging personalities lay the great debate over America's relationship to the war in Europe. The America First Committee, with the support of prominent men like Herbert Hoover and Charles Lindbergh, attacked Roosevelt's provocative attitude toward the Axis and Japan and called for confining America's armed defense to the Western Hemisphere. Roosevelt seemed to them to be a warmonger. For his part, Roosevelt solemnly promised that there would be no war. However, the contest was more over leadership than issues, and the people showed that they had continuing faith in Roosevelt's capacity to lead them during a crisis. Roosevelt's victory was smaller than his others, yet he won by 27 million votes to 22 million, 54 percent of the vote.

LEND-LEASE

Shortly after the election, Churchill notified Roosevelt that Great Britain had already seriously depleted her cash reserves in paying for weapons. He asked for continued support in spite of his inability to pay. Roosevelt, already in the process of appointing Republicans to his new administration in order to boost national unity, responded to the appeal by formulating the "Lend-Lease" program. In a fireside chat to the American people on December 29, 1940, he described the fascists and their

Pro-Lend-Lease

“ *First, by an impressive expression of the public will and without regard to partisanship, we are committed to all-inclusive national defense.*

Second, by an impressive expression of the public will and without regard to partisanship, we are committed to full support of all those resolute peoples, everywhere, who are resisting aggression and are thereby keeping war away from our hemisphere. By this support, we express our determination that the democratic cause shall prevail; and we strengthen the defense and security of our own Nation.

Third, by an impressive expression of the public will and without regard to partisanship, we are committed to the proposition that principles of morality and considerations for our own security will never permit us to acquiesce in a peace dictated by aggressors and sponsored by appeasers. We know that enduring peace cannot be bought at the cost of other people's freedom. . . .

Our most useful and immediate role is to act as an arsenal for them as well as for ourselves. They do not need man power. They do need billions of dollars' worth of the weapons of defense. . . .

Let us say to the democracies, "We Americans are vitally concerned in your defense of freedom. We are putting forth our energies, our resources, and our organizing powers to give you the strength to regain and maintain a free world. We shall send you, in ever-increasing numbers, ships, planes, tanks, guns. This is our purpose and our pledge." ”

—*Franklin D. Roosevelt,*
Message to Congress

Anti-Lend-Lease

“ *Mr. President, what are you going to tell your people when you go back home? Are you going to say, "I wanted to balance the Budget; I did not want to give money to the workers; I did not want to give money to the farmers; I did not want to give money to the widows or to the aged; but I was willing to vote to permit the President of the United States to give $1,300,000,000 to any or all countries in the whole wide world. . . ."*

Senators, read some of the letters which come into your offices from patriotic mothers—mothers, some of whose husbands were killed in the last war, and who now have sons just the right age for cannon fodder who are now being drafted. It is time that the Senate, the Congress, and the people of this country displayed sanity. This country is being torn to pieces by insidious, warminded propaganda. They are subversive who want to get this country into war. They are subversive because war will mean the end of what we have known as constitutional government. War will mean dictatorship during the course of the war, could mean the permanent end of parliamentary government in the United States. . . .

On somewhat the same premise, somewhat paradoxically, we are asked in this bill to authorize the President to commit acts of war which would be tantamount to delegating to him the power to declare war. One such provision is the authorization to use our harbors as havens of refuge and repair for the naval vessels of one belligerent and not the other. There can be no reasonable doubt as to the warlike character of such an act. . . . ”

—*Senator Burton K. Wheeler*

methods. Pointing to American industrial might, he concluded that the United States "must be the great arsenal of democracy." Popular response to the speech was favorable. Thereupon Roosevelt proposed that Congress appropriate 7 billion dollars for the production of weapons and other war materials. The President was to be given authority to sell, lend, lease, or exchange these materials, as he saw fit, to any nation in danger whose security was linked to that of the United States. The plan was specifically intended for Great Britain.

Isolationist opposition was feverish, because Lend-Lease brought the United States closer to involvement in an undeclared war. Senator Burton K. Wheeler remarked, "The Lend-Lease program is the New Deal's Triple A foreign policy; it will plow under every fourth American boy." Unification across party lines was already taking place, however. While Lindbergh and others, such as the historian Charles Beard, testified against the bill, Wendell Willkie campaigned for it. Lend-Lease became law on March 11, 1941. However, the selective service system instituted the year before was renewed by only one vote.

WAR CONTINUES

GERMANY INVADES RUSSIA

On June 22, Hitler, frustrated in his attempt to overwhelm an England aided by the United States, invaded the Soviet Union. Stalin, who until the last moment had been shipping Hitler raw materials,

was taken by surprise. There was widespread fear that Hitler might succeed where Napoleon had failed. But Hitler's decision in fact marked the end of the systematic and successful policy of conquest pursued thus far by the Nazis.

Faced with popular dislike of Stalin in the United States, Roosevelt moved slowly, but eventually extended Lend-Lease to the Soviet Union. He was already working closely with Churchill who, though fiercely anticommunist, was more than happy to regard any of Hitler's foes as an ally. "If Hitler invaded Hell," Churchill remarked, "I would make at least a favorable reference to the Devil in the House of Commons." Gradually, the American people accepted Russia as a military ally.

In the month of August, 1941, the Anglo-American bond was dramatized by a meeting between Roosevelt and Churchill off the coast of Newfoundland. There they issued a joint statement known as the Atlantic Charter. It renounced any desire for new territories and reiterated the democratic longings of the British and American peoples in affirming the right of peoples to choose their own governments and national boundaries, praised the idea of free trade, and called for disarmament of the aggressor nations after the Nazis had been destroyed.

WAR IN THE ATLANTIC

But the practical problem which the Anglo-American alliance had to face was that of German attacks on arms shipments. The President's actions in this crisis unilaterally destroyed American neutrality. The Nazi submarine fleet had become devastatingly efficient in the Atlantic. It now engaged in direct attacks on American ships, which were patrolling the North Atlantic and illegally engaged in convoying British ships in the area. The attacks were an acknowledgment of an undeclared state of war. In September the Germans attacked the Amer-

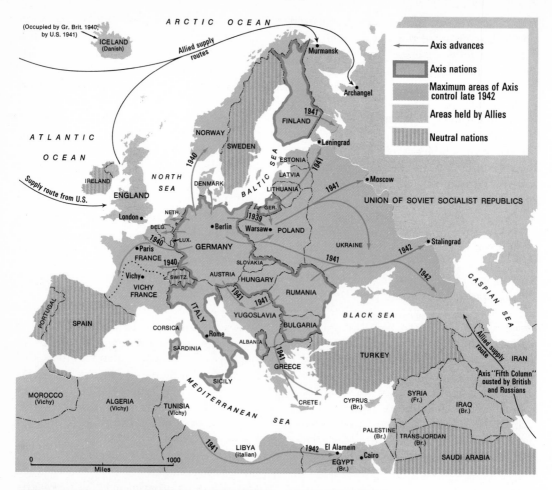

WORLD WAR II • EUROPEAN THEATER • 1939 TO 1942

ican destroyer *Greer,* and Roosevelt ordered retaliation on German and Italian ships in American-patrolled waters. Before this attack the United States was also repairing British ships and seizing Axis vessels in American ports and giving them to the Allies. In October the Nazis sank the destroyer *Reuben James,* killing many Americans, and in November Congress provided arms for merchant vessels. "The attack on the *Greer,*" Roosevelt said on September 11, "was no localized military operation in the North Atlantic. This was no mere episode in a struggle between two nations.

This was one determined step toward creating a permanent world system based on force, terror, and on murder . . ." Roosevelt had abandoned diplomatic and peaceful language.

WAR IN THE PACIFIC

Meanwhile the United States was as preoccupied with the Far East as she was with Europe. Either area eventually could have plunged the United States into war, but Hitler's hesitation, combined with antiwar sentiment at home, made it unlikely that the United States would openly have entered the European conflict for many months. Only when the Japanese directly attacked the United States did she enter the global conflict.

The Japanese military regime, having declared the Open Door Policy irrelevant to her plans for Asia, continued its assault on China. At first the United States imposed no sanctions, though threats were made in 1939. But she did loan China 25 million dollars and fortified Guam and Alaska. The sanctions finally came in 1940, after Japan, taking advantage of the defeat of France, threatened to invade French Indochina. The United States fleet was sent to Pearl Harbor and a new American embargo in July, 1940, cut off supplies of raw materials urgently needed by the military government of Japan such as gas, oil, and steel scrap. Isolationists protested that the embargo was a provocation to war. The Japa-

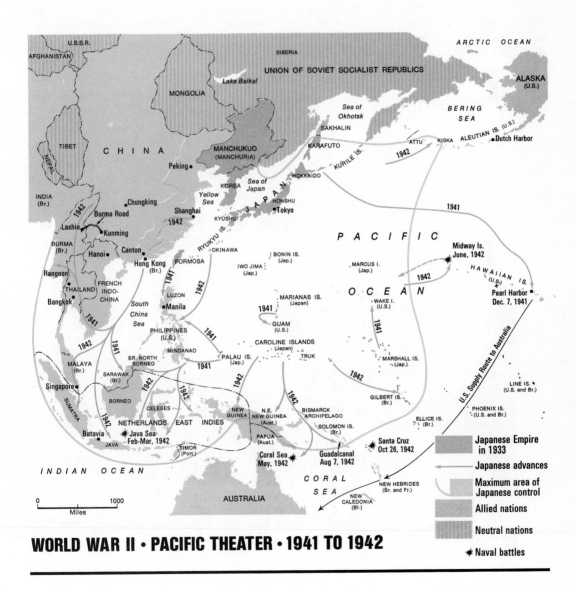

WORLD WAR II · PACIFIC THEATER · 1941 TO 1942

nese now concluded a tripartite pact with the Axis and began moving into northern Indochina.

Some historians view the pact with the Axis powers as a natural and inevitable one for the Japanese since they were planning to increase their penetration of Asia even at the risk of war with the United States. Others insist that the Japanese wished to avoid war with the United States, and adopted the pact as a bargaining point. There was an ongoing split within Japan, and the treaty might have been regarded as offensive by militants, and as defensive by moderates. As the squeeze of the embargo tightened, the Japanese made their last diplomatic gesture toward the United States in late 1941. Japan called for an end to the economic sanctions against her. Secretary of State Cordell Hull took a hard line, and rebuffed the Japanese by insisting there were no grounds for negotiations as long as military operations continued in China and the Axis alliance remained. In Japan, Premier Fumimaro Konoye, eager to abandon the Axis and come to terms with America, was losing ground. When his appeal for a summit conference with Roosevelt was rejected by the United States until he made a commitment on China, he fell and was replaced by General Hideki Tojo, an ardent militarist who made preparations for war while keeping up a front of nego-

The Japanese attack on Pearl Harbor, Hawaii, although not unexpected by the United States government, caught the navy by surprise. This photograph shows the destroyer Shaw *at the moment of explosion.*

tiations. War plans were discussed in October and on November 5 the Japanese Cabinet decided on war with the United States. A fleet of ships secretly training in the Kurile Islands left for Hawaii on November 25.

Meanwhile, in late November, the Japanese offered to withdraw from Indochina in exchange for a renewal of trade with the United States. Because the offer made no provision for stopping hostilities against China, Secretary of State Hull again refused to consider this proposal though aware that the rebuff made war almost inevitable.

PEARL HARBOR

War warnings were sent out to the Pacific on November 27, ordering American forces to be on the alert. The Japanese code had been deciphered, and when, on December 6, Tojo instructed his ambassadors to break with the United States the following day, Roosevelt knew that war was imminent.

Even so, he sent one final appeal to the Emperor. Despite later charges that he anticipated the Pearl Harbor attack and welcomed it as a dramatic and unifying excuse for war, there is little doubt that the site of the raid was a surprise. An attack somewhere in the South Pacific was anticipated, but not at Pearl Harbor. During the attack which began early Sunday morning, December 7, the Japanese killed 2,500 men, crippled the fleet, and destroyed hundreds of planes.

On December 8 Roosevelt in his war message announced that the American people would always "remember the character of the onslaught against us." December 7 was a day that would "live in infamy." The Axis powers honored the tripartite pact and declared war on the United States within a few days. The debate between isolationists and interventionists was now in the past. Energies were focused on victory and on the unprecedented mobilization required to achieve it.

AMERICAN MOBILIZATION

The social revolution begun by the New Deal was accelerated by the Second World War, the greatest mobilization of her resources ever undertaken by the United States. Just a few statistics suggest the scope of mobilization. Sixteen million people served in the armed forces with total casualties numbering over one million. War production accounted for more than one third of the Gross National Product while the conflict continued. The new demand

for labor erased unemployment and brought black people in increasing numbers into industrial centers. Women went to work in factories or joined newly organized women's branches of the military. The Gross National Product almost doubled during the five-year period of 1940 to 1945. The national debt amounted to 280 billion dollars in 1945, compared to 40 billion dollars in 1940—a figure then thought to be astoundingly large. Federal spending during the war totaled more than 320 billion dollars or twice as much as had been spent since the federal government was founded.

FINANCING THE WAR

The government adopted several methods of financing the war, which cost 300 billion dollars as compared to the 32 billion dollars of World War I. Congress expanded the income tax to cover nearly all white-collar and industrial workers. But the burden of the war did not fall mainly on those of moderate and low incomes. The tax was graduated, so that no one could earn more than 25,000 dollars a year after taxes. As a result, some of the wealthiest citizens paid as much as 94 percent of their income to the federal government, and the distribution of wealth, which had begun to level off during the New Deal, shifted until the top 1 percent of the nation earned only about 7 percent of the total income, a relatively modest proportion.

Yet, taxation financed only about 40 percent of the war effort, leaving a large deficit at the end of the conflict. The administration, as in World War I, also conducted many bond drives calling for people to put aside 10 percent of their income for the purchase of war bonds. The response was enthusiastic and over 40 billion dollars worth of war bonds were sold.

INDUSTRIAL MOBILIZATION

Paying for the war was a less complex challenge than administering it. Efficiency in this sphere was an all-important requirement. The armed forces were built up quickly, but in a society oriented toward unregulated trade, industrial mobilization called for elaborate planning and inevitably brought conflicts. The President was the only figure capable of uniting all the branches of the military and the productive units of private industry into a coordinated whole. Under various laws the President was given sweeping powers, such as had been delegated by Congress to Wilson in World War I. Roosevelt consulted with Congress but believed that as Commander-in-Chief he had the responsibility to manage the war effort. The Truman Senate War Investigating Committee on the efficiency of the war effort kept Congress in the forefront of events, however. Nevertheless, Roosevelt had exercised great scope in the conduct of American foreign policy before the war began and conducted the war effort partly by powers he considered inherent in his office and partly under those delegated to him by law. Under such laws as the two War Powers Acts, Roosevelt had vast authority to reorganize the federal government for war, and to regulate all industrial plants, overseas communications, alien property, and defense contracts. By the end of 1942, he had created more than 700 wartime offices, boards, and commissions. There was much overlapping and inefficiency, and the Office of Emergency Management under Harry Hopkins tried to bring some order out of the chaotic conditions.

When the war began Roosevelt already had created the Office of Production Management (OPM), and it immediately began to supervise the transition to a war economy in early 1941. Thus mobilization was under way before the bombing of Pearl Harbor. The production of aircraft, only one key factor, quadrupled during 1941. After Pearl Harbor, Roosevelt announced newer and bigger goals. In January, 1942, he set very high production levels for the year, including 60,000 airplanes and 45,000 tanks. He created the War Production Board (WPB) to replace the OPM, and appointed Donald Nelson to head it.

Nelson's task was enormous. He had to coordinate the new system of priorities on the allocation of materials both for industry and for the different branches of the armed service. Production grew so rapidly that it was barely possible to keep the WPB operating above the level of chaos. Nelson met with considerable opposition from those who believed that he delegated too much authority. But despite the Board's inefficiency, industrial mobilization was successful and by the end of 1942, goals were being substantially met.

LIFE ON THE HOME FRONT

While the government allocated war materials, a parallel system of controls on rents, wages, salaries, profits, rationing, and prices was developed for the civilian economy. At the beginning of the war there was poor control over wages and farm prices. Increases in food prices created worker demands for increased wages. The War Labor Board of 1942 had tried to solve the problem with the Little Steel formula under which wages were allowed to rise to keep pace with the 15 percent increase in the cost of living since early 1941. But inflation continued until the creation of the Office of War Mobilization under Supreme Court Justice James F. Byrnes. Wages were stabilized in 1943 with prices being the special province of the Office of Price Administration (OPA) run by Chester Bowles. Items such as sugar and gasoline were rationed.

Employment and income increased and strikes were rare after the middle of 1943. When the war began, union leaders had pledged not to strike if there were reasonable guarantees against a cost-of-living inflation. Though this pledge was generally kept, a major exception was the United Mine Workers Union under John L. Lewis. Public indignation at the production halt was so great that Congress passed the Smith-Connally War Labor Disputes Act over Roosevelt's veto. The June, 1943, legislation provided for government take-over of plants involved in essential war industries in the event that they were struck.

RACIAL TENSIONS

The acceleration in industrial output radically changed the lives of many black people, drawing them out of rural areas in the South and into industrial cities like Chicago, Detroit, and Los Angeles. The growing presence of black people in industry, like the increase of women, was largely the result of emergency needs. Segregation in the armed forces and at home persisted despite official notices from the White House decrying it. Roosevelt issued an executive order in 1941 forbidding discrimination in hiring in defense plants and establishing a Fair Employment Practices Commission. While there was some progress under the Commission, black demands also led to racial tensions. In June, 1943, severe race riots struck Detroit. Twenty-five blacks and nine whites were killed. In 1944, the War Department ordered an end to the segregation of military facilities, but the order was largely ineffective.

While on the whole there was little Axis sympathy in the United States and little curtailment of civil liberties during the war, in its dealings with Japanese-Americans, the federal government abandoned even democratic rhetoric. Many Americans, especially on the West Coast, were very fearful of a Japanese invasion of the country which they thought would be aided by a Japanese fifth column within the United States. Areas with a high concentration of Japanese were put under curfew and more than a hundred thousand people were rounded up and crowded into relocation centers hundreds of miles away from the West Coast. Although these actions were a complete violation of the civil rights of Japanese-Americans, the Supreme Court upheld both the curfew and relocation policies as justified measures of preventing activities such as spying and sabotage during wartime. Ironically, many Japanese-Americans were in the armed forces, fighting and winning decorations in Europe.

971

THE ELECTION OF 1944

Even global war did not interrupt the American political process. Though Roosevelt was exhausted, there was no opposition to his renomination in 1944. The fateful decision of the Democratic convention was to replace Henry Wallace with Senator Harry S. Truman of Missouri as Roosevelt's running mate. The Republicans nominated the young and efficient governor of New York, Thomas E. Dewey, as a contrast to the fading President. Nevertheless, Roosevelt won for the fourth time, 25.6 million to 22 million and 432 to 99 in the electoral college.

MILITARY VICTORY AND UNCERTAIN DIPLOMACY

WAR IN THE PACIFIC BEGINS

In the months following Pearl Harbor, Japan embarked on a takeover of the South Pacific. Since the Allies planned to give the Asian front only secondary attention until substantial inroads had been made against Hitler, American forces in Asia were forced to retreat toward the mid-Pacific and stage nuisance air raids on the enemy.

The immediate aftermath of Pearl Harbor was not the seizure of Hawaii and bombardment of the California coast that many Americans feared, but a rounding-out of the Japanese hegemony in Asia. Step by step Japan invaded and conquered the Philippines, Thailand, British Malaya, and The Netherlands East Indies. Thus established on the Malay Peninsula, Japan took the western extreme of her new territory, Hong Kong, and then went on to capture the eastern extreme, Guam, the Gilbert and Solomon islands, and Wake Island.

During this grim period for the Allies, General Douglas MacArthur staged a major defense of the Philippines against Japanese invasion. While Japanese troops took over most of the islands, MacArthur formed an enclave at Bataan and Corregidor, overlooking Manila Bay. Although their situation was hopeless, the American and Filipino force held out until April, 1942. Their surrender resulted in a long march to prison during which many died. MacArthur had been ordered out of the Philippines in mid-March by the President, but vowed he would return to the islands. Roosevelt had removed MacArthur largely because his military skills were needed in defense of Australia.

The next Japanese move proved to be an attempt to cut off communications between the Allies and Australia. Having made vast territorial gains in only a few months, the Japanese might have concentrated on a program of empire consolidation and development, fortifying their organization before engaging in a new phase of war. The wisest men in the Japanese military apparently did argue that the period of expansion was complete, at least for the time being. But the majority of the Japanese military leaders were overconfident.

In May, 1942, the Japanese advanced a fleet toward Port Moresby, on the southern coast of New Guinea in the Coral Sea, a region crucial to Australian security and as a contact point with the Allies. Although the Japanese attack on Pearl Harbor had crippled the Pacific fleet, it had failed to destroy even one aircraft carrier. As Japanese warships approached Port Moresby from the north, the carriers *Lexington* and *Yorktown* launched an aerial bombardment which caused the enemy to retreat.

The Battle of the Coral Sea was significant since the failure of the Japanese to reach New Guinea marked the end of their easy expansion. The battle itself demonstrated the central importance of aerial bombardment in naval warfare.

The Japanese, still blinded by overconfidence, now launched an attack in the mid-Pacific on Midway Island, an American base. This was to be the decisive naval battle of the war. Japan's objective was to destroy the already weak Pacific fleet before the United States had time to rebuild. Their strategy had been deciphered by the Navy, however, and Admiral Chester W. Nimitz succeeded in turning the Japanese initiative into a massive defeat. Confident of victory, the Japanese had deployed a substantial part of their navy to the mid-Pacific, where it was routed by a smaller American force. Midway marked the turning point of the war. After their defeat there, the Japanese fell into a defensive posture while they undertook repairs and reconstruction.

Even without massive supplies during the second half of 1942, the Americans were able to oust the Japanese from New Guinea and the Solomon Islands. Though supply routes between Hawaii and Australia were still open, they had been endangered by the Japanese presence in these outposts. The fighting culminated in the battle of Guadalcanal, which lasted more than six months. When the hard-fighting Japanese finally retreated from Guadalcanal in February, 1943, Allied forces in Asia were ready to begin a full-scale offensive.

WAR AGAINST THE AXIS

The Japanese advance in Asia did not alter Allied resolve to concentrate at first on Europe. During the first months of 1942, while trying to reach agreement on overall strategy for the invasion of Europe, the Allies were limited to specific offensive and defensive actions. The German submarine force in the Atlantic, wreaking havoc on Anglo-American convoys and also disrupting hemispheric trade, had to be stopped. Patrols were set up, scanning devices improved, and efforts made to devise systems of air attack lethal to submarines. But the problem of destroying submarines from the air seemed almost insurmountable. Though by the end of 1943 the submarine menace had been substantially reduced, it continued to do great harm.

Meanwhile the British Royal Air Force, assisted by the American Air Force, began saturation bombing raids on mass targets in Germany. Theoretically, the objective of these raids was to cripple German industries by bringing cities such as Cologne to their knees. At least as important, however, were the motives of demoralization of the German population and revenge for the blitz on Britain. In Hamburg 60,000 civilians were killed during one week of bombing in July, 1943.

NORTH AFRICA

Allied plans finally were worked out in the last months of 1942. Stalin had asked for a second front, an immediate invasion of Europe from the north. But American forces were not ready for such an attack, though Roosevelt gave it considerable thought. Churchill insisted that the German defense of continental Europe was for the moment impermeable, that a too early

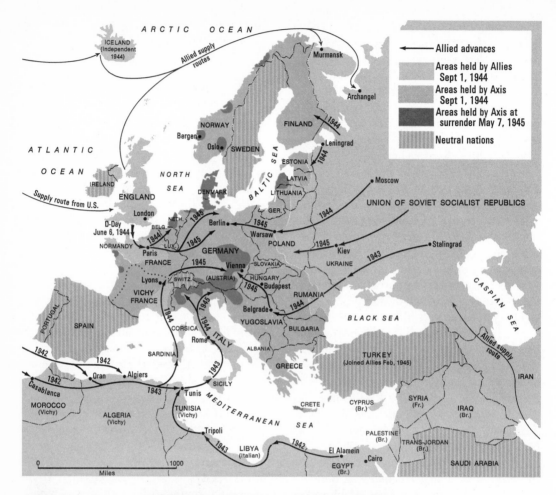

ARCTIC OCEAN

ICELAND (Independent 1944)

Allied supply routes

Murmansk

Archangel

← Allied advances

Areas held by Allies Sept 1, 1944

Areas held by Axis Sept 1, 1944

Areas held by Axis at surrender May 7, 1945

Neutral nations

NORWAY
Bergen
Oslo SWEDEN
FINLAND
1944
Leningrad
1944
ESTONIA
LATVIA
Moscow

ATLANTIC OCEAN

IRELAND
NORTH SEA
ENGLAND
London
D-Day June 6, 1944
NORMANDY
Paris
FRANCE

DENMARK
LITHUANIA
GER.
1944

UNION OF SOVIET SOCIALIST REPUBLICS

BALTIC SEA

NETH.
BELG.
LUX.
1944
1945
1945
Berlin
1945
Warsaw
POLAND
1945
Kiev
UKRAINE
1943
Stalingrad
1944

GERMANY
1945
Vienna
(AUSTRIA)
Lyons
SWITZ.
1945 Budapest
HUNGARY
VICHY FRANCE
1944
1945
Belgrade
1944
RUMANIA
YUGOSLAVIA
BULGARIA
BLACK SEA

CASPIAN SEA

PORTUGAL
SPAIN
CORSICA
Rome
SARDINIA
1944
ITALY
1943
ALBANIA
GREECE
TURKEY (Joined Allies Feb, 1945)

Allied supply route

IRAN

1942
Oran
Algiers
1942
SICILY
1943
Tunis
MEDITERRANEAN SEA
CRETE
CYPRUS (Br.)
SYRIA (Fr.)
IRAQ (Br.)

Casablanca
1942
MOROCCO (Vichy)
ALGERIA (Vichy)
TUNISIA (Vichy)
Tripoli
1943
LIBYA (Italian)
1942
El Alamein
Cairo
EGYPT (Br.)
PALESTINE (Br.)
TRANS-JORDAN (Br.)
SAUDI ARABIA

Supply route from U.S.

0   1000
Miles

WORLD WAR II • EUROPEAN THEATER • 1942 TO 1945

invasion of the Continent would be disastrous. New German operations in North Africa determined the final plans. Field Marshal Erwin Rommel had captured Tobruk, Libya, in May, 1942, and then made inroads into Egypt toward the Suez Canal, threatening to cut off vital supplies. The Allies agreed on Operation TORCH, a plan to invade North Africa, destroy Rommel's forces, and use the area as a base for a northward assault on Italy.

British and German forces were stalled in a confrontation with each other for months around El Alamein, 70 miles from Alexandria. In late October, however, battle began, and General Bernard Montgomery let Rommel think that the major blow would come from the south. The Germans were routed and began a retreat westward. British forces recaptured Tobruk in November, 1942, and were in Tripoli by January, 1943. Meanwhile the Axis had been caught off-guard and dismayed when, exactly at the time that the battle of El Alamein had begun, the Allies commenced amphibious landings at three key points in

North Africa, around Casablanca, Oran and Algiers. Allied forces from the west and east now began to converge on Rommel in Tunisia.

The African campaign was an apparent success when Roosevelt and Churchill met in Casablanca in January, 1943, to discuss future strategy. The British favored an attack through Sicily, and the Americans were again interested in an attack on the northern coast of France, using Great Britain as a base. The conference resulted in a compromise plan to do both, with the attack from the south coming first. The two leaders also issued a statement demanding "unconditional surrender" from the Axis powers.

Unmoved by Allied demands, Hitler rushed more troops to Tunisia. Several months of hard fighting culminated at last in Allied victory and possession of the coastal cities of Bizerte and Tunis. With the southern Mediterranean thus recaptured by May, 1943, the Allies now undertook the invasion of southern Europe.

INVASION OF SICILY

The Allies did not have a thorough grasp of the serious feud that had long gone on between German and Italian fascists. While the demand for unconditional surrender reinforced German determination to win, it frightened Italians and gave inspiration to internal opposition to Mussolini. Axis unity had been a keynote of Hitler's propaganda, and the Allies had believed it. As a consequence, when Mussolini was deposed shortly after the Allied invasion of Sicily in July, 1943, Hitler's own invincibility became suspect.

After Sicily fell in a matter of six weeks to the Allied forces under General Dwight Eisenhower, the Italian king informed Mussolini of his dismissal and replaced him with Marshal Pietro Badoglio. Hitler, to overcome German demoralization, began a frantic effort to reinstate Mussolini as a puppet ruler, backed by German rather than Italian troops. The once popular and powerful dictator had become a political pawn. In the middle of negotiations over Italian surrender, Hitler sent the German army deep into Italy, south of Rome. Nevertheless, in September the Italian government finally surrendered and declared war on Germany.

Allied forces landed in Italy on September 9, 1943, one day after the official surrender. The first beachhead, at Salerno, endured severe bombardment before it finally broke through tenacious German encirclement. The Germans began a slow retreat toward Rome, leaving Naples in ruins behind them. It took eight months for the Allies to advance the short distance from Naples to Rome. Anzio and Monte Cassino were the sites of the worst fighting. Finally in May, 1944, Monte Cassino fell and the troops trapped in Anzio broke

ITALIAN CAMPAIGN · 1943 TO 1945

loose. On June 4 the battered, exhausted men reached Rome and won a joyous reception from its liberated inhabitants.

"BIG THREE" CONFERENCE AT TEHERAN

While the United States had reluctantly accepted Russia as an ally, the American people were encouraged by the Soviet acceptance of the principles of the Atlantic Charter, and her agreement not to make a separate peace with the Axis powers. Yet, realistically, while the United States had no territorial aims, the British were determined to preserve the British Empire, and Russia already had control over the Baltic states, eastern Poland, part of Finland, and Rumania, and was not likely to give them up.

Before meeting at Teheran with Stalin, Roosevelt and Churchill stopped at Cairo for a conference with Chiang Kai-shek. At this meeting they promised the beleaguered Chinese leader more supplies and promised China Formosa, the Pescadores, and Manchuria after the war, with Korea left independent. These commitments were later accepted by Stalin at Teheran.

Late in 1943, the "Big Three"—Roosevelt, Churchill, and Stalin—met in Teheran, Iran, to discuss plans for a Second Front, an invasion of Europe from the north. Some historians have suggested that Churchill encouraged the Allied invasion of Italy, and stalled on a Second Front, because he was already interested in countering Soviet influence in eastern Europe. Churchill himself has denied this and argued that before 1944 the northern attack was impossible to

The "Big Three" at Teheran. Stalin and Churchill had been allied since 1941, when Hitler had invaded the Soviet Union. Although Roosevelt was reluctant to accept Russia as an ally, he was encouraged when Stalin agreed to terms of the Atlantic Charter.

Allied convoys offshore at Omaha Beach on the Normandy coast of France. Behind the D-Day forces were almost three million troops assembled in England for the invasion of Nazi-held Europe.

execute successfully. At Teheran he was still hesitant, but plans went ahead. The three leaders worked closely together and emerged from the conference apparently united and vowing to "work together in the war and in the peace that will follow." Stalin was deeply gratified that the northern invasion was at last about to begin and Roosevelt was very impressed with the Russian leader. Teheran marked a high point of cooperation in the Soviet-Western wartime alliance.

THE WESTERN FRONT

The plan approved at Teheran was called Operation OVERLORD, and it was largely an American project. Churchill still feared that a Second Front invasion might fail but gave it his full support after the conference. His fears were understandable. The German line of defense on the northern coast of France presented an enormous, unbroken obstacle. However, communica-

tion deceptions succeeded in misleading the German high command as to the time and place of the inevitable landings. On D-Day, June 6, the largest amphibious operation in history began under the command of General Dwight Eisenhower. The Allied forces landed at Normandy, on the northwest coast of France rather than farther east, where Hitler's intelligence was persuaded the landing would take place. One hundred and seventy-six thousand men poured from 600 warships and 4,000 smaller vessels. General George Patton's Third Army took Brittany. By mid-July the Allies had won control of a long stretch of coast, a base from which to move inward through France and on toward Germany. Stalin called the invasion "grandiose" and "masterly."

American troops dig in near the French town of Brest in 1944.

From Normandy, where more than a million men had landed by the end of July, the Allies began their movement toward Paris. A simultaneous Allied invasion of southern France from bases on the Africa coast also began working its way north. As the Allied forces approached Paris, the Parisians themselves began to attack their German conquerors, and the city was liberated on August 25 amid great rejoicing.

On the eastern front, the Soviet Union had first stopped Hitler in 1942, when the German army failed to take Stalingrad. At an enormous cost of human life (the Russian death toll by the end of the war was nearly eight million) the Russians forced the Germans to retreat. After the liberation of Paris the drive intensified. With important consequences for the future the Red Army on its way toward Germany invaded or cooperated with resistance forces in Hungary, Yugoslavia, Rumania, Bulgaria, Czechoslovakia, and Austria.

In southern Europe the Allies had continued their drive northward after the liberation of Rome, and finally reached the Gothic line south of the Po Valley, which remained impenetrable for the time being.

Allied forces in France, stalled by problems of supply, now faced the most difficult phase of their assault, meeting hard-core German resistance in their drive toward the Rhine and into Germany. After a series of difficult and costly battles, the Allies reached the Rhine toward the end of 1944.

Anti-aircraft batteries guard against enemy planes, while army tanks move across the Remagen Bridge over the Rhine River into Germany.

Since their forces were stretched out over a long front, they were vulnerable to enemy attack. Hitler then attempted his last major counterattack in the thinly defended Ardennes forest region of Belgium and Luxembourg. His first surprise moves met with success, and for a while it looked as if the Germans might retake Antwerp. A bulge had been created by Germany in the Allied line of defense, and the effort to force a German retreat was named "The Battle of the Bulge." The Germans met their first reversal when Allied reinforcements finally smashed through to the Ardennes. Another month of fighting and the Germans were pushed back to the Rhine. They had gained some time but at the cost of over 100,000 men. Hitler was thereafter unable to stage any major offensives.

Crossing the Rhine to invade Germany involved another spectacular amphibious operation in March, 1944. Aerial bombardment, which had already done so much damage to German cities, now rose to a fierce pitch. Combined with Hitler's scorched-earth policy undertaken by German troops, it reduced Germany to rubble.

The march across Germany and eastern Europe led to the discovery of concentration camps such as those at Dachau, Auschwitz, Buchenwald, and Belsen. The Nazi extermination campaign against the Jews had been rumored since the early 1930s but never completely believed. During the war, people in Denmark and Holland had begun to recognize that Hitler's anti-Semitism was not mere oratory and that their Jewish fellow citizens were being exported to be murdered. This recognition had helped to spark resistance in these countries. In 1945 the extent of the atrocities became apparent when Allied forces liberated survivors of the camps, found mass graves, and learned about the Nazis' methods of mass murder. In the very last months of the war, realizing the certainty of defeat, Hitler ordered an intensification of the extermination policy. Well over a half million Jews were murdered in a seven-week period in Hungary alone in the spring of 1945.

The last months of the war also brought chaos within the Third Reich. Many German politicians were convinced that Hitler's presence blocked a more reasonable and less destructive conclusion to the war, and some even hoped that the United States and Great Britain would still look to Germany as a useful element in any future power struggle with the Soviet Union. Hitler himself, convinced that most of his staff had betrayed him, committed suicide in Berlin on April 30, two days after Mussolini was killed and mutilated by a mob in northern Italy. On May 2 Berlin surrendered.

WAR IN THE PACIFIC CONTINUES

Throughout the war years, the dual purpose of the United States in the Far East was to defeat Japan while at the same time preventing the collapse of China. By the time the United States entered the war, China had been fighting the Japanese for four years. She was war-weary and low on supplies. Roosevelt believed in the potential of China and the leadership of Chiang, little realizing the country's weakness and the internal corruption and intrigue that characterized Chiang's regime.

American supplies flown from India over the Himalayas by General Claire Chenault's Flying Tigers were all the United States could give at first, but in 1942 the administration also assigned General Joseph W. Stilwell to China as the commander of American forces there. Stilwell was able to build a road through northern Burma to facilitate the movement of supplies, but the rest of his mission was a failure. Chiang was more concerned about hoarding his supplies and troops for a future engagement with the rising Chinese communist forces in northwest China than with fighting the Japanese.

979

The Allied invasion of Germany disclosed concentration camps where over six million Jews had been murdered. This photograph shows row upon row of dead bodies, victims of the Germans at the Belsen concentration camp, awaiting burial in common graves.

Stilwell protested to Chiang about the increasing danger from the Japanese and warned the Joint Chiefs that the Generalissimo was undermining the war effort in China. The administration asked Chiang to put Stilwell in command of the Chinese army, but the Generalissimo countered by asking for Stilwell's dismissal. Roosevelt had to recall him, and the Chinese war effort was left in disarray.

A combination of the wishes of two military leaders, General MacArthur and Admiral Nimitz, determined the final strategy of the Asian war. MacArthur adhered to his conviction that the only way to beat Japan was by making headway northward through the Philippines. Nimitz believed such a campaign would only bring unnecessary difficulties. He suggested an attack farther out in the Pacific, where the Japanese had bases—through the Caroline Islands, Guam, the Marianas, and Iwo Jima. MacArthur countered with a passion-

ate plea to Roosevelt stressing the moral commitment of the United States to liberate the Philippines. The result, like the two-front action against Hitler, was a decision in Washington to combine routes. MacArthur and Nimitz thus commanded parallel campaigns.

Between 1943 and 1945, suffering a great number of casualties all along the way, Americans inched toward Japan. After a full year of fighting, Admiral Nimitz's arm of the war had taken the Gilbert and Marshall islands, staging large and complex amphibious landings and then using the islands as bases for bombing raids farther north. This was to be the repeated pattern of the Asian war, moving northward from

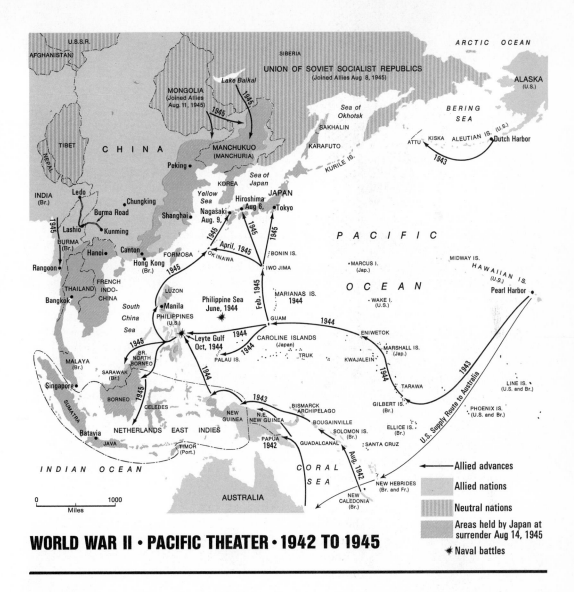

WORLD WAR II · PACIFIC THEATER · 1942 TO 1945

one island group to another in the Pacific. Meanwhile MacArthur's forces moved into vulnerable areas of the Japanese occupation of northern New Guinea and were able to take the Admiralty Islands in March, 1944. Nimitz next captured Guam and the Marianas and commenced bombing raids on Japan. Fire bombs were a particularly effective harassment which by the end of the war had taken 330,000 Japanese lives.

There were three major landmarks in the battle to defeat Japan prior to the use of the atomic bomb: the battle for the Philippines, the battle for Iwo Jima, and the battle for Okinawa. On October 20, 1944, MacArthur realized his long-cherished dream, and landed in the heart of the Philippines on the beach at Leyte Gulf declaring, "I have returned." The Japanese believed that this invasion was a key one and committed the bulk of their navy to it. MacArthur reached Manila in February, 1945, but there were still months, perhaps years, of fighting ahead before the dense

981

cluster of islands would be completely cleared of enemy troops.

Admiral Nimitz focused on tiny Iwo Jima because the Japanese had built airfields there and used it as a lookout for approaching American bombers. The Japanese, however, had anticipated Nimitz's attack on the island and poured in vast numbers of men and armaments. As a result, the battle cost the United States 20,000 casualties, though the island was won. From Iwo Jima still more fire bombs were dropped on the Japanese home islands. The landing on Okinawa again brought long casualty lists.

On August 2, 1939, the physicist Albert Einstein had written to Roosevelt: ". . . the element uranium may be turned into a new and important source of energy in the immediate future." Einstein warned that "watchfulness" and "quick action" were called for. Roosevelt heeded the advice. The Manhattan Project, a secret wartime operation, placed a workable atomic bomb in the hands of President Harry Truman in midsummer, 1945. It had been successfully tested on July 17.

Meeting at Potsdam on July 26, the Allied leaders informed the Japanese that total destruction would be the result of a refusal to surrender instantly. Churchill had given Truman his consent to use the new weapon, should the Japanese refuse to surrender. The Japanese government hesitated, and on August 6, a single plane dropped an atomic bomb on Hiroshima devastating the city. More than 78,000 people were killed and many more either wounded or doomed to suffer the delayed consequences of radioactivity. Two days later, Stalin, keeping a pledge he had made earlier, declared war on Japan and began an invasion of Manchuria. The Japanese still hesitated, and on August 9, the United States dropped a second bomb on the city of Nagasaki. Threatened now by the bombings and by the looming presence of the Soviet Union in Manchuria, on August 15 the Japanese surrendered. The Allies finally overlooked their Casablanca demand for "unconditional surrender," and agreed that Emperor Hirohito might remain on the throne in the months ahead.

Was the United States right in using such a devastating weapon? Defenders of the

Marines attacking a Japanese pillbox on Tarawa.

policy argued that it was used as a military measure. Its destructive effect hastened the end of the war by many months and probably saved half a million American lives. Protesters of the policy countered that Japan was already defeated. Since no land invasion of the Japanese islands was scheduled before November, the United States could have given more warning of the destructiveness of an atomic attack.

YALTA CONFERENCE

At Yalta in February, 1945, the Big Three leadership had met for the last time, to make final war plans, arrange for the fate of Germany, and settle international boundaries. There Churchill and Roosevelt had been willing to grant Stalin a dominant influence in Manchuria as well as the Kurile Islands, Outer Mongolia, and southern Sakhalin Island. In return, Russia agreed to enter the war against Japan a few months after the defeat of Germany.

The Soviet Union insisted on the permanent and complete dissolution of Germany. Seeking further revenge, Stalin also asked for reparations in the form of what amounted to slave labor to rebuild Russia. Roosevelt and Churchill resisted these extreme demands, and the final agreement

On August 6, 1945, an atomic bomb destroyed the city of Hiroshima, killing 200,000 people according to Japanese estimates — 80,000 according to the Americans. Three days later, a second atomic bomb leveled the city of Nagasaki, shown here after the blast.

was for a presumably temporary partition of Germany among the Big Three and France. John L. Snell has described the foreign policy crisis for the Western Powers succinctly: ". . . the prospect of Germany's early collapse had brought the Western statesmen face to face at last with the greatest European dilemma of the twentieth century: how can the threat of German power be eliminated from Europe without leaving Soviet power dominant throughout the continent?"

According to the Yalta agreements, Stalin was to hold much of the Polish territory Russia had taken in 1939, and Poland was to be compensated with a comparable amount of territory inhabited by German-speaking peoples to the west. A Polish government-in-exile, situated in London, seemed to have more genuine support from the Polish people than the one in actual power, which was under Soviet influence. Roosevelt and Churchill, however, accepted a provision specifying merely that the Polish government would be enlarged to include "democratic leaders from Poland itself and . . . Poles abroad." In the eyes of critics, this amounted to a concession to totalitarianism, which paved the way for the Soviet Union's subsequent acquisition of a buffer of satellite countries in eastern Europe, whose "revolutions" she supported. Defenders of the Yalta agreement have pointed out that Roosevelt and Churchill could not have stopped the course of events in eastern Europe without a great sacrifice of human life. The Red Army was already in control of large sections of that area by the time of the Yalta conference. Shortly after the conference Churchill had urged that British and American armies should march as swiftly as possible through Germany into eastern Europe to counter Soviet power. But the United States, considering the military but not the political aspects of such a plan, did not consider it feasible.

The Yalta agreements over Manchuria and central and eastern Europe were later criticized because of postwar Russian action, but, at the time, they were received with jubilation. The war was not yet won and a protracted conflict with Japan was expected. The Big Three emerged from Yalta declaring their solidarity. Roosevelt and his advisers were hopeful that the postwar international climate would be truly peaceful. Some critics have attributed this hope to feeblemindedness and have pointed out that Roosevelt and his most important adviser, Harry Hopkins, were both ailing and tired. But neither Roosevelt, nor Hopkins, nor Churchill, saw themselves as appeasing Stalin in eastern Europe. They believed they had worked long and hard to limit, on paper at least, the extent of Soviet control there.

It was only when the Yalta agreement was made public in 1946 and the Cold War had begun, that its provisions began to look so undesirable. By then the American people knew Russia had not been needed in the war against Japan since America already had the atomic bomb. By then Americans saw that Chiang Kai-shek was in a perilous struggle with the communists in China. Of most importance, it was the subsequent Russian violations of the agreements on eastern Europe that put the conference in such a bad light to Americans.

THE UNITED NATIONS

For a brief period after Germany's defeat, Westerners felt a kind of exultation, and hoped that the world might be entering a new era of peace. Many believed that past mistakes would be instructive, and that the failures of the League of Nations would offer guidelines for a better international organization. The greatest failure of the League had been the nonparticipation of the United States. At Yalta some progress had already been made toward outlining the structure of a new organization and guaranteeing the presence of all the major powers.

Economic instability and the American failure to meet the war debt crises in Europe with a responsible policy had been one factor encouraging the rise of European fascism. In 1944, steps were also taken to avoid a repetition of that failure. At Bretton Woods, New Hampshire, United Nations representatives met and created the International Monetary Fund and the International Bank for Reconstruction. The purpose of these new agencies was to stabilize international currency and speed economic recovery in Europe.

In the midst of these preparations to deal with the postwar world, Franklin Roosevelt died of a cerebral hemorrhage at Warm Springs, Georgia, on April 12, 1945. Responsibility for handling the complexities of the situation now passed into the hands of Harry Truman.

Readings

GENERAL WORKS

Adler, Selig, *The Isolationist Impulse, Its Twentieth Century Reaction*. New York: Abelard-Schuman, 1957—An analysis of the social background and motivations of isolationists since World War I.

Buchanan, A. Russell, *The United States and World War II*, Vols. I–II. New York: Harper & Row, 1964—A general history of the United States in the Second World War which stresses military and administrative matters.

Churchill, Winston, *The Second World War*, Vols. I–VI. Boston: Houghton Mifflin, 1948–1953—The prime minister's own account of World War II which combines historical perspective and an intimate involvement in crucial wartime decisions.

DeConde, Alexander, ed., *Isolation and Security: Ideas and Interests in Twentieth Century American Foreign Policy*. Durham, N.C.: Duke University Press, 1957—A collection of readings on recent American foreign policy.

Dulles, Foster R., *America's Rise to World Power*. New York: Harper & Row, 1955—A general history of American foreign relations from the Spanish-American War to 1954.

Goodman, Jack, ed., *While You Were Gone: A Report on Wartime Life in the United States*. New York: Simon & Schuster, 1946—A collection of short essays on different facets of American life during World War II. The subjects range from sports and comics to veterans and racial problems.

Janeway, Eliot, *The Struggle for Survival*. New York: Weybright & Talley, 1968—An account of economic mobilization for World War II which stresses the political, administrative, and social issues which the transformation to a war economy entailed.

Morison, Samuel E., *The Two-Ocean War*. Boston: Little, Brown, 1963—A short account of the naval operations of the Second World War. Morison is both a leading historian and an admiral.

Nevins, Allan, *The New Deal and World Affairs*. New York: United States Publishers Association, 1970—A brief description of diplomatic relations under Roosevelt in peace and war.

Nevins, Allan, *The United States in a Chaotic World: Chronicle of International Affairs 1918–1933*. New York: United States Publishers Association, 1970—A short history of American involvement in world affairs during the fifteen years following World War I. Nevins asserts that the major diplomatic issues of the period reflected the disruptions the war had caused.

SPECIAL STUDIES

Beard, Charles A., *President Roosevelt and the Coming of the War*. Hamden, Conn.: Shoe String, 1968—A sharply hostile account of Roosevelt's diplomacy and political maneuverings before United States entry into World War II. In this, the great historian's last book, he accuses Roosevelt of deceit and dictatorial ambitions.

Borg, Dorothy, *The United States and the Far Eastern Crisis of 1933–1938*. Cambridge, Mass.: Harvard University Press, 1964—As well as studying United States policy toward Japan's war against China, the book investigates such matters as United States naval policy in the Pacific and reactions to internal Chinese political developments.

DeConde, Alexander, *Herber Hoover's Latin American Policy*. New York: Octagon, 1970 —DeConde maintains that Herbert Hoover began moves to ease relations with Latin American and put them on a more equal footing. These policies were later elaborated upon and carried out in Roosevelt's Good Neighbor Policy.

Ellis, L. Ethan, *Republican Foreign Policy 1921–1933*. New Brunswick, N.J.: Rutgers University Press, 1968—Ellis argues that foreign policy in the 1920s was not isolationist but that Secretaries of State and Presidents feared making strong commitments.

Feis, Herbert, *Churchill, Roosevelt, Stalin*. Princeton, N.J.: Princeton University Press, 1967—A detailed narrative of diplomacy among the three Allied leaders, concentrating on the great summit conferences at which they met.

Feis, Herbert, *The Road to Pearl Harbor*. Princeton, N.J.: Princeton University Press, 1950—Feis, a former State Department official, presents a detailed account of the growing tension between the United States and Japan which culminated in Pearl Harbor.

Ferrell, Robert H., *American Diplomacy in the Great Depression*. Hamden, Conn.: Shoe String, 1969—An analysis of foreign policy under Herbert Hoover. Ferrell devotes considerable attention to Henry Stimson's tentative moves away from American isolationism.

Girdner, Audrie, and Anne Loftis, *The Great Betrayal*. New York: Macmillan, 1969—A study of the evacuation of Japanese-Americans to detention camps during World War II.

Langer, William L., and S. E. Gleason, *The Challenge to Isolation 1937–1940*. New York: Harper & Row, 1952—The first volume of the authors' two-volume study of American diplomacy in the years before Pearl Harbor. Langer and Gleason write from an internationalist perspective and criticize isolationism as a force to be overcome.

Langer, William L., and S. E. Gleason, *Undeclared War 1940–1941*. New York: Harper & Row, 1953—The second and final volume of Langer and Gleason's study of the diplomatic origins of America's entry into World War II.

Snell, John L., ed., *The Meaning of Yalta.* Baton Rouge: Louisiana State University Press, 1956—Four essays on different aspects of the diplomacy of the 1945 Yalta Conference. The authors rebut the accusation that Yalta was a United States sell-out to the Soviet Union.

Wohlstetter, Roberta, *Pearl Harbor, Warning and Decision.* Stanford, Calif.: Stanford University Press, 1962—A political scientist's analysis of American intelligence and strategy at Pearl Harbor. The author claims that too much contradictory information was being received for the President to have acted on the assumption that the Japanese were actually planning to attack Pearl Harbor.

Wood, Bryce, *The Making of the Good Neighbor Policy.* New York: Columbia University Press, 1961—Dealing more with ideas about diplomacy rather than Latin American relations themselves, Wood places the Good Neighbor policy in the context of the difficulties in ties between great and small powers.

PRIMARY SOURCES

Bradley, Omar N., *A Soldier's Story.* New York: Popular Library, 1970—War memoirs of a leading American general in the European Theater of World War II. Bradley gives detailed accounts of United States military strategy.

Eisenhower, Dwight D., *Crusade in Europe.* Garden City, N.Y.: Doubleday, 1948—Eisenhower's own account of his experiences in World War II.

Grew, Joseph C., *Turbulent Era,* Vols. I–II. Freeport, N.Y.: Books for Libraries, 1970—As the American ambassador to Japan, Grew played an important role in American-Japanese diplomacy before Pearl Harbor. This is his memoir.

Hull, Cordell, *Memoirs,* Vols. I–II. New York: Macmillan, 1948—A long, detailed memoir of Hull's life from youth to retirement. The focus is on Hull's twelve years as Roosevelt's Secretary of State.

MacArthur, Douglas, *Reminiscences.* New York: McGraw-Hill, 1964—Published after his death, MacArthur's memoirs cover half defends his political views.

Pyle, Ernie, *Here's Your War: The Story of G.I. Joe.* Cleveland: World, 1945—A famous war correspondent who died in action in the Pacific, Pyle's reports concentrate on the day-to-day experiences of the average G.I.

Stimson, Henry L., and McGeorge Bundy, *On Active Service in Peace and War.* New York: Harper & Row, 1948—Over a period of more than four decades, Henry Stimson held virtually every important position in the defense and foreign policy establishment. These are his memoirs.

BIOGRAPHIES

Blum, John M., *From the Diaries of Henry Morgenthau*, Vols. I–II. Boston: Houghton Mifflin, 1959–1967—Morgenthau was Roosevelt's Secretary of the Treasury, and his diaries are a valuable source for studying both the depression and World War II. The diaries show Morgenthau's role in such important questions as wartime finance and the planning for postwar Germany.

Burns, James M., *Roosevelt: Soldier of Freedom*. New York: Harcourt Brace Jovanovich, 1970—A sequel to Burns's *Roosevelt: The Lion and the Fox*. This volume deals with the President's role as wartime leader and stresses the conflict between short-term military and political expediency and the need for long-range planning for both war and peace.

Morison, Elting E., *Turmoil and Tradition, A Study of the Life and Times of Henry L. Stimson*. New York: Atheneum, 1964—A sympathetic biography of the Republican political leader who served Franklin D. Roosevelt as Secretary of War during World War II.

Pogue, Forrest, *George C. Marshall*, Vols. I–II. New York: Viking, 1963–1966—The definitive biography of the general and statesman. The two volumes published cover through 1943.

Pratt, Julius W., *Cordell Hull*, Vols. I–II. New York: Cooper Square, 1964—A detailed record of Hull's years as Secretary of State. Pratt portrays Hull as a dedicated believer in Woodrow Wilson's internationalist ideals.

Tuchman, Barbara, *Stilwell and the American Experience in China*. New York: Macmillan, 1970—Both a biography of the acid-tongued American general and an account of internal and external revolution and war in China during World War II. Tuchman tends to share Stilwell's harsh evaluation of Chiang Kai-shek.

FICTION

Cozzens, James G., *Guard of Honor*. New York: Harcourt, Brace, 1949—A novel which takes place during three days in an air force training camp in Florida during World War II.

Heller, Joseph, *Catch-22*. New York: Simon & Schuster, 1965—A novel of black humor concerning a group of airmen flying bombing raids on Italy during World War II.

Jones, James, *From Here to Eternity*. New York: Scribner's, 1951—A novel of army life in Hawaii. The time is late 1941, the month before Pearl Harbor. The plot revolves around two soldiers and their women.

Mailer, Norman, *The Naked and the Dead*. New York: New American Library, 1960—Mailer's first novel, concerning the lives and deaths of a platoon of soldiers on a Pacific island. The action centers around a futile and bloody mission against the Japanese.

28

President Truman and the Cold War Years

I believe that it must be the policy of the United States to support free peoples who are resisting attempted subjugation by armed minorities or by outside pressures.

I believe that we must assist free peoples to work out their own destinies in their own way.

I believe that our help should be primarily through economic and financial aid which is essential to economic stability and orderly political processes. . . .

The free peoples of the world look to us for support in maintaining their freedoms.

If we falter in our leadership, we may endanger the peace of the world—and we shall surely endanger the welfare of our own nation.

—Harry S. Truman

When Berlin fell to the Allied forces, Russian troops occupied and held the western section of the city, creating a Russian Zone in which American trade was prohibited. The Berlin Airlift, shown here, became the lifeline of the West Berlin people, bringing in supplies to the blockaded city.

At the time of Franklin Roosevelt's death, Harry S. Truman commented, "Last night the moon, the stars and all the planets fell on me." Gradually Truman began to learn the extent of his own lack of information—he had not even been kept informed about research on the atomic bomb. However, the problems confronting Truman were not as much inherent in his sudden elevation to the Presidency as in the historical situation. Almost immediately he had to cope with foreign policy questions of crucial importance. The meaning and significance of the international events during Truman's Presidency have become one of the most debated topics among historians of modern America.

TRUMAN AS PRESIDENT

Nothing in Truman's personal background hinted at his national destiny. Born in Lamar, Missouri, in 1884, he grew up in Independence, worked for the Santa Fe Railroad, was a dirt farmer for twelve years, served as a captain of artillery in World War I, and became a partner in a haberdashery store that failed. Then he went into politics under the wing of the Democratic boss of Kansas City, Tom Pendergast. It was an association that brought Truman much criticism when Pendergast's career ended in prison, but he was never personally implicated in any of the machine's corrupt activities. Elected to the Senate in 1934, Truman won another term in 1940,

and was prominent enough in his party to be selected by FDR for Vice President four years later.

Truman was a forthright, quick-tempered man who was informal and accessible in his manner. He was more concerned with doing his duty than with the power of his office. He liked making decisions. He was a loyal party man who gained more self-confidence the longer he was in the Presidency.

THE POTSDAM CONFERENCE

Truman became President shortly before the collapse of Germany, and V-E Day on May 7 was celebrated less than a month after the new President's inauguration. Although Truman was reluctant to attend an international conference, postwar problems made it necessary for him to meet with America's major allies. To that end he journeyed to Potsdam in July to confer with Stalin and Churchill (who was replaced by Clement Attlee following the election victory by the British Labour Party in July, 1945).

Events immediately preceding the Potsdam meeting were not encouraging to those who hoped for postwar cooperation among the Allies. Shortly after the Yalta Conference, Russia not only began consolidating her hold on eastern Europe but charged that the Western Allies were secretly negotiating with Germany. Truman seems to have initially believed that he could work with Stalin, but W. Averell Harriman and George Kennan warned that the Russians were bent on an expansionist policy which would not be easy to control. The Russians, for their part, were indignant when Truman abruptly terminated Lend-Lease in May, 1945, after sidetracking a Russian request for a large loan.

With the Japanese conflict still raging, Truman opened the conference by giving his colleagues a briefing on the progress of

Stalin and Truman during an informal moment at the Potsdam Conference. Although Truman believed he could come to terms with Stalin regarding post-war expansionism, Truman's advisors warned him against dealing with the Russians.

American arms under General MacArthur, agreed with them on the unconditional surrender policy, and, fearful of a last-ditch defense of the home islands by the Japanese, welcomed Stalin's renewed promise to enter the war. On July 24, Truman, after receiving word of the successful testing of an atomic device, told Stalin that the United States had detonated an atomic bomb, but the Russian dictator showed very little interest in it. Two days later the British and Americans, without consulting the Soviet Union, issued the Potsdam Declaration calling on Japan to surrender.

POLAND AND THE SATELLITES

The issue of Poland's postwar government came up again at Potsdam and was the point at which Soviet intransigence blocked all progress. Without consulting their Allies, the Soviets had extended the western boundary of Poland to the Oder and Neisse rivers, inside pre-war Germany. The Allies refused to accept this claim to German territory, but there was nothing they could do to reverse the decision. The

Russians also had imposed a pro-communist puppet regime on the Poles despite Stalin's pledges to permit free elections there. Stalin had made a gesture of allowing members of the Polish government-in-exile to return to Warsaw from London, but they were elbowed out in a few months, leaving the communists in full control.

The other nations of eastern Europe suffered a similar fate. During the second half of 1945 the Russians installed pro-communist regimes in Poland, Rumania, Bulgaria, and Albania. Since Russian troops were still camped on the soil of these countries, the Allies were powerless to do anything about it short of an all-out war. To their protests in behalf of democratic government in the area of eastern Europe, Stalin retorted coldly: "Any government not fascist is democratic." There were free elections in Hungary in November, 1945, and the communists, left in a minority position, were not able to attain power until 1947 when they were backed by Soviet power. Yugoslavia, though communist, was freer of Russian influence and broke openly with the Soviet Union in 1948.

GERMANY

To disarm and de-Nazify Germany, and to try the remaining Nazi leaders for war crimes, were points easily agreed upon. Direction of German affairs was to be placed under an Allied Control Council in Berlin, made up of British, French, Russian, and American representatives of the four occupied zones. It was to manage the defeated nation as a single economic unit. The precise nature of a German government remained vague, and the verbal agreement on German unity concealed Stalin's determination to keep the Soviet zone under communist control. Russia finally gave way on her most extreme demands for reparations from Germany when she was promised a percentage of industrial equipment from the western zones. The United States fulfilled this promise until May, 1946.

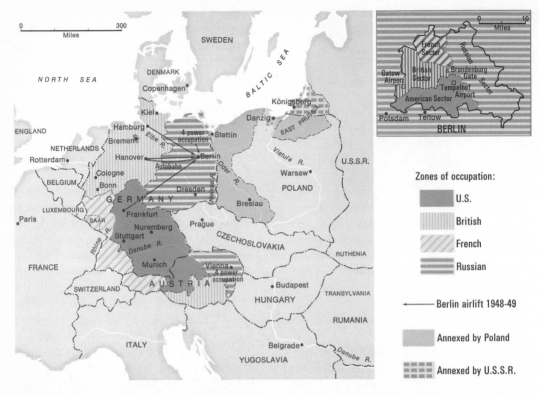

OCCUPATION ZONES GERMANY AND AUSTRIA • 1945 TO 1950

More ominous for the future, the Allies agreed to a division of Berlin into four sectors. The city lay inside the Soviet Zone, and the Allies did not demand a land corridor to guarantee access rights to their respective zones.

The men who had surrounded Hitler went on trial in Nuremberg on November 20, 1945, accused of crimes against peace, humanity, and the laws of war. Of those found guilty, twelve were sentenced to death, but only ten went to the gallows. Goering had committed suicide and Bormann escaped capture, his fate a mystery. Similar war crimes trials in Japan between 1946 and 1948 sentenced seven officials to death.

An important agreement which came out of the Potsdam Conference was the creation of a Council of Foreign Ministers to work out the peace treaties for Italy, Austria, Hungary, Rumania, Bulgaria, and Finland. Meetings between July and August, 1946, produced peace treaties with all these countries but Austria. A treaty with that nation was finally worked out in 1955 and only then were Soviet troops removed.

THE UNITED NATIONS

An international organization to replace the League of Nations had been fashioned under Roosevelt's guidance. Truman had the satisfaction of seeing the plan become a reality. He addressed the opening session of the San Francisco Conference to work out the details of its Charter in April, 1945, and was present for the signing of the Charter on June 26. The Senate ratified it on July 28. Both the United States and the Soviet Union blocked a plan for an international police force although the Charter provided for police action against an aggressor. Still, the UN was the best hope for world peace available, and Truman hailed the Charter as "a solid structure upon which we can build a better world."

THE CHARTER

In its quest for peace through negotiation rather than war, the United Nations established a General Assembly, a world forum for the discussion of issues representing all members, and a Security Council with six temporary and five permanent members: Britain, France, the Soviet Union, China, and the United States. The Economic and Social Council, the Trusteeship Council, and the International Court of Justice were three of the more significant bodies founded under the Charter. A Secretariat, headed by a Secretary General, performed the administrative work of the organization.

THE VETO

The most troublesome element in the United Nations structure as laid out in the Charter proved to be the use of the veto. Since none of the great powers would per-

Hitler's associates were brought to trial in Nuremberg in 1945 for crimes against humanity. Twelve men were sentenced to death for their part in the war. This photograph shows (left to right) Hermann Goering (taking notes), Rudolph Hess, and Joachim Von Ribbentrop, Hitler's Foreign Minister.

mit the assembled representatives to meddle in its important affairs, unanimity of the five major world powers on the Security Council was required before action could be approved. But in the first few years of the UN's operation, the Soviet representative used the veto repeatedly, nine times in 1946 alone.

ATOMIC ENERGY

The men at the United Nations also labored under the sinister shadow of a new era of atomic power. While President Truman believed he had made the correct decision in using the bomb against Japan, he wanted Hiroshima and Nagasaki to be the last examples of nuclear destruction. Controls, national and international, dominated his thinking.

THE ATOMIC ENERGY COMMISSION

To supervise this new source of energy, Truman signed the Atomic Energy Act on August 1, 1945. Under its provisions the Atomic Energy Commission was established with David Lilienthal as its first chairman. Further tests were scheduled so that scientists might learn how to harness nuclear power more effectively. The most dramatic test was the explosion at Bikini in the Marshall Islands in 1946.

THE BARUCH PLAN

In addition, Truman moved to place the development of atomic energy under international control. Bernard Baruch, the American member of the United Nations Atomic Energy Commission, offered a plan by which American atomic bombs would be destroyed, all nations would be barred from making atomic bombs, and the United Nations given the authority to supervise the uses of atomic power. The Baruch Plan also called for on-site inspection to see that the agreement was carried out. Andrei Gromyko, the Soviet representative, said *"nyet."* Thus, the plan was rejected because Russia did not want the world to see the progress of her nuclear research.

TRUMAN'S RECONVERSION POLICY

Truman's task was to shift the national economy from wartime to peacetime production, and to do it with as little turmoil as possible.

Most Americans wanted the soldiers brought home from Europe and Asia as quickly as possible. Therefore, even though a certain number had to remain in uniform to man bases and provide occupation forces, by the end of 1945 five million men had been returned to civilian life. In July, 1946, there were 1.5 million men in the Army. The draft was discontinued from March, 1947, to June, 1948, when tensions with the Soviet Union prevailed on a reluctant Congress to reinstate it.

Truman spelled out his plans in a message to Congress on September 6, 1945. His long array of proposals included full and fair employment, unemployment insurance, the building of at least one million homes a year for ten years, public works, farm price supports, an increase in the minimum wage from 40 cents to 65 cents, and development of natural resources. In later messages he pressed for a strong civil rights bill, health insurance, and improved social security. The program, a forerunner of his Fair Deal proposals, seemed overwhelming to the conservative coalition in Congress, and died on Capitol Hill.

Some social analysts predicted that the American economy, after an excessive wartime expansion, would suffer a severe depression in changing over to peacetime demands. They were wrong for several reasons. The end of hostilities caused an army of consumers to besiege the stores demanding goods that had virtually disappeared from the market during the previous five years. Factories and businesses worked overtime to meet the demand, turning out cars instead of tanks and civilian shoes instead of military boots. Tax reductions also aided the business transition. War taxes were lifted, easing the country's tax burden by 6 billion dollars. The G.I. Bill took up much of the slack in education, allowing former servicemen to attend schools or colleges at government expense. In April, 1946, unemployment was at a low of three million people and the Employment Act of 1946, following the theories of John Maynard Keynes, committed the government to use its powers to prevent any return to the "boom-and-bust" cycles of the past. Truman appointed a Council of Economic Advisors under this law. The function of the three members was "to analyze and interpret economic developments" and make a yearly report. It was a further move in the direction of government planning within the free enterprise system.

INFLATION

As the fear of depression receded, the fear of inflation replaced it in the minds of government economists. They were afraid of a spiral of increased wages, followed by higher prices, which in turn would be followed by increased wages.

STRIKES

The war was hardly over before the unions began to push for an end to wage controls. Since prices had risen about 33 percent since 1944, the unions asked for raises of about 30 percent. Their demands, rejected by management as unrealistic, produced a rash of strikes. Millions of working hours were lost during the first year of peace. There were 1.6 million men on strike in January, 1946, and the Steel and Electrical workers obtained raises of 18 to 20 cents an hour. Two strikes of 1946 shook the nation. The United Mine Workers under John L. Lewis created a coal shortage amounting to a "national disaster." When the government seized the mines, Lewis jibed: "You can't mine coal with bayonets." The final settlement of the dispute gave him much of what he demanded in wage increases, safety rules, and a welfare fund. Truman also seized the railroads when the workers went on strike, and most unions accepted a compromise settlement. However, a few unions were recalcitrant. They also finally came to terms, but not before Truman had threatened to draft into the armed forces all those who struck against the government. Not only did Congress deny him such power when he asked for it, but some of the President's friends had warned him that his stand had gained him nothing but a legacy of enmity within the ranks of labor.

OPA

The Office of Price Administration, after holding the lid on prices during the war, expired under Truman, in spite of his efforts to save it. He wanted to keep wartime controls until the reconversion process was completed. However, both businessmen and farmers wanted higher prices and called for an end to OPA. Truman had to decide whether to accept a badly watered down version passed by Congress over his objections in 1946. The measure would have extended the life of OPA minus what Truman considered its essential powers. He vetoed the bill and prices soared at once. Then Congress passed a new OPA bill which Truman accepted in July, 1946, but all controls except on rents were gradually lifted by the end of the year. The cost of living rose from 83.4 in 1946 to 102.8 in 1948.

THE CONGRESSIONAL ELECTIONS OF 1946

The domestic troubles of the first Truman administration gave the Republicans the battle cry of "Had enough?" for the Congressional elections of 1946. They charged that the President simply was not a big enough man for the job. Consumers were angry about high prices, labor about low wages, management about government policies toward business, and many individuals about Truman's earthy personality. As a result, the Democrats lost control of Congress for the first time since Franklin Roosevelt became President. The Republicans gained eleven seats in the Senate and 54 seats in the House. They dominated the Eightieth Congress, presenting so thorny a problem to the Democratic President that he soon was calling it "the worst Congress in history."

THE TAFT-HARTLEY ACT

While the Republicans cut government expenses and taxes, the Eightieth Congress gave Truman the chance to win back some of the popularity he had lost with the labor unions in trying to curb strikes. Senator Robert A. Taft of Ohio, often under attack by labor, was one sponsor of a new labor act which passed the last Congressional hurdles in 1947. Its most highly criticized provisions outlawed the closed shop which compelled workers to be union members, and approved 80-day government injunctions by which the President could enforce a cooling-off period during any strike affecting the national welfare. It also provided that unions could be sued by employers for breach of contract, and prohibited unions from using coercion against nonunion members. Unions were also required to publish a financial statement and they were forbidden to make contributions to political parties.

Truman vetoed the Taft-Hartley Act in stinging terms. He charged that "it would go far toward weakening our trade-union movement." The unions agreed with him but Congress did not. The Presidential veto was overridden on Capitol Hill.

THE TWENTY-SECOND AMENDMENT

The old enemies of Franklin Roosevelt on the Hill, still smarting from his four terms in office and anxious to prevent a repetition, maneuvered through Congress a document that, when ratified by the states in 1951, became the Twenty-second Amendment to the Constitution. According to this amendment, "No person shall be elected to the office of the President more than twice." Truman, explicitly excluded by this prohibition, commented satirically that FDR's place in history was now secure since he alone would be more than a two-term President, unless and until some future amendment should change the requirements.

CIVIL RIGHTS

In 1946 Truman appointed a Committee on Civil Rights. Toward the end of 1947, the Committee issued a report, *To Secure*

These Rights, covering a broad spectrum of existing problems and possible solutions. Education, housing, employment, health, and public services were all covered in the survey, which suggested laws and legal actions to curtail if not end discrimination in American life. Truman followed this fundamental document with a strong legislative proposal on civil rights but never was able to secure any legislation from the Congress. However, he strengthened the Civil Rights Section of the Justice Department and began desegregation of the armed forces and government departments by executive order. Herein lay the seeds of Southern disenchantment with, and the support of black Americans for, the President in the coming election.

THE COLD WAR

For two decades following the end of World War II, historians saw the Cold War purely as an American response to Soviet aggression. By the 1960s, however, some students of the period began to wonder whether the United States did not share at least part of the responsibility for the international tensions which developed rapidly during 1945. Truman, say these revisionists, was influenced by the Joint Chiefs and his State Department advisers to take a hard line, whereas Roosevelt had been able to cooperate with Russia. Truman told Stalin about the atomic bomb at Potsdam to try to alter her expansionist policy in the Far East and in eastern Europe. According to the revisionists, the United States wanted to keep these areas out of Soviet control in order that American businessmen could expand their markets there. Truman's hard-line policy was self-defeating, however, since Stalin was not deterred from extending Russian power into either Manchuria or eastern Europe. In fact, the Soviet Union moved into Manchuria and acted to prevent democratic elements from having any political control in the Balkans. Thus, all of eastern Europe and the Russian zone in Germany were out of the reach of American trade. This economic interpretation of the Cold War has in turn been challenged by those who see the conflict more in political and ideological terms. They point out that regardless of the course of American policy, the Soviet Union was guided by her centuries-old desire to dominate eastern Europe for her own security and by the Marxist drive to spread communism.

By the beginning of 1946, the conflicting interests and ideals of the Soviet Union and the Western democracies, earlier doubted by some, were obvious to men in power in both camps. The Cold War was underway.

On February 9, 1946, Stalin addressed the Soviet people regarding the state of the world. He pictured western Europe as weak and ripe for a communist take-over. The Soviet Union, he declared, would do everything possible to bring the old order down in ruins and bring them the benefits of communism.

On March 5, less than a month after Stalin's chilling analysis, Winston Churchill also reviewed the international situation at Westminster College in Fulton, Missouri. He concluded that wartime amity was a thing of the past, killed by the Russians for their own purposes. "From Stettin in the Baltic to Trieste in the Adriatic," he told his audience, "an iron curtain has descended across the Continent. This is certainly not the liberated Europe we fought to build up. Nor is it one which contains the essentials of permanent peace."

THE IRANIAN CRISIS

Even as Stalin spoke, the Soviet Union was making a test case of Iran. Allied forces in the domain of the Shah had promised to withdraw by March 2, 1946. The Russians refused to honor the evacuation deadline. Allied diplomacy failed to budge them. Only when Iran took the matter to the United Nations, and at the same time agreed to let the Soviets have a hand in the control of Iranian oil, did Stalin's troops finally withdraw. The Shah then turned to America for help, rejected the oil agreement with Russia, and hastened to make military preparations in case of another Soviet threat.

PRESSURE ON GREECE AND TURKEY

Russia now shifted her pressure to the eastern Mediterranean and an old ambition to control the Turkish Straits. In March, 1945, she demanded territory in eastern Turkey on the border of Russia and bases in the straits. Turkey refused and the United States backed her by sending a naval force to the Mediterranean, threatening to take the matter to the Security Council.

The Soviets were also active in another traditional area of Russian interest—the Balkan Peninsula. Greece, convulsed by civil war, nearly fell to Soviet expansionism as the internal confusion there at the end of the war gave the communists their opportunity to bid for power. But British troops had entered Greece on the heels of the retreating Nazis, and Churchill ordered them to prevent any Moscow-inspired coup. The conservative government drove the communists from Athens, but there were two ominous developments. Guerrilla fighting in the provinces became full-fledged civil war as the communist bloc demanded part of the Greek territory and sent aid to the rebels across the Yugoslav border. In

addition, London could no longer afford the expense of defending Greek liberty in spite of a large American loan to Britain in December, 1945. She started withdrawing her troops in early 1947.

THE TRUMAN DOCTRINE

Believing that the United States must fill the vacuum caused by British withdrawal of aid from both Turkey and Greece, President Truman outlined an important shift in American foreign policy. In his message to Congress on March 12, 1947, he declared: "The free peoples of the world look to us for support in maintaining their freedoms. If we falter in our leadership, we may endanger the peace of the world—and we shall surely endanger the welfare of our own nation."

Congress agreed with the President, earmarking 400 million dollars in aid to Greece and Turkey, and accepting the principle that America had to assist other nations that might be threatened by communism. The policy which became known as the "Truman Doctrine" saved Greece, although the civil war went on until 1948 when Tito's feud with Stalin put an end to Russia's use of Yugoslavia as a base for interfering in Greek affairs.

THE CONTAINMENT POLICY

The Truman Doctrine was a turning point in American foreign policy. The President shifted gears suddenly and committed the nation to global responsibilities never before undertaken. Truman had bluntly claimed that Soviet moves in the eastern Mediterranean were a threat to American security. He did not speak of ideology—neither Greece nor Turkey were democracies. He also appeared to be calling on the American people for a long-range effort to hold the line against communist expansion everywhere. It was an open recognition on the part of the United States that, despite her hopes, the United Nations could not be counted on to protect American national security. The critics of the containment policy attacked it for its lack of idealism in aiding such reactionary governments as those in Greece and Turkey. It was also criticized as a unilateral bypassing of the United Nations, an aggressive act by the United States rather than Russia. Some argued that American money would be better spent in feeding the world's poor.

KENNAN'S ARTICLE

A member of the State Department, formerly with the American Embassy in Moscow, gave the new strategy its basic formulation and its familiar name. George Kennan called it "containment" in an article in the July, 1947, issue of *Foreign Affairs*. According to Kennan, the Soviets, believing in the inevitable triumph of communism, felt no compulsion to take chances for the sake of a quick victory. Their ideology made them flexible. Therefore, while creating trouble for the free world wherever they safely could, they would not be unyielding when met by resolute opposition. Thus, it was a mistake to fear that firmness in dealing with them would lead to war. On the contrary, the safest strategy was "a policy designed to confront the Russians with unalterable counterforce at every point where they show signs of encroaching upon the interests of a peaceful and stable world."

THE MARSHALL PLAN

As Kennan outlined a diplomatic strategy for dealing with Moscow, so Secretary of State Marshall sketched an economic strategy for the restoration of Europe. A revitalized western Europe would also help contain Soviet expansion.

Marshall's ideas were the culmination of earlier thinking. Even before the Cold War with Russia became America's main foreign policy problem, she was concerned with the dangerous economic situation in Europe and Asia. In 1943, the United States had taken the lead in organizing the United Nations Relief and Rehabilitation Administration (UNRRA) which between 1945 and 1947 distributed more than 11 billion dollars in food, clothing, and medical supplies in Europe and the Far East.

The United States withdrew from the UNRRA in 1947 fearing that some of the money being spent was being used by communist countries for ulterior purposes. In 1946, however, the United States had made a unilateral loan to Great Britain of 4 billion dollars. But the winter of 1946 was cruel, and food and coal shortages were evident all over Europe. Speaking at Harvard on June 5, 1947, Marshall suggested raising American aid to war-torn and starving Europe from a piecemeal affair to a general scheme. "Any assistance this country may render in the future," he said, "should provide a cure rather than a mere palliative. Any government that is willing to assist in the task of recovery will find full cooperation, I am sure, on the part of the United States government. Any government which maneuvers to block the recovery of other countries cannot expect help from us."

Marshall's words created a sensation in Europe, giving hope to despairing nations. Sixteen representatives of western European nations met in Paris on July 12, 1947, and worked out arrangements for making the best use of the massive economic aid being offered by the United States.

Americans were not so unified in their support of the plan. Senator Taft and other isolationists sniped at the scheme as a "handout." Henry Wallace called it another device to divide Europe which would lead to war. But Congressional approval came overwhelmingly in March, 1948, with the backing of farm, labor, and business groups. By the end of Truman's Presidency, approximately 13.2 billion dollars had been put into European recovery. The burgeoning prosperity of the participating nations proved the effectiveness of the plan.

Russia had not only forbidden her eastern European satellites to participate in the plan, but she took several countermeasures after the plan was announced. In October, 1947, she set up the Cominform, a web of communist agencies designed to sabotage the economic recovery of Europe. In January, 1949, she initiated an economic assistance plan of her own for eastern Europe.

THE COMMUNIST COUP IN CZECHOSLOVAKIA

One of the first nations to accept the Marshall Plan had been Czechoslovakia, a nation run by a coalition of communists and noncommunists. But Prague was forced to withdraw under Russian pressure, and Stalin became determined to have a more compliant regime. Under the Soviet occupation, the communists had deeply infiltrated the government departments. Foreign Minister Jan Masaryk, who was the strongest noncommunist figure in the government, was found dead beneath his office window on May 10, 1948. The Russians called it suicide, but the suspicious nature of the tragedy provoked a belief that Soviet agents had murdered him. The Russians quickly staged a one-party election, ousted noncommunist Eduard Beneš, and set up a puppet regime headed by their faithful supporter Klement Gottwald.

THE FIRST BERLIN CRISIS

At the suggestion of the United States, European nations also began planning a military union to defend themselves against possible Russian aggression. On March 17, 1948, Britain, France, and the Benelux countries (Belgium, The Netherlands, and

Luxembourg) signed the Brussels Pact, a 50-year military alliance. The United States stood behind it. The United States, Britain, and France also agreed to coordinate their economic policies in their zones in Germany and give them Marshall Plan aid. An unarmed West German government, with control over its own domestic policies, was also set up. The institution of a West German currency over Soviet protest brought on the first Berlin crisis.

The one point at which Stalin felt free to harass the free world openly was the western section of Berlin, more than a hundred miles inside communist territory. On April 1, 1948, border guards began to interfere with traffic to West Berlin and on July 24 stopped all passage along the roads and railways. The Allied governments sent protests to Moscow, but Stalin remained adamant.

Ground transportation being denied them, the Allies took to the air rather than risk conflict with the Soviets. Planes roared into West Berlin on a round-the-clock schedule, ferrying supplies and passengers. At first considered only a temporary expedient, the Berlin airlift became a fact of life for two million people. The planes brought to West Berlin about 8,000 tons of supplies a day for nearly a year, until Stalin gave up the blockade and restored normal traffic on May 12, 1949. The Western Powers proclaimed the German Federal Republic in May, 1949, and East Germany became the German Democratic Republic in October.

NATO

The aggressive Russian behavior in eastern Europe brought the Western Powers closer together in military as well as economic planning. Following the formation of the Brussels Pact, the United States made her own commitment to the military security of Europe in the Vandenberg Resolution. Approved June 11, 1948, by a vote of

64 to 4, the resolution sponsored by Arthur H. Vandenberg declared the nation's willingness to join regional defense arrangements as provided for under the United Nations Charter "should any armed attack occur threatening its national security."

The Vandenberg Resolution with its bipartisan support helped the President to take the further step of proposing a 20-year free world military alliance, the North Atlantic Treaty Organization, concluded in London on April 4, 1949. Twelve nations agreed that an attack on one would be an attack on all. In addition they agreed to raise an army to ensure security. The treaty passed the Senate on July 21, 82 to 13, over strong isolationist opposition to further commitments outside the Western Hemisphere. The United States agreed to supply not only men and arms, but also a Supreme Commander, General Eisenhower, who established his headquarters in Paris. The Mutual Defense Assistance Act provided about one billion dollars for NATO.

In the late 1940s, America revamped her own military organization through the National Security Act. The Department of Defense replaced the War and Navy Departments, with James Forrestal as its first Secretary. The Joint Chiefs of Staff gained a formal status and convened for the first time under Chairman Omar Bradley. The draft was extended, and the National Security Council and the Central Intelligence Agency were also created.

THE CHINESE REVOLUTION

At the same time that the United States was concerned with the Soviet threat in Europe, momentous events were also occurring in China. The Kuomintang under Chiang Kai-shek still held the southwestern provinces after the Japanese retreat, but in the north, the communists under Mao Tsetung were entrenched and gaining daily

66 *The broad picture is that after the war, Chiang Kai-shek emerged as the undisputed leader of the Chinese people. Only one faction, the Communists, up in the hills, ill-equipped, ragged, a very small military force, was determinedly opposed to his position. He had overwhelming military power, greater military power than any ruler had ever had in the entire history of China. He had tremendous economic and military support and backing from the United States. He had the acceptance of all other foreign countries, whether sincerely or insincerely in the case of the Soviet Union is not really material to this matter. Here he was in this position, and four years later what do we find? We find that his armies have melted away. His support in the country has melted away. His support largely outside the country has melted away, and he is a refugee on a small island off the coast of China with the remnants of his forces.*

As I said, no one says that vast armies moved out of the hills and defeated him. To attribute this to the inadequacy of American aid is only to point out the depth and power of the forces which were miscalculated or ignored. What has happened in my judgment is that the almost inexhaustible patience of the Chinese people in their misery ended. They did not bother to overthrow this government. There was really nothing to overthrow. They simply ignored it throughout the country. . . .

. . . Added to the grossest incompetence ever experienced by any military command was this total lack of support both in the armies and in the country, and so the whole matter just simply disintegrated.

The Communists did not create this. The Communists did not create this condition. They did not create this revolutionary spirit. They did not create a great force which moved out from under

1003

Chiang Kai-shek. But they were shrewd and cunning to mount it, to ride this thing into victory and into power. **99**

—*Secretary of State Dean Acheson*

Taft on China

66 *In China for some reason, the State Department has pursued a different policy from that followed throughout the rest of the world. There is not the slightest doubt in my mind that the proper kind of sincere aid to the Nationalist Government a few years ago could have stopped communism in China. But the State Department has been guided by a left-wing group who obviously have wanted to get rid of Chiang, and were willing at least to turn China over to the Communists for that purpose. They have, in effect, defied the general policy in China laid down by Congress. In recent months it has, of course, been very doubtful whether aid to the Nationalist Government could be effective, and no one desires to waste American efforts.* **99**

—*Senator Robert Taft*

support among the Chinese peasantry. Chiang enjoyed the prestige which came from being the national leader who had fought the invaders (but in north China he was considered a coward). He suffered, however, from the corruption inside the Kuomintang, from his international alliances which aroused the age-old xenophobia of the Chinese people, and from the popularity of Mao's promise to institute basic agrarian reforms in China.

American policy during the war and immediately following it was to work for a united China under Chiang Kai-shek, but the weakness of the Nationalist government made such a prospect unlikely. When Japan asked for peace, the United States ordered the Japanese to hold their positions until she could transport Nationalist troops to northern China in an effort to prevent a communist take-over as the Japanese left. With the aid of American marines, Chiang's forces were able to receive the Japanese surrender. Meanwhile the communists were seizing a large quantity of Japanese arms and supplies.

The attitude of the Soviet Union was also a vital factor because Russian troops had entered Manchuria just before the Japanese surrender. In battles in northern China, the Soviet Union cooperated with the communists against the Nationalists in spite of Stalin's promise at Yalta to support the Nationalist government.

THE CHINESE CIVIL WAR

Chiang asked for more American aid. The United States would not cooperate in attacking the communists directly but did continue Lend-Lease. Talks arranged by the American Ambassador, Patrick Hurley, between Chiang and Mao Tse-tung also were fruitless. General Marshall, the new American ambassador to China, arranged a truce early in 1946 but it collapsed in April and the civil war spread.

Another trip by Marshall in April failed to halt the fighting and continued shipment of American military supplies did not turn the tide in favor of Chiang's forces. His supporters in Congress demanded even greater appropriations. A report by General Albert C. Wedemeyer after a trip to China in 1947 confirmed the weakness of the Nationalist military position and called for more military aid to Chiang. Truman and Marshall did not believe more aid would change the situation. China was so huge that they calculated it would take billions of dollars and millions of American troops to make a dent in the problem. Moreover, by that time the United States was deeply committed to spending its foreign aid in Europe. Critics argued that the nation should have as strong an aid program in the Far East as in Europe.

Pushed out of Manchuria, the Nationalists fell back slowly. When the dust had settled in December, 1949, Mao victoriously proclaimed the People's Republic of China. He had driven Chiang from mainland China and the Generalissimo was forced to set up his government in exile on Formosa (Taiwan). In subsequent years he continued

Emperor Hirohito is received by General Douglas MacArthur at the United States Embassy in Tokyo.

to plan his return to the mainland, where he felt sure the Chinese people would rally to him.

The immediate problem for the United States was whether to recognize the new regime. By 1950, twenty-five nations had done so and the Soviet Union had made an alliance with the new government. But the American people were antagonistic to such a move and the administration refused recognition and blocked Red China's bid for membership in the United Nations. Many Republicans wanted continued military aid to Chiang in Formosa, but Truman only sent economic assistance.

Communist power was in the ascendant in Asia, and the United States now turned more attention to rebuilding Japan as a counterbalance to China. General Douglas MacArthur was made Supreme Commander for the Allied Powers and acted as absolute ruler of the islands. He was austere and hard working and demanded obedience and loyalty from the Japanese people. Military societies were banned, the country was disarmed and demobilized, and she lost all her territories. Russia and even the Western Allies, however, resented America's unilateral actions there.

The Japanese government and economy were transformed under the pressure of the Cold War. A new, Western-style constitution was instituted under which the emperor became a figurehead and people were given political liberties they had never had before. The economy had to be completely rebuilt since urban areas and industrial production were at a very low level.

After the communist victory in China, the United States determined on a policy of helping Japan regain her prewar industrial supremacy. She also wanted to be able to use bases in Japan in case of war in the Far East. In 1951, the United States signed a peace treaty with Japan whereby Japan's full sovereignty was recognized. Russian alarm was heightened as Japan became the informal ally of the United States.

ELECTION OF 1948 AND THE FAIR DEAL

"Truman is a gone goose," said Clare Boothe Luce. She appeared to be right. The President was beleaguered as he sought another term in the White House, under fire from left, right, and center of the Democratic Party as well as from the Republicans. The left wing of the Democratic Party, angered by his hard line toward the Russians, rallied behind Henry Wallace whom Truman had forced out of the Commerce Department for his criticism of the administration's foreign policy. Wallace, assuming leadership of a new Progressive Party, stumped the country promising, if elected, to work for accommodations with Moscow on fundamental world issues. The conservative Southern wing, angered by Truman's civil rights program, formed the states' rights party (the Dixiecrats), and nominated Senator Strom Thurmond of South Carolina for President. The moderates were convinced that Truman could not win and carried on an unsuccessful pre-convention campaign to "Dump Truman," with the hope of replacing him on the ticket with a more attractive candidate. The public opinion polls declared Thomas E. Dewey, nominated by the Republicans for the second time, an almost certain winner in the coming election. Dewey ran on a platform to reduce taxes, to root out any communists in the government, and maintain a bipartisan foreign policy.

THE WHISTLESTOP CAMPAIGN

Truman reacted with characteristic spirit. Having nothing to lose, he decided to run forthrightly on his record and to go directly to the people. During the campaign he criss-crossed the country, pausing wherever he could speak effectively from the rear platform of his train, addressing big crowds and small groups. Those who criticized him for running a "whistlestop campaign" overlooked the fact that he was getting a hearing from ordinary citizens. Over and over the President heard the cry, "Give 'em hell, Harry!" as he lambasted Congress and his election opponents. He made 356 speeches in thirty-five days.

THE ELECTION OF 1948

Dewey did nothing to slow down the whistlestop campaign. Feeling assured of victory, the GOP standard bearer decided not to rock the boat. His message was lost in a mass of nonpolitical verbiage. Meanwhile, critical groups were moving to Truman's side, recalling what he had done, or tried to do, for them—labor, farmers, and minority groups. The polls were not sensitive enough to register this shift shortly before the election. They prophesied a Dewey victory right down to election night. The Chicago *Tribune* even printed the headline: "Dewey Defeats Truman." A picture of Truman holding up the paper with this headline the morning after the election remains one of the most familiar photos in the history of journalism.

Truman's victory was substantial in spite of the four-way race. He took the popular vote 24,104,836 to 21,969,500, the electoral vote 303 to 189. Thurmond got 1,169,312 popular votes and Wallace 1,157,172.

THE FAIR DEAL

Back in the White House, Truman vigorously backed the measures that, taken as a package, became known as the Fair Deal. It was an enlargement of the program he had introduced when he first became President and it met a similar response from a Congress still dominated by a coalition of Southern Democrats and Northern Republicans. The men on Capitol Hill refused to give him the new civil rights legislation he asked for. Truman's accomplishments included a housing bill in 1949, improvements in social security benefits, and the minimum wage raised to 75 cents an hour. His Federal Security Administrator, Oscar Ewing, backed an insurance program to make sure of "proper medical care" for all Americans, and his Secretary of Agriculture, Charles F. Brannan, suggested shifting the emphasis in farm policy to a guaranteed income to a certain level while at the same time allowing food prices to seek their own level. Ewing and Brannan were denounced for "promoting socialism," and their bills remained buried in the Congress. The previous farm support policy was continued.

Truman had made the Taft-Hartley Act a major issue of his whistlestop campaign, terming it a measure that oppressed the

A jubilant Truman, who has just defeated Dewey in the election of 1948, holds a copy of the Chicago Daily Tribune. *The newspaper was sure Dewey would win, although Truman led in the balloting from the start.*

workers of America and promised to work for its repeal if reelected. Labor had responded with support at the polls. The President, therefore, returned to the attack in 1949, demanding repeal of the Taft-Hartley Act. Congress turned him down on this issue as well.

The creation of the Point Four Program was one of his few legislative successes. It took its popular name from his second inaugural address, in which after mentioning support for the United Nations, the Marshall Plan, and NATO, the President advocated "a bold new program for making the benefits of our scientific advances and industrial progress available for the improvement and growth of underdeveloped areas." Congress approved with 155 million dollars in 1950.

THE MILITARY PREDICAMENT

The dismantling of America's war machine, and the subsequent establishment of the Department of Defense, left the nation's defense planning in confusion. There was much interservice rivalry until Louis Johnson became Secretary of Defense in 1949 with a mandate to take a firm position in getting genuine unification of the Army, Navy, and Air Force. The Strategic Air Command had assumed a central role in the entire defense program. Its long-range bombers flying from bases at home and abroad made it the prime carrier of atomic bombs. There was a tendency to view SAC as the first line of defense.

Tactical nuclear weapons had not yet been devised and little defense spending went into preparing for limited brush-fire wars. America's manpower strength was barely enough to meet the most limited international responsibilities between 1946 and 1950. Military thinking on national defense was oriented toward all-out war at a time when a war with limited objectives lay just over the horizon.

THE KOREAN WAR

Seen from the vantage point of Washington, the world seemed a relatively safe place until the fall of 1949 because the United States alone possessed atomic weapons. This feeling was rudely shattered by Truman's announcement of September 23, 1949: "We have evidence that within recent weeks an atomic explosion occurred in the U.S.S.R." The Russians were drawing closer to the Americans in their ability to harness atomic energy and there was little doubt that they would stockpile atomic bombs until they had an arsenal of their own. Under these circumstances, the President went a step further. On January 31, 1950, he announced: "I have directed the Atomic Energy Commission to continue its work on all forms of atomic weapons, including the so-called hydrogen or super-bomb."

The first hydrogen bomb, exploded at Eniwetok in the Marshall Islands on November 1, 1952, proved to be a far more devastating weapon than the atomic bomb. Truman's strategy was to develop such weapons, not for use in war, but as a deterrent against war. He accepted the fact that humanity would henceforth live under an "umbrella of terror" because an all-out conflict with these ultimate weapons would be too horrible to contemplate. The age of limited wars had begun.

THE PROBLEM OF KOREA

Korea, freed of Japanese occupation at the end of W.W. II, had been occupied by the Russians in the north and the Amer-

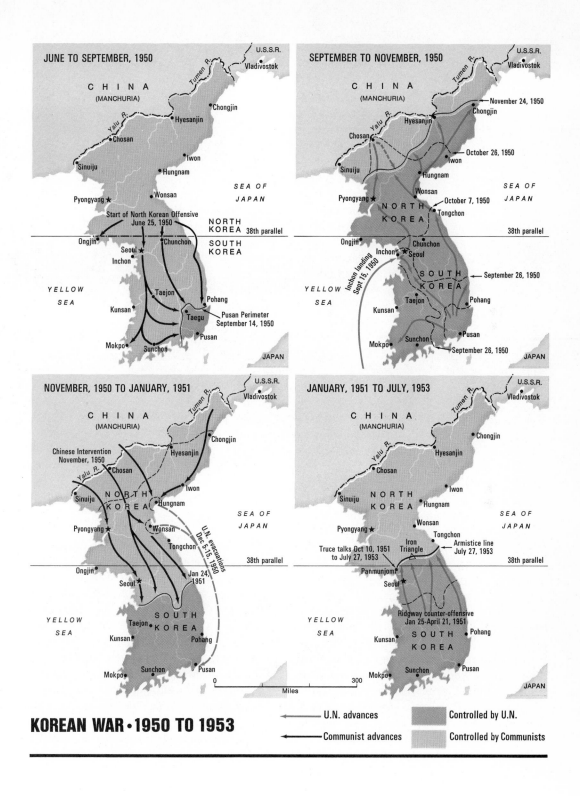

JUNE TO SEPTEMBER, 1950

U.S.S.R.
Vladivostok

C H I N A
(MANCHURIA)

Chongjin

Yalu R.
Hyesanjin

Tumen R.

Chosan

Iwon

Sinuiju

Hungnam

SEA OF
JAPAN

Pyongyang ★   Wonsan

Start of North Korean Offensive
June 25, 1950   NORTH
KOREA   38th parallel

Ongjin   Chunchon   SOUTH
Seoul ★   KOREA

Inchon

YELLOW
SEA   Taejon

Kunsan   Taegu   Pohang

Mokpo   Pusan Perimeter
        Sunchon   Pusan   September 14, 1950

JAPAN

SEPTEMBER TO NOVEMBER, 1950

U.S.S.R.
Vladivostok

C H I N A
(MANCHURIA)

Yalu R.   November 24, 1950
        Hyesanjin   Chongjin

Chosan

October 26, 1950
Sinuiju   Iwon

Hungnam   SEA OF
Pyongyang ★   NORTH   JAPAN
              KOREA   October 7, 1950
                      Tongchon

38th parallel

Ongjin   Chunchon
        Inchon   Seoul ★

Inchon landing   SOUTH
Sept. 15, 1950   KOREA   September 26, 1950

YELLOW
SEA   Taejon   Pohang

Kunsan

Mokpo   Sunchon   Pusan

September 26, 1950

JAPAN

NOVEMBER, 1950 TO JANUARY, 1951

U.S.S.R.
Vladivostok

C H I N A
(MANCHURIA)   Tumen R.

Chongjin

Chinese Intervention   Hyesanjin
November, 1950

Chosan   Iwon

Sinuiju   NORTH
        KOREA   Hungnam

Pyongyang ★   Wonsan   SEA OF
                          JAPAN
        Tongchon
                      U.N. evacuations
                      Dec 5-15, 1950
Ongjin   Jan 24,
        Seoul ★   1951   38th parallel

YELLOW   SOUTH
SEA   Taejon   KOREA

Kunsan

Mokpo   Sunchon   Pohang

Pusan

0   300
        Miles

JANUARY, 1951 TO JULY, 1953

U.S.S.R.
Vladivostok

C H I N A
(MANCHURIA)   Tumen R.

Chongjin

Hyesanjin

Chosan

Sinuiju   NORTH   Iwon
        KOREA   Hungnam

Pyongyang ★   Wonsan   SEA OF
                          JAPAN
              Tongchon
              Iron   Armistice line
Truce talks Oct 10, 1951 Triangle July 27, 1953
to July 27, 1953
Panmunjom   38th parallel
        Seoul ★

Ridgway counter-offensive
Jan 25-April 21, 1951
        SOUTH
YELLOW   KOREA   Pohang
SEA
        Kunsan

Mokpo   Sunchon   Pusan

JAPAN

KOREAN WAR · 1950 TO 1953

⟵ U.N. advances   ▮ Controlled by U.N.

◀— Communist advances   ▮ Controlled by Communists

South Korean refugees faced a long cold march which led them further south in their flight from the North Korean forces. The refugees were forced to stay off the main roads to avoid hindering military traffic.

icans in the south, with the temporary military line of the 38th parallel between them. The Americans accepted the 38th parallel as a military convenience, to be respected until a Korean government could be set up. The Russians considered it a permanent barrier behind which they placed a regime of local communists in power.

The United Nations voted to send a mission to Korea in 1947 after the United States and Russia could not reach agreement on a provisional government for the country. However, the North Koreans refused to accept the mission. As a result, a general election held in 1948 took place below the 38th parallel only, and the new president, Syngman Rhee, presided over a Republic of Korea that covered only South Korea. North Korea remained communist.

In 1949, the Russians and Americans both withdrew officially from divided Korea, but enough Russian advisers remained in the Korean capital, Pyongyang, to guide and prompt the government of the Democratic People's Republic. In a speech a year later, the new Secretary of State Dean Acheson, backed by the judgment of the Joint Chiefs left Korea outside the free world's defense perimeter as plotted on the

PRESIDENT TRUMAN AND THE COLD WAR YEARS

map of the Far East. It is likely that from this unfortunate statement Stalin drew the inference that the United States would not defend South Korea in case of attack from the north.

COMMUNIST AGGRESSION

On Sunday, June 25, 1950, Russian-built tanks rumbled across the 38th parallel from North Korea. Russian-made artillery opened fire on South Korean positions. Masses of infantry roared south in military trucks from the Soviet Union. The radio in Pyongyang summoned the people of South Korea to rise against Syngman Rhee, "the running dog of American imperialism."

Under the hammering of this surprise assault, South Korean defenses crumbled. As refugees fled in terror, the communists broke through and drove on into Seoul, the South Korean capital. Syngman Rhee also fled and entire South Korean divisions were shattered and dispersed. The North Koreans swept south virtually unimpeded.

MacARTHUR'S REACTION

As the fury of the communist attack mounted, General MacArthur flew from Japan to Korea to view the situation for himself. Returning to Tokyo, he reported to Washington that American troops would have to be thrown in immediately or the whole peninsula would fall. President Truman took his advice, made MacArthur commander-in-chief, and ordered the Seventh Fleet to the Formosa Straits. Within a few days the President ordered air and naval forces to aid South Korea.

The first American ground forces sent in by MacArthur could not halt the communist offensive. General Walton Walker fought a delaying action, using his few troops ineffectually against massive attacks that swamped his positions with tragic regularity. At last he retreated to Pusan at the

tip of the peninsula where he fortified a beachhead and waited. Some observers thought the outcome would be a Dunkirk-style evacuation of Pusan by Walker's American and Korean forces.

UNITED NATIONS INTERVENTION

President Truman considered the use of American troops in Korea not an act of war but "a police action" to restrain "a bunch of bandits." The communist attack was, in his view, precisely the type of international conflict that fell within the jurisdiction of the United Nations.

Ordinarily the Security Council would have become a forum for bitter communist invective against the American demand for an international force to be sent to Korea. But due to an astonishing miscalculation in Moscow, Gromyko was not there. He had walked out and was boycotting the Security Council over the exclusion of Red China from membership. The Security Council found North Korea guilty of "a breach of the peace" on June 25 and called on the member nations to go to the aid of South Korea on June 27. Sixteen nations eventually complied with the Resolution and the defense of South Korea thus became a matter of mutual defense authorized by and under the flag of the United Nations. The fear in Washington had been that the Americans might have to "go it alone" in Korea. That fear was now dispelled although less than 10 percent of the troops were sent by nations other than the United States and South Korea.

SUCCESS AND FAILURE IN KOREA

The communists expected MacArthur to land his reinforcements at besieged Pusan. Instead, he sent a powerful combined force by sea around the peninsula and up to

Inchon, far to the north near Seoul. These American troops stormed ashore on September 15. The invaders at the Pusan perimeter, caught in the jaws of a two-pronged attack as General Walker broke out of his beachhead, fled in disarray. Walker pushed after them, and linked up with the Inchon landing. MacArthur's men continued north, liberated Seoul, reached the 38th parallel, and cleared South Korea of the enemy in two weeks.

Truman sent MacArthur a message: "Well and nobly done." Shortly thereafter less cordial messages began to be exchanged on the question of what to do north of the

38th parallel. MacArthur, thinking in traditionally military terms, wanted to win the war by destroying the possibility of another invasion from North Korea. He proposed to go all the way to the Yalu River, employing troops offered by Chiang Kai-shek. Truman accepted a National Security Council plan for military unification of Korea if there was no threat of Chinese intervention. The United Nations also supported such a plan and MacArthur's forces crossed into North Korea on October 9. Truman was quite concerned about the Chinese and summoned the General to a meeting at Wake Island on October 15. MacArthur stressed his skepticism about an invasion from China, and spoke of having the war over "by Thanksgiving." Truman

U.S. Marines toss grenades at North Korean fighters in Seoul, while two other American soldiers look on.

told the press: "The General and I are in full agreement."

MacArthur continued his offensive toward the Yalu, but on November 26, his forces were hit by an onslaught of Chinese soldiers. They pushed the American forces south of the 38th parallel and recaptured Seoul. Later the General denied that he was proven wrong in his prediction, insisting that he meant the Chinese would not come in if he had the right to bomb their Manchurian bases. Whatever the truth, that right was denied him because neither the United States nor the United Nations was prepared for war with China. As MacArthur's forces reeled back, he told the President, "We face an entirely new war" and demanded the right to use atomic weapons against China. Truman rejected the plea and by early 1951 had returned to the first objective of the war, the holding of South Korea.

MacARTHUR'S DISMISSAL

Despite the gradual stabilization of his lines in Korea, MacArthur remained exasperated by the limitations placed on him. He began to make stronger public declarations, expressing his disapproval of the President's policies and even his authority. He wanted to enlarge the war and pressed for the overthrow of communism in the Far East. His words were picked up by opponents of the administration, who by now were calling the Korean impasse: "Mr. Truman's war."

Ironically, the final break between the President and the General came over a letter that MacArthur never intended to be made public. In reply to a query from Joe Martin, GOP leader of the House, on March 20, 1951, MacArthur called for a showdown with the communists in Asia, and concluded: "There is no substitute for victory." He supposed this to be a private communication, but Martin released the contents to the press.

Having repeatedly ordered MacArthur to stop making policy statements, Truman felt that he had no alternative but to remove him in order to maintain civilian control of the military. He consulted his advisers, military and civilian, all of whom felt that the General should be replaced. Truman relieved MacArthur of his command on April 4, and named General Matthew Ridgway, the second in command, to lead the war effort.

The President made the decision even though he could foresee the anger he would arouse by the dismissal of a great national hero. MacArthur came home to great emotional acclaim and delivered an energetic and moving defense of himself before a joint session of Congress on June 19, in which he applied to himself the old line he had heard as a West Point cadet: "Old soldiers never die, they just fade away."

President Truman now continued the policy of a limited war in Korea with the objective of a return to the 38th parallel. General Ridgway conducted successful military operations on the battlefield within the guidelines set by Washington. In addition, the top military men testifying before Congress disagreed with MacArthur's military judgment. They believed the main threat of communism was in Europe. As General Bradley put it, MacArthur's projected war with China would have been "the wrong war at the wrong place at the wrong time with the wrong enemy."

The Korean War ultimately bogged down into a stalemate. The Chinese military capability was weakened and in June, 1951, the Soviets asked for peace negotiations at the United Nations. The United States agreed and negotiations began with Chinese and North Korean representatives in July. They dealt with the cease-fire line, enforcement of an armistice, and the repatriation of war prisoners. The United States refused to repatriate 46,000 war prisoners against their will and the talks stalled just before the 1952 Presidential election.

FEAR OF SUBVERSION

CONSEQUENCES OF THE KOREAN WAR

The United States, which had fought World War II on the basis of unconditional surrender, had been forced to accept the policy of a limited war of containment in Korea. It was a painful adjustment to the limited ability of the country to make the rest of the world conform to her ideals. Communism had not spread further in Asia and there had been no World War III, but the United States had not reduced the power of either Russia or China. The war had, in fact, reinforced the rigid, international stalemate of the Cold War which made diplomatic agreements with the communist world even more difficult to attain.

President Truman had placed the nation on a partial wartime footing to meet the situation. He was given power by Congress to impose wage and price controls if he thought it necessary. On July 20, 1950, he outlined a 10-billion-dollar rearmament program, and the draft was speeded up. There was a solemnity about the proposals because it was not simply a temporary expedient, but a long-range plan to increase America's defense posture.

Under threat of a strike, the President also seized the steel mills in 1951 to prevent a slowdown in the war effort. Truman acted as commander-in-chief but had no legal backing for his action. Congress refused to pass legislation and the company took its case to the courts. In *Youngstown Sheet and Tube Co. v. Snyder,* the Supreme Court ruled that the President had acted unconstitutionally by usurping power not delegated to him under the Constitution. The result was a 53-day steel strike and a loss of $2 billion to the economy.

Although there were only 20,000 members in the American Communist Party, the administration's strategy in Korea and the fall of China to the communists made many Americans fear that there was communist influence in high government circles. Suspicion of treasonous activity already existed. In 1945, a raid on the magazine *Amerasia,* a left-wing publication, had revealed a cache of secret government documents. In 1946 a Canadian Royal Commission uncovered communist spy operations in which at least twenty-three persons "in positions of trust" were implicated. Information that the network had extended into the United States sent shock waves through the nation. In 1947 President Truman established new procedures for weeding out any government employees with communist affiliations by the FBI and Civil Service Commission. Job applicants were to be subjected to a "loyalty investigation." A Loyalty Review Board would maintain a master index of persons investigated and groups considered subversive by the Attorney General. Under this order 2,000 employees resigned and 560 were dismissed.

THE HISS CASE

In spite of Truman's program, Congress also took a hand in the question. Disloyalty investigations on Capitol Hill centered in the House Un-American Activities Committee whose most energetic member was Richard M. Nixon of California. This group, on testimony of former communist agents, turned up evidence of pro-Soviet activity by men in high government positions. The most prominent person accused of communist activities was Alger Hiss, who, while in the State Department, had been an aide to Roosevelt at Yalta and to Secretary of State Stettinius at the San Francisco conference on the United Nations. In 1948, he headed the Carnegie Foundation for International Peace. Accused by a former communist agent, Whittaker Chambers, of passing government documents to a ring of communist couriers, Hiss defended his innocence to

Communism in the United States

" At war's end we were physically the strongest nation on earth and, at least potentially, the most powerful intellectually and morally. Ours could have been the honor of being a beacon in the desert of destruction, a shining living proof that civilization was not yet ready to destroy itself. Unfortunately, we have failed miserably and tragically to arise to the opportunity.

The reason why we find ourselves in a position of impotency is not because our only powerful potential enemy has sent men to invade our shores, but rather because of the traitorous actions of those who have been treated so well by this Nation. . . .

This is glaringly true in the State Department. There the bright young men who are born with silver spoons in their mouths are the ones who have been the worst. . . . In my opinion the State Department, which is one of the most important government departments, is thoroughly infested with Communists.

I have in my hand 57 cases of individuals who would appear to be either card carrying members or certainly loyal to the Communist Party, but who nevertheless are still helping to shape our foreign policy. "

—*Senator Joseph McCarthy*

Communism in the United States

" *It is to the official representatives of the United States abroad that foreign Governments and peoples have the right to look with confidence for the most authentic interpretation of American values and the American point of view, and it is upon these same representatives that the President, the Secretary of State and others engaged in formulating our foreign policy must rely for accurate information concerning persons and events abroad.*

Recently the Foreign Service has been subjected to a series of attacks from outside sources which have questioned the loyalty and the moral standards of its members. With rare exceptions the justification for these attacks has been so flimsy as to have no standing in a court of law or in the mind of any individual capable of differentiating repeated accusation from even a reasonable presumption of guilt. Nevertheless these attacks have had sinister results.

The conclusion has become inescapable, for instance, that a Foreign Service officer who reports on persons and events to the very best of his ability and who makes recommendations which at the time he conscientiously believes to be in the interest of the United States may subsequently find his loyalty and integrity challenged and may even be forced out of the service and discredited forever as a private citizen after many years of distinguished service. A premium therefore has been put upon reporting and upon recommendations which are ambiguously stated or so cautiously set forth as to be deceiving. "

Letter to The New York Times

1015

the end. However, the circumstantial evidence against him was formidable and discrepancies in his testimony brought him a prison term for perjury.

The Hiss conviction came in January, 1950. A month later another startling case broke. The British arrested Klaus Fuchs, a nuclear physicist who had worked on the atomic bomb at Los Alamos. Fuchs confessed to having passed American atomic secrets to the Russians. Further investigation led to Julius and Ethel Rosenberg, both of whom were found guilty of working with a Soviet network in the United States, giving classified information to its agents. They were executed in 1953.

The disclosures of disloyalty within the federal government brought popular demands for new federal legislation to curb the Communist Party. The result was the harsh McCarren Internal Security Act passed in September, 1950, over President Truman's veto. It required all communist and communist-controlled organizations, as well as their individual members, to register with the Attorney General. Communists could not work in defense plants, obtain a passport, and could be interned in case of war. It also set up a Subversive Activities Control Board to investigate loyalty cases. The Supreme Court, following popular sentiment, held in *Dennis et al. v. United States* that even the teaching or advocacy of a revolutionary doctrine created a "clear and present danger" to the country.

McCARTHYISM

With some evidence of and much speculation about espionage in Washington, the junior Senator from Wisconsin found his opportunity to become a national figure. Joseph McCarthy, speaking at a February, 1950, meeting of Republican women in Wheeling, West Virginia, told his audience: "In my opinion, the State Department, which is one of the most important government departments, is thoroughly infested with Communists." From there he went on to attack those he considered "soft on Communism," beginning with the President of the United States, and including a list of prominent public figures such as Acheson and Marshall. Many who spoke out against his unsubstantiated charges became victims of "McCarthyism" as McCarthy took the issue of communist subversion and turned it to his own self-serving purposes, making wild charges against those he disliked or opposed. According to President Truman, who was angered by McCarthy's tactics, the issue of communist subversion was nothing but a "red herring."

A senate subcommittee under Millard Tydings of Maryland investigated McCarthy's charges and pronounced them "a fraud and a hoax." But public fears produced continued support for McCarthy and he helped secure Tydings' defeat in 1950 by the use of smear tactics. For a few years McCarthy was a great power in American politics. He was the spokesman for all those fearful of communist subversion, those who were confused and frustrated by the lack of a clear-cut resolution of the Cold War, and perhaps even those who resented the intellectuals who ran the State Department.

ELECTION OF 1952

By the time Harry Truman officially declared himself out of the Presidential race in 1952, he was in the deepest political trouble of his career. His adversaries called it "the mess in Washington." The Republicans said: "It's time for a change."

Not only communism, Korea, and inflation, but the issue of corruption in Washington monopolized the headlines in 1951. Persons close to the President were shown to have benefited from their White House connection. The freezer bestowed on Presidential military aide General Harry Vaughn by a grateful friend became notorious. Another aide, Donald Dawson, was charged with soliciting favors for certain individuals from the Reconstruction Finance Corporation. At the Justice Department, Assistant Attorney General T. Lamar Caudle, using his position in the Internal Revenue Service, was caught in a tax-fixing scandal and eventually went to prison. Senator Estes Kefauver had also shown in his investigations that there were links between a few Democratic Party bosses and organized crime.

THE CAMPAIGN OF 1952

As the 1952 elections approached, the Republicans were jubilant. They had gained seats in both houses of Congress in 1950. Conservative Republicans backed Senator Robert Taft of Ohio, a long-time foe of New Deal legislation and a staunch isolationist. But he was opposed by the Eastern moderate wing which had been in the ascendant in the party since 1940. They persuaded General Eisenhower to enter the race. Rivalry between the Taft and Eisenhower camps was intense, but after a tremendous battle over the seating of delegates at the convention, Eisenhower was nominated on the first ballot. Senator Nixon was chosen as his running mate. The Republican platform called for reduced taxes and a foreign policy directed toward the liberation of countries under Soviet rule. Eisenhower had to conciliate the conservative wing of the party by promising an all-out fight against the Democrats' "socialistic policies."

The Democrats decided on Governor Adlai E. Stevenson of Illinois, who was at first reluctant to run. Senator John Sparkman of Alabama was chosen as his running mate. Once nominated, Stevenson proved to be an eloquent speaker and an enthusiastic campaigner.

The climax of the campaign came in October when Eisenhower promised to personally go to Korea if elected to help bring an end to the war. The enthusiasm for Eisenhower's promise was temporarily dimmed for the Republicans when Nixon was accused of having accepted contributions from businessmen to a private expense account. Some party leaders called for him to withdraw, but Eisenhower kept Nixon on the ticket after he made an effective defense of his conduct on national television in what came to be known as his "Checkers" speech.

ELECTION RESULTS

The General's personal popularity carried the Republicans to victory. To the people he was "Ike," the idol with the friendly grin and unimpeachable moral standards. Stevenson, despite his personal ability, seemed too intellectual, talking over the heads of many Americans. He was hampered by the unpopularity of much of the Truman record, from which he tried vainly to dissociate himself. Sparkman also could not hold the South against Eisenhower's appeal.

Eisenhower won easily, with 33,937,252 votes to Stevenson's 27,314,992. The electoral vote margin was 442 to 89. The Republicans also controlled both houses of Congress by a very small margin.

Readings

GENERAL WORKS

Agar, Herbert, *The Price of Power: America Since 1945*. Chicago: University of Chicago Press, 1957—An appraisal of the position of the United States in world politics since 1945.

Fairbank, John K., *The United States and China*. New York: Viking, 1971—A history of United States–China relations by a leading scholar. Fairbank considers the historical background but concentrates on recent years.

Goldman, Eric F., *The Crucial Decade*. New York: Knopf, 1956—A popular history of the ten years following the conclusion of World War II.

Graebner, Norman, *Cold War Diplomacy: American Foreign Policy 1945–1960*. New York: Van Nostrand, 1962—A short essay and collection of documents on a decade and a half of postwar foreign relations.

Gunther, John, *Inside U.S.A.* New York: Harper & Row, 1951—A state-by-state report on the political and social trends in the United States shortly after World War II.

Halle, Louis, *The Cold War as History*. New York: Harper & Row, 1967—An attempt at a dispassionate history of the Cold War. Halle criticizes excessive American idealism and moralism and indicates that the strategic positions of the United States and the Soviet Union after World War II made the Cold War virtually inevitable.

Kennan, George F., *American Diplomacy 1900–1950*. Chicago: University of Chicago Press, 1951—A leading American diplomat's reflections on the conduct of American foreign policy in the first half of the twentieth century. Kennan criticizes the forces of isolationism and excessive idealism which he feels have been too strong an influence on American diplomacy.

Lubell, Samuel, *The Future of American Politics*. New York: Harper & Row, 1965—Lubell, a leading expert on public opinion, ties together evidence from polls and voting patterns and predicts important trends that will emerge in American political life.

Neustadt, Richard E., *Presidential Power*. New York: Wiley, 1960—A series of case studies of how Roosevelt, Truman, and Eisenhower handled crises in their Presidencies. Neustadt draws implications from these studies on how a President can best gain and hold personal power.

Phillips, Cabell, *The Truman Presidency*. New York: Macmillan, 1966—A history of Truman's years in the White House which praises his conduct of both domestic and foreign policy.

Reischauer, Edward O., *The United States and Japan*. Cambridge, Mass.: Harvard University Press, 1965—A survey of relations between the two nations by a scholar who became the United States Ambassador to Japan.

Spanier, John, *American Foreign Policy Since World War II*. New York: Praeger, 1968— A standard account of American foreign relations.

SPECIAL STUDIES

Alperowitz, Gar, *Atomic Diplomacy: Hiroshima and Potsdam*. New York: Simon & Schuster, 1965—A major reinterpretation of American foreign policy after FDR's death. Alperowitz argues that America's use of the atomic bomb at Hiroshima and Nagasaki was motivated more by an effort to gain political leverage over the Soviet Union in eastern Europe than by military necessities.

Carr, Robert K., *The House Un-American Activities Committee, 1945–1950*. Ithaca, N.Y.: Cornell University Press, 1952—A history of HUAC's investigations during the late 1940s. Carr's emphasis is on the committee's procedures which he criticizes as jeopardizing witnesses' rights.

Feis, Herbert, *Between War and Peace: The Potsdam Conference*. Princeton, N.J.: Princeton University Press, 1960—The Potsdam Conference of July, 1945, at which Truman confronted Stalin for the first time, was an important milestone on the road to the Cold War. Feis's account defends Truman's policies during the spring and summer of 1945.

Latham, Earl, *The Communist Controversy in Washington*. Cambridge, Mass.: Harvard University Press, 1966—A general account of the McCarthy period. Latham minimizes the influence of the Communist Party in the formation of American policies, even when the Party was at the height of its strength.

Lee, R. Alton, *Truman and Taft-Hartley*. Lexington: University Press of Kentucky, 1966—A case study of the passage of the Taft-Hartley Act despite Truman's opposition. Lee places the struggle in the context of efforts to maintain the Democratic labor union alliance formed in the New Deal era.

Neumann, William L., *After Victory*. New York: Harper & Row, 1967—A revisionist study of diplomacy among the Great Powers following the defeat of Hitler.

Rees, David, *Korea, the Limited War*. Baltimore: Penguin, 1970—Rees believes that President Truman's containment policy made the Korean War almost inevitable. The book concentrates on military developments.

Rorty, James, and Moshe Decter, *McCarthy and the Communists*. Botson: Beacon, 1954 —An analysis of McCarthy's charges which claims that the Wisconsin Senator was fundamentally correct although guilty of distortions and exaggerations.

Rose, Arnold M., *The Negro in Postwar America*. New York: Anti-Defamation League of B'nai B'rith, 1950—A short pamphlet on the status of black Americans by a leading sociologist.

Ross, Irwin, *The Loneliest Campaign: The Truman Victory of 1948*. New York: New American Library, 1968—A narrative of Truman's upset victory over Dewey in 1946. Ross maintains that Truman had many political assets which the poll takers

did not recognize at the time.

Spanier, J. W., *The Truman-MacArthur Controversy and the Korean War*. Cambridge, Mass.: Harvard University Press, 1959—A study of Truman's removal of General MacArthur as an example of difficulties in civilian-military relations during wartime. Spanier argues that MacArthur went beyond the bounds of reasonable disagreement with his Commander-in-Chief.

Zink, Harold, *The United States in Germany*. Princeton, N.J.: Van Nostrand, 1957—A critical study of the United States military occupation of West Germany from 1945 to 1955.

PRIMARY SOURCES

Acheson, Dean, *Present at the Creation*. New York: Norton, 1969—Memoirs of the author's years as Secretary of State under Truman. Acheson's memoirs are a good case study of the foreign policy assumptions of American liberalism during the Cold War years.

Bernstein, Barton J., and Alan I. Matusow, *The Truman Administration: A Documentary Record*. New York: Harper & Row, 1968—A collection of documents relating to the foreign and domestic policies of the Truman administration.

Chambers, Whittaker, *Witness*. New York: Random House, 1952—A highly personal autobiography of the accuser of Alger Hiss describing Chambers' journey from Communist Party member to political conservative.

Kennan, George F. *Memoirs*. Boston: Little, Brown, 1957—Spanning about a quarter century of the author's diplomatic career, Kennan's memoirs are a valuable source for a study of the origins of the Cold War.

Stevenson, Adlai E., *Speeches*. New York: Random House, 1952—Addresses by the Illinois governor during his first unsuccessful race for the White House in 1952.

Trefousse, Hans L., *The Cold War: A Book of Documents*. New York: Putnam, 1965 —Eighty-six documents concerning the course of the Cold War, from the 1942 United Nations Declaration to the 1964 Tonkin Gulf resolution.

Truman, Harry S., *Memoirs,* Vols. I–II. Garden City, N.Y.: Doubleday, 1955–1956—A valuable source for the history of mid-twentieth century America. The first volume covers the events of 1945, the second deals with Truman's last six years as President.

BIOGRAPHIES

Davis, K. S., *The Politics of Honor*. New York: Putnam, 1967—A sympathetic biography of Adlai E. Stevenson, the twice-defeated Democratic Presidential candidate.

Rovere, Richard H., *Senator Joe McCarthy*. New York: World, 1959—Rovere depicts McCarthy as a man totally lacking in scruples or principles who seized on the communist issue for purely opportunistic reasons and achieved considerable power because of his willingness to resort to any tactic.

Schmidt, K. M., *Henry Wallace: Quixotic Crusader*. Syracuse, N.Y.: Syracuse University Press, 1960—A sympathetic biography of Roosevelt's Secretary of Agriculture and Vice President who broke with the Truman administration over the Cold War and ran for President on the Progressive Party ticket in 1948.

Steinberg, Alfred, *The Man from Missouri*. New York: Putnam, 1962—A sympathetic biography of Harry Truman.

White, William S., *The Taft Story*. New York: Harper & Row, 1954—An admiring biography of the late Republican Senator from Ohio.

During the Eisenhower administration, civil rights became a national issue, with blacks demanding an end to segregation. This photo shows black students integrating the Little Rock Central High School under the protection of federal troops.

Eisenhower: 29
The
Politics
of Moderation

There is, in world affairs, a steady course to be followed between an assertion of strength that is truculent and a confession of helplessness that is cowardly.

There is, in our affairs at home, a middle way between untrammeled freedom of the individual and the demands for the welfare of the whole nation. This way must avoid government by bureaucracy as carefully as it avoids neglect of the helpless.

In every area of political action, free men must think before they can expect to win.

—President Dwight D. Eisenhower

The above passage from President Eisenhower's first State of the Union message, on February 2, 1953, reveals his basic thinking about politics. He was a man of the "middle way," and the conflicts over important events during the next eight years would test both the President's philosophy of avoiding extremes and the nation's willingness to have him do so.

THE EISENHOWER STYLE

The Republicans had attained a landslide victory in 1952 due to Eisenhower's personal magnetism. Although Eisenhower was not a party politician, he shared so many beliefs with middle-of-the-road Republicanism that he felt comfortable amid his political colleagues. The President and the party advocated fiscal responsibility, the protection of private enterprise, individual initiative, and a strong stand against communism. Eisenhower's approach to power was that of a chairman of the board. He was simple, direct, and listened to all sides in a controversy. He preferred not to exercise power directly, but to delegate broad authority to his subordinates, reserving for himself the role of coordinator. He made recommendations to Congress but infrequently used his influence to get his programs passed. Throughout most of his Presidency he was not a strong-willed, independent executive and seldom exercised the powers inherent in the office of President. He was always a team man, and the Republican Party was his team.

BACKGROUND

Dwight David Eisenhower was a child of middle America, born in Texas, and raised in Abilene, Kansas. Entering West Point in 1911, he became one of the most popular cadets at the military academy, although he ranked well below the top academically in the graduating class of 1915. Between the two world wars he served on MacArthur's staff, first in Washington and then in the Philippines.

World War II gave Eisenhower his opportunity for command. Catching the eye of General Marshall, the Chief of Staff, at the Louisiana maneuvers of 1941, he began a rapid rise to the top. He was made commander of United States forces in Europe. After the North African campaign had revealed his ability to command and inspire international armies, he was sent to London to plan and direct the titanic assault against the Nazis in northern Europe. He was an American hero and a world figure after he launched the Allied cross-Channel invasion of France on June 6, 1944. After the war, Eisenhower held the posts of Army Chief of Staff, president of Columbia University, and later Supreme Commander of the NATO forces in Europe.

Eisenhower's background was notably devoid of political experience. He termed himself "a horse in a corral," which he explained thus: "As a boy I used to watch the horse being lassoed for the daily work. I rooted for him but observed that he was always caught. In 1952 I found myself in much the position of that horse."

EISENHOWER THE ADMINISTRATOR

Dwight Eisenhower held a high opinion of businessmen. He admired the qualities necessary for success in the world of industry and finance—the skill, planning, tenacity, and public relations that spelled the difference between profit and loss. Moreover, his party had always had strong support from the business community. It was natural that he would recruit successful businessmen for his Cabinet, and that, given his military background, he would appoint a chief of staff to assist him.

SHERMAN ADAMS

As Assistant to the President, Eisenhower appointed Sherman Adams, a taciturn, flinty New Englander who had gone from business into politics and had become governor of New Hampshire. Adams held Cabinet rank at the express wish of the President. He ran the Executive Office until 1958, when he was forced to resign over charges that he had used his position to gain government favors for a friend. He sometimes exasperated members of Con-

gress because he filtered out men and measures he did not consider important enough to occupy the President's time. Even members of the Cabinet usually had to get past Adams before reaching the White House study. Only Secretary of State John Foster Dulles was permitted to see the President whenever he chose. Eisenhower had said, "I don't want people springing things on me," and Sherman Adams saw to it that this happened infrequently. If he could not make a decision himself, he stated the question clearly and succinctly before passing it on to the President.

If Sherman Adams was the President's chief of staff, the members of the Cabinet

World problems brought the leaders of England and America together in 1954. Seated on the White House lawn are (left to right): Secretary of State John Foster Dulles, Prime Minister Winston Churchill, President Eisenhower, and British Foreign Secretary Anthony Eden.

were the commanding generals of the administration. During the war, Eisenhower had given his generals their military objectives, which they were expected to reach without calling his attention to every tactical problem of the battlefield. He now applied the same thinking to his Cabinet. His aversion to what he termed "a faceful of paperwork" was great, whether in the military or political spheres.

John Foster Dulles, Secretary of State, headed the nine Cabinet officers. Eisenhower's friend as well as his most trusted counselor, Dulles directed American foreign policy until his death in 1959. He came with good credentials—a corporation lawyer who had been close to diplomacy since his youth, he was the grandson of John W. Foster, Harrison's Secretary of State, and nephew of Robert Lansing, Wilson's Secretary of State.

Six successful businessmen took over key departments—Charles E. Wilson, Defense; George Humphrey, Treasury; Sinclair Weeks, Commerce; Douglas McKay, Interior; Arthur Summerfield, Postmaster General; and Ezra Taft Benson, Agriculture. A well-known lawyer, Herbert Brownell, became Attorney General. Martin Durkin, president of the Plumbers and Steamfitters Union, became Secretary of Labor. These were the "eight millionaires and a plumber." Durkin, a Stevenson Democrat as well as a labor leader, soon resigned with the complaint that he was not getting a fair hearing at Cabinet meetings on revisions of the Taft-Hartley Act. James P. Mitchell, a businessman and specialist in labor relations, replaced him.

MODERATE PROGRESSIVISM

This phrase was Eisenhower's own description of his Presidential policies. Sometimes he reversed the terms and spoke of "progressive moderation" or "modern Republicanism." Some students of this period have called his policies "dynamic conservatism." He considered the Democrats guilty of excessive spending, irresponsible promises, and a desire to have the government do everything. Yet he was more moderate than the conservative wing of his party, which he believed had put a balanced budget over social justice and had failed to understand the necessity of American commitments abroad.

Eisenhower's philosophy called for humane programs without passionate crusades. No intellectual, he tended to follow his common sense in dealing with national problems. He tried to balance opposing forces and reach a compromise, accepting half a loaf when the whole loaf seemed beyond reach. What this meant in practice was a retreat from New Deal–Fair Deal policies in some areas and an extension of those policies in other areas. In fiscal policy, public power, and the conservation of natural resources the trend was conservative. In labor, farm, and welfare legislation the trend was to extend rather than reverse the New Deal.

His critics insisted that his moderate progressivism was not a strong enough remedy for severe national ills, and blamed him for allowing the growth of problems that shook the country under subsequent administrations. The people in general, however, were of a different opinion. They wanted a breathing spell after the turmoil of the previous decade and the Eisenhower administration gave it to them. He was as popular when he left the White House as when he entered it.

The reason for Eisenhower's great popularity throughout eight years of domestic and international controversy was not only his almost nonpartisan approach to the Presidency, but also was related to the confused and unstable state of American politics in the 1950s. He was a symbol of stability in an era of fluctuating political alignments. It was an era in which traditional party allegiance declined and a huge independent vote developed. The United States was a nation of moderates who feared inflation and government spending but at the same time did not want to give up New Deal legislation.

The parties themselves were nearly equal in voting strength. The fear of communism drew many Roman Catholics to the Republicans and many farmers also voted Republican again now that inflation and not debts was their main economic worry. Many workers, now in the middle class, were also fearful of inflation and voted for Eisenhower. The rising urban and suburban middle class in the South gave the Republicans solid support in 1952 as did those who were against the strong civil rights stand of the Democratic Party. Only black Americans could be counted on to vote solidly Democratic.

The Congress generally reflected the national temper during the decade. The Republicans had a very thin majority in 1953 and 1954. After 1954 the Congress was in Democratic hands and there were also more moderate Republicans represented. The 1958 elections showed a strong Democratic voting trend throughout the country. Toward the end of Eisenhower's second term the Congress was more liberal than the President. But there was generally good cooperation between the White House and Capitol Hill since the latter was dominated by two moderate Southern Democrats from Texas: Sam Rayburn, the Speaker of the House, and Lyndon Johnson, the Senate Majority Leader.

INTERNAL SECURITY

In the early 1950s the internal communist threat still ranked high among the issues that disturbed the American people. Eisenhower shared the concern, although he refused to be stampeded by the wild accusations of certain professional anticommunists. He set out to give solid assurances that the communist conspiracy was being watched and controlled.

DEPARTMENTAL AUTHORITY

In April, 1953, the President ordered the FBI to assemble files on all those who worked for the government, and to send the file on anyone suspected of disloyalty, alcoholism, drug addiction, or immorality to the proper departmental head, who would decide whether the individual should be retained. A board was empowered to hear appeals and make suggestions, but the final decision was up to the man who ran the department. Although 2,600 people were dismissed, only 315 were released as disloyal.

These stringent rules led to the bitterly debated case of Robert Oppenheimer, the "father of the atomic bomb," and a distinguished member of the Atomic Energy Commission. When the FBI presented derogatory information about Oppenheimer and designated him as a security risk, he was dropped from the AEC although never charged with disloyalty. Lewis Strauss, as chairman, absolved him of treason or espionage, but agreed that he suffered from "fundamental defects in his character" and had shown poor judgment by associating with communists and arguing against development of the hydrogen bomb. The other members of the AEC supported the verdict four to one.

THE DECLINE OF McCARTHYISM

In 1952, Senator Joseph McCarthy rode the wave of anticommunism, loudly castigating the two previous administrations for "twenty years of treason." He made much of the terms Roosevelt accepted at Yalta, and continued to charge that there were communist spies in Washington under Truman. He played upon fears created by Cold War tensions, and although a Republican, did not hesitate to attack the new administration. However, Eisenhower refused to make a direct countercharge to McCarthy's charges of traitorous activities in the State Department.

The President had chosen as the new ambassador to Moscow a knowledgeable and experienced member of the diplomatic corps, Charles Bohlen. However, since Bohlen had been at Yalta with FDR, McCarthy demanded that the President withdraw the nomination. Eisenhower stood his ground, and Bohlen was confirmed after an investigation by two of McCarthy's most respected colleagues on the Hill, Senators Taft and Sparkman.

McCarthy was not cowed. He next accused the government's information agencies, especially the Voice of America, of being "soft on Communism." He sent two of his staff members, Roy Cohn and David Schine, to Europe to inspect the overseas libraries of the United States Information Agency and, after their report, demanded the removal of books of which he disapproved. The State Department then removed books McCarthy said were by subversive authors.

Now McCarthy took on the United States Army. He first insulted General Ralph Zwicker over the handling of a security case at Fort Monmouth, New Jersey. The Army retorted that McCarthy had tried to wangle favored treatment for Private Schine, a former member of McCarthy's staff. The whole nation was able to watch televised hearings in which the two sides aired their complaints. The spectacle ruined McCarthy, who appeared as a vulgar bully in his confrontation with the gentlemanly Secretary of the Army, Robert Stevens. As a result of the Army-McCarthy hearings, the Senate censured the junior Senator from Wisconsin in December, 1954. McCarthy's power was gone, and he died in 1957.

EISENHOWER'S DOMESTIC POLICY

By 1952, the American economy had recovered from the war. Most of the old shortages were gone. The factories that had hurriedly converted from peacetime production to satisfy the requirements of the battlefield had gone through a process of reconversion. The postwar boom had gained a momentum that continued with the Cold War. There was almost full employment and wages were good even with high prices. Visitors from abroad were amazed at the number of buildings under construction, the countless miles of new roads and highways, and the multiplication of airports. The majority of Americans had money and were eager to spend it.

Despite efforts, first by progressives and then New Dealers, the tendency of American capitalism was still toward consolidation. Along with increased government regulation, the trend was toward oligopoly. A few big corporations dominated major industries such as steel and automobiles. Of the foreign cars, only Volkswagen had large sales. It was more and more difficult for small companies to compete with the large corporations. One hundred and thirty-five corporations owned 45 percent of the industrial assets. Within this arrangement the emphasis was not on price competition but on outdoing one's competitor in quality, style, and luxury. Advertising and packaging of a commodity were thus very important factors.

The trend was also away from businesses owned and run by one family. The day of the business tycoon was gone. New managers were college-educated men who had risen to positions of power in a company by climbing the managerial ladder. Good salaries, retirement benefits, and company pride were replacing the goal of immense wealth. Company policies were frequently worked out by a team of men. Thus, the corporation was more powerful than ever, but the managers were anonymous.

FISCAL POLICY

Harry Truman had been quoted as saying: "Dollars may not be worth as much, but they're easier for the average man to get." Dwight Eisenhower took the opposite viewpoint. He doubted the economy of possessing dollars of dwindling value, and insisted on the need to curtail inflation while balancing the budget. Wage and price controls still existed as a result of the Korean War. There were ceilings on an array of domestic items from shoes to farm machinery. The Eisenhower administration got rid of the ceilings on the basis that they were not preventing the erosion of the dollar. The result convinced Eisenhower that he had been right. He wrote: "Prices were holding steady. They continued to hold remarkably steady through the administration's eight years."

When a recession developed in 1953, the President, supported by Secretary Humphrey, asked Congress to lower taxes rather than increase spending as the Democrats had done. The administration cut both the federal payroll and defense spending. An end to the Korean War also allowed the

administration to end excess profits taxes and cut the income tax. Nevertheless, conservatives were irritated that it took three years before the budget could be brought into balance.

While the economy was generally prosperous during Eisenhower's eight years in office, it was sluggish after 1958. Between 1954 and 1956 the country was riding the crest of an economic boom with inflation under control. But by 1957 the cost of living went up again and many believed it was caused by wages rising faster than production. The administration's policy was to tighten the money supply which helped to bring on a recession in 1958. Unemployment rose and there was a decrease in consumer spending and cuts in production. Now, contrary to Secretary Humphrey's wishes, Eisenhower supported greater appropriations for defense and public works, relaxed credit controls, and reduced down payments for housing. There was an economic spurt in 1959, but the economy was lagging again by 1960. The country's economic growth rate was never over 3 percent during the Eisenhower years.

FARM POLICY

Agriculture was one of the most vexing of the nation's economic problems. The dilemma of overproduction had not changed since the 1920s. The farmers of America were producing more food than they could sell on the market, and when they were able to dispose of their produce, prices held at a disappointingly low level. Government price supports protected the farmer but also allowed immense surpluses to pile up in storage bins and grain elevators, with the consequent drain of federal money to pay the cost of storage.

The Eisenhower-Benson agricultural plan called for reducing surpluses by replacing rigid price supports with more flexible supports, a slight modification of the New Deal approach. According to the Agricultural Act of 1954, the Secretary of Agriculture could use a sliding scale as he saw fit. The "parity" price of a farm product was supposed to be fair in relation to the farmer's costs. The Agricultural Act allowed supports to be pegged between 75 and 90 percent of parity on major crops after 1955. Actually, less was achieved than had been anticipated because of declining farm prices and pressure by farm organizations to keep the supports high.

In 1956 the administration turned to a "soil bank" plan. This measure permitted payments to farmers who would turn some of their land into forests or pastures. The farmers were supposed to make money while surpluses fell along with storage costs. In fact, farm production per acre increased and "soil bank" payments could not compensate for it by reducing the number of acres under cultivation. Surpluses continued to grow until the government decided to dispose of some products in a school lunch program and by shipping them abroad.

Eisenhower disliked price supports, and would have done away with them altogether. However, he realized that without supports, there would have been panic on the nation's commercial farms. Even with the supports the farmer's share of the national income dropped. The tendency toward fewer and larger farms continued. Every year the number of family farms declined as rural people moved to urban centers.

UNIONS

Even though labor feared that it would be undermined in the postwar period by the Taft-Hartley Act and state right-to-work laws, the union movement was more powerful than ever. Laborers were demanding higher wages, which, in turn, were being paid for by higher prices on consumer goods. The result was an inflationary spiral.

The unions also wanted wage security and advanced several plans to achieve it. In 1948, General Motors agreed to an escalator clause which tied wage rates to the cost-of-living index. In 1950, General Motors also agreed for the first time to a five-year rather than a one-year contract. There were to be annual wage increases and cost-of-living adjustments. Other companies followed. By the middle 1950s Ford and other companies also accepted a version of Walter Reuther's idea for a guaranteed annual wage. It provided for a company fund out of which state unemployment benefits would be supplemented. Workers laid off would receive 65 percent of their take-home pay for four weeks and 60 percent for 22 additional weeks. But the biggest problem for the unions as the nation approached the 1960s was automation. It was difficult to be against such technological innovation since the result was increased production which in turn resulted in higher wages. At the same time unions were determined to protect the jobs of their men.

There was a reconciliation in the labor movement during the first Eisenhower administration. The AF of L and the CIO had gone their separate ways under William Green and Philip Murray. George Meany and Walter Reuther, stepping forward at the death of these old antagonists in 1952, ended the quarrel in 1955. The two labor groups merged into a single organization, the AFL-CIO, of 15 million members, with only the United Mine Workers and the railroad unions remaining independent. Meany as president and Reuther as vice president attained a more powerful place in national life, taking public positions on issues of concern to all Americans.

In the 1950s, corrupt activities were uncovered in a few important unions. Corruption in the Teamsters Union was disclosed in 1951 by a Senate Committee. Connections with local politicians on the West Coast gave the union control of gambling and vice in the area. The Teamsters stood behind their president, James Hoffa, who was alleged to have misused union funds and to have close ties with gamblers. The AFL-CIO expelled the union in 1957. However, it was not until 1964 that the Justice Department got a conviction against Hoffa for misusing union funds and he went to prison.

Aroused by the events, the Congress passed the Landrum-Griffin Act of 1959. Aimed at certain labor abuses, the measure limited picketing, demanded publication of union finances, and gave the states jurisdiction over disputes not covered by the National Labor Relations Board.

THE STEEL STRIKE

The worst strike of the Eisenhower years came in 1959, when his Presidency was coming to a close. The United Steel Workers of America went off their jobs following management's rejection of their demands for job security. The steel shortage had immediate repercussions throughout the economy. Automobile manufacturers, for example, had to curtail purchases of rubber. The entire economic life of the nation was so gravely affected that the President decided to act. He asked the courts for an 80-day injunction under the Taft-Hartley Act, enforcing a cooling-off period during which negotiations could proceed. He began a strenuous round of talks at the White House with both sides, and dispatched both Secretary Mitchell and Vice President Nixon to do the same at labor and management headquarters. The result was an agreement providing for wage increases and additional fringe benefits. But the company's demand to be able to lay off men as a result of automation was not settled.

BUSINESS

The administration instituted few antitrust suits. However, Eisenhower did take action against certain executives of the electrical industry who tried to prevent competition. Shocked by their alleged conduct, the President ordered the Antitrust Division of the Justice Department to prosecute these men, who in 1960 were found guilty of price-fixing at clandestine meetings. The Du Pont Company was compelled to sell massive holdings of General Motors stock because the independence and control of the latter company was at stake. Nevertheless, businessmen felt satisfied that they had a friend in the White House and that feeling contributed to the optimism of the business community for the eight years Eisenhower served as Chief Executive.

SOCIAL WELFARE

The President committed himself to increased social welfare. "Along with the protection of freedom and maintenance of a strong and growing economy," he wrote, "this administration recognizes a third great purpose of government—care for the human problems of our citizens." One of his early appointments made Oveta Culp Hobby, wartime head of the WAC, the Secretary of Health, Education and Welfare, a new Cabinet post long advocated by President Truman.

In 1954 and 1956, Social Security benefits were extended to four million workers, including farmers, state and local government workers, the clergy, professional people, domestics and members of the armed forces. Old-age pensions were raised. The federal minimum wage also was raised to one dollar an hour in 1956.

The administration spent about one billion dollars on education between 1953 and 1956, mainly on school lunches, student aid, and research facilities, although the school program was bedeviled by protests against integration, aid to parochial institutions, and government regulations.

The National Defense Education Act of 1958 provided for federal aid in the teaching of sciences and languages. This measure authorized student loans and grants enabling schools to upgrade their standards in these subjects.

There were also appropriations to aid home building and the construction of interstate highways. In 1954, down payments on homes were reduced and there were appropriations for federal housing units.

The Interstate Highway Act of 1956 led to the greatest road-building program in the nation's history. The cost ran to over thirty billion dollars in the next thirteen years. As the government increased its share of the expense from 60 percent to 90 percent, new highway construction added up to more than 40,000 miles.

PRESIDENTIAL POWER

As early as 1954, the Bricker amendment forced Eisenhower to clarify his theory of Presidential power in foreign affairs. Senator John Bricker called on Congress to limit the President's ability to make executive agreements in order to prevent any future Yaltas. Many conservative Senators supported the amendment. Eisenhower forthrightly opposed the measure because he believed it would violate the separation of powers written into the Constitution and hamper the conduct of foreign policy. The Bricker amendment was defeated when it came up for a vote, but only a minority of Republican Senators supported the President.

PRIVATE VERSUS PUBLIC CONTROL

The proposal for building of a St. Lawrence Seaway touched the Eisenhower political philosophy in another way. Strong private business interests wanted to have private control or no Seaway. Eisenhower favored private development in the power field, but he supported public control of the

Seaway on the grounds that only state and national governments on both sides of the border could ensure its construction. The matter could not be put on the shelf because Canada was threatening to build the Seaway by herself. The President won this domestic battle and inaugurated the Seaway in 1959.

On other proposals to construct power plants, Eisenhower followed a more conservative philosophy. He turned the damming of the Snake River at Hells Canyon in Idaho into a private project. The Idaho Power Company built three small dams there. Ruling out public ownership except in areas too large for local action, he outraged many Westerners who charged that on the Snake and elsewhere public lands were being plundered by big businessmen.

The willingness of the President to go along with the expansion of private power interests provoked a major quarrel. In 1954, the Tennessee Valley Authority was planning to build a generating plant to provide power for the Atomic Energy Commission. When the Congress refused to appropriate money, Eisenhower backed a plan under which two companies headed by Edgar H. Dixon and Eugene Yates would build a plant in Arkansas. An uproar broke out immediately. The President's critics maintained that the Dixon-Yates plan would cost more than that of TVA and the syndicate's profits would be guaranteed by the government. But the contract was signed anyway in 1954. Then, a consultant to the Bureau of the Budget who helped draw up the contract was found to have a major conflict of interest since he was a member of the banking firm financing the project. Finally the city of Memphis decided to build the plant, to the relief of the President. He hastened to withdraw the Dixon-Yates agreement.

The President's handling of the question of how best to develop the nation's offshore resources also caused dispute. In 1947, the Supreme Court had denied California ownership of the three-mile offshore area, a decision applauded by those fearing a give-away by the state of rich natural resources. However, in 1953 Congress enacted the Sub-merged Lands Act, granting offshore oil and natural gas properties in the Pacific and the Gulf Coast to the states. California, Louisiana, Texas, and Florida proceeded to pass the rights on to private companies. Senator Wayne Morse of Oregon protested the "surrender of resources belonging to all the people," but Eisenhower signed the bill. He believed private interests could develop the offshore continental shelf better and less expensively than the government. He also pointed out that the government retained title to the biggest portion of the shelf and the wealthiest in natural resources.

THE ELECTION OF 1956

Eisenhower was certain of renomination in 1956. He had suffered a heart attack in 1955 but seemed fully recovered by the middle of 1956. Richard Nixon's renomination was not as certain, however. His enemies castigated his hard campaigning against political rivals in the 1954 Congressional elections and accused him of exploiting the communist issue for his own purpose. A "Dump Nixon" movement tried to gather momentum behind Harold Stassen, who considered the Vice President a political liability to the party. The President did not directly intervene in the intraparty dispute. Many businessmen and party workers were for Nixon, however, and the GOP convention went solidly for another Eisenhower-Nixon ticket.

The Democrats held a more boisterous convention. There was a tough contest for the Presidential nomination. Former President Truman, charging that "Stevenson can't win," backed Averell Harriman. Senator Estes Kefauver of Tennessee had won several primaries. But most delegates wanted Stevenson again and this time

he sought the nomination. Kefauver was chosen as his Vice Presidential running mate in a contest with Senator John F. Kennedy of Massachusetts.

The Democratic standard-bearer fared worse than he had four years before at the hands of the national hero. Stevenson carried seven states, two less than in 1952. Eisenhower's popular vote was 35,590,472 to Stevenson's 26,022,752. The difference in the electoral vote was 457 to 73.

CIVIL RIGHTS AND CIVIL LIBERTIES

The central domestic issue of the Eisenhower era was civil rights for black Americans. Many black Americans had fought in large numbers in World War II and now wanted recognition for their contribution to the nation's security. On the home front black people had worked in defense plants as a result of a government order for equal hiring practices. They had raised their standard of living and many were also active union members. After the war these workers wanted the same rights as their white counterparts. Moreover, as blacks had moved to Northern cities, they had of necessity settled solidly in certain sections which they could now use as a base for political organization and power. For exam-

Race Relations: Segregation

66 *When the Constitution of the United States was enacted, a Government was formed upon the premise that people, as individuals, are endowed with the rights of life, liberty and property, and with the right of local self-government. The people and their local self-governments formed a Central Government and conferred upon it certain stated and limited powers. All other powers were reserved to the states and to the people.*

Strong local government is the foundation of our system and must be continually guarded and maintained. . . .

I stand here today, as Governor of this sovereign state, and refuse to willingly submit to illegal usurpation of power by the Central Government. I claim today for all the people of the State of Alabama those rights reserved to them under the Constitution of the United States. Among those powers so reserved and claimed is the right of state authority in the operation of the public schools, colleges and universities. . . .

Now, therefore, I, George C. Wallace, as Governor of the State of Alabama, have by my action raised issues between the Central Government and the sovereign State of Alabama, which said issues should be adjudicated in the manner prescribed by the Constitution of the United States; and now being mindful of my duties and responsibilities under the Constitution of the United States, the Constitution of the State of Alabama, and seeking to preserve and maintain the peace and dignity of this state, and the individual freedoms of the citizens thereof, do hereby denounce and forbid this illegal and unwarranted action by the Central Government. 99

—*Governor George C. Wallace*

Race Relations: Integration

66 *In each of the cases, minors of the Negro race, through their legal representatives, seek the aid of the courts in obtaining admission to the public schools of their community on a nonsegregated basis. In each instance, they had been denied admission to schools attended by white children under laws requiring or permitting segregation according to race. This segregation was alleged to deprive the plaintiffs of the equal protection of the laws under the Fourteenth Amendment. . . .*

The plaintiffs, contend that segregated public schools are not "equal" and cannot be made "equal," and that hence they are deprived of the equal protection of the laws. . . .

We come then to the question presented. Does segregation of children in public schools solely on the basis of race, even though the physical facilities and other "tangible" factors may be equal, deprive the children of the minority group of equal educational opportunities? We believe that it does. . . .

We conclude that in the field of public education the doctrine of "separate but equal" has no place. Separate educational facilities are inherently unequal. . . .

—**Brown v. Board of Education of Topeka**

ple, Representative Adam Clayton Powell of Harlem became a power in the Democratic Party.

The problem was a complex one because, while idealism and humanitarianism were powerful factors in America, so was racism. The independence movements in Africa against European colonialism gave encouragement to the civil rights movement in the United States. Many an individual, con-

vinced of the morality of equal rights for black people, could not actually accept the practical changes that must ensue for integration to succeed. Moreover, wherever a black majority existed locally, white people were fearful of giving them real political power. At first, opposition centered in the South, with its deep attachment to segregation of the races. White Citizens Councils appeared as Southerners closed ranks against integration. Then the North began to awaken to the facts of ghetto life in big cities from New York to Los Angeles. Here, too, the race question became explosive.

By the time Eisenhower entered the White House, black Americans would wait no longer for their rights. They pushed harder for legal guarantees of racial equality. The President supported the civil rights movement morally and politically: "There must be no second class citizens in this country." But it was the Supreme Court that initiated a new era in the battle for racial equality in the United States.

THE SUPREME COURT

EARL WARREN

Chief Justice Earl Warren belonged to the moderate wing of the Republican Party and had been Thomas E. Dewey's running mate in 1948. Before that, he had been a moderate reformer while serving as governor of California. He was considered to be a level-headed person devoid of extremism, and even Republican conservatives raised no outcry against his appointment to America's highest tribunal. Only political liberals were uneasy remembering his support of Japanese internment in World War II.

THE "SEPARATE BUT EQUAL" DOCTRINE

The NAACP was in the forefront of the campaign to eradicate the legal basis of segregation. They pressed for the Supreme Court to overturn the decision in *Plessey v. Ferguson,* under which, in 1896, the "separate but equal" doctrine had been established as the law of the land.

Several Supreme Court decisions beginning in the late 1930s laid the groundwork for the legal overthrow of segregated education in the United States. They had ruled against separate dining cars on railroads, racial covenants in housing, segregation in buses, and had declared separate law school facilities in Texas unequal. In *Brown v. Board of Education,* which came before the Warren Court in 1954, the Court ruled on the case of Linda Brown of Topeka, Kansas, who had to travel five miles because the nearby school refused to enroll her on the grounds of race. Her father decided to sue the school board and the NAACP decided to make segregation as such the target. The Court's ruling in the case concluded: ". . . that in the field of public education the doctrine of 'separate but equal' has no place. Separate educational facilities are inherently unequal." The decision was based on the equal protection clause of the Fourteenth Amendment and on sociological evidence that segregation imposed a "feeling of inferiority" on black children.

In the second Brown case in 1955, the Chief Justice spoke for a united Court in directing school authorities everywhere to implement the desegregation decision "with all deliberate speed."

THE CIVIL RIGHTS ACT

President Eisenhower provoked an ambivalent attitude among black Americans. Although they wanted him to use his moral authority more decisively on the side of civil rights, they applauded his executive action ending segregation in the armed forces and in the District of Columbia. J. Ernest Wilkins, Assistant Secretary of Labor, became, in the President's words, "the first Negro in United States history ever to sit officially at the President's Cabinet table."

Most of all they appreciated Eisenhower's signing of the Civil Rights Act of 1957, a broad assault on the laws and practices that had justified discrimination ever since the end of Reconstruction. The Civil Rights Commission was founded to investigate violations of voting rights and the Justice Department gained a new Civil Rights Division. The Attorney General also received authority to use injunctions to defend voting rights for all the citizens of the country. A 1960 law made it a crime to interfere with voting rights and school desegregation.

THE LITTLE ROCK CRISIS

In the South, where racial segregation was deeply entrenched, there was massive resistance to desegregation of the schools. Schools were closed, compulsory attendance was abolished, and some states even passed acts for indirect state aid to private schools rather than obey the Supreme Court ruling.

Virulent opposition to integrated education culminated in 1957 when Orval Faubus, governor of Arkansas, intervened to prevent black students from entering the all-white high school in Little Rock under a Federal District Court order. President Eisenhower responded by putting the Arkansas National Guard under federal control and sending in a hundred army paratroopers to protect the students. Faubus had to give way. But his allies fulminated against the President, terming him a "dictator" and an enemy of American liberties. They distributed pictures of soldiers holding back crowds of angry parents.

Eisenhower might not have pressed for civil rights laws as hard as some had

When Southern white schools were faced with federally supported desegregation, compulsory attendance was abolished and many schools closed in resistance to the federal order. Eisenhower sent troops to Little Rock to escort black students to class.

Alain Locke, a leading intellectual and professor at Howard University, advised his fellow black Americans in the twenties that their greatest opportunities in America lay in the arts. Locke pointed out that blacks had shaped American society as much as they were shaped by it, particularly through their culture. In a Harper's *article in 1928, another important black writer of the period, James Weldon Johnson, observed, "It is perhaps a startling thought that America would not be peculiarly the America it is today except for the powerful, if silent influence the Negro has exerted upon it—both positively and negatively."*

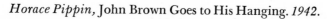

Horace Pippin, John Brown Goes to His Hanging. *1942.*

America as Seen by the Black Artist

The first effects of slavery were moral rather than cul-
tural. To ease his conscience, the slave owner convinced
himself that all blacks were born inferior and, hence,
were incapable of caring for themselves in a free society.
In place of liberty, dignity, education, and legal protec-
tion, the slave owner offered paternalism, while in the
second century of slavery in America, he himself em-
braced the Declaration of Independence. Hypocrisy
thus became socially acceptable in plantation society,
and the slave learned to play the master's game—he
avoided the lash by pretending to have the characteris-
tics the white man attributed to him. In the only theater
known to the plantation, blacks who could sing, enter-
tained by creating the minstrel character. White per-
formers learned to mimic them and gave American
audiences the minstrel show in blackface, perpetuating a

Aaron Douglas, mural, Countee Cullen Branch, New York Public Library. 1934.

degrading stereotype, until protests brought this kind of entertainment to disrepute in the mid-twenties.

Torn from their rich African culture and deprived of the means for self-expression, plantation slaves gave America songs, folklore, and dance. Bill Robinson's tap dancing and the great African based modern dances of Katherine Dunham and Alvin Ailey all have the same roots. Out of the slave's work songs and folk songs came the music that all the world associates with America—ragtime, the blues, jazz and, later, rock. In his deeply stirring spirituals, the black man expressed his religious feelings, his hope for an easier life in the next world, and his suffering in this one. "No More Auction Block," "Nobody Knows the Troubles I've Seen," and "Go Down Moses" expressed the anguish of an oppressed people.

In the eighteenth century, a few black craftsmen and an occasional painter developed, usually favored slaves. Typical was Joshua Johnson, an enslaved blacksmith-painter, who turned out portraits of the Maryland aristocracy. At about the same time, a talented black poet, Phillis Wheatley, attracted attention. The slave of a Northern family, she also avoided racial subjects, favoring religious and sentimental themes.

Emancipation brought no immediate freedom from the restraints on the artist's spirit imposed by an environment which continued to make the black man feel inferior, and upheld time-worn conventions as the standard for art. When black artists and writers at last began to appear in number, their work was largely imitative and they tended to shun racial subjects. Long after the Civil War, an important black painter emerged. Henry O. Tanner of Philadelphia achieved an international reputation at the end of the century for his landscapes and genre pictures. Angered by the attention American critics gave to his race, Tanner spent most of his life abroad.

The change in the black man's view of himself, and, in turn, its reflection in his art, began with the migrations from the South to the North. They started in

1900 and grew out of the black man's rising resentment of his treatment in the South and his awakened hopes for better opportunities in the North. With the North as a base, countless gifted performers have developed, such as Marion Anderson, Louis Armstrong, and James Earl Jones; great jazz composers, such as W. C. Handy and Duke Ellington, and symphonic composers of the stature of William Grant Still and Howard Swanson; poets such as Countee Cullen, Langston Hughes, and Pulitzer-Prize-winning Gwendolyn Brooks, and novel-

Charles White, The Contribution of the Negro to American Democracy. *1943.*

ists like Richard Wright, James Baldwin, and Ralph Ellison. One of the greatest black artists, singer-actor Paul Robeson, no longer able to accept racial injustice, left America for the Soviet Union.

In painting and sculpture, the black artist came to the fore in the mid-thirties. Opportunities offered by the Work Projects Administration in the New Deal Era, and the civil rights movement, strengthened his self-image and freed his art. The black people of America developed a new mood of assertiveness, mirrored in the work of such major talents as Archibald Motley, Hale Woodruff, and Jacob Lawrence. Like the writer and the musician, the painter has succeeded in being judged, not on the basis of his color, but for his talent. He has entered the mainstream of his profession, yet he cannot help but be affected by a society that remains largely segregated. Romare Bearden, a New York painter whose works hang in the nation's museums has said, "I do not need to go looking for 'happenings,' the absurd, surreal, because I have seen things out of my studio window on 125th Street in Harlem that neither Dali nor Beckett nor Ionesco would have ever thought possible."

Jacob Lawrence, from The Migration of the Negro. *1941.*

Jacob Lawrence, Ambulance Call.

Allan Crite, street scene.

Palmer Hayden, Virginia Teamster.

Russ Thompson, Poor Room, Rich Room. *1968.*

Romare Bearden, Three Folk Musicians. *1967.*

Alma Thomas, Tenement Scene, Harlem.

Arthur L. Britt, Jr., The Dream.

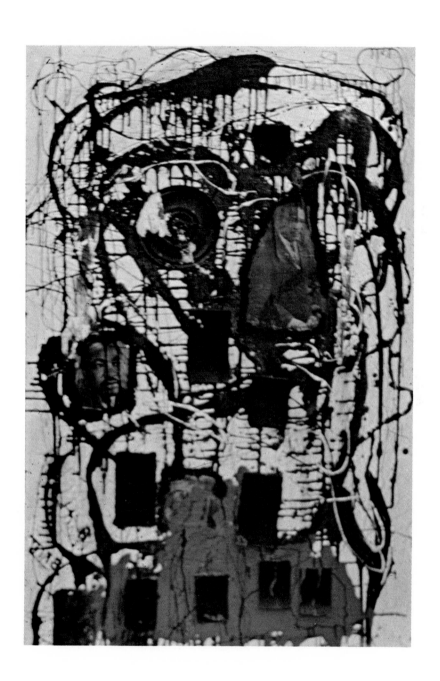

George Carter, Ghetto. *1968.*

George Carter, Le Roi. *1969.*

Dana C. Chandler, Jr., Land of the Free #1. *1967.*

Dana C. Chandler, Jr., Fred Hampton's Door. *1970.*

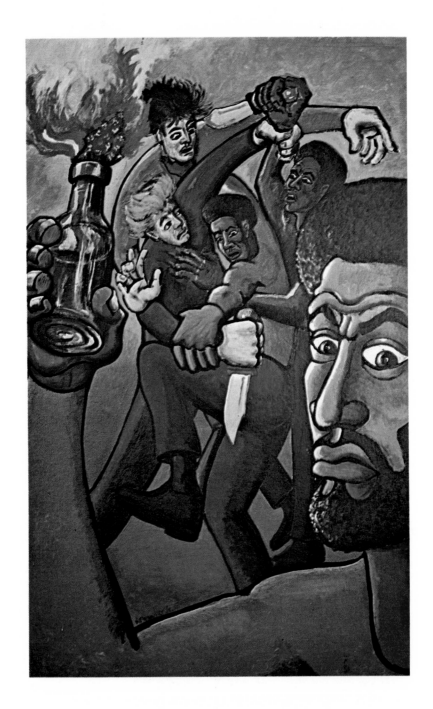

Dana C. Chandler, Jr., Rebellion '72.

wanted, but once the Supreme Court had ruled, he accepted the moral obligation of enforcing the law. As he said of Little Rock: "Failure to act in such a case would be tantamount to acquiescence in anarchy and the dissolution of the Union." In 1958, the case of *Cooper v. Aaron,* brought by the Little Rock school board, ended in a Supreme Court decision favoring desegregation of the high school immediately.

CIVIL LIBERTIES DECISIONS

On June 17, 1957, the Warren Court handed down several important rulings on civil liberties in an effort to end an era of judicial support of conformity and suppression of dissent while not undermining the government's ability to protect itself from subversion. In *Yates v. United States,* the Court made a sharp distinction between words and acts. An advocate of the forceful overthrow of the American government could be convicted henceforth only if he advocated revolutionary action rather than the doctrine of revolution. In *Watkins v. United States,* the Court upheld the right of a labor official, John T. Watkins, not to reveal his past associations to the House Un-American Activities Committee. It further stated that the Congressional power to investigate was not unlimited, especially when the aims were excessively vague. The witness had been denied "a fair opportunity to determine whether he was within his rights in refusing to answer, and his conviction is necessarily invalid under the Due Process Clause of the Fifth Amendment." Less noticed was a subsequent ruling in *Barenblatt v. United States,* which declared that a valid legislative purpose justified forcing a witness to turn over relevant documents and answer relevant questions because "the balance between the individual and the governmental interests here at stake must be struck in favor of the latter."

NEW LOOK DIPLOMACY

JOHN FOSTER DULLES

No man in the Eisenhower administration, other than the President himself, had more authority than the Secretary of State. An experienced diplomat who adhered to strong moral principles and a firm religious faith, Dulles took over the office with a determination to apply his beliefs to international affairs. During the 1952 election campaign he had spoken of ending the policy of containment and initiating a policy to bring about the eventual liberation of the nations which were the captives of the Russian and Chinese communists. While Secretary of State Dulles' admirers credited him with the toughness and perspicacity to handle American foreign policy, his critics charged him with an inflexibility harmful to the nation's diplomacy.

The rigid polarity of the Truman years continued into the Eisenhower administration. The hard lines between the communist bloc and the Western allies were established in both Europe and most of Asia. Stalin's policies did not change in the early 1950s and the Eisenhower administration guided by John Foster Dulles took an equally tough approach to world politics.

PEACEFUL COEXISTENCE

The world was shocked to learn of Stalin's death in 1953. After a short period of collective leadership, Nikita Khrushchev emerged from a power struggle in the Kremlin as the leader of the Soviet Union. Gregarious, ebullient, given to the quotation of Russian proverbs, Khrushchev gave

Russian diplomacy a new look. In 1956, Nikita Khrushchev announced a comprehensive program of furthering communism without war. His slogan was "peaceful co-existence," by which he meant that ideological competition would replace the threatened use of force to spread communism. Khrushchev saw the danger of a nuclear war, which, he declared, must be avoided at all costs.

Although he crushed the 1956 Hungarian uprising by force, he preferred diplomatic and economic warfare. He traveled abroad —to China, to England, to Yugoslavia, where he apologized to Tito for Stalin's hostility. He pushed Soviet-American rivalry into Asia, Africa, and the Middle East,

where colonial regimes were pulling out. Russian technical assistance was used to help raise the standard of living in these areas, and Russian propaganda claimed that communism provided a formula for rapid modernization of their economies.

Dulles, however, still thought of communism as aggressively militaristic. He did not believe Russia would change from within. He began to work out international alliances and agreements to interpose sufficient military power between vulnerable areas and the might of the Soviet war machine.

MASSIVE RETALIATION

Nevertheless, Dulles saw that forming alliances on a piecemeal basis was not a panacea. The Russians and the Chinese could organize and finance brush-fire wars in which they themselves would, ostensibly, not be involved. This was the rationale behind the Dulles policy of "massive retaliation" when it warned that America would not simply wring her hands while the communists used war-by-proxy as an instrument of their foreign policy. America would, if driven to it, retaliate with her full power against the major communist powers themselves rather than see the free world eroded slowly away.

Moreover, this kind of defense policy would allow America to get a "bigger bang for a buck"—that is, to reduce spending on conventional arms and training and to concentrate on strategic air power able to use nuclear weapons. The United States would get bogged down in no more limited wars. The policy was designed to prevent either Moscow or Peking from blundering into war through a misunderstanding of American intentions.

One of the most famous remarks ever made by John Foster Dulles was that the United States had to have "the ability to get to the verge without getting into war." His policy was to take a chance on war for

In 1956, Hungarian resistance to Soviet control of Hungary resulted in revolt. Here, Hungarians burn pictures of Stalin during the uprising.

Policy of Liberation

There are a number of policy matters which I would prefer to discuss with the committee in executive session, but I have no objection to saying in open session what I have said before: namely, that we shall never have a secure peace or a happy world so long as Soviet communism dominates one-third of all of the peoples that there are, and is in the process of trying at least to extend its rule to many others. . . .

Therefore, we must always have in mind the liberation of these captive peoples. Now, liberation does not mean a war of liberation. Liberation can be accomplished by processes short of war. We have, as one example, not an ideal example, but it illustrates my point, the defection of Yugoslavia, under Tito, from the domination of Soviet communism. . . .

. . . But all of this can be done and must be done in ways which will not provoke a general war, or in ways which will not provoke an insurrection which would be crushed with bloody violence, such as the case, for example, when the Russians instigated the Polish revolt, under General Bor, and merely sat by and watched them when the Germans exterminated those who were revolting.

It must be and can be a peaceful process, but those who do not believe that results can be accomplished by moral pressures, by the weight of propaganda, just do not know what they are talking about.

—*John Foster Dulles*

Policy of Liberation

A further requisite of the art of peacemaking is a keen sense of the possible, coupled with constructive imagination. No imaginable peace settlement can remove the deep ideological differences between Communism and Western liberalism—it was Roosevelt's fatal error to believe that this was possible. All that a peace settlement can remove is the foreseeable causes of war, and the fear of war, between States. Further, no peace settlement based on the existing balance of power can have as its condition the liberation of the Communist countries in Eastern Europe. It might have as its result some liberalization both in their external relations and in their internal regimes.

The best we can hope for—and this is not a wholly unreasonable or unrealistic hope—is that a period of peace may reduce Russia's iron grip on her neighbors which six years of cold war have merely tightened—just as in Aesop's fable of the gale and the sun betting which of them could strip a wanderer of his coat, the sun succeeded, where all the violent tuggings of the gale had only made the wanderer grip his wrappings more firmly.

—*The London* Observer

the sake of peace. A good example of Dulles' approach can be seen in America's policy toward communist China during the Eisenhower years. A strong supporter of Chiang Kai-shek as the legitimate ruler of China, Dulles proclaimed that the islands of Matsu and Quemoi were vital to the defense of Formosa and therefore would be defended despite denunciations from Peking. However, when the United States made a mutual defense treaty with Taiwan in 1955, it included no mention of defending the two islands. Red China shelled the islands in 1955 and 1958, but the United States did nothing when she found her European allies would not support her in case of war.

As appealing as Dulles' ideas were to an economy-minded public weary of international tensions, they were of limited practical use. The threat of massive retaliation against any communist aggression in the world and a realistic policy to liberate Russia's satellites contained the danger of world war with the communist bloc. The Soviet Union also had nuclear weapons and a strong air force. As a result, the United States did nothing when there were uprisings against Soviet rule in East Berlin in 1953 and in Hungary in 1956. In spite of Dulles' pronouncements, the United States continued to rely on a policy of alliances and foreign aid to contain world communism.

PROBLEMS IN THE FAR EAST

KOREA

Eisenhower kept his promise to go to Korea. He agreed with Dulles on a tough line toward the communists, even hinting at the use of atomic weapons should they refuse to resume negotiations. The North Koreans decided to re-enter the peace talks.

REPATRIATION

Prisoners of war on both sides still refused to return home. Thousands of North Korean combat troops asked for asylum in South Korea, and twenty-one Americans captured by the North Koreans or Chinese refused to come home. Their attitude stirred protests on the Allied side that they had been brainwashed by their captors. But they stuck to their refusal and went to China. The North Korean defectors were able to remain in South Korea when Syngman Rhee

released 27,000 prisoners, although no armistice agreement had yet been signed.

THE ARMISTICE

With the repatriation matter taken out of the hands of the negotiators, an armistice ending the Korean hostilities was signed on July 27, 1953. It provided for a withdrawal of troops and divided the Korean Peninsula at the 38th parallel leaving the country as it had been before the war. The United States had lost over 33,000 men and had spent about 22 billion dollars in the three-year defense of the area.

THE WAR IN INDOCHINA

During the 1880s, France had taken over the Indochina peninsula, which included Laos, Cambodia, and Vietnam. French culture and French policies prevailed. Saigon was called the "Paris of the Orient." World War II shattered French colonial rule as the Japanese pushed the French out. When they tried to return at the end of the war, the French were met with stiff resistance from an indigenous anticolonial movement. In Ho Chi Minh, they faced a communist leader fanatically convinced of the inevitable victory of his nationalist cause. In August, 1945, Ho Chi Minh was designated president of the Democratic Republic of Vietnam.

The French initially agreed to recognize Ho's government but then reneged and set up a puppet state under former Emperor Bao Dai. Now war broke out between Ho's army and the French forces. The French kept pouring men and weapons into Vietnam in quest of a victory that proved elusive. Ho's forces attacked suddenly and then melted back into the jungle, where they skillfully dodged large French military columns. Postwar France could not stand the strain. Paris looked to Washington for aid. Both Truman and Eisenhower supported aid to the French forces out of fear of the spread of communism in Asia. By 1954 the United States was paying 80 percent of the cost of the war.

Despite American aid, the French were tired and baffled. Something more than American financial help was required, and Paris sent to Washington a plea for military assistance. The fate of French Indochina was sealed at a fortress selected by the French military command near the Laotian border. Dien Bien Phu was an isolated place that had to be supplied by air. Eisenhower warned the French about sending their best troops into so exposed a position. The French countered that Dien Bien Phu could be held because Ho's forces lacked artillery, and would be decimated if they attacked without the covering fire of big guns on the surrounding hills. The theory proved wrong. Ho Chi Minh got his guns from China, placed them on the nearby hills, and pounded the defenders mercilessly. Only a heavy air attack on Ho's supply lines could avert French surrender. Dulles and Admiral Arthur W. Radford, Chairman of the Joint Chiefs, called for Congressional support of such a move. But the President, the rest of the Joint Chiefs, and the British were all against intervening, and Congress did not act. Dien Bien Phu fell to the North Vietnamese in May, 1954.

GENEVA SETTLEMENT

With the French now pulling out, a conference at Geneva forged a precarious division of the peninsula in July. Vietnam was partitioned temporarily in the manner of Korea, North Vietnam above the 17th parallel was left to communist domination under Ho Chi Minh, while South Vietnam was left under the government of Bao Dai. The rest of the peninsula was divided into two small nations which were to remain neutral—Laos and Cambodia. Free elections to bring about the unification of North and South Vietnam were to be held under international supervision in 1956.

The United States was not a party to the Geneva agreement out of antagonism to any agreement with the communists. President Eisenhower did, however, issue a statement accepting the terms, pledging support for them under the United Nations Charter, and warning that "any renewal of Communist aggression would be viewed by us as a matter of grave concern."

SEATO

The French debacle in Indochina followed by the diplomatic settlement at Geneva convinced Dulles that a completely new defense alignment had to be formed among the free nations of Asia. The pattern already existed in Europe in the form of the North Atlantic Treaty Organization (NATO). The concerned nations now came together in the Southeast Asia Treaty Organization (SEATO), in September, 1954. Great Britain, France, Australia, New Zealand, Pakistan, the Philippines, Thailand, and the United States signed the treaty. South Vietnam, Laos, and Cambodia were not signatories, yet under a protocol added to the document they were included within the region guarded by SEATO. All signatories agreed that an attack on any one of them would be an attack on all. There would be consultation on measures for common defense if there were other than military threats to the treaty area.

Unlike NATO, there was never a joint military force under the SEATO pact; it depended on American air and sea power. Another drawback in the treaty resulted from the fact that important and newly independent nations, such as India, Burma, and Indonesia were not members. These countries wanted more emphasis on anti-colonialism and less on military resistance to communism. The United States was not in a position to make such a commitment since it would have alienated her European allies.

UNION OF SOVIET SOCIALIST REPUBLICS

BERING SEA

Lake Baikal

Irkutsk•

Sea of Okhotsk

(U.S.S.R.)
(U.S.) ATTU

KISKA

SAKHALIN I.
(U.S.S.R.)

Ulan Bator•

MONGOLIA

MANCHURIA

KURILE IS.
(U.S.S.R.)

Vladivostok•

Peking•

NORTH KOREA

Pyongyang•

Sea of Japan

Seoul• SOUTH KOREA

J A P A N

•Tokyo

C H I N A

TIBET

Shanghai•

BONIN IS.

RYUKYU IS. (Jap.)

IWO JIMA

TACHEN IS.

MATSU I.

QUEMOY I.

OKINAWA

MARCUS I.

NEPAL

E. PAKISTAN

Calcutta•

BURMA

Hanoi•

LAOS

NORTH VIETNAM

Hong Kong (Br.)

TAIWAN (FORMOSA)

PESCADORES IS.

P A C I F I C

INDIA

Rangoon•

Vientiane•

THAILAND

Bangkok•

CAMBODIA

SOUTH VIETNAM

Saigon•

South China Sea

•Manila

PHILIPPINES (also member of SEATO)

PHILIPPINE SEA

MARIANAS IS.

O C E A N

WAKE I. (U.S.)

BAY OF BENGAL

GUAM (U.S.)

M I C R O N E S I A

MARSHALL IS. (U.S. trust)

CEYLON

BRUNEI (Br.)

Kuala Lumpur•

MALAYSIA

SARAWAK

SINGAPORE

SUMATRA

KALIMANTAN

SULAWESI

CAROLINE ISLANDS (U.S. trust)

GILBERT IS. (Br.)

M E L A N E S I A

I N D O N E S I A

IRIAN (To U.N. 1962, Indonesia 1963)

NEW GUINEA (Aust.)

•Djakarta

JAVA

TIMOR (Port.)

PAPUA (Aust.)

SOLOMON IS. (Br.)

ELLICE IS. (Br.)

I N D I A N

O C E A N

C O R A L S E A

NEW HEBRIDES IS. (Br. and Fr.)

FIJI IS. (Br.)

NEW CALEDONIA (Fr.)

A U S T R A L I A

Brisbane•

T A S M A N S E A

•Perth

•Sidney

Canberra•

NEW ZEALAND

Melbourne•

•Wellington

TASMANIA

Members of SEATO

Nations having bilateral treaties with the U.S.

Communist bloc

POSTWAR ALLIANCES · THE FAR EAST

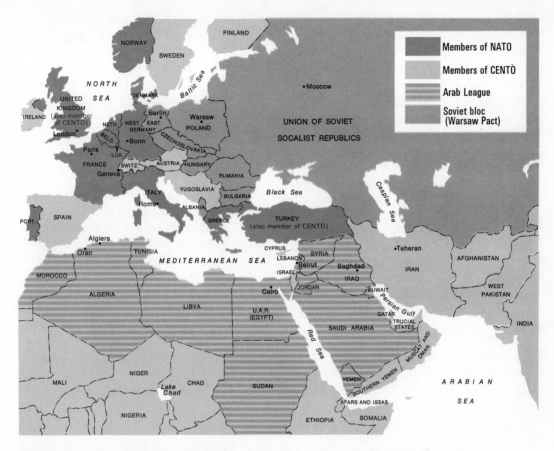

POSTWAR ALLIANCES · EUROPE, NORTH AFRICA, THE MIDDLE EAST

THE MIDDLE EAST

Before World War II American interest in the Middle East had been limited to her oil investments. Britain and France dominated the area and it was not until after the war that the United States began to play a larger role in the Middle East. Since the Middle East was on the periphery of the Soviet Union, it became a link in the containment of world communism.

The effort to protect American oil interests and curb Soviet power was undermined by the equally strong desire of the United States to support the Jewish state of Israel, the focal point of Arab hostility. As early as 1922 Congress had approved the Balfour Declaration in which Great Britain had put her support behind a "national home for the Jewish people." By the end of World

1043

War II much of the American public supported creation of a Jewish state because of the persecution of the Jews in Nazi Germany. A United Nations plan to partition Palestine between the Jews and Arabs was accepted by the Jews, but the Arabs immediately initiated a guerrilla war in Palestine to prevent the partition. The Jews proclaimed the state of Israel on May 14, 1948, and Truman recognized it immediately. After a short and bloody war, the Jews controlled the area. About a million Arabs had fled the country and have subsequently lived in refugee camps. By July, 1949, an armistice had been worked out between the two sides by Dr. Ralph J. Bunche, under United Nations auspices. Raids continued, however, and the Arabs bitterly resented the United States for her pro-Israeli policy.

No international problem seemed more intractable than that of Israel's place in an area of hostile Arab neighbors. They continued to deny her right to exist, demanded the return to Palestine of the refugees exiled at the time of the Arab-Israeli war, and continued to threaten another armed conflict. For their part the Israelis refused to let the refugees return, and turned to the West, especially the United States, for support.

NASSER

Arab resentment and intransigence focused on the Egypt of Gamal Abdel Nasser, who saw himself as the leader of an Arab coalition against Israel. In an agreement with Egypt, the British withdrew from the Suez Canal. Dulles, in an effort to placate the Arabs, offered Nasser economic and military aid, but the Egyptian ruler turned it down.

Nasser was further alienated when the United States threw her support behind an alliance to counter Soviet influence in oil-rich Iran. While the United States was not a signatory, she stood behind the Baghdad

Pact of February, 1955, signed by Britain, Turkey, Pakistan, Iran, and Iraq. The so-called Middle East Treaty Organization was to act as a barrier where they had common frontiers with the Soviet Union. Nasser decried the Baghdad Pact as an attack on Arab unity.

THE ASWAN DAM AND THE SUEZ CANAL

In an effort to better relations with Nasser while not supplying him with arms, the United States offered to help him build a High Dam at Aswan in central Egypt. At the same time Nasser had negotiated an arms deal with the Russians to protect Egypt against Israeli raids. He also tried to get better terms from Russia for a loan to build the dam. As a result, Dulles canceled American participation in the project under pressure from Congress.

The late President of Egypt, Gamal Abdel Nasser, greets an enthusiastic crowd of Egyptians after announcing the nationalization of the Suez Canal in 1956.

In retaliation for America's action, Nasser seized the Suez Canal, nationalized the waterway, and applied the assets to the financing of the Aswan High Dam. Nasser then increased raids on Israel, thereby touching off an international crisis. Britain, France, and Israel felt their economic interests were directly threatened. They mounted military operations and bombed Egyptian targets in October, 1956, to occupy Suez and keep the canal open. Nasser closed the canal and blew up oil pipelines. Eisenhower and Dulles believed British and French tactics had no legal basis and were angered by their acting without American advice. The United States sponsored a resolution in the United Nations for a cease-fire and Russia threatened intervention. Britain, France, and Israel had to back down. The United Nations sent a peace-keeping force to Suez to supervise troop withdrawals. United States relations with both Britain and France had been undermined—a fact which damaged cooperation within the NATO alliance. On the other hand, the United States had earned new respect among the anticolonial powers of Asia.

THE EISENHOWER DOCTRINE

The United States now gave up the idea of cooperating with the Arabs to stabilize the Middle East against Soviet influence. Her main concern was to protect Israel and curb Nasser. The outgrowth of this policy of maintaining the status quo was the Eisenhower Doctrine. In March, 1957, as a result of fear of growing Soviet influence in the area, a Congressional resolution declared that the United States would unilaterally protect the independence of all Middle East nations with military aid to prevent aggression from any nation "controlled by international communism."

The doctrine was soon initiated. The United States sent economic aid to Jordan in April to help King Hussein stamp out pro-Nasser opposition. In early 1958, Nasser formed the United Arab Republic with Syria and pro-Nasser rebellions broke out in Iraq and Lebanon. A pro-Nasser government came to power in Iraq and joined the UAR. Eisenhower sent American troops to Lebanon where they stayed for a few months to prevent full-scale civil war between pro- and anti-Nasser factions. The pro-Nasser group did not obtain power and Russia refused to aid Nasser in a direct confrontation with the United States. At the same time, American influence in the Arab world was at a low ebb by the late 1950s as a result of her interventionist policy and friendship with Israel.

LATIN AMERICA

Immediately following World War II the United States and her Latin American neighbors appeared to be on the friendliest of terms. At Rio in 1947 the nations of the Western Hemisphere signed a defensive military alliance for the collective security of the region. At Bogotá, the following year, the Organization of American States was created with a Council of Ministers of Foreign Affairs to consider urgent problems.

In spite of these pacts, however, the Good Neighbor Policy began to decline. The United States counted on Latin American support at the United Nations, but paid little attention to her internal problems of poverty and overpopulation. American pressure for support against communism did not seem as important to Latin Americans as their chronic economic difficulties.

GUATEMALA

Although the Eisenhower administration in theory wanted to extend more economic aid to Latin America, in practice it pursued an unpopular interventionist policy in Guatemala in the name of anticommunism. A pro-communist government had come to power there in 1951. The government expropriated American property without compensation. An American protest was, however, considered by most Guatemalans as a cover for American economic imperialism. An inter-American conference meeting at Caracas in 1954 reluctantly supported a United States resolution calling international communism a threat to the Western Hemisphere. At the same time, communist arms were arriving in Guatemala and the United States countered with arms to neighboring Honduras and Nicaragua. Before the Organization of American States could consult on the situation, an armed band invaded Guatemala from Honduras and overthrew the pro-communist government. The United States immediately recognized the new government and gave it economic aid. She also blocked any appeal to the United Nations by the overthrown government of Guatemala. Even America's European allies criticized her and anti-Americanism was rejuvenated in Latin America.

NIXON IN SOUTH AMERICA

The United States received a stringent warning of her unpopularity in Latin America when Vice President Nixon visited Peru, Colombia, and Venezuela in 1958 on a goodwill tour. Students in Lima threw stones at him and in Caracas, protesters smashed the windows of the car in which he was riding. Booing and obscenities were common on the trip. During the worst phase in Caracas, Eisenhower even thought of sending American forces to the aid of the Vice President and his wife.

The United States was at last jolted out of its complacent attitude toward her neighbors. She agreed to an Inter-American Development Bank in 1959 to aid the economic development of the hemisphere. As a result of even more alarming events in Cuba a new program of economic aid was also authorized by the Congress in 1960.

THE CUBAN REVOLUTION

As the administration was pondering ways to improve its image in Latin America, its worst fears were realized in Cuba. The dictator Fulgencio Batista had been driven out by Fidel Castro. Castro came to Washington, was received by the President at the White House, and firmly declared that he was not a communist. Back in Cuba, however, Castro sent his opponents before firing squads, drew closer to Moscow, brusquely seized American firms without compensation, and delivered long tirades against American imperialism. He signed an economic pact with Russia in February, 1960. In retaliation, the United States placed an embargo on Cuban sugar in June and Russia threatened a missile attack on the United States if she intervened in Cuba. On January 3, 1961, the United States severed diplomatic relations with Cuba.

EUROPEAN SECURITY

The main concern of American foreign policy continued to be Europe. The NATO alliance was weak because most United States arms were committed elsewhere and because France was against the rearming of West Germany. Plans to integrate German troops into NATO were defeated by France. Nevertheless, in October, 1954, West Germany was finally brought into NATO as a sovereign nation by including her in the Brussels Pact. Allied occupation of Germany came to an end. The buildup of the NATO forces was also undermined by the relaxation of the hard communist line in the Kremlin and the tensions in Sino-Soviet relations by 1960.

The United States was encouraged enough by Soviet flexibility to agree to a summit conference in July, 1955, at Geneva. There were no dramatic results from the meeting, but the spirit of cordiality helped to further relax world anxiety about a nuclear war.

BERLIN

Yet the arms race continued. Russia launched a space satellite in 1957 (Sputnik), and the new leader in the Kremlin wanted to oust the Western Powers from Berlin as much as had his predecessors. Khrushchev was fond of terming West Berlin "a bone in my throat." Buoyed by Russia's scientific feats, he set a deadline in 1959, after which Allied rights in the city would lapse. Washington, London, and Paris refused to be intimidated, and Khrushchev prudently allowed the deadline to pass without incident.

KHRUSHCHEV AND THE UNITED STATES

Khrushchev expressed a desire to visit the United States. Hoping to relax international tensions, Eisenhower extended an invitation. The American people were hosts to the Soviet leader in September, 1959. Khrushchev visited a farm in Iowa and a Hollywood set, argued with American labor leaders about working conditions in Russia, and conferred with Eisenhower at the Camp David Presidential retreat, a meeting

that gave birth to a short period of amity called the "spirit of Camp David."

The two men agreed on another summit conference in 1960. However, by the time of the meeting in Paris in May, the "spirit of Camp David" had evaporated. Only days before the scheduled Paris meeting, the Russians shot down an American U-2, a spy plane making an overflight of the Soviet Union. The pilot, Gary Francis Powers, was captured. Eisenhower took personal responsibility for Powers' flight but would not apologize for it. In retaliation, Khrushchev refused to attend the Paris summit conference and withdrew an invitation to Eisenhower to visit Russia.

ELECTION OF 1960

THE CANDIDATES

In his choice of Richard M. Nixon as the Republican Presidential candidate, Eisenhower was backed by the vast majority of Republican party workers. Nixon won on the first ballot and Henry Cabot Lodge, Jr., ambassador to the United Nations, was his running mate.

Looking back in disappointment at the election outcome, Eisenhower passed this self-judgment: "As of that time, I did what I thought best, and even more than the Vice President planned for. But I participated, on an intensively partisan basis, only in the final week of the campaign. I shall never cease to wonder whether a more extensive program of political speaking on my part might have had a favorable effect on the outcome."

Adlai Stevenson seemed a likely Democratic choice for a third attempt at the

White House but he never declared his candidacy and made little effort to get the nomination. Senator John F. Kennedy of Massachusetts had put together a strong and enthusiastic organization, and it now carried him to victory in the Wisconsin and West Virginia primaries and then at the convention. Lyndon Baines Johnson of Texas gained the second place on the ticket in the hope that he could carry the South in November.

THE ISSUES

Nixon stood on the Eisenhower record, one of mixed success, identifying himself with it, and promising only to enlarge on it, especially in the area of civil rights. Kennedy launched a broad offensive against the Eisenhower administration, claiming that America had virtually stood still for eight years. Kennedy promised to better conditions for all Americans, restore America's military supremacy which he claimed Russia had surpassed, and repair the Amer-

ican image abroad. His most controversial charge concerned what he termed "the missile gap." He maintained that the Soviet Union was ahead of America in nuclear weapons development, a charge which the administration flatly denied.

THE TELEVISION DEBATES

Perhaps Nixon's greatest mistake in 1960 was his acceptance of Kennedy's challenge to a series of debates on television. The Vice President, a well-known national figure of wide experience in government, seemed to be going out of his way to make a national figure of his less well-known opponent. Kennedy gained a nation-wide exposure he would not otherwise have had. The debates gave Kennedy another advantage—he was a skilled debater. Finally, and perhaps decisively, Kennedy's personality came across onto television screens throughout the country. Viewers reacted favorably to his youth, vigorous manner, and engag-

Readings

GENERAL WORKS

Baldwin, D. A., *Economic Development and American Foreign Policy*. Chicago: University of Chicago Press, 1966—An analysis of the impact of American technical and economic aid programs on the donor and on the recipients. Baldwin concludes that many political obstacles remain in the path of an effective foreign-aid program.

Bell, Daniel, *The End of Ideology*. New York: Macmillan, 1960—A series of essays on different aspects of American life since World War II connected by the theme that

ideologies, especially orthodox Marxism, have lost their relevance for contemporary American life.

Dozer, Donald M., *Are We Good Neighbors? Three Decades of Inter-American Relations, 1930–1960*. Gainesville: University of Florida Press, 1959—Dozer believes that while the Good Neighbor policy improved United States–Latin American relations in the 1930s, United States insensitivity and indifference led to a growth of hostility in the 1940s and 1950s.

Eulau, Heinz, *Class and Party in the Eisenhower Years*. New York: Macmillan, 1962—A political scientist's analysis of the effects of social class and party loyalty on voters for Eisenhower in 1952 and 1956.

Key, V. O., Jr., *The Responsible Electorate*,

ing smile. Nixon, on the other hand, often appeared tense and tired. In the minds of the American people, Kennedy won the debates and with them, quite possibly, the election.

ELECTION RESULTS

Election night created bedlam in the United States. The political analysts had generally forecast a close contest. All night long the American people followed a race that could go either way. Around noon the next day Nixon conceded defeat. He actually carried more states than Kennedy, trailed him in the popular vote by only 113,000 out of some 70 million votes and lost by an electoral margin of 303 to 219. The Democratic strongholds were still the Deep South and the East. Nixon carried the Midwest, Far West, and upper South.

John Kennedy became the thirty-fifth President of the United States. At 43, he was the youngest man ever elected to the office, and the first Roman Catholic.

John F. Kennedy began his political career in 1946, when he ran for Congress, and culminated it fourteen years later when he was elected the thirty-fifth President of the United States.

Rationality in Presidential Voting, 1936–1960. Cambridge, Mass.: Harvard University Press, 1966—A leading political scientist explores voting behavior and finds that most Americans voted in a way that expressed the best interests of the groups to which they belonged.

La Feber, Walter, *America, Russia and the Cold War.* New York: Wiley, 1967—A general history of the Cold War from a moderately revisionist standpoint, covering the first two decades of the post-World War II era.

Lubell, Samuel, *The Revolt of the Moderates.* New York: Harper, 1956—Lubell analyzes Eisenhower's Presidency as being peculiarly suited to the cautious, unimaginative political temper of the times.

Neustadt, Richard E., *Presidential Power.* New York: Wiley, 1960—A series of case studies of how Roosevelt, Truman, and Eisenhower handled crises in their Presidencies. Neustadt draws implications from these studies on how a President can best gain and hold personal power.

Shannon, David A., *The Decline of American Communism: A History of the Communist Party of the United States since 1945.* New York: Harcourt, Brace, 1959—At the close of World War II, the United States Communist Party was relatively strong. By the late 1950s, Shannon argues, it had declined because of the party's own failures.

Vatter, Harold G., *The U.S. Economy in the 1950s.* New York: Norton, 1963—A general survey of the United States economy noting the sluggish growth rate and inconsistent fiscal policies of the Eisenhower years.

SPECIAL STUDIES

Clark, Thomas D., *The Emerging South.* New York: Oxford University Press, 1968—Clark finds the South since 1920 to have combined rapid change with a lingering nostalgia for an older, agrarian way of life.

Draper, Theodore, *Castro's Revolution: Myths and Realities.* New York: Praeger, 1962—An account of American relations with the Cuban revolutionaries which accuses Castro of betraying a revolution originally made for democratic purposes by taking his nation into the Soviet camp.

Eisenhower, Milton, *The Wine Is Bitter.* Garden City, N.Y.: Doubleday, 1963—The former President's brother reports on American policy in Latin America.

Fall, Bernard B., *Two Vietnams: A Political and Military Analysis.* New York: Praeger, 1967—A firsthand analysis of North and South Vietnam by a leading expert on Vietnam who was killed while covering the war.

Finer, Herman, *Dulles over Suez.* Chicago: Quadrangle, 1964—A political scientist's study of the Secretary of State's policy during the Suez invasion crisis of 1956. Finer criticizes Dulles for failing to follow a consistent policy.

Galbraith, John K., *The Affluent Society.* Boston: Houghton Mifflin, 1969—A popular statement of the liberal economist's views of American economic problems. Galbraith argues that the ideology of the free market economy is outmoded and forces the United States into spending billions on wasteful private consumption while starving the public sector's social programs.

Kissinger, Henry A., *Nuclear Weapons and Foreign Policy.* New York: Norton, 1969—A treatise on military and diplomatic policy which recommends preparations for limited wars as well as all-out nuclear destruction.

Lomax, Louis E., *The Negro Revolt.* New York: Harper & Row, 1962—A black journalist's analysis of the growth of the civil rights movement.

Miller, Loren, *The Petitioners.* New York: Pantheon, 1956—Between 1789 and the present, the Supreme Court has issued many important rulings on the rights of blacks. Miller argues that racism permeated the legal thinking of the Court until the most recent era.

Parsons, Talcott, and Kenneth B. Clark, eds., *The American Negro.* Boston: Beacon, 1966—A collection of essays by leading social scientists on the position of blacks in American society.

Soth, Lauren, *Farm Trouble in an Age of Plenty.* Princeton, N.J.: Princeton University Press, 1957—An economic study of the farm problem in the 1950s along with an analysis of why existing government aid programs were ineffectual.

White, Theodore H., *The Making of the*

President, 1960. New York: Atheneum, 1961—A detailed popular account of the 1960 Presidential race between John F. Kennedy and Richard M. Nixon.

Widick, B. J., *Labor Today*. Boston: Houghton Mifflin, 1964—Essays on the state of the labor movement which accuse it of having abandoned its militant past in favor of gaining a share of the pie in an affluent society.

PRIMARY SOURCES

Adams, Sherman, *Firsthand Report*. New York: Harper & Row, 1961—The memoirs of Eisenhower's special assistant. Sherman Adams was one of the most powerful men in Washington during the earlier years of the Eisenhower administration.

Benson, Ezra T., *Crossfire: The Eight Years with Eisenhower*. Garden City, N.Y.: Doubleday, 1962—These are the memoirs of Eisenhower's highly conservative Secretary of Agriculture.

Eisenhower, Dwight D., *Mandate for Change*. Garden City, N.Y.: Doubleday, 1963—The first volume of Eisenhower's memoirs of his years in the White House. This volume covers 1953 through 1956.

Hughes, Emmet J., *The Ordeal of Power*. New York: Atheneum, 1963—A memoir by a former speechwriter for Eisenhower which is critical of the President for his lack of leadership in foreign and domestic affairs.

Nixon, Richard, *Six Crises*. New York: Pyramid, 1970—This book deals with six of the turning points in the career of the author.

BIOGRAPHIES

Childs, Marquis, *Eisenhower: Captive Hero*. New York: Harcourt, Brace, 1958—An analysis of Eisenhower as general and as President which concludes that he was bound by his heroic image and incapable of strong decisive leadership.

Dayton, E. L., *Walter Reuther*. New York: Devin-Adair, 1958—A hostile biography of the late president of the United Auto Workers Union.

Donovan, Robert J., *Eisenhower: the Inside Story*. New York: Harper & Row, 1956—A White House correspondent's narrative of Eisenhower's first three years in office. The author had access to many high-level administration documents.

Goold-Adams, Richard, *John Foster Dulles: A Reappraisal*. New York: Appleton-Century-Crofts, 1962—A British journalist gives a mixed appraisal of Dulles' service as Secretary of State. The author concentrates on the effect of Dulles' policies on the Atlantic Alliance.

Pusey, Merlo J., *Eisenhower: the President*. New York: Macmillan, 1956—An extremely favorable appraisal of Eisenhower's first term as President.

Weaver, John D., *Warren*. Boston: Little, Brown, 1967—A sympathetic biography of the Chief Justice of the Supreme Court and an analysis of the role of the Court he headed.

30

Foreign and Domestic Dilemmas of the 1960s

So, let us not be blind to our differences—but let us also direct attention to our common interests and to the means by which those differences can be resolved. And if we cannot end now our differences, at least we can help make the world safe for diversity. For, in the final analysis, our most basic common link is that we all inhabit this small planet. We all breathe the same air. We all cherish our children's future. And we are all mortal.

—President John F. Kennedy

America in the 1960s was a land of growing suburbs and urban crisis.

John F. Kennedy was the descendent of Irish families deeply involved in Boston politics. His father, Joseph P. Kennedy, had decided against a career in Boston politics, graduated from Harvard, and became a millionaire while still young. As first Chairman of the SEC during the 1930s, he had served as go-between for New Dealers and the business community. He raised his sons to be well-bred, athletic, and tough. They went to good prep schools and to Harvard.

The eldest of the four Kennedy sons was killed in the Second World War. John, the second, returned home from the South Pacific with a medal for bravery and was chosen to carry on the family tradition in politics. He was elected to the House of Representatives in 1946 and reached the Senate in 1952 by defeating Henry Cabot Lodge, Jr. By 1956 Kennedy was being considered for the Vice Presidential nomination on Stevenson's ticket.

THE KENNEDY YEARS

Kennedy's personal beliefs and public stature developed considerably during the period he was in Congress. During the late 1940s and early 1950s, Joseph Kennedy had shown a fondness for McCarthyism, and in his first Senate years John Kennedy never opposed the Wisconsin Republican. Back troubles, the result of war injuries, kept him in the hospital in 1954 for a long spell, and he missed the voting on McCarthy's

censure. However, Kennedy later said that he would have voted for censure. While in the hospital, Kennedy wrote his prize-winning study of American leaders, *Profiles in Courage*. The book displayed both his stylistic gifts and his development of a liberal political philosophy. His image was soon enhanced by a marriage to the attractive socialite Jacqueline Bouvier. By 1960, JFK was a popular public figure with a reputation as war hero and liberal, young husband and father, hard-fighting but humane politician. He was a realist who disliked rhetoric and stereotypes.

Kennedy's most-quoted words in his inaugural address were ". . . my fellow Americans: ask not what your country can do for you—ask what you can do for your country." Many had claimed that Kennedy's personality and glamour, rather than his ideas, had won him the election. Now he asked people to work constructively to solve the country's massive problems of poverty, unemployment, urban decay, poor housing and health care. Doubters and critics, annoyed by Kennedy spending, wealth, and image-making during the campaign, characterized the rhetoric of the New Frontier as just public relations. There could be no doubt, however, that like FDR in 1933, he had caught the popular imagination and brought a mood of optimism to the country.

Kennedy disliked the type of formal Cabinet meetings that had characterized the Eisenhower years and substituted more flexible meetings with small groups of political leaders and experts. He made himself open to many sources of information. He also sought direct contact with the public through speeches and press conferences. Yet his style was characterized not just by flexibility and buoyancy but self-criticism, a mordant wit, and a certain fatalism about moving the Congress to accept his New Frontier program of social reform.

Kennedy's Cabinet was characterized by youth, drive, and technical brilliance. Douglas Dillon, a Republican and Wall Street banker, became Secretary of the Treasury as a reassurance to the business community. Robert S. McNamara, another Republican, previously president of Ford Motor Company, became Secretary of Defense. McNamara had the reputation for being a managerial genius. Like Kennedy he feared the growth of power in the Pentagon. He was always distrusted by those in the Pentagon who resented his efforts to assert civilian control over its organization, limit defense spending, and streamline government operations through the introduction of computers. Dean Rusk, president of the Rockefeller Foundation, became Secretary of State rather than the more prestigious Adlai Stevenson. Though Rusk was instrumental in formulating policy, he was quiet, and tended to remain behind the scenes. Stevenson was made American Ambassador to the United Nations. Other appointments included Arthur J. Goldberg, a well-known labor lawyer, as Secretary of Labor; and Robert F. Kennedy, the President's brother, became Attorney General and was the President's closest confidant. Several economic and political experts, such as Walter Heller and McGeorge Bundy, were also added to the President's staff.

Kennedy, for all the brilliance of his personality, was young and not taken too seriously by old-timers on Capitol Hill. The President had never been a student of the legislative process and was at his best as an executive and as a speaker. Therefore, to push his legislative program, Kennedy relied on the aging Speaker of the House, Sam Rayburn, and on Vice President Lyndon Baines Johnson, probably the greatest modern master of Congressional politics.

The conservative coalition of Southern Democrats and Northern Republicans continued in the House, and conservative control of committees was an important factor weakening chances for passage of Kennedy's legislative program. Most important was the House Rules Committee which, under the chairmanship of Howard W. Smith of Virginia, controlled the flow of bills to the floor for a vote. As currently constituted it had twelve members, and its conservative majority killed or crippled key legislation on civil rights and the economy. Shortly before he died, Speaker Rayburn presented a Kennedy proposal to expand the Committee by three members. Conservative opposition was fierce and to the last, the outcome was uncertain. Kennedy was forced to exert all the pressure available to his office to get the result he wanted. The final margin of five votes gave him an expanded Rules Committee, but it was a pyrrhic victory. The high-pressure fight had alienated many legislators, and bills which now found their way to the floor of the House also found a consolidated and determined opposition led by Minority Leader Charles Halleck of Indiana. Sam Rayburn died in November, 1961, another blow to Kennedy's legislative goals.

RECESSION AND UNEMPLOYMENT

At the time Kennedy took office, more than 8 percent of the working population, about 5.7 million people, were unemployed, and the Gross National Product was falling. The President did not want to antagonize business by massive government spending, so he used his Presidential prerogative to accelerate federal construction projects, released money for building state highways, and ordered 1 billion dollars in credit advanced to the residential construction industry. On February 2, 1961, the President also delivered an Economic Message to Congress, requesting new legislation. But since there was no emergency situation comparable to that in 1932, the response was subdued. Only about half of Kennedy's suggestions were passed and often with major alterations.

The most significant of the new bills passed were (1) the Housing Act of 1961, appropriating 5.6 billion dollars for public housing, with emphasis on urban renewal, and other funds for the preservation and upkeep of park areas in cities; (2) an Area Redevelopment Act, empowering a newly created agency to stimulate economic growth in chronically depressed areas, through loans to new businesses and training of workers unemployed as a result of automation; (3) a Minimum Wage Law applicable to over 3.5 million workers not covered before and raising the minimum from 1.00 dollar to 1.25 dollars an hour; (4) a liberalized Social Security Law, with increased benefits and increased payments to unemployed workers with children.

These laws, in the spirit of the second New Deal, attempted to speed recovery and encourage spending by giving money directly to the poorer citizen, and fostered development and reconstruction in poverty-stricken sectors of the economy. At the same time, they resulted in relatively slight spending, amounting only to some 900 million dollars while about 4 billion dollars were added to the defense budget. By the end of 1961 the economy was picking up, but unemployment remained high.

Despite his initial hopes Kennedy did antagonize big business. In 1962, responding to Kennedy's plea for anti-inflationary measures, steelworkers had accepted a contract with a small pay increase and emphasis on fringe benefits. Nevertheless, the steel industry, ignoring the President's plea for price stability, declared substantial price increases shortly thereafter. Leaders of the industry argued that the raise in consumer prices would be slight and that they needed new capital for modernization. Kennedy was enraged and commented: "My father always told me that all businessmen were sons-of-bitches, but I never believed it till now." The remark became public and caused widespread criticism of the President. Kennedy, undeterred, threatened antitrust suits and instituted intensive federal investigations of the industry. The com-

panies finally backtracked and rescinded the increases. Kennedy's swift action to get results where he believed it was in the national interest worked in the short run but boomeranged quickly. Business hostility over the fight was so great that the stock market dropped, bringing enormous losses and damaging the economy in a way antithetical to Kennedy's hopes. Moreover, the steel industry raised prices the next year and the President offered no resistance.

LAST LEGISLATIVE PROPOSALS

The continuing recession encouraged Kennedy in 1963 to make a proposal that he had considered earlier and rejected. He had already suffered a defeat in his attempt to reform the tax structure in a way that would make it more difficult for vested interests to profit from loopholes. He now proposed an across-the-board cut in taxes amounting to 13 billion dollars to encourage business investment and greater production and employment. He had committed himself to Keynesian economics which called for increased government spending in a recession period. However, Republican leaders such as Nelson Rockefeller and Dwight Eisenhower suggested that cuts in federal spending should accompany any major tax cut. Kennedy rejected this argument on the grounds that a reduction in federal spending would worsen the recession. At the time of his death, the issue was still under debate in the Senate, but the economy was beginning to enter a long boom period in part due to government tax credits to business.

An important proposal which was passed in October, 1962, was the Trade Expansion Act. It gave the President power to reduce tariffs by 50 percent on some items and completely on others whenever he thought lowering barriers would stimulate trade. Such flexibility might be a valuable tool in improving the balance-of-payments deficit and in dealing with the European Common Market. The so-called "Kennedy Round" of tariff negotiations with Europe was successfully completed by 1967.

Kennedy lost two key legislative battles on the issues of medical care for the aged and massive increases in federal aid to public schools. By the early 1960s, both hospital services and public schools in urban areas had deteriorated drastically. The Medicare program, though later passed, met defeat during the Kennedy era largely because lobbyists for the American Medical Association (AMA) continued to decry the program as a step in the direction of socialized medicine. The AMA denied that the poor and aged were not getting adequate treatment in the United States and pointed to public hospitals and workers' health insurance programs. The only appropriation was a small one for aid to medical schools and loans to medical students. Supporters of aid to parochial schools organized effectively against the school aid bill because, given the constitutional separation of church and state, they had been excluded from its provisions. Those who defended the omission argued that parochial education was a private religious choice for which the rest of the community was not responsible. Proponents of aid to parochial schools argued that they were ill-funded and undersupplied, even while they reduced the expenses of public school boards by taking care of large numbers of children. President Kennedy upheld the separation of church and state. Parochial schools received no aid in the proposed bill and it went down to defeat.

KENNEDY'S FOREIGN POLICY

President Kennedy, sharing the worldwide fear of nuclear confrontation, considered it the main task of his administration to contain communist aggression while at the same time working out a nuclear détente with the Soviets. It would be an effort to avoid what the political scientist Richard E. Neustadt has called "holocaust by mutual miscalculation." However, the first phase of Kennedy's foreign policy was concentrated on building American prestige and on shifts in the structure of the military which would later turn out to be highly significant.

The Pentagon under Eisenhower had been preoccupied with a strategy of massive retaliation and missile warfare. Once in office, Kennedy discovered that the "missile gap" he had warned of during his campaign did not exist, as Eisenhower had repeatedly insisted. Nuclear defenses were sufficient. The Kennedy administration shifted the emphasis in defense planning to military preparation for possible limited wars and ground fighting. It was a realistic move since Moscow had warned that it intended to support "wars of national liberation" such as colonial uprisings. The Defense Department also sold weapons to other nations through private firms.

Kennedy quickly moved to divert public attention from the nuclear missile race to the space race. He announced Project Apollo in 1961, and asked Congress for approximately 20 billion dollars over the next decade with the goal of putting a man on the moon before 1970. Congress approved the funds. However, during the Kennedy years American space feats lagged behind those of the Soviets, although Alan Shepard was the first American in space in May, 1961, and John Glenn made a three-day orbital flight around the earth in 1962.

Several international programs proposed in the first months of the administration also aimed at improving America's image abroad. On March 1, 1961, the President announced the creation of the Peace Corps, which enlisted educators and techicians to help train people in less economically developed areas. The Alliance for Progress, initiated the same month, was a project for massive and effective financial aid to Latin America in the spirit of the Good Neighbor policy. Kennedy proposed that the United States provide about one half of a 20-billion-dollar program to improve living conditions in the area over the next ten years. Theoretically, the funds were to go directly for public projects rather than to public officials. As the decade progressed, however, the Alliance did not live up to its promises. Public corruption was not easy to fight, and several South American governments fell under military rule in the sixties. Not only did Latin American governments resist social change, but private investors did not want to put their money in uncertain projects. Political stability and nonviolent social changes were hard to effect in an area of overpopulation, poverty, illiteracy, and disease. A number of projects were completed, but they made only a dent in the overwhelming problems of Latin America.

CUBA AND THE MISSILE CRISIS

When Kennedy came to office, he discovered that Cuban exiles in Guatemala were being organized under the aegis of the Central Intelligence Agency for an invasion of Cuba. Although he had authorized the plan, President Eisenhower had been hesitant about going ahead with it. Castro had warned the world that an American invasion was imminent and vowed that Cuba would defend herself. Americans generally dismissed this as propaganda, attributing it to Castro's need for an outside enemy in order to justify repressive policies within Cuba.

Having been in office only a few months, Kennedy felt pressured to continue his predecessor's plan. CIA men assured him that the Cuban people resented Castro and would cooperate in his overthrow once the exiles' invasion force had established a beachhead. The Joint Chiefs of Staff joined in the chorus urging him to score an easy

victory over communism. Although dubious, Kennedy authorized the project in early April.

On April 17, 1961, a force of about fifteen hundred men landed on the southern coast of Cuba, in the Bahia de Cochinos (Bay of Pigs). Even the landing site had been insisted upon by Kennedy because it was inconspicuous. This was to be a Cuban revolution. Two days prior to the landing, B-26s piloted by Cuban exiles had staged small and ineffective raids on the island. International reaction had been so negative that Kennedy halted the raids. Meanwhile, the Cuban army quickly defeated the invaders, who had no air or naval artillery support, and took twelve hundred men prisoners. The projected popular uprising did not take place.

Kennedy had made several serious mistakes. First, he chose to let the CIA execute its plan, unaware that it was founded on a distorted picture of the Cuban scene. At the same time, in an effort to avoid possible embarrassment, he refused to put full American support behind the plan. The United States role in the invasion was to be concealed. He seemed to have believed that the Cuban people were ready to rise up with only a little help, and that the world would believe that the United States had not been involved. Americans were in heated disagreement about the invasion. Conservatives argued that Kennedy had erred grievously by not committing the air force to insure victory over Castroite oppression. Moderates and liberals saw the whole affair as an unjustified intervention in Cuba. Castro now moved even closer to the Soviet Union.

Kennedy was deeply stung by the failure but within a few days acknowledged his personal responsibility for the fiasco, a move that won him acclaim since he could easily have blamed others. The President now also believed he should be more wary of advice from the military and the CIA.

THE BERLIN CRISIS

The tensions created by the Soviet-American space race and the Cuban debacle caused Kennedy to desire a face-to-face meeting with Khrushchev in an effort to calm world anxiety. From June 3 to 4, 1961, the two leaders met in Vienna, and Kennedy asked for more peaceful relations between the two powers to avoid war. But the Russian leader said communism was expanding through wars of liberation, and he refused to discuss disarmament or an end to nuclear testing. He also warned the President that the United States had to sign a peace treaty with Germany or face the possibility of being forced out of Berlin.

Khrushchev soon gave substance to his harsh line at Vienna. The city of West Berlin was the most vulnerable part of free Europe, locked in the middle of East Germany. The success of the West German economy and a desire for political freedom spurred thousands of East Germans to take the relatively open route of escape from the Soviet sector into West Berlin. Shortly after both leaders returned from Vienna, Khrushchev announced that he would recognize the sovereignty of East Germany by the end of the year and leave Berlin to her mercy unless the Western Powers recognized East Germany as an independent power. The Western Powers unanimously refused. Khrushchev increased the size of his armed forces. Kennedy responded in kind. Fear of war mounted, and Kennedy asked Americans to construct bomb shelters. During the crisis the number of refugees from East Germany fleeing into West Berlin tripled.

Khrushchev, realizing that he could not go on with his bluff, ordered the construction of the Berlin Wall, a barbed wire and concrete obstruction running through divided Berlin. By October, the blustering was still on, but Khrushchev had withdrawn his end-of-the-year ultimatum. The freedom of West Berlin had been saved, but the Soviets had succeeded in violating the international agreement that there would be free movement within Berlin. Soviet propaganda called the wall a barrier against capitalist infection. A minority in the United States urged that the wall be destroyed, but that alternative was extremely dangerous and the Western Powers confined themselves to outbursts of indignation. Visiting Berlin in June, 1963, Kennedy implied that the isolated situation of the city's people, free but surrounded by a police state, might well be a symbol for all free people.

THE CUBAN BLOCKADE

Khrushchev now tried a daring maneuver to seize the initiative in the Cold War from the United States. Cuba had been expelled from the Organization of American States in January through American pressure, and during the summer of 1962 Soviet technicians and apparently defensive military equipment began pouring into Cuba. Reconnaissance flights confirmed Soviet assurances that there were no offensive installations being built, but Cuban refugees and some members of the Senate disputed the reports. Kennedy then warned that "significant offensive capability either in Cuban hands or under Soviet direction" would precipitate the "gravest" international crisis. On October 14, aerial photographs of Cuba revealed installations of short-range and medium-range ballistic missiles.

The delicacy and extreme danger of the situation required careful planning. An overly aggressive move, such as bombardment of the sites, might well have pushed Russia into a nuclear war. A weak policy might have failed to oust the Soviets—a political as well as strategic calamity for the United States in the hemisphere. Latin American countries might have seen the installations as a Soviet victory and realigned themselves. Strategically, the sites reduced the warning time on a nuclear attack to two or three minutes.

After a week's deliberation with top advisers, on October 22, Kennedy made the crisis public, and announced his plan: to blockade Cuba and prevent further Soviet shipments of military equipment coupled with a demand that the bases be removed. He requested and received approval of the blockade from the Organization of American States on October 23.

The world feared a nuclear war but America's allies backed her stand. The American navy encircled Cuba, while the Soviets at first refused to change their policy and sent further shipments. Foreign critics charged that Kennedy's reaction was hysterical and irresponsible and that the United States had missile bases in Turkey within similar range of the Soviet heartland. Continual negotiation by cablegram engrossed Kennedy and Khrushchev for three days, with no progress. U Thant, Secretary General of the United Nations, proposed an end to Soviet shipments in exchange for a withdrawal of the blockade, followed by negotiations. Kennedy rejected the bid. On October 24, the Soviet ships turned back, however, and Khrushchev agreed on October 28 to remove the missiles in exchange for an end to the blockade and an American promise not to invade Cuba.

Kennedy's popularity in the United States rocketed. Some critics charged that he had taken an insane risk, but the conclusion of the episode took the steam out of their charge. Further, though Kennedy had used the technique of brinkmanship, the policy had proven that the leaders of the Soviet Union would back down to avoid total war. Khrushchev, for his part, had been forced to see that the threat of nuclear war could not be used to bully the United States.

TEST-BAN TREATY

In his inaugural address, Kennedy had provided a formula for American posture in the Cold War: "Let us never negotiate out of fear. But let us never fear to negotiate." After the lesson of the Bay of Pigs, the President had proceeded to insure the first part of the formula, taking a strong stand on Berlin and in the Cuban missile crisis. He next tried to use the second part of the formula to reduce the possibility of nuclear war.

Speaking at American University in June, 1963, Kennedy called for a change in the attitude toward negotiations with the Soviet Union; he urged Americans "not to see only a distorted and desperate view of the other side, not to see conflict as inevitable." There was, he maintained, "a mutually deep interest in a just and genuine peace and in halting the arms race. . . . If we cannot end now all our differences, at least we can help make the world safe for diversity."

With the Soviet setback in Cuba and relations with Communist China in a state of deterioration, Khrushchev was ready to respond favorably to Kennedy's advances. After some haggling in Geneva, representatives of the Soviet Union and the United States agreed on a test-ban treaty. During the Berlin crisis Khrushchev had announced resumption of aboveground nuclear tests, but the new ban signed on August 5 prohibited tests under water, in space, or in the air. Underground tests might continue. On September 24, a skeptical Senate ratified the treaty by a vote of 80 to 19. Many other nations signed, with the exception of France and Communist China who were developing their own nuclear weapons.

SOUTHEAST ASIA

Following the Geneva Conference in 1954, the ruler of South Vietnam, Bao Dai, abdicated in favor of Ngo Dinh Diem, whose family was a leader of the powerful Roman Catholic minority in the country. Although there were supposed to be elections throughout North and South Vietnam in 1956 to determine the presidency of the entire country, Diem maneuvered a rigged election in 1955 and the elections scheduled for the following year never materialized. Diem ruled South Vietnam between 1954 and 1963 with authoritarian and corrupt methods, destroying all vestiges of popular government in the rural villages and ignoring pressures from the United States for political and economic reforms.

By the time Kennedy took office, the situation in Vietnam was becoming extremely grave. The Diem government had its political base in the old elite which had risen to power under French colonial rule. A small portion of the Vietnamese population was Catholic, the majority was Buddhist. Most of the resistance to Diem organized itself into the National Liberation Front (NLF), the political arm of the Viet Cong. The Viet Cong, organized in 1957 to overthrow Diem, were mainly South Vietnamese, but many had training in communist ideology and guerrilla tactics in North Vietnam. They were well organized and used terror and sabotage in the villages to undermine government control. There may have been more than 200,000 people associated with the movement. There were also other South Vietnamese who opposed their government's policies. In 1963, to attract the attention of the world, a number of Buddhists immolated themselves in protest against Diem.

In 1961, President Kennedy sent Lyndon Johnson to Vietnam, and he reported that it was important for the United States to stay in Southeast Asia and continue economic aid to South Vietnam. General Maxwell Taylor and Walt W. Rostow, a White House assistant, also undertook a mission preparatory to advising Kennedy about the military situation. They encouraged an initial commitment of about eight thousand ground troops to support Diem. These soldiers, while called advisers, did take part in combat operations.

The President was also concerned about Laos, where the local communist organization, the Pathet Lao, was gaining ground.

Since 1954 the United States had poured enormous sums of money into Laos, and virtually taken control of the economy in an effort to prevent a communist takeover. The fall of Laos would endanger both South Vietnam and Thailand. Yet the Pathet Lao still held the advantage in the fighting, and by 1961 the situation had deteriorated to the extent that Kennedy proposed new negotiations at Geneva in the hope of averting American intervention. But the situation continued to deteriorate rapidly so that as a warning to the communists, the United States sent the Seventh Fleet to the South China Sea and four thousand more American soldiers to Thailand in May, 1962. In June, at Geneva, the three Laotian leaders—neutralist, pro-Western, and leftist—agreed to a coalition government and official neutrality.

In spite of Kennedy's desire for a hands-off approach in Southeast Asia, his practical policy was determined by his acceptance of the "domino" theory first formulated by Eisenhower in a speech on April 7, 1954. According to this theory, if communist terrorism overran one part of the area, the rest of Southeast Asia would collapse like a row of dominoes. The President was convinced that revolutionary activity there was not local in inspiration but represented only one phase of a communist plan to gain influence over the whole continent of Asia and the mid-Pacific, with its raw materials and immense strategic value.

Nevertheless, by 1963, the President, supported by the advice of the ambassador to Saigon, Henry Cabot Lodge, Jr., encouraged the downfall of Ngo Dinh Diem by a withdrawal of United States aid. Vice President Johnson thought it was a mistake, and from a practical standpoint, Diem's fall brought grave governmental instability and a rapid succession of coups. But the President found Diem's corruption and despotism intolerable. He hoped that a democratic noncommunist regime would emerge. Some historians believe that had Kennedy made his decision two years ear-

*Defense of American
Involvement in Vietnam*

---

66 *When all the foregoing factors had been
taken into account, the Administration
made its decision. Fundamentally, that
decision was based upon a willingness to
accept Khrushchev's challenge of Jan. 6,
1961, and to see the struggle in Southeast
Asia pursued on "political, social and
psychological" grounds. Our willingness to
accept the challenge is based not only on
our desire to see the evolutionary struggle
of Southeast Asia resolved peacefully, but
also on our confidence that communism is
not "the wave of the future" and that free
peoples can devise more attractive solutions
to the problems of Southeast Asia than
can Communists. The fact is, however, that
in Southeast Asia the North Vietnamese
are not pursuing "peaceful coexistence"
but instead are engaged in armed
aggression. Therefore, before we can
respond to Khrushchev's challenge on
political, social and economic grounds, it is
necessary that the North Vietnamese stop
their armed aggression.*

   *The decision with respect to the
Republic of Vietnam was to undertake
military responsibilities there in a
prolonged, substantive effort to assist the
Republic in freeing itself from the
northern aggression.* 99

—*Averell Harriman*

*Attack on American
Involvement in Vietnam*

---

66 *"We can never again stand aside prideful
in isolation." So spoke Lyndon B. Johnson
at his inauguration, and all Americans
should agree. Head-in-the-sand isolationism
died a generation ago. The American
retaliatory bombing of North Vietnam
last week was dramatic evidence of our
present-day stand—and of the worldwide
scope of our involvement. . . . We have
come to treat "Communism," regardless of
what form it may take in any given
country, as the enemy. We fancy ourselves
as guardian of the "free" world, though
most of it is not free, and never has been.*

   *We seek to immunize this world against
further Communist infection through
massive injections of American aid and,
wherever necessary, through direct
American intervention. Such a vast
undertaking has at least two defects:
First, it exceeds our national capability;
second, among the newly emerging
nations, where the specter of Western
imperialism is dreaded more than
Communism, such a policy can be
self-defeating. As a seasoned, friendly
foreign diplomat recently put it: "The
United States is getting involved in
situations where no one—not even a nation
of saints—would be welcome."* 99

—*Frank Church*

lier, in 1961, it might have worked. However, by 1963, the battle lines were drawn
too clearly. Diem was murdered a few weeks
before Kennedy's death by a group of army
officers. By then there were 15,500 American military advisers in South Vietnam and
sixty American soldiers had been killed in
combat.

THE ASSASSINATION

President Kennedy's popularity was sag-
ging in some sections of the country in late
1963. Growing civil rights agitation made
him especially disliked in parts of the
South. On June 12, 1963, Medgar W. Evers,

NAACP organizer in Mississippi, was shot to death by a sniper in Jackson. Looking forward to the national election in 1964, and seeking to increase his support in Texas, a half-Southern, half-Western state which was the political stronghold of his Vice President, Kennedy ignored the advice of associates, and decided to tour the state. Some Texas Democrats had been angered by rumors that Johnson would be left off the ticket in 1964, and a joint appearance there might heal political wounds.

Riding in an open car through banks of cheering crowds in Dallas on November 22 with the First Lady at his side, the President was shot twice by a sniper. Also wounded was Governor John Connally who was sitting in the front seat. Kennedy was pronounced dead shortly after arrival at Parkland Memorial Hospital. The Vice President, visibly shaken, was rushed to the Presidential plane and sworn in as President en route to Washington with his wife and Jacqueline Kennedy standing next to him.

Meanwhile in Dallas, police had arrested Lee Harvey Oswald for the murder of a policeman and were also charging him with the assassination. Though circumstantial evidence pointed to Oswald, he never confessed guilt. Then, two days later, while millions of people were viewing on television his transfer from one prison to another under police guard, a man named Jack Ruby broke through the line of spectators and fatally shot Oswald. Ruby was a Dallas night-club owner who said his action had been motivated by outrage at the assassination.

The country was swept with shock and grief. The young President had been barraged with criticism, had not been successful in getting his legislative program accepted, and had been the object of considerable hatred in some sections of the nation. But after his death the great majority of Americans were struck by an acute sense of loss.

The bizarre circumstances of the assassination and its aftermath brought suspicions of an elaborate plot. President Johnson appointed Chief Justice Warren to head an investigatory commission. Warren and the other members, after close and tedious examination of the evidence, concluded in the Warren Commission Report that Oswald had indeed been the assassin and had acted alone.

JOHNSON'S SUCCESSION

JOHNSON'S BACKGROUND

Lyndon Johnson emerged from a political and economic background quite different from Kennedy's. Johnson's family were farmers in south-central Texas, and he had worked his way through school. He was not urbane or polished, and his personal capability could not be captured by the television cameras. He was a staunch New Dealer with a great respect for FDR and the programs that aided debtor farmers. Johnson reached the top of the political pyramid through unequaled skill and sheer hard work. He entered the House of Representatives in 1937 in a special election. His first Senate victory in 1948 was close and marked by a bitter struggle; a little less than a million voters gave him a margin of 87 votes. In 1953, after the Democratic leader was defeated in the wake of machine scandals in Chicago, Lyndon Johnson received the post, moving from Minority Leader to Majority Leader after the 1954 elections. Johnson observers were unanimous in their awe of his ability as a legislator and Capitol Hill organizer. He

Lyndon Johnson, well known for his effectiveness as Majority Leader of the Senate, became President on November 22 following Kennedy's assassination.

is generally considered the most effective Majority Leader of the Senate in modern times.

As a result, when Lyndon Baines Johnson assumed the Presidency on November 22, he was well known and well liked on Capitol Hill, which he called "my home for thirty-two years." But he was not so well-known to the American public. Kennedy's main strength had been his public image. Johnson's strength was by its very nature half public and half hidden by the workings of the political process. He only partly succeeded in reaching the public, though he succeeded magnificently in getting things done. Johnson was at once ruthless and compassionate, proud and yet sensitive to attack. He was a man of great energy and determination, direct, earthy, and sometimes crude in his manner. Politics was his only real interest.

"LET US CONTINUE"

In the aftermath of the assassination Congress was in no mood to offer resistance to the late President's program. Johnson made full use of the moment and of his own legislative genius, and pushed through most of the legislation he wanted. On November 27, taking into account the fact that public sentiment was focused on Kennedy, and that he himself had as yet no personal mandate, Johnson offered to complete the Kennedy program. "Let us continue," he said.

The Revenue Act passed early in 1964 reduced taxes by 11.5 billion dollars—about 2 billion dollars short of what Kennedy had asked for. Johnson appeased conservative fears that reduced taxes would bring a federal deficit by trimming down the federal budget for the coming year. In the next few months the business community, which had opposed the measure at first, began to admit that it was working. The longest economic boom in American history was underway and unemployment had fallen to a level of 5 percent. Johnson enjoyed a good relationship with both business and labor until the late 1960s.

Though he was a Southerner, President Johnson now risked the enmity of the deep South by working for a civil rights bill with teeth. For almost three months Southern Senators filibustered against it. During this period demonstrations, sometimes dissolving into violence, occurred both in the South and North, as black people demanded passage of the bill. Finally a cloture vote succeeded in silencing the filibuster, the first time in Senate history.

The bill passed on June 19, 1964, by a vote of 73 to 27. A few conservative Republicans voted with the South against the bill. Senator Barry Goldwater of Arizona argued that it involved too much federal interference in the nation's social life, and that traditions, no matter how wrong, could not be changed by legislation.

The Civil Rights Act of 1964 was a landmark piece of legislation. The key provisions attempted to insure the following rights: voting, the use of public facilities and accommodations, equal treatment by employers and unions, integrated schooling, and a fair trial. The new law required that literacy tests be in writing, and made a sixth-grade education adequate proof of literacy. An important provision was that programs receiving federal aid must be integrated and that continued discrimination would bring a withdrawal of funds. It also extended the life of the Civil Rights Commission.

THE WAR ON POVERTY

Another program which was opposed by conservatives was Johnson's "War on Poverty." Social criticism of poverty in a supposedly affluent society had been generated by government figures which put 18 percent (34.1 million) of the population below the poverty line in 1964. The Economic Opportunity Act of 1964, though by no means the full realization of Johnson's requests to Congress, created VISTA, a domestic Peace Corps, recruiting Americans, especially between the ages of 18 and 25, to work on neighborhood projects in areas of urban and rural distress to try to reduce illiteracy, unemployment, and lack of social services. Much of VISTA's activity was educational. The "Head Start" program created under the act provided preschool training for disadvantaged children. Johnson's 1964 request for aid to the Appalachian area went unheeded, but he did get a wilderness conservation act and federal aid to urban mass transit.

The goals of Johnson's domestic program were wide-ranging: an end to poverty, an end to discrimination, programs to fight pollution and encourage conservation and beautification of the environment, Medicare for the aged, aid to education, and an end to urban deterioration. It was the Presi-

dent's vision of how to improve the quality of American life. Johnson decided to use the program as the basis of his election campaign in 1964, and hoped that a strong showing of national "consensus" would give him the go-ahead to build the "Great Society."

ELECTION OF 1964

Successful though Johnson was in beginning to secure legislation for his program, there were still a large number of conservatives in the country who disapproved of the effort to solve internal problems through increased federal action. They also opposed any policy of negotiation with the communist bloc. Since the late 1950s, one of the most eloquent and appealing spokesmen of the conservative cause had been Barry Goldwater. By the time of the 1964 Republican convention, the extreme right wing of the GOP had gained a majority of the delegates. Goldwater was nominated easily for the Presidency over Nelson A. Rockefeller of New York and William Scranton of Pennsylvania. There was no concession to party moderates in the selection of the Vice Presidential candidate, William Miller, a conservative New York Congressman, nor in the party platform. The party was split so badly that moderates did almost no work for the ticket.

Southern segregationists and some whites elsewhere in the country considered Goldwater's candidacy a "backlash" against the civil rights movement and jumped on the bandwagon. Senator Strom Thurmond, a hard-core segregationist from South Carolina, abandoned the Democratic Party to support Goldwater. Some pundits suggested that the cracks in the solid South were irreparable and that segregationists would move over into the Republican Party.

Goldwater's critique of the liberal governance of the United States since 1933 (he roughly included Eisenhower in this pattern and accused him of running a "dime store New Deal") was unadulterated. He spoke of gradually dismantling such New Deal innovations as Social Security and TVA and called for decentralization of government power. State governments should resume control of many programs.

At the same time, Goldwater demanded a stronger military posture toward world communism. He believed negotiations with the Soviets were hopeless, and charged that the Kennedy-Johnson administration had adopted a "no-win" policy in Southeast Asia. Escalation there was inevitable and Goldwater advocated the use of tactical nuclear weapons to avoid a long and fruitless commitment of United States troops. This proposal, though it shocked and frightened many voters, had in fact been bandied about by the Kennedy administration, and there was a faction in the Pentagon which strongly supported it.

President Johnson was overwhelmingly nominated by the Democrats to take over in his own right. He chose Hubert H. Humphrey, a liberal from Minnesota, who might possibly draw some of the farm vote in the Midwest away from Goldwater, to be his running mate. The Democratic platform urged moderation in foreign affairs and enactment of the Great Society program. There was a battle over civil rights, and the resulting plank was not overly strong.

The campaign, which might have been an interesting philosophical debate, turned out to be dull and muddled. The important issues Goldwater raised—dangerous centralization of government, breakdown of traditional values, programs of high government spending that concealed corruption—never earned the full discussion they deserved. Neither did American involvement in Vietnam. At the time only conservatives like Goldwater, and knowledgeable leftists, were predicting a long, drawn-out conflict. The majority of Americans believed the administration promise that escalation would be avoided.

The results of the election showed that most Americans had been frightened by Goldwater's "extremism." Johnson took full advantage of Goldwater's tendency to make blunt statements which sometimes seemed contradictory, as well as the fear of nuclear catastrophe that Goldwater aroused, by remaining benign, friendly, reassuring, and moderate in his statements. Only Arizona and five Southern states went for Goldwater. The electoral balance was 486 to 52 with the Democrats receiving 62 percent of the vote. Johnson had the largest popular plurality in American history—almost 16 million votes. Johnson had secured wide support from business, labor, farm areas, the suburbs, and black Americans.

THE EIGHTY-NINTH CONGRESS

Johnson's landslide put the Congress in his "hip pocket." In addition, a large number of Democrats were elected to the House and Senate. Conservatives found themselves unable to put together their traditionally effective coalition, and one by one, Great Society bills were passed.

Aid to education, stalled previously by the parochial school dilemma, was restructured in an effort to avoid the constitutional barrier. The Elementary and Secondary Education Act of 1965 provided aid on the basis of the numbers of poor children in any school, regardless of the school's status. By this means of focusing on individual students and on poverty, 1.3 billion dollars was poured into the country's deteriorating school systems. In other legislation, money to assist higher education was also appropriated.

Medicare, despite continued opposition from the AMA, was finally launched, although it met with administrative difficulties and resistance from some doctors. Medicare was the most dramatic achievement of the new legislation. Since the days of the

New Deal the economic suffering of the elderly had been a major problem. In the sixties rising medical and pharmaceutical costs proved to be a crippling burden on the aged, many of whom had nothing but small Social Security checks to live on. The Medicare allowance financed through Social Security provided for hospital and nursing home care.

The Appalachian Regional Development Act, rejected in 1964, was now approved and appropriated 1.1 billion dollars for the large impoverished region from Pennsylvania to Alabama where hungry children, chronic unemployment, and desperate working conditions in mines had become a nationally publicized scandal. There were also appropriations for more public works, Youth Corps camps, and job retraining programs. Speaking about his war on poverty, Johnson sometimes referred to personal memories of the depression of the 1930s and acknowledged that there was still a problem of starvation in the United States. Costs of basic items such as food and utilities were rising dramatically. Poor whites in areas such as Appalachia, blacks in urban slums, Indians, Puerto Ricans, and migrant farm workers, including the Mexican-Americans or Chicanos of the Southwest, were among the large groups who did not benefit from the affluent economic conditions of middle-class America.

The Great Society program also contained new civil rights legislation. Not only had the literacy test provisions of the 1964 act proved complex and costly, but some people criticized it as an arbitrary criterion. Moreover, resistance to allowing blacks to vote continued in the South. There was violence in Alabama when Governor George Wallace refused to give state protection to a civil rights march from Selma to Montgomery protesting voting restrictions. As a result, Congress passed the Civil Rights Act of 1965 which abolished literacy and other tests for voting. It authorized federal registrars to enroll eligible voters in states where they had been refused registration and where less than half the voting age population was registered.

A further expansion of civil rights legislation came in 1968, after the death of Martin Luther King, Jr., with a far-reaching ban on racial discrimination in federally owned and multi-unit housing and single units sold by a real estate broker. Reacting to increasing racial violence in the country, the law also provided penalties for injuring civil rights workers, traveling between states to incite riots, and manufacturing or selling firearms for civil disorders.

The Housing and Urban Development Act of 1965 appropriated 7.8 billion dollars for urban renewal. The bill was expected to produce 240,000 units of low rent public housing and urban renewal. However, in Chicago, for example, newly constructed apartment buildings were often not used for the people who had been dislocated, mainly blacks. In 1966, the Congress reluctantly provided federal rent supplements to low-income families.

There was other important legislation. Congress created a new Cabinet post, the Department of Housing and Urban Development, whose first Secretary was Robert C. Weaver. Another important act scrapped the 1929 national quota system on immigration and Asian exclusion. It substituted hemispheric quotas with no country sending more than twenty thousand people a year and ended the dominant place of Anglo-Saxon immigration. The first laws for environmental control were passed, though they were extremely slight in their effect. Among these were a water-pollution control law, a highway beautification program that tried to limit the number of signs and billboards obstructing the natural beauty of the American countryside, and a token effort to reduce vehicle exhaust fumes. Finally, the National Foundation on the Arts and Humanities was formed to stimulate and finance creative endeavors in the arts.

By 1966, the momentum of Johnson's domestic program had slowed almost to a halt. Not only were the programs costly, but many had reservations about the massive bureaucratic expansion needed to administer them. Of even greater importance was the growing preoccupation of the President and the country with urban riots, the disaffection of American youth, and, above all, the Vietnam war.

THE WARREN COURT

At the end of October, 1963, a few weeks before John F. Kennedy's death, Supreme Court Chief Justice Earl Warren was harassed in New York by pickets who hit him with their flimsy signs. It was a minor episode of violence that nevertheless demonstrated the strong dislike of the Warren Court's libertarian decisions among the right wing of American politics. Calls for Warren's impeachment rang out regularly throughout the decade.

One of the most controversial decisions was the 1962 Court ban on local and state laws which required prayers and Bible readings in public schools, as contrary to the First Amendment's protection of the separation of church and state (*Engel v. Vitale*). Opponents of the ruling argued that the Founding Fathers did not mean that the public order would be godless but that it would permit all forms of worship. School prayers were always generalized and interdenominational, at least within the

In the South, segregation laws called for "separate but equal" facilities for blacks. Drinking fountains, public rest rooms, and other facilities were usually labeled "colored" or "white only." Blacks were forced to sit at the back in public buses and were not served in restaurants.

limits of the Judeo-Christian faith. They also saw the decision as part of a new decadence in American life, excessive tolerance for atheism and attendant immorality that would bring the collapse of society. Those who had advocated the ban rejoiced at the Court decision as a defense of religious freedom for children as well as the separation of church and state.

In *Baker v. Carr* (1962), the Supreme Court paved the way for state reapportionment of election districts by ruling that federal courts might have jurisdiction where unfairness in state apportionment was charged under the equal protection clause of the Fourteenth Amendment. The problem of representation had been aggravated by the growth of urban America. In many states rural representatives dominated the legislature. They banded together to prevent redistricting that would reduce their power. Demands for reapportionment arose because urban areas were more and more blighted, and yet were getting a proportionally smaller amount of state money. The only way to change the balance of power would be by enforcing representation according to population. Reluctantly, the Supreme Court accepted the responsibility for this political crisis, and widespread redistricting to create equal electoral districts resulted.

Probably the most controversial decisions were, however, in the area of criminal law. In *Gideon v. Wainwright* (1963), the Court held that under the Sixth Amendment states must provide defense counsel for indigent defendants in all cases. The following year the Court ruled in *Escobedo v. Illinois* that a conviction was invalid if the police had refused a suspect counsel during an interrogation or failed to inform him of his right to remain silent under the Fifth Amendment. The case of *Miranda v. Arizona* (1966) reinforced this demand on the police. The Court's efforts to protect suspected criminals from self-incrimination ran head on into the rising crime rate in the country during the 1960s. A poll taken during the decade showed that 63 percent of those questioned considered the Supreme Court too lenient toward criminals.

CIVIL RIGHTS AND BLACK POWER

Industrial mobilization during the Second World War had only accelerated a shift already taking place in the distribution of population within the United States, with black Americans moving increasingly to the cities, to the North, and to the West. By the sixties, almost half of the black population lived outside the South, and the great majority had become urban. Cities such as Los Angeles, Detroit, Washington, New York, Chicago, Gary, and Newark, had expanding black ghettos, neighborhoods whose living conditions remained largely invisible to those who lived in the suburbs or worked in well-kept business districts. In the 1960s, black Americans moved to destroy the old, legal order of discrimination in the South, to achieve autonomy within the ghettos of the great cities, and to win political power. More and more they bypassed appeals to the courts and resorted to boycotts, sit-ins, and demonstrations.

THE BEGINNING OF RESISTANCE

Late in 1955, a public bus in Montgomery, Alabama, became the unlikely focus of the first phase of the struggle to end discrimination, when Mrs. Rosa Parks was told by the driver to give up her seat in the back or black section of the bus so that a standing white commuter might have it. Mrs. Parks, who had neither anticipated nor planned any resistance, suddenly decided that she had had enough, and refused. She had decided, she said later, "never to move again." She was arrested. Montgomery blacks took up the cause, and led by Martin Luther King, Jr., a young clergyman, they staged a year-long boycott of city buses. King and some of his supporters were arrested and sent to jail, but in December, 1956, a federal court ordered desegregation of the whole city system. Other Southern cities followed this lead.

This series of events brought King national recognition. His Southern Christian Leadership Conference (SCLC) stood at the center of much civil rights activity for the next ten years. King's technique of non-violent resistance and civil disobedience, modeled on Mahatma Gandhi's philosophy, was considered extreme and daring in the 1950s. Critics berated King for advocating illegal or extralegal acts of civil disobedience which could bring the disintegration of society; and in some quarters he was even denounced as a communist. His answer was that people cannot be forced to obey unjust laws. Black Americans had to be freed from psychological death. King was passionately religious, and spoke in a prophetic style, but his boldness consisted in bringing the black movement out of the phase of a purely legal struggle represented by the NAACP, and into a phase of nonviolent civil disobedience characterized by highly effective public demonstrations.

The success of the Montgomery boycott encouraged others to organize in support of racial equality. Younger people who did not share King's religious orientation or-

In August, 1963, NAACP leader Martin Luther King led a march on Washington, D.C., demanding an end to segregation and equal employment opportunities for blacks.

ganized the Student Non-violent Coordinating Committee (SNCC), which later became more militant, and the Congress of Racial Equality (CORE). Both these organizations became increasingly interested in political power in the North, but in the early sixties awareness was still focused on the Southern dilemma. Sit-ins were staged en masse by black youths at segregated restaurants and luncheonettes which brought charges that they were trespassing on private property. This target was more open and accessible than racial bigotry in the North. Simply by being at the counter blacks could create havoc and threaten the traditional assumptions of racism in the South. With violent results, civil rights groups also sponsored "freedom rides" in 1961 to open up mass transportation. The reaction to the first freedom ride—burning of the bus and the beating of the riders in Alabama—only brought a swarm of new integrated rides. But the federal government finally had to intervene to prevent mass bloodshed in Montgomery.

CIVIL RIGHTS UNDER KENNEDY

The Kennedy administration was at first reluctant to become involved but then decided on a stricter enforcement of civil rights. Kennedy created a committee on Equal Employment Opportunity to enforce nondiscrimination where federal contracts were involved and appointed a large number of blacks to high federal positions. He also issued an Executive Order against discrimination in federal housing.

In 1962, the University of Mississippi was tcehnically "desegregated" when one man, James Meredith, walked through an angry mob under the protection of federal authorities. It had taken him three nights of effort, during which whites rioted in protest. Attorney General Robert F. Kennedy won the everlasting dislike of Southern

segregationists by using his office to enforce the Supreme Court ruling with the United States Army and the Mississippi National Guard. A subsequent effort in 1963 by Governor Wallace of Alabama to prevent desegregation of the University of Alabama was also a failure.

The culmination of civil rights activities during the Kennedy years occurred in the spring and summer of 1963. Massive demonstrations, sit-ins, and picketing took place to open up public accommodations in Birmingham, Alabama. Police dispersed the marchers with dogs, electric cattle prods, and fire hoses; hundreds of arrests followed. The nation was shocked at the sight of these incidents on television.

Now President Kennedy called for new civil rights legislation. The measure, which ultimately passed under his successor, was the most far-reaching civil rights bill ever proposed. But even with the public opinion polls showing widespread white support, Southern resistance in Congress was stiff and the beginning of a white backlash among Northern workers was evident. A massive and orderly March on Washington by civil rights advocates in August, 1963, had no effect on passage of the bill.

ENFORCEMENT OF CIVIL RIGHTS

Enforcement of civil rights was an ambiguous question in the rest of the country. For the most part, public forms of discrimination, such as segregated restaurants and public toilets, were nonexistent. But it was all too easy for whites outside the South to express outrage and indignation at Southern bias and refuse to take action against, or even admit the existence of, subtler but very real forms of discrimination in their own communities. When Martin Luther King, Jr., staged marches in Chicago for open housing he met with outbursts of hatred no less vehement than those he had been accustomed to in the South. Neighborhood schools were just as segregated because black and white communities were segregated, and were almost always kept separate by districting ordinances wherever there was a chance of fusion. The seniority system for teaching staffs often allowed the better and more experienced teachers to choose not to teach in the ghetto where schools were allowed to run down, supplies such as books and cafeteria food were poor or scanty, and the attitude of the white administration toward the black children was defeatist and sometimes hostile. Too often black children picked up the message that they were neither able nor expected to get anywhere. Rundown communities where crime, filth, and the use of drugs abounded also did not provide an atmosphere conducive to an orderly learning process.

The first major strategy adopted by blacks to fight these conditions in Northern schools was the boycott. The demand was: "quality integrated education." Mothers kept their children out of school. Leaders of boycotts, such as the Reverend Milton Galamison in New York, were sometimes charged with illegally encouraging truancy, and arrested. But the school boycott was self-defeating because what parents wanted for their children was better education, not no education at all. During the boycotts, temporary schoolrooms were usually set up by the boycotters, both to counteract charges that they were depriving their own children of education and to experiment with more creative classrooms. In the process some parents decided that these "freedom schools" were preferable to public schools. Others disagreed. But the "freedom schools" were among the activities that planted the seeds of "black power." More and more black activists came to the conclusion that it was useless to keep making demands on white authorities, especially when the techniques required to get attention from the white community often re-

Nonviolence and Black Power

" *. . . It was stones yesterday, Molotov cocktails today; it will be hand grenades tomorrow and whatever else is available the next day. The seriousness of this situation must be faced up to. You should not feel that I am inciting someone to violence. I'm only warning of a powder-keg situation. You can take it or leave it. If you take the warning perhaps you can still save yourself. But if you ignore it or ridicule it, well, death is already at your doorstep. There are 22,000,000 African-Americans who are ready to fight for independence right here. When I say fight for independence right here, I don't mean any non-violent fight, or turn-the-other-cheek fight. Those days are gone. Those days are over.*

If George Washington didn't get independence for this country non-violently, and if Patrick Henry didn't come up with a non-violent statement, and you taught me to look upon them as patriots and heroes, then it's time for you to realize that I have studied your books well.

. . . When George Washington and the others got ready to declare or come up with the Declaration of Independence, they didn't care anything about the odds of the British Empire. They were fed up with taxation without representation. And you've got 22,000,000 black people in this country today, 1964, who are fed up with taxation without representation, and will do the same thing. Who are ready, willing and justified to do the same thing today to bring about independence for our people that your forefathers did to bring about independence for your people. . . .

And the only way without bloodshed that this can be brought about is that the black man has to be given full use of the

Nonviolence and Black Power

The Negro people can organize socially to initiate many forms of struggle which can drive their enemies back without resort to futile and harmful violence. In the history of the movement for racial advancement, many creative forms have been developed —the mass boycott, sitdown protests and strikes, sit-ins,—refusal to pay fines and bail for unjust arrests—mass marches— mass meetings—prayer pilgrimages, etc. . . .

There is more power in socially organized masses on the march than there is in guns in the hands of a few desperate men. Our enemies would prefer to deal with a small armed group rather than with a huge, unarmed but resolute mass of people. . . .

It is this form of struggle— non-cooperation with evil through mass actions—"never letting them rest"— which offers the more effective road for those who have been tempted and goaded to violence. It needs the bold and the brave because it is not free of danger. It faces the vicious and evil enemies squarely. It requires dedicated people, because it is a backbreaking task to arouse, to organize, and to educate tens of thousands for disciplined, sustained action. From this form of struggle more emerges that is permanent and damaging to the enemy than from a few acts of organized violence. . . .

—*Reverend Martin Luther King, Jr.*

ballot in every one of the 50 states. But if the black man doesn't get the ballot, then you are going to be faced with another man who forgets the ballot and starts using the bullet.

—*Malcolm X*

sulted in getting beaten or killed. The answer, some began to think, would be black control of black communities. Integration had always been resisted by white society and it would be better at least to have power in the ghettos, if nowhere else. Others in the black community continued to press for political and economic integration as their prime objective.

But even getting more power in the ghettos would not be an easy task. While Stokely Carmichael of SNCC spoke ardently of black power, the great mass of capital invested in the black neighborhoods did not lie in black hands. Black people in general were rarely hired for better jobs, and when they were it was often tokenism. Entrenched white control of the economy and the government combined with ingrained prejudice to place obstacles in the way of black control of their own communities. Some of the agencies of the Johnson administration, however, such as the Office of Economic Opportunity, did pour funds into black areas. But these federal programs were often poorly administered. They succeeded in raising the living standard of some blacks but not in altering the overall poverty of the slums.

URBAN RIOTS

The black ghettos of New York, Los Angeles, Cleveland, Newark, Detroit, and Kansas City were swept by violence and destruction between 1964 and 1968. The pent-up rage and frustration of black Americans was not just a Southern problem but a national problem. The disturbances may have been intensified by advocates of black power who called for the use of force and violence not only as therapy but also to gain social and economic goals. But the main cause was impatience at the slow progress for blacks in obtaining the promised equality in education, housing, and good jobs. Blacks felt more and more isolated from the rest of society as their demands were resisted by white America. Trapped in urban slums, they lashed out against white society and the representatives of white society in their midst—the police. The Kerner Commission Report of 1968 on these disorders placed the greatest blame for the riots on white racism. But much of white America looked on the riots as a manifestation of the wave of crime and lawlessness sweeping the nation. Fear of additional urban riots was created by the murder of Martin Luther King in April, 1968.

THE NEW SPOKESMEN

At the same time, many of the younger spokesmen in the black community no longer believed in King's methods of dealing with racism in America. The belief among the most extreme blacks that white

violence must be met by black violence resulted in the creation of the Black Panther Party in 1966. It stressed black self-determination, black strength, and pride in being black. Eldridge Cleaver, the author of *Soul on Ice* and member of the Black Panther Party, described his own ecstasy at seeing the party leader, Huey Newton, stand up to a policeman and dare him to shoot. When the policeman backed down, Cleaver was amazed. What impressed him most about Newton was not his willingness to be shot, but his courage to refuse to play Uncle Tom, and to prove that the oppressor was afraid. Such were the terms in which an increasing number of young black people were persuaded to see their lives.

The first and most formidable of the figures in stressing black militance and pride in being black had been Malcolm X. His *Autobiography,* published posthumously, was widely read and had great influence on the younger black leadership. Malcolm X was born to a family that had suffered persecution by the Ku Klux Klan because of his father's civil rights activities. He had a wild adolescence in Boston and then in Harlem, quickly became involved in crime, and ended up in prison. There he developed a passionate allegiance to the Black Muslim faith which preached separatism for black people. After ten years in

Trapped in a white supremacist society, blacks began lashing out in rage and violence against the city and the urban ghettos they were chained to.

The plane bearing the body of Martin Luther King receives the Black Power salute from two mourners. With the assassination of their leader, civil rights supporters became increasingly embittered with the slow pace of government action. Militant factions arose, calling for revolution by violence.

prison, he emerged as Malcolm X, and rose rapidly in the church hierarchy. As a Muslim he abandoned all vices, which he regarded as the deliberate creation of white oppression.

He was the first important black spokesman to call for black control of the economic and political sources of power in their communities. The struggle by black Americans for dignity was part of a worldwide struggle of depressed peoples. If violence was necessary to obtain freedom, justice, and human dignity, then it must be employed. Yet when Malcolm X traveled through the Near East, he underwent a spiritual rebirth. Many Arabs were white, but they treated him with respect. He was amazed. He realized that it was possible for whites and blacks to live together, and that racism was not a God-ordained attitude.

On returning home he founded the Organization of Afro-American Unity, emphasizing an interest in the African cultural heritage and self-defense. Malcolm X was assassinated in February, 1965, apparently by a faction of the Muslim movement with which he had broken.

JOHNSON'S FOREIGN POLICY

Kennedy's popularity in Latin America did not continue under his successor. Two crises, one minor and one major, created problems for the administration in the Caribbean and ill will in Latin America.

In Panama, where the Canal Zone was managed by the United States under the provisions of the Hay–Bunau-Varilla Treaty of 1903, demands arose for a new settlement on the question of higher revenues to Panama. A short period of nationalistic disturbances in 1964 preceded the negotiation of a new agreement in 1967 which recognized Panamanian sovereignty over the Canal Zone and more control and joint defense of the canal with the United States. Panama rejected the agreement, however, and the United States began plans to build another sea level canal outside of Panama.

Much more serious was President Johnson's decision to intervene in the Dominican Republic in 1965, on the grounds that there was a communist coup in the offing. Juan Bosch, a leftist but not a communist, had become president of the island in December, 1962, during free and fair elections conducted a year after the assassination of the long-time dictator of the island, General Trujillo. A military coup ousted Bosch's weak government in 1963, but the new junta, far to the right of Bosch, also proved flimsy. By 1965, there was virtual civil war between the two factions and the economy was in chaos. Supporters of Bosch bloodied the streets, and it appeared that rightists were losing. At this point, President Johnson, acting on information that showed that the rebels were infiltrated with communists and fearing another Cuba in the Caribbean, unilaterally sent a force of 22,000 men to the island in April. President Johnson told the American people the Marines had been sent to protect American lives. Latin Americans and many liberals in the United States were furious at this reversal of the Good Neighbor policy and that the administration never offered convincing proof of communist infiltration of Bosch's group. In order to try to repair the damage to her relations with Latin America, the United States now asked the OAS to send an Inter-American Peace Force to keep order in the Dominican Republic.

This team under a Brazilian general took over responsibility from the Americans. Juan Bosch was not reelected, but a right-wing politician named Joaquín Balaguer did come to power. The United States had poured not only troops but also about 25 million dollars' worth of aid into the Dominican Republic. The elections appeared to be fair, and the defeat of Bosch assisted those who argued that the President had intervened to protect democracy. However, what was left of the Alliance for Progress suffered a grave setback. Latin Americans charged that Johnson had returned to Big Stick diplomacy. Critics in the United States and in Europe regarded the intervention as a blatant move to keep Bosch out, and decried what seemed to them American inability to distinguish between forward-looking leaders in underdeveloped nations and a communist plot.

VIETNAM

"The Pentagon Papers disclose," wrote Neil Sheehan of *The New York Times,* "that for six months before the Tonkin Gulf incident in August, 1964, the United States had been mounting clandestine military attacks against North Vietnam while planning to obtain a Congressional resolution that the Administration regarded as the equivalent of a declaration of war." The events surrounding the escalation of the Vietnam war, and Johnson's decision to bomb North Vietnam, were the subject of controversy at the time, and are still in dispute among historians.

The Gulf of Tonkin lies directly to the east of North Vietnam. On August 2 and 4, 1964, North Vietnamese torpedo boats attacked the American destroyers *Maddox* and *Turner Joy* as they patrolled the Gulf waters. The White House then ordered retaliatory bombing raids on strategic targets in North Vietnam.

On August 7, a Congressional resolution gave the President the power to take all

VIETNAM

Major battles

U.S. bases

Areas of guerilla activity

Communist countries

Allied with U.S.

Neutral countries

The Tonkin Gulf Resolution marked the official beginning of the escalation of the war in Vietnam. The secret strategy of the administration in 1964 was the beginning of what was later called the "credibility gap," resulting mainly from the discrepancy between Johnson's promise that American men would not be sent to Vietnam and the fact that they soon were sent in increasing numbers. At the end of 1965, about 165,000 United States troops were in Vietnam. That figure had doubled a year later. By 1968, it was 550,000, with about 30,000 American deaths. The financial cost of the war had also become enormous, estimated at 24 billion dollars in fiscal 1968, and growing.

REASONS FOR ESCALATION

The economic and human strain of the conflict inevitably brought on a full-scale debate within the United States about American involvement. The administration seemed to have two basic reasons for its escalation of American participation in the war. The most far-reaching one was its continued adherence to the domino theory and determination to prevent the expansion of world communism. It seemed particularly fearful of the possibility of Chinese aggression in Southeast Asia as only the first step in pushing the United States out of Asia entirely and back to the Hawaiian Islands. Administration spokesmen frequently referred to the Soviet and Chinese aid to North Vietnam to substantiate this viewpoint. The United States in their view had to stay in Asia to prevent her own decline as a world power and protect the free world. The second rationale for American intervention was a more limited one—to protect the independence of South Vietnam against aggression. The people of South Vietnam had a right to select their own government and live their own lives free from outside interference.

During the early phase of the war, debate was focused primarily on the issue of the

necessary measures "to repel any armed attack against the forces of the United States and to prevent further aggression." The vote for the resolution was 416 to 0 in the House of Representatives, and 88 to 2 in the Senate. The wording was general, but many Senators later said they had no intention of authorizing a full-scale war. Moreover, most of the Senators were unaware that throughout 1964 the United States had engaged in spy missions, sabotage, and PT-boat bombardment of North Vietnamese coastal installations. The White House insisted publicly that the raids, which had been reported, were conducted independently by the South Vietnamese.

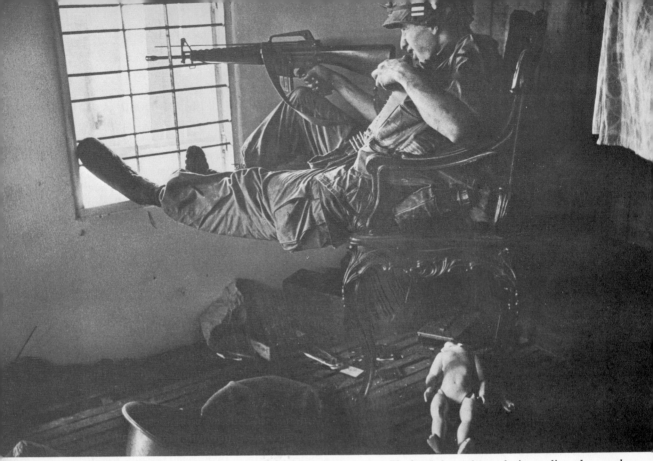

Under Johnson's escalation policy, the number of American troops in Vietnam almost quadrupled in three years.

bombing of North Vietnam which began on February 7, 1965. The administration, and supporters of the war, argued that a good part of stubborn resistance in the South was the result of supply lines from North Vietnam, convoying both guerrilla fighters and material. According to this view, the North was supervising the war. The main supply route did not pass through Vietnam, but slightly to the west, through "neutral" Laos, on the so-called "Ho Chi Minh Trail." Bombing of the trail and of industrial areas in the North would reduce the fighting capacity of the Viet Cong and shorten the war considerably. The administration conviction that the war was primarily caused by outside forces was summed up by Dean Rusk in his Vietnam Hearing testimony in 1966, when he said, "It could end literally in twenty-four hours . . . if these people in Hanoi should come to the conclusion that they are not going to try to seize Vietnam and Laos by force."

OPPOSITION TO THE WAR

Those who opposed the war offered a radically different description of what was going on in Vietnam. According to the war's opponents, such as William Fulbright, Chairman of the Senate Foreign Relations Committee, the Viet Cong, with its political arm, the National Liberation Front, was a largely indigenous and nationalistic movement. There had been some help from the North, which, they charged, increased after the bombing began. The reason the United States and South Vietnamese armies failed to defeat the enemy was that what was going on was an insurrection against the government supported by or acquiesced in by a majority of the Vietnamese people.

Since the Viet Cong was largely independent of Ho's influence, the critics

Hundreds of thousands of Vietnamese have been made homeless by the war, creating a flood of refugees to the cities.

South Vietnamese help a wounded child. NLF reports state that in order to destroy the enemy, the United States would have to destroy the Vietnamese people. It is estimated that around 125,000 civilians have been killed each year in the war.

charged that bombing the North would have little effect on the outcome of the war. To destroy the NLF, the United States would be obliged to destroy the Vietnamese people. George F. Kennan, long a government adviser, put the argument this way: "Any total rooting out of the Viet Cong from the territory of South Vietnam could be achieved, if it could be achieved at all, only at the cost of a degree of damage to civilian life and of civilian suffering, generally, for which I would not like to see this country responsible."

In addition, the war's opponents argued that South Vietnam's independence was not essential to American security. The United States had overcommitted herself in Asia when her major concerns were still in Eu-

1079

rope. Some argued that America's commitment to Asia should extend only to the offshore islands—Japan, the Philippines, Indonesia, Australia, and New Zealand. They also charged that the United States was not really protecting the political freedom of South Vietnam since the government there was weak and had shown little interest in economic reforms or protection of the civil liberties of the people.

STALEMATE

By 1966 the war was a stalemate. American intervention had prevented the collapse of the Saigon government and kept the Viet Cong from winning. Yet the United States could not end the war with the current level of fighting. During the course of his administration, Johnson halted the bombing of North Vietnam several times as a peace gesture, awaiting a response from Hanoi. The President also offered to withdraw American troops if North Vietnam withdrew hers. Meanwhile, Hanoi persistently demanded that the United States withdraw from South Vietnam and insisted that it could not represent the NLF, which was autonomous. The administration cited this reaction as evidence of Hanoi's intransigence and lying. Peace critics countered that Johnson was secretly escalating the war while making these peace gestures. More significantly, they charged that the President's willingness to halt bombing raids resulted from the fact that they were useless, and always had been. The ground war in the South was continuing at the same level.

The more extreme elements in the peace movement made additional charges: racist genocide; "ecocide" (systematic destruction of Vietnamese land and ecological culture); and the use of atrocious weapons such as napalm and fragmentation bombs which inflicted slow and painful death or mutilation on civilians and children. These accusations amounted to a vision of the United States as an imperialist aggressor that was absolutely inconceivable to most Americans. Nevertheless in some parts of the United States the peace movement grew, notably on campuses. Supporters of the war countered that the Viet Cong was responsible for most of the terrorism and that, though occasional and tragic mistakes occurred, they were extremely rare: the American effort was directed against communist aggression, not against the people of Vietnam.

A debate of this dimension was, of course, divisive, and there were many demonstrations and much civil disobedience by members of the peace movement. College students went on strike and at some universities students demanded an end to university research contracts with the federal government. The President and other administration officials found it difficult to appear anywhere unless under heavy guard. America's friends around the world called for de-escalation.

POLITICAL SITUATION

After the fall of Diem and a rapid succession of unstable governments, the United States succeeded in getting the South Vietnamese government to draft a constitution, and hold elections, in September, 1967. A combination of two military men, General Thieu and Marshal Ky, was elected, but by only 34.8 percent of the vote. Little more responsive to demands for civil liberties and economic reform than their predecessors, they nevertheless brought some governmental stability.

THE MIDDLE EAST AND EUROPE

The Johnson administration, caught in the morass of an ugly and divisive war, had little time to think about international problems in other areas. There was administration relief that Israel was easily able to defend herself against the Arab world in the lightning six-day conflict of June,

1967. Within a week, Israel held decisive control of territory on the Syrian border, West Jordan (including Jerusalem), and the entire Sinai Peninsula. The war ended with a United Nations cease-fire, but real peace in the Middle East was further away than ever. The Arabs, though militarily humiliated, were unwilling to recognize Israel's existence and demanded a return of all territories.

In its relations with Europe, the Johnson administration was unable to stem the movement away from American leadership led by General Charles de Gaulle of France. The European Economic Community, created in 1959, was giving its six western European members new economic prosperity. President de Gaulle kept Great Britain out of the Common Market on the grounds that England was only a front for continued American political and economic domination of Europe. Further angered by American refusal to share nuclear secrets with her, France built up her own nuclear capability. She then recognized Red China and between 1964 and 1966 removed all French naval forces and troops from NATO. President de Gaulle also forced the removal of NATO headquarters from France in April, 1967.

ELECTION OF 1968

For the first two years after the Tonkin Gulf Resolution, the peace movement comprised a harassed minority. Demonstrations were highly unpopular, and gestures such as draft-card burning were widely criticized as not only illegal but treasonous. As the election year of 1968 approached, however,

various factors had contributed to growing national disillusionment with the war. The human cost was enormous. Taxes had risen also, and the economic strain on the American citizen was becoming apparent. Johnson had promised that there would be both "guns and butter," but the war had produced a cutback in domestic recovery programs. Finally, in January, 1968, during Tet, the Vietnamese lunar New Year, all administration assurances that progress was being made were countered by a sudden and terrifying Viet Cong offensive. The enemy even made inroads into Saigon, as well as about thirty other cities and towns. They seemed to have taken over the whole country, though they clearly would not be able to hold most of their new positions. General Westmoreland, after the Viet Cong had been pushed back, requested about 200,000 more troops. This would have brought the total to about three-quarters of a million men to defend an area about half the size of Texas. Many Americans rebelled against the suggestion. Now many hitherto uncommitted people began to advocate either a negotiated withdrawal, or a rapid "Vietnamization" of the war which would leave the fighting in the hands of the South Vietnamese themselves—something that had always been the official aim of the State Department.

DIVISION IN THE DEMOCRATIC PARTY

The dove group in the Senate included Senator Eugene McCarthy of Minnesota. Not a typical politician, he was quiet, meditative, and soft-spoken, with little power in Congressional circles. He reminded many people of Stevenson, but he was even less aggressive. As a result, when he announced in November, 1967, that he would run against the President in the Democratic primaries to test the popular mood concerning the war, many, including McCarthy himself, considered it a political gesture only.

But the McCarthy campaign gained wide support, especially after the disastrous Tet offensive. Many students canvassed communities for his support. The March primary in New Hampshire, a moderate state often used as an indicator of national trends, gave McCarthy a startling 42 percent of the vote.

McCarthy's showing in New Hampshire encouraged Robert Kennedy to also seek the nomination. The younger brother of the assassinated President had run successfully for Senator from New York in 1964. It was well known that he and Johnson nursed a mutual personal dislike, and Kennedy had openly opposed the President on the war. Until McCarthy's strong showing in New Hampshire, however, RFK had remained out of the Presidential race for he feared that if he challenged Johnson's candidacy he would be beaten within the party ranks and lose all hope of being nominated in 1972. Now Kennedy announced his entry into the race.

Democratic Party politics were further complicated when, on March 31, 1968, Johnson appeared on television, visibly exhausted, and told the American people that he would not seek or accept renomination. He also announced a de-escalation of the war in Vietnam, with bombing raids limited to below the 20th parallel, and new overtures to Hanoi. The latter eventually brought about the beginning of peace talks in Paris in May.

There was a terrific intraparty scramble for the nomination. Vice President Hubert Humphrey announced his candidacy, with the blessings of the White House; and Kennedy and McCarthy, disagreeing over who was the real peace candidate, fought for convention votes in Indiana, Nebraska, and Oregon. Kennedy supporters at his campaign headquarters in Los Angeles were celebrating his primary victory in California in early June, which would give him a strong base at the coming convention, when

he was shot by Sirhan Sirhan, an Arab nationalist who resented Kennedy's pro-Israel stand. Kennedy died within a few hours. President Johnson declared a period of national mourning during which campaigning ceased. The assassination of Robert Kennedy was the decisive event of the preconvention period. It pitted Humphrey, backed by an unpopular but powerful President, against McCarthy.

REPUBLICAN CANDIDATES

In contrast to the chaos within the Democratic Party, the Republican landscape was fairly serene. An early front-runner, Governor George Romney of Michigan, dropped out to leave Richard Nixon facing weak and belated opposition from Nelson Rockefeller, a Republican moderate. Nixon took the nomination on the first ballot at the Miami convention in August.

Nixon's chosen running mate was Governor Spiro T. Agnew of Maryland. Agnew was relatively unknown at the time, but his home state and his fairly conservative stance on crime and black militancy made him a valuable addition to the Republican ticket in the South. Faced by a potential coalition of ethnic groups in Northern cities, liberals and other traditional supporters of the Democratic Party, the Republicans decided to move to consolidate their Southern support. Goldwater had taken five Southern states in 1964; and this crucial electoral bloc seemed invaluable, although threatened by Governor George Wallace of Alabama.

The Alabama governor had a passionate following in his home state and elsewhere in the country. Though he abjured outspoken expressions of racism, he had long been an active segregationist. He also called for decentralization of government with a return to states' rights, lower taxes, and a clampdown on criminals. Wallace's Amer-

Richard Nixon, campaigning on the issues of law and order and the war in Vietnam, won the 1968 Presidential election with 301 electoral votes.

Anti-war demonstrators in Grant Park, Chicago, during the Democratic National Convention, in 1968.

ican Independent Party threatened to cut a big chunk out of Nixon's conservative support, possibly enough to put any Democratic opponent into the White House as a minority President.

Nixon's campaign approach was to promise an end to the Vietnam war and to undercut support for Wallace by playing up the idea that "law and order" was the most important current crisis in the United States. Both he and Agnew also emphasized that violent radicals had stolen a great deal of national attention in the media, especially television. Nixon insisted that "the forgotten Americans, the non-shouters, the non-demonstrators, that are not racists or sick, that are not guilty of the crime that plagues the land," wanted a new and more vigorous administration in Washington.

THE CONVENTION IN CHICAGO

Meanwhile the Democratic Party was in a shambles. The convention was held in Chicago in deference to the politically powerful Mayor Richard Daley. Antiwar youths —both those who favored McCarthy and the radical "Yippies"—descended on the city to demonstrate and protest the domination of the convention by what they saw as the pro-war Democratic leadership. During the convention television cameras showed demonstrators being clubbed and gassed by the police in the streets of Chicago. Within the convention itself, delegates also were harassed by Mayor Daley's henchmen. Senator Abraham A. Ribicoff of Connecticut even denounced the mayor from the podium for "Gestapo tactics on the streets of Chicago."

The Democrats finally nominated Johnson's candidate, Hubert Humphrey, for President and Senator Edmund Muskie of Maine for Vice President. Humphrey was in a most difficult position; he could not oppose the Vietnam war since he had for four years backed administration policy there. On the other hand, he needed liberal support to be elected, and his own private sympathies were now for an end to the conflict. Humphrey entered the campaign far behind, and while he gradually narrowed the gap, it was not enough even with the Johnson announcement of a bombing halt on October 31.

ELECTION OUTCOME

In a campaign without great popular enthusiasm for either ticket, Nixon won by about half a million votes, or 43 percent of the total. But he secured the great majority of states so that the electoral vote was 301 to 191. Governor Wallace, with about 10 million popular votes and 46 electoral votes, was the most successful third party candidate in history. He had swept the deep South.

NIXON'S DOMESTIC AND FOREIGN PROGRAMS

The election had brought to power a moderately conservative political leadership at a time when many groups were striving for economic dignity and social equality. Traditional patterns of living and thinking had been challenged and often overthrown by the early 1940s. The new economic opportunities for black Americans and women during World War II had created aspirations for social and economic equality which intensified rather than diminished over the next twenty-five years. Moreover, the post-World War II affluence of middle-class America encouraged boredom with material things and even feelings of guilt among many young people when they compared their economic conditions with the numbers of Americans who lived in poverty. The expansion of the mass media, especially television, greatly accelerated the spread of information about the nation's problems and the ways Americans were trying to combat them. The civil rights movement and the opposition to the war in Vietnam channeled the energies of many Americans, especially the young, into causes they felt worthwhile. Other movements began to exert a greater influence on American thought and actions, notably the women's liberation movement, equal rights for Indians, Puerto Ricans, and Mexican-Americans, penal and political reform, and ecological controls. It remained to be seen how the new administration, whose leader had asked for "lowered voices" during the campaign, would balance the desire for order and stability of middle America with the diverse demands for change.

DOMESTIC POLICIES

While many of Nixon's appointments were conservative, his Cabinet was balanced between moderate and conservative politicians. There were several Republican moderates: Secretary of State William Rogers; Secretary of Health, Education and Welfare Robert Finch; and Secretary of Housing and Urban Development George Romney. Probably the most controversial figure was the Attorney General, John Mitchell, a former law partner of Nixon's and a staunch "law and order" man.

More controversial were Nixon's appointments to the Supreme Court. When Chief Justice Earl Warren retired in 1969, Nixon appointed Warren E. Burger as his successor, a respected jurist who met with the easy approval of the Senate. But the President's next nomination to replace Abe Fortas was Judge Clement F. Haynesworth of South Carolina, who was rejected by the Senate, opponents claiming that his record showed conflicts of interest. Undaunted by the Senate's action, the President tried to appoint another Southerner, Judge G. Harold Carswell of Florida, and was again turned down on the grounds that Carswell had a mediocre judicial record and was a racist. Finally, the Senate accepted Judge Harry A. Blackmun of Minnesota. The President had wanted to please the South with an appointment from that section, but the men he had designated had not appeared to the Senate to be of Supreme Court caliber.

The Nixon administration tried to appeal to both liberals and conservatives by developing moderate domestic policies. The President sponsored a moderately liberal proposal on welfare reform which would put welfare funds under the federal government, thus equalizing payments throughout the country. The bill would also provide assistance to employed fathers whose incomes were below the poverty level, and a work training program for those on welfare capable of holding a job. In addition, the administration offered comprehensive bills to clean up the nation's air and water and increase the number of parks, and

a multi-billion-dollar health program to finance medical insurance, increase the number of doctors, and establish prepaid group medical centers. Nixon also called on Congress to continue federal aid to the Indians while at the same time allowing them to supervise any aid themselves, a longtime Indian demand. He renounced the policy of "termination," which would have ended the federal role of trustee of the tribes, and endorsed return to the Taos Pueblos of 48,000 acres of New Mexico land taken without compensation in 1906.

At the same time, the President advocated several policies more appealing to conservatives. He backed a plan for "revenue sharing." States were to receive more federally collected revenues and use them for their own purposes without federal intervention, with the hope of encouraging more local government responsibility. The District of Columbia Crime bill was passed which had provisions for preventive detention in certain cases, court reform, authorized wider use of wiretaps, and police entrance to a home, in certain instances, without a search warrant. Nixon also appeared to want to move away from public statements about the question of race relations. The administration continued to authorize increased appropriations for civil rights programs, and federal employment of minority citizens increased. The administration pursued support of integrated schooling in areas where it could be achieved without disrupting the neighborhood school system. However, the Commission on Civil Rights strongly criticized what it termed Nixon's inadequate policy on school integration.

Other legislation included the Twenty-sixth Amendment lowering the voting age to 18, bypassing the traditional state determination of that requirement; and a revision of the draft with the institution of a national lottery of birthdates as part of the selective service system in an effort to reduce inequities in the system.

1085

The economy meanwhile was plagued both by inflation and by unemployment. Nixon's economic strategy was to cut back government spending and tighten interest rates. Nevertheless, the country continued to suffer from high unemployment at the same time that prices continued to rise at least in part because wages continued to rise without increases in industrial productivity. For two and one-half years, Nixon insisted that his policy would work. However, in August, 1971, the administration suddenly reversed itself and ordered a temporary 90-day wage-price freeze. Businessmen and consumers generally hailed the new initiative. But labor leaders, notably George Meany, earlier angered by the Administration's failure to lower unemployment, now charged that the freeze was mainly being felt by workers, whereas profits and interest rates were untouched.

One indicator of inflation, and of the growing power of the "military-industrial complex," as Eisenhower had called the link between the armed services and the arms industry, was the fact that since 1964, when the Vietnam war had begun in force, the budget had grown about 100 percent, from about 100 billion dollars to about 200 billion dollars in 1970. About half the budget, when veterans' benefits and war debts were included, went for military costs. The President moved to reduce spending and succeeded in eliminating the deficit for the first time in years. However, a much-touted 4 percent reduction in military allocations was denounced by critics as meaningless because it involved calling a few military appropriations by a different name. There were also incessant charges that not enough money was being spent on urgent domestic social problems.

FOREIGN POLICIES

President Nixon's foreign policy stressed a realistic appraisal of the realities of international power. He wanted to base his pol-icy on what he considered possible given the country's military strength. The Nixon doctrine advocated a low posture abroad through the reduction of commitments wherever possible. For example, although he indicated that the United States would remain a power in the Pacific and would fulfill her treaty obligations, she would not augment those responsibilities.

VIETNAM

In his campaign, Nixon had promised to make every effort to "end the war," without outlining a specific plan. During the year after he took office, he elaborated a plan for gradual withdrawal of American troops which became known as "Vietnamization." After meeting with President Thieu of South Vietnam at Midway Island in June, 1969, the President announced that 25,000 American troops would soon be able to go home. By the end of the year over 100,000 men had been scheduled to leave, and the implication was that the process would continue. The South Vietnamese army was to take over the defense of the country.

Though these announcements tended to dampen nationwide antiwar sentiment, and made Nixon popular with the majority, who felt that any realistic withdrawal must be slow, advocates of the peace movement continued to call for immediate withdrawal. Members of the movement insisted that (1) hundreds of thousands of American troops were still in Vietnam; (2) aerial bombardment and defoliation was still continuing; and (3) the President's policy was bypassing the Paris peace talks. Protesters scheduled a series of "Moratorium" days in the fall of 1969. The moratorium gathered a quarter of a million people in Washington, D.C., but the President remained unmoved. On November 3, Nixon reiterated his policy of "Vietnamization" of the war, promised that eventually all American troops would be withdrawn, and coined a new phrase—the "silent majority"—to describe his own consensus.

CAMBODIA

In May, 1970, the President, after informing the country that the Viet Cong were using Cambodia as a haven from which to make raids into South Vietnam, announced that a temporary incursion by American troops into Cambodia would begin for the purpose of clearing out the Viet Cong "sanctuaries."

Peace groups accepted neither Nixon's description of the Cambodian situation nor his suggestion that the entire operation was aimed at shortening the conflict. Here, to them, was proof that Nixon was actually escalating the war. There was unprecedented and heated protest across the nation, especially among students. At one of these protests, the Ohio National Guard opened fire on rioting students at Kent State University. Four students were killed and several wounded. None had weapons on them. It seemed that at least three of those killed had been observers and that the troops had overreacted, since tear gas, which was in their possession, was never used. Protests at

Student anti-war demonstrators in Berkeley, California, suggest that Americans "make love, not war."

a black college, Jackson State in Mississippi, brought two student deaths from police fire.

Protests against the policy were so widespread and Congressional criticism so insistent that the President promised that ground troops would be withdrawn from Cambodia within six weeks.

FREEDOM OF THE PRESS

One of the most controversial aspects of the early Nixon years was the hard-hitting speeches of Vice President Agnew. The President remained relatively benign even when speaking about his opponents, but Agnew charged that those who denounced United States foreign policy in Southeast Asia as imperialistic were suffering from and contributing to a mood of "national masochism." He described the antiwar critics as an "effete corps of impudent snobs who characterize themselves as intellectuals." Moreover, he termed coverage of the war by the news media "misleading."

In defense, spokesmen for the media charged that the administration was attempting repression and censorship of news coverage. Some liberals were also horrified by Agnew's suggestion that radical students should be removed from the scene "with no more regret than we should feel over discarding rotten apples from a barrel." They dismissed the Vice President as a decoy, set up by the administration, to divert attention from serious issues. However, the President insisted repeatedly that Agnew's words were his own and he was free to say what he liked.

The fact was that television and press coverage of the war in Vietnam had shown and continued to reveal information which undermined popular support for American involvement. For several years, television cameras had shown South Vietnamese army atrocities, interviews with antiwar American soldiers, and the increased use of hard drugs by American servicemen in South Vietnam.

1087

The first months of 1970 brought press reports of massacres of civilians by American soldiers in the Vietnamese hamlets of My Lai and Son My. Then in June, 1971, a major battle erupted between the press and the administration when *The New York Times* published the first of the *Pentagon Papers.* An administration attempt to stop publication on the grounds that it threatened national security was ended by the Supreme Court, which ruled that the government had not proved its case for restraint on free expression.

BALANCE OF POWER

In the latter half of the 1960s, it was widely acknowledged that the Sino-Soviet split within the communist world would be a major factor determining the balance of power in the future. The idea of "monolithic" communism had faded so thoroughly that it became possible for President Nixon, though denounced for it by extreme conservatives, to move toward the establishment of diplomatic relations with Communist China.

The balance of power in the world was changing. In July, 1969, Nixon passed through Rumania, a Soviet satellite which had managed to preserve a little more autonomy than its neighbors since the days of Stalinism. The Rumanians gave Nixon an extremely warm welcome. By contrast, in the same year that the President entered this Soviet "sphere of influence," Nelson Rockefeller, on a fact-finding trip for Nixon through Latin America met with mobs and riots expressing their hatred for alleged "Yankee imperialism."

It was in Asia, however, that the most important changes were taking place. Japan, under the economic wing of the United States after World War II, had grown by the 1970s into a major economic competitor. Moreover, Japanese nationalism had revived, although without a military accompaniment. She had long demanded the return of Okinawa, the major military base of the United States in Asia during the postwar period. In November, 1969, Nixon agreed to return Okinawa by 1972, and plans were under way for a transfer of American installations, forces, and nuclear strike capability to a base in the Marianas.

In spite of America's long-time support of Chiang Kai-shek, Communist China had already received a trade nod from the Nixon administration when the President relaxed the embargo of American purchases of Chinese goods in 1969. Communist China, influenced by her fears of the Soviet Union and of new Japanese militarism, was also more open to a shift in the international balance of power. Following the visit of an American ping-pong team to Communist China, the President astounded the nation and the world when he announced in mid-1971 that on a secret journey to China, Henry Kissinger, his chief adviser on foreign policy, had arranged for a journey there by the President himself. Nixon was to visit China sometime before the middle of 1972.

Nixon's initiative toward Communist China further affected the shifting power relationships in the world. The Soviets invited the President to visit Russia and signed the Soviet-West German treaty affirming the territorial status quo in Europe. A few days later, the Soviet Union and India also signed a treaty of cooperation as a counter to American friendship with India's hostile neighbor, Pakistan. In East Pakistan, meanwhile, the government of General Yahya Khan was embarrassing the United States by carrying out a ruthless campaign to suppress a move for autonomy. Refugees from East Pakistan poured into India, telling stories of atrocities and burdening the already suffering Indian economy.

Despite the diplomatic maneuvering to reduce world tensions, the arms race still accelerated. The anti-ballistic missile program, costing about 8 billion dollars to begin with, was designed to provide the United States with a "second strike" capacity (ability to destroy the Soviet Union even after large parts of the United States had been destroyed). This ability theoretically would act as a deterrent to a Soviet "first strike." Although supported by the administration, this plan met with vocal opposition from Senators who saw it as a waste of money and argued that it would probably be outmoded by the time it was complete. But the Congress finally passed a modified project in October, 1969.

A nuclear nonproliferation treaty sponsored by the United Nations was ratified by the Senate in March, 1969. Its most important stipulation was that nuclear powers would not spread their weapons to nonnuclear nations. Strategic Arms Limitation Talks (SALT) began at the end of 1969 in Helsinki between the Soviet Union and the United States, but progress was slow and nothing substantial had emerged as of 1971.

A decade which had begun with John F. Kennedy's campaign charge that there was a "missile gap" ended with a decisive victory for the United States in the space race. On July 20, 1969, mission Apollo 11 gently set down two men on the surface of the moon. Astronauts Neil Armstrong and Edwin Aldrin, Jr., the first men on the moon, moved about the lunar surface and saw the earth through the sky. Other moon landings followed. Critics charged that the 24-billion-dollar Apollo program represented a misappropriation of funds needed for domestic recovery. Others regretted only that the efficiency and technological aura which surrounded the landings made it difficult for many spectators to absorb fully the awesomeness of the adventure. A new age of space exploration had begun.

From the days of the first settlements at Jamestown and Plymouth to the space flights of the 1960s, Americans had shown great energy and inventiveness in overcoming environmental and technological problems and in spreading political freedom. Yet, efforts spanning three centuries have not provided the equality of opportunity for all Americans which has been the nation's highest ideal throughout her history. It remains to be seen whether the American dream will ever be completely realized.

According to some observers, the population explosion and the growth of technology have obscured the essence of America, leaving the American dream yet to be realized.

Readings

GENERAL WORKS

Anderson, Patrick, *The President's Men*. Garden City, N.Y.: Doubleday, 1968—A study of the changing roles of Presidential advisors from Franklin Roosevelt through Lyndon Johnson.

Douglas, Paul, *America in the Market Place: Trade, Tariffs and the Balance of Payments*. New York: Holt, Rinehart & Winston, 1966—The former Illinois Senator, a professional economist, calls for a reaffirmation of the principles of free trade in United States foreign economic relations.

Evans, Rowland, and Robert Novak, *Lyndon B. Johnson: The Exercise of Power*. New York: New American Library, 1966—A description of Johnson's career in public office since 1931. The authors admire his political skills as Senate Majority Leader but point out that the Presidency requires a broader range of talents.

Geyelin, Philip L., *Lyndon B. Johnson and the World*. New York: Praeger, 1966—A study of Johnson's foreign policies in his first years in office. Geyelin claims that Johnson could not realize that his domestic political talents would not work in foreign affairs.

Goldman, Eric F., *The Tragedy of Lyndon Johnson*. New York: Knopf, 1969—Goldman, an historian who served as an adviser to Lyndon Johnson, discusses the President's failure to confront the objections of young people and intellectuals, especially in regard to Vietnam.

Heller, Walter, *New Dimensions of Political Economy*. Cambridge, Mass.: Harvard University Press, 1969—A defense of active government fiscal policy to regulate the economy and prevent recessions.

Hilsman, Roger, *To Move a Nation*. Garden City, N.Y.: Doubleday, 1967—A State Department and White House official under Kennedy and Johnson, Hilsman in this volume offers an interpretation of Kennedy's goals and methods in foreign and military policy.

Hilsman, Roger, and R. C. Good, eds., *Foreign Policy in the Sixties*. Baltimore, Md.: Johns Hopkins Press, 1965—A collection of fifteen articles on modern American foreign policy.

Sorenson, Theodore C., *Kennedy*. New York: Harper & Row, 1965—Sorenson was Special Counsel to the late President and long-term adviser. This memoir concentrates on Kennedy's personal characteristics and his skill as a political leader.

Schlesinger, Arthur M., *A Thousand Days: John F. Kennedy in the White House*. Boston: Houghton Mifflin, 1965—A memoir and history of Kennedy's administration by an historian who was also an adviser to the President.

Schwarz, Urs, *American Strategy: A New Perspective*. Garden City, N.Y.: Doubleday, 1966—An analysis of the fusion of political and military theory in foreign affairs. Schwarz devotes considerable attention to the development of limited war and counterinsurgency theories.

Waskow, Arthur I., *From Race Riot to Sit-in*. Garden City, N.Y.: Doubleday, 1966—An analysis of the race riots which followed World War I and a comparison of them to the nonviolent social disruption espoused and practiced by the civil rights movement in the 1950s and early 1960s. Waskow draws several implications about how change can be achieved best in modern American society.

SPECIAL STUDIES

Abel, Elie, *The Missile Crisis*. Philadelphia: Lippincott, 1965—A journalist's narrative of the incidents leading up to and surrounding the October, 1962, crisis in which the United States blockaded Cuba and demanded the removal of Soviet missiles which had been placed there.

Burns, James M., *The Deadlock of Democracy*. Englewood Cliffs, N.J.: Prentice-Hall, 1963—Burns, a well-known political scientist, advances the thesis that the American political system is hampered by the fact that both of our major parties are in reality divided between an activist "Presidential" wing and an obstructionist "Congressional" wing.

Cooper, Chester L., *The Lost Crusade: the U.S. in Vietnam*. New York: Dodd, Mead, 1970—A former State Department official's critique of American policy in Vietnam.

Epstein, Edward J., *Inquest*. New York: Viking, 1966—A critique of the methods of investigation used by the Warren Commission in probing President Kennedy's assassination. Epstein concludes that the Commission did not conclusively prove that Oswald acted alone.

Faber, Harold, ed., *The Road to the White House*. New York: McGraw-Hill, 1965—An account of the 1964 Presidential campaign prepared by *The New York Times*.

Fuchs, Lawrence H., *John F. Kennedy and American Catholicism*. New York: Meredith Press, 1967—Fuchs explores the background of anti-Catholicism in American life and politics and discusses Kennedy's own feelings about the proper role of the Catholic Church. He feels Kennedy's election was a blow for religious freedom.

Hoopes, Townsend, *The Limits of Interven-*

tion. New York: McKay, 1970—A former Defense Department official explores America's failure to win a victory in Vietnam and recommends an immediate withdrawal of United States troops.

Johnson, Haynes B., *The Bay of Pigs*. New York: Norton, 1964—An account of the Bay of Pigs written in collaboration with leaders of the Cuban exile invaders.

Levinson, Jerome, and Juan de Onis, *The Alliance that Lost Its Way*. Chicago: Quadrangle, 1970—The authors charge that the Alliance for Progress has brought more disillusionment than progress in Latin America.

Lewis, Anthony, *Portrait of a Decade: The Second American Revolution*. New York: Random House, 1964—A journalistic summary of a decade of civil rights activity, beginning with the Supreme Court school desegregation decision.

Manchester, William, *The Death of a President*. New York: Harper & Row, 1967—A minutely-detailed recounting of the events leading up to the assassination of President Kennedy.

Martin, John B., *Overtaken by Events*. Garden City, N.Y.: Doubleday, 1966—Ambassador to the Dominican Republic from 1962 to 1965 and a Presidential envoy during the 1965 invasion, Martin portrays that invasion as a highly complex question of power and morality.

White, Theodore H., *The Making of the President, 1964*. New York: Atheneum, 1965—The second of White's detailed narratives of Presidential election campaigns, this one describes Johnson's landslide victory over Barry Goldwater.

White, Theodore H., *The Making of the President, 1968*. New York: Atheneum, 1969—White's most recent account of a Presidential election campaign. The author's narration is highly critical of the peace and radical forces which demonstrated at the Chicago Democratic Convention.

PRIMARY SOURCES

Baldwin, James, *The Fire Next Time*. New York: Dial, 1963—Two essays by the well-known black novelist. Baldwin blends social analysis and autobiography in his indictment of white racism and his warning to American society.

Baldwin, James, *Nobody Knows My Name*. New York: Dial, 1961—A collection of essays by the noted black novelist dealing with themes of race relations in life and in literature.

Fulbright, J. William, *The Arrogance of*

Power. New York: Random House, 1967—
An indictment of much of American foreign policy by the Arkansas Democrat who is Chairman of the Senate Foreign Relations Committee. Fulbright accuses policymakers of trying to impose an American mold on the rest of the world.

Gardner, John W., ed., *To Turn the Tide.* New York: Harper & Row, 1962—A collection of President Kennedy's speeches during his first year in office.

King, Martin Luther, Jr., *Why We Can't Wait.* New York: Harper & Row, 1964—A statement of purpose by the late civil rights leader. While holding to a course of nonviolence, King is insistent in demanding the achievement of full civil rights for American blacks.

Malcolm X, *The Autobiography of Malcolm X.* New York: Grove Press, 1966—Published after his murder in 1965, Malcolm X's autobiography tells the story of his life as a street criminal, Black Muslim minister, and finally as a black nationalist leader on his own. Malcolm X makes a powerful indictment of American racism.

Salinger, Pierre, *With Kennedy.* Garden City, N.Y.: Doubleday, 1965—Salinger, as Kennedy's press secretary, was a close associate of the late President. This is an account of his years in the White House.

BIOGRAPHIES

Burns, James M., *John Kennedy: A Political Profile.* New York: Harcourt, Brace, 1959—Written shortly before the 1960 Presidential election, Burns's book is nevertheless more balanced than most campaign biographies.

Steinberg, Alfred, *Sam Johnson's Boy.* New York: Macmillan, 1968—A long biography, emphasizing the Texas political background of Lyndon B. Johnson. The book contains a great deal of political gossip about what Steinberg calls Johnson's ruthless drive for power.

Whalen, Richard J., *The Founding Father, the Story of Joseph E. Kennedy.* New York: New American Library, 1964—Though well known during FDR's administration as Ambassador to Great Britain and later as an isolationist, Joseph Kennedy is better known in his role as father of President John F. Kennedy and Senators Robert and Edward Kennedy. This is a popular biography of the Boston millionaire.

White, William S., *The Professional: Lyndon B. Johnson.* Boston: Houghton Mifflin, 1964—A laudatory political biography by a veteran Washington columnist. White writes admiringly of Johnson as a party leader.

APPENDIX

Supplementary Readings

General Books

The American Heritage Atlas of United States History (1966). Bailey, T. A., A Diplomatic History of the American People (1969). Bemis, S. F., ed., American Secretaries of State and Their Diplomacy (10 vols., 1927–1929). Binkley, W. E., American Political Parties, Their Natural History (1963). Boorstin, D. J., ed., An American Primer (11 vols., 1969). Boorstin, D. J., ed., Chicago History of American Civilization Series (21 vols., 1956). Commager, H. S., ed., Documents of American History (1969). Commager, H. S., and R. B. Morris, eds., The New American Nation Series (50 vols., 1954). Curti, Merle, The Growth of American Thought (1964). David, Henry, et al., eds., The Economic History of the United States (10 vols. projected. 1945). DeConde, Alexander, A History of American Foreign Policy (1970). Handlin, Oscar, et al., eds., Harvard Guide to American History (1954). Hartz, Louis, The Liberal Tradition in America (1955). Hofstadter, Richard, The American Political Tradition (1948). Hofstadter, Richard, The Progressive Historians (1968). Hofstadter, Richard, Anti-Intellectualism in American Life (1963). Hofstadter, Richard, and Michael Wallace, American Violence: A Documentary History (1970). Hudson, W. S., Religion in America (1965). Johnson, Allen, ed., Chronicles of America (50 vols., 1918–1921; 6 additional vols. 1950–1951). Johnson, Allen, and Dumas Malone, eds., Dictionary of American Biography (22 vols., 1928–1958). Josephy, A. M., Jr., The Indian Heritage of America (1968). Kelly, A. H., and W. A. Harbison, The American Constitution (1963). Kirkland, E. C., A History of American Economic Life (1951). Quarles, Benjamin, The Negro in the Making of America (1964). Schlesinger, A. M., and D. R. Fox, eds., A History of American Life, (vols. I–XII, 1950). Schneider, H. W., A History of American Philosophy (1946). Simkins, F. B., A History of the South (1963). Spiller, R. E., et al., Literary History of the United States (3 vols., 1963). Stephenson, W. H., and E. M. Coulter, eds., A History of the South (10 vols., 1947–1967). Sweet, W. W., The Story of Religions in America (1950).

Journals

The American Historical Review. The Journal of American History. The Journal of Negro History. The Journal of Southern History. The Pacific Historical Review. The William and Mary Quarterly.

Section 1: From Colonies to Independent Nation

Bridenbaugh, Carl, Mitre and Sceptre (1962). Bridenbaugh, Carl, Vexed and Troubled Englishmen, 1590–1642 (1968). Bronner, E. D., William Penn's Holy Experiment, The Founding of Pennsylvania 1681–1701 (1962). Cremin, L. A., American Education: The Colonial Experience 1607–1783 (1971). Douglass, E. P., Rebels and Democrats (1955). Ferguson, E. J., The Power of the Purse (1961). Freeman, D. S., George Washington: A Biography (6 vols., 1948–1954). Hansen, Chadwick, Witchcraft in Salem (1969). Labaree, Leonard, Royal Government in America (1930). Main, J. T., The Social Structure of Revolutionary America (1965). Miller, Perry, The New England Mind: From Colony to Province (1953). Miller, Perry, The New England Mind: The Seventeenth Century (1939). Morison, S. E., The European Discovery of America, The Northern Voyages, 500–1600 (1971). Morris, R. B., The Peacemakers, The Great Powers and American Independence (1965). Pomfret, John E., Founding the American Colonies, 1583–1660 (1971). Robbins, Caroline, The Eighteenth Century Commonwealth Man (1959). Shipton, C. K., New England Life in the Eighteenth Century (1963). Smith, J. M., ed., Seventeenth Century America, Essays on Colonial History (1959). Stourzh, Gerald, Benjamin Franklin and American Policy (1954).

Section 2: The Evolution of Democracy

Ammon, Harry, James Monroe (1971). Cunningham, N. E., Jr., The Jeffersonian Republicans in Power (1963). Hofstadter, Richard, The Idea of a Party System: The Rise of Legitimate Opposition in the United States 1780–1840 (1969). Ketcham, Robert, James Madison (1971). Levy, L. W., Jefferson and Civil Liberties (1963). Mitchell, Broadus, Alexander Hamilton (2 vols., 1957, 1962). Prucha, F. P., American Indian Policy in the Formative Years (1962). Risjord, N. K., The Old Republicans (1965). Rossiter, Clinton, Alexander Hamilton and the Constitution (1964). Seager, Robert, II, And Tyler Too (1963). White, L. D., The Federalists (1948). White L. D., The Jeffersonians (1951). Wilkins, Thurman, Cherokee Tragedy (1970). Young, J. S., The Washington Community, 1800–1829 (1966).

Section 3: Nationalism and Sectionalism

Bruchey, Stuart, Cotton and the Growth of the American Economy 1790–1860 (1967). Conrad, A. H., and J. R. Meyer, The Economics of Slavery (1964). Gilchrist, D. T., and W. D. Lewis, eds., Economic Change in the Civil War Era (1965). Hamilton, Holman, The Compromise of 1850 (1964). Miller, Perry, The Life of the Mind in America (1966). Phillips, U. B., Life and Labor in the Old South (1929). Silbey, J. H., The Transformation of American Politics, 1840–1860 (1967). Wade, R. C., Slavery in the Cities (1964).

Section 4: Emergence of Industrial America

Donald, David, Charles Sumner and the Rights of Man (1970). Donald, David, The Politics of Reconstruction 1864–1867 (1965). Fritz, H. E., The Movement for Indian Assimilation 1860–1890 (1963). Gillette, William, The Right to Vote (1965). Glad, P. W., The Trumpet Soundeth: William J. Bryan and His Democracy (1960). Grodinsky, Julius, Jay Gould, His Business Career, 1867–1892

(1957). Hacker, L. M., *The World of Andrew Carnegie 1865–1901* (1968). Martin, Jay, *Harvest of Change: American Literature 1865–1914* (1967). Muzzey, D. S., *James G. Blaine* (1934). Wall, J. F., *Andrew Carnegie* (1971).

Section 5: World Power and Domestic Reform

Bendiner, Robert, *Just Around the Corner* (1968). Bowers, C. G., *Beveridge and the Progressive Era* (1932). Bremner, R. H., *From the Depths: The Discovery of Poverty in the United States* (1956). Filene, P. G., *Americans and the Soviet Experiment 1917–1933* (1967). Garrett, Charles, *The LaGuardia Years* (1961). Ginger, Ray, *The Bending Cross, A Biography of Eugene Victor Debs* (1949). Jackson, K. T., *The Ku Klux Klan in the City* (1967). Kraditor, A. S., *The Ideas of the Woman's Suffrage Movement 1890–1920* (1965). Mason, A. T., *Brandeis* (1946). Mason, A. T., *The Supreme Court From Taft to Warren* (1958). McKenna, M. C., *Borah* (1961). Osgood, Robert, *Ideals and Self-Interest in America's Foreign Relations* (1953). Sullivan, Mark, *Our Times: The United States 1900–1925* (6 vols., 1920–1935). White, W. A., *A Puritan in Babylon* (1938).

Section 6: The Challenges of Maturity

Divine, R. A., *The Illusion of Neutrality* (1962). Feis, Herbert, *The China Tangle* (1953). Ferrell, R. H., *George C. Marshall* (1966). Graebner, N. A., *American Secretaries of State in the Twentieth Century* (1961). Kennan, G. F., *Russia and the West Under Lenin and Stalin* (1960). Kolko, Gabriel, *The Politics of War* (1968). Offner, A. A., *American Appeasement, United States Foreign Policy and Germany, 1933–1938* (1969). Osgood, R. E., *NATO: The Entangling Alliance* (1962). Rappaport, Armin, *Henry L. Stimson and Japan, 1931–1933* (1963). Ulam, A. B., *Expansion and Coexistence: The History of Soviet Foreign Policy 1917–1967* (1968). Vinson, J. C., *The Parchment Peace* (1950).

Articles and Papers

Aeschbacher, W. D., "Historical Organization on the Great Plains." *North Dakota History*, 34:93–104(1967). Albers, Carl W., "America Immigration Policy Since 1945: A Comparative Study." Ph.D. dissertation, Columbia University, 1972. Aldridge, Frederick Stoikes, "Organization and Administration of the Militia System of Colonial Virginia." Ph.D. dissertation, The American University, 1964. Allen, James B., "The Company Town: A Passing Phase of Utah's Industrial Development." *Utah Historian Quarterly*, 34:138–60(1966). Allen, Walser H., "George Washington: Premier 18th Century American." *The Lower Cape Fear Historical Society Bulletin*, 14:1–6(1967). Allmendinger, David Frederick, Jr., "Indigent Students and Their Institutions, 1800–1860." Ph.D. dissertation, University of Wisconsin, 1968. Amundson, Richard J., "The Florida Land and Colonization Company." *Florida Historical Quarterly*, 44:153–68(1966). Andrews, Richard Allen, "Years of Frustration: William T. Sherman, the Army and Reform, 1968–1883." Ph.D. dissertation, Northwestern University, 1968. Astorina, Samuel J., "Senator Albert B. Fall and Wilson's Last Crisis with Mexico." *Duquesne Review*, 13:3–17(1968). Aurand, Harold W., "The Workingmen's Benevolent Association." *Labor History*, 7:19–34(1966).

Bader, Ernest B., "Some Aspects of American Public Reaction to Franklin D. Roosevelt's Japanese Policy, 1933–1941." Ph.D. dissertation, University of Nebraska, 1957. Barber, Tom, "Stephen Arnold Douglas and the Presidential Election of 1860 in Illinois." Master's thesis, Chicago State Teacher's College, 1965. Bates, Whitney K., "Northern Speculators and Southern State Debts." *William and Mary Quarterly* (January, 1962). Beck, Paul, "Daniel Drake and the Interior Valley." Ph.D. dissertation, University of Nebraska, 1961. Beck, Paul A., "Lowering the Voting Age: The Case of the Reluctant Electorate." *Public Opinion Quarterly*, 370–79 (Fall, 1969). Bell, Frank Carter, "Federal Legislation Concerning the Disposition of Grazing Lands (1862–1900)." Ph.D. dissertation, Indiana University, 1959. Berman, Milton, "John Fiske and the Evolution of American Religion, 1842–1902." Ph.D. dissertation, Harvard University, 1959. Bill, Shirley A., "The Meaning and Background of the Interstate Comity Clause of Federal Constitution." Ph.D. dissertation, The University of Chicago, 1950. Billias, George A., "The American Revolution: A Measure of America's Maturity." *New England Social Studies Bulletin*, 22:7–9(1964). Billings, Warren Martin, " 'Virginia's Deplored Condition,' 1660–1676: The Coming of Bacon's Rebellion." Ph.D. dissertation, Northern Illinois University, 1969. Billman, Calvin J., "Backgrounds and Policies of Selected United States Diplomats to Latin America, 1898–1938." Ph.D. dissertation, Tulane University, 1954. Billman, Calvin J., ed., "Joseph M. Ellison: War Letters (1862)." *Georgia Historical Quarterly*, 48:229–38(1964). Black, Wilfred W., "Marching with Sherman Through Georgia and the Carolinas: Civil War Diary of Jesse L. Dozer." *Georgia Historian Quarterly*, 52:308–36(1968). Boeck, George A., "Senator Grimes and the Iowa Press, 1867–1868." *Mid-America*, 48: 147–61(1966). Boller, Paul F., Jr., "Calhoun on Liberty." *South Atlantic Quarterly*, 66:395–408(1967). Born, John D. Jr., "Charles Strachon in Mobile: The Frontier of a Scottish Factor 1764–1768." *Alabama Historical Quarterly*, 27: 23–42(1966). Boyd, William H., "The Shasta Route, 1863–1887: The Rail Road Link Between the Sacramento and the Columbia." Ph.D. dissertation, University of California, 1942. Branyon, Robert Lester, "Antimonopoly Activities During the Truman Administration." Ph.D. dissertation, Oklahoma State University, 1961. Brown, Dorothy M., "Politics of Crisis." *Maryland Historical Magazine* (September, 1962). Brown, Thomas H., "Theodore Roosevelt and the Great White Fleet." Master's thesis, New York University, 1965. Bultmann, William A., "The Society for the Propagation of the Gospel in Foreign Ports and the Foreign Settler in the American Colonies." Ph.D. dissertation, University of California at Los Angeles, 1950. Burke, Bernard Vincent, "American Diplomats and Hitler's Rise to Power, 1930–1933: The Mission of Ambassador Sackett." Ph.D. dissertation, University of Washington, 1966. Burnette, Rand, "The Quest for Union in the American Colonies, 1689–1701." Ph.D. dissertation, Indiana University, 1968. Bush, Mary T., "American Historians Interpret Manifest Destiny." Ph.D. dissertation, University of Ottawa, 1963. Buzanski, Peter M., "The Knowledge Explosion and the Teaching of American History: The Cromwell American History Series." *Studies in History and Sociology*, 1:41–46(1969).

Carageorge, Ted, "An Evaluation of Hoke Smith and Thomas E. Watson as Georgia Reformers." Ph.D. dissertation, University of Georgia, 1963. Carlstedt, E. T., "The Congress of Berlin, 1878." Master's thesis, University of Iowa, 1929. Carlstedt, E. T., "When Fond Du Lac was British." *Minnesota History Quarterly* (1938). Carriker, Robert Charles, "Fort Supply, Indian Territory Frontier Outpost on the Southern Plains, 1868–1894." Ph.D. dissertation, The University of Oklahoma, 1967. Carroll, Peter Neil, "Puritanism and the Wilderness: The Intellectual Significance of the New England Frontier—1629–1675." Ph.D. dissertation, Northeastern University, 1968. Cater, Harold Dean, "Some Unpublished Letters of Henry

Adams." Ph.D. dissertation, Columbia University, 1946. Cave, Alfred A., "The Case of Calvin Colton: White Racism in Northern Antislavery Thought." *New York Historical Society Quarterly*, 53:214–29(1969). Chasteen, Robert J., "American Foreign Aid and Public Opinion, 1945–1952." Ph.D. dissertation, University of North Carolina, 1958. Chiles, Paul N., "The Puerto Rican Press Reaction to the United States, 1888–1898." Ph.D. dissertation, University of Pennsylvania, 1942. Christian, John Willis, "The Kootenay Gold Rush: The Placer Decade, 1863–1872." Ph. D. dissertation, Washington State University, 1967. Clark, Clifford E., Jr., "The Changing Nature of Protestantism in Mid–19th Century America: Henry Ward Beecher's *Seven Lectures to Young Men.*" *Journal of American History* (March, 1971). Clark, Clifford E. Jr., "Henry Ward Beecher: Revivalist and Anti-slavery Leader, 1813–1867." Ph.D. dissertation, Harvard University, 1967. Clark, Clifford E., Jr., "Religious Beliefs and Social Reforms in the Gilded Age: The Case of Henry Whitney Bellows." *The New England Quarterly* (March, 1970). Clemmer, Robert Rugh, "Enlightenment Church History in the United States, 1800–1850." Ph.D. dissertation, University of Pennsylvania, 1961. Coady, Joseph William, "Franklin D. Roosevelt's Early Washington Years (1913–1920)." Ph.D. dissertation, Saint John's University, 1969. Cochrane, William G., "Freedom Without Equality: A Study of Northern Opinion and the Negro Issue: 1861–1870." Ph.D. dissertation, University of Minnesota, 1957. Cogswell, Sedi, "Land Tenancy and Ethnic Factors in Iowa Agriculture, 1850–1870—A Computer Study." Ph.D. dissertation, University of Iowa, 1972. Cohen, Donald D., "The Hartford Treaty of 1650: Anglo-Dutch Cooperation in the Seventeenth Century." *New York Historical Society Quarterly*, 53:310–32(1969). Combs, Barry B., "The Union Pacific Railroad and the Early Settlement of Nebraska. 1868–1880." *Nebraska History*, 50:1–26(1969). Combs, Jerald Arthur, "Power Politics and Ideology: A Case Study of the Jay Treaty." Ph.D. dissertation, University of California at Los Angeles, 1964. Comegys, Robert G., "The Agrarian and Rural Tradition as Reflected in National Periodical Literature, 1919–1929." Ph.D. dissertation, Stanford University, 1958. Cooke, John White, "Some Aspects of the Concept of the Free Individual in the United States, 1800–1860." Ph.D. dissertation, Vanderbilt University, 1967. Cowing, Cedric B., "Speculation on the American Exchanges: The Principal Ideas Affecting the Evolution of Trading, 1892–1936." Ph.D. dissertation, University of Wisconsin, 1955. Crooks, James Benedict, "Politics and Progress: The Rise of Urban Progressivism in Baltimore, 1895–1911." Ph.D. dissertation, Johns Hopkins University, 1965. Curl, Donald Walter, "The Long Memory of the United States Senate." *Ohio History*, 76: 103–13(1967).

Danielson, Jean Marie, "The Evolution of the Political Thought of Reinhold Niebuhr." Ph.D. dissertation, University of Kansas, 1965. Davis, Gerald H., "The 'Ancona' Affair: A Case of Preventative Diplomacy." *Journal of Modern History*, 38:267–77(1966). Davis, Gerald H., "The 'Petrolite' Incident: A World War I Case Study on the Limitations of Warfare." *Historian*, 29:238–48(1967). Davis, John A., "The Influence of Africans on American Culture." *Annals of the American Academy of Political and Social Science*, 75–83(1964). Dickinson, William, and John Barsness, "The Sully Expedition of 1864." *Montana*, 16: 23–29(1966). Dickson, Charles, "Politics in a New Nation: The Early Career of James Monroe." Ph.D. dissertation, Ohio University, 1971. Dinkin, Robert Joseph, "Provincial Massachusetts: A Deferential or a Democratic Society?" Ph.D. dissertation, Columbia University, 1968. Doster, James F., "Alabama's First Railroad Commission, 1881–

1885." Ph.D. dissertation, University of Chicago, 1948. Duncan, Richard Ray, "The Impact of the Civil War on Education in Maryland." *Maryland Historical Magazine* (March, 1966).

Earnhart, Hugh G., "Aboard a Blockade Runner: Some Civil War Experiences of Jerome Duchane." *North Carolina Historic Review*, 44:392–99(1967). Eisenman, Harry James, "Charles F. Brush: Pioneer Innovator in Electrical Technology." Ph.D. disertation, Case Western Reserve University, 1965. Ernst, Eldon Gilbert, "The Interchurch World Movement of North America, 1919–1920." Ph.D. dissertation, Yale University, 1968. Ernst, Robert, "Immigrant Life in New York City, 1825–1863." Ph.D. dissertation, Columbia University, 1947. Essin, Emmett M., "The Cavalry and the Horse." Ph.D. dissertation, Texas Christian University, 1968.

Faulk, Odie B., "A Letter From John R. Bartlett at Camp Yuma, 1852." *Journal of Arizona History*, 6:204–13 (1965). Ferguson, Clyde R., "General Andrew Pickens." Ph.D. dissertation, Duke University, 1960. Fischer, David H., "The Myth of the Essex Junto." *William and Mary Quarterly*, 21:191–235(1964). Fischer, Harold, "Family and Social Life During the Jackson Period." Master's Thesis, University of Southern California, 1943. Flaherty, David H., "A Select Guide to the Manuscrip Court Records of Colonial New England." *American Journal of Legal History*, 11:107–26(1967). Folmar, John Kent, "Pre-Civil War Sentiment From Belmont County: Correspondence of Hugh Anderson." *Ohio Historian*, 78:202–10(1969). Fordham, Jefferson B., "The Implications of the Supreme Court Decisions Dealing with Religious Practices in the Public Schools." *Journal of Church and State*, 6:44–60 (1964). Foster, Kent, "Peace Moves During the World War: The Search for a Negotiated Peace, 1914–1918." Ph.D. dissertation, University of Pennsylvania, 1941.

Gamson, Ian C., "The American Historian and the Concepts of Manifest Destiny, 1846–1898." Ph.D. dissertation, University of Minnesota, 1971. Gardner, James Alexander, "The Life of Moses Austin, 1761–1821." Ph.D. dissertation, Washington University at Missouri, 1963. Gelfand, Lawrence E., "The Inquiry: A Study of American Preparations for Peace, 1917–1919." Ph.D. dissertation, Washington University, 1958. Gerrity, Francis X., "American Editorial Opinion of the French Intervention in Mexico, 1861–1867." Ph.D. dissertation, Georgetown University, 1952. Gilmore, Jesse Lee, "A Pioneer History of Southern Oregon, 1860." Ph.D. dissertation, University of California at Berkeley, 1952. Gilmore, Jesse Lee, "The Political Emergence of William Jennings Bryan, 1887–1896." Master's thesis, University of California at Berkeley, 1948. Goodwin, Gerald J., "The Anglican Reaction to the Great Awakening." *Historical Magazine of the Protestant Episcopal Church*, 35:343–71(1966). Graebner, Norman A., "The Limits of Military Aid." *Current History*, 50:353–57(1966). Graebner, Norman A., "Obligation vs. Interest in American Foreign Policy." *Australian Journal of Politics and History*, 2:137–49(1695). Gruger, B. Madeline, "The Genesis of the Republican Party as Reflected in Northern Illinois Newspapers." Master's thesis, Catholic University of America, Washington, D.C., June, 1955. Guice, John D., "Colorado's Territorial Courts." *Colorado Magazine*, 45: 204–24(1968). Guidorizzi, Richard Peter, "Timothy Peckering: Opposite Politics in the Early Years of the Republic." Ph.D. dissertation, Saint John's University, 1968.

Hakola, John William, "Samuel T. Houser and the Economic Development of Montana: A Case Study in 19th Century Frontier Capitalism." Ph.D. dissertation, Indiana University, 1961. Hansen, James E., "A Study of Prohibition in Denver." Master's thesis, University of Denver, 1965. Harris, Merne Arthur, "The MacArthur Dismissal: A Study in Political Mail." Ph.D. dissertation, University of Iowa, 1966. Harris, Sally Ann, "The Inter-American Conferences of the 1930's." Ph.D. dissertation, University of Missouri, 1968. Hartwig, Edwin, "Origin and Evolution of Mandates System." Master's thesis, Wayne State University, 1956. Hebb, Douglas, "The Woman in the California Grange, 1870–1880." Master's thesis, University of California at Berkeley, 1950. Hendrich, J. Joseph, "Jefferson's Naval Policy." Ph.D. dissertation, Duke University, 1971. Hendrickson, Kenneth E., Jr., "The Socialists of Reading, Pennsylvania, and World War 1—A Question of Loyalty." *Pennsylvania History*, 36:430–50(1969). Hill, Frederick G., "Veblen, Berle and the Modern Corporation." *American Journal of Economics and Sociology*, 26:279–96(1967). Hilligas, Ernest L., "Chester Rowell and His Conflict with Johnson and the League of Nations Hiram Treaty—1918–1920." Master's thesis, University of California at Berkeley, 1955. Hinton, Wayne K., "Civil Rights Controversy of 1948." Ph.D. dissertation, South Utah State University, 1967. Hinton, Wayne K., "The Horn Silver Bonanza." *American West*, 32:35–56(1966). Hinton, Wayne K., "Origin of the Welfare Plan of the Church of Jesus Christ of Latter Day Saints." *Brigham Young University Studies*, 67–86(1964). Hoffman, George, "The Fight to Re-Charter the Second Bank of the United States." Master's thesis, University of Southern California, 1941. Hoffman, George, "The Political Career of Senator McNary." *Oregon Historical Quarterly* (1967). Horowitz, David, "Visions of Harmonious Abundance: Corporate Ideology in the 1920's." Ph.D. dissertation, University of Minnesota, 1971. Hout, Frederick Gilman, "The Wood-Forbes Mission to the Philippines, 1921." Ph.D. dissertation, Claremont Graduate School and University Center, 1963. Hoyt, Franklyn, "Railroad Development in Southern California, 1868–1900." Ph.D. dissertation, University of Southern California, 1951. Hughes, Richard Bennett, "Texas Churches and Presidential Politics, 1928 and 1960." Ph.D. dissertation, Saint Louis University, 1969. Hunt, Robert, "Domestic Slave Trade in the Old South, 1850–1860." Paper for West Virginia Historical Association of the University and College Professors of History, 1962. Hunt, Robert, "Strip Mining in 17 North Central Counties of West Virginia, 1939–1957." Paper for West Virginia Historical Association of University and College Professors of History, 1971. Hurst, James W., "The Fenians, a Bibliography." *Eire-Ireland Journal of the American-Irish Cultural Institute in St. Paul, Minnesota* (1969–1970). Hybels, Robert, "Lake Superior Copper Fever." Master's thesis, published in *Michigan History Magazine* (1950).

Illick, Joseph Edward, "William Penn's Relations with the British Government." Ph.D. dissertation, University of Pennsylvania, 1963.

Jaebker, Orville J., "Henry Hamilton: British Soldier and Colonial Governor." Ph.D. dissertation, Indiana University, 1954. Jarvis, Charles, "John Greenleaf Whittier and the Anti-Slavery Movement, 1828–1860." Ph.D. dissertation, University of Missouri, 1970. Jines, Lewis P., "Carolinians and Cubans: The Elliotts and Gonzales Families." Ph.D. dissertation, University of North Carolina, 1951. Jines, Lewis P., "Evolution of Political Subdivisions in South Carolina." Master's thesis, Wofford College, 1940. Jonas, Manfred, "The Clairborne-Calvert Controversy: An Episode in the Colonization of North America." *Jahrbuck für Amerika-studien*, 11:241–59(1966). Jonas, Manfred, "Pro-Axis Sentiment and American Isolationism." *Historian*, 29:221–37(1967). Jones, Newton B., "Charlottesville and Albemarle County, Virginia, 1819–1860." Ph.D. dissertation, University of Virginia, 1950.

Kammen, Michael G., "Colonial Court Records and the Study of Early American History: A Bibliographical Review." *American Historical Review*, 70:732–39(1965). Keltner, Hubert W., "De-Nazification (After World War II)." Master's thesis, University of Montana, 1954. Klement, Frank L., "Middle-Western Copperheadism: Jeffersonian Democracy in Revolt." Ph.D. dissertation, University of Wisconsin, 1945. Knapp, Wesley, "The Indian Nationalist Movement, 1916–1921." Master's thesis, University of Wisconsin, 1948. Knepper, George W., Jr., "The Convention Army, 1777–1783." Ph.D. dissertation, University of Michigan, 1954. Kottman, Richard N., "The Diplomatic Relations of the United States and Canada, 1927–1941." Ph.D. dissertation, Vanderbilt University, 1959. Kyte, George Wallace, "Victory in the South: An Appraisal of General Greene's Strategy in the Carolinas." *North Carolina Historical Review* (July, 1960).

Lacy, Eric Russell, "Tennessee Teetotalism: Social Forces and the Politics of Progressivism." *Tennessee Historical Quarterly*, 24:219–40(1965). Lambert, Robert S., "The Democratic Party, 1841–1844." Ph.D. dissertation, University of North Carolina, 1950. Lamnke, Wayne, "Unemployment in the Truman Administration: Social, Economic, Political Aspects." Ph.D. dissertation, Ohio State University, 1972. Lane, Ann J., "Recent Literature on the Molly Maguires." *Science and Society*, 30:309–19(1966). Lanier, Osmos, Jr., "Anti-Annexationists of the 1890's." Ph.D. dissertation, University of Georgia, 1965. Latham, Robert C., "The Dirt Farmer in Politics: A Study of Webster County, Mississippi During the Rise of Democratic Factionalism 1880–1910." Master's thesis, Mississippi State University, 1951. Linford, Lawrence L., "Conrad Weiser and the Frontier History of Colonial Pennsylvania." Master's thesis, University of Utah, 1967. Loveless, J. Alton, "The Dixiecrat Revolt—1948." Master's thesis, Stetson University, 1968. Lybarger, Mike, "The Origins and Spread of the Irish Volunteer Movement, 1778–1782." Master's thesis, University of Notre Dame, 1961. Lybarger, Mike, "Significance of the Catholic J. F. K.'s Vote in Wisconsin's Primary of 1960—A Commentary." *Wisconsin Association of Teachers of College History* (October, 1970).

Macomson, E. M., "Diplomatic Relations Between the United States and Argentina, 1919–1924." Master's thesis, Atlanta University, 1938. Malone, Miles S., "Distribution of Population on the Virginia Frontier." Ph.D. dissertation, Princeton University, 1935. Manek, Thomas, "Some Characteristics of Union Members in the 1880's." *Labor History*, 5:57–66(1964). Marcum, Richard Tandy, "'Fort Brown, Texas': The History of a Border Post." Ph.D. dissertation, Texas Technical University, 1965. Maschmann, Marita, "The American Diplomatic Relations with Turkey, 1919–1923." Master's thesis, Catholic University of America, 1959. McCarthy, John L., "Reconstruction Legislation and Voting Alignments in the U.S. House of Representatives, 1863–1869." Ph.D. dissertation, Yale University, 1970. McClintock, Thomas C., "Seth Lewelling, William S. U'ren and the Birth of the Oregon Progressive Movement." *Oregon Historical Quarterly*, 68:197–220 (1967). McConnell, Roland C., "The Negro in North Carolina Since Reconstruction." Ph.D. dissertation, New York University, 1945. McCurry, Allan J., "The North Administration and America, 1774–1778." Ph.D. dissertation, Cornell University, 1952. McDonald, Archie P., "The Illinois Commission of 'Major' Jedediah Hotchkiss." *Virginia Magazine of History and Biology*, 75:181–85 (1967). McDonald, Archie P., "Washington in February, 1861." *West Virginia History*, 27:201–10(1966). McFarlane, Larry

Allan, "The Missouri Land and Live Stock Company, Limited, of Scotland: Foreign Investment of the Missouri Farming Frontier, 1882–1908." Ph.D. dissertation, University of Missouri, 1963. McKee, James B., "Urbanism and the Problem of Social Order." *Centennial Review*, 10:382–99(1966). McLaughlin, Tom L., "Sectional Responses of Free Negroes to the Idea of Colonization." *Research Studies*, 34:123–34(1966). Meier, August, and Elliot M. Rudwick, "Early Boycotts of Segregated Schools: The Alton Illinois Case, 1897–1908." *Journal of Negro Education*, 36:394–402(1967). Meire, Matt S., "Folsom Letter." *Sacramento Historical Society Journal* (1955). Meyer, Freeman W., "A Note on the Origins of the 'Hamiltonian System.'" *William and Mary Quarterly*, 21:579–88(1964). Millet, Allan R., "The General Staff and the Cuban Intervention of 1960." *Military Affairs*, 31:113–19(1967). Morgner, Fred, "Ultraconservative Response to Supreme Court Judicial Behavior: A Study in Political Alienation, 1935–65." Ph.D. dissertation, University of Minnesota, 1970. Morice, Joseph, "The Contribuitons of W. F. Dumas to the Cause of American Independence." *Duquesne Review*, 7:17–28(1961). Morrill, James R., "The Presidential Election of 1852: Death Knell of the Whig Party of North Carolina." *North Carolina Historical Review*, 44:342–59 (1967). Morris, Harry W., "The Republicans in a Minority Role, 1933–1938." Ph.D. dissertation, The University of Iowa, 1960. Morris, Thomas, "The Personal Liberty Laws: Constitutional and Legal Aspect, 1780–1861." Ph.D. dissertation, University of Washington, 1969. Moseley, Thomas Vernon, "Evolution of the American Civil War Infantry Tactics." Ph.D. dissertation, University of North Carolina, 1967.

Nagasawa, Arthur, "The Governance of Hawaii from Annexation to 1908: Major Problems and Developments." Ph.D. dissertation, University of Denver, 1969. Nash, Gerald David, "The Role of State Government in the Economy of California, 1849–1911." Ph.D. dissertation, University of California at Berkeley, 1957. Nelsen, Clair E., "The Image of Herbert Hoover as Reflected in the American Press." Ph.D. dissertation, Stanford University, 1956. Nordin, Dennis S., "Graduate Studies in American Agricultural History." *Agricultural History*, 41:275–312 (1967). Norris, James D., "The Missouri and Kansas Zinc Miners' Association, 1899–1905." *Pacific Historical Review*, 36:189–207(1967). Nutting, Bradford, "Connecticut Relations with the British Government, 1662–1776." Ph.D. dissertation, University of North Carolina, 1972.

Olm, Lee E., "The Chatham Ministry and the American Colonies, 1766–1768." Ph.D. dissertation, University of Michigan, 1960. Oster, Donald B., "Community Image in the History of Saint Louis and Kansas City." Master's thesis, University of Missouri, 1969. Oviatt, Alton B., "Pacific Coast Competition for the Gold Camp Trade of Montana." *Pacific Northwest Quarterly*, 56:168–76(1965).

Pancake, John S., "The General From Baltimore: A Biography of Samuel Smith." Ph.D. dissertation, University of Virginia, 1949. Passi, Michael, "Mandarins and Immigrants, the Irony of Ethnic Studies in America Since Turner." Ph.D. dissertation, University of Minnesota, 1971. Penick, James L., Jr., "The Age of the Bureaucrat: Another View of the Ballinger-Pinchot Controversy." *Forest History*, 7:15–20(1963). Perman, Michael, "The South and Congress' Reconstruction Policy of 1866–1867." *Journal of American Studies*, IV:181–200(1971). Phillips, Edward Hake, "Timothy Pickering at His Best: Indian Commissioner, 1790–1794." *Essex Institute of Historical Collections*, 102:163–202(1966). Polenberg, Richard, "The National Committee to Uphold Constitutional Government, 1937–1941." *Journal of American History*, 52:582–98

(1965). Potts, David Bronson, "A Historical Perspective." *Cambridge Historical Society Proceedings* (October, 1967). Preyer, Kathryn, "Federalist Policy and the Judiciary Act of 1801." *William and Mary Quarterly* (January, 1965).

Quinten, B. T., "Oklahoma Tribes, The Great Depression and the Indian Bureau." *Mid-America*, 49:29–43(1967).

Rainbolt, John C., "A New Look at Stuart 'Tyranny': The Crown's Attack on the Virginia Assembly, 1676–1689." *Virginia Magazine of History and Biology*, 75:387–406 (1967). Ranson, James, "General James Robertson: Father of Tennessee." Master's thesis, University of Tennessee, 1966. Redmond, Kent C., "Henry L. Stimson and the Question of League Membership." *Historian*, 25:200–12 (1963). Reese, James V., "The Early History of Labor Organizations in Texas: 1838–1876." *Southwestern Historical Quarterly*, 72:1–20(1968). Reeve, Thomas V., "From Resistance to Independence: A Period of Changing Attitudes, 1775–1776." *The Thetian* (April, 1967). Reeves, Thomas C., "John Checkley and the Emergence of the Episcopal Church in New England." *Historical Magazine of the Protestant Episcopal Church*, 34:349–60(1965). Reid, Bill G., "The Concept of Soldier Settlement in American History." *North Dakota Quarterly*, 36:41–51(1968). Riley, William A., "Presidential Popularity, Leadership and Sectional Issues in the Nineteenth Century." Ph.D. dissertation, Syracuse University, 1969. Risjord, Norman K., "The Virginia Federalists." *Journal of Southern History*, 33: 486–517(1967). Rissler, Howard F., "The State Capitol." *Journal of the Illinois State Historical Society*, 61:397–452(1968). Roberts, Robert R., "Economic and Political Ideas Expressed in the Early Social Gospel Movement: 1875–1900." Ph.D. dissertation, University of Chicago, 1952. Ross, Oliver Dell, "Studies of Selected Mexican Communal Institutions: Colonial Period." Ph.D. dissertation, Ohio State University, 1953. Ruppel, George J., "The Council and Its Activities in Business, Politics and Law, in New York, 1664–1760." Ph.D. dissertation, University of Pittsburgh, 1955. Ryden, Daniel, "Civil Liberty in War Time, Comparing Administrations of Abraham Lincoln and Woodrow Wilson, the Civil War and World War One." Master's thesis, Oklahoma University, 1963.

Sanders, Albert N., "Jim Crow Comes to South Carolina." *Proceedings of the South Carolina Historical Association*, 27–39(1966). Savage, Richard A., "Maine Steam-boating: 1818–1868." *Steamboat Bill*, 196–203(1970). Schaefers, Mortina, "Development of Pan-American Policy in American Tradition, 1810–1820 (Genesis of the Organization of American States)." Master's thesis, Catholic University of America, 1953. Schelbert, Leo, "Swiss Migration to America: the Swiss Mennonites." Ph.D. dissertation, Columbia University, 1966. Schmeltekopf, Donald D., "The Dimensions of History." *Corn College Social Science Quarterly* (1971). Schmeltekopf, Donald D., "The Impact of Puritan Thoughts Upon the Early American Political Tradition." Ph.D. dissertation, Drew University, 1972. Schmidtlein, Gene, "Harry S. Truman and the Pendergast Machine." *Mid-Continent American Studies Journal*, 7:3–39(1966). Schwartzkopf, Calvin, "Rush County Seat War." *Kansas Historical Quarterly* (June, 1970). Scroggs, Jack B., "Carpetbagger Influence in the Political Reconstruction of the South Atlantic States: 1865–1876." Ph.D. dissertation, University of North Carolina, 1951. Sewell, Richard H., "John P. Hale and the Liberty Party, 1847–1848." *New England Quarterly*, 37:200–23(1964). Sewry, Charles L., "The Alleged 'Un-Americanism' of the Church as a Factor in Anti-Catholicism in the United States, 1860–1914." Ph.D. dissertation, University of Minnesota, 1955. Shepperson, Wilbers, "British Views of Emigration to North America, 1837–1860." Ph.D. dissertation, Western Reserve University, 1951. Sherman, Richard B., "Progressive Politics in Massachusetts: 1908–1916." Ph.D. dissertation, Harvard University, 1959. Shruben, Francis W., "The Kansas State Refinery Law of 1905." Kansas Historical Quarterly, 34: 299–324(1968). Sibley, Joel H., "The Slavery Extension Controversy and Illinois Congressmen, 1846–50." Journal of the Illinois State Historical Society, 58:378–95(1965). Smith, Thomas H., "Crawford County 'Ez Trooly Dime-cratic': A Study of Mid-western Copperheadism." Ohio Historian, 76:33–55(1967). Smith, Wayne W., "An Experiment in Counterinsurgency: The Assessment of Confederate Sympathizers in Missouri." Journal of Southern History, 35:361–80(1969). Smith, Wilda M., "Reactions of Kansas Farmers to the New Deal Program." Ph.D. dissertation, University of Illinois, 1960. Smith, Wilson, "The Teacher in Puritan Culture." Harvard Educational Review, 36:394–411(1966). Snodgrass, William, "The History of the Cherokee Outlet." Ph.D. dissertation in progress, Oklahoma State University at Stillwater, 1971. Soady, Fred W., Jr., "The Making of the Shawnee." Forest History, 9: 10–23(1965). Sparks, Dade, "The Career of Henry Lane Wilson as American Ambassador to Mexico, 1910–1913." Master's thesis, University of Texas, 1931. Sparks, Dade, "Central America and Its Diplomatic Relation with the United States, 1860–1893." Ph.D. dissertation, Duke University, 1934. Steckl, William R., "Pietist in Colonial Pennsylvania: Christopher Sauer, Printer, 1738–1758." Ph.D. dissertation, Stanford University, 1949. Sterling, Robert E., "Civil War Draft Resistance in Illinois." Journal of the Illinois State Historical Society (Fall, 1971). Sternsiter, Bernard, "The New Deal 'Revolution'." Social Studies, Vol. 57 (1966), pp. 157–62. Susskind, Jacob, "The Use of Protest Songs During the Depression." International Review of History and Political Science (February, 1971). Suter, John, "The Slave Trade into Virginia and South Carolina." Master's thesis, University of Wisconsin, 1960.

Tasher, Lucy L., "The Missouri Democrat and the Civil War." Ph.D. dissertation, University of Chicago, 1934. Taylor, A. Elizabeth, "The Woman Suffrage Movement in North Carolina." North Carolina Historical Review, 38: 45–62(1961). Taylor, Joe Gray, "Slavery in Louisiana During the Civil War." Lousiana History, 8:27–33(1967). Thomas, John L., "Romantic Reform in America, 1815–65." American Quarterly, 17:656–81(1965). Thomson, Robert Polk, "The Merchant in Virginia, 1700–1775." Ph.D. dissertation, University of Wisconsin, 1955. Thurston, George, "The Iron Industry in Connecticut, 1630–1850." Ph.D. dissertation, University of Pennsylvania, 1971. Timmons, Gordon, "Economic Aspects of Air Power." Master's thesis, Montana State, June, 1958. Tomberlin, Joseph Aaron, "The Negro and Florida's System of Education; The Aftermath of the Brown Case." Ph.D. disseration, Florida State University, 1968. Toscano, V., "Anthracite Coal Strike, 1902—A Study of Executive Leadership." Master's thesis, Seton Hall University, 1962. Tricamo, John Edgar, "Tennessee Politics, 1845–1861." Ph.D. dissertation, Columbia University, 1964.

Venza, James Raymond, Jr., "Federalists in Congress, 1800–1812." Ph.D. dissertation, Vanderbilt University, 1967.

Walsh, Walter Richard, "Charleston's Sons of Liberty: A Study of the Mechanics, 1760–1785." Ph.D. dissertation, University of South Carolina, 1954. Waters, John J., and John A. Schutz, "Paterns of Massachusetts Colonial Politics: The Writs of Assistance and the Rivalry Between the Otis and the Hutchinson Families." William and Mary Quarterly, 24:543–67(1967). Watson, Alan B., "Ordinaries in Colonial Eastern N. Carolina." North Carolina Historic Review, 45:67–83(1968). Watson, Alan B., "The Quitrent System in Royal South Carolina." Ph.D. dissertation, University of South Carolina, 1971. Wechman, Robert, "The Eager Immigrants." The Torch, 44:22–26 (1971). Weinstein, Allan, "Was There a 'Crime of 1873'?: The Case of the Demonetized Dollar." Journal of American History, 54:307–26(1967). Weisberg, Maurice, "An Economic History of Tungsten Mining in Colorado." Master's thesis, University of Colorado, 1943. Wheller, William Bruce, "Urban Politics in Nature's Republic: The Development of Political Parties in the Seaport Cities in the Federalist Era." Ph.D. dissertation, University of Virginia, 1968. White, John B., "Published Sources on Territorial Nebraska: An Essay and Bibliography." Ph.D. dissertation, University of Nebraska, 1953. White, Lonnie J., "The Hancock and Custer Expeditions of 1867." Journal of the West, 5:355–78(1966). White, Lonnie J., "Winter Campaigning with Sheridan and Custer: The Expedition of the Nineteenth Kansas Volunteer Cavalry." Journal of the West, 6:68–98(1967). Whiteside, Henry Overton, "Kennedy and the Kremlin: Soviet American Relations, 1961–1963." Ph.D. dissertation, Stanford University, 1969. Wiebe, Robert H., "The Response of American Businessmen to the National Progressive Movement." Ph.D. dissertation, University of Rochester, 1957. Wiggins, Sarah Woolfolk, "Unionist Efforts to Control Alabama Reconstruction: 1865–1867." Alabama Historical Quarterly, 30: 51–64(1968). Williams, Frank B., Jr., "Samuel Harvey Laughlin, Polk's Political Handyman." Tennessee Historical Quarterly, 24:356–92(1965). Williams, Frederick De Forrest, "The Career of J.F.H. Clairborne, State's Rights Unionist." Ph.D. dissertation, Indiana University, 1953. Wilson, R. Jackson, "United States: The Reassessment of Liberalism." Journal of Contemporary History, 2:93–105(1967). Winchester, Richard Carlyle, "James G. Blaine and the Ideology of American Expansionism." Ph.D. dissertation, University of Rochester, 1966. Winston, Noma Dix, "The Session Movement in Kentucky, 1859–1860." Master's thesis, University of Chicago, 1930. Wright, John Dean, Jr., "Robert Peter and Early Science in Kentucky." Ph.D. dissertation, Columbia University, 1955. Wyman, Roger, "Insurgency and the Elections of 1910 in the Middle West." Master's thesis, University of Wisconsin, 1964. Wyman, Roger, "Wisconsin Ethnic Groups and the Election of 1890." Wisconsin Magazine of History (1968).

Yackuboskey, John, "The Impact of Federal Legislation on Textile Mills in the South." Master's thesis, Emory University, 1949. Yarborough, Kemp Plummer, "Chisholm v. Georgia: A Study of the Minority Opinion." Ph.D. dissertation, Columbia University, 1964.

Zabel, Orville H., "Church and State in Nebraska, 1854–1950: A Study of the Legal Relationship." Ph.D. dissertation, University of Nebraska, 1954. Zilversmit, Arthur, "Slavery and Its Abolition in the Northern States." Ph.D. dissertation, University of California at Berkeley, 1963. Zimmerman, John Joseph, "Benjamin Franklin: A Study of Pennsylvania Politics and the Colonial Agency, 1755–1775." Ph.D. dissertation, University of Michigan, 1957. Zornow, William F., "The Re-Election of Abraham Lincoln." Ph.D. dissertation, Western Reserve University, 1952.

The Declaration of Independence

When in the Course of human events, it becomes necessary for one people to dissolve the political bands which have connected them with another, and to assume among the Powers of the earth, the separate and equal station to which the Laws of Nature and of Nature's God entitle them, a decent respect to the opinions of mankind requires that they should declare the causes which impel them to the separation.

We hold these truths to be self-evident, that all men are created equal, that they are endowed by their Creator with certain unalienable Rights, that among these are Life, Liberty and the pursuit of Happiness. That to secure these rights, Governments are instituted among Men, deriving their just powers from the consent of the governed, That whenever any Form of Government becomes destructive of these ends, it is the Right of the People to alter or to abolish it, and to institute new Government, laying its foundation on such principles and organizing its powers in such form, as to them shall seem most likely to effect their Safety and Happiness. Prudence, indeed, will dictate that Governments long established should not be changed for light and transient causes; and accordingly all experience hath shown, that mankind are more disposed to suffer, while evils are sufferable, than to right themselves by abolishing the forms to which they are accustomed. But when a long train of abuses and usurpations, pursuing invariably the same Object evinces a design to reduce them under absolute Despotism, it is their right, it is their duty, to throw off such Government, and to provide new Guards for their future security.—Such has been the patient sufferance of these Colonies; and such is now the necessity which constrains them to alter their former Systems of Government. The history of the present King of Great Britain is a history of repeated injuries and usurpations, all having in direct object the establishment of an absolute Tyranny over these States. To prove this, let Facts be submitted to a candid world.

He has refused his Assent to Laws, the most wholesome and necessary for the public good.

He has forbidden his Governors to pass Laws of immediate and pressing importance, unless suspended in their operation till his Assent should be obtained; and when so suspended, he has utterly neglected to attend to them.

He has refused to pass other Laws for the accommodation of large districts of people, unless those people would relinquish the right of Representation in the Legislature, a right inestimable to them and formidable to tyrants only.

He has called together legislative bodies at places unusual, uncomfortable, and distant from the depository of their public Records, for the sole purpose of fatiguing them into compliance with his measures.

He has dissolved Representative Houses repeatedly, for opposing with manly firmness his invasions on the rights of the people.

He has refused for a long time, after such dissolutions, to cause others to be elected; whereby the Legislative Powers, incapable of Annihilation, have returned to the People at large for their exercise; the State remaining in the mean time exposed to all the dangers of invasion from without, and convulsions within.

He has endeavoured to prevent the population of these States; for that purpose obstructing the Laws of Naturalization of Foreigners; refusing to pass others to encourage their migration hither, and raising the conditions of new Appropriations of Lands.

He has obstructed the Administration of Justice, by refusing his Assent to Laws for establishing Judiciary powers.

He has made Judges dependent on his Will alone, for the tenure of their offices, and the amount and payment of their salaries.

He has erected a multitude of New Offices, and sent hither swarms of Officers to harass our People, and eat out their substance.

He has kept among us in times of peace, Standing Armies without the Consent of our legislature.

He has affected to render the Military independent of and superior to the Civil power.

He has combined with others to subject us to a jurisdiction foreign to our constitution, and unacknowledged by our laws; giving his Assent to their acts of pretended Legislation:

For quartering large bodies of armed troops among us:

For protecting them, by a mock Trial, from punishment for any Murders which they should commit on the Inhabitants of these States:

For cutting off our Trade with all parts of the world:

For imposing taxes on us without our Consent:

For depriving us in many cases, of the benefits of Trial by Jury:

For transporting us beyond Seas to be tried for pretended offences:

For abolishing the free System of English Laws in a neighbouring Province, establishing therein an Arbitrary government, and enlarging its Boundaries so as to render it at once an example and fit instrument for introducing the same absolute rule into these Colonies:

For taking away our Charters, abolishing our most valuable Laws, and altering fundamentally the Forms of our Governments:

For suspending our own Legislature, and declaring themselves invested with Power to legislate for us in all cases whatsoever.

He has abdicated Government here, by declaring us out of his Protection and waging War against us.

He has plundered our seas, ravaged our Coasts, burnt our towns, and destroyed the lives of our people.

He is at this time transporting large Armies of foreign Mercenaries to compleat the works of death, desolation and tyranny, already begun with circumstances of Cruelty & perfidy scarcely paralleled in the most barbarous ages, and totally unworthy the Head of a civilized nation.

He has constrained our fellow Citizens taken Captive on the high Seas to bear Arms against their Country, to become the executioners of their friends and Brethren, or to fall themselves by their Hands.

He has excited domestic insurrections amongst us, and has endeavoured to bring on the inhabitants of our frontiers, the merciless Indian Savages, whose known rule of warfare, is an undistinguished destruction of all ages, sexes and conditions.

In every stage of these Oppressions We have Petitioned for Redress in the most humble terms: Our repeated Petitions have been answered only by repeated injury. A Prince, whose character is thus marked by every act which may define a Tyrant, is unfit to be the ruler of a free People.

Nor have We been wanting in attention to our British brethren. We have warned them from time to time of attempts by their legislature to extend an unwarrantable jurisdiction over us. We have reminded them of the circumstances of our emigration and settlement here. We have appealed to their native justice and magnanimity, and we have conjured them by the ties of our common kindred to disavow these usurpations, which, would inevitably interrupt our connections and correspondence. They too have been deaf to the voice of justice and of consanguinity. We must, therefore, acquiesce in the necessity, which denounces our Separation, and hold them, as we hold the rest of mankind, Enemies in War, in Peace Friends.

We, therefore, the Representatives of the united States of America, in General Congress, Assembled, appealing to the Supreme Judge of the world for the rectitude of our intentions, do, in the Name, and by Authority of the good People of these Colonies, solemnly publish and declare, That these United Colonies are, and of Right ought to be Free and Independent States; that they are Absolved from all Allegiance to the British Crown, and that all political connection between them and the State of Great Britain, is and ought to be totally dissolved; and that as Free and Independent States, they have full Power to levy War, conclude Peace, contract Alliances, establish Commerce, and to do all other Acts and Things which Independent States may of right do. And for the support of this Declaration, with a firm reliance on the protection of divine Providence, we mutually pledge to each other our Lives, our Fortunes and our sacred Honor.

The Constitution of the United States

We the people of the United States, in Order to form a more perfect Union, establish Justice, insure domestic Tranquility, provide for the common defence, promote the general Welfare, and secure the Blessings of Liberty to ourselves and our Posterity, do ordain and establish this CONSTITUTION for the United States of America.

ARTICLE I

Section 1. All legislative Powers herein granted shall be vested in a Congress of the United States, which shall consist of a Senate and House of Representatives.

Section 2. The House of Representatives shall be composed of Members chosen every second Year by the People of the several States, and the Electors in each State shall have the Qualifications requisite for Electors of the most numerous Branch of the State Legislature.

No Person shall be a Representative who shall not have attained to the Age of twenty-five Years, and been seven Years a Citizen of the United States, and who shall not, when elected, be an Inhabitant of that State in which he shall be chosen.

Representatives and direct Taxes shall be apportioned among the several States which may be included within this Union, according to their respective Numbers, which shall be determined by adding to the whole Number of free Persons, including those bound to Service for a Term of Years, and excluding Indians not taxed, three fifths of all other Persons. The actual Enumeration shall be made within three Years after the first Meeting of the Congress of the United States, and within every subsequent Term of ten Years, in such Manner as they shall by Law direct. The Number of Representatives shall not exceed one for every thirty Thousand, but each State shall have at Least one Representative; and until such enumeration shall be made, the State of New Hampshire shall be entitled to chuse three, Massachusetts eight, Rhode-Island and Providence Plantations one, Connecticut five, New-York six, New Jersey four, Pennsylvania eight, Delaware one, Maryland six, Virginia ten, North Carolina five, South Carolina five, and Georgia three.

When vacancies happen in the Representation from any State, the Executive Authority thereof shall issue Writs of Election to fill such Vacancies.

The House of Representatives shall chuse their Speaker and other Officers; and shall have the sole Power of Impeachment.

Section 3. The Senate of the United States shall be composed of two Senators from each State, chosen by the Legislature thereof, for six Years; and each Senator shall have one Vote.

Immediately after they shall be assembled in Consequence of the first Election, they shall be divided as equally as may be into three Classes. The Seats of the Senators of the first Class shall be vacated at the Expiration of the second Year, of the second Class at the Expiration of the fourth Year, and of the third Class at the Expiration of the sixth Year, so that one-third may be chosen every second Year; and if Vacancies happen by Resignation, or otherwise, during the Recess of the Legislature of any State, the Executive thereof may make temporary Appointments until the next Meeting of the Legislature, which shall then fill such Vacancies.

No Person shall be a Senator who shall not have attained to the Age of thirty Years, and been nine Years a Citizen of the United States, and who shall not, when elected, be an Inhabitant of that State in which he shall be chosen.

The Vice President of the United States shall be President of the Senate, but shall have no vote, unless they be equally divided.

The Senate shall chuse their other Officers, and also a President pro tempore, in the absence of the Vice President, or when he shall exercise the Office of the President of the United States.

The Senate shall have the sole Power to try all Impeachments. When sitting for that purpose, they shall be on Oath or Affirmation. When the President of the United States is tried, the Chief Justice shall preside: And no person shall be convicted without the Concurrence of two thirds of the Members present.

Judgment in Cases of Impeachment shall not extend further than to removal from Office, and disqualification to hold and enjoy any Office of honor, Trust, or Profit under the United States: but the Party convicted shall nevertheless be liable and subject to Indictment, Trial, Judgment, and Punishment, according to Law.

Section 4. The Times, Places and Manner of holding Elections for Senators and Representatives, shall be prescribed in each state by the Legislature thereof; but the Congress may at any time by Law make or alter such Regulations, except as to the Places of Chusing Senators.

The Congress shall assemble at least once in every Year, and such Meeting shall be on the first Monday in December, unless they shall by Law appoint a different Day.

Section 5. Each House shall be the Judge of the Elections, Returns and Qualifications of its own Members, and a Majority of each shall constitute a Quorum to do Business; but a smaller number may adjourn from day to day, and may be authorized to compel the Attendance of absent Members, in such Manner, and under such Penalties, as each House may provide.

Each House may determine the Rules of its Proceedings, punish its Members for disorderly Behaviour, and, with the Concurrence of two thirds, expel a Member.

Each House shall keep a Journal of its Proceedings, and from time to time publish the same, excepting such Parts as may in their Judgment require Secrecy; and the Yeas and Nays of the Members of either House on any question shall, at the Desire of one fifth of those Present, be entered on the Journal.

Neither House, during the Session of Congress, shall,

without the Consent of the other, adjourn for more than three days, nor to any other Place than that in which the two Houses shall be sitting.

Section 6. The Senators and Representatives shall receive a Compensation for their Services, to be ascertained by Law, and paid out of the Treasury of the United States. They shall in all Cases, except Treason, Felony, and Breach of the Peace, be privileged from Arrest during their Attendance at the Session of their respective Houses, and in going to and returning from the same; and for any Speech or Debate in either House, they shall not be questioned in any other Place.

No Senator or Representative shall, during the Time for which he was elected, be appointed to any civil Office under the Authority of the United States, which shall have been created, or the Emoluments whereof shall have been increased, during such time; and no Person holding any Office under the United States shall be a Member of either House during his continuance in Office.

Section 7. All Bills for raising Revenue shall originate in the House of Representatives; but the Senate may propose or concur with Amendments as on other Bills.

Every Bill which shall have passed the House of Representatives and the Senate, shall, before it become a Law, be presented to the President of the United States; If he approve he shall sign it, but if not he shall return it, with his Objections, to that House in which it shall have originated, who shall enter the Objections at large on their Journal, and proceed to reconsider it. If after such Reconsideration two thirds of that House shall agree to pass the Bill, it shall be sent, together with the Objections, to the other House, by which it shall likewise be reconsidered, and if approved by two thirds of that House, it shall become a Law. But in all such Cases the Votes of both Houses shall be determined by Yeas and Nays, and the Names of the Persons voting for and against the Bill shall be entered on the Journal of each House respectively. If any Bill shall not be returned by the President within ten Days (Sundays excepted) after it shall have been presented to him, the Same shall be a Law, in like Manner as if he had signed it, unless the Congress by their Adjournment prevent its Return, in which Case it shall not be a Law.

Every Order, Resolution, or Vote to which the Concurrence of the Senate and House of Representatives may be necessary (except on a question of Adjournment) shall be presented to the President of the United States; and before the Same shall take Effect, shall be approved by him, or being disapproved by him, shall be repassed by two thirds of the Senate and House of Representatives, according to the Rules and Limitations prescribed in the Case of a Bill.

Section 8. The Congress shall have Power To lay and collect Taxes, Duties, Imposts and Excises, to pay the Debts and provide for the common Defence and general Welfare of the United States; but all Duties, Imposts and Excises shall be uniform throughout the United States;

To borrow money on the credit of the United States;

To regulate Commerce with foreign Nations, and among the several States, and with the Indian Tribes;

To establish an uniform Rule of Naturalization, and uniform Laws on the subject of Bankruptcies throughout the United States;

To coin Money, regulate the Value thereof, and of foreign Coin, and fix the Standard of Weights and Measures;

To provide for the Punishment of counterfeiting the Securities and current Coin of the United States;

To establish Post Offices and post Roads;

To promote the Progress of Science and useful Arts, by securing for limited Times to Authors and Inventors the exclusive Right to their respective Writings and Discoveries;

To constitute Tribunals inferior to the Supreme Court;

To define and punish Piracies and Felonies committed on the high Seas, and Offenses against the Law of Nations;

To declare War, grant Letters of Marque and Reprisal, and make Rules concerning Captures on Land and Water;

To raise and support Armies, but no Appropriation of Money to that Use shall be for a longer Term than two Years;

To provide and maintain a Navy;

To make Rules for the Government and Regulation of the land and naval forces;

To provide for calling forth the Militia to execute the Laws of the Union, suppress Insurrections and repel Invasions;

To provide for organizing, arming, and disciplining the Militia, and for governing such Part of them as may be employed in the Service of the United States, reserving to the States respectively, the Appointment of the Officers, and the Authority of training the Militia according to the discipline prescribed by Congress;

To exercise exclusive Legislation in all Cases whatsoever, over such District (not exceeding ten Miles square) as may, by Cession of particular States, and the acceptance of Congress, become the Seat of Government of the United States, and to exercise like Authority over all Places purchased by the Consent of the Legislature of the State in which the Same shall be, for the Erection of Forts, Magazines, Arsenals, dock-Yards, and other needful Buildings;—And

To make all Laws which shall be necessary and proper for carrying into Execution the foregoing Powers, and all other Powers vested by this Constitution in the Government of the United States, or in any Department or Officer thereof.

Section 9. The Migration or Importation of such Persons as any of the States now existing shall think proper to admit, shall not be prohibited by the Congress prior to the Year one thousand eight hundred and eight, but a tax or duty may be imposed on such Importation, not exceeding ten dollars for each Person.

The privilege of the Writ of Habeas Corpus shall not be suspended, unless when in Cases of Rebellion or Invasion the public Safety may require it.

No Bill of Attainder or ex post facto Law shall be passed.

No Capitation, or other direct, Tax shall be laid unless in Proportion to the Census or Enumeration herein before directed to be taken.

No Tax or Duty shall be laid on Articles exported from any State.

No Preference shall be given by any Regulation of Revenue to the Ports of one State over those of another: nor shall Vessels bound to, or from, one State, be obliged to enter, clear, or pay Duties in another.

No Money shall be drawn from the Treasury, but in Consequence of Appropriations made by Law; and a regular Statement and Account of the Receipts and Expenditures of all public Money shall be published from time to time.

No Title of Nobility shall be granted by the United States: And no Person holding any Office of Profit or Trust under them, shall, without the Consent of the Congress, accept of any present, Emolument, Office, or Title, of any kind whatever, from any King, Prince, or foreign State.

Section 10. No State shall enter into any Treaty Alliance, or Confederation; grant Letters of Marque and Reprisal; coin Money; emit Bills of Credit; make any Thing but gold and silver Coin a Tender in Payment of

Debts; pass any Bill of Attainder, ex post facto Law, or Law impairing the Obligation of Contracts, or grant any Title of Nobility.

No State shall, without the Consent of the Congress, lay any Imposts or Duties on Imports or Exports, except what may be absolutely necessary for executing its inspection Laws: and the net Produce of all Duties and Imposts, laid by any State on Imports or Exports, shall be for the Use of the Treasury of the United States; and all such Laws shall be subject to the Revision and Control of the Congress.

No State shall, without the Consent of Congress, lay any duty of Tonnage, keep Troops, or Ships of War in time of Peace, enter into any Agreement or Compact with another State, or with a foreign Power, or engage in War, unless actually invaded, or in such imminent Danger as will not admit of delay.

ARTICLE II

Section 1. The executive Power shall be vested in a President of the United States of America. He shall hold his Office during the Term of four Years, and, together with the Vice President, chosen for the same Term, be elected, as follows:

Each State shall appoint, in such Manner as the Legislature thereof may direct, a Number of Electors, equal to the whole Number of Senators and Representatives to which the State may be entitled in the Congress: but no Senator or Representative, or Person holding an Office of Trust or Profit under the United States, shall be appointed an Elector.

The Electors shall meet in their respective States, and vote by Ballot for two Persons, of whom one at least shall not be an Inhabitant of the same State with themselves. And they shall make a List of all the Persons voted for, and of the Number of Votes for each; which List they shall sign and certify, and transmit sealed to the Seat of the Government of the United States, directed to the President of the Senate. The President of the Senate shall, in the Presence of the Senate and House of Representatives, open all the Certificates, and the Votes shall then be counted. The Person having the greatest Number of Votes shall be the President, if such Number be a Majority of the whole Number of Electors appointed; and if there be more than one who have such Majority, and have an equal Number of Votes, then the House of Representatives shall immediately chuse by Ballot one of them for President; and if no Person have a Majority, then from the five highest on the List the said House shall in like Manner chuse the President. But in chusing the President, the Votes shall be taken by States, the Representation from each State having one Vote; a quorum for this Purpose shall consist of a Member or Members from two-thirds of the States, and a Majority of all the States shall be necessary to a Choice. In every Case, after the Choice of the President, the Person having the greatest Number of Votes of the Electors shall be the Vice President. But if there should remain two or more who have equal votes, the Senate shall chuse from them by Ballot the Vice President.

The Congress may determine the Time of chusing the Electors, and the Day on which they shall give their Votes; which Day shall be the same throughout the United States.

No person except a natural-born Citizen, or a Citizen of the United States, at the time of the Adoption of this Constitution, shall be eligible to the Office of President; neither shall any Person be eligible to that Office who shall not have attained to the Age of thirty-five Years, and been fourteen Years a Resident within the United States.

In Case of the Removal of the President from Office, or of his Death, Resignation, or Inability to discharge the Powers and Duties of the said Office, the same shall devolve on the Vice President, and the Congress may by Law provide for the Case of Removal, Death, Resignation, or Inability, both of the President and Vice President, declaring what Officer shall then act as President, and such Officer shall act accordingly, until the Disability be removed, or a President shall be elected.

The President shall, at stated Times, receive for his Services a Compensation, which shall neither be increased nor diminished during the Period for which he shall have been elected, and he shall not receive within that Period any other Emolument from the United States, or any of them.

Before he enter on the Execution of his Office, he shall take the following Oath or Affirmation:— "I do solemnly swear (or affirm) that I will faithfully execute the Office of President of the United States, and will, to the best of my Ability, preserve, protect, and defend the Constitution of the United States."

Section 2. The President shall be Commander in Chief of the Army and Navy of the United States, and of the Militia of the several States, when called into the actual Service of the United States; he may require the Opinion, in writing, of the principal Officer in each of the executive Departments, upon any subject relating to the Duties of their respective Offices, and he shall have Power to Grant Reprieves and Pardons for Offences against the United States, except in Cases of Impeachment.

He shall have Power, by and with the Advice and Consent of the Senate, to make Treaties, provided two thirds of the Senators present concur; and he shall nominate, and by and with the Advice and Consent of the Senate, shall appoint Ambassadors, other public Ministers and Consuls, Judges of the supreme Court, and all other Officers of the United States, whose Appointments are not herein otherwise provided for, and which shall be established by Law: but the Congress may by Law vest the Appointment of such inferior Officers, as they think proper, in the President alone, in the Courts of Law, or in the Heads of Departments.

The President shall have Power to fill up all Vacancies that may happen during the Recess of the Senate, by granting Commissions which shall expire at the End of their next Session.

Section 3. He shall from time to time give to the Congress Information of the State of the Union, and recommend to their Consideration such Measures as he shall judge necessary and expedient; he may, on extraordinary occasions, convene both Houses, or either of them, and in Case of Disagreement between them, with respect to the Time of Adjournment, he may adjourn them to such Time as he shall think proper; he shall receive Ambassadors and other public Ministers; he shall take Care that the Laws be faithfully executed, and shall Commission all the Officers of the United States.

Section 4. The President, Vice President and all civil Officers of the United States, shall be removed from Office on Impeachment for, and Conviction of, Treason, Bribery, or other high Crimes and Misdemeanors.

ARTICLE III

Section 1. The judicial Power of the United States, shall be vested in one supreme Court, and in such inferior Courts as the Congress may from time to time ordain and establish. The Judges, both of the supreme and inferior Courts, shall hold their Offices during good Behaviour, and shall, at stated Times, receive for their Services, a Compensation, which shall not be diminished during their Continuance in Office.

Section 2. The judicial Power shall extend to all Cases, in Law and Equity, arising under this Constitution, the Laws of the United States, and Treaties made, or which shall be made, under their Authority;—to all Cases affecting Ambassadors, other public Ministers and Consuls;—to all Cases of admiralty and maritime Jurisdiction;—to Controversies to which the United States shall be a Party;—to Controversies between two or more States;—between a State and Citizens of another State;—between Citizens of the same State claiming Lands under Grants of different States, and between a State, or the Citizens thereof, and foreign States, Citizens or Subjects.

In all Cases affecting Ambassadors, other public Ministers and Consuls, and those in which a State shall be Party, the supreme Court shall have original Jurisdiction. In all the other Cases before mentioned, the supreme Court shall have appellate Jurisdiction, both as to Law and Fact, with such Exceptions, and under such Regulations as the Congress shall make.

The trial of all Crimes, except in Cases of Impeachment, shall be by Jury; and such Trial shall be held in the State where the said Crimes shall have been committed; but when not committed within any State, the Trial shall be at such Place or Places as the Congress may by Law have directed.

Section 3. Treason against the United States, shall consist only in levying War against them, or in adhering to their Enemies, giving them Aid and Comfort. No Person shall be convicted of Treason unless on the Testimony of two Witnesses to the same overt Act, or on Confession in open Court.

The Congress shall have power to declare the Punishment of Treason, but no Attainder of Treason shall work Corruption of Blood, or Forfeiture except during the Life of the Person attainted.

ARTICLE IV

Section 1. Full Faith and Credit shall be given in each State to the public Acts, Records, and judicial Proceedings of every other State. And the Congress may by general Laws prescribe the Manner in which such Acts, Records and Proceedings shall be proved, and the Effect thereof.

Section 2. The Citizens of each State shall be entitled to all Privileges and Immunities of Citizens in the several States.

A Person charged in any State with Treason, Felony, or other Crime, who shall flee from Justice, and be found in another State, shall on demand of the executive Authority of the State from which he fled, be delivered up, to be removed to the State having Jurisdiction of the crime.

No Person held to Service or Labour in one State, under the Laws thereof, escaping into another, shall, in Consequence of any Law or Regulation therein, be discharged from such Service or Labour, but shall be delivered up on Claim of the Party to whom such Service or Labour may be due.

Section 3. New States may be admitted by the Congress into this Union; but no new State shall be formed or erected within the Jurisdiction of any other State; nor any State be formed by the Junction of two or more States, or parts of States, without the Consent of the Legislatures of the States concerned as well as of the Congress.

The Congress shall have Power to dispose of and make all needful Rules and Regulations respecting the Territory or other Property belonging to the United States; and nothing in this Constitution shall be so construed as to Prejudice any Claims of the United States, or of any particular State.

Section 4. The United States shall guarantee to every State in this Union a Republican Form of Government, and shall protect each of them against Invasion; and on Application of the Legislature, or of the Executive (when the Legislature cannot be convened) against domestic Violence.

ARTICLE V

The Congress, whenever two thirds of both Houses shall deem it necessary, shall propose Amendments to this Constitution, or, on the Application of the Legislatures of two thirds of the several States, shall call a Convention for proposing Amendments, which, in either Case, shall be valid to all Intents and Purposes, as part of this Constitution, when ratified by the Legislatures of three fourths of the several States, or by Conventions in three fourths thereof, as the one or the other Mode of Ratification may be proposed by the Congress; Provided that no Amendment which may be made prior to the Year One thousand eight hundred and eight shall in any Manner affect the first and fourth Clauses in the Ninth Section of the first Article; and that no State, without its Consent, shall be deprived of its equal Suffrage in the Senate.

ARTICLE VI

All Debts contracted and Engagements entered into, before the Adoption of this Constitution, shall be as valid against the United States under this Constitution, as under the Confederation.

This Constitution, and the Laws of the United States which shall be made in Pursuance thereof; and all Treaties made, or which shall be made, under the Authority of the United States, shall be the supreme Law of the Land; and the Judges in every State shall be bound thereby, any Thing in the Constitution or Laws of any State to the Contrary notwithstanding.

The Senators and Representatives before mentioned, and the Members of the several State Legislatures, and all executive and judicial Officers, both of the United States and of the several States, shall be bound by Oath or Affirmation to support this Constitution; but no religious Test shall ever be required as a qualification to any Office or public Trust under the United States.

ARTICLE VII

The Ratification of the Conventions of nine States shall be sufficient for the Establishment of this Constitution between the States so ratifying the same.

Done in Convention by the Unanimous Consent of the States present the Seventeenth Day of September in the Year of our Lord one thousand seven hundred and Eighty seven, and of the Independence of the United States of America the Twelfth. In Witness whereof We have hereunto subscribed our Names.

Articles in Addition to, and Amendment of, the Constitution of the United States of America, Proposed by Congress, and Ratified by the Legislatures of the Several States, Pursuant to the Fifth Article of the Original Constitution.

AMENDMENT I [1791]

Congress shall make no law respecting an establishment of religion, or prohibiting the free exercsie thereof; or abridging the freedom of speech, or of the press; or the right of the people peaceably to assemble, and to petition the Government for a redress of grievances.

AMENDMENT II [1791]

A well regulated Militia, being necessary to the security of a free State, the right of the people to keep and bear Arms, shall not be infringed.

AMENDMENT III [1791]

No Soldier shall, in time of peace, be quartered in any house, without the consent of the Owner, nor in time of war, but in a manner to be prescribed by law.

AMENDMENT IV [1791]

The right of the people to be secure in their persons, houses, papers, and effects, against unreasonable searches and seizures, shall not be violated, and no Warrants shall issue, but upon probable cause, supported by Oath or affirmation, and particularly describing the place to be searched, and the persons or things to be seized.

AMENDMENT V [1791]

No person shall be held to answer for a capital or otherwise infamous crime, unless on a presentment or indictment of a Grand Jury, except in cases arising in the land or naval forces, or in the Militia, when in actual service in time of War or public danger; nor shall any person be subject for the same offence to be twice put in jeopardy of life or limb; nor shall be compelled in any criminal case to be a witness against himself, nor be deprived of life, liberty, or property, without due process of law; nor shall private property be taken for public use, without just compensation.

AMENDMENT VI [1791]

In all criminal prosecutions, the accused shall enjoy the right to a speedy and public trial, by an impartial jury of the State and district wherein the crime shall have been committed, which district shall have been previously ascertained by law, and to be informed of the nature and cause of the accusation; to be confronted with the witnesses against him; to have compulsory process for obtaining witnesses in his favor, and to have the Assistance of Counsel for his defence.

AMENDMENT VII [1791]

In Suits at common law, where the value in controversy shall exceed twenty dollars, the right of trial by jury shall be preserved, and no fact tried by a jury, shall be otherwsie re-examined in any Court of the United States, than according to the rules of the common law.

AMENDMENT VIII [1791]

Excessive bail shall not be required, nor excessive fines imposed, nor cruel and unusual punishments inflicted.

AMENDMENT IX [1791]

The enumeration in the Constitution, of certain rights, shall not be construed to deny or disparage others retained by the people.

AMENDMENT X [1791]

The powers not delegated to the United States by the Constitution, nor prohibited by it to the States, are reserved to the States respectively, or to the people.

AMENDMENT XI [1798]

The Judicial power of the United States shall not be construed to extend to any suit in law or equity, commenced or prosecuted against one of the United States by Citizens of another State, or by Citizens or Subjects of any Foreign State.

AMENDMENT XII [1804]

The Electors shall meet in their respective States and vote by ballot for President and Vice President, one of whom, at least, shall not be an inhabitant of the same States with themselves; they shall name in their ballots the person voted for as President, and in distinct ballots the person voted for as Vice-President, and they shall make distinct lists of all persons voted for as President, and of all persons voted for as Vice-President, and of the number of votes for each, which lists they shall sign and certify, and transmit sealed to the seat of the government of the United States, directed to the President of the Senate;—The President of the Senate shall, in the presence of the Senate and House of Representatives, open all the certificates and the votes shall then be counted;—The person having the greatest number of votes for President, shall be the President, if such number be a majority of the whole number of Electors appointed; and if no person have such majority, then from the persons having the highest numbers not exceeding three on the list of those voted for as President, the House of Representatives shall choose immediately, by ballot, the President. But in choosing the President, the votes shall be taken by states, the representation from each state having one vote; a quorum for this purpose shall consist of a member or members from two-thirds of the states, and a majority of all the states shall be necessary to a choice. And if the House of Representatives shall not choose a President whenever the right of choice shall devolve upon them, before the fourth day of March next following, then the Vice-President shall act as President, as in the case of the death or other constitutional disability of the President.—The person having the greatest number of votes as Vice-President, shall be the Vice-President, if such number be a majority of the whole number of Electors appointed, and if no person have a majority, then from the two highest numbers on the list, the Senate shall choose the Vice-President; a quorum for the purpose shall consist of two-thirds of the whole number of Senators, and a majority of the whole number shall be necessary to a choice. But no person constitutionally ineligible to the office of President shall be eligible to that of Vice-President of the United States.

AMENDMENT XIII [1865]

Seciton 1. Neither slavery nor involuntary servitude, except as a punishment for crime whereof the party shall have been duly convicted, shall existed within the United States, or any place subject to their jurisdiction.

Section 2. Congress shall have power to enforce this article by appropriate legislation.

AMENDMENT XIV [1868]

Section 1. All persons born or naturalized in the United States, and subject to the jurisdiction thereof, are citizens of the United States and of the State wherein they reside. No State shall make or enforce any law which shall abridge the privileges or immunities of citizens of the United States; nor shall any State deprive any person of life, liberty, or property, without due process of law; nor deny to any person within its jurisdiction the equal protection of the laws.

Section 2. Representatives shall be apportioned among the several States according to their respective numbers, counting the whole number of persons in each State, excluding Indians not taxed. But when the right to vote at any election for the choice of electors for President and Vice President of the United States, Representatives in Congress, the Executive and Judicial officers of a State, or the members of the Legislature thereof, is denied to any of the male inhabitants of such State, being twenty-one years of age, and citizens of the United States, or in any way abridged, except for participation in rebellion, or other crime, the basis of representation therein shall be reduced in the proportion which the number of such male citizens shall bear to the whole number of male citizens twenty-one years of age in such State.

Section 3. No person shall be a Senator or Representative in Congress, or elector of Presiednt and Vice President, or hold any office, civil or military, under the United States, or under any State, who, having previously taken an oath, as a member of Congress, or as an officer of the United States, or as a member of any State legislature, or as an executive or judicial officer of any State, to support the Constitution of the United States, shall have engaged in insurrection or rebellion against the same, or given aid or comfort to the enemies thereof. But Congress may by a vote of two-thirds of each House, remove such disability.

Section 4. The validity of the public debt of the United States, authorized by law, including debts incurred for payment of pensions and bounties for services in suppressing insurrection or rebellion, shall not be questioned. But neither the United States nor any State shall assume or pay any debt or obligation incurred in aid of insurrection or rebellion against the United States, or any claim for the loss or emancipation of any slave; but all such debts, obligations, and claims shall be held illegal and void.

Section 5. The Congress shall have the power to enforce, by appropriate legislation, the provisions of this article.

AMENDMENT XV [1870]

Section 1. The right of citizens of the United States to vote shall not be denied or abridged by the United States or by any State on account of race, color, or previous condition of servitude—

Section 2. The Congress shall have power to enforce this article by appropriate legislation.

AMENDMENT XVI [1913]

The Congress shall have power to lay and collect taxes on incomes, from whatever source derived, without apportionment among the several States, and without regard to any census or enumeration.

AMENDMENT XVII [1913]

The Senate of the United States shall be composed of two Senators from each State, elected by the people thereof, for six years; and each Senator shall have one vote. The electors in each State shall have the qualifications requisite for electors of the most numerous branch of the State legislatures.

When vacancies happen in the representation of any State in the Senate, the executive authority of such State shall issue writs of election to fill such vacancies: *Provided,* That the legislature of any State may empower the executive thereof to make temporary appointments until the people fill the vacancies by election as the legislature may direct.

This amendment shall not be so construed as to affect the election or term of any Senator chosen before it becomes valid as part of the Constitution.

AMENDMENT XVIII [1919]

Section 1. After one year from the ratification of this article the manufacture, sale, or transportation of intoxicating liquors within, the importation thereof into, or the exportation thereof from the United States and all territory subject to the jurisdiction thereof for beverage purposes is hereby prohibited.

Section 2. The Congress and the several States shall have concurrent power to enforce this article by appropriate legislation.

Section 3. This article shall be inoperative unless it shall have been ratified as an amendment to the Constitution by the legislatures of the several States, as provided in the Constitution, within seven years from the date of the submission hereof to the States by the Congress.

AMENDMENT XIX [1920]

The right of citizens of the United States to vote shall not be denied or abridged by the United States or by any State on account of sex.

Congress shall have power to enforce this article by appropriate legislation.

AMENDMENT XX [1933]

Section 1. The terms of the President and Vice President shall end at noon on the 20th day of January, and the terms of Senators and Representatives at noon on the 3d day of January, of the years in which such terms would have ended if this article had not been ratified; and the terms of their successors shall then begin.

Section 2. The Congress shall assemble at least once in every year, and such meeting shall begin at noon on the 3d day of January, unless they shall by law appoint a different day.

Section 3. If, at the time fixed for the beginning of the term of the President, the President elect shall have died, the Vice President elect shall become President. If a President shall not have been chosen before the time fixed for the beginning of his term, or if the President elect shall have failed to qualify, then the Vice President elect shall act as President until a President shall have qualified; and the Congress may by law provide for the case wherein neither a President elect nor a Vice President elect shall have qualified, declaring who shall then act as President, or the manner in which one who is to act shall be selected, and such person shall act accordingly until a President or Vice President shall have qualified.

Section 4. The Congress may by law provide for the case of the death of any of the persons from whom the House of Representatives may choose a President whenever the right of choice shall have devolved upon them, and for the case of the death of any of the persons from whom the Senate may choose a Vice President whenever the right of choice shall have devolved upon them.

Section 5. Sections 1 and 2 shall take effect on the 15th day of October following the ratification of this article.

Section 6. This article shall be inoperative unless it shall have been ratified as an amendment to the Constitution by the legislatures of three-fourths of the several States within seven years from the date of its submission.

AMENDMENT XXI [1933]

Section 1. The eighteenth article of amendment to the Constitution of the United States is hereby repealed.

Section 2. The transportation or importation into any State, Territory, or possession of the United States for delivery or use therein of intoxicating liquors, in violation of the laws thereof, is hereby prohibited.

Section 3. This article shall be inoperative unless it shall have been ratified as an amendment to the Constitution by conventions in the several States, as provided in the Constitution, within seven years from the date of the submission hereof to the States by the Congress.

AMENDMENT XXII [1951]

No person shall be elected to the office of the President more than twice, and no person who has held the office of President, or acted as President, for more than two years of a term to which some other person was elected President shall be elected to the office of the President more than once.

But this Article shall not apply to any person holding the office of President when this Article was proposed by the Congress, and shall not prevent any person who may be holding the office of President, or acting as President, during the term within which this Article becomes operative from holding the office of President or acting as President during the remainder of such term.

AMENDMENT XXIII [1961]

Section 1. The District constituting the seat of Government of the United States shall appoint in such manner as the Congress may direct:

A number of electors of President and Vice President equal to the whole number of Senators and Representatives in Congress to which the District would be entitled if it were a State, but in no event more than the least populous State; they shall be in addition to those appointed by the States, but they shall be considered, for the purposes of the election of President and Vice President, to be electors appointed by a State; and they shall meet in the District and perform such duties as provided by the twelfth article of amendment.

Section 2. The Congress shall have power to enforce this article by appropriate legislation.

AMENDMENT XXIV [1964]

Section 1. The right of citizens of the United States to vote in any primary or other election for President or Vice President, for electors for President or Vice President, or for Senator or Representative in Congress, shall not be denied or abridged by the United States or any State by reason of failure to pay any poll tax or other tax.

Section 2. The Congress shall have the power to enforce this article by appropriate legislation.

AMENDMENT XXV [1967]

Section 1. In case of the removal of the President from office or his death or resignation, the Vice President shall become President.

Section 2. Whenever there is a vacancy in the office of the Vice President, the President shall nominate a Vice President who shall take the office upon confirmation by a majority vote of both houses of Congress.

Section 3. Whenever the President transmits to the President pro tempore of the Senate and the Speaker of the House of Representatives his written declaration that he is unable to discharge the powers and duties of his office, and until he transmits to them a written declaration to the contrary, such powers and duties shall be discharged by the Vice President as Acting President.

Section 4. Whenever the Vice President and a majority of either the principal officers of the executive departments, or of such other body as Congress may by law provide, transmit to the President pro tempore of the Senate and the Speaker of the House of Representatives their written declaration that the President is unable to discharge the powers and duties of his office, the Vice President shall immediately assume the powers and duties of the office as Acting President.

Thereafter, when the President transmits to the President pro tempore of the Senate and the Speaker of the House of Representatives his written declaration that no inability exists, he shall resume the powers and duties of his office unless the Vice President and a majority of either the principal officers of the executive departments, or of such other body as Congress may by law provide, transmit within four days to the President pro tempore of the Senate and the Speaker of the House of Representatives their written declaration that the President is unable to discharge the powers and duties of his office. Thereupon Congress shall decide the issue, assembling within 48 hours for that purpose if not in session. If the Congress, within 21 days after receipt of the latter written declaration, or, if Congress is not in session, within 21 days after Congress is required to assemble, determines by two-thirds vote of both houses that the President is unable to discharge the powers and duties of his office, the Vice President shall continue to discharge the same as Acting President; otherwise, the President shall resume the powers and duties of his office.

AMENDMENT XXVI [1971]

Section 1. The right of citizens of the United States, who are 18 years of age or older, to vote shall not be denied or abridged by the United States or any state on account of age.

Section 2. The Congress shall have the power to enforce this article by appropriate legislation.

Presidential Elections

Year	Candidates	Party	Popular Vote	Electoral Vote
1789	**George Washington**			69
	John Adams			34
	Others			35
1792	**George Washington**			132
	John Adams			77
	George Clinton			50
	Others			5
1796	**John Adams**	Federalist		71
	Thomas Jefferson	Democratic-Republican		68
	Thomas Pinckney	Federalist		59
	Aaron Burr	Democratic-Republican		30
	Others			48
1800	**Thomas Jefferson**	Democratic-Republican		73
	Aaron Burr	Democratic-Republican		73
	John Adams	Federalist		65
	Charles C. Pinckney	Federalist		64
1804	**Thomas Jefferson**	Democratic-Republican		162
	Charles C. Pinckney	Federalist		14
1808	**James Madison**	Democratic-Republican		122
	Charles C. Pinckney	Federalist		47
	George Clinton	Independent-Republican		6
1812	**James Madison**	Democratic-Republican		128
	DeWitt Clinton	Federalist		89
1816	**James Monroe**	Democratic-Republican		183
	Rufus King	Federalist		34
1820	**James Monroe**	Democratic-Republican		231
	John Quincy Adams	Independent-Republican		1
1824	**John Quincy Adams**	Democratic-Republican	108,740	84
	Andrew Jackson	Democratic-Republican	153,544	99
	Henry Clay	Democratic-Republican	47,136	37
	William H. Crawford	Democratic-Republican	46,618	41
1828	**Andrew Jackson**	Democratic	647,231	178
	John Quincy Adams	National Republican	509,097	83
1832	**Andrew Jackson**	Democratic	687,502	219
	Henry Clay	National Republican	530,189	49
	William Wirt	Anti-Masonic	33,108	7
	John Floyd	National Republican		11
1836	**Martin Van Buren**	Democratic	761,549	170
	William H. Harrison	Whig	549,567	73
	Hugh L. White	Whig	145,396	26
	Daniel Webster	Whig	41,287	14

Year	Candidates	Party	Popular Vote	Electoral Vote
1840	**William H. Harrison**	Whig	1,275,017	234
	Martin Van Buren	Democratic	1,128,702	60
1844	**James K. Polk**	Democratic	1,337,243	170
	Henry Clay	Whig	1,299,068	105
	James G. Birney	Liberty	62,300	
1848	**Zachary Taylor**	Whig	1,360,101	163
	Lewis Cass	Democratic	1,220,544	127
	Martin Van Buren	Free Soil	291,263	
1852	**Franklin Pierce**	Democratic	1,601,474	254
	Winfield Scott	Whig	1,386,578	42
1856	**James Buchanan**	Democratic	1,838,169	174
	John C. Frémont	Republican	1,335,264	114
	Millard Fillmore	American	874,534	8
1860	**Abraham Lincoln**	Republican	1,865,593	180
	Stephen A. Douglas	Democratic	1,382,713	12
	John C. Breckinridge	Democratic	848,356	72
	John Bell	Constitutional Union	592,906	39
1864	**Abraham Lincoln**	Republican	2,206,938	212
	George B. McClellan	Democratic	1,803,787	21
1868	**Ulysses S. Grant**	Republican	3,013,421	214
	Horatio Seymour	Democratic	2,706,829	80
1872	**Ulysses S. Grant**	Republican	3,596,745	286
	Horace Greeley	Democratic	2,843,446	66
1876	**Rutherford B. Hayes**	Republican	4,036,572	185
	Samuel J. Tilden	Democratic	4,284,020	184
1880	**James A. Garfield**	Republican	4,449,053	214
	Winfield S. Hancock	Democratic	4,442,035	155
	James B. Weaver	Greenback-Labor	308,578	
1884	**Grover Cleveland**	Democratic	4,874,986	219
	James G. Blaine	Republican	4,851,981	182
	Benjamin F. Butler	Greenback-Labor	175,370	
1888	**Benjamin Harrison**	Republican	5,444,337	233
	Grover Cleveland	Democratic	5,540,050	168
1892	**Grover Cleveland**	Democratic	5,554,414	277
	Benjamin Harrison	Republican	5,190,802	145
	James B. Weaver	People's	1,027,329	22
1896	**William McKinley**	Republican	7,035,638	271
	William J. Bryan	Democratic; Populist	6,467,946	176
1900	**William McKinley**	Republican	7,219,530	292
	William J. Bryan	Democratic; Populist	6,356,734	155
1904	**Theodore Roosevelt**	Republican	7,628,834	336
	Alton B. Parker	Democratic	5,084,401	140
	Eugene V. Debs	Socialist	402,460	
1908	**William H. Taft**	Republican	7,679,006	321
	William J. Bryan	Democratic	6,409,106	162
	Eugene V. Debs	Socialist	420,820	
1912	**Woodrow Wilson**	Democratic	6,286,820	435
	Theodore Roosevelt	Progressive	4,126,020	88
	William H. Taft	Republican	3,483,922	8
	Eugene V. Debs	Socialist	897,011	

Year	Candidates	Party	Popular Vote	Electoral Vote
1916	**Woodrow Wilson**	Democratic	9,129,606	277
	Charles E. Hughes	Republican	8,538,221	254
1920	**Warren G. Harding**	Republican	16,152,200	404
	James M. Cox	Democratic	9,147,353	127
	Eugene V. Debs	Socialist	919,799	
1924	**Calvin Coolidge**	Republican	15,725,016	382
	John W. Davis	Democratic	8,385,586	136
	Robert M. LaFollette	Progressive	4,822,856	13
1928	**Herbert C. Hoover**	Republican	21,392,190	444
	Alfred E. Smith	Democratic	15,016,443	87
1932	**Franklin D. Roosevelt**	Democratic	22,809,638	472
	Herbert C. Hoover	Republican	15,758,901	59
	Norman Thomas	Socialist	881,951	
1936	**Franklin D. Roosevelt**	Democratic	27,751,612	523
	Alfred M. Landon	Republican	16,681,913	8
	William Lemke	Union	891,858	
1940	**Franklin D. Roosevelt**	Democratic	27,243,466	449
	Wendell L. Willkie	Republican	22,304,755	82
1944	**Franklin D. Roosevelt** **(Harry S. Truman,** 1945)	Democratic	25,602,505	432
	Thomas E. Dewey	Republican	22,006,278	99
1948	**Harry S. Truman**	Democratic	24,105,812	303
	Thomas E. Dewey	Republican	21,970,065	189
	J. Strom Thurmond	States' Rights	1,169,063	39
	Henry A. Wallace	Progressive	1,157,172	
1952	**Dwight D. Eisenhower**	Republican	33,936,234	442
	Adlai E. Stevenson	Democratic	27,314,992	89
1956	**Dwight D. Eisenhower**	Republican	35,590,472	457
	Adlai E. Stevenson	Democratic	26,022,752	73
1960	**John F. Kennedy** **(Lyndon B. Johnson,** 1963)	Democratic	34,227,096	303
	Richard M. Nixon	Republican	34,108,546	219
1964	**Lyndon B. Johnson**	Democratic	43,126,233	486
	Barry M. Goldwater	Republican	27,174,989	52
1968	**Richard M. Nixon**	Republican	31,783,783	301
	Hubert H. Humphrey	Democratic	31,271,839	191
	George C. Wallace	Amer. Independent	9,899,557	46

Date of Statehood

State	Date	State	Date
Delaware	December 7, 1787	Michigan	January 16, 1837
Pennsylvania	December 12, 1787	Florida	March 3, 1845
New Jersey	December 18, 1787	Texas	December 29, 1845
Georgia	January 2, 1788	Iowa	December 28, 1846
Connecticut	January 9, 1788	Wisconsin	May 29, 1848
Massachusetts	February 6, 1788	California	September 9, 1850
Maryland	April 28, 1788	Minnesota	May 11, 1858
South Carolina	May 23, 1788	Oregon	February 14, 1859
New Hampshire	June 21, 1788	Kansas	January 29, 1861
Virginia	June 25, 1788	West Virginia	June 19, 1863
New York	July 26, 1788	Nevada	October 31, 1864
North Carolina	November 21, 1789	Nebraska	March 1, 1867
Rhode Island	May 29, 1790	Colorado	August 1, 1876
Vermont	March 4, 1791	North Dakota	November 2, 1889
Kentucky	June 1, 1792	South Dakota	November 2, 1889
Tennessee	June 1, 1796	Montana	November 8, 1889
Ohio	March 1, 1803	Washington	November 11, 1889
Louisiana	April 30, 1812	Idaho	July 3, 1890
Indiana	December 11, 1816	Wyoming	July 10, 1890
Mississippi	December 10, 1817	Utah	January 4, 1896
Illinois	December 3, 1818	Oklahoma	November 16, 1907
Alabama	December 14, 1819	New Mexico	January 6, 1912
Maine	March 15, 1820	Arizona	February 14, 1912
Missouri	August 10, 1821	Alaska	January 3, 1959
Arkansas	June 15, 1836	Hawaii	August 21, 1959

Population of the United States

Year	Population
1790	3,929,214
1800	5,308,483
1810	7,239,881
1820	9,638,453
1830	12,860,692
1840	17,063,353
1850	23,191,876
1860	31,443,321
1870	38,558,371
1880	50,155,783
1890	62,947,714
1900	75,994,575
1910	91,972,266
1920	105,710,620
1930	122,775,046
1940	131,669,275
1950	150,697,361
1960	179,323,175
1970	204,765,770

PRESIDENT		VICE PRESIDENT		SECRETARY OF STATE		SECRETARY OF TREASURY	
1. George Washington, Federalist	1789	John Adams	1789	T. Jefferson E. Randolph T. Pickering	1789 1794 1795	Alex. Hamilton Oliver Wolcott	1789 1795
2. John Adams, Federalist	1797	Thomas Jefferson	1797	T. Pickering John Marshall	1797 1800	Oliver Wolcott Samuel Dexter	1797 1801
3. Thomas Jefferson, Republican	1801	Aaron Burr George Clinton	1801 1805	James Madison	1801	Samuel Dexter Albert Gallatin	1801 1801
4. James Madison, Republican	1809	George Clinton Elbridge Gerry	1809 1813	Robert Smith James Monroe	1809 1811	Albert Gallatin G. W. Campbell A. J. Dallas W H. Crawford	1809 1814 1814 1816
5. James Monroe, Republican	1817	D. D. Tompkins	1817	J. Q. Adams	1817	W. H. Crawford	1817
6. John Quincy Adams, Nat'l Rep.	1825	John C. Calhoun	1825	Henry Clay	1825	Richard Rush	1825
7. Andrew Jackson, Democrat	1829	John C. Calhoun Martin Van Buren	1829 1833	M. Van Buren E. Livingston Louis McLane John Forsyth	1829 1831 1833 1834	Sam D. Ingham Louis McLane W. J. Duane Roger B. Taney Levi Woodbury	1820 1831 1833 1833 1834
8. Martin Van Buren, Democratic	1837	Richard M. Johnson	1837	John Forsyth	1837	Levi Woodbury	1837
9. William H. Harrison, Whig	1841	John Tyler	1841	Daniel Webster	1841	Thos. Ewing	1841
10. John Tyler, Whig and Democrat	1841			Daniel Webster Hugh S. Legare Abel P. Upshur John C. Calhoun	1841 1843 1843 1844	Thos. Ewing Walter Forward John C. Spencer Geo. M. Bibb	1841 1841 1843 1844
11. James K. Polk, Democrat	1845	George M. Dallas	1845	James Buchanan	1845	Robt. J. Walker	1845
12. Zachary Taylor, Whig	1849	Millard Fillmore	1849	John M. Clayton	1849	Wm. M. Meredith	1849
13. Millard Fillmore, Whig	1850			Daniel Webster Edward Everett	1850 1852	Thomas Corwin	1850
14. Franklin Pierce, Democratic	1853	William R. D. King	1853	W. L. Marcy	1853	James Guthrie	1853
15. James Buchanan, Democratic	1857	John C. Breckinridge	1857	Lewis Cass J. S. Black	1857 1860	Howell Cobb Philip F. Thomas John A. Dix	1857 1860 1861
16. Abraham Lincoln, Republican	1861	Hannibal Hamlin Andrew Johnson	1861 1865	W. H. Seward	1861	Salmon P. Chase W. P. Fessenden Hugh McCulloch	1861 1864 1865

SECRETARY OF WAR		ATTORNEY GENERAL		POSTMASTER GENERAL*		SECRETARY OF NAVY		SECRETARY OF INTERIOR	
Henry Knox	1789	E. Randolph	1789	Samuel Osgood	1789				
T. Pickering	1795	Wm. Bradford	1794	Tim Pickering	1791				
Jas. McHenry	1796	Charles Lee	1795	Jos. Habersham	1795				
Jas. McHenry	1797	Charles Lee	1797	Jos. Habersham	1797	Benj. Stoddert	1798		
John Marshall	1800	Theo. Parsons	1801						
Sam'l Dexter	1800								
R. Griswold	1801								
H. Dearborn	1801	Levi Lincoln	1801	Jos. Habersham	1801	Benj. Stoddert	1801		
		Robert Smith	1805	Gideon Granger	1801	Robert Smith	1801		
		J. Breckinridge	1805			J. Crowninshield	1805		
		C. A. Rodney	1807						
Wm. Eustis	1809	C. A. Rodney	1809	Gideon Granger	1809	Paul Hamilton	1809		
J. Armstrong	1813	Wm. Pinkney	1811	R. J. Meigs, Jr.	1814	William Jones	1813		
James Monroe	1814	Richard Rush	1814			B. W. Crowninshield	1814		
W. H. Crawford	1815								
Isaac Shelby	1817	Richard Rush	1817	R. J. Meigs, Jr.	1817	B. W. Crowninshield	1817		
Geo. Graham	1817	William Wirt	1817	John McLean	1823	Smith Thompson	1818		
J. C. Calhoun	1817					S. L. Southard	1823		
Jas. Barbour	1825	William Wirt	1825	John McLean	1825	S. L. Southard	1825		
Peter B. Porter	1828								
John H. Eaton	1829	John M. Berrien	1829	Wm. T. Barry	1829	John Branch	1829		
Lewis Cass	1831	Roger B. Taney	1831	Amos Kendall	1835	Levi Woodbury	1831		
B. F. Butler	1837	B. F. Butler	1833			Mahlon Dickerson	1834		
Joel R. Poinsett	1837	B. F. Butler	1837	Amos Kendall	1837	Mahlon Dickerson	1837		
		Felix Grundy	1838	John M. Niles	1840	Jas. K. Paulding	1838		
		H. D. Gilpin	1840						
John Bell	1841	J. J. Crittenden	1841	Francis Granger	1841	George E. Badger	1841		
John Bell	1841	J. J. Crittenden	1841	Francis Granger	1841	George E. Badger	1841		
John McLean	1841	Hugh S. Legare	1841	C. A. Wickliffe	1841	Abel Upshur	1841		
J. C. Spencer	1841	John Nelson	1843			David Henshaw	1843		
Jas. M. Porter	1843					Thomas W. Gilmer	1844		
Wm. Wilkins	1844					John Y. Mason	1844		
Wm. L. Marcy	1845	John Y. Mason	1845	Cave Johnson	1845	George Bancroft	1845		
		Nathan Clifford	1846			John Y. Mason	1846		
		Isaac Toucey	1848						
G. W. Crawford	1849	Reverdy Johnson	1849	Jacob Collamer	1849	Wm. B. Preston	1849	Thomas Ewing	1849
C. M. Conrad	1850	J. J. Crittenden	1850	Nathan K. Hall	1850	Wm. A. Graham	1850	A. H. Stuart	1850
				Sam D. Hubbard	1852	John P. Kennedy	1852		
Jefferson Davis	1853	Caleb Cushing	1853	James Campbell	1853	James C. Dobbin	1853	Rob't. McClelland	1853
John B. Floyd	1857	J. S. Black	1857	Aaron V. Brown	1857	Isaac Toucey	1857	Jacob Thompson	1857
Joseph Holt	1861	Edw. M. Stanton	1860	Joseph Holt	1859				
S. Cameron	1861	Edward Bates	1861	Horatio King	1861	Gideon Welles	1861	Caleb B. Smith	1861
E. M. Stanton	1862	Titian J Coffey	1863	M'tgomery Blair	1861			John P. Usher	1863
		James Speed	1864	Wm. Dennison	1864				

*Not in Cabinet until 1829.

PRESIDENT		VICE PRESIDENT		SECRETARY OF STATE		SECRETARY OF TREASURY		SECRETARY OF WAR	
17. Andrew Johnson Unionist	1865			Wm. H. Seward	1865	Hugh McCulloch	1865	E. M. Stanton	1865
								U. S. Grant	1867
								L. Thomas	1868
								J. M. Schofield	1868
18. Ulysses S. Grant Republican	1869	Schuyler Colfax	1869	E. B. Washburne	1869	Geo. S. Boutwell	1869	J. A. Rawlins	1869
		Henry Wilson	1873	Hamilton Fish	1869	W. A. Richardson	1873	W. T. Sherman	1869
						Benj. H. Bristow	1874	W. W. Belknap	1869
						Lot M. Morrill	1876	Alphonso Taft	1876
								J. D. Cameron	1876
19. Rutherford B. Hayes Republican	1877	William A. Wheeler	1877	W. M. Evarts	1877	John Sherman	1877	G. W. McCrary	1877
								Alex. Ramsey	1879
20. James A. Garfield Republican	1881	Chester A. Arthur	1881	James G. Blaine	1881	Wm. Windom	1881	R. T. Lincoln	1881
21. Chester A. Arthur Republican	1881			F. T. Frelinghuysen	1881	Chas. J. Folger	1881	R. T. Lincoln	1881
						W. Q. Gresham	1884		
						Hugh McCulloch	1884		
22. Grover Cleveland Democratic	1885	T. A. Hendricks	1885	Thos. F. Bayard	1885	Daniel Manning	1885	W. C. Endicott	1885
						Chas. S. Fairchild	1887		
23. Benjamin Harrison Republican	1889	Levi P. Morton	1889	James G Blaine	1889	Wm. Windom	1889	R. Proctor	1889
				John W. Foster	1892	Charles Foster	1891	S. B. Elkins	1891
24. Grover Cleveland Democratic	1893	Adlai E. Stevenson	1893	W. Q. Gresham	1893	John G. Carlisle	1893	D. S. Lamont	1893
				Richard Olney	1895				
25. William McKinley Republican	1897	Garret A. Hobart	1897	John Sherman	1897	Lyman J. Gage	1897	R. A. Alger	1897
		Theodore Roosevelt	1901	Wm. R. Day	1897			Elihu Root	1899
				John Hay	1898				
26. Theodore Roosevelt Republican	1901	Chas. W. Fairbanks	1905	John Hay	1901	Lyman J. Gage	1901	Elihu Root	1901
				Elihu Root	1905	Leslie M. Shaw	1902	Wm. H. Taft	1904
				Robert Bacon	1909	G. B. Cortelyou	1907	Luke E. Wright	1908
27. William H. Taft Republican	1909	James S. Sherman	1909	P. C. Knox	1909	F. MacVeagh	1909	J. M. Dickinson	1909
								H. L. Stimson	1911
28. Woodrow Wilson Democratic	1913	Thomas R. Marshall	1913	Wm. J. Bryan	1913	W. G. McAdoo	1913	L. M. Garrison	1913
				Robert Lansing	1915	Carter Glass	1918	N. D. Baker	1916
				Bainbridge Colby	1920	D. F. Houston	1920		
29. Warren G. Harding Republican	1921	Calvin Coolidge	1921	Chas. E Hughes	1921	Andrew W. Mellon	1921	John W. Weeks	1921
30. Calvin Coolidge Republican	1923	Charles G. Dawes	1925	Chas. E. Hughes	1923	Andrew W. Mellon	1923	John W. Weeks	1923
				Frank B. Kellogg	1925			Dwight F. Davis	1925
31. Herbert Hoover Republican	1929	Charles Curtis	1929	H. L. Stimson	1929	Andrew W. Mellon	1929	James W. Good	1929
						Ogden L. Mills	1932	P. J. Hurley	1929
32. Franklin D. Roosevelt Democratic	1933	John Nance Garner	1933	Cordell Hull	1933	Wm. H. Woodin	1933	Geo. H. Dern	1933
		Henry A. Wallace	1941	E. R. Stettinius, Jr.	1944	Henry Morgenthau, Jr.	1934	H A. Woodring	1936
		Harry S. Truman	1945					H. L. Stimson	1940
33. Harry S. Truman Democratic	1945	Alben W. Barkley	1949	James F. Byrnes	1945	Fred M. Vinson	1945	Robt. H. Patterson	1945
				Geo. C. Marshall	1947	John W. Snyder	1946	K. C. Royall	1947
				Dean G. Acheson	1949			*	
34. Dwight D. Eisenhower Republican	1953	Richard M. Nixon	1953	John Foster Dulles	1953	George C. Humphrey	1953		
				Christian Herter	1959	Robert B. Anderson	1957		
35. John F. Kennedy Democratic	1961	Lyndon B. Johnson	1961	Dean Rusk	1961	C. Douglas Dillon	1961		
36. Lyndon B. Johnson Democratic	1963	Hubert H. Humphrey	1965			Henry H. Fowler	1965		
37. Richard M. Nixon Republican	1969	Spiro T. Agnew	1969	William P. Rogers	1969	David M. Kennedy	1969		

Lost Cabinet status in 1947.

ATTORNEY GENERAL		POSTMASTER GENERAL		SECRETARY OF NAVY		SECRETARY OF INTERIOR		SECRETARY OF AGRICULTURE		OTHER MEMBERS
James Speed	1865	Wm. Dennison	1865	Gideon Welles	1865	John P. Usher	1865			*Secretary of Commerce and Labor*
Henry Stanbery	1866	A. W. Randall	1866			James Harlan	1865	Cabinet status		G. B. Cortelyou 1903
Wm. M. Evarts	1868					O. H. Browning	1866	since 1889.		Victor H. Metcalf 1904
										O. S. Straus 1907
E. R. Hoar	1869	J. A. J. Creswell	1869	Adolph E. Borie	1869	Jacob D. Cox	1869			Chas. Nagel 1909
A. T. Ackerman	1870	Jas. W. Marshall	1874	Geo. M. Robeson	1869	C. Delano	1870			(Department divided, 1913)
Geo. H. Williams	1871	Marshall Jewell	1874			Zach. Chandler	1875			
Edw. Pierrepont	1875	Jas. N. Tyner	1876							*Secretary of Commerce*
Alphonso Taft	1876									W. C. Redfield 1913
Chas. Devens	1877	David M. Key	1877	R. W. Thompson	1887	Carl Schurz	1877			J. W. Alexander 1919
		H. Maynard	1880	Nathan Goff, Jr.	1881					H. C. Hoover 1921
W. MacVeagh	1881	T. L. James	1881	W. H. Hunt	1881	S. J. Kirkwood	1881			H. C. Hoover 1925
										W. F. Whiting 1928
B. H. Brewster	1881	T. O. Howe	1881	W. E. Chandler	1881	Henry M. Teller	1881			R. P. Lamont 1929
		W. Q. Gresham	1883							R. D. Chapin 1932
		Frank Hatton	1884							D. C. Roper 1933
A. H. Garland	1885	Wm. F. Vilas	1885	W. C. Whitney	1885	L. Q. C. Lamar	1885	N. J. Colman	1889	H. L. Hopkins 1939
		D. M. Dickinson	1888			Wm. F. Vilas	1888			Jesse Jones 1940
W. H. H. Miller	1889	J. Wanamaker	1889	Benj. F. Tracy	1889	John W. Noble	1889	J. M. Rusk	1889	Henry A. Wallace 1945
										W. Averell Harriman 1946
R. Olney	1893	W. S. Bissell	1893	Hilary A.		Hoke Smith	1893	J. S. Morton	1893	Charles W. Sawyer 1948
J. Harmon	1895	W. L. Wilson	1895	Herbert		D. R. Francis	1896			Sinclair Weeks 1953
										Lewis L. Strauss 1958
J. McKenna	1897	James A. Gary	1897	John D. Long	1897	C. N. Bliss	1897	James Wilson	1897	Frederick H. Mueller 1959
J. W. Griggs	1897	Chas E. Smith	1898			E. A. Hitchcock	1899			Luther H. Hodges 1961
P. C. Knox	1901									J. Thomas Connor 1964
P. C. Knox	1901	Chas. E. Smith	1901	John D. Long	1901	E. A. Hitchcock	1901	James Wilson	1901	A. B. Trowbridge 1967
W. H. Moody	1904	Henry C. Payne	1902	Wm. H. Moody	1902	J. R. Garfield	1907			C. R. Smith 1968
C. J. Bonaparte	1907	Robt. J. Wynne	1904	Paul Morton	1904					Maurice H. Stans 1969
		G. B. Cortelyou	1905	C. J. Bonaparte	1905					
		G. von L. Meyer	1907	V. H. Metcalf	1907					*Secretary of Labor*
				T. H. Newberry	1908					W. B. Wilson 1913
G. W. Wicker-		F. H. Hitchcock	1909	G. von L. Meyer	1909	R. A. Ballinger	1909	James Wilson	1909	J. J. Davis 1921
sham	1909					W. L. Fisher	1911			W. N. Doak 1930
										Frences Perkins 1933
J. C. Mc-		A. S. Burleson	1913	Josephus Daniels	1913	F. K. Lane	1913	D. F. Houston	1913	L. B. Schwellenbach 1945
Reynolds	1913					J. B. Payne	1920	E. T. Meredith	1920	M. J. Tobin 1948
T. W. Gregory	1914									M. P. Durkin 1953
A. M. Palmer	1919									James P. Mitchell 1953
H. M.		Will H. Hays	1921	Edwin Denby	1921	Albert B. Fall	1921	H. C. Wallace	1921	Arthur J. Goldberg 1961
Daugherty	1921	Hubert Work	1922			Hubert Work	1923			W. Willard Wirtz 1962
		Harry S. New	1923							George P. Shultz 1969
										James D. Hodgson 1970
H. M.		Harry S. New	1923	Edwin Denby	1923	Hubert Work	1923	H. M. Gore	1924	
Daugherty	1923			Curtis D.		Roy O. West	1928	W. M. Jardine	1925	*Secretary of Defense*
Harlan F. Stone	1924			Wilbur	1924					James V. Forrestal 1947
John G. Sargent	1925									Louis A. Johnson 1949
Wm. D. Mitchell	1929	Walter F.		Chas. F. Adams	1929	Ray L. Wilbur	1929	Arthur M.		George C. Marshall 1950
		Brown	1929					Hyde	1929	Robert A. Lovett 1951
H. S. Cummings	1933	James A. Farley	1933	Claude A.		Harold L. Ickes	1933	H. A. Wallace	1933	Charles E. Wison 1953
Frank Murphy	1939	Frank C.		Swanson	1933			C. R. Wickard	1940	Neil McElroy 1957
Robt. H.		Walker	1940	Chas. Edison	1940					Thomas Gates 1960
Jackson	1940			Frank Knox	1940					Robert S. McNamara 1961
Francis Biddle	1941			James V.						Clark M. Clifford 1968
				Forrestal	1944					Melvin R. Laird 1969
Tom C. Clark	1945	Robt. E.		James V.		Harold L. Ickes	1945	C. P. Anderson	1945	*Secretary of Health, Education, and Welfare*
J. H. McGrath	1949	Hannegan	1945	Forrestal	1945	Julius A. Krug	1946	C. F. Brannan	1948	Oveta Culp Hobby 1953
James P.		Jesse L.		†		O. L. Chapman	1951			Marion B. Folsom 1955
McGranery	1952	Donaldson	1947							Arthur S. Flemming 1958
Herbert		Arthur E.				Douglas		Ezra T.		Abraham A. Ribicoff 1961
Brownell, Jr.	1953	Summerfield	1953			McKay	1953	Benson	1953	A. J. Celebrezze 1962
William P.						Fred Seaton	1956			John W. Gardner 1965
Rogers	1957									Wilbur J. Cohen 1968
Robert F.		J. Edward Day	1961			Stewart L.		Orville L.		Robert H. Finch 1969
Kennedy	1961	John A.				Udall	1961	Freeman	1961	E. L. Richardson 1970
		Gronouski	1963							*Secretary of Housing and Urban Development*
Nicholas deB.		Lawrence F.								Robert C. Weaver 1966
Katzenbach	1965	O'Brien	1965							George W. Romney 1969
Ramsey Clark	1967	W. Marvin				Walter J. Hickel	1969	Clifford M.		*Secretary of Transportation*
John N. Mitchell	1969	Watson	1968					Hardin	1969	Alan S. Boyd 1967
		Winton M.								John A. Volpe 1969
		Blount	1969							

†*Lost Cabinet status in 1947.*

ILLUSTRATION CREDITS

Numbers refer to portfolio and text pages.

Early American Folk Art

1. Massachusetts Historical Society, Boston. 4. New York State Historical Assoc., Cooperstown, N.Y. 5. Abby Aldrich Rockefeller Folk Art Collection, Williamsburg, Va. 6. Downtown Gallery, New York. Photo: Hermann Kessler. 6. Index of American Design, National Gallery of Art, Washington, D.C. 6. National Gallery of Art, Washington, D.C. Gift of Edgar William and Bernice Chrysler Garbisch. 7. Index of American Design, National Gallery of Art, Washington D.C. 8. Abby Aldrich Rockefeller Folk Art Collection, Williamsburg, Va. 9. Downtown Gallery, New York. Photo: Hermann Kessler. 10. Index of American Design, National Gallery of Art, Washington, D.C. 10. Abby Aldrich Rockefeller Folk Art Collection, Williamsburg, Va. 11. Downtown Gallery, New York. Photo: Hermann Kessler. 12. Photo: Edith Reichmann. 12. Photo: Edith Reichmann. 12. Essex Institute, Salem, Mass. 13. Wadsworth Atheneum, Hartford, Conn. 14. Museum of the City of New York. Courtesy of Newark Museum. 14. Museum of Fine Arts, Boston. 15. Index of American Design, National Gallery of Art, Washington, D.C. 16. Index of American Design, National Gallery of Art, Washington, D.C. 16. Owned by the Henry Ford Museum, Dearborn, Mich. 16. Index of American Design, National Gallery of Art, Washington, D.C.

The Spanish In the Southwest

1. Royal Ontario Museum, Toronto, Canada. 5. M. H. DeYoung Museum, San Francisco, on loan to the Society of California Pioneers, J. Schopplein, photographer. 6. The John Carter Brown Library, Brown University. 7. Manuscript Division, The New York Public Library. 8. Index of American Design, National Gallery of Art, Washington, D.C. 9. Index of American Design, National Gallery of Art, Washington, D.C. 10. Index of American Design, National Gallery of Art, Washington, D.C. 11. Index of American Design, National Gallery of Art, Washington, D.C. 12. Bancroft Library, University of California. 13. Photo: Edith Reichmann. 14. Photo: Edith Reichmann. 15. Index of American Design, National Gallery of Art, Washington, D.C. 16. Index of American Design, National Gallery of Art, Washington, D.C.

Nineteenth-Century Posters

1. Library of Congress. 5. Library of Congress. 6. Culver Pictures, Inc. 7. The New York Historical Society. 8. The New York Historical Society. 9. Marine Historical Association, Mystic, Conn. 10. Rutherford B. Hayes Library. 11. Library of Congress. 12. Library of Congress. 13. New Hampshire Historical Society. 14. The New York Historical Society. 15. The New York Historical Society. 16. The New York Historical Society.

A Land of Immigrants

1. Culver Pictures, Inc. 3. The New York Public Library. 3. Sy Seidman. 4. Library of Congress. 4. Brown Brothers. 7. Brown Brothers. 7. George Eastman House Collection, Lewis W. Hine, photographer. 8. Library of Congress. 9. Library of Congress. 10. Brown Brothers. 11. Index of American Design, National Gallery of Art, Washington, D.C. 12. Henri Cartier-Bresson, Magnum. 13. World Wide Photos. 14. Weyerhaeuser Company. 15. Weyerhaeuser Company. 16. Culver Pictures, Inc.

America as Seen by the Black Artist

1. Pennsylvania Academy of Fine Arts. 2. Lloyd Yearwood. 5. Hampton Institute, Va. 7. The Phillips Collection, Washington, D.C. 8. The Robert Carlen Galleries, Collection of Dr. & Mrs. Bernard J. Ronis, Philadelphia. 9. Boston Atheneum. 9. Fisk University, Nashville, Tenn. 10. Collection of the artist, Photo: Sandak, Inc., New York. 11. Cordier & Ekstrom, New York, Photo: Robert S. Crandall. 12. Barnett Aden Gallery, Washington, D.C. 13. Southern University, New Orleans. 14. Collection of the artist, Photo: Sandak, Inc., New York. 15. Courtesy of the artist, Photo: Abdul Hakim RaQuib. 16. Courtesy of the artist, Photo: Abdul Hakim RaQuib.

Text

1. Culver Pictures, Inc. 2. The American Museum of Natural History. 3. The American Museum of Natural History. 6. The British Museum. 8. Rare Book Division, The New York Public Library. 10. Rare Book Division, The New York Public Library. 11. Rare Book Division, The New York Public Library. 14. The Museum of Natural History. 16. Culver Pictures, Inc. 19. Culver Pictures, Inc. 20. Print Division, The New York Public Library. 24. The Bettmann Archive. 25. The Granger Collection. 26. The Granger Collection. 30. The British Museum. 33. Prints Division, The New York Public Library. 40. The New York Historical Society. 42. Culver Pictures, Inc. 44. Rare Book Division, The New York Public Library. 55. Culver Pictures, Inc. 56. Plimoth Plantation. 61. Edith Reichmann. 70. Library of Congress. 71. I. N. Phelps Stokes Collection, The New York Public Library. 73. I. N. Phelps Stokes Collection, The New York Public Library. 84. The Metropolitan Museum of Art. 89. Culver Pictures, Inc. 90. Library of Congress. 91. The New York Historical Society, Landauer Collection. 94. Continental Distilling Corp. of Philadelphia. 101. Massachusetts Historical Society. 103. The Bettmann Archive. 106. Essex Institute, Salem, Mass. 108. Essex Institute, Salem, Mass. 114. Philadelphia Museum of Art. 115. Culver Pictures, Inc. 115. Culver Pictures, Inc. 117. Museum of Fine Arts, Boston. 119. Prints Division, The New York Public Library. 124. Prints Division, The New York Public Library. 131. The New Brunswick Museum. 133. Library of Congress. 136. Prints Division, The New York Public Library. 137. Public Archives of Canada. 141. Piaget—Washington University Gallery of Art, St. Louis. 143. Culver Pictures, Inc. 146. The Granger Collection. 148. Museum of Fine Arts, Boston. 150. The Rhode Island Historical Society. 152. Culver Pictures, Inc. 155. The Metropolitan Museum of Art, New York. 156. The Metropolitan Museum of Art, New York. 166. The Metropolitan Museum of Art, New York. 169. The

Metropolitan Museum of Art, New York. 170. The New York Historical Society. 170. American Antiquarian Society, Mass. 174. Culver Pictures, Inc. 175. The Historical Society of Pennsylvania. 175. The Metropolitan Museum of Art, New York. 178. Culver Pictures, Inc. 179. Brown Brothers. 181. American Antiquarian Society, Mass. 184. The Historical Society of Pennsylvania. 190. Culver Pictures, Inc. 200. Culver Pictures, Inc. 206. I. N. Phelps Stokes Collection, The New York Public Library. 209. Virginia Museum of Fine Arts. 216. New History of the United States. 219. Brown Brothers. 222. Colonial Williamsburg Collection. 223. Museum of Fine Arts, Boston. 226. I. N. Phelps Stokes Collection, The New York Public Library. 231. The New York Historical Society. 239. Fogg Art Museum, Harvard University. 240. Brown Brothers. 243. The Henry Francis du Pont Winterthur Museum. 245. Culver Pictures, Inc. 250. The Granger Collection. 253. Collection of Mrs. T. Coolidge. 255. Culver Pictures, Inc. 263. Montana Historical Society. 263. Missouri Historical Society. 265. Culver Pictures, Inc. 268. The Bettmann Archive. 270. The New York Historical Society. 276. Brown Brothers. 278. Brown Brothers. 279. The New York Historical Society. 283. The New York Public Library, Astor, Lenox and Tilden Foundations. 286. National Portrait Gallery, Washington, D.C. 292. The New York Historical Society. 302. Smithsonian Institution. 303. Smithsonian Institution. 305. Yale University Art Gallery, the Mabel Brady Garvan Collection. 307. The Virginia Museum of Fine Arts. 312. The New York Public Library. 315. Maryland Historical Society. 317. Harry T. Peters Collection, Museum of the City of New York. 319. The New York Historical Society. 326. The Historical Society of Pennsylvania. 331. New York Historical Association, Cooperstown. 332. The New York Public Library, Rare Book Division. 333. National Gallery of Art, Andrew Mellon Collection. 334. Addison Gallery of Art, Phillips Academy, Andover, Mass. 338. J. N. Bartfield Galley, Inc. 339. Missouri Historical Society. 342. The Corcoran Gallery of Art, Washington, D.C. 343. The Virginia Museum of Fine Arts. 345. National Portrait Gallery. 346. The Virginia Museum of Fine Arts. 358. Culver Pictures, Inc. 361. Culver Pictures, Inc. 363. The collection of the Boatmen's National Bank of St. Louis. 365. Houghton Library, Harvard University. 371. Woolaroo Museum, Batlesville, Okla. 378. The New York Public Library. 385. National Gallery of Art, Andrew Mellon Collection. 388. Culver Pictures, Inc. 389. The New York Historical Society.

396. The Baltimore and Ohio Railroad. 400. The New York Public Library. 401. Solomon D. Butcher Collection, Nebraska State Historical Society. 405. Culver Pictures, Inc. 406. The New York Historical Society. 410. Duke University Library. 416. The Bettmann Archive. 417. Honolulu Academy of Arts. 417. Honolulu Academy of Arts. 418. New York Graphic Society, Greenwich, Conn. 420. The Baltimore and Ohio Railroad. 425. The Bettmann Archive. 432. Old Print Shop. 437. Culver Pictures, Inc. 438. The Bettmann Archive. 442. Brown Brothers. 445. The New York Public Library, Rare Book Room. 446. Library of Congress. 447. Harvard University. 450. The New York Public Library. 451. City Art Museum of St. Louis. 451. National Portrait Gallery, Smithsonian Institution. 459. Culver Pictures, Inc. 462. Library of Congress. 468. Harry T. Peters Collection, Museum of the City of New York. 481. Brown Brothers. 489. Brown Brothers. 496. The New York Historical Society. 504. Sy Seidman. 511. Brown Brothers. 512. Culver Pictures, Inc. 517. Brown Brothers. 522. Sy Seidman. 530. Brown Brothers. 540. Sy Seidman. 547. Library of Congress. 554. Library of Congress. 555. Brown Brothers. 562. Library of Congress. 564. The Bett-

mann Archive. 570. Brown Brothers. 580. Illinois State Historical Society. 583. U.S. Signal Corps, Brady Collection in the National Archives. 584. Sy Seidman. 588. Sy Seidman. 598. Library of Congress. 600. The Bettmann Archive. 601. Culver Pictures, Inc. 607. Brown Brothers. 610. The New York Public Library, Stromberg Collection. 616. The Bettmann Archive. 620. Library of Congress. 622. State Historical Society of Colorado. 628. Western History Collections, University of Oklahoma Library. 630. Denver Public Library, Western Collection. 631. Montana Historical Society, Helena. 646. Brown Brothers. 650. The Bettmann Archive. 656. The Pierpont Morgan Library. 659. Culver Pictures, Inc. 660. Brown Brothers. 662. Culver Pictures, Inc. 665. Culver Pictures, Inc. 676. Brown Brothers. 681. Brown Brothers. 687. George Eastman House Collection, Lewis Hine, photographer. 688. Library of Congress. 692. The Bettmann Archive. 700. The Bettmann Archive. 700. Jacob A. Riis Collection, Museum of the City of New York. 703. Brown Brothers. 706. Sy Seidman. 723. The New York Public Library. 725. Brown Brothers. 726. Library of Congress. 728. The Metropolitan Museum of Art, New York. 729. Jefferson College and Medical Center. 730. Ezra Stoller © ESTO. 736. Culver Pictures, Inc. 744. Library of Congress. 747. Brown Brothers. 751. Library of Congress. 756. Library of Congress. 763. The Bettmann Archive. 765. The Bettmann Archive. 766. The Bettmann Archive. 774. Library of Congress. 783. Brown Brothers. 791. The New York Public Library. 793. Theodore Roosevelt Association. 794. United Press International. 797. Library of Congress. 812. Brown Brothers. 819. State Historical Society of Wisconsin. 821. Culver Pictures, Inc. 824. Brown Brothers. 827. Underwood and Underwood. 828. Culver Pictures, Inc. 834. United Press International. 835. U.S. Signal Corps, The National Archives. 842. Culver Pictures, Inc. 847. Culver Pictures, Inc. 850. Culver Pictures, Inc. 859. Brown Brothers. 859. The Bettmann Archive. 861. U.S. Signal Corps, The National Archives. 866. Brown Brothers. 878. Culver Pictures, Inc. 885. Culver Pictures, Inc. 886. Brown Brothers. 887. Culver Pictures, Inc. 895. Culver Pictures, Inc. 898. Culver Pictures, Inc. 900. Culver Pictures, Inc. 902. The Newark Museum. 902. Whitney Museum of American Art. 910. Brown Brothers. 913. Wide World Photos. 919. Wide World Photos. 920. Culver Pictures, Inc. 922. United Press International. 928. The New York Historical Society. 933. Library of Congress. 934. Library of Congress, Dorothea Lange, photographer. 948. On loan from the artist to the Museum of Modern Art, New York. 958. Brown Brothers. 968. United Press International. 976. The National Archives. 977. United Press International. 978. United Press International. 978. Wide World Photos. 980. Wide World Photos. 982. United Press International, Official Marine Corps Photo. 983. United Press International. 990. Fermo Jacobs, Black Star. 993. Brown Brothers. 995. Brown Brothers. 1005. Underwood and Underwood. 1007. United Press International. 1010. UNATIONS (from U.S. Army). 1012. United Press International, Stanley Tretick, photographer. 1023. United Press International. 1025. United Press International. 1036. Burt Glinn, Magnum. 1038. Erich Lessing, Magnum. 1044. Wide World Photos. 1049. United Press International. 1052. Elliott Erwitt, Magnum. 1064. United Press International. 1068. Fred Ward, Black Star. 1070. United Press International. 1074. Burt Glinn, Magnum. 1075. Burk Uzzle, Magnum. 1078. Philip Jones Griffiths, Magnum. 1079. Philip Jones Griffiths, Magnum. 1079. Philip Jones Griffiths, Magnum. 1083. United Press International. 1083. Roger Malloch, Magnum. 1087. Wayne Miller, Magnum. 1089. Bruce Davidson, Magnum.

INDEX

Page numbers in italics refer to illustrations with or without text.

International Cigar Makers Union, 695
international finance in 1920s, 912
International Monetary Fund, 985
Interstate Commerce Act (1887), 656
Interstate Commerce Commission, 656, 664, 881, 889; legislation on, 826, 829
Interstate Highway Act (1956), 1032
"intolerable acts," 152–4
inventions, 301–3, 405, 422, 453; industrialization and, 649, 665; in printing, 723–4
Invincible Armada, 31
Iowa, 406, 478, 818
Iran, 1044; Soviet forces in, 1000
Iraq, 1044, 1045
Irish immigrants, 95, 426, 439, 636, 650, 652, 678–80, 684; anti-British feeling, 750, 752, 777; raids in Canada, 777
Iron Act (1750), 76
iron industry, 422, 423, 481; railroads and, 421; see also steel industry
iron ore, 422, 475, 658–9
Iroquois Indians (Iroquois League), 4, 118, 130–2, 136, 140, 329
Irving, Washington, 332; Sketchbook, 332, 333
Isabella, Queen of Spain, 10–13, 22
isolationism: neutrality legislation, 958–9; nineteenth century, 776–7; after World War I, 949; before World War II, 957–60; in World War II, 963–5, 967
Israel, 1043–4; Arabs in, 1044; Egypt and, 1044–5; U.S. relations with, 1044–5; war with Arabs (1967), 1080–1
Italian immigrants, 678–84
Italy, 801, 804; Albania invaded, 960; Ethiopia invaded, 959; with Germany and Japan, Axis powers, 957, 959, 968; Mussolini's dictatorship, 957; territory after World War I, 867; in Triple Alliance, 843; in World War I, 860; in World War II, 962, 975–6, 994, map, 981
Itata (Chilean ship), 786
Iwo Jima, 980–2
IWW (Industrial Workers of the World), 856, 883

Jackson, Andrew, 313, 346, 475; background and career, 363; and Bank of the United States, 377–83; veto message, 379–80; battle of New Orleans, 280, 282; campaign against Adams, 364–5; character, 365–6; in Democratic Party, 368, 384; in Democratic Republican Party, 344, 364; Eaton affair, 376; in election of 1824, 352; in election of 1828, 362–5, map, 364; in election of 1832, 377, 380–1, map, 281; Florida campaign, 286; in foreign affairs, 367–8; historians' opinions of, 385–6; inauguration, 360, 361; Indian removal policy, 369–72, 402; Kitchen Cabinet, 366–7; portraits, 358, 385;

Jackson, Andrew (cont.)
President, 360, 365–86; South Carolina nullification controversy, 372–7, quotations, 373; spoils system, 366; Supreme Court appointments, 389; and Texas Republic, 478; veto power used, 367; in War of 1812, 280, 282, 284
Jackson, Mrs. Andrew (Rachel), 365
Jackson, Francis James, 272
Jackson, Helen Hunt, A Century of Dishonor, 624
Jackson, Gen. Thomas J. (Stonewall), 554, 557–60, 562–3, 566
Jacksonian democracy, 360–2, 383–6, 442, 834, 941
Jackson State College, 1087
Jamaica, 72, 100; as slave market, 89
James I, King of England, 32, 34, 37, 48, 54, 86; on divine right of kings, 35
James II, King of England, 71, 77, 78; as Duke of York, land grant to, 66, 67
James, Henry, 713, 726–7
James, Marquis, 385
James, William, 438, 713–14, 795
Jameson, J. Franklin, 160
James River, 557
Jamestown, 43–8; Bacon's Rebellion in, 51, 118; slaves in, 89
Japan: atomic bombs on, 982, 983, 984, 993; in Boxer Rebellion, 806; China invaded, 959, 960, 967; disarmament, 950–51; economic growth, 1088; Five Power Treaty (1922), 951; Four Power Treaty (1921), 951; Gentlemen's Agreement with U.S., 684; with Germany and Italy, Axis powers, 957, 959, 968; Hawaii and, 785; immigration from, 679, 684, 884, 955; Lansing–Ishii agreement, 807; Manchuria invaded, 956–7; Okinawa returned to, 1088; Open Door Policy, 807; Panay sinking, 960; Perry's visit to, 416, 417, 776; Philippine fear of, 955; rise of militarism, 955–6; trade with U.S., 482, 776; treaties abrogated by, 957; treaty after World War II, 1005; Twenty-one Demands on China, 807; U.S. policy after World War II, 1005; U.S. relations with, 807; war crimes trials, 994; war with China (1895), 804; war with Russia, 806–7; withdraws from League of Nations, 957; in World War I, 807, 868; in World War II, 967–9, 972–3, 979–83, 1004
Japanese–Americans in World War II, 971
Japanese Exclusion League, 684
Jarratt, Devereaux, on social classes, 97
Java, 416
Java, H.M.S., 280
Jay, John, 209, 476; Chief Justice, 221; Federalist papers, 216; in First Continental Congress, 154; letter to Washington, 192; in Paris treaty negotiations, 181–2; treaty (Jay's

Jay, John (cont.)
Treaty), 233–5, 238, 240, 267; treaty with Spain proposed, 194
Jay, Mrs. John, 194
Jay's Treaty (Treaty of London, 1794), 233–5, 238, 240, 267
jazz, 899
Jazz Age, 897–904
Jazz Singer, The, 899
Jefferson, Thomas, 112, 148, 191, 192, 195, 209, 217, 233, 239, 245, 276, 277, 279, 294, 342, 351, 366, 370, 470; and Adams, friendship renewed, 300; agrarian philosophy, 228, 237, 255, 295, 648; and Bank of the United States, 226–7, 295, 321; and Barbary pirates, 255–6; beliefs and ideas, 237; on Boston Port Bill, 152; and Burr's trial, 266; Constitution, interpretation of, 227, 242, 262; on debts in Virginia, 141; Declaration of Independence, 158–9; democracy of, compared with Jackson's, 360; democratic informality, 252; economic policies, 254–5; in election of 1800, 242, 244; in election of 1804, 264; and embargo, 268–70; family, 253; and Federalists, 237–8; first inaugural address, 253–4, quoted, 251; foreign policy, 229–30; France, admiration for, 229–30; on French Revolution, 229; on Genêt, 230–1; Hamilton as enemy of, 228–9, 236–7; and Hamilton's plan for state debts, 225; interests and talents, 252–3; and judiciary system, 256–7, 310; Kentucky Resolutions, 242, 375; letter from Adams, 351; letter to Breckinridge, 260; letters to Adams, 321, 351; letter to Livingston, 261; letter to Madison, 236; Lewis and Clark expedition sent, 262–3; Louisiana Purchase, 258–62, map, 259; and Madison's nomination for Presidency, 271; minister to France, 192; on Northerners and Southerners, 116–17; Notes on Virginia, 228; President, 244, 252–66, 269–70; retires from politics, 233, 237; in Second Continental Congress, 156; Secretary of State, 220, 221, 229, 233, 237; on Shays's Rebellion, 200; slavery, attitude toward, 255; states' rights, principle, 242; A Summary View of the Rights of British America, 156; Vice President, 238; Virginia education plan, 336; Virginia statute of religious freedom, 187; on Whiskey Rebellion, 236
Jeffersonian party, see Democratic Republicans
Jervis, John B., 318
Jesuits (Society of Jesus), 30
Jewel (ship), 58
Jews: in colonies, 104; as immigrants, 679, 680, 682–4; Nazi extermination of, 979, 980
Johns Hopkins University, 721
Johnson, Andrew: candidate in 1868, 595; early life, 588–9; impeachment

Reid, Whitelaw, 783

relief: for blacks, 917; in Great Depression, 914, 916–18; Hoover's program, 916–18; New Deal measures, 929; Roosevelt's policies, 921, 929

religion: church and state separated, 186–7; evangelism, 440; on frontier, 104; fundamentalism and Scopes trial, 885–6; Great Awakening, 107–11, 434, second, 340–1, 434; middle nineteenth century, 434–5, 439–40, 454, 458, 464; in reform movements, 454, 455, 457, 702; revival meetings, 340–1, *432*, 440, 454; Social Gospel, 702

religion in colonies, 48–50, 54, 59–62, 79, 104–10, 186–7; Pennsylvania, 67–70; Puritan government and, 59–60; Rhode Island, 61–2

religious freedom: in colonies, 50, 62, 70, 79; in state constitutions, 187; Virginia statute, 187

Remagen Bridge, *978*

Rensselaerswyck, 66

representative government: in British possessions, 139–40; in colonies, 32, 46, 50, 57, 59–60, 62–3, 70–1, 127–9; in England, 32–3, 78–9

Republican conventions: 1860, 523–4; 1920, 887

Republican Party: beginning of, 510; blacks in, 739; Compromise of 1877, 606–7, 612; in Eightieth Congress, 998; in elections, *see* elections; elephant as symbol, 730; in Grant administration, 600, 602–3; Halfbreeds, 605, 738, 746–8; in Harding and Coolidge administrations, 888–92; late nineteenth century, 738, 753; Liberal Republicans, 602–3; progressive, 823; Progressive Party: (1911), 831–3, (1924), 892; Radical Republicans, 550–1, 573, 585–93, 596–600; in Reconstruction, 582, 585–96, 600; in Roosevelt administration, 933; slavery opposed, 523–4; Stalwarts, 605, 738, 746–8; tariff and, 520, 524, 739; Union Party in 1864, 572, 588–9

Republican Party, National, *see* National Republican Party; Whigs

Republicans (Jeffersonian), *see* Democratic Republicans

Republic Steel Company, 936

Resaca, Ga., 570

Resettlement Administration, 934

Reuben James (destroyer), 966

Reuther, Walter, 1030

Revels, H. R., *610*

Revenue Act: (1916), 850; (1921), 889, 896; (1964), 1064

Revere, Paul: Boston Massacre, engraving, *124;* Copley's portrait of, 116, *117;* ride, 157, *158*

revisionist historians, 535–6, 612, 999

revival meetings, 340–1, *432*, 440, 454

Revolution, 167–83, maps, *172–3;* beginning of, 155; British troops first sent, 157; events leading to, 125–65; financing, 169–70; French alliance, 177–8; historical interpretation of,

Revolution *(cont.)*
159–61; peace negotiations, 180–82; Treaty of Paris (1783), 182–3, 193, 235, map, *183*

revolver, 453

Reynaud, Paul, 962

Rhee, Syngman, 1010, 1011, 1040

Rheims, 862

Rhett, Robert Barnwell, 529

Rhine River in World War II, *978,* 979

Rhode Island: colony, 60–3, 126, 129, 186; Constitution opposed, 209, 214, 215, 217; paper money, 199; religious freedom, 61–2; slavery in, 90

Rhodes, James Ford, 532–3

Ribbentrop, Joachim von, *995*

Ribicoff, Abraham A., 1083–4

Rice, David, 341

rice culture, 90, 407

Richardson, Joseph, 116

Richardson, Samuel, 331

Richmond, Va., 335; in Civil War, 551, 553, 556, 557, 559, 571, *580*

Rickenbacker, Edward, 863

Ridgway, Gen. Matthew, 1013

Riegel, Robert, 639–40

Rifle Clubs (against blacks), 600

Riis, Jacob, 813, 814, 822; *How the Other Half Lives*, 813, quoted, 700–1, 813

Rillieux, Norbert, 460

Rio de Janeiro, 1045

Rio Grande, Texas boundary, 492–3, 496

riots: black, 1073, *1074;* race (against blacks), 598, 884, 971

Ripley, George, 455

roads: building in 1950s, 1032; Coxey's proposal on, 762; early nineteenth century, 298, 313, 315–16, map, *314;* expenditures for, 895; Jackson's policy on, 368–9

Roanoke Island: in Civil War, 553; colony, 33

Robber Barons, 669–70; in railroads, 653–4

Roberts, Owen J., 939

Robinson, Charles, 511

Robinson, Edwin Arlington, 903

Robinson, James Harvey, 719

Robinson, Joseph T., 904

Rochester, N.Y., *Democrat*, 474

Rockefeller, John D., 423, 654, 658, *660,* 661–5, 671, 672, 789, 883; quotations on, 62–3; quoted, 671

Rockefeller, John D., Jr., 661

Rockefeller, Nelson A., 1065, 1082, 1088

Rockhill, William W., 805

Rockingham, Lord, 181

Rockingham Whigs, 139, 145

Rocky Mountain Company, 489

Rocky Mountains, 618, 651; as western boundary of Louisiana, 286

Roebling, John, 649

Rogers, William, 1085

Rolfe, John, 46

Roman Catholic Church, *see* Catholic Church

Romanticism, 332, 435; in art, 449–52; in literature, 445; Southern inter-

Romanticism *(cont.)*
pretation of, 464; Transcendentalism and, 440–1

Rome in World War II, 976

Rommel, Field Marshal Erwin, 974

Romney, George, 1082, 1085

Roosevelt, Franklin D., 998, 999, 1015; Atlantic Charter, 965; Brain Trust, 922, 923, 927, 931; character, 922–3; Churchill and, 963, 965, 975; death, 985, 992; destroyers-for-bases deal, 963; early career, 922–3; economic and social theories, 923–5; Einstein's letter to, 982; election of 1932, 921–2; election of 1936, 937–8; election of 1940, 963; election of 1944, 972; financial policy, 925, 931, 936–7, 940; fireside chats, 924, 963, 965; first inauguration, *922,* 923; Good Neighbor Policy, 952, 954; hatred and criticism of, 931, 937, 939; "Hundred Days," 923–30; Lend–Lease program, 963–5, quotations, 964; and neutrality, 959; New Deal, 921–42, quotations, 911; "quarantine the aggressor" speech, 959; relief policies, 921, 929; second inaugural address, 938; Soviet Union recognized, 955; Teheran conference, *976,* 977; and United Nations, 994; Vice Presidential candidate, 887; war declared, 969; in World War II, 961–6, 969–73, 976, 979–80, 982–5; Yalta conference, 983–4, 1027

Roosevelt, Mrs. Franklin D. (Eleanor), 925

Roosevelt, Theodore, 670, 709, 783, 799, *812, 821,* 838, 922; in Ballinger-Pinchot affair, 831; Caribbean policy, 801–2; character, 823; in Civil Service Commission, 752; early life, 821–2; election of 1904, election of 1912, 834; evaluation of, 827; Gentlemen's Agreement on Japanese immigration, 684; Latin American policy, 801–2, quotation, 801; Monroe Doctrine Corollary, 801–2, 954; and muckrakers, 815; New Deal influenced by, 941; New Nationalism, 831, 833; in New York City Police Board, 822; Nobel Peace Prize, 807; and Panama Canal, 798; President, 798, 823–7; Progressive Party, campaign of 1912, 831–3; Rough Riders at San Juan Hill, 792, *793;* in Russo–Japanese War, 806–7; on Socialists, 834; in Spanish–American War, 789, 791–2, *793;* Square Deal, 825; Taft influenced by, 827–8; as trust buster, 823–5; Vice President, 821–3; in World War I, 848, 849, 851, 858, 865

Roosevelt Corollary of Monroe Doctrine, 801–2, 954

Root, Elihu, 856, 866

Rosecrans, Maj. Gen. William S., 565–6, 568

Rosenberg, Ethel, 1016

Rosenberg, Julius, 1016

Ross, Edward A., 817

Rostow, Walt W., 1061